The
Hutchinson Paperback
Dictionary of Biography

Arrow Books

Arrow Books Ltd
20 Vauxhall Bridge Road
London SW1V 2SA

An imprint of Random Century Group

London Melbourne Sydney Auckland
Johannesburg and agencies throughout
the world

First published in Great Britain in 1990

Set in Century Old Style

Data prepared on Telos and typeset
by Falcon Typographic Art Ltd, Edinburgh

Automatic Page Make-up
Digital Publications Ltd, Edinburgh

ISBN 0 09 978210 3

Printed and bound in Great Britain by
Courier International Ltd, Tiptree, Essex

Editors

Editor
Michael Upshall

Project Editor
Penny Hext

Database Editors
Jane Dickins
Claire Debenham
Gian Douglas Home
Claire Jenkins
Pamela Sharpe

Text Editors
Ingrid von Essen
Liz Heron

Office Administration
Anne von Broen

Designed by
Tek Art Ltd

Administration & Production
Edna A Moore, Tek Art

Database Software
BRS Software Products Ltd

Computers
Radstone Technology

Page Make-Up
Marie-Anges Banidol
Rosalia Pardina Seśe
Alex N Watson (Advisor)

Picture Research
Michael Nicholson
Anna Smith

Contributors

David Armstrong MSc, PhD
Christine Avery MA, PhS
John Ayto MA
Lionel Bender BSc, ChBiol, MLBiol
David Benest
Malcolm Bradbury BA, MA, PhD,
  Hon D Litt, FRSL
Brendan P Bradley MA, MSc, PhD
Roy Brigden
John O E Clark BSc
Mike Corbishley BA, FSA, MIFA
Barbara Taylor Cork
David Cotton BA, PhD
Nigel Davis MSc
Ian D Derbyshire MA, PhD
J Denis Derbyshire BSc, PhD, FBIM

Peter Dews PhD
Dougal Dixon, BSc, MSc
Professor George du Boulay FRCR,
  FRCP, Hon FACR
Robin Dunbar BA, PhD
Suzanne Duke
Jane Farron BA
Peter Fleming BA, PhD
Linda Gamlin BSc, MSc
Derek Gjertsen BA
Andrew Gleeson
Larence Garner BA
Michael Hitchcock PhD
Jane Insley MSc
H G Jerrard PhD
Brian Jones
Ros Kaveney BA
Robin Kerrod FRAS
Charles Kidd
Stephen Kite B Arch, RIBA
Peter Lafferty
Chris Lawn BA
Judith Lewis LLB
Mike Lewis MBCS
Graham Ley BA, MPhil
Carol Lister BSc, PhD
Graham Littler, DSc, MSc, FSS
Robin Maconie MA
Roslin Mair MA
Morven MacKilop
Tom McArthur PhD
Karin I. A Mogg BSc, MSc
Bob Moore BA, PhD
Ian Morrison
David Munro BSc, PhD
Danial O'Brien MA
Robert Piasley PhD
Carol Place NSc, PhD
Mike Pudlo MSc, PhD
Ian Ridpath
Adrian Room MA
John Rowlinson BSc, MSc, CChem, FRSC
Jack Schofield BA, MA
Mark Slade MA
Angela Smith BA
Imogen Stooke Wheeler, Director of
  Choreography
Glyn A Stone
Ingrid von Essen
Stephen Webster BSc, MPhil
Liz Whitelegg BSc
John Woodruff

with special thanks to E M Horsley

Acknowledgements

Allsport Photographic
BBC Hulton Picture Library
British Tourist Authority
Camera Press
Cavendish Laboratory, University of Cambridge
Indian Tourist Office Information Service
Keystone Photos
Lacock Abbey Collection
Mansell Collection
Maxim
National Library of Australia
National Portrait Gallery, London
Peter Newark's Western Americana
Novosti Press Agency
Popperfoto
Beatrix Potter Trust
REX Features
Royal Danish Ministry of Foreign Affairs
Sachem Publishing Associates
Science Museum, London
Society for Anglo-Chinese Understanding
Sotheby Parke Barnet & Co
Mireille Vautier
Victoria and Albert Museum, London
Virago Press
Wallace Collection

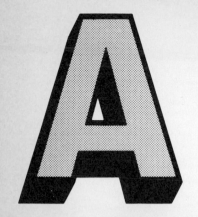

Aalto Alvar 1898–1976. Finnish architect and designer. One of Finland's first modernists, his architectural style was unique, characterized by asymmetry, curved walls, and contrast of natural materials. Buildings include the Hall of Residence, Massachusetts Institute of Technology, Cambridge, Massachusetts 1947–49; Technical High School, Otaniemi 1962–65; Finlandia Hall, Helsinki 1972. He also invented a new form of laminated bent plywood furniture in 1932.

Aaltonen Wäinö 1894–1966. Finnish sculptor and painter, best known for his monumental figures and busts portraying citizens of modern Finland, following the country's independence in 1917. He was one of the early 20th-century pioneers of direct carving, and favoured granite as his medium.

The bronze monument to the athlete Nurmi (1925, Helsinki Stadium) and the bust of the composer Sibelius (1928) are good examples of his work. He also developed a more sombre style of modern classicism, well suited to his public commissions, such as the allegorical figures in the Finnish Parliament House (1930–32).

Aaron in the Bible, the elder brother of Moses and co-leader of the Israelites in their march from Egypt to the Promised Land of Canaan. He made the Golden Calf for the Israelites to worship when they despaired of Moses' return from Mount Sinai.

Aaron Hank 1934– . US baseball player. He played for 23 years with the Milwaukee (later Atlanta) Braves (1954–74) and the Milwaukee Brewers (1975–76), hitting a major-league record 755 home runs and 2,297 runs batted in. He was elected to the Baseball Hall of Fame 1982.

Aasen Ivar Andreas 1813–1896. Norwegian philologist, poet and playwright. Through a study of rural dialects he evolved by 1853 a native 'country language', which he called

Landsmaal, to take the place of literary Dano-Norwegian.

Abbado Claudio 1933– . Italian conductor, long associated with La Scala, Milan. Principal conductor of London Symphony Orchestra from 1979, he also worked with the European Community Youth Orchestra from 1977.

Abbas I *the Great* c.1557–1629. Shah of Persia from 1588. He expanded Persian territory by conquest, defeating the Uzbeks near Herat in 1597 and also the Turks. The port of Bandar-Abbas is named after him. At his death his empire reached from the river Tigris to the Indus. He was a patron of the arts.

Abbas II Hilmi 1874–1944. Last Okhedive (viceroy) of Egypt, 1892–1914. On the outbreak of war between Britain and Turkey in 1914, he sided with Turkey and was deposed following the establishment of a British protectorate over Egypt.

Abbasid dynasty dynasty of the Islamic empire who reigned as caliphs in Baghdad 750–1258. They were descended from Abbas, the prophet Muhammad's uncle, and some of them, such as Harun al-Rashid and Mamun (reigned 813–33), were outstanding patrons of cultural development. Later their power dwindled, and in 1258 Baghdad was burned by the Tatars.

From then until 1517 the Abbasids retained limited power as caliphs of Egypt.

Abd el-Krim el-Khettabi 1881–1963. Moroccan chief known as the 'Wolf of the Riff'. With his brother Muhammad, he led the *Riff revolt* against the

Abbas I *Called the Great, Abbas I was Shah of Persia 1588–1629. This is an engraving from Herbett's* Travels *1638.*

French and Spanish invaders, inflicting disastrous defeat on the Spanish at Anual in 1921, but surrendered to a large French army under Pétain in 1926. Banished to the island of Réunion, he was released in 1947 and died in voluntary exile in Cairo.

Abdul-Hamid II 1842–1918. Last sultan of Turkey 1876–1909. In 1908 the reformist Young Turks under Enver Pasha forced Abdul-Hamid to restore the constitution of 1876, and in 1909 insisted on his deposition. He died in confinement. For his part in the Armenian massacres suppressing the revolt of 1894–96 he was known as the Great Assassin.

Abdullah ibn Hussein 1882–1951. King of Jordan from 1946. He worked with the British guerrilla leader T E ◊Lawrence in the Arab revolt of World War I. Abdullah became king of Transjordan 1946; on the incorporation of Arab Palestine (after the 1948–49 Arab-Israeli War) he renamed the country the Hashemite Kingdom of Jordan. He was assassinated.

Abdullah Sheikh Muhammad 1905–1982. Indian politician, known as the 'Lion of Kashmir'. He headed the struggle for constitutional government against the Maharajah of Kashmir, and in 1948 became prime minister of Kashmir. He agreed to the accession of the state to India to halt ethnic infiltration, but was dismissed and imprisoned from 1953 (with brief intervals) until 1966, when he reaffirmed the right of the people 'to decide the future of the state'. He became chief minister of Jammu and Kashmir 1975, accepting the sovereignty of India.

Abel in the Old Testament, second son of Adam and Eve; as a shepherd, he made burnt offerings of meat to God which were more acceptable than the fruits offered by his brother Cain; he was killed by the jealous Cain.

Abel Frederick Augustus 1827–1902. British scientist and inventor, who developed explosives. As a chemist to the War Department, he introduced a method of making gun-cotton and was joint inventor with ◊Dewar of cordite. He also invented the Abel close-test instrument for determining the flash point (ignition temperature) of petroleum.

Abel John Jacob 1857–1938. US biochemist. He studied the chemical composition of body tissues, and this led, in 1898, to the discovery of adrenaline, the first hormone to be identified, which Abel called epinephrine. He later became the first to isolate amino acids from blood.

Abel Niels Henrik 1802–1829. Norwegian mathematician. He demonstrated that the general quintic equation

$$ax^5 + bx^4 + cx^3 + dx^2 + ex + f = 0$$

could not be solved algebraically.

His other work covered elliptic functions, integral equations, infinite series, and the binomial theorem. He lived a life of poverty and ill-health, dying of tuberculosis shortly before the arrival

of an offer of a position at the University of Berlin.

Abelard Peter 1079–1142. French scholastic philosopher noted for his work on logic and theology and for his love affair with ◊Heloise. Details of his controversial life are contained in the autobiographical *Historia Calamitatum Mearum/The History of My Misfortunes.*

Born near Nantes, he became canon of Notre Dame in Paris, and master of the cathedral school 1115. When his seduction of, and secret marriage to, his pupil ◊Héloïse became known, she entered a convent and he was castrated at the instigation of her uncle, Canon Fulbert, and became a monk. Resuming teaching a year later, he was cited for heresy and became a hermit at Nogent, where he built the oratory of the Paraclete, and later abbot of a monastery in Brittany. He opposed realism in the debate over universals, and propounded 'conceptualism' whereby universal terms have only a mental existence. His love letters from Héloïse survive. He died at Châlon-sur-Saône, on his way to defend himself against a new charge of heresy. Héloïse was buried beside him at the Paraclete 1164, their remains being taken to Père Lachaise, Paris 1817.

Abercrombie Leslie Patrick 1879–1957. Pioneer of British town planning. He is known for his work of replanning British cities after damage in World War II (such as the Greater London Plan, 1944) and for the policy of building new towns.

Abercromby Ralph 1734–1801. Scots soldier who in 1801 commanded an expedition to the Mediterranean, charged with the liquidation of the French forces left behind by Napoleon in Egypt. He fought a brilliant action against the French at Aboukir Bay in 1801, but was mortally wounded at the battle of Alexandria a few days later.

Aberdeen George Hamilton Gordon, 4th Earl of Aberdeen 1784–1860. British Tory politician, prime minister 1852–55, resigned because of the Crimean War losses. Although a Tory, he supported Catholic emancipation and followed Robert Peel in his conversion to free trade.

Born in Edinburgh, he succeeded his grandfather as earl in 1801, and was a prominent diplomat. In 1828 and again in 1841 he was foreign secretary under Wellington. In 1852 he became prime minister in a government of Peelites and Whigs (Liberals), but resigned in 1855 because of the hostile criticism aroused by the miseries and mismanagement of the Crimean War.

Abraham *c.* 2300 BC. According to the Old Testament, founder of the Jewish nation. Jehovah promised him heirs and land for his people in Canaan, renamed him Abraham ('father of many nations') and once tested him by a command (later retracted) to sacrifice his son Isaac or, in the Koran, Ishmael.

Abraham was born in Ur, Sumeria, the son of Terah. With his father, wife Sarah, and nephew Lot, he migrated to Haran, N Mesopotamia. While in Canaan he received Jehovah's promise of land. After visiting Egypt he separated from Lot at Bethel and settled in Hebron. He was still childless at the age of 76, subsequently had a son (Ishmael) with his wife's maidservant Hagar, and then, at the age of 100, a son Isaac with his wife Sarah. Abraham was buried in Machpelah Cave, Hebron.

Abraham Edward Penley 1913– . British biochemist, who isolated the antibiotic cephalosporin, capable of destroying penicillin-resistant bacteria.

Absalom in the Old Testament, favourite son of King David; when defeated in a revolt against his father he fled on a mule, but was caught up by his hair in a tree branch and killed by Joab, one of David's officers.

Abu Bakr or *Abu-Bekr* 573–634. 'Father of the virgin', name used by Abd-el-Ka'aba from about 618 when the prophet Muhammad married his daughter Ayelsha. He was a close adviser to Muhammad in the period 622–32. On the prophet's death, he became the first caliph adding Mesopotamia to the Muslim world and instigating expansion into Iraq and Syria.

Traditionally he is supposed to have encouraged some of those who had known Muhammad to memorize his teachings; these words were later written down to form the Koran.

Abu Nuwas Hasan ibn Hani 762–c.815. Arab poet. His work was based on old forms, but the new freedom with which he used them, his eroticism, and his ironic humour, have contributed to his reputation as perhaps the greatest of Arab poets.

Achaemenid dynasty dynasty ruling the Persian Empire 550–330 BC, and named after Achaemenes, ancestor of Cyrus the Great, founder of the empire. His successors included Cambyses, Darius I, Xerxes, and Darius III, who, as the last Achaemenid ruler, was killed after defeat in battle against Alexander the Great in 330 BC.

Achebe Chinua 1930– . Nigerian novelist, whose themes include the social and political impact of European colonialism on African people, and the problems of newly independent African nations. His first novel, *Things Fall Apart* 1958, was widely acclaimed; *Anthills of the Savannah* 1987 is also set in a fictional African country.

Acheson Dean (Gooderham) 1893–1971. US politician; as undersecretary of state 1945–47 in ◊Truman's Democratic administration, he was associated with George C ◊Marshall in preparing the Marshall Plan, and succeeded him as secretary of state 1949–53.

He helped establish NATO, and criticized Britain for having 'lost an empire and not yet found a role'.

Acquaviva Claudius 1543–1615. Neapolitan general of the Jesuits from 1581 and one of their most able organizers and educators.

Acton Eliza 1799–1859. English cookery writer and poet, whose *Modern Cookery for Private Families* 1845 influenced Mrs Beeton.

Acton John Emerich Edward Dalberg-Acton, 1st Baron Acton 1834–1902. British historian and Liberal politician. Elected to Parliament in 1859, he was a friend and adviser of Gladstone. Appointed professor of modern history at Cambridge in 1895, he planned and edited the *Cambridge Modern History*, but died after completing the first two volumes.

Adam (Hebrew *adham* 'man') in the Old Testament, founder of the human race. Formed by God from the dust and given the breath of life, Adam was placed in the Garden of Eden, where ◊Eve was given to him as a companion. With her, he tasted the forbidden fruit of the Tree of Knowledge of Good and Evil, and they were expelled from the Garden.

Adam family of Scottish architects and designers. *William Adam* (1689–1748), the leading Scottish architect of his day, trained his three sons in his Edinburgh office. *Robert Adam* (1728–92), the most distinguished member of the family, is considered the greatest British architect of the late 18th century and leader of the Neo-Classical revival. He was born at Kirkcaldy, travelled in Italy and Dalmatia, and was appointed architect to King George in 1762. In the interiors of Harewood House, Luton Hoo, Syon House, Osterley Park and others, he employed delicate stucco decoration with Neo-Classical motifs. With the assistance of his brothers *James Adam* (1732–94) and *John Adam* (1721–92) he designed and speculatively developed the district of London between Charing Cross and the Thames, which was named after them the Adelphi (Greek for 'brothers'). The area was largely rebuilt in 1936. He was also a furniture designer.

Adam Adolphe Charles 1803–1856. French composer of light operas. Some 50 of his works were staged, including the classic ballet *Giselle*.

Adam de la Halle c.1240–c.1290. French poet and composer. His *Jeu de Robin et Marion*, written in Italy about 1282, is a theatrical work with dialogue and songs set to what were apparently popular tunes of the day. It is sometimes called the forerunner of comic opera.

Adams Ansel 1902–1984. US photographer, known for his printed images of dramatic landscapes and organic forms of the American West. He was associated with the Zone System of exposure estimation.

Adams Gerry (Gerard) 1948– . Northern Ireland politician, president of Provisional Sinn Féin (the political wing of the IRA). He was elected a member of Parliament 1983 but declined to take up

Adams US photographer Ansel Adams.

his Westminster seat. He has been criticized for failing to denounce IRA violence. In the 1970s, because of his connections with the IRA, he was interned and later released.

Adams Henry Brooks 1838–1918. US historian, the grandson of President John Quincy Adams; he wrote *Mont-Saint-Michel and Chartres* 1904, and a classic autobiography *The Education of Henry Adams* 1907.

Adams John 1735–1826. 2nd president of the USA 1797–1801, and vice president 1789–97. Born at Quincy, Massachusetts. He was a member of the Continental Congress, 1774–78, and signed the Declaration of Independence. In 1779 he went to France and negotiated the treaties that ended the War of American Independence. In 1785 he became the first US ambassador in London.

Adams John Coolidge 1947–. US composer and conductor, director of the New Music Ensemble 1972–81, and artistic adviser to the San Francisco Symphony Orchestra from 1978. His works include *Electric Wake* 1968, *Heavy Metal* 1971, *Bridge of Dreams* 1982, and the opera *Nixon in China* 1988.

Adams John Couch 1819–1892. English astronomer, who deduced the existence of the planet Neptune 1845.

Adams John Quincy 1767–1848. 6th president of the USA 1825–29. Eldest son of President John ◊Adams, he was born at Quincy, Massachusetts, and became US minister in The Hague, Berlin,

St Petersburg, and London. In 1817 he became ◊Monroe's secretary of state, formulated the Monroe doctrine 1823, and succeeded him in the presidency, despite receiving fewer votes than his main rival, Andrew ◊Jackson. As president, Adams was an advocate of strong federal government.

Adams Neil 1958– . English judo champion. He won two junior and five senior European titles 1974–85, eight senior national titles, and two Olympic silver medals 1980, 1984. In 1981 he was world champion in the 78 kg class.

Adams Richard 1920– . British novelist. A civil servant 1948–72, he wrote *Watership Down* 1972, a tale of a rabbit community, which is read by adults and children. Later novels include *The Plague Dogs* 1977 and *Girl on a Swing* 1980.

Adams Roger 1889–1971. US organic chemist, known for his painstaking analytical work to determine the composition of naturally occuring substances such as complex vegetable oils and plant alkaloids (chemically basic and physiologically active substances such as morphine).

Adams Samuel 1722–1803. US politician, second cousin of President John Adams; he was the chief prompter of the Boston Tea Party in the War of American Independence. He was also a signatory of the Declaration of Independence, and anticipated the French emperor Napoleon in calling the British a 'nation of shopkeepers'.

Adamson Joy 1910–1985. German-born author and painter, who worked with wildlife in Kenya, including the lioness Elsa described in *Born Free* 1960. She was murdered at her home in Kenya. She worked with her third husband, British game warden *George Adamson* (1906–1989), who was murdered by bandits.

Adamson Robert R 1821–1848. Scottish photographer who, with David Octavius Hill, produced 2,500 calotypes (mostly portraits) in five years from 1843.

Addams Charles 1912–1988. US cartoonist, creator of the Gothically ghoulish Addams family in the *New Yorker* magazine. There was a successful television series based on the cartoon in the 1960s.

Addams Jane 1860–1935. US sociologist and feminist, who in 1889 founded and led the social settlement of Hull House, Chicago, one of the earliest community centres. She was vice president of the National American Woman Suffrage Association 1911–14, and in 1915 led the Woman's Peace Party and the first Women's Peace Congress. She shared a Nobel Prize for Peace in 1931. Her publications include *Newer Ideals of Peace* 1907 and *Twenty Years at Hull House* 1910.

Addington Henry 1757–1844. British Tory prime minister 1801–04, later Viscount ◊Sidmouth.

Addison Joseph 1672–1719. British writer. In 1704 he celebrated ◊Marlborough's victory at Blenheim in a poem, 'The Campaign', and subsequently held political appointments, including under-secretary of state and secretary to the Lord-Lieutenant of Ireland 1708. In 1709 he contributed to the *Tatler*, begun by Richard ◊Steele, with whom he was cofounder in 1711 of the *Spectator*.

Addison Thomas 1793–1863. British physician who first recognized the condition affecting the adrenal glands known as Addison's disease in 1855.

Adelaide 1792–1849. Queen consort of ◊William IV of England. Daughter of the Duke of Saxe-Meiningen, she married William, then Duke of Clarence, in 1818. No children of the marriage survived infancy.

Adenauer Konrad 1876–1967. German Christian Democrat politician, chancellor of West Germany 1949–63. With the French president de Gaulle he achieved the postwar reconciliation of France and Germany and strongly supported all measures designed to strengthen the Western bloc in Europe.

Adenauer was mayor of his native city of Cologne from 1917 until his imprisonment by Hitler in 1933 for opposition to the Nazi regime. After the war he headed the Christian Democratic Union and became chancellor; he was known as the 'Old Fox'. He supported the UK's entry into the European Community.

Ader Clement 1841–1925. French aviation pioneer whose steam-driven aeroplane, the *Éole*, made the first powered take-off in history (1890), but it could not fly. In 1897, with his *Avion III*, he failed completely, despite false claims made later.

Adjani Isabelle 1955–. French film actress of Algerian-German descent. She played the title role in Truffaut's *L'Histoire d'Adèle H/The Story of Adèle H* 1975 and has since appeared in international productions including *Le Locataire/The Tenant*; *Nosferatu Phantom der Nacht* 1979; *Ishtar* 1987.

Adler Alfred 1870–1937. Austrian psychologist. Adler saw the 'will to power' as more influential in accounting for human behaviour than the sexual drive theory. Over this theory he parted company with ◊Freud after a ten-year collaboration.

Born in Vienna, he was a general practitioner and nerve specialist there 1897–1927, serving as an army doctor in World War I. He joined the circle of Freudian doctors in Vienna about 1900. The concepts of inferiority complex and over-compensation originated with Adler, for example in his books *Organic Inferiority and Psychic Compensation* 1907 and *Understanding Human Nature* 1927.

Adler Larry 1914– . US musician, a virtuoso performer on the harmonica.

Adrian Edgar, 1st Baron Adrian 1889–1977. British physiologist. He received the Nobel Prize for Medicine in 1932 for his work with Sherrington in the field of nerve impulses.

Adrian IV (Nicholas Breakspear) *c.*1100–1159. Pope 1154–59, the only British pope. He secured the execution of ◊Arnold of Brescia; crowned Frederick I Barbarossa as German emperor; refused Henry II's request that Ireland should be granted to the English crown in absolute ownership; and was at the height of a quarrel with the emperor when he died.

Aehrenthal Count Aloys von 1854–1912. Foreign minister of Austria-Hungary during the Bosnian crisis of 1908.

Aelfric *c.*955–1020. English writer, author of two collections of homilies and the *Lives of the Saints*, written in vernacular Old English prose.

Aeschines lived 4th century BC. An orator of ancient Athens, a rival of ◊Demosthenes.

Aeschylus *c.*525–*c.*456 BC. Greek dramatist, widely regarded as the founder of Greek tragedy. By the introduction of a second actor he made true dialogue and dramatic action possible. Aeschylus wrote some 90 plays between 499 and 458 BC of which seven survive. These are: *The Suppliant Women* peformed about 490, *The Persians* 472, *Seven against Thebes* 467, *Prometheus Bound* (about 460) and the *Oresteia* trilogy 458.

Aeschylus was born at Eleusis, near Athens, of a noble family. He took part in the Persian Wars and fought at Marathon (490). He twice visited the court of Hieron I, king of Syracuse, and died at Gela in Sicily.

Aesop traditional writer of Greek fables. According to Herodotus he lived in the reign of Amasis of Egypt (mid-6th century BC) and was a slave of Iadmon, a Thracian. The fables, for which no evidence of his authorship exists, are anecdotal stories using animal characters to illustrate moral or satirical points.

Aga Khan IV 1936– . Spiritual head (*imam*) of the Ismaili Muslim sect. He succeeded his grandfather in 1957.

Agassiz (Jean) Louis 1807–1873. Swiss naturalist who emigrated to the US and became one of the foremost scientists of the 19th century. He established his name through work on the classification of the fossil fishes, and is credited with the discovery of the ice ages. Unlike Darwin, he did not believe that individual species themselves changed, but that new species were created from time to time. He is now criticized for holding racist views concerning the position of blacks in American society.

Agate James Evershed 1877–1947. British writer, known for *Ego*, a diary in nine volumes 1935–49.

Agnew Spiro 1918– . US vice president 1969–73. A Republican, he was governor of Maryland 1966–69, and vice president under ◊Richard Nixon. He resigned in 1973, shortly before pleading 'no contest' to a charge of income-tax evasion.

Agnon Shmuel Yosef 1888–1970. Israeli novelist. Born in Buczacz, Galicia (now in the USSR), the setting of his most famous book, *A Guest for the Night*. He shared a Nobel prize 1966.

Agostini Giacomo 1943–. Italian motorcyclist. He won a record 122 grands prix and 15 world titles. His world titles were at 350cc and 500cc and he was five times a dual champion. In addition he won 10 races at the Isle of Man TT races; a figure bettered only by Mike ◊Hailwood and Joey Dunlop.

Agricola Gnaeus Julius AD 37–93. Roman general and politician. Born in Provence, he became Consul of the Roman Republic AD 77, and then governor of Britain AD 78–85. He extended Roman rule to the Firth of Forth in Scotland and won the battle of Mons Graupius. His fleet sailed round the N of Scotland and proved Britain an island.

Agrippa Marcus Vipsanius 63–12 BC. Roman general. He commanded the victorious fleet at the battle of Actium and married Julia, daughter of ◊Augustus.

Ahab *c.*875–854 BC. King of Israel. His empire included the suzerainty of Moab, and Judah was his subordinate ally, but his kingdom was weakened by constant wars with Syria. By his marriage with Jezebel, princess of Sidon, Ahab introduced into Israel the worship of the Phoenician god Baal, thus provoking the hostility of Elijah and other prophets. Ahab died in battle against the Syrians at Ramoth Gilead.

Ahasuerus (Latinized Hebrew form of the Persian Khshayarsha, Greek *Xerxes*). Name of several Persian kings in the Bible, notably the husband of ◊Esther. Traditionally it was also the name of the Wandering Jew, a legendary figure said to have insulted Jesus before the crucifixion and condemned to wander the world until Christ's return to Earth.

Ahmad Shah 1724–1773. First ruler of Afghanistan. Elected king in 1747, he had made himself master of the Punjab by 1751. He defeated the Mahrattas at Panipat in 1761, and then the Sikhs.

Aidan, St *c.*600–651. Irish monk from Iona who converted Northumbria to Christianity and founded Lindisfarne monastery on Holy Island. His feast day is 31 Aug.

Aidoo Ama Ata 1940– . Ghanaian writer of plays, *Dilemma of a Ghost* 1965, novels, *Our Sister Killjoy* 1977, and short stories.

Aiken Conrad (Potter) 1899–1973. US poet and novelist, whose *Collected Poems* appeared 1953.

Aiken Howard 1900– . US mathematician. In 1939, in conjunction with engineers from IBM, he started work on the design of an automatic calculator using standard business machine components. In 1944 they completed one of the first computers, the Automatic Sequence Controlled Calculator (known as the Mark 1), a programmable computer controlled by punched paper tape and using punched cards.

Ainsworth William Harrison 1805–1882. British historical novelist. He produced in all some 40 novels and helped popularize the legends of Dick ◊Turpin in *Rookwood* 1834 and ◊Herne the Hunter in *Windsor Castle* 1834.

Airy George Biddell 1801–1892. English astronomer. At Greenwich he installed a transit telescope for accurately measuring time by the stars. The position of this instrument defines the Greenwich meridian, internationally accepted as the line of zero longitude in 1884.

Airy was made director of the Cambridge University Observatory in 1828 and became the seventh Astronomer Royal in 1835. He began the distribution of Greenwich time signals by telegraph, and Greenwich Mean Time as measured by Airy's telescope was adopted as legal time in Britain in 1880.

Akbar Jellaladin Muhammad 1542–1605. Mughal emperor of N India from 1556, when he succeeded his father. He gradually established his rule throughout the whole of India N of the Deccan. He is considered the greatest of the Mughal emperors, and the firmness and wisdom of his rule won him the title 'Guardian of Mankind'; he was a patron of the arts.

Akhmatova Anna. Pen name of Anna Andreevna Gorenko 1889–1966. Russian poet. Among her works are the cycle *Requiem* 1963 (written in the 1930s), which deals with the Stalinist terror, and *Poem without a hero* 1962 (begun 1940).

In the 1920s she published several collections of poetry in the realist style of ◊Mandelshtam, but her lack of sympathy with the post-revolutionary regimes inhibited her writing, and her work was banned 1922 40 and again from 1946. From the mid-1950s her work was gradually rehabilitated in the USSR. In 1989 an Akhmatova Museum was opened in Leningrad.

Akihito 1933– . Emperor of Japan from 1989, succeeding his father Hirohito (Showa). His reign is called the Heisei ('achievement of universal peace') era. Unlike previous crown princes, Akihito was educated alongside commoners at the elite Gakushuin school and in 1959 he married Michiko Shoda (1934–), the daughter of a flour-company president. Their three children, the Oxford University educated Crown Prince Hiro, Prince Aya, and Princess Nori, were raised at Akihito's home instead of being reared by tutors and chamberlains in a separate imperial dormitory.

Akins Zoe 1886–1958. US writer. Born in Missouri, she wrote poems, literary criticism, and plays, of which the best known is *The Greeks Had a Word for It* 1930.

Aksakov Sergei Timofeyevich 1791–1859. Russian writer, born at Ufa, in the Urals. Under the influence of ◊Gogol, he wrote autobiographical novels, including *Chronicles of a Russian Family* 1856, and *Years of Childhood* 1858.

Alain-Fournier pen name of Henri-Alban Fournier 1886–1914. French novelist. His haunting semi-autobiographical fantasy *Le Grand Meaulnes/The Lost Domain* 1913 was a cult novel of the 1920s and 1930s. His life is intimately recorded in his correspondence with his brother-in-law Jacques Rivière.

Alanbrooke Alan Francis Brooke, 1st Viscount Alanbrooke 1883–1963. British army officer, chief of staff in World War II and largely responsible for the strategy that led to the German defeat.
He was born in Ireland. He served in the artillery in World War I, and in World War II, as commander of the 2nd Corps 1939–40, did much to aid the extrication of the British Expeditionary Force from Dunkirk.

Alarcón Pedro Antonio de 1833–1891. Spanish journalist and writer. The acclaimed *Diario/Diary* was based upon his experiences as a soldier in Morocco. His *El Sombrero de tres picos/The Three-Cornered Hat* 1874 was the basis of Manuel de Falla's ballet.

Alaric *c.*370–410. King of the Visigoths. In 396 he invaded Greece and retired with much booty to Illyria. In 400 and 408 he invaded Italy, and in 410 captured and sacked Rome, but he died the same year on his way to invade Sicily.
The river Busento was diverted by his soldiers so that he could be buried in its course with his treasures; the labourers were killed to keep the secret.

Albee Edward 1928– . US playwright. His internationally performed plays are associated with the theatre of the absurd and include *The Zoo Story* 1960, *The American Dream* 1961, *Who's Afraid of Virginia Woolf?* 1962 (filmed with Elizabeth Taylor and Richard Burton as the quarrelling, alcoholic, academic couple 1966), *Tiny Alice* 1965, and *A Delicate Balance* 1966.

Albéniz Isaac 1860–1909. Spanish composer and pianist, born in Catalonia. He composed the suite *Iberia* and other piano pieces, making use of traditional Spanish tunes.

Alberoni Giulio 1664–1752. Spanish-Italian priest and politician. Born in Parma, Italy. Philip V made him prime minister of Spain in 1715. In 1717 he became a cardinal. He introduced many reforms, but was forced to flee to Italy in 1719, when his foreign policies failed.

Albert Prince Consort 1819–1861. Husband of British Queen ◊Victoria from 1840; a patron of arts and science. Albert was the second son of the Duke of Saxe-Coburg-Gotha and first cousin to Queen Victoria. He planned the Great Exhibition of 1851, which made a handsome profit (£186,000); Albert popularized the Christmas tree in England. He was regarded by the British people with groundless suspicion because of his German connections. He died of typhoid.

Albert I 1875–1934. King of the Belgians from 1909, the younger son of Philip, Count of Flanders, and the nephew of Leopold II. In 1900 he married Duchess Elisabeth of Bavaria. In World War I he commanded the Allied army that conquered the Belgian coast in 1918, re-entering Brussels in triumph on 22 Nov. He was killed while mountaineering.

Alberti Leon Battista 1404–1472. Italian Renaissance architect and theorist, noted for his recognition of the principles of classical architecture and their modification for Renaissance practice in *On Architecture* 1452.

Albertus Magnus, St 1206–1280. Scholar of theology, philosophy (especially Aristotle), natural science, chemistry, and physics. He was known as 'doctor universalis' because of the breadth of his knowledge. Feast day 15 Nov.
He studied at Bologna and Padua, and entered the Dominican order 1223. He taught at Cologne and lectured from 1245 in Paris University. St Thomas Aquinas was his pupil there, and followed him to Cologne 1248. He became provincial of the Dominicans in Germany 1254, and was made bishop of Ratisbon 1260. Two years later he resigned and eventually retired to his convent at Cologne. He was canonized 1932.

Albinoni Tomaso 1671–1751. Italian Baroque composer and violinist, whose work was studied and adapted by JS ◊Bach. He composed over 40 operas. *Adagio*, often described as being by Albinoni, was actually composed by his biographer Remo Giazotto (1910–).

Alboin 6th century. King of the Lombards about 561–573. At that time the Lombards were settled north of the Alps. Early in his reign he attacked the Gepidae, a Germanic tribe occupying Romania, killing their king and taking his daughter Rosamund to be his wife. About 568 he invaded Italy, conquering the country as far as Rome. He was murdered at the instigation of his wife, whom he had forced to drink from a wine-cup made from her father's skull.

Albone Dan 1860–1906. English inventor of one of the first commercially available farm tractors, the Ivel, in 1902. It was a three-wheeled vehicle with a midmounted twin-cylinder petrol engine that could plough an acre in 1.5 hours.

Albuquerque Alfonso de 1453–1515. Viceroy and founder of the Portuguese East Indies 1508–15, when the king of Portugal replaced him by his worst enemy and he died at sea on the way home; his ship *Flor del Mar* was lost between Malaysia and India with all his treasure.

Alcaeus *c.*611–*c.*580 BC. Greek lyric poet. Born at Mytilene in Lesvos, he was a member of the aristocratic party and went into exile when the popular party triumphed. He wrote odes, and the Alcaic stanza is named after him.

Alcibiades 450–404 BC. Athenian general. Handsome and dissolute, he became the archetype of capricious treachery for his military intrigues against his native state with Sparta and Persia; the Persians eventually had him assassinated. He was brought up by ◊Pericles and was a friend of ◊Socrates, whose reputation as a teacher suffered from the association.

Alcock John William 1892–1919. British aviator. On 14 June 1919 in a Vickers-Vimy biplane, he and Lt Whitten-Brown made the first nonstop transatlantic flight. Alcock died after an aeroplane accident in the same year.

Alcoforado Marianna 1640–1723. Portuguese nun. The *Letters of a Portuguese Nun* 1699, supposedly written by her to a young French nobleman (who abandoned her when their relations became known), are no longer accepted as authentic.

Alcott Louisa M(ay) 1832–1888. US author of the children's classic *Little Women* 1869, which drew on her own home circumstances, the heroine Jo being a partial self-portrait. *Good Wives* 1869 was among its sequels.

Alcuin 735–804. English scholar. Born in York, he went to Rome in 780, and in 782 took up residence at Charlemagne's court in Aachen. From 796 he was abbot of Tours. He disseminated Anglo-Saxon scholarship, organized education and learning in the Frankish empire, gave a strong impulse to the Carolingian Renaissance, and was a prominent member of Charlemagne's academy.

Aldhelm, St *c.* 640–709. English prelate and scholar. He was abbot of Malmesbury from 673 and bishop of Sherborne from 705. Of his poems and treatises in Latin, some survive, notably his *Riddles* in hexameters, but his English verse has been lost. He was also known as a skilled architect.

Aldington Richard 1892–1962. British Imagist poet, novelist and critic, who was married to Hilda ◊Doolittle from 1913 to 1937. He wrote biographies of D H Lawrence and T E Lawrence. His novels include *Death of a Hero* 1929 and *All Men are Enemies* 1933.

Aldiss Brian 1925– . English science-fiction writer, anthologist, and critic. His novels include *Non-Stop* 1958, *The Malacia Tapestry* 1976, and the 'Helliconia' trilogy. *Trillion Year Spree* 1986 is a history of science fiction.

Aleixandre Vicente 1898–1984. Spanish lyric poet, born in Seville. His verse, which was influential with younger Spanish writers, showed Republican sympathies, and his work was for a time banned by Franco's government. Nobel Prize for Literature 1977.

Alembert Jean le Rond d' 1717–1783. French mathematician and encyclopedist. He was associated with ◊Diderot in planning the great *Encyclopédie*.

Alençon François, Duke of, later Duke of Anjou 1554–1584. Fourth son of Henry II of France and Catherine de' Medici. At one time he was considered as a suitor to Elizabeth I of England.

Alexander Frederick Matthias 1869–1955. Australian founder and teacher of the Alexander Technique, a psycho-physical relaxation method named after him. At one time a professional reciter, he developed throat and voice trouble, and his experiments in curing himself led him to work out the system of mental and bodily control described in his book *Use of the Self*.

Alexander Harold Rupert Leofric George, 1st Earl Alexander of Tunis 1891–1969. British field marshal, a commander in World War II in Burma, N Africa, and the Mediterranean. He was governor general of Canada 1946–52 and minister of defence 1952–54.

In World War II he was the last person to leave in the evacuation of Dunkirk. In Burma he fought a delaying action for five months against superior Japanese forces. In Aug 1942 he went to N Africa, and in 1943 became deputy to Eisenhower in charge of the Allied forces in Tunisia. After the Axis forces in N Africa surrendered, Alexander became supreme Allied commander in the Mediterranean and, in 1944, field marshal.

Alexander Samuel 1859–1938. Australian philosopher, who originated the theory of emergent evolution: that the space-time matrix evolved matter; matter evolved life; life evolved mind; and finally God emerged from mind.

His books include *Space, Time and Deity* 1920. He was professor at Manchester University 1893–1924.

Alexander eight popes, including:

Alexander VI (Rodrigo Borgia) 1431–1503. Pope 1492–1503. He was of Spanish origin, and bribed his way to the papacy, where he furthered the advancement of his illegitimate children, who included Cesare and Lucrezia ◊Borgia. When ◊Savonarola preached against his corrupt practices Alexander had him executed, and he is said to have died of poison he had prepared for his cardinals. He was a great patron of the arts.

Alexander three tsars of Russia:

Alexander I 1777–1825. Tsar from 1801. Defeated by Napoleon at Austerlitz 1805, he made peace at Tilsit 1807, but economic crisis led to a break with Napoleon's continental system, and the opening of Russian ports to British trade; this led to Napoleon's ill-fated invasion of Russia. After the Congress of Vienna in 1815, Alexander hoped through the Holy Alliance with Austria and Prussia to establish a new Christian order in Europe. He gave a constitution to Poland.

Alexander II 1818–1881. Tsar from 1855. He embarked on reforms of the army, the government, and education, and is remembered as 'the Liberator' for his emancipation of the serfs 1861. However, the revolutionary element remained unsatisfied, and Alexander became increasingly autocratic and reactionary. He was assassinated by Nihilists.

Alexander III 1845–1894. Tsar from 1881, when he succeeded his father, Alexander II. He pursued a reactionary policy, persecuting the Jews and promoting Russification. He married Dagmar (1847–1928), daughter of Christian IX of Denmark and sister of Queen Alexandra of the UK, in 1866.

Alexander three kings of Scotland:

Alexander I *c.*1078–1124. King of Scotland from 1107, known as the *Fierce*.

Alexander II 1198–1249. King of Scotland from 1214, when he succeeded his father William the Lion. Alexander supported the English barons in their struggle with King John after Magna Carta. By the treaty of Newcastle 1244 he acknowledged Henry III of England as his liege lord.

Alexander III 1241–1285. King of Scotland from 1249, son of Alexander II. In 1263 he extended his authority over the Western Isles, which had been dependent on Norway, and strengthened the power of the central Scottish government. He died as the result of a fall from his horse, leaving his granddaughter Margaret, the Maid of Norway, to become queen of Scotland.

Alexander I Karageorgevich 1888–1934. Regent of Serbia 1912–21 and king of Yugoslavia 1921–34, as dictator from 1929; assassinated, possibly by Italian Fascists.

Alexander II Despite his nickname 'the Liberator', the latter part of the reign of Alexander II of Russia was notable for conflict between the tsar and his government.

Second son of ◊Peter I, king of Serbia, he was declared regent for his father in 1912, and on his father's death became king of the state of South Slavs – Yugoslavia – which had come into being in 1918. Rivalries of neighbouring powers and of the Croats, Serbs, and Slovenes within the country led Alexander to establish a personal dictatorship. He was assassinated on a state visit to France, and Mussolini's government was later declared to have instigated the crime.

Alexander Nevski, St 1220–1263. Russian military leader, son of the grand duke of Novgorod; in 1240 he defeated the Swedes on the banks of the Neva (hence Nevski), and in 1242 defeated the Teutonic Knights on frozen Lake Peipus.

Alexander Obrenovich 1876–1903. King of Serbia from 1889 while still a minor, on the abdication of his father, King Milan. He took power into his own hands in 1893, and in 1900 married a widow, Draga Mashin. In 1903 Alexander and his queen were murdered, and ◊Peter I Karageorgevich was placed on the throne.

Alexander Severus AD 208–235. Roman emperor from 222, when he succeeded his cousin Heliogabalus. He was born in Palestine. His campaign against the Persians in 232 achieved some success, but in 235, while proceeding to defend Gaul against German invaders, he was killed in a mutiny.

Alexander the Great 356–323 BC. King of Macedonia and conqueror of the large Persian empire. As commander of the vast Macedonian army he conquered Greece 336. He defeated the Persian king Darius in Asia Minor 333, then moved on to Egypt, where he founded Alexandria. He defeated the Persians again in Assyria 331, then advanced further east to reach the Indus. He conquered the Punjab before dwindling troops forced his retreat.

The son of King Philip of Macedonia and Queen Olympias, Alexander was educated by the philosopher Aristotle. At the age of 20, when his father was murdered, the Macedonian throne and army passed into his hands. He secured his northern frontier, suppressed an attempted rising in Greece by his capture of Thebes, and in 334 crossed the Dardanelles for the campaign against the vast Persian empire. In 333 he routed the Darius at Issus, and then set out for Egypt, where he was greeted as Pharaoh, son of the god Ra, and hailed as son of Zeus. Meanwhile, Darius assembled half a million men for a final battle, but at Arbela on the Tigris in 331 Alexander, with 47,000 men, drove the Persians into retreat.

In Afghanistan he founded colonies at Herat and Kandahar, and in 328 reached the plains of Sogdiana, where he married Roxana, daughter of King Oxyartes. India now lay before him, and he pressed on to the Indus. Near the river Hydaspes (now Jhelum) he fought one of his fiercest battles against the rajah Porus. At the river Hyphasis (now Beas) his men refused to go farther, and reluctantly he turned back down the Indus and along the coast. They reached Susa in 324, where Alexander made Darius's daughter his second wife. He died in Babylon of a malarial fever.

Alexandra 1844–1925. Queen consort of ◊Edward VII of the UK, whom she married in 1863. She was the daughter of Christian IX of Denmark. An annual Alexandra Rose Day in aid of hospitals commemorates her charitable work.

Alexandra 1936–. Princess of the UK. Daughter of the Duke of Kent and Princess Marina, she married Angus Ogilvy (1928–), younger son of the earl of Airlie. They have two children, James (1964–) and Marina (1966–).

Alexandra 1872–1918. Last tsarina of Russia 1894–1917. She was the former Princess Alix of Hessen, and granddaughter of Queen Victoria. She married ◊Nicholas II and, from 1907, fell under the spell of ◊Rasputin, brought to the palace to try to cure her son of haemophilia. She was shot with the rest of her family by the Bolsheviks in the Russian Revolution.

Alexeev Vasiliy 1942– . Soviet weightlifter who broke 80 world records 1970–77, a record for any sport. He was Olympic super-heavyweight champion twice, world champion seven times, and European champion on eight occasions. At one time the most decorated man in the USSR, he was regarded as the strongest man in the world. He carried the Soviet flag at the 1980 Moscow Olympics opening ceremony, but retired shortly afterwards.

Alexius five emperors of Byzantium, including:

Alexius I (Comnenus) 1048–1118. Byzantine emperor 1081–1118. The Latin (W European) Crusaders helped him repel Norman and Turkish invasions, and he devoted great skill to buttressing the threatened empire. His daughter ◊Anna Comnena chronicled his reign.

Alexius IV (Angelos) 1182–1204. Byzantine emperor from 1203, when, with the aid of the army of the Fourth Crusade, he deposed his uncle Alexius III. He soon lost the support of the Crusaders (by that time occupying Constantinople), and he was overthrown and murdered by another Alexius, Alexius Mourtzouphlus (son-in-law of Alexius III) in 1204, an act which the Crusaders used as a pretext to sack the city the same year.

Alfieri Vittorio, Count Alfieri 1749–1803. Italian dramatist. The best of his 28 plays, most of them tragedies, are *Saul* 1782 and *Mirra* 1786.

Alfonsín Foulkes Raúl Ricardo 1927–. Argentinian politician, president 1983–89, leader of the Radical Union Party (UCR). As president from the country's return to civilian government, he set up an investigation of the army's human-rights violations. Economic problems forced him to seek help from the International Monetary Fund and introduce austerity measures.

Educated at a military academy and a university law school, Alfonsín joined the UCR at the age of 18 and eventually went on to lead it. He was active in local politics 1951–62, being imprisoned 1953 by the right-wing Perón regime, and was a member of the national congress 1963–66. With the return to civilian government in 1983 and the legalization of political activity, Alfonsín and the UCR won convincing victories and he became president. He was succeeded by the Perónist Carlos Menem.

Alfonso six kings of Portugal, including:

Alfonso I 1094–1185. King of Portugal from 1112, who made Portugal independent from León.

Alfonso 13 kings of León, Castile, and Spain, including:

Alfonso VII *c.*1106–1157. King of León and Castile from 1126, who attempted to unite Spain. Although he protected the Moors, he was killed trying to check a Moorish rising.

Alfonso X called *el Sabio* 'the Wise' 1221–1284. King of Castile from 1252. His reign was politically unsuccessful but he contributed to learning: he made Castilian the official language of the country, and commissioned a history of Spain and an encyclopedia, as well as several translations from Arabic, concerning, among other subjects, astronomy and games.

Alfonso XI 'the Avenger' 1312–1350. King of Castile from 1312 who ruled cruelly, repressed a rebellion by his nobles, and defeated the last Moorish invasion 1340.

Alfonso XII 1857–1885. King of Spain from 1875, son of ◊Isabella II. He assumed the throne after a period of republican government following his mother's flight and effective abdication 1868.

Alfonso XIII 1886–1941. King of Spain 1886–1931. He assumed power 1906 and married Princess Ena, granddaughter of Queen Victoria of the UK, in the same year. He abdicated soon after the fall of the Primo de Rivera dictatorship (which he supported), and Spain became a republic. His assassination was attempted several times.

Alfred the Great *c.*848–*c.*900. King of Wessex from 871. He defended England against Danish invasion, founded the first English navy, and put into operation a legal code. He encouraged the translation of works from Latin (some of which he translated himself), and promoted the development of the Anglo-Saxon Chronicle. Alfred was born at Wantage, Berkshire, the youngest son of Ethelwulf (died 858), king of the West Saxons. In 870 Alfred and his brother Ethelred fought many battles against the Danes. He gained a victory over the Danes at Ashdown 871, and succeeded Ethelred as king in Apr after a series of defeats. Five years of uneasy peace followed while the Danes were occupied in other parts of England. In 876 the Danes attacked again, and in 878 Alfred was forced to retire to the stronghold of Athelney, from where he finally emerged to win the victory of Edington, Wiltshire. By the Peace of Wedmore 878 the Danish leader Guthrum (died 890) agreed to withdraw from Wessex and from Mercia west of Watling Street. A new landing in Kent encouraged a revolt of the East Anglian Danes, which was suppressed 884–86, and after the final foreign invasion was defeated 892–96, Alfred strengthened the navy to prevent fresh incursions.

Algardi Alessandro c.1595–1654. Italian Baroque sculptor, active in Rome and at the papal court. His greatest work, on which he was intermittently occupied from 1634 to 1652, is the tomb of Pope Leo XI (Medici), in St Peter's, Rome.

He is known for church monuments and bronze portrait busts, such as *St Philip Neri* 1640 (Sta Maria Vallicella, Rome).

Alger Horatio 1834–1899. US writer of children's books. He wrote over 100 didactic moral tales in which the heroes rise from poverty to riches through hard work and good deeds, including the series 'Ragged Dick' from 1867 and 'Tattered Tom' from 1871.

It is estimated that his books sold more than 20 million copies. In US usage a 'Horatio Alger tale' has now come to mean any rags-to-riches story, often an implausible one.

Alhazen Latinized name of Ibn al Haytham 965–1038. Arab scientist, author of the *Kitab al Manazir/Book of Optics*, translated into Latin as *Perspectiva*. For centuries it remained the most comprehensive and authoritative treatment of optics in both East and West.

Ali c.600–661. 4th caliph of Islam. He was born in Mecca, the son of Abu Talib, uncle to the prophet Muhammad, who gave him his daughter Fatima in marriage. On Muhammad's death 632, Ali had a claim to succeed him, but this was not conceded until 656. After a stormy reign, he was assassinated. Around Ali's name has raged the sectarian controversy of the Sunnites and the Shi'ites, the former denying his right to the caliphate and the latter supporting it.

Ali (Ali Pasha) 1741–1822. Turkish politician, known as *Arslan* ('the Lion'). An Albanian, he was appointed pasha (governor) of the Janina region (now Ioánnina, Greece) 1788. His court was visited by the British poet Byron. He was murdered by the sultan's order.

Ali Muhammad. Born Cassius Marcellus Clay 1942– . US boxer. Olympic light-heavyweight champion 1960, he went on to become world professional heavyweight champion 1964, and was the only man to regain the title twice. He was known for his quickness and extroversion. He had his title stripped from him 1967 for refusing to be drafted into the US Army. He regained his title 1974, lost it Feb 1978. and regained it seven months later.

Alia Ramiz 1925–. Albanian communist politician,

head of state from 1982 and party leader from 1985. He has slightly modified the isolationist policies of his predecessor Hoxha.

Born in Shkodër in NW Albania, the son of poor Muslim peasants, Alia joined the National Liberation Army 1944, actively opposing Nazi control. After a period in charge of agitation and propaganda ('agitprop') work, Alia was inducted into the secretariat and Politburo of the ruling Party of Labour of Albania (APL) 1960–61. On the death of Enver Hoxha he became party leader.

Ali Pasha Mehmed Emin 1815–1871. Grand vizier (chief minister) of the Ottoman empire 1855–56, 1858–59, 1861, and 1867–71, noted for his attempts to Westernize the Ottoman Empire.

After a career as ambassador to the UK, minister of foreign affairs 1846, delegate to the Congress of Vienna 1855 and of Paris 1856, he was grand vizier a total of five times. While promoting friendship with Britain and France, he defended the vizier's powers against those of the sultan.

Allan David 1744–1796. Scottish historical painter, director of the Academy of Arts in Edinburgh from 1786. He is noted for portrait and genre paintings such as *Scotch Wedding*.

Allan William 1782–1850. Scottish historical painter, born in Edinburgh, who spent several years in Russia and neighbouring countries, and returned to Edinburgh in 1814. He was elected president of the Royal Scottish Academy in 1838. His paintings include scenes from Walter Scott's Waverley novels.

Allbutt Thomas Clifford 1836–1925. British physician. He invented a compact medical thermometer, proved that angina is caused by narrowing of the coronary artery, and studied hydrophobia and tetanus.

Allegri Gregorio 1582–1652. Italian Baroque composer, born in Rome, who became a priest and entered the Sistine chapel choir 1629. His *Miserere* for nine voices was reserved for performance by the chapel choir until Mozart, at the age of 14, wrote out the music from memory.

Allen Woody. Adopted name of Allen Stewart Konigsberg 1935– . US film director and actor, known for his cynical, witty, often self-deprecating parody and off-beat humour. His films include *Sleeper* 1973, *Annie Hall* 1977 (for which he won three Academy Awards), and *Hannah and her Sisters* 1986, all of which he directed, wrote, and appeared in. From the late 1970s, Allen has mixed his output of comedies with straight dramas in which he does not appear, such as *Interiors* 1978 and *Another Woman* 1988.

Allenby Henry Hynman, 1st Viscount Allenby 1861–1936. British field marshal. In World War I he served in France before taking command in 1917–19 of the British forces in the Middle East. His defeat of the Turkish forces at Megiddo in Palestine in Sept 1918 was followed almost at once by the capitulation of Turkey. He was high commissioner in Egypt 1919–35.

Allende (Gossens) Salvador 1908–1973. Chilean left-wing politician. Elected president 1970 as the candidate of the Popular Front alliance, Allende never succeeded in keeping the electoral alliance together in government. His failure to solve the country's economic problems or to deal with political subversion allowed the army, backed by the CIA, to stage the 1973 coup which brought about the death of Allende and many of his supporters.

Allende, born in Valparaiso, became a Marxist activist in the 1930s and rose to prominence as a presidential candidate 1952, 1958, and 1964. In each election he had the support of the socialist and communist movements but was defeated by the Christian Democrats and Nationalists. As president, his socialism and nationalization of US-owned copper mines made the CIA regard him as a communist and take part in engineering the coup that replaced him by Gen Pinochet.

Allingham Margery (Louise) 1904–1966. British detective novelist, creator of detective Albert Campion, as in *More Work for the Undertaker* 1949.

Allston Washington 1779–1843. US painter, a pioneer of the Romantic movement in the USA with his sea- and landscapes. His handling of light and colour earned him the title 'the American Titian'. He also painted classical, religious, and historical subjects.

Allyson June. Stage name of Ella Geisman 1917–. US film actress, popular in musicals and straight drama in the 1940s and 1950s. Her work includes *Music for Millions* 1945, *The Three Musketeers* 1948, and *The Glenn Miller Story* 1954.

Alma-Tadema Laurence 1836–1912. Dutch painter who settled in the UK 1870. He painted romantic, idealized scenes from Greek, Roman, and Egyptian life in a distinctive, detailed style.

Almeida Francisco de c.1450–1510. First viceroy of Portuguese India 1505–08. He was killed in a skirmish with the Hottentots at Table Bay, S Africa.

Almohad a Berber dynasty 1130–1269 founded by the Berber prophet Muhammad ibn Tumart (c.1080–1130). They ruled much of Morocco and Spain, which they took by defeating the Almoravids; they later took the area which today forms Algeria and Tunis. Their policy of religious 'purity' involved the forced conversion and massacre of the Jewish population of Spain. They were themselves defeated by the Christian kings of Spain in 1212, and in Morocco in 1269.

Almoravid a Berber dynasty 1056–1147 founded by the prophet Abdullah ibn Tashfin, ruling much of Morocco and Spain in the 11th–12th centuries. They came from the Sahara and in the 11th century began laying the foundations of an empire covering the whole of Morocco and parts

of Algeria; their capital was the newly founded Marrakesh. In 1086 they defeated Alfonso VI of Castile to gain much of Spain. They were later overthrown by the ◊Almohads.

Aloysius, St 1568–1591. Italian Jesuit who died while nursing plague victims. He is the patron saint of youth. Feast day 21 June.

Alphege, St 954–1012. Anglo-Saxon priest, bishop of Winchester from 984, archbishop of Canterbury from 1006. When the Danes attacked Canterbury he tried to protect the city, was thrown into prison, and, refusing to deliver the treasures of his cathedral, was stoned and beheaded at Greenwich on 19 Apr, his feast day.

Altdorfer Albrecht c.1480–1538. German painter and printmaker, active in Regensburg, Bavaria. Altdorfer's work, influenced by the linear, classical style of the Italian Renaissance, often depicts dramatic landscapes that are out of scale with the figures in the paintings. His use of light creates tension and effects of movement. Many of his works are of religious subjects.

With ◊Dürer and ◊Cranach, Altdorfer is regarded as one of the leaders of the German Renaissance. *St George and the Dragon* 1510 (Alte Pinakothek, Munich) is an example of his landscape style; *The Battle of Issus* 1529 (also Munich) is a dramatic panorama.

Altgeld John Peter 1847–1902. US political and social reformer. Born in Prussia, he was taken in infancy to the USA. During the Civil War he served in the Union army. He was a judge of the Supreme Court in Chicago 1886–91, and as governor of Illinois 1893–97 was a champion of the worker against the government-backed power of big business.

Althusser Louis 1918– . French philosopher and Marxist, born in Algeria, who from 1968 argued that the idea that economic systems determine family and political systems is too simple. He attempted to show how the ruling class ideology of a particular era is a crucial form of class control.

Works include *For Marx* 1965, *Lenin and Philosophy* 1969, and *Essays in Self-Criticism* 1976.

Altman Robert 1922–. US film director. His antiwar comedy *M.A.S.H.* 1970 was a critical and commercial success; subsequent films include *McCabe and Mrs Miller* 1971, *Nashville* 1975, and *Popeye* 1980. He has a distinctive style as a director.

Alva or *Alba* Ferdinand Alvarez de Toledo, Duke of Alva 1508–1582. Spanish politician and general. He commanded the Spanish armies of the Holy Roman emperor Charles V and his son Philip II of Spain, and in 1567 was appointed governor of the Netherlands, where he set up a reign of terror to suppress the revolt against increased taxation, reductions in local autonomy, and the Inquisition. In 1573 he retired, and returned to Spain.

Alvarado Pedro de c.1485–1541. Spanish conquistador. In 1519 he accompanied Hernándo Cortés in the conquest of Mexico. In 1523–24 he conquered Guatemala.

Alvarez Luis Walter 1911–1988. US physicist. He received the 1968 Nobel Prize for Physics for developing the liquid hydrogen bubble chamber, a device for studying interactions between high-energy elementary particles. In 1980 he and his son *Walter Alvarez* originated the idea that the extinction of dinosaurs and other species 70 million years ago was linked with the impact of an asteroid about 10 km/15 mm in diameter.

He was professor of physics at the University of California from 1945 as well as associate director of the Lawrence Radiation Laboratory 1954–59, and worked on the US atomic bomb project for two years, at Chicago and Los Alamos, during World War II.

Alvárez Quintero Serafin 1871–1938 and Joaquin 1873–1945. Spanish dramatists. The brothers, born near Seville, always worked together and from 1897 produced some 200 plays, principally dealing with Andalusia. Among them are *Papá Juan: Centenario* 1909 and *Los Mosquitos* 1928.

Alwyn William 1905–1985. British composer. Professor of composition at the Royal Academy of Music 1926–55, he wrote film music (*Desert Victory, The Way Ahead*) and composed symphonies and chamber music.

Amalia Anna 1739–1807. Duchess of Saxe-Weimar-Eisenach. As widow of Duke Ernest, she reigned form 1758 to 1775 (when her son Karl August succeeded her) with prudence and skill, making the court of Weimar a literary centre of Germany. She was a friend of the writers Wieland, Goethe, and Herder.

Amanullah Khan 1892–1960. Emir (ruler) of Afghanistan 1919–29. Third son of Habibullah Khan, he seized the throne on his father's assassination and concluded a treaty with the British, but his policy of Westernization led to rebellion 1928. Amanullah had to flee, abdicated 1929, and settled in Rome, Italy.

Amar Das 1495–1574. Indian religious leader, third guru (teacher) of Sikhism 1552–74. He laid emphasis on equality and opposed the caste system. He initiated the custom of the *langar* (communal meal).

Amati Italian family of violin-makers, who worked in Cremona, about 1550–1700. Niccolo Amati (1596–1684) taught Andrea ◊Guarneri and Antonio ◊Stradivari.

Ambler Eric 1909–1986. British novelist. Born in London, he used Balkan/Levant settings in the thrillers *The Mask of Dimitrios* 1939 and *Journey into Fear* 1940.

Ambrose, St *c.*340–397. One of the early Christian leaders and writers known as the Fathers of the Church. He was bishop of Milan, Italy, and wrote on theological subjects. Feast day 7 Dec.

Born at Trèves, in S Gaul, the son of a Roman prefect, Ambrose became governor of N Italy. In 374 he was chosen bishop of Milan, although he was not yet a member of the church. He was then baptized and consecrated. He wrote many hymns, and devised the arrangement of church music known as the *Ambrosian Chant*, which is still used in Milan.

Amenhotep four Egyptian pharaohs, including:
Amenhotep III *c.*1400 BC. King of Egypt who built great monuments at Thebes, including the temples at Luxor. Two portrait statues at his tomb were known to the Greeks as the colossi of Memnon; one was cracked, and when the temperature changed at dawn it gave out an eerie sound, then thought supernatural. His son *Amenhotep IV* subsequently changed his name to ◊Ikhnaton.

Amery Leo(pold Stennett) 1873–1955. British Conservative politician, First Lord of the Admiralty 1922–24, secretary for the colonies 1924–29, secretary for the dominions 1925–29, and secretary of state for India and Burma 1940–45.

Ames Adelbert 1880–1955. US scientist, who studied optics and the psychology of visual perception. He concluded that much of what a person sees depends on what he or she expects to see, based (consciously or unconsciously) on previous experience.

Amiel Henri Frédéric 1821–1881. Swiss philosopher and writer, who wrote *Journal Intime* 1882–84. Born at Geneva, he became professor of philosophy at the university there.

Amies Hardy 1909– . British couturier, one of Queen Elizabeth II's dressmakers. Noted from 1934 for his tailored clothes for women, he also designed for men from 1959.

Amin Dada Idi 1925– . Ugandan politician, president 1971–79. He led the coup that deposed Milton Obote 1971, expelled the Asian community 1972, and exercised a reign of terror over his people. He fled when insurgent Ugandan and Tanzanian troops invaded the country 1979.

Amis Kingsley 1922– . English novelist and poet. His works include *Lucky Jim* 1954, a comic portrayal of life in a provincial university, and *Take a Girl Like You* 1960. He won the Booker Prize 1986 for *The Old Devils*. He is the father of Martin Amis.

Amis Martin 1949– . English novelist, son of Kingsley Amis. His works include *The Rachel Papers* 1974 and *Money* 1984.

Ampère André Marie 1775–1836. French physicist and mathematician who made many discoveries in electromagnetism and electrodymanics. He followed up the work of Hans ◊Oersted on the interaction between magnets and electric currents, developing a rule for determining the direction of the magnetic field associated with an electric current. The *ampere*, the unit of electric

Amundsen *Norwegian explorer Roald Amundsen. He devoted his life to polar exploration and in 1911 became the first man to reach the South Pole.*

Amin Dada *Idi Amin, Ugandan president from 1971 until his overthrow in 1979, surrounded by his bodyguard. He is being asked to explain to reporters how the archbishop of Uganda and two cabinet ministers met a violent death while they were in custody in 1977.*

current, is named after him.

Amundsen Roald 1872–1928. Norwegian explorer who in 1903–06, was the first person to navigate the Northwest Passage. Beaten to the North Pole by Robert Peary 1910, he reached the South Pole ahead of Robert Falcon Scott 1911.

In 1918, Amundsen made an unsuccessful attempt to drift across the North Pole in the airship *Maud* and in 1925 tried unsuccessfully to fly from Spitsbergen, in the Arctic Ocean N of Norway, to the Pole by aeroplane. The following year he joined the Italian explorer Umberto Nobile in the airship *Norge*, which circled the North Pole twice and landed in Alaska. Amundsen was killed in a plane crash over the Arctic Ocean while searching for Nobile and his airship *Italia*.

Ananda 5th century BC. Favourite disciple of the Buddha. At his plea, a separate order was established for women. He played a major part in collecting the teachings of the Buddha after his death.

Anastasia 1901–1918. Russian Grand Duchess, youngest daughter of ◊Nicholas II. She was murdered with her parents but it has been alleged that

Anastasia escaped. Those who claimed her identity included Anna Anderson (1902–1984). Alleged by some to be a Pole, Franziska Schanzkowski, she was rescued from a Berlin canal 1920. The German Federal Supreme Court found no proof of her claim 1970.

Anaximander 610–*c.*547 BC. Greek astronomer and philosopher. He is thought to have been the first to determine the solstices and equinoxes, to have invented the sundial, and to have produced the first geographical map. He believed that the universe originated as a formless mass (*apeiron,* 'indefinite') containing within itself the contraries of hot and cold, and wet and dry, from which land, sea, and air were formed out of the union and separation of these opposites.

Andersen Hans Christian 1805–1875. Danish writer. His fairy tales such as 'The Ugly Duckling', 'The Emperor's New Clothes', and 'The Snow Queen', gained him international fame and have been translated into many languages.

Andersen was born the son of a shoemaker in Odense, Fyn. His first children's stories were published 1835. Some are based on folklore; others are original. His other works include the novel *The Improvisatore* 1845, romances, and an autobiography *Mit livs eventyr/The Tale of My Life*.

Anderson Carl David 1905– . US physicist, who

Andersen The Danish writer Hans Christian Andersen. He was admired by Charles Dickens, whom he visited in 1857.

discovered the positive electron (positron) 1932; he shared a Nobel prize 1936.

Anderson Elizabeth Garrett 1836–1917. The first English woman to qualify in medicine. Refused entry into medical school, Anderson studied privately and was licensed by the Society of Apothecaries in London 1865. She was physician to the Marylebone Dispensary for Women and Children (later renamed the Elizabeth Garrett Anderson Hospital), now staffed by women and serving women patients.

She helped found the London School of Medicine. She was the first woman member of the British Medical Association and the first woman mayor in Britain.

Anderson Marian 1902– . US contralto, whose voice is remarkable for its range and richness. She toured Europe 1930, but in 1939 she was barred from singing at Constitution Hall, Washington, DC, because she was black. In 1955 she sang at the Metropolitan Opera, the first black singer to appear there. In 1958 she was appointed an alternate delegate to the United Nations.

Anderson Maxwell 1888–1959. US playwright, whose *What Price Glory?* 1924, written with Laurence Stallings, was a realistic portrayal of the US soldier in action during World War I.

Anderson Sherwood 1876–1941. US writer of sensitive, experimental, and poetic stories of small-town Midwestern life, *Winesburg, Ohio* 1919.

Ando Tadao. Japanese architect. His houses are a continuation of the refined Japanese domestic tradition in materials of bare concrete and glass.

Andrássy Gyula, Count Andrássy 1823–1890. Prime minister and foreign minister of the Austro-Hungarian Empire 1871–79.

André Carl 1935–. US sculptor, a Minimalist, who often uses industrial materials and basic geometrical forms. An example is the notorious *Equivalent VIII* 1976, a simple rectangle of bricks (Tate Gallery, London), much criticized at the time for its alleged lack of artistic merit.

André John 1751–1880. British army major in the War of American Independence, who covertly negotiated the surrender of West Point with Benedict ◊Arnold, and was caught and hanged by the Americans.

Andrea del Sarto (Andrea d'Agnola) 1486–1531. Italian Renaissance painter active in Florence, one of the finest portraitists and religious painters of his time. His style is serene and noble, characteristic of High Renaissance art.

Del Sarto was the foremost painter in Florence after about 1510, along with Fra Bartolommeo, although gradually superseded by the emerging Mannerists during the 1520s. Apart from portraits, such as *A Young Man* (National Gallery, London), he painted many religious works, including the *Madonna of the Harpies* (Uffizi, Florence), an example of classical beauty reminiscent of Raphael. He painted frescoes at SS Annunziata and the Chiostro dello Scalzo, both in Florence.

Andress Ursula 1936–. Swiss actress specializing in glamour leads. Her international career started with *Dr No* 1962. Other films include *She* 1965, *Casino Royale* 1967, *Red Sun* 1971, and *Clash of the Titans* 1981.

Andrew (full name Andrew Albert Christian Edward) 1960– . Prince of the United Kingdom, duke of York, second son of Queen Elizabeth II. He married Sarah Ferguson 1986, and they have two daughters, Princess Beatrice, born 1988 and Princess Eugenie, born 1990. He is a naval helicopter pilot.

Andrewes Lancelot 1555–1626. Church of England bishop successively of Chichester (1605), Ely (1609), and Winchester (1618). He helped prepare the text of the Authorized Version of the Bible, and was known for his fine preaching.

Andrews John 1813–1885. Irish chemist, who conducted a series of experiments on the behaviour of carbon dioxide under varying temperature and pressure. In 1869 he introduced the idea of a critical temperature, 30.9°C in the case of carbon dioxide, beyond which no amount of pressure will liquefy the gas.

Andrews Julie 1935– . British singer and actress. Formerly a child performer with her mother and father in a music-hall act, she was the original 'My Fair Lady' on stage 1956. Her films include *Mary Poppins* 1964, *The Sound of Music* 1965, *10* 1979, and *Victor/Victoria* 1982.

Andrew, St New Testament apostle, martyred on an X-shaped cross (*St Andrew's cross*). He is the patron saint of Scotland. Feast day 30 Nov.

A native of Bethsaida, he was Simon Peter's

brother. With Peter, James, and John, who worked with him as fisherfolk at Capernaum, he formed the inner circle of Jesus' 12 disciples. According to tradition he went with John to Ephesus, preached in Scythia, and was crucified at Patras.

Andreyev Leonid Nicolaievich 1871–1919. Russian author. Many of his works show an obsession with death and madness including the symbolic drama *Life of Man* 1907, the melodrama *He Who Gets Slapped* 1915; and the novels *Red Laugh* 1904, and *S.O.S.* 1919 published in Finland, where he fled after the Russian Revolution.

Andrić Ivo 1892–1974. Yugoslavian novelist and nationalist. He became a diplomat, and was ambassador to Berlin 1940. *Na Drini ćuprija/The Bridge on the Drina* 1945 is an epic history of a small Bosnian town. Nobel prize 1961.

He was a member of the Young Bosnia organization, and spent World War I in an internment camp because of his politics.

Androcles Traditionally, a Roman slave who fled from a cruel master into the African desert, where he withdrew a thorn from the paw of a crippled lion. Recaptured and sentenced to combat a lion in the arena, he found his adversary was his old friend. The emperor Tiberius was said to have freed them both.

Andropov Yuri 1914–1984. Soviet communist politician, president 1983–84. As chief of the KGB 1967–82, he established a reputation for efficiently suppressing dissent.

Andropov was politically active from the 1930s. His part in quelling the Hungarian national rising 1956, when he was Soviet ambassador, brought him into the Communist Party secretariat 1962 as a specialist on Eastern European affairs. He became a member of the Politburo 1973 and succeeded Brezhnev as party general secretary 1982. Elected president 1983, he introduced economic reforms, but died Feb 1984.

Angad 1504–1552. Indian religious leader, second guru (teacher) of Sikhism 1539–52, succeeding Nanak. He popularized the alphabet known as *Gurmukhi*, in which the Sikh scriptures are written.

Angelico Fra (Guido di Pietro) *c.*1400–1455. Italian painter of religious scenes, active in Florence. He was a monk and painted a series of frescoes at the monastery of San Marco, Florence, begun after 1436. He also produced several altarpieces in a simple style.

His other fresco sequences, *Scenes from the Life of Christ* (Orvieto Cathedral) and *Scenes from the Lives of SS Stephen and Lawrence* 1440s (Chapel of Nicholas V, Vatican Palace), are more elaborate.

Angell Norman 1872–1967. British writer on politics and economics. In 1910 he acquired an international reputation with his book *The Great Illusion*, in which he maintained that any war must prove ruinous to the victors as well as to the vanquished. Nobel Peace Prize 1933.

Angelou Maya (born Marguerite Johnson) 1928– . US novelist, poet, playwright, and short-story writer. Her powerful autobiographical work, *I Know Why the Caged Bird Sings* 1970 and its sequels, tell of the struggles towards physical and spiritual liberation of a black woman growing up in the US South.

Anger Kenneth 1932–. US avant-garde filmmaker, brought up in Hollywood. His films, which dispense with conventional narrative, often portray homosexual iconography and a personal form of mysticism. They include *Fireworks* 1947, *Scorpio Rising* 1964, and *Lucifer Rising* 1973.

Anglesey Henry William Paget 1768–1854. British cavalry leader during the Napoleonic wars. He was twice Lord Lieutenant of Ireland, and succeeded his father as Earl of Uxbridge 1812. At the Battle of Waterloo he led a charge, lost a leg, and was made a marquess.

Ångström Anders Jonas 1814–1874. Swedish physicist, who worked in spectroscopy and solar physics. The *angstrom unit*, until recently widely used as a measure of the wavelength of light and other electromagnetic radiation, was named after him.

Anna Comnena 1083–after 1148. Byzantine historian, daughter of the emperor ◊Alexius I, who chronicled her father's reign. After a number of abortive attempts to alter the imperial succession in favour of her husband, Nicephorus Bryennius (*c.*1062–1137), she retired to a convent to write her major work, the *Alexiad*. It describes the

Angelou *US writer Maya Angelou.*

Byzantine view of public office, as well as the religious and intellectual life of the period.

Anne 1665–1714. Queen of Great Britain and Ireland 1702–14. Second daughter of James, Duke of York, who became James II, and Anne Hyde. She succeeded William III on the throne 1702. Events of her reign include the War of the Spanish Succession, Marlborough's victories at Blenheim, Ramillies, Oudenarde, and Malplaquet, and the union of the English and Scottish parliaments 1707. She was succeeded by George I.

She received a Protestant upbringing, and in 1683 married Prince George of Denmark. Of their many children only one survived infancy, William, Duke of Gloucester, who died at the age of 11. For the greater part of her life Anne was a close friend of Sarah Churchill, wife of John Churchill, afterwards Duke of Marlborough; the Churchills' influence helped lead her to desert her father for her brother-in-law, William of Orange, during the Revolution of 1688, and later to engage in Jacobite intrigues. Her replacement of the Tories by a Whig government 1703–04 was her own act, not due to Churchillian influence. Anne finally broke with the Marlboroughs 1710, when Mrs Masham succeeded the duchess as her favourite, and supported the Tory government of the same year.

Anne (full name Anne Elizabeth Alice Louise) 1950 . Princess of the UK, second child of Queen Elizabeth II, declared Princess Royal 1987. She is an excellent horsewoman, winning a gold medal at the 1976 Olympics, and is actively involved in global charity work, especially for children. In 1973 she married Captain Mark Phillips (1949–), of the Queen's Dragoon Guards; they separated in 1989. Their son Peter (1977–) was the first direct descendant of the Queen not to bear a title. They also have a daughter Zara (1981–).

Anne of Austria 1601–1666. Queen of France from 1615 and regent 1643–61. Daughter of Philip III of Spain, she married Louis XIII of France and on his death became regent for their son, Louis XIV, until his majority.

She was much under the influence of Cardinal Mazarin, her chief minister, to whom she was supposed to be secretly married. She is one of the main characters in Alexandre Dumas' novel *The Three Musketeers* 1844.

Anne of Cleves 1515–1557. Fourth wife of ◊Henry VIII of England. She was the daughter of the Duke of Cleves, and was recommended to Henry as a wife by Thomas ◊Cromwell, who wanted an alliance with German Protestantism against the Holy Roman Emperor. Henry did not like her looks, had the marriage declared void after six months, and pensioned her.

Anne of Denmark 1574–1619. Queen consort of James VI of Scotland (later James I of Great Britain 1603). She was the daughter of Frederick II of Denmark and Norway, and married James 1589. Anne was suspected of Catholic leanings, and was notably extravagant.

Annigoni Pietro 1910–1988. Italian portrait painter. His style is influenced by Italian Renaissance portraiture. Sitters have included John F. Kennedy and Queen Elizabeth II, 1969 (National Portrait Gallery, London).

Anouilh Jean 1910–1987. French playwright. His plays, influenced by the Neo-Classical tradition, include *Antigone* 1942, *L'Invitation au château/Ring Round the Moon* 1947, *Colombe* 1950, and *Becket* 1959, about St Thomas Becket and Henry II.

Anquetil Jacques 1934–1988. French cyclist, the first person to win the Tour de France five times (between 1957 and 1964), a record later equalled by Eddie ◊Merckx and Bernard ◊Hinault.

Anselm, St c. 1033–1109. Medieval priest. Educated at the abbey of Bec in Normandy, which as an abbot (from 1078) he made a centre of scholarship in Europe, he was appointed archbishop of Canterbury by William II 1093, but was later forced into exile. He holds an important place in the development of ◊Scholasticism.

Anselm was born near Aosta in Piedmont. As archbishop of Canterbury he was recalled from exile by Henry I, with whom he bitterly disagreed on the investiture of the clergy; a final agreement gave the king the right of temporal investiture and the clergy that of spiritual investiture. Anselm was canonized 1494. In his *Proslogion* he developed the ontological proof of theism, which infers God's existence from our capacity to conceive of a perfect Being. His *Cur deus homo* deals with the Atonement.

Ansermet Ernest 1883–1969. Swiss conductor with Diaghilev's Russian Ballet 1915–23. In 1918 he founded the Swiss Romande Orchestra, conducting many first performances of ◊Stravinsky.

Anson George, 1st Baron Anson 1697–1762. English admiral who sailed around the world 1740–44. In 1740 he commanded the squadron attacking the Spanish colonies and shipping in South America; he returned home by circumnavigating the world, with £500,000 of Spanish treasure; his chaplain recorded the events in *Voyage Round the World* 1748. He carried out reforms at the Admiralty.

Antheil George 1900–1959. US composer and pianist, the son of a Polish political exile. He is known for his *Ballet mécanique* 1926, scored for anvils, aeroplane propellers, electric bells, automobile horns, and pianos.

Anthony Susan B(rownell) 1820–1906. US pioneering feminist, who also worked for the anti-slavery and temperance movements. Her campaigns included demands for equality of pay for female teachers, the married women's property act, and women's suffrage. In 1869, with Elizabeth

Cady Stanton, she founded the National Woman Suffrage Association.

She edited and published a radical women's newspaper *The Revolution* 1868–70, and worked on the *History of Woman Suffrage* 1881–86. She organized the International Council of Women and founded the International Woman Suffrage Alliance in Berlin 1904.

Anthony of Padua, St 1195–1231. Portuguese Franciscan preacher who opposed the relaxations introduced into the order. Born in Lisbon, the son of a nobleman, he became an Augustinian monk, but in 1220 joined the Franciscans. He died in Padua, Italy, and was canonized in 1232. Like St Francis, he is said to have preached to animals.

Anthony, St *c.*251–356. Also known as Anthony of Thebes. Founder of Christian monasticism. Born in Egypt, at the age of 20 he renounced all his possessions and lived in a tomb, and at 35 sought further solitude on a mountain in the desert.

In 305 Anthony founded the first cenobitic order, or community of Christians following a rule of life under a superior. When he was about 100 he went to Alexandria and preached against the Arians (see ◊Arius). Anthony's temptations in the desert were a popular subject in art; he is also often depicted with a pig.

Antigonus 382–301 BC. A general of Alexander the Great, after whose death 323 he made himself master of Asia Minor. He was defeated and slain by ◊Seleucus I at the battle of Ipsus.

Antiochus four kings of Commagene (69 BC–AD 72), affiliated to the Seleucid dynasty, including:

Anthony Early American feminist Susan B Anthony. She founded the National Woman Suffrage Association in 1869 and edited a radical women's newspaper The Revolution.

Antiochus IV Epiphanes 1st century AD. King of Commagene, son of Antiochus III. He was made king in 38 by Caligula, who deposed him immediately. He was restored in 41 by Claudius, and reigned as an ally of Rome against Parthia. He was deposed on suspicion of treason in 72.

Antiochus I *c.*324–*c.*261 BC. King of Syria from 281 BC, son of Seleucus I, one of the generals of Alexander the Great. He earned the title of Antiochus Soter or Saviour by his defeat of the Gauls in Galatia 278 BC.

Antiochus II *c.*286–*c.*246 BC. King of Syria 261–246 BC, son of Antiochus I. He was known as Antiochus Theos, the Divine. During his reign the eastern provinces broke away from the Graeco-Macedonian rule and set up native princes. He made peace with Egypt by marrying the daughter of Ptolemy Philadelphus, but was a tyrant among his own people.

Antiochus III the Great *c.*241–187 BC. King of Syria from 223 BC, nephew of Antiochus II. He secured a loose suzerainty over Armenia and Parthia 209, overcame Bactria, received the homage of the Indian king of the Kabul valley, and returned by way of the Persian Gulf 204. He took possession of Palestine, entering Jerusalem 198. He crossed into NW Greece, but was decisively defeated by the Romans at Thermopylae 191 and at Magnesia 190. He had to abandon his domains in Anatolia, and perished at the hands of the people of Elymais.

Antiochus IV *c.*215–164 BC. King of Syria from 175 BC, known as Antiochus Epiphanes, the Illustrious; second son of Antiochus III. He occupied Jerusalem about 170 BC, seizing much of the Temple treasure, and instituted worship of the Greek type in the Temple in an attempt to eradicate Judaism. This produced the revolt of the Jewish people under the Maccabees, and Antiochus died before he could suppress it.

Antiochus XIII Asiaticus 1st century BC. King of Syria 69–65 BC, the last of the Seleucid dynasty. During his reign Syria was made a Roman province by Pompey the Great.

Antonello da Messina *c.*1430–1479. Italian painter, born in Messina, Sicily, a pioneer of the technique of oil painting, which he is said to have introduced to Italy from N Europe.

He visited Venice in the 1470s where his work inspired, among other Venetian painters, the young Giovanni Bellini. *St Jerome in his Study* about 1460 (National Gallery, London) and *A Young Man* 1478 (Staatliche Museen, West Berlin) are examples of his work.

Antonescu Ion 1882–1946. Romanian general and politician who headed a pro-German government during World War II and was executed for war crimes in 1946.

Antoninus Pius AD 86–161. Roman emperor who had been adopted 138 as Hadrian's heir, and succeeded him later that year. He enjoyed a prosperous reign, during which he built the Antonine Wall in Scotland. His daughter married ◊Marcus Aurelius Antoninus.

Antonioni Michelangelo 1912– . Italian film director, famous for his subtle analysis of neuroses and personal relationships of the leisured classes. His work includes *L'Avventura* 1960, *Blow Up* 1966, and *The Passenger* 1975.

Aouita Said 1960– . Moroccan runner. Outstanding at middle and long distances, he won the 1984 Olympic and 1987 World Championship 5000 metres title, and has set many world records.

In 1985 he held world records at both 1500 and 5000 metres, the first man for 30 years to hold both. He has since broken the 2 miles, 3000 metres and 2000 metres world records.

Aoun Michel 1935– . Lebanese soldier and Maronite Christian politician. As commander of the Lebanese army, in 1988 he was made president without Muslim support, his appointment precipitating a civil war between Christians and Muslims. His unwillingness to accept a 1989 Arab League sponsored peace agreement increased his isolation.

Born in Beirut, he joined the Lebanese army and rose to become, in 1984, its youngest commander. When, in 1988, the Christian and Muslim communities failed to agree on a Maronite successor to the outgoing president, Amin Gemayel (as required by the constitution) Gemayel unilaterally appointed Aoun. This precipitated the creation of a rival Muslim government, and, eventually, a civil war. Aoun, dedicated to freeing his country from Syrian domination, became isolated in the presidential palace and staunchly opposed the 1989 peace plan worked out by parliamentarians under the auspices of the Arab League.

Apelles 4th century BC. Greek painter, said to have been the greatest in antiquity. He was court painter to Philip of Macedonia and his son Alexander the Great. None of his work survives, only descriptions of his portraits and nude Venuses.

Apollinaire Guillaume. Pen name of Guillaume Apollinaire de Kostrowitsky 1880–1918. French poet of aristocratic Polish descent. He was a leader of the *avant garde* in Parisian literary and artistic circles. His novella *Le Poète assassiné/The Poet Assassinated* 1916, along with the experimental poems *Alcools/Alcohols* 1913 and *Calligrammes/Word Pictures* 1918, show him as a representative of the Cubist and Futurist movements.

Born in Rome and educated in Monaco, Apollinaire went to Paris in 1898. His work greatly influenced younger French writers, such as ◊Aragon. He coined the word 'surrealism' to describe his play *Les Mamelles de Tirésias/The Breasts of Tiresias* 1917.

Apollonius of Perga *c.260–c.190* BC. Greek mathematician, known as 'the Great Geometer'. In his work *Conics* he showed that a plane intersecting a cone will generate an ellipse, a parabola, or a hyperbola, depending on the angle of intersection. In astronomy, he used a system of circles called epicycles and deferents to explain the motion of the planets; this system, as refined by Ptolemy, was to survive until the Renaissance.

Apollonius of Rhodes *c.220–180* BC. Greek poet, author of the epic *Argonautica*, which tells the story of Jason and the Argonauts.

Appert Nicolas 1750–1841. French pioneer of food preservation by canning. He devised a system of sealing food in glass bottles and subjecting it to heat. His book *L'art de conserver les substances animales et végétales* appeared in 1810. Shortly after, others employed the same principles to iron or sheet steel containers plated with tin.

Appleton Edward Victor 1892–1965. British physicist, who worked at Cambridge under Ernest ◊Rutherford from 1920. He proved the existence of the Kennelly–Heaviside layer in the atmosphere, and the Appleton layer beyond it (both important in radio communication), and was involved in the initial work on the atomic bomb. He won a Nobel prize 1947.

Aquaviva Claudius (Claudio) 1543–1615. Fifth general of the Roman Catholic monastic order of Jesuits. Born in Naples, of noble family, he entered the order in 1567 and became its head in 1581. Under his rule they greatly increased in numbers, and the revolt of the Spanish Jesuits was put down. He published a treatise on education.

Aquinas St Thomas *c.1226–1274*. Neapolitan philosopher and theologian. His *Summa contra gentiles/Against the Errors of the Infidels* 1259–64 argues that reason and faith are compatible. His most significant contribution to philosophy was to synthesize the philosophy of Aristotle and Christian doctrine.

His unfinished *Summa Theologica*, begun 1265, deals with the nature of God, morality, and the work of Jesus. His works embodied the world view taught in universities up until the mid-17th century, and include scientific ideas derived from Aristotle. In 1879, they were recognized as the basis of Catholic theology by Pope Leo XIII, who had launched a modern edition of his works. He was a Dominican monk, known as the 'Angelic Doctor', and was canonized 1323.

Aquino (Maria) Corazón (born Cojuangco) 1933– . President of the Philippines from 1986, when she was instrumental in the nonviolent overthrow of President Marcos. She has sought to rule in a conciliatory manner, but has encountered opposition from left (communist guerrillas) and right (army coup attempts), and her land reforms have been seen as inadequate.

The daughter of a sugar baron, she studied

Aquino *President Corazón Aquino campaigning in Angeles City, Philippines, Jan 1987.*

in the USA and married the politician Benigno Aquino 1956. The chief political opponent of the right-wing president Marcos, he was assassinated by a military guard at Manila airport 1983. Corazón Aquino was drafted by the opposition to contest the Feb 1986 presidential election and claimed victory over Marcos, accusing the government of ballot-rigging. She led a nonviolent 'people's power' campaign which overthrew Marcos 25 Feb. A devout Roman Catholic, Aquino enjoyed strong church backing in her 1986 campaign.

Aquino Arafat Yasser 1929– . Palestinian nationalist politician, cofounder of al-Fatah 1956 and president of the Palestine Liberation Organization (PLO) from 1969. In the 1970s his activities in pursuit of an independent homeland for Palestinians made him a prominent figure in world politics, but in the 1980s the growth of factions within the PLO effectively reduced his power. He was forced to evacuate Lebanon 1983, but remained leader of most of the PLO.

Arago Dominique 1786–1853. French physicist and astronomer who made major contributions to the early study of electromagnetism. In 1820 he found out that iron enclosed in a wire coil could be magnetized by the passage of an electric current. Later in 1824 he was the first to observe the ability of a floating copper disc to deflect a magnetic needle, the phenomenon of magnetic rotation.

Aragon Louis 1897–1982. French poet and novelist. Beginning as a Dadaist, he became one of the leaders of Surrealism, published volumes of verse and in 1930 joined the Communist Party. Taken prisoner in World War II he escaped to join the Resistance, experiences reflected in the poetry of *Le Crève-coeur* 1942 and *Les Yeux d'Elsa* 1944.

Arafat *The leader of the Palestine Liberation Organization from 1969, Yasser Arafat.*

Aram Eugene 1704–1759. British murderer, the subject of works by the novelist Bulwer Lytton, the poet Thomas Hood, and others.

Arany János 1817–1882. Hungarian writer. His comic epic *The Lost Constitution* 1846 was followed in 1847 by *Toldi*, a product of the popular nationalist school. In 1864 his epic masterpiece *The Death of King Buda* appeared. During his last years Arany produced the rest of the *Toldi* trilogy, and his most personal lyrics.

Arbenz Guzmán Jácobo 1913–1971. Guatemalan social democratic politician and president from 1951 until his overthrow in 1954 by rebels operating with the help of the US Central Intelligence Agency.

Guzmán brought in policies to redistribute land, much of which was owned by overseas companies, to landless peasants and encouraged labour organization. He was exiled in Mexico, Uruguay, and Cuba until his death.

Arbuckle (Roscoe Conkling) 'Fatty' 1887–1933. Big-framed US silent-film comedian, also a writer and director. His successful career in such films as *The Butcher Boy* 1917 and *The Hayseed* 1919 ended in 1921 after a sex-murder scandal. Although acquitted, he was spurned by the public and his films banned.

Arbuthnot John 1667–1735. Scottish physician, attendant on Queen Anne 1705–14. He was a friend of Pope, Gray, and Swift, and was the chief author of the satiric *Memoirs of Martinus*

Scriblerus. He created the national character of John Bull, a prosperous farmer, in his *The History of John Bull* 1712, pamphlets advocating peace with France.

Arch Joseph 1826-1919. English Radical member of Parliament and trade unionist, founder of the National Agricultural Union (the first of its kind) 1872.

Joseph Arch started work at the age of nine, and travelled all over England for 40 years as an agricultural labourer. Appalled at the poor working conditions, he became politically active, first as a trade unionist and later as a Liberal-Labour MP for NW Norfolk.

Archer Frederick 1857-1886. English jockey. He rode 2,748 winners in 8,084 races 1870-86, including 21 classic winners.

He won the Derby five times, Oaks four times, St Leger six times, the Two Thousand Guineas four times, and the One Thousand Guineas twice. He rode 246 winners in the 1885 season, a record that stood until 1933. Archer shot himself in a fit of depression.

Archer Jeffrey 1940- . English writer and politician. A Conservative member of Parliament 1969-74, he lost a fortune in a disastrous investment, but recouped it as a best-selling novelist. Works include *Not a Penny More, Not a Penny Less* 1975 and *First Among Equals* 1984. In 1985 he became deputy chair of the Conservative Party but resigned Nov 1986 after a scandal involving an alleged payment to a prostitute.

Archimedes *c.*287-212 BC. Greek mathematician, who made important discoveries in geometry, hydrostatics, and mechanics. He formulated a law of fluid displacement (*Archimedes' principle*), and is credited with the invention of the *Archimedes screw*, a cylindrical device for raising water.

He was born at Syracuse in Sicily. It is alleged that Archimedes' principle was discovered when he stepped into the public bath and saw the water overflow. He used his discovery to prove that the goldsmith of the king of Syracuse had adulterated a gold crown with silver. The Archimedes screw is still used to raise water in the Nile delta. He designed engines of war for the defence of Syracuse, and was killed when the Romans besieged the town.

Archipenko Alexander 1887-1964. Russian-born abstract sculptor, who lived in France from 1908 and in the USA from 1923. He pioneered Cubist works composed of angular forms and spaces, and later experimented with clear plastic and sculptures incorporating lights.

Arden John 1930- . English playwright. His early plays *Serjeant Musgrave's Dance* 1959 and *The Workhouse Donkey* 1963 show the influence of Brecht. Subsequent works, often written in collaboration with his wife, Margaretta D'Arcy, show

increasing concern with the political situation in Northern Ireland and a dissatisfaction with the professional and subsidized theatre world.

Aretino Pietro 1492-1556. Italian writer, born in Arezzo. He earned his living, both in Rome and Venice, by publishing satirical pamphlets while under the protection of a highly placed family. His *Letters* 1537-57 are a unique record of the cultural and political events of his time, and illustrate his vivacious, exuberant character. He also wrote poems and comedies.

Argentina La Antonia Merce 1890-1936. Spanish dancer, choreographer and director. She took her artistic name from the land of her birth. She toured the world as a concert artist with Vicente Escudero and her techniques of castanet playing were revolutionary.

Argyll earls and dukes of Argyll line of Scottish peers who trace their descent to the Campbells of Lochow. The earldom dates from 1457. They include:

Argyll Archibald Campbell, 5th Earl of, 1530-1573. Adherent of the Scottish presbyterian, John ◊Knox. A supporter of Mary Queen of Scots from 1561 on her return from France, he commanded her forces during the days following her escape from Lochleven Castle in 1568. He revised his position and became Lord High Chancellor of Scotland in 157?

Arias Sanchez Oscar 1940-. Costa Rican politician, president from 1986, secretary-general of the left-wing National Liberation Party (PLN). He advocated a neutralist policy and in 1987 was the leading promoter of the Central American Peace Plan.

Ariosto Ludovico 1474-1533. Italian poet, born in Reggio. He wrote Latin poems and comedies on Classical lines, including the epic poem *Orlando Furioso* 1516, 1532.

Ariosto joined the household of Cardinal Ippolito d'Este 1503, and was frequently engaged in embassies and diplomacy for the Duke of Ferrara. In 1521 he became governor of a province in the Apennines, and after three years retired to Ferrara, where he died.

Aristarchus of Samos *c.*310-264 BC. Greek astronomer. The first to argue that the Earth moves round the Sun, he was ridiculed for his beliefs.

Aristides *c.*530-468 BC. Athenian politician. He was one of the ten Athenian generals at the battle of Marathon 490 BC and was elected chief archon, or magistrate. Later he came into conflict with the democratic leader Themistocles, and was exiled about 483 BC. He returned to fight against the Persians at Salamis 480 BC and in the following year commanded the Athenians at Plataea.

Aristippus *c.*435-356 BC. Greek philosopher, founder of the Cyrenaic or hedonist school. A pupil of Socrates, he developed the doctrine that pleasure is the only good in life. He lived at the court of ◊Dionysius of Syracuse, and then with his mistress Laïs, the courtesan, at Corinth.

Aristophanes c.448–380 BC. Greek dramatist. Of his 11 extant plays (of a total of over 40), the early comedies are remarkable for the violent satire with which he ridiculed the democratic war leaders. He also satirized contemporary issues such as the new learning of Socrates in *The Clouds* 423, and the power of women in *Lysistrata* 411. The chorus plays a prominent role, frequently giving the play its title, as in *The Wasps* 422, *The Birds* 414, and *The Frogs* 405.

Aristotle 384–322 BC. Greek philosopher, who advocated reason and moderation. Aristotle maintained that sense experience is our only source of knowledge, and that by reasoning we can discover the essences of things, that is, their distinguishing qualities. In his works on ethics and politics, Aristotle suggested that human happiness consists in living in conformity with nature. He derived his political theory from the recognition that mutual aid is natural to humankind, and refused to set up any one constitution as universally ideal. Of Aristotle's works some 22 treatises survive, dealing with logic, metaphysics, physics, astronomy, meteorology, biology, psychology, ethics, politics, and literary criticism.

Born in Stagira in Thrace, he studied in Athens, became tutor to ◊Alexander the Great, and in 335 opened a school in the Lyceum (grove sacred to Apollo) in Athens. It became known as the 'peripatetic school' because he walked up and down as he talked, and his works are a collection of his lecture notes. When Alexander died, Aristotle was forced to flee to Chalcis, where he died.

In the Middle Ages, Aristotle's philosophy first became the foundation of Islamic philosophy, and was then incorporated into Christian theology; medieval scholars tended to accept his vast output without question.

He is sometimes referred to as 'the Stagirite', after his birthplace.

Arius c.256–336. Egyptian priest whose ideas gave rise to Arianism, a Christian belief which denied the complete divinity of Jesus. He was condemned at the Council of Nicaea 325.

He was born in Libya, and became a priest of Alexandria 311. In 318 he was excommunicated and fled to Palestine, but his theology spread to such an extent that the emperor Constantine called a council at Nicaea to resolve the question. Arius and his adherents were banished, though later he was allowed to return.

Arkwright Richard 1732–1792. English inventor and manufacturing pioneer. He developed a machine for spinning cotton, the 'spinning frame' in Preston, Lancashire 1768. He installed steam power in his Nottingham works 1790.

Arkwright was born in Preston and experimented in machine-designing with a watchmaker, John Kay of Warrington, until, with Kay and John Smalley, he set up the 'spinning frame'. Soon afterwards he moved to Nottingham to escape the fury of the spinners, who feared that their handicraft skills would become redundant. In 1771 he went into partnership with Jedediah Strutt, a Derby man who had improved the stocking frame, and Samuel Need, and built a water-powered factory at Cromford in Derbyshire.

Arlen Michael. Adopted name of Dikran Kuyumjian 1895–1956. Bulgarian novelist of Armenian descent, who became a naturalized British subject 1922. His greatest success was the cynical *The Green Hat* 1924, the story of a *femme fatale*. He died in New York.

Arminius 17 BC–AD 21. German chieftain. An ex-soldier of the Roman army, he annihilated a Roman force led by Varus in the Teutoburger Forest area AD 9, and saved Germany from becoming a Roman province. He thus ensured that the empire's frontier did not extend beyond the Rhine.

Arminius Jacobus. Latinized name of Jakob Harmensen 1560–1609. Dutch Protestant priest who founded Arminianism, a school of Christian theology opposed to Calvin's doctrine of predestination. His views were developed by Simon Episcopius (1583–1643). Arminianism is the basis of Wesleyan Methodism in the UK.

Armstrong born Henry Jackson, nicknamed 'Homicide Hank'. 1912–1988. US boxer. He was the only man to hold world titles at three different weights simultaneously. Between May and Nov 1938 he held the featherweight, welterweight and lightweight titles. He retired in 1945 and became a Baptist minister.

Armstrong Edwin Howard 1890–1954. US radio engineer, who developed superheterodyne tuning for reception over a very wide spectrum of radio frequencies and frequency modulation (FM) for static-free reception.

Armstrong Louis ('Satchmo') 1901–1971. US jazz trumpet player and singer, born in New Orleans, the first solo jazz virtuoso. He is credited with the invention of scat singing (meaningless syllables chosen for their sound). His Chicago recordings in the 1920s with the Hot Five and Hot Seven made him known for his warm and pure trumpet tone, his improvisation and gravelly voice.

In 1923 Armstrong joined the Creole Jazz Band led by the cornet player Joe 'King' Oliver (1885–1938) in Chicago, but soon broke away and fronted various line-ups of his own. From the 1930s he became equally widely known as a singer and entertainer. In 1947 he formed the Louis Armstrong All Stars and gained wide popularity.

Armstrong Neil Alden 1930– . US astronaut. On 20 July 1969, he was the first person to set foot on the Moon, saying, 'That's one small step for a man, one giant leap for mankind.'

Born in Ohio, he gained his pilot's licence at 16, and served as a naval pilot in Korea 1949–52 before joining NASA as a test pilot. He was selected to be an astronaut in 1962.

Armstrong Robert, Baron Armstrong of Ilminster 1927–. British civil servant. After Oxford University he joined the civil service and rose rapidly to deputy-secretary rank. In 1970 he became Prime Minister Heath's principal private secretary; Thatcher later made him cabinet secretary and head of the home civil service. He achieved considerable attention as a witness in the 'Spycatcher' trial in Australia when he admitted to having been sometimes 'economical with the truth'. He retired in 1988 and was made a life peer.

Armstrong William George 1810–1900. English engineer, who developed a revolutionary method of making gun barrels 1855, by building a breech-loading artillery piece with a steel and wrought iron barrel (previous guns were muzzle loaded and had cast bronze barrels). By 1880 the 150 mm/16 in Armstrong gun was the standard for all British ordnance.

Arnauld French family closely associated with Jansenism, a Christian church movement in the 17th century. *Antoine Arnauld* (1560–1619) was a Paris advocate and pamphleteer, strongly critical of the Jesuits. Many of his 20 children were associated with the abbey of Port Royal, which became the centre of Jansenism. His youngest child, *Antoine* (1612–94), the 'great Arnauld', was religious director of the nuns there.

With the philosopher Pascal and others, the elder Antoine produced not only Jansenist pamphlets, but works on logic, grammar, and geometry. For years he had to live in hiding, and the last 16 years of his life were spent in Brussels. Port Royal was a convent of Cistercian nuns near Versailles where his second daughter, *Angélique* (1591–1661), became abbess through her father's influence at the age of 11. Later she served as prioress under her sister *Agnes* (1593–1671), and her niece, *La Mère Angélique* (1624–84), succeeded to both positions.

Arne Thomas Augustus 1710–1778. English composer, whose musical drama *Alfred* 1740 includes the song 'Rule Britannia!'.

Arnim Ludwig Achim von 1781–1831. German Romantic poet and novelist. Born in Berlin, he wrote short stories, a romance, *Gräfin Dolores/Countess Dolores* 1810, and plays, but left the historical novel *Die Kronenwächter* 1817 unfinished. With Clemens Brentano he

Armstrong *Seen here with fellow Apollo 11 crew-members Michael Collins and Edwin 'Buzz' Aldrin, Neil Armstrong was the first person to set foot on the Moon, on 20 July 1969.*

collected the German folk-songs in *Des Knaben Wunderhorn/The Boy's Magic Horn* 1805–08.

Arnold Benedict 1741–1801. US soldier and traitor to the American side in the War of American Independence. A merchant in New Haven, Connecticut, he joined the colonial forces but in 1780 plotted to betray the strategic post at West Point to the British. Maj André was sent by the British to discuss terms with him, but was caught and hanged as a spy. Arnold escaped to the British, who gave him an army command.

Arnold Edwin 1832–1904. English scholar and poet. He wrote the *Light of Asia* 1879, a rendering of the life and teaching of the Buddha in blank verse. *The Light of the World* 1891 retells the life of Jesus.

Arnold Malcolm (Henry) 1921– . English composer. His work is tonal and includes a large amount of orchestral, chamber, ballet, and vocal music. His operas include *The Dancing Master* 1951, and he has written music for more than 80 films, including *The Bridge on the River Kwai* 1957, for which he won an Academy Award.

Born in Northampton, he began his career as a trumpeter, becoming principal trumpet in the London Philharmonic Orchestra.

Arnold Matthew 1822–1888. English poet and critic, son of Thomas Arnold. His poems, characterized by their elegiac mood and pastoral themes, include *The Forsaken Merman* 1849, *Thyrsis* 1867 (commemorating his friend Arthur Hugh Clough), *Dover Beach* 1867 and *The Scholar Gypsy* 1853. Arnold's critical works include *Essays in Criticism* 1865 and 1888, and *Culture and Anarchy* 1869, which attacks 19th-century philistinism.

He was educated at public schools and Oxford University. After a short spell as an assistant master at Rugby, Arnold became a school inspector 1851–86. He published two unsuccessful volumes of anonymous poetry, but two further publications under his own name 1853 and 1855 led to his appointment as professor of poetry at Oxford. Arnold first used the word 'philistine' in its present sense in his attack on the cultural values of the middle classes.

Arnold Thomas 1795–1842. English schoolmaster, father of Matthew Arnold. Ordained in the Church of England 1818, he was headmaster of Rugby School 1828–42. His regime has been graphically described in Thomas Hughes' *Tom Brown's Schooldays* 1857. He emphasized training of character, and his influence on public school education was profound.

Arnold of Brescia 1100–1155. Italian Augustinian monk, who attacked the holding of property by the Catholic church; he was hanged and burned, and his ashes were thrown into the Tiber.

Arp Hans or Jean 1887–1966. French abstract painter and sculptor. He was one of the founders of Dada about 1917, and later associated with the Surrealists. His innovative wood sculptures use organic shapes in bright colours.

In his early experimental works, such as collages, he collaborated with his wife **Sophie Taeuber-Arp** (1889–1943).

Arrau Claudio 1903– . Chilean pianist. A concert performer since the age of five, he excels in 19th-century music, and is known for his thoughtful interpretation.

Arrhenius Svante August 1859–1927. Swedish scientist, the founder of physical chemistry. Born near Uppsala, he became a professor at Stockholm in 1895, and made a special study of electrolysis. He wrote *Worlds in the Making* and *Destinies of the Stars*, and in 1903 received the Nobel Prize for Chemistry.

Artaud Antonin 1896–1948. French theatre director. Although his play, *Les Cenci/The Cenci* 1935, was a failure, his concept of the *Theatre of Cruelty*, intended to release feelings usually repressed in the unconscious, has been an important influence on modern dramatists such as Camus and Genet and on directors and producers. Declared insane 1936, Artaud was confined in an asylum.

Arthur 6th century AD . Legendary English 'king' and hero in stories of the legendary castle Camelot and the quest for the Holy Grail. Arthur is said to have been born at Tintagel and buried at Glastonbury. He may have been a Romano-British leader against pagan Saxon invaders.

The legends of Arthur and the knights of the Round Table (so shaped to avoid strife over precedence) was developed in the 12th century by Geoffrey of Monmouth and the Norman writer Wace. Later writers on the theme include the anonymous author of *Sir Gawayne and the Greene Knight* 1346, Sir Thomas Malory, Tennyson, T H White, and Mark Twain.

Arthur Chester Alan 1830–1886. 21st president of the USA. He was born in Vermont, son of a Baptist minister, and became a lawyer and Republican political appointee in New York. In 1880, Arthur was chosen as ◊Garfield's vice president, and was his successor when Garfield was assassinated the following year. Arthur held office until 1885.

Arthur Duke of Brittany 1187–1203. Grandson of Henry II of England and nephew of King ◊John, who is supposed to have had him murdered, 13 Apr 1203, as a rival for the crown.

Arthur Prince of Wales 1486–1502. Eldest son of Henry VII of England. He married ◊Catherine of Aragon 1501, when he was 16 and she was 15, but died the next year.

Arundel Thomas Howard, 2nd Earl of Arundel 1586–1646. English politician and patron of the arts. The Arundel Marbles, part of his collection of Italian sculptures, were given to Oxford University in 1667 by his grandson.

Ascham Roger *c.*1515–1568. English scholar and royal tutor, author of *The Scholemaster* 1570 on the art of education.

After writing a treatise on archery, King Henry VIII's favourite sport, Ascham was appointed tutor to Princess Elizabeth in 1548. He retained favour under Edward VI and Queen Mary (despite his Protestant views), and returned to Elizabeth's service as her secretary after she became queen.

Ashbee C(harles) R(obert) 1863–1942. British designer, architect, and writer, one of the major figures of the Arts and Crafts movement. He founded a 'Guild and School of Handicraft' in the East End of London in 1888, but later modified his views, accepting the importance of machinery and design for industry.

Ashbery John 1927– . US poet and art critic. His collections of poetry, including *Self-Portrait in a Convex Mirror* 1975 , which won a Pulitzer prize, are distinguished by their strong visual element and narrative power.

Ashcroft Peggy 1907– . English actress. Her many leading roles include Desdemona in *Othello* (with Paul Robeson), Juliet in *Romeo and Juliet* 1935 (with Laurence Olivier and John Gielgud), and appearances in the British TV play *Caught on a Train* 1980 (BAFTA award), the series *The Jewel in the Crown* 1984, and the film *A Passage to India* 1985.

Ashdown (Jeremy John Durham) 'Paddy' 1941–. British politician. Originally a Liberal MP, he became leader of the Social and Liberal Democrats 1988. He served in the Royal Marines as a commando, leading a Special Boat Section in Borneo, and was a member of the Diplomatic Service 1971–76.

Ashford Daisy 1881–1972. English author of *The Young Visiters* 1919, a classic of unconscious humour written when she was nine.

Ashkenazy Vladimir 1937– . Soviet-born pianist and conductor. After studying in Moscow, he toured the USA in 1958. He settled in England in 1963 and moved to Iceland in 1968. He excels in Rachmaninov, Prokofiev, and Liszt.

In 1962 he was joint winner of the Tchaikovsky Competition with John Ogdon. He was musical director of the Royal Philharmonic, London, from 1987. His keyboard technique differs slightly from standard Western technique.

Ashley Laura (born Mountney) 1925–1985. Welsh designer, who established and gave her name to a Neo-Victorian country style in clothes and furnishings beginning in 1953. She started an international chain of shops.

Ashmole Elias 1617–1692. English antiquary, whose collection forms the basis of the Ashmolean Museum, Oxford.

He wrote books on alchemy and on antiquarian subjects, and amassed a fine library and a collection of curiosities, both of which he presented to Oxford University 1682. His collection was housed in the 'Old Ashmolean' (built 1679–83); the present Ashmolean Museum was erected 1897.

Ashton Frederick 1904–1988. British dancer and choreographer. He studied with Léoide Massine and Marie Rambert before joining the Vic-Wells Ballet 1935 as chief choreographer, creating several roles for Margot Fonteyn. He was director of the Royal Ballet, London, 1963–70.

His major works include *Façade* 1931, *Cinderella* 1948, *La Fille mal gardée* 1960, *Marguerite and Armand* – for Fonteyn and Nureyev – 1963, and *A Month in the Country* 1976. He contributed much to the popularity of ballet in the mid-20th century.

Asimov Isaac 1920– . US science-fiction writer and writer on science, born in the USSR. He has published about 200 books, and is possibly best known for his *I, Robot* 1950 and the 'Foundation' trilogy 1951–53, continued in *Foundation's Edge* 1983.

Asoka reigned 264–228 BC. Indian emperor, who was a Buddhist convert. He had edicts enjoining the adoption of his new faith carved on pillars and rock faces throughout his dominions, and many survive. In Patna there are the remains of a hall built by him.

Aspasia *c.*440 BC. Greek courtesan, the mistress of the Athenian politician ◊Pericles. As a 'foreigner' from Miletus, she could not be recognized as his wife, but their son was later legitimized. The philosopher Socrates visited her salon, a meeting place for the celebrities of Athens. Her free thinking led to a charge of impiety, from which Pericles had to defend her.

Asplund (Erik) Gunnar 1885–1940. Swedish architect. His early work, for example at the Stockholm South Cemetery 1914, was in the Neo-Classical tradition. Later buildings, such as the Stockholm City Library 1924–27 and Gothenburg City Hall 1934–37, developed a refined Modern-Classical style, culminating in the Stockholm South Cemetery Crematorium 1935–40.

Asquith H(erbert) H(enry), 1st Earl of Oxford and Asquith 1852–1928. British Liberal politician, prime minister 1908–16. As chancellor of the Exchequer he introduced old-age pensions 1908. He limited the powers of the House of Lords and attempted to give Ireland Home Rule.

Asquith was born in Yorkshire. Elected member of Parliament 1886, he was home secretary in Gladstone's 1892–95 government. He was chancellor of the Exchequer 1905–08 and succeeded Campbell-Bannerman as prime minister. Forcing through the radical budget of his chancellor (Lloyd George) led him into two elections 1910, which resulted in the Parliament Act 1911, limiting the right of the Lords to veto legislation. His endeavours to pass the Home Rule for Ireland Bill led to the Curragh 'mutiny' and incipient civil war. Unity

was re-established by the outbreak of World War
I, and a coalition government was formed May
1915. However, his attitude of 'wait and see' was
not adapted to all-out war, and in Dec 1916 he was
replaced by Lloyd George. In 1918 the Liberal
election defeat led to the eclipse of the party.

Asquith Cynthia 1887–1960. British author, born
Charteris. She married Herbert, second son of H
H Asquith, and wrote a diary of the World War I
years.

Assad Hafez al 1930–   . Syrian Ba'athist politician.
He became prime minister after a bloodless military coup 1970, and in 1971 was the first president
of Syria to be elected by popular vote. He was
re-elected 1978. He is a Shia (Alawite) Muslim.

Astaire Fred. Stage name of Frederick Austerlitz 1899–1987. US dancer, actor, singer, and
choreographer, who starred in numerous films,
including *Top Hat* 1935, *Easter Parade* 1948, and
Funny Face 1957, many of which contained inventive sequences he designed himself. He made ten
classic films with the most popular of his dancing partners, Ginger Rogers. He later played
straight dramatic roles, in films such as *On the
Beach* 1959.

Born in Omaha, Nebraska, he danced in partnership with his sister Adele (1898–1981) from
1904 until her marriage in 1932. He entered films
in 1933. Among his many other films are *Roberta*
1935 and *Follow the Fleet* 1936. Astaire was a
virtuoso dancer and perfectionist known for his
elegant style.

Aston Francis William 1877–1945. English physicist, who developed the mass spectrometer, which
separates isotopes (atoms of the same element
but of different masses) by projecting their ions
(charged atoms) through a magnetic field.

From 1910, he worked in the Cavendish Laboratory, Cambridge. He published *Isotopes*, and
received the Nobel Prize for Chemistry 1922.
His researches were of the utmost value in the
development of atomic theory.

Astor prominent US and British family. *John Jacob
Astor* (1763–1848) was a US millionaire. *Wal-
dorf Astor*, 2nd Viscount Astor (1879–-1952),
was Conservative member of Parliament for
Plymouth 1910–19, when he succeeded to the
peerage. He was chief proprietor of the British *Observer* newspaper. His wife was Nancy
Witcher Langhorne (1879–1964) *Lady Astor*,
the first woman member of Parliament to take
a seat in the House of Commons 1919, when
she succeeded her husband for the constituency
of Plymouth. She was also a temperance fanatic
and political hostess. Government policy was
said to be decided at Cliveden, their country
home.

Astor Mary. Stage name of Lucille Langhanke
1906–1987. US film actress, whose many films
included *Don Juan* 1926 and *The Maltese Falcon*

Astaire *Stylish American dancer Fred Astaire and his
most frequent partner, Ginger Rogers.*

1941. Her memoirs *My Story* 1959 were notorious
for their frankness.

Asturias Miguel Ángel 1899–1974. Guatemalan
author and diplomat. He published poetry,
Guatemalan legends, and novels, such as *El
Señor Presidente/The President* 1946, *Men of
Corn* 1949, and *Strong Wind* 1950, attacking
Latin-American dictatorships and 'Yankee imperi-
alism'. Nobel prize 1967.

Atahualpa *c.*1502–1533. Last emperor of the Incas
of Peru. He was taken prisoner 1532 when the
Spaniards arrived, and agreed to pay a huge ransom, but was accused of plotting against the conquistador Pizarro and sentenced to be burned. On
his consenting to Christian baptism, the sentence
was commuted to strangulation.

Atatürk Kemal. Name assumed 1934 by Mustafa
Kemal Pasha 1881–1938. Turkish politician and
general, first president of Turkey from 1923.
After World War I he established a provisional
rebel government and in 1921–22 the Turkish
armies under his leadership expelled the Greeks
who were occupying Turkey. He is the founder
of the modern republic, which he ruled as virtual
dictator, with a policy of consistent and radical
westernization.

Kemal, born in Thessaloniki, was banished 1904
for joining a revolutionary society. Later he was
pardoned and promoted in the army, and was

largely responsible for the successful defence of the Dardanelles against the British 1915. In 1918, after Turkey had been defeated, he was sent into Anatolia to carry through the demobilization of the Turkish forces in accordance with the armistice terms, but instead established a provisional government opposed to that of Constantinople (under Allied control), and in 1921 led the Turkish armies against the Greeks, who had occupied a large part of Anatolia. He checked them at the Battle of the Sakaria, 23 Aug–13 Sept 1921, for which he was granted the title of Ghazi (the Victorious), and within a year had expelled the Greeks from Turkish soil. War with the British was averted by his diplomacy and Turkey in Europe passed under Kemal's control. On 29 Oct 1923, Turkey was proclaimed a republic with Kemal as first president.

Atget Eugène 1857–1927. French photographer. He took up photography at the age of 40, and for 30 years documented urban Paris, leaving some 10,000 photos.

Athanasius, St 298–373. Christian bishop of Alexandria, supporter of the doctrines of the Trinity and incarnation. He was a disciple of St Anthony the hermit, and an opponent of Arianism (see ◊Arius) in the great Arian controversy. Arianism was officially condemned at the Council of Nicaea 325, and Athanasius was appointed bishop of Alexandria 328. The Athanasian creed was not actually written by him, although it reflects his views.

Banished 335 by the emperor Constantine because of his intransigence towards the defeated Arians, in 346 he was recalled but suffered three more banishments before his final reinstatement about 366.

Athelstan c.895–939. King of the Mercians and West Saxons. Son of Edward the Elder and grandson of Alfred the Great, he was crowned king 925 at Kingston-upon-Thames. He subdued parts of Cornwall and Wales, and in 937 defeated the Welsh, Scots, and Danes at Brunanburh.

Attenborough David 1926– . English traveller and zoologist, brother of Richard Attenborough. He was director of programmes for BBC television 1969–72, and commentator in the television series *Life on Earth* 1979 and *The Living Planet* 1983. He was knighted 1985.

Attenborough Richard 1923– . English film actor and director. His films include *Brighton Rock* 1947 and *10 Rillington Place* 1970 (as actor), and *Oh! What a Lovely War* 1968, *Gandhi* 1982, and *Cry Freedom* 1987 (as director).

Atterbury Francis 1662–1732. English bishop and Jacobite politician. In 1687 he was appointed a royal chaplain by William III. Under Queen Anne he received rapid promotion, becoming bishop of Rochester 1713. His Jacobite sympathies prevented his further rise, and in 1722 he was sent to the Tower of London and subsequently banished. He was a friend of the writers Pope and Swift.

Attila c.406–453. King of the Huns from 434, called the 'Scourge of God'. He embarked on a career of vast conquests ranging from the Rhine to Persia. In 451 he invaded Gaul, but was defeated on the Catalaunian Fields near Troyes, France, by the Roman and Visigothic armies under Aëtius (died 454) and Theodoric I. In 452 he led his Huns into Italy and only the personal intervention of Pope Leo I prevented the sacking of Rome.

He returned to Pannonia, west of the Danube, and died on the night of his marriage with Ildico, poison being suspected as the cause. He was said to have been buried with a vast treasure.

Attlee Clement (Richard), 1st Earl 1883–1967. British Labour politician. In the coalition government during World War II he was Lord Privy Seal 1940–42, dominions secretary 1942–43, and Lord President of the Council 1943–45, as well as deputy prime minister from 1942. As prime minister 1945–51 he introduced a sweeping programme of nationalization and a whole new system of social services.

Attlee was educated at Oxford and practised at the Bar 1906–09. Social work in London's East End and cooperation in poor-law reform led him to become a socialist; he joined the Fabian Society and the Independent Labour Party 1908. He became lecturer in social science at the London School of Economics 1913. After service in World War I he was mayor of Stepney, E London, 1919–20; Labour member of Parliament for Limehouse 1922–50 and for W Walthamstow 1950–55.

In the first and second Labour governments he was undersecretary for war 1924 and chancellor of the Duchy of Lancaster and postmaster general 1929–31. In 1935 he became leader of the opposition. In July 1945 he became prime minister after a Labour landslide in the general election. The government was returned to power with a much reduced majority 1950 and was defeated 1951. In 1955 he accepted an earldom on retirement as leader of the opposition.

Attwell Mabel Lucie 1879–1964. British artist, illustrator of many books for children, including her own stories and verse.

Atwood Margaret (Eleanor) 1939– . Canadian novelist, short-story writer, and poet. Her novels, which often treat feminist themes with wit and irony, include *The Edible Woman* 1969, *Life Before Man* 1979, *Bodily Harm* 1981, *The Handmaid's Tale* 1986, and *Cat's Eye* 1989. Collections of poetry include *Power Politics* 1971, *You are Happy* 1974, and *Interlunar*.

Auber Daniel François Esprit 1782–1871. French operatic composer who studied under the Italian composer and teacher Luigi Cherubini. He wrote about 50 operas, including *La Muette de Portici/The Mute Girl of Portici* 1828 and the comic opera *Fra Diavolo* 1830.

Atwood Canadian novelist and poet Margaret Atwood.

Aubrey John 1626–1697. English antiquary. His *Brief Lives* 1898 (edited by A Clark) contains gossip and anecdotes on celebrities of his time. Aubrey was the first to claim Stonehenge as a Druid temple.

Aubrey was born in Wiltshire. He studied law but became dependent on patrons, including the antiquary Ashmole and the philosopher Hobbes. He published *Miscellanies* 1696 of folklore and ghost stories. *Lives of Eminent Men* appeared 1813 and *Remaines of Gentilisme and Judaisme* 1881. His observations on the natural history of Surrey and Wiltshire were also posthumously published.

Auchinleck Claude John Eyre 1884–1981. British commander in World War II. He won the First Battle of El Alamein 1942 in N Egypt. In 1943 he became commander in chief of India and founded the modern Indian and Pakistani armies.

Auckland George Eden, 1st Earl of Auckland 1784–1849. British Tory politician for whom Auckland, New Zealand, is named. He became a Member of Parliament 1810, and 1835–41 was governor general of India.

Auden W(ystan) H(ugh) 1907–1973. English poet. He wrote some of his most original poetry, such as *Look, Stranger!* 1936, in the 1930s when he led the influential left-wing literary group that included MacNeice, Spender, and Day Lewis. He moved to the USA 1939, became a citizen 1946, and adopted a more conservative and Christian viewpoint, such as in *The Age of Anxiety* 1947.

Born in York, Auden was associate professor of English literature at the University of Michigan from 1939, and professor of poetry at Oxford 1956–61. He also wrote verse dramas with ◊Isherwood such as *The Dog Beneath the Skin* and *The Ascent of F6* 1951 and opera librettos, notably for Stravinsky's *The Rake's Progress* 1951.

Audubon John James 1785–1851. US naturalist. In 1827, he published the first part of his *Birds of*

North America, with a remarkable series of colour plates. Later, he produced a similar work on North American quadrupeds.

He was born in Santo Domingo (now Haiti) and educated in Paris. The National Audubon Society (originating 1886) has branches throughout the USA and Canada for the study and protection of birds.

Auerbach Frank Helmuth 1931– . British artist, whose portraits and landscapes blend figurative and abstract work.

Augier Émile 1820–1889. French dramatist. He wrote *Le Gendre de M Poirier* 1854, in collaboration with Jules Sandeau, a realistic delineation of bourgeois society.

Augustin Eugène 1791–1861. French dramatist, the originator and exponent of the 'well-made' plays, which achieved success but were subsequently forgotten. He wrote *Une Nuit de la Garde Nationale* 1815.

Augustine of Hippo, St 354–430. One of the early Christian leaders and writers known as the Fathers of the Church. He was converted to Christianity by Ambrose in Milan and became bishop of Hippo (modern Annaba, Algeria) 396. Among Augustine's many writings are his *Confessions*, a spiritual autobiography, and the influential *De Civitate Dei/The City of God* vindicating the Christian church and divine providence in 22 books.

Born in Tagaste, Numidia (modern Algeria), of Roman descent, he studied rhetoric in Carthage where he became the father of an illegitimate son, Adeodatus. He lectured in Tagaste and Carthage and for ten years was attached to the Manichaeist belief. In 383 he went to Rome, and on moving to Milan came under the influence of Ambrose. After prolonged study of neo-Platonism he was baptized by Ambrose together with his son. Resigning his chair in rhetoric, he returned to Africa, his mother, St Monica, dying in Ostia on the journey, and settled in Tagaste. His son died at 17. In 391, while visiting Hippo, Augustine was ordained priest. In 395 he was given the right of succession to the bishopric of Hippo and died there during its siege by the Vandals.

Many of Augustine's books resulted from his share in three great controversies: he refuted Manichaeism; attacked and did much to eliminate the exclusive N African Donatist sect at the conference of Carthage 411; and devoted the last 20 years of his life to refute ◊Pelagius, maintaining the doctrine of original sin and the necessity of divine grace. He estimated the number of his works at 230, and also wrote many sermons, as well as pastoral letters.

Augustus 63 BC–AD 14. Title of Octavian (Gaius Julius Caesar Octavianus), first of the Roman emperors. He joined forces with Mark Antony

Augustus *Great-nephew of Julius Caesar, the 'venerable' Augustus was the first Roman emperor. He was a ruler of great administrative ability and initative, and his reign marks the golden age of Roman literature.*

and Lepidus in the Second Triumvirate. Following Mark Antony's liaison with the Egyptian Queeen Cleopatra, Augustus defeated her troops at Actium 31 BC. As emperor (from 27 BC) he reformed the government of the empire, the army, and Rome's public services, and was a patron of the arts. The period of his rule is known as the Augustan Age.

He was the son of a senator who married a niece of Julius Caesar, and he became his great-uncle's adopted son and principal heir. Following Caesar's murder, Octavian formed with Mark Antony and Lepidus the Triumvirate that divided the Roman world between them and proceeded to eliminate the opposition. Antony's victory 42 BC over Brutus and Cassius had brought the republic to an end. Antony then fell in love with Cleopatra and spent most of his time at Alexandria, while Octavian consolidated his hold on the western part of the Roman dominion. War was declared against Cleopatra, and the naval victory at Actium left Octavian in unchallenged supremacy, since Lepidus had been forced to retire.

After his return to Rome 29 BC, Octavian was created *princeps senatus*, and in 27 BC he was given the title of Augustus ('venerable'). He then resigned his extraordinary powers and received

from the Senate, in return, the proconsular command, which gave him control of the army, and the tribunician power, whereby he could initiate or veto legislation. In his programme of reforms Augustus received the support of three loyal and capable helpers, Agrippa, Maecenas, and his wife, Livia, while Virgil and Horace acted as the poets laureate of the new regime.

Under Augustus the empire's frontiers were secured. The provinces were governed either by imperial legates responsible to the *princeps* or by proconsuls appointed by the Senate. The army was made a profession, with fixed pay and length of service, and a permanent fleet was established. Finally, Rome itself received an adequate water supply, a fire brigade, a police force, and a large number of public buildings.

The years after 12 BC were marked by private and public calamities: the marriage of Augustus' daughter Julia to his stepson Tiberius proved disastrous; a serious revolt occurred in Pannonia AD 6; and in Germany three legions under Varus were annihilated in the Teutoburg Forest AD 9. Augustus died a broken man, but his work remained secure.

Aung San 1914–1947. Burmese politician. As leader of the Anti-Fascist People's Freedom League he became vice president of the executive council Sept 1946. During World War II he had collaborated first with Japan and then with the UK.

Imprisoned for his nationalist activities while a student in Rangoon, Aung escaped to Japan 1940. He returned to lead the Burma Independence Army, which assisted the Japanese invasion 1942, and became defence minister in the puppet government set up. Before long, however, he secretly contacted the Resistance movement, and from Mar 1945 openly cooperated with the British in the expulsion of the Japanese. He was assassinated by political opponents July 1947.

Aurangzeb or *Aurungzebe* 1618–1707. Mughal emperor of N India from 1658. Third son of Shah Jehan, he made himself master of the court by a palace revolution. His reign was the most brilliant period of the Mughal dynasty, but by despotic tendencies and Muslim fanaticism he aroused much opposition. His latter years were spent in war with the princes of Rajputana and Mahrattas.

Aurelian (Lucius Domitius Aurelianus) c. AD 214–275. Roman emperor from 270. A successful soldier, he was chosen emperor by his troops on the death of Claudius II. He defeated the Goths and Vandals, defeated and captured ◊Zenobia of Palmyra, and was planning a campaign against Parthia when he was murdered.

Auric Georges 1899–1983. French composer. He was one of the musical group called *Les Six*. Auric composed a comic opera, several ballets, and incidental music to films of Jaques Cocteau.

Auriol Vincent 1884–1966. French socialist politician. He was president of the two Constituent

Austen Jane Austen, based on a drawing by her sister Cassandra. Her work appeared anonymously in her lifetime, and she received very little recognition or payment for it, but she has since become one of the most popular English novelists.

Assemblies of 1946 and first president of the Fourth Republic 1947–54.

Austen Jane 1775–1817. English novelist, noted for her domestic novels of manners. All her novels are set within the confines of middle-class provincial society, and show her skill at drawing characters and situations with delicate irony. These include *Sense and Sensibility* 1811, *Pride and Prejudice* 1813, *Mansfield Park* 1814, *Emma* 1816, and published posthumously, *Persuasion* 1817 and *Northanger Abbey* 1818.

She was born at Steventon, Hampshire, where her father was rector, and began writing early; the burlesque *Love and Freindship* (sic), published 1922, was written 1790. In 1801 the family moved to Bath, and, after the death of her father 1805, to Southampton, finally settling in Chawton, Hampshire with her brother Edward.

Between 1795 and 1798 she worked on three novels. The first to be published (like its successors, anonymously) was *Sense and Sensibility* (drafted in letter form 1797–98). *Pride and Prejudice* (written 1796–97) followed, but *Northanger Abbey*, a skit on the contemporary Gothic novel (written 1798, sold to a London publisher 1803, and bought back 1816), did not appear until 1818. The fragmentary *Watsons* and *Lady Susan* written about 1803–05 remained unfinished. The success of her published works, however, stimulated Jane Austen to write in rapid succession *Mansfield Park*, *Emma*, *Persuasion*, and the final fragment

Sanditon written 1817. She died in Winchester, and is buried in the cathedral.

Auster Paul 1947–. US novelist. His experimental use of detective story techniques to explore modern urban identity is exemplified in his *New York Trilogy: City of Glass* 1985, *Ghosts* 1986, and *The Locked Room* 1986.

Austin Alfred 1835–1913. British poet. He made his name with the satirical poem *The Season* 1861, which was followed by plays and volumes of poetry little read today; from 1896 he was Poet Laureate.

Austin Herbert, 1st Baron Austin 1866–1941. English industrialist, who began manufacturing cars 1905 at Northfield, Birmingham, notably the 'Austin Seven' 1921.

Austin J(ohn) L(angshaw) 1911–1960. British philosopher. Influential in later work on the philosophy of language, Austin was a pioneer in the investigation of the way words are used in everyday speech. His lectures *Sense and Sensibilia* and *How to do Things with Words* were published posthumously in 1962.

Avebury John Lubbock, 1st Baron Avebury 1834–1913. British banker. A Liberal (from 1886 Liberal Unionist) member of Parliament 1870–1900, he was largely responsible for the Bank Holidays Act 1871 introducing statutory public holidays.

Avedon Richard 1923– . US photographer. A fashion photographer with *Harper's Bazaar* magazine in New York in the mid-1940s, he later became one of the highest-paid commercial photographers.

Averroes (Arabic **Ibn Rushd**) 1126–1198. Arabian philosopher, who argued for the eternity of matter, and denied the immortality of the individual soul. His philosophical writings, including commentaries on Aristotle and Plato's *Republic*, became known to the West through Latin translations. He influenced Christian and Jewish writers, and reconciled Islamic and Greek thought.

Born in Córdoba, Spain, he was trained in medicine, and became physician to the caliph as well as judge of Seville and Córdoba. He was accused of heresy by the Islamic authorities and banished 1195. Later he was recalled, and died in Marrakesh.

Avery 'Tex' (Frederick Bean) 1907–1980. US cartoon-film director who used violent, sometimes surreal humour. At Warner Brothers he helped develop the characters Bugs Bunny and Daffy Duck before moving to MGM in 1942 where he created, among others, Droopy and Screwball Squirrel.

Avicenna (Arabic **Ibn Sina**) 979–1037. Arabian philosopher and physician, who studied the Koran, philosophy, and the science of his day. His *Canon Medicinae* was a standard work for centuries. His philosophical writings were influenced by al-Farabi, Aristotle, and the Neo-Platonists, and influenced the scholastics of the 13th century.

Avogadro Amedeo Conte di Quaregna 1776–1856. Italian physicist. His work on gases still has relevance for modern atomic studies.

Axelrod Julius 1912–. US neuropharmacologist, who shared the 1970 Nobel Prize for Medicine with the biophysicists Bernard Katz and Ulf von Euler for his work on neurotransmitters (the chemical messengers of the brain).

Axelrod wanted to know why the messengers, once transmitted, ever stopped operating. Through his studies he found a number of specific enzymes that rapidly degraded the neurotransmitters.

Ayckbourn Alan 1939– . English playwright. His prolific output, characterized by his acute ear for comic dialogue, includes *Absurd Person Singular* 1973, the trilogy *The Norman Conquests* 1974, *A Woman in Mind* 1986, *A Small Family Business* 1987, *Man of the Moment* 1988, and scripts for television.

Ayer A(lfred) J(ules) 1910–1989. English philosopher. He wrote *Language, Truth and Logic* 1936, an exposition of the theory of 'logical positivism', presenting a criterion by which meaningful statements (essentially truths of logic, as well as statements derived from experience) could be distinguished from meaningless metaphysical utterances (for example, claims that there is a God, or that the world external to our own minds is illusory).

He was Wykeham professor of logic at Oxford 1959–78. Later works included *Probability and Evidence* 1972 and *Philosophy in the Twentieth Century* 1982.

Ayesha 611–678. Third and favourite wife of the prophet Muhammad, who married her when she was nine. Her father, Abu Bakr, became caliph on Muhammad's death 632, and she bitterly opposed the later succession to the caliphate of Ali, who had once accused her of infidelity.

Ayrton Michael 1921–1975. British painter, sculptor, illustrator, and writer. From 1961, Ayrton developed an obsession with the Daedalus myth, producing bronzes of Icarus and a fictional autobiography of Daedalus, *The Maze Maker* 1967.

Aytoun Robert 1570–1638. Scottish poet employed and knighted by James I; he was noted for his love poems. Aytoun is the reputed author of the lines on which Robert Burns based 'Auld Lang Syne'.

Aytoun William Edmonstoune 1813–1865. Scottish poet, born in Edinburgh, chiefly remembered for his *Lays of the Scottish Cavaliers* 1848, and for the *Bon Gaultier Ballads* 1855, which he wrote in collaboration with Sir Theodore Martin.

Azaña Manuel 1880–1940. Spanish politician and first prime minister 1931–33 of the second Spanish republic. He was last president of the republic during the civil war 1936–39, before the establishment of a dictatorship under Francisco Franco.

Azorín. Pen name of José Martínez Ruiz 1873–1967. Spanish writer. His works include volumes of critical essays and short stories, plays and novels, such as the autobiographical *La voluntad/The Choice* 1902 and *Antonio Azorín* 1903 – the author adopted the name of the eponymous hero of the latter as his pen name.

Baade Walter 1893–1960. US astronomer, who made observations that doubled the distance scale and the age of the universe. Born in Germany, during World War II Baade worked at Mount Wilson observatory (USA), where he discovered that stars are in two distinct populations according to their age, known as Population I (the youngest) and Population II (the oldest). Later, he found that Cepheid variable stars of Population I are brighter than had been supposed, and that distances calculated from them were wrong.

Baader Andreas 1943–1977. West German extreme left-wing guerrilla. A former left-wing student activist, he formed, with Ulrike ◊Meinhof, the Red Army Faction, an underground urban guerrilla organization that carried out a succession of terrorist acts in West Germany during the 1970s. Sentenced to life imprisonment in Apr 1977, he took his own life in Oct 1977, following the failure of the Faction's hostage-swap attempt at Mogadishu airport.

Bab Mirza Ali Mohammad 1819–1850. Persian religious leader, born in Shiraz, founder of Babism, an offshoot of Islam. In 1844 he proclaimed that he was a gateway to the Hidden Imam, a new messenger of Allah who was to come. He gained a large following whose activities caused the Persian authorities to fear a rebellion, and who were therefore persecuted. Bab was executed for heresy.

Babangida Ibrahim 1941– . Nigerian politician and soldier. After training in the UK and the USA, he became head of the Nigerian army in 1983 and in 1985 led a coup against President Buhari, assuming the presidency himself.

Born in Minna, Niger state, he trained at military schools in Nigeria and the UK. He became an instructor in the Nigerian Defence Academy and by 1983 had reached the rank of major-general. In 1983, after taking part in the overthrow of

President Shehu Shagari, he was made army commander-in-chief.

Babbage Charles 1792–1871. English mathematician credited with being the inventor of the computer. He designed an 'analytical engine', a general-purpose mechanical computing device for performing different calculations according to a program input on punched cards (an idea borrowed from the Jacquard loom). This device was never built, but it embodied many of the principles on which modern digital computers are based.

As a young man Babbage assisted John Herschel with his astronomical calculations. He became involved with calculating machines when he worked on his mechanical 'difference' engine for the British Admiralty, though this was never completed.

Babbitt Milton 1916– . US composer. After studying with Roger ◊Sessions he developed a personal style of serialism influenced by jazz. He became leading composer of electronic music using the 1960 RCA Mark II synthesizer, which he helped to design.

Babel Isaak Emmanuilovich 1894–1939/40. Russian writer. Born in Odessa, he was an ardent supporter of the Revolution and fought with Budyenny's cavalry in the Polish campaign of 1921–22, an experience which inspired *Konarmiya/Red Cavalry* 1926. His other works include *Odesskie rasskazy/Stories from Odessa* 1924, which portrays the life of the Odessa Jews.

Baber (Arabic 'lion') title given to ◊Zahir ud-din Muhammad, founder of the Mughal Empire in N India.

Babeuf François Noël 1760–1797. French revolutionary journalist, a pioneer of practical socialism. In 1794 he founded a newspaper in Paris, later known as the *Tribune of the People*, in which he demanded the equality of all people. He was guillotined for conspiring against the ruling Directory during the French Revolution.

Babington Anthony 1561–1586. English traitor who hatched a plot to assassinate Elizabeth I and replace her by ◊Mary, Queen of Scots; its discovery led to Mary's execution and his own.

Babrius lived about 3rd century AD. Roman writer of fables, written in Greek. He probably lived in Syria, where his fables first gained popularity. In 1842 a manuscript of his fables was discovered in a convent on Mount Athos, Greece. There were 123 fables, arranged alphabetically, but discontinued at the letter O.

Bacall Lauren. Stage name of Betty Joan Perske 1924– . Striking US actress who became an overnight star when cast by Howard Hawks opposite Humphrey Bogart in *To Have and Have Not* 1944. She and Bogart married in 1945, and starred together in *The Big Sleep* 1946. Her other films include *The Cobweb* 1955 and *Harper* 1966.

Bach Carl Philip Emmanuel 1714–1788. German composer, son of J S Bach. He introduced a new 'homophonic' style, lighter and easier to follow, which influenced Mozart, Haydn, and Beethoven. In the service of Frederick the Great 1740–67, he left to become Master of church music at Hamburg in 1768. He wrote over 200 pieces for keyboard instruments, and published a guide to playing the piano. Through his music and concert performances he helped to establish a leading solo role for the piano in Western music.

Bach Johann Christian 1735–1782. German composer, the 11th son of J S Bach, who became well known in Italy as a composer of operas. In 1762 he was invited to London, where he became music master to the royal family. He remained in England until his death, enjoying great popularity both as a composer and performer.

Bach Johann Sebastian 1685–1750. German composer. His appointments included positions at the courts of Weimar and Anhalt-Köther, and from 1723 until his death, he was musical director at St Thomas's choir school in Leipzig. Bach was a master of counterpoint, and his music epitomizes the Baroque polyphonic style. His orchestral music includes the six *Brandenburg Concertos*, other concertos for clavier and for violin, and four orchestral suites. Bach's keyboard music, for clavier and for organ, his fugues and his choral music are of equal importance. He also wrote chamber music and songs.

Born at Eisenach, he came from a distinguished musical family. At 15 he became a chorister at Lüneburg, and at 19 he was organist at Arnstadt. Bach married twice and had over 20 children, (although several died in infancy). His second wife, Anna Magdalena Wülkens, was a soprano; she also acted as his amanuensis when his sight failed in later years.

Bach's sacred music includes 200 church cantatas, the Easter and Christmas oratorios, the two great Passions, of St Matthew and St John, and the Mass in B minor. His keyboard music includes a collection of 48 preludes and fugues known as the *Well-Tempered Clavier*, the *Goldberg Variations*, and the *Italian Concerto*. Of his organ music the most important examples are the chorale preludes. Two works written in his later years illustrate the principles and potential of his polyphonic art – the *Musical Offering* and *The Art of Fugue*.

Bach Wilhelm Friedemann 1710–1784. German composer, who was also an organist, improviser, and master of counterpoint. He was the eldest son of J S Bach.

Bacon Francis 1561–1626. English politician, philosopher, and essayist. He became Lord Chancellor 1618, and the same year confessed to bribe-taking, was fined £40,000 (which was paid by the king), and spent four days in the Tower of London. Although he admitted taking the money, he claimed that he had not always given the verdict to his paymasters. His works include *Essays* 1597,

Bacon *Sir Francis Bacon was a long-serving adviser to Elizabeth I and James I, and and a writer on scientific thought and method.*

notable for pith and brevity; *The Advancement of Learning* 1605, a seminal work discussing scientific method; the *Novum Organum* 1620, in which he redefined the task of natural science, seeing it as a means of empirical discovery and a method of increasing human power over nature; and *The New Atlantis* 1626, describing a Utopian state in which scientific knowledge is systematically sought and exploited.

Bacon was born in London, studied law at Cambridge from 1573, was part of the embassy in France until 1579, and became a member of Parliament 1584. He was the nephew of Queen Elizabeth's adviser Lord ◊Burghley, but turned against him when he failed to provide Bacon with patronage. He helped secure the execution of the Earl of Essex as a traitor 1601, after formerly being his follower. Bacon was accused of ingratitude, but he defended himself in *Apology* 1604. The satirist Pope called Bacon 'the wisest, brightest, and meanest of mankind'. Knighted on the accession of James I 1603, he became Baron Verulam 1618 and Viscount St Albans 1621.

His writing helped to inspire the founding of the Royal Society. The *Baconian Theory*, originated by James Willmot in 1785, suggesting that the works of Shakespeare were written by Bacon, probably has no validity.

Bacon Francis 1909– . British painter, born in Dublin. He came to London in 1925 and taught himself to paint. He practised abstract art, then developed a distorted Expressionist style, with tortured figures presented in loosely defined space. Since 1945 he has focused on studies of figures, as in his series of screaming popes based on the portrait of Innocent X by Velázquez.

Bacon began to paint about 1930 and held his first show in London in 1949. He destroyed much of his early work. *Three Studies for Figures at the Base of a Crucifixion* 1944 (Tate Gallery, London) is an early example of his mature syle. Bacon distorts and mutilates his human figures to express the complexity of their emotions.

Bacon Roger 1214–1292. English philosopher and scientist. In 1266, at the invitation of his friend Pope Clement IV, he began his *Opus Majus*, a compendium of all branches of knowledge. In 1268 he sent this with his *Opus Minus* and other writings to the Pope. In 1277 he was condemned and imprisoned by the church for 'certain novelties' (heresy) and not released until 1292. He foresaw the magnifying properties of convex lenses, the extensive use of gunpowder, and the possibility of mechanical cars, boats, and flying machines.

Born in Somerset, and educated at Oxford and Paris, he became a Franciscan friar and was in Paris until about 1251 lecturing on Aristotle. His works include *On Mirrors*, *Metaphysical Questions*, and *On the Multiplication of Species*. He followed the maxim 'Cease to be ruled by dogmas and authorities; look at the world!'

Baden-Powell Agnes 1854–1945. Sister of Robert Baden-Powell, she helped him found the Girl Guides.

Baden-Powell Lady Olave 1889–1977. Wife of Robert Baden-Powell from 1912, she was the first and only World Chief Guide 1918–1977.

Baden-Powell Robert Stephenson Smyth, 1st Baron Baden-Powell 1857–1941. British general, founder of the Scout Association. He fought in defence of Mafeking (now Mafikeng) during the Second South African War. After 1907 he devoted his time to developing the Scout movement, which rapidly spread throughout the world. He was created a peer in 1929.

Bader Douglas 1910–1982. British fighter pilot. He lost both legs in a flying accident 1931, but had a distinguished flying career in World War II. He was knighted 1976 for his work with disabled people.

Badoglio Pietro 1871–1956. Italian soldier and Fascist politician. A veteran of campaigns against the peoples of Tripoli and Cyrenaica, in 1935 he became commander in chief in Ethiopia, adopting ruthless measures to break patriot resistance, and being created viceroy of Ethiopia and duke of Addis Ababa in 1936. He succeeded Mussolini as prime minister of Italy from July 1943 to June 1944.

Baedeker Karl 1801–1859. German publisher of foreign-travel guides; these are now based in Hamburg (before World War II in Leipzig).

Baekeland Leo Hendrik 1863–1944. US chemist, the inventor of Bakelite, the first commercial plastic. He later made a photographic paper, Velox, which could be developed in artificial light.

Baer Karl Ernst von 1792–1876. German zoologist, who was the founder of comparative embryology.

Baez Joan 1941– . US folk singer who came to prominence in the early 1960s with her versions of traditional English and American folk songs such as 'Silver Dagger'. She introduced Bob Dylan to a wide audience and has remained active as a pacifist and antiwar campaigner.

Baffin William 1584–1622. English explorer and navigator. In 1616, he and Robert Bylot explored Baffin Bay, NE Canada, and reached latitude 77° 45′ N, which for 236 years remained the 'furthest north'.

In 1612, Baffin was chief pilot of an expedition in search of the Northwest passage, and in 1613–14 commanded a whaling fleet near Spitsbergen, Norway. He piloted the *Discovery* on an expedition to Hudson Bay lead by Bylot in 1615. After 1617, Baffin worked for the East India Company and made surveys of the Red Sea and Persian Gulf. In 1622 he was killed in an Anglo-Persian attack on Hormuz.

Bagehot Walter 1826–1877. British writer and economist, author of *The English Constitution* 1867, a classic analysis of the British political system. He was editor of *The Economist* magazine 1860–77.

Bagnold Enid 1889–1981. British author of *National Velvet* 1935, a novel about horse racing that was also successful as a film (1944).

Bagritsky Eduard. Pen name of Eduard Dzyubin 1895–1934. Soviet poet. One of the Constructivist group, he published the heroic poem *Lay About Opanas* 1926, and collections of verse called *The Victors* 1932 and *The Last Night* 1932.

Bahadur Shah II 1775–1862. Last of the Mughal emperors of India. He reigned, though in name only (including under the British), as king of Delhi 1837–57, when he was hailed by the mutineers in the Indian Mutiny as an independent emperor at Delhi. After the mutiny he was deported to Rangoon, Burma, with his family.

Baha'ullah title of Mirza Hosein Ali 1817–1892. Persian founder of the Baha'i religion. Baha'ullah, 'God's Glory', proclaimed himself as the prophet the ◊Bab had foretold.

Bailey Donald Coleman 1901–1985. English engineer, inventor in World War II of the portable *Bailey bridge*, made of interlocking, interchangeable, adjustable and easily transportable units.

Baillie Isobel 1895–1983. British soprano. Born in Hawick, Scotland, she became celebrated for her work in oratorio. She was professor of singing at Cornell University in New York 1960-61. She became a Dame of the British Empire 1978.

Bailly Jean Sylvain 1736-1793. French astronomer, who wrote about the satellites of Jupiter and the history of astronomy. Early in the French Revolution he was president of the National Assembly and mayor of Paris, but resigned in 1791, and was guillotined during the Terror.

Bainbridge Beryl 1933- . English novelist, originally an actress, whose works have the drama and economy of a stage-play. They include *The Dressmaker* 1973, *The Bottle Factory Outing* 1974, and the collected short stories in *Mum and Mr Armitage* 1985.

Bainbridge Kenneth Tompkins 1904- . US physicist, who was director of the first atomic bomb test at Alamagordo, USA, in 1945.

He worked at the Cavendish Laboratory, Cambridge, England, in the 1930s. He also carried out research in radar. From 1961, he was George Vasmer Everett Professor of Physics at Harvard University, USA.

Baird John Logie 1888-1946. Scottish electrical engineer, who pioneered television. In 1925 he gave the first public demonstration of television, and in 1926 pioneered fibre optics, radar (in advance of Robert ◊Watson-Watt), and 'noctovision', a system for seeing at night by using infrared rays.

Born at Helensburgh, Scotland, Baird studied electrical engineering in Glasgow at what is now the University of Strathclyde, at the same time serving several practical apprenticeships. He was working on television possibly as early as 1912, and he took out his first provisional patent 1923. He also developed video recording on both wax records and magnetic steel discs (1926-27), colour television (1925-28), 3D colour television (1925-46), and transatlantic television (1928). In 1936 his mechanically scanned 240-line system competed with EMI-Marconi's 405-line, but the latter was preferred for the BBC service from 1937, partly because it used electronic scanning and partly because it handled live indoor scenes with smaller, more manoeuvrable cameras. In 1944 he developed facsimile television, the forerunner of Ceefax, and demonstrated the world's first all-electronic colour and 3D-colour receiver (500 lines).

Bairnsfather Bruce 1888-1959. British artist, celebrated for his 'Old Bill' cartoons of World War I. In World War II he was official cartoonist to the US Army in Europe 1942-44.

Baker Benjamin 1840-1907. English engineer, who designed (with English engineer John Fowler 1817-1898) London's first underground railway (the Metropolitan and District) in 1869, the Forth Bridge, Scotland, 1890, and the original Aswan Dam on the River Nile, Egypt.

Baker James (Addison) Baker III 1930- . US Republican politician. Under President Reagan, he was White House Chief of Staff 1981-85 and Treasury secretary 1985-88. After managing Bush's successful presidential campaign 1988, Baker was appointed secretary of state 1989.

Baker, a lawyer from Houston, Texas, entered politics 1970 as one of the managers of his friend George Bush's unsuccessful campaign for the Senate. He served as undersecretary of commerce 1975-76 in the Ford administration and was deputy manager of the 1976 and 1980 Ford and Bush presidential campaigns. Baker was inducted into the Reagan administration 1981. He has been criticized for the unscrupulousness of the 1988 Bush campaign. The most influential member of the 'Bush team', he has been described as an effective 'prime minister'.

Baker Janet 1933- . English mezzo-soprano who excels in lied, oratorio, and opera. Her performances include Dido in both *Dido and Aeneas* and *The Trojans*, and Marguerite in *Faust*. She retired from the stage in 1981 but continues to perform recitals, oratorio, and concerts.

Baker Kenneth (Wilfrid) 1934- . British Conservative politician, education secretary 1986-89, and chair of the Conservative Party from 1989.

He was elected to the House of Commons 1968; from 1983 he represented Mole Valley. Undergoing national service in N Africa Baker was, for a time, a gunnery instructor to the Libyan army. He then read history at Oxford. Despite a reputation of being on the liberal wing of the Conservative Party, he became a minister of state in Thatcher's 1979 Administration.

Baker Samuel White 1821-1893. English explorer, in 1864 the first European to sight Lake Albert Nyanza (now Lake Mobutu Sese Seko) in central Africa, and discover that the Nile flowed through it.

He founded an agricultural colony in Ceylon (now Sri Lanka), built a railway across the Dobruja, and in 1861 set out to discover the source of the Nile. His wife, Florence von Sass, accompanied him. From 1869 to 1873 he was governor-general of the Nile equatorial regions.

Bakewell Robert 1725-1795. Pioneer improver of farm livestock. From his home in Leicestershire, England, he developed the Dishley or New Leicester breed of sheep and also worked on raising the beef-producing qualities of Longhorn cattle.

Bakhuyzen Ludolf 1631-1708. Dutch painter of seascapes. *Stormy Sea* 1697 (Rijksmuseum, Amsterdam) is typically dramatic.

Bakke Allan 1940- . US student who, in 1978, gave his name to a test case claiming 'reverse discrimination' when appealing against his exclusion from medical school, since less well-qualified blacks were to be admitted as part of a special programme for ethnic minorities. He won his case against quotas before the Supreme Court, although other affirmative action for minority groups was still endorsed.

Bakst Leon. Stage name of Leon Rosenberg 1866–1924. Russian theatre designer. From 1900–09 he was scenic artist to the imperial theatres; then scenery painter and costume designer for ◊Diaghilev's Ballets Russes.

In later life, when living in Paris, he exercised worldwide influence on the decorative arts of the theatre.

Bakunin Mikhail 1814–1876. Russian anarchist, active in Europe. In 1848 he was expelled from France as a revolutionary agitator. In Switzerland in the 1860s he became recognized as the leader of the anarchist movement. In 1869 he joined the First International (a coordinating socialist body) but, after stormy conflicts with Karl Marx, was expelled 1872.

Born of a noble family, Bakunin served in the Imperial Guard but, disgusted with tsarist methods in Poland, resigned his commission and travelled abroad. For his share in a brief revolt at Dresden 1849 he was sentenced to death. The sentence was commuted to imprisonment, and he was handed over to the tsar's government and sent to Siberia 1855. In 1861 he managed to escape to Switzerland. He had a large following, particularly in the Latin American countries. He wrote books and pamphlets, including *God and the State*.

Balakirev Mily Alexeyevich 1837–1910. Russian composer. He wrote orchestral and piano music, songs, and a symphonic poem *Tamara*, all imbued with the Russian national character and spirit. He was leader of the group known as The Five and taught its members, Mussorgsky, Cui, Rimsky-Korsakov, and Borodin.

Balakirev was born at Nijni-Novgorod. At St Petersburg he worked with Mikhail ◊Glinka, established the Free School of Music 1862, which stressed the national element, and was director of the Imperial Chapel 1883–95.

Balanchine George 1904–1983. Russian-born choreographer. After leaving the USSR in 1924, he worked with Diaghilev in France. Moving to the USA in 1933, he became a major influence on modern dance, starting the New York City Ballet in 1948. His many works include *Apollon Musagète* 1928 and *The Prodigal Son* 1929 for Diaghilev, several works for music by Stravinsky such as *Agon* 1957 and *Duo Concertante* 1972, and musicals such as *On Your Toes* 1936 and *The Boys from Syracuse* 1938.

Balboa Vasco Núñez de 1475–1517. Spanish conquistador, the first European to see the Pacific Ocean, on 29 Sept 1513, from the isthmus of Darien (now Panama). He was made admiral of the Pacific and governor of Panama, but was removed by Spanish court intrigue, imprisoned and executed.

Balcon Michael 1896–1977. British film producer, responsible for the 'Ealing Comedies' of the 1940s and early 1950s, such as *Kind Hearts and Coronets* 1949, and *The Lavender Hill Mob* 1951.

Baldung Grien Hans 1484/85–1545. German Renaissance painter, engraver, and designer, based in Strasbourg. He painted the theme *Death and the Maiden* in several versions.

Baldwin James 1924–1987. US writer, born in Harlem, New York, who portrayed the condition of black Americans in contemporary society. His works include the novels *Go Tell It on the Mountain* 1953, *Another Country* 1962, and *Just Above My Head* 1979; the play *The Amen Corner* 1955; and the autobiographical essays *Notes of a Native Son* 1955 and *The Fire Next Time* 1963.

Baldwin Stanley, 1st Earl Baldwin of Bewdley 1867–1947. British Conservative politician, prime minister 1923–24, 1924–29, and 1935–37; he weathered the general strike 1926, secured complete adult suffrage 1928, and handled the abdication crisis of Edward VIII 1936.

Born in Bewdley, Worcestershire, the son of an iron and steel magnate, in 1908 he was elected Unionist member of Parliament for Bewdley, and in 1916 he became parliamentary private secretary to Bonar Law. He was financial secretary to the Treasury 1917–21, and then appointed to the presidency of the Board of Trade. In 1919 he gave the Treasury £150,000 of War Loan for cancellation, representing about 20% of his fortune. He was a leader in the disruption of the Lloyd George coalition 1922, and, as chancellor under Bonar Law, achieved a settlement of war debts with the USA.

As prime minister 1923–24 and again 1924–29, Baldwin passed the Trades Disputes Act of 1927 after the general strike, granted widows' and orphans' pensions, and complete adult suffrage 1928. He joined the national government of Ramsay MacDonald 1931 as Lord President of the Council. He handled the abdication crisis during his third premiership 1935–37, but was later much criticized for his failures to resist popular desire for an accommodation with the dictators Hitler and Mussolini, and to rearm more effectively.

Baldwin I 1058–1118. King of Jerusalem. A French nobleman, who joined his brother ◊Godfrey de Bouillon on the First Crusade in 1096, he established the kingdom in 1100. It was destroyed by Islamic conquest in 1187.

Balfe Michael William 1808–1870. Irish composer and singer. He was a violinist and baritone at Drury Lane, London, when only 16. In 1825 he went to Italy, where he sang in Palermo and at La Scala, and in 1846 he was appointed conductor at Her Majesty's Theatre. He composed operas, including *The Bohemian Girl* 1843.

Balfour Arthur James, 1st Earl of Balfour 1848–1930. British Conservative politician, prime minister 1902–05 and foreign secretary 1916–19, when he issued the Balfour Declaration and was involved in peace negotiations after World War I.

Son of a Scottish landowner, he was elected a Conservative member of Parliament in 1874. In Lord Salisbury's ministry he was secretary for Ireland 1887, and for his ruthless vigour was called 'Bloody Balfour' by Irish nationalists. In 1891 and again in 1895 he became First Lord of the Treasury and leader of the Commons, and in 1902 he succeeded Salisbury as prime minister. His cabinet was divided over Joseph Chamberlain's tariff-reform proposals, and in the 1905 elections suffered a crushing defeat.

Balfour retired from the party leadership in 1911. In 1915 he joined the Asquith coalition as First Lord of the Admiralty. As foreign secretary 1916–19 he issued the Balfour Declaration of 1917 in favour of a national home in Palestine for the Jews and signed the Treaty of Versailles.

Baliol John de c.1250–1314. King of Scotland 1292–96. As an heir to the Scottish throne on the death of Margaret, the Maid of Norway, his cause was supported by the English king, Edward I, against 12 other claimants. Having paid homage to Edward, he was proclaimed king but soon rebelled and gave up the kingdom when English forces attacked Scotland.

Ball John died 1381. English priest, one of the leaders of the Peasants' Revolt 1381, known as 'the mad priest of Kent'. A follower of John Wycliffe and a believer in social equality, he was imprisoned for disagreeing with the archbishop of Canterbury, and was probably excommunicated. During the revolt, he was released from prison, and when in Blackheath, London, preached from the text 'When Adam delved and Eve span, who was then the gentleman?' When the revolt collapsed he escaped but was captured near Coventry and executed.

Ball Lucille 'Lucy' 1911–1989. US comedy actress. From 1951–57 she starred with her husband, Cuban bandleader Desi Arnaz, in *I Love Lucy*, the first US television show filmed before an audience. It was followed by *The Lucy Show* 1962–68 and *Here's Lucy* 1968–74.

She entered films as a bit player 1933, and appeared in dozens of films over the next few years, including *Room Service* 1938 (with the Marx Brothers) and *Fancy Pants* 1950 (with Bob Hope). Her TV success limited her film output after 1950; her later films include *Mame* 1974. The television series are still transmitted in many countries.

Ballance John 1839–1893. New Zealand politician, born in Northern Ireland; prime minister 1891–93. He emigrated to New Zealand, founded and edited the *Wanganui Herald*, and held many cabinet posts.

Ballantyne R(obert) M(ichael) 1825–1894. Scottish writer of children's books. Childhood visits to Canada and six years as a trapper for the Hudson's Bay company provided material for his adventure stories, which include *The Young Fur Traders* 1856, *Coral Island* 1857, and *Martin Rattler* 1858.

Ballard J(ames) G(raham) 1930– . British novelist, whose works include science fiction on the theme of disaster, such as *The Drowned World* 1962, and *High-Rise* 1975, and the partly autobiographical *Empire of the Sun* 1984, dealing with his internment in China during World War II.

Ballesteros Severiano 'Seve' 1957– . Spanish golfer who came to prominence 1976 and has been dominant in Europe, as well as winning leading tournaments in the USA. He has won the British Open three times 1979, 1984, 1988.

Born in Pedrena, N Spain, he is one of four golf-playing brothers. Seve has won more than 60 tournaments worldwide and more than £1 million on the European Tour.

Balmer Johann 1825–1898. Swiss physicist and mathematician who developed a formula that gave the wavelengths of the hydrogen atom spectrum. This formula played a central role in the development of spectral theory.

Balzac Honoré de 1799–1850. French novelist. His first success was *Les Chouans*/*The Chouans* and *La Physiologie du mariage*/*The Physiology of Marriage* 1829, inspired by Scott. This was the beginning of the long series of novels *La Comédie humaine*/*The Human Comedy*. He also

Balzac *French novelist Honoré de Balzac planned to depict every aspect of French life in* La Comédie humaine, *but only managed to complete about 80 of the planned 143 volumes.*

wrote Rabelaisian *Contes drolatiques/Ribald Tales* 1833.

Born in Tours, Balzac studied law and worked as a notary's clerk in Paris, before turning to literature. His first attempts included tragedies such as *Cromwell* and novels published pseudonymously with no great success. A venture in printing and publishing 1825–28 involved him in a lifelong web of debt. His patroness, Madame de Berny, figures in *Le Lys dans la vallée/The Lily in the Valley* 1836. Balzac planned for his major work *La Comédie humaine/The Human Comedy* to comprise 143 volumes, depicting every aspect of society in 19th-century France, but he only managed to complete 80. The series includes *Eugénie Grandet* 1833, *Le Père Goriot* 1834, and *Cousine Bette* 1846. Balzac corresponded constantly with the Polish countess Evelina Hanska after meeting her in 1833, but they only married four months before his death in Paris. He was buried in Père Lachaise cemetery.

Bancroft George 1800–1891. US diplomat and historian. A Democrat, he was secretary of the navy 1845, when he established the US Naval Academy at Annapolis, Maryland, and as acting secretary of war (May 1846) was instrumental in bringing about the occupation of California and war with Mexico. He wrote a *History of the United States* 1834–76.

Banda Hastings Kamuzu *c.*1902– . Malawi politician, president from 1966. He led his country's independence movement, was prime minister of Nyasaland (the former name of Malawi) from 1963, and became the first president of the one-party republic.

Banda studied in the USA and was a medical practitioner in Britain until 1953. His rule has been authoritarian, and in 1971 he made himself life president.

Bandaranaike Sirimavo (born Ratwatte) 1916– . Sri Lankan politician, who succeeded her husband Solomon Bandaranaike to become the world's first woman prime minister 1960–65 and 1970–77, but was expelled from parliament 1980 for abuse of her powers while in office. She was largely responsible for the new constitution 1972.

Bandaranaike Solomon West Ridgeway Dias 1899–1959. Sri Lankan nationalist politician. In 1951 he founded the Sri Lanka Freedom Party and in 1956 became prime minister, pledged to a socialist programme and a neutral foreign policy. He failed to satisfy extremists and was assassinated by a Buddhist monk.

Bankhead Tallulah 1903–1968. US actress, noted for her wit and flamboyant lifestyle. Her stage appearances include *Dark Victory* 1934, *The Little Foxes* 1939, and *The Skin of Our Teeth* 1942.

Her films include Hitchcock's *Lifeboat* 1943.

Banks Joseph 1744–1820. British naturalist and explorer. He accompanied Capt James ◊Cook on his voyage round the world 1768–71 and brought

Bandaranaike *Sirimavo Bandaranaike became in 1960 the world's first woman prime minister.*

back 3,600 plants, 1,400 of them never before classified. A founder of the Botanical Gardens, Kew, he was President of the Royal Society from 1778–1819. The *banksia* genus of shrubs is named after him.

Bannister Roger Gilbert 1929– . English athlete, the first person to run the mile in under four minutes. He achieved this feat at Oxford, England, on 6 May 1954 in a time of 3 min 59.4 sec.

Studying at Oxford to be a doctor at the time, Bannister broke the four-minute barrier on one more occasion: at the 1954 Commonwealth Games in Vancouver, Canada, when he was involved in the 'Mile of the Century' with John Landy (Australia).

Banting Frederick Grant 1891–1941. Canadian physician who discovered the hormone insulin in 1921 when, experimentally, he tied off the ducts of the pancreas in order to determine the function of the cells known as the islets of Langerhans. He was helped by Charles ◊Best and John J R Macleod, with whom he shared the 1923 Nobel Prize for Medicine.

Barbellion W N P, pseudonym of Bruce Frederick Cummings 1889–1919. English diarist, author of *The Journal of a Disappointed Man* 1919, an account of his struggle with the illness multiple sclerosis.

Barber Samuel 1910–1981. US composer of works in a restrained neo-classical style, including *Adagio for Strings* 1936 and the opera *Vanessa* 1958.

Barbie Klaus 1913– . German Nazi, a member of the SS from 1936. During World War II he was involved in the deportation of Jews from the occupied Netherlands 1940–42 and in tracking down Jews and Resistance workers in France 1942–45. He was arrested 1983 and convicted of crimes against humanity in France 1987.

His work as SS commander, based in Lyon, included the rounding-up of Jewish children from an orphanage at Izieu and the torture of the Resistance leader Jean Moulin. During this time, his ruthlessness earned him the epithet 'Butcher of Lyon'. Having escaped capture in 1945, Barbie was employed by the US intelligence services in Germany before moving to Bolivia in 1951. Expelled from there in 1983, he was returned to France where he was tried by a court in Lyon.

Barbirolli John 1899–1970. English conductor. He made a name as a cellist, and in 1937 succeeded Toscanini as conductor of the New York Philharmonic Orchestra. He returned to England in 1943, where he remained conductor of the Hallé Orchestra, Manchester until his death.

Barbour John c.1316–1395. Scottish poet whose chronicle-poem *The Brus* is among the earliest Scottish poetry.

Bardeen John 1908– . US physicist, who won a Nobel prize 1956, with Walter Brattain and William Shockley, for the development of the transistor in 1948. In 1972, he was the first double winner of a Nobel prize in the same subject (with Leon Cooper and John Schrieffer) for his work on superconductivity.

Bardot Brigitte 1934– . French film actress, whose sensual appeal did much to popularize French cinema internationally. Her films include *Et Dieu créa la Femme/And God Created Woman* 1950 and *Shalako* 1968.

Barenboim Daniel 1942– . Israeli pianist and conductor, born in Argentina. Pianist/conductor with the English Chamber Orchestra from 1964, he became conductor of the New York Philharmonic Orchestra 1970 and musical director of the Orchestre de Paris 1975. Appointed artistic director of the Opéra Bastille, Paris, July 1987, he was fired from his post a few months before its opening in July 1989. He is a celebrated interpreter of Mozart and Beethoven.

Barents Willem c.1550–1597. Dutch explorer and navigator. He made three expeditions to seek the Northeast Passage; he died on the last voyage. The Barents Sea, part of the Arctic Ocean N of Norway, is named after him.

Barham Richard Harris 1788–1845. British writer and clergyman, author of verse tales of the supernatural, and *The Ingoldsby Legends*, published under his pen name Thomas Ingoldsby.

Baring-Gould Sabine 1834–1924. British writer, rector of Lew Trenchard in N Devon from 1881. He was a prolific writer of novels, books of travel, mythology and folklore, and wrote the words of 'Onward, Christian Soldiers'.

Barker Clive 1952– . British horror writer, whose *Books of Blood* 1984–85 are in the sensationalist tradition of horror fiction.

Barker George 1913– . British poet, noted for his vivid imagery, as in *Calamiterror* 1937, *The*

True Confessions of George Barker 1950, and *Collected Poems* 1930–50.

Barker Herbert 1869–1950. British manipulative surgeon, whose work established the popular standing of orthopaedics (the study and treatment of disorders of the spine and joints), but who was never recognized by the world of orthodox medicine.

Barlach Ernst 1870–1938. German Expressionist sculptor, painter, and poet. His simple, evocative figures carved in wood (for example in St Catherine's, Lübeck, 1930–32) often express melancholy.

Barnard Christiaan Neethling 1922– . South African surgeon who performed the first human heart transplant in 1967 in Cape Town. The patient, 54-year-old Louis Washkansky, lived for 18 days.

Barnardo Thomas John 1845–1905. British philanthropist, who was known as Dr Barnardo, although not medically qualified. He opened the first of a series of homes for destitute children 1867 in Stepney, E London.

Barnes Ernest William 1874–1953. British cleric. A lecturer in mathematics at Cambridge 1902–15, he was an ardent advocate of the significance of scientific thought on modern religion. In 1924 he became bishop of Birmingham and published the controversial work *The Rise of Christianity* 1947.

Barnes Thomas 1785–1841. British journalist, editor of *The Times* from 1817, during which time it became known as the 'Thunderer'.

Barnes William 1800–1886. English poet and cleric who published volumes of poems in the Dorset dialect.

Barnum Phineas T(aylor) 1810–1891. US showman. In 1871, after an adventurous career, he established the 'Greatest Show on Earth' (which included the midget 'Tom Thumb') comprising circus, menagerie, and exhibition of 'freaks', conveyed in 100 rail cars. He coined the phrase 'there's a sucker born every minute'.

Barocci Federico c.1535–1612. Italian artist, born and based in Urbino. He painted religious themes in a highly coloured, sensitive style that falls between Renaissance and Baroque. The *Madonna del Graffo* (National Gallery, London) shows the influence of Raphael (also from Urbino) and Correggio on his art.

Baroja Pio 1872–1956. Spanish novelist of Basque extraction whose works include a trilogy dealing with the Madrid underworld, *La lucha por la vida/The Struggle for Life* 1904–05, and the multi-volume *Memorias de un hombre de acción/Memoirs of a Man of Action* 1913–28.

Barragán Luis 1902–1988. Mexican architect, known for his use of rough wooden beams, cobbles, lava, and adobe, his simple houses with walled gardens, and his fountains.

Barras Paul François Jean Nicolas, Count Barras 1755–1829. French revolutionary. He was elected to the National Convention 1792, and helped to overthrow Robespierre 1794. In 1795 he became a member of the ruling Directory. In 1796 he brought about the marriage of his former mistress, Joséphine de Beauharnais, with Napoleon, and assumed dictatorial powers. After Napoleon's coup d'état 19 Nov 1799, Barras fell into disgrace.

Barrault Jean Louis 1910– . French actor and director. His films include *La Symphonie fantastique* 1942, *Les Enfants du Paradis* 1944, and *La Ronde* 1950.

He was producer and director to the Comédie Française 1940–46, and director of the Théâtre de France (formerly Odéon) from 1959 until dismissed 1968 because of statements made during the occupation of the theatre by student rebels.

Barre Raymond 1924– . French politician, member of the centre-right Union pour la Démocratie Française; prime minister 1976–81, when he also held the Finance Ministry portfolio and gained a reputation as a tough and determined budget-cutter (nicknamed Monsieur Economy).

Barre, born on the French dependency of Réunion, was a liberal economist at the Sorbonne and vice president of the European Commission 1967–72. He served as minister of foreign trade to President Giscard d'Estaing and became prime minister on the resignation of Chirac 1976. He built up a strong political base in the Lyon region during the early 1980s.

Barrie J(ames) M(atthew) 1860–1937. Scottish playwright and novelist, author of *The Admirable Crichton* 1902 and the children's fantasy *Peter Pan* 1904.

He became known by his studies of Scottish rural life in plays such as *A Window in Thrums* 1889. His reputation as a playwright was established with *The Professor's Love Story* 1894 and *The Little Minister*. His later plays include *Quality Street* 1901 and *What Every Woman Knows* 1908.

Barrow Isaac 1630–1677. British mathematician, theologian, and classicist. His *Lectiones geometricae* 1670 contains the essence of the theory of calculus, which was later expanded by Isaac ◊Newton and Gottfried ◊Leibniz.

Barry Charles 1795–1860. English architect of the Neo-Gothic Houses of Parliament at Westminster, London, 1840–60, in collaboration with ◊Pugin.

Barry Comtesse du see ◊Du Barry, mistress of Louis XV of France.

Barrymore US family of actors. *Lionel Barrymore* (1878–1954) played numerous film roles but was perhaps best known for his portrayal of Scrooge in Dickens's *A Christmas Carol*. *Ethel Barrymore* (1879–1959) played with British actor Henry Irving in London in 1898 and in 1928 opened the Ethe Barrymore Theatre in New York. *John Barrymore* (1882–1942), acted in films, including *Dinner at Eight* 1933,

and became a screen idol, nicknamed 'the Profile'.

Barstow Stan 1928– . English novelist. Born in W Yorkshire, his novels describe northern working-class life, including *A Kind of Loving* 1960.

Bart Jean 1651–1702. French naval hero. The son of a fisherman, he served in the French navy, and harassed the British fleet in many daring exploits.

Bart Lionel 1930– . English composer, author of both words and music for many musicals including *Fings Ain't Wot They Us'd T'Be* 1959 and *Oliver!* 1960.

Barth Heinrich 1821–1865. German geographer and explorer who in explorations of N Africa between 1844 and 1855 established the exact course of the river Niger.

He studied the coast of N Africa from Tunis to Egypt 1844–45, travelled in the Middle East 1845–47, crossed the Sahara from Tripoli 1850, and then spent five years exploring the country between Lake Chad and Cameroon which he described in the five-volume *Travels and Discoveries in Central Africa* 1857–58.

Barth John 1930– . US novelist, born in Baltimore, influential in experimental writing in the 1960s. Chief works include *The Sot-Weed Factor* 1960, *Giles Goat-Boy* 1966, and *Lost in the Funhouse* 1968, interwoven fictions based on language games.

Barth Karl 1886–1968. Swiss Protestant theologian. Socialist in his political views, he attacked the Nazis. His *Church Dogmatics* 1932–62 makes the resurrection of Jesus the focal point of Christianity.

Barthes Roland 1915–1980. French critic. He was an influential theorist of semiology, the science of signs and symbols. One of the French 'new critics', he attacked traditional literary criticism in his early works, including *Sur Racine/On Racine* 1963, and set out his own theories in *Eléments de sémiologie* 1964. He also wrote an autobiographical novel, *Roland Barthes sur Roland Barthes* 1975.

Bartholdi Frédéric Auguste 1834–1904. French sculptor. He designed the **Statue of Liberty** overlooking New York harbour, 1884.

Bartók Béla 1881–1945. Hungarian composer. Regarded as a child prodigy, he studied music at the Budapest Conservatory later working with ◊Kodály in recording and and transcribing local folk music for a government project. This led him to develop a personal musical language combining folk elements with mathematical concepts of tone and rhythmic proportion. His large output includes six string quartets, a ballet *The Miraculous Mandarin* 1919, which was banned because of its subject matter, concertos, an opera, and graded teaching pieces for piano. He died in the US having fled from Hungary in 1940.

Bartók Hungarian composer Béla Bartók.

Bartolommeo Fra, also called Baccio della Porta C. 1472–c.1517. Italian religious painter of the High Renaissance, active in Florence. His painting of the *Last Judgment* 1499 (Museo di S Marco, Florence) influenced Raphael.

Barton Edmund 1849–1920. Australian politician. He was leader of the federation movement from 1896 and first prime minister of Australia 1901–03.

Baruch Bernard (Mannes) 1870–1965. US financier. He was a friend of British prime minister Churchill and a self-appointed, unpaid adviser to US presidents Wilson, F D Roosevelt, and Truman. He strongly advocated international control of nuclear energy.

Baryshnikov Mikhail 1948– . Soviet dancer, now in the USA. He joined the Kirov Ballet in 1967 and soon gained fame worldwide as a soloist. After defecting 'on artistic, not political grounds' while in Canada in 1974, he danced with various companies, becoming director of the American Ballet Theatre in 1980.

He has created many roles, notably in Twyla Tharp's *Push Comes to Shove* 1976 (music by Haydn/Lamb) and in Jerome Robbins's *Opus 19* 1979 (Prokofiev). He made his film debut in *The Turning Point* 1978 and has since acted in other films, including *White Nights* 1985. He made his dramatic stage debut in *Metamorphosis* 1989.

Bashkirtseff Marie 1860–1884. Russian diarist and painter whose journals, written in French, were cited by Simone de Beauvoir as the archetypal example of 'self-centred female narcissism', but also as the discovery by the female of her independent existence. She died of tuberculosis at 24.

Bashō pen name of Matsuo Munefusa, Japanese poet. 1644–1694. He was master of the *haiku*,

a 17-syllable poetic form with lines of 5, 7, and 5 syllables, which he infused with subtle allusiveness and made the accepted form of poetic expression in Japan. His most famous work is *Oku-no-hosomichi/The Narrow Road to the Deep North* 1694, an account of a visit to N Japan, which consists of haikus interspersed with prose passages.

Basie 'Count' (William) 1904–1984. US jazz band leader, pianist, and organist who developed the big-band sound and a simplified, swinging style of music. He led impressive groups of musicians in a career spanning more than 50 years.

Basil II c.958–1025. Byzantine emperor from 976. His achievement as emperor was to contain, and later decisively defeat, the Bulgarians, earning for himself the title *Bulgar-Slayer* after a victory 1014. After the battle he blinded almost all 15,000 of the defeated, leaving only a few men with one eye to lead their fellows home. The Byzantine empire reached its greatest extent at the time of his death.

Basil, St c.330–379. Cappadocian monk, known as 'the Great', founder of the Basilian monks. Elected bishop of Caesarea 370, Basil opposed the heresy of Arianism (see ◊Arius). He wrote many theological works and composed the 'Liturgy of St Basil', in use in the Eastern Orthodox Church. Feast day 2 Jan.

Born in Caesarea, Anatolia, he studied in Constantinople and Athens, visited the hermit saints of the Egyptian desert, entered a monastery in Anatolia about 358, and developed a monastic rule based on community life, work, and prayer. These ideas form the basis of monasticism in the Greek Orthodox church, and influenced the foundation of similar monasteries by St Benedict.

Baskerville John 1706–1775. English printer and typographer, who experimented in casting types from 1750 onwards. The Baskerville typeface is named after him.

He manufactured fine printing paper and inks, and in 1756 published a quarto edition of the Classical poet Virgil, which was followed by 54 highly crafted books.

Basov Nikolai Gennadievich 1912– . Soviet physicist who in 1953, with his compatriot Alexander Prokhorov, developed the microwave amplifier called a maser. They were awarded the Nobel Prize for Physics 1964, which they shared with Charles Townes of the USA.

Bass George 1763–c.1808. English naval surgeon who with Matthew ◊Flinders explored the coast of New South Wales and the strait that bears his name between Tasmania and Australia 1795–98.

Bastos Augusto Roa 1917– . Paraguayan writer of short stories and novels, including *Son of Man* 1960 about the Chaco War between Bolivia and Paraguay, in which he fought.

Bateman H(enry) M(ayo) 1887–1970. Australian cartoonist, lived in England. His cartoons were based on themes of social embarrassment and confusion, in such series as *The Man who. ...* (as in *The Guardsman who dropped his rifle*).

Bates Alan 1934– . English actor. A versatile male lead in over 60 plays and films, his roles include *Zorba the Greek* 1965; *Far from the Madding Crowd* 1967; *Women in Love* 1970; *The Go-Between* 1971; *The Shout* 1978 and *Duet for One* 1986.

Bates H(enry) W(alter) 1825–1892. English naturalist and explorer, who identified 8,000 new species of insects. He made a special study of camouflage in animals, and his observation of insect imitation of species unpleasant to predators is known as 'Batesian mimicry'.

Báthory Stephen 1533–1586. King of Poland, elected by a diet convened 1575 and crowned 1576. Báthory proved extremely sucessful in driving the Russian troops of Ivan the Terrible out of his country. His military successes brought potential conflicts with Sweden, but he died before these could develop.

Batista Fulgencio 1901–1973. Cuban dictator 1933–44 and 1952–59, whose authoritarian methods enabled him to jail his opponents and amass a large personal fortune. He was overthrown by rebel forces led by Fidel ◊Castro 1959.

Batoni Pompeo 1708–1787. Italian painter, celebrated for his detailed portraits of princes and gentlemen visiting Rome on the Grand Tour.

Batten Jean 1909–1982. New Zealand aviator, who made the first return solo flight by a woman Australia–Britain 1935, and established speed records.

Battenberg title (conferred 1851) of German noble family; its members included ◊Louis, Prince of Battenberg, and Louis Alexander, Prince of Battenberg, who changed his name to Mountbatten 1917.

Baudelaire Charles Pierre 1821–1867. French poet, whose work combined rhythmical and musical perfection with a morbid romanticism and eroticism, finding beauty in decadence and evil. His first book of verse was *Les Fleurs du mal/Flowers of Evil* 1857.

Baudouin 1930– . King of the Belgians from 1951. In 1950 his father, ◊Leopold III, abdicated and Baudouin was known until his succession in July 1951 as *Le Prince Royal*. In 1960 he married Fabiola de Mora y Aragó (1928–), member of a Spanish noble family.

Baum L(yman) Frank 1856–1919. US writer, best known for the children's fantasy *The Wonderful Wizard of Oz* 1900.

Bausch Pina 1940– . German dance choreographer and director of the unique Wuppertal Tanztheater. Her works incorporate dialogue, elements of psychoanalysis, comedy and drama.

She never accepts requests to restage her creations.

Bawa Geoffrey 1919– . Sri Lankan architect, formerly a barrister. His buildings are a contemporary interpretation of vernacular traditions, and include houses, hotels, and gardens. More recently he has designed public buildings such as the New Parliamentary Complex, Kotte, Colombo, Sri Lanka (1982), and Ruhuru University, Matara, Sri Lanka (1984).

Bax Arnold Edward Trevor 1883–1953. English composer. His works were often based on Celtic legends and include seven symphonies, *The Garden of Fand* (a symphonic poem), and *Tintagel* (an orchestral tone poem). He was Master of the King's Musick 1942–53.

Baxter George 1804–1867. English engraver and printmaker; inventor in 1834 of a special process for printing in oil colours, which he applied successfully in book illustrations.

Baxter Richard 1615–1691. English cleric. During the English Civil War he was a chaplain in the Parliamentary army, and after the Restoration he became a royal chaplain. In 1662 the Act of Uniformity drove him out of the church. In 1685 he was imprisoned for nearly 18 months for alleged sedition.

Bayard Pierre du Terrail (Chevalier) 1473–1524. French soldier. He served under Charles VIII, Louis XII, and Francis I, and was killed in action at the crossing of the Sesia in Italy. His heroic exploits in battle and in tournaments, his chivalry and magnanimity won him the name of 'knight without fear and without reproach'.

Bayes Thomas 1702–1761. English mathematician, noted particularly for his work in probability now known as Bayes' theorem.

Bayle Pierre 1647–1706. French critic and philosopher. He was suspended from the chair of philosophy at Rotterdam under suspicion of religious scepticism in 1693. Three years later his *Dictionnaire historique et critique* appeared, which had a wide influence, particularly on the French Encyclopedists.

Bayliss William Maddock 1860–1924. English physiologist, who discovered the hormone secretin with E H ◊Starling in 1902. Secretin plays an important part in digestion. During World War I, he introduced the use of saline (salt water) injections to help the injured recover from shock.

Bazaine Achille François 1811–1888. Marshal of France. From being a private soldier in 1831 he rose to command the French troops in Mexico 1862–67, and was made a marshal in 1864. In the Franco-Prussian War Bazaine commanded the Third Corps of the Army of the Rhine, allowed himself to be taken in the fortress of Metz, and surrendered on 27 Oct 1870 with nearly 180,000 men. For this he was court-martialled 1873 and imprisoned, but in 1874 escaped to Spain.

Bazalgette Joseph 1819–1890. British civil engineer who, as Chief Engineer to the London Board of Works, designed London's sewer system, a total of 155 km/83 mi of sewers, covering an area of 256 sq km/100 sq mi. It was completed 1865. He also designed the Victoria Embankment 1864–70, which was built over the river Thames and combined a main sewer, a water frontage, an underground railway, and a road.

Beaconsfield title taken by Benjamin ◊Disraeli, prime minister of Britain 1868 and 1874–80.

Beadle George Wells 1903– . US biologist. Born in Wahoo, Nebraska, he was professor of biology at the California Institute of Technology 1946–61, and in 1958 shared a Nobel prize with Edward L Tatum for his work in biochemical genetics.

Beale Dorothea 1831–1906. British pioneer in women's education. She was influential in raising the standard of women's education and the status of women teachers. She was headmistress of the Ladies' College at Cheltenham from 1858, and founder of St Hilda's Hall, Oxford, 1892.

Beardsley Aubrey (Vincent) 1872–1898. British illustrator, whose meticulously executed black-and-white work displays the sinuous line and decorative mannerisms of Art Nouveau and was often charged with being grotesque and decadent. He became known through the *Yellow Book* magazine and his drawings for Oscar Wilde's *Salome* 1893.

Beaton Cecil 1904–1980. English portrait and fashion photographer, designer, illustrator, diarist, and conversationalist. He produced portrait studies and also designed scenery and costumes for ballets, and sets for plays and films.

Beaton David 1494–1546. Scottish nationalist cardinal and politician, adviser to James V. Under Mary, Queen of Scots, he was opposed to the alliance with England and persecuted reformers such as George Wishart, who was condemned to the stake; he was killed by Wishart's friends.

Beatrix 1936– . Queen of the Netherlands. The eldest daughter of Queen ◊Juliana, she succeeded to the throne on her mother's abdication 1980. In 1966, she married W German diplomat, Claus von Amsberg (1926–), who was created Prince of the Netherlands. Her heir is Prince Willem Alexander (1967–).

Beatty David, 1st Earl 1871–1936. British admiral in World War I. He commanded the cruiser squadron 1912–16 and bore the brunt of the Battle of Jutland. In 1916 he became commander of the fleet, and in 1918 received the surrender of the German fleet.

Beatty Warren. Stage name of Warren Beaty 1937– . US film actor and director, popular for such films as *Bonnie and Clyde* 1967 and *Heaven Can Wait* 1978. His more recent productions include *Reds* 1981 and *Dick Tracy* 1990.

Beauclerk family name of the Dukes of St Albans; descended from King Charles II by his mistress Eleanor Gwyn.

Beaufort Francis 1774–1857. British admiral, hydrographer to the Royal Navy from 1829; the Beaufort scale and the Beaufort Sea in the Arctic Ocean are named after him.

Beaufort Henry 1375–1447. English priest, bishop of Lincoln from 1398, Winchester from 1405. As chancellor of England, he supported his half-brother Henry IV, and made enormous personal loans to Henry V to finance war against France. As a guardian of Henry VI from 1421, he was in effective control of the country until 1426. In the same year he was created a cardinal. In 1431 he crowned Henry VI as king of France in Paris.

Beauharnais Alexandre, Vicomte de Beauharnais 1760–1794. French liberal aristocrat. He served in the American War of Independence, and became a member of the National Convention in the early days of the French Revolution. He was the first husband of Josephine, consort of Napoleon I. Their daughter Hortense (1783–1837) married Louis, a younger brother of Napoleon, and their son became ◊Napoleon III. Beauharnais was guillotined during the Terror.

Beaumarchais Pierre Augustin Caron de 1732–1799. French dramatist. His great comedies *Le Barbier de Seville/The Barber of Seville* 1775 and *Le Mariage de Figaro/The Marriage of Figaro* (1778, but prohibited until 1784) form the basis of operas by ◊Rossini and ◊Mozart.

Louis XVI entrusted Beaumarchais with secret missions, notably for the profitable shipment of arms to the American colonies during the War of Independence. Accused of treason in 1792, he fled to Holland and England, but in 1799 he returned to Paris.

Beaumont Francis 1584–1616. English dramatist and poet. From about 1608 he collaborated with John ◊Fletcher. Their joint plays include *Philaster* 1610, *The Maid's Tragedy* c.1611, and *A King and No King* c.1611. *The Woman Hater* c.1606 and *The Knight of the Burning Pestle* c.1607 are ascribed to Beaumont alone.

Beaumont William 1785–1853. US surgeon who conducted pioneering experiments on the digestive system. In 1882 he saved the life of a Canadian trapper wounded in the side by a gun blast; the wound only partially healed and through an opening in the stomach wall, Beaumont was able to observe the workings of the stomach. His *Experiments and Observations on the Gastric Juice and the Physiology of Digestion* was published in 1833.

Beauregard Pierre 1818–1893. US Confederate general whose opening fire on Fort Sumter, South Carolina, started the American Civil War 1861.

Beauvoir Simone de 1908–1986. French socialist, feminist, and writer, who taught philosophy at the

Beauvoir *Simone de Beauvoir, the distinguished French literary figure and philosopher of the feminist movement.*

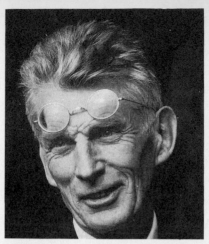

Beckett *Irish novelist and dramatist Samuel Beckett, winner of the Nobel Prize for Literature in 1969.*

Sorbonne university in Paris 1931–43. Her book *Le Deuxième sexe/The Second Sex* 1949 became a seminal work for many feminists.

Her novel of postwar Paris, *Les Mandarins/The Mandarins* 1954, has characters resembling the writers Camus, Koestler, and ◊Sartre. She also published autobiographical volumes.

Beaverbrook William Maxwell Aitken, 1st Baron Beaverbrook 1879–1964. British newspaper proprietor and politician, born in Canada. Between World War I and II he used his newspapers, especially the *Daily Express*, to campaign for Empire, free trade, and against Prime Minister Baldwin.

Bebel August 1840–1913. German socialist and founding member of the *Verband deutsche Arbeitervereine* (League of Workers' Clubs), together with Wilhelm Liebknecht. Also known as the Eisenach Party, it was based in Saxony and SW Germany before being incorporated into the SPD (*Sozialdemokratische Partei Deutschlands)* 1875.

Beccaria Cesare, Marese di Beccaria 1738–1794. Italian philanthropist, born in Milan. He opposed capital punishment and torture; advocated education as a crime preventative; influenced ◊Bentham; and coined the phrase 'the greatest happiness of the greatest number', the tenet of utilitarianism.

Bechet Sidney (Joseph) 1897–1959. US jazz musician, born in New Orleans. He played clarinet and was the first to forge an individual style on soprano saxophone. He was based in Paris in the late 1920s and the 1950s.

Becker Boris 1967– . West German lawn-tennis player. In 1985 he became the youngest winner of a singles title at Wimbledon at the age of 17 years. He has won the title three times and helped West Germany to win the Davis Cup 1988.

Becker Lydia 1827–1890. English botanist and campaigner for women's rights. In 1865 she established the Manchester Ladies Literary Society as a forum for women to study scientific subjects. In 1867 she cofounded and became secretary of the National Society for Women's Suffrage. In 1870 she founded a monthly newsletter, *The Women's Suffrage Journal.*

Becket St Thomas á 1118–1170. English priest and politician. He was chancellor to ◊Henry II 1155–62, when he was appointed archbishop of Canterbury. The interests of the church soon conflicted with those of the crown, and Becket was assassinated; he was canonized 1172.

A friend of Henry II, Becket was his chancellor, but on becoming archbishop of Canterbury 1162 transferred his allegiance to the church. In 1164 he opposed Henry's attempt to regulate the relations between church and state, and had to flee the country; he returned in 1170, but the reconciliation soon broke down. Encouraged by a hasty outburst of the king's, four knights murdered Becket before the altar of Canterbury cathedral. He was declared a saint, and his shrine became the busiest centre of pilgrimage in England until the Reformation.

Beckett Samuel 1906–1989. Irish novelist and dramatist, who wrote in French and English. *En attendant Godot/Waiting for Godot* 1952 is possibly the best-known example of Theatre of the Absurd (in which life is taken to be meaningless). This genre is taken to further extremes in *Fin de Partie/Endgame* 1957 and *Happy Days* 1961. Nobel Prize for Literature 1969.

Beckford William 1760–1844. British author and eccentric. Forced out of England by scandals about his private life, he published *Vathek* 1787 in Paris, a fantastic Arabian Nights tale, and on returning to England in 1796, rebuilt his home, Fonthill Abbey in Wiltshire, as a Gothic fantasy.

Beckmann Max 1884–1950. German Expressionist painter, who fled the Nazi regime in 1933 for the USA. After World War I his art was devoted to themes of cruelty in human society, portraying sadists and their victims with a harsh style of realism.

Beckmann was born in Leipzig. He fought in World War I, and was discharged following a breakdown, reflected in the agony of his work; pictures include *Carnival* and *The Titanic*. He later painted huge triptychs, full of symbolic detail. He died in New York.

Becquerel Antoine Henri 1852–1908. French physicist, who discovered penetrating radiation coming from uranium salts, the first indication of radioactivity, and shared a Nobel prize with Marie and Pierre ◊Curie in 1903.

Beddoes Thomas Lovell 1803–1849. British poet and dramatist. His play *Death's Jest Book* was begun in 1825, but it was not published until 1850, much revised.

Bede *c.*673–735. English theologian and historian, known as the Venerable Bede, active in Durham and Northumbria. He wrote many scientific, theological, and historical works. His *Historia Ecclesiastica Gentis Anglorum/Ecclesiastical History of the English People* 731 is an important source for early English history.

Born at Monkwearmouth, Durham, he entered the local monastery at the age of seven, later transferring to Jarrow, where he became a priest in about 703. He devoted his life to writing and teaching; among his pupils was Egbert, archbishop of York.

Beebe Charles 1877–1962. US naturalist, explorer, and writer. His interest in deep-sea exploration led to a collaboration with the engineer Otis Barton and the development of a spherical diving vessel: the bathysphere. In 1934 the two men made a record-breaking dive to 923 m/3028 ft. His expeditions are described in a series of memoirs.

Beecham Thomas 1879–1961. British conductor and impresario. He established the Royal Philharmonic Orchestra in 1946 and fostered the works of composers such as Delius, Sibelius, and Stravinsky.

Beecher Henry Ward 1813–1887. US Congregational minister and opponent of slavery, son of the pulpit orator Lyman ◊Beecher and brother of the writer Harriet Beecher ◊Stowe.

Beecher Lyman 1775–1863. US Presbyterian minister, the father of Harriet Beecher ◊Stowe and Henry Ward Beecher. As pastor from 1847 of Plymouth church, Brooklyn, New York, he was a leader in the movement for the abolition of slavery.

Beeching Richard, Baron Beeching 1913–1985. British scientist and administrator. He was chair of British Railways Board 1963–65, producing the controversial *Beeching Report* 1963 planning concentration on inter-city passenger traffic and a freight system at the expense of rural and branch lines.

Beerbohm Max 1872–1956. British caricaturist and author, the half-brother of the actor and manager Herbert Beerbohm Tree (1853–1917). A perfectionist in style, he contributed to *The Yellow Book*; wrote the novel of Oxford undergraduate life *Zuleika Dobson* 1911; and published volumes of caricature, including *Rossetti and his Circle* 1922.

Beethoven Ludwig van 1770–1827. German composer and pianist, whose mastery of musical expression in every genre made him the dominant influence on 19th-century music. Beethoven's repertoire includes concert overtures; the opera *Fidelio*; five piano concertos and two for violin (one unfinished); 32 piano sonatas, including the *Moonlight* and *Appassionata*; 17 string quartets; the *Mass in D* (*Missa solemnis*); and nine symphonies, as well many youthful works. He usually played his own piano pieces and conducted his orchestral works until he was hampered by deafness 1801; nevertheless he continued to compose.

Born in Bonn, the son and grandson of musicians, Beethoven became deputy organist at the court of the Elector of Cologne at Bonn before he was 12; later he studied under ◊Haydn and possibly ◊Mozart, whose influence dominated his early work. Beginning in 1809 he received a small allowance from aristocratic patrons.

Beeton, Mrs (Isabella Mary Mayson) 1836–1865. British writer on cookery and domestic management. Wife of a publisher, she produced *Beeton's Household Management* 1859, the first comprehensive work on domestic science.

Begin Menachem 1913– . Israeli politician, born in Poland. He was a leader of the extremist Irgun Zvai Leumi organization in Palestine from 1942; prime minister of Israel 1977–83, as head of the right-wing Likud party; and in 1978 shared a Nobel Peace Prize with President Sadat of Egypt for work on the Camp David Agreements for a Middle East peace settlement.

Behan Brendan 1923–1964. Irish dramatist. His early experience of prison and knowledge of the workings of the IRA (recounted in his autobiography *Borstal Boy* 1958) provided him with two recurrent themes in his plays. *The Quare Fellow* 1954 was followed by the tragicomedy *The Hostage* 1958, first written in Gaelic.

Behn Aphra 1640–1689. English novelist and playwright, the first professional English writer. She

Beeton, Mrs Isabella Beeton, whose name became a byword for household management.

was often criticized for her sexual explicitness, and tended to present her novels and plays from a woman's point of view. In 1688 her novel *Oronooko*, an attack on slavery, was published.

Between 1670 and 1687 fifteen of her plays were produced including *The Rover*, which attacked forced and mercenary marriages. She had the patronage of James I and was employed as a government spy in Holland in 1666.

Behrens Peter 1868–1940. German architect. He pioneered the adaptation of architecture to industry, and designed the AEG turbine factory in Berlin 1909, a landmark in industrial design. He influenced ◊Le Corbusier and ◊Gropius.

Behring Emil von 1854–1917. German physician who discovered that the body produces antitoxins, substances able to counteract poisons released by bacteria. Using this knowledge, he developed new treatments for diseases such as diphtheria.

Educated in Berlin, Behring was Robert ◊Koch's assistant before becoming professor of hygiene at Halle and Marburg. He won the 1901 Nobel Prize for Medicine.

Beiderbecke Bix (Leon Bismarck) 1903–1931. US jazz cornetist, composer, and pianist. A romantic soloist with Paul Whiteman's orchestra, he was inspired by the classical composers Debussy, Ravel, and Stravinsky.

Belasco David 1859–1931. US playwright. His works include *Madame Butterfly* 1900 and *The Girl of the Golden West* 1905, both of which Puccini used as libretti for operas.

Belaúnde Terry Fernando 1913– . President of Peru 1963–68 and 1980–85. He championed land reform and the construction of roads to open up the Amazon valley. He fled to the USA in 1968 after being deposed by a military junta. After his

return, his second term in office was marked by rampant inflation, huge foreign debts, terrorism, mass killings, and human-rights violations by the armed forces.

Belgrano Manuel 1770–1820. Argentinian revolutionary. He was a member of the military group that led the 1810 revolt against Spain. Later, he commanded the revolutionary army until he was replaced by José de ◊San Martín in 1814.

Bell Alexander Graham 1847–1922. British scientist, and inventor of the telephone. He patented his invention in 1876, and later experimented with a type of phonograph and in aeronautics invented the tricycle undercarriage.

Born in Edinburgh, he was educated at the universities of Edinburgh and London, and in 1870 went first to Canada and then to the USA where he opened a school for teachers of the deaf in Boston in 1872, and in 1873 became professor of vocal physiology at the university.

Bell Patrick *c.*1800–1869. Scottish inventor of a reaping machine, developed around 1828. It was pushed by two horses and used a rotating cylinder of horizontal bars to bend the standing corn on to a reciprocating cutter that was driven off the machine's wheels (in much the same way as on a combine harvester).

Bellarmine Roberto Francesco Romolo 1542–1621. Italian Christian theologian, cardinal, and controversialist. He taught at the Jesuit College in Rome, and became archbishop of Capua 1602. His *Disputationes de controversersiis fidei christianae* 1581–93 was an important defence of Catholicism in the 16th century. He was canonized in 1930.

Bellay Joaquim du *c.*1522–1560. French poet and prose-writer, who published the great manifesto of the new school of French poetry, the Pléiade: *Défense et illustration de la langue française* 1549.

Bell Burnell Jocelyn 1943– . British astronomer. In 1967 she discovered the first pulsar (rapidly flashing star) with Antony ◊Hewish and colleagues at Cambridge University, England.

Bellingshausen Fabian Gottlieb von 1779–1852. Russian Antarctic explorer, the first to sight and circumnavigate the Antarctic continent 1819–21, although he did not realize what it was.

Bellini family of Italian painters, founders of the Venetian school. *Jacopo Bellini* (*c.*1400–70) was father to Gentile and Giovanni. Little of his work has survived, but two of his sketchbooks (exhibited in the British Museum and the Louvre) contain his ideas and designs.

Gentile (*c.*1429–1507) assisted in the decoration of the Doge's Palace 1474 and worked in the court of Muhammad II at Constantinople (a portrait of the sultan is in the National Gallery, London). His also painted processional groups (Accademia, Venice).

Gentile's younger brother, *Giovanni* (*c.*1430–1516), studied under his father, and painted portraits and various religious subjects. Giovanni Bellini's early works show the influence of his brother-in-law, Mantegna. His style developed from the static manner of mid-15th-century Venetian work towards a High Renaissance harmony and grandeur, as in the altarpiece 1505 in S Zaccaria, Venice. He introduced softness in tone, harmony in composition, and a use of luminous colour that influenced the next generation of painters (including his pupils Giorgione and Titian). He worked in oil rather than tempera, a technique adopted from Antonello da Messina.

Bellini Vincenzo 1801–1835. Italian composer, born in Catania, Sicily. His operas include *La sonnambula* 1831, *Norma* 1831, and *I puritani* 1835.

Belloc (Joseph) Hilaire Pierre 1870–1953. British author, best remembered for his nonsense verse for children, *The Bad Child's Book of Beasts* 1896 and *Cautionary Tales* 1907. With G K ◊Chesterton, he advocated a return to the guild system of commercial association in the late Middle Ages in place of capitalism or socialism.

Bellot Joseph René 1826–1853. French Arctic explorer, who reached the Bellot Strait in 1852, and lost his life while searching for John ◊Franklin.

Bellow Saul 1915– . US novelist of Russian descent, born in Canada, who settled in Chicago with his family in 1924. His works include the picaresque *The Adventures of Augie March* 1953, the philosophically speculative *Herzog* 1964, *Humboldt's Gift* 1975, *The Dean's December* 1982, and *More Die of Heartbreak* 1987. Nobel prize 1976.

Belmondo Jean Paul 1933– . French film actor who played the leading role of Godard's *A bout de souffle/Breathless* 1959. Despite appearances in some international films, he remains best known in France.

Beloff Max 1913– . British historian. From 1974 to 1979 he was principal of the University College at Buckingham, Britain's first independent institution at university level. He was created a life peer 1981.

Benali Zine el Abidine 1936– . Tunisian politician, president from 1987. After training in France and the USA, he returned to Tunisia and became director-general of national security. He was made minister of the interior and then prime minister under the ageing president for life, Habib ◊Bourguiba, in 1987 whom he deposed by a bloodless coup with the aid of ministerial colleagues. He assumed the presidency, promising greater democracy through constitutional reform.

Ben Barka Mehdi 1920–1965. Moroccan politician. He became president of the National Consultative Assembly in 1956 on the country's independence from France. He was assassinated in France. The case disturbed Franco-Moroccan relations, and

led to de Gaulle's reorganization of the French secret service.

Ben Bella Ahmed 1916– . Algerian leader of the National Liberation Front (FLN) from 1952; prime minister of independent Algeria 1962–65, when he was overthrown by ◊Boumédienne and detained until 1980. He founded a new party, Mouvement pour la Démocratie en Algérie, 1985.

Benbow John 1653–1702. English admiral, hero of several battles with France. He ran away to sea as a boy, and from 1689 served in the navy. He fought at Beachy Head 1690 and La Hogue 1692, and died of wounds received in a long fight with the French off Jamaica.

Benchley Robert 1889–1945. US humorist and actor, born in Massachusetts. He was associated with the writer Dorothy Parker, the *New Yorker*, and the circle of wits at the Algonquin Round Table in New York.

His books include *Of All Things* 1921 and *Benchley Beside Himself* 1943, and his film skit *How to Sleep* illustrates his ability to extract humour from daily living.

Benda Julien 1867–1956. French writer and philosopher. He was an outspoken opponent of the philosophy of Bergson, and in 1927 published a manifesto on the necessity of devotion to the absolute truth which he felt his contemporaries had betrayed, *La Trahison des clercs/The Treason of the Intellectuals*.

Benedict XV 1854–1922. Pope from 1914. During World War I he endeavoured to remain neutral, and his papacy is noted for the renewal of British official relations with the Vatican, suspended since the 17th century.

Benedict, St c.480–c.547. Founder of Christian monasticism in the West, and of the Benedictine order. He founded the monastery of Monte Cassino, Italy. Here he wrote out his rule for monastic life, and was visited shortly before his death by the Ostrogothic king Totila, whom he converted to the Christian faith. Feast day 11 July.

Beneš Eduard 1884–1948. Czech politician. He was president of the republic from 1935 until forced to resign by the Germans, and headed a government in exile in London during World War II. He returned home as president 1945, but resigned again after the communist coup 1948.

Benét Stephen Vincent 1898–1943. US poet, noted for his narrative poem of the Civil War *John Brown's Body* 1928.

Ben-Gurion David. Adopted name of David Gruen 1886–1973. Israeli socialist politician, the country's first prime minister 1948–53, and again in 1955–63. He was born in Poland.

Benjamin Arthur 1893–1960. Australian pianist and composer who taught composition at the Royal College of Music in London from 1925,

Benedict, St *Italian St Benedict, the founder of Western monasticism.*

where ◊Britten was one of his pupils. His works include *Jamaican Rumba*, inspired by a visit to the West Indies in 1937.

Benn Tony (Anthony Wedgwood) 1925– . British Labour politician, formerly the most influential figure on the party's left wing. He was minister of technology 1966–70 and of industry 1974–75, but his campaign against entry to the European Community led to his transfer to the Department of Energy 1975–79. He unsuccessfully contested Neil Kinnock for the party leadership 1988.

Son of Lord Stansgate, a Labour peer, he succeeded his father 1960, though he never used his title and in 1963 was the first person to disclaim a title under the Peerage Act. In 1981 he challenged Denis Healey for the deputy leadership of the party and was so narrowly defeated that he established himself as the acknowledged leader of the left.

Bennett (Enoch) Arnold 1867–1931. English novelist. Coming from one of the 'five towns' of the Potteries which formed the setting of his major books, he became a London journalist 1893 and editor of *Woman* 1896. His books include *Anna of the Five Towns* 1904, *The Old Wives' Tale* 1908, and the trilogy *Clayhanger, Hilda Lessways*, and *These Twain* 1910–15.

Bennett Alan 1934– . English playwright. His works (set in his native north of England), treat subjects such as senility, illness, and death with macabre comedy. They include TV films, for example, *An Englishman Abroad* 1982; the cinema film *A Private Function* 1984; and plays like *Forty Years On* 1968 and *Getting On* 1971.

Bennett Richard Rodney 1936– . English composer of jazz, film music, symphonies, and operas. His film scores for *Far from the Madding Crowd* 1967, *Nicholas and Alexandra* 1971, and *Murder on the Orient Express* 1974 all received Oscar nominations. His operas include *The Mines of Sulphur* 1963 and *Victory* 1970.

Benny Jack. Stage name of Benjamin Kubelsky 1894–1974. US comedian, active mainly in radio and television. His film appearances, mostly in the 1930s and 1940s, included a starring role in *To Be or Not To Be* 1942. He also played in *Charley's Aunt* 1941, *It's In the Bag* 1945, and *A Guide for the Married Man* 1967.

Benson E(dward) F(rederic) 1867–1940. British writer. He specialized in novels gently satirizing the foibles of upper-middle-class society, and is best known for his series of books featuring the formidable female antagonists Mapp and Lucia, including *Queen Lucia* 1920. He was the son of Edward White Benson.

Benson Edward White 1829–1896. British cleric, first headmaster of Wellington College 1859–68, and, as archbishop of Canterbury from 1883, responsible for the 'Lincoln Judgment' on questions of ritual in 1887.

Bentham Jeremy 1748–1832. English philosopher, legal and social reformer, and founder of utilitarianism. The essence of his moral philosophy is found in the pronouncement of his *Principles of Morals and Legislation* (written 1780, published 1789), that the object of all legislation should be 'the greatest happiness for the greatest number'.

He declared that the 'utility' of any law is to be measured by the extent to which it promotes the pleasure, good, and happiness of the people concerned. In 1776, he published *Fragments on Government*. He made suggestions for the reform of the poor law 1798, which formed the basis of the reforms enacted in 1834, and in his *Catechism of Parliamentary Reform* 1817, he proposed annual elections, the secret ballot, and universal male suffrage. He was also a pioneer of prison reform. In economics Bentham was an apostle of *laissez-faire*, and in his *Defence of Usury* 1787 and *Manual of Political Economy* 1798, he contended that his principle of 'utility' was best served by allowing every man (sic) to pursue his own interests unhindered by restrictive legislation. He was made a citizen of the French Republic in 1792.

Bentinck Lord William Cavendish 1774–1839. British colonial administrator, first governor general of India 1828–35. He acted against the ancient Indian rituals of thuggee and suttee, and established English as the medium of instruction.

Bentley Edmund Clerihew 1875–1956. British author. He invented the four-line humorous verse form known as the *clerihew*, first used in *Biography for Beginners* 1905 and in *Baseless Biography* 1939. He was also the author of the classic detective story *Trent's Last Case* 1912.

Bentley John Francis 1839–1902. British architect, a convert to Catholicism, who designed Westminster Cathedral, London (1895–1903). It is outwardly Byzantine but inwardly shaped by shadowy vaults of bare brickwork. The campanile is the tallest church tower in London.

Bentley Richard 1662–1742. British classical scholar, whose textual criticism includes *Dissertation upon the Epistles of Phalaris* 1699. He was Master of Trinity College, Cambridge University, from 1700.

Benz Karl 1844–1929. German automobile engineer, who produced the world's first petrol-driven motorcar. He built his first model engine 1878 and the petrol-driven car 1885.

Ben Zvi Izhak 1884–1963. Israeli politician, president 1952–63. He was born in Atpoltava, Russia, and became active in the Zionist movement in Ukraine. In 1907 he went to Palestine but was deported 1915 with ◊Ben Gurion. They served in the Jewish Legion under Gen Allenby, who commanded the British forces in the Middle East.

Béranger Pierre Jean de 1780–1857. French poet, famous for his light satirical lyrics, dealing with love, wine, popular philosophy, and politics.

Berchtold Count Leopold von 1863–1942. Prime minister and foreign minister of Austria-Hungary 1912–15, and a crucial figure in the events that led to World War I.

Berdyaev Nikolai Alexandrovich 1874–1948. Russian philosopher, who often challenged official viewpoints. Although appointed professor of philosophy in 1919 at the university of Moscow, his defence of Orthodox Christian religion caused his exile in 1922. His books include *The Meaning of History* 1923 and *The Destiny of Man* 1935.

Berenson Bernard 1865–1959. US art expert, born in Lithuania, once revered as a leading scholar of the Italian Renaissance. He amassed a great fortune, and many of his attributions of previously anonymous Italian paintings were later disproved.

Berg Alban 1885–1935. Austrian composer. He studied under ◊Schoenberg and was associated with him as one of the leaders of the serial, or 12-tone, school of composition. His output includes orchestral, chamber and vocal music as well as two operas, *Wozzeck* 1925, a grim story of working-class life and the unfinished *Lulu* 1929–35.

His music is emotionally expressive, and sometimes anguished, but can also be lyrical, as in the *Violin Concerto* 1935.

Berg Paul 1926– . US molecular biologist. In 1972, using gene-splicing techniques developed

Bergius *German chemist and Nobel prizewinner for chemistry in 1931.*

by others, Berg spliced and combined into a single hybrid DNA from an animal tumour virus (SV40) and DNA from a bacterial virus. Berg's work aroused fears in other workers and excited continuing controversy. For his work on recombinant DNA, Berg shared the 1980 Nobel Chemistry Prize with Walter ◊Gilbert and Frederick ◊Sanger.

Bergius Friedrich Karl Rudolph 1884–1949. German research chemist who invented processes for converting coal into oil, and wood into sugar. Nobel prize 1931.

Bergman Ingmar 1918– . Swedish film producer and director. His work deals with complex moral, psychological, and metaphysical problems and is often heavily tinged with pessimism. His films include *Wild Strawberries* 1957, *Persona* 1966, and *Fanny and Alexander* 1982.

Bergman Ingrid 1917–1982. Swedish actress, whose early films include *Casablanca* and *For Whom the Bell Tolls* both 1943. By leaving her husband for film producer Roberto Rossellini, she broke an unofficial moral code of Hollywood 'star' behaviour and was ostracized for many years. During her 'exile', she made films in Europe such as *Stromboli* 1949 (directed by Rossellini). Later films include *Anastasia* 1956, for which she won an Academy Award.

Bergson Henri 1859–1941. French philosopher, who believed that time, change, and development were the essence of reality. He thought that time was not a succession of distinct and separate instants, but a continuous process in which one period merged imperceptibly into the next.

He was professor of philosophy at the Collège de France (1900–21). Nobel Prize for Literature 1928.

Beria Lavrenti 1899–1953. Soviet politician, who became head of the Soviet police force and minister of the interior in 1938. On Stalin's death in 1953, he was shot after a secret trial.

Bering Vitus 1681–1741. Danish explorer, the first European to sight Alaska. He died on Bering Island in the Bering Sea, both named after him, as is the Bering Strait, which separates Asia (USSR) from North America (Alaska).

Berio Luciano 1925– . Italian composer. His style has been described as graceful serialism, and he has frequently experimented with electronic music and taped sound. His works include nine *Sequenzas/Sequences* 1957–75 for various solo instruments or voice, *Sinfonia* 1969 for voices and orchestra, *Points on the curve to find...* 1974, and a number of dramatic works, including the opera *Un re in ascolto/A King Listens* 1984, loosely based on Shakespeare's *The Tempest*.

Beriosova Svetlana 1932– . British ballerina. Born in Lithuania and brought up partly in the USA she danced with the Royal Ballet from 1952. Her style had a lyrical dignity and she excelled in *The Lady and the Fool, Ondine*, and *Giselle*.

Berkeley Busby 1895–1976. US film choreographer and director, famous for his ingeniously extravagant sets and his use of female dancers to create large-scale pattern effects through movement and costume, as in *Gold Diggers of 1933*.

Berkeley George 1685–1753. Irish philosopher, who believed that nothing exists apart from perception, that a thing which is not perceived cannot be known, and therefore cannot exist. For Berkeley, everyday objects are collections of ideas or sensations, hence the dictum *esse est percipi* ('to exist is to be perceived'). He became Bishop of Cloyne 1734.

Berkeley Lennox (Randal Francis) 1903–1989. English composer. His works for the voice include *The Hill of the Graces* 1975, verses from Spenser's *Fairie Queene* set for eight-part unaccompanied chorus; and his operas *Nelson* 1953 and *Ruth* 1956.

Berlin Irving. Adopted name of Israel Baline 1888–1989. Russian-born US composer, whose hits include 'Alexander's Ragtime Band', 'Always', 'God Bless America', and 'White Christmas', and the musicals *Top Hat* 1935, *Annie Get Your Gun* 1950, and *Call Me Madam* 1953. He also wrote film scores such as *Blue Skies* and *Easter Parade*.

Berlin Isaiah 1909– . British philosopher. The son of a refugee from the Russian Revolution, he was professor of social and political theory at Oxford 1957–67. His books include *Historical Inevitability* 1954 and *Four Essays on Liberty* 1969. He was awarded the Order of Merit in 1971.

Berlinguer Enrico 1922–1984. Italian Communist who freed the party from Soviet influence. By 1976 he was near to the premiership, but the murder of Aldo Moro, the prime minister, by Red Brigade guerrillas revived the socialist vote.

Bernadette, St 1844–1879. French saint, born in Lourdes in the French Pyrenees. In Feb 1858 she had a vision of the Virgin Mary in a grotto, and it became a centre of pilgrimage. Many sick people who were dipped in the water of a spring there were said to have been cured. Feast day 16 Apr.

At the age of 20 Bernadette became a nun at Nevers, and nursed the wounded of the Franco-Prussian War.

Bernadotte Count Folke 1895–1948. Swedish diplomat and president of the Swedish Red Cross. In 1945 he conveyed the Nazi commander Himmler's offer of capitulation to the British and US governments, and in 1948 was United Nations mediator in Palestine, where he was assassinated by Stern Gang guerrillas. He was a nephew of Gustaf VI of Sweden.

Bernadotte Jean-Baptiste Jules 1764–1844. Marshal in Napoleon's army, who in 1818 became ◊Charles XIV of Sweden. Hence, Bernadotte is the family name of the present royal house of Sweden.

Bernanos Georges 1888–1948. French author. Born in Paris, he achieved fame in 1926 with *Sous le soleil de Satan/The Star of Satan*. His strongly Catholic viewpoint emerged equally in his *Journal d'un curé de campagne/The Diary of a Country Priest* 1936.

Bernard Claude 1813–1878. French physiologist and founder of experimental medicine. Bernard first demonstrated that digestion is not restricted to the stomach, but takes place throughout the small intestine. He discovered the digestive input of the pancreas, several functions of the liver, and the vasomotor nerves which dilate and contract the blood vessels and thus regulate body temperature.

This led him to the important concept of the *milieu intérieur* ('internal environment') whose stability is essential to good health. Bernard was a member of the Académie Française and served in the Senate.

Bernard of Clairvaux, St 1090–1153. Christian founder in 1115 of Clairvaux monastery in Champagne, France. He reinvigorated the Cistercian order, preached in support of the Second Crusade in 1146, and had the scholastic philosopher Abelard condemned for heresy. He is often depicted with a beehive. Feast day 20 Aug.

Bernard of Menthon, St (or *Bernard of Montjoux*) 923–1008. Christian priest, founder of the hospices for travellers on the Alpine passes that bear his name. The large, heavily built *St Bernard dogs* formerly used to find travellers lost in the snow were also called after him. He is the patron saint of mountaineers. Feast day 28 May.

Bernhard Prince of the Netherlands 1911– . Formerly Prince Bernhard of Lippe-Biesterfeld, he married Princess ◊Juliana in 1937. When Germany invaded the Netherlands in 1940, he escaped to England and became liaison officer for the Dutch and British forces, playing a part in the organization of the Dutch Resistance. In 1976 he was widely censured for his involvement in the purchase of Lockheed aircraft by the Netherlands.

Bernhardt Sarah. Stage name of Rosine Bernard 1845–1923. French actress who dominated the stage of her day, frequently performing at the Comédie-Française in Paris. She excelled in tragic roles, including Cordelia in Shakespeare's *King Lear*, the title role in Racine's *Phèdre*, and the male roles of Hamlet and of Napoleon's son in Edmond ◊Rostand's *L'Aiglon*.

Bernini Giovanni Lorenzo 1598–1680. Italian sculptor, architect, and painter, a leading figure in the development of the Baroque style. His work in Rome includes the colonnaded piazza in front of St Peter's Basilica (1656), fountains (as in the Piazza Navona), and papal monuments. His sculpture includes *The Ecstasy of St Theresa* 1645–52 (Sta Maria della Vittoria, Rome), and numerous portrait busts. Inside St Peter's, he created several marble monuments and the elaborate canopy over the high altar. He also produced many fine portrait busts, one of Louis XIV of France.

Bernoulli Swiss family which produced many capable mathematicians and scientists in the 17th, 18th, and 19th centuries, in particular the brothers *Jakob* (1654–1705) and *Johann* (1667–1748), and Johann's son *Daniel* (1700–1782).

Jakob and Johann were pioneer's of ◊Leibniz's calculus. Jakob used calculus to study the forms of many curves arising in practical situations, and studied mathematical probability (his *Ars conjectandi* appearing in 1713). Many things mathematical now bear his name, including the series of fractions called *Bernoulli numbers*. Johann, a great teacher, developed the exponential calculus and contributed to many areas of applied mathematics, including the problem of a particle moving in a gravitational field. His three sons all became professors of mathematics. The most famous, Daniel, worked on calculus and probability, and in physics proposed *Bernoulli's principle*, which states that the pressure of a moving fluid decreases the faster it flows (which explains the origin of lift on the aerofoil of an aircraft's wing). This and other work on hydrodynamics was published in *Hydrodynamica* 1738.

Bernstein Edouard 1850–1932. German socialist thinker, proponent of reformist rather than revolutionary socialism, whereby a socialist society could be achieved within an existing parliamentary structure, merely by workers' parties obtaining a majority.

Bernstein Leonard 1918– . US composer, conductor, and pianist. He has conducted major orchestras throughout the world. His works, which established a vogue for realistic, contemporary themes, include symphonies such as *The Age of Anxiety* 1949; ballets such as *Fancy Free* 1944; scores for musicals including *Wonderful Town* 1953 and *West Side Story* 1957; and *Mass* 1971 in memory of President J F Kennedy.

Born in Lawrence, Massachussetts, he was educated at Harvard University and the Curtis Institute of Music. From 1958–1970 he was musical director of the New York Philharmonic. Among his other works are *Jeremiah* 1944, *Facsimile* 1946, *Candide* 1956, and the *Chichester Psalms* 1965.

Berri Nabih 1939– . Lebanese politician and soldier, leader of Amal ('Hope'), the Syrian-backed Shi'ite nationalist movement. He was minister of justice in government of President ◊Gemayel from 1984. In 1988 Amal was disbanded after defeat by the Iranian-backed Hezbollah ('Children of God') during the Lebanese civil wars.

Berrigan Daniel 1921– and Philip 1924– . US Roman Catholic priests. The brothers, opponents of the Vietnam War, broke into the draft-records offices at Catonsville, Maryland, to burn the files with napalm, and were sentenced in 1968 to three and six years' imprisonment, but went underground.

Berry Family name of Viscount Camrose, Viscount Kemsley and Lord Hartwell.

Berry Chuck (Charles Edward) 1926– . US rock-and-roll singer, prolific songwriter, and guitarist. His characteristic guitar riffs became staples of rock music, and his humorous storytelling lyrics were also influential. He had a string of hits in the 1950s and 1960s beginning with 'Maybellene' 1955.

Berryman John 1914–1972. US poet, whose complex and personal works include *Homage to Mistress Bradstreet* 1956, *77 Dream Songs* 1964 (Pulitzer Prize), and *His Toy, His Dream, His Rest* 1968.

Berthelot Pierre Eugène Marcellin 1827–1907. French chemist and politician, who carried out research into dyes and explosives, and proved that hydrocarbons and other organic compounds can be synthesized from inorganic materials.

Bertholet Claude Louis 1748–1822. French chemist, who carried out research on dyes and bleaches (introducing the use of chlorine as a bleach) and determined the composition of ammonia.

Modern chemical nomenclature is based on a system worked out by Bertholet and Antoine ◊Lavoisier.

Bertolucci Bernardo 1940– . Italian film director, whose work combines political and historical satire with an elegant visual appeal. His films include *The Spider's Stratagem* 1970, *Last Tango in Paris* 1972, and *The Last Emperor* 1987, for which he received an Academy Award.

Bertrand de Born *c.*1140–*c.*1215. Provençal troubadour. He was viscount of Hautefort in Périgord, accompanied Richard Lionheart to Palestine, and died a monk.

Berwick James Fitzjames, Duke of Berwick 1670–1734. French marshal, illegitimate son of the Duke of York (afterwards James II of England) and Arabella Churchill (1648–1730), sister of the great duke of Marlborough, his enemy in battle. He was made duke of Berwick in 1687. After the revolution of 1688 he served under his father in Ireland, joined the French army, fought against William III and Marlborough, and in 1707 defeated the English at Almansa in Spain. He was killed at the siege of Philippsburg.

Berzelius Jöns Jakob 1779–1848. Swedish chemist, whose accurate determination of atomic and molecular weights helped to establish the laws of combination and the atomic theory. He invented (1813–14) the system of chemical symbols now in use and did valuable work on catalysts.

Besant Annie 1847–1933. British socialist and feminist activist. Separated from her clerical husband in 1873 because of her freethinking views, she was associated with the radical atheist Charles Bradlaugh and the socialist Fabian group. She and Bradlaugh published a treatise advocating birth control and were prosecuted; as a result she lost custody of her daughter. In 1889 she became a disciple of Mme ◊Blavatsky. She thereafter preached theosophy and, as a supporter of Indian independence, became president of the Hindu National Congress in 1917.

Besant Walter 1836–1901. British writer. He wrote novels in partnership with James Rice (1844–82), and produced an attack on the social evils of the East End of London, *All Sorts and Conditions of Men* 1882, and an unfinished *Survey of London* 1902–12.

Bessel Friedrich Wilhelm 1784–1846. German astronomer and mathematician, the first person to find the approximate distance to a star by direct methods when he measured the parallax (annual displacement) of the star 61 Cygni in 1838. In mathematics, he introduced the series of functions now known as *Bessel functions*.

Bessemer Henry 1813–1898. British civil engineer, who invented a method of converting molten pig-iron into steel (the *Bessemer process*).

Best Charles Herbert 1899–1978. Canadian physiologist, one of the team of Canadian scientists including Frederick ◊Banting, whose researches resulted in 1922 in the discovery of insulin as a treatment for diabetes.

A Banting–Best Department of Medical Research was founded in Toronto, and Best was its director from 1941 to 1967.

Best George 1946– . Irish footballer. He won two League championship medals and was a member of the Manchester United side that won the European Cup in 1968.

Born in Belfast, he joined Manchester United as a youth and made his debut at 17; seven months later he made his international debut for Northern Ireland.

Bethe Hans Albrecht 1906– . German-born US physicist. He worked on the first atomic bomb, and was in 1967 awarded a Nobel prize for his discoveries concerning energy production in stars.

Bethe left Germany for England in 1933, working at Manchester and Bristol universities. In 1935 he moved to the USA where he became professor of theoretical physics at Cornell University; his research was interrupted by the war and by his appointment as head of the theoretical division of the Los Alamos atomic bomb project. He has since become a leading peace campaigner, and opposed the US government's Strategic Defense Initiative or 'Star Wars' programme.

Bethmann Hollweg Theobald von 1856–1921. German politician, imperial chancellor 1909–17, largely responsible for engineering popular support for World War I in Germany, but his power was gradually superseded by a military dictatorship under ◊Ludendorff.

Betjeman John 1906–1984. English poet and essayist, originator of a peculiarly English light verse, nostalgic and delighting in Victorian and Edwardian architecture. His *Collected Poems* appeared in 1968 and a verse autobiography *Summoned by Bells* in 1960. He was knighted in 1969 and became poet laureate in 1972.

Betterton Thomas *c.*1635–1710. British actor, a member of the Duke of York's company after the Restoration. He was greatly admired in many Shakespeare parts, including Hamlet and Othello.

Betti Ugo 1892–1953. Italian poet and dramatist. His best-known plays are *Delitto all'isola delle capre/Crime on Goat Island* 1948 and *La regina e gli insorte/The Queen and the Rebels* 1949.

Betty William Henry West 1791–1874. British boy actor, called the 'Young Roscius' after the greatest comic actor of ancient Rome. He was famous, particularly in Shakespearean roles, from the ages of 11 to 17.

Beuys Joseph 1921–1986. German sculptor and performance artist. By the 1970s he had gained an international reputation. His sculpture makes use of unusual materials such as felt and fat. He was strongly influenced by his wartime experiences.

Bevan Aneurin 1897–1960. British Labour politician. Son of a Welsh miner, and himself a miner at 13, he became member of Parliament for Ebbw

Vale 1929–60. As minister of health 1945–51, he inaugurated the National Health Service (NHS); he was minister of labour Jan–Apr 1951, when he resigned (with Harold Wilson) on the introduction of NHS charges and led a Bevanite faction against the government. He was noted as an orator.

Beveridge William Henry, 1st Baron Beveridge 1879–1963. British economist. A civil servant, he acted as Lloyd George's lieutenant in the social legislation of the Liberal government before World War I. The *Beveridge Report* 1942 formed the basis of the welfare state in Britain.

Bevin Ernest 1881–1951. British Labour politician. Chief creator of the Transport and General Workers' Union, he was its general secretary 1921–40, when he entered the war cabinet as minister of labour and National Service. He organized the 'Bevin boys', chosen by ballot to work in the coal mines as war service, and was foreign secretary in the Labour government 1945–51.

Bewick Thomas 1753–1828. British wood engraver, excelling in animal subjects. His illustrated *General History of Quadrupeds* 1790 and *History of British Birds* 1797, 1804 display his skill.

Beza Théodore (properly De Bèsze) 1519–1605. French church reformer. He settled in Geneva, Switzerland, where he worked with the Protestant leader John Calvin and succeeded him in 1564 as head of the reformed church there. He wrote in defence of the burning of ◊Servetus (1554) and translated the New Testament into Latin.

Bhindranwale Sant Jarnail Singh 1947–1984. Indian Sikh fundamentalist leader, who campaigned for the creation of a separate state of Khalistan during the early 1980s, precipitating a bloody Hindu-Sikh conflict in the Punjab.

Having taken refuge in the Golden Temple complex in Amritsar and built up an arms cache for guerrilla activities, Bhindranwale, along with around 500 followers, died at the hands of Indian security forces who stormed the temple in 'Operation Blue Star' June 1984.

Bhumibol Adulyadej 1927– . King of Thailand from 1946. Educated in Bangkok and Switzerland, he succeeded on the assassination of his brother, formally taking the throne 1950. In 1973 he was active, with popular support, in overthrowing the military government of Field Marshal Kittikachorn and ending a sequence of army-dominated regimes in power from 1932.

Bhutto Benazir 1953– . Pakistani politician, leader of the Pakistan People's Party (PPP) from 1984 (in exile until 1986), and prime minister of Pakistan from 1988. She is the first female leader of a Muslim state.

Benazir Bhutto was educated at Harvard and Oxford universities. She returned to Pakistan 1977 but was placed under house arrest after Gen ◊Zia ul Haq seized power from her father, Prime Minister Zulfiqar Ali Bhutto. On her release she

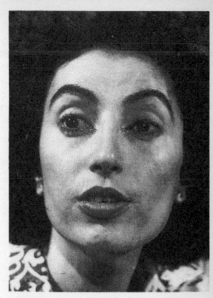

Bhutto *Benazir Bhutto at a press conference in Islamabad, 01 Dec 1900.*

moved to the UK and became, with her mother Nusrat (1934–), the joint leader in exile of the opposition PPP. When martial law had been lifted, she returned to Pakistan Apr 1986 to launch a campaign for open elections. In her first year in office she struck an uneasy balance with the military establishment and improved Pakistan's relations with India. She led her country back into the Commonwealth 1989 and became in 1990 the first head of government to bear a child while in office.

Bhutto Zulfiqar Ali 1928–1979. Pakistani politician, president 1971–73 and then prime minister until the 1977 military coup led by Gen ◊Zia ul Haq. In 1978 he was sentenced to death for conspiracy to murder a political opponent, and was hanged.

Biber Heinrich von 1644–1704. Bohemian composer, kapellmeister at the archbishop of Salzburg's court. A virtuoso violinist, he composed a wide variety of musical pieces including the *Nightwatchman Serenade*.

Bichat Marie François Xavier 1771–1802. French physician and founder of histology, the study of tissues. He studied the organs of the body, their structure, and the ways in which they are affected by disease. This led to his discovery and naming of 'tissues', a basic medical concept. He argued that disease does not affect the whole organ but only certain of its constituent tissues.

He was physician at the Hôtel-Dieu hospital in Paris, and here, in a single year, he carried out 600 autopsies. He identified 21 types of tissue.

Bidault Georges 1899–1983. French politician. As a leader of the Movement Républicaine Populaire, he held office as prime minister and foreign minister in a number of unstable administrations of 1944–54. He was head of the *Organisation de l'Armée Secrète* an underground organization formed 1961 by French settlers devoted to pepetuating their own rule in Algeria. In 1962 he left the country, but was allowed to return in 1968.

Bierce Ambrose (Gwinett) 1842–1914. US author. He established his reputation as a master of supernatural and psychological horror with his *Tales of Soldiers and Civilians* 1891 and *Can Such Things Be?* 1893. He also wrote *The Devil's Dictionary* 1906, a collection of ironic definitions. He disappeared on a secret mission to Mexico.

Bierstadt Albert 1830–1902. US landscape painter. His spectacular panoramas fell out of favour after the American Civil War. A classic work is *Thunderstorm in the Rocky Mountains* 1859 (Museum of Fine Arts, Boston).

***Billy the Kid** The US outlaw William Bonney, Billy the Kid, who was shot by Sheriff Pat Garrett in 1881.*

Biffen (William) John 1930– . British Conservative politician. In 1971 Biffen was elected to Parliament for a Shropshire seat. Despite being to the left of Margaret Thatcher, he held key positions in government from 1979, including leader of the House of Commons from 1982, but was dropped after the general election of 1987.

Biko Steve (Stephen) 1946–1977. South African civil rights leader. An active opponent of apartheid, he was arrested in Sept 1977 and died in detention six days later.

He founded the South African Students Organization (SASO) in 1968 and was cofounder in 1972 of the Black People's Convention, also called the Black Consciousness movement, a radical association of South African students that aimed to develop black pride. Since his death in the custody of South African police he has been a symbol of the anti-apartheid movement.

Billy the Kid nickname of William H Bonney 1859–1881. US outlaw, a leader in the Lincoln County cattle war in New Mexico, who allegedly killed his first man at 12 and 22 people in total. He was sentenced to death for murdering a sheriff, but escaped (killing two guards), and was finally shot by Sheriff Pat Garrett while trying to avoid recapture.

Bingham Hiram 1875–1919. US explorer and politician, who from 1907 visited Latin America, discovering Machu Picchu, Vitcos, and other Inca settlements in Peru. He later entered politics, becoming a senator.

Binyon Laurence 1869–1943. British poet. His verse volumes include *Lyric Poems* 1894 and *London Visions*, but he is best remembered for his ode *For the Fallen* 1914.

Biot Jean 1774–1862. French physicist who studied the polarization of light. In 1804 he made a balloon ascent to a height of three miles, in an early investigation of the Earth's atmosphere.

Birch John M 1918–1945. US Baptist missionary, commissioned by the US Air Force to carry out intelligence work behind the Chinese lines, where he was killed by the communists; the US extreme right-wing nationalist *John Birch Society* 1958 is named after him.

Bird Isabella 1832–1904. British traveller and writer who wrote extensively of her journeys in the USA, Persia, Tibet, Kurdistan, China, Japan, and Korea. She suffered from a spinal illness, and many expeditions were 'test' cures.

Her published works include *The Englishwoman in America* 1856, *A Lady's Life in the Rocky Mountains* 1874, *Unbeaten Tracks in Japan* 1880, *Among the Tibetans* 1894, and *Pictures from China* 1900. Her last great journey was made in 1901 when she travelled over 1,600 km/1,000 mi in Morocco.

Birdseye Clarence 1886–1956. US inventor who pioneered food refrigeration processes. While working as a fur trader in Labrador in 1912–16

Bismarck Prusso-German politician Prince Otto von Bismarck in army uniform.

he was struck by the ease with which food could be preserved in an Arctic climate. Back in the USA he found that the same effect could be obtained by rapidly freezing prepared food between two refrigerated metal plates.

Birkenhead Frederick Edwin Smith, 1st Earl of Birkenhead 1872–1930. British Conservative politician. A flamboyant character, known as 'FE', he joined with Baron Carson in organizing armed resistance in Ulster to Irish Home Rule; he was Lord Chancellor 1919–22, and a much criticized secretary for India 1924–28.

Biro Lazlo 1900–1985. Hungarian-born Argentinian who invented a ballpoint pen in 1944. His name became generic for ballpoint pens in the UK.

Birtwistle Harrison 1934– . English avant-garde composer. He has specialized in chamber music: for example, his chamber opera *Punch and Judy* 1967 and *Down by the Greenwood Side* 1969.

Birtwistle's early music was influenced by ◊Stravinsky and by the medieval and renaissance masters, and for many years he worked alongside Maxwell ◊Davies. Orchestral works include *The Triumph of Time* 1972 and *Silbury Air* 1977; he has also written one large-scale opera *The Mask of Orpheus* 1986 and has experimented with electronic music. His *Chronometer* 1972 is based on clock sounds.

Bishop Ronald Eric 1903–1989. British aircraft designer. He joined the De Havilland Aircraft Company 1931 as an apprentice, and designed the Mosquito bomber, the Vampire fighter, and the Comet jet airliner.

Bishop William Avery 1894–1956. Canadian air ace, who won the Victoria Cross in 1917.

Bismarck Otto Eduard Leopold, Prince von Bismarck 1815–1898. German politician, prime minister of Prussia 1862–90 and chancellor of the German Empire 1871–90. He pursued an aggressively expansionist policy, with wars against Denmark 1863–64, Austria 1866, and France 1870–71, which brought about the unification of Germany.

Bismarck was ambitious to establish Prussia's hegemony inside Germany and eliminate the influence of Austria. He secured Austria's support for his successful war against Denmark, then in 1866 went to war against Austria and its allies (the Seven Weeks' War), his victory forcing Austria out of the German Bund and unifying the N German states in the North German Confederation under his own chancellorship 1867. He then defeated France, under Napoleon III, in the Franco-Prussian War 1870–71, proclaimed the German Empire 1871, and annexed Alsace-Lorraine. He tried to secure his work by the Triple Alliance 1881 with Austria and Italy, but ran into difficulties at home with the Roman Catholic church and the socialist movement, and was forced to resign by Wilhelm II 18 Mar 1890.

Bizet Georges (Alexandre César Léopold) 1838–1875. French composer of operas, among them *Les Pêcheurs de perles/The Pearl Fishers* 1863, and *La jolie Fille de Perth/The Fair Maid of Perth* 1866. He also wrote the concert overture *Patrie* and incidental music to Daudet's *L'Arlésienne*. His operatic masterpiece *Carmen* was produced a few months before his death in 1875.

Bjelke-Patterson Joh(annes) 1911– . Australian right-wing politician, leader of the Queensland National Party (QNP) and premier of Queensland 1968–87.

Björnson Björnstjerne 1832–1910. Norwegian novelist, playwright, poet, and journalist. His plays included *The Newly Married Couple* 1865 and *Beyond Human Power* 1883, dealing with politics and sexual morality. Among his novels is *In God's Way* 1889. Nobel Prize for Literature 1903.

Black Davidson 1884–1934. Canadian anatomist. In 1927, when professor of anatomy at the Union Medical College, Peking, he unearthed the remains of Peking man, a very early human.

Black James 1924– . British physiologist, director of therapeutic research at Wellcome Laboratories (near London) from 1978. He was active in the development of beta-blockers (which reduce the rate of heartbeat) and anti-ulcer drugs. Nobel Prize for Medicine 1988.

Black Joseph 1728–1799. Scottish physicist and chemist, who in 1754 discovered carbon dioxide (which he called 'fixed air'). By his investigations in 1761 of latent heat and specific heat, he laid the foundation for the work of his pupil James Watt.

Born in Bordeaux, France, he qualified as a doctor in Edinburgh. In chemistry, he prepared the way for the scientists Cavendish, Priestley, and Lavoisier.

Blackett Patrick Maynard Stuart, Baron Blackett 1897–1974. British physicist. He was awarded a Nobel prize in 1948 for work in cosmic radiation and his perfection of the Wilson cloud chamber.

Blackmore R(ichard) D(oddridge) 1825–1900. English novelist, author of *Lorna Doone* 1869, a romance set on Exmoor, SW England, in the late 17th century.

Black Prince name given to ◊Edward, Prince of Wales, eldest son of Edward III of England.

Blackstone William 1723–1780. English jurist, who published his *Commentaries on the Laws of England* 1765–70. Called to the Bar in 1746, he became professor of law at Oxford 1758, and a Justice of the Court of Common Pleas 1770.

Blackwell Elizabeth 1821–1910. First British woman to qualify in medicine, in 1849. Blackwell studied medicine at the University of Geneva in New York State. On her return to Britain, she became the first woman to appear in the Medical Register. Her example inspired Elizabeth Garrett ◊Anderson and many other aspiring female doctors.

Blagonravov Anatoly Arkadievich 1894–1975. Russian engineer, a specialist in rocketry and instrumentation. He directed the earth satellite programme leading to the launching of Sputniks 1 and 2.

Blake Robert 1599–1657. British admiral of the Parliamentary forces. Appointed 'general-at-sea' 1649, he destroyed Prince Rupert's privateering fleet off Cartagena, Spain, in the following year. In 1652 he won several engagements against the Dutch. In 1654 he bombarded Tunis, the stronghold of the Barbary corsairs, and in 1657 captured the Spanish treasure fleet in Santa Cruz.

Blake William 1757–1827. English painter, engraver, poet, and mystic, a leading figure in the Romantic period. His visionary, symbolic poems include *Songs of Innocence* 1789 and *Songs of Experience* 1794. He engraved the text and illustrations for his works and hand-coloured them, mostly in watercolour. He also illustrated works by others, including the poet Milton, and created a highly personal style.

He was born in Soho, London, and apprenticed to an engraver 1771–78. Blake illustrated the Bible, works by Dante and Shakespeare, and his own poems. His figures are heavily muscled with elongated proportions. In his later years he attracted a group of followers including Samuel

Palmer, who called themselves the Ancients. Henry Fuseli was another admirer. Blake's poem *Jerusalem* 1820 was set to music by Charles Parry (1848–1918).

Blakey Art (Muslim name Abdullah Ibn Buhaina) 1919– . US jazz drummer, known for his dynamic style with rolls and explosions. He formed and led the Jazz Messengers from 1955, and widely expanded percussion possibilities, including the assimilation of African rhythms.

Blamey Thomas Albert 1884–1951. The first Australian field marshal. Born in New South Wales, he served at Gallipoli, Turkey, and on the Western Front in World War I. In World War II he was commander in chief of the Allied Land Forces in the SW Pacific 1942–45.

Blanc Louis 1811–1882. French socialist and journalist. In 1839 he founded the *Revue du progrès*, in which he published his *Organisation du travail*, advocating the establishment of cooperative workshops and other socialist schemes. He was a member of the provisional government of 1848 and from its fall lived in the UK until 1871.

Blanchard Jean Pierre 1753–1809. French balloonist, who made the first balloon flight across the English Channel with Dr John Jeffries in 1785. He made the first balloon flight in the USA in 1793.

Blanche of Castile 1188–1252. Queen of France, wife of ◊Louis VIII of France, and regent for her son Louis IX (St Louis of France) from the death of her husband in 1226 until Louis IX's majority in 1234, and again from 1247 while he was on a Crusade.

She effectively quelled a series of revolts by the barons, and in 1229 negotiated the Treaty of Paris, by which Toulouse came under control of the monarchy.

Blanqui Louis Auguste 1805–1881. French revolutionary politician. He formulated the theory of the 'dictatorship of the proletariat', used by Karl Marx, and spent a total of 33 years in prison for insurrection. He became a martyr figure for the French workers' movement.

Blashford-Snell John 1936– . British explorer and soldier. His expeditions have included the first descent and exploration of the Blue Nile 1968; the journey N to S from Alaska to Cape Horn, crossing the Darien Gap between Panama and Colombia for the first time 1971–72; and the first complete navigation of the Zaïre river, Africa 1974–75.

From 1963 he organized adventure training at Sandhurst military academy. He was director of Operation Drake 1977–81 and Operation Raleigh 1978–82. His books include *A Taste for Adventure* 1978.

Blasis Carlo 1797–1878. Italian ballet teacher of French extraction. He was successful as a dancer in Paris and in Milan, where he established a dancing school in 1837. His celebrated treatise on the art of dancing, *Traité élémentaire, théoretique et pratique de l'art de la danse* 1820, forms the basis of classical dance training.

Blavatsky Helena Petrovna (born Hahn) 1831–1891. Russian spiritualist and mystic, co-founder of the Theosophical Society 1875, which has its head-quarters near Madras. In Tibet she underwent spiritual training, and later became a Buddhist. Her books include *Isis Unveiled* 1877 and *The Secret Doctrine* 1888. She was declared a fraud by the London Society for Psychical Research 1885.

Blériot Louis 1872–1936. French aviator who, in a 24-horsepower monoplane of his own construction, made the first flight across the English Channel on 25 July 1909.

Blessington Marguerite, Countess of Blessington 1789–1849. Irish writer. A doyenne of literary society, she published *Conversations with Lord Byron* 1834, travel sketches, and novels.

Bligh William 1754–1817. British admiral. Bligh accompanied Capt James ◊Cook on his second voyage 1772–74, and in 1787 commanded HMS *Bounty* on an expedition to the Pacific. On the return voyage the crew mutinied 1789, and Bligh was cast adrift in a boat with 18 men. He was appointed governor of New South Wales in 1805, where his discipline again provoked a mutiny 1808. He returned to Britain, and was made an admiral in 1811.

He went to Tahiti with the *Bounty* to collect breadfruit shortly before the mutiny, and gained the nickname 'Breadfruit Bligh'. In protest against harsh treatment, he and those who supported him were put in a small craft with no map and few provisions. They survived after drifting 5,822 km/3,618 mi.

Bliss Arthur (Drummond) 1891–1975. English composer, who became Master of the Queen's Musick in 1953. Works include *A Colour Symphony* 1922, music for ballets *Checkmate* 1937, *Miracle in the Gorbals* 1944, and *Adam Zero* 1946; an opera *The Olympians* 1949; and dramatic film music, including *Things to Come* 1935.

Blitzstein Marc 1905–1964. US composer. Born in Philadelphia, he was a child prodigy as a pianist at the age of six. He served with the US Army 8th Air Force 1942–45, for which he wrote *The Airborne* 1946, a choral symphony. His operas include *The Cradle Will Rock* 1937.

Blixen Karen, born Karen Dinesen 1885–1962. Danish writer. Her autobiography *Out of Africa* 1937 is based on her experience of running a coffee plantation in Kenya. She wrote fiction, mainly in English, under the pen name Isak Dinesen.

Bloch Ernest 1880–1959. US composer, born in Geneva, Switzerland. He went to the US in 1916 and became founder-director of the Cleveland Institute of Music 1920–25. Among his works are the lyrical drama *Macbeth* 1910, *Schelomo* for cello and orchestra 1916, five string quartets, and *Suite*

Hébraique, for viola and orchestra 1953. He often used themes based on Jewish liturgical music and folk song.

Bloch Felix 1905–1983. Swiss–US physicist. He received a Nobel prize jointly with E M Purcell in 1952 for his work on nuclear magnetic resonance (NMR) spectroscopy.

He was born in Zürich, and was professor of physics at Stanford University, USA, 1934–71.

Bloch Konrad 1912– . US chemist whose research, lasting more than a decade, concerned cholesterol. Making use of the radioisotope carbon-14 (the radioactive form of carbon), Bloch was able to follow the complex steps by which the body chemically transforms acetic acid into cholesterol. For his ability in this field Bloch shared the 1964 Nobel Prize for Medicine with Feodor Lynen (1911–).

Blok Alexander Alexandrovich 1880–1921. Russian poet who, as a follower of the French Symbolist movement, used words for their symbolic rather than actual meaning. He backed the 1917 revolution, as in his most famous poems *The Twelve* 1918, and *The Scythians* 1918, the latter appealing to the West to join in the revolution.

Blomberg Werner von 1878–1946. German soldier and Nazi politician, minister of defence 1933–35 and minister of war and head of the *Wehrmacht* (army) 1935–38 under Hitler's chancellorship. He was discredited by his marriage to a prostitute and dismissed in Jan 1938, enabling Hitler to exercise more direct control over the armed forces. In spite of his removal from office, Blomberg was put on trial for war crimes in 1946 at Nuremberg.

Blomdahl Karl-Birger 1916–1968. Swedish composer of ballets and symphonies in expressionist style. His opera *Aniara* 1959 incorporates electronic music and is set in a spaceship.

Blondin Charles. Assumed name of Jean François Gravelet 1824–1897. French tightrope walker, who walked across a rope suspended above Niagara Falls, USA. He first crossed the falls 1859 at a height of 48.75 m/160 ft, and later repeated the feat blindfolded and then pushing a wheelbarrow.

Blood Thomas 1618–1680. Irish adventurer, known as Colonel Blood, who attempted to steal the Crown Jewels from the Tower of London, England, 1671.

Bloom Claire 1931– . British actress. Born in London, she first made her reputation on the stage in Shakespearean roles. Her films include *Richard III* 1956 and *The Brothers Karamazov* 1958, and television appearances include *Brideshead Revisited* 1980.

Bloomer Amelia Jenks 1818–1894. US campaigner for women's rights. She introduced in 1849, when unwieldy crinolines were the fashion, a knee-length skirt combined with loose trousers gathered at the ankles, which became known as *bloomers* (also called 'rational dress'). She published the magazine *The Lily* 1849–54, which campaigned for women's rights and dress reform, and lectured with Susan B ◊Anthony in New York.

Blow John 1648–1708. British composer. He taught ◊Purcell, and wrote church music, for example the anthem 'I Was Glad when They Said unto Me' 1697. His *Venus and Adonis* 1685 is sometimes called the first English opera.

Bloy Léon-Marie 1846–1917. French author. He achieved a considerable reputation with his literary lampoons in the 1880s.

Blücher Gebhard Leberecht von 1742–1819. Prussian general and field marshal, popular as 'Marshal Forward'. He took an active part in the patriotic movement, and in the War of German Liberation defeated the French as commander in chief at Leipzig 1813, crossed the Rhine to Paris 1814, and was made prince of Wahlstadt (Silesia). In 1815 he was defeated by Napoleon at Ligny, but played a crucial role in the British commander Wellington's triumph at Waterloo, near Brussels.

Blum Léon 1872–1950. French politician. He was converted to socialism by the Dreyfus affair 1899, and in 1936 became the first socialist prime minister of France. He was again premier for a few weeks 1938. Imprisoned under the Vichy government 1942 as a danger to French security, he was released by the Allies 1945. He again became premier for a few weeks 1946.

Blunden Edmund 1896–1974. English poet. He served in World War I, and published the prose work *Undertones of War* 1928. His poetry is mainly about rural life. Among his scholarly contributions was the discovery and publication of some poems by the 19th-century poet John ◊Clare.

Blunt Anthony 1907–1983. British art historian and double agent. As a Cambridge lecturer, he recruited for the Soviet secret service, and, as a member of the British Secret Service 1940–45, passed information to the Russians. In 1951 he assisted the defection to the USSR of the British agents Guy ◊Burgess and Donald Maclean (1913–83). He was author of many respected works on French and Italian art.

Unmasked in 1964, he was given immunity after his confession, but was stripped of his knighthood in 1979 when the affair became public. He was director of the Courtauld Institute of Art 1947–74 and Surveyor of the Queen's Pictures 1945–1972.

Blunt Wilfrid Scawen 1840–1922. British poet. He married Lady Anne Noel, Byron's granddaughter, and travelled with her in the Middle East, becoming a supporter of Arab nationalism. He also supported Irish Home Rule (imprisoned 1887–88), and wrote anti-imperialist books, poetry and diaries.

Blyth Charles 'Chay' 1940– . British sailing adventurer who rowed across the Atlantic with

Capt John Ridgeway in 1966 and sailed solo around the world in a westerly direction during 1970–71. In 1973–74 he sailed around the world with a crew in the opposite direction, and in 1977 he made a record-breaking transatlantic crossing from Cape Verde to Antigua.

Blyton Enid 1897–1968. British writer of children's books. She created the character Noddy and the adventures of the 'Famous Five' and 'Secret Seven', but has been criticized by educationalists for social, racial, and sexual stereotyping.

Boadicea alternative spelling of British queen ◊Boudicca.

Boateng Paul 1951– . British Labour politician. He became member of Parliament for Brent South 1987. He has served on numerous committees on crime and race relations.

Boccaccio Giovanni 1313–1375. Italian poet, author of a collection of tales called the ◊*Decameron* 1348–53.

Son of a Florentine merchant, he lived in Naples 1328–41, where he fell in love with the unfaithful 'Fiametta', who inspired his early poetry. Before returning to Florence in 1341 he had written *Filostrato* and *Teseide* (used by Chaucer in his *Troilus and Criseyde* and *Knight's Tale*).

Boccherini (Ridolfo) Luigi 1743–1805. Italian composer and cellist. He studied in Rome, made his mark in Paris in 1768, and was court composer in Prussia and Spain. Boccherini composed some 350 instrumental works, an opera, and oratorios.

Boccioni Umberto 1882–1916. Italian painter and sculptor. One of the founders of the Futurist movement, he was a pioneer of abstract art.

Böcklin Arnold 1827–1901. Swiss Romantic painter. His mainly imaginary landscapes have a dreamlike atmosphere, for example *Island of the Dead* 1880 (Metropolitan Museum of Art, New York).

He was strongly attracted to Italy, and lived for years in Rome. Many of his paintings are peopled with mythical beings such as nymphs and naiads.

Bode Johann Elert 1747–1826. German astronomer, director of the Berlin observatory. He published the first atlas of all stars visible to the naked eye, *Uranographia* 1801.

He also popularized *Bode's law*, a numerical sequence that gives the approximate distances of the planets from the Sun. Bode's law predicted the existence of a planet between Mars and Jupiter, which led to the discovery of the asteroids.

Bodhidharma 6th century AD. Indian Buddhist. He entered China from S India *c.*520, and was the founder of Zen, the school of Mahāyāna Buddhism in which intuitive meditation, prompted by contemplation, leads to enlightenment.

According to one legend, Bodhidharma sat in uninterrupted meditation until after nine years his legs withered and fell off.

Bodichon Barbara (born Leigh-Smith) 1827–1891. English feminist and campaigner for women's education and suffrage. She wrote *Women and Work* 1857, and was a founder of the magazine *The Englishwoman's Journal* in 1858.

Born into a radical family that believed in female equality, she attended Bedford College, London. She was a founder of the college for women that became Girton College, Cambridge.

Bodin Jean 1530–1596. French political philosopher, whose six-volume *De la République* 1576 is considered the first work on political economy.

An attorney in Paris, in 1574 he published a tract explaining that prevalent high prices were due to the influx of precious metals from the New World. His theory of an ideal government emphasized obedience to a sovereign ruler.

Bodley Thomas 1545–1613. English scholar and diplomat, after whom the Bodleian Library in Oxford is named. After retiring from Queen Elizabeth I's service in 1597, he restored the library, which was opened as the Bodleian Library 1602. The library had originally been founded in the 15th century by Humphrey, Duke of Gloucester (1391–1447).

Bodoni Giambattista 1740–1813. Italian printer who managed the printing-press of the Duke of Parma and produced high-quality editions of the classics. He designed several typefaces, including one bearing his name, which is in use today.

Bodichon English feminist Barbara Bodichon, probably the model for the heroine of George Eliot's novel Romola.

Boehme Jakob 1575–1624. German mystic. He claimed divine revelation of the unity of everything and nothing, and found in God's eternal nature a

Bogart US film actor Humphrey Bogart.

principle to reconcile good and evil. He was the author of the treatise *Aurora* 1612. By trade he was a shoemaker.

Boeing William Edward 1881–1956. US industrialist, founder of the Boeing Airplane Company 1917. Its military aircraft include the flying fortress bombers used in World War II, and the Chinook helicopter; its commercial craft include the jetfoil (a hydrofoil powered by water jets), and the Boeing 747 and 707 jets.

Boethius Anicius Manlius Severinus AD 480–524. Roman philosopher. While imprisoned on suspicion of treason by ◊Theodoric, he wrote treatises on music and mathematics and *De Consolatione Philosophiae/The Consolation of Philosophy*, a dialogue in prose. It was translated into European languages during the Middle Ages and into English by Alfred the Great, Geoffrey Chaucer, and Queen Elizabeth I.

Bogarde Dirk. Stage-name of Derek van den Bogaerde 1921– . British film actor, who appeared in comedies and adventure films such as *Doctor in the House* 1954 and *Campbell's Kingdom* 1957, before acquiring international recognition for complex roles in films such as *The Servant* 1963. He distinguished himself in films made with director Joseph Losey, such as *Accident* 1967, and with Luchino Visconti in *Death in Venice* 1971.

He has also written autobiographical books and novels, for example *A Postillion Struck by Lightning* 1977, *Snakes and Ladders* 1978, *Orderly Man* 1983, and *Backcloth* 1986.

Bogart Humphrey 1899–1957. US film actor, who achieved fame with his portrayal of a gangster in *The Petrified Forest* 1936. He became a cult figure as the romantic, tough 'loner' in such films as *The Maltese Falcon* 1941 and *Casablanca* 1943. He won an Academy Award for his role in *The African Queen* 1952.

Bogdanovich Peter 1939– . US film director, screenwriter, and producer, formerly a critic. *The Last Picture Show* 1971 was followed by two films that attempted to capture the style of old Hollywood, *What's Up Doc?* 1972 and *Paper Moon* 1973. Both made money but neither was a critical success.

Bohlen Charles 'Chip' 1904–1974. US diplomat. Educated at Harvard, he entered the foreign service in 1929. Interpreter and adviser to presidents Roosevelt at Tehran and Yalta, and Truman at Potsdam, he served as ambassador to the USSR 1953–57.

Böhm Karl 1894–1981. Austrian conductor, known for his interpretation of Beethoven, and of the Mozart and Strauss operas.

Bohr Aage Niels 1922– . Danish physicist, the son of Niels Bohr. He produced a new model of the nucleus in 1952, known as the collective model. For this work, he shared the 1975 Nobel Prize for Physics.

Bohr Niels Henrik David 1885–1962. Danish physicist. He founded the Institute of Theoretical Physics in Copenhagen, of which he became director in 1920. Nobel prize 1922. In 1952, he helped to set up CERN, the European nuclear research organization, in Geneva.

After work with Ernest ◊Rutherford at Manchester, he became professor at Copenhagen in 1916. He fled from the Nazis in World War II and took part in work on the atomic bomb in the USA.

Boiardo Matteo Maria, Count 1434–1494. Italian poet, famed for his *Orlando Innamorato/Roland in Love* 1486.

Boileau Nicolas 1636–1711. French poet and critic. After a series of contemporary satires, his *Epîtres/Epistles* 1669–77 led to his joint appointment with Racine as royal historiographer in 1677. Later works include *L'Art poétique/The Art of Poetry* 1674 and the mock-heroic *Le Lutrin/The Lectern* 1674–83.

Bokassa Jean-Bédel 1921– . President and later self-proclaimed emperor of the Central African Republic 1966–79. Commander in chief from 1963, in Dec 1965 he led a military coup which gave him the presidency, and on 4 Dec 1977 he proclaimed the Central African Empire with himself as emperor for life. His regime was characterized by arbitrary state violence and cruelty. In exile 1979–86, he was tried and imprisoned.

Bol Ferdinand 1610–1680. Dutch painter, a pupil and for many years an imitator of ◊Rembrandt. There is uncertainty in attributing some works between them. After the 1660s Bol developed a more independent style and prospered as a portraitist.

Boldrewood Rolf. Pen name of Thomas Alexander Browne 1826–1915. Australian writer, born in London, he was taken to Australia as a child in 1830. He became a pioneer squatter, and a police magistrate in the goldfields. His books include *Robbery Under Arms* 1888.

Boleyn Anne 1507–1536. Queen of England. Second wife of King Henry VIII, she was married to him in 1533 and gave birth to the future Queen Elizabeth I in the same year. Accused of adultery and incest with her half-brother (a charge invented by Thomas Cromwell), she was beheaded.

Bolingbroke Henry John, Viscount Bolingbroke 1678–1751. British Tory politician and philosopher. He was secretary of war 1704–08, became foreign secretary in Robert ◊Harley's ministry in 1710, and in 1713 negotiated the Treaty of Utrecht. His plans to restore the 'Old Pretender' James Francis Edward Stuart were ruined by Queen Anne's death only five days after he had secured the dismissal of Harley in 1714. He fled abroad, returning in 1723, when he worked to overthrow Robert Walpole. His books, such as *Idea of a Patriot King* 1738, influenced the 19th-century prime minister Disraeli.

Bolingbroke title of, Henry of Bolingbroke ◊Henry IV of England.

Bolívar Simón 1783–1830. South American nationalist, leader of revolutionary armies, known as *the Liberator*. He fought the Spanish colonial forces in several uprisings and eventually liberated his native Venezuela 1821, Colombia and Ecuador 1822, Peru 1824, and Bolivia (a new state named after him, formerly Upper Peru) 1825.

Born in Venezuela, Bolívar joined the nationalists working for Venezuelan independence, and was sent to Britain in 1810 as the representative of their government. Forced to flee to Colombia in 1812, he joined the revolutionaries there, and invaded Venezuela in 1811. A bloody civil war followed and in 1814 Bolívar had to withdraw to Colombia, and eventually to the West Indies, from where he raided the Spanish-American coasts. In 1817 he returned to Venezuela to set up a provisional government, crossed into Colombia 1819, where he defeated the Spaniards, and returning to Angostura proclaimed the republic of Colombia, comprising Venezuela, New Granada (present-day Colombia), and Quito (Ecuador), with himself as president. The independence of Venezuela was finally secured in 1821, and 1822 Bolívar (along with Antonio ◊Sucre) liberated Ecuador. He was invited to lead the Peruvian struggle in 1823; and, final victory having been won by Sucre at Ayacucho in 1824, he turned his attention to framing a constitution. In 1825 the independence of Upper Peru was proclaimed, and the country adopted the name Bolivia in Bolívar's honour.

Bolkiah Hassanal 1946– . Sultan of Brunei from 1967, following the abdication of his father, Omar Ali Saifuddin (1916–86). On independence, in 1984, Bolkiah also assumed the posts of prime minister and defence minister.

As head of an oil- and gas-rich micro-state, the sultan is reputedly the world's richest individual, with an estimated total wealth of $2 billion, which includes the Dorchester and Beverly Hills hotels in London and Los Angeles, and, at a cost of $40 million, the world's largest palace. He was educated at a British military academy.

Böll Heinrich 1917–1985. West German novelist. A radical Catholic and anti-Nazi, he attacked Germany's political past and the materialism of its contemporary society. His many publications include poems, short stories, and novels which satirize German society, for example *Billard um Halbzehn/Billiards at Half-Past Nine* 1959 and *Gruppenbild mit Dame/Group Portrait with Lady* 1971. Nobel Prize for Literature 1972.

Bolt Robert (Oxton) 1924– . British dramatist, noted for his historical plays, especially *A Man for All Seasons* 1960, about Thomas More (filmed 1967), and for his screenplays, including *Lawrence of Arabia* 1962 and *Dr Zhivago* 1965.

Boltzmann Ludwig 1844–1906. Austrian physicist who studied the kinetic theory of gases, which explains the properties of gases by reference to the motion of their constituent atoms and molecules.

He derived a formula, the *Boltzmann distribution*, which gives the number of atoms or molecules with a given energy at a specific temperature. This involves a constant, called the *Boltzmann constant*.

Bonaparte Corsican family of Italian origin, which gave rise to the Napoleonic dynasty: see ◊Napoleon I, ◊Napoleon II, and ◊Napoleon III. Other well-known members were the brothers and sister of Napoleon I:

Joseph 1768–1844, whom Napoleon made king of Naples 1806 and Spain 1808.

Lucien 1775–1840, whose handling of the Council of Five Hundred on 10 Nov 1799 ensured Napoleon's future.

Louis 1778–1846, made king of Holland 1806–10, who was the father of Napoleon III.

Caroline 1782–1839, who married Joachim ◊Murat in 1800.

Jerome 1784–1860, made king of Westphalia in 1807.

Bonar Law British Conservative politician. See ◊Law, Andrew Bonar.

Bonaventura, St (John of Fidanza) 1221–1274. Italian Roman Catholic theologian. He entered the Franciscan order in 1243, became professor of theology at Paris, France, and in 1256 general of his order. In 1273 he was created cardinal and bishop of Albano. His eloquent writings earned him the title of the 'Seraphic Doctor'. Feast day 15 July.

Bond Edward 1935– . British dramatist, whose work has aroused controversy because of the savagery of some of his themes, for example the brutal killing of a baby, symbolic of a society producing unwanted children, in *Saved* 1965. His later works

include *Black Mass* 1970 about apartheid, *Bingo* 1973, and *The Sea* 1973.

Bondfield Margaret Grace 1873–1953. British socialist who became a trade-union organizer to improve working conditions for women. She was a Labour member of Parliament 1923–24 and 1926–31, and was the first woman to enter the cabinet – as Minister of Labour, 1929–31.

Bondi Hermann 1919– . British cosmologist, born in Austria. In 1948 he joined with Fred ◊Hoyle and Thomas Gold (1920–) in developing the steady-state theory of cosmology, which suggested that matter is continuously created in the universe.

Bonham-Carter Violet, Lady Asquith of Yarnbury 1887–1969. British peeress, president of the Liberal party 1945–47.

Bonheur Rosa (Marie Rosalie) 1822–1899. French painter, noted for her realistic animal portraits, such as *Horse Fair* 1853 (Metropolitan Museum of Art, New York).

Bonhoeffer Dietrich 1906–1945. German Lutheran theologian and opponent of Nazism. Involved in an anti-Hitler plot, he was executed by the Nazis in Flossenburg concentration camp. His *Letters and Papers from Prison* 1953 advocate the idea of 'religionless' Christianity.

Boniface VIII Benedict Caetani *c.* 1228–1303. Pope from 1294. He clashed unsuccessfully with Philip IV of France over his taxation of the clergy, and also with Henry III of England.

Boniface exempted the clergy from taxation by the secular government in a bull (edict) in 1296, but was forced to give way when the clergy were excluded from certain lay privileges. His bull of 1302 *Unam Sanctam*, asserting the complete temporal and spiritual power of the papacy, was equally ineffective.

Boniface, St 680–754. English Benedictine monk, known as the 'Apostle of Germany'; originally named Wynfrith. After a missionary journey to Frisia in 716, he was given the task of bringing Christianity to Germany by Pope Gregory II in 718, and was appointed archbishop of Mainz in 746. He returned to Frisia in 754 and was martyred near Dockum. Feast day 5 June.

Bonington Chris(tian) 1934– . British mountaineer. He took part in the first ascent of Annapurna II 1960, Nuptse 1961, and the first British ascent of the N face of the Eiger 1962, climbed the central Tower of Paine in Patagonia 1963, and was the leader of an Everest expedition 1975 and again in 1985, reaching the summit.

Bonington Richard Parkes 1801–1828. British painter, noted for fresh, atmospheric seascapes and landscapes in oil and watercolour. He was much admired by Delacroix.

Bonnard Pierre 1867–1947. French Post-Impressionist painter. With other members of *les Nabis* (a group following Gaugin's simplicity of style and colour), he explored the decorative arts (posters, stained glass, furniture). He painted domestic interiors and nudes.

Bonnie and Clyde Popular names of Bonnie Parker 1911–34 and Clyde Barrow. Infamous US criminals who carried out a series of small-scale robberies, primarily in Texas, Oklahoma, New Mexico, and Missouri between Aug 1932 and May 1934. Much of their fame emanated from encounters with the police and their coverage by the press. They were eventually betrayed and then killed in a police ambush. Their story was filmed as *Bonnie and Clyde* 1967 by the US director Arthur Penn.

Bonner Yelena 1923– . Soviet human-rights campaigner. Disillusioned by the Soviet invasion of Czechoslovakia 1968, she resigned from the Communist Party (CPSU) after marrying her second husband Dr Andrei ◊Sakharov in 1971, and became active in the dissident movement.

Bonner was brought up in Leningrad by her grandmother after the arrest and subsequent imprisonment and execution of her parents in Stalin's 'great purge' of 1937. She suffered serious eye injuries while fighting for the Red Army during World War II and afterwards worked as a doctor. She joined the CPSU in 1965. Following hunger strikes by Sakharov, she was granted permission to travel to Italy for specialist eye treatment in 1981 and 1984, but was placed in internal exile in Gorky 1984–86.

Boole George 1814–1864. English mathematician, whose work *The Mathematical Analysis of Logic* 1847 established the basis of modern mathematical logic, and whose *Boolean algebra* can be used in designing computers.

Boone Daniel 1734–1820. US pioneer, who explored the Wilderness Road (East Virginia/–Kentucky) 1775 and paved the way for the first westward migration of settlers.

Boorman John 1933– . British film director who, after working in television, subsequently directed successful films both in Hollywood (*Deliverance* 1972, *Point Blank* 1967) and in Britain (*Excalibur* 1981, *Hope and Glory* 1987).

Boot Jesse 1850–1931. British entrepreneur and founder of pharmacy chain. In 1863 Boot took over his father's small Nottingham shop trading in medicinal herbs. Recognizing that the future lay with patent medicines, he concentrated on selling cheaply, advertising widely, and offering a wide range of medicines. In 1892, Boot also began to manufacture drugs. He had 126 shops by 1900 and more than 1,000 by his death.

Booth Charles 1840–1916. British sociologist, author of the study *Life and Labour of the People in London* 1891–1903, and pioneer of an old-age pension scheme.

Booth John Wilkes 1839–1865. US actor and fanatical Confederate who assassinated President Abraham ◊Lincoln 14 Apr 1865; he escaped with a broken leg and was later shot in a barn in Virginia when he refused to surrender.

Booth William 1829–1912. British founder of the Salvation Army in 1878, and its first 'general'. Born in Nottingham, the son of a builder, he experienced religious conversion at the age of 15. In 1865 he founded the Christian Mission, in Whitechapel, E London, which in 1878 became the Salvation Army. *In Darkest England, and the Way Out* 1890 contained proposals for the physical and spiritual redemption of the many down-and-outs.

His wife Catherine (1829–90, born Mumford), whom he married in 1855, became a public preacher in about 1860, initiating the ministry of women. Their eldest son, *William Bramwell Booth* (1856–1929), became chief of staff of the Salvation Army in 1880 and was general from 1912 until his deposition 1929. *Evangeline Booth* (1865–1950), 7th child of Gen William Booth, was a prominent Salvation Army officer, and 1934–39 was general. She became a US citizen. *Catherine Bramwell Booth* (1884–1987), a granddaughter of William Booth, was a commissioner in the Salvation Army.

Boothe Luce Clare 1903–1987. US journalist, playwright, and politician. She was managing editor of the magazine *Vanity Fair* 1933–34, and wrote several successful plays, including *The Women* 1936 and *Margin for Error* 1939.

She was born in New York, was a Republican member of Congress 1943–47 and ambassador to Italy 1953–57. She was married to the magazine publisher Henry Robinson Luce.

Borchert Wolfgang 1921–1947. German playwright and prose writer. Borchert was sent home wounded during World War II while serving on the Russian front, for alleged anti-Nazi comments. *Draussen vor der Tür/The Outsider* 1947 is a surreal play about the chaotic conditions that a German soldier finds when he returns to Germany after walking home from the Russian front.

Border Allan 1955– . Australian cricketer, captain of the Australian team from 1985. He has played for New South Wales and Queensland, and in England for Gloucestershire and Essex. He made his test debut for Australia 1978–79.

Bordet Jules 1870–1961. Belgian bacteriologist and immunologist who researched the role of blood serum in the human immune response. He was the first to isolate, in 1906, the whooping cough bacillus.

Borelli Giovanni Alfonso 1608–1679. Italian scientist who explored the links between physics and medicine, and showed how mechanical principles could be applied to animal physiology. This approach has proved basic to understanding how the mammalian body works.

Borges *The Argentinian author and former university professor is seen here after receiving an honorary degree at the University of Oxford in 1970.*

Borg Björn 1956– . Swedish lawn-tennis player who won the men's singles title at Wimbledon five times 1976–80, a record since the abolition of the challenge system 1922.

Borges Jorge Luis 1899–1986. Argentinian poet and short-story writer. In 1961 he became director of the National Library, Buenos Aires, and was professor of English literature at the university there. He is known for his fantastic and paradoxical work *Ficciones/Fictions* 1944.

Borgia Cesare 1476–1507. Italian general, illegitimate son of Pope ◊Alexander VI. Made a cardinal at 17 by his father, he resigned to become captain-general of the papacy, campaigning successfully against the city republics of Italy. Ruthless and treacherous in war, he was an able ruler (the model of Machiavelli's *The Prince*), but his power crumbled on the death of his father. He was a patron of artists, including Leonardo da Vinci.

Borgia Lucrezia 1480–1519. Duchess of Ferrara from 1501. She was the illegitimate daughter of Pope ◊Alexander VI and sister of Cesare Borgia. She was married at 12 and again at 13 to further her father's ambitions, both marriages being annulled by him. At 18 she was again married, but her husband was murdered in 1500 on the order of her brother, with whom (as well as with her father) she was said to have committed incest. Her final marriage was to the son and heir of the

Duke of Ferrara. She made the court a centre of culture and was a patron of authors and artists such as Ariosto and Titian.

Borglum Gutzon 1871–1941. US sculptor. He created a six-tonne marble head of Lincoln in Washington DC and a series of giant heads of presidents Washington, Jefferson, Lincoln, and Theodore Roosevelt carved on *Mount Rushmore*, South Dakota (begun 1930).

Boris III 1894–1943. Tsar of Bulgaria from 1918, when he succeeded his father, Ferdinand I. From 1934 he was virtual dictator until his sudden and mysterious death following a visit to Hitler. His son Simeon II was tsar until deposed in 1946.

Boris Godunov see Boris ◊Godunov, tsar of Russia from 1598.

Borlaug Norman Ernest 1914– . US microbiologist and agronomist. He developed high-yielding varieties of wheat and other grain crops to be grown in Third World countries, and was the first to use the term 'Green Revolution'. Nobel Prize for Peace 1970.

Bormann Martin 1900–1945. German Nazi leader. He took part in the abortive Munich putsch (uprising) of 1923, and rose to high positions in the National Socialist Party, becoming party chancellor in May 1941. He was believed to have escaped the fall of Berlin in May 1945, and was tried in his absence and sentenced to death at Nuremberg 1945–46, but a skeleton uncovered by a mechanical excavator in Berlin in 1972 was officially recognized as his by forensic experts in 1973.

Born Max 1882–1970. German physicist, who received a Nobel prize in 1954 for fundamental work on the quantum theory. He left Germany for Britain during the Nazi era.

Borodin Alexander Porfir'yevich 1833–1887. Russian composer. Born in St Petersburg the illegitimate son of a Russian prince, he became by profession an expert in medical chemistry, but in his spare time devoted himself to music. His principal work is the opera *Prince Igor*; left unfinished, it was completed by Rimsky-Korsakov and Glazunov and includes the Polovtsian Dances.

Borromeo Carlo 1538–1584. Italian Roman Catholic saint and cardinal. He wound up the affairs of the Council of Trent, and largely drew up the catechism that contained its findings. Feast day 4 Nov.

Borromini Francesco 1599–1667. Italian Baroque architect. He worked under Bernini, later his rival, on St Peter's Basilica, Rome, and created the oval-shaped church of San Carlo alle Quattro Fontane, Rome.

Borrow George Henry 1803–1881. British author and traveller. He travelled on foot through Europe and the East. His books, incorporating his knowledge of languages and Romany lore, include *Zincali* 1840, *The Bible in Spain* 1843, *Lavengro*

1851, *The Romany Rye* 1857, and *Wild Wales* 1862.

Boscawen Edward 1711–1761. English admiral who served against the French in the mid-18th century wars. To his men he was known as 'Old Dreadnought'.

Bosch Hieronymus (Jerome) 1460–1516. Early Netherlandish painter. His fantastic visions of weird and hellish creatures, as shown in *The Garden of Earthly Delights* about 1505–10 (Prado, Madrid), show astonishing imagination and a complex imagery. His religious subjects focused not on the holy figures but on the mass of ordinary witnesses, placing the religious event in a contemporary Netherlandish context and creating cruel caricatures of human sinfulness.

Bosch is named from his birthplace, Hertogenbosch, in Brabant (now in Belgium). His work foreshadowed Surrealism and was probably inspired by a local religious brotherhood. However, he was an orthodox Catholic and a prosperous painter, not a heretic, as was once believed. After his death, his work was collected by Philip II of Spain.

Bosch Juan 1909– . President of the Dominican Republic 1963. His left-wing Partido Revolucionario Dominicano won a landslide victory in the 1962 elections. In office, he attempted agrarian reform and labour legislation. Opposed by the USA, he was overthrown by the army. His achievement was to establish a democratic political party after three decades of dictatorship.

Boscovich Ruggiero 1711–1787. Italian scientist. An early supporter of Newton, he developed a theory of the atom as a single point with surrounding fields of repulsive and attractive forces that was popular in the 19th century.

Bose Jagadis Chunder 1858–1937. Indian physicist and plant physiologist. Born near Dacca, he was professor of physical science at Calcutta 1885–1915, and studied plant life, especially the growth and minute movements of plants, and their reaction to electrical stimuli. He founded the Bose Research Institute, Calcutta.

Bose Satyendra Nath 1894–1974. Indian physicist. With ◊Einstein, he formulated the Bose–Einstein law of quantum mechanics, and was professor of physics at the University of Calcutta 1945–58.

Bossuet Jacques Bénigne 1627–1704. French Roman Catholic priest and theologian. Appointed to the Chapel Royal in 1662, he became known for his funeral orations. He was bishop of Meaux from 1681.

Bossuet was tutor to the young dauphin (crown prince). He became involved in a controversy between Louis XIV and the Pope and did his best to effect a compromise. He wrote an *Exposition de la foi catholique* 1670 and *Histoire des variations des églises protestantes* 1688.

Boswell James 1740–1795. Scottish biographer and diarist. He was a member of Samuel ◊Johnson's London Literary Club, and in 1773 the two men travelled to Scotland together, as recorded in Boswell's *Journal of the Tour to the Hebrides* 1785. His *Life of Samuel Johnson* was published 1791.

Born in Edinburgh, Boswell studied law but centred his ambitions on literature and politics. He first met Johnson 1763, before setting out on a European tour during which he met the French thinkers Rousseau and Voltaire, and the Corsican nationalist general Paoli (1726–1807), whom he commemorated in his popular *Account of Corsica* 1768. In 1766 he became a lawyer, and in 1772 renewed his acquaintance with Johnson in London. Establishing a place in his intimate circle, he became a member of the Literary Club 1773, and in the same year accompanied Johnson on the journey later recorded in the *Journal of the Tour to the Hebrides* 1785. On his succession to his father's estate 1782, he made further attempts to enter Parliament, was called to the English bar 1786, and was recorder of Carlisle 1788–90. In 1789 he settled in London, and in 1791 produced the classic English biography, the *Life of Samuel Johnson*. His long-lost personal papers were acquired for publication by Yale University 1949, and the *Journals* are of exceptional interest.

Botero Fernando 1932– . Colombian painter. He studied in Spain and gained an international reputation for his paintings of fat, vulgar figures, often of women, parodies of conventional sensuality.

Botha Louis 1862–1919. South African soldier and politician, a commander in the Second South

Botha *South African Politician P W Botha prime minister 1978–84 and president 1984–89.*

Botham *English cricketer Ian Botham batting for England at the Benson and Hedges challenge at Perth, 1986.*

African War. In 1907 Botha became premier of the Transvaal and in 1910 of the first Union government. On the outbreak of World War I in 1914 he rallied South Africa to the Commonwealth, suppressed a Boer revolt under Gen de Wet, and conquered German South West Africa.

Botha P(ieter) W(illem) 1916– . South African politician. Prime minister from 1978, he initiated a modification of apartheid, which later slowed in the face of Afrikaner (Boer) opposition. In 1984 he became the first executive state president. In 1989 he unwillingly resigned both party leadership and presidency after suffering a stroke, and was succeeded by F W de Klerk.

Botham Ian (Terrence) 1955– . English cricketer, a prolific all-rounder. His 373 test wickets, 109 catches, and 5,057 runs in 94 appearances by the end of the 1988 English season were a record until surpassed by Richard Hadlee (New Zealand) in 1989. He has played county cricket for Somerset and Worcestershire as well as playing in Australia.

Bothe Walther 1891–1957. German physicist, who showed in 1929 that the cosmic rays bombarding the Earth are composed not of photons but of more massive particles. Nobel Prize for Physics 1954.

Bothwell James Hepburn, 4th Earl of Bothwell *c.* 1536–1578. Scottish nobleman, husband of ◊Mary, Queen of Scots, 1567–70, alleged to

have arranged the explosion that killed Darnley, her previous husband, in 1567.

Tried and acquitted a few weeks after the assassination, he abducted Mary, and (having divorced his wife) married her on 15 May. A revolt ensued, and Bothwell was forced to flee to Norway and on to Sweden. In 1570 Mary obtained a divorce on the ground that she had been ravished by Bothwell before marriage. Later, Bothwell was confined in a castle in Zeeland, the Netherlands, where he died insane.

Botticelli Sandro 1445–1510. Florentine painter of religious and mythological subjects. He was patronized by the ruling Medici family, for whom he painted *Primavera* 1478 and *The Birth of Venus* about 1482–84 (both in the Uffizi, Florence). From the 1490s he was influenced by the religious fanatic ◊Savonarola and developed a harshly expressive and emotional style.

His real name was Filipepi, but his elder brother's nickname Botticelli 'little barrel' was passed on to him. His work for the Medicis was designed to cater to the educated classical tastes of the day. As well as his sentimental, beautiful young Madonnas, he produced a series of inventive compositions, including *tondi*, circular paintings. He broke with the Medicis after their execution of Savonarola.

Boucher François 1703–1770. French Rococo painter, court painter from 1765. He was much patronized for his light-hearted, decorative scenes, for example *Diana Bathing* 1742 (Louvre, Paris). He also painted portraits and decorative chinoiserie for Parisian palaces. He became director of the Gobelin tapestry works, Paris, in 1755.

Boucher de Crèvecoeur de Perthes Jacques 1788–1868. French geologist, whose discovery of Palaeolithic hand-axes in 1837 challenged the acccepted view of human history dating only from 4004 BC, as proclaimed by the calculations of Bishop James ◊Usher.

Boudicca died AD 60. Queen of the Iceni (native Britons), often referred to by the Latin form *Boadicea*. Her husband, King Prasutagus, had been a tributary of the Romans, but on his death AD 60 the territory of the Iceni was violently annexed, Boudicca was scourged and her daughters raped. Boudicca raised the whole of SE England in revolt, and before the main Roman armies could return from campaigning in Wales she burned London and Colchester. Later the British were virtually annihilated somewhere between London and Chester, and Boudicca poisoned herself.

Boudin Eugène 1824–1898. French painter, a forerunner of Impressionism, noted for his fresh seaside scenes painted in the open air.

Bougainville Louis Antoine de 1729–1811. French navigator. After service with the French in Canada during the Seven Years' War, he made the first

French circumnavigation of the world in 1766–69 and the first systematic observations of longitude. Several Pacific islands are named after him, as is the climbing plant *bougainvillea*.

Bouguereau Adolphe William 1825–1905. French academic painter of historical and mythological subjects. He was respected in his day but his style is now thought to be insipid.

Boulanger George Ernest Jean Marie 1837–1891. French general. He became minister of war 1886, and his anti-German speeches nearly provoked a war with Germany 1887. In 1889 he was suspected of aspiring to dictatorship by a coup d'état. Accused of treason, he fled into exile and committed suicide.

Boulanger Lili (Juliette Marie Olga) 1893–1918. French composer, the younger sister of Nadia Boulanger. At the age of 19, she won the Prix de Rome with the cantata *Faust et Halkne* for voices and orchestra.

Boulanger Nadia (Juliette) 1887–1979. French music teacher and conductor. A pupil of Fauré, and admirer of Stravinsky, she included among her composition pupils at the American Conservatory in Fontainebleau (from 1921) Aaron Copland, Roy Harris, Walter Piston, and Philip Glass.

Boulestin Marcel 1878–1943. French cookery writer and restaurateur. He was influential in spreading the principles of simple but high-quality French cooking in Britain in the first half of the 20th century, with a succession of popular books such as *What Shall We Have Today?* (1931).

Boulez Pierre 1925– . French composer and conductor. He studied with ◊Messiaen and has promoted contemporary music with a series of innovative *Domaine Musical* concerts and recordings. His music, strictly serial and expressionistic in style, includes the cantatas *Le Visage nuptial* 1946–52 and *Le Marteau sans maître* 1955, both to texts by René Char; *Pli selon pli* 1962 for soprano and orchestra; and *Répons* 1981 for soloists, orchestra, tapes and computer-generated sounds.

Boult Adrian (Cedric) 1889–1983. British conductor of the BBC Symphony Orchestra 1930–50 and the London Philharmonic 1950–57. He promoted the work of Holst and Vaughan Williams, and was a noted interpreter of Elgar.

Boulting John 1913–85 and Roy 1913– . British director-producer team that was particularly influential in the years following World War II. Their films include *Brighton Rock* 1947, *Lucky Jim* 1957, and *I'm All Right Jack* 1959. They were twins.

Boulton Matthew 1728–1809. British factory-owner, who helped to finance James ◊Watt's development of the steam engine.

Boulton had an engineering works at Soho near Birmingham, and in 1775 he went into partnership with Watt to develop engines to power factory machines that had previously been driven by water.

Boumédienne Houari. Adopted name of Mohammed Boukharouba 1925–1978. Algerian politician who brought the nationalist leader Ben Bella to power by a revolt 1962, and superseded him as president 1965–78 by a further coup.

Bourbon French royal house (succeeding that of ◊Valois) beginning with Henry IV, and ending with Louis XVI, with a brief revival under Louis XVIII, Charles X, and Louis Philippe. The Bourbons also ruled Spain almost uninterruptedly from Philip V to Alfonso XIII, and were restored in 1975 (◊Juan Carlos); as well as Naples and several Italian duchies. The Grand Duke of Luxembourg is also a Bourbon by male descent.

Bourbon Charles, Duke of Bourbon 1490–1527. Constable of France, honoured for his courage at the Battle of Marignano 1515. Later he served the Holy Roman Emperor Charles V, and helped to drive the French from Italy. In 1526 he was made duke of Milan, and in 1527 allowed his troops to sack Rome. He was killed by a shot the artist Cellini claimed to have fired.

Bourdon Eugène 1808–1884. French engineer and instrument maker, who invented the pressure gauge which bears his name.

Bourgeois Léon Victor Auguste 1851–1925. French politician. Entering politics as a Radical, he was prime minister in 1895, and later served in many cabinets. He was one of the pioneer advocates of the League of Nations. Nobel Prize for Peace 1920.

Bourguiba Habib ben Ali 1903– . Tunisian politician, first president of Tunisia 1957–87. Educated at the University of Paris, he became a journalist and was frequently imprisoned by the French for his nationalist aims as leader of the Néo-Destour party. He became prime minister 1956, president (for life from 1974) and prime minister of the Tunisian republic 1957, and was overthrown in a coup 1987.

Bournonville August 1805–1879. Danish dancer and choreographer. He worked with the Royal Danish Ballet for most of his life, giving Danish ballet a worldwide importance. His ballets, many of which have been revived in the last 50 years, include *La Sylphide* 1836 (music by Lövenskjöld) and *Napoli* 1842.

Bouts Dierick *c.*1420–1475. Early Netherlandish painter. Born in Haarlem, he settled in Louvain, painting portraits and religious scenes influenced by Rogier van der Weyden. *The Last Supper* 1464–68 (St Pierre, Louvain) is one of his finest works.

Bovet Daniel 1907– . Swiss physiologist. He pioneered research into antihistamine drugs used in the treatment of nettle rash and hay fever, and was awarded a Nobel Prize for Medicine 1957 for his production of a synthetic form of curare, used as a muscle relaxant in anaesthesia.

Bow Clara 1905–1965. US silent-film actress, known as the 'It' girl after her vivacious performance in *It* 1927. Her other films included *Wings* 1927 and *The Wild Party* 1929. Scandals about her romances and her mental and physical fragility led to the end of her career, and she spent many of her post-career years in sanatoriums.

Bowdler Thomas 1754–1825. British editor, whose prudishly expurgated versions of Shakespeare and other authors gave rise to the verb *bowdlerize*.

Bowen Elizabeth 1899–1973. Irish novelist. She published her first volume of short stories, *Encounters* in 1923. Her novels include *The Death of the Heart* 1938, *The Heat of the Day* 1949, and *The Little Girls* 1964.

Bowie David. Stage name of David Jones 1947– . British pop singer and songwriter, born in Brixton, London. He became a glitter-rock star with the album *The Rise and Fall of Ziggy Stardust and the Spiders from Mars* 1972, and collaborated in the mid-1970s with the electronic virtuoso Brian Eno (1948–) and Iggy Pop. He has also acted in plays and films, including Nicolas Roeg's *The Man Who Fell to Earth* 1976.

Bowie James 'Jim' 1796–1836. US frontiersman and folk hero. A colonel in the Texan forces during the Mexican War, he is said to have invented the single-edge, guarded hunting and throwing knife known as a *Bowie knife*. He was killed in the battle of the Alamo.

Bowles Paul 1910– . US novelist and composer. Born in New York, he settled in Morocco, the setting of novels like *Let It Come Down* 1952 and the stories of *The Delicate Prey* 1950.

Boycott Charles Cunningham 1832–1897. English land agent in County Mayo, Ireland, who strongly opposed the demands for agrarian reform by the Irish Land League 1879–81, with the result that the peasants refused to work for him; hence the word *boycott*.

Boycott Geoffrey 1940– . England cricketer born in Yorkshire, England's most prolific run-maker with 8,114 runs in test cricket. He was banned as a test player in 1982 for taking part in matches against South Africa.

He played in 108 test matches and in 1981 overtook Gary Sober's world record total of test runs. Twice, in 1971 and 1979, his average was over 100 runs in an English season.

Boyd-Orr John 1880–1971. British nutritionist and health campaigner. He was awarded the Nobel Prize for Peace in 1949 in recognition of his work towards alleviating world hunger.

Boyer Charles 1899–1978. French film actor, who made his name in Hollywood in the 1930s as a screen 'lover' in films such as *Mayerling* 1937 and *The Garden of Allah* 1936.

Boyle Charles, 4th Earl of Orrery 1676–1731. Irish soldier and diplomat. The *orrery*, a mechanical model of the solar system in which the planets move at the correct relative velocities, is named after him.

Boyle Robert 1627–1691. Irish physicist and chemist, who published the seminal *The Skeptical Chymist* 1661.

He was the first chemist to collect a gas, enunciated *Boyle's law* on the compressibility of a gas in 1662, was one of the founders of the Royal Society, and endowed the Boyle Lectures for the defence of Christianity.

Bo Zhu Yi 772–846. Chinese poet (formerly known as *Po Chü-i*). President from 841 of the imperial war department, he criticized government policy. He is said to have checked his work with an old peasant woman for clarity of expression.

Bracegirdle Anne *c*.1663–1748. British actress, the mistress of ◊Congreve, and possibly his wife; she played Millamant in his *The Way of the World*.

Bracton Henry de, died 1268. English judge, writer on English law, and chancellor of Exeter cathedral from 1264. He compiled an account of the laws and customs of the English, *De Legibus et Consuetudinibus Anglie*, the first of its kind.

Bradbury Malcolm 1932– . British novelist and critic, noted for his comic and satiric portrayals of academic life. His best-known work is *The History Man* 1975, set in a provincial English university. Other works include *Rates of Exchange* 1983.

Bradbury Ray 1920– . US writer, born in Illinois. He was one of the first science-fiction writers to make the genre 'respectable' to a wider readership. His work shows nostalgia for small-town Midwestern life, and includes *The Martian Chronicles* 1950, *Something Wicked This Way Comes* 1962, and *Fahrenheit 451* 1953.

Bradlaugh Charles 1833–1891. British freethinker and radical politician. In 1880 he was elected Liberal member of Parliament for Northampton, but was not allowed to take his seat until 1886 because, as an atheist, he (unsuccessfully) claimed the right to affirm instead of taking the oath. He was associated with the feminist Annie Besant.

He served in the army, was a lawyer's clerk, became well known as a speaker and journalist under the name of Iconoclast, and from 1860 ran the *National Reformer*. He advocated the freedom of the press, contraception, and other social reforms.

Bradley Francis Herbert 1846–1924. British philosopher. In *Ethical Studies* 1876 and *Principles of Logic* 1883 he attacked the utilitarianism of J S Mill, and in *Appearance and Reality* 1893 and *Truth and Reality* 1914 he outlined his Neo-Hegelian doctrine of the universe as a single ultimate reality.

Bradley James 1693–1762. English astronomer, who in 1728 discovered the aberration of starlight. From the amount of aberration in star positions, he was able to calculate the speed of light. In 1748 he announced the discovery of nutation (variation in the Earth's axial tilt). He became Astronomer Royal 1742.

Bradley Omar Nelson 1893–1981. US general in World War II. In 1943 he commanded the 2nd US Corps in Tunisia and Sicily, and in 1944 led the US troops in the invasion of France.

Bradman Donald George 1908– . Australian test cricketer with the highest average in test history. From 52 test matches he averaged 99.94 runs per innings. He only needed four runs from his final test innings to average 100 but was dismissed at second ball.

Bradman was born in New South Wales, came to prominence at an early age, and made his test debut in 1928. He played for Australia for 20 years and was captain 1936–48. He twice scored triple centuries against England and in 1930 scored 452 not out for New South Wales against Queensland, the highest first-class innings until 1959.

Bradshaw George 1801–1853. British publisher who brought out the first railway timetable in 1839. Thereafter *Bradshaw's Railway Companion* appeared at regular intervals.

He was apprenticed to an engraver on leaving school, and set up his own printing and engraving business in the 1820s, beginning in 1827 with an engraved map of Lancashire.

Bragança name of the royal house of Portugal whose members reigned 1640–1853; another branch were emperors of Brazil 1822–89.

Bragg William Henry 1862–1942. British physicist. In 1915 he shared with his son *(William) Lawrence Bragg* (1890–1971) the Nobel Prize for Physics for their research work on X-rays and crystals.

Brahe Tycho 1546–1601. Danish astronomer, who made accurate observations of the planets from which ◊Kepler proved that planets orbit the Sun in ellipses. His discovery and report of the 1572 supernova made him famous, and his observations of the comet of 1577 proved that it moved on an orbit among the planets, thus disproving the Greek view that comets were in the Earth's atmosphere.

Brahe was a colourful figure who had to wear a metal nose after his own was cut off in a duel, and who took an interest in alchemy. Brahe was the greatest observer in the days before telescopes, making the most accurate measurements of the positions of stars and planets.

Brahms Johannes 1833–1897. German composer, pianist, and conductor. Considered one of the greatest composers of symphonic music and of songs, his works include four symphonies; *lieder* (songs); concertos for piano and for violin; cham-

Brahms *The composer in his study.*

ber music; sonatas; and the choral *A German Requiem* 1868. He performed and conducted his own works.

In 1853 the violinist Joachim introduced him to Liszt and Schumann. From 1868 Brahms made his home in Vienna. Although his music has romantic qualities, it is essentially a sophistication of the classical tradition from the point to which Beethoven had brought it.

Braine John 1922–1986. English novelist. His novel *Room at the Top* 1957 created the character of Joe Lampton, one of the first of the northern working-class anti-heroes.

Braithwaite Eustace Adolph 1912– . Guyanese author. His experiences as a teacher in London prompted *To Sir With Love* 1959. His *Reluctant Neighbours* 1972 deals with black/white relations.

Braithwaite Richard Bevan 1900– . British philosopher, who experimented in the provision of a rational basis for religion and moral choice. Originally a physicist and mathematician, he was Knightbridge professor of moral philosophy at Cambridge 1953–67.

Bramah Ernest. Pen name of Ernest Bramah Smith 1868–1948. British short-story writer, creator of Kai Lung, and of Max Carrados, a blind detective.

Bramah Joseph 1748–1814. British inventor of a flushing water closet (1778), an 'unpickable' lock (1784), and the hydraulic press (1795). The press made use of Pascal's principle (that pressure in fluid contained in a vessel is evenly distributed) and employed water as the hydraulic fluid; it enabled the 19th-century bridge-builders to lift massive girders.

Bramante Donato *c.*1444–1514. Italian Renaissance architect and artist. Inspired by Classical designs, he was employed by Pope Julius II in rebuilding part of the Vatican and St Peter's in Rome.

Branagh Kenneth 1960– . British actor and director. He launched his Renaissance Theatre Company in 1987, was a notable Hamlet and Touchstone in 1988, and in 1989 directed and starred in a film of Shakespeare's *Henry V.*

Brancusi Constantin 1876–1957. Romanian sculptor, active in Paris from 1904, a pioneer of abstract forms and conceptual art. He was one of the first sculptors in the 20th century to carve directly from his material, working with marble, granite, wood, and other materials. He developed increasingly simplified natural or organic forms, such as the sculpted head that gradually came to resemble an egg (*Sleeping Muse* 1910, Musée National d'Art Moderne, Paris).

By the 1930s he had achieved monumental simplicity with structures of simple repeated forms (*Endless Column* and other works in Tirgu Jiu public park, Romania). Brancusi was revered by his contemporaries, and remains a seminal figure in 20th-century sculpture.

Brand 'Dollar' (Adolf Johannes) 1934– . Former name of the South African jazz musician Abdullah ◊Ibrahim.

Brando Marlon 1924– . US actor, whose casual, mumbling speech and use of Method acting earned him a place as one of the most distinctive screen actors. His films include *A Streetcar Named Desire* 1951, *On the Waterfront* 1954 (Academy Award), *The Godfather*, and *Last Tango in Paris* both 1972.

Brandt Bill 1905–1983. British photographer who produced a large body of richly printed and romantic black and white studies of people, London life, and social behaviour.

Brandt Willy. Adopted name of Karl Herbert Frahm 1913– . West German socialist politician, federal chancellor (premier) 1969–74. He played a key role in the remoulding of the Social Democratic Party (SPD) as a moderate socialist force (leader 1964–87). As mayor of West Berlin 1957–66, Brandt became internationally known during the Berlin Wall crisis 1961. In the 'grand coalition' 1966–69 he served as foreign minister and introduced *Ostpolitik*, a policy of reconciliation between East and West Europe, which was continued when he became federal chancellor 1969, and culminated in the 1972 signing of the Basic Treaty with East Germany. He resigned from the chancellorship 1974 following the discovery that a close aide, Günther Guillaume, had been an East German spy. Brandt continued to wield considerable influence in the SPD, especially over the party's new radical left wing. He chaired the Brandt Commission on Third-World problems 1977–83, and was a member of the European Parliament 1979–83. Nobel Prize for Peace 1971.

Brangwyn Frank 1867–1956. British artist. Of Welsh extraction, he was born in Bruges, Belgium. He initially worked for William Morris as a textile designer. He produced furniture, pottery, carpets, schemes for interior decoration and architectural designs, as well as book illustrations, lithographs and etchings.

Branson Richard 1950– . British entrepreneur, whose Virgin company developed quickly, diversifying from retailing records to the airline business.

Braque Georges 1882–1963. French painter, who, with Picasso, founded the Cubist movement around 1907–10. They worked together at L'Estaque in the south of France and in Paris. Braque soon began to experiment in collages, and invented a technique of gluing paper, wood, and other materials to canvas. His later work became more decorative.

Brassäi Adopted name of Gyula Halesz 1899–1986. French photographer of Hungarian origin. From the early 1930s on he documented, mainly by flash, the nightlife of Paris, before turning to more abstract work.

Bratby John 1928– . British artist, one of the leaders of the 'kitchen-sink' school of the 1950s because of a preoccupation in early work with working-class domestic interiors.

Brattain Walter Houser 1902–1987. US physicist. In 1956, he was awarded a Nobel prize jointly with William Shockley and John Bardeen for their work on the development of the transistor, which replaced the comparatively costly and clumsy vacuum tube in electronics.

Brauchitsch Walther von 1881–1948. German field marshal. A staff officer in World War I, he became in 1938 commander in chief of the army and a member of Hitler's secret cabinet council. He was dismissed after his failure to invade Moscow 1941. Captured in 1945, he died before being tried.

Braun Eva 1910–1945. German Nazi. Born in Munich. Secretary to Hitler's photographer and personal friend, Heinrich Hoffmann, she was Hitler's mistress for years, and married him in the air-raid shelter of the Chancellery in Berlin on 29 Apr 1945. They then committed suicide together.

Brautigan Richard 1935–1984. US novelist, most noted for his playful fictions of modern California, like *Trout Fishing in America* 1967, and Gothic works like *The Hawkline Monster* 1974.

Breakspear Nicholas. Original name of ◊Adrian IV, the only English pope.

Bream Julian (Alexander) 1933– . British virtuoso of the guitar and lute. He has revived much Elizabethan lute music and encouraged composition by contemporaries for both instruments. Britten and Henze have written for him.

Brecht Bertolt 1898–1956. German dramatist and

Brecht *German dramatist and poet Bertolt Brecht.*

poet, who aimed to destroy the 'suspension of disbelief' usual in the theatre and to express Marxist ideas. He adapted John Gay's *Beggar's Opera* as *Die Dreigroschenoper/The Threepenny Opera* 1928, set to music by Kurt Weill. Later plays include *Mutter Courage/Mother Courage* 1941, set in the Thirty Years' War, and *Der kaukasische Kreidekreis/The Caucasian Chalk Circle* 1949.

As an anti-Nazi, he left Germany in 1933 for Scandinavia and the USA. He became an Austrian citizen after World War II, and in 1949 established the Berliner Ensemble theatre group in East Germany.

Brennan Christopher (John) 1870–1932. Australian Symbolist poet, influenced by Baudelaire and Mallarmé. Although one of Australia's greatest poets, he is virtually unknown outside his native country. His complex, idiosyncratic verse includes *Poems* 1914 and *A Chant of Doom and Other Verses* 1918.

Brennan Walter 1894–1974. US actor, often seen in Westerns as the hero's sidekick. His work includes *The Westerner* 1940, *Bad Day at Black Rock* 1955, and *Rio Bravo* 1959.

Brenner Sidney 1927– . South African scientist, one of the pioneers of genetic engineering. Brenner discovered messenger RNA (a link between DNA and ribosomes, where proteins are synthesized) 1960.

Brenner studied medicine at university, but then moved into molecular biology at Oxford. He worked for many years with Francis Crick, doing much research on the nematode worm.

Brentano Franz 1838–1916. German-Austrian philosopher, whose *Psychology from the Empirical Standpoint* 1874 developed the concept of 'intentionality', the directing of the mind to an object, for example in perception.

Brentano Klemens 1778–1842. German writer,

leader of the Young Romantics. He published a seminal collection of folktales and songs with Ludwig von ◊Arnim (*Des Knaben Wunderhorn*) 1805–08, and popularized the legend of the Lorelei (a rock in the river Rhine). He also wrote mystic religious verse *Romanzen vom Rosenkranz* 1852.

Brenton Howard 1942– . British dramatist, noted for *The Romans in Britain* 1980, and a translation of Brecht's *The Life of Galileo*.

Breton André 1896–1966. French author, among the leaders of the Dada art movement. *Les Champs magnétiques/Magnetic Fields* 1921, an experiment in automatic writing, was one of the most notable products of the movement He was also a founder of Surrealism, publishing *Le Manifeste de surréalisme/Surrealist Manifesto* 1924. Other works include *Najda* 1928, the story of his love affair with a medium.

Breuer Josef 1842–1925. Viennese physician, one of the pioneers of psychoanalysis. He applied it successfully to cases of hysteria, and collaborated with Freud in *Studien über Hysterie/Studies in Hysteria* 1895.

Breuer Marcel 1902– . Hungarian-born architect and designer, who studied and taught at the Bauhaus school in Germany. His tubular steel chair 1925 was the first of its kind. He moved to England, then to the USA, where he was in partnership with Walter Gropius 1937–40. His buildings show an affinity with natural materials; the best known is the Bijenkorf, Rotterdam (with Elzas) 1953.

Breuil Henri 1877–1961. French prehistorian, professor of historic ethnography and director of research at the Institute of Human Palaeontology, Paris, from 1910. He established the genuine antiquity of Palaeolithic cave art and stressed the anthropological approach to early human history.

Brewster David 1781–1868. Scottish physicist, who made discoveries regarding the diffraction and polarization of light, and invented the kaleidoscope.

Brezhnev Leonid Ilyich 1906–1982. Soviet leader. A protégé of Stalin and Khrushchev, he came into power as general secretary of the Soviet Communist Party (CPSU) 1964–82 and was president 1977–82. Domestically he was conservative; abroad the USSR was established as a military and political superpower during the Brezhnev era, extending its influence in Africa and Asia.

Brezhnev, born in Ukraine, joined the CPSU in the 1920s. After World War II he caught the attention of the CPSU leader Stalin, who inducted Brezhnev into the secretariat and Politburo 1952. In 1960 he was moved to the ceremonial post of state president and began to criticize Khrushchev's policies.

Brezhnev stepped down as president 1963, was elected CPSU general secretary 1964, when Khrushchev was ousted, and gradually came to dominate the conservative and consensual coalition. In 1977 he regained the additional title of state president under the new constitution. He suffered an illness Mar–Apr 1976 which was believed to have affected his thought and speech so severely that he was not able to make decisions. These were made by his entourage, for example committing the troops to Afghanistan to prop up the government. Within the USSR, economic difficulties mounted; the Brezhnev era was a period of caution and stagnation, although outwardly imperialist.

Brian Havergal 1876–1972. English composer of 32 symphonies in visionary romantic style, including the *Gothic* 1919–27 for large choral and orchestral forces.

Brian known as *Brian Boru* ('Brian of the Tribute') 926–1014. King of Ireland from 976, who took Munster, Leinster, and Connacht, to become ruler of all Ireland. He defeated the Norse at Clontarf, thus ending Norse control of Dublin, although he was himself killed. His exploits were celebrated in several chronicles.

Briand Aristide 1862–1932. French radical socialist politician. He was prime minister 1909–11, 1913, 1915–17, 1921–22, 1925–26, and 1929, and foreign minister 1925–32. In 1925 he concluded the Locarno Pact (settling Germany's Western frontiers) and in 1928 the Kellogg Briand Pact (renouncing war); in 1930 he outlined a scheme for a United States of Europe.

Bridge Frank 1879–1941. English composer, the teacher of Benjamin Britten. His works include the orchestral *The Sea* 1912, and *Oration* 1930 for cello and orchestra.

Bridges Robert (Seymour) 1844–1930. British poet, poet laureate from 1913, author of *The Testament of Beauty* 1929, a long philosophical poem. In 1918 he edited and published posthumously the poems of Gerard Manley ◊Hopkins.

Bridget, St 453–523. A patron saint of Ireland, also known as *St Brigit* or *St Bride*. She founded a church and monastery at Kildare, and is said to have been the daughter of a prince of Ulster. Feast day 1 Feb.

Bridgewater Francis Egerton, 3rd Duke of 1736–1803. Pioneer of British inland navigation. With James ◊Brindley as his engineer, he constructed 1762–72 the Bridgewater canal from Worsley to Manchester, and thence to the Mersey, a distance of 67.5 km/42 mi.

Bridgman Percy Williams 1882–1961. US physicist. His research into machinery producing high pressure led in 1955 to the creation of synthetic diamonds by General Electric.

Born in Cambridge, Massachusetts, he was educated at Harvard, where he was Hollis professor of mathematics and natural philosophy 1926–50 and Higgins university professor 1950–54.

Bridie James. Pen name of Osborne Henry Mavor

1888–1951. Dramatist and professor of medicine, and a founder of Glasgow Citizens' Theatre. His plays include *Tobias and the Angel* 1930, and *The Anatomist* 1931.

Brieux Eugène 1858–1932. French dramatist, an exponent of the naturalistic problem play attacking social evils. His most powerful plays are *Les trois filles de M Dupont* 1897; *Les Avariés/Damaged Goods* 1901, long banned for its outspoken treatment of syphilis; and *Maternité*.

Briggs Barry 1934– . New Zealand motorcyclist who won four individual world speedway titles 1957–66 and took part in a record 87 world championship races.

Brighouse Harold 1882–1958. English playwright. Born and bred in Lancashire, in his most famous play, *Hobson's Choice* 1916, he dealt with a Salford bootmaker's courtship, using the local idiom.

Bright John 1811–1889. British Liberal politician, a campaigner for free trade, peace, and social reform. A Quaker millowner, he was among the founders of the Anti-Corn Law League in 1839, and was largely instrumental in securing the passage of the Reform Bill of 1867.

After entering Parliament in 1843 Bright led the struggle there for free trade, together with Richard ◊Cobden, which achieved success in 1846. His *laissez-faire* principles also made him a prominent opponent of factory reform. His influence was constantly exerted on behalf of peace, as when he opposed the Crimean War, Palmerston's aggressive policy in China, Disraeli's anti-Russian policy, and the bombardment of Alexandria. During the American Civil War he was outspoken in support of the North. He sat in Gladstone's cabinets as president of the Board of Trade 1868–70 and chancellor of the Duchy of Lancaster 1873–74 and 1880–82, but broke with him over the Irish Home Rule Bill. Bright owed much of his influence to his skill as a speaker.

Bright Richard 1789–1858. British physician. He was for many years on the staff of Guy's Hospital, London; *Bright's disease*, an inflammation of the kidneys, is named after him.

Brillat-Savarin Jean Anthelme 1755–1826. French gastronome, author of *La Physiologie du Goût* 1825, a compilation of observations on food and drink regarded as the first great classic of gastronomic literature. Most of his professional life was spent as a politician.

Brindley James 1716–1772. British canal builder, the first to employ tunnels and aqueducts extensively, in order to reduce the number of locks on a direct-route canal. His 580 km/360 mi of canals included the Bridgewater (Manchester-Liverpool) and Grand Union (Manchester-Potteries) canals.

Brinell Johann Auguste 1849–1925. Swedish engineer, who devised the Brinell hardness test for measuring the hardness of substances in 1900.

Brisbane Thomas Makdougall 1773–1860. Scottish soldier, colonial administrator, and astronomer. After serving in the Napoleonic Wars under Wellington, he was governor of New South Wales 1821–25, and Brisbane in Queensland is named after him. He catalogued over 7,000 stars.

Brissot Jacques Pierre 1754–1793. French revolutionary leader, born in Chartres. He became a member of the legislative assembly and the National Convention, but his party of moderate republicans, the Girondins, or Brissotins, fell foul of Robespierre and Brissot was guillotined.

Bristow Eric 1957– . English darts player, nicknamed 'the Crafty Cockney'. He has won all the game's major titles, including the world professional title a record five times between 1980 and 1986.

Britannicus Tiberius Claudius *c.*AD 41–55. Roman prince, son of the Emperor Claudius and Messalina; so-called from his father's expedition to Britain. He was poisoned by Nero.

Brittain Vera 1894–1970. English socialist writer, a nurse to the troops overseas 1915–19, as told in her *Testament of Youth* 1933; *Testament of Friendship* 1950 commemorated Winifred ◊Holtby. She married political scientist Sir George Catlin (1896–1979); their daughter is Shirley ◊Williams.

Brittan Leon 1939– . British Conservative politician and lawyer. Chief secretary to the Treasury 1981–83, home secretary 1983–85, secretary for trade and industry 1985–86 (resigned over his part in the Westland affair) and senior European Commissioner from 1988.

Britten (Edward) Benjamin 1913–1976. English composer. He often wrote for the individual voice, for example the role of Peter Pears in the opera *Peter Grimes* 1945, based on verses by Crabbe. Among his many works are the *Young Person's Guide to the Orchestra* 1946; the chamber opera *The Rape of Lucretia* 1946; *Billy Budd* 1951; *A Midsummer Night's Dream* 1960; and *Death in Venice* 1973.

He studied at the Royal College of Music. From 1939–42 he worked in the USA, then returned to England and devoted himself to composing at his home in Aldeburgh, Suffolk, where he established an annual music festival. His oratorio *War Requiem* 1962 was written for the re-dedication of Coventry Cathedral.

Broad Charles Dunbar 1887–1971. British philosopher. His books include *Perception, Physics and Reality* 1914, and *Lectures on Psychic Research* 1962, discussing modern scientific evidence for survival after death.

Born in London, he was educated at Trinity College, Cambridge, and was Knightbridge professor of moral philosophy at the university 1933–53.

Broch Hermann 1886–1951. Austrian novelist, who used experimental techniques in *Die Schlafwandler/The Sleepwalkers* 1932, *Der Tod des Vergil/The Death of Virgil* 1945, and *Die Schuldlosen/The Guiltless*, a novel in 11 stories. He went to the USA 1938 after being persecuted by the Nazis.

Brodsky Joseph 1940– . Russian poet, who emigrated to the USA in 1972. His work, often dealing with themes of exile, is admired for its wit and economy of language, particularly in its use of understatement. Many of his poems, written in Russian, have been translated into English (*A Part of Speech* 1980). More recently he has also written in English. Nobel prize 1987.

Broglie, de see ◊de Broglie.

Bromfield Louis 1896–1956. US novelist. His most notable books are *The Strange Case of Miss Annie Spragg* 1928, and *Mrs Parkington* 1943, dealing with the golden age of New York society.

Bronson Charles. Stage name of Charles Bunchinsky 1922– . US film actor. His films are mainly violent thrillers such as *Death Wish* 1974. He was one of *The Magnificent Seven* 1960.

Brontë family of English writers, including the three sisters *Charlotte* (1816–55), *Emily Jane* (1818–48) and *Anne* (1820–49), and their brother *Patrick Branwell* (1817–48). Their best-known works are Charlotte Brontë's *Jane Eyre* 1847 and Emily Brontë's *Wuthering Heights* 1847. Later works include Anne's *The Tenant of Wildfell Hall* 1848 and Charlotte's *Shirley* 1849 and *Villette* 1853.

The Brontës were brought up by an aunt at Haworth rectory (now a museum) in Yorkshire. In 1846 the sisters published a volume of poems under the pen names Currer (Charlotte), Ellis (Emily) and Acton (Anne) Bell. In 1847 (using the same names), they published the novels *Jane Eyre*, *Wuthering Heights*, and *Agnes Grey*, Anne's much weaker work. During 1848–49 Branwell, Emily, and Anne all died of tuberculosis, aided in Branwell's case by alcohol and opium addic-

Brontë *Emily, Anne, and Charlotte Brontë painted by their brother, Patrick Branwell, c.1835.*

tion; he is remembered for his portrait of the sisters. Charlotte married her father's curate, A B Nicholls, in 1854, and died during pregnancy.

Bronzino Agnolo 1503–1572. Italian painter active in Florence, court painter to Cosimo I, Duke of Tuscany. He painted in an elegant, Mannerist style, and is best known for portraits and the allegory *Venus, Cupid, Folly and Time* about 1545 (National Gallery, London).

Brook Peter 1925– . British theatrical producer and director. Known for his experimental productions with the Royal Shakespeare Company in England, he began working with the Paris-based Le Centre International de Créations Théâtrales in 1970. Films he has directed include *Lord of the Flies* 1962 and *Meetings with Remarkable Men* 1979.

Brooke James 1803–1868. British administrator who became rajah of Sarawak, on Borneo, 1841.

Born near Benares, he served in the army of the East India Company. In 1838 he headed a private expedition to Borneo, where he helped to suppress a revolt, and when the sultan gave him the title of rajah of Sarawak, Brooke became known as the 'the white rajah'. He was succeeded as rajah by his nephew, Sir Charles Johnson (1829–1917), whose son Sir Charles Vyner (1874–1963) in 1946 arranged for the transfer of Sarawak to the British crown.

Brooke Peter Leonard 1934– . British Conservative politician. The son of a former home secretary, Lord Brooke of Cumnor, he became an MP in 1977 and entered Thatcher's government in 1979. Following a number of junior appointments, he succeeded Norman Tebbit as chair of the Conservative Party in 1987. After an undistinguished two years in that office, he succeeded Tom King as Northern Ireland secretary in 1989. He aroused criticism for observing that at some future time negotiations with the IRA might take place.

Brooke Rupert Chawner 1887–1915. English poet, symbol of the World War I 'lost generation'. His poems, the best-known being the five war sonnets (including 'Grantchester' and 'The Great Lover'), were published posthumously.

Born in Rugby, where he was educated, Brooke travelled abroad after a nervous breakdown in 1911, but in 1913 won a fellowship at King's College, Cambridge. Later that year he toured America (*Letters from America* 1916), New Zealand, and the South Seas, and in 1914 became an officer in the Royal Naval Division. After fighting at Antwerp, he sailed for the Dardanelles, but died of blood-poisoning on the Greek island of Skyros, where he is buried.

Brookeborough Basil Brooke, Viscount Brookeborough 1888–1973. Unionist politician of Northern Ireland. He entered Parliament in 1929, held ministerial posts 1933–45, and was prime minister of Northern Ireland 1943–63. He was a staunch advocate of strong links with Britain.

Brookner Anita 1928– . British novelist and art historian, whose novels include *Hotel du Lac* 1984, winner of the Booker prize, *A Misalliance* 1986, and *Latecomers* 1988.

Brooks Louise 1906–1985. US actress, known for her roles in silent films such as *Die Büchse der Pandora/Pandora's Box* and *Das Tagebuch einer Verlorenen/Diary of a Lost Girl* both 1929, and directed by G W ◊Pabst. She retired from the screen 1938.

Brooks Mel. Assumed name of Melvin Kaminsky 1926– . US film director, whose comic films include *Blazing Saddles* 1974 and *History of the World Part I* 1981.

Broome David 1940– . British show jumper. He won the 1970 world title on a horse named *Beethoven*. His sister Liz (now Edgar) is also a top class show jumper.

Brougham Henry Peter, 1st Baron Brougham and Vaux 1778–1868. British Whig politician and lawyer. From 1811 he was chief adviser to the Princess of Wales (afterwards Queen Caroline), and in 1820 he defeated the attempt of George IV to divorce her. He was lord chancellor 1830–34, supporting the Reform Bill.

Brouwer Adriaen 1605–1638. Flemish painter who studied with Frans Hals. He excelled in scenes of peasant revelry.

Brown 'Capability' (Lancelot) 1715–1783. English landscape gardener. He acquired his nickname because of his continual enthusiam for the 'capabilities' of natural landscapes.

He advised on gardens of stately homes including Blenheim, Stowe, and Petworth, sometimes also contributing to the architectural designs.

Brown (James) Gordon 1951– . British Labour politician. He entered Parliament in 1983, rising quickly to the opposition front bench, with a reputation as an outstanding debater.

Brown, the son of a Church of Scotland minister, won a first in history at Edinburgh University before he was 20. After four years as a college lecturer and three as a television journalist, he entered the House of Commons, for Dunfermline East in 1983. He topped the Labour Party shadow-cabinet poll in 1989.

Brown Charles Brockden 1771–1810. US novelist and magazine editor. He is called the 'father of the American novel' for his *Wieland* 1798, *Ormond* 1799, *Edgar Huntly* 1799, and *Arthur Mervyn* 1800. His works also pioneered the Gothic and fantastic tradition of US fiction.

Brown Earle 1926– . US composer who pioneered graphic notation and mobile form during the 1950s. He was an associate of ◊Cage.

Brown Ford Madox 1821–1893. British painter, associated with the Pre-Raphaelite Brotherhood. His pictures include *The Last of England* 1855 (Birmingham Art Gallery) and *Work* 1852–65

(City Art Gallery, Manchester), packed with realistic detail and symbolic incident.

Brown George, Baron George-Brown 1914–1985. British Labour politician. He entered Parliament 1945, was briefly minister of works 1951, and contested the leadership of the party on the death of Gaitskell, but was defeated by Harold Wilson. He was secretary for economic affairs 1964–66 and foreign secretary 1966–68. He was created a life peer 1970.

Brown John 1800–1859. US slavery abolitionist. With 18 men, he seized, on the night of 16 Oct 1859, the government arsenal at Harper's Ferry in W Virginia, apparently intending to distribute weapons to runaway slaves who would then defend the mountain stronghold, which Brown hoped would become a republic of former slaves. On 18 Oct the arsenal was stormed by US Marines under Col Robert E ◊Lee. Brown was tried and hanged on 2 Dec, becoming a martyr and the hero of the popular song 'John Brown's Body' *c.* 1860.

Brown John 1825–1883. Scottish servant, a personal confidant of Queen Victoria from 1858 until his death.

Brown Robert 1773–1858. Scottish botanist, a pioneer of plant classification and the first to describe and name the cell nucleus.

On an expedition to Australia in 1801 he collected 4,000 species of plant and later classified them using the 'natural' system of Bernard de Jussieu (1699–1777) rather than relying upon the system of Carolus ◊Linnaeus. The agitated movement of small particles suspended in water, now explained by kinetic theory, was described by Brown in 1827 and later became known as *Brownian motion.*

Browne Hablot Knight 1815–1882. British illustrator, pseudonym Phiz, known for his illustrations of Dickens's works.

Browne Robert 1550–1633. English Puritan religious leader, founder of the Brownists. He was imprisoned several times in 1581–82 for attacking Episcopalianism (church government by bishops). He founded a community in Norwich, East Anglia and in the Netherlands which continued on Nonconformist lines, developing into modern Congregationalism.

Browne Thomas 1605–1682. English author and physician. Born in London, he travelled widely in Europe before settling in Norwich in 1637. He is noted for his personal richness of style in *Religio Medici/The Religion of a Doctor* 1643, a justification of his profession; *Vulgar Errors* 1646, an examination of popular legend and superstition; *Urn Burial* and *The Garden of Cyrus* 1658; and *Christian Morals* 1717. He was knighted in 1671.

Browning Elizabeth Barrett 1806–1861. English poet. In 1844 she published *Poems* (including 'The Cry of the Children'), which led to her friendship and secret marriage with Robert Browning in 1846. The *Sonnets from the Portuguese* 1847 were written during their courtship. Later works include *Casa Guidi Windows* 1851 and the poetic novel *Aurora Leigh* 1857.

Barrett Browning was born near Durham. As a child she fell from her pony and injured her spine, and was subsequently treated by her father as a confirmed invalid. Freed from her father's oppressive influence, her health improved, she wrote strong verse about social injustice and oppression in Victorian England.

Browning Robert 1812–1889. English poet, married to Elizabeth Barrett Browning. His work is characterized by the use of dramatic monologue and an interest in obscure literary and historical figures. It includes the play *Pippa Passes* 1841, and the poems 'The Pied Piper of Hamelin' 1842, 'My Last Duchess' 1842, 'Home Thoughts from Abroad' 1845, and 'Rabbi Ben Ezra' 1864.

Browning, born in Camberwell, London, wrote his first poem 'Pauline' 1833 under the influence of Shelley; it was followed by 'Paracelsus' 1835 and 'Sordello' 1840. In 1837 he achieved moderate success with his play *Strafford*, and in the pamphlet series of *Bells and Pomegranates* 1841–46, which contained *Pippa Passes, Dramatic Lyrics* 1842 and *Dramatic Romances* 1845, he included the dramas *King Victor and King Charles, Return of the Druses*, and *Colombe's Birthday*.

In 1846 he met Elizabeth Barrett; they married the same year and went to Italy. There he wrote *Christmas Eve and Easter Day* 1850 and *Men and Women* 1855, the latter containing some of his finest love-poems and dramatic monologues, which were followed by *Dramatis Personae* 1864, and *The Ring and the Book* 1868–69, based on an Italian murder story. After his wife's death in 1861 Browning settled in England and enjoyed an established reputation, although his late works, such as *Red-Cotton Night-Cap Country* 1873, *Dramatic Idylls* 1879–80, and *Asolando* 1889, still prompted opposition by their rugged obscurity of style.

Brubeck Dave (David Warren) 1920– . US jazz pianist, a student of the French composer Milhaud. The Dave Brubeck Quartet (formed 1951) combined improvisation with modern classical discipline.

Bruce one of the most important Scottish noble houses. Robert I and his son David II were both kings of Scotland descended from Robert de Bruis (died 1094), a Norman knight who came to England with William the Conqueror 1066.

Bruce James 1730–1794. Scottish explorer, the first European to reach the source of the Blue Nile 1770, and to follow the river downstream to Cairo 1773.

Bruce Robert de, 5th Lord of Annandale 1210–1295. Scottish noble, one of the unsuccessful claimants to the throne at the death of Alexander II 1290. His grandson was ◊Robert I (the Bruce).

Bruce Robert the, king of Scotland; see ◊Robert I.

Bruce Stanley Melbourne, 1st Viscount Bruce of
Melbourne 1883–1967. Australian National Party
politician, prime minister 1923–29. He was elected
to parliament in 1918. As prime minister he introduced a number of social welfare measures.

Bruch Max 1838–1920. German composer, professor at the Berlin Academy 1891. He wrote
three operas including *Hermoine* 1872, *Kol Nidrei*
for cello and orchestra, violin concertos, and many
choral works.

Bruckner (Joseph) Anton 1824–1896. Austrian
Romantic composer. He was cathedral organist
at Linz 1856–68, and from 1868 he was professor
at the Vienna Conservatoire. His works include
many choral pieces, and ten symphonies, the last
unfinished. His compositions were influenced by
Richard ◊Wagner and Beethoven.

Brueghel family of Flemish painters. *Pieter
Brueghel* (*c.*1525–69), was one of the greatest
artists of his time. He painted satirical and humorous pictures of peasant life, many of which include
symbolic details illustrating folly and inhumanity,
and a series of Months (five survive), including
Hunters in the Snow (Kunsthistorisches Museum,
Vienna).

The elder Pieter was nicknamed 'Peasant'
Brueghel. Two of his sons were painters. *Pieter
Brueghel the Younger* (1564–1638), called
'Hell' Brueghel, specialized in religious subjects,
and another son, *Jan Brueghel* (1568–1625),
called 'Velvet' Brueghel, painted flowers and land-
and seascapes.

Brulé 1592–1632. French adventurer and explorer.
He travelled with ◊Champlain to the New World in
1608 and settled in Quebec, where he lived with
the Algonquin Indians. He explored the Great
Lakes and travelled as far south as Chesapeake
Bay. Returning north, he was killed and eaten by
Huron Indians.

Brummell George Bryan 'Beau' 1778–1840. British dandy and leader of fashion. A friend of the
Prince of Wales, the future George IV, he later
quarrelled with him, and was driven by gambling
losses to exile in France in 1816.

Brundtland Gro Harlem 1939– . Norwegian
Labour politician, prime minister 1981 and from
1986, environment minister 1974–76.

The *Brundtland Report* 1987, produced by the
World Commission on Environment and Development, was chaired by her.

Brunel Isambard Kingdom 1806–1859. British
engineer and inventor. In 1833 he became engineer to the Great Western Railway, which adopted
the 2.1 m/7 ft gauge on his advice. He built the
Clifton Suspension Bridge over the river Avon
at Bristol and the Saltash Bridge over the river
Tamar near Plymouth. His ship-building designs
include the *Great Western* 1838, the first steam-

ship to cross the Atlantic regularly; the *Great
Britain* 1845, the first large iron ship to have
a screw propeller; and the *Great Eastern* 1858,
which laid the first transatlantic telegraph cable.

The son of Marc Brunel, he made major contributions in ship-building and bridge construction,
and assisted his father in the Thames tunnel project. Brunel University in Uxbridge, London, is
named after both father and son.

Brunel Marc Isambard 1769–1849. British engineer and inventor, and father of Isambard Kingdom Brunel. He constructed the Rotherhithe
tunnel under the river Thames in London from
Wapping to Rotherhithe 1825–43.

Born in France, he came to England in 1799, did
engineering work for the Admiralty, and improved
the port of Liverpool.

Brunelleschi Filippo 1377–1446. Italian Renaissance architect. One of the earliest and greatest
Renaissance architects, he pioneered the scientific
use of perspective. He was responsible for the
construction of the dome of Florence Cathedral
(completed 1438), a feat deemed impossible by
many of his contemporaries.

Bruning Heinrich 1885–1970. German politician.
Elected to the Reichstag (parliament) 1924, he led
the Catholic Centre Party from 1929 and was federal chancellor (premier) 1930–32, when political
and economic crisis forced his resignation.

Bruno Giordano 1548–1600. Italian philosopher.
He became a Dominican friar 1563, but his sceptical attitude to Catholic doctrines forced him to
flee Italy 1577. After visiting Geneva and Paris, he
lived in England 1583–85, where he wrote some
of his finest works. After returning to Europe, he
was arrested by the Inquisition 1593 in Venice,
and burned at the stake for his adoption of
Copernican astronomy and his heretical religious
views.

Bruno, St 1030–1101. German founder of the
monastic Catholic Carthusian order. He was born
in Cologne, became a priest, and controlled the
cathedral school of Rheims 1057–76. Withdrawing
to the mountains near Grenoble after an ecclesiastical controversy, he founded the monastery at
Chartreuse in 1084. Feast day 6 Oct.

Brussilov Aleksei Alekseevich 1853–1926. Russian general, military leader in World War I,
who achieved major sucesses against the Austro-
Hungarian forces in 1916. Later he was commander of the Red Army 1920 which drove the
Poles to within a few miles of Warsaw before being
repulsed.

Brutus Marcus Junius *c.*78–42 BC. Roman soldier,
a supporter of ◊Pompey (against Caesar) in the
civil war. Pardoned by ◊Caesar and raised to high
office by him, he nevertheless plotted Caesar's
assassination to restore the purity of the Republic.
Brutus committed suicide when he was defeated
(with ◊Cassius) by ◊Mark Antony, Caesar's lieu-

tenant, at Philippi 42 BC.

Bryan William Jennings 1860–1925. US politician who campaigned unsuccessfully for the presidency three times: as the Populist and Democratic nominee 1896, as an anti-imperialist Democrat 1900, and as a Democratic tariff reformer 1908. He served as President Wilson's secretary of state 1913–15. In the early 1920s he was a leading fundamentalist and opponent of Clarence Darrow in the Scopes monkey trial in which John Scopes was accused of teaching Darwin's theory of evolution.

Bryant Arthur 1899–1985. British historian, noted for his studies of Restoration figures such as Pepys and Charles II, and a series covering the Napoleonic Wars including *The Age of Elegance* 1950. He was knighted in 1954.

Bryant David 1931– . English flat-green (lawn) bowls player. He has won every honour the game has offered, including four outdoor world titles (three singles and one triples) 1966–88 and three indoor titles 1979–81.

Bryce James, 1st Viscount Bryce 1838–1922. British Liberal politician, and professor of civil law at Oxford University 1870–93. He entered Parliament 1880, holding office under Gladstone and Rosebery. He was author of *The American Commonwealth* 1888, was ambassador to Washington 1907–13, and improved US-Canadian relations.

Brynner Yul. Stage name of Youl Bryner 1915–1985. US actor who made baldness his trademark. He played the king in *The King and I* both on stage 1951 and on film 1956; he is also memorable as the leader of *The Magnificent Seven* 1960.

Bryusov Valery 1873–1924. Russian Symbolist poet, novelist and critic, author of the *The Fiery Angel* 1908.

Brzezinski Zbigniew 1928– . US Democrat politician, born in Poland; he taught at Harvard University, USA, and became a US citizen 1949. He was national-security adviser to President Carter 1977–81 and chief architect of Carter's human-rights policy.

Buber Martin 1878–1965. Israeli philosopher, a Zionist and advocate of the reappraisal of ancient Jewish thought in modern terms. Born in Vienna, he was forced to abandon a professorship in comparative religion at Frankfurt by the Nazis, and taught social philosophy at the Hebrew University, Jerusalem, 1937–51.

Bucer Martin 1491–1551. German Protestant reformer, regius professor of divinity at Cambridge University from 1549, who tried to reconcile the views of his fellow Protestants Luther and Zwingli and the significance of the eucharist.

Buchan John, Baron Tweedsmuir 1875–1940. Scottish politician and author. Called to the Bar in 1901, he was Conservative member of Parliament for the Scottish universities 1927–35, and governor

general of Canada 1934–40. His adventure stories include *The Thirty-Nine Steps* 1915, *Greenmantle* 1916, and *The Three Hostages* 1924.

Buchanan George 1506–1582. Scottish humanist. Forced to flee to France in 1539 owing to some satirical verses on the Franciscans, he returned to Scotland about 1562 as tutor to Mary Queen of Scots. He became principal of St Leonard's College, St Andrews, in 1566, and wrote *Rerum Scoticarum Historia/A History of Scotland* 1582, which was biased against ◊Mary Queen of Scots.

Buchanan Jack 1891–1957. British musical-comedy actor. His songs such as 'Good-Night Vienna' epitomized the period between World Wars I and II.

Buchman Frank N D 1878–1961. US right-wing Christian evangelist. In 1938 he launched in London the anticommunist campaign, the *Moral Re-Armament* movement.

Buchner Eduard 1860–1917. German chemist who researched the process of fermentation. In 1897 Buchner observed that fermentation could be produced mechanically, by cell-free extracts. Buchner argued that it was not the whole yeast cell which produced fermentation, only the presence of the enzyme he named zymase. Nobel prize 1907.

Buck Pearl S 1892–1973. US novelist. Daughter of missionaries to China, she wrote novels about Chinese life, such as *East Wind-West Wind* 1930 and *The Good Earth* 1931. Nobel Prize for Literature 1938.

Buckingham George Villiers, 1st Duke of Buckingham 1592–1628. English courtier, adviser to James I and later Charles I. After Charles's accession, Buckingham attempted to form a Protestant coalition in Europe which led to war with France, but he failed to relieve the Protestants besieged in La Rochelle 1627. This added to his unpopularity with Parliament, and he was assassinated.

Introduced to the court of James I in 1614, he soon became his favourite and was made Earl of Buckingham in 1617 and a duke in 1623. He failed to arrange the marriage of Prince Charles and the Infanta of Spain 1623, but on returning to England negotiated Charles's alliance with Henrietta Maria, sister to the French king. His policy on the French Protestants was attacked in Parliament, and when about to sail again for La Rochelle he was assassinated in Portsmouth.

Buckingham George Villiers, 2nd Duke of Buckingham 1628–1687. English politician, a member of the powerful clique known as the Cabal under Charles II. A dissolute son of the 1st duke, he was brought up with the royal children. His play *The Rehearsal* satirized the style of the poet Dryden, who portrayed him as Zimri in *Absalom and Achitophel*.

Buckley William 1780–1856. Australian convict, who escaped from Port Phillip and lived 1803–35 among the Aborigines before giving himself up, hence **Buckley's chance** meaning an 'outside chance'.

Buckley William F(rank) 1925– . US conservative political writer, novelist, and founder-editor of the *National Review* 1955. In such books as *Up from Liberalism* 1959, and in a weekly television debate 'Firing Line', he represented the 'intellectual' right-wing, anti-liberal stance in US political thought.

Budaeus Latin form of the name of Guillaume Budé 1467–1540. French scholar. He persuaded Francis I to found the Collège de France, and also the library that formed the nucleus of the French national library, the Bibliothèque Nationale.

Buddha 'enlightened one', title of Prince *Gautama Siddhãrtha* c.563–483 BC. Religious leader, founder of Buddhism, born at Lumbini in Nepal. At the age of 29, he left a life of luxury, and his wife and son, to escape from the burdens of existence. After six years of austerity he realized that asceticism, like overindulgence, was futile, and chose the middle way of meditation. He became enlightened under a bo tree near Buddh Gaya in Bihar, India. He began teaching at Varanasi, and founded the Sangha, or order of monks. He spent the rest of his life moving around N India and died at Kusinagara in Uttar Pradesh.

Buddha acquired the *Four Noble Truths*: the fact of frustration or suffering; that suffering has a cause; that it can be ended; and that it can be ended by following the *Noble Eightfold Path* – right views, right intention, right speech, right action, right livelihood, right effort, right mindfulness, and right concentration – and so arriving at nirvana, the extinction of all craving for things of the senses.

Budge Donald 1915– . US tennis player, the first to perform the Grand Slam when he won the Wimbledon, French, US, and Australian championships 1938. Altogether he won 14 Grand Slam events. including Wimbledon singles twice. He turned professional 1938.

Buffet Bernard 1928– . French figurative painter who created distinctive thin, spiky forms with bold, dark outlines. He was a precocious talent in the late 1940s.

Bugatti Etore 1881–1947. Italian car manufacturer, who designed his first car 1899, and founded the Bugatti company in Strasbourg 1907.

Bukharin Nikolai Ivanovich 1888–1938. Russian politician and theorist. A moderate, he was the most influential Bolshevik thinker after Lenin. Executed on Stalin's orders for treason in 1938, he was posthumously rehabilitated in 1988.

He wrote the major defence of war communism in his *Economics of the Transition Period* 1920. He drafted the Soviet constitution of 1936, but in 1938 was imprisoned and tried for treason in one of Stalin's 'show trials'. He pleaded guilty

to treason, but defended his moderate policies and denied criminal charges. He was nonetheless executed, as were all other former members of Lenin's Politburo except Trotsky, who was murdered, and Stalin himself.

Bulgakov Mikhail Afanasyevich 1891–1940. Russian novelist and playwright. His novel *The White Guard* 1924, dramatized as *The Days of the Turbins* 1926, deals with the Revolution and the civil war. His satiric approach made him unpopular with the Stalin regime, and he was unpublished from the 1930s. *The Master and Margarita*, a fantasy about the devil in Moscow, was not published until 1967.

Bulganin Nikolai 1895–1975. Russian military leader and politician. He helped to organize Moscow's defence in World War II, became a marshal of the USSR 1947, and was minister of defence 1947–49 and 1953–55. On the fall of Malenkov he became prime minister (chair of Council of Ministers) 1955–58 until ousted by Khrushchev.

Bull John c.1562–1628. British composer, organist, and virginalist. Most of his output is for keyboard, and includes 'God Save the King'. He also wrote sacred vocal music.

Bull Olaf 1883–1933. Norwegian lyric poet, son of humourist and fiction writer Jacob Breda Bull (1853–1930). He often celebrated his birthplace Christiania (now Oslo) in his poetry.

Buller Redvers Henry 1839–1908. British commander against the Boers in the South African War 1899–1902. He was defeated at Colenso and Spion Kop, but relieved Ladysmith; he was superseded by Lord Roberts.

Bülow Hans (Guido) Frieherr von 1830–1894. German conductor and pianist. He studied with Richard ◊Wagner and ◊Liszt, and in 1857 married Cosima, daughter of Liszt. From 1864 he served Ludwig II of Bavaria, conducting first performances of Wagner's *Tristan und Isolde* and *Die Meistersinger*. His wife left him and married Wagner in 1870.

Bülow Prince Bernhard von 1849–1929. German diplomat and politician. He was chancellor of the German Empire 1900–09 under Kaiser Wilhelm II and, holding that self-interest was the only rule for any state, adopted attitudes to France and Russia which unintentionally reinforced the trend towards opposing European power groups: the Triple Entente (Britain, France, Russia) and Triple Alliance (Germany, Austria-Hungary, Italy).

Bulwer-Lytton Edward George Earle Lytton, Ist Baron Lytton 1803–1873. See ◊Lytton.

Bunche Ralph 1904–1971. US diplomat. Grandson of a slave, he was principal director of the UN Department of Trusteeship 1947–54, and UN undersecretary acting as mediator in Palestine 1948–49 and as special representative in the Congo 1960. Nobel Prize for Peace 1950.

Bundelas Rajput clan prominent in the 14th century, which gave its name to the Bundelkhand in N central India. The clan had replaced the Chandelā dynasty in the 11th century and continued to resist the attacks of other Indian rulers until coming under British control after 1812.

Bunin Ivan Alexeyevich 1870–1953. Russian writer, author of *Derevnya/The Village* 1910, which tells of the passing of peasant life; and *Gospodin iz San Frantsisko/The Gentleman from San Francisco* 1916, about the death of a millionaire on Capri, which won him a Nobel prize in 1933. He was also a poet and translated Byron into Russian.

Bunsen Robert Wilhelm von 1811–1899. German chemist, credited with the invention of the *Bunsen burner*. His name is also given to the carbon–zinc electric cell, which he invented in 1841 for use in arc-lamps. In 1859 he discovered two new elements, caesium and rubidium.

Buñuel Luis 1900–1983. Spanish Surrealist film director. He collaborated with Salvador Dali in *Un Chien Andalou* 1928, and established his solo career with *Los Olvidados/The Young and the Damned* 1950. His works are often controversial and anticlerical, with black humour and erotic imagery.

Later films include *Le Charme discret de la Bourgeoisie/The Discreet Charm of the Bourgeoisie* 1972 (Academy Award winner) and *Cet Obscur Objet du Désir/That Obscure Object of Desire* 1977.

Bunyan John 1628–1688. English author. A Baptist, he was imprisoned in Bedford 1660–72 for preaching. During a second jail sentence in 1675 he started to write *Pilgrim's Progress*, the first part of which was published in 1678. Other works include *Grace Abounding* 1666, *The Life and Death of Mr Badman* 1680, and *The Holy War* 1682.

At 16, during the Civil War, he was conscripted into the Parliamentary army. Released in 1646, he passed through a period of religious doubt before joining the Baptists in 1653. In 1660 he was committed to Bedford county jail for preaching, where he remained for 12 years, refusing all offers of release conditional on his not preaching again. During his confinement he wrote *Grace Abounding* describing his early spiritual struggles. Set free in 1672, he was elected pastor of the Bedford congregation, but in 1675 was again arrested and imprisoned for six months in the jail on Bedford Bridge, where he began *The Pilgrim's Progress*. The book was an instant success, and a second part followed in 1684.

Burbage Richard *c.*1567–1619. English actor, thought to have been Shakespeare's original Hamlet, Othello, and Lear. He also appeared in first productions of works by Ben Jonson, Thomas Kyd, and John Webster. His father *James Burbage* (*c.* 1530–97) built the first English playhouse, known as 'the Theatre'; his brother **Cuthbert Burbage** (*c.*1566–1636) built the original Globe Theatre 1599 in London.

Burckhardt Jacob 1818–1897. Swiss art historian, professor of history at Basel University 1858–93. His *The Civilization of the Renaissance in Italy* 1860, intended as part of a study of world cultural history, has been highly influential.

Burckhardt Johann Ludwig 1784–1817. Swiss traveller whose knowledge of Arabic enabled him to travel throughout the Middle East, visiting Mecca disguised as a Muslim pilgrim in 1814. In 1817 he discovered the ruins of Petra.

Bürger Gottfried 1747–1794. German Romantic poet, remembered for his ballad 'Lenore' 1773.

Burges William 1827–1881. British Gothic revivalist architect. His chief works are Cork Cathedral 1862–76, additions to and remodelling of Cardiff Castle 1865, and Castle Coch near Cardiff 1875. His style is characterized by sumptuous interiors with carving, painting, and gilding.

Burgess Anthony. Pen name of Anthony John Burgess Wilson 1917– . British novelist, critic, and composer. His prolific work includes *A Clockwork Orange* 1962, set in a future London terrorized by teenage gangs, and the panoramic *Earthly Powers* 1980. His vision has been described as bleak and pessimistic, but his work is also comic and satiric, as in his novels featuring the poet Enderby.

Burgess Guy (Francis de Moncy) 1910–1963. British spy, a diplomat recruited by the USSR as agent; linked with Kim ◊Philby, Donald Maclean (1913–83), and Anthony ◊Blunt.

Burghley William Cecil, Baron Burghley 1520–1598. English politician, chief adviser to Elizabeth I as secretary of state from 1558 and Lord High Treasurer from 1572. He was largely responsible for the religious settlement of 1559, and took a leading role in the events preceding the execution of Mary, Queen of Scots, in 1587.

One of Edward VI's secretaries, he lost office under Queen Mary, but on Queen Elizabeth's succession became one of her most trusted ministers. He carefully avoided a premature breach with Spain in the difficult period leading up to the attack by the Spanish Armada in 1588, did a great deal towards abolishing monopolies and opening up trade, and was created Baron Burghley 1571.

Burgoyne John 1722–1792. British general and dramatist. He served in the American War of Independence and surrendered 1777 to the colonists at Saratoga, New York State, in one of the pivotal battles of the war. He wrote comedies, among them *The Maid of the Oaks* 1775 and

The Heiress 1786. He figures in George Bernard Shaw's play *The Devil's Disciple*.

Burke Edmund 1729-1797. British Whig politician and political theorist, born in Dublin, Ireland. In Parliament from 1765, he opposed the government's attempts to coerce the American colonists, for example in *Thoughts on the Present Discontents* 1770, and supported the emancipation of Ireland, but denounced the French Revolution, for example in *Reflections on the Revolution in France* 1790.

Burke wrote *A Philosophical Inquiry into the Origin of our Ideas on the Sublime and Beautiful* 1756, on aesthetics. He was paymaster of the forces in Rockingham's government 1782 and in the Fox–North coalition 1783, and after the collapse of the latter spent the rest of his career in opposition. He attacked Warren Hastings's misgovernment in India and promoted his impeachment. Burke defended his inconsistency in supporting the American but not the French Revolution in his *Appeal from the New to the Old Whigs* 1791 and *Letter to a Noble Lord* 1796, and attacked the suggestion of peace with France in *Letters on a Regicide Peace* 1795-97. He retired 1794. He was a noted orator and is regarded by modern Conservatives as the greatest of their political theorists.

Burke John 1787-1848. First publisher, in 1826, of *Burke's, Peerage*, a regularly updated genealogy of Britain's nobility.

Burke Martha Jane *c.*1852-1903. Real name of US heroine ◊Calamity Jane.

Burke Robert O'Hara 1820-1861. Australian explorer who made the first south-north crossing of Australia (from Victoria to the Gulf of Carpentaria), with William Wills (1834-61). Both died on the return journey, and only one of their party survived.

He was born in Galway, Ireland, and became a police inspector in the goldfields of Victoria.

Burke William 1792-1829. Irish murderer. He and his partner **William Hare**, living in Edinburgh, dug up the dead to sell for dissection. They increased their supplies by murdering at least 15 people. Burke was hanged on the evidence of Hare. Hare is said to have died a beggar in London in the 1860s.

Burlington Richard Boyle, 3rd Earl of 1694-1753. British architectural patron and architect; one of the premier exponents of the Palladian style in Britain. His buildings, such as Chiswick House in London (1725-29), are characterized by absolute adherence to the Classical rules. His major protégé was William ◊Kent.

Burnaby Frederick 1842-1885. English soldier, traveller, and founder of the weekly critical journal *Vanity Fair*. He travelled to Spain, Sudan, and Russian Asia during his leave from the Horse Guards. His books include *A Ride to Khiva*

1876 and *On Horseback through Asia Minor* 1877. Burnaby joined the British Nile expedition to relieve General Gordon, under seige in Khartoum, Sudan, and was killed in action at the battle of Abu Klea.

Burne-Jones Edward Coley 1833-1898. British painter. Influenced by William Morris and the Pre-Raphaelite Rossetti, he was inspired by legend and myth, as in *King Cophetua and the Beggar Maid* 1880-84 (Tate Gallery, London), but moved towards Symbolism. He also designed tapestries and stained glass.

Burnes Alexander 1805-1841. Scottish soldier, linguist, diplomat, and traveller in Central Asia. Following journeys to Rajputana and Lajhore he led an expedition across the Hindu Kush to Bokhara described in his *Travels into Bokhara* 1834. In 1836-37 he led a diplomatic mission to the Afghan leader Dost Mohammed, described in his book *Kabul* 1842. He was killed in Kabul during a rising that sparked off the first Afghan War.

Burnet Gilbert 1643-1715. British historian and bishop, author of *History of His Own Time* 1723-24. His Whig views having brought him into disfavour, he retired to The Hague on the accession of James II, and became the confidential adviser of William of Orange, with whom he sailed to England in 1688. He was appointed bishop of Salisbury in 1689.

Burnet Macfarlane 1899-1985. Australian physician, authority on immunology and viral diseases. He was awarded the Order of Merit in 1958 in recognition of his work on such diseases as influenza, polio and cholera.

Burnett Frances Eliza Hodgson 1849-1924. English writer, living in the USA from 1865, whose novels for children include the rags-to-riches tale *Little Lord Fauntleroy* 1886 and the sentimental *The Secret Garden* 1909.

Burney Frances (Fanny) 1752-1840. English novelist and diarist, daughter of the musician Dr Charles Burney (1726-1814). She achieved success with *Evelina*, published anonymously 1778, became a member of Dr ◊Johnson's circle, received a post at court from Queen Charlotte, and in 1793 married the émigré General D'Arblay. She published two further novels, *Cecilia* 1782, and *Camilla* 1796, and her diaries and letters appeared in 1842.

Burnham Forbes 1923-1985. Guyanese Marxist-Leninist politician. He was prime minister 1964-80, leading the country to independence 1966 and declaring it the world's first cooperative republic 1970. He was executive president 1980-85. Resistance to the US landing in Grenada 1983 was said to be due to his forewarning the Grenadans of the attack.

Burnham James 1905- . US philosopher, who argued in *The Managerial Revolution* 1941 that world control is passing from politicians and capitalists to the new class of business executives, the managers.

Burns John 1858–1943. British labour leader, sentenced to six weeks' imprisonment for his part in the Trafalgar Square demonstration on 'Bloody Sunday' 13 Nov 1887, and leader of the strike in 1889 securing the dockers' tanner (wage of 6d per hour). An Independent Labour member of parliament 1892–1918, he was the first person from the labouring classes to be a member of the Cabinet, as president of the Local Government Board 1906–14.

Burns Robert 1759–1796. Scottish poet, notable for his use of the Scots dialect at a time when it was not considered suitably 'elevated' for literature. Burns's first volume, *Poems, Chiefly in the Scottish Dialect*, appeared in 1786. In addition to his poetry Burns wrote or adapted many songs, including 'Auld Lang Syne'.

Born at Alloway near Ayr, he became joint tenant with his brother of his late father's farm at Mossgiel in 1784, but it was unsuccessful. Following the success of his first volume of poems in 1786 he farmed at Ellisland, near Dumfries. He became district excise officer, on the failure of his farm in 1791. His fame rests equally on his poems (such as 'Holy Willie's Prayer', 'Tam o'Shanter', 'The Jolly Beggars', and 'To a Mouse') and his songs – sometimes wholly original, sometimes adaptations – of which he contributed some 300 to Johnson's *Scots Musical Museum* 1787–1803 and Thomson's *Scottish Airs with Poetry* 1793–1811.

Burns Terence 1944– . British economist. A monetarist, he was director of the London Business School for Economic Forecasting 1976–79, and became chief economic adviser to the Thatcher government 1980.

Burr Aaron 1756–1836. US politician. He was on George Washington's staff during the War of Independence. He tied with Thomas Jefferson in the presidential election of 1800, but Alexander ◊Hamilton influenced the House of Representatives to vote Jefferson in, Burr becoming vice president. He killed Hamilton in a duel in 1804, became a social outcast, and had to leave the USA for some years following the 'Burr conspiracy', which implicated him variously in a scheme to conquer Mexico, or part of Florida, or to rule over a seceded Louisiana.

Burr Raymond 1917– . Canadian character actor who played Perry Mason in the television series of the same name and in several films. He played the murderer in Alfred Hitchcock's *Rear Window* 1954, and his other films include *The Adventures of Don Juan* 1948 and *Godzilla* (English-language version) 1956.

Burra Edward 1905–1976. British painter devoted to themes of city life, its hustle, humour, and grimy squalor. His watercolour scenes of Harlem,

New York, 1933–34, are characteristic. Postwar works include religious paintings and landscapes.

Burroughs Edgar Rice 1875–1950. US novelist, born in Chicago. He wrote *Tarzan of the Apes* 1914, the story of an aristocratic child lost in the jungle and reared by apes, and many other thrillers.

Burroughs William S 1914– . US novelist, born in St Louis, Missouri. He dropped out and, as part of the beat generation, wrote *Junkie* 1953, *The Naked Lunch* 1959, *The Soft Machine* 1961, and *Dead Fingers Talk* 1963. Later novels include *Queer* 1986.

Burroughs William Steward 1857–1898. US industrialist, who invented the first hand-operated adding machine to give printed results.

Burt Cyril Lodowic 1883–1971. British psychologist. A specialist in child and mental development, he argued in *The Young Delinquent* 1925 the importance of social and environmental factors in delinquency. After his death it was discovered that he falsified some of his experimental results in an attempt to prove his theory that intelligence is largely inherited.

Burton Richard Francis 1821–1890. British traveller, master of 35 oriental languages, and translator of the *Arabian Nights* 1885–88. In 1853 he made the pilgrimage to Mecca in disguise; in 1856 he was commissioned by the Foreign Office to explore the sources of the Nile, and (with Speke) reached Lake Tanganyika 1858.

He translated the *Kama Sutra* and *The Perfumed Garden* 1886. His wife burned his other manuscripts after his death.

Burton Richard. Stage name of Richard Jenkins 1925–1984. Welsh actor. He was remarkable for his voice, as in the radio adaptation of Dylan Thomas's *Under Milk Wood*, and for his marital and acting partnership with Elizabeth Taylor, with whom he appeared in the films *Cleopatra* 1962 and *Who's Afraid of Virginia Woolf?* 1966. His later works include *Equus* 1977 and *1984* 1984.

Burton Robert 1577–1640. English philosopher, who wrote an analysis of depression, *Anatomy of Melancholy* 1621, a compendium of information on the medical and religious opinions of the time, much used by later authors. Born in Leicester, he was educated at Oxford, and remained there for the rest of his life as a fellow of Christ Church.

Busby Richard 1606–1695. English headmaster of Westminster school from 1640, renowned for his use of flogging. Among his pupils were Dryden, Locke, Atterbury, and Prior.

Bush Alan (Dudley) 1900– . British composer. A student of John ◊Ireland, he later adopted a didactic simplicity in his compositions in line with his Marxist beliefs. He has written a large number of works for orchestra, voice, and chamber groups.

His operas include *Wat Tyler* 1952, and *Men of Blackmoor* 1956.

Bush US President from 1989, George Bush.

Bush George 1924– . US Republican president from 1989. He was director of the Central Intelligence Agency (CIA) 1976–81 and US vice president 1981–89. Evidence came to light in 1987 linking him with the Irangate scandal. His responses as president to the Soviet leader Gorbachev's diplomatic initiatives were criticized as inadequate but sending US troops to depose his former ally, Gen Noriega of Panama, proved a popular move at home.

Bush, son of a Connecticut senator, moved to Texas in 1948 to build up an oil-drilling company. A congressman 1967–70, he was appointed US ambassador to the United Nations (1971–73) and Republican national chair (1973–74) by President Nixon. During the Ford administration, Bush was a special envoy to China 1974–75. During his time as head of the CIA he is alleged to have supported the cocaine-trafficking Gen Noriega of Panama as a US ally. Panama was also used as a channel for the secret supply of arms to Iran and the Nicaraguan Contra guerrillas, of which Bush, then vice president, claimed to have been unaware. In the trial of Oliver ◊North evidence emerged that Bush had visited the president of Honduras in 1985 and offered him extra US aid in exchange for help to the Contras. When, in Dec 1989, Noriega proved uncontrollable, Bush sent an invasion force to Panama and set up a puppet government; Noriega was sent to the US to stand trial.

Busoni Ferruccio (Dante Benvenuto) 1866–1924. Italian pianist, composer, and music critic. Much of his music was for the piano, but he also composed several operas including *Doktor Faust*, completed by a pupil after his death.

Buss Frances Mary 1827–1894. British pioneer in education for women. She first taught in a school run by her mother, and at 18, she founded her own school for girls in London, which became the North London Collegiate School in 1850. She founded the Camden School for Girls in 1871.

She was influential in raising the status of women teachers and the academic standard of women's education in the UK. She is often associated with Dorothea ◊Beale, a fellow pioneer.

Bustamante (William) Alexander (born Clarke) 1884–1977. Jamaican socialist politician. As leader of the Labour Party, he was the first prime minister of independent Jamaica 1962–67.

Bute John Stuart, 3rd Earl of Bute 1713–1792. British Tory politician, prime minister 1762–63. On the accession of George III in 1760, he became the chief instrument in the king's policy for breaking the power of the Whigs and establishing the personal rule of the monarch through Parliament.

Buthelezi Chief Gatsha 1928– . Zulu leader and politician, chief minister of KwaZulu, a black homeland in the Republic of South Africa from 1070. He is founder and president of Inkatha 1975, a paramilitary organization for attaining a nonracial democratic political system.

Great-grandson of King ◊Cetewayo, Buthelezi is strongly opposed to KwaZulu becoming a Black National State, but envisages a confederation of the black areas, with eventual majority rule over all South Africa under a one-party socialist system.

Butler Joseph 1692–1752. British priest, who became dean of St Paul's in 1740 and bishop of Durham in 1750; his *Analogy of Religion* 1736 argued that it is no more rational to accept deism, arguing for God as the first cause, than revealed religion (not arrived at by reasoning).

Butler Josephine (born Gray) 1828–1906. British social reformer. She promoted women's education and the Married Women's Property Act, and campaigned against the Contagious Diseases Acts of 1862–70, which made women in garrison towns liable to compulsory examination for venereal disease. As a result of her campaigns the acts were repealed in 1883.

Butler Reg 1913–1981. British sculptor, once an architect and a blacksmith, best known for cast or forged iron works, abstract and figurative. In 1953 he won the international competition for a monument to The Unknown Political Prisoner (a model is in the Tate Gallery, London).

Butler Richard Austen, Baron Butler 1902–1982. British Conservative politician, known from his initials as Rab. As minister of education 1941–45, he was responsible for the Education Act 1944; he was chancellor of the Exchequer 1951–55, Lord Privy Seal 1955–59, and foreign minister 1963–64. As a candidate for the premiership, he was defeated by Harold Macmillan in 1957 (under whom he was home secretary 1957–62), and by Douglas-Home in 1963. He was master of Trinity College, Cambridge, 1965–78.

Butler Samuel 1612–1680. English satirist. His poem *Hudibras*, published in three parts in 1663, 1664 and 1678, became immediately popular for its biting satire against the Puritans.

Butler Samuel 1835–1902. English author, who made his name in 1872 with his satiric attack on contemporary utopianism, *Erewhon* ('nowhere' reversed), but is now remembered for his autobiographical *The Way of All Flesh* written 1872–85 and published 1903.

The Fair Haven examined the miraculous element in Christianity. *Life and Habit* 1877 and other works were devoted to a criticism of the theory of natural selection. In *The Authoress of the Odyssey* 1897 he maintained that Homer's *Odyssey* was the work of a woman.

Butlin William 'Billy' 1899–1980. British holiday-camp entrepreneur. Born in South Africa, he went in early life to Canada, but later entered the fairground business in the UK. He originated a chain of camps that provide accommodation, meals, and amusements at an inclusive price.

Butor Michel 1926– . French writer, a practitioner of the 'anti-novel'. His works include *Passage de Milan/Passage from Milan* 1954, *Dégrès/Degrees* 1960, and *L'Emploi du temps/Passing Time* 1963. *Mobile* 1962 is a volume of essays.

Butterfield William 1814–1900. English architect. His work is Gothic Revival characterized by vigorous, aggressive forms and multicoloured striped and patterned brickwork, as in the church of All Saints, Margaret Street, London, and Keble College, Oxford.

Buxtehude Diderik 1637–1707. Danish composer and organist at Lübeck, Germany, who influenced ◊Bach and ◊Handel. He is remembered for his organ works and cantatas, written for his evening concerts or *Abendmusiken*.

Byng George, Viscount Torrington 1663–1733. British admiral. He captured Gibraltar 1704, commanded the fleet that prevented an invasion of England by the 'Old Pretender' James Francis Edward Stuart 1708, and destroyed the Spanish fleet at Messina 1718. John ◊Byng was his fourth son.

Byng John 1704–1757. British admiral. Byng failed in the attempt to relieve Fort St Philip when in 1756 the island of Minorca was invaded by France. He was court-martialled and shot. As the French writer Voltaire commented, it was done 'to encourage the others'.

Byng Julian, 1st Viscount of Vimy 1862–1935. British general in World War I, commanding troops in Turkey and France, where, after a victory at Vimy Ridge, he took command of the Third Army.

Byrd Richard Evelyn 1888–1957. US aviator and explorer. The first to fly over the North Pole (1926), he also flew over the South Pole (1929), and led five overland expeditions in Antarctica.

Byrd William 1543–1623. British composer. His church choral music (set to Latin words, as he was a firm Catholic) represents his most important work. He also composed secular vocal and instrumental music.

He became organist at Lincoln cathedral in 1563. He shared with ◊Tallis the honorary post of organist in Queen Elizabeth's Chapel Royal, and in 1575 he and Tallis were granted a monopoly in the printing and selling of music.

Byron George Gordon, 6th Baron Byron 1788–1824. English poet, who became the symbol of Romanticism and political liberalism throughout Europe in the 19th century. His reputation was established with the first two cantos of *Childe Harold* 1812. Later works include *The Prisoner of Chillon* 1816, *Beppo* 1818, *Mazeppa* 1819, and, most notably, *Don Juan* 1819–24. He left England in 1816, spending most of his later life in Italy.

Born in London, Byron succeeded his great-uncle to the title in 1798. Educated at Harrow and Cambridge, he published his first volume *Hours of Idleness* 1807, and attacked its harsh critics in *English Bards and Scotch Reviewers* 1809. Overnight fame came with the first two cantos of *Childe Harold*, romantically describing his tours in Portugal, Spain, and the Balkans (third canto 1816, fourth 1818). In 1815 he married the mathematician Anne Milbanke (1792–1860) by whom he had a daughter, Augusta Ada Byron, separating from her a year later amid much scandal. He then went to Europe where he became friendly with Percy and Mary ◊Shelley. He engaged in Italian revolutionary politics, and sailed for Greece in 1823 to further the Greek struggle for independence, but died of fever at Missolonghi. He is remembered for his lyrics, his colloquially easy *Letters*, and, particularly in Europe, as the 'patron saint' of romantic liberalism. His friend Thomas ◊Moore wrote one of the first biographies of Byron.

Byron Robert 1904–1941. British writer on travel and architecture, including *The Byzantine Achievement* 1929 and *The Road to Oxiana* 1937, an account of a journey Iran–Afghanistan in 1933–34.

Cabot Sebastian 1474–1557. Italian navigator and cartographer, the second son of Giovanni ◊Caboto. He explored the Brazilian coast and the River Plate for Charles V 1526–30.

He was also employed by Henry VIII, Edward VI, and Ferdinand of Spain. He planned a voyage to China by way of the Northeast Passage, the sea route along the N Eurasian coast, encouraged the formation of the Company of Merchant Adventurers of London 1551, and in 1553 and 1556 directed the Company's expeditions to Russia, where he opened British trade.

Caboto Giovanni or *John Cabot* 1450–1498. Italian navigator. Commissioned with his three sons by Henry VII of England to discover unknown lands, he arrived at Cape Breton Island on 24 June 1497, thus becoming the first European to reach the North American mainland (he thought he was in NE Asia). In 1498 he sailed again, touching Greenland, and probably died on the voyage.

Cabral Pedro Alvarez 1460–1526. Portuguese explorer. He set sail from Lisbon for the East Indies Mar 1500, and accidentally reached Brazil by taking a course too far W. He claimed the country for Portugal 25 Apr, as Spain had not followed up Vicente Pinzón's (*c.* 1460–*c.* 1523) landing there earlier in the year. Continuing around Africa, he lost seven of his fleet of 13 ships (Bartolomeu ◊Diaz being one of those drowned), and landed in Mozambique. Proceeding to India, he negotiated the first Indo-Portuguese treaties for trade, and returned to Lisbon July 1501.

Cabrini Frances or Francesca 1850–1917. First Roman Catholic saint in the USA. Born in Lombardy, Italy, she founded the Missionary Sisters of the Sacred Heart, and established many schools and hospitals in the care of her nuns. She was canonized 1946.

Cadwalader 7th century. Welsh hero. The son of Cadwallon, king of Gwynedd, N Wales, he defeated and killed Eadwine of Northumbria in 633. About a year later he was killed in battle.

Caedmon 7th century. Earliest known English poet. According to the Northumbrian historian Bede, when Caedmon was a cowherd at the Christian monastery of Whitby, he was commanded to sing by a stranger in a dream, and on waking produced a hymn on the Creation. The original poem is preserved in some manuscripts. Caedmon became a monk and may have composed other religious poems.

Caesar powerful family of ancient Rome, which included Gaius Julius ◊Caesar, whose grand-nephew and adopted son ◊Augustus assumed the name of Caesar and passed it on to his adopted son ◊Tiberius. Henceforth, it was used by the successive emperors, becoming a title of the Roman rulers. The titles 'tsar' in Russia and 'kaiser' in Germany were both derived from the name Caesar.

Caesar Gaius Julius *c.* 102–44 BC. Roman statesman and general. He formed with Pompey and Crassus the First Triumvirate in 60 BC. He conquered Gaul 58–50 and invaded Britain 55 and 54. He fought against Pompey 49–48 defeating him at Pharsalus. After a period in Egypt Caesar returned to Rome as dictator from 46. He was assassinated by conspirators on the Ides of March 44.

A patrician, Caesar allied himself with the popular party, and when elected Aedile 65 nearly ruined himself with lavish amusements for the Roman populace. Although a free thinker, he was elected chief pontiff 63 and appointed governor of Spain 61. Returning to Rome 60, he

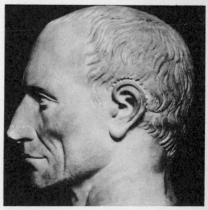

Caesar Roman statesman and military commander, Gaius Julius Caesar.

formed with Pompey and Crassus the First Triumvirate. As governor of Gaul, he was engaged
in its subjugation 58–50, defeating the Germans
under Ariovistus and selling thousands of the
Belgic tribes into slavery. In 55 he crossed into
Britain, returning for a further campaigning visit
54. A revolt by the Gauls under Vercingetorix 52
was crushed 51. His own commentaries on the
campaigns show a mastery worthy of fiction, as
does his account of the ensuing Civil War. His
governorship of Spain was to end 49, and, Crassus
being dead, Pompey became his rival. Declaring
'the die is cast', Caesar crossed the Rubicon (the
small river separating Gaul from Italy) to meet
the army raised against him by Pompey. In the
ensuing civil war, he followed Pompey to Epirus
48, defeated him at Pharsalus, and chased him to
Egypt, where he was murdered. Caesar stayed
some months in Egypt, where Cleopatra, queen
of Egypt, gave birth to his son, Caesarion. He
executed a lightning campaign 47 against King
Pharnaces II (ruled 63–47 BC) in Asia Minor,
which he summarized: *Veni vidi vici* 'I came,
I saw, I conquered'. With his final victory over
the sons of Pompey at Munda in Spain 45, he
established his position, having been awarded a
ten-year dictatorship 46. On 15 Mar 44 he was
stabbed to death at the foot of Pompey's statue
(see ◊Brutus, ◊Cassius) in the Senate house.

Caetano Marcello 1906–1980. Portuguese right-
wing politician. Professor of administrative law
at Lisbon from 1940, he succeeded the dictator
Salazar as prime minister from 1968 until his exile
after the revolution of 1974. He was granted political asylum in Brazil.

Cage John 1912– . US composer. A pupil of
◊Schoenberg and ◊Cowell, he joined others in
reacting against the European art music tradition in favour of a more realistic idiom open to
non-Western attitudes. Working in films during
the 1930s he asssembled and toured a percussion
orchestra incorporating ethnic instruments and
noise-makers, for which the *First Construcion
in Metal* 1930 was composed. He also invented
the prepared piano (in which the tonal qualities of
some strings are changed) to tour as accompanist
with the dancer Merce Cunningham, a lifelong
collaborator.

His effect on contemporary musical thinking is
summed up by the piano piece *4 minutes 33 seconds* 1952, in which a performer holds an audience
in expectation without playing a note.

Cagney James 1899–1986. US actor who moved
to films from Broadway. Usually associated with
gangster roles in films such as *The Public Enemy*
1931, he was an actor of great versatility, playing
Bottom in *A Midsummer Night's Dream* 1935 and
singing and dancing in *Yankee Doodle Dandy* 1942.

Cain in the Old Testament, the first-born son of
Adam and Eve. He murdered his brother Abel

*Calamity Jane Martha Jane Burke, known as
'Calamity Jane'. She made her name as a sharpshooter in the mining camps of South Dakota.*

from motives of jealousy, as Abel's sacrifice was
more acceptable to God than his own.

Cain James M(allahan) 1892–1977. US novelist.
He was the author of thrillers, including *The
Postman Always Rings Twice* 1934, *Mildred Pierce*
1941, and *Double Indemnity* 1943.

Caine Michael. Stage-name of Maurice Micklewhite
1933– . British actor, noted for his dry, laconic
Cockney style. His long cinematic career includes
the films *Alfie* 1966, *California Suite* 1978,
Educating Rita 1983, and *Hannah and her Sisters* 1986.

Calamity Jane nickname of Martha Jane Burke
c. 1852–1903. US heroine of Deadwood, South
Dakota, mining camps. She worked as a teamster,
transporting supplies to the camps, adopted male
dress and, as an excellent shot, promised 'calamity' to any aggressor. Her renown was spread
by many fictional accounts of the 'wild west' that
featured her exploits.

Caldecott Randolph 1846–1886. British artist and
illustrator of books for children, for example *John
Gilpin* 1848.

Calder Alexander 1898–1976. US abstract sculptor, the inventor of *mobiles*, suspended shapes

that move in the lightest current of air. In the 1920s he began making wire sculptures with movable parts; in the 1960s he created *stabiles*, large coloured sculptures of sheet metal.

Calderón de la Barca Pedro 1600–1681. Spanish dramatist and poet. After the death of Lope de Vega, he was considered to be the leading Spanish dramatist. Most famous of some 118 plays is the philosophical *La Vida es sueño/Life is a Dream* 1635.

Born in Madrid, Calderón studied law at Salamanca (1613–19). By 1636 his first volume of plays was published and he had been made master of the revels at the court of Philip IV. He became a Franciscan in 1650, was ordained in 1651, and appointed to a prebend of Toledo in 1653. As honorary chaplain to the king in 1663, he produced outdoor religious plays for the festival of the Holy Eucharist. His works include the tragedies *El pintor de su deshonra/The Painter of his own Dishonour* 1645, *El Alcalde de Zalamea/The Mayor of Zalamea* 1640, and *El Médico de su honra/The Surgeon of his Honour* 1635; the historical *El Príncipe constante/The Constant Prince* 1629; and the dashing intrigue *La Dama duende/The Phantom Lady* 1629.

Caldwell Erskine (Preston) 1903–1987. US novelist, whose *Tobacco Road* 1932 and *God's Little Acre* 1933 are earthy and vivid presentations of poverty-stricken Southern sharecroppers.

Calhoun John Caldwell 1782–1850. US politician, born in South Carolina. He was vice president 1825–29 under John Quincy Adams and 1829–33 under Andrew Jackson. Throughout he was a defender of the *states' rights* against the federal government, and of the institution of black slavery.

Caligula Gaius Caesar AD 12–41. Roman emperor, son of Germanicus and successor to Tiberius in AD 37. Caligula was a cruel tyrant and was assassinated by an officer of his guard. Believed to have been mentally unstable, he is remembered for giving a consulship to his horse Incitatus.

Callaghan (Leonard) James 1912– . British Labour politician. As chancellor of the Exchequer 1964–67, he introduced corporation and capital-gains tax, and resigned following devaluation. He was home secretary 1967–70 and prime minister 1976–79 in a period of increasing economic stress.

As foreign secretary 1974 Callaghan renegotiated Britain's membership of the European Community. In 1976 he succeeded Harold Wilson as prime minister and in 1977 entered into a pact with the Liberals to maintain his government in office. Strikes in the winter of 1978–79 led to his being the first prime minister since Ramsay MacDonald 1924 to be forced into an election by the will of the Commons, and he was defeated at the polls May 1979. In 1980 he resigned the party leadership under left-wing pressure.

Callaghan Morley 1903– . Canadian novelist and short story writer, whose realistic novels include *Such Is My Beloved* 1934, *More Joy In Heaven* 1937, and *Close To The Sun Again* 1977.

Callas Maria. Adopted name of Maria Kalogeropoulos 1923–1977. US lyric soprano, born in New York of Greek parents. With a voice of fine range and a gift for dramatic expression, she excelled in operas including *Norma, Madame Butterfly, Aïda, Lucia di Lammermoor* and *Medea*.

Callimachus 310–240 BC. Greek poet and critic known for his epigrams. Born in Cyrene, he taught in Alexandria where he is reputed to have been head of the great library.

Callot Jacques 1592/93–1635. French engraver and painter. His series of etchings *Great Miseries of War* 1632–33, prompted by his own experience of the Thirty Years' War, are brilliantly composed, full of horrific detail.

Calmette Albert 1863–1933. French bacteriologist. A student of Pasteur, he developed, with ◊Guérin, the BCG (bacille Calmette–Guérin) vaccine against tuberculosis in 1921.

Calvin John 1509–1564. French-born Swiss Protestant church reformer and theologian. He was a leader of the Reformation in Geneva and set up a strict religious community there. His theological system is known as *Calvinism*, and his church government as Presbyterianism. Calvin wrote (in Latin) *Institutes of the Christian Religion* 1536 and commentaries on the New Testament and much of the Old Testament.

Calvin *The founder of Presbyterianism John Calvin.*

Calvin, born in Noyon, Picardie, studied theology and then law, and about 1533 became prominent in Paris as an evangelical preacher. In 1534 he was obliged to leave Paris and retired to Basel, where he studied Hebrew. In 1536 he accepted an invitation to go to Geneva, Switzerland, and assist in the Reformation, but was expelled 1538 because of public resentment at the many and too drastic changes he introduced. He returned to Geneva 1541 and established in the face of strong opposition a rigorous theocracy (government by priests). In 1553 he had the Spanish theologian Servetus burned for heresy. He supported the Huguenots in their struggle in France and the English Protestants persecuted by Queen Mary I.

Calvin Melvin 1911– . US chemist who, using radioactive carbon-14 as a tracer, determined the biochemical processes of photosynthesis, in which green plants use sunlight and chlorophyll to convert carbon dioxide and water into sugar and oxygen. Nobel prize 1961.

Camargo Marie-Anne de Cupis de 1710–1770. French ballerina of Spanish descent, the first ballerina to attain the 'batterie' (movements involving beating the legs together), previously danced only by men. She caused a scandal by shortening her skirt to expose her ankles, showing her brilliant footwork and giving more liberty of movement.

Cambon Paul 1843–1924. French diplomat who was ambassador to London during the years leading to the outbreak of World War I, and a major figure in the creation of the Anglo-French entente during 1903–04.

Cambyses 6th century BC. Emperor of Persia 529–522 BC. Succeeding his father Cyrus, he assassinated his brother Smerdis and conquered Egypt in 525. Here he outraged many of the local religious customs, and was said to have become mad. He died in Syria on his journey home, probably by suicide.

Camden William 1551–1623. English antiquary. He published his topographical survey *Britannia* 1586, and was headmaster of Westminster School from 1593. The *Camden Society* (1838) commemorates his work.

Cameron Charles 1746–1812. Scottish architect. He trained under Isaac Ware in the Palladian tradition before being summoned to Russia in 1779. He created the palace complex at Tsarskoe Selo (Pushkin), planned the town of Sofia, and from 1803 as Chief Architect of the Admiralty executed many buildings, including the Naval Hospital and barracks at Kronstadt.

Cameron Julia Margaret 1815–1879. British photographer. She made lively, revealing portraits of the Victorian intelligentsia using a large camera, five-minute exposures, and wet plates. Her subjects included Darwin and Tennyson.

Camoëns or *Camões*, Luís Vaz de 1524–1580. Portuguese poet and soldier. He went on various military expeditions, and was shipwrecked in 1558. His poem, *Os Lusiades/The Lusiads*, published 1572, tells the story of the explorer Vasco da Gama and incorporates much Portuguese history; it has become the country's national epic. His posthumously published lyric poetry is also now valued.

Campbell family name of Dukes of Argyll; seated at Inveraray Castle, Argyll.

Campbell Colin, 1st Baron Clyde 1792–1863. British field marshal. He commanded the Highland Brigade at Balaclava in the Crimean War, and as commander in chief during the Indian Mutiny raised the siege of Lucknow and captured Cawnpore.

Campbell Donald Malcolm 1921–1967. British car and speedboat enthusiast, son of Malcolm Campbell. He simultaneously held the land-speed and water-speed records. In 1964 he set the world water-speed record of 444.57 kph/276.3 mph on Lake Dumbleyung, Australia, with the turbo-jet hydroplane *Bluebird*, and achieved the land-speed record of 648.7 kph/403.1 mph at Lake Eyre salt flats, Australia. He was killed in an attempt to raise his water-speed record on Coniston Water, England.

Campbell Gordon 1886–1953. British admiral in World War I. He commanded Q-ships, which were armed vessels that masqueraded as merchant ships to decoy German U-boats to destruction.

Campbell Malcolm 1885–1948. British racing driver who at one time held both land- and water-speed records. His car and boat were both called *Bluebird*.

He nine times set the land-speed record, pushing it up to 484.5 kph/301.1 mph at Bonneville, USA, in 1935, and three times broke the water-speed record, the best being 228.1 kph/141.74 mph on Coniston Water, England, in 1939. His son Donald Campbell emulated his feats.

Campbell Mrs Patrick (born Beatrice Stella Tanner) 1865–1940. British actress, whose roles included Paula in Pinero's *The Second Mrs Tanqueray* 1893 and Eliza in *Pygmalion*, written for her by G B Shaw, with whom she had an amusing correspondence.

Campbell Roy 1901–1957. South African poet, who established his reputation with the *The Flaming Terrapin* 1924. Born in Durban, he became a professional jouster and bull-fighter in Spain and Provence, France. He fought for Franco in the Spanish Civil War, and was with the Commonwealth forces in World War II.

Campbell Thomas 1777–1844. Scottish poet. Following the successful publication of his *Pleasures of Hope* in 1799, he travelled in Europe, and there wrote his war poems *Hohenlinden* and *Ye Mariners of England*.

Camus French novelist and dramatist Albert Camus.

Campbell-Bannerman Henry 1836–1908. British Liberal politician, prime minister 1905–08. He granted self-government to the South African colonies, and passed the Trades Disputes Act 1906.

Campbell-Bannerman, born in Glasgow, was chief secretary for Ireland 1884–85, war minister 1886 and again 1892–95, and leader of the Liberals in the House of Commons from 1899. In 1905 he became prime minister, and led the Liberals to an overwhelming electoral victory 1906. He began the conflict between Commons and Lords that led to the Parliament Act of 1911. He resigned 1908.

Campin Robert active 1406–1444. Netherlandish painter of the early Renaissance, active in Tournai, one of the first northern masters to use oil. His outstanding work is *Mérode altarpiece*, about 1425 (Metropolitan Museum of Art, New York), which shows a distinctly naturalistic style, with a new subtlety in modelling and a grasp of pictorial space.

Campion Edmund 1540–1581. English Jesuit and Roman Catholic martyr. He took deacon's orders in the English church, but fled to Douai, France, where in 1571 he recanted Protestantism. In 1573 he became a Jesuit in Rome, and in 1580 was sent to England as a missionary. He was betrayed as a spy in 1581, imprisoned in the Tower of London, and hanged, drawn, and quartered as a traitor.

Campion Thomas 1567–1620. English poet and musician. He was the author of the critical *Art of English Poesie* 1602, and four *Bookes of Ayres*, for which he composed both words and music.

Camus Albert 1913–1960. Algerian-born French writer. A journalist in France, he was active in the Resistance during World War II. His novels, which owe much to existentialism, include *L'Etranger/The Outsider* 1942, *La Peste/The Plague* 1948, and *L'Homme Révolté/The Rebel* 1952. Nobel prize 1957.

Canaletto Antonio (Giovanni Antoni Canal) 1697–1768. Italian painter celebrated for his paintings of views (*vedute*) of Venice (where he

lived for some years) and of the Thames and London 1746–56.

Much of his work is very detailed and precise, with a warm light and a sparkling of tiny highlights on the green waters of canals and rivers. His later style became clumsier and more static.

Candela Felix 1910– . Spanish-born Mexican architect, originator of the hypar (hyperbolic paraboloid) from 1951, in which doubly curved surfaces are built up on a framework of planks sprayed with cement. Professor at the National School of Architecture, University of Mexico, from 1953.

Canetti Elias 1905– . Bulgarian-born writer. He was exiled from Austria as a Jew 1938, and settled in England 1939. His books, written in German, include the novel *Die Blendung/Auto da Fé*; and an autobiography *The Tongue Set Free* (translated 1988). He was concerned with crowd behaviour and the psychology of power. Nobel prize 1981.

Canning Charles John, 1st Earl 1812–1862. British administrator, first viceroy of India from 1858. As governor-general of India from 1856, he suppressed the Indian Mutiny with an unvindictive firmness which earned him the nickname 'Clemency Canning'. He was the son of George Canning.

Canning George 1770–1827. British Tory politician, foreign secretary 1807–10 and 1822–27, and prime minister 1827 in coalition with the Whigs. He was largely responsible during the Napoleonic Wars for the seizure of the Danish fleet and British intervention in the Spanish peninsula.

Canning entered Parliament 1793. His verse, satires, and parodies for the *Anti-Jacobin* 1797–98 led to his advancement by Pitt the Younger. His disapproval of the abortive military expedition to Walcheren in the Netherlands 1809 involved him in a duel with Castlereagh and led to his resignation as foreign secretary. He was president of the Board of Control 1816–20. On Castlereagh's death 1822, he again became foreign secretary, supported the national movements in Greece and South America, and was made prime minister 1827. When Wellington, Peel, and other Tories refused to serve under him, he formed a coalition with the Whigs. He died in office.

Cannizzaro Stanislao 1826–1910. Italian chemist who revived interest in the work of Avogadro 1811 which had revealed the difference between atoms and molecules, and so established atomic and molecular weights as the basis of chemical calculations.

Cannizzaro also worked in organic chemistry, and reactions of the type he discovered in 1853 for making benzyl alcohol and benzoic acid from benzaldehyde are named after him.

Cannon Annie Jump 1863–1941. US astronomer who, from 1896, worked at Harvard College Observatory, most notably on the classification of stars by examining their spectra. She also discovered over 300 variable stars and five novae.

Cano Alonso 1601–1667. Spanish sculptor, painter, and architect, an exponent of the Baroque style in Spain. He was active in Seville, Madrid, and Granada, and designed the façade of Granada Cathedral 1667.

Cano Juan Sebastian del *c.*1476–1526. Spanish voyager. It is claimed that he was the first sea captain to sail around the world. He sailed with Magellan in 1519 and, after the latter's death in the Philippines, brought the *Victoria* safely home to Spain.

Canova Antonio 1757–1822. Italian Neo-Classical sculptor, based in Rome from 1781. He received commissions from popes, kings, and emperors for his highly finished marble portrait busts and groups. He made several portraits of Napoleon. His reclining marble *Pauline Borghese* 1805–07 (Borghese Gallery, Rome) is a fine example of cool, polished Classicism.

Cánovas del Castillo Antonio 1828–1897. Spanish politician and chief architect of the political system known as the *turno politico*, through which his own conservative party, and that of the liberals under Práxedes Sagasta, alternated in power. Elections were rigged to ensure the appropriate majorities. Cánovas was assassinated in 1897 in an attack carried out by anarchists.

Cantor Georg Ferdinand Ludwig Philip 1845–1918. German mathematician, born in Russia. He developed a rigorous and consistent theory of infinite numbers ('transfinite' in his terminology), strongly opposed by Leopold Kronecker (1823–1891). This was part of a broader theory of sets, which has permeated most of modern mathematics. He taught at the University of Halle, Germany 1869–1905.

Canute *c.*995–1035. King of England from 1016, Denmark from 1018, and Norway from 1028. Having invaded England 1013 with his father, Sweyn, king of Denmark, he was acclaimed king on his father's death 1014 by his Viking army. Canute defeated ◊Edmund Ironside at Assandun, Essex, 1016, and became king of all England on Edmund's death. He succeeded his brother Harold as king of Denmark 1018, compelled King Malcolm to pay homage by invading Scotland about 1027, and conquered Norway 1028. He was succeeded by his illegitimate son Harold I.

The legend of Canute disenchanting his flattering courtiers by showing that the sea would not retreat at his command was first told by Henry of Huntingdon in 1130.

Canute (Cnut VI) 1163–1202. King of Denmark from 1182, son and successor of Waldemar Knudsson. With the aid of his brother and successor, Waldemar II, and Absalon, archbishop of Lund, he resisted Frederick Barbarossa's northward expansion, and established Denmark as the dominant power in the Baltic.

Cao Chan or *Ts'ao Chan* 1719–1763. Chinese novelist whose tragic love story *Hung Lou Meng/The Dream of the Red Chamber* published 1792, which involves the downfall of a Manchu family, is semi-autobiographical.

Čapek Karel (Matelj) 1890–1938. Czech writer whose works often deal with social injustice in an imaginative, satirical way. *R.U.R.* 1921 is a play in which robots (a term he coined) rebel against their controllers; the novel *Valka s Mloky/War With the Newts* 1936 is a science-fiction classic.

Capet Hugh 938–996. King of France from 987, when he claimed the throne on the death of Louis V. He founded the *Capetian dynasty*, of which various branches continued to reign until the French Revolution, for example, ◊Valois and ◊Bourbon.

Capone Al(phonse) 1898–1947. US gangster, born in Brooklyn, New York, the son of an Italian barber. During the Prohibition period Capone built up a criminal organization in the city of Chicago. He was imprisoned 1931–39 for income-tax evasion, the only charge that could be sustained against him. His nickname was *Scarface*.

Capote Truman. Pen name of Truman Streckfuss Persons 1924–1984. US novelist. He wrote *Breakfast at Tiffany's* 1958; set a trend with *In Cold Blood* 1966, reconstructing a Kansas killing; and mingled recollection and fiction in *Music for Chameleons* 1980.

Capra Frank 1897– . US film director. His films, which often have idealistic heroes, include *It Happened One Night* 1934, *Mr Deeds Goes to Town* 1936, and *You Can't Take It With You* 1938.

Caracalla Marcus Aurelius Antoninus AD 186–217. Roman emperor, so named from the celtic cloak (caracalla) that he wore. He succeeded his father

Caracalla Marcus Aurelius Antoninus Caracalla, Roman emperor AD 211–17.

Septimus Severus in 211, ruled with cruelty and extravagance, and was assassinated.

With the support of the army he murdered his brother Geta and thousands of his followers to secure sole possession of the throne. During his reign Roman citizenship was given to all subjects of the Empire, and he built on a grandiose scale, for example the Baths of Caracalla in Rome.

Caractacus died *c.* AD 54. British chieftain, who headed resistance to the Romans in SE England AD 43–51, but was defeated on the Welsh border. Shown in Claudius's triumphal procession, he was released in tribute to his courage and died in Rome.

Caradon Baron title of Hugh ◊Foot, British Labour politician.

Caravaggio Michelangelo Merisi da 1573–1610. Italian early Baroque painter, active in Rome 1592–1606, then in Naples and finally Malta. His life was as dramatic as his art (he had to leave Rome after killing a man). He created a forceful style, using contrasts of light and shade and focusing closely on the subject figures, sometimes using dramatic foreshortening.

He was born in Caravaggio, near Milan. His compositions were unusual, with little extraneous setting, making strong designs in the two-dimensional plane. He painted from models, making portraits of real Roman people as saints and Madonnas, which caused outrage. An example is *The Conversion of St Paul* (Sta Maria del Popolo, Rome).

He had a number of direct imitators (Caravaggisti), and a group of Dutch and Flemish artists who visted Rome, including Honthorst and Terbrugghen were inspired by him.

Cardano Girolamo 1501–1576. Italian physician, mathematician, philosopher, astrologer, and gambler. He is remembered for his theory of chance, his use of algebra, and many medical publications, notably the first clinical description of typhus fever.

Born at Pavia, he became professor of medicine there in 1543, and wrote two works on physics and natural science, *De Subtilitate rerum* 1551 and *De Varietate rerum* 1557.

Cárdenas Lázaro 1895–1970. Mexican centre-left politician and general, president 1934–40. In early life a civil servant, Cárdenas took part in the revolutionary campaigns 1915–29 that followed the fall of President Díaz (1830–1915). As president of the republic, he attempted to achieve the goals of the revolution by building schools, distributing land to the peasants, and developing transport and industry. He was minister of defence 1943–45.

Cardiff Jack 1914– . British director of photography. He is regarded as one of cinema's finest colour cameramen for *A Matter of Life and Death* 1946; *The African Queen* 1951; *Conan the Destroyer* 1984. He also directed the film *Sons and Lovers* 1960.

Cardin Pierre 1922– . French fashion designer; the first women's designer to show a collection for men, in 1960.

Carducci Giosuè 1835–1907. Italian poet. Born in Tuscany, he was appointed in 1860 professor of Italian literature in Bologna, and won a distinguished place by his lecturing, critical work, and poetry. His revolutionary *Inno a Satana/Hymn to Satan* 1865 was followed by several other volumes of verse, in which his nationalist sympathies are apparent. Nobel prize 1906.

Cardwell Edward, Viscount Cardwell 1813–1886. British Liberal politician. He entered Parliament as a supporter of the Conservative prime minister ◊Peel in 1842, and 1868–74 was secretary for war under Gladstone, when he carried out many reforms, including the abolition of the purchase of military commissions and promotions.

Carême Antonin 1784–1833. French chef who is regarded as the founder of classical French *haute cuisine*. At various times he was chief cook to the Prince Regent in England and Tsar Alexander I in Russia.

Carew Thomas *c.*1595–*c.*1640. English poet. He was a gentleman of the privy chamber to Charles I in 1628, and a lyricist as well as craftsman of the school of Cavalier Poets.

Carey Henry 1690–1743. British poet and musician, remembered for the song 'Sally in Our Alley'. 'God Save the King' (both words and music) has also been attributed to him.

Carey Peter 1943– . Australian novelist. He has combined work in advertising with a writing career since 1962, and his novels include *Bliss* 1981, *Illywhacker* (Australian slang for 'con man') 1985, and *Oscar and Lucinda* 1988, which won the Booker prize.

Carissimi Giacomo 1605–1674. Italian composer, a pioneer of the oratorio.

Carl XVI Gustaf 1946– . King of Sweden from 1973. He succeeded his grandfather Gustaf VI, his father having been killed in an air crash in 1947. Under the new Swedish constitution which became effective on his grandfather's death, the monarchy was effectively stripped of all power at his accession.

Carlos I 1863–1908. King of Portugal, of the Braganza-Coburg line, from 1889 until he was assassinated in Lisbon with his elder son Luis. He was succeeded by his younger son Manoel.

Carlos Don 1545–1568. Spanish prince. Son of Philip II, he was recognized as heir to the thrones of Castile and Aragon, but became mentally unstable and had to be placed under restraint following a plot to assassinate his father. His story was the subject of plays by Schiller, Alfieri, Otway, and others.

Carlson Chester 1906–1968. US scientist, who invented the xerography photocopying process. A research worker with Bell Telephone, he was sacked from his post in 1930 during the Depression, and set to work on his own to develop an efficient copying machine. By 1938 he had invented the Xerox photocopier.

Carlsson Ingvar (Gösta) 1934– . Swedish socialist politician, leader of the Social Democratic Party, deputy prime minister 1982–86 and prime minister from 1986.

After studying in Sweden and the USA, Carlsson became president of the Swedish Social-Democratic Youth League in 1961. He was elected to the Riksdag (parliament) in 1964 and became a minister in 1969. With the return to power of the Social Democrats in 1982, Carlsson became deputy to Prime Minister Palme and on his assassination in 1986 succeeded him.

Carlucci Frank (Charles) 1930– . US politician, a pragmatic moderate. A former diplomat and deputy director of the CIA, he was national security adviser 1986–87 and defence secretary from Nov 1987 under Reagan, supporting Soviet-US arms reduction. Carlucci found himself out of step with the hawks in the Reagan administration, and left to work in industry after barely a year as deputy secretary of defence. In Dec 1986, after the Irangate arms-sales scandal, he replaced John ◊Poindexter as national security adviser.

Carlyle Thomas 1795–1881. Scottish essayist and social historian. His work included *Sartor Resartus* 1836, describing his loss of Christian belief, *French Revolution* 1837, *Chartism* 1839, and *Past and Present* 1843. He was a friend of J S ◊Mill and Ralph Waldo ◊Emerson.

Carlyle was born at Ecclefechan in Dumfriesshire. In 1821 he passed through the spiritual crisis described in *Sartor Resartus*. He married Jane Baillie Welsh (1801–66) in 1826 and they moved to her farm at Craigenputtock, where *Sartor Resartus* was written. His reputation was established with the *French Revolution*. The series of lectures he gave 1837–40 included *On Heroes, Hero-Worship*, and *The Heroic in History* 1841. He also wrote several pamphlets, including *Chartism* 1839, attacking the free-market doctrine of *laissez-faire*; the notable *Letters and Speeches of Cromwell* 1845; and the miniature life of his friend John Sterling 1851. Carlyle then began his *History of Frederick the Great* 1858–65, and after the death of his wife in 1866 edited her letters 1883 and prepared his *Reminiscences* 1881, which shed an unfavourable light on his character and his neglect of her, for which he could not forgive himself. His house in Cheyne Row, Chelsea, London, is a museum.

Carmichael 'Hoagy' (Hoagland Howard) 1899–1981. US jazz composer, pianist, singer, and actor. His songs include 'Stardust' 1927, 'Rockin' Chair' 1930, 'Lazy River' 1931, and 'In the Cool, Cool, Cool of the Evening' 1951 (Academy Award).

Carnap Rudolf 1891–1970. German philosopher, and exponent of logical empiricism (the belief that knowledge is derived from experience). He was a member of the Vienna Circle who adopted Ernst ◊Mach as their guide. His books include *The Logical Syntax of Language* 1934, and *Meaning and Necessity* 1956. He was born in Wuppertal, Germany, and went to the United States 1935, where he was professor of philosophy at the University of California 1954–62.

Carné Marcel 1906– . French director of the films *Le Jour se lève* 1939 and *Les Enfants du Paradis* 1944.

Carnegie family name of the earls of Northesk and Southesk and of the Duke of Fife, who is descended from Queen Victoria.

Carnegie Andrew 1835–1919. US industrialist and philanthropist, who developed the Pittsburgh iron and steel industries. He endowed public libraries, education, and various research trusts.

Born in Dunfermline, Scotland, he was taken by his parents to the USA in 1848, and at 14 became a telegraph boy in Pittsburgh. Subsequently he became a railway employee, rose to be superintendent, introduced sleeping-cars and invested successfully in oil. He developed the Pittsburgh iron and steel industries, and built up a vast empire which he disposed of to the United States Steel Trust in 1901. Then he moved to Skibo castle in Sutherland, Scotland, and devoted his wealth to endowing libraries and universities, the Carnegie Hero Fund, and other good causes. On his death the Carnegie Trusts continued his benevolent activities. Carnegie Hall in New York, opened in 1891 as The Music Hall, was renamed in 1898 because of his large contribution to its construction.

Carnegie Dale 1888–1955. US author and teacher, a former YMCA public-speaking instructor, who wrote *How to Win Friends and Influence People* 1938.

Carnot Lazare 1753–1823. French general and politician. A member of the National Convention in the French Revolution, he organized the armies of the republic. He was war minister 1800–01 and minister of the interior 1815 under Napoleon. His work on fortification, *De la défense de places fortes* 1810, became a military textbook.

Carnot Marie François Sadi 1837–1894. French president from 1887, grandson of Lazare Carnot. He successfully countered the Boulangist anti-German movement (see ◊Boulanger) and in 1892 the scandals arising out of French financial activities in Panama. He was assassinated by an Italian anarchist at Lyons.

Carnot Nicolas Leonard Sadi 1796–1832. French scientist and military engineer, son of Lazare Carnot. He founded thermodynamics with his pioneering work on heat engines, *Réflexions sur* *la puissance motrice du feu/On the Motive Power of Fire* 1824.

Caro Anthony 1924– . British sculptor, noted for bold, large abstracts, using ready-made angular metal shapes, often without bases. Works include *Fathom* (outside the Economist Building, London).

Carol I 1839–1914. First king of Romania, 1881–1914. A prince of the house of Hohenzollern-Sigmaringen, he was invited to become prince of Romania, then under Turkish suzerainty, 1866. In 1877, in alliance with Russia, he declared war on Turkey, and the Congress of Berlin 1878 recognized Romanian independence.

Carol II 1893–1953. King of Romania 1930–40. Son of King Ferdinand, he married Princess Helen of Greece and they had a son, Michael. In 1925 he renounced the succession and settled in Paris with his mistress, Mme Lupescu. Michael succeeded to the throne 1927, but in 1930 Carol returned to Romania and was proclaimed king. In 1938 he introduced a new constitution under which he became practically absolute. He was forced to abdicate by the pro-Nazi Iron Guard Sept 1940, and went to Mexico and married his mistress 1947.

Caroline of Anspach 1683–1737. Queen of George II of Great Britain. The daughter of the Margrave of Brandenburg-Anspach, she married George, Electoral Prince of Hanover, in 1705, and followed him to England in 1714 when his father became King George I. She was the patron of many leading writers and politicians.

Caroline of Brunswick 1768–1821. Queen of George IV of Great Britain, who unsuccessfully attempted to divorce her on his accession to the throne 1820.

Second daughter of Karl Wilhelm, duke of Brunswick, and Augusta, sister of George III, she married her first cousin the Prince of Wales in 1795, but after the birth of Princess ◊Charlotte Augusta a separation was arranged. When her husband ascended the throne in 1820 she was offered an annuity of £50,000 provided she agreed to renounce the title of queen and to continue to live abroad. She returned forthwith to London, where she assumed royal state. In July 1820 the government brought in a bill to dissolve the marriage, but Lord ◊Brougham's splendid defence led to the bill's abandonment. On 19 July 1821 Caroline was prevented by royal order from entering Westminster Abbey for the coronation. She died on 7 Aug, and her funeral was the occasion of popular riots.

Carothers Wallace 1896–1937. US chemist, who carried out research into polymerization. By 1930 he had discovered that some polymers were fibre-forming, and in 1937 produced nylon.

Carpaccio Vittorio 1450/60–1525/26. Italian painter, known for scenes of his native Venice.

His series *The Legend of St Ursula* 1490–98 (Accademia, Venice) is full of detail of contemporary Venetian life. His other great series is the lives of saints George and Jerome 1502–07 (S Giorgio degli Schiavone, Venice).

Carpeaux Jean-Baptiste 1827–1875. French sculptor, whose lively naturalistic subjects include *La Danse* 1865–69 for the Opéra, Paris.

Another example is the *Neapolitan Fisherboy* 1858 (Louvre, Paris). Their Romantic charm belies his admiration of Michelangelo. He studied in Italy 1856–62 and won the Prix de Rome 1854.

Carpenter Edward 1844–1929. English socialist and writer. Inspired by reading ◊Thoreau, he resigned his post as tutor at Cambridge University 1874 to write poems and books, such as *Civilization: Its Cause and Cure* 1889 and *Love's Coming of Age* 1896, a plea for toleration of homosexuality.

Carpenter John 1948– . US director of horror and science fiction films. His career began with *Dark Star* 1974 and *Halloween* 1978, and continued with such films as *The Thing* 1981 and *They Live* 1988.

Carpini Johannes de Plano 1182–1252. Franciscan friar and traveller. Sent by Pope Innocent IV on a mission to the Great Khan, he visited Mongolia 1245–47 and wrote a history of the Mongols.

Carracci Italian family of painters in Bologna, noted for murals and ceilings. The foremost of them, *Annibale Carracci* (1560–1609), decorated the Farnese Palace, Rome, with a series of mythological paintings united by simulated architectural ornamental surrounds (completed 1604).

Ludovico Carracci (1555–1619) with his cousin *Agostino Carracci* (1557–1602) founded an Academy of Art in Bologna . Agostino collaborated with his brother Annibale on the Farnese Palace decorative scheme, which paved the way for a host of elaborate murals in Rome's palaces and churches, ever more inventive illusions of pictorial depth and architectural ornament. Annibale also painted early landscapes like *Flight into Egypt* 1603 (Doria Gallery, Rome).

Carradine Richmond Reed ('John') 1906–1988. US film actor who often played sinister roles. He appeared in many major Hollywood films, such as *Stagecoach* 1939 and *The Grapes of Wrath* 1940, but was later seen mostly in 'B' horror films, including *House of Frankenstein* 1944.

Carrel Alexis 1873–1944. US surgeon born in France, whose experiments paved the way for organ transplantation. Working at the Rockefeller Institute, Carrel devised a way of joining blood vessels end to end (anastomosing). This was important in the development of transplant surgery, as was his work on keeping organs viable outside the body. He was awarded the Nobel Prize for Medicine in 1912.

Carreras José 1947– . Spanish tenor, whose roles include Handel's Samson, and whose recordings include *West Side Story* 1984. In 1987, he became seriously ill with leukaemia, but returned and resumed his career 1988.

Carrington Peter Alexander Rupert, 6th Baron Carrington 1919– . British Conservative politician. He was defence secretary 1970–74, and led the opposition in the House of Lords 1964–70 and 1974–79. While foreign secretary 1979–82, he negotiated independence for Zimbabwe, but resigned after failing to anticipate the Falklands crisis. He was secretary-general of NATO 1984–88.

Carroll Lewis. Pen name of Charles Lutwidge Dodgson 1832–1898. English mathematician and writer of children's books. He wrote the children's classics *Alice's Adventures in Wonderland* 1865, and its sequel *Through the Looking Glass* 1872, published under the pen name Lewis Carroll. He also published mathematics books under his own name.

Born in Daresbury, Cheshire, Dodgson was a mathematics lecturer at Oxford 1855–1881. *Alice's Adventures in Wonderland* grew out of a story told by Dodgson to amuse three little girls, including the original 'Alice', the daughter of Dean Liddell, dean of Christ Church. During his lifetime Dodgson refused to acknowledge any connection with any books not published under his own name. Among later works was the mock-heroic nonsense poem 'The Hunting of the Snark' 1876. He was among the pioneers of portrait photography.

Carson Christopher 'Kit' 1809–68. US frontiersman, guide, and Indian agent, who later fought for the Federal side in the Civil War. Carson City was named after him.

Carson Edward Henry, Baron Carson 1854–1935. Irish politician and lawyer, who played a decisive part in the trial of the writer Oscar Wilde. In the years before World War I he led the movement in Ulster to resist Irish Home Rule by force of arms if need be.

Carson was a well-known barrister both in England and Ireland. On the outbreak of war he campaigned in Ulster in support of the government, and took office under both Asquith and Lloyd George (attorney general 1915, First Lord of the Admiralty 1916, member of the war cabinet 1917–18).

Carson Rachel 1907–1964. US naturalist. An aquatic biologist with the US Fish and Wildlife Service 1936–49, she then became its editor-in-chief until 1952. In 1951, she published *The Sea Around Us*, and in 1963 *Silent Spring*, attacking the indiscriminate use of pesticides.

Carson William (Willie) 1942– . British jockey, born in Scotland, who has ridden three Epsom Derby winners as well as the winners of most major races in England and abroad.

The top flat race jockey on five occasions, he has ridden over 2,500 winners in Britain. For many years he has ridden for the Royal trainer, Major Dick Hern.

Carter Angela 1940– . English writer of the magic realist ('realistic fantasy') school. Her novels include *The Magic Toyshop* 1967 (filmed by David Wheatley 1987) and *Nights at the Circus* 1984. She co-wrote the script for the film *The Company of Wolves* 1984, based on one of her stories.

Carter Elliott (Cook) 1908– . US composer. His early music shows the influence of ◊Stravinsky, but after 1950 it became increasingly intricate and densely written in a manner resembling Charles ◊Ives. He invented 'metrical modulation' which allows different instruments or groups to stay in touch while playing at different speeds. He has written four string quartets, the *Symphony for Three Orchestras* 1967, and the song cycle *A Mirror on Which to Dwell* 1975.

Carter Jimmy (James Earl) 1924– . 39th president of the USA 1977–81, a Democrat. In 1976 he narrowly wrested the presidency from Ford. Features of his presidency were the return of the Panama Canal Zone to Panama, the Camp David Agreements for peace in the Middle East, and the Iranian seizure of US embassy hostages. He was defeated by Reagan 1980.

Carteret Philip died 1796. English navigator who discovered the Pitcairn Islands in 1767 during a round-the-world expedition 1766–69. He retired in 1794 with the rank of rear-admiral.

Cartier Georges Étienne 1814–1873. French-Canadian politician. He fought against the British in the rebellion 1837, was elected to the Canadian parliament 1848, and was joint prime minister with John A Macdonald 1858–62. He brought Québec into the Canadian federation 1867.

Cartier Jacques 1491–1557. French navigator who was the first European to sail up the St Lawrence river in 1534. He named the site of Montreal.

Cartier-Bresson Henri 1908– . French photographer, considered the greatest of photographic artists. His documentary work was achieved in black and white, using a small format camera. He was noted for his ability to structure the image and to capture the decisive moment.

Cartland Barbara 1904– . English romantic novelist. She published her first book *Jigsaw* in 1921, and since then has produced a prolific stream of stories of chastely romantic love, usually in idealized or exotic settings, for a mainly female audience (such as *Love Climbs In* 1978 and *Moments of Love* 1981).

Cartwright Edmund 1743–1823. British inventor. He patented the power loom 1785, built a weaving mill 1787, and patented a wool-combing machine 1789.

Carter 39th President of the USA Jimmy (James Earl) Carter who sponsored the Camp David Agreements but failed to achieve the release of US hostages in Iran.

Born in Nottinghamshire, he studied at Oxford and became a country rector (and also a farmer). He went bankrupt in 1793.

Caruso Enrico 1873–1921. Italian operatic tenor. In 1902 he starred in Monte Carlo, in Puccini's *La Bohème*. He is chiefly remembered for performances as Canio in Leoncavallo's *Pagliacci*, and the Duke in Verdi's *Rigoletto*.

Carver George Washington 1864–1943. US agricultural chemist. Born a slave in Missouri, he devoted his life to improving the economy of the US South and the condition of blacks. He advocated the diversification of crops, promoted peanut production, and was a pioneer in the field of plastics.

Carver Raymond 1939–1988. US story writer and poet, author of vivid stories of contemporary US life. *Cathedral* 1983 collects many of his stories; *Fires* 1985 also has essays and poems.

Cary (Arthur) Joyce (Lunel) 1888–1957. British novelist. In 1918 he entered the Colonial Service, and Nigeria, where he had served, gave a background to such novels as *Mister Johnson* 1939. Other books include *The Horse's Mouth* 1944.

Casals Pablo 1876–1973. Catalan cellist, composer, and conductor. As a cellist, he was renowned for his interpretations of J S Bach's unaccompanied suites. He left Spain in 1939 to live in Prades, in the French Pyrenees, where he founded an annual music festival. He wrote instrumental and choral works, including the Christmas oratorio *The Manger*.

In 1919 Casals founded the Barcelona orchestra, which he conducted until leaving Spain at the outbreak of the Spanish Civil War in 1936. He was an outspoken critic of fascism, and a tireless crusader for peace. In 1956 he moved to Puerto Rico where he launched the Casals Festival 1957 and toured extensively in the US. He married three times; his first wife was the Portuguese cellist Guilhermina Suggia.

Casanova de Seingalt Giovanni Jacopo 1725–1798. Italian adventurer, spy, violinist, librarian, and, according to his *Memoirs*, one of the world's great lovers. From 1774 he was a spy in the Venetian police service. In 1782 a libel got him into trouble, and after more wanderings he was in 1785 appointed Count Waldstein's librarian at his castle of Dûx in Bohemia, where he wrote his *Memoirs* (published 1826–38, although the complete text did not appear until 1960–61).

Casement Roger David 1864–1916. Irish nationalist. While in the British consular service he exposed the ruthless exploitation of the people of the Belgian Congo and in Peru, for which he was knighted in 1911 (degraded 1916). He was hanged for treason by the British for his part in the Irish republican Easter Rising.

In 1914 Casement went to Germany and attempted to induce Irish prisoners of war to form an Irish brigade to take part in a republican insurrection. He returned to Ireland in a submarine in 1916 (actually to postpone, not start, the Easter Rising), was arrested, tried for treason, and hanged.

Cash Johnny 1932– . US country singer, songwriter, and guitarist. His early hits, recorded for Sun Records in Memphis, Tennessee, include the million-selling 'I Walk the Line' 1956. Many of his songs have become classics.

Caslavska Vera 1943– . Czechoslovak gymnast, the first of the great modern-day stylists. She won a record 21 world, Olympic and European gold medals 1959–68; she also won eight silver and three bronze medals.

Cassatt Mary 1845–1926. US Impressionist painter and printmaker. In 1868 she settled in Paris. Her popular, colourful pictures of mothers and children show the influence of Japanese prints, for example *The Bath* 1892 (Art Institute, Chicago).

Cassavetes John 1929–1989. US film director and actor, who directed experimental, apparently improvised films, including *Shadows* 1960, and

The Killing of a Chinese Bookie 1980. His acting appearances included *The Dirty Dozen* 1967, and *Rosemary's Baby* 1968.

Cassini Giovanni Domenico 1625–1712. Italian-French astronomer, who discovered four moons of Saturn and the gap in the rings of Saturn now called the *Cassini division*.

Born in Italy, he became director of the Paris Observatory in 1671. His son, grandson, and great-grandson in turn became directors of the Paris Observatory.

Cassius Gaius died 42 BC. Roman soldier, one of the conspirators who killed Julius ◊Caesar in 44. He fought at Carrhae 53, and with the republicans against Caesar at Pharsalus 48, was pardoned and appointed praetor, but became a leader in the conspiracy of 44, and after Caesar's death joined Brutus. He committed suicide after his defeat at the battle of Philippi 42 BC.

Cassivelaunus 1st century BC. Chieftain of the British tribe, the Catuvellauni, who led the British resistance to Caesar in 54 BC.

Casson Hugh 1910– . British architect, professor at the Royal College of Art 1953–75, and president of the Royal Academy 1976–84. His books include *Victorian Architecture* 1948. He was director of architecture for the Festival of Britain 1948–51.

Castagno Andrea del *c.* 1421–1457. Italian Renaissance painter, active in Florence. In his frescoes in Sta Apollonia, Florence, he adapted the pictorial space to the architectural framework and followed ◊Masaccio's lead in perspective.

Castagno's work is sculptural and strongly expressive, anticipating the Florentine late-15th-century style, as in his *David* about 1450–57 (National Gallery, Washington DC).

Castelo Branco Camilo 1825–1890. Portuguese novelist. His work fluctuates between mysticism and Bohemianism, and includes *Amor de perdição/Love of Perdition* 1862, written during his imprisonment for adultery, and *Novelas do Minho* 1875, stories of the rural north.

Illegitimate and then orphaned, he led a dramatic life. Other works include *Onde está a felicidade?/Where is Happiness?* 1856 and *A brazileira de Prazins/The Brazilian girl from Prazins* 1882. Created a viscount in 1885, he committed suicide when overtaken by blindness.

Castiglione Baldassare, Count Castiglione 1478–1529. Italian author and diplomat, who described the perfect Renaissance gentleman in *Il Cortegiano/The Courtier* 1528.

Born near Mantua, Castiglione served the Duke of Milan, and in 1506 was engaged by the Duke of Albino on a mission to Henry VII of England. While in Spain in 1524 he was created bishop of Avila.

Castilla Ramón 1797–1867. President of Peru 1841–51 and 1855–62. He dominated Peruvian politics for over two decades, bringing political

stability. Income from guano exports was used to reduce the national debt and improve transport and educational facilities. He abolished black slavery and the head tax on Indians.

Castle Barbara, Baroness Castle (born Betts) 1911– . British Labour politician, a cabinet minister in the Labour governments of the 1960s and 1970s. She led the Labour group in the European Parliament 1979–89.

She was minister of overseas development 1964–65, transport 1965–68, employment 1968–70 (when her White Paper 'In Place of Strife', on trade-union reform, was abandoned as too controversial), and social services 1974–76, when she was dropped from the cabinet by prime minister James Callaghan. She criticized Callaghan in her *Diaries* 1980.

Castlemaine Lady (born Barbara Villiers) 1641–1709. Mistress of Charles II of England 1660–70 and mother of his son the Duke of Grafton (1663–90).

She was the wife from 1659 of Roger Palmer (1634–1705), created Earl of Castlemaine in 1661. She was the chief mistress of Charles II 1660–70, when she was created Duchess of Cleveland. Among her descendants through the Duke of Grafton is Diana, Princess of Wales.

Castlereagh Robert Stewart, Viscount Castlereagh 1769–1822. British Tory politician. As chief secretary for Ireland 1797–1801, he suppressed the rebellion of 1798, and helped the younger Pitt secure the union of England, Scotland, and Ireland in 1801. As foreign secretary 1812–22 he coordinated European opposition to Napoleon and represented Britain at the Congress of Vienna 1814–15.

When his father, an Ulster landowner, was made an earl in 1796, he took the courtesy title of Viscount Castlereagh. In 1821 he succeeded his father as Marquess of Londonderry. He sat in the Irish House of Commons from 1790.

In Parliament at Westminster he was war secretary 1805–06 and 1807–09, when he had to resign after a duel with foreign secretary George ◊Canning. Castlereagh was foreign secretary from 1812, when he devoted himself to the overthrow of Napoleon and subsequently to the Congress of Vienna and the congress system. Abroad his policy favoured the development of material liberalism, but at home he repressed the Reform movement, and popular opinion held him responsible for the Peterloo massacre of peaceful demonstrators in 1819.

Castro Cipriano 1858–1924. Venezuelan dictator 1899–1908, known as 'the Lion of the Andes'. When he refused to pay off foreign debts in 1902, British, German, and Italian ships blockaded the country. He presided over a corrupt government. There were frequent rebellions during his rule,

Castro (Ruz) *Cuban revolutionary and premier, Fidel Castro.*

and opponents of his regime were exiled or murdered.

Castro (Ruz) Fidel 1927– . Cuban Communist politician, prime minister 1959–76 and president from 1976. He led two unsuccessful coups against the right-wing Batista regime and led the revolution that overthrew the dictator 1959. From 1979 he was also president of the non-aligned movement, although promoting the line of the USSR, which subsidized his regime.

Of wealthy parentage, Castro was educated at Jesuit schools and, after studying law at the University of Havana, he gained a reputation through his work for poor clients. He opposed the Batista dictatorship, and took part in an unsuccessful attack on the army barracks at Santiago de Cuba in 1953. After some time in exile in the USA and Mexico, Castro attempted a secret landing in Cuba in 1956 in which all but 11 of his supporters were killed. He eventually gathered an army of over 5,000 which overthrew Batista in 1959 and he became prime minister a few months later. His brother Raúl was appointed minister of armed forces.

The Castro regime introduced a centrally planned economy based on the production for export of sugar, tobacco, and nickel. Aid for developmemt has been provided by the USSR while Cuba joined COMECON, the economic association of Communist countries, in 1972. By nationalizing US-owned businesses in 1960 Castro gained the enmity of the USA, which came to a head in the Cuban missile crisis of 1962. His regime became socialist and he epoused Marxism-Leninism until in 1974 he rejected Marx's formula 'from each according to his ability and to each according to his need' and decreed that each Cuban should 'receive according to his work'.

Cather Willa (Sibert) 1876–1947. US novelist. Born in Virginia, she moved as a child to Nebraska. Her novels and short stories frequently explore life in the pioneer West, for example in *Death Comes for the Archbishop* 1927, set in New Mexico. Other chief works are *My Antonia* 1918 and *A Lost Lady* 1923.

Catherine I 1683–1727. Empress of Russia from 1724. A Lithuanian peasant girl, born Martha Skavronsky, she married a Swedish dragoon and eventually became the mistress of Peter the Great. In 1703 she was rechristened as Katarina Alexeievna, and in 1711 the tsar divorced his wife and married Catherine. She accompanied him in his campaigns, and showed tact and shrewdness. In 1724 she was proclaimed empress, and after Peter's death 1725 she ruled capably with the help of her ministers. She allied Russia with Austria and Spain in an anti-English bloc.

Catherine II *the Great* 1729–1796. Empress of Russia from 1762, and daughter of the German prince of Anhalt-Zerbst. In 1745, she married the Russian grand duke Peter. Catherine was able to dominate him, and six months after he became tsar 1762 she ruled alone. During her reign Russia extended its boundaries to include territory from Turkey 1774, and profited also by the partitions of Poland.

Catherine's private life was notorious throughout Europe, but she did not permit her lovers to influence her policy. She admired and aided the French Encyclopédistes (see ◊Diderot), including d'Alembert, and corresponded with the radical writer Voltaire.

Catherine de' Medici 1519–1589. French queen consort of Henry II, whom she married 1533, and mother of Francis II, Charles IX, and Henry III. At first outshone by Henry's mistress Diane de Poitiers (1490–1566), she became regent 1560–63 for Charles IX, and was politically powerful until his death 1574.

At first scheming with the Huguenots, she later opposed them, instigating the murders known as the Massacre of St Bartholomew 1572.

Catherine of Alexandria, St Christian martyr. According to legend she disputed with 50 scholars, refusing to give up her faith and marry Emperor Maxentius. Her emblem is a wheel, on which her persecutors tried to kill her (the wheel broke and she was beheaded). Feast day 25 Nov.

Catherine of Aragon 1485–1536. First queen of Henry VIII of England, 1509–33, and mother of Mary I; Henry divorced her without papal approval.

Catherine de' Medici During her regency Catherine de' Medici virtually ruled France.

She married Henry's elder brother Prince Arthur 1501 (the marriage was allegedly unconsummated), and on his death 1502 was betrothed to Henry, marrying him on his accession 1509. Of their six children, only a daughter lived. Wanting a male heir, Henry sought an annulment 1526 on the grounds that the union with his brother's widow was invalid despite a papal dispensation. When the Pope demanded that the case be referred to him, Henry married Anne Boleyn, afterwards receiving the desired decree of nullity from ◊Cranmer, the archbishop of Canterbury, in 1533. The Reformation in England followed, and Catherine went into retirement until her death.

Catherine of Braganza 1638–1705. Queen of Charles II of England 1662–85. The daughter of John IV of Portugal (1604–56), she brought the Portuguese possessions of Bombay and Tangier as her dowry. Her childlessness and practice of her Catholic faith were unpopular, but Charles resisted pressure for divorce. She returned to Lisbon 1692.

Catherine of Genoa, St 1447–1510. Italian mystic, who devoted herself to the sick and to meditation. Her feast day is 15 Sept.

Catherine of Siena, St 1347–1380. Catholic mystic, born in Siena, Italy. She attempted to reconcile the Florentines with the Pope, and persuaded Gregory XI to return to Rome from Avignon 1376. In 1375 she is said to have received on her body the stigmata, the impression of Jesus' wounds. Her *Dialogue* is a classic mystical work. Feast day 29 Apr.

Catherine of Valois 1401–1437. Queen of Henry V of England, whom she married 1420, and the mother of Henry VI. After the death of Henry V, she secretly married Owen Tudor (c.1400–61) about 1425, and their son became the father of Henry VII.

Catherwood Frederick 1799–1854. British topographical artist and archaeological illustrator, who

accompanied John Lloyd ◊Stephens in his exploration of central America 1839–40 and the Yucatan 1841–42. His engravings, published 1844, were the first accurate representation of Mayan civilization in the West.

Catiline (Lucius Sergius Catilina) *c.*108–62 BC. Roman politician. Twice failing to be elected to the consulship in 64/63 BC, he planned a military coup, but ◊Cicero exposed his conspiracy. He died at the head of the insurgents.

Catlin George 1796–1872. US painter and explorer. From the 1830s he made a series of visits to the Great Plains, painting landscapes and scenes of American Indian life.

He produced an exhibition of over 500 paintings with which he toured America and Europe. His style is factual, with close attention to detail. Many of his pictures are in the Smithsonian Institute, Washington DC.

Cato Marcus Porcius 234–149 BC. Roman politician. Appointed censor (senior magistrate) in 184, he excluded from the Senate those who did not meet his high standards. He was so impressed by the power of Carthage, on a visit in 157, that he ended every speech by saying 'Carthage must be destroyed.' His farming manual is the earliest surviving work in Latin prose.

Catullus Gaius Valerius *c.*84–54 BC. Roman lyric poet, born in Verona of a well-to-do family. He moved in the literary and political society of Rome and wrote lyrics describing his unhappy love affair with Clodia, probably the wife of the consul Metellus, calling her Lesbia. His longer poems include two wedding-songs. Many of his poems are short verses to his friends.

Cauchy Augustin Louis 1789–1857. French mathematician, noted for his rigorous methods of analysis. His prolific output included work on complex functions, determinants and probability, and on the convergence of infinite series. In calculus, he refined the concepts of the limit and the definite integral. Although bigoted in his religion and conceited in his work, he published 1843 a defence of academic freedom of thought which was instrumental in the abolition of the oath of allegiance soon after the fall of Louis Phillipe 1848.

Causley Charles Stanley 1917– . British poet, born in Launceston, Cornwall. He published his first volume *Hands to Dance* in 1951; his ballad 'Samuel Sweet' is noteworthy.

Cauthen Steve 1960– . US jockey. He has ridden in England since 1979 and has twice won the Derby, on Slip Anchor in 1985 and on Reference Point in 1987. He rode Affirmed to the US Triple Crown in 1978 at the age of 18 and won 487 races in 1977. He was UK champion jockey in 1984, 1985, and 1987.

Cavaco Silva Anibal 1939– . Portuguese politician, finance minister 1980–81, and prime minister and Social Democratic Party (PSD) leader from 1985. Under his leadership Portugal joined the European Community (EC) 1985 and the Western European Union (WEU) 1988.

Born at Loule, he studied economics in Britain and the USA, and was a university teacher and research director in the Bank of Portugal. In 1978, with the return of constitutional government, he was persuaded to enter politics. His government fell in 1987, but an election later that year gave him Portugal's first absolute majority since democracy was restored.

Cavafy Constantinos. Pen name of Konstantínos Pétrou 1863–1933. Greek poet. An Alexandrian, he threw light on the Greek past, recreating the classical period with zest. He published only one book of poetry, and remained almost unknown until translations appeared in 1952.

Cavalli (Pietro) Francesco 1602–1676. Italian composer, organist at St Mark's, Venice, and the first to make opera a popular entertainment with such works as *Xerxes* 1654, later performed in honour of Louis XIV's wedding in Paris. Twenty-seven of his operas survive.

Cave Edward 1691–1754. British printer, founder under the pseudonym Sylvanus Urban of *The Gentleman's Magazine* 1731–1914, the first periodical to be called a magazine. Dr Samuel Johnson was an influential contributor 1738–44.

Cavell Edith Louisa 1865–1915. British matron of a Red Cross hospital in Brussels, Belgium, in World War I, who helped Allied soldiers escape to the Dutch frontier. She was court-martialled by the Germans and condemned to death. Her last words were: 'Patriotism is not enough. I

Cavour As prime minister of Piedmont, Cavour was largely responsible for achieving the unification of Italy in 1861.

must have no hatred or bitterness towards anyone.'

Cavendish family name of dukes of Devonshire; the family seat is at Chatsworth, Derbyshire.

Cavendish Frederick Charles, Lord Cavendish 1836–1882. British administrator, second son of the 7th duke of Devonshire. He was appointed chief secretary to the lord-lieutenant of Ireland in 1882. On the evening of his arrival in Dublin he was murdered in Phoenix Park with Burke, the permanent Irish undersecretary, by members of the Irish Invincibles, a group of Irish Fenian extremists founded 1881.

Cavendish Henry 1731–1810. British physicist. He discovered hydrogen, which he called 'inflammable air' 1766, and determined the compositions of water and of nitric acid.

A grandson of the 2nd Duke of Devonshire, he devoted his life to scientific pursuits, living in rigorous seclusion at Clapham Common, London. The *Cavendish experiment* was a device of his to discover the mass and density of the Earth.

Cavendish Thomas 1555–1592. English navigator, and commander of the third circumnavigation of the world. He sailed in July 1586, touched Brazil, sailed down the coast to Patagonia, passed through the Straits of Magellan, and returned to Britain via the Philippines, the Cape of Good Hope, and St Helena, reaching Plymouth after two years and 50 days.

Cavendish-Bentinck family name of Dukes of Portland.

Cavour Camillo Benso, Count 1810–1861. Italian nationalist politician, editor of the pro-nationalist *Il Risorgimento* from 1847.

Cavour was born in Turin, and served in the army in early life; he entered politics in 1847. From 1848 he sat in the Piedmontese parliament, and held cabinet posts 1850–52. As prime minister, he sought to secure French and British sympathy for the cause of Italian unity by sending Piedmontese troops to fight in the Crimean War. In 1858 he had a secret meeting with Napoleon III at Plombières, where they planned the war of 1859 against Austria, which resulted in the union of Lombardy with Piedmont. The central Italian states also joined the kingdom of Italy, although Savoy and Nice were to be ceded to France. With Cavour's approval Garibaldi overthrew the Neapolitan monarchy, but to prevent him from marching on Rome Cavour occupied part of the Papal States, which with Naples and Sicily were annexed to Italy.

Caxton William c.1422–1491. First English printer. He learned the art of printing in Cologne, Germany 1471 and set up a press in Belgium, where he produced the first book printed in English, his own version of a French romance, *Recuyell of the Historyes of Troye* 1474. Returning to England in 1476 he established himself in London, where he produced the first book printed in England, *Dictes or Sayengis of the Philosophres* 1477.

Born in Kent, Caxton was apprenticed to a London cloth dealer 1438, and set up his own business in Bruges 1441–70; he became governor of the English merchants there, negotiating on their behalf with the dukes of Burgundy. In 1471 he went to Cologne, where he learned the art of printing, and then set up his own press in Bruges in partnership with Colard Mansion, a calligrapher. The books from Caxton's press in Westminster included editions of the poets Chaucer, Gower, and John Lydgate (*c*. 1370–1449). He translated many texts from French and Latin and revised some English ones, such as Malory's *Morte d'Arthur*. Altogether he printed about 100 books.

Cayley Arthur 1821–1895. British mathematician, who developed matrix algebra, used by ◊Heisenberg in his elucidation of quantum mechanics.

Cayley George 1773–1857. British aviation pioneer, inventor of the first piloted glider in 1853, and the caterpillar tractor.

Ceauşescu Nicolae 1918–1989. Romanian politician, leader of Romanian Communist Party (RCP), in power 1965–89. He pursued a policy line independent of and critical of the USSR. He appointed family members, including his wife, to senior state and party posts, and governed in a personalized and increasingly repressive manner, zealously implementing schemes that impoverished the nation. He was overthrown in a bloody revolutionary coup Dec 1989 and executed, along with his wife Elena, on Christmas Day 1989.

Ceauşescu joined the underground RCP in 1933 and was imprisoned for antifascist activities 1936–38 and 1940–44. After World War II he was elected to the Grand National Assembly and was soon given ministerial posts. He was inducted into the party secretariat and Politburo in 1954–55. In 1965 Ceauşescu became leader of the RCP and from 1967 chair of the state council. He was elected president in 1974. Following his execution, the full extent of his repressive rule and personal extravagance became public.

Cecil Henry Richard Amherst 1943– . Scottish-born racehorse trainer with stables at Warren Place, Newmarket. The most successful English trainer of all time in terms of prize money, he was the first trainer to win over £1 million in a season 1985. He trained Slip Anchor and Reference Point to win the Epsom Derby.

Cecil Robert, 1st Earl of Salisbury 1563–1612. Secretary of state to Elizabeth I of England, succeeding his father, Lord Burghley; he was afterwards chief minister to James I, who created him Earl of Salisbury 1605.

Cecilia, St Christian patron saint of music, martyred in Rome in the 2nd or 3rd century, who is said to have sung hymns while undergoing torture. Feast day 22 Nov.

Céline Louis Ferdinand. Pen name of Louis Destouches 1884–1961. French novelist, whose writings (the first of which was *Voyage au bout de la nuit/Journey to the End of the Night* 1932) were controversial for their cynicism and misanthropy.

Cellini Benvenuto 1500–1571. Italian sculptor and goldsmith working in the Mannerist style; author of an arrogant autobiography (begun 1558). Among his works is a graceful bronze *Perseus* 1545–54 (Loggia dei Lanzi, Florence) and a magnificent gold salt cellar made for Francis I of France 1540–43 (Kunsthistorisches Museum, Vienna), topped by nude reclining figures.

Cervantes Saavedra Miguel de 1547–1616. Spanish novelist, playwright, and poet, whose masterpiece, *Don Quixote* (in full *El ingenioso hidalgo Don Quixote de la Mancha*) was published 1605. In 1613, his *Novelas Ejemplares/Exemplary Novels* appeared, followed by *Viaje del Parnaso/The Voyage to Parnassus* 1614. A spurious second part of *Don Quixote* prompted Cervantes to bring out his own authentic second part in 1615, considered by many to be superior to the first in construction and characterization.

Born at Alcalá de Henares, he entered the army in Italy, and was wounded in the battle of Lepanto 1571. While on his way back to Spain 1575, he was captured by Barbary pirates and was taken to Algiers, where he became a slave until ransomed 1580. Returning to Spain, he wrote several plays, and in 1585 his pastoral romance *Galatea* was printed. He was employed in Seville 1587 provisioning the Armada. While working as a tax collector, he was imprisoned more than once for deficiencies in his accounts. He sank into poverty, and little is known of him until 1605 when he published *Don Quixote*. It immediately achieved great success and was soon translated into English and French.

César adopted name of César Baldaccini 1921– . French sculptor who uses iron and scrap metal and, in the 1960s, crushed car bodies. His subjects are imaginary insects and animals.

Cetewayo (Cetshwayo) *c*. 1829–1884. King of Zululand, S Africa 1873–83, whose rule was threatened by British annexation of the Transvaal 1877. Although he defeated the British at Isandhlwana 1879, he was later that year defeated by them at Ulundi. Restored to his throne 1883, he was then expelled by his subjects.

Cézanne Paul 1839–1906. French Post-Impressionist painter, a leading figure in the development of modern art. He broke away from the Impressionists' spontaneous vision to develop a style that captured not only light and life, but the structure of natural forms, in landscapes, still lifes, portraits, and his series of bathers.

He was born in Aix-en-Provence, where he studied, and was a friend of the novelist Emile Zola. In 1872 Cézanne met Pissarro and settled near him in Pontoise, outside Paris, but soon abandoned Impressionism. His series of paintings of Mont Sainte-Victoire in Provence from the 1880s into the 1900s show an increasing fragmentation of the painting's surface and a movement towards abstraction, with layers of colour and square brushstrokes achieving monumental solidity. He was greatly revered by early abstract painters, notably Picasso and Braque.

Chabrier (Alexis) Emmanuel 1841–1894. French composer who wrote *España* 1883, an orchestral rhapsody, and the light opera *Le Roi malgré lui/King Against His Will* 1887. His orchestration inspired Debussy and Ravel.

Chabrol Claude 1930– . French film director. Originally a critic, he was one of the French 'new wave' of directors. His works of murder and suspense, which owe much to Hitchcock, include *Les Biches/The Girlfriends* 1968; *Le Boucher/The Butcher* 1970; *Cop au Vin* 1984.

Chadli Benjedid 1929– . Algerian socialist politician, president from 1979. An army colonel, he supported ◊Boumédienne in the overthrow of ◊Ben Bella 1965, and succeeded Boumédienne 1979, pursuing more moderate policies.

Chadwick Edwin 1800–1890. English social reformer, author of the Poor Law Report of 1834. He played a prominent part in the campaign which resulted in the Public Health Act 1848. He was commissioner of the first Board of Health 1848–54.

A self-educated protégé of Jeremy ◊Bentham and advocate of utilitarianism, he used his influence to implement measures to eradicate cholera, improve sanitation in urban areas, and clear slums in British cities.

Chadwick James 1891–1974. British physicist. In 1932, he discovered the particle in an atomic nucleus which became known as the neutron because it has no electric charge. He was awarded a Nobel prize 1935, and in 1940 was one of the British scientists reporting on the atomic bomb.

Chadwick studied at Cambridge under ◊Rutherford. He was Lyon Jones professor of physics at Liverpool 1935–48, and master of Gonville and Caius College, Cambridge, 1948–59.

Chadwick Lynn 1914– . British abstract sculptor, known for mobiles (influenced by Calder) in the 1940s and welded ironwork from the 1950s.

Chagall Marc 1887–1985. French painter and designer, born in Russia; much of his highly coloured, fantastic imagery was inspired by the village life of his boyhood. He also designed stained glass, mosaics (for Israel's Knesset in the 1960s), tapestries, and stage sets.

Chagall is an original figure, often seen as a precursor of Surrealism, as in *The Dream* (Met-

ropolitan Museum of Art, New York). He lived mainly in France from 1922. His stained glass can be found notably in a chapel in Vence, in the south of France, and in a synagogue near Jerusalem. He also produced illustrated books.

Chaillu Paul Belloni du 1835–1903. French-born US explorer. In 1855 he began a four year journey of exploration in West Africa. His *Explorations and Adventures in Equatorial Africa* 1861 describes his discovery of the gorilla in Gabon.

Chain Ernst Boris 1906–1979. German biochemist who worked on the development of penicillin. Chain was born in Germany but fled to Britain 1933. After the discovery of penicillin by Alexander ◊Fleming, Chain worked to isolate and purify it. For this work, he shared the 1945 Nobel Prize for Medicine with Fleming and Howard Florey. He also discovered penicillinase, an enzyme which destroys penicillin.

Chaka alternative spelling of ◊Shaka, Zulu chief.

Chaliapin Fyodor Ivanovich 1873–1938. Russian bass singer, born in Kazan of peasant parentage. His greatest role was that of Boris Godunov in Mussorgsky's opera of the same name. Chaliapin left the USSR in 1921 to live and sing in the world's capitals.

Chalmers Thomas 1780–1847. Scottish theologian. At the 'Disruption' of the Church of Scotland 1843, Chalmers withdrew from the church along with a large body of other priests, and became principal of the Free Church college, thus founding the Free Church of Scotland.

As minister of Tron Church, Glasgow, from 1815, Chalmers became noted for his eloquence and for his proposals for social reform. In 1823 he became professor of moral philosophy at St Andrews, and in 1828 of theology at Edinburgh.

Chamberlain (Arthur) Neville 1869–1940. British Conservative politician, son of Joseph Chamberlain. He was prime minister 1937–40; his policy of appeasement towards the fascist dictators Mussolini and Hitler (with whom he concluded the Munich Agreement 1938) failed to prevent the outbreak of World War II. He resigned 1940 following the defeat of the British forces in Norway.

Younger son of Joseph Chamberlain and half-brother of Austen Chamberlain, he was born in Birmingham, of which he was lord mayor in 1915. He was minister of health in 1923 and 1924–29 and worked at slum clearance. In 1931 he was chancellor of the Exchequer in the national government, and in 1937 succeeded Baldwin as prime minister. Trying to close the old Anglo-Irish feud, he agreed to return to Eire those ports that had been occupied by the navy. He also attempted to appease the demands of the European dictators, particularly Mussolini. In 1938 he went to Munich and negotiated with Hitler the settlement of the Czechoslovak question, by which the Czeck

Sudeten districts were ceded to Germany. He was ecstatically received on his return, and claimed that the Munich Agreement brought 'peace in our time'. Within a year, however, Britain was at war with Germany.

Chamberlain Joseph 1836–1914. British politician, reformist mayor of and member of Parliament for Birmingham. In 1886 he resigned from the cabinet over Gladstone's policy of home rule for Ireland, and led the revolt of the Liberal-Unionists.

By 1874 Chamberlain had adopted radical views, and took an active part in local affairs. Three times mayor of Birmingham, he carried through many schemes of municipal development. In 1876 he was elected to Parliament and joined the republican group led by Charles Dilke, the extreme left wing of the Liberal Party. The climax of his radical period was reached with an unauthorized programme, advocating, among other things, free education, graduated taxation, and smallholdings of 'three acres and a cow'.

As colonial secretary in Salisbury's Conservative government, Chamberlain was responsible for relations with the Boer republics up to the outbreak of war in 1899. In 1903 he resigned to campaign for imperial preference or tariff reform as a means of consolidating the empire. From 1906 he was incapacitated by a stroke. Chamberlain was one of the most colourful figures of British politics, and his monocle and orchid made him a favourite subject for political cartoonists.

Chamberlain (Joseph) Austen 1863–1937. British Conservative politician, elder son of Joseph Chamberlain; as foreign secretary 1924–29 he negotiated the Pact of Locarno (settling Germany's W frontiers), for which he won the Nobel Peace Prize 1925, and signed the Kellogg–Briand pact (renouncing war) 1928.

He was elected to Parliament 1892 as a Liberal-Unionist, and after holding several minor posts was chancellor of the Exchequer 1903–06. During World War I he was secretary of state for India 1915–17 and member of the war cabinet 1918. He was chancellor of the Exchequer 1919–21 and Lord Privy Seal 1921–22, but failed to secure the leadership of the party 1922, as many Conservatives resented the part he had taken in the Irish settlement of 1921. He was foreign secretary in the Baldwin government 1924–29.

Chamberlain Owen 1920– . US physicist whose graduate studies were interrupted by wartime work on the Manhattan project at Los Alamos. After World War II, working with Italian physicist Emilio Segrè (1905–1989), he discovered the existence of the anti-proton. Both men were awarded the Nobel Prize for Physics in 1959.

Chamberlain Wilton Norman 'Wilt' 1936– . US basketball player, who set a record by averaging 50.4 points a game during the 1962 season, and was the only man to score 100 points in a game.

He was known as 'Wilt the Stilt' because of his height 2.16 m/7ft 1¹/8 in.

Chambers William 1726–1796. British architect, popularizer of Chinese influence (as in the pagoda in Kew Gardens, London) and designer of Somerset House, London.

Chamisso Adelbert von. Pen name of Louis-Charles-Adélaide Chamisso de Boncourt 1781–1831. German writer of the story 'Peter Schlemihl', the man who sold his shadow. The son of a French family who left France because of the French Revolution, he was subsequently a botanist with Otto von Kotzebue's trip around the world 1815–18, recounted in *Reise um de Welt* 1821. His verse includes the cycle of lyrics *Frauenliebe und Frauenleben* 1831, set to music by Schumann.

Champaigne Philippe de 1602–1674. French artist, the leading portrait painter of the court of Louis XIII. Of Flemish origin, he went to Paris 1621, and gained the patronage of Cardinal Richelieu. His style is elegant, cool, and restrained.

Champlain Samuel de 1567–1635. French pioneer, soldier, and explorer in Canada. Having served in the army of Henry IV and on an expedition to the West Indies, he began his exploration of Canada 1603. On a further expedition 1608 he founded and named Québec, and was appointed lieutenant-governor of French Canada 1612.

Champollion Jean François, le Jeune 1790–1832. French Egyptologist who in 1822 deciphered Egyptian hieroglyphics with the aid of the Rosetta Stone (an ancient slab inscribed in Egyptian and Greek).

Chandler Raymond 1888–1959. US crime writer, who created the 'private eye' hero Philip Marlowe, a hard-boiled detective, in books which include *The Big Sleep* 1939, *Farewell, My Lovely* 1940, and *The Long Goodbye* 1954.

Chandrasekhar Subrahmanyan 1910– . Indian-born US astrophysicist, who made pioneering studies of the structure and evolution of stars. Born in Lahore, he studied in Madras, India, and Cambridge, England, before emigrating to the USA. He was awarded the 1983 Nobel Prize for Physics.

Chanel Coco (Gabrielle) 1883–1971. French fashion designer, creator of the 'little black dress', informal cardigan suit, costume jewellery, and perfumes.

Chaney Alonso ('Lon') 1883–1930. US star of silent films, often in grotesque or monstrous roles such as *The Phantom of the Opera* 1925. A master of make-up, he sometimes employed extremely painful devices for added effectiveness, as in the title role in *The Hunchback of Notre Dame* 1923.

Chaney Creighton ('Lon Jr') 1906–1973. US actor, son of Lon Chaney, who gave an acclaimed performance as Lennie in *Of Mice and Men* 1940.

He went on to star in many 1940s horror films, including the title role in *The Wolfman* 1941. His other work includes *My Favorite Brunette* 1947 and *The Haunted Palace* 1963.

Chang Michael 1972– . US tennis player who, at the age of 17 years 3 months, became the youngest ever winner of a Grand Slam event when he beat Stefan Edberg to win the French Open in 1989. He beat the top seed Ivan Lendl on his way to the title.

Chang Ch'ien 2nd century BC. Chinese explorer who pioneered the Silk Route, the trade route by which the Chinese traded silk for European wool and metals.

Chantrey Francis Legatt 1781–1841. British sculptor, known for portrait busts and monuments. His unaffected studies of children were much loved in his day, notably *Sleeping Children* 1817 (in Lichfield cathedral).

Chaplin Charles Spencer ('Charlie') 1889–1977. English actor-director. He made his reputation as a tramp with smudge moustache, bowler hat, and cane in silent films from the mid-1910s, including *The Rink* 1916, *The Kid* 1921, and *The Gold Rush* 1925. His works often contrast buffoonery with pathos, and later films combine dialogue with mime and music, such as *The Great Dictator* 1940, and *Limelight* 1952.

Born in South London, he first appeared on the stage at the age of five. His other films include *City Lights* 1931, *Modern Times* 1936, and *Monsieur Verdoux* (in which he spoke for the first time) 1947. *Limelight* 1952 was awarded an Oscar for Chaplin's musical theme. He left the USA in 1952 when accused of Communist sympathies in the McCarthy era, and moved to Switzerland. He was four times married, his third wife being Paulette Goddard, and the fourth, Oona, daughter of Eugene O'Neill. He received special Oscars 1928 and 1972, and was knighted 1975.

Chaplin *Comic film actor Charlie Chaplin, seen here with Jackie Coogan in the silent film* The Kid *1920.*

Chapman Frederick Spencer 1907–1971. British explorer, mountaineer, and writer, who explored Greenland, the Himalayas, and Malaya. He accompanied Gino Watkins on the British Arctic Air Routes Expedition 1930–31, recalled in *Northern Lights* 1932, and in 1935 he joined a climbing expedition to the Himalayas. For two years he participated in a government mission to Tibet described in *Lhasa, the Holy City* 1938, before setting out to climb the 7,300 m/24,000 ft peak, Chomollari.

Chapman George 1559–1634. English poet and dramatist. His translations of Homer (completed 1616) were celebrated; his plays include the comedy *Eastward Ho!* (with Jonson and Marston) 1605, and the tragedy *Bussy d'Amboise* 1607.

Charcot Jean-Martin 1825–1893. French neurologist who studied diseases of the nervous system. He became known for his work on hysteria, sclerosis, locomotor ataxia, and senile diseases.

Charcot worked at a hospital in Paris where he studied the way certain mental illnesses cause physical changes in the brain. He exhibited hysteria patients at weekly public lectures, which became highly fashionable events. Among his pupils was Sigmund ◊Freud.

Chardin Jean-Baptiste-Siméon 1699–1779. French painter of naturalistic still lifes and quiet domestic scenes that recall the Dutch tradition. His work is a complete contrast to that of contemporary

Chanel *French couturier 'Coco' Chanel in 1929.*

Rococo painters. He developed his own technique using succesive layers of paint to achieve depth of tone and is generally considered one of the finest exponents of the genre.

Chardonnet Hilaire Bernigaud 1839–1924. French chemist who developed artificial silk in 1883, the first artificial fibre.

Charlemagne Charles I, the Great 742–814. King of the Franks from 768 and Holy Roman emperor from 800. By inheritance (his father was ◊Pepin the Short) and extensive campaigns of conquest, he united most of W Europe by 804, when after 30 years of war the Saxons came under his control. He reformed the legal, judicial, and military systems, established schools, promoted Christianity, commerce, agriculture, arts, and literature. In his capital Aachen, scholars gathered from all over Europe.

He was engaged in his first Saxon campaign when the Pope's call for help against the Lombards reached him; he crossed the Alps, captured Pavia, and took the title of king of the Lombards.

The pacification and christianizing of the Saxon peoples occupied the greater part of Charlemagne's reign. The Westphalian leader Widukind did not submit until 785, when he received baptism. From 792 N Saxony was subdued, and in 804 the country was finally pacified. In 777 the emir of Zaragoza asked for Charlemagne's help against the emir of Córdoba. Charlemagne crossed the Pyrenees 778, and reached the Ebro, but had to turn back from Zaragoza. In 801 the district between the Pyrenees and the Llobregat was organized as the Spanish March. The independent duchy of Bavaria was incorporated in the kingdom 788, and the Avar people were subdued 791–96, and accepted Christianity. Charlemagne's last campaign was against a Danish attack on his northern frontier 810.

The supremacy of the Frankish king in the western world found outward expression in the bestowal of the imperial title: in Rome, during Mass on Christmas Day 800, Pope Leo III crowned Charlemagne emperor. He enjoyed diplomatic relations with Byzantium, Baghdad, Mercia, Northumbria, and other countries. Jury courts were introduced, the laws of the Franks revised, and other peoples' laws written down. A new coinage was introduced, weights and measures were reformed, and communications were improved. Charlemagne also took a lively interest in theology, organized the church in his dominions, and furthered missionary enterprises and monastic reform.

The *Carolingian Renaissance* of learning began when he persuaded the Northumbrian scholar Alcuin to enter his service 781. Charlemagne gathered a kind of academy around him. Although he never learned to read, he collected the old heroic sagas, began a Frankish grammar, and

Charlemagne *The Frankish king who became a hero of medieval romances.*

promoted religious instruction in the vernacular. He died 28 Jan 814 in Aachen, where he was buried. Soon a cycle of heroic legends and romances developed around him, including epics by Ariosto, Boiardo, and Tasso.

Charles Jacques Alexandre César 1746–1823. French physicist, who studied gases and made the first ascent in a hydrogen-filled balloon 1783. His work on the expansion of gases led to the formulation of Charles' law.

Charles (Mary) Eugenia 1919– . Dominican politician, prime minister from 1980.

Born at Pointe Michel, she qualified as a barrister in England and returned to practise in the Windward and Leeward Islands in the West Indies. She was co-founder and first leader of the centrist Dominica Freedom Party (DFP). Two years after Dominica's independence the DFP won the 1980 general election and she became the Caribbean's first female prime minister.

Charles Ray 1930– . US singer, songwriter, and pianist, whose first hits were 'I've Got A Woman' 1955, 'What'd I Say' 1959, and 'Georgia on My Mind' 1960. He has recorded gospel, blues, rock, soul, country, and rhythm and blues.

Charles two kings of Britain:

Charles I 1600–1649. King of Great Britain and Ireland from 1625, son of James I of England (James VI of Scotland). He accepted the Petition of Right 1628, but then dissolved Parliament and ruled without one 1629–40. His advisers were ◊Strafford and ◊Laud, who persecuted the Puritans and provoked the Scots to revolt. The 'Short Parliament', summoned 1640, refused funds, and the 'Long Parliament' later that year rebelled. Charles declared war on Parliament 1642 but surrendered 1646 and was beheaded 1649. He was the father of Charles II.

Charles was born at Dunfermline, and became heir to the throne on the death of his brother

Henry 1612. He married Henrietta Maria, daughter of Henry IV of France. When he succeeded his father, friction with Parliament began at once. The parliaments of 1625 and 1626 were dissolved, and that of 1628 refused supplies until Charles had accepted the Petition of Right, which limited his powers. In 1629 it attacked Charles' illegal taxation and support of the Arminians (see Jacobus ◊Arminius) in the church, whereupon he dissolved Parliament and imprisoned its leaders.

For 11 years he ruled without a parliament, the Eleven Years' Tyranny, raising money by expedients, such as ship money (a tax for the navy which the king attempted to levy in inland as well as coastal districts), that alienated the nation, while the Star Chamber court suppressed opposition by persecuting the Puritans. When Charles attempted in 1637 to force a prayer book on the English model on Presbyterian Scotland he found himself confronted with a nation in arms. The Short Parliament, which met Apr 1640, refused to grant money until grievances were redressed, and was speedily dissolved. The Scots then advanced into England and forced their own terms on Charles. The Long Parliament met 3 Nov 1640 and declared extra-parliamentary taxation illegal, abolished the Star Chamber and other prerogative courts, and voted that Parliament could not be dissolved without its own consent. Laud and other ministers were imprisoned, and Strafford condemned to death. After the failure of his attempt to arrest the parliamentary leaders 4 Jan 1642, Charles, confident that he had substantial support among those who felt that Parliament was becoming too radical and zealous, withdrew from London, and on 22 Aug declared war on Parliament by raising his standard at Nottingham.

Charles's defeat at Naseby June 1645 ended all hopes of victory; in May 1646 he surrendered at Newark to the Scots, who handed him over to Parliament Jan 1647. In June the army seized him and carried him off to Hampton Court. While the army leaders strove to find a settlement, Charles secretly intrigued for a Scottish invasion. In Nov he escaped, but was recaptured and held at Carisbrooke Castle; a Scottish invasion followed 1648, and was shattered by Oliver ◊Cromwell at Preston. In Jan 1649 the House of Commons set up a high court of justice, which tried Charles and condemned him to death. He was beheaded 30 Jan before the Banqueting Hall in Whitehall.

Charles II 1630–1685. King of Great Britain and Ireland from 1660, when Parliament accepted the restoration of the monarchy; son of Charles I. His chief minister Clarendon arranged his marriage 1662 with Catherine of Braganza, but was replaced 1667 with the 'Cabal' of advisers. His plans to restore Catholicism in Britain led to war with the Netherlands 1672–74 and a break with

Parliament, which he dissolved 1681. He was succeeded by James II.

Charles was born in St James's Palace, London; during the Civil War he lived with his father at Oxford 1642–45, and after the victory of Cromwell's Parliamentary forces withdrew to the Continent. Accepting a Scottish offer to make him king, he landed in Scotland 1650, and was crowned at Scone 1 Jan 1651. An attempt to invade England was ended 3 Sept by Cromwell's victory at Worcester. Charles escaped, and for nine years he wandered through France, Germany, Flanders, Spain, and Holland until the opening of negotiations by George Monck (1608–70) 1660. In Apr Charles issued the Declaration of Breda, promising a general amnesty and freedom of conscience. Parliament accepted the Declaration and he was proclaimed king 8 May 1660, landed at Dover on the 26th, and entered London three days later.

Charles wanted to make himself absolute, and favoured Catholicism for his subjects as most consistent with absolute monarchy. The disasters of the Dutch war furnished an excuse for banishing Clarendon 1667, and he was replaced by the Cabal of Clifford and Arlington, both secret Catholics, and ◊Buckingham, Ashley (Lord ◊Shaftesbury), and ◊Lauderdale, who had links with the Dissenters (non-conformists). In 1670 Charles signed the Secret Treaty of Dover, the full details of which were known only to Clifford and Arlington, whereby he promised Louis XIV of France he would declare himself a Catholic, re-establish Catholicism in England, and support Louis's projected war against the Dutch; in return Louis was to finance Charles and in the event of resistance to supply him with troops. War with the Netherlands followed 1672, and at the same time Charles issued the Declaration of Indulgence, suspending all penal laws against Catholics and Dissenters.

In 1673, Parliament forced Charles to withdraw the Indulgence and accept a Test Act exluding all Catholics from office, and in 1674 to end the Dutch war. The Test Act broke up the Cabal, while Shaftesbury, who had learned the truth about the treaty, assumed the leadership of the opposition. ◊Danby, the new chief minister, built up a court party in the Commons by bribery, while subsidies from Louis relieved Charles from dependence on Parliament. In 1678 Titus ◊Oates's announcement of a 'popish plot' released a general panic, which Shaftesbury exploited to introduce his Exclusion Bill, excluding James, Duke of York, from the succession as a Catholic; instead he hoped to substitute Charles' illegitimate son ◊Monmouth.

In 1681 Parliament was summoned at Oxford, which had been the Royalist headquarters during the Civil War. The Whigs attended armed, but when Shaftesbury rejected a last compromise, Charles dissolved Parliament and the Whigs fled in terror. Charles now ruled without a Parliament, financed by Louis XIV. When the Whigs plotted a revolt their leaders were executed, while Shaftesbury and Monmouth fled to the Netherlands.

Charles was a patron of the arts and science. His mistresses included Lady ◊Castlemaine, Nell ◊Gwyn, Lady ◊Portsmouth, and Lucy ◊Walter.

Charles (full name Charles Philip Arthur George) 1948– . Prince of the United Kingdom, heir to the British throne, and Prince of Wales since 1958 (invested 1969). He is the first-born child of Queen Elizabeth II and the Duke of Edinburgh. He studied at Trinity College, Cambridge, 1967–70, before serving in the RAF and Royal Navy. He is the first royal heir since 1659 to have an English wife, Lady Diana Spencer, daughter of the 8th Earl Spencer. They have two sons: Prince William, born 1982, and Prince Henry, born 1984.

Prince Charles's concern for social and environmental issues has led to many self-help projects for the young and underprivileged, and he is a leading critic of unsympathetic features of contemporary architecture.

Charles ten kings of France, including:

Charles I better known as the emperor ◊Charlemagne.

Charles II *the Bald*; see ◊Charles II, Holy Roman emperor.

Charles III *the Simple* 879–929. King of France 893–922, son of Louis the Stammerer. He was crowned at Reims. In 911 he ceded what later became the duchy of Normandy to the Norman chief Rollo.

Charles IV *the Fair* 1294–1328. King of France from 1322, when he succeeded Philip V as the last of the direct Capetian line.

Charles V *the Wise* 1337–1380. King of France from 1364. He was regent during the captivity of his father, John II, in England 1356–60, and became king on John's death. He reconquered nearly all France from England 1369–80.

Charles VI *the Mad* or *the Well-Beloved* 1368–1422. King of France from 1380, succeeding his father Charles V, he was under the regency of his uncles until 1388. He became mentally unstable 1392, and civil war broke out between the dukes of Orleans and Burgundy. Henry V of England invaded France 1415, conquering Normandy, and in 1420 forcing Charles to sign the Treaty of Troyes, recognizing Henry as his successor.

Charles VII 1403–1461. King of France from 1429. Son of Charles VI, he was excluded from the succession by the Treaty of Troyes, but recognized by the South of France. In 1429 Joan of Arc raised the siege of Orléans and had him crowned at Reims. He organized France's first standing army and by 1453 he had expelled the English from all of France except Calais.

Charles VIII 1470–1498. King of France from 1483, when he succeeded his father, Louis XI. In 1494 he unsuccessfully tried to claim the Neapolitan crown, and when he entered Naples 1495 was forced to withdraw by a coalition of Milan, Venice, Spain, and the Holy Roman Empire. He defeated them at Fornovo, but lost Naples. He died while preparing a second expedition.

Charles IX 1550–1574. King of France from 1560. Second son of Henry II and Catherine de' Medici, he succeeded his brother Francis II at the age of ten, but remained under the domination of his mother for ten years while France was torn by religious wars. In 1570 he fell under the influence of the Huguenot leader Admiral Coligny (1517–72); alarmed by this, Catherine instigated his order for the Huguenot murders known as the Massacre of St Bartholomew, which led to a new religious war.

Charles X 1757–1836. King of France from 1824. Grandson of Louis XV and brother of Louis XVI and Louis XVIII, he was known as the Count of Artois before his accession. He fled to England at the beginning of the French Revolution, and when he came to the throne on the death of Louis XVIII, he attempted to reverse the achievements of the Revolution. A revolt ensued 1830, and he again fled to England.

Charles seven rulers of the Holy Roman Empire:

Charles I better known as ◊Charlemagne.

Charles II *the Bald* 823–877. Holy Roman emperor from 875 and (as Charles II) king of France from 843. Younger son of Louis I (the Pious), he warred against his eldest brother, Emperor Lothair I. The Treaty of Verdun 843 made him king of the West Frankish Kingdom (modern France and the Spanish Marches).

Charles III *the Fat* 839–888. Holy Roman emperor 881–87; he became king of the West Franks 885, thus uniting for the last time the whole of Charlemagne's dominions, but was deposed.

Charles IV 1316–1378. Holy Roman emperor from 1355 and king of Bohemia from 1346. Son of John of Luxembourg, king of Bohemia, he was elected king of Germany 1346 and ruled all Germany from 1347. He was the founder of the first German university in Prague 1348.

Charles V 1500–1558. Holy Roman emperor 1519–56. Son of Philip of Burgundy and Joanna of Castile, he inherited vast possessions which led to rivalry from Francis I of France, whose alliance with the Ottoman Empire brought Vienna under siege 1529 and 1532. Charles was also in conflict with the Protestants in Germany until the Treaty of Passau 1552, which allowed the Lutherans religious liberty.

Charles was born in Ghent and received the Netherlands from his father 1506; Spain, Naples, Sicily, Sardinia, and the Spanish dominions in N Africa and America on the death of his maternal grandfather, Ferdinand V of Castile (1452–1516); and from his paternal grandfather, Maximilian I, the Habsburg dominions 1519, when he was elected emperor. He was crowned in Aachen 1520. From 1517 the empire was split by the rise of Lutheranism, Charles making unsuccessful attempts to reach a settlement at Augsburg 1530, and being forced by the Treaty of Passau to yield most of the Protestant demands. Worn out, he abdicated in favour of his son Philip II in the Netherlands 1555 and Spain 1556. He yielded the imperial crown to his brother Ferdinand I, and retired to the monastery of Yuste, Spain.

Charles VI 1685–1740. Holy Roman emperor from 1711, father of ◊Maria Theresa, whose succession to his Austrian dominions he tried to ensure, and himself claimant to the Spanish throne 1700, thus causing the War of the Spanish Succession.

Charles VII 1697–1745. Holy Roman emperor from 1742, opponent of ◊Maria Theresa's claim to the Austrian dominions of Charles VI.

Charles (Karl Franz Josef) 1887–1922. Emperor of Austria and king of Hungary from 1916, the last of the Habsburg emperors. He succeeded his great-uncle, Franz Josef, in 1916, but was forced to withdraw to Switzerland 1918, although he refused to abdicate. In 1921 he attempted unsuccessfully to regain the crown of Hungary and was deported to Madeira, where he died.

Charles (Spanish *Carlos*) four kings of Spain:

Charles I 1500–1558. see ◊Charles V, Holy Roman emperor.

Charles II 1661–1700. King of Spain from 1665; second son of Philip IV, he was the last of the Spanish Habsburg kings. Mentally handicapped from birth, he bequeathed his dominions to Philip of Anjou, grandson of Louis XIV, which led to the War of the Spanish Succession.

Charles III 1716–1788. King of Spain from 1759. Son of Philip V, he became duke of Parma in 1732, and in 1734 conquered Naples and Sicily. On the death of his half-brother Ferdinand VI (1713–1759), he became king of Spain, handing over Naples and Sicily to his son Ferdinand (1751–1825). During his reign Spain was twice at war with Britain: during the Seven Years' War, when he sided with France and lost Florida; and when he backed the Americans in the War of Independence and regained it. At home he carried out a programme of reforms and expelled the Jesuits.

Charles IV 1748–1819. King of Spain from 1788, when he succeeded his father, Charles III, but left the government in the hands of his wife and her lover, the minister Manuel de Godoy (1767–1851). In 1808 Charles was induced to abdicate by Napoleon's machinations in favour of his son Ferdinand VII (1784–1833), who was subsequently deposed by Napoleon's brother Joseph. Charles was awarded a pension by Napoleon, and died in Rome.

Charles (Swedish *Carl*) 15 kings of Sweden. The first six were local chieftains:

Charles IX 1550–1611. King of Sweden from 1604, the youngest son of Gustavus Vasa. In 1568 he and his brother John led the rebellion against Eric XIV (1533–77); John became king as John III, and attempted to Catholicize Sweden, and Charles led the opposition. John's son Sigismund, king of Poland and a Catholic, succeeded to the Swedish throne 1592, and Charles led the Protestants. He was made regent 1595, and deposed Sigismund 1599. Charles was elected king of Sweden 1604. He was involved in unsuccessful wars with Russia, Poland, and Denmark. He was the father of Gustavus Adolphus.

Charles X 1622–1660. King of Sweden from 1654, when he succeeded his cousin Christina. He waged war with Poland and Denmark, and in 1657 invaded Denmark by leading his army over the frozen sea.

Charles XI 1655–1697. King of Sweden from 1660, when he succeeded his father Charles X. His mother acted as regent until 1672 when Charles took over the government. He was a remarkable general, and reformed the administration.

Charles XII 1682–1718. King of Sweden from 1697, when he succeeded his father, Charles XI. From 1700 he was involved in wars with Denmark, Poland, and Russia. He won a succession of victories, until in 1709 while invading Russia, he was defeated at Poltava in Ukraine, and forced to take refuge in Turkey until 1714. He was killed while besieging Fredrikshall.

Charles XIII 1748–1818. King of Sweden from 1809, when he was elected; he became the first king of Sweden and Norway 1814.

Charles XIV (Jean Baptiste Jules ◊Bernadotte) 1763–1844. King of Sweden and Norway from 1818. A former marshal in the French army, in 1810 he was elected crown prince of Sweden, under the name of Charles John (*Carl Johan*). Loyal to his adopted country, he brought Sweden into the alliance against Napoleon 1813, as a reward for which Sweden received Norway. He was the founder of the present dynasty.

Charles XV 1826–1872. King of Sweden and Norway from 1859, when he succeeded his father Oscar I. A popular and liberal monarch, his main achievement was the reform of the constitution.

Charles Albert 1798–1849. King of Sardinia from 1831. He showed liberal sympathies in early life, and after his accession introduced some reforms. On the outbreak of the 1848 revolution he granted a constitution and declared war on Austria. His troops were defeated at Custozza and Novara. In 1849 he abdicated in favour of his son Victor Emmanuel and retired to a monastery, where he died.

Charles Augustus 1757–1828. Grand Duke of Saxe-Weimar in Germany. He succeeded his father in infancy, fought against the French in 1792–94 and 1806, and was the patron and friend of the writer Goethe.

Charles Edward Stuart 1720–1788. British prince, known as the *Young Pretender* or *Bonnie Prince Charlie*, grandson of James II. In the Jacobite rebellion 1745 Charles won the support of the Scottish Highlanders and his army invaded England, but was beaten back by the Duke of ◊Cumberland and routed at the battle of Culloden 1746.

He was born in Rome, the son of James, the Old Pretender, and created Prince of Wales at birth. In July 1745 he sailed for Scotland, and landed in Inverness-shire with seven companions. On 19 Aug he raised his father's standard, and within a week had rallied an army of 2,000 Highlanders. He entered Edinburgh almost without resistance, won an easy victory at Prestonpans, invaded England, and by 4 Dec had reached Derby, where his officers insisted on a retreat. The army returned to Scotland and won a victory at Falkirk, but was forced to retire to the Highlands before Cumberland's advance. On 16 Apr at Culloden Charles's army was routed by Cumberland, and he fled. For five months he wandered through the Highlands with a price of £30,000 on his head before escaping to France. He visited England secretly in 1750, and may have made other visits. In later life he degenerated into a friendless drunkard. He settled in Italy 1766.

Charles Martel *c.* 688–741. Frankish ruler of the east of the Frankish kingdom from 717 and the whole kingdom from 731. His victory against the Moors 732 between Poitiers and Tours earned him his nickname of Martel, 'the Hammer', and halted the Islamic advance into Europe. An illegitimate son of Pepin of Heristal (Pepin II, *c.* 640–714), he was grandfather of Charlemagne.

Charles the Bold Duke of Burgundy 1433–1477. Son of Philip the Good, he inherited Burgundy and the Low Countries from him 1465. He waged wars attempting to free the duchy from dependence on France and restore it as a kingdom. He was killed in battle.

Charles' ambition was to create a kingdom stretching from the mouth of the Rhine to the mouth of the Rhône. He formed the League of the Public Weal against Louis XI of France, invaded France 1471, and conquered the country as far as Rouen. The Holy Roman emperor, Lorraine, and the Swiss united against him; he captured Nancy, but was defeated at Granson, and again at Morat 1476. Nancy was lost and he was killed while attempting to recapture it. His possessions in the Netherlands passed to the Habsburgs by the marriage of his daughter Mary to Maximilian I of Austria.

Charlotte Augusta Princess 1796–1817. Only child of George IV and Caroline of Brunswick, and heir to the British throne. In 1816 she

married Prince Leopold of Saxe-Coburg (later Leopold I of the Belgians), but died in childbirth 18 months later.

Charlotte Sophia 1744–1818. British queen consort. The daughter of the German duke of Mecklenburg-Strelitz, she married George III of Great Britain and Ireland 1761; they had nine sons and six daughters.

Charlton Jack 1935– . English footballer, older brother of Robert (Bobby) and nephew of Jackie Milburn. He spent all his playing career with Leeds United and played more than 750 games for them.

He and his brother both appeared in the England team that won the World Cup 1966. After retiring, Charlton managed Middlesborough to the 2nd division title. Appointed manager of the Republic of Ireland national squad in 1986, he took the team to the 1988 European Championship finals after which he was made an 'Honorary Irishman'. He led Ireland to the World Cup finals for the first time in 1990.

Charlton Robert 'Bobby' 1937– . English footballer, younger brother of Jack Charlton, who scored a record 49 goals in 106 appearances. He spent most of his playing career with Manchester United.

With Manchester United he won two League championship medals, one FA Cup winner's medal and a European Cup winner's medal. He was Footballer of the Year and European Footballer of the Year. On retiring he had an unsuccessful spell as manager of Preston North End. He later became a director of Manchester United.

Charpentier Gustave 1860–1956. French composer who wrote an opera about Paris working-class life, *Louise* 1900.

Charpentier Marc-Antoine 1645–1704. French composer. He wrote sacred music including a number of masses; other works include instrumental theatre music and the opera *Médée* 1693.

Charrière Isabelle Van Zuylen de 1740–1805. Dutch aristocrat, who settled in Colombier, Switzerland, in 1761. Her works include plays, tracts, and novels, including *Caliste* 1786. She had many early feminist ideas.

Charteris Leslie 1907– . British novelist. Born in Singapore, his varied career in many exotic occupations gave authentic background to some 40 novels about Simon Templar, the 'Saint', a gentleman-adventurer on the wrong side of the law, which have been adapted for films, radio and television. The first was *The Saint Meets the Tiger* 1928. He became a US citizen 1946.

Chase James Hadley. Pen name of René Raymond 1906–1985. He served in the Royal Air Force during World War II, and wrote *No Orchids for Miss Blandish* 1939, and other popular novels.

Chateaubriand François René, Vicomte de 1768–1848. French author. In exile from the

French Revolution 1794–99, he wrote *Atala* 1801 (written after his encounters with North American Indians); and the autobiographical *René*, which formed part of *Le Génie de Christianisme/The Genius of Christianity* 1802.

He visited the USA 1791 and, on his return to France, fought for the royalist side which was defeated at Thionville 1792. He lived in exile in England until 1800. When he returned to France, he held diplomatic appointments under Louis XVIII. He later wrote *Mémoires d'outre tombe/Memoirs from Beyond the Tomb* 1849–50.

Châtelet Emilie de Breteuil, Marquise du 1706–1749. French scientific writer, mistress of ◊Voltaire, and translator into French of Newton's *Principia*.

Her marriage to the Marquis du Châtelet in 1725 gave her the leisure to study physics and mathematics. She met Voltaire in 1733, and settled with him at her husband's estate at Cirey, in the Duchy of Lorraine. Her study of Newton, with whom she collaborated on various scientific works, influenced Voltaire's work. She independently produced the first (and only) French translation of Newton's *Principia Mathematica* (published posthumously in 1759).

Chatterji Bankim Chandra 1838–1894. Indian novelist. Born in Bengal, where he established his reputation with his first book, *Durges-Nandini* 1864, he became a favourite of the nationalists. *Ananda Math* 1882 contains the Indian national song 'Bande-Mataram'.

Chatterton Thomas 1752–1770. English poet, whose medieval-style poems and brief life were to inspire English Romanticism. Born in Bristol, he studied ancient documents he found in the Church of St Mary Redcliffe, and composed poems he ascribed to a 15th-century monk, 'Thomas Rowley', which were accepted as genuine. He committed suicide in London, after becoming destitute.

Chatwin Bruce 1940–1989. English writer. His works include *The Songlines* 1987, written after living with nomadic Aborigines, and *Utz* 1988, a novel about a manic porcelain collector in Prague.

Chaucer Geoffrey *c.*1340–1400. English poet. Author of *The Canterbury Tales* about 1387, a collection of tales told by pilgrims on their way to the Thomas Becket shrine, he was the most influential English poet of the Middle Ages. The popularity of his work assured the dominance of southern English in literature. Chaucer's other work includes the French-influenced *Romance of the Rose* and an adaptation of Boccaccio's *Troilus and Criseyde*.

Chaucer was born in London. Taken prisoner in the French wars, he had to be ransomed by Edward III 1360. He married Philippa Roet 1366, becoming in later life the brother-in-law of ◊John

of Gaunt. He achieved various appointments, for example, controller of London customs, and was sent on missions to Italy (where he may have met ◊Boccaccio and ◊Petrarch), France, and Flanders.

His early work showed formal French influence, as in his adaptation of the French allegorical poem on courtly love *Romance of the Rose*; more mature works reflected the influence of Italian realism, as in his long narrative poem *Troilus and Criseyde*, adapted from Boccaccio. In *The Canterbury Tales* he showed his own genius for metre and characterization.

Chávez Carlos 1899–1978. Mexican composer. A student of the piano and of the complex rhythms of his country's folk music, he founded the Mexico Symphony Orchestra. His composed a number of ballets, seven symphonies, and concertos for both violin and piano.

Chayefsky (Sidney) 'Paddy' 1923–1981. US writer. He established his reputation with the television plays *Marty* 1955 (for which he won an Oscar when he turned it into a film), and *Bachelor Party* 1957. He also won Oscars for *The Hospital* 1971 and *Network* 1976.

Cheever John 1912–1982. US writer. His short stories and novels include *The Wapshot Chronicle* 1937, *Bullet Park* 1969, *World of Apples* 1973, and *Falconer* 1977.

Chekhov Anton (Pavlovich) 1860–1904. Russian dramatist and writer. He began to write short stories and comic sketches as a medical student. His plays concentrate on the creation of atmosphere and delineation of internal development, rather than external action. His first play *Ivanov* 1887 was a failure, as was *The Seagull* 1896 until revived by Stanislavsky 1898 at the Moscow Arts Theatre, for which Chekhov went on to write his major plays *Uncle Vanya* 1899, *The Three Sisters* 1901 and *The Cherry Orchard* 1904.

Born at Taganrog, he qualified as a doctor 1884, but devoted himself to writing short stories rather than medical practice. A collection *Particoloured Stories* 1886 consolidated his reputation, and gave him leisure to develop his style: *My Life* 1895, *The Lady with the Dog* 1898 and *In the Ravine* 1900.

Chénier André de 1762–1794. French poet, born in Constantinople. His lyrical poetry was later to inspire the Romantic movement, but he was known in his own time for his uncompromising support of the constitutional royalists after the Revolution. In 1793 he went into hiding, but finally he was arrested, and on 25 July 1794, guillotined. While in prison he wrote *Jeune Captive/Captive Girl* and the political *Iambes*, published after his death.

Cherenkov Pavel 1904– . Soviet physicist. In 1934, he discovered *Cherenkov radiation*; this occurs as a bluish light when charged atomic particles pass through water or other media at a speed faster than the speed of light in that medium. He shared a Nobel prize 1958 with his colleagues Ilya ◊Frank and Igor Tamm (1895–1971).

Chéret Jules 1836–1932. One of the first French poster artists.

Chernenko Konstantin 1911–1985. Soviet politician, leader of the Soviet Communist Party (CPSU) and president 1984–85. He was a protégé of Brezhnev and from 1978 a member of the Politburo.

Chernenko, born in central Siberia, joined the Komsomol (Communist Youth League) 1929 and the CPSU 1931. The future CPSU leader Brezhnev brought him to Moscow to work in the central apparatus 1956 and later sought to establish Chernenko as his successor, but he was passed over in favour of the KGB chief Andropov. When Andropov died Feb 1984 Chernenko was selected as the CPSU's stop-gap leader by cautious party colleagues, and was also elected president. From July 1984 he gradually retired from public life because of failing health.

Cherubini Luigi (Carlo Zanobi Salvadore Maria) 1760–1842. Italian composer. His first opera *Quinto Fabio* 1779 was produced at Alessandria. In 1784 he went to London and became composer to King George III, but from 1788 he lived in Paris, where he produced a number of dramatic works including *Médée* 1797, *Les Deux Journées* 1800, and the ballet *Anacréon* 1803. After 1809 he devoted himself largely to church music.

Cherwell Frederick Alexander Lindemann Winston 1886– 1957. British physicist. He was director of the Physical Laboratory of the RAF at Farnborough in World War I, and personal adviser to ◊Churchill on scientific and statistical matters during World War II. He was professor of experimental philosophy at the Clarendon Laboratory, Oxford 1919–56.

Cheshire (Geoffrey) Leonard 1917– . British pilot. Commissioned with the Royal Air Force on the outbreak of the World War II, he won the Victoria Cross, Distinguished Service Order (with 2 bars), and Distinguished Flying Cross. A devout Roman Catholic, he founded the first Cheshire Foundation Home for the Incurably Sick 1948. In 1959 he married Susan Ryder (1923–) who established a foundation for the sick and disabled of all ages and became a life peeress 1978.

Chesterfield Philip Dormer Stanhope, 4th Earl of Chesterfield 1694–1773. English politician and writer, author of *Letters to his Son* 1774 – his illegitimate son, Philip Stanhope (1732–68).

Born in London, he was ambassador to Holland 1728–32 and 1744. In Ireland, he established schools, helped to reconcile Protestants and Catholics, and encouraged manufacturing. An opponent of Walpole, he was a Whig MP 1715–26, Lord-Lieutenant of Ireland 1745–46, and Secretary of State 1746–48. A member of the literary circle of Swift, Pope, and Bolingbroke, he incurred

the wrath of Dr Samuel ◊Johnson by failing to carry out an offer of patronage.

Chesterton G(ilbert) K(eith) 1874–1936. English novelist, essayist, and satirical poet, author of a series of novels featuring the naive priest-detective 'Father Brown'. Other novels include *The Napoleon of Notting Hill* 1904 and *The Man Who Knew Too Much* 1922.

Born in London, he studied art but quickly turned to journalism. Like Hilaire Belloc he was initially a Socialist sympathizer and joined the Catholic Church 1922.

Chevalier Maurice 1888–1972. French singer and actor. He began as dancing partner to the revue artiste ◊Mistinguett at the Folies-Bergère music-hall, and made numerous films including *Innocents of Paris* 1929, which revived his song 'Louise', *The Merry Widow* 1934, and *Gigi* 1958.

Chevreul Michel-Eugene 1786–1889. French chemist who studied the composition of fats and identified a number of fatty acids, including 'margaric acid', which became the basis of margarine.

Chevreul was Director of the Natural History Museum and Director of Dyeing at the Gobelin tapestry factory.

Chiang Ching former name of the Chinese actress ◊Jiang Qing, third wife of Mao Zedong.

Chiang Ching-kuo 1910–1988. Taiwanese politician, son of Chiang Kai-shek. Prime minister from 1971, he became president 1978.

Chiang Kai-shek Pinyin *Jiang Jie Shi* 1887–1975. Chinese Guomindang (nationalist) general and politician, president of China 1928–31 and 1943–49, and of Taiwan from 1949, where he set up a breakaway right-wing government on his expulsion from the mainland by the communist forces. He was a commander in the civil war that lasted from the end of imperial rule 1911 to the Second Sino-Japanese War and beyond, having split with the communist leader Mao Zedong 1927.

̄Chiang took part in the revolution of 1911 that overthrew the Manchu Ch'ing dynasty, and on the death of the Guomindang leader Sun Yat-sen was made commander in chief of the nationalist armies in S China 1925. Collaboration with the communists, broken in 1927, was resumed in 1936, and Chiang nominally headed the struggle against the Japanese invaders, receiving the Japanese surrender 1945. In Dec 1949 he took refuge on the island of Taiwan, maintaining a large army in the hope of reclaiming the mainland. His authoritarian regime enjoyed US support until his death. He was succeeded as president by his son Chiang Ching-kuo.

Chichester Francis 1901–1972. English sailor and navigator. In 1931, he made the first E–W crossing of the Tasman Sea in *Gipsy Moth*, and in 1966–67 circumnavigated the world in his yacht *Gipsy Moth IV*.

Chifley Joseph Benedict 'Ben' 1885–1951. Australian Labor prime minister 1945–49. He united the party in fulfilling a welfare and nationalization programme 1945–49 (although he failed in an attempt to nationalize the banks 1947) and initiated an immigration programme and the Snowy Mountains hydroelectric project.

Childe Gordon 1892–1957. Australian archaeologist, director of the London Institute of Archaeology 1946–57. He discovered the prehistoric village of Skara Brae in the Orkneys, and published *The Dawn of European Civilization* 1939.

Childers (Robert) Erskine 1870–1922. Irish Sinn Féin politician, author of the spy novel *The Riddle of the Sands* 1903. He was executed as a Republican terrorist.

Before turning to Irish politics, Childers was a clerk in the House of Commons in London. In 1921 he was elected to the Irish Parliament as a supporter of the Sinn Féin leader de Valera, and took up arms against the Irish Free State 1922. Shortly afterwards he was captured, court-martialled, and shot by the Irish Free State government of William T Cosgrave.

Chippendale Thomas *c.*1718–1779. English furniture designer. He set up his workshop in St Martin's Lane, London 1753. His book *The Gentleman and Cabinet Maker's Director* 1754, was a significant contribution to furniture design. He favoured Louis XVI, Chinese, Gothic, and Neo-Classical styles, and worked mainly in mahogany.

Chirac Jacques 1932– . French conservative politician, prime minister 1974–76 and 1986–88. He established the neo-Gaullist Rassemblement pour la République (RPR) 1976, and became mayor of Paris 1977.

Chirac held ministerial posts during the Pompidou presidency and gained the nickname 'the Bulldozer'. In 1974 he became prime minister to President Giscard d'Estaing, but the relationship was uneasy. Chirac contested the 1981 presidential election and emerged as the National Assembly leader for the parties of the right during the socialist administration of 1981–86. Following the rightist coalition's victory 1986, Chirac was appointed prime minister by President Mitterrand in a 'cohabitation' experiment. The term was marked by economic decline, nationality reforms, and student unrest. Student demonstrations in autumn 1986 forced him to scrap controversial plans for educational reform. He was defeated in the May 1988 elections, and replaced by the moderate Socialist Michel Rocard.

Chirico Giorgio di 1888–1978. Italian painter, born in Greece, the founder of Metaphysical painting, a style that presaged Surrealism in its use of enigmatic imagery and dreamlike settings. Early examples date from 1910.

Chissano Joaquim 1939– . Mozambique politician, president from 1986. He was secretary to

Chirac French politician Jacques Chirac, 1986.

Samora ◊Machel, who led the National Front for the Liberation of Mozambique (Frelimo) during the campaign for independence in the early 1960s. When Mozambique was given internal self-government in 1974 Chissano was appointed prime minister. After independence in 1975 he served under Machel as foreign minister and on Machel's death in 1986 succeeded him as president.

Chladni Ernest Florens Friedrich 1756–1827. German physicist, a pioneer in the field of acoustics.

Chodowiecki Daniel Nicolas 1726–1801. German painter and engraver. His works include engravings of scenes from the Seven Years' War and the life of Christ, and the portrait *Jean Calas and his family*.

Choiseul Étienne François, Duc de Choiseul 1719–1785. French politician. Originally a protégé of Mme de Pompadour, the mistress of Louis XV, he became minister for foreign affairs 1758, and held this and other offices until 1770. He banished the Jesuits, and was a supporter of the Enlightenment philosophers Diderot and Voltaire.

Chomsky Noam 1928– . US professor of linguistics. He proposed a theory of transformational generative grammar, which attracted widespread interest because of the claims it made about the relationship between language and the mind, and the universality of an underlying language structure. He is also a leading spokesman against imperialist tendencies of the US government.

Choong Ewe Beng 'Eddy' 1930– . Malayan bad-minton player. Only 157 cm/5ft 2 in tall, he was a dynamic player and won most major honours in a career between 1950–1957, including All-England singles title four times 1953–1957.

Choonhavan Major-General Chatichai 1922– . Thai politician, prime minister of Thailand from 1988. He has promoted a peace settlement in neighbouring Cambodia as part of a broader vision of transforming Indochina into a thriving, open-trading zone.

Chopin Frédéric (François) 1810–1849. Polish composer and pianist. He made his debut as a pianist at the age of eight. As a performer, Chopin revolutionized the technique of pianoforte-playing, and concentrated on solo piano pieces. His compositions for piano are characterized by their lyrical and poetic quality.

Chopin A daguerreotype of the composer.

Born the son of a French father and a Polish mother, from 1831 he made his home in Paris, where he became known in the fashionable salons, although he rarely performed in public. In 1836 Liszt introduced him to Mme Dudevant (George ◊Sand), with whom he had a close relationship 1838–46. During this time she nursed him in Majorca for tuberculosis, while he composed intensively and for a time regained his health. He died 17 Oct 1849 and was buried in Père Lachaise cemetery in Paris.

Chopin Kate 1851–1904. US novelist and story writer. Her novel *The Awakening* 1899 is now regarded as a classic of feminist sensibility.

Chou En-lai former name for Chinese politician ◊Zhou Enlai.

Chrétien de Troyes medieval French poet, born in Champagne about the middle of the 12th century. His epics, which include *Le Chevalier de la Charrette*; *Perceval*, written for Philip, Count of Flanders; *Erec*; *Yvain*; and other Arthurian romances, introduced the concept of the Holy Grail.

Christ (Greek *khristos* 'anointed one') the Messiah as prophesied in the Hebrew Bible, or Old Testament. See ◊Jesus.

Christian ten kings of Denmark and Norway, including:

Christian I 1426–1481. King of Denmark from 1448, and founder of the Oldenburg dynasty. In 1450 he established the union of Denmark and Norway that lasted until 1814.

Christian III 1503–1559. King of Denmark and Norway from 1535. Under his reign the Reformation was introduced.

Christian IV 1577–1648. King of Denmark and Norway from 1588. He sided with the Protestants in the Thirty Years' War (1618–48), and founded Christiania (now Oslo, capital of Norway). He was succeeded by Frederick II 1648.

Christian VIII 1786–1848. King of Denmark 1839–48. He was unpopular because of his opposition to reform. His attempt to encourage the Danish language and culture in Schleswig and Holstein led to an insurrection there shortly after his death. He was succeeded by Frederick VII.

Christian IX 1818–1906. King of Denmark from 1863. His daughter Alexandra married Edward VII of the UK and another, Dagmar, married Tsar Alexander III of Russia; his second son, George, became king of Greece. In 1864 he lost the duchies of Schleswig and Holstein after a war with Austria and Prussia.

Christian X 1870–1947. King of Denmark and Iceland from 1912, when he succeeded his father Frederick VIII. He married Alexandrine, Duchess of Mecklenburg-Schwerin, and was popular for his democratic attitude. During World War II he was held prisoner by the Germans in Copenhagen. He was succeeded by Frederick IX.

Christie Agatha 1890–1976. English detective novelist who created the characters Hercule Poirot and Miss Jane Marple. Her prolific output included the novels *The Murder of Roger Ackroyd* 1926 and *Ten Little Indians* 1939, and the play *The Mousetrap* 1952.

Born in Torquay as Agatha Miller, she married Colonel Archibald Christie 1914 and served during World War I as a nurse. Her first crime novel, *The Mysterious Affair at Styles* 1920, introduced Hercule Poirot. She often broke 'purist' rules, as in *The Murder of Roger Ackroyd* 1926 in which the narrator is the murderer. She caused a nationwide sensation 1926 by disappearing for ten days (possibly because of amnesia) when her husband fell in love with another woman. After a divorce 1928, she married the archaeologist Max Mallowan (1904–78) 1930.

Christie Julie 1940– . British film actress, who became a star in the 1960s following her award-winning performance in *Darling* 1965. She also appeared in *Doctor Zhivago* 1965; *The Go-Between* 1971; *Don't Look Now* 1973; *Memoirs of a Survivor* 1982; and *Power* 1986.

Christina 1626–1689. Queen of Sweden 1632–54. Succeeding her father Gustavus Adolphus at the age of six, she assumed power 1644, but disagreed with the former regent ◊Oxenstjerna. Refusing to marry, she eventually nominated her cousin Charles Gustavus (Charles X) as her successor. As a secret convert to Roman Catholicism, which was then illegal in Sweden, she had to abdicate 1654, and went to live in Rome, twice returning to Sweden unsuccessfully to claim the throne.

Christine de Pisan 1364–1430. French poet and historian. Her works include love lyrics, philosophical poems, a poem in praise of Joan of Arc, a history of Charles V, and various defences of women, including *La cité des dames/The City of Ladies*.

Born in Venice, she was brought to France as a child when her father entered the service of Charles V. In 1389, after the death of her husband, the Picardian nobleman Etienne Castel, she began writing to support herself and her family,

Christo adopted name of Christo Javacheff 1935– . US sculptor, born in Bulgaria, active in Paris in the 1950s and in New York from 1964. He is known for his wrapped works: structures such as bridges and buildings, and even areas of coastline, are temporarily wrapped in synthetic fabric tied down with rope. The *Running Fence* 1976 across California was another temporary work.

Christoff Boris 1918– . Bulgarian bass who made his operatic debut in 1946. His roles included Boris Godunov, Ivan the Terrible, and Mephistopheles.

Christophe Henri 1767–1820. West Indian slave, one of the leaders of the revolt against the French 1791, who was proclaimed king of Haiti 1811. His government distributed plantations to military leaders. He shot himself when his troops deserted him because of his alleged cruelty.

Christopher, St the patron saint of travellers. His feast day on 25 July was dropped from the Roman Catholic liturgical calendar 1969.

Traditionally he was a martyr in Syria in the 3rd century, and legend describes his carrying the Christ child over the stream; despite his great strength he found the burden increasingly heavy, and was told that the child was Christ bearing the sins of all the world.

Chukovsky Kornei Ivanovitch 1882–1969. Russian critic and poet. The leading authority on the 19th century Russian poet Nekrasov, he was also an expert on the Russian language, for example *Zhivoi kak zhizn/A Life as Life* 1963, and beloved as 'Grandpa' Kornei Chukovsky for his nonsense poems which owe much to the English nursery rhymes and nonsense verse that he admired.

Chun Doo-hwan 1931– . South Korean military ruler who seized power 1979; president 1981–88 as head of the newly formed Democratic Justice Party.

Chun, trained in Korea and the USA, served as an army commander from 1967 and was in charge of military intelligence 1979 when President Park was assassinated by the chief of the Korean Central Intelligence Agency (KCIA). Gen Chun took charge of the KCIA and, in a coup, assumed control of the army and the South Korean government. In 1981 Chun was appointed president, and oversaw a period of rapid economic growth, governing in an authoritarian manner.

Church Frederic Edwin 1826–1900. US painter, a follower of the Hudson River school's style of grand landscape. During the 1850s he visited South America and the Arctic.

Churchill Caryl 1938– . British playwright, whose predominantly radical and feminist works include *Cloud Nine* 1979, *Top Girls* 1982, and *Serious Money* 1987.

Churchill Charles 1731–1764. British satiric poet. Once a priest in the Church of England, he wrote coarse and highly personal satires dealing with political issues.

Churchill Randolph (Henry Spencer) 1849–1895. British Conservative politician, chancellor of the Exchequer and leader of the House of Commons 1886, father of Winston Churchill.

Born at Blenheim Palace, son of the 7th duke of Marlborough, he entered Parliament 1874. In 1880 he formed a Conservative group known as the Fourth Party with Drummond Wolff (1830–1908), J E Gorst, and Arthur Balfour, and in 1885 his policy of Tory democracy was widely accepted by the party. In 1886 he became chancellor of the Exchequer, but resigned within six months because he did not agree with the demands made on the Treasury by the War Office and the Admiralty. In 1874, he married Jennie Jerome (1854–1921), daughter of a wealthy New Yorker.

Churchill Winston (Leonard Spencer) 1874–1965. British Conservative politician. In Parliament from 1900, as a Liberal until 1923, he held a number of ministerial offices, including First Lord of the Admiralty 1911–15 and chancellor of the Exchequer 1924–29. Absent from the cabinet in the 1930s, he returned Sept 1939 to lead a coalition government 1940–45, negotiating with Allied leaders in World War II; he was again prime minister 1951–55. Nobel Prize for Literature 1953.

He was born at Blenheim Palace, the elder son of Lord Randolph Churchill. During the Boer War he was a war correspondent and made a dramatic escape from imprisonment in Pretoria. In 1900 he was elected Conservative Member of Parliament for Oldham, but he disagreed with Chamberlain's tariff-reform policy, and joined the Liberals. Asquith made him president of the Board of Trade 1908, where he introduced legislation for the establishment of labour exchanges. He became home secretary 1910.

In 1911 Asquith appointed him First Lord of the Admiralty. In 1915–16 he served in the trenches in France, but then resumed his parliamentary duties and was minister of munitions under Lloyd George 1917, when he was concerned with the development of the tank. After the armistice he was secretary for war 1918–21, and then as colonial secretary played a leading part in the establishment of the Irish Free State. During the post-war years he was active in support of the Whites (anti-Bolsheviks) in Russia.

In 1922–24 Churchill was out of Parliament. He left the Liberals 1923, and was returned for Epping as a Constitutionalist 1924. Baldwin made him chancellor of the Exchequer, andm he brought about Britain's return to the gold standard and was prominent in the defeat of the General Strike of 1926. In 1929–39 he was out of office as he disagreed with the Conservatives on India, rearmament, and Chamberlain's policy of appeasement.

On the first day of World War II he went back to his old post at the Admiralty. In May 1940 he was called to the premiership as head of an all-party administration and made a much-quoted 'blood, tears, toil, and sweat' speech to the House of Commons. He had a close relationship with US president Roosevelt, reflected in the Atlantic Charter they concluded in Aug 1941. He travelled to Washington, Casablanca, Cairo, Moscow, and Tehran, meeting the other leaders of the Allied war effort. In Feb 1945 he met Stalin and Roosevelt in the Crimea and agreed on the final plans for victory. On 8 May he announced the unconditional surrender of Germany.

On 23 May 1945 the coalition was dissolved, and Churchill formed a caretaker government drawn mainly from the Conservatives. Defeated in the general election in July, he became leader of the opposition until the election Oct 1951, in which he again became prime minister. In Apr 1955 he resigned. His home from 1922, Chartwell in Kent, is a museum.

His books include a six-volume history of World War II (1948–54) and a four-volume *History of the English-Speaking Peoples* (1956–58).

Ciano Galeazzo 1903–1944. Italian Fascist politician. Son-in-law of Mussolini, he was foreign minister 1936–43, when his loyalty became suspect. He voted against Mussolini at the meeting of the Grand Council 25 July 1943 that overthrew the dictator, but was later tried for treason and shot by the Fascists.

Cicero 106–43 BC. Roman orator, writer, and statesman. His speeches, and philosophical and rhetorical works are models of Latin prose, and his letters provide a picture of contemporary Roman life. As consul 63 BC he exposed Catiline's conspiracy in four major orations.

Born in Arpinium, Cicero became an advocate in Rome, spent three years in Greece studying

Churchill *British Conservative politician Winston Churchill, 1955.*

oratory, and after the dictator Sulla's death distinguished himself in Rome on the side of the popular party. When the First Triumvirate was formed 59, Cicero was exiled and devoted himself to literature. He sided with Pompey during the civil war (49–48 BC) but was pardoned by Caesar and returned to Rome. After Caesar's assassination 44 he supported Octavian (the future Emperor Augustus) and violently attacked Antony in speeches known as the Philippics. On the reconciliation of Antony and Octavian he was executed by Antony's agents.

Cid Rodrigo Díaz de Bivar 1040–1099. Spanish soldier, nicknamed *El Cid* ('the lord') by the Moors. Born in Castile of a noble family, he fought against the king of Navarre, and won his nickname *el Campeador* (the Champion) by killing the Navarrese champion in single combat. Essentially a mercenary, fighting both with and against the Moors, he died while defending Valencia against them, and in subsequent romances became Spain's national hero.

Cierva Juan de la 1895–1936. Spanish engineer. In trying to produce an aircraft that would not stall and could fly slowly, he invented the autogyro, the forerunner of the helicopter, but differing from it in having unpowered rotors that revolve freely.

Cimabue Giovanni (Cenni de Peppi) *c.*1240–1302. Italian painter, active in Florence, traditionally styled the 'father of Italian painting'. Among the works attributed to him are *Madonna and Child* (Uffizi, Florence), a huge Gothic image of the Virgin which nevertheless has a new softness and solidity that leads forwards to Giotto.

Cimarosa Domenico 1749–1801. Italian composer of operas that include *Il Matrimonio segreto/The Secret Marriage* 1792.

Cimino Michael 1943– . US film director, who established his reputation with *The Deer Hunter* 1978 (which won five Academy Awards). His other films include *Heaven's Gate* 1981, and *The Year of the Dragon* 1986.

Cincinnatus Lucius Quintus lived 5th century BC. Early Roman general. Appointed dictator in 458 BC he defeated the Aequi (an Italian people) in a brief campaign, then resumed life as a yeoman farmer.

Clair René, pseudonym of René-Lucien Chomette 1898–1981. French film-maker, originally a poet, novelist, and journalist. His *Sous les Toits de Paris/Under the Roofs of Paris* 1930 was one of the first sound films.

Clapperton Hugh 1788–1827. English explorer who crossed the Sahara from Tripli with Dixon Denham and discovered Lake Chad 1823. With his servant, Richard Lander, he attempted to reach the Niger, but died at Sokoto. Lander eventually reached the mouth of the river Niger in 1830.

Clapton Eric 1945– . English blues and rock guitarist, singer, and composer, member of the groups Yardbirds and Cream in the 1960s. One of the pioneers of heavy rock and an influence on younger musicians, he later adopted a more subdued style.

Clare John 1793–1864. English poet. His work includes *Poems Descriptive of Rural Life* 1820, *The Village Minstrel* 1821, and *Shepherd's Calendar* 1827. Clare's work was largely rediscovered in the 20th century.

Born at Helpstone, near Peterborough, the son of a farm labourer, Clare spent most of his life in poverty. He was given an annuity from the Duke of Exeter and other patrons, but had to turn to work on the land. He spent his last 20 years in Northampton asylum. His early life is described in his autobiography, first published 1931.

Clarence English ducal title, which has been conferred on a number of princes. The last was Albert Victor 1864–92, eldest son of Edward VII.

Clarendon Edward Hyde, 1st Earl of Clarendon 1609–1674. English politician and historian, chief adviser to Charles II 1651–67. A member of Parliament 1640, he joined the Royalist side 1641. The *Clarendon Code* (1661–65) was designed to secure the supremacy of the Church of England.

In 1641 he broke with the revolutionary party and became one of the royal advisers. When civil war began he followed Charles to Oxford, and was knighted and made chancellor of the Exchequer. On the king's defeat in 1646 he followed Prince Charles to Jersey, where he began his *History of the Rebellion*, published 1702–04, which provides memorable portraits of his contemporaries.

In 1651 he became chief adviser to the exiled Charles II. At the Restoration he was created earl of Clarendon, while his influence was further increased by the marriage of his daughter Anne to James, Duke of York. His moderation earned the hatred of the extremists, however, and he lost Charles's support by openly expressing disapproval of the king's private life. After the disasters of the Dutch war 1667, he went into exile.

Clarendon George William Frederick Villiers, 4th Earl of Clarendon 1800–1870. British Liberal diplomat, Lord Lieutenant of Ireland 1847–52, foreign secretary 1853–58, 1865–66, and 1868–70.

Clare, St *c.* 1194–1253. Christian saint. Born in Assisi, Italy, she became at 18 a follower of St Francis, who founded for her the convent of San Damiano. Here she gathered the first members of the *Order of Poor Clares*. In 1958 she was proclaimed by Pius XII the patron saint of television, since in 1252 she saw from her convent sickbed the services celebrating Christmas in the basilica of St Francis in Assisi. Feast day 12 Aug.

Clark James 'Jim' 1936–1968. Scottish-born motor racing driver, one of the finest in the post-war era. He was twice world champion in 1963 and 1965. He spent all his Formula One career with Lotus.

His partnership with Lotus boss Colin Chapman was one of the closest in the sport. He won 25 Formula One Grand Prix races, a record at the time, before losing his life at Hockenheim, West Germany, in April 1968 during a Formula Two race.

Clark Joe (Joseph) Charles 1939– . Canadian Progressive Conservative politician, born in Alberta. He became party leader 1976, and in May 1979 defeated ◊Trudeau at the polls to become the youngest prime minister in Canada's history. Following the rejection of his government's budget, he was defeated in a second election Feb 1980. He became Secretary of State for External Affairs (foreign minister) in the ◊Mulroney government from 1984.

Clark Kenneth, Lord Clark 1903–1983. British art historian, director of the National Gallery, London, 1934–45. He popularized the history of art through his television series *Civilisation* 1969. His books include *Leonardo da Vinci* 1939 and *The Nude* 1956.

Clark Mark (Wayne) 1896–1984. US general in World War II. In 1942 he became chief of staff for ground forces, led a successful secret mission by submarine to get information in N Africa preparatory to the Allied invasion, and commanded the 5th Army in the invasion of Italy. He was commander in chief of the United Nations forces in the Korean War 1952–53.

Clarke Arthur C(harles) 1917– . English science fiction and non-fiction writer, who originated the plan for the modern system of communications satellites 1945. His works include *Childhood's End* 1953 and the screenplay of *2001: A Space Odyssey* 1968.

Clarke Jeremiah 1659–1707. English composer. Organist at St Paul's, he composed 'The Prince of Denmark's March', a harpsichord piece that was arranged by Sir Henry ◊Wood as a 'Trumpet Voluntary' and wrongly attributed to Purcell.

Clarke Kenneth (Harry) 1940– . British Conservative politician, member of Parliament from 1970, a cabinet minister from 1985, and minister of Health from 1988.

Clarke was politically active as a law student at Cambridge. He was elected to Parliament for Rushcliff, Nottinghamshire, in 1970. In 1982 he became a minister of state, in 1985 paymaster general, with special responsibility for employment, in 1987 chancellor of the Duchy of Lancaster, and in 1988 was given the newly independent Department of Health. Clarke was once secretary of the left-of-centre Bow Group.

Clarke Marcus Andrew Hislop 1846–1881. Australian writer. Born in London, he went to Australia when he was 18, and worked as a journalist in Victoria. He wrote *For the Term of his Natural Life* in 1874, a novel dealing with life in the early Australian prison settlements.

Clarke Ron (ald William) 1937– . Australian middle- and long-distance runner. A prolific record breaker, he broke 17 world records ranging from 2 miles to the one-hour run.

The first man to break 13 min for the 3 miles (1966), he was also the first to better 28 min for the 10,000 metres. Despite his record-breaking achievements, he never won a gold medal at a major championship.

Clarkson Thomas 1760–1846. British philanthropist. From 1785 he devoted himself to a campaign against slavery. He was one of the founders of the Anti-Slavery Society 1823 and was largely responsible for the abolition of slavery in British colonies 1833.

Claude Georges 1870–1960. French industrial chemist, responsible for inventing neon signs. He discovered in 1896 that acetylene, normally explosive, could be safely transported when disolved in acetone. He later demonstrated that neon gas could be used to provide a bright red light in signs. These were displayed publicly for the first time at the Paris Motor Show 1910.

As an old man, Claude spent the period 1945–49 in prison as a collaborator.

Claudel Paul 1868–1955. French poet and dramatist. A fervent Catholic, he was influenced by the Symbolists and achieved an effect of mystic allegory in such plays as *L'Annonce faite à Marie/Tidings Brought to Mary* 1912 and *Le Soulier de satin/The Satin Slipper* 1929, set in 16th-century Spain. His verse includes *Cinq Grandes Odes/Five Great Odes* 1910.

Claude Lorrain (Claude Gellée) 1600–1682. French landscape painter, active in Rome from 1627. His distinctive, luminous, Classical style had great influence on late 17th- and 18th-century taste. His subjects are mostly mythological and historical, with insignificant figures lost in great expanses of poetic scenery, as in *The Enchanted Castle* 1664 (National Gallery, London).

Claudian or *Claudius Claudianus* c.370–404. Last of the great Latin poets of the Roman empire. He was probably born at Alexandria, and wrote official panegyrics, epigrams, and the epic *The Rape of Proserpine*.

Claudius Tiberius Claudius Nero 10 BC–AD 54. Nephew of ◊Tiberius, made Roman emperor by his troops AD 41, after the murder of his nephew Caligula. Claudius was a scholar, historian, and able administrator. During his reign the Roman Empire was considerably extended, and in 43 he took part in the invasion of Britain.

Lame and suffering from a speech impediment, he was frequently an object of ridicule. He was dominated by his third wife, ◊Messalina, whom he ultimately had executed, and is thought to have been poisoned by his fourth wife, Agrippina the Younger. His life is described by the novelist Robert Graves in his books *I Claudius* 1934 and *Claudius the God* 1934.

Clausewitz Karl von 1780–1831. Prussian officer and writer on war, born near Magdeburg. He is known mainly for his book *Vom Kriege/On War* 1833. Translated into English 1873, the book gave a new philosophical foundation to the science of war, and put forward a concept of strategy that was influential until World War I.

Clausius Rudolf Julius Emanuel 1822–1888. German physicist, one of the founders of the science of thermodynamics. In 1850, he enunciated its second law: heat cannot of itself pass from a colder to a hotter body.

Claverhouse John Graham, Viscount Dundee 1649–1689. Scottish soldier. Appointed by Charles II to suppress the Covenanters from 1677, he was routed at Drumclog 1679, but three weeks later won the battle of Bothwell Bridge, by which the rebellion was crushed. Until 1688 he was engaged in continued persecution and became known as 'Bloody Clavers', regarded by the Scottish people as a figure of evil. Then his army joined the first Jacobite rebellion and defeated the loyalist forces in the pass of Killiecrankie, where he was mortally wounded.

Clay Cassius Marcellus original name of boxer Muhammad ◊Ali.

Clay Frederic 1838–1889. British composer. Born in Paris, he wrote light operas and the cantata *Lalla Rookh* 1877, based on the poem by Thomas Moore.

Clay Henry 1777–1852. US politician. He stood three times unsuccessfully for the presidency, as a Democratic-Republican 1824, as a National Republican 1832, and as a Whig 1844. He supported the War of 1812 against Britain, and tried to hold the Union together on the slavery issue by the Missouri Compromise of 1820, and again in the compromise of 1850. He was secretary of state 1825–29, and is also remembered for his 'American system', which favoured the national bank, internal improvements to facilitate commercial and industrial development, and the raising of protective tariffs.

Clay Lucius DuBignon 1897–1978. US commander-in chief of the US occupation forces in Germany 1947–49. He broke the Soviet blockade of Berlin 1948 after 327 days, with an *airlift* – a term he brought into general use – which involved bringing all supplies into West Berlin by air.

Clayton Jack 1921–   . British film director, originally a producer. His first feature, *Room at the Top* 1958, heralded a new maturity in British cinema. Other works include *The Great Gatsby* 1974; *The Lonely Passion of Judith Hearne* 1987.

Cleese John 1939–   . English actor and comedian. For television he has written for and/or appeared in the satirical *That Was The Week That Was* and *The Frost Report*, and the comic *Monty Python's Flying Circus* and *Fawlty Towers*. His films include *A Fish Called Wanda* 1988.

Cleisthenes ruler of Athens. Inspired by Solon, he is credited with the establishment of democracy in Athens 507 BC.

Cleland John 1709–1789. English author. He wrote *Fanny Hill, the Memoirs of a Woman of Pleasure* 1748–49 to try to extract himself from the grip of his London creditors. The book was considered immoral, and Cleland was called before the Privy Council, but was granted a pension to prevent further misdemeanours.

Clemenceau Georges 1841–1929. French politician and journalist (prominent in the defence of ◊Dreyfus). He was prime minister 1906–09 and 1917–20. After World War I he presided over the Peace Conference in Paris that drew up the Treaty of ◊Versailles, but failed to secure for France the Rhine as a frontier.

Clemenceau was mayor of Montmartre, Paris, in the war of 1870, and in 1871 was elected a member of the National Assembly at Bordeaux. He was elected a deputy in 1876 after the formation of the Third Republic. An extreme radical, he soon earned the nickname of 'the Tiger' on account of his ferocious attacks on politicians whom he disliked. In 1893 he lost his seat and spent the next ten years in journalism. In 1902 he was elected senator for the Var, and was soon one of the most powerful politicians in France. He became prime minister for the second time in 1917, and made the decisive appointment of Marshal ◊Foch as supreme commander.

Clemens Samuel Langhorne. Real name of the US writer Mark ◊Twain.

Clement VII 1478–1534. Pope 1523–34. He refused to allow the divorce of Henry VIII of England and Catherine of Aragon. Illegitimate son of a brother of Lorenzo di Medici, the ruler of Florence, he commissioned monuments for the Medici chapel in Florence from the Renaissance artist Michelangelo.

Clemente Roberto (Walker) 1934–1972. Puerto Rican baseball player, born in Carolina, who played for the Pittsburgh Pirates 1955–72. He had a career batting average of 0.317, was the 11th player in history to reach 3,000 hits, and was a right fielder of outstanding talent. He died in a plane crash while flying to aid Nicaraguan earthquake victims.

Clementi Muzio 1752–1832. Italian pianist and composer. He settled in London in 1782 as a teacher and then as proprietor of a successful pianoforte and music business. He was the founder of the new technique of piano playing, and his series of studies, *Gradus ad Parnassum* 1817 is still in use.

Clement of Alexandria c. AD 150–c. 215. Greek theologian who applied Greek philosophical ideas to Christian doctrine, and was the teacher of the theologian Origen.

Clement of Rome, St late 1st century AD. One of the early Christian leaders and writers known as the Fathers of the Church. According to tradition he was the third or fourth bishop of Rome, and a disciple of St Peter. He wrote a letter addressed to the church at Corinth (First Epistle of Clement), and many other writings have been attributed to him.

Clements John 1910–   . British actor and director, whose productions included revivals of Restoration comedies and the plays of G B Shaw.

Cleon Athenian demagogue and military leader in the Peloponnesian War (431–404 BC). After the death of Pericles, to whom he was opposed, he won power as representative of the commercial classes and leader of the party, advocating a vigorous war policy. He was killed fighting the Spartans at Amphipolis.

Cleopatra c.68–30 BC. Queen of Egypt 51–48 BC and 47–30 BC. When Julius Caesar arrived in Egypt, he restored her to the throne from which she had been ousted in favour of her brother, Ptolemy XIII, and Ptolemy was killed. Cleopatra became Caesar's mistress, returned with him to Rome, and gave birth to a son, Caesarion. After Caesar's assassination 44 BC she returned to Alexandria and resumed her position as queen of Egypt. In 41 BC she met Mark Antony, and subsequently bore him three sons. In 32 BC Rome declared war on Egypt and scored a decisive victory in the naval Battle of Actium off the W coast of Greece 31 BC. Cleopatra fled with her 60 ships to Egypt; Antony abandoned the struggle and followed her. Both he and Cleopatra committed suicide.

Cleopatra was Macedonian, and the last ruler of the Macedonian dynasty, which ruled Egypt from 323 BC until annexation by Rome 31 BC. She succeeded her father jointly with her younger brother Ptolemy XIII, whom she married according to Pharaonic custom. Shakespeare's play *Antony and Cleopatra* recounts how Cleopatra killed herself with an asp (poisonous snake) after Antony's suicide.

Cleveland (Stephen) Grover 1837–1908. 22nd and 24th president of the USA, 1885–89 and 1893–97; the first Democratic president elected after the Civil War, and the only president to hold office for two nonconsecutive terms. He attempted to check corruption in public life, and in 1895 initiated arbitration proceedings that eventually settled a territorial dispute with Britain concerning the Venezuelan boundary.

Cliff Clarice 1899–1972. English pottery designer. Her Bizarre ware, characterized by brightly coloured floral and geometric decoration on often geometrically shaped china, became increasingly popular in the 1930s.

Clift (Edward) Montgomery 1920–1966. US film and theatre actor. A star of the late 1940s and 1950s in films such as *Red River* 1948 and *A Place in the Sun* 1951, he was disfigured in a car accident in 1957 but continued to make films. He played the title role in *Freud* 1962.

Clive Robert, Baron Clive of Plassey 1725–1774. British general and administrator, who established British rule in India by victories over the French at Arcot in the Carnatic (a region in SE India) 1751 and over the nawab of Bengal, Suraj-ud-Dowlah, at Calcutta and Plassey 1757. On his return to Britain his wealth led to allegations that he had abused his power.

Clouet François *c.* 1515–1572. French portrait painter, who succeeded his father Jean Clouet as court painter. He worked in the Italian style of Mannerism. His half-nude portrait of Diane de Poitiers, *The Lady in her Bath* 1499–1566 (National Gallery, Washington), is also thought to to be a likeness of Marie Touchet, mistress of Charles IX.

Clouet Jean (known as *Janet*) 1486–1541. French artist, court painter to Francis I. His portraits, often compared to Holbein's, show an outstanding naturalism, particularly his drawings.

Clough Arthur Hugh 1819–1861. English poet. Many of his lyrics are marked by a melancholy scepticism that reflects his struggle with his religious doubt.

Clovis 465–511. Merovingian king of the Franks from 481. He succeeded his father Childeric as king of the Salian (northern) Franks, defeated the Gallo-Romans (Romanized Gauls) near Soissons 486, ending their rule in France, and defeated the Alemanni, a confederation of Germanic tribes, near Cologne 496. He embraced Christianity and subsequently proved a powerful defender of orthodoxy against the Arian Visigoths, whom he defeated at Poitiers 507. He made Paris his capital.

Clunies-Ross family that established a benevolently paternal rule in the Cocos Islands. John Clunies-Ross settled on Home Island in 1827: the family's rule ended in 1978 with the purchase of the Cocos by the Australian government.

Coates Eric 1886–1957. English composer. He is remembered for the orchestral suites *London* 1933, including the 'Knightsbridge' march; 'By the Sleepy Lagoon' 1939; 'The Dam Busters March' 1942; and the songs 'Bird Songs at Eventide' and 'The Green Hills of Somerset'.

Cobb Ty(rus Raymond), nicknamed 'the Georgia Peach' 1886–1961. US baseball player, one of the greatest batters and base runners of all time. He played for Detroit and Philadelphia 1905–28, and won the American League batting average championship 12 times. He holds the all-time record for runs scored, 2,254, and batting average, .367. He had 4,191 hits in his career, a record that stood for almost 60 years.

Cobbett William 1763–1835. British Radical politician and journalist, who published the weekly *Political Register* 1802–35. He spent much time in North America. His crusading essays on farmers' conditions were collected as *Rural Rides* 1830.

Born in Surrey, the self-taught son of a farmer, Cobbett enlisted in the army 1784 and saw service in Canada. He subsequently lived in the USA as a teacher of English, and became a vigorous pamphleteer, at this time supporting the Tories. In 1800 he returned to England. With increasing knowledge of the sufferings of the farm labourers, he became a Radical and leader of the working-class movement. He was imprisoned 1809–11 for criticizing the flogging of British troops by German mercenaries. He visited the USA again 1817–19. He became a strong advocate of parliamentary reform, and represented Oldham in the Reformed Parliament after 1832.

Cobden Richard 1804–1865. British Liberal politician and economist, co-founder with John Bright of the Anti-Corn Law League 1839. A member of Parliament from 1841, he opposed class and religious privileges and believed in disarmament and free trade.

Born in Sussex, the son of a farmer, Cobden became a calico manufacturer in Manchester. With other businessmen he founded the Anti-Corn Law League and began his lifelong association with John Bright, until 1845 devoting himself to the repeal of the Corn Laws. A typical early Victorian radical, he believed in the abolition of privileges, a minimum of government interference, and the securing of international peace through free trade and by disarmament and arbitration. He opposed trade unionism and most of the factory legislation of his time, because he regarded them as opposed to liberty of contract. His opposition to the Crimean War made him unpopular. He was largely responsible for the commercial treaty with France in 1860.

Cobden-Sanderson Thomas James 1840–1922. British bookbinder and painter. Influenced by William ◊Morris and ◊Burne-Jones, he opened his own workshop in Maiden Lane, Strand, London, 1884.

Coburn James 1928– . US film actor, popular in the 1960s and 1970s. His films include *The Magnificent Seven* 1960, *Our Man Flint* 1966, and *Cross of Iron* 1977.

Cochran C(harles) B(lake) 1872–1951. British impresario who promoted entertainment ranging from wrestling and roller-skating to Diaghilev's *Ballets Russes*.

Cockcroft John Douglas 1897–1967. British physicist. In 1932, he and E T S Walton succeeded in splitting the nucleus of the atom for the first time. In 1951 they were jointly awarded a Nobel prize.

Born in Todmorden, W Yorkshire, Cockcroft held an engineering appointment with Metropolitan-Vickers, and took up research work under ◊Rutherford at the Cavendish Laboratory, Cambridge. He succeeded ◊Appleton as Jacksonian professor of natural philosophy, Cambridge (1939–46), and did work on the atomic bomb during World War II.

Cockerell Charles Robert 1788–1863. English architect, whose works display a logical, assured classicism inspired by ancient Greece. Their finesse parallels that of the French *Beaux-Arts*. His buildings include the Ashmolean Museum, Oxford (1839–45), and Bank of England branch buildings in Manchester and Liverpool (begun 1845).

Cockerell Christopher 1910– . British engineer, who invented the hovercraft 1959.

From a first interest in radio, he switched to electronics, working with the Marconi Company from 1935 to 1950. In 1953 he began work on the hovercraft, carrying out his early experiments on Oulton Broad, Norfolk.

Cocteau Jean 1889–1963. French poet, dramatist, and film director. A leading figure in European modernism, he worked with Picasso, Diaghilev, and Stravinsky. He produced many volumes of poetry, ballets such as *Le Boeuf sur le toit/The Nothing Doing Bar* 1920, plays, for example, *Orphée/Orpheus* 1926, and a mature novel of bourgeois French life, *Les Enfants terribles/Children of the Game* 1929, which he made into a film 1950.

Coe Sebastian 1956– . English middle-distance runner. He was Olympic 1500 metre champion 1980 and 1984. Between 1979 and 1981 he broke eight individual world records at 800 m, 1000 m, 1500 m, and one mile.

Coetzee J(ohn) M 1940– . South African author whose novel *In the Heart of the Country* 1975 dealt with the rape of a white woman by a black man. In 1983 he won the Booker Prize for *The Life and Times of Michael K.*

Coke Edward 1552–1634. Lord Chief Justice of England 1613–17. Against Charles I he drew up the Petition of Right 1628 to curb the king's power. His *Institutes* are a legal classic, and he ranks as the supreme common lawyer.

Coke was called to the Bar in 1578, and in 1592 became speaker of the House of Commons and solicitor-general. As attorney-general from 1594 he conducted the prosecution of Elizabeth I's former favourites Essex and Raleigh, and of the Gunpowder Plot conspirators. In 1606 he became Chief Justice of the Common Pleas, and began his struggle, as champion of the common law, against James I's attempts to exalt the royal prerogative. An attempt to silence him by promoting him to the dignity of Lord Chief Justice proved unsuccessful, and from 1620 he led the parliamentary opposition and the attack on Charles I's adviser Buckingham.

Coke Thomas William 1754–1842. English pioneer and promoter of the improvements associated with the Agricultural Revolution. His innovations included regular manuring of the soil, the cultivation of fodder crops in association with corn, and the drilling of wheat and turnips.

He also developed a fine flock of Southdown sheep at Holkham, Norfolk, which were superior to the native Norfolks, and encouraged his farm tenants to do likewise. These ideas attracted attention at the annual sheep shearings, an early form of agricultural show, which Coke held on his home farm from 1776. By the end of the century these had become major events, with many visitors coming to see and discuss new stock, crops, and equipment.

Colbert Claudette. Stage name of Claudette Lily Cauchoin 1905– . French-born film actress, who lived in Hollywood from childhood. She was ideally cast in sophisticated, romantic roles, but had a natural instinct for comedy and appeared in several of Hollywood's finest, including *It Happened One Night* 1934 and *The Palm Beach Story* 1942.

Colbert Jean-Baptiste 1619–1683. French politician, chief minister to Louis XIV, and controller-general (finance minister) from 1665. He reformed the Treasury, promoted French industry and commerce by protectionist measures, and tried to make France a naval power equal to England or the Netherlands, while favouring a peaceful foreign policy.

Colbert, born in Reims, entered the service of Cardinal Mazarin and succeeded him as chief minister to Louis XIV. In 1661 he set to work to reform the Treasury. The national debt was largely repaid, and the system of tax collection was drastically reformed. Industry was brought under state control, shipbuilding was encouraged by bounties, companies were established to trade with India and America, and colonies were founded in Louisiana, Guiana, and Madagascar. In his later years Colbert was supplanted in Louis's favour by the war minister Louvois (1641–91), who supported a policy of conquests.

Cole Thomas 1801–1848. US painter, founder of the *Hudson River school* of landscape artists.

Cole wrote *An Essay on American Scenery* in 1835. Apart from panoramic views such as *The Oxbow* 1836 (Metropolitan Museum of Art, New York), he painted a dramatic historical series, *The Course of the Empire* 1830s, influenced by Claude, Turner, and John Martin.

Coleman Ornette 1930– . US alto saxophonist and jazz composer. In the late 1950s he rejected the established structural principles of jazz for free avant-garde improvisation.

Colenso John William 1814–1883. Bishop of Natal, South Africa, from 1853. He was the first to write down the Zulu language. He championed the Zulu way of life (including polygamy) in relation to Christianity, and applied Christian morality to race relations in South Africa.

Coleridge Samuel Taylor 1772–1834. English poet, one of the founders of the Romantic movement. A friend of Southey and Wordsworth, he collaborated with the latter on *Lyrical Ballads* 1798. His poems include 'The Ancient Mariner', 'Christabel', and 'Kubla Khan'; critical works include *Biographia Literaria* 1817.

While at Cambridge, Coleridge was driven by debt to enlist in the Dragoons, and then in 1795, as part of an abortive plan to found a communist colony in the USA with Robert Southey, married Sarah Fricker, from whom he afterwards separated. He became addicted to opium and from 1816 lived at Highgate under medical care. As a philosopher, he argued inferentially that even in registering sense-perceptions the mind was performing acts of creative imagination, rather than being a passive arena in which ideas interacted mechanistically. As a critic, he used psychological insight to brilliant effect in his *Biographia Literaria* and Shakespearean criticism.

Coleridge-Taylor Samuel 1875–1912. English composer, the son of a West African doctor and an English mother. He wrote the cantata *Hiawatha's Wedding Feast* 1898, a setting in three parts of Longfellow's poem. He was a student and champion of traditional black music.

Colet John *c.*1467–1519. English humanist, influenced by the Italian reformer Savonarola and the Dutch scholar Erasmus. He reacted against the scholastic tradition in his interpretation of the Bible, and founded modern biblical exegesis. In 1505 he became dean of St Paul's Cathedral, London.

Colette Sidonie-Gabrielle 1873–1954. French writer. At 20 she married Henri Gauthier-Villars, a journalist known as 'Willy'. Her four 'Claudine' novels, based on her own early life, were written under her husband's direction and signed by him. Divorced in 1906, she was a striptease and mime artist for a while, but continued to write, for example, *Chéri* 1920, *La Fin de Chéri/The End of Chéri* 1926, and *Gigi* 1944.

Coligny Gaspard de 1517–1572. French admiral and soldier, and prominent Huguenot. About 1557 he joined the Protestant party, helping to lead the Huguenot forces during the Wars of Religion. After the Treaty of St Germain 1570, he became a favourite of the young king Charles IX, but was killed on the first night of the massacre of St Bartholomew.

Collier Jeremy 1650–1726. British Anglican cleric, a Nonjuror (refusing to take the oath of allegiance to William and Mary), who was outlawed 1696 for granting absolution on the scaffold to two men who had tried to assassinate William III. His *Short View of the Immorality and Profaneness of the English Stage* 1698 was aimed at the dramatists Congreve and Vanbrugh.

Collier Lesley 1947– . British ballerina, a principal dancer of the Royal Ballet from 1972.

She had major roles in MacMillan's *Anastasia* 1971, and *Four Seasons* 1975, van Manen's *Four Schumann Pieces* 1975, Ashton's *Rhapsody* and Tetley's *Dance of Albion* both 1980.

Collingwood Cuthbert, Baron Collingwood 1748–1810. British admiral, who served with Horatio Nelson in the West Indies against France and blockaded French ports 1803–05; after Nelson's death he took command at the Battle of Trafalgar.

Collingwood Robin George 1889–1943. English philosopher, who believed that any philosophical theory or position could only be properly understood within its own historical context and not from the point of view of the present. His aesthetic theory is outlined in *Principles of Art* 1938.

Collins Michael 1890–1922. Irish Sinn Féin leader, a founder and director of intelligence of the Irish Republican Army 1919, minister for finance in the Provisional government of the Irish Free State 1922, commander of the Free State forces and for ten days head of state; killed in the civil war.

Born in County Cork, Collins became an active member of the Irish Republican Brotherhood, and in 1916 fought in the Easter Rising. In 1918 he was elected a Sinn Féin member to the Dáil, and became a minister in the Republican Provisional government. In 1921 he and Arthur Griffith (1872–1922) were mainly responsible for the treaty that established the Irish Free State. During the ensuing civil war, Collins took command and crushed the opposition in Dublin and the large towns within a few weeks. When Griffith died on 12 Aug Collins became head of the state and the army, but he was ambushed near Cork by fellow Irishmen on 22 Aug and killed.

Collins Phil 1951– . English pop singer, drummer, and actor. A member of the group Genesis from 1970, he has also pursued a successful solo career from 1981, with hits (often new versions of old songs) including 'In the Air Tonight' 1981 and 'Groovy Kind of Love' 1988.

Collins William 1721–1759. British poet. His *Persian Eclogues* 1742 were followed in 1746 by his series 'Odes', the best-known being 'To Evening'.

Collins (William) Wilkie 1824–1889. English novelist, author of mystery and suspense novels, including *The Woman in White* 1860 (with its fat villain Count Fosco), and *The Moonstone* 1868 (with Sergeant Cuff, one of the first detectives in English literature).

Collodi Carlo. Pen name of Carlo Lorenzini 1826–1890. Italian journalist and writer, who in 1881–83 wrote *The Adventure of Pinocchio*, the children's story of a wooden puppet who became a human boy.

Colman Ronald 1891–1958. British actor. Born in Richmond, Surrey, he went to the USA in 1920 where his charm, good looks and speaking voice soon brought success in romantic Hollywood roles. His films include *Beau Geste* 1924, *The Prisoner of Zenda* 1937, *Lost Horizon* 1937, and *A Double Life* 1947, for which he received an Academy Award.

Colombo Matteo Realdo *c.*1516–1559. Italian anatomist who discovered pulmonary circulation, the process of blood circulating from the heart to the lungs and back.

This showed that ◊Galen's teachings were wrong, and was of help to ◊Harvey in his work on the heart and cirulation. Colombo was a pupil of Vesalius, and became his successor at Padua.

Colonna Vittoria *c.*1492–1547. Roman poet. Many of her Petrarchan poems idealize her husband, killed at the battle of Paria 1525. She was a friend of Michelangelo, who addressed sonnets to her.

Colt Samuel 1814–1862. US gunsmith who invented the revolver 1835 that bears his name. He built up an immense arms-manufacturing business at Hartford, Connecticut, his birthplace, and subsequentlyin England.

Coltrane John (William) 1926–1967. US jazz saxophonist, a member of the Miles ◊Davis quintet. His performances were noted for experimentation, and his quartet was highly regarded for its innovations in melody and harmony.

Colum Padraic 1881–1972. Irish poet and playwright. He was associated with the foundation of the Abbey Theatre, Dublin, where his plays *Land* 1905, and *Thomas Muskerry* 1910, were

performed. His *Collected Poems* 1932 show his gift for lyrical expression.

Columba, St 521–597. Irish Christian abbot, missionary to Scotland. He was born in County Donegal of royal descent, and founded monasteries and churches in Ireland. In 563 he sailed with 12 companions to Iona, and built a monastery there that was to play an important part in the conversion of Britain. Feast day 9 June.

From his base on Iona St Columba made missionary journeys to the mainland. Legend has it that he drove a monster from the river Ness, and he crowned Aidan, an Irish king of Argyll.

Columban, St 543–615. Irish Christian abbot. He was born in Leinster, studied at Bangor, and about 585 went to the Vosges, France, with 12 other monks and founded the monastery of Luxeuil. He preached in Switzerland, then went to Italy, where he built the abbey of Bobbio in the Apennines. Feast day 23 Nov.

Columbus Christopher (Spanish *Cristóbal Colón*) 1451–1506. Italian navigator and explorer who made four voyages to the New World: 1492 to San Salvador Island, Cuba, and Haiti; 1493–96 to Guadaloupe, Montserrat, Antigua, Puerto Rico, and Jamaica; 1498 to Trinidad and the mainland of South America; 1502–04 to Honduras and Nicaragua.

Born in Genoa, Columbus went to sea at an early age, and settled in Portugal 1478 where he became a mapmaker. Believing that the earth was round and Asia could be reached by sailing westward, he eventually won the support of King Ferdinand and Queen Isabella of Spain and on 3 Aug 1492 sailed from Palos with three small ships, the *Niña*, the *Pinta*, and his flagship the *Santa Maria*. On 12 Oct

***Columbus** An engraving of the portrait by Sebastiano del Piombo; the original is in the Uffizi, Florence.*

land was sighted, probably Watling Island (now San Salvador Island), and within a few weeks he reached Cuba and Haiti, returning to Spain in Mar 1493. After his third voyage in 1498, he became involved in quarrels among the colonists sent to Haiti, and in 1500 the governor sent him back to Spain in chains. Released and compensated by the king, he made his last voyage 1502–04, during which he hoped to find a strait leading to India. He died in poverty in Valladolid and is buried in Seville cathedral.

Comaneci Nadia 1961– . Romanian gymnast. She won three gold medals at the 1976 Olympics at the age of 14, and was the first gymnast to record a perfect score of 10 in international competition.

Comines Philippe de *c.*1445–1509. French diplomat in the service of Charles the Bold, Louis XI, and Charles VIII; author of *Mémoires* 1489–98.

Commodus Lucius Aelius Aurelius AD 161–192. Roman emperor from 180, son of Marcus Aurelius Antoninus. He was a tyrant, spending lavishly on gladiatorial combats, confiscating the property of the wealthy, persecuting the Senate, and renaming Rome 'Colonia Commodia'. There were many attempts against his life, and he was finally strangled at the instigation of his mistress and advisors, who had discovered themselves on the emperor's death list.

Compton Arthur Holly 1892–1962. US physicist known for his work on X-rays. Working at Chicago 1923 he found that X-rays scattered by such light elements as carbon increased their wavelengths. Compton could only conclude from this unexpected result that the X-rays were displaying both wave-like and particle-like properties. For this discovery since named the *Compton effect*, he shared the 1927 Nobel Prize for Physics with Charles ◊Wilson.

Compton-Burnett Ivy 1892–1969. English novelist. She used dialogue to show reactions of small groups of characters dominated by the tyranny of family relationships. Her novels, set at the turn of the century, include *Pastors and Masters* 1925, *More Women than Men* 1933, and *Mother and Son* 1955.

Comte Auguste 1798–1857. French philosopher, regarded as the founder of sociology, a term he coined 1830. He sought to establish sociology as an intellectual discipline, using a scientific approach, 'positivism', as the basis of a new science of social order and social development.

Comte, born in Montpellier, was expelled from the Paris Ecole Polytechnique for leading a student revolt in 1816. In 1818 he became secretary to the socialist Saint-Simon and was much influenced by him. He began lecturing on the 'Positive Philosophy' in 1826, but almost immediately succumbed to a nervous disorder and once tried to commit suicide in the Seine. On his recovery he resumed his lectures and mathematical teaching.

In his six-volume *Cours de philosophie positive* 1830–42 he argued that human thought and social development evolve through three stages: the theological, the metaphysical, and the positive or scientific. Though he originally sought to proclaim society's evolution to a new golden age of science, industry, and rational morality, his radical ideas were increasingly tempered by the political and social upheavals of his time.

Condé Louis II 1621–1686. Prince of Condé, called the *Great Condé*. French commander, who won brilliant victories during the Thirty Years' War at Rocroi 1643 and Lens 1648, but rebelled 1651 and entered the Spanish service. Pardoned 1660, he commanded Louis XIV's armies against the Spanish and the Dutch.

Condé Louis de Bourbon, Prince of Condé 1530–1569. A prominent French Huguenot leader, founder of the house of Condé and uncle of Henry IV of France. He distinguished himself in the wars between Henry II and the Holy Roman emperor Charles V, particularly in the defence of Metz.

Conder Charles 1868–1909. English artist, who painted in watercolour and oil, and executed a number of lithographs including the *Balzac* 1899 and the *Carnival* sets 1905.

Condillac Étienne Bonnot de 1715–1780. French philosopher. He mainly followed ◊Locke, but his *Traité de sensations* 1754 claims that all mental activity stems from the transformation of sensations. He was a collaborator in the French *Encyclopédie* (see ◊Diderot). Born in Grenoble of noble parentage, he entered the Church and was appointed tutor to Louis XV's grandson, the Duke of Parma.

Condorcet Marie Jean Antoine Nicolas Caritat, Marquis de Condorcet 1743–1794. French philosopher and politician, associated with the Encyclopédistes (see ◊Diderot). One of the right-wing Girondins, he opposed the execution of Louis XVI, and was imprisoned and poisoned himself. His *Esquisse d'un tableau des progrès de l'esprit humain*/*Historical Survey of the Progress of Human Understanding* 1795 envisaged inevitable future progress, though not the perfectibility of human nature.

Confucius Latinized form of *Kong Zi*, 'Kong the master' 551–479 BC. Chinese philosopher whose name is given to Confucianism. He devoted his life to relieving suffering of the poor through governmental and administrative reform. His emphasis on tradition and ethics attracted a growing number of pupils during his lifetime; *The Analects of Confucius*, a compilation of his teachings, was published after his death.

Confucius was born in Lu, in what is now the province of Shangdong, and his early years were spent in poverty. Married at 19, he worked as a minor official, then as a teacher. In 517 there was an uprising in Lu, and Confucius spent the next year or two in the adjoining state of Ch'i. As a teacher he was able to place many of his pupils in government posts but a powerful position eluded him. Only in his fifties was he given an office but soon resigned at the lack of power it conveyed. Then for 14 years he wandered from state to state looking for a ruler who could give him a post where he could put his reforms into practice. At the age of 67 he returned to Lu and devoted himself to teaching. At his death five years later he was buried with great pomp, and his grave outside Qufu has remained a centre of pilgrimage.

Congreve William 1670–1729. English dramatist and poet. His first success was the comedy *The Old Bachelor* 1693, followed by *The Double Dealer* 1694, *Love for Love* 1695, the tragedy *The Mourning Bride* 1697, and *The Way of the World* 1700. His plays, which satirize the social affectations of the time, are noted for their elegant wit and wordplay.

Connery Sean 1930– . Scottish film actor, the most famous interpreter of James Bond in several films based on the novels of Ian Fleming. His films include *Dr No* 1962, *From Russia with Love* 1963, *Marnie* 1964, *Goldfinger* 1964, *Diamonds are Forever* 1971, *A Bridge too Far* 1977, and *The Untouchables* 1987.

Connolly Cyril 1903–1974. English critic and author. As founder-editor of the literary magazine *Horizon* 1930–50, he had considerable critical influence. His books include *The Rock Pool* 1935, a novel of artists on the Riviera, and *The Unquiet Grave* 1945.

Connolly Maureen 1934–1969. US lawn-tennis player, nicknamed 'Little Mo' because she stood only 1.57 m/5 ft 2 in tall. In 1953 she became the first woman to complete the Grand Slam by winning all four major tournaments.

All her singles titles (won at nine major championships) and her Grand Slam titles were won between 1951 and 1954. She also represented the USA in the Wightman Cup. After a riding accident 1954 her career was ended.

Connors Jimmy 1952– . US lawn tennis player. A popular and entertaining player, he became well known for his 'grunting' during play. He won the Wimbledon title 1974, and has since won ten Grand Slam events. He was one of the first players to popularize the two-handed backhand.

Conrad Joseph 1857–1924. British novelist, of Polish parentage, born Teodor Jozef Konrad Korzeniowski in the Ukraine. His novels include *Almayer's Folly* 1895, *Lord Jim* 1900, *Heart of Darkness* 1902, *Nostromo* 1904, *The Secret Agent* 1907, and *Under Western Eyes* 1911. His works vividly evoked for English readers the mysteries of sea life and exotic foreign settings, and explored the psychological isolation of the 'outsider'.

Conrad several kings of the Germans and Holy Roman Emperors, including:

Conrad III 1093–1152. Holy Roman emperor from 1138, the first king of the Hohenstaufen dynasty. Throughout his reign there was a fierce struggle between his followers, the *Ghibellines*, and the *Guelphs*, the followers of Henry the Proud, duke of Saxony and Bavaria (1108–1139), and later of his son Henry the Lion (1129–1195).

Conrad IV 1228–1254. Elected king of the Germans 1237. Son of the Holy Roman emperor Frederick II, he had to defend his right of succession against Henry Raspe of Thuringia (died 1247) and William of Holland (1227–1256).

Conrad V (Conradin) 1252–1268. Son of Conrad IV, recognized as king of the Germans, Sicily, and Jerusalem by German supporters of the Hohenstaufens dynasty 1254. He led Ghibelline forces against Charles of Anjou at the battle of Tagliacozzo, N Italy 1266, and was captured and executed.

Conran Terence 1931– . British designer and retailer of furnishings, fashion, and household goods. He was founder of the Habitat and Conran companies, with retail outlets in the UK, USA, and elsewhere.

In 1964 he started the Habitat company, then developed Mothercare. His Storehouse group of companies gained control of British Home Stores 1986.

Constable John 1776–1837. English landscape painter. The scenes of his native Suffolk are well loved and include *The Haywain* 1821 (National Gallery, London), but he travelled widely in Britain, depicting castles, cathedrals, landscapes, and coastal scenes. His many sketches, worked in the open air, are often considered among his best work. The paintings are remarkable for their freshness and were influential in France as well as Britain.

Constable first worked in his father's mills in East Bergholt, Suffolk, but in 1795 was sent to study art in London. He inherited the Dutch tradition of sombre realism, particularly the style of Jacob ◊Ruysdael, but he aimed to capture the momentary changes of nature as well as to create monumental images of British scenery, such as *The White Horse* 1819 (Frick Collection, New York) and *Flatford Mill* 1825. He was finally elected to the Royal Academy in 1829 but his greatest impact was in France, where his admirers included Delacroix.

Constant de Rebecque (Henri) Benjamin 1767–1830. French writer and politician. An advocate of the Revolution, he opposed Napoleon and in 1803 went into exile. Returning to Paris after the fall of Napoleon in 1814 he proposed a constitutional monarchy. He published the autobiographical novel *Adolphe* 1816, which reflects his affair with Madame de ◊Stael, and later wrote the monumental study *De la Religion* 1825–31.

Constantine II 1940– . King of the Hellenes (Greece). In 1964 he succeeded his father Paul I, went into exile 1967, and was formally deposed 1973.

Constantine the Great AD 274–337. First Christian emperor of Rome and founder of Constantinople. Born at Naissus (Nish, Yugoslavia), Constantine was the son of Constantius. He was already well known as a soldier when his father died at York in 306 and he was acclaimed by the troops there as joint emperor in his father's place. A few years later Maxentius, the joint emperor in Rome (whose sister had married Constantine), challenged his authority and mobilized his armies to invade Gaul. Constantine won a crushing victory outside Rome in 312. During this campaign he was said to have seen a vision of the cross of Jesus superimposed upon the sun, accompanied by the words, 'In this sign conquer'. By the Edict of Milan 313 he formally recognized Christianity as one of the religions legally permitted within the Roman Empire, and in 314 summoned the bishops of the Western world to the Council of Arles. Sole emperor of the West since 321, by defeating Licinius, the emperor in the East, Constantine became sole Roman emperor 324. He increased the autocratic power of the emperor, issued legislation to tie the farmers and workers to their crafts in a sort of caste system, and enlisted the support of the Christian Church. He summoned, and presided over, the first general council of the Church at Nicaea 325. Constantine moved his capital to Byzantium on the Bosporus 330 and renamed it Constantinople (now Istanbul).

Conti Tom 1945– . British stage and film actor specializing in character roles. His films include *The Duellists* 1976; *Merry Christmas Mr Lawrence* 1983; *Reuben, Reuben* 1983; *Beyond Therapy* 1987; *Shirley Valentine* 1989.

Cook James 1728–1779. English naval explorer. After surveying the St Lawrence 1759, he made three voyages: 1769–71 to Tahiti, New Zealand, and Australia; 1772–75 to the South Pacific; and 1776–79 to the South and North Pacific, attempting to find the Northwest Passage and charting the Siberian coast. He was killed in Hawaii.

In 1768 Cook was given command of an expedition to the South Pacific to witness Venus eclipsing the sun. He sailed in the *Endeavour* with Joseph ◊Banks and other scientists, reaching Tahiti Apr 1769. He then sailed around New Zealand and made a detailed survey of the E coast of Australia, naming New South Wales and Botany Bay. He returned to England 12 June 1771. Now a commander, Cook set out 1772 with the *Resolution* and *Adventure* to search for the Southern Continent. The location of Easter Island was determined, and the Marquesas and Tonga Islands plotted. He also went to New Caledonia and Norfolk Island. Cook returned 25 July

Cook *English navigator and explorer Captain James Cook.*

1775, having sailed about 100,000 km/60,000 mi in three years. On 25 June 1776, he began his third and last voyage with the *Resolution* and *Discovery*. On the way to New Zealand, he visited several of the Cook or Hervey Islands and revisited the Hawaiian or Sandwich Islands. The ships sighted the North American coast at latitude 45° N and sailed N hoping to discover the Northwest Passage. He made a continuous survey as far as the Bering Strait, where the way was blocked by ice. Cook then surveyed the opposite coast of the strait (Siberia), and returned to Hawaii early 1779, where he was killed in a scuffle with islanders.

Cook Peter 1937– . English comic actor and writer best known for his partnership with Dudley Moore (1935–). Together they appeared in revue (*Beyond the Fringe* 1959–64) and opened London's first satirical nightclub, the Establishment, in 1960. His films include *The Wrong Box* 1966; *Bedazzled* 1968; *The Bed Sitting Room* 1969; a parody of *The Hound of the Baskervilles* 1977; and *Supergirl* 1984.

Cook Robin Finlayson 1946– . English Labour politician. A member of the moderate-left Tribune Group, he entered Parliament in 1974 and became a leading member of Labour's shadow cabinet.

Cook Thomas 1808–1892. Pioneer British travel agent and founder of Thomas Cook & Son. He introduced traveller's cheques (then called 'circular notes'), in the early 1870s.

Cooke Alistair 1908– . US journalist. Born in the UK, he was *Guardian* correspondent in the USA 1948–72, and contributed a weekly *Letter from America* to BBC radio.

Cooke Sam 1931–1964. US soul singer and songwriter, who began his career as a gospel singer and turned to pop music in 1956. His hits include

'You Send Me' 1957 and 'Wonderful World' 1960 (re-released 1986).

Coolidge (John) Calvin 1872–1933. 30th president of the USA 1923–29, a Republican. As governor of Massachusetts 1919, he was responsible for crushing a Boston police strike. He became vice president 1921 and president on the death of Warren Harding. He was re-elected 1924, and his period of office was marked by economic prosperity.

Cooney Ray (Raymond) 1932– . British actor, director, and playwright, known for his farces *Two into One* 1981 and *Run for Your Wife* 1983.

Cooper Gary 1901–1962. US actor. He epitomized the lean, true-hearted Yankee, slow of speech but capable of outdoing the 'badmen' in *Lives of a Bengal Lancer* 1935, *Mr Deeds Goes to Town* 1936, *Sergeant York* 1940 (Academy Award 1941), and *High Noon* 1952.

Cooper Henry 1934– . English heavyweight boxer, the only man to win three Lonsdale Belts outright, 1961, 1965, and 1970. He fought for the world heavyweight title but lost in the 6th round to Muhammad Ali 1966.

A former greengrocer, Cooper was famed for his left-hook known as 'Henry's hammer', and for an eye that bled easily. He held the British heavyweight title 1959–71 and lost it to Joe Bugner in a controversial fight

Cooper James Fenimore 1789–1851. US writer of 50 novels, becoming popular with *The Spy* 1821. He wrote volumes of *Leatherstocking Tales* about the frontier hero Leatherstocking and American Indians before and after the American Revolution, including *The Last of the Mohicans* 1826.

Cooper was born in New Jersey, grew up on the family frontier settlement of Cooperstown, New York State, and sailed as an apprentice seaman to Europe. After success as a writer, he lived in Paris for seven years before returning to Cooperstown.

Cooper Leon 1930– . UK physicist who in 1955 began work on the puzzling phenomenon of superconductivity (very high conductivity at very low temperature). He proposed that at low temperatures electrons would be bound in pairs (since known as *Cooper pairs*) and in this state electrical resistance to their flow through solids would disappear. He shared the 1972 Nobel Prize for Physics with ◊Bardeen and Schrieffer.

Cooper Samuel 1609–1672. English miniaturist. His subjects included Milton, members of Charles II's court, Samuel Pepys's wife, and Oliver Cromwell.

Cooper Susie. Married name Susan Vera Barker 1902– . English pottery designer. Her style has varied from colourful Art Deco to softer, pastel decoration on more classical shapes. She started her own company 1929, which later became part of the Wedgwood factory, where she was senior designer from 1966.

Coote Eyre 1726–1783. Irish general in British India. His victory 1760 at Wandiwash, followed by the capture of Pondicherry, ended French hopes of supremacy. He returned to India as commander in chief 1779, and several times defeated ◊Hyder Ali, sultan of Mysore.

Coper Hans 1920–1981. German potter, originally an engineer. His work resembles Cycladic Greek pots in its monumental quality.

Coperario John *c.*1570–1626. English composer of songs with lute or viol accompaniment.

Born John Cooper, he changed his name after studying in Italy. His works include several masques, such as *The Masque of Flowers* 1614, and sets of fantasies for organ and solo viol.

Copernicus Nicolaus 1473–1543. Polish astronomer, who believed that the Sun, not Earth, is at the centre of the solar system, thus defying established doctrine. For 30 years he worked on the hypothesis that the rotation and the orbital motion of Earth were responsible for the apparent movement of the heavenly bodies. His great work *De revolutionibus orbium coelestium* was not published until the year of his death.

Born at Torun on the Vistula, then under the Polish king, he studied at Cracow and in Italy, and lectured on astronomy at Rome. On his return to Pomerania 1505 he became physician to his uncle, the bishop of Ermland, and was made canon at Frauenburg, although he did not take holy orders. Living there until his death, he interspersed astronomical work with the duties of various civil offices.

Copland Aaron 1900– . US composer. Copland's early works, such as the piano concerto of 1926, were in the jazz idiom but he gradually developed a gentler style with a regional flavour drawn from American folk music.

Born in New York, he studied in France with Nadia Boulanger, and in 1940 became instructor in composition at the Berkshire Music Center. After 1945 he was the assistant director. Among his later works are the ballets *Billy the Kid* 1939; *Rodeo* 1942; and *Appalachian Spring* 1944, based on a poem by Hart Crane; and *Inscape for Orchestra* 1967.

Copley John Singleton 1738–1815. American painter. He was the leading portraitist of the colonial period, but from 1775 he lived mainly in London, where he painted lively historical scenes such as *The Death of Major Pierson* 1783 (Tate Gallery, London).

Copley was born in Boston, Massachussetts. Some of his history paintings are unusual in portraying recent dramatic events, such as *Brook Watson and the Shark* 1778 (National Gallery, Washington).

Coppola Francis Ford 1939– . US film director and screenwriter. He directed *The Godfather*

1972, which became one of the biggest money-makers of all time. Other successes include *Apocalypse Now* 1979, and *The Cotton Club* 1984.

Coralli Jean 1779–1854. French dancer and choreographer of Italian descent. He made his debut as a dancer in 1802. He choreographed *Le Diable boîteux* 1836 for the Austrian ballerina Fanny Elssler, *Giselle* 1841 and *La Péri* 1843 for the Italian ballerina Grisi; and many other well-known ballets.

Coram Thomas 1668–1751. English philanthropist, who established the Foundling Hospital for orphaned and abandoned children in Holborn, London, 1741. The site, now Coram's Fields, is still a children's foundation.

Corbière Tristan 1845–1875. French poet. His *Les Amours jaunes/Yellow Loves* 1873 went unrecognized until Verlaine called attention to it in 1884. Many of his poems, such as *La Rhapsodie Foraine/Wandering Rhapsody*, deal with life in his native Brittany.

Corday Charlotte 1768–1793. French Girondin (right-wing republican during the French Revolution). After the overthrow of the Girondins by the more extreme Jacobins May 1793, she stabbed to death the Jacobin leader, Marat, with a bread knife as he sat in his bath in July of the same year. She was guillotined.

Corelli Arcangelo 1653–1713. Italian composer and violinist. He was one of the first virtuoso violinists and his music, marked by graceful melody, includes a set of *concerti grossi* and five sets of chamber sonatas.

Corelli Marie. Pseudonym of British novelist Mary Mackay 1855–1924. Trained for a musical career, she turned instead to writing (she was said to be Queen Victoria's favourite novelist) and published *The Romance of Two Worlds* 1886. Her works were later ridiculed for their pretentious style.

Cori Carl (1896–) and Gerty 1896–1957. Husband and wife team of US biochemists, both born in Prague. Together with Bernardo Houssay, they received a Nobel prize 1947 for their discovery of how glycogen – a derivative of glucose – is broken down and resynthesized in the body, for use as a store and source of energy.

Corinna 6th century BC. Greek lyric poet, said to have instructed Pindar. Only fragments of her poetry survive.

Corman Roger 1926– . US film director and producer. He directed a stylish series of Edgar Allan Poe films starring Vincent Price that began with *House of Usher* 1960. After 1970 Corman confined himself to production and distribution.

Corneille Pierre 1606–1684. French dramatist. His many tragedies, such as *Oedipe* 1659, glorify the strength of will governed by reason, and established the French classical dramatic tradition for the next two centuries. His first play, *Mélite*, was performed 1629, followed by others that gained him a brief period of favour with Cardinal Richelieu. *Le Cid* 1636 was attacked by the Academicians although it achieved huge public success. Later plays were based on Aristotle's unities.

Although Corneille enjoyed public popularity, periodic disfavour with Richelieu marred his career, and it was not until 1639 that Corneille (again in favour) produced plays such as *Horace* 1639, *Polyeucte* 1643, *Le Menteur* 1643, and *Rodogune* 1645, leading to his election to the Académie 1647. His later plays were approved by Louis XIV.

Cornforth John 1917– . Australian chemist who settled in England 1941. In 1975 he shared a Nobel prize with Vladimir Prelog for work utilizing radioisotopes (the radioactive form of a chemical element) as 'markers' to find out how enzymes synthesize chemicals that are mirror images of one another (stereoisomers).

Cornwallis Charles, 1st Marquess Cornwallis 1738–1805. British soldier, eldest son of the 1st Earl Cornwallis. He led the British forces in the War of American Independence until 1781, when his surrender at Yorktown ended the war. Subsequently he was twice governor general of India, and viceroy of Ireland, and was made a marquess 1793.

Coronado Francisco de *c.*1500–1554. Spanish explorer who sailed to the New World in 1535 in search of gold. In 1540 he set out with several hundred men from the Gulf of California on an exploration of what are today the Southern states. Although he failed to discover any gold, his expedition came across the impressive Grand Canyon of the Colorado and introduced the use of the horse to the indigenous Indians.

Corot Jean-Baptiste-Camille 1796–1875. French painter, creator of a distinctive landscape style with cool colours and soft focus. His early work, particularly Italian scenes in the 1820s, influenced the Barbizon school of painters. Like them, Corot worked out of doors, but he also continued a conventional academic tradition with more romanticized paintings.

Correggio Antonio Allegri da *c.*1494–1534. Italian painter of the High Renaissance, whose style followed the classical grandeur of Leonardo and Titian but anticipated the Baroque in its emphasis on movement, softer forms, and contrasts of light and shade.

Based in Parma, he painted splendid illusionistic visions in the cathedral there. His religious paintings, including the night scene *Adoration of the Shepherds* about 1527–30 (Gemäldegalerie, Dresden), and mythological scenes, such as *The Loves of Jupiter* (Wallace Collection, London), were much admired in the 18th century.

Cort Henry 1740–1800. British iron manufacturer. For the manufacture of wrought iron, he invented the puddling process (by which iron is heated in a furnace with ferric oxide to remove carbon) and developed the rolling mill, both of which were significant in the Industrial Revolution.

Cortázar Julio 1914– . Argentine writer, born in Brussels, whose novels include *The Winners* 1960, *Hopscotch* 1963, and *A Model Kit* 1968. His several volumes of short stories include 'Blow-up', adapted for a film by the Italian director Antonioni.

Cortés Hernándo (Ferdinand) 1485–1547. Spanish conquistador. He overthrew the Aztec empire 1519–21, and secured Mexico for Spain.

He went to the West Indies as a young man, and in 1518 was given command of an expedition to Mexico. Landing with only 600 men, he was at first received as a god by the Aztec emperor ◊Montezuma II, but was finally expelled from Tenochtitlán (Mexico City) by a revolt. With the aid of Indian allies he recaptured the city 1521, and overthrew the Aztec empire. His conquests eventually included most of Mexico and N Central America.

Corvo Baron 1860–1913. Assumed name of British writer Frederick ◊Rolfe.

Cosgrave Liam 1920– . Irish Fine Gael politician, prime minister of the Republic of Ireland 1973–77. As party leader 1965–77, he headed a Fine Gael–Labour coalition government from 1973. Relations between the Irish and UK governments improved under his premiership.

Cosgrave William Thomas 1880–1965. Irish politician. He took part in the Easter Rising 1916, and sat in the Sinn Féin cabinet of 1919–21. Head of the Free State government 1922–33, he founded and led the Fine Gael opposition 1933–44. His eldest son is Liam Cosgrave.

Costello Elvis. Stage name of Declan McManus 1954– . English rock singer, songwriter, and guitarist, noted for his stylistic range and intricate lyrics. His albums with his group the Attractions include *Armed Forces* 1979, *Trust* 1981, and *Blood and Chocolate* 1986.

Coster Laurens Janszoon 1370–1440. Dutch printer. According to some sources, he invented movable type, but after his death an apprentice ran off to Mainz with the blocks and, taking ◊Gutenberg into his confidence, began a printing business with him.

Cotman John Sell 1782–1842. British landscape painter, with Crome a founder of the *Norwich school*, a group of realistic landscape painters influenced by Dutch examples. Cotman is best known for his early watercolour style, bold designs in simple flat washes of colour, such as *Greta Bridge, Yorkshire* 1805 (British Museum, London).

Cotton Joseph 1905– . US actor, who was brought into films by Orson Welles. He appeared in many international productions, often in leading roles, until the early 1980s, including *Citizen Kane* 1941,

The Third Man 1949, and *The Abominable Dr Phibes* 1971.

Cotton Robert Bruce 1571–1631. English antiquary. At his home in Westminster he built up a fine collection of manuscripts and coins, many of which had come from the despoiled monasteries. His son, *Thomas Cotton* (1594–1662), added to the library. The collection is now in the British Museum.

Coulomb Charles Auguste de 1736–1806. French scientist, inventor of the torsion balance for measuring the force of electric and magnetic attraction. The *coulomb*, the unit of electric charge, was named after him.

Couperin François *le Grand* 1668–1733. French composer. He held various court appointments under Louis XIV and wrote vocal, chamber, and harpsichord music.

Courbet Gustave 1819–1877. French artist, a portrait, genre, and landscape painter. Reacting against academic trends, both Classicist and Romantic, he sought to establish a new realism based on contemporary life. His *Burial at Ornans* 1850 (Louvre, Paris), showing ordinary working people gathered round a village grave, shocked the public and the critics with its 'vulgarity'.

His spirit of realism was to be continued by Manet. In 1871 Courbet was active in the shortlived Paris Commune and was later imprisoned for six months for his part in it.

Courrèges André 1923– . French couturier. Originally with Balenciaga, he founded his own firm 1961 and is credited with inventing the mini-skirt in 1964.

Court Margaret (born Smith) 1942– . Australian tennis player. The most prolific winner in the women's game, she won a record 64 Grand Slam titles, including 24 at singles.

She was the first from her country to win the ladies title at Wimbledon 1963, and the second woman after Maureen Connolly to complete the Grand Slam 1970.

Courtauld Samuel 1793–1881. British industrialist who developed the production of viscose rayon and other synthetic fibres from 1904. He founded the firm of Courtaulds in 1816 at Bocking, Essex, which at first specialized in silk and crepe manufacture.

His great-nephew, *Samuel Courtauld* (1876–1947), was chairman of the firm from 1921, and in 1931 gave his house and art collection to the University of London as the Courtauld Institute.

Courtneidge Cicely 1893–1980. British comic actress and singer, who appeared both on stage and in films. She married comedian Jack Hulbert (1892–1978), with whom she formed a successful variety partnership.

Cousin Victor 1792–1867. French philosopher, who helped to introduce German philosophical ideas into France. In 1840 he was minister of public instruction and reorganized the system of elementary education.

Cousteau Jacques-Yves 1910– . French oceanographer, celebrated for his researches in command of the *Calypso* from 1951; he was one of the inventors of the aqualung 1943, and he pioneered techniques in underwater filming.

Coutts Thomas 1735–1822. British banker. He established with his brother the firm of Coutts & Co (one of London's oldest banking houses, founded in 1692 in the Strand), becoming sole head on the latter's death in 1778. Since the reign of George III an account has been maintained there by every succeeding sovereign; other customers have included Chatham, William Pitt, Fox, Wellington, Reynolds, and Boswell.

Coverdale Miles 1488–1569. English Protestant priest whose translation of the Bible 1535 was the first to be printed in English. His translation of the psalms is that retained in the Book of Common Prayer.

Coverdale, born in Yorkshire, became a Catholic priest, but turned to Protestantism and in 1528 went abroad to avoid persecution. In 1539 he edited the Great Bible which was ordered to be placed in churches. After some years in Germany, he returned to England in 1548, and in 1551 was made bishop of Exeter. During the reign of Mary he left the country.

Coward Noël 1899–1973. English playwright, actor, producer, director, and composer, who epitomized the witty and sophisticated man of the theatre. From his first success with *The Young Idea* 1923, he wrote and appeared in plays and comedies on both sides of the Atlantic such as *Hay Fever* 1925, *Private Lives* 1930 with Gertrude Lawrence, *Design for Living* 1933, and *Blithe Spirit* 1941.

Coward also wrote for and acted in films, including the patriotic *In Which We Serve* 1942 and the sentimental *Brief Encounter* 1945. After World War II he became a nightclub and cabaret entertainer, performing songs like 'Mad Dogs and Englishmen'.

Cowell Henry 1897–1965. US composer and writer. He experimented with new ways of playing the piano, strumming the strings in *Aeolian Harp* 1923 and introducing clusters, using a ruler on the keys in *The Banshee* 1925.

Cowell also wrote chamber and orchestral music and was active as a critic and publisher of 20th-century music.

Cowley Abraham 1618–1667. English poet. He introduced the Pindaric ode (based on the Greek poet Pindar) to English poetry, and published metaphysical verse with elaborate imagery, as well as essays.

Cowper William 1731–1800. English poet. He trained as a lawyer, but suffered a mental breakdown 1763 and entered an asylum, where he

underwent an evangelical conversion. He later wrote hymns (including 'God moves in a mysterious way'). His verse includes the six books of *The Task* 1785.

Cox David 1783–1859. British artist. Born near Birmingham, the son of a blacksmith, he studied under John ◊Varley and made a living as a drawing master. His watercolour landscapes, many of scenes in N Wales, have attractive cloud effects, and are characterized by broad colour washes on a rough, tinted paper.

Coysevox Antoine 1640–1720. French Baroque sculptor. He was employed at the palace of Versailles, contributing a stucco relief of a triumphant Louis XIV to the Salon de la Guerre.

He also produced portrait busts, for example a terracotta of the artist Le Brun 1676 (Wallace Collection, London), and more sombre monuments, such as the *Tomb of Cardinal Mazarin* 1689–93 (Louvre, Paris).

Cozens John Robert 1752–1797. British landscape painter, a watercolourist, whose Romantic views of Europe, painted on tours in the 1770s and 1780s, were popular in his day and influenced both Girtin and Turner.

His father, *Alexander Cozens* (*c.*1717–86), also a landscape painter, taught drawing at Eton public school and produced books on landscape drawing.

Crabbe George 1754–1832. English poet. Originally a doctor, he became a clergyman 1781, and wrote grimly realistic verse of the poor of his own time: *The Village* 1783, *The Parish Register* 1807, *The Borough* 1810 (which includes the story used in the Britten opera *Peter Grimes*), and *Tales of the Hall* 1819.

Craig Edward Gordon 1872–1966. British director and stage designer. His innovations and theories on stage design and lighting effects, expounded in *On the Art of the Theatre* 1911, had a huge influence on stage production in Europe and the USA.

Craig James 1871–1940. Ulster Unionist politician, the first prime minister of Northern Ireland 1921–40. Craig became a member of Parliament 1906, and was a highly effective organizer of Unionist resistance to Home Rule. As prime minister he carried out systematic discrimination against the Catholic minority, abolishing proportional representation 1929 and redrawing constituency boundaries to ensure Protestant majorities.

Craik Dinah Maria (born Mulock) 1826–1887. British novelist, author of *John Halifax, Gentleman* 1857, the story of the social betterment of a poor orphan through his own efforts.

Cranach Lucas 1472–1553. German painter, etcher, and woodcut artist, a leading light in the German Renaissance. He painted many full-length nudes and precise and polished portraits, such as *Martin Luther* 1521 (Uffizi, Florence).

Born at Kronach in Bavaria, he settled at Wittenberg in 1504 to work for the elector of Saxony. He is associated with Dürer and Altdorfer, and was a close friend of Luther, whose portrait he painted several times. His religious paintings feature splendid landscapes.

His second son *Lucas Cranach the Younger* (1515–86) had a similar style, and succeeded his father as director of the Cranach workshop.

Crane (Harold) Hart 1899–1932. US poet. His long mystical poem *The Bridge* (1930) uses the Brooklyn Bridge as a symbol. He drowned after jumping overboard from a steamer bringing him back to the USA after a visit to Mexico.

Crane Stephen 1871–1900. US journalist and writer, who introduced grim realism into the US novel. His book *The Red Badge of Courage* 1895 deals vividly with the US Civil War.

Crane Walter 1845–1915. British artist and designer, mainly known as a book illustrator. He was influenced by William Morris and became an active socialist in the 1880s.

While apprenticed to W J Linton, a wood engraver, he came under the influence of the Pre-Raphaelites. His book illustration, both for children's and for adult books, included an edition of Spenser's *Faerie Queene* 1894–96.

Cranko John 1927–1973. British choreographer. Born in South Africa, he joined Sadler's Wells in 1946, and excelled in the creation of comedy characters, as in the *Tritsch-Tratsch Polka* 1946 and *Pineapple Poll* 1951.

Cranmer Thomas 1489–1556. English cleric, archbishop of Canterbury from 1533. A Protestant convert, under Edward VI he helped to shape the doctrines of the Church of England. He was responsible for the issue of the Prayer Books of 1549 and 1552, and supported the succession of Lady Jane Grey. He was burned at the stake as a heretic by Mary I.

Cranmer suggested in 1529 that the question of Henry VIII's marriage to Catherine of Aragon should be referred to the universities of Europe rather than to the Pope, and in 1533 he declared it null and void. Condemned for heresy under the Catholic Mary Tudor, he at first recanted, but when his life was not spared, resumed his position and was burned, first holding to the fire the hand which had signed his recantation.

Crashaw Richard 1613–1649. English religious poet of the metaphysical school. He published a book of Latin sacred epigrams in 1634, then went to Paris, where he joined the Roman Catholic Church; his collection of poems *Steps to the Temple* appeared in 1646.

Crassus Marcus Licinius *c.*108–53 BC. Roman general who crushed the ◊Spartacus uprising 71 BC. In 60 BC he joined with Caesar and Pompey in the First Triumvirate and obtained command in the East 55 BC. Invading Mesopotamia, he was defeated by the Parthians at the battle of Carrhae, captured, and put to death.

Crawford Joan 1908–1977. US film actress, who made her name from 1925 in dramatic films such as *Mildred Pierce* 1945, and *Whatever Happened to Baby Jane?* 1962.

Crawford Osbert Guy Stanhope 1886–1957. British archaeologist, who introduced aerial survey as a means of finding and interpreting remains, an idea conceived in World War I.

Craxi Bettino 1934–   . Italian socialist politician, leader of the Italian Socialist Party (PSI) from 1976, prime minister 1983–87.

Craxi, born in Milan, became a member of the Chamber of Deputies 1968 and in 1976 general secretary of the PSI. In 1983 he became Italy's first socialist prime minister, successfully leading a broad coalition until 1987.

Crazy Horse 1849–1877. Sioux Indian chief, one of the Indian leaders at the massacre of Little Bighorn. He was killed when captured.

Creed Frederick George 1871–1957. Canadian inventor, who developed the teleprinter. He perfected the Creed telegraphy system (teleprinter), first used in Fleet Street 1912 and now, usually known as Telex, in offices throughout the world.

Creevey Thomas 1768–1838. British Whig politician and diarist, whose lively letters and journals give information on early 19th-century society and politics. He was a member of Parliament and opposed the slave trade.

Crichton James *c.*1560–1582. Scottish scholar, known as 'the Admirable Crichton' because of his extraordinary gifts as a poet, scholar, and linguist. He was also an athlete and fencer. According to one account he was killed at Mantua in a street brawl by his pupil, a son of the Duke of Mantua, who resented Crichton's popularity.

Crick Francis 1916–   . British molecular biologist. From 1949 he researched into DNA's molecular structure, and the means whereby characteristics are transmitted from one generation to another. For this work he was awarded a Nobel prize (with Maurice Wilkins (1916–   ) and James D ◊Watson).

Crippen Hawley Harvey 1861–1910. US murderer of his wife, variety artist Belle Elmore. He buried her remains in the cellar of his London home and tried to escape to the USA with his mistress Ethel le Neve (dressed as a boy). He was arrested on board ship following a radio message, the first criminal captured 'by radio', and was hanged.

Cripps (Richard) Stafford 1889–1952. British Labour politician, expelled from the Labour party 1939–45 for supporting a 'Popular Front' against Chamberlain's appeasement policy. He was ambassador to Moscow 1940–42, minister of aircraft production 1942–45, and chancellor of the Exchequer 1947–50.

Crispi Francesco 1819–1907. Italian prime minister 1887–91 and 1893–96. He advocated the Triple Alliance of Italy with Germany and Austria, but was deposed 1896.

Crivelli Carlo 1435/40–1495/1500. Italian painter in the early Renaissance style, active in Venice. He painted extremely detailed, decorated religious works, sometimes festooned with garlands of fruit. His figure style is strongly N Italian, reflecting the influence of Mantegna.

Croce Benedetto 1866–1952. Italian philosopher and literary critic, an opponent of fascism. Like Hegel, he held that ideas do not represent reality but *are* reality; but unlike Hegel, he rejected every kind of transcendence.

Crockett Davy 1786–1836. US folk hero, a Democrat Congressman 1827–31 and 1833–35. A series of books, of which he may have been part-author, made him into a mythical hero of the frontier, but their Whig associations cost him his office.

He died in the battle of the Alamo during the war for Texan independence.

Crockford William 1775–1844. British gambler, founder in 1827 of Crockford's Club in St James's Street, which became the fashionable place for London society to gamble.

Croker Richard 1841–1922. US politician, 'boss' of Tammany Hall, the Democratic party political machine in New York 1886–1902.

Crome John 1768–1821. British landscape painter, founder of the **Norwich school** with Cotman 1803. His works include *The Poringland Oak* c.1818 (Tate Gallery, London), showing Dutch influence.

Crompton Richmal, Pen name of British writer R C Lamburn 1890–1969. She is remembered for her stories about the mischievous schoolboy 'William'.

Crompton Samuel 1753–1827. British inventor at the time of the Industrial Revolution. He invented the 'spinning mule' 1779, combining the ideas of ◊Arkwright and ◊Hargreaves. Though widely adopted, his invention brought him little financial return.

Cromwell Oliver 1599–1658. English general and politician, Puritan leader of the Parliamentary side in the Civil War. He raised cavalry forces (later called *Ironsides*) which aided the victories at Edgehill 1642 and Marston Moor 1644, and organized the New Model Army, which he led (with Gen Fairfax) to victory at Naseby 1645. As Lord Protector (ruler) from 1653, he established religious toleration, and Britain's prestige in Europe on the basis of an alliance with France against Spain.

Cromwell was born at Huntingdon, NW of Cambridge, son of a small landowner. He entered Parliament 1629 and became active in events leading to the Civil War. Failing to secure a constitutional settlement with Charles I 1646–48, he defeated the 1648 Scottish invasion at Preston. A special

commission, of which Cromwell was a member, tried the king and condemned him to death, and a republic was set up.

The democratic Leveller party demanded radical reforms, but he executed their leaders in 1649. He used terror to crush Irish clan resistance 1649–50; and defeated the Scots (who had acknowledged Charles II) at Dunbar 1650 and Worcester 1651. In 1653, having forcibly expelled the corrupt 'Rump' Parliament, he summoned a convention ('Barebone's Parliament'), soon dissolved as too radical, and under a constitution (Instrument of Government) drawn up by the army leaders, became Protector (king in all but name). The Parliament of 1654–55 was dissolved as uncooperative, and after a period of military dictatorship, his last parliament offered him the crown; he refused because he feared the army's republicanism.

Cromwell Richard 1626–1712. Son of Oliver Cromwell, he succeeded his father as Protector, but resigned May 1659, living in exile after the Restoration until 1680, when he returned to England.

Cromwell Thomas, Earl of Essex c.1485–1540. English politician. Originally in Lord Chancellor Wolsey's service, he became secretary to Henry VIII 1534 and the real director of government policy. He had Henry proclaimed head of the church, suppressed the monasteries, ruthlessly crushed all opposition, and favoured Protestantism, which denied the divine right of the pope. His mistake in arranging Henry's marriage to Anne of Cleves (to cement an alliance with the German Protestant princes against France and the Holy Roman Empire) led to his being accused of treason and beheaded.

Cronkite Walter 1916– . US broadcast journalist, who became a household name and face throughout the USA as anchorman of the national evening news programme for CBS, a US television network, from 1962 to 1981.

Crookes William 1832–1919. English scientist, whose many chemical and physical discoveries included the metal thallium 1861, the radiometer 1875, and Crooke's high vacuum tube used in X-ray techniques.

Crosby 'Bing' (Harry Lillis) 1904–1977. US film actor and singer, who achieved world success with his distinctive style of crooning in such songs as 'Pennies from Heaven', and 'White Christmas'. He won an acting Oscar for *Going My Way* 1944, and made a series of 'road' film comedies with Dorothy Lamour and Bob Hope, the last being *Road to Hong Kong* 1962.

Crossman Richard (Howard Stafford) 1907–1974. British Labour politician. He was minister of housing and local government 1964–66 and of health and social security 1968–70. His posthumous *Crossman Papers* 1975 revealed confidential cabinet discussion.

Crowley Aleister (Edward Alexander) 1875–1947. British occultist, a member of the theosophical Order of the Golden Dawn; he claimed to practise black magic, and his books include the novel *Diary of a Drug Fiend* 1923. He designed a tarot pack that bears his name.

Crowley John 1942– . US writer of science fiction and fantasy, notably *Little, Big* 1980 and *Aegypt* 1987, which contain esoteric knowledge and theoretical puzzles.

Cruden Alexander 1701–1770. Scottish compiler of a Biblical *Concordance* 1737.

Cruft Charles 1852–1938. British dog expert. He organized his first dog show 1886, and from that year annual shows bearing his name were held in Islington, London.

Cruikshank George 1792–1878. British painter and illustrator, remembered especially for his political cartoons and illustrations to Dickens's *Oliver Twist* and Defoe's *Robinson Crusoe*.

Cubitt Thomas 1788–1855. English builder and property developer. One of the earliest speculators, Cubitt rebuilt much of Belgravia, London, an area of Brighton, and the east front of Buckingham Palace.

Cugnot Nicolas 1728–1804. French engineer who produced the first high-pressure steam engine. While serving in the French army, he was asked to design a steam-operated gun-carriage. After several years' labour, he produced a three-wheeled, high-pressure carriage capable of carrying 1,800 litres/400 gallons of water and four passengers at a speed of 5 kph/3 mph. Although he worked further on the carriage, political conditions mitigated against much progress being made and his invention was ignored.

Cui Casar Antonovich 1853–1918. Russian composer of operas and chamber music. A professional soldier, he joined ◊Balakirev's Group of Five and promoted a Russian national style.

Cukor George 1899–1983. US film director. He moved to the cinema from the theatre, and was praised for his skilled handling of stars such as Greta ◊Garbo (in *Camille* 1937) and Katherine Hepburn (in *The Philadelphia Story* 1940, among others). His films were usually civilized dramas or light comedies.

Culshaw John 1924–1980. British record producer, who developed recording techniques. Managing classical recordings for the Decca record company in the 1950s and 1960s, he introduced echo chambers, and the speeding and slowing of tapes, to achieve effects not possible in live performance. He produced the first complete recordings of Wagner's *Ring* cycle.

Cumberland Ernest Augustus, Duke of Cumberland 1771–1851. King of Hanover from 1837, the fifth son of George III of Britain. A high Tory and an opponent of all reforms, his attempts to suppress the constitution met with open resistance that had to be put down by force.

Cumberland William Augustus, Duke of Cumberland 1721–1765. British general, who ended the Jacobite rising in Scotland with the Battle of Culloden 1746; his brutal repression of the Highlanders earned him the nickname of 'Butcher'. Third son of George II, he was created Duke of Cumberland 1726. In the Seven Years' War he surrendered with his army at Kloster-Zeven 1757.

Cumming Mansfield 1859–1923. British naval officer, first head of the British Secret Intelligence Service. The head of the service has always since been known by the initial letter 'C'.

cummings e(dward) e(stlin) 1894–1962. US poet, whose published collections of poetry include *Tulips and Chimneys* 1923. His poems were initially notorious for their idiosyncratic punctuation and typography (he always wrote his name in lower-case letters, for example), but their lyric power has gradually been recognized.

Cunha Euclydes da 1866–1909. Brazilian writer. His novel *Os Sertoes/Rebellion in the Backlands* 1902 describes the Brazilian *sertao* (backlands), and how a small group of rebels resisted government troops.

Cunningham Andrew Browne, 1st Viscount Cunningham of Hyndhope 1883–1963. British admiral in World War II; as commander in chief of the Allied Naval Forces in the Mediterranean Feb–Oct 1943 he received the surrender of the Italian fleet.

Cunningham John 1885–1962. British admiral in World War II. In 1940 he assisted in the evacuation of Norway and prepared the way for the N African invasion in 1942.

Cunningham Merce 1919– . US dancer and choreographer. Influenced by Martha ◊Graham, with whose company he was soloist from 1939–45; he formed his own dance company and school in New York in 1953. His works include *The Seasons* 1947, *Antic Meet* 1958, *Squaregame* 1976, and *Arcade* 1985.

Cunninghame-Graham Robert Bontine 1852–1936. Scottish writer, politician, and adventurer. He wrote essays and short stories such as *Success* 1902, *Faith* 1909, *Hope* 1910, and *Charity* 1912, and many travel books based on his experiences as a rancher in Texas and Argentina 1869–83, and as a traveller in Spain and Morocco 1893–98. He was president of the Scottish Labour Party in 1888 and became first president of the Scottish National Party in 1928.

Curie Marie (born Sklodovska) 1867–1934. Polish scientist, who investigated radioactivity, and with her husband Pierre (1859–1906) discovered radium.

Born in Warsaw, she studied in Paris from 1891. Impressed by the publication of ◊Becquerel's experiments, Marie Curie decided to investigate the nature of uranium rays. In 1898 she

Curie Marie Curie in her Paris laboratory.

reported the possible existence of some new powerful radioactive element in pitchblende ores. Her husband abandoned his own researches to assist her, and in the same year they announced the existence of polonium and radium. They isolated the pure elements in 1902.

Both scientists refused to take out a patent on their discovery, and were jointly awarded the Davy Medal (1903) and the Nobel Prize for Physics (1903; with Becquerel). In 1904 Pierre was appointed to a chair in physics at the Sorbonne, and on his death in a street accident was succeeded by his wife. She wrote a *Treatise on Radioactivity* in 1910, and was awarded the Nobel Prize for Chemistry in 1911. She died a victim of the radiation among which she had worked in her laboratory.

Curnonsky pseudonym of Maurice Edmond Sailland 1872–1956. French gastronome and cookery writer, who was a pioneer in the cataloguing of French regional cuisine.

Curtin John 1885–1945. Australian Labor politician, prime minister and minister of defence 1941–45. He was elected leader of the Labor Party 1935. As prime minister, he organized the mobilization of Australia's resources to meet the danger of Japanese invasion during World War II.

Curtis Tony. Stage name of Bernard Schwartz 1925– . US actor, who starred in the 1950s and 1960s in such films as *The Vikings* 1959 and *Some Like it Hot* 1959, with Jack Lemmon and Marilyn Monroe.

Curtiz Michael (Mihaly Kersesz) 1888–1962. Hungarian-born film director who worked in Austria, Germany, and France before moving to the USA where he made several Errol Flynn films and *Casablanca* 1942. His wide range of films includes *Doctor* 1932; *The Adventures of Robin Hood* 1938; *Mildred Pierce* 1945; and *The Comancheros* 1962.

Curwen John 1816–1880. English musician. In about 1840 he established the *tonic sol-fa* system of music notation (originated in the 11th century by

Guido d'Arezzo) in which the notes of a scale are named by syllables (doh, ray, me, fah, soh, lah, te) to simplify singing by sight.

Curzon George Nathaniel, 1st Marquess Curzon of Kedleston 1859–1925. British Conservative politician. Viceroy of India from 1899, he resigned 1905 following a controversy with Kitchener. He was foreign secretary 1919–22.

Curzon Robert, Lord Zouche 1810–1873. English diplomat and traveller, author of *Monasteries in the Levant* 1849.

Cusack Cyril 1910– . Irish actor who joined the Abbey Theatre, Dublin, 1932 and appeared in many of its productions, including Synge's *The Playboy of the Western World*. In Paris he won an award for his solo performance in Beckett's *Krapp's Last Tape*. In the UK he has played many roles as a member of the Royal Shakespeare Company and the National Theatre Company.

Cushing Harvey Williams 1869–1939. US neurologist who pioneered neurosurgery. He developed a range of techniques for the surgical treatment of brain tumours, and also studied the link between the pituitary gland (which controls, among other things, growth) and conditions such as dwarfism.

Cushing Peter 1913– . British actor who specialized in horror roles in films made at Hammer studios 1957–73, including *Dracula* 1958; *Cash on Demand* 1963; *Frankenstein Must be Destroyed* 1969. Other films include *Star Wars* 1977 and *Top Secret* 1984.

Cuvier Georges, Baron Cuvier 1769–1832. French comparative anatomist. In 1799 he showed that some species have become extinct by reconstructing extinct giant animals that he believed were destroyed in a series of giant deluges. These ideas are expressed in *Recherches sur les ossements fossiles de quadrupèdes* 1812 and *Discours sur les revolutions de la surface du globe 1825*.

In 1798 Cuvier produced *Tableau élémentaire de l'histoire naturelle des animaux*, in which his scheme of classification is outlined. He was professor of natural history in the Collège de France from 1799, and at the Jardin des Plantes from 1802; and at the Restoration in 1815 he was elected chancellor of the University of Paris. Cuvier was the first to relate the structure of fossil animals to that of their living relatives. His great work, *Le Règne animal/ The Animal Kingdom* 1817 is a systematic survey.

Cuyp Aelbert 1620–1691. Dutch painter of countryside scenes, seascapes, and portraits. His idyllically peaceful landscapes are bathed in golden light, for example *A Herdsman with Cows by a River* (*c.*1650 National Gallery, London). His father was *Jacob Gerritsz Cuyp* (1594–1652), also a landscape and portrait painter.

Cynewulf lived early 8th century. Anglo-Saxon poet. He is thought to have been a Northumbrian monk, and is the undoubted author of 'Juliana' and part of the 'Christ' in the Exeter Book (a collection of poems now in Exeter Cathedral), and of the 'Fates of the Apostles' and 'Elene' in the Vercelli Book (a collection of Old English manuscripts housed at Vercelli, Italy), in all of which he inserted his name by using runic acrostics.

Cyprian, St *c.* 210–258. Christian martyr, one of the earliest Christian writers, and bishop of Carthage about 249. He wrote a treatise on the unity of the church. Feast day 16 Sept.

Cyrano de Bergerac Savinien de 1619–1655. French writer. He joined a corps of guards at 19, and performed heroic feats which made him famous. He is the hero of a classic play by ◊Rostand, in which his notoriously long nose is used as a counterpoint to his chivalrous character.

Cyril and Methodius two brothers, both Christian saints: Cyril 826–869 and Methodius 815–885. Born in Thessalonica, they were sent as missionaries to what is today Moravia. They invented a Slavonic alphabet, and translated the Bible and the liturgy from Greek to Slavonic. The language (known as *Old Church Slavonic*)

remained in use in churches and for literature among Bulgars, Serbs, and Russians up to the 17th century. The *cyrillic alphabet* is named after Cyril and may also have been invented by him. Feast day 14 Feb.

Cyril of Alexandria, St 376–444. Bishop of Alexandria from 412, persecutor of Jews and other non-Christians, and suspected of ordering the murder of Hypatia (*c.* 370–*c.* 415), a philosopher whose influence was increasing at the expense of his.

Cyrus the Great died 529 BC. Founder of the Persian Empire. As king of Persia, originally subject to the Medes, whose empire he overthrew 550 BC. He captured Croesus, king of Lydia 546 BC, and conquered all Asia Minor, adding Babylonia (including Syria and Palestine) to his empire 539 BC, allowing exiled Jews to return to Jerusalem. He died fighting in Afghanistan.

Czerny Carl 1791–1857. Austrian composer and pianist. He wrote an enormous quantity of religious and concert music, but is chiefly remembered for his books of graded studies and technical exercises used in piano teaching.

improvement of the range of opportunities open to the individual.

Daimler Gottlieb 1834–1900. German engineer who pioneered the modern motorcar. In 1886 he produced his first motor vehicle and a motor-bicycle. He later joined forces with Karl ◊Benz and was one of the pioneers of the high-speed 4-stroke petrol engine.

Born in Württemberg, he had engineering experience at the Whitworth works, Manchester, England, before joining N A Otto of Cologne in the production of an internal-combustion gas engine 1872.

Daladier Edouard 1884–1970. French Radical politician. As prime minister Apr 1938–Mar 1940, he was largely responsible both for the Munich Agreement (by which the Sudeten districts of Czeckoslovakia were ceded to Germany) and France's declaration of war on Germany. Arrested on the fall of France, he was a prisoner in Germany 1943–45. He was re-elected to the Chamber of Deputies 1946–58.

Dalai Lama 14th incarnation 1935– . Spiritual and temporal head of the Tibetan state until 1959, when he went into exile in protest against Chinese annexation and oppression. Tibetan Buddhists believe that each Dalai Lama is a reincarnation of his predecessor and also of Avalokiteśvara. Nobel peace prize 1989 in recognition of his

Dadd Richard 1817–1887. British painter. In 1843 he murdered his father and was committed to an insane asylum, but continued to paint minutely detailed pictures of fantasies and fairy tales, such as *The Fairy Feller's Master-Stroke* 1855–64 (Tate Gallery, London).

Dafydd ap Gwilym c.1340–c.1400. Welsh poet. His work is notable for its complex but graceful style, its concern with nature and love rather than with heroic martial deeds, and for its references to Classical and Italian poetry. He was born into an influential Dyfed gentry family, and is traditionally believed to have led a life packed with amorous adventures.

Daguerre Louis Jacques Mande 1789–1851. French pioneer of photography. Together with Niepce, he is credited with the invention of photography (though others were reaching the same point simultaneously). In 1839 he invented the daguerreotype, a single-image process, superseded ten years later by ◊Talbot's negative/positive process.

Dahl Johann Christian 1788–1857. Norwegian landscape painter in the Romantic style. He trained in Copenhagen but was active chiefly in Dresden from 1818. He was the first great painter of the Norwegian landscape, in a style that recalls the Dutch artist ◊Ruisdael.

Dahl Roald 1916– . British writer, celebrated for short stories with a twist, for example, *Tales of the Unexpected* 1979, and for children's books including *Charlie and the Chocolate Factory* 1964.

Dahrendorf Ralf (Gustav) 1929– . German sociologist, director of the London School of Economics 1974–84. His works include *Life Chances* 1980, which sees the aim of society as the

Daguerre *Frenchman Louis Daguerre discovered how to produce a single photographic image as a result of accidentally spilt iodine on some of his silvered plates.*

commitment to the nonviolent liberation of his homeland.

Enthroned 1940, the Dalai Lama temporarily fled 1950–51 when the Chinese overran Tibet, and in Mar 1959 made a dramatic escape from Lhasa to India, when a local uprising against Chinese rule was suppressed. He then settled at Dharmsala in the Punjab. His people continue to demand his return, and the Chinese offered to lift the ban on his living in Tibet, providing he refrained from calling for Tibet's independence. His deputy, the Panchen Lama, has cooperated with the Chinese but failed to protect the monks.

Dalcroze Emile Jaques see ◊Jaques-Dalcroze, Emile.

Dale Henry Hallett 1875–1968. British physiologist, who in 1936 shared a Nobel prize with Otto Loewi (1873–1961) for work on the chemical transmission of nervous effects.

d'Alembert see ◊Alembert, French mathematician.

Dalen Nils 1869–1937. Swedish industrial engineer who invented the light-controlled valve. This allowed lighthouses to operate automatically and won him the 1912 Nobel Prize for Physics.

Dalgarno George 1626–1687. Scottish schoolteacher and inventor of the first sign-language alphabet 1680.

Dalglish Kenneth 'Kenny' 1951– . Scottish footballer, the only man to play 200 League games in England and Scotland, and score 100 goals in each country.

Born in Glasgow, he made over 200 appearances for Glasgow Celtic before joining Liverpool 1977. He won all domestic honours as a player and since becoming Liverpool manager in 1985 has led the club to similar successes. He played for Scotland 102 times.

Dalhousie James Andrew Broun Ramsay, 1st Marquess and 10th Earl of Dalhousie 1812–1860. British administrator, governor general of India 1848–56. In the second Sikh War he annexed the Punjab 1849, and, after the second Burmese War, Lower Burma 1853. He reformed the Indian army and civil service and furthered social and economic progress.

Dali Salvador 1904–1989. Spanish painter. In 1928 he collaborated with Buñuel on the film *Un chien andalou*. In 1929 he joined the Surrealists and became notorious for his flamboyant eccentricity. Influenced by the psychoanalytic theories of Freud, he developed a repertoire of dramatic images, such as the distorted human body, limp watches, and burning giraffes. These are painted with a meticulous, polished clarity. He also painted religious themes and many portraits of his wife Gala.

Dali, born near Barcelona, initially came under the influence of the Italian Futurists. He is credited as co-creator of *Un chien andalou* but his role is thought to have been subordinate; he abandoned film after collaborating on the script for Buñuel's *L'Age d'Or* 1930. He designed ballet costumes, scenery, jewellery, and furniture. The books *Secret Life of Salvador Dali* 1942 and *Diary of a Genius* 1966 are autobiographical. He is buried beneath a crystal dome in the museum of his work at Figueras on the Costa Brava, Spain.

Dallapiccola Luigi 1904–1975. Italian composer. In his early years he was a Neo-Classicist in the manner of Stravinsky, but he soon turned to Serialism, which he adapted to his own style. His works include the operas *Il Prigioniero/The Prisoner* 1949 and *Ulisse/Ulysses* 1968, as well as many vocal and instrumental compositions.

Dalton Hugh, Baron Dalton 1887–1962. British Labour politician and economist. Chancellor of the Exchequer from 1945, he oversaw nationalization of the Bank of England, but resigned 1947 after making a disclosure to a lobby correspondent before a budget speech.

Dalton John 1776–1844. British chemist, the first in modern times to propose the existence of atoms, which he considered to be the smallest parts of matter. He produced the first list of relative atomic masses, *Absorption of Gases* 1805. He was also the first scientist to note and record colour-blindness.

From experiments with gases he noted that the proportions of two components combining to form another gas were always consistent. From this he suggested that if substances combine in simple numerical ratios then the macroscopic weight proportions represent the relative atomic masses of those substances.

Daly Augustin 1838–1899. US theatre manager. He began as a drama critic and playwright before building his own theatre in New York 1879 and another, Daly's, in Leicester Square, London (1893–1937).

Dalziel family British wood-engravers. *George* (1815–1902), *Edward* (1817–1905), *John* (1822–60), and *Thomas Bolton* (1823–1906) were all sons of Alexander Dalziel of Wooler, Northumberland. George went to London in 1835 and was joined by his brothers. They produced a large number of illustrations of the classics and for magazines.

Dam Carl 1895–1976. Danish biochemist who discovered vitamin K. For his success in this field he shared the 1943 Nobel Prize for Medicine with Edward Doisy.

In 1928 Dam began a series of experiments to see if chickens could live on a cholesterol-free diet. The birds, it turned out, were able to metabolize their own supply. Yet they continued to die from spontaneous haemorrhages. Dam concluded that their diet lacked an unknown essential ingredient, which he eventually found in abundance in green leaves. As it controlled coagulation, Dam named the new compound vitamin K.

Damien, Father 1840–1889. Name adopted by Belgian missionary Joseph de ◊Veuster.

Damocles lived 4th century BC. In Classical legend, a courtier of the elder Dionysius, ruler of Syracuse, Sicily. Having extolled the happiness of his sovereign, Damocles was invited by him to a feast, during which he saw above his head a sword suspended by a single hair. He recognized this as a symbol of the insecurity of the great.

Dampier William 1652–1715. English explorer and hydrographic surveyor who circumnavigated the world three times.

He was born in Somerset, and went to sea in 1668. He led a life of buccaneering adventure, circumnavigated the globe, and published his *New Voyage Round the World* in 1697. In 1699 he was sent by the government on a voyage to Australia and New Guinea, and again circled the world. He accomplished a third circumnavigation 1703–07, and on his final voyage 1708–11 rescued Alexander ◊Selkirk (on whose life Defoe's *Robinson Crusoe* is based) from Juan Fernandez in the S Pacific.

Dana Richard Henry 1815–1882. US author who went to sea and worked his passage round Cape Horn to California and back, writing an account in *Two Years before the Mast* 1840.

Danby Thomas Osborne, Earl of Danby 1631–1712. British Tory politician. He entered Parliament 1665, acted 1673–78 as Charles II's chief minister and in 1674 was created earl of Danby, but was imprisoned in the Tower of London 1678–84. In 1688 he signed the invitation to William of Orange to take the throne. Danby was again chief minister 1690–95, and in 1694 was created duke of Leeds.

Dance Charles 1946– . British film and television actor who achieved fame in *The Jewel in the Crown* 1984. He has also appeared in *Plenty* 1986, *Good Morning Babylon*, *The Golden Child* 1987, and *White Mischief* 1988.

Dandolo Venetian family that produced four doges (rulers), of whom the most outstanding, *Enrico Dandolo* (*c.* 1120–1205), became doge in 1193. He greatly increased the dominions of the Venetian republic and accompanied the crusading army that took Constantinople in 1203.

Daniel 6th century BC. Jewish folk hero and prophet at the court of Nebuchadnezzar. One of the best-known stories is that of Daniel in the den of lions, where he was thrown for refusing to compromise his beliefs, and was preserved by divine intervention.

Daniel Glyn 1914– . British archaeologist. Prominent in the development of the subject, he was Disney professor of archaeology, Cambridge, 1974–81. His books include *Megaliths in History* 1973 and *A Short History of Archaeology* 1981.

Daniel Samuel 1562–1619. English poet, author of the sonnet collection *Delia* 1592. He was master of the revels at court from 1603, for which he wrote masques.

Daniell John Frederic 1790–1845. British chemist and meteorologist who invented a primary electrical cell, the *Daniell cell*, in 1836.

Dankworth John 1927– . British jazz musician, composer, and bandleader, influential in the development of British jazz from about 1950. His film scores include *Saturday Night and Sunday Morning* 1960 and *The Servant* 1963.

D'Annunzio Gabriele 1863–1938. Italian poet, novelist, and playwright. He wrote the play *La Gioconda* for the actress Eleonora ◊Duse in 1898. His mystic nationalism prepared the way for Fascism.

Dante Alighieri 1265–1321. Italian poet. His masterpiece is *Divina Commedia/The Divine Comedy* 1300–21. Other works include the

Dante Alighieri *Italian poet Dante Alighieri by Andrea del Castagno.*

prose philosophical treatise *Convivio* 1306–08; *Monarchia* 1310–13, expounding his political theories; *De vulgari eloquentia/Concerning the Vulgar Tongue* 1304–06, an original Latin work on Italian, its dialects, and kindred languages; and *Canzoniere/Lyrics*, containing his scattered lyrics. Dante was born in Florence. He first met Beatrice (Portinari) in 1274 and conceived a love for her that survived her marriage to another and her death in 1290, as he described in *Vita Nuova/New Life* about 1295. In 1289 Dante fought in the battle of Campaldino, won by Florence against Arezzo, and from 1295 took an active part in Florentine politics. In 1300 he was one of the six Priors of the Republic, and, since he favoured the moderate White Guelph party rather than the Black, was convicted in his absence of misapplication of public moneys in 1302 when the Black Guelphs became predominant. He spent the remainder of his life in exile, in central and northern Italy.

Danton Georges Jacques 1759–1794. French revolutionary. Originally a lawyer, during the early years of the Revolution he was one of the most influential people in Paris. He organized the rising 10 Aug 1792 that overthrew the monarchy, roused the country to expel the Prussian invaders, and in Apr 1793 formed the revolutionary tribunal and the *Committee of Public Safety*, of which he was the real leader until July. Thereafter he lost power, and when he attempted to recover it, he was arrested and guillotined.

D'Arblay, Madame married name of British writer Fanny ◊Burney.

Darby Abraham 1677–1717. English iron manufacturer who developed a process for smelting iron ore using coke instead of the more expensive charcoal.

He employed the cheaper iron to cast strong thin pots for domestic use as well as the huge cylinders required by the new steam pumping-engines. In 1779 his son (also Abraham) constructed the world's first iron bridge, over the river Severn at Coalbrookdale.

Darío Rubén. Pen name of Félix Rubén García Sarmiento 1867–1916. Nicaraguan poet. His *Azul/Azure* 1888, a collection of prose and verse influenced by French Symbolism, created a sensation. He went on to establish *modernismo*, the Spanish-American modernist literary movement, and his vitality and eclecticism influenced every poet writing in Spanish after him, both in the New World and in Spain.

Darius I *the Great* c.558–486 BC. King of Persia 521–485 BC. A member of a younger branch of the Achaemenid dynasty, he won the throne from the usurper Gaumata (died 522 BC), reorganized the government, and in 512 BC marched against the Scythians, a people north of the Black Sea, and subjugated Thrace and Macedonia.

An expedition in 492 BC to crush a rebellion in Greece failed, and the army sent into Attica 490 BC was defeated at the battle of Marathon. Darius had an account of his reign inscribed on the mountain at Behistun, Persia.

Darlan Jean François 1881–1942. French admiral and politician. He entered the navy 1899, and was appointed admiral and commander in chief 1939. He commanded the French navy 1939–40, took part in the evacuation of Dunkirk, and entered the Pétain cabinet as naval minister. In 1941 he was appointed vice-premier, and became strongly anti-British and pro-German, but in 1942 he was dropped from the cabinet by Laval and sent to N Africa, where he was assassinated.

Darling Grace 1815–1842. British heroine. She was the daughter of a lighthouse keeper on the Farne Islands, off Northumberland. On 7 Sept 1838 the *Forfarshire* was wrecked, and Grace Darling and her father rowed through a storm to the wreck, saving nine lives. She was awarded a medal for her bravery.

Darnley Henry Stewart or Stuart, Lord Darnley 1545–1567. British aristocrat, second husband of Mary Queen of Scots from 1565, and father of James I of England (James VI of Scotland). On the advice of her secretary, David ◊Rizzio, Mary refused Darnley the crown matrimonial; in revenge Darnley led a band of nobles who murdered Rizzio in Mary's presence. Darnley was assassinated 1567.

He was born in England, the son of the 4th Earl of Lennox (1516–71) and Lady Margaret Douglas (1515–78), through whom he inherited a claim to the English throne. Mary was his first cousin. Mary and Darnley were reconciled after the murder of Rizzio 1566, but soon Darnley alienated all parties and a plot to kill him was formed by ◊Bothwell. Mary's part in it remains a subject of controversy.

Darrow Clarence (Seward) 1857–1938. US lawyer, born in Ohio, a champion of liberal causes and defender of the underdog. He defended many trade-union leaders, including Eugene ◊Debs 1894. He was counsel for the defence in the Nathan Leopold and Richard Loeb murder trial in Chicago 1924.

Dart Raymond 1893–1988. Australian anthropologist. He discovered the fossil remains of the 'southern African ape' *Australopithecus africanus* 1924, near Taungs in Botswana.

Darwin Charles Robert 1809–1882. English scientist, who developed the modern theory of evolution and proposed the principle of natural selection. After much research in South America and the Galápagos Islands as naturalist on HMS *Beagle* 1831–36, Darwin published *On the Origin of Species by Means of Natural Selection or the Preservation of Favoured Races in the Struggle for Life* 1859. This explained the evolutionary

CHARLES ROBERT DARWIN, LL.D., F.R.S.

In his *Descent of Man* he brought his own Species down as low as possible—*i.e.*, to "A Hairy Quadruped furnished with a Tail and Pointed Ears, and probably *Arboreal* in its habits"—which is a reason for the very general Interest in a "Family Tree." He has lately been turning his attention to the "Politic Worm."

Darwin Cartoon of Charles Robert Darwin by Linley Sambourne.

process through the principles of natural and sexual selection, refuting earlier theories. It aroused bitter controversy because it disagreed with the literal interpretation of the Book of Genesis in the Bible.

Darwin Erasmus 1731–1802. British poet, physician, naturalist, and grandfather of Charles Darwin. He wrote *The Botanic Garden* 1792, which included a versification of the Linnaean system entitled 'The Loves of the Plants', and *Zoonomia* 1794–96, which anticipated aspects of evolutionary theory, but tended to ◊Lamarck's interpretation.

Daudet Alphonse 1840–1897. French novelist. He wrote about his native Provence in *Lettres de mon moulin/Letters from My Mill* 1866, and created the character Tartarin, a hero epitomizing southern temperament, in *Tartarin de Tarascon* 1872 and two sequels.

Daudet Léon 1867–1942. French writer and journalist, who founded the militant right-wing royalist periodical *Action française* in 1899 after the Dreyfus case. During World War II he was a collaborator with the Germans. He was the son of Alphonse Daudet.

Daumier Honoré 1808–1879. French artist. His sharply dramatic and satirical cartoons dissected

Parisian society. His output was enormous and included 4,000 lithographs and, mainly after 1860, powerful satirical oil paintings that were little appreciated in his lifetime.

Daumier drew for *La Caricature, Charivari* and other periodicals. He created several fictitious stereotypes of contemporary figures, and was once imprisoned for an attack on Louis Philippe.

Davenant William 1606–1668. English poet and dramatist, poet laureate from 1638. His *Siege of Rhodes* 1656 is sometimes considered the first English opera. He was rumoured to be an illegitimate son of Shakespeare.

David *c.*1060–970 BC. Second king of Israel. According to the Bible he played the harp before King Saul to banish his melancholy, and later slew the Philistine giant Goliath with a sling and stone. After Saul's death David was anointed king at Hebron, took Jerusalem and made it his capital. David probably wrote a few of the psalms and was celebrated as a secular poet.

David Elizabeth 1914– . British cookery writer. Her *Mediterranean Food* 1950 and *French Country Cooking* 1951 helped to spark an interest in foreign cuisine in Britain, and also inspired a growing school of informed, highly literate writing on food and wine.

David Félicien César 1810–1876. French composer. His symphonic fantasy *Desert* 1844 was inspired by travels in Palestine. He was one of the first Western composers to introduce oriental scales and melodies into his music.

David Gerard *c.*1450–1523. Netherlandish painter active chiefly in Bruges from about 1484. His style follows that of van der Weyden, but he was also influenced by the new taste in Antwerp for Italianate ornament. *The Marriage at Cana* about 1503 (Louvre, Paris) is a good example of his work.

David Jacques Louis 1748–1825. French painter in the Neo-Classical style. He was an active supporter of and unofficial painter to the republic during the French Revolution, for which he was imprisoned 1794–95. He was later appointed court painter to the emperor Napoleon, of whom he created well-known images such as the horseback figure of *Napoleon Crossing the Alps* 1800 (Louvre, Paris).

During the Revolution he was elected to the Convention and a member of the Committee of Public Safety, and narrowly escaped the guillotine. In his *Death of Marat* 1793, he turned political murder into a classical tragedy. Later he devoted himself to the empire in paintings like the enormous, pompous *Coronation of Napoleon* 1805–07 (Louvre, Paris). After Napoleon's fall, David was banished by the Bourbons and settled in Brussels.

David two kings of Scotland:

David I 1084–1153. King of Scotland from 1124. The youngest son of Malcolm III Canmore and

St ◊Margaret, he was brought up in the English court of Henry I, and in 1113 married ◊Matilda, widow of the 1st earl of Northampton. He invaded England 1138 in support of Queen Matilda, but was defeated at Northallerton in the Battle of the Standard, and again 1141.

David II 1324–1371. King of Scotland from 1329, son of ◊Robert I (the Bruce). David was married at the age of four to Joanna, daughter of Edward II of England. After the defeat of the Scots by Edward III at Halidon Hill, David and Joanna were sent to France for safety. They returned 1341. In 1346 David invaded England, was captured at the battle of Neville's Cross and imprisoned for 11 years. On Joanna's death 1362 David married Margaret Logie, but divorced her 1370.

David, St or *Dewi* 5th–6th century. Patron saint of Wales, Christian abbot and bishop. According to legend he was the son of a prince of Dyfed and uncle of King Arthur, and responsible for the adoption of the leek as the national emblem of Wales, but his own emblem is a dove. Feast day 1 Mar.

Tradition has it that David made a pilgrimage to Jerusalem, where he was consecrated bishop. He founded 12 monasteries in Wales, including one at Menevia, which he made his bishop's seat; he presided over a synod at Brefi and condemned the ideas of the British theologian Pelagius.

Davidson John 1857–1909. Scottish poet whose modern, realistic idiom, as in 'Thirty Bob a Week', influenced T S ◊Eliot.

Davies Henry Walford 1869–1941. English composer and broadcaster. From 1934 he was Master of the King's Musick, and he contributed to the musical education of Britain through his radio talks.

His compositions include the cantata *Everyman* 1904, the 'Solemn Melody' 1908 for organ and strings, chamber music, and part songs.

Davies Peter Maxwell 1934– . English composer and conductor. His music combines medieval and serial codes of practice with a heightened Expressionism as in his opera *Taverner* 1962–68.

After training alongside the British composers Goehr and Birtwistle, he studied with Petrassi and later with the US composer Sessions. He has composed music-theatre works for the group the Pierrot Players, later the Fires of London. He moved to Orkney in the 1970s where he has done much to revitalize music, composing for local groups and on local themes.

Davies Robertson 1913– . Canadian novelist. He gained an international reputation with *Fifth Business* 1970, the first novel of his Deptford trilogy, a panoramic work blending philosophy, humour, the occult, and ordinary life. Other works include *A Mixture of Frailties* 1958, *The Rebel Angels* 1981, and *What's Bred in the Bone* 1986.

Davis Hollywood legend Bette Davis.

Davies W(illiam) H(enry) 1871–1940. Welsh poet, born in Monmouth. He went to the USA where he lived the life of a hobo, or vagrant, and lost his right foot 'riding the rods'. His first volume of poems was *Soul's Destroyer* 1906. He published his *Autobiography of a Super-Tramp* 1908.

Da Vinci see ◊Leonardo da Vinci, Italian Renaissance artist.

Davis Angela 1944– . US left-wing activist for black rights, prominent in the student movement of the 1960s. In 1970 she went into hiding after being accused of supplying guns used in the murder of a judge who had been seized as a hostage in an attempt to secure the release of three black convicts. She was captured, tried, and acquitted. In 1980 she stood as the Communist vice-presidential candidate.

At the University of California she studied under Marcuse, and was assistant professor of philosophy at UCLA 1969–70.

Davis Bette 1908–1989. US actress. She entered films in 1930, and established a reputation with *Of Human Bondage* 1934 as a forceful dramatic actress. Later films included *Dangerous* 1935 and *Jezebel* 1938, both winning her Academy Awards, and *Whatever Happened to Baby Jane?* 1962.

Davis Colin 1927– . English conductor. He was musical director at Sadler's Wells 1961–65, chief conductor of the BBC Symphony Orchestra 1967–71, musical director of the Royal Opera 1971–86, and chief conductor of the Bavarian Radio Symphony Orchestra 1983.

Davis Jefferson 1808–1889. US politician, president of the short-lived Confederate States of America 1861–65. He was a leader of the Southern Democrats in the US Senate from 1857, and a defender of 'humane' slavery; in 1860 he issued a declaration in favour of secession from the USA. During the Civil War he assumed strong political leadership, but often disagreed with military policy. He was imprisoned for two years after the war, one of the very few cases of judicial retribution against Confederate leaders.

Born in Kentucky, he served in the US army before becoming a cotton planter in Mississippi. He sat in the US Senate 1847–51, was secretary of war 1853–57, and returned to the Senate 1857.

Davis Joe 1901–1978. British billiards and snooker player. World snooker champion a record 15 times 1927–46, he was responsible for much of the popularity of the modern game. His brother Fred was also a billiards and snooker world champion.

Davis John 1550–1605. English navigator and explorer. He sailed in search of the Northwest Passage through the Canadian Arctic to the Pacific Ocean 1585, and in 1587 sailed to Baffin Bay through the straits named after him. He was the first European to see the Falkland Islands 1592.

Davis Miles (Dewey Jr) 1926– . US jazz trumpeter, composer, and band leader. He recorded bebop with Charlie Parker 1945, pioneered cool jazz in the 1950s and jazz-rock fusion from the late 1960s. His influential albums include *Birth of the Cool* 1949, *Sketches of Spain* 1959, and *Bitches' Brew* 1970.

Davis Steve 1957– . English snooker player. He has won every major honour in the game since turning professional 1978. He has been world champion six times, including 1989. He has won as many major titles as all the other professionals between them.

Davis won his first major title 1980 when he won the Coral UK Championship. He has also won world titles at Pairs and with the England team. His earnings regularly top £1 million through on- and off-the-table prize money and endorsements.

Davis Stuart 1894–1964. US abstract painter. He used hard-edged geometric shapes in primary colours and experimented with collage. In the 1920s he produced paintings of commercial packaging, such as *Lucky Strike* 1921 (Museum of Modern Art, New York), which foreshadow Pop art.

Davison Emily 1872–1913. English militant suffragette, who died while trying to stop the king's horse at the Derby at Epsom (she was trampled by the horse). She joined the Women's Social and Political Union in 1906 and served several prison sentences for militant action such as stone throwing, setting fire to pillar boxes, and bombing Lloyd George's country house.

Her coffin was carried through London draped in the colours of the suffragette movement, purple, white and green. It was escorted by 2,000 uniformed suffragettes.

Davisson Clinton 1881–1958. US physicist. With Lester Germer (1896–1971), he discovered that electrons can undergo diffraction, so proving Louis ◊de Broglie's theory that electrons, and

therefore all matter, can show wave-like behaviour. G P ◊Thomson carried through the same research independently, and in 1937 the two men shared a Nobel prize.

Davitt Michael 1846–1906. Irish Fenian revolutionary. He joined the Fenians (forerunners of the Irish Republican Army) 1865, and was imprisoned for treason 1870–77. After his release, he and Charles Parnell founded the Land League 1879. Davitt was jailed several times for his share in the land-reform agitation. He was a member of Parliament 1895–99.

Davy Humphry 1778–1829. English chemist. As a laboratory assistant in Bristol in 1799, he discovered the respiratory effects of laughing gas (nitrous oxide). He discovered, by electrolysis, the elements sodium, potassium, calcium, magnesium, strontium, and barium. He invented the 'safety lamp' for use in mines where methane was present, in effect enabling the miners to work in previously unsafe conditions.

Dawes Charles Gates 1865–1951. US Republican politician. In 1923 he was appointed by the Allied Reparations Commission president of the committee that produced the *Dawes Plan*, a $200 million loan that enabled Germany to pay enormous war debts after World War I.

Dawes was elected vice president of the USA 1924, received the Nobel Peace Prize 1925, and was ambassador to Britain 1929–32.

Dawkins Richard 1941– . British zoologist, whose book *The Selfish Gene* 1976 popularized the theories of sociobiology (social behaviour in humans and animals in the context of evolution). A second book, *The Blind Watchmaker* 1986, explains the modern theory of evolution.

Dawson Peter 1882–1961. Australian baritone, remembered for his singing of marching songs and ballads.

Day Doris. Stage name of Doris von Kappelhoff 1924– . US film actress and singing star of the 1950s and early 1960s, mostly in musicals and, later, rather coy sex comedies. Her films include *Tea for Two* 1950, *Calamity Jane* 1953, and *Lover Come Back* 1962.

Day Robin 1923– . British broadcasting journalist. A barrister, he pioneered the probing political interview, notably when he questioned Harold Macmillan on the composition of his cabinet in 1958.

Dayan Moshe 1915–1981. Israeli general and politician. As minister of defence 1967 and 1969–74, he was largely responsible for the victory over neighbouring Arab states in the 1967 Six-Day War, but was criticized for Israel's alleged unpreparedness in the 1973 October War, and resigned with Golda Meir. Foreign minister from 1977, he resigned in 1979 in protest over the refusal of the Begin government to negotiate with the Palestinians.

Day Lewis Cecil 1904–1972. Irish poet, British poet laureate 1968–1972. With Auden and Spender, he was one of the influential left-wing poets of the 1930s. He also wrote detective novels under the pseudonym Nicholas Blake.

His work, which includes *From Feathers to Iron* 1931, and *Overtures to Death* 1938, is marked by accomplished lyrics and sustained narrative power. Professor of poetry at Oxford 1951–56, he published critical works and translations from Latin of Virgil's *Georgics* and *Aeneid*. In 1968 he succeeded Masefield as poet laureate. His autobiography, *The Buried Day* 1960, was followed by a biography written by his eldest son Sean 1980.

Dazai Osamu, pen name of Shuji Tsushima 1909–1948. Japanese novelist. The title of his novel *The Setting Sun* 1947 became in Japanese synonymous with the dead of World War II. He committed suicide.

Deakin Alfred 1856–1919. Australian Liberal politician, prime minister 1903–04, 1905–08, and 1909–10. In his second administration, he enacted legislation on defence and pensions.

Dean Basil 1888–1978. British founder and director-general of the English National Service Association 1939, which provided entertainment for the Allied forces in World War II.

Dean James (Byron) 1931–1955. US actor. Killed in a road accident after only his first film, *East of Eden* 1955, had been shown, he posthumously became a cult hero with *Rebel Without a Cause* and *Giant*, both 1956. He became a symbol of teenage rebellion against American middle-class values.

de Bono Edward 1933– . British medical doctor and psychologist, best known for his concept of lateral thinking, first expounded in *The Use of Lateral Thinking* 1967; it involves thinking round a problem rather than tackling it head on.

Deborah in the Old Testament or Jewish Bible, a prophet and judge (leader). She helped lead an Israelite army against the Canaanite general Sisera, who was killed trying to flee; her song of triumph at his death is regarded as an excellent example of early Hebrew poetry.

Debray Régis 1941– . French Marxist theorist. He was associated with Che Guevara in the revolutionary movement in Latin America in the 1960s, and in 1967 was sentenced to 30 years' imprisonment in Bolivia, but was released after three years. His writings on Latin American politics include *Strategy for Revolution* 1970. He became a specialist adviser to President Mitterrand of France on Latin American affairs.

Debrett John 1753–1822. London publisher of a directory of the peerage from 1802, baronetage in 1808, and knightage 1866–73/4; the books are still called by his name.

de Broglie Louis, 7th Duc de Broglie 1892–1987. French theoretical physicist. He established that

Dean *American cult hero James Dean.*

all subatomic particles can be described either by particle equations or by wave equations, thus laying the foundations of wave mechanics. Nobel prize 1929.

de Broglie Maurice, 6th Duc de Broglie 1875–1960. French physicist. He worked on X-rays and gamma rays, and helped to establish the Einsteinian

Debray *One of the influential theorists of the revolutionary liberation movements in Latin America, Debray was a friend of Che Guevara and was imprisoned in Bolivia in the 1960s.*

description of light in terms of photons. He was the brother of Louis de Broglie.

Debs Eugene V(ictor) 1855–1926. US labour leader and socialist, who organized the Social Democratic Party 1897. He was the founder and first president of the American Railway Union in 1893, and was imprisoned for six months in 1894 for defying a federal injunction to end the Pullman strike in Chicago. He was socialist candidate for the presidency in every election from 1900 to 1920, except that of 1916.

Debs was born in Terre Haute, Indiana. He opposed US intervention in World War I and was imprisoned 1918–21 for allegedly advocating resistance to conscription. In 1920 he polled nearly one million votes, the highest socialist vote ever in US presidential elections, despite having to conduct the campaign from a federal penitentiary in Atlanta, Georgia.

Debussy (Achille-) Claude 1862–1918. French composer. He broke with the dominant tradition of German Romanticism and introduced new qualities of melody and harmony based on the whole-tone scale, evoking oriental music. His work includes *Prélude à l'après-midi d'un faune* 1894 and the opera *Pelléas et Mélisande* 1902.

Among his other works are numerous piano pieces, songs, orchestral pieces such as *La Mer* 1903–05, and the ballet *Jeux* 1910–13. Debussy also wrote with humour about the music of his day, using the fictional character Monsieur Croche 'anti-dilettante' (professional debunker).

Debye Peter 1884–1966. Dutch physicist. A pioneer of X-ray powder crystallography, he also worked on polar molecules, dipole moments, and molecular structure. Nobel Prize for Chemistry 1936.

In 1940, he went to the USA where he was professor of chemistry at Cornell University 1940–52.

Decatur Stephen 1779–1820. US naval hero, who distinguished himself in the war with Tripoli (1801–05), when he succeeded in burning the *Philadelphia*, which the enemy had captured. During the War of 1812 with Britain, he surrendered only after a desperate resistance in 1814. In 1815, he was active against Algerian pirates. He was killed in a duel. Decatur coined the phrase 'our country, right or wrong'.

Decius Gaius Messius Quintus Traianus AD 201–251. Roman emperor from 249. He fought a number of campaigns against the Goths but was finally beaten and killed by them near Abritum. He ruthlessly persecuted the Christians.

Dedekind Richard 1831–1916. German mathematician who made contributions to number theory. In 1872, he introduced the *Dedekind cut* (which divides a line of infinite length representing all real numbers) to define irrational numbers (those not expressible as the quotient of two integers).

Dee John 1527–1608. English alchemist, astrologer, and mathematician, who claimed to have transmuted metals into gold, although he died in poverty. He long enjoyed the favour of Elizabeth I, and was employed as a secret diplomatic agent.

de Falla Manuel Spanish composer. See ◊Falla, Manuel de.

Defoe Daniel 1660–1731. English novelist and journalist, who wrote *Robinson Crusoe* 1719, which was greatly influential in the development of the novel. An active pamphleteer and political critic, he was imprisoned 1702–1704 following publication of the ironic *The Shortest Way With Dissenters*. Fictional works include *Moll Flanders* 1722 and *A Journal of the Plague Year* 1724. Altogether he produced over 500 books, pamphlets, and journals.

Born in Cripplegate, the son of a butcher, James Foe, Defoe was educated for the Nonconformist ministry, but became a hosier. He took part in Monmouth's rebellion, and joined William of Orange 1688. After his business had failed, he held a civil-service post 1695–99. He wrote numerous pamphlets, and first achieved fame with the satire *The True-Born Englishman* 1701, followed in 1702 by the ironic *The Shortest Way with Dissenters*, for which he was fined, imprisoned, and pilloried. In Newgate he wrote his 'Hymn to the Pillory' and started a paper, *The Review* 1704–13. Released in 1704, he travelled in Scotland 1706–07, working to promote the Union, and published *A History of the Union* 1709. During the next ten years he was almost constantly employed as a political controversialist and pamphleteer. His version of the contemporary short story 'True Relation of the Apparition of one Mrs Veal' 1706 had revealed a gift for realistic narrative, and *Robinson Crusoe*, based on the story of Alexander Selkirk, appeared 1719. It was followed among others by the pirate story *Captain Singleton* 1720, and the picaresque *Colonel Jack* 1722 and *Roxana* 1724.

De Forest Lee 1873–1961. US physicist who succeeded in exploiting the commercial value of radio. Ambrose ◊Fleming invented the diode valve 1904. De Forest saw that if a third electrode were added, the triode valve would serve as an amplifier and radio communications would become a practical possibility. He patented his discovery 1906.

Degas (Hilaire Germain) Edgar 1834–1917. French Impressionist painter and sculptor. He devoted himself to lively, informal studies of ballet, horse racing, and young women working, often using pastels. From the 1890s he turned increasingly to sculpture, modelling figures in wax in a fluent, naturalistic style.

Degas studied under a pupil of Ingres and worked in Italy in the 1850s, painting Classical themes. In 1861 he met Manet, and they developed Impressionism. Degas' characteristic style soon emerged, showing influence of Japanese prints and of photography in inventive compositions and unusual viewpoints. An example of his sculpture is *The Little Dancer* 1881 (Tate Gallery, London).

de Gaulle Charles 1890–1970. French conservative politician and general. He organized the Free French troops fighting the Nazis 1940–44, was head of the provisional French government 1944–46, and leader of his own Gaullist party. In 1958 the national assembly asked him to form a government during France's economic recovery, and to solve the crisis in Algeria. He was president 1959–69, having changed the constitution.

Born in Lille, he graduated from Saint-Cyr 1911 and was severely wounded and captured by the Germans 1916. In June 1940 he refused to accept the new prime minister Pétain's truce with the Germans, and became leader of the Free French in England. In 1944 he entered Paris in triumph and was briefly head of the provisional government before resigning over the new constitution of the Fourth Republic 1946. In 1947 he founded the Rassemblement du Peuple Français, a non-party constitutional reform movement, and when national bankruptcy and civil war loomed 1958, de Gaulle was called to form a government.

As premier he promulgated a constitution subordinating the legislature to the presidency, and took office as president 1959. Economic recovery and Algerian independence after a bloody war followed. A nationalist, he opposed 'Anglo-Saxon' influence in Europe. Re-elected president 1965, he violently quelled student demonstrations May 1968 when they were joined by workers. The Gaullist party, reorganized as Union des Democrats pour la Cinquième République, won an overwhelming majority in the elections of the same year. In 1969 he resigned after the defeat of the government in a referendum on constitutional reform.

de Havilland Geoffrey 1882–1965. British aircraft designer who designed the Moth Biplane, the Mosquito fighter-bomber of World War II, and the postwar Comet – the world's first jet-driven airliner to enter commercial service.

De Havilland Olivia 1916– . US actress, a star in Hollywood from the age of 19, when she appeared in *A Midsummer Night's Dream* 1935. She later successfully played more challenging dramatic roles in films such as *Gone with the Wind* 1939, *Dark Mirror* 1946, and *The Snake Pit* 1948.

Deighton Len 1929– . British author of spy fiction, including *The Ipcress File* 1963, and the trilogy *Berlin Game, Mexico Set, London Match* 1983–85, featuring the spy Bernard Samson.

de Gaulle French general and wartime leader Charles de Gaulle.

Dekker Thomas *c.*1572–*c.*1632. English dramatist and pamphleteer, who wrote mainly in collaboration with others. His play *The Shoemaker's Holiday* 1600 was followed by collaborations with Thomas Middleton, John Webster, Philip Massinger, and others. His pamphlets include *The Gull's Hornbook* 1609, a lively satire on the fashions of the day.

De Klerk F(rederik) W(illem) 1936– . South African National Party politician, president from 1989. Trained as a lawyer, he entered the South African parliament in 1972. He served in the cabinets of B J Vorster and P W Botha 1978–89, and in Feb and Aug 1989 successively replaced Botha as National Party leader and state president. Projecting himself as a pragmatic conservative who sought gradual reform of the apartheid system, he won the Sept 1989 elections for his party, but with a reduced majority. In Feb 1990 he ended the ban on the African National Congress opposition movement and released its effective leader, Nelson Mandela.

Delacroix Eugène 1798–1863. French painter in the Romantic style. His prolific output included religious and historical subjects and portraits of friends, among them the musicians Paganini and Chopin. Against French academic tradition, he evolved a highly coloured, fluid style, as in *The Death of Sardanapalus* 1827 (Louvre, Paris).

The *Massacre at Chios* 1824 (Louvre, Paris) shows Greeks enslaved by wild Turkish horsemen, a contemporary atrocity (his use of a contemporary theme recalls Géricault's example). His style was influenced by the English landscape painter Constable. Delacroix also produced illustrations from Shakespeare, Dante, and Byron. His *Journal* is a fascinating record of his times.

Delafield E M, pen name of Edmée Elizabeth Monica de la Pasture 1890–1931. British writer, best remembered for her amusing *Diary of a Provincial Lady* 1931, skilfully exploiting the foibles of middle-class life.

de la Mare Walter 1873–1956. English poet, best known for his verse for children, such as *Songs of Childhood* 1902, and the novels *The Three Royal Monkeys* 1910 for children and, for adults, *The Memoirs of a Midget* 1921.

His debut, *Songs of Childhood*, appeared under the pseudonym Walter Ramal. Later works include poetry for adults (*The Listeners* 1912 and *Collected Poems* 1942), anthologies (*Come Hither* 1923 and *Behold this Dreamer* 1939), and short stories.

Delane John Thaddeus 1817–1879. British journalist. As editor of *The Times* (1841–77), he first gave it international standing.

de la Ramée Louise. British novelist who wrote under the name of ◊Ouida.

de la Roche Mazo 1885–1961. Canadian novelist, author of the 'Whiteoaks' family saga.

Delaroche Paul 1797–1856. French historical artist. His melodramatic, often sentimental, historical paintings achieved great contemporary popularity; an example is *Lady Jane Grey* 1833 (National Gallery, London).

Delaunay Robert 1885–1941. French painter, a pioneer in abstract art. With his wife Sonia Delaunay-Terk he invented *Orphism*, an early variation on Cubism, focusing on the effects of pure colour.

He painted several series, notably *Circular Forms* (almost purely abstract) and *Windows* (inspired by Parisian cityscapes).

Delaunay-Terk Sonia 1885–1979. French painter and textile designer born in Russia, active in Paris from 1905. With her husband Robert Delaunay she was a pioneer of abstract art.

De Laurentis Dino 1919– . Italian producer. His earlier efforts, including Fellini's *La Strada/The Street* 1954, brought more acclaim than later epics such as *Waterloo* 1970. He then produced a series of Hollywood films: *Death Wish* 1974, *King Kong* (remake) 1976, *Dune* 1984.

de la Warr Thomas West, Baron de la Warr 1577–1618. US colonial administrator, known as Delaware. Appointed governor of Virginia 1609, he arrived 1610 just in time to prevent the desertion of the Jamestown colonists, and by 1611 had reorganized the settlement. Both the river and state are named after him.

Delbruck Max 1906–1981. German-born US biologist who pioneered techniques in molecular biology, studying genetic changes occurring when viruses invade bacteria. Nobel Prize for Medicine 1969.

Delcassé Théophile 1852–1923. French politician. He became foreign minister 1898, but had to resign 1905 because of German hostility; he held that post again 1914–15. To a large extent he was

responsible for the Entente Cordiale alliance with Britain.

De Lesseps Ferdinand, Vicomte 1805–1894. French engineer, who constructed the Suez Canal 1859–1869. He reluctantly began the Panama Canal 1881, but failed when he tried to construct it without locks.

Delibes (Clament Philibert) Léo 1836–1891. French composer. His works include the ballet *Coppélia* and the opera *Lakma*.

Delilah in the Old Testament or Jewish Bible, the Philistine mistress of ◊Samson.

Delius Frederick (Theodore Albert) 1862–1934. English composer. His works include the opera *A Village Romeo and Juliet* 1901; the choral pieces *Appalachia* 1903, *Sea Drift* 1904, *A Mass of Life* 1905; orchestral works such as *In a Summer Garden* 1908, *A Song of the High Hills* 1911; chamber music; and songs.

Born at Bradford, he tried orange-growing in Florida, before studying music in Leipzig in 1888, where he met Grieg. From 1890 Delius lived mainly in France and in 1903 married the artist Jelka Rosen. Although blind and paralysed for the last ten years of his life, he continued to compose.

Dell Ethel M(ary) 1881–1939. British writer of romantic fiction. Her commercially successful novels usually included a hero who was ugly: *Way of an Eagle* 1912, *The Keeper of the Door* 1915, and *Storm Drift* 1930.

Deller Alfred 1912–1979. English singer, a countertenor. He founded the Deller Consort 1950, a group that performed 16th–18th century music.

Delon Alain 1935– . French actor, who appeared in the films *Rocco e i suoi Fratelli/Rocco and his Brothers* 1960, *Il Gattopardi/The Leopard* 1963, *Texas across the River* 1966, *Scorpio* 1972, and *Swann in Love* 1984.

Delors Jacques 1925– . French socialist politician, finance minister 1981–84. As president of the European Commission from 1984 he has overseen significant budgetary reform and the move towards a free European Community market in 1992, with increased powers residing in Brussels.

Delors, the son of a Paris banker, worked as social-affairs adviser to Prime Minister Jacques Chaban-Delmas 1969–72 before joining the Socialist Party 1973. He served as minister of economy and finance (and, later, budget) in the administration of President Mitterrand 1981–84, overseeing an austerity programme (*'rigueur'*) from June 1982. Having been passed over for the post of prime minister, Delors left to become president of the European Commission.

del Sarto Andrea 1486–1531. See ◊Andrea del Sarto, Italian Renaissance painter.

Demetrius Donskoi ('of the Don') 1350–1389. Grand prince of Moscow from 1363. He achieved the first Russian victory over the Tatars on the plain of Kulikovo, next to the Don (hence his nickname) 1380.

De Mille Agnes 1909– . US dancer and choreographer. One of the most significant contributors to the American Ballet Theater with dramatic ballets like *Fall River Legend* 1948, she also led the change on Broadway to new-style musicals with her choreography of *Oklahoma!* 1943, *Carousel* 1945, and others.

de Mille Cecil B(lount) 1881–1959. US film director. He entered films with Jesse L Lasky 1913 (with whom he later established Paramount), and was one of the founders of Hollywood. He specialized in biblical epics, such as *The Sign of the Cross* 1932 and *The Ten Commandments* 1956.

Demirel Suleyman 1924– . Turkish politician. Leader from 1964 of the Justice Party, he was prime minister 1965–71, 1975 –77, and 1979–80. He favoured links with the West, full membership of the European Community, and foreign investment in Turkish industry.

De Mita Luigi Ciriaco 1928– . Italian conservative politician, leader of the Christian Democratic Party (DC) from 1982, prime minister from 1988. He entered the Chamber of Deputies in 1963 and held a number of ministerial posts in the 1970s before becoming DC secretary-general.

Democritus c. 460–361 BC. Greek philosopher and speculative scientist. His most important contribution to metaphysics is his atomic theory of the universe: all things originate from a vortex of atoms, and differ according to the shape and arrangement of its atoms.

de Morgan William Frend 1839–1917. English pottery designer. He set up his own factory 1888 in Fulham, London, producing tiles and pottery painted with flora and fauna in a style typical of the Arts and Crafts Movement.

Inspired by William ◊Morris and Edward ◊Burne-Jones, he started designing tiles and glass for Morris's Merton Abbey factory. Influenced by Persian and Italian styles – he spent many months in Italy in later years – he also developed lustre techniques (a way of covering pottery with an iridescent metallic surface).

Demosthenes c. 384–322 BC. Athenian orator and politician. From 351 BC he led the party that advocated resistance to the growing power of ◊Philip of Macedon, and in his *Philippics* incited the Athenians to war. This policy resulted in the defeat of Chaeronea 338, and the establishment of Macedonian supremacy. After the death of Alexander he organized a revolt; when it failed, he took poison to avoid capture by the Macedonians.

Dempsey Jack ('the Manassa Mauler') 1895–1983. US heavyweight boxing champion. He beat Jess Willard 1919 to win the title and held it until losing to Gene Tunney 1926. He engaged in the 'Battle of the Long Count' with Tunney 1927. of

his 79 fights, he won 64, and was defeated only six times.

Dench Judi 1934– . British actress who made her debut as Ophelia in *Hamlet* 1957 with the Old Vic Company. Her Shakespearean roles include Portia in *Twelfth Night*, Lady Macbeth, and Cleopatra. She is also a versatile comedy actress and has appeared in films, for example *A Room with a View*, and on television.

Deneuve Catherine 1943– . French actress acclaimed for her performance in Polanski's film *Repulsion* 1965. She also appeared in *Les Parapluies de Cherbourg/Umbrellas of Cherbourg* 1964, *Belle de jour* 1967, *Hustle* 1975, *The Hunger* 1983.

Deng Xiaoping formerly *Teng Hsiao-ping* 1904– . Chinese political leader. A member of the Chinese Communist Party (CCP) from the 1920s, he took part in the Long March 1934–36. He was in the Politburo from 1955 until ousted in the Cultural Revolution 1966–69. Reinstated in the 1970s, he gradually took power and introduced a radical economic modernization programme. He retired from the Politburo in 1987 and from his last official position (as chair of Central Military Commission) Nov 1989, but remained influential behind the scenes.

Deng, born in Sichuan province into a middle-class landlord family, joined the CCP as a student in Paris where he adopted the name Xiaoping (Little Peace) 1925, and studied in Moscow 1926. After the Long March, he served as a political commissar to the People's Liberation Army during the civil war of 1937–49. He entered the CCP Politburo 1955 and headed the secretariat during the early 1960s, working closely with President Liu Shaoqi. During the Cultural Revolution Deng was dismissed as a 'capitalist roader' and sent to work in a tractor factory in Nanchang for 're-education'.

Deng was rehabilitated by his patron Zhou Enlai 1973 and served as acting prime minister after Zhou's heart attack 1974. On Zhou's death Jan 1976 he was forced into hiding but returned to office as vice premier July 1977. By Dec 1978, although nominally a CCP vice chair, state vice premier, and Chief of Staff to the PLA, Deng was the controlling force in China. He helped to oust ◊Hua Guofeng in favour of his protégés Hu Yaobang and Zhao Ziyang.

Despite repeated suggestions of retirement, Deng remained the dominant decision-maker in China. His policy of 'socialism with Chinese characteristics', misinterpreted in the West as a drift to capitalism, had success in rural areas. Deng's reputation, both at home and in the West, was tarnished by his sanctioning of the army's massacre of more than 2,000 pro-democracy demonstrators in Tiananmen Square, Beijing, in June 1989.

Deng Xiaoping *China's 'paramount ruler', Deng Xiaoping. In effective charge of the country since 1978, he has promoted greater economic, but not political liberalization.*

Denikin Anton Ivanovich 1872–1946. Russian general. He distinguished himself in the Russo-Japanese War 1904–05 and World War I. After the outbreak of the Bolshevik Revolution 1917 he organized a volunteer army of 60,000 Whites (counter-revolutionaries), but in 1919 was routed and escaped to France. He wrote a history of the Revolution and the Civil War.

De Niro Robert 1943– . US actor. He won Oscars for *The Godfather Part II* 1974 and *Raging Bull* 1979. Other films include *Taxi Driver* 1976, *The Deer Hunter* 1978, and *The Untouchables* 1987.

Denis, St 3rd century. First bishop of Paris and one of the patron saints of France, who was martyred by the Romans. Feast day 9 Oct.

He is often represented as carrying his head in his hands, and is often confused with Dionysius the Areopagite, who was the first bishop of Athens, and died about AD 95.

Denktash Rauf R 1924– . Turkish-Cypriot politician. In 1975 the Turkish Federated State of Cyprus (TFSC) was formed in the northern third of the island, with Denktash as its head, and in 1983 he became president of the breakaway Turkish Republic of Northern Cyprus (TRNC).

Denktash held law-officer posts under the crown before independence, in 1960. Relations between the Greek and Turkish communities progressively deteriorated, leading to the formation of the TFSC. In 1983 the TRNC, with Denktash as its president, was formally constituted, but recognized internationally only by Turkey. The accession of the independent politician Georgios Vassilou to the Cyprus presidency offered hopes of reconciliation, but meetings between him and Denktash,

under UN auspices, during 1989 failed to produce an agreement.

Denning Alfred Thompson, Baron Denning of Whitchurch 1899– . British judge, Master of the Rolls 1962–82. In 1963 he conducted the inquiry into the Profumo scandal. A vigorous and highly innovative civil lawyer, he was controversial in his defence of the rights of the individual against the state, the unions, and big business.

De Palma Brian 1941– . US film director, especially of thrillers. His technical mastery and enthusiasm for spilling blood are shown in films such as *Sisters* 1973, *Carrie* 1976, and *The Untouchables* 1987.

Depardieu Gerard 1948– . Versatile French actor who has appeared in such films as *Deux Hommes dans la Ville* 1973, *Le Camion* 1977, *Mon Oncle d'Amérique* 1980, *The Moon in the Gutter* 1983, and *Jean de Florette* 1985.

de Quincey Thomas 1785–1859. English author, whose works include *Confessions of an English Opium-Eater* 1821 and the essays 'On the Knocking at the Gate in Macbeth' 1823 and 'On Murder Considered as One of the Fine Arts' 1827. He was a friend of the poets Wordsworth and Coleridge.

Born in Manchester, de Quincey ran away from school there to wander and study in Wales. He then went to London, where he lived in extreme poverty but with the constant companionship of the young orphan Ann, of whom he writes in the *Confessions*. In 1803 he was reconciled to his guardians and was sent to university at Oxford, where his opium habit began. In 1809 he settled with the Wordsworths and Coleridge in the Lake District. He moved to Edinburgh 1828, where he eventually died. De Quincey's work had a powerful influence on ◊Baudelaire and ◊Poe among others.

Derain André 1880–1954. French painter, who experimented with strong, almost primary colours and exhibited with the Fauves, but later developed a more sombre landscape style. His work includes costumes and scenery for Diaghilev's Ballets Russes.

Derby Edward Geoffrey Smith Stanley, 14th Earl of Derby 1799–1869. British politician, prime minister 1852, 1858–59, and 1866–68. Originally a Whig, he became secretary for the colonies 1830, and introduced the bill for the abolition of slavery. He joined the Tories 1834, and the split in the Tory Party over Robert Peel's free-trade policy gave Derby the leadership for 20 years.

Derby Edward George Villiers Stanley, 17th Earl of Derby 1865–1948. British Conservative politician, member of Parliament from 1892. He was secretary of war 1916–18 and 1922–24, and ambassador to France 1918–20.

De Roburt Hammer 1923– . President of Nauru from 1968, out of office 1976–78 and briefly in 1986. During the country's occupation 1942–45, he was deported to Japan. He became head chief of Nauru in 1956 and was elected the country's first president in 1968.

Desai Morarji 1896– . Indian politician. An early follower of Mahatma Gandhi, he was prime minister, a leader 1977–79 of the Janata Party, after toppling Indira Gandhi's Congress Party. Party infighting led to his resignation of both the premiership and the party leadership.

de Savary Peter 1944– . British entrepreneur. He acquired Land's End, Cornwall, England, in 1987 and built a theme park there. He revived Falmouth dock and the port of Hayle in N Cornwall. A yachting enthusiast, he sponsored the Blue Arrow America's Cup challenge team.

Descartes René 1596–1650. French mathematician and philosopher. He believed that commonly accepted knowledge was doubtful because of the subjective nature of the senses, and attempted to rebuild human knowledge using as foundation *'cogito ergo sum'* ('I think, therefore I am'). He also believed that the entire material universe could be explained in terms of mathematical physics. He is regarded as the discoverer of analytical geometry and the founder of the science of optics. He was also influential in shaping contemporary theories of astronomy and animal behaviour.

Descartes was born near Tours. He served in the army of Prince Maurice of Orange, and in 1619, while travelling through Europe, decided to apply the methods of mathematics to metaphysics and science. He settled in the Netherlands in 1628, where he was more likely to be free from interference by the ecclesiastical authorities. In 1649 he visited the court of Queen Christina of Sweden, and died in Stockholm.

His works include *Discourse on Method* 1637, *Meditations on the First Philosophy* 1641, and *Principles of Philosophy* 1644, and numerous books on physiology, optics, and geometry.

Coordinate geometry, as a way of defining and manipulating geometrical shapes by means of algebraic expressions, was determined by Leibniz, and only later called **Cartesian coordinates** in honour of Descartes.

Deschamps Eustache 1346–1406. French poet, born in Champagne. He was the author of more than 1,000 ballades, and the *Miroir de Mariage/The Mirror of Marriage*, an attack on women.

de Sica Vittorio 1902–1974. Italian director and actor. He won his first Oscar with *Bicycle Thieves* 1948, a film of subtle realism. Later films included *Umberto D* 1952, *Two Women* 1960, and *The Garden of the Finzi-Continis* 1971.

Desmoulins Camille 1760–1794. French revolutionary, who summoned the mob to arms on 12 July 1789, so precipitating the revolt that culminated in the storming of the Bastille. A prominent Jacobin (republican), he was elected to the National Convention 1792. His *Histoire des*

Descartes *An engraving of French philosopher and mathematician René Descartes after a portrait by Frans Hals.*

Brissotins was largely responsible for the overthrow of the right-wing Girondins, but shortly after he was sent to the guillotine as too moderate.

de Soto Hernando *c.*1496–1542. Spanish explorer who sailed with d'Avila (1440–1531) to Darien, Central America, 1519, explored the Yucatán Peninsula 1528, and travelled with Pizarro in Peru 1530–35. In 1538 he was made governor of Cuba and Florida. In his expedition of 1539, he explored Florida, Georgia, and the Mississippi River.

Desprez Josquin *c.*1440–1521. Franco-Flemish composer; see ◊Josquin Desprez.

Dessalines Jean Jacques *c.*1758–1806. Emperor of Haiti 1804–1806. Born in Guinea, he was taken to Haiti as a slave, where in 1802 he succeeded ◊Toussaint L'Ouverture as leader of the black revolt against the French. After defeating the French, he proclaimed Haiti's independence and made himself emperor. He was killed when trying to suppress an uprising provoked by his cruelty.

Dessau Paul 1894–1979. German composer. He work includes incidental music to the playwright Bertolt Brecht's theatre pieces, an opera, *Der Verurteilung des Lukullus*, also to a libretto by Brecht, and numerous choral works and songs.

de Tocqueville Alexis 1805–1859. French politician, see ◊Tocqueville, Alexis de.

de Valera Eamon 1882–1975. Irish nationalist politician, prime minister of the Republic of Ireland 1932–48, 1951–54, and 1957–59, and president 1959–73. Repeatedly imprisoned, he participated in the Easter Rising 1916 and was leader of the nationalist Sinn Féin party 1917–26, when he formed the republican Fianna Fáil ('soldiers of destiny' party; he directed negotiations with Britain 1921 but refused to accept the partition of Ireland until 1937.

He was born in New York, the son of a Spanish father and an Irish mother, and sent to Ireland as a child, where he became a teacher of mathematics. He was sentenced to death for his part in the Easter Rising, but the sentence was commuted, and he was released under an amnesty 1917. In the same year he was elected member of Parliament for E Clare, and president of Sinn Féin. He was rearrested May 1918, but escaped to the USA 1919. He returned to Ireland 1920 and directed the struggle against the British government from a hiding place in Dublin. He authorized the negotiations of 1921, but refused to accept the ensuing treaty which divided Ireland into the Free State and the North.

Civil war followed. De Valera was arrested by the Free State government 1923, and spent a year in prison. He formed a new party, Fianna Fáil 1926, which secured a majority 1932. De Valera became prime minister and foreign minister of the Free State, and at once abolished the oath of allegiance and suspended payment of the annuities due under the Land Purchase Acts. In 1938 he negotiated an agreement with Britain, under which all outstanding points were settled. Throughout World War II he maintained a strict neutrality, rejecting an offer by Churchill 1940 to recognize the principle of a united Ireland in return for Eire's entry into the war. He resigned after his defeat at the 1948 elections, but was again prime minister in the 1950s, and then president of the republic.

de Valois Ninette. Stage name of Edris Stannus 1898– . Irish dancer, choreographer, and teacher. A pioneer of British national ballet, she worked with Diaghilev in Paris before opening a dance academy in London 1926. Collaborating with Lilian Baylis at the Old Vic theatre, she founded the Vic-Wells Ballet 1931, which later became the Royal Ballet and Royal Ballet School. Among her works are *Job* 1931 and *Checkmate* 1937.

Devonshire Spencer Compton Cavendish, 8th Duke of Devonshire 1833–1908. British Liberal politician, known as Lord Hartington 1858–91, and leader of the Liberal Party 1874–80. He broke with Gladstone over Irish Home Rule 1885, and was president of the council 1895–1903 under Salisbury and Balfour. As a free-trader, he resigned from Balfour's cabinet.

de Valera Eamon de Valera, Irish politician, shortly before his imprisonment 1923.

Devonshire William Cavendish, 7th Duke of Devonshire 1808–1891. British aristocrat, whose development of Eastbourne, Sussex, England, was an early example of town planning.

Dewar James 1842–1923. Scottish chemist and physicist who invented the vacuum flask 1872, during his research into the properties of matter at extremely low temperatures.

de Wet Christiaan Rudolf 1854–1922. Boer general and politician. In 1907 he became minister of agriculture in the Orange River Colony; when World War I began, he headed a pro-German rising of 12,000 Afrikaners that was soon suppressed by Prime Minister Louis Botha.

Dewey John 1859–1952. US philosopher, who believed that the exigencies of a modern democratic and industrial society demanded new educational techniques. He expounded his ideas in numerous writings, including *School and Society* 1899, and founded a progressive school in Chicago.

Dewey Melvil 1851–1931. US librarian. In 1876, he devised the *Dewey decimal system* of classification for books, now widely used in libraries.

de Wint Peter 1784–1849. English landscape artist, of Dutch descent. He was a notable watercolourist.

Diaghilev Sergei Pavlovich 1872–1929. Russian ballet impresario, who in 1909 founded the *Ballets Russes*/Russian Ballet (headquarters in Monaco), which he directed for 20 years. Through this company he brought Russian ballet to the West, introducing and encouraging a dazzling array of dancers, choreographers, and composers, such as Pavlova, Nijinsky, Fokine, Massine, Balanchine, Stravinsky, and Prokofiev.

Diana Princess of Wales 1961– . The daughter of the 8th Earl Spencer, she married Prince Charles at St Paul's Cathedral 1981, the first English bride of a royal heir since 1659. She is descended from

Dickens English novelist Charles Dickens.

the only sovereigns from whom Prince Charles is not descended, Charles II and James II.

Diaz Bartolomeu *c.*1450–1500. Portuguese explorer, the first European to reach the Cape of Good Hope 1488, and to establish a route around Africa. He drowned during an expedition with Pedro ◊Cabral.

Díaz Porfirio 1830–1915. Dictator of Mexico 1877–80 and 1884–1911. After losing the 1876 election, he overthrew the government and seized power. He was supported by conservative landowners and foreign capitalists, who invested in railways and mines. He centralized the state at the expense of the peasants and Indians, and dismantled all local and regional leadership. He faced mounting and revolutionary opposition in his final years and was forced into exile 1911.

Diaz de Solís Juan 1471–*c.*1516. Spanish explorer in South America, who reached the estuary of the River Plate and was killed and eaten by cannibals.

Dick Philip K(endred) 1928–1982. US science-fiction writer, whose works often deal with religion and the subjectivity of reality; his novels include *The Man in the High Castle* 1962 and *Do Androids Dream of Electric Sheep?* 1968.

Dickens Charles 1812–1870. English novelist, popular for his memorable characters and his portrayals of the social evils of Victorian England. In 1836 he published the first number of the *Pickwick Papers*, followed by *Oliver Twist* 1838, the first of his 'reforming' novels; *Nicholas Nickleby* 1839; *Barnaby Rudge* 1840; *The Old Curiosity Shop* 1841; and *David Copperfield* 1849. Among his later

books are *A Tale of Two Cities* 1859 and *Great Expectations* 1861, and *Our Mutual Friend* 1864.

Born in Portsea, Hampshire, the son of a clerk, Dickens received little formal education, although a short period spent working in a blacking factory in S London, while his father was imprisoned for debt in the Marshalsea prison during 1824, was followed by three years in a private school. In 1827 he became a lawyer's clerk, and then after four years a reporter for the *Morning Chronicle*, to which he contributed the *Sketches by Boz*. In 1836 he married Katherine Hogarth, three days after the publication of the first number of the *Pickwick Papers*. Originally intended merely as an accompaniment to a series of sporting illustrations, the adventures of Pickwick outgrew their setting and established Dickens' reputation.

In 1842 he visited the USA, where his attack on the pirating of English books by US publishers chilled his welcome; his experiences are reflected in *American Notes* and *Martin Chuzzlewit* 1843. In 1843 he published the first of his Christmas books, *A Christmas Carol*, followed in 1844 by *The Chimes*, written in Genoa during his first long sojourn abroad, and in 1845 by the even more successful *Cricket on the Hearth*. A venture as editor of the Liberal *Daily News* in 1846 was shortlived, and *Dombey and Son* 1848 was largely written abroad. *David Copperfield*, his most popular novel, appeared 1849, and contains many autobiographical incidents and characters.

Returning to journalism, Dickens inaugurated the weekly magazine *Household Words* 1850, reorganizing it 1859 as *All the Year Round*; many of his later stories were published serially in these periodicals.

In 1856 he agreed with his wife on a separation; his sister-in-law remained with him to care for his children, while Dickens formed an association with the actress Ellen Ternan. In 1858 he began making public readings from his novels, which proved such a success that he was invited to make a second US tour 1867. Among his later novels are *Bleak House* 1853, *Hard Times* 1854, *Little Dorrit* 1857, and *Our Mutual Friend* 1864. *Edwin Drood*, a mystery story influenced by the style of his friend Wilkie ◊Collins, was left incomplete on his death.

Dickens Monica (Enid) 1915– . British writer. Her first books were humorous accounts of her experiences in various jobs, beginning as a cook (*One Pair of Hands* 1939); she went on to become a novelist. She is a great-granddaughter of Charles Dickens.

Dickinson Emily 1830–1886. US poet. Born in Amherst, Massachusetts, she lived in near seclusion there from 1862. Almost none of her many short, mystical poems were published during her lifetime. Her work became well known only in the 20th century.

Dick-Read Grantly 1890–1959. British gynaecologist. In private practice in London 1923–48, he developed the theory of natural childbirth, that is, that by the elimination of fear and tension, childbirth pain could be minimized and anaesthetics rendered unnecessary.

Diderot Denis 1713–1784. French philosopher. He is closely associated with the Enlightenment, the European intellectual movement for social and scientific progress, as editor of the *Encyclopédie* 1751–1780. An expanded and politicized version of Ephraim Chamber's English encyclopedia of 1728, this work exerted an enormous influence on contemporary social thinking with its materialism and anti-clericalism. Its compilers were known as the *Encyclopédistes*.

His materialism, most articulately expressed in *D'Alembert's Dream*, sees the natural world as nothing more than matter and motion. He gave an account of the origin and development of life which is purely mechanical.

Didion Joan 1934– . US novelist and journalist. Her sharp, culturally evocative writing includes the novel *The Book of Common Prayer* 1970 and the essays of *The White Album* 1979.

Diefenbaker John George 1895–1979. Canadian Progressive Conservative politician, prime minister 1957–63, when he was defeated after criticism of the proposed manufacture of nuclear weapons in Canada.

He was born in Ontario, and moved to Saskatchewan. A brilliant defence counsel, he became known as the 'prairie lawyer'. He became leader of his party 1956 and prime minister 1957. In 1958 he achieved the greatest landslide victory in Canadian history.

Diels Otto 1876–1954. German chemist. In 1950 he and his former assistant, Kurt Alder (1902–1958), were jointly awarded the Nobel Prize for Chemistry for their research into the synthesis of organic chemical compounds.

Diemen Anthony van 1593–1645. Dutch admiral. In 1636 he was appointed governor general of Dutch settlements in the E Indies, and wrested Ceylon and Malacca from the Portuguese. In 1636 and 1642 he supervised expeditions to Australia, on the second of which the navigator Abel Tasman discovered land not charted by Europeans, and named it *Van Diemen's Land*, now Tasmania.

Diesel Rudolf 1858–1913. German engineer who patented the diesel engine. He began his career as a refrigerator engineer and, like many engineers of the period, sought to develop a more efficient power source than the conventional steam engine. Able to operate with greater efficiency and economy, the diesel engine soon found a ready market.

Dietrich Marlene Dietrich In The Blue Angel 1930, the film that won her international fame.

Dietrich Marlene. Stage name of Magdalene von Losch 1904– . German actress and singer, born in Berlin, who first won fame by her appearance with Emil Jannings in the film *The Blue Angel* 1930. She went to Hollywood, becoming a US citizen in 1937. Her husky, sultry singing voice added to her appeal. Her other films include *Blonde Venus* 1932 and *Destry Rides Again* 1939.

Dilke Charles Wentworth 1843–1911. British Liberal politician, member of Parliament 1868–86 and 1892–1911. A Radical, he supported a minimum wage and legalization of trade unions.

Dillinger John 1903–1934. US criminal who undertook a series of bank robberies between June 1933 and July 1934 in several states. Although captured in Ohio and Arizona, he was able to escape on both occasions before being trapped and shot by the Federal Bureau of Investigation outside the Biograph Theater in Chicago. After the shooting, rumours circulated that he was not the man killed by the federal agents.

Dilthey Wilhelm 1833–1911. German philosopher, a major figure in the interpretive tradition of hermeneutics. He argued that the 'human sciences' (*Geisteswissenschaften*) could not employ the same methods as the natural sciences, but must use the procedure of 'understanding' (*Verstehen*) to grasp the inner life of an alien culture or past historical period. Thus Dilthey extended the significance of hermeneutics far beyond the interpretation of texts to the whole of human history and culture.

DiMaggio Joe 1914– . US baseball player who spent his whole career with the New York Yankees 1936–51. In 1941 he set a record by getting hits in 56 consecutive games. He was an outstanding fielder, hit 361 home runs, and had a career average of .325. He was once married to the actress Marilyn Monroe.

Dimbleby Richard 1913–1965. British broadcaster and provincial newspaper owner. He joined the

British Broadcasting Corporation in 1936 and established himself as the foremost commentator on royal and state events and current affairs (*Panorama*) on radio and television. He is commemorated by the *Dimbleby lectures*.

Dimitrov Georgi 1882–1949. Bulgarian Communist, prime minister from 1946. He was elected a deputy in 1913, and from 1919 was a member of the executive of the Comintern, an international Communist organization. In 1933 he was arrested in Berlin and tried with others in Leipzig for allegedly setting fire to the Reichstag, the parliament building. Acquitted, he went to the USSR, where he became general secretary of the Comintern until its dissolution in 1943.

Dine Jim 1935– , US Pop artist. He experimented with combinations of paintings and objects, such as a washbasin attached to a canvas.

Dine was a pioneer of happenings (art as live performance) in the 1950s and of environment art (three-dimensional works that attempt active interaction with the spectator, sometimes using sound or movement).

Dinesen Isak 1885–1962. Pen name of Danish writer Karen ◊Blixen, born Karen Christentze Dinesen.

Dingaan Zulu chief from 1828. He obtained the throne by murdering his predecessor, Shaka, and became noted for his cruelty. In warfare with the Boer immigrants into Natal he was defeated on 16 Dec 1838 – 'Dingaan's Day'. He escaped to Swaziland, where he was deposed by his brother Mpande and subsequently murdered.

Ding Ling 1904–1986. Chinese novelist. Her works include *Wei Hu* 1930 and *The Sun Shines over the Sanggan River* 1951.

She was imprisoned by the Guomindang (Chiang Kai-Shek's Nationalists) in the 1930s, wrongly labelled as rightist and expelled from the Communist Party 1957, imprisoned in the 1960s and intellectually exiled for not keeping to Maoist literary rules; she was rehabilitated 1979. Her husband was the writer Hu Yapin, executed by Chiang Kai-Shek's police 1931.

Dinkins David 1927– . Mayor of New York City from Jan 1990, a Democrat. He won a reputation as a moderate and consensual community politician and was Manhattan borough president before succeeding Ed Koch to become New York's first black mayor.

Diocletian Gaius Valerius Diocletianus AD 245–313. Roman emperor 284–305, when he abdicated in favour of Galerius. He reorganized and subdivided the empire, with two joint and two subordinate emperors, and in 303 initiated severe persecution of the Christians.

Diogenes c.412–323 BC. Ascetic Greek philosopher of the Cynic school. He believed in freedom and self-sufficiency for the individual, and did not believe in social mores.

He was born at Sinope, captured by pirates and sold as a slave to a Corinthian named Xeniades, who appointed Diogenes tutor to his two sons. He spent the rest of his life in Corinth. He is said to have carried a lamp during the daytime, looking for one honest man. The story of his having lived in a barrel arose only from Seneca having said that was where a man so crabbed ought to have lived. His writings do not survive.

Dion Cassius AD 150–235. Roman historian. He wrote, in Greek, a Roman history in 80 books (of which 26 survive), covering the period from the founding of the city to AD 229, including the only surviving account of the invasion of Britain by Claudius in 43 BC.

Diophantus Greek mathematician lived 3rd century AD whose *Arithmetica c.* 275 is one of the first known works on problem-solving by algebra, in which both words and symbols were used.

Dior Christian 1905–1957. French couturier. He established his own Paris salon in 1947 and made an impact with the 'New Look' – long, cinch-waisted, and full-skirted – after wartime austerity.

Diouf Abdou 1935– . Senegalese politician, president from 1980. He became prime minister 1970 under President Leopold Senghor and, on his retirement, succeeded him, being re-elected in 1983 and 1988.

Born at Louga in NW Senegal, Diouf studied at Paris University and was a civil servant before entering politics. He was chair of the Organization of African Unity 1985–86.

Dirac Paul Adrien Maurice 1902–1984. British physicist who worked out a version of quantum mechanics consistent with special relativity. The existence of the positron (positive electron) was one of its predictions. He shared a Nobel prize 1933.

Dirichlet Peter Gustav Lejeune 1805–1859. German mathematician, who made major contributions to number theory. His most important work, though, was on the convergence of ◊Fourier series, and this led to the modern notion of a generalized function as represented in the form $f(x)$.

Disch Thomas M(ichael) 1940– . US writer and poet, noted for science-fiction novels such as *Camp Concentration* 1968 and *334* 1972.

Disney Walt(er Elias) 1901–1966. US filmmaker and animator, a pioneer of family entertainment. He established his own studio in Hollywood 1923, and his first Mickey Mouse cartoon (*Plane Crazy*) appeared 1928. In addition to short cartoons the studio made feature-length animated films, including *Snow White and the Seven Dwarfs* 1938, *Pinocchio* 1940, and *Dumbo* 1941. Disney's cartoon figures, for example Donald Duck, also appeared in comic books worldwide. In 1955 Disney opened the first theme park, Disneyland, in California.

Using the new medium of sound film, Disney developed the 'Silly Symphony', a type of cartoon based on the close association of music with visual images, producing them in colour from 1932 and culminating in the feature-length *Fantasia* 1940. The Disney studio also made nature-study films such as *The Living Desert* 1953, which have been criticized for their fictionalization of nature: wild animals would be placed in unnatural situations to create 'drama'. Feature films with human casts were made from 1946, such as *The Swiss Family Robinson* 1960 and *Mary Poppins* 1964.

Disraeli Benjamin, Earl of Beaconsfield 1804–1881. British Conservative politician and novelist. Elected to Parliament 1837, he was chancellor of the Exchequer under Lord ◊Derby 1852, 1858–59, and 1866–68, and prime minister 1868 and 1874–80. His imperialist policies brought India directly under the crown and he personally purchased control of the Suez Canal. The central Conservative Party organization is his creation. His popular, political novels reflect an interest in social reform and include *Coningsby* 1844 and *Sybil* 1845.

He was the son of Isaac ◊D'Israeli. After a period in a solicitor's office, Disraeli wrote the novels *Vivian Grey* 1826, *Contarini Fleming* 1832, and others, and the pamphlet *Vindication of the English Constitution* 1835. Entering Parliament in 1837 after four unsuccessful attempts, he was laughed at as a dandy, but when his maiden speech was shouted down, he said: 'The time will come when you will hear me.'

Excluded from Peel's government of 1841–46, Disraeli formed his Young England group to keep a critical eye on Peel's conservatism. Its ideas were expounded in the novel trilogy *Coningsby*, *Sybil*, and *Tancred* 1847. When Peel decided in 1846 to repeal the Corn Laws, Disraeli opposed the measure in a series of witty and effective speeches; Peel's government fell soon after, and Disraeli gradually came to be recognized as the leader of the Conservative Party in the Commons.

During the next 20 years the Conservatives formed short-lived minority governments in 1852, 1858–59, and 1866–68, with Lord Derby as prime minister and Disraeli as chancellor of the Exchequer and leader of the Commons. In 1852 Disraeli first proposed discrimination in income tax between earned and unearned income, but without success. The 1858–59 government legalized the admission of Jews to Parliament. On Lord Derby's retirement in 1868 Disraeli became prime minister, but a few months later he was defeated by Gladstone in a general election. During the six years of opposition that followed he published another novel, *Lothair* 1870, and established Conservative Central Office, the prototype of modern party organizations.

In 1874 Disraeli took office for the second time, with a majority of 100. The outstanding feature of the government's policy was its imperialism. It was Disraeli's personal initiative that purchased from the Khedive of Egypt a controlling interest in the Suez Canal, conferred on the Queen the title of Empress of India, and sent the Prince of Wales on the first royal tour of that country. He accepted an earldom 1876. The Bulgarian revolt of 1876 and the subsequent Russo-Turkish War of 1877–78 provoked one of many political duels between Disraeli and Gladstone, the Liberal leader, and was concluded by the Congress of Berlin 1878, where Disraeli was the principal British delegate and brought home 'peace with honour' and Cyprus. The government was defeated in 1880, and a year later Disraeli died.

D'Israeli Isaac 1766–1848. British scholar, father of Benjamin ◊Disraeli and author of *Curiosities of Literature* 1791–93 and 1823.

Djilas Milovan 1911– . Yugoslav political writer and dissident. A former close wartime colleague of Marshal Tito, in 1953 he was dismissed from high office and subsequently imprisoned because of his advocacy of greater political pluralism. He was released in 1966 and formally rehabilitated in 1989.

Djilas was born in Montenegro and was a partisan during World War II. He rose to a senior position in Yugoslavia's postwar communist government before being ousted in 1953. His writings, including the books *The New Class* 1957 and *The Undivided Society* 1969, were banned until May 1989.

Dobell William 1899–1970. Australian portraitist and genre painter, born in New South Wales. In 1929–39 he studied art in the UK and the Netherlands. His portrait of *Joshua Smith* 1943 (Sir Edward Hayward, Adelaide) provoked a court case (Dobell was accused of caricaturing his subject).

Döblin Alfred 1878–1957. German novelist. *Berlin-Alexanderplatz* 1929 owes much to James Joyce in its minutely detailed depiction of the inner lives of a city's inhabitants, and is considered by many to be the finest 20th-century German novel. Other works include *November 1918: Eine deutsche Revolution/A German Revolution* 1939–50 (published in four parts) about the formation of the Weimar Republic.

Dobrynin Anataloy Fedorovich 1919– . Soviet diplomat, ambassador to the USA 1962–86, emerging during the 1970s as a warm supporter of detente.

Dobrynin trained as an engineer before joining the Soviet diplomatic service in 1941, and was appointed Soviet ambassador to Washington in 1962. He remained at this post for 25 years. Brought back to Moscow by the new Soviet leader, Mikhail Gorbachev, he was appointed to the Communist Party's Secretariat as head of the International Department, before retiring in 1988.

Dobzhansky Theodosius 1900–1975. US geneticist of Ukrainian origin. A pioneer of modern genetics and evolutionary theory, he showed that genetic variability between individuals of the same species is very high and that this diversity is vital to the process of evolution. His book *Genetics and the Origin of Species* was published in 1937.

Doctorow E L 1931– . US novelist. Politically acute, artistically experimental author of the bestseller *Ragtime* 1976, set in the Jazz Age, and *World's Fair* 1985, about a Jewish New York boyhood.

Dodds Charles 1899–1973. English biochemist. He was largely responsible for the discovery of stilboestrol, a powerful synthetic hormone used in treating prostate conditions and also for fattening cattle.

Dodds Johnny 1892–1940. US clarinetist, generally ranked among the top New Orleans jazz clarinetists. He was most successful with the New Orleans Wanderers and noted for his warmth of tone and improvisation.

Doe Samuel Kenyon 1950– . Liberian politician and soldier. He joined the army as a private in 1969 and rose to the rank of master sergeant ten years later. In 1980 he led a coup in which President Tolbert was killed. Doe replaced him as head of state, and in 1981 made himself general and army commander in chief. In 1985 he was narrowly elected president, as leader of the newly formed National Democratic Party of Liberia (NDPL).

Dōgen 1200–1253. Japanese Buddhist monk, pupil of Eisai; founder of the Sōtō school of Zen. He did not reject study, but stressed the importance of *zazen*, seated meditation for its own sake.

Doi Takako 1929– . Japanese socialist politician, leader of the Japan Socialist Party (JSP) from 1986 and responsible for much of its recent revival. She is the country's first female major party leader.

Doi was a law lecturer before being elected to Japan's House of Representatives in 1969. She assumed leadership of the JSP at a low point in the party's fortunes, and proceeded to moderate and modernize its image. With the help of 'housewife volunteers' she established herself as a charismatic political leader, and at a time when the ruling Liberal Democrats were beset by scandals, the JSP vote increased to make Doi the leader of an effective opposition.

Doisy Edward 1893–1986. US biochemist. In 1939 Doisy succeeded in synthesizing vitamin K, a compound earlier discovered by Carl ◊Dam, with whom he shared the 1943 Nobel Prize for Medicine.

Dolci Carlo 1616–1686. Italian painter of the late Baroque period, active in Florence. He created intensely emotional versions of religious subjects, such as *The Last Communion of St Jerome*.

Dolin Anton. Stage name of Patrick Healey-Kay 1904–1983. British dancer and choreographer, a pioneer of British ballet. After studying under Nijinsky, he was a leading member of Diaghilev's company 1924–27. He formed the Markova–Dolin Ballet with Alicia Markova 1935–38, and was a guest soloist with the American Ballet Theater 1940–46.

Doll William Richard 1912– . British physician who proved the link between smoking and lung cancer.

Working with Professor Bradford Hill, he provided the first statistical proof of the link in 1950. In a later study of the smoking habits of doctors, they were able to show that stopping smoking immediately reduces the risk of cancer.

Dollfuss Engelbert 1892–1934. Austrian Christian Socialist politician. He was appointed chancellor in 1932, and in 1933 suppressed parliament and ruled by decree. In Feb 1934 he crushed the Social Democrats by force, and in May Austria was declared a 'corporative' state. The Nazis attempted a coup d'état on 25 July; the Chancellery was seized and Dollfuss murdered.

Dolmetsch Arnold 1858–1940.. French-born musician and instrument-maker who settled in England in 1914 and became a leading figure in the revival of early music.

Domagk Gerhard 1895–1964. German pathologist, discoverer of antibacterial drugs. He found that a dye substance called prontosil red contains chemicals with powerful antibacterial properties. This became the first of the sulphonamide drugs, used to treat a wide range of conditions, including pneumonia and septic wounds. Nobel Prize for Medicine 1939.

Domenichino name given to Domenico Zampieri 1582–1641. Italian Baroque painter and architect, active in Bologna, Naples, and Rome. He began as an assistant to the ◊Carracci family of painters and continued their early Baroque style in, for example, frescoes 1624–28 in the choir of S Andrea della Valle, Rome.

Domenico Veneziano *c*.1400–1461. Italian painter, active in Florence. His few surviving frescoes and altarpieces show a remarkably delicate use of colour and light (which recurs in the work of Piero della Francesca, who worked with him).

Domingo Placido 1937– . Spanish tenor who excels in romantic operatic roles. A member of a musical family, he emigrated with them to Mexico in 1950. He made his debut in 1960 as Alfredo in Verdi's *La Traviata*, then spent four years with the Israel National Opera. He sang at the New York City Opera in 1965 and has since performed diverse roles in opera houses worldwide. In 1986 he starred in the film version of *Otello*.

Domingo Spanish opera singer Placido Domingo at the Royal Opera House, Covent Garden, London, in 1985.

Dominic, St 1170–1221. Founder of the Roman Catholic Dominican order of preaching friars. Feast day 7 Aug.

Dominic, born in Old Castile, was sent by Pope Innocent III in 1205 to preach among the heretic Albigensian sect in Provence. In 1208 the pope instigated the Albigensian crusade to suppress the heretics by force, and this was supported by Dominic. In 1215 the Dominican order was given premises at Toulouse. Pope Honorius III, in 1218, permitted Dominic to constitute his 'holy preaching' as an order, and by the time of his death it was established all over W Europe.

Domino 'Fats' (Antoine) 1928– . US rock-and-roll pianist, singer, and songwriter, exponent of the New Orleans style. His hits include 'Ain't That A Shame' 1955 and 'Blueberry Hill' 1956.

Domitian Titus Flavius Domitianus AD 51–96. Roman emperor from AD 81. He finalized the conquest of Britain (see ◊Agricola), strengthened the Rhine–Danube frontier, and suppressed immorality as well as freedom of thought (see ◊Epictetus) in philosophy and religion (Christians were persecuted). His reign of terror led to his assassination.

Donald Ian 1910–1987. English obstetrician who introduced ultrasound (very high frequency sound waves) scanning. He pioneered its use in obstetrics as a means of scanning the growing fetus without exposure to X-rays.

Donald's experience of using radar in World War II suggested to him the use of ultrasound for medical purposes.

Donaldson Stephen 1947– . US fantasy writer, best known for two Thomas Covenant trilogies in six volumes 1978–1983.

Donat Robert 1905–1958. British actor of Anglo-Polish parents. He started out in the theatre, made one film in Hollywood (*The Count of Monte Cristo* 1934), and his other films include *The Thirty-Nine Steps* 1935, *Goodbye, Mr Chips* 1939, and *The Winslow Boy* 1948.

Donatello (Donato di Niccolo) 1386–1466. Italian sculptor of the early Renaissance, born in Florence. He was instrumental in reviving the Classical style, as in his graceful bronze statue of the youthful *David* (Bargello, Florence) and his equestrian statue of the general *Gattamelata* 1443 (Padua). The course of Florentine art in the 15th century was strongly influenced by his style.

Donatello introduced true perspective in his relief sculptures, like the panel of *St George Slaying the Dragon* about 1415–17 (Orsanmichele, Florence).

Donen Stanley 1924– . US film director, formerly a dancer, who co-directed two of Gene Kelly's best musicals, *On the Town* 1949 and *Singin' in the Rain* 1952. His other films include *Charade* 1963 and *Two for the Road* 1968.

Dönitz Karl 1891–1980. German admiral, originator of the wolf-pack submarine technique, which sank 15 million tonnes of Allied shipping in World War II. He succeeded Hitler in 1945, capitulated, and was imprisoned 1946–56.

Donizetti Gaetano 1797–1848. Italian composer who created more than 60 operas, including *Lucrezia Borgia* 1833, *Lucia di Lammermoor* 1835, *La Fille du régiment* 1840, *La Favorite* 1840, and *Don Pasquale* 1843. They show the influence of Rossini and Bellini, and are characterized by a flow of expressive melodies.

Donne John 1571–1631. English metaphysical poet, whose work is characterized by subtle imagery and figurative language. In 1615 Donne took orders in the Church of England and as dean of St Paul's Cathedral, London, was noted for his sermons. His poetry includes the sonnets 'No man is an island' and 'Death be not proud', elegies, and satires.

Donne was brought up in the Roman Catholic faith, and matriculated early at Oxford to avoid taking the oath of supremacy. Before entering Lincoln's Inn as a law student 1592 he travelled in Europe. During his four years at the law courts he was notorious for his wit and reckless living. In 1596 he sailed as a volunteer with Essex and Raleigh, and on his return became private secretary to Sir Thomas Egerton, Keeper of the Seal. This appointment was ended by his secret marriage to Ann More (died 1617), niece of Egerton's wife, and they endured many years of poverty. The more passionate and tender of his love poems were probably written to her.

From 1621 to his death Donne was dean of St Paul's. His sermons rank him with the century's greatest orators, and his fervent poems of love and hate, violent, tender, or abusive, give him a unique position among English poets. His verse was not published in collected form until after his death, and was long out of favour, but he is now recognized as one of the greatest English poets.

Donoghue Stephen ('Steve') 1884–1945. British jockey. Between 1915 and 1925 he won the Epsom Derby six times, equalling the record of Jem Robinson (since beaten by Lester Piggott). Donoghue is the only jockey to win the race in three successive years.

Doolittle Hilda, pen name *HD* 1886–1961. US poet. She went to Europe in 1911, and was associated with Ezra Pound and the British writer Richard ◊Aldington (to whom she was married 1913–37) in founding the Imagist school of poets, advocating simplicity, precision, and brevity. Her work includes the *Sea Garden* 1916 and *Helen in Egypt* 1916.

Doone English family of freebooters who according to legend lived on Exmoor, Devon, until they were exterminated in the 17th century. They feature in R D ◊Blackmore's novel *Lorna Doone* 1869.

Doppler Christian Johann 1803–1853. Austrian physicist. He became professor of experimental physics at Vienna. He described the *Doppler effect*, the change in frequency (and thus also wavelength) of a wave due to relative motion of its source and observer, as for example in the change in pitch of an ambulance's siren as it approaches and then recedes.

Dorati Antal 1906–1988. US conductor, born in Hungary. He toured with ballet companies 1933–45 and went on to conduct orchestras in the USA and Europe in a career spanning more than half a century. Dorati gave many first performances of Bartók's music and recorded all Haydn's symphonies with the Philharmonia Hungarica.

Doré Gustave 1832–1883. French artist, chiefly known as a prolific illustrator, and also active as a painter, etcher, and sculptor. He produced closely worked engravings of scenes from, for example, Rabelais, Dante, Cervantes, the Bible, Milton, and Poe.

Doré was born in Strasbourg. His views of Victorian London 1869–71, concentrating on desperate poverty and overcrowding in the swollen city, were admired by van Gogh.

Dornier Claude 1884–1969. German aircraft designer who invented the seaplane and during World War II supplied the Luftwaffe with the 'flying pencil' bomber.

Born in Bavaria, he founded the Dornier Metallbau works at Friedrichshafen, Lake Constance, in 1922.

d'Orsay Alfred Guillaume Gabriel, Count d'Orsay 1801–1857. French dandy. For 20 years he resided with Lady ◊Blessington in London at Gore House, where he became known as an arbiter of taste.

Dos Passos John 1896–1970. US author, born in Chicago. He made a reputation with the war novels *One Man's Initiation* 1919 and *Three Soldiers* 1921. His greatest work is the *USA* trilogy 1930–36, which gives a panoramic view of US life through the device of placing fictitious characters against the real setting of newspaper headlines and contemporary events.

Dossantos Jose Eduardo 1942– . Angolan leftwing politician, president from 1979, a member of the People's Movement for the Liberation of Angola (MPLA). He was in exile 1961–70 during the civil war between the MPLA and the National Union for the Total Independence of Angola (UNITA). He returned to Angola in 1970 and rejoined the war, which continued after independence in 1975. He held key positions under President Agostinho Neto, and succeeded him on his death. By 1989, he had negotiated the withdrawal of South African and Cuban forces, and a ceasefire between MPLA and UNITA.

Dostoievsky Fyodor Mihailovich 1821–1881. Russian novelist. Remarkable for their profound psychological insight, Dostoievsky's novels have greatly influenced Russian writers, and since the beginning of the 20th century have been increasingly influential abroad. In 1849 he was sentenced to four years' hard labour in Siberia, followed by army service, for printing socialist propaganda. *The House of the Dead* 1861 recalls his prison experiences, followed by his major works *Crime and Punishment* 1866, *The Idiot* 1868–69, and *The Brothers Karamazov* 1880.

Born in Moscow, the son of a physician, he was for a short time an army officer. His first novel, *Poor Folk*, appeared in 1846. In 1849 Dostoievsky was arrested as a member of a free-thinking literary circle during a period of intense tsarist censorship, and after being reprieved from death at the last moment was sent to the penal settlement at Omsk for four years, where the terrible conditions increased his epileptic tendency. Finally pardoned in 1859, he published the humorous *Village of Stepanchikovo*, *The House of the Dead*, and *The Insulted and the Injured* 1862. Meanwhile he had launched two unsuccessful liberal periodicals, in the second of which his *Letters from the Underworld* 1864 appeared. Compelled to work by pressure of debt, he quickly produced *Crime and Punishment* 1866 and *The Gambler* 1867, before fleeing abroad from his creditors. He then wrote *The Idiot*, in which the hero is an epileptic like himself; *The Eternal Husband* 1870; and *The Possessed* 1871–72.

Returning to Russia in 1871, he again entered journalism and issued the personal miscellany

Dostoievsky Russian novelist Fyodor Dostoievsky.

Journal of an Author, in which he discussed contemporary problems. In 1875 he published *A Raw Youth*, but the great work of his last years is *The Brothers Karamazov*.

Dou Gerard 1613–1675. Dutch genre painter, a pupil of Rembrandt. He is known for small domestic interiors, minutely observed. He was born in Leiden, where he founded a painters' guild with Jan Steen. He had many pupils, including Metsu.

Doughty Charles Montagu 1843–1926. English travel writer, author of the verbose *Travels in Arabia Deserta* 1888, written after two years in the Middle East searching for Biblical relics. He was a role model for T E ◊Lawrence ('Lawrence of Arabia').

Douglas Alfred (Bruce) 1870–1945. English poet who became closely associated in London with Oscar ◊Wilde. Douglas's father, the 9th Marquess of Queensberry, strongly disapproved of the relationship and called Wilde a 'posing Somdomite' (sic). Wilde's action for libel ultimately resulted in his own imprisonment.

Douglas Gavin (or Gawain) 1475–1522. Scottish poet whose translation of Virgil's *Aeneid* 1515 into Scots was the first translation from the classics into an English-based language.

Douglas Kirk. Stage name of Issur Danielovitch 1916– . US film actor, of Russian parents. Usually cast as a dynamic and intelligent hero, as in *Spartacus* 1960, he was a major star of the 1950s and 1960s in such films as *Ace in the Hole/The Big Carnival* 1951, *Lust for Life* 1956, and *The War Wagon* 1967.

Douglas Major (Clifford Hugh) 1879–1952. English social reformer, founder of the economic theory of *Social Credit*, which held that interest should be abolished, and credit should become a state monopoly. During a depression, the state

should provide purchasing power by subsidizing manufacture, and paying dividends to individuals; as long as there was spare capacity in the economy, this credit would not cause inflation.

Douglas Norman 1868–1952. British diplomat and travel writer (*Siren Land* 1911 and *Old Calabria* 1915, dealing with Italy); his novel *South Wind* 1917 is set in his adopted island of Capri.

Douglas-Hamilton family name of dukes of Hamilton: seated at Lennoxlove, East Lothian, Scotland.

Douglas-Home William 1912– . British playwright, younger brother of Lord ◊Home of the Hirsel. His plays include *The Chiltern Hundreds* 1947 and *Lloyd George Knew My Father* 1972.

Douglas of Kirtleside William Sholto Douglas, 1st Baron Douglas of Kirtleside 1893–1969. British air marshal. During World War II he was air officer commander in chief of Fighter Command 1940–42, Middle East Command 1943–44, and Coastal Command 1944–45.

Douglass Frederick *c.* 1817–1895. US anti-slavery campaigner. Born a slave in Maryland, he escaped 1838. His autobiographical *Narrative of the Life of Frederick Douglass* 1845 aroused support in northern states for the abolition of slavery. After the Civil War, he held several US government posts, including minister to Haiti.

Doulton Henry 1820–1897. English ceramicist. He developed special wares for the chemical, electrical, and building industries, and established the world's first stoneware drainpipe factory 1846. From 1870 he created a reputation for art pottery and domestic tablewares in Lambeth, S London, and Burslem, near Stoke-on-Trent.

Doumer Paul 1857–1932. French politician. He was elected president of the Chamber in 1905, president of the Senate in 1927, and president of the republic in 1931. He was assassinated by Gorgulov, a White Russian emigré.

Doumergue Gaston 1863–1937. French prime minister Dec 1913–June 1914 (during the time leading up to World War I); president 1924–31; and premier again Feb–Nov 1934 at head of 'national union' government.

Dowding Hugh Caswall Tremenheere, 1st Baron Dowding 1882–1970. British air chief marshal. He was chief of Fighter Command at the outbreak of World War II in 1939, a post he held through the Battle of Britain. He wrote works on spiritualism.

Dowell Anthony 1943– . British ballet dancer in the classical style. He was principal dancer with the Royal Ballet 1966–86, and director 1986–89. Dowell joined the Royal Ballet in 1961. The choreographer Ashton chose him to create the role of Oberon in *The Dream* 1964 opposite Antoinette Sibley, the start of an outstanding partnership.

Dowland John 1563–1626. English composer. He is remembered for his songs to lute accompaniment as well as music for lute alone, such as *Lachrymae* 1605.

Dowson Ernest 1867–1900. British poet, one of the 'decadent' poets of the 1890s. He is best remembered for the lyric with the refrain 'I have been faithful to thee, Cynara! in my fashion'.

Doxiadis Constantinos 1913–1975. Greek architect and town planner. He designed Islamabad, from 1967 the capital of Pakistan.

Doyle Arthur Conan 1859–1930. British writer, creator of the detective Sherlock Holmes and his assistant Dr Watson, who featured in a number of stories, including *The Hound of the Baskervilles* 1902. Conan Doyle is also known for his romances, for example *The Lost World* 1912.

Born in Edinburgh, he qualified as a doctor, and during the Second South African War was senior physician of a field hospital. He wrote *The Great Boer War* 1900, and was knighted in 1902. The first of his books, *A Study in Scarlet*, appeared in 1887 and introduced Sherlock Holmes and his ingenuous companion, Dr Watson. Other books featuring the same characters followed, including *The Sign of Four* 1889 and *The Valley of Fear* 1915, as well as several volumes of short stories, first published in the *Strand Magazine*. Conan Doyle also wrote historical romances (*Micah Clarke* 1889, and *The White Company* 1891) and the scientific romance *The Lost World* 1912 with an irascible hero Professor Challenger. In his later years he became a spiritualist.

Doyle Richard 1824–1883. British caricaturist and book illustrator. In 1849 he designed the original cover for the humorous magazine *Punch*.

D'Oyly Carte Richard 1844–1901. British producer of the Gilbert and Sullivan operas at the Savoy Theatre, London, which he built. The old D'Oyly Carte Opera Company founded 1876 was disbanded 1982, but a new one opened its first season 1988.

Drabble Margaret 1939– . British writer. Her novels include *The Millstone* 1966 (filmed as *The Touch of Love*), *The Middle Ground* 1980, and *The Radiant Way* 1987. She edited the 1985 edition of the *Oxford Companion to English Literature*.

Draco 7th century BC. Athenian politician, the first to codify the laws of the Athenian city-state. These were notorious for their severity; hence *draconian*, meaning particularly harsh.

Drake Francis *c.*1545–1596. English buccaneer and explorer. Having enriched himself as a pirate against Spanish interests in the Caribbean 1567–72, he was sponsored by Elizabeth I for an expedition to the Pacific, sailing round the world 1577–80 in the *Golden Hind*, robbing Spanish ships as he went. He was mayor of Plymouth 1582 and member of Parliament 1584–85. In 1587 he raided the Spanish port of Cádiz. Against the invasion fleet of the Spanish Armada 1588 he was vice admiral.

He was born in Devon and apprenticed to the master of a coasting vessel, who left him the ship at his death. He accompanied his relative, the navigator John Hawkins, in 1567 and 1572 to plunder the Caribbean, and returned to England 1573 with considerable booty. After serving in Ireland as a volunteer, he suggested to Queen Elizabeth I an expedition to the Pacific, and in Dec 1577 he sailed in the *Pelican* with four other ships and 166 men towards South America. In Aug 1578 the fleet passed through the Straits of Magellan and was then blown south to Cape Horn. The ships became separated and returned to England, all but the *Pelican*, now renamed the *Golden Hind*. Drake sailed north along the coast of Chile and Peru, robbing Spanish ships as far north as California, and then, in July 1579, SW across the Pacific. He rounded the South African Cape June 1580, and reached England Sept 1580. Thus the second voyage around the world, and the first made by an English person, was completed in a little under three years. When the Spanish ambassador demanded Drake's punishment, the Queen knighted him on the deck of the *Golden Hind* at Deptford, London.

In 1581 Drake was chosen mayor of Plymouth, and in 1584–85 he represented Bossinney in Parliament. In a raid on Cádiz 1587 he burned 10,000 tons of shipping, 'singed the King of Spain's beard', and delayed the Armada for a year. He was stationed off Ushant 1588 to intercept the Armada, but was driven back to England by unfavourable winds. During the fight in the Channel he served as a vice admiral in the *Revenge*. Drake sailed on his last expedition to the West Indies with Hawkins 1595, and in Jan 1596 died on his ship off Nombre de Dios.

Drayton Michael 1563–1631. English poet. His volume of poems *The Harmony of the Church* 1591 was destroyed by order of the archbishop of Canterbury. His greatest poetical work was the topographical survey of England, *Polyolbion* 1613–22, in 30 books.

Drees Willem 1886–1988. Dutch socialist politician, prime minister 1948–58. Chair of the Socialist Democratic Workers' Party from 1911 until the German invasion of 1940, he returned to politics in 1947, after being active in the resistance movement.

Dreiser Theodore 1871–1945. US novelist, formerly a Chicago journalist. He wrote the naturalistic novels *Sister Carrie* 1900 and *An American Tragedy* 1925, based on the real-life crime of a young man who in 'making good' kills a shop assistant he has made pregnant. It was filmed as *Splendor in the Grass* 1961.

Dreyer Carl Theodor 1889–1968. Danish director. His wide range of films include the silent classic *La Passion de Jeanne d'Arc/The Passion of Joan of Arc* 1928 and the Expressionist horror film *Vampyr*

1932, after the failure of which Dreyer made no films until *Vredens Dag/Day of Wrath* 1943.

Dreyfus Alfred 1859–1935. French army officer, victim of miscarriage of justice, anti-Semitism, and cover-up. Employed in the War Ministry, in 1894 he was accused of betraying military secrets to Germany, court-martialled, and sent to the penal colony on Devil's Island. When his innocence was discovered 1896 the military establishment tried to conceal it, and the implications of the Dreyfus affair were passionately discussed in the press until in 1906 he was exonerated.

Dreyfus was born in Mulhouse, E France, of a Jewish family. He had been a prisoner in the French Guiana penal colony for two years when it emerged that the real criminal was a Maj Esterhazy; the high command nevertheless attempted to suppress the facts, and used forged documents to strengthen their case. After a violent controversy, in which the future prime minister Clemenceau and the novelist ◊Zola championed Dreyfus, he was brought back for a retrial 1899, found guilty with extenuating circumstances, and received a pardon. In 1906 the court of appeal declared him innocent, and he was reinstated in his military rank.

Drinkwater John 1882–1937. British poet and playwright. He was a prolific writer of lyrical and reflective verse, and also wrote many historical plays, including *Abraham Lincoln* 1918.

Drummond William 1585–1649. Scottish poet, laird of his native Hawthornden, hence known as Drummond of Hawthornden. He was the first Scottish poet of note to use southern English.

Drummond de Andrade Carlos 1902–1987. Brazilian writer, generally considered the greatest modern Brazilian poet, and a prominent member of the Modernist school. His verse, often seemingly casual, continually confounds the reader's expectation of the 'poetical'.

Dryden John 1631–1700. English poet and dramatist, noted for his satirical verse and for his use of the heroic couplet. His poetry includes the verse satire *Absalom and Achitophel* 1681, *Annus Mirabilis* 1667, and 'St Cecilia's Day' 1687. Plays include the comedy *Marriage à la Mode* 1671 and *All for Love* 1678, a reworking of Shakespeare's *Antony and Cleopatra*.

On occasion, Dryden trimmed his politics and his religion to the prevailing wind, and, as a Roman Catholic convert under James II, lost the post of poet laureate (to which he had been appointed 1688) at the Revolution of 1688. Critical works include *Essay on Dramatic Poesy* 1668. Later ventures to support himself include a translation of Virgil 1697.

Drysdale George Russell 1912–1969. Australian artist, born in England. His drawings and paintings often depict the Australian outback, its drought, desolation, and poverty, and Aboriginal life.

Duarte José Napoleon 1925– . El Salvadorean politican, president 1980–82 and 1984–88. He was mayor of San Salvador 1964–70, and was elected president 1972, but exiled by the army in 1982. On becoming president again in 1984, he sought a negotiated settlement with the left-wing guerrillas 1986, but resigned following diagnosis of cancer.

Du Barry Marie Jeanne Bécu, Comtesse Du Barry 1743–1793. Mistress of ◊Louis XV of France from 1768. At his death in 1774 she was banished to a convent, and at the Revolution fled to London. Returning to Paris in 1793, she was guillotined.

Dubček Alexander 1921– . Czech politician, chair of the federal assembly from 1989. As first secretary of the Communist Party 1967–69, he launched a liberalization campaign (the Prague Spring). He was arrested by invading Soviet troops, and expelled from the party 1970. In 1989 he gave speeches at pro-democracy rallies, and in Dec, after the overthrow of the hardline regime, he was elected speaker of the Czech parliament.

Dubos René Jules 1901–1981. French-US microbiologist and forerunner of Alexander ◊Fleming. Dubos studied soil microorganisms and became interested in their antibacterial properties.

The antibacterials he discovered had limited therapeutic use since they were toxic. Nevertheless, he opened up a new field of research which eventually led to the discovery of major drugs like penicillin and streptomycin.

Dubuffet Jean 1901–1985. French artist. He originated *l'art brut*, raw or brutal art, in the 1940s. He used a variety of materials in his paintings and sculptures – plaster, steel wool, straw, and so on – and was inspired by graffiti and children's drawings.

L'art brut emerged in 1945 with an exhibition of Dubuffet's own work and of paintings by psychiatric patients and naive or untrained artists. His own paintings and sculptural works have a similar quality, primitive and expressive.

Duccio di Buoninsegna *c.*1255–1319. Italian painter, a major figure in the Sienese school. His greatest work is his altarpiece for Siena Cathedral, the *Maestà* 1308–11; the figure of the Virgin is Byzantine in style, with much gold detail, but Duccio also created a graceful linear harmony in drapery hems, for example, and this proved a lasting characteristic of Sienese style.

Duchamp Marcel 1887–1968. US artist, born in France. He achieved notoriety with his *Nude Descending a Staircase* 1912 (Philadelphia Museum of Art), influenced by Cubism and Futurism. An active member of the Dada movement, he invented **ready-mades**, everyday items like a bicycle wheel on a kitchen stool, which he displayed as works of art.

Duchamp exhibited at the Armory Show in New York 1913. A major early work which focuses on mechanical objects endowed with mysterious significance is *La Mariée mise à nu par ses célibataires, même/The Bride Stripped Bare by her Bachelors, Even* 1915–23 (Philadelphia Museum of Art). Duchamp continued to experiment with collage, mechanical imagery, and abstract sculpture throughout his career. He lived mostly in New York and became a US citizen in 1954.

Dudintsev Vladimir Dmitriyevich 1918– . Soviet novelist, author of the remarkably frank *Not by Bread Alone* 1956, a depiction of Soviet bureaucracy and inefficiency.

Dufay Guillaume 1400–1474. Flemish composer. He is recognized as the foremost composer of his time, of both secular songs and sacred music (including 84 songs and eight masses). His work marks a transition between the music of the Middle Ages and that of the Renaissance and is characterized by expressive melodies and rich harmonies.

Dufy Raoul 1877–1953. French painter and designer. He originated a fluent, brightly coloured style in watercolour and oils, painting scenes of gaiety and leisure, such as horse racing, yachting, and life on the beach.

Duiker Johannes 1890–1935. Dutch architect of the 1920s and 1930s avant-garde period. His works demonstrate great structural vigour, and include the Zonnestraal sanatorium 1926, Open Air School, Amsterdam 1932, and the Cineac News Cinema, Amsterdam 1933.

Dukakis Michael 1933– . US Democrat politician, governor of Massachusetts 1974–78 and from 1982, presiding over a high-tech economic boom, the 'Massachusetts miracle'. He was a presidential candidate in 1988.

Dukakis was born in Boston, Massachusetts, the son of Greek immigrants. After studying law at Harvard and serving in Korea (1955–57), he concentrated on a political career in his home state. Elected as a Democrat to the Massachusetts legislature in 1962, he became state governor in 1974. After an unsuccessful first term, marred by his unwillingness to compromise, he was defeated in 1978. Dukakis returned as governor in 1982, committed to working in a more consensual manner. He was re-elected in 1986 and captured the Democratic Party's presidential nomination in 1988. After a poor campaign, the diligent but uncharismatic Dukakis was defeated by the incumbent vice president George Bush.

Dukas Paul (Abraham) 1865–1935. French composer. His orchestral scherzo *L'Apprenti Sorcier/The Sorcerer's Apprentice* 1897 is full of the colour and energy that characterizes much of his work.

He was professor of composition at the Paris Conservatoire and composed the opera *Ariane et Barbe-Bleue/Ariane and Bluebeard* 1907, and the ballet *La Péri* 1912.

Dulles Alan 1893–1969. US lawyer, director of the Central Intelligence Agency (CIA) 1953–61. He was the brother of John Foster Dulles.

Dulles John Foster 1888–1959. US politician. Senior US adviser at the founding of the United Nations, he was largely responsible for drafting the Japanese peace treaty of 1951. As secretary of state 1952–59, he secured US intervention in support of South Vietnam following the expulsion of the French in 1954, and was critical of Britain in the Suez Crisis 1956.

Dulong Pierre 1785–1838. French chemist and physicist who, along with ◊Petit, discovered in 1819 the law that, for many elements solid at room temperature, the product of the atomic weight and specific heat capacity is approximately constant. He had earlier, in 1811, and at the cost of an eye, discovered the explosive nitrogen trichloride.

Dumas Alexandre 1802–1870. French author, known as Dumas *père* (the father). His play *Henri III et sa cour/Henry III and his Court* 1829 established French romantic historical drama, but today he is remembered for his romances, the reworked output of a 'fiction-factory' of collaborators. They include *Les trois mousquetaires/The Three Musketeers* 1844 and its sequels. Dumas *fils* was his illegitimate son.

Dumas Alexandre 1824–1895. French author, known as Dumas *fils* (the son), son of Dumas *père* and remembered for the play *La Dame aux camélias/The Lady of the Camellias* 1852, based on his own novel and source of Verdi's opera *La Traviata*.

Du Maurier Daphne 1907–1989. British novelist, whose romantic fiction includes *Jamaica Inn* 1936, *Rebecca* 1938, and *My Cousin Rachel* 1951.

Du Maurier George (Louis Palmella Busson) 1834–1896. French-born British author of the novel *Trilby* 1894 – the story of a natural singer able to perform only under the hypnosis of Svengali, her tutor.

Dumont D'Urville Jean 1780–1842. French explorer in Australasia and the Pacific. In 1838–40 he sailed round Cape Horn on a voyage to study terrestial magnetism and reached Adélie Land in Antarctica.

Dumouriez Charles François du Périer 1739–1823. French general during the Revolution. In 1792 he was appointed foreign minister, supported the declaration of war against Austria, and after the fall of the monarchy was given command of the army defending Paris; later he won the battle of Jemappes, but was defeated at Neerwinden (Austrian Netherlands) in 1793. After intriguing with the royalists he had to flee for his life, and from 1804 he lived in England.

Dunant Jean Henri 1828–1910. Swiss philanthropist; the originator of the Red Cross. At the Battle of Solferino 1859 he helped to tend the wounded, and in *Un Souvenir de Solferino* 1862 he proposed the establishment of an international body for the aid of the wounded – an idea that was realized in the Geneva Convention 1864. He shared the Nobel Peace Prize 1901.

Dunaway Faye 1941– . US actress whose first starring role was in *Bonnie and Clyde* 1967. Her subsequent films, including *Network* 1976 and *Mommie Dearest* 1981, received a varying critical reception.

Dunbar William *c.*1460–*c.*1520. Scottish poet at the court of James IV. His poems include a political allegory, 'The Thrissel and the Rose' 1503, and the elegy with the refrain '*Timor mortis conturbat me*'.

Duncan Isadora 1878–1927. US dancer and teacher. An influential pioneer of modern dance, she adopted an expressive, free form, dancing barefoot and wearing a loose tunic, inspired by the ideal of Hellenic beauty. She toured extensively, often returning to Russia after her initial success there 1905. She died in an accident when her long scarf caught in the wheel of the car in which she was travelling.

Duncan-Sandys Duncan Edwin Sandys, Baron Duncan-Sandys 1908–1987. British Conservative politician. As minister for Commonwealth Relations 1960–64, he negotiated the independence of Malaysia 1963. He was created a life peer 1974.

Dundas Henry, 1st Viscount Melville 1742–1811. British Tory politician. In 1791 he became home secretary, and with revolution raging in France, carried through the prosecution of the English and Scottish radicals. After holding other high cabinet posts, he was impeached in 1806 for corruption and, although acquitted on the main charge, held no further office.

Dunham Katherine 1912– . US dancer, born in Chicago, noted for a free, strongly emotional method. She founded her own school and company 1945.

Dunlop John Boyd 1840–1921. Scottish inventor, who founded the rubber company that bears his name. In 1887, to help his child win a tricycle race, he bound an inflated rubber hose to the wheels. The same year he developed commercially practical pneumatic tyres (first patented by R W Thomson in 1846) for bicycles and cars.

Dunsany Edward, 18th Baron Dunsany 1878–1957. Irish writer. His works include short ironic heroic fantasies, collected in *The Gods of Pegana* 1905 and other books, but he is best known for employing the convention of a narrator sitting in a club or bar (his narrator was called Jorkens).

Duns Scotus John *c.*1265–*c.*1308. Franciscan monk, an important figure of medieval scholasticism. On many points he turned against the orthodoxy of ◊Aquinas; for example, he rejected the idea of a necessary world, favouring a concept of God as absolute freedom capable of spontaneous activity.

The church rejected his ideas, hence the word *dunce.*

Dunstable John *c.*1385–1453. English composer. He wrote songs and anthems, and is generally considered one of the founders of Renaissance music.

Dunstan, St *c.*924–988. English priest and politician, archbishop of Canterbury from 960. As abbot of Glastonbury from 945, he made it a centre of learning. Feast day 19 May.

Duparc (Marie Eugène) Henri Fouques 1848–1933. French composer. He studied under César ◊Franck. His songs, though only 15 in number, are memorable for their craft and for their place in the history of French songwriting.

Du Pré Jacqueline 1945–1987. English cellist. Celebrated for her proficient technique and powerful interpretations of the Classical cello repertory, particularly of ◊Elgar. She had an international concert career while still in her teens and made many recordings.

She married Daniel ◊Barenboim in 1967 and worked with him in concerts, as a duo, and in a conductor-soloist relationship until her playing career was ended by multiple sclerosis. Although confined to a wheelchair for the last 14 years of her life, she continued to work as a teacher and to campaign on behalf of other sufferers of the disease.

Duras Marguerite 1914– . French writer. Her works include short stories (*Des Journées entières dans les arbres*), plays (*La Musica*), film scripts (*Hiroshima mon amour* 1960), and novels such as *Le Vice-Consul* 1966, evoking an existentialist world from the actual setting of Calcutta. Her autobiographical novel, *La Douleur*, is set in Paris in 1945.

Dürer Albrecht 1471–1528. German artist, the leading figure of the northern Renaissance. He was born in Nuremberg and travelled widely in Europe. Highly skilled in drawing and a keen student of nature, he perfected the technique of woodcut and engraving, producing woodcut series such as the *Apocalypse* 1498 and copperplate engravings such as *The Knight, Death and the Devil* 1513 and *Melancholia* 1514; he may also have invented etching. His paintings include altarpieces and meticulously observed portraits (including many self-portraits).

He was apprenticed first to his father, a goldsmith, then in 1486 to Michael Wolgemut, a painter, woodcut artist, and master of a large workshop in Nuremberg. From 1490 he travelled widely, studying Netherlandish and Italian art, then visited Colmar, Basel, and Strasbourg, and returned to Nuremberg in 1495. Another notable journey was to Venice 1505–07, where he met Giovanni Bellini, and in 1520 to Antwerp, where he was made court painter to Charles V of Spain and the Netherlands (a journey recorded in detail in his diary).

Durham John George Lambton, 1st Earl of Durham 1792–1840. British politician. Appointed Lord Privy Seal in 1830, he drew up the first Reform Bill of 1832, and as governor general of Canada briefly in 1837 drafted the Durham Report which led to the union of Upper and Lower Canada.

Durkheim Emile 1858–1917. French sociologist, one of the founders of modern sociology, who also influenced social anthropology.

He examined the bases of social order and the effects of industrialization on traditional social and moral order, and attempted to establish sociology as a respectable and scientific discipline, capable of diagnosing social ills and recommending possible cures.

His four key works are *The Division of Labour in Society* 1893, comparing social order in small-scale societies with that in industrial ones; *The Rules of Sociological Method* 1895, outlining his own brand of functionalism and proclaiming positivism as the way forward for sociology as a science; *Suicide* 1897, showing social causes of this apparently individual act; and *The Elementary Forms of Religion*, a study of the beliefs of Australian aborigines, showing the importance of religion in social solidarity.

Durrell Gerald (Malcolm) 1925– . British naturalist, Director of Jersey Zoological Park, he is the author of travel and natural history books, and the humorous memoir *My Family and Other Animals* 1956. He is the brother of Lawrence Durrell.

Durrell Lawrence (George) 1912– . British novelist and poet. Born in India, he joined the foreign service, and has lived mainly in the E Mediterranean, the setting of his novels, including the Alexandria Quartet: *Justine*, *Balthazar*, *Mountolive*, and *Clea* 1957–60; he has also written travel books. He is the brother of Gerald Durrell.

Dürrenmatt Friedrich 1921– . Swiss dramatist, author of grotesquely farcical tragicomedies, for example *The Visit* 1956 and *The Physicists* 1962.

Duse Eleonora 1859–1924. Italian actress. She was the mistress of the poet ọD'Annunzio from 1897, as recorded in his novel *Il Fuoco/The Flame of Life*.

Dutilleux Henri 1916– . French composer of instrumental music in elegant Neo-Romantic style. His works include *Mataboles* 1962–65 for orchestra and *Ainsi la Nuit* 1975–76 for string quartet.

Duval Claude 1643–1670. English criminal. He was born in Normandy and turned highwayman after coming to England at the Restoration. His gallantry was famous. He was hanged at Tyburn, London.

Duvalier François 1907–1971. Right-wing president of Haiti 1957–71. Known as *Papa Doc*,

he ruled as a dictator, organizing the Tontons Macoutes ('bogeymen') as a private security force to intimidate and assassinate opponents of his regime. He rigged the 1961 elections in order to have his term of office extended until 1967, and in 1964 declared himself president for life. He was excommunicated by the Vatican for harassing the church, and was succeeded on his death by his son Jean-Claude Duvalier.

Duvalier Jean-Claude 1951– . Right-wing president of Haiti 1971–86. Known as *Baby Doc*, he succeeded his father François Duvalier, becoming, at the age of 19, the youngest president in the world. He was forced by the USA to moderate his father's tyrannical regime, yet he tolerated no opposition. In 1986, with Haiti's economy stagnating and with increasing civil disorder, Duvalier fled to France.

Duve Christian de 1917– . Belgian scientist, who shared the Nobel prize for Medicine in 1974 for his work on the structural and functional organization of the biological cell.

Duvivier Julien 1896–1967. French film director, whose work includes *Un Carnet de Bal* 1937 and *La Fin du Jour* 1938.

Duwez Pol 1907– . US scientist, born in Belgium, who in 1959 developed metallic glasses (alloys rapidly cooled from the melt which combine properties of glass and metal) with his team at the California Institute of Technology.

Dvořák Antonin (Leopold) 1841–1904. Czech composer. International recognition came with his series of Slavonic Dances 1877–86, and he was director of the National Conservatory, New York, 1892–95. Works such as his *New World Symphony* 1893 reflect his interest in American folk themes, including black and Native American. He wrote nine symphonies; tone poems; operas, including

Dvořák *Czech composer Antonin Dvořák.*

Rusalka 1901; large-scale choral works; the *Carnival* and other overtures; violin and cello concertos; chamber music; piano pieces; and songs. His Romantic music extends the classical tradition of Beethoven and Brahms and displays the influence of Czech folk music.

Dyck Anthony van 1599–1641. Flemish painter. Born in Antwerp, he was an assistant to Rubens 1618–20, then briefly worked in England at the court of James I, and moved to Italy in 1622. In 1626 he returned to Antwerp, where he continued to paint religious works and portraits. He painted his best-known portraits during his second period in England from 1632, for example, *Charles I on Horseback* about 1638 (National Gallery, London).

His characteristic portrait style emerged in the 1620s. In England he produced numerous portraits of royalty and aristocrats (some of them doomed to extinction in the Civil War), and was knighted by Charles I. His work influenced the course of British portraiture.

Dylan Bob. Adopted name of Robert Allen Zimmerman 1941– . US singer and songwriter, whose work in the 1960s, first in the folk-music tradition and from 1965 in an individualistic rock style, was influential on later pop music.

Dylan's early songs, on his albums *Freewheelin'* 1963 and *The Times They Are A-Changin'* 1964, were associated with the US civil-rights movement and antiwar protest. When he first used an electric rock band he was criticized by purists, but the albums *Highway 61 Revisited* 1965 and *Blonde on Blonde* 1966 are often cited as his best work. His increasingly obscure lyrics provided catchphrases for a generation and influenced innumerable songwriters.

Eagling Wayne 1950– . Canadian dancer. He joined the Royal Ballet in London, appearing in *Gloria* 1980, and other productions.

Eakins Thomas 1844–1916. US painter. He studied in Europe and developed a realistic style with strong contrasts between light and shade, as in *The Gross Clinic* 1875 (Jefferson Medical College, Philadelphia), a group portrait of a surgeon, his assistants and students.

Eanes António dos Santos Ramalho 1935– . Portuguese politician. He helped plan the 1974 coup which ended the Caetano regime, and as army chief of staff put down a left-wing revolt in Nov 1975. He was president 1976–86.

Earhart Amelia 1898–1937. American aviator, born in Kansas. In 1932 she was the first woman to fly the Atlantic alone, and in 1937 disappeared without trace while making a Pacific flight. Clues found on Nikumuroro island in Kiribati in 1989 suggest that she and her male navigator might have survived a crash only to die of thirst.

Eastman George 1854–1932. US entrepreneur and inventor who founded the Kodak photographic company. From 1888 he marketed daylight-loading flexible roll films (to replace the glass plates used previously) and portable cameras. By 1900 his company was selling a pocket camera for as little as $1.

Eastwood Clint 1930– . US film actor and director. As the 'man with no name' caught up in Wild West lawlessness in *A Fistful of Dollars* 1964, he started the vogue for 'spaghetti westerns'. Later westerns include *The Good, the Bad, and the Ugly* 1966 and *High Plains Drifter* 1973. He also starred in the 'Dirty Harry' series, and directed *Bird* 1988.

Eban Abba 1915– . Israeli diplomat and politician, Israeli ambassador in Washington 1950–59 and foreign minister 1966–74.

Born in Cape Town, and educated in England, he taught at Cambridge University before serving at Allied HQ during World War II. He subsequently settled in Israel.

Eccles John Carew 1903– . Australian physiologist, who in 1963 shared a Nobel prize (with Alan ◊Hodgkin and Andrew ◊Huxley) for work on conduction in the central nervous system. He argued that the mind has an existence independent of the brain.

Echegaray José 1832–1916. Spanish dramatist. His dramas include *O locura o santidad/Madman or Saint* 1877, and *El gran Galeoto/The World and his Wife* 1881. Nobel prize 1904.

Eckert John Presper Jr 1919– . US mathematician who collaborated with John ◊Mauchly on the development of the ENIAC and Univac 1 computers.

Eckhart Johannes, called Meister Eckhart *c.*1260–1327. German theologian, leader of a popular mystical movement. In 1326 he was accused of heresy, and in 1329 a number of his doctrines were condemned by the pope as heretical.

Eco Umberto 1932– . Italian cultural and literary critic (*The Role of the Reader* 1979), and author of the 'philosophical thriller' *The Name of the Rose* 1983.

Eddery Patrick (Pat) 1952– . Irish-born flat racing jockey who has won the jockey's championship seven times including four in succession.

He has won all the major races, including the Epsom Derby twice. He won the Prix de L'Arc de Triomphe four times, including three in succession 1985–87.

Eddington Arthur Stanley 1882–1944. British astrophysicist, who studied the motions and equilibrium of stars, their luminosity and atomic structure, and became a leading exponent of Einstein's relativity theory. In 1919 his observation of stars during an eclipse of the sun confirmed Einstein's prediction that light is bent when passing near the Sun. In *The Expanding Universe* 1933 he expressed the theory that the galaxies are receding from one another.

Eddy Mary Baker 1821–1910. US founder of the Christian Science movement. Her faith in divine healing was confirmed by her recovery from injuries caused by a fall 1866, and she based a religious sect on this belief, set out in her pamphlet *Science and Health with Key to the Scriptures* 1875.

She was born in New Hampshire and brought up as a Congregationalist. Her pamphlet *Science of Man* 1869 was followed by *Science and Health* which she constantly revised. In 1876 she founded the Christian Science Association. In 1879 the Church of Christ, Scientist, was established, and although living in retirement after 1892 she continued to direct the activities of the movement until her death.

Edelman Gerald 1929– . US biochemist. The structure of the antibody gamma globulin (one of the body's defences) was worked out by Rodney ◊Porter by 1962. Edelman tackled the related problem of working out the sequence of 1330 amino acids which compose the antibody. The task was completed by 1969 and won for Edelman a share of the 1972 Nobel Prize for Medicine with Porter.

Eden Anthony, 1st Earl of Avon 1897–1977. British Conservative politician, foreign secretary 1935–38, 1940–45, and 1951–55; prime minister 1955–57, when he resigned after the failure of the Anglo-French military intervention in the Suez Crisis.

Upset by his prime minister's rejection of a peace plan secretly proposed by Roosevelt in Jan 1938, Eden resigned as foreign secretary in Feb 1938 in protest against Chamberlain's decision to open conversations with the Fascist dictator Mussolini, but was foreign secretary again in the wartime coalition formed Dec 1940 and in the Conservative government elected 1951. With the Soviets, he negotiated an interim peace in Vietnam 1954. In Apr 1955 he succeeded Churchill as prime minister. His use of force in the Suez Crisis led to his resignation in Jan 1957, but he continued to maintain that his action was justified.

Edgar c.1050–c.1130. English prince, born in Hungary, known as the *Atheling* ('of royal blood'). Grandson of Edmund Ironside, he was supplanted as heir to Edward the Confessor by William the Conqueror. He led two rebellions against William 1068 and 1069, but made peace 1074.

Edgar the Peaceful 944–975. King of all England from 959. He was the younger son of Edmund I, and strove successfully to unite English and Danes as fellow subjects.

Edgeworth Maria 1767–1849. Irish novelist. Her first novel, *Castle Rackrent* 1800, dealt with Anglo-Irish country society, and was followed by the similar *The Absentee* 1812 and *Ormond* 1817.

Edison Thomas Alva 1847–1931. US scientist and inventor. Born in Ohio, of Dutch-Scottish parentage, he became first a newsboy and then a telegraph operator. His first invention was an automatic repeater for telegraphic messages. Later came the carbon transmitter (used as a microphone in the production of the Bell telephone), the phonograph, the electric filament lamp, a new type of storage battery, and the kinetoscopic camera, an early film camera. He also anticipated the Fleming thermionic valve. He supported direct current (DC) transmission, but alternating current (AC) was eventually found to be more efficient and economical.

Edmund Ironside c.989–1016. King of England, the son of Ethelred the Unready. He led the resistance to ◊Canute's invasion 1015, and on Ethelred's death 1016 was chosen as king by the citizens of London, while the Witan (the king's council) elected Canute. Edmund was defeated by Canute at Assandun (Ashington), Essex, and they divided the kingdom between them.

Edmund, St c.840–870. King of East Anglia from 855. In 870 he was defeated and captured by the Danes at Hoxne, Suffolk, and martyred on refusing to renounce Christianity. He was canonized and his shrine at Bury St Edmunds became a place of pilgrimage.

Edward the Black Prince 1330–1376. Prince of Wales, eldest son of Edward III of England. The epithet supposedly derived from his black armour. During the Hundred Years' War he fought at the Battle of Crécy 1346 and captured the French king at Poitiers 1356. In 1367 he invaded Castile and restored to the throne the deposed king, Pedro the Cruel (1334–69).

Edward (full name Edward Antony Richard Louis) 1964– . Prince of the UK, third son of Queen Elizabeth II. He is seventh in line to the throne after Charles, Charles' two sons, Andrew, and Andrew's two daughters.

Edward ten kings of England or the UK:

Edward the Martyr c.963–978. King of England from 975. Son of King Edgar, he was murdered at Corfe Castle, Dorset, probably at his stepmother Aelfthryth's instigation (she wished to secure the crown for her son, Ethelred). He was canonized 1001.

Edward the Confessor c.1003–1066. King of England from 1042, the son of Ethelred II. He lived in Normandy until shortly before his accession. During his reign power was held by Earl ◊Godwin and his son ◊Harold, while the king devoted himself to religion. He was buried in Westminster Abbey, which he had rebuilt. He was canonized 1161.

Edward I 1239–1307. King of England from 1272, son of Henry III. Edward led the royal forces against Simon de Montfort in the Barons' War 1264–67, and was on a crusade when he succeeded to the throne. He established English rule over all Wales 1282–84, and secured recognition of his overlordship from the Scottish king, though the Scots (under Wallace and Bruce) fiercely resisted actual conquest. In his reign Parliament took its approximate modern form with the Model Parliament 1295. He was succeeded by his son, Edward II.

Edward II 1284–1327. King of England from 1307. Son of Edward I and born at Caernarvon Castle, he was created the first Prince of Wales 1301. His invasion of Scotland 1314 to suppress revolt resulted in defeat at Bannockburn. He was deposed 1327 by his wife Isabella (1292–1358), daughter of Philip IV of France, and her lover Roger de ◊Mortimer, and murdered in Berkeley Castle, Gloucestershire. He was succeeded by his son, Edward III.

Incompetent and frivolous, and entirely under the influence of his favourites, he struggled throughout his reign with discontented barons.

Edward III 1312–1377. King of England from 1327, son of Edward II. He assumed the government 1330 from his mother, through whom in 1337 he laid claim to the French throne and thus began the Hundred Years' War with France. He was succeeded by Richard II.

Edward began his reign by attempting to force his rule on Scotland, winning a victory at Halidon Hill 1333. During the first stage of the Hundred Years' War, the English victories included the Battle of Crécy 1346 and the capture of Calais 1347. In 1360 Edward surrendered his claim to the French throne but the war resumed 1369.

Edward IV 1442–1483. King of England 1461–70 and from 1471. He was the son of Richard, Duke of York, and succeeded Henry VI in the Wars of the Roses, temporarily losing the throne to Henry when Edward fell out with his adviser ◊Warwick but regaining it at the Battle of Barnet. He was succeeded by his son Edward V.

Edward was known as Earl of March until his accession. After his father's death he occupied London 1461, and was proclaimed king in place of Henry VI by a council of peers. His position was secured by the defeat of the Lancastrians at Towton 1461 and by the capture of Henry. He quarrelled, however, with Warwick, his strongest supporter, who in 1470–71 temporarily restored Henry, until Edward recovered the throne by his victories at Barnet and Tewkesbury.

Edward V 1470–1483. King of England 1483. Son of Edward IV, he was deposed three months after his accession in favour of his uncle (◊Richard III), and is traditionally believed to have been murdered (with his brother) in the Tower of London on Richard's orders.

Edward VI 1537–1553. King of England from 1547, son of Henry VIII and Jane Seymour. The government was entrusted to his uncle the Duke of Somerset (who fell 1549), and then to the Earl of Warwick, later created Duke of Northumberland. He was succeeded by his sister, Mary I.

Edward VII 1841–1910. King of Great Britain and Ireland from 1901. As Prince of Wales he was a prominent social figure, but his mother Queen Victoria considered him too frivolous to take part in political life. In 1860 he made the first tour of Canada and the USA ever undertaken by a British prince.

Edward was born at Buckingham Palace, the eldest son of Queen Victoria and Prince Albert. After his father's death 1861 he undertook many public duties, took a close interest in politics, and

Edward VIII *The Duke and Duchess of Windsor in a Sussex village, Sept 1939.*

was on friendly terms with the party leaders. In 1863 he married Princess ◊Alexandra of Denmark, by whom he had six children. He toured India 1875–76. He succeeded to the throne 1901, and was crowned 1902. Although he overrated his political influence, he contributed to the Entente Cordiale 1904 with France and the Anglo-Russian agreement 1907.

Edward VIII 1894–1972. King of Great Britain and Northern Ireland Jan–Dec 1936, when he abdicated to marry Wallis Warfield ◊Simpson. He was created duke of Windsor and was governor of the Bahamas 1940–45, subsequently settling in France.

Eldest son of George V, he received the title of Prince of Wales 1910 and succeeded to the throne 20 Jan 1936. In Nov 1936 a constitutional crisis arose when Edward wished to marry Mrs Simpson; it was felt that, as a divorcee, she would be unacceptable as queen. On 11 Dec Edward abdicated and left for France, where the couple were married 1937. Papers found 1987 revealed he offered to accept the presidency of a British socialist state. He was succeeded by his brother, George VI.

Edwards Blake. Adopted name of William Blake McEdwards 1922– . US film director and writer, formerly an actor. Specializing in lively comedies, he directed the series of *Pink Panther* films (1963–1978), starring Peter Sellers. His other work includes *Breakfast at Tiffany's* 1961 and *Blind Date* 1986.

Edwards Gareth 1947– . Welsh rugby union player. He was appointed captain of his country when only 20 years old.

He appeared in seven championship winning teams, five Triple Crown winning teams, and two Grand Slam winning teams. In 53 international matches he scored a record 20 tries. He toured with the British Lions three times.

Edwards George 1908– . British civil and military aircraft designer, associated with the *Viking, Viscount, Valiant V-bomber, VC-10*, and *Concorde.*

Edwards Jonathan 1703–1758. US theologian, who took a Calvinist view of predestination, and initiated a religious revival, the 'Great Awakening'; author of *The Freedom of the Will* (defending determinism) 1754.

Edward the Elder *c.*870–924. King of the West Saxons. He succeeded his father ◊Alfred the Great 899. He reconquered SE England and the Midlands from the Danes, uniting Wessex and Mercia with the help of his sister, Athelflad. By the time Edward died, his kingdom was the most powerful in the British Isles. He was succeeded by his son ◊Athelstan.

Edwin *c.*585–633. King of Northumbria from 617. He captured and fortified Edinburgh, which was named after him, and was killed in battle with Penda of Mercia, 632.

Egerton family name of Dukes of Sutherland; seated at Mertoun, Roxburghshire, Scotland.

Egmont Lamoral, Count of Egmont 1522–1568. Flemish nobleman, born in Hainault. As a servant of the Spanish crown, he defeated the French at St Quentin 1557 and Gravelines 1558, and became stadholder (chief magistrate) of Flanders and Artois. From 1561 he helped to lead the movement against Spanish misrule, but in 1567 the Duke of Alva was sent to crush the Resistance, and Egmont was beheaded.

Ehrlich Paul 1854–1915. German bacteriologist and immunologist, who developed the first cure for syphilis. He developed the arsenic compounds, in particular salvarsan, used in the treatment of syphilis before the discovery of antibiotics. He shared the 1908 Nobel prize.

Eichendorff Joseph Freiherr von 1788–1857. German lyric poet and romantic novelist, born in Upper Silesia. His work was set to music by Schumann, Mendelssohn, and Wolf. He held various judicial posts.

Eichmann (Karl) Adolf 1906–1962. Austrian Nazi. As an SS official during Hitler's regime he was responsible for atrocities against Jews and others, including the implementation of genocide. He managed to escape at the fall of Germany 1945, but was discovered in Argentina 1960, abducted by Israeli agents, tried in Israel 1961, and executed.

Eiffel Gustave Alexandre 1832–1923. French engineer who constructed the Eiffel Tower for the 1889 Paris exhibition.

He set up his own business in Paris and quickly established his reputation with the construction of a series of ambitious railway bridges of which the 160 m/525 ft span across the Duoro at Oporto, Portugal was the longest. In 1881 he provided the iron skeleton for the Statue of Liberty.

Eijkman Christiaan 1858–1930. Dutch bacteriologist, who identified vitamin B_1 deficiency as the cause of beri-beri, and pioneered the recognition of vitamins as essential to health. Nobel prize 1929.

Einstein Albert 1879–1955. German-Swiss physicist, who formulated the theories of relativity, and did important work in radiation physics and thermodynamics. In 1905 he published the special theory of relativity, and in 1915 issued his general theory of relativity. His latest conception of the basic laws governing the universe was outlined in his unified field theory, made public 1953; and of the 'relativistic theory of the non-symmetric field', completed 1955.

Born at Ulm, in Württemberg, West Germany, he lived with his parents in Munich and then in Italy. After teaching at the polytechnic school at Zürich, he became a Swiss citizen and was appointed an inspector of patents in Berne. In his spare time, he took his PhD at Zürich. In 1909 he was given a chairmanship of theoretical physics at the university. After holding a similar post at Prague 1911, he returned to teach at Zürich 1912, and in 1913 took up a specially created post as director of the Kaiser Wilhelm Institute

Einstein Physicist Albert Einstein, 1944.

for Physics, Berlin. He received the Nobel Prize for Physics 1921. After being deprived of his post at Berlin by the Nazis, he emigrated to the USA 1933, and became professor of mathematics and a permanent member of the Institute for Advanced Study at Princeton, New Jersey. During World War II he worked for the US Navy Ordnance Bureau.

Einthoven Willem 1860–1927. Dutch physiologist and inventor of the electrocardiograph. He was able to show that particular disorders of the heart alter its electrical activity in characteristic ways. Einthoven combined his medical studies with an interest in physics. This led him to investigate the electrical activity of the heart. He invented a machine for detecting and recording this activity, the string galvanometer, or electrocardiograph.

Eisai 1141–1215. Japanese Buddhist monk who introduced Zen and tea from China to Japan and founded the Rinzai school.

Eisenhower Dwight D(avid) ('Ike') 1890–1969. 34th president of the USA 1953–60, a Republican. A general in World War II, he commanded the Allied forces in Italy 1943, then the Allied invasion of Europe, and from Oct 1944 all the Allied armies in the West.

He resigned from the army 1952 to campaign for the presidency; he was elected, and re-elected 1956. A popular politician, Eisenhower hold office during a period of domestic and international tension, with the growing civil rights movement at home and the Cold War dominating international politics.

Eisenstein Sergei Mikhailovich 1898–1948. Latvian film director. He pioneered the use of montage (a technique of deliberately juxtaposing shots to create a particular meaning) as a means of propaganda, as in *The Battleship Potemkin* 1925. His *Alexander Nevsky* 1938 was the first part of an uncompleted trilogy, the second part, *Ivan the Terrible* 1944, being banned in Russia.

Eldem Sedad Hakki 1908– . Turkish architect. His work is inspired by the spatial harmony and regular rhythms of the traditional Turkish house. These qualities are reinterpreted in modern forms with great sensitivity to context, as in the Social Security Agency Complex, Zeyrek, Istanbul (1962–64), and the Ataturk Library, Istanbul (1973).

Eldon John Scott, 1st Earl of Eldon 1751–1838. English politician, born in Newcastle. He became a Member of Parliament 1782, and Lord Chancellor 1801–05 and 1807–27. During his period the rules of the Lord Chancellor's court governing the use of the injunction and precedent in equity finally became fixed.

Eleanor of Aquitaine c.1122–1204. Queen of France 1137–51 and of England from 1154. She was the daughter of William X, Duke of Aquitaine, and was married 1137–52 to Louis VII of France,

Eisenhower US soldier and politician Dwight D Eisenhower. After commanding Allied forces in Europe during World War II, he became 34th President of the US in 1952.

but the marriage was annulled. The same year she married Henry of Anjou, who became king of England 1154. Henry imprisoned her 1174–89 for supporting their sons, the future Richard I and King John, in revolt against him.

Eleanor of Castile c.1245–1290. Queen of Edward I of England, the daughter of Ferdinand III of Castile. She married Prince Edward 1254, and accompanied him on his crusade 1270. She died at Harby, Nottinghamshire, and Edward erected stone crosses in towns where her body rested on the funeral journey to London. Several *Eleanor Crosses* are still standing, for example at Northampton.

Elgar Edward (William) 1857–1934. English composer. His *Enigma Variations* appeared 1899, and although his celebrated choral work, the oratorio setting of Newman's *The Dream of Gerontius*, was initially a failure, it was well received at Düsseldorf in 1902. Many of his earlier works were then performed, including the *Pomp and Circumstance* marches. Among his later works are oratorios, two symphonies, a violin concerto, a cello concerto, chamber music, songs, and the tone-poem *Falstaff* 1913.

Elijah c. mid-9th century BC. In the Old Testament or Jewish Bible, a Hebrew prophet during the reigns of the Israelite kings Ahab and Ahaziah. He came from Gilead. He defeated the prophets of the fertility god Baal, and was said to have been carried up to heaven in a fiery chariot in a whirlwind. In Jewish belief, Elijah will return to Earth to herald the coming of the messiah.

Eliot George. Pen name of Mary Ann Evans 1819–1880. English novelist, who portrayed Victorian society, particularly its intellectual hypocrisy, with realism and irony. In 1857 she published the story 'Amos Barton', the first of the *Scenes of Clerical Life*. This was followed by the novels *Adam Bede* 1859, *The Mill on the Floss* 1860, and *Silas Marner* 1861. *Middlemarch* 1872 is now considered one of the greatest novels of the 19th century. Her final book *Daniel Deronda* 1876 was concerned with anti-Semitism. She also wrote poetry.

Born at Chilvers Coton, Warwickshire, she had a strict evangelical upbringing, but on moving to Coventry with her father in 1841 was converted to free thought (a movement opposed to Christian dogma). As assistant editor of the *Westminster Review* under John Chapman 1851–53, she made the acquaintance of Carlyle, Harriet Martineau, Herbert Spencer, and the philosopher and critic George Henry Lewes (1817–1878). Lewes was married but separated from his wife, and from 1854 he and Eliot lived together in a relationship which she regarded as a true marriage and which continued until his death. In 1880 she married John Cross (1840–1924).

Eliot John 1592–1632. English politician, born in Cornwall. He became a member of Parliament 1614, and with the Earl of Buckingham's patronage was made a vice-admiral 1619. In 1626 he was imprisoned in the Tower of London for demanding Buckingham's impeachment. In 1628 he was a formidable supporter of the Petition of Right opposing Charles I, and with other parliamentary leaders was again imprisoned in the Tower of London 1629, where he died.

Eliot T(homas) S(tearns) 1888–1965. US poet, playwright, and critic, who lived in London from 1915. His first volume of poetry, *Prufrock and Other Observations* 1917, introduced new verse forms and rhythms; further collections include *The Waste Land* 1922, *The Hollow Men* 1925, and *Old Possum's Book of Practical Cats* 1939. His plays include *Murder in the Cathedral* 1935 and *The Cocktail Party* 1949. His critical works include *The Sacred Wood* 1920. Nobel prize 1948.

Eliot was born in St Louis, Missouri, and was educated at Harvard, Paris, and Oxford. He settled in London 1915, and became a British subject 1927. As editor of *The Criterion* 1922–39, he exercised a moulding influence on the thought of his generation. In 1948 he received the Order of Merit.

Prufrock and other Observations expressed the disillusionment of the generation affected by World War I and caused a sensation by its

Eliot Mary Ann Evans, otherwise known as the English novelist George Eliot.

experimental form and rhythms. His reputation was established by the desolate modernity of *The Waste Land*. Among his other works are *Four Quartets* 1943, a religious sequence in which he seeks the eternal reality, and the poetic dramas *Murder in the Cathedral* about Thomas Becket, *The Cocktail Party*, *The Confidential Clerk* 1953, and *The Elder Statesman* 1958. His collection *Old Possum's Book of Practical Cats* was used for the popular British composer Lloyd Webber's musical *Cats* 1981. His critical works include *Notes toward the Definition of Culture* 1949.

Elizabeth the Queen Mother 1900– . Wife of King George VI of England. She was born Lady Elizabeth Angela Marguerite Bowes-Lyon, and on 26 Apr 1923, she married Albert, Duke of York. Their children are Queen Elizabeth II and Princess Margaret.

She is the youngest daughter of the 14th Earl of Strathmore and Kinghorne (died 1944), through whom she is descended from Robert Bruce, king of Scotland. When her husband became King George VI 1936 she became Queen Consort, and was crowned with him 1937. She adopted the title Queen Elizabeth the Queen Mother after his death.

Elizabeth two queens of England or the UK:

Elizabeth I 1533–1603. Queen of England 1558–1603, the daughter of Henry VIII and Anne Boleyn. Through her Religious Settlement of 1559 she enforced the Protestant religion by law and she had ◊Mary, Queen of Scots, executed 1587. Her conflict with Catholic Spain led to the defeat of the Spanish Armada 1588. The Elizabethan age was expansionist in commerce and geographical exploration, and arts and literature flourished. The rulers of many European states made unsuccessful bids to marry Elizabeth, and she used these bids to strengthen her power. She was succeeded by James I.

Elizabeth was born at Greenwich, London, 7 Sept 1533. She was well educated in several languages. During her Catholic half-sister Mary's reign, Elizabeth's Protestant sympathies brought her under suspicion, and she lived in seclusion at Hatfield, Hertfordshire, until on Mary's death she became queen. Her first task was to bring about a broad religious settlement.

Many unsuccessful attempts were made by Parliament to persuade Elizabeth to marry or settle the succession. Courtship she found a useful political weapon, and she maintained friendships with, among others, the courtiers ◊Leicester, Sir Walter ◊Raleigh, and ◊Essex.

The arrival in England 1568 of Mary, Queen of Scots, and her imprisonment by Elizabeth caused a political crisis and a rebellion of the feudal nobility of the north followed 1569. Friction between English and Spanish sailors hastened the breach with Spain. When the Dutch rebelled against Spanish tyranny Elizabeth secretly encouraged them; Philip II retaliated by aiding Catholic conspiracies against her. This undeclared war continued for many years, until the landing of an English army in the Netherlands 1585, and Mary's execution 1587, brought it into the open. Philip's Armada met with total disaster.

The war with Spain continued with varying fortunes to the end of the reign, while events at home foreshadowed the conflicts of the 17th century. Among the Puritans discontent was developing with Elizabeth's religious settlement, and several were imprisoned or executed. Yet her prestige remained unabated, as was shown by the failure of Essex's rebellion 1601.

Elizabeth II 1926– . Queen of Great Britain and Northern Ireland from 1952, the elder daughter of George VI. She married her third cousin, Philip, the Duke of Edinburgh, 1947. They have four children: Charles, Anne, Andrew, and Edward.

Princess Elizabeth Alexandra Mary was born in London 21 Apr 1926, educated privately, and assumed official duties at 16. During World War II she served in the Auxiliary Territorial Service, and by an amendment to the Regency Act she became a state counsellor on her 18th birthday. On the death of George VI she succeeded to the throne while in Kenya with her husband. She is the richest woman in the world, with an estimated wealth of £5.3 billion.

Elizabeth 1709–1762. Empress of Russia from 1741, daughter of Peter the Great. She carried through a palace revolution and supplanted her cousin, the infant Ivan VI (1730–1764), on the throne. She continued the policy of westernization begun by Peter, and allied herself with Austria against Prussia.

Ellington 'Duke' (Edward Kennedy) 1899–1974. US pianist, who had an outstanding career as a composer and arranger of jazz. He wrote numerous pieces for his own jazz orchestra, and became one of the most important figures in jazz over a 55-year span. Compositions include 'Mood Indigo', 'Sophisticated Lady', 'Solitude', and 'Black and Tan Fantasy'.

Ellis (Henry) Havelock 1859–1939. English psychologist and writer of many works on the psychology of sex, including *Studies in the Psychology of Sex* (seven volumes) 1898–1928.

Ellison Ralph 1914– . US novelist. His *Invisible Man* 1952 portrays with humour and energy the plight of a black man whom society cannot acknowledge; it is regarded as one of the most impressive novels published in the USA in the 1950s.

Elsheimer Adam 1578–1610. German painter and etcher, active in Rome from 1600. His small paintings, nearly all on copper, depict landscapes darkened by storm or night, with figures picked out by beams of light, as in *The Rest on the Flight into Egypt* 1609 (Alte Pinakothek, Munich).

Elton Charles 1900– . British ecologist, a pioneer of the study of animal and plant forms in their natural environments, and of animal behaviour as part of the complex pattern of life. Elton published *Animal Ecology and Evolution* 1930 and *The Pattern of Animal Communities* 1966.

Eluard Paul. Pen name of Eugène Grindel 1895–1952. French poet, born in Paris. He expressed the suffering of poverty in his verse, and was a leader of the Surrealists. He fought in

Elizabeth II Her Majesty Queen Elizabeth II of the United Kingdom and head of the Commonwealth.

World War I, the inspiration for *Poèmes pour la paix/Poems for Peace* 1918, and was a member of the Resistance in World War II. His books include *Poésie et vérité/Poetry and Truth* 1942 and *Au Rendezvous allemand/To the German Rendezvous* 1944.

Elyot Thomas 1490–1546. English diplomat and scholar. In 1531 he published *The Governour*, the first treatise on education in English.

Elzevir Louis 1540–1617. Founder of the Dutch printing house of Elzevir in the the 17th century. Among the firm's publications were editions of Latin, Greek, and Hebrew works, and French and Italian classics.

Born at Louvain, Elzevir was obliged to leave Belgium in 1580 because of his Protestant and political views. He settled at Leyden as a bookseller and printer.

Emerson Ralph Waldo 1803–1882. US philosopher, essayist, and poet. He settled in Concord, Massachusetts, which he made a centre of transcendentalism, and wrote *Nature* 1836, which states the movement's main principles emphasizing the value of self-reliance and the God-like nature of human souls. His two volumes of *Essays* (1841, 1844) made his reputation.

Born in Boston, Massachusetts, and educated at Harvard, Emerson became a Unitarian minister. In 1832 he resigned and travelled to Europe, meeting the British writers Carlyle, Coleridge, and Wordsworth. On his return to the USA 1833 he settled in Concord. He made a second visit to England 1847 and incorporated his impressions in *English Traits* 1856. Much of his verse was published in the literary magazine the *Dial*. His work includes *Representative Life* 1850 and *The Conduct of Life* 1870.

Emin Pasha Mehmed, born Eduard Schnitzer 1849–1892. German explorer, doctor and linguist. Appointed by General Gordon as chief medical officer and then governor of the Equatorial Province, he carried out extensive research in anthropology, botany, zoology, and meteorology.

Isolated by his remote location and cut off from the outside world by Arab slave traders, he was 'rescued' by an expedition led by H M Stanley in 1889. He travelled with Stanley as far as Zanzibar but returned to continue his work near Lake Victoria. Three years later he was killed by Arabs while leading an expedition to the W coast of Africa.

Emmet Robert 1778–1803. Irish nationalist leader. In 1803 he led an unsuccessful revolt in Dublin against British rule, and was captured, tried, and hanged. His youth and courage made him an Irish hero.

Empedocles *c.* 490–430 BC. Greek philosopher and scientist. He lived at Acragas (Agrigentum) in Sicily, and is known for his analysis of the universe into the four elements - fire, air, earth, and water – which through the action of love

and discord are eternally constructed, destroyed, and constructed anew. According to tradition, he committed suicide by throwing himself into the crater of Mount Etna.

Ender Kornelia 1958– . West German swimmer. She won a record-equalling four gold medals at the 1976 Olympics at freestyle, butterfly, and relay. She won a total of eight Olympic medals 1972–76. She also won a record ten world championship medals 1973 and 1975.

Enders John Franklin 1897–1985. US virologist. With Thomas Weller and Frederick Robbins, he discovered the ability of the polio virus to grow in cultures of different tissues, which led to the perfection of an effective vaccine. They were awarded the Nobel Prize for Medicine 1954. He also succeeded in isolating the measles virus.

Engel Carl Ludwig 1778–1840. German architect, who from 1815 worked in Finland. His great Neo-Classical achievement is the Senate Square in Helsinki, which is defined by his Senate House 1818–22 and University Building 1828–32, and crowned by the domed Lutheran cathedral 1830–40.

Engels Friedrich 1820–1895. German social and political philosopher, a friend of, and collaborator with, Karl ◊Marx on *The Communist Manifesto* 1848 and other key works. His later interpretations of Marxism, and his own philosophical and historical studies such as *Origins of the Family, Private Property, and the State* 1884 (which linked patriarchy with the development of private property), developed such concepts as historical materialism. His use of positivism and Darwinian ideas gave Marxism a scientific and deterministic flavour which was to influence Soviet thinking.

In 1842 Engels's father sent him to work in the cotton factory owned by his family in Manchester, England, where he became involved with the working-class Chartist reform movement. In 1844

Engels *The German socialist philosopher Friedrich Engels.*

began his lifelong friendship with Karl Marx, and together they worked out the materialist interpretation of history and in 1847–48 wrote the *Communist Manifesto*.

Engels's first book was *The Condition of the Working Classes in England* 1845. The lessons of 1848 he summed up in *The Peasants' War in Germany* 1850 and *Revolution and Counter-Revolution in Germany* 1851. After Marx's death Engels was largely responsible for the wider dissemination of his ideas; he edited the second and third volumes of Marx's *Capital* 1885 and 1894. Although Engels himself regarded his ideas as identical with those of Marx, discrepancies between their works are the basis of many modern Marxist debates.

Ennius Quintus 239–169 BC. Early Roman poet. Born near Tarentum in S Italy, he wrote tragedies based on the Greek pattern. His epic poem, the *Annales*, deals with Roman history.

Ensor James 1860–1949. Belgian painter and printmaker. His bold style uses strong colours to explore themes of human cruelty and the macabre, as in the *Entry of Christ into Brussels in 1889* 1888 (Musée Royale des Beaux-Arts, Brussels), and anticipated German Expressionism.

Enver Pasha 1881–1922. Turkish politician and soldier. He led the military revolt 1908 that resulted in the Young Turks' revolution (a reformist group of army officers). He was killed fighting the Bolsheviks in Turkestan.

Eötvös Roland von, Baron 1848–1919. Hungarian scientist, born in Budapest, who investigated problems of gravitation, and constructed the double-armed torsion balance for determining variations of gravity.

Epaminondas *c.* 420–362 BC. Theban general and politician who won a decisive victory over the Spartans at Leuctra 371. He was killed at the moment of victory at Mantinea.

Epictetus *c.* AD 55–135. Greek Stoic philosopher, who encouraged people to refrain from self-interest, and to promote the common good of humanity. He believed that people were in the hands of an all-wise providence, and that they should endeavour to do their duty in the position to which they were called.

Born at Hierapolis in Phrygia, he lived for many years in Rome as a slave, but eventually secured his freedom. He was banished by ◊Domitian from Rome in 89.

Epicurus 341–270 BC. Greek philosopher, founder of Epicureanism (that human happiness is the highest good), who taught at Athens from 306 BC.

Epstein Jacob 1880–1959. British sculptor, born in New York. He experimented with abstract forms, but is better known for muscular nude figures such as *Genesis* 1931 (Whitworth Art Gallery, Manchester).

In 1904 he moved to the UK, where most of his major work was done. An early example showing the strong influence of ancient sculptural styles is the angel over the tomb of Oscar Wilde 1912 (Père Lachaise, Paris), while *Rock Drill* 1913–14 (Tate Gallery, London) is Modernist and semi-abstract. Such figures outraged public sensibilities.

Equiano Olaudah 1745–1797. African anti-slavery campaigner and writer. He travelled widely both as a slave and a free man. His autobiography, *The Interesting Narrative of the Life of Olaudah Equiano or Gustavus Vassa the African* 1789, is one of the earliest significant works by an African written in English.

Equiano was born near the Niger River in what is now Nigeria, captured at the age of ten and sold to slavers, who transported him to the West Indies. He learned English and bought his freedom at the age of 21. He was an active campaigner against slavery.

Epstein *British sculptor who worked in stone and marble. He is photographed next to his statue* Lazarus.

Erasmus Desiderius *c.*1466–1536. Dutch scholar and humanist. Born at Rotterdam, the illegitimate son of Rogerius Gerardus; he adopted the Latin-Greek name which means 'beloved'. As a youth he was a monk in an Augustinian monastery near Gouda. After becoming a priest, he went to study in Paris 1495 and paid the first of a number of visits to England 1499. Here he met Linacre, More, and Colet, and for a time he was professor of Divinity and Greek at Cambridge University. His pioneer edition of the Greek New Testament was published 1516, and an edition of the writings of St Jerome, and his own *Colloquia* (dialogues on contemporary subjects) in 1519. He went to Basle 1521, where he edited the writings of the early Christian leaders.

Eratosthenes *c.*276–194 BC. Greek geographer and mathematician, whose map of the ancient world was the first to contain lines of latitude and longitude, and who calculated the earth's circumference with an error of less than 322 km/ 200 mi. His mathematical achievements include a method for duplicating the cube, and for finding prime numbers (Eratosthenes' 'sieve').

Erhard Ludwig 1897–1977. West German Christian Democrat politician, chancellor of the Federal Republic 1963–66. The 'economic miracle' of West Germany's recovery after World War II is largely attributed to Erhard's policy of social free enterprise (German *Marktwirtschaft*).

Eric the Red AD 940–1010. Allegedly the first European to find Greenland. According to a 13th-century saga, he was the son of a Norwegian chieftain, who was banished from Iceland about 982 for murder and then sailed westward and discovered a land that he called Greenland.

Ericsson John 1803–1889. Swedish born, US engineer who took out a patent to produce screw-propeller powered paddle-wheel ships in 1836. He built a number of such ships, including the *Monitor*, which was successfully deployed during the Civil War.

Ericsson Leif lived *c.* AD 1000. Norse explorer, son of Eric 'the Red', who sailed west from Greenland about 1000 to find a country first sighted by Norsemen 986. Landing with 35 companions in North America, he called it Vinland, because he discovered grape vines growing there.

The story was confirmed 1963 when a Norwegian expedition, led by Helge Ingstad, discovered remains of a Viking settlement (dated about 1000) near the fishing village of L'Anse-aux-Meadows at the northern tip of Newfoundland.

Erigena Johannes Scotus 815–877. Medieval philosopher. He was probably Irish and, according to tradition, travelled in Greece and Italy. The French king Charles II (the Bald) invited him to France (before 847), where he became head of the court school. He is said to have visited Oxford, to have taught at Malmesbury, and to

have been stabbed to death by his pupils. In his philosophy, he tried to combine Christianity with Neo-Platonism.

Ernst Max 1891–1976. German artist, who worked in France 1922–38 and in the USA from 1941. He was an active Dadaist, experimenting with collage, photomontage, and surreal images, and helped found the Surrealist movement 1924. His paintings are highly diverse.

Ernst first exhibited in Berlin in 1916. He produced a collage novel, *La Femme Cent Têtes* 1929, worked on films with Dali and Buñuel, and designed sets and costumes for Diaghilev's Ballets Russes. His pictures range from smooth Surrealist images to highly textured emotive abstracts, from 1925 making use of frottage (rubbing over textured materials).

Ershad Hussain Mohammad 1930– . Military ruler of Bangladesh from 1982. He became chief of staff of the Bangladeshi army 1979 and assumed power in a military coup 1982. As president from 1983, Ershad introduced a successful rural-orientated economic programme. He was re-elected 1986 and lifted martial law, but faced continuing political opposition.

Erskine Thomas, 1st Baron Erskine 1750–1823. British barrister and Lord Chancellor. He was called to the Bar in 1778 and appeared for the defence in a number of trials of parliamentary reformers for sedition. When the Whigs returned to power in 1806 he became Lord Chancellor and a baron. Among his speeches were those in defence of Lord George Gordon, Thomas Paine, and Queen Caroline.

Esaki Leo 1925– . Japanese physicist who in 1957 noticed that electrons could sometimes 'tunnel' through the barrier formed at the junctions of certain semiconductors. The effect is now widely used in the electronics industry and for this early success Esaaki shared the 1973 Nobel Prize for Physics with ◊Josephson and Giaver.

Esarhaddon died 669 BC. King of Assyria from 680, when he succeeded his father ◊Sennacherib. He conquered Egypt 671–74.

Esau in the Old Testament or Jewish Bible, the son of Isaac and Rebekah, and the elder twin brother of Jacob, who tricked Isaac into giving him the blessing intended for Esau. Earlier Esau had sold his birthright to Jacob for a 'mess of red pottage'. He was the ancestor of the Edomites.

Escher Maurits Cornelis 1902–1972. Dutch graphic artist. His prints are often based on mathematical concepts and contain paradoxes and illusions. The lithograph *Ascending and Descending* 1960, with interlocking staircases creating a perspective puzzle, is typical.

Esenin Sergey 1895–1925. Soviet poet, born in Konstantinovo (renamed Esenino in his honour). He went to Petrograd 1915, attached himself to the Symbolists, welcomed the Russian

Revolution, revived peasant traditions and folk-lore, and initiated the Imaginist group of poets 1919. A selection of his poetry was translated in *Confessions of a Hooligan* 1973. He was married briefly to the US dancer Isadora Duncan 1922–23.

Espronceda José de 1808–1842. Spanish poet. Originally one of the Queen's guards, he lost his commission because of his political activity, and was involved in the Republican risings of 1835 and 1836. His lyric poetry and life style both owed much to Byron.

Esquivel Adolfo 1932– . Argentinian sculptor and architect. As leader of the Servicio de Paz y Justicia (Peace and Justice Service), a Catholic-Protestant human-rights organization, he was awarded a Nobel Peace Prize in 1980.

Essex Robert Devereux, 2nd Earl of Essex 1566–1601. English soldier and politician. He fought in the Netherlands 1585–86 and distinguished himself at the Battle of Zutphen. In 1596 he jointly commanded a force that seized and sacked Cádiz. He became a favourite with Elizabeth I from 1587, but was executed because of his policies in Ireland.

In 1599 he became Lieutenant of Ireland and led an army against Irish rebels under the Earl of Tyrone in Ulster, but was unsuccessful, made an unauthorized truce with Tyrone, and returned without permission to England. He was forbidden to return to court, and when he marched into the City of London at the head of a body of supporters, he was promptly arrested, tried for treason, and beheaded on Tower Green.

Essex Robert Devereux, 3rd Earl of Essex 1591–1646. English soldier. Eldest son of the 2nd earl, he commanded the Parliamentary army at the inconclusive English Civil War Battle of Edgehill 1642. Following a disastrous campaign in Cornwall, he resigned his command 1645.

Esteve-Coll Elizabeth Anne Loosemore 1938– . British museum administrator. Keeper of the National Art Library at the Victoria and Albert Museum 1985–88, she became director of the museum itself in 1988. Her reorganization of it in 1989, when she split the administrative and research roles, led to widespread criticism and the resignation of several senior staff.

Esther in the Old Testament or Jewish Bible, the wife of the Persian king Ahasuerus, who prevented the extermination of her people by the vizier Haman, a deliverance celebrated in the Jewish festival of Purim. Her story is told in the Old Testament book Esther.

Ethelred II *the Unready* c.968–1016. King of England from 978. The son of King Edgar, he became king after the murder of his half-brother, Edward the Martyr. He tried to buy off the Danish raiders by paying Danegeld, and in 1002 ordered the massacre of the Danish settlers, provoking an

invasion by Sweyn I of Denmark. War with Sweyn and Sweyn's son, Canute, occupied the rest of Ethelred's reign. He was nicknamed the 'Unready' because of his apparent lack of foresight.

Etherege George c.1635–c.1691. English Restoration dramatist whose play *Love in a Tub* 1664 was the first attempt at the *comedy of manners* (a genre further developed by Congreve and Sheridan). Later plays include *She Would if She Could* 1668 and *The Man of Mode, or Sir Fopling Flutter* 1676.

Etty William 1787–1849. British academic painter. He first gained success with *Telemachus Rescuing Antiope* 1811. He was a prolific painter of female nudes.

Euclid c.330–c.260 BC. Greek mathematician, who lived at Alexandria and wrote the *Stoicheia/Elements* in 13 books, of which nine deal with plane and solid geometry, and four with number theory. His main work lay in the systematic arrangement of previous discoveries, based on axioms, definitions, and theorems.

Euclid's geometry texts have remained in common usage for over 2,000 years until recent times.

Eugène Prince of Savoy 1663–1736. Austrian general, who had many victories against the Turkish invaders (whom he expelled from Hungary 1697 in the Battle of Zenta) and against France, especially in the War of the Spanish Succession (battles of Blenheim, Oudenaarde, and Malplaquet).

The son of Prince Eugène Maurice of Savoy-Carignano, he was born in Paris. When Louis XIV refused him a commission he entered the Austrian army, and served against the Turks at the defence of Vienna 1683, and against the French on the Rhine and in Italy ten years later. In the War of the Spanish Succession 1701–14 he shared with the British commander Marlborough in his great victories against the French and won many successes as an independent commander in Italy. He again defeated the Turks 1716–18, and fought a last campaign against the French 1734–35.

Eugénie Marie Ignace Augustine de Montijo 1826–1920. Empress of France, daughter of the Spanish count of Montijo. In 1853 she married Louis Napoleon, who had become emperor as ◊Napoleon III. She encouraged court extravagance, Napoleon III's intervention in Mexico, and urged him to fight the Prussians. After his surrender to the Germans at Sedan, NE France, 1870 she fled to England.

Euler Leonhard 1707–1783. Swiss mathematician. He developed the theory of differential equations, the calculus of variations, and did important work in astronomy and optics. He was a pupil of Johann ◊Bernoulli.

He became professor of physics at the University of St Petersburg in 1730. In 1741 he was invited to Berlin by Frederick the Great, where he spent 25 years before returning to Russia.

Eusebio (Eusebio Ferreira da Silva) 1942– . Portuguese footballer, born in Lourenco Marques. He made his international debut 1961 and played for his country 77 times. He spent most of his league career with Benfica, and also played in the USA.

Eusebius *c.*260–*c.*340. Bishop of Caesarea (modern Qisarya, Israel); author of a history of the Christian church to 324.

Eustachio Bartolommeo 1520–1574. Italian anatomist, the discoverer of the Eustachian tube, leading from the middle ear to the pharynx, and of the Eustachian valve in the right auricles of the heart.

Eutyches *c.*384–*c.*456. Christian theologian. An archimandrite (monastic head) in Constantinople, he held that Jesus had only one nature, the human nature being subsumed in the divine (a belief which became known as Monophysitism). He was exiled after his ideas were condemned as heretical by the Council of Chalcedon 451.

Evans Arthur John 1851–1941. English archaeologist. His excavation of Knossos on Crete resulted in the discovery of pre-Phoenician Minoan script and proved the existence of the legendary Minoan civilization.

Evans Edith 1888–1976. English character actress, who performed on the London stage and on Broadway. She is particularly remembered for the film role of Lady Bracknell in Oscar Wilde's comedy *The Importance of Being Earnest* 1952.

Evans Walker 1903–1975. US photographer, known for his documentary photographs of the people in the rural US south during the Great Depression of the 1930s. Many of his photographs appeared in James Agee's book *Let Us Now Praise Famous Men* 1941.

Evelyn John 1620–1706. English diarist and author. He was a friend of Pepys, and like him remained in London during the Plague and the Great Fire. He wrote 300-odd books, noted of which is his diary, first published 1818, which covers the period 1640–1706.

Born in Surrey, he enlisted for three years in the Royalist army 1624, but withdrew on finding his estate exposed to the enemy and lived mostly abroad until 1652. He declined all office under the Commonwealth, but after the Restoration enjoyed great favour, received court appointments, and was one of the founders of the Royal Society.

Evert Chris 1954– . US lawn tennis player. She won her first Wimbledon title 1974, and has since won 21 Grand Slam titles. She became the first woman tennis player to win $1 million in prize money.

Eyck Jan van *c.* 1390–1441. Flemish painter of the early northern Renaissance, one of the first to work in oil. His paintings are technically brilliant and sumptuously rich in detail and colour. Little is known of his brother **Hubert van Eyck** (died 1426), who is supposed to have begun the huge and complex altarpiece in St Bavo's cathedral, Ghent, *The Adoration of the Mystical Lamb*, completed by Jan 1432.

Jan van Eyck is known to have worked in The Hague 1422–24 for John of Bavaria, Count of Holland. He served as court painter to Philip the Good, Duke of Burgundy, from 1425, and worked in Bruges from 1430.

Oil painting allowed for much subtler effects of tone and colour and greater command of detail than the egg-tempera technique then in common use, and van Eyck took full advantage of this. In his *Arnolfini Wedding* 1434 (National Gallery, London) the bride and groom appear in a domestic interior crammed with disguised symbols, as a kind of pictorial marriage certificate. Another notable work is the *Madonna with Chancellor Rolin* probably 1435/37 (Louvre, Paris).

Eyre Edward John 1815–1901. English explorer who wrote *Expeditions into Central Australia* 1845. He was Governor of Jamaica 1864–65.

Eyre Richard (Charles Hastings) 1943– . English stage and film director. He succeeded Peter Hall as artistic director of the National Theatre, London, 1988. His films include *The Ploughman's Lunch* 1983.

Eysenck Hans Jurgen 1916– , English psychologist. He concentrated on personality theory and testing by developing behaviour therapy. He is an outspoken critic of psychoanalysis as a therapeutic method.

Ezekiel lived *c.*600 BC. In the Old Testament, a Hebrew prophet. Carried into captivity in Babylon by ◊Nebuchadnezzar 597, he preached that Jerusalem's fall was due to the sins of Israel. The book of Ezekiel begins with a description of a vision of supernatural beings.

Ezra in the Old Testament, a Jewish scribe who was allowed by Artaxerxes, king of Persia (probably Artaxerxes I, 464–423 BC), to lead his people back to Jerusalem from Babylon 458 BC. He re-established the Mosaic law (laid down by Moses) and eradicated intermarriage.

Fabergé Peter Carl 1846–1920. Russian goldsmith and jeweller. His workshops in St Petersburg and Moscow were celebrated for the exquisite delicacy of their products, especially the use of gold in various shades. Among his masterpieces was a series of jewelled Easter eggs, the first of which was commissioned by Alexander III for the tsarina 1884. Fabergé died in exile in Switzerland.

Fabius Laurent 1946– . French socialist politician, prime minister 1984–86. He introduced a liberal, free-market economic programme.

Fabius became economic adviser to the Socialist Party (PS) leader Mitterrand in 1976, entered the National Assembly 1978, and was a member of the socialist government from 1981. In 1984, at a time of economic crisis, he was appointed prime minister. He resigned after his party's electoral defeat in Mar 1986.

Fabre Jean Henri Casimir 1823–1915. French entomologist, noted for his vivid and intimate descriptions and paintings of the life of wasps, bees, and other insects.

Fabricius Geronimo 1537–1619. Italian anatomist and embryologist. He made a detailed study of the veins, and discovered the valves which direct the bloodflow towards the heart. He also studied the development of chick embryos.

A professor of surgery and anatomy at Padua, his work greatly influenced and helped his pupil William ◊Harvey. Despite many errors, he raised anatomy and embryology to a higher scientific level.

Fabritius Carel 1622–1654. Dutch painter, a pupil of Rembrandt. His own style, lighter and with more precise detail than his master's, is evident for example in *The Goldfinch* 1654. He painted religious scenes and portraits.

Fadden Arthur 'Artie' 1895–1973. Australian politician, born in Queensland. He was leader of the Country Party 1941–58 and prime minister Aug–Oct 1941.

Fahd 1921– . King of Saudi Arabia from 1982, when he succeeded his half-brother Khalid. As head of government he has been active in trying to bring about a solution to the Middle East conflicts.

Fahrenheit Gabriel Daniel 1686–1736. German physicist who lived mainly in England and Holland. He devised the Fahrenheit temperature scale.

Fairbanks Douglas. Stage name of Douglas Elton Ulman 1883–1939. US actor. He played swashbuckling heroes in silent films such as *The Mark of Zorro* 1920, *The Three Musketeers* 1921, *Robin Hood* 1922, *The Thief of Baghdad* 1924, and *Don Quixote* 1925. He was married to the film star Mary Pickford 1920–33.

Fairbanks Douglas, Jr 1909– . US actor who appeared in the same type of swashbuckling film roles as his father, Douglas Fairbanks; for example, in *Catherine the Great* 1934 and *The Prisoner of Zenda* 1937.

Fairfax Thomas, 3rd Baron Fairfax of Cameron 1612–1671. English general, commander in chief of the Parliamentary army in the English Civil War. With Cromwell he formed the New Model Army, defeated Charles I at Naseby, and suppressed the Royalist and Presbyterian risings 1648.

Faisal Ibn Abdul Aziz 1905–1975. King of Saudi Arabia from 1964. The younger brother of King Saud, on whose accession 1953 he was declared crown prince. He was prime minister 1953–60 and from 1962 until his assassination by a nephew. In 1964 he emerged victorious from a lengthy conflict with his brother and adopted a policy of steady modernization of his country.

Falconet Etienne-Maurice 1716–1791. French sculptor whose works range from formal Baroque to gentle Rococo in style. He directed sculpture at the Sèvres porcelain factory 1757–66. His bronze equestrian statue of *Peter the Great* in Leningrad was commissioned 1766 by Catherine II.

Falkender Marcia, Baroness Falkender (Marcia Williams) 1932– . British political secretary to Labour prime minister Harold Wilson from 1956, she was influential in the 'kitchen cabinet' of the 1964–70 government, as described in her book *Inside No 10* 1972.

Falkland Lucius Cary, 2nd Viscount Falkland *c.* 1610–1643. English soldier and politician. He was elected to the Long Parliament 1640. Falkland was opposed to absolute monarchy but alienated by Puritan extremism, and tried hard to secure a compromise peace between Royalists and Parliamentarians.

Falla Manuel de 1876–1946. Spanish composer. His opera *La vida breve/Brief Life* 1905 (performed 1913) was followed by the ballets *El amor brujo/Love the Magician* 1915 and *El sombrero de tres picos/The Three-Cornered Hat* 1919, and his most ambitious concert work, *Noches en los jardines de España/Nights in the Gardens of Spain* 1916. The folk idiom of southern Spain is an integral part of his compositions. He also wrote songs and pieces for piano and guitar.

Fallopius Gabriel. Latinized name of Gabriello Fallopio 1523–1562. Italian anatomist who discovered the *Fallopian tubes*, which in mammals carry eggs from the ovary to the uterus. He studied the anatomy of the brain, eyes, and reproductive organs, and gave the first accurate description of the inner ear.

Fallopius studied at Padua under Andreas ◊Vesalius, and later taught there and at Ferrara and Pisa.

Fangio Juan Manuel 1911– . Argentinian motor-racing driver who won the world driver's title a record five times 1951–57. He drove a blue and yellow Maserati.

Fanon Frantz 1925–1961. French political writer. His experiences in Algeria during the war for liberation in the 1950s led to the writing of *Les Damnés de la terre/The Wretched of the Earth* 1964, which calls for violent revolution by the peasants of the Third World.

Fantin-Latour (Ignace) Henri (Joseph Théodore) 1836–1904. French painter, excelling in delicate still lifes, flower paintings, and portraits.

Homage à Delacroix 1864 (Musée d'Orsay, Paris) is a portrait group with many poets, authors, and painters, including Baudelaire and Whistler.

Faraday Michael 1791–1867. English chemist and physicist. In 1821 he began experimenting with electromagnetism, and ten years later discovered the induction of electric currents and made the first dynamo. He subsequently found that a magnetic field will rotate the plane of polarization of light. Faraday also investigated electrolysis.

In 1812 he began researches into electricity, and made his first electric battery. He became a laboratory assistant to Sir Humphry Davy at the Royal Institution 1813, and in 1833 succeeded him as professor of chemistry there. He delivered highly popular lectures at the Royal Institution, and published many treatises on scientific subjects.

Fargo William George 1818–1881. US transport pioneer. In 1844 he established with Henry Wells (1805–78) and Daniel Dunning the first express company to carry freight west of Buffalo. Its success led to his appointment 1850 as secretary of the newly established American Express Company, of which he was president 1868–81. He also established *Wells Fargo & Company*

1851, carrying goods express between New York and San Francisco via Panama.

Farman Henry 1874–1958. Anglo-French aviation pioneer. He designed a biplane 1907–08 and in 1909 flew a record 160 km/100 mi.

With his brother **Maurice Farman** (1878–1964), he founded an aircraft works at Billancourt, supplying the army in France and other countries. The UK also made use of Farman's inventions, for example, air-screw reduction gears, in World War II.

Farmer Frances 1913–1970. US actress who starred in such films as *Come and Get It* 1936, *The Toast of New York* 1937, and *Son of Fury* 1942, before her career was ended by alcoholism and mental illness.

Farnaby Giles 1563–1640. English composer. He composed pieces for the virginal (an early keyboard instrument), psalms for Ravenscroft's Psalter 1621, and madrigals for voices.

Farnese an Italian family who held the duchy of Parma 1545–1731.

Farouk 1920–1965. King of Egypt 1936–52. He succeeded his father Fuad I. In 1952 he was compelled to abdicate, his son Fuad II being temporarily proclaimed in his stead.

Farquhar George 1677–1707. Irish dramatist. His plays *The Recruiting Officer* 1706 and *The Beaux' Stratagem* 1707 are in the tradition of the Restoration comedy of manners, although less robust.

Farragut David (Glasgow) 1801–1870. US admiral, born near Knoxville, Tennessee. During the US Civil War he took New Orleans 1862, after destroying the Confederate fleet, and in 1864 effectively put an end to blockade-running at Mobile.

Farrell J(ames) G(ordon) 1935–1979. British historical novelist, born in Liverpool, author of *Troubles* 1970, set in Ireland, and *The Siege of Krishnapur* 1973.

Farrell James T(homas) 1904–1979. US novelist. His naturalistic *Studs Lonigan* trilogy 1932–35, comprising *Young Lonigan, The Young Manhood of Studs Lonigan*, and *Judgement Day*, describes the growing-up of a young Catholic man in Chicago after World War I.

Farrow Mia 1945– . US film and television actress. Popular since the late 1960s, she was associated with the director Woody Allen from 1982, both on and off screen. She starred in his films *Zelig* 1983 and *Hannah and her Sisters* 1986, as well as in Polanski's *Rosemary's Baby* 1968.

Fassbinder Rainer Werner 1946–1982. West German film director, who began his career as a fringe actor and founded his own 'anti-theatre' before moving into films. His works are mainly stylized indictments of contemporary German society. He made over 30 films, including *Die bitteren Tränen der Petra von Kant/The Bitter Tears of Petra von Kant* 1972 and *Die Ehe*

CONCILIVM SEPTEM NOBILIVM ANGLORVM CONIVRANTIVM IN NECEM IACOBI ·I·
MAGNÆ BRITANNIÆ. REGIS TOTIVSQ· ANGLICI CONVOCATI PARLEMENTI·

Fawkes *England's most famous subversive, Guy Fawkes, joined the Gunpowder Plot to blow up James I and both Houses of Parliament in 1605. Fireworks and bonfires on which his effigy, the guy, is burned still celebrate the failure of the plot on 5 Nov every year.*

von Maria Braun/The Marriage of Maria Braun 1979.

Fathy Hassan 1900–1989. Egyptian architect. In his work at the village of New Gouma in Upper Egypt he demonstrated the value of native building technology and natural materials in solving contemporary housing problems. This, together with his book *The Architecture of the Poor* 1973, influenced the growth of community architecture around the world.

Fatimid dynasty of Muslim Shi'ite caliphs founded in 909 by Obaidallah, who claimed to be a descendent of Fatima, the prophet Muhammad's daughter, and her husband Ali, in N Africa. In 969 the Fatimids conquered Egypt, and the dynasty continued until overthrown by Saladin in 1171

Faulkner Brian 1921–1977. Northern Ireland Unionist politician. He was the last prime minister of Northern Ireland 1971–72 before the Stormont Parliament was suspended.

Faulkner William 1897–1962. US novelist who wrote in an experimental stream-of-consciousness style. His works include *The Sound and the Fury* 1929, dealing with a Southern US family in decline; *As I Lay Dying* 1930; *Light in August* 1932, a study of segregation; *The Unvanquished* 1938, stories of the Civil War; and *The Hamlet* 1940, *The Town* 1957, and *The Mansion* 1959, a trilogy

covering the rise of the materialist Snopes family. Nobel Prize 1949.

Faulkner served in World War I and his first novel, *Soldier's Pay* 1929, is about a war veteran. After the war he returned to Oxford, Mississippi, on which he was to model Jefferson in the county of Yoknapatawpha, the setting of his major novels.

Fauré Gabriel (Urbain) 1845–1924. French composer of songs, chamber music, and *Requiem* 1888. He was a pupil of Saint-Saëns, became professor of composition at the Paris Conservatoire 1896 and was director 1905–20.

Fawcett Millicent Garrett 1847–1929. English suffragette, younger sister of Elizabeth Garrett ◊Anderson. A non-militant, she rejected the violent acts of some of her contemporaries in the suffrage movement. She joined the first Women's Suffrage Committee 1867 and became president of the Women's Unionist Association 1889.

Fawcett Percy Harrison 1867–1925. British explorer. After several expeditions to delineate frontiers in South America during the rubber boom, he set off in 1925, with his eldest son John and a friend, into the Mato Grosso to find the the legendary 'lost cities' of the ancient Indians, the 'cradle of Brazilian civilization'. They were never seen again.

Fawkes Guy 1570–1606. English conspirator in the Gunpowder Plot to blow up King James I and the members of both Houses of Parliament. Fawkes, a Roman Catholic convert, was arrested in the cellar underneath the House 4 Nov 1605, tortured, and executed. The event is still commemorated in Britain every 5 Nov with bonfires, fireworks, and the burning of the 'guy', an effigy.

Fechner Gustav 1801–1887. German psychologist. He became professor of physics at Leipzig in 1834, but in 1839 turned to the study of psychophysics (the relationship between physiology and psychology). He devised *Fechner's law*, a method for the exact measurement of sensation.

Feininger Lyonel 1871–1956. US abstract artist, an early Cubist. He worked at the Bauhaus, a key centre of modern design in Germany, 1919–33, and later helped to found the Bauhaus in Chicago.

While in Germany, he formed the *Blaue Vier* (Blue Four) in 1924 with the painters Alexei von Jawlensky (1864–1941), Kandinsky, and Klee.

Feldman Morton 1926–1988. US composer. An associate of ◊Cage and Earle ◊Brown in the 1950s, he composed large-scale set pieces using the orchestra mainly as a source of colour and texture.

Fellini *Italian film director Federico Fellini was a cartoonist and journalist before he began directing films in the 1950s. La Dolce Vita caused a scandal when it won the Grand Prix at the 1960 Cannes Film Festival.*

Fellini Federico 1920– . Italian director, whose films include *I vitelloni/The Young and the Passionate* 1953, *La dolce vita* 1960, and *La città delle donne/City of Women* 1981.

Fénelon François de Salignac de la Mothe 1651–1715. French writer and ecclesiastic. He entered the priesthood 1675 and in 1689 was appointed tutor to the Duke of Burgundy, grandson of Louis XIV. For him he wrote his *Fables* and *Dialogues des morts/Dialogues of the Dead* 1690, *Télémaque/Telemachus* 1699, and *Plans de gouvernement/Plans of Government*.

Télémaque, with its picture of an ideal commonwealth, had the effect of a political manifesto, and Louis banished Fénelon to Cambrai, where he had been consecrated archbishop 1695. Fénelon's mystical *Maximes des Saints/Sayings of the Saints* 1697 had also led to a quarrel with the Jansenists, and condemnation by Pope Innocent XII.

Fenton Roger 1819–1869. English photographer. The world's first war photographer, he went to the Crimea 1855; he also founded the Royal Photographic Society in London.

Ferber Edna 1887–1968. US novelist and playwright. Her novel *Show Boat* 1926 was adapted as an operetta by Jerome Kern and Oscar Hammerstein II.

Ferdinand 1861–1948. King of Bulgaria 1908–18. Son of Prince Augustus of Saxe-Coburg- Gotha, he was elected prince of Bulgaria 1887, and in 1908 proclaimed Bulgaria's independence of Turkey and assumed the title of tsar. In 1915 he

Fawcett *An educational reformer and leader of the women's suffrage movement, Millicent Garrett Fawcett was one of the founders of Newnham College, Cambridge.*

entered World War I as Germany's ally, and in 1918 abdicated.

Ferdinand five kings of Castile, including:

Ferdinand I the Great c.1016–1065. King of Castile from 1035. He began the reconquest of Spain from the Moors and united all NW Spain under his and his brothers' rule.

Ferdinand V 1452–1516. King of Castile from 1474, **Ferdinand II** of Aragon from 1479, and **Ferdinand III** of Naples from 1504; first king of all Spain. In 1469 he married his cousin ◊Isabella I, who succeeded to the throne of Castile 1474; together they were known as **the Catholic Monarchs**. They introduced the anti-heretic Inquisition tribunal in 1480, expelled the Jews, forced the surrender of the Moors at Granada 1492, and financed Columbus' expedition to the Americas.

Ferdinand three Holy Roman emperors:

Ferdinand I 1503–1564. Holy Roman emperor who succeeded his brother Charles V 1558; king of Bohemia and Hungary from 1526, king of the Germans from 1531. He reformed the German monetary system, and reorganized the judicial Aulic council (*Reichshofrat*). He was the son of Philip the Handsome and grandson of Maximilian I.

Ferdinand II 1578–1637. Holy Roman emperor from 1619, when he succeeded his uncle Matthias; king of Bohemia from 1617 and Hungary from 1618. A zealous Catholic, he provoked the Bohemian revolt that led to the Thirty Years' War. He was a grandson of Ferdinand I.

Ferdinand III 1608–1657. Holy Roman emperor from 1637 when he succeeded his father Ferdinand II; king of Hungary from 1625. Although anxious to conclude the Thirty Years' War, he did not give religious liberty to Protestants.

Ferdinand `1865–1927. King of Romania from 1914, when he succeeded his uncle Charles I. In 1916 he declared war on Austria. After the Allied victory in World War I, Ferdinand acquired Transylvania and Bukovina from Austria-Hungary, and Bessarabia from Russia. In 1922 he became king of Greater Romania.

Ferguson Harry 1884–1960. Irish engineer who pioneered the development of the tractor, joining forces with Henry Ford 1938 to manufacture it in the USA. He also experimented in automobile and aircraft development.

Fermat Pierre de 1601–1665. French mathematician, who with Pascal founded the theory of probability and the modern theory of numbers, and made contributions to analytical geometry.

Fermat's last theorem states that equations of the form $x^n + y^n = z^n$ where x, y, z, and n are all integers have no solutions if $n > 2$. There is no general proof of this, so it constitutes a conjecture rather than a theorem.

Fermi Enrico 1901–1954. Italian physicist, who proved the existence of new radioactive elements produced by bombardment with neutrons, and discovered nuclear reactions produced by low-energy neutrons. Nobel prize 1938.

Born in Rome, he was professor of theoretical physics there 1926–38. He was professor at Columbia University, New York, USA, 1939–42 and from 1946 at Chicago.

Fermor Patrick (Michael) Leigh 1915– . English travel writer who joined the Irish Guards in 1939 after four years' travel in central Europe and the Balkans. His books include *The Traveller's Tree* 1950, *Mani* 1958, *Roumeli* 1966, *A Time of Gifts* 1977, and *Between the Woods and the Water* 1986.

Fernández Juan c.1536–c.1604. Spanish explorer and navigator. As a pilot on the Pacific coast of South America 1563, he reached the islands off the coast of Chile that now bear his name. On one of these islands was later marooned Alexander ◊Selkirk, on whose life Defoe's *Robinson Crusoe* is based.

Fernandez de Quirós Pedro 1565–1614. Spanish navigator, one of the first Europeans to search for the great southern continent that Ferdinand ◊Magellan believed lay to the south of the Magellan Strait. Despite a series of disastrous expeditions, he took part in the discovery of the Marquesas Islands and the main island of Espíritu Santo in the New Hebrides.

Fernel Jean François 1497–1558. French physician who introduced the words physiology and pathology into medicine.

Ferneyhough Brian 1943– . English composer. His uncompromising, detailed compositions include *Carceri d'Invenzione*, a cycle of seven works inspired by the engravings of Piranesi, *Time and Motion Studies* 1974–77, and string quartets.

Ferranti Sebastian de 1864–1930. British electrical engineer who electrified central London. He made and sold his first alternator 1881. He worked on the design of a large power station at Deptford but legislation permitting low-powered stations to operate killed the scheme and in 1896 he opened his business to develop high-voltage systems for long-distance transmission.

Ferrar Nicolas 1592–1637. English mystic and founder in 1625 of the Anglican monastic community at Little Gidding, Cambridgeshire, in 1625, which devoted itself to work and prayer. It was broken up by the Puritans in 1647.

Ferrari Enzo 1898–1988. Italian founder of the Ferrari car company, which specializes in Grand Prix racing cars and high-quality sports cars. He was a racing driver for Alfa Romeo in the 1920s, went on to become one of their designers, and in 1929 took over their racing division. In 1947 the first 'true' Ferrari was seen. The Ferrari car has won more world championship Grand Prix races than any other car.

Ferraro Geraldine 1935– . US Democrat politician, vice-presidential candidate in the 1984 election.

Ferraro, a lawyer, was elected to Congress in 1981 and was selected in 1984 by Walter Mondale to be the USA's first female vice-presidential candidate from one of the major parties. The Democrats were defeated by the incumbent president Reagan, and Ferraro, damaged by investigations of her husband's affairs, retired from politics.

Ferrier Kathleen (Mary) 1912–1953. English contralto who sang oratorio and opera. In Britten's *The Rape of Lucretia* 1946 she created the role of Lucretia, and she appeared in Mahler's *Das Lied von der Erde* 1947.

Ferrier Susan Edmundstone 1782–1854. Scottish novelist, born in Edinburgh. Her anonymously published books include *Marriage* 1818, *Inheritance* 1824, and *Destiny* 1831, all of which give a lively picture of Scottish manners and society.

Ferry Jules François Camille 1832–1893. French republican politician, mayor of Paris during the siege of 1870–71. As a member of the republican governments of 1879–85 (prime minister 1880–81 and 1883–85) he was responsible for the law of 1882 making primary education free, compulsory, and secular.

Fessenden Reginald Aubrey 1866–1932. Canadian physicist who worked in the USA, first for Thomas Edison and then for Westinghouse. He patented the modulation of radio waves (transmission of a signal using a carrier wave), an essential technique for voice transmission. At the time of his death, he held 500 patents.

Feyerabend Paul K 1924– . US philosopher of science, who rejected the attempt by certain philosophers (for instance ◊Popper) to find a methodology applicable to all scientific research. His works include *Against Method* 1975.

Although his work relies on historical evidence, he argues that successive theories that apparently concern the same subject (for instance the motion of the planets) cannot in principle be subjected to any comparison that would aim at finding the truer explanation.

Feynman Richard Phillips 1918–1988. US physicist. He provided the foundations for the quantum theory of radiation, for which he was awarded a share of the 1965 Nobel Prize for Physics. As a member of the committee investigating the *Challenger* space-shuttle disaster 1986, he demonstrated the lethal faults in the rubber seals on the shuttle's booster rocket.

Fibonacci also known as *Leonardo of Pisa* c.1175–c.1250. Italian mathematician. He published *Liber abaci* in Pisa 1202, which was instrumental in the introduction of Arabic numerals into Europe. One of the book's problems featured what are now called *Fibonacci numbers*, in their simplest form a sequence in which each

number is the sum of its two predecessors (1, 1, 2, 3, 5, 8, 13, …). They have unusual characteristics and are known to have applications in botany, psychology, and astronomy.

Fichte Johann Gottlieb 1762–1814. German philosopher who developed a comprehensive form of subjective idealism, expounded in *The Science of Knowledge* 1794. He was an admirer of ◊Kant.

In 1792, Fichte published *Critique of Religious Revelation*, a critical study of Kant's doctrine of the 'thing-in-itself'. For Fichte, the absolute ego posits both the external world (the non-ego) and finite self. Morality consists in the striving of this finite self to rejoin the absolute. In 1799 he was accused of atheism, and was forced to resign his post as professor of philosophy at Jena.

Field Sally 1946– . US film and television actress. She won an Academy Award for *Norma Rae* 1979 and again for *Places in the Heart* 1984. Her other films include *Hooper* 1978, *Absence of Malice* 1981, and *Murphy's Romance* 1985.

Fielding Henry 1707–1754. English novelist, whose narrative power influenced the form and technique of the novel and helped to make it the most popular form of literature in England. In 1742 he parodied Richardson's novel *Pamela* in his *Joseph Andrews*, which was followed by *Jonathan Wild the Great* 1743; his masterpiece *Tom Jones* 1749, which he described as a 'comic epic in prose'; and *Amelia* 1751.

He was appointed Justice of the Peace for Middlesex and Westminster in 1748. In failing health, he went to recuperate in Lisbon in 1754, writing on the way *A Journal of a Voyage to Lisbon*.

Fields Gracie. Stage name of Grace Stansfield 1898–1979. English comedian and singer. Her humourously sentimental films include *Sally in our Alley* 1931 and *Sing as We Go* 1934.

Fields W C. Stage name of William Claude Dukenfield 1879–1946. US actor and screenwriter. His distinctive speech and professed attitudes such as hatred of children and dogs gained him enormous popularity in films such as *David Copperfield* 1935, *My Little Chickadee* (co-written with Mae West) and *The Bank Dick* both 1940, and *Never Give a Sucker an Even Break* 1941.

Fiennes Ranulph Twisleton-Wykeham 1944– . British explorer who made the first surface journey around the world's polar axis 1979–82. Earlier expeditions included explorations of the White Nile 1969, Jostedalsbre Glacier, Norway, 1970, and the Headless Valley, Canada, 1971. Accounts of his adventures include *A Talent for Trouble* 1970, *Hell on Ice* 1979, and the autobiographical *Living Dangerously* 1987.

Filchner Wilhelm 1877–1957. German explorer who travelled extensively in Central Asia, but is remembered for his expedition into the Weddell

Sea of Antarctica, where his ship became ice-bound for a whole winter. He landed a party and built a hut on the floating ice shelf, which eventually broke up and floated northwards.

Fillmore Millard 1800–1874. 13th president of the USA 1850–53, a Whig. He was Zachary Taylor's vice president from 1849, and succeeded him on Taylor's death. Fillmore supported a compromise on slavery 1850 to reconcile North and South, and failed to be renominated.

Finch Peter 1916–1977. British cinema actor who began his career in Australia before becoming internationally known for his roles in *A Town Like Alice* 1956; *The Trials of Oscar Wilde* 1960; *Sunday, Bloody, Sunday* 1971; *Network* 1976.

Finney Albert 1936– . English stage and film actor. He created the title roles in Keith Waterhouse's *Billy Liar* 1960 and John Osborne's *Luther* 1961, and was artistic director of the Royal Court Theatre 1972–75. His films include *Saturday Night and Sunday Morning* 1960, *Tom Jones* 1963, *Murder on the Orient Express* 1974, and *The Dresser* 1984.

Finney Thomas 'Tom' 1922– . English footballer, known as the 'Preston Plumber'. He played for England 76 times, and in every forward position. He was noted for his ball control and goal-scoring skills, and was the first person to win the Footballer of the Year award twice.

Finsen Niels Ryberg 1860–1904. Danish physician, the first to use ultraviolet light treatment for skin diseases. Nobel Prize for Medicine in 1903.

Firbank Ronald 1886–1926. English novelist. His work, set in the Edwardian decadent period, has

Fitzgerald US novelist F Scott Fitzgerald.

a malicious humour, and includes *Caprice* 1916, *Valmouth* 1918, and the posthumous *Concerning the Eccentricities of Cardinal Pirelli* 1926.

Firdausi Abdul Qasim Mansur *c.*935–*c.*1020. Persian poet, whose epic *Shahnama/The Book of Kings* relates the history of Persia in 60,000 verses.

Firestone Shulamith 1945– . Canadian feminist writer, whose book *The Dialectic of Sex: the Case for Feminist Revolution* 1970 exerted considerable influence on feminist thought. She was also one of the most influential early organizers of the women's liberation movement in the USA.

Fischer Emil Hermann 1852–1919. German chemist who produced synthetic sugars and from these the various enzymes. His descriptions of the chemistry of the carbohydrates and peptides laid the foundations for the science of biochemistry. Nobel prize 1902.

Fischer Hans 1881–1945. German chemist awarded a Nobel prize 1930 for his discovery of haemoglobin in blood.

Fischer-Dieskau Dietrich 1925– . German baritone, renowned for his interpretation of Schubert's songs.

Fisher Andrew 1862–1928. Australian Labor politician. Born in Scotland, he went to Australia 1885, and entered the Australian parliament 1901. He was prime minister 1908–09, 1910–13, and 1914–15, and Australian high commissioner to the UK 1916–21.

Fisher Geoffrey, Baron Fisher of Lambeth 1887–1972. English priest, archbishop of Canterbury 1945–61. He was the first holder of this office to visit the pope for 600 years.

Fisher John Arbuthnot, 1st Baron Fisher 1841–1920. British admiral, First Sea Lord 1904–10, when he carried out many radical reforms and innovations, including the introduction of the dreadnought battleship.

He held various commands before becoming First Sea Lord, and returned to the post 1914, but resigned the following year, disagreeing with Churchill over sending more ships to the Dardanelles, Turkey, in World War I.

Fisher John, St *c.*1469–1535. English bishop, created bishop of Rochester 1504. He was an enthusiastic supporter of the revival in the study of Greek, and a friend of the humanists More and Erasmus. In 1535 he was tried on a charge of denying the royal supremacy and beheaded.

Fisher Ronald Aylmer 1890–1962. English statistician and geneticist. He modernized Charles Darwin's theory of evolution, thus securing the key biological concept of genetic change by natural selection. Fisher developed several new statistical techniques and, applying his methods to genetics, published *The Genetical Theory of Natural Selection* in 1930.

Fitzgerald family name of the dukes of Leinster.

Fitzgerald F(rancis) Scott (Key) 1896–1940. US novelist. His autobiographical novel *This Side of Paradise* 1920 made him known in the postwar society of the East Coast, and *The Great Gatsby* 1925 epitomizes the Jazz Age. His wife Zelda's descent into mental illness forms the subject of *Tender is the Night* 1934.

Fitzgerald was born in Minnesota. His first book, *This Side of Paradise*, reflected his experiences at Princeton University. In *The Great Gatsby* 1925 the narrator resembles his author, and Gatsby, the self-made millionaire, is lost in the soulless society he enters. Fitzgerald's wife Zelda Sayre (1900–47), a schizophrenic, entered an asylum 1930, after which he declined into alcoholism. His other works include numerous short stories and the novels *The Beautiful and the Damned* 1922 and *The Last Tycoon*, which was unfinished at his death.

FitzGerald Garret 1926– . Irish politician. As *Taoiseach* (prime minister) 1981–82 and again 1982–86, he was noted for his attempts to solve the Northern Ireland dispute, ultimately by participating in the Anglo-Irish agreement 1985. He tried to remove some of the overtly Catholic features of the constitution to make the Republic more attractive to Northern Protestants. He retired as leader of the Fine Gael Party 1987.

Fitzherbert Maria Anne 1756–1837. Wife of the Prince of Wales, later George IV. She became Mrs Fitzherbert by her second marriage 1778 and, after her husband's death 1781, entered London society. She secretly married the Prince of Wales 1785, and finally parted from him 1803.

Fitzroy family name of dukes of Grafton; descended from King Charles II by his mistress Barbara Villiers; seated at Euston Hall, Norfolk.

Fitzroy Robert 1805–1865. British vice-admiral and meteorologist. In 1828 he succeeded to the command of HMS *Beagle*, then engaged on a survey of the Patagonian coast of South America, and in 1831 was accompanied by the naturalist Charles Darwin on a five-year survey. From 1843 to 45 he was governor of New Zealand.

Fixx James 1932–1984. US popularizer of jogging with his book *The Complete Book of Running* 1978. He died of a heart attack while jogging.

Flagstad Kirsten (Malfrid) 1895–1962. Norwegian soprano who specialized in Wagnerian opera.

Flaherty Robert 1884–1951. US film director. He exerted great influence through his silent film of Inuit (Eskimo) life *Nanook of the North* 1920. Later films include *Man of Aran* 1934 and *Elephant Boy* 1937.

Flamsteed John 1646–1719. First Astronomer Royal of England, who began systematic observations of the positions of the stars, Moon, and planets at Greenwich, London, 1676. His observations were published 1725.

Flanagan Bud. Stage name of Robert Winthrop 1896–1968. British comedian, leader of the 'Crazy Gang' 1931–62. He played in variety theatre all over the world and, with his partner Chesney Allen, popularized such songs as 'Underneath the Arches'.

Flaubert Gustave 1821–1880. French novelist, author of *Madame Bovary* 1857. *Salammbô* 1862 earned him the Legion of Honour 1866, and was followed by *L'Education sentimentale/Sentimental Education* 1869, and *La Tentation de Saint Antoine/The Temptation of St Anthony* 1874. Flaubert also wrote the short stories *Trois contes/Three Tales* 1877.

He entered Paris literary circles 1840, but in 1846 retired to Rouen, where he remained for the rest of his life.

Flaxman John 1755–1826. English sculptor and illustrator in the Neo-Classical style. From 1775 he worked for the Wedgwood pottery as a designer. His public works include the monuments of Nelson 1808–10 in St Paul's Cathedral, London, and of Burns and Kemble in Westminster Abbey.

Flecker James Elroy 1884–1915. English poet. During a career in the consular service, he wrote several volumes of verse, including *The Bridge of Fire* 1907, *The Golden Journey to Samarkand* 1913, and *The Old Ships* 1915.

Fleming Alexander 1881–1955. Scottish bacteriologist who discovered lysozyme (a nasal enzyme with antibacterial properties) 1922, and in 1928 the antibiotic drug penicillin. With H W Florey and E B Chain, he won the Nobel Prize for Medicine 1945.

After a false start as a shipping clerk, Fleming retrained in medicine. Lysozyme was an early discovery. While studying this, he found an unusual mould growing on a neglected culture dish. He isolated and grew it in pure culture. However, its full value was not realized until Florey and Chain isolated the active ingredient, penicillin, and tested it clinically.

Fleming Ian 1908–1964. English author of suspense novels featuring the ruthless, laconic James Bond, UK Secret Service agent No. 007.

Fleming John Ambrose 1849–1945. English electrical physicist and engineer, who invented the thermionic valve 1904.

Fleming Peter 1907–1971. British journalist and travel writer, remembered for his journeys up the Amazon and across the Gobi Desert recounted in *Brazilian Adventure* 1933 and *News from Tartary* 1941.

Fletcher John 1579–1625. English dramatist. He collaborated with ◊Beaumont, producing, most notably, *Philaster* 1609 and *The Maid's Tragedy* 1610–11. He is alleged to have collaborated with Shakespeare on *The Two Noble Kinsmen* and *Henry VIII* in 1612.

Flinders Matthew 1774–1814. English navigator who explored the Australian coasts 1795–99 and 1801–03.

Florey Howard Walter, Baron Florey 1898–1968. Australian pathologist whose research into lysozyme, an antibacterial enzyme discovered by ◊Fleming, led him to study penicillin, which he and ◊Chain isolated and prepared for widespread use. With Fleming, they were awarded the Nobel Prize for Medicine 1945.

Florio Giovanni *c.*1553–1625. English translator, born in London, the son of Italian refugees. He is best known for his translation of ◊Montaigne 1603.

Flotow Friedrich (Adolf Ferdinand), Freiherr von 1812–1883. German composer who wrote 18 operas, including *Martha* 1847.

Fludd Robert 1574–1637. British physician and scientist. He was educated at Oxford and, later, after several years travel through Europe, he practised medicine in London. He published numerous works, of which the best known remains *The History of the Macrocosm and the Microcosm* 1617, his attempt to present a comprehensive account of the universe based on hermeticism, an ancient (possibly Egyptian) cosmic religion.

Flynn Errol 1909–1959. Australian actor. He is renowned for his portrayal of swashbuckling heroes in such films as *Captain Blood* 1935, *The Sea Hawk* 1940, and *The Master of Ballantrae* 1953.

Flynn John 1880–1951. Australian missionary. Inspired by the use of aircraft to transport the wounded of World War I, he instituted in 1928 the *flying doctor* service in Australia, which can be summoned to the outback by radios in individual homesteads.

Fo Dario 1926– . Italian playwright. His plays are predominantly political satires combining black humour with slapstick. They include *Morte accidentale di un anarchico/Accidental Death of an Anarchist* 1970, and *Non si paga non si paga/Can't Pay? Won't Pay!* 1975/1981.

Foch Ferdinand 1851–1929. Marshal of France during World War I. He was largely responsible for the Allied victory at the first battle of the Marne Sept 1914, and commanded on the NW front Oct 1914–Sep 1916. He was appointed commander in chief of the Allied armies in the spring of 1918, and launched the Allied counter-offensive in July that brought about the negotiation of an armistice to end the war.

Fokine Mikhail 1880–1942. Russian dancer and choreographer, born in St Petersburg. He was chief choreographer to the *Ballets Russes* 1909–14, and with ◊Diaghilev revitalized and reformed the art of ballet.

His creations for Diaghilev include *Les Sylphides* 1907, *Carnival* 1910, *The Firebird* 1910, *Le Spectre de la Rose* 1911, and *Petrushka* 1911.

Fonda Henry 1905–1982. US actor whose engaging acting style made him ideal in the role of the American pioneer and honourable man. His many films include *The Grapes of Wrath* 1940, *My Darling Clementine* 1946, and *On Golden Pond* 1981. He was the father of the actress Jane Fonda and the actor and director *Peter Fonda* (1939–).

Fonda Jane 1937– . US film actress. Her early films include *Cat Ballou* 1965 and *Barbarella* 1968, and she won Academy Awards for *Klute* 1971 and *Coming Home* 1979. She is also active in left-wing politics and in promoting physical fitness. She is the daughter of Henry Fonda.

Fontana Domenico 1543–1607. Italian architect. He was employed by Pope Sixtus V, and his principal works include the Vatican library and the completion of the dome of St Peter's in Rome, and the royal palace in Naples.

Fontana Lucio 1899–1968. Italian painter and sculptor. He developed a unique abstract style, presenting bare canvases with straight parallel slashes.

Fontanne Lynn 1887–1983. US actress, one half of the husband-and-wife acting partnership known as the 'Lunts' with her husband Alfred ◊Lunt.

Fonteyn Margot. Stage name of Margaret Hookham 1919– . English ballet dancer. She

Fonteyn One of the greatest partnerships in the history of ballet – Margot Fonteyn and Rudolf Nureyev in Giselle.

made her debut with the Vic-Wells Ballet in *Nutcracker* 1934 and first appeared as Giselle 1937, eventually becoming prima ballerina of the Royal Ballet, London. Renowned for her perfect physique, musicality, and interpretive powers, she created several roles in ◊Ashton's ballets and formed a successful partnership with ◊Nureyev.

Foot Dingle 1905–1978. British lawyer and Labour politician, solicitor-general 1964–67. He was the brother of Michael Foot.

Foot Hugh, Baron Caradon 1907– . British Labour politician. As governor of Cyprus 1957–60, he guided the independence negotiations, and he represented the UK at the United Nations 1964–70. He is the son of Isaac Foot and brother of Michael Foot.

Foot Isaac 1880–1960. British Liberal politician. A staunch Nonconformist, he was minister of mines 1931–32. He was the father of Dingle, Hugh, and Michael Foot.

Foot Michael 1913– . British Labour politician. A leader of the left-wing Tribune Group; he was secretary of state for employment 1974–76, Lord President of the Council and leader of the House 1976–79, and succeeded James Callaghan as Labour Party leader 1980–83.

Forbes Bryan (John Clarke) 1926– . British film producer, director, and screenwriter. After acting in films like *An Inspector Calls* 1954, he made his directorial debut with *Whistle Down the Wind* 1961; among his other films is *The L-Shaped Room* 1962.

Ford Ford Madox. Adopted name of Ford Madox Hueffer 1873–1939. English writer of the novel *The Good Soldier* 1915, and editor of the *English Review* 1908, to which Thomas Hardy, D H Lawrence, and Joseph Conrad contributed. He was a grandson of the painter Ford Madox Brown.

Ford Gerald R(udolph) 1913– . 38th president of the USA 1974–77, a Republican. He was elected to the House of Representatives 1949, was nominated to the vice-presidency by Richard Nixon 1973 following the resignation of Spiro ◊Agnew, and in 1974, when Nixon resigned, Ford became president. He pardoned Nixon, and gave amnesty to those who had resisted the draft for the Vietnam War.

Ford's visit to Vladivostok 1974 resulted in agreement with the USSR on strategic arms limitation. He was defeated by Carter in the 1976 election by a narrow margin.

Ford Glenn (Gwyllym Samuel Newton) 1916– . Canadian actor, active in Hollywood during the 1940s–1960s. Usually cast as the tough but good-natured hero, he was equally at home in westerns, thrillers, and comedies. His films include *Gilda* 1946, *The Big Heat* 1953, and *Dear Heart* 1965.

Ford Henry 1863–1947. US automobile manufacturer, who built his first car 1893 and founded the Ford Motor Company 1903. His Model T (1908–27) was the first car to be constructed by purely mass-production methods, and 15 million of these cars were made.

He was a pacifist, and visited Europe 1915–16 in an attempt to end World War I. In 1936 he founded, with his son *Edsel Ford* (1893–1943), the philanthropic *Ford Foundation*.

Ford John 1586–c.1640. English poet and dramatist. His play *'Tis Pity She's a Whore* (performed about 1626, printed 1633) is a study of incest between brother and sister.

Among his other plays are *The Witch of Edmonton* (1621, 1658), *The Broken Heart* (about 1629, 1633), *The Chronicle History of Perkin Warbeck* 1634, and *The Lady's Trial* (about 1638, 1639).

Ford John. Assumed name of Sean O'Fearn 1895–1973. US film director. His films, especially his westerns, were of great influence, and include *Stagecoach* 1939, *The Grapes of Wrath* 1940, and *The Man who Shot Liberty Valance* 1962.

Ford made many silent films, including *The Iron Horse* 1924 and *Four Sons* 1928. After the introduction of sound, he went on to make films such as *The Informer* 1935, *She Wore a Yellow Ribbon* 1949, and *The Quiet Man* 1952. He won six directing Oscars, two of them for wartime documentaries.

Forest Lee de 1873–1961. US inventor who perfected the audion tube (triode valve) and contributed to the development of radio, radar, and television.

Ford *Henry Ford, founder of the Ford Motor Company.*

Forester C(ecil) S(cott) 1899–1966. English novelist, born in Egypt. He wrote a series of historical novels set in the Napoleonic era which, beginning with *The Happy Return* 1937, cover the career – from midshipman to admiral – of Horatio Hornblower.

He also wrote *Payment Deferred* 1926, a subtle crime novel, and *The African Queen* 1938, later filmed with Humphrey Bogart.

Formby George 1904–1961. English comedian. He established a stage and screen reputation as an apparently simple Lancashire working lad, and sang such songs as 'Mr Wu' and 'Cleaning Windows', accompanying himself on the ukulele. His father was a music-hall star of the same name.

Forrest John, 1st Baron Forrest 1847–1918. Australian explorer and politician. He crossed Western Australia W–E in 1870, when he went along the southern coast route, and in 1874, when he crossed much further N, exploring the Musgrave Ranges. He was born in Western Australia, and was its first premier 1890–1901.

Forrestal James Vincent 1892–1949. US Democratic politician. As secretary of the navy from 1944, he organized its war effort, accompanying the US landings on the Japanese island Iwo Jima.

Forssmann Werner 1904–1979. West German heart specialist. In 1929 he originated, by experiment on himself, the technique of cardiac catheterization (passing a thin tube from an arm artery into the heart itself for diagnostic purposes). He shared the Nobel Prize for Medicine 1956.

Forster E(dward) M(organ) 1879–1970. English novelist, concerned with the interplay of personality and the conflict between convention and instinct. His novels include *A Room with a View* 1908, *Howards End* 1910, and *A Passage to India* 1924. He also wrote short stories, for example 'The Eternal Omnibus' 1914; criticism, including *Aspects of the Novel* 1927; and essays, including *Abinger Harvest* 1936.

Forster published his first novel, *Where Angels Fear to Tread*, 1905. His many years spent in India and as secretary to the Maharajah of Dewas in 1921 provided him with the material for *A Passage to India*, which explores the relationship between the English and the Indians. *Maurice*, published 1971, has a homosexual theme.

Forster William Edward 1818–1886. British Liberal reformer. In Gladstone's government 1868–74 he was vice president of the council, and secured the passing of the Education Act 1870 and the Ballot Act 1872. He was chief secretary for Ireland 1880–82.

Forsyth Frederick 1938– . English thriller writer. His books include *The Day of the Jackal* 1970, *The Dogs of War* 1974, and *The Fourth Protocol* 1984.

Fortin Jean 1750–1831. French physicist and instrument-maker who invented a mercury barometer that bears his name. On this scale, normal atmospheric pressure is 760 mm of mercury.

Foss Lukas 1922– . US composer and conductor. He wrote the cantata *The Prairie* 1942 and *Time Cycle* for soprano and orchestra 1960.

Born in Germany, he studied in Europe before settling in the USA in 1937. A student of ◊Hindemith, his vocal music is composed in Neo-Classical style; in the mid-1950s he began increasingly to employ improvisation. Foss has also written chamber and orchestral music in which the players reproduce tape-recorded effects.

Fosse Robert ('Bob') 1927–1987. US film director who entered films as a dancer and choreographer from Broadway, making his directorial debut with *Sweet Charity* 1968. He gained an Academy Award for his second film as director, *Cabaret* 1972. His other work includes *All That Jazz* 1979.

Foster Jodie 1962– . US film actress, who began as a child in a great variety of roles. Her work includes *Taxi Driver* 1976, *Bugsy Malone* 1976, and *The Accused* 1988.

Foster Norman 1935– . British architect of the high-tech school. His works include the Willis Faber office, Ipswich, 1978, the Sainsbury Centre for Visual Arts at the University of East Anglia 1979, and the headquarters of the Hongkong and Shanghai Bank, Hong Kong, 1986.

Foster Stephen Collins 1826–1864. US songwriter. He wrote sentimental popular songs including 'My Old Kentucky Home' 1853 and 'Beautiful Dreamer' 1864, and rhythmic minstrel songs such as 'Oh! Susanna' 1848 and 'Camptown Races' 1850.

Foucault Jean Bernard Léon 1819–1868. French physicist who used a pendulum to demonstrate the rotation of the Earth on its axis, and invented the gyroscope.

He investigated heat and light, discovered eddy currents induced in a copper disc moving in a magnetic field, invented a polarizer, and made improvements in the electric arc.

Foucault Michel 1926–1984. French philosopher, who rejected phenomenology and existentialism. His work was concerned with how forms of knowledge and forms of human subjectivity are constructed by specific institutions and practices. Foucault was deeply influenced by ◊Nietzsche, and developed a novel analysis of the operation of power in modern society using Nietzschean concepts.

Fouché Joseph, Duke of Otranto 1759–1820. French politician. He was elected to the National Convention (the post-Revolutionary legislature), and organized the conspiracy which overthrew the Jacobin leader Robespierre. Napoleon employed him as police minister.

Fouquet Jean *c.* 1420–1481. French painter. He became court painter to Charles VIII in 1448 and to Louis XI in 1475. His *Melun diptych* about 1450 (Musées Royaux, Antwerp, and Staatliche

Museen, Berlin), shows Italian Renaissance influence.

Fouquet Nicolas 1615–1680. French politician, a rival to Louis XIV's minister ♦Colbert. Fouquet became *procureur général* of the Paris parliament 1650 and *surintendant des finances* 1651, responsible for raising funds for the long war against Spain, a post he held until arrested and imprisoned for embezzlement (at the instigation of Colbert, who succeeded him) from 1661 until his death.

Fourier François Charles Marie 1772–1837. French socialist. In *Le Nouveau monde industriel/The New Industrial World* 1829–30, he advocated that society should be organized in self-sufficient cooperative units of about 1,500 people. Conventional marriage was to be abandoned.

Fourier Jean Baptiste Joseph 1768–1830. French applied mathematician. His mathematical formulation of heat flow in 1807 contains the proposal that, with certain constraints, any mathematical function can be represented by a trigonometrical series. This principle forms the basis of *Fourier analysis*, used in many fields of physics, and is embodied in his *Théorie analytique de la chaleur/The Analytical Theory of Heat* 1822.

Fowler Henry Watson 1858–1933 and his brother Francis George 1870–1918. English scholars and authors of a number of English dictionaries. *Modern English Usage* 1926, the work of Henry Fowler, has become a classic reference work for advice on matters of style and disputed usage.

Fowler (Peter) Norman 1938– . British Conservative politician. He was a junior minister in the Heath government, transport secretary in the first Thatcher administration 1979, social services secretary 1981, and employment secretary 1987–89.

Fowler William 1911– . US astrophysicist. In 1983, he and Subrahmanyan Chandrasekhar were awarded the Nobel Prize for Physics for their work on the life cycle of stars and the origin of chemical elements.

Fowles John 1926– . English writer whose novels, often concerned with illusion and reality, and with the creative process, include *The Collector* 1963, *The Magus* 1965, *The French Lieutenant's Woman* 1969, *Daniel Martin* 1977, *Mantissa* 1982, and *A Maggot* 1985.

Fox Charles James 1749–1806. English Whig politician, son of the 1st Baron Holland. He entered Parliament 1769 as a supporter of the court, but went over to the opposition 1774. In 1782 he became secretary of state in Rockingham's government, but resigned when Shelburne succeeded Rockingham. He allied with North 1783 to overthrow Shelburne, and formed a coalition ministry with himself as secretary of state. When the Lords threw out Fox's bill to reform the government of India, George III dismissed the ministry, and in their place installed Pitt.

Fourier French socialist François Fourier.

Fox now became leader of the opposition, although cooperating with Pitt in the impeachment of Warren Hastings, the governor general of India. The 'Old Whigs' deserted to the government 1792 over the French Revolution, leaving Fox and a small group of 'New Whigs' to oppose Pitt's war of intervention and his persecution of the reformers. On Pitt's death 1806 a ministry was formed with Fox as foreign secretary, which at Fox's insistence abolished the slave trade. He opened peace negotiations with France, but died before their completion, and was buried in Westminster Abbey, London.

Fox George 1624–1691. English founder of the Society of Friends. He became a travelling preacher 1647, and in 1650 was imprisoned for blasphemy at Derby, where the name Quakers was first applied derogatorily to him and his followers, supposedly because he enjoined Judge Bennet to 'quake at the word of the Lord'.

Fox James 1939– . British film actor, usually cast in upper-class, refined roles, but renowned for his portrayal of a psychotic gangster in Nicolas Roeg's *Performance* 1970, which was followed by a ten-year break from acting.

In the 1960s Fox appeared in films like *The Servant* 1963 and *Isadora* 1968. He returned to the screen in, for example, *A Passage to India* 1984 and *Absolute Beginners* 1985.

Foxe John 1516–1587. English Protestant propagandist. He became a canon of Salisbury 1563.

His *Book of Martyrs* 1563 luridly described persecutions under Queen Mary, reinforcing popular hatred of Roman Catholicism.

Fracastoro Girolamo *c.*1478–1553. Italian physician known for his two medical books. His first book was written in verse, *Syphilis sive morbus gallicus/Syphilis or the French disease* 1530. It was one of the earliest texts on syphilis, a disease Fracastoro named. In a second work, *De contagione/ On contagion* 1546, he wrote, far ahead of his time, about 'seeds of contagion'.

Fra Diavolo nickname of Michele Pezza 1771–1806. Italian brigand. He was a renegade monk, led a gang in the mountains of Calabria for many years, and was eventually executed in Naples.

Fragonard Jean Honoré 1732–1806. French painter, the leading exponent of the Rococo style (along with his master Boucher). His lighthearted subjects include *The Swing* about 1766 (Wallace Collection, London).

Frame Janet. Pen name of Janet Paterson Frame Clutha 1924– . New Zealand novelist. After being wrongly diagnosed as schizophrenic, she reflected her experiences 1945–54 in the novel *Faces in the Water* 1961 and the autobiographical *An Angel at My Table* 1984.

Frampton George James 1860–1928. British sculptor. His work includes the statue of Peter Pan in Kensington Gardens and the Nurse Cavell memorial near St Martin's, London.

Francis or *François* two kings of France:

Francis I 1494–1547. King of France from 1515. He succeeded his cousin Louis XII, and from 1519 European politics turned on the rivalry between him and the Holy Roman emperor Charles V, which led to war 1521–29, 1536–38, and 1542–44. In 1525 Francis was defeated and captured at Pavia, and released only after signing a humiliating treaty. At home, he developed absolute monarchy.

Francis II 1544–1560. King of France from 1559 when he succeeded his father, Henry II. He married Mary Queen of Scots 1558. He was completely under the influence of his mother, ◊Catherine de' Medici.

Francis II 1768–1835. Holy Roman emperor 1792–1806. He succeeded his father Leopold II. He became Francis I, Emperor of Austria 1804, and abandoned the title of Holy Roman emperor 1806. During his reign Austria was five times involved in war with France, 1792–97, 1798–1801, 1805, 1809, and 1813–14.

Francis Ferdinand English name for ◊Franz Ferdinand, archduke of Austria.

Francis Joseph English name for ◊Franz Joseph, emperor of Austria-Hungary.

Francis of Assisi, St 1182–1226. Italian founder of the Roman Catholic Franciscan order of friars 1209 and, with St Clare, of the Poor Clares 1212. In 1224 he is said to have undergone a mystical experience during which he received the *stigmata*

Francis I Unstable and vacillating as a ruler, he is remembered for the brilliance of the artists and writers of his court.

(five wounds of Jesus). Many stories are told of his ability to charm wild animals, and he is the patron saint of ecologists. His feast day is 4 Oct.

The son of a wealthy merchant, Francis changed his life after two dreams during an illness following spells of military service when he was in his early twenties. He resolved to follow literally the behests of the New Testament and live a life of poverty and service while preaching a simple form of the Christian gospel. In 1219 he went to Egypt to convert the sultan, and lived for a month in his camp. Returning to Italy, he resigned his leadership of the friars.

Francis of Sales, St 1567–1622. French bishop and theologian. He became bishop of Geneva 1602, and in 1610 founded the order of the Visitation, an order of nuns. He is the patron saint of journalists and other writers. Feast day 24 Jan.

Franck César Auguste 1822–1890. Belgian composer. His music, mainly religious, and Romantic in style, includes the Symphony in D minor 1866–68, *Symphonic Variations* 1885 for piano and orchestra, the Violin Sonata 1886, the oratorio *Les Béatitudes/The Beatitudes* 1879, and many organ pieces.

Franck James 1882–1964. US physicist influential in atom technology. He was awarded the 1925 Nobel prize for his 1914 experiments on the energy transferred by colliding electrons to mercury atoms, showing that the transfer was governed by the rules of quantum theory.

Franck participated in the wartime atomic-bomb project at Los Alamos but organized the 'Franck petition' 1945, which argued that the bomb should not be used against Japanese cities.

Franco (Bahamonde) Francisco (Paulino Hermenegildo Teódulo) 1892–1975. Spanish dictator from 1939. As a general, he led the insurgent Nationalists to victory in the Spanish Civil War 1936–39, supported by Fascist Italy and Nazi Germany, and established a dictatorship. In 1942 Franco reinstated the Cortes (Spanish parliament), which in 1947 passed an act by which he became head of state for life.

Franco was born in Galicia, NW Spain. He entered the army 1910, served in Morocco 1920–26, and was appointed chief of staff 1935, but demoted to governor of the Canary Islands 1936. Dismissed from this post by the Popular Front (Republican) government, he plotted an uprising with German and Italian assistance, and on the outbreak of the Civil War organized the invasion of Spain by N African troops and foreign legionaries. After the death of Gen Sanjurjo, he took command of the Nationalists, proclaiming himself *Caudillo* (leader) of Spain. The defeat of the Republic with the surrender of Madrid 1939 brought all Spain under his government. On the outbreak of World War II, in spite of Spain's official attitude of 'strictest neutrality', his pro-Axis sympathies led him to send aid, later withdrawn, to the German side.

At home, he curbed the growing power of the Falange (the fascist party), and in later years slightly liberalized his regime. In 1969 he nominated ◊Juan Carlos as his successor and future king of Spain. He relinquished the premiership 1973, but remained head of state until his death.

François French form of ◊Francis, two kings of France.

Francome John 1952– . British jockey. He holds the record for the most National Hunt winners (over hurdles or fences). Between 1970 and 1985 he rode 1,138 winners from 5,061 mounts – the second person (after Stan Mellor) to ride 1,000 winners. He took up training after retiring from riding.

Frank Anne 1929–1945. German diarist who fled to the Netherlands with her family 1933 to escape Nazi anti-semitism. During the German occupation of Amsterdam, they remained in a sealed-off room 1942–44, when betrayal resulted in Anne's deportation and death in Belsen concentration camp. Her diary of her time in hiding was published 1947.

Frank Ilya 1908– . Russian physicist known for his work on radiation. In 1934, ◊Cherenkov had noted a blue radiation sometimes emitted as electrons passed through water. Frank and his colleague Igor Tamm (1895–1971), realized that this form of radiation was produced by charged particles travelling faster through the medium than the speed of light in the medium. Franck shared the 1958 Nobel Prize for Physics with Cherenkov and Tamm.

Frankel Benjamin 1906–1973. English composer. He studied the piano in Germany and continued his studies in London while playing jazz violin in nightclubs. He wrote chamber music and numerous film scores.

Frankenthaler Helen 1928– . US Abstract Expressionist painter, inventor of the colour-staining technique whereby the unprimed, absorbent canvas is stained or soaked with thinned-out paint, creating deep, soft veils of translucent colour.

Franklin Benjamin 1706–1790. US scientist and politician. He proved that lightning is a form of electricity by the experiment of flying a kite in a storm, distinguished between positive and negative electricity, and invented the lightning conductor. He helped to draft the Declaration of Independence and the US constitution, and was ambassador to France 1776–85.

Franklin, born in Boston, combined a successful printing business with scientific experiment and inventions; he published the popular *Poor Richard's Almanac* 1733–58. A member of the Pennsylvania Assembly 1751–64, he was sent to Britain to lobby Parliament about tax grievances and achieved the repeal of the Stamp Act, by which Britain had imposed a tax on all US documents; on his return to the USA he was prominent in the deliberations leading up to independence. As ambassador in Paris, he negotiated an alliance with France and the peace settlement with Britain. His autobiography appeared in 1781.

Franklin John 1786–1847. English naval explorer who took part in expeditions to Australia, the Arctic, and N Canada, and in 1845 commanded an expedition to look for the Northwest Passage from the Atlantic to the Pacific, during which he and his crew perished.

The 1845 expedition had virtually found the Passage when it became trapped in the ice. In 1984, two of its members, buried on King Edward Island, were found to be perfectly preserved in the frozen ground of their graves.

Franklin Rosalind 1920–1958. English biophysicist whose research on X-ray diffraction of DNA crystals helped Francis Crick and James D Watson to deduce the chemical structure of DNA.

Franz Joseph Emperor of Austria who precipitated
World War I.

Franz Ferdinand or Francis Ferdinand 1863–1914.
Archduke of Austria. He became heir to his uncle,
Emperor Franz Joseph, from 1884 but while visiting Sarajevo 28 June 1914, he and his wife were
assassinated by Serbian nationalists. Austria used
the episode to make unreasonable demands on
Serbia that ultimately precipitated World War I.

Franz Joseph or Francis Joseph 1830–1916.
Emperor of Austria-Hungary from 1848, when
his uncle, Ferdinand I, abdicated. After the suppression of the 1848 revolution, Franz Joseph
tried to establish an absolute monarchy, but had
to grant Austria a parliamentary constitution 1861,
and Hungary equality with Austria 1867. He was
defeated in the Italian War 1859 and the Prussian
War 1866. In 1914 he made the assassination of his
nephew, Franz Ferdinand, the excuse for attacking
Serbia, precipitating World War I.

Fraser Antonia 1932– . English author of biographies, including *Mary Queen of Scots* 1969; historical works, such as *The Weaker Vessel* 1984; and
a series of detective novels featuring investigator
Jemima Shore.
    She is married to the playwright Harold Pinter,
and is the daughter of Lord Longford.

Fraser Dawn 1937– . Australian swimmer. The
only person to win the same swimming event at
three consecutive Olympic Games: 100 metres
freestyle in 1956, 1960, and 1964. The holder
of 27 world records, she was the first woman
to break the one-minute barrier for the 100
metres.

Fraser (John) Malcolm 1930– . Australian Liberal
politician, prime minister 1975–83; nicknamed
'the Prefect' because of a supposed disregard of
subordinates.

In 1975, following the Whitlam government's
economic difficulties, he blocked finance bills in
the Senate, became prime minister of a caretaker
government and in the consequent general election won a large majority. He lost to Hawke in the
1983 election.

Fraser Peter 1884–1950. New Zealand Labour
politician, born in Scotland. He held various cabinet posts 1935–40, and was prime minister
1940–49.

Fraser Simon 1776–1862. Canadian explorer and
surveyor for the Hudson Bay Company who
crossed the Rockies and travelled most of the way
down the river that bears his name 1805–07.

Fraunhofer Joseph von 1787–1826. German physicist who did important work in optics. The
dark lines in the solar spectrum (*Fraunhofer
lines*), which revealed the chemical composition
of the Sun's atmosphere, were accurately mapped
by him.

Frazer James George 1854–1941. Scottish anthropologist, author of *The Golden Bough* 1890, a pioneer study of the origins of religion and sociology
on a comparative basis. It exerted considerable
influence on writers such as T S Eliot and D
H Lawrence, but by the standards of modern
anthropology many of its methods and findings
are unsound.

Frederick V known as *the Winter King*
1596–1632. Elector palatine of the Rhine
1610–23 and king of Bohemia 1619–20 (for one
winter, hence the name 'winter king'), having been
chosen by the Protestant Bohemians as ruler after
the deposition of Catholic emperor ◊Ferdinand II.
His selection was the cause of the Thirty Years'
War. Frederick was defeated at the Battle of the
White Mountain, near Prague, in Nov 1620 by the
army of the Catholic League, and fled to Holland.
He was the son-in-law of James I of England.

Frederick IX 1899–1972. King of Denmark from
1947. He was succeeded by his daughter who
became Queen ◊Margrethe II.

Frederick two Holy Roman emperors:

Frederick I c.1123–1190. Holy Roman emperor
from 1152, known as *Barbarossa*, 'red-beard'.
Originally duke of Swabia, he was elected emperor
1152, and was engaged in a struggle with Pope
Alexander III 1159–77, which ended in his sub-
mission; the Lombard cities, headed by Milan,
took advantage of this to establish their independence of imperial control. Frederick joined the
Third Crusade, and was drowned in Anatolia.

Frederick II 1194–1250. Holy Roman emperor
from his election 1212, called 'the Wonder of the
World'. He led a crusade 1228–29 that recovered
Jerusalem by treaty without fighting. He quarrelled with the pope, who excommunicated him
three times, and a feud began which lasted at
intervals until the end of his reign. Frederick,
who was a complete sceptic in religion, is often

considered the most cultured man of his age. He was the son of Henry VI.

Frederick three kings of Prussia:

Frederick I 1657–1713. King of Prussia from 1701. He became elector of Brandenburg 1688.

Frederick II *the Great* 1712–1786. King of Prussia from 1740, when he succeeded his father Frederick William I. In that year he started the War of the Austrian Succession by his attack on Austria. In the peace of 1745 he secured Silesia. The struggle was renewed in the Seven Years' War 1756–63. He acquired West Prussia in the first partition of Poland 1772, and left Prussia as Germany's foremost state. He was an efficient and just ruler in the spirit of the Enlightenment, and a patron of the arts.

He received a harsh military education from his father, and in 1730 was threatened with death for attempting to run away. In the Seven Years' War, in spite of assistance from Britain, Frederick had a hard task holding his own against the Austrians and their Russian allies; the skill with which he did so proved him to be one of the great soldiers of history. In his domestic policy he was one of the 'enlightened despots' of the Age of Reason; he encouraged industry and agriculture, reformed the judicial system, fostered education, and established religious toleration. He corresponded with the French writer Voltaire, and was a talented musician.

Frederick III 1831–1888. King of Prussia and emperor of Germany 1888. The son of Wilhelm I, he married the eldest daughter (Victoria) of Queen Victoria of the UK 1858, and, as a liberal, frequently opposed Chancellor Bismarck. He died three months after his accession.

Frederick William 1620–1688. Elector of Brandenburg from 1640, 'the Great Elector'. By successful wars against Sweden and Poland, he prepared the way for Prussian power in the 18th century.

Frederick William 1882–1951. Last crown prince of Germany, eldest son of Wilhelm II. During World War I he commanded a group of armies on the western front. In 1918, he retired into private life.

Frederick William four kings of Prussia:

Frederick William I 1688–1740. King of Prussia from 1713, who developed Prussia's military might and commerce.

Frederick William II 1744–1797. King of Prussia from 1786. He was a nephew of Frederick II, but had little of his relative's military skill. He was unsuccessful in waging war on the French 1792–95, and lost all Prussia west of the Rhine.

Frederick William III 1770–1840. King of Prussia from 1797. He was defeated by Napoleon 1806, but contributed to his final overthrow 1813–15, and profited in territory allotted at the Congress of Vienna.

Frederick William IV 1795–1861. King of Prussia from 1840. He upheld the principle of the divine right of kings, but was forced to grant a constitution 1850 after the Prussian revolution 1848. He suffered two strokes 1857, and became mentally debilitated. His brother William (later emperor) took over his duties.

Frege Gottlob 1848–1925. German philosopher. The founder of modern mathematical logic, he published *Die Grundlagen der Arithmetik/The Foundations of Arithmetic* 1884, which was to influence Bertrand ◊Russell and ◊Wittgenstein.

The *Grundgesetze* was a less successful work, published 1903. His work, neglected for a time, has attracted renewed attention in recent years in Britain and the USA.

Frémont John Charles 1813–1890. US explorer and politician who travelled extensively throughout the western USA. He surveyed much of the territory between the Mississippi River and the coast of California with the aim of establishing an overland route E–W across the continent. In 1842 he crossed the Rocky Mountains, climbing a peak that is named after him.

French Daniel Chester 1850–1931. US sculptor, designer of the seated figure of Abraham Lincoln 1922 for the Lincoln Memorial, Washington DC. The imposing classical style continued academic tradition.

French John Denton Pinkstone, 1st Earl of Ypres 1852–1925. British field marshal. In the second South African War 1899–1902, he relieved Kimberley and took Bloemfontein; in World War I he was commander in chief of the British Expeditionary Force in France 1914–15; he resigned after being criticized as indecisive.

Freneau Philip Morin 1752–1832. US poet whose *A Political Litany* 1775 was a mock prayer for deliverance from British tyranny.

Frere John 1740–1807. English archaeologist, high sheriff of Suffolk and Member of Parliament for Norwich. He discovered Palaeolithic tools at Hoxne, Suffolk, in 1790 and suggested that they predated the conventional biblical timescale.

Frescobaldi Girolamo 1583–1643. Italian composer of virtuoso pieces for the organ and harpsichord.

Fresnel Augustin 1788–1827. French physicist who refined the theory of polarized light. Fresnel realized in 1821 that light waves did not vibrate like sound waves longitudinally in the direction of their motion, but transversely, at right angles to the direction of the propagated wave.

Freud Clement 1924– . British journalist, television personality, and until 1987 Liberal member of Parliament; a grandson of Sigmund Freud.

Freud Lucian 1922– . British painter, known for realist portraits with the subject staring intently from an almost masklike face, for example *Francis*

Freud Austrian psychiatrist and pioneer of psycho-analysis, Sigmund Freud.

Bacon 1952 (Tate Gallery, London). He is a grand-son of Sigmund Freud.

Freud Sigmund 1865–1939. Austrian psychiatrist who pioneered study of the unconscious mind. He developed the methods of free association and interpretation of dreams that are still techniques of psychoanalysis. His books include *Die Traumdeutung/The Interpretation of Dreams* 1900, *Totem and Taboo* 1913, and *Das Unbehagen in der Kultur/Civilization and its Discontents* 1930.

Freud studied medicine in Vienna and was a member of the research team that discovered the local anaesthetic effects of cocaine. From 1886 to 1938 he had a private practice in Vienna, and his theories and writings drew largely on case studies of his own patients. He was also influenced by the research into hysteria of the Viennese physician ◊Breuer. In the early 1900s a group of psychoanalysts gathered around Freud. Some of these later broke away and formed their own influential schools: Alfred ◊Adler in 1911 and Carl ◊Jung in 1913. Following the Nazi occupation of Austria in 1938, Freud left for London, where he died.

The word 'psychoanalysis' was, like much of its terminology, coined by Freud, and many terms have passed into popular usage, not without distortion. The way that unconscious forces influence people's thoughts and actions was Freud's discovery, and his theory of the repression of infantile sexuality as the root of neuroses in the adult was particularly controversial. Later he also stressed the significance of aggressive drives. His work, long accepted as definitive by many, has been criticized particularly from a feminist point of view.

Freyberg Bernard Cyril, Baron Freyberg 1889–1963. New Zealand soldier and administrator. He fought in World War I, and during World War II he commanded the New Zealand expeditionary force. He was governor-general of New Zealand 1946–52.

Friedan Betty 1921– . US liberal feminist. Her book *The Feminine Mystique* 1963 was one of the most influential books for the women's movement in both the USA and the UK. She founded the National Organization for Women (NOW) 1966, the National Women's Political Caucus 1971, the First Women's Bank 1973, and called the First International Feminist Congress 1973.

Friedman Milton 1912– . US economist. The foremost exponent of monetarism, the argument that a country's economy, and hence inflation, can be controlled through its money supply, although most governments lack the 'political will' to control inflation by cutting government spending and thereby increasing unemployment.

Friedrich German form of ◊Frederick.

Friedrich Caspar David 1774–1840. German landscape painter in the Romantic style, active mainly in Dresden. He imbued his subjects – mountain scenes and moonlit seas – with great poetic melancholy, and was later admired by Symbolist painters.

Frink Elisabeth 1930– . British sculptor of rugged, naturalistic bronzes, mainly based on animal forms.

Frisch Karl von 1886–1982. German zoologist, founder with Konrad Lorenz of ethology, the study of animal behaviour. He specialized in bees, discovering how they communicate the location of sources of nectar by movements called 'dances'. He shared the Nobel Prize for Medicine 1973 with Lorenz and Nikolaas ◊Tinbergen.

Frisch Max 1911– . Swiss dramatist. Influenced by ◊Brecht, his early plays such as *Als der Krieg zu Ende war/When the War Is Over* 1949 are more romantic in tone than his later symbolic dramas, such as *Andorra* 1962, dealing with questions of identity. His best-known play is *Biedermann und die Brandstifter/The Fire Raisers* 1958.

Frisch Otto 1904–1979. Austrian physicist who coined the term 'nuclear fission'. A refugee from Nazi Germany, he worked from 1943 on the atom bomb at Los Alamos, USA, then at Cambridge, England. He was the nephew of Lise ◊Meitner.

Frisch Ragnar 1895–1973. Norwegian economist, pioneer of econometrics (the application of mathematical and statistical methods in economics). He shared the first Nobel Prize for Economics in 1969 with Jan ◊Tinbergen.

Frith William Powell 1819–1909. British painter, especially noted for large contemporary scenes with numerous figures and incidental detail. Examples are *Ramsgate Sands*, bought by Queen Victoria, and *Derby Day* 1856–58 (both Tate Gallery, London).

Frobisher Martin 1535–1594. English navigator. He made his first voyage to Guinea, West Africa, 1554. In 1576 he set out in search of the Northwest Passage, and visited Labrador, and Frobisher Bay, Baffin island. A second and third expedition sailed 1577 and 1578.

He served as vice admiral in Drake's West Indian expedition 1585. In 1588, he was knighted for helping to defeat the Armada. He was mortally wounded 1594 fighting against the Spanish off the coast of France.

Froebel Friedrich August Wilhelm 1782–1852. German educationist. He evolved a new system of education using instructive play, described in *Education of Man* 1826 and other works. In 1836 he founded the first kindergarten (German 'garden for children') in Blankenburg. He was influenced by ◊Pestalozzi.

Fromm Erich 1900–1980. German psychoanalyst who moved to the USA 1933 to escape the Nazis. His *The Fear of Freedom* 1941 and *The Sane Society* 1955 were source books for modern alternative lifestyles.

Frontenac et Palluau Louis de Buade, Comte de Frontenac et Palluau 1622–1698. French colonial governor. He was appointed governor of the French possessions in North America 1672, but was recalled 1682. After the Iroquois, supported by the English, won several military victories, Frontenac was reinstated 1689. He defended Quebec against the English 1690 and defeated the Iroquois 1696.

Frost Robert (Lee) 1874–1963. US poet whose verse, in traditional form, is written with an individual voice and penetrating vision; his best-known poems include 'Mending Wall' ('Something there is that does not love a wall'), 'The Road Not Taken', and 'Stopping by Woods on a Snowy Evening'.

Froude James Anthony 1818–1894. British historian, whose *History of England from the Fall of Wolsey to the Defeat of the Spanish Armada* 1856–70 was a classic Victorian work.

Fry Christopher 1907– . English dramatist. He was a leader of the revival of verse drama after World War II with *The Lady's Not for Burning* 1948, *Venus Observed* 1950, and *A Sleep of Prisoners* 1951.

Fry Elizabeth (born Gurney) 1780–1845. English Quaker philanthropist. She formed an association for the improvement of female prisoners 1817, and worked with her brother, *Joseph Gurney* (1788–1847), on an influential report 1819 on prison reform.

Fry Roger Eliot 1866–1934. British artist and art critic, a champion of Post-Impressionism and a great admirer of Cézanne. He founded the *Omega Workshops* to improve design and to encourage young artists working in modern styles.

Fuad two kings of Egypt:

Fuad I 1868–1936. King of Egypt from 1922. Son of the Khedive Ismail, he succeeded his elder brother, Hussein Kiamil, as sultan of Egypt 1917, and when Egypt was declared independent 1922 he assumed the title of king.

Fuad II 1952– . King of Egypt 1952–53, between the abdication of his father ◊Farouk and the establishment of the republic. He was a grandson of Fuad I.

Fuchs Klaus (Emil Julius) 1911–1988. German spy who worked on atom-bomb research in the UK in World War II. He was imprisoned 1950–59 for passing information to the USSR and resettled in East Germany.

Fuchs Vivian 1908– . British explorer and geologist. Before World War II, he accompanied several Cambridge University expeditions to Greenland, Africa, and Antarctica. In 1957–58, he led the Commonwealth Trans-Antarctic Expedition.

Fuentes Carlos 1928– . Mexican novelist, whose first novel *La región más transparente/Where the Air is Clear* 1958 encompasses the history of the country from the Aztecs to the present day.

Führer or *Fuehrer* title adopted by Adolf ◊Hitler as leader of the Nazi Party.

Fulbright William 1905– . US Democratic politician. He was responsible for the *Fulbright Act* 1946 which provided grants for thousands of Americans to study overseas and for overseas students to enter the USA; he had studied at Oxford, UK, on a Rhodes scholarship.

Fuller John Frederick Charles 1878–1966. British major general and military theorist who propounded the concept of armoured warfare, or *blitzkrieg*, as adopted by the Germans 1939.

Fuller (Richard) Buckminster 1895–1983. US architect and engineer. In 1947 he invented the lightweight *geodesic dome*, a self-supporting hemispherical structure of triangular components. It combines the maximum strength with the minimum structure. Within 30 years over 50,000 had been built.

Fuller Roy 1912– . English poet and novelist. His collections of poetry include *Poems* 1939, *Epitaphs and Occasions* 1951, *Brutus's Orchard* 1957, *Collected Poems* 1962, and *The Reign of Sparrows* 1980. Novels include *My Child, My Sister* 1965 and *The Carnal Island* 1970.

Fuller Thomas 1608–1661. English writer. He served as a chaplain to the Royalist army during the Civil War, and at the Restoration became the king's chaplain. He wrote *History of the Holy War* 1639, *Good Thoughts in Bad Times* 1645, its sequel *Good Thoughts in Worse Times* 1647, and the biographical *Worthies of England* 1662.

Fulton Robert 1765–1815. US engineer and inventor, who designed the first successful steamships. He produced a submarine, the *Nautilus*, in Paris, France, 1797, and experimented with steam navigation on the Seine, then returned to the USA. The first steam vessel of note, the *Clermont*, appeared on the Hudson 1807, sailing between New York and Albany. The first steam warship was the *Fulton*, of 38 tonnes, built 1814–15.

Funk Casimir 1884–1967. US biochemist, born in Poland, who did pioneering research into vitamins.

Funk proposed that certain diseases are caused by dietary deficiencies. In 1912 he demonstrated that rice extracts cure beriberi in pigeons. As the extract contains an amine (ammonia-based organic compound), he mistakenly concluded that he had discovered a class of 'vital amines', a phrase soon reduced to 'vitamins'.

Furtwängler (Gustav Heinrich Ernst Martin) Wilhelm 1886–1954. German conductor; leader of the Berlin Philharmonic Orchestra 1922–54. His interpretations of the German Romantic composers, especially Wagner, were regarded as classically definitive. He remained in Germany during the Nazi regime.

Fusell Henry 1741–1825. British artist born in Switzerland, working in the Romantic style. He painted macabre and dreamlike images such as *The Nightmare* 1781 (Detroit Institute of Arts).

Fyfe David Maxwell, 1st Earl of Kilmuir. British lawyer and Conservative politician; see ◊Kilmuir.

Fyffe Will 1885–1947. Scots music-hall comedian remembered for his vivid character sketches and for his song 'I Belong to Glasgow'.

Gable Clark 1901–1960. US film actor. He was a star for more than 30 years in 90 films, including *It Happened One Night* 1934, *Gone with the Wind* 1939, and *The Misfits* 1961. He was nicknamed the 'King' of Hollywood.

Gabo Naum. Adopted name of Naum Neemia Pevsner 1890–1977. US abstract sculptor, born in Russia. One of the leading exponents of *Constructivism*, he left the USSR in 1922 for Germany and taught at the Bauhaus (a key centre of modern design). He lived in the UK in the 1930s, then in the USA from 1946. He often used transparent coloured plastics in his sculptures.

Gabor Dennis 1900–1979. Hungarian-born British physicist. In 1947, he invented the holographic method of three-dimensional photography and in 1958 invented a type of colour TV tube of greatly reduced depth.

Gabrieli Giovanni *c.*1555–1612. Italian composer and organist. Although he composed secular music, and madrigals, he is best known for his motets, which are frequently dramatic and often use several choirs and groups of instruments. In 1585 he became organist at St Mark's, Venice.

Gadamer Hans-Georg 1900– . German philosopher. In *Truth and Method* 1960, he argued that 'understanding' is fundamental to human existence, and that all understanding takes place within a tradition. The relation between text and interpreter can be viewed as a dialogue, in which the interpreter must remain open to the truth of the text.

Gaddafi alternative form of ◊Khaddhafi, Libyan leader.

Gaddi family of Italian painters in Florence: *Gaddo Gaddi* (*c.*1250–*c.*1330); his son *Taddeo Gaddi* (*c.*1300–*c.*1366), who was influenced by Giotto and

painted the fresco cycle *Life of the Virgin* in Santa Croce, Florence; and grandson *Agnolo Gaddi* (active 1369–96), who also painted frescoes in Santa Croce, *The Story of the Cross*, 1380s, and produced panel paintings in characteristic pale pastel colours.

Gaddis William 1922– . Experimental US novelist, whose *The Recognitions* 1955, is about artistic counterfeiting. His other novels are *JR* 1976 and *Carpenter's Gothic* 1985.

Gagarin Yuri (Alexeyevich) 1934–1968. Soviet cosmonaut, who in 1961 became the first human in space aboard the spacecraft Vostok 1.

Born in the Smolensk Region, son of a farmer, he qualified as a foundryman. He became a pilot 1957, and on 12 Apr 1961, completed one orbit of the Earth, taking 108 minutes from launch to landing. He died in a plane crash while training for the Soyuz 3 mission.

Gainsborough Thomas 1727–1788. English landscape and portrait painter. He was born in Sudbury, Suffolk; in 1759 he settled in Bath, gaining fame as a painter of high society. In 1774 he went to London and became one of the original members of the Royal Academy. He was one of the first British artists to follow the Dutch in painting realistic landscapes rather than imaginative Italianate scenery.

Gainsborough began to paint while still at school and in 1741 went to London where he learnt etching and studied at the Academy of Arts, but remained largely self-taught. His portraits of Sir Charles Holte and the actor Garrick belong to this period. His sitters included the royal family, Mrs Siddons, Dr Johnson, Burke, and Sheridan.

Gaitskell Hugh Todd Naylor 1906–1963. British Labour politician. In 1950 he became minister of economic affairs, and then chancellor of the Exchequer until Oct 1951. In 1955 he defeated Aneurin Bevan for the succession to Attlee as party leader, and tried to reconcile internal differences on nationalization and disarmament. He was re-elected leader in 1960.

Galbraith John Kenneth 1908– . Canadian economist of the Keynesian school whose major works include *The Affluent Society* 1958 and *Economics and the Public Purpose* 1974. In the former he argued that industrialized societies like the USA were suffering from private affluence accompanied by public squalor.

Galen AD *c.*130–*c.*200. Greek physician whose ideas dominated Western medicine for almost 1,500 years. Born at Pergamum in Asia Minor, he personally attended the Roman emperor Marcus Aurelius. Central to his thinking were the theories of humours (that human characteristics followed from the balance of the 'humours' – phlegm, blood, choler and melancholy – thought to constitute the body) and the threefold circulation of the blood.

Galen made relatively few discoveries and relied heavily on the teachings of ◊Hippocrates. He wrote a large number of books, over 100 of which are known.

Galileo properly Galileo Galilei 1564–1642. Italian mathematician, astronomer, and physicist. He developed the astronomical telescope and was the first to see sunspots, the four main satellites of Jupiter, mountains and craters on the Moon, and the appearance of Venus going through 'phases', thus proving it was orbiting the Sun. In mechanics, Galileo discovered that freely falling bodies, heavy or light, had the same, constant acceleration (though the story of his dropping cannonballs from the Leaning Tower of Pisa is questionable), and that a body moving on a perfectly smooth horizontal surface would neither speed up nor slow down.

He discovered in 1583 that each oscillation of a pendulum takes the same amount of time despite the difference in amplitude. He invented a hydrostatic balance, and discovered that the path of a projectile was a parabola.

Galileo was born in Pisa, and in 1589 became professor of mathematics at the university there; in 1592 he became a professor at Padua; and in 1610 was appointed chief mathematician to the Grand Duke of Tuscany, Florence. Galileo's observations and arguments were an unwelcome refutation of the ideas of ◊Aristotle taught at the (Church-run) universities, especially because they made plausible for the first time the heliocentric (Sun-centred) theory of ◊Copernicus. Galileo's persuasive *Dialogues on the Two Chief Systems of the World* 1632 was banned by the Church authorities at Rome; he was made to recant by the anti-heretical Inquisition and put under house arrest for his last years.

Gall Franz Joseph 1758–1828. Austrian anatomist, instigator of the discredited theory of phrenology (in which minor variations in skull shape determine a person's character).

Gallé Emile 1846–1904. French Art Nouveau glassmaker. He produced glass in sinuous forms or rounded, solid-looking shapes almost as heavy as stone, typically decorated with flowers or leaves in colour on colour.

After training in various parts of Europe, he worked at his father's glass factory and eventually took it over. A founder of the Ecole de Nancy, he designed furniture as well as achieving significant developments in the techniques of glassmaking.

Galle Johann Gottfried 1812–1910. German astronomer who located the planet Neptune 1846, close to the position predicted by French mathematician Urbain Leverrier.

Gallegos Rómulo 1884–1969. Venezuelan politican and writer. He was Venezuela's first democratically elected president 1948 before being overthrown by a military coup the same year. He was also a

Galileo *The Italian mathematician, astronomer, and physicist, Galileo Galilei.*

professor of philosophy and literature. His novels include *La trepadora/The Climber* 1925 and *Doña Barbara* 1929.

Gallico Paul (William) 1897–1976. US author. Originally a sports columnist, he began writing fiction in 1936. His books include *The Snow Goose* 1941.

Gallup George Horace 1901–1984. US journalist and statistician, founder in 1935 of the American Institute of Public Opinion and deviser of the **Gallup Polls**, in which public opinion is gauged by questioning a number of representative individuals.

Galois Évariste 1811–1832. French mathematician who orginated the theory of groups. Galois was killed in a duel before he was 21. The night before, he had put his unpublished discoveries in writing. Galois's attempts to gain recognition for his work were largely thwarted by the French mathematical establishment, who saw not his genius but his lack of formal qualifications. The importance of his discoveries came to be appreciated later.

Galsworthy John 1867–1933. British novelist and dramatist, whose work examines the social issues of the Victorian period. He is famous for *The Forsyte Saga* 1922, and its sequel *A Modern Comedy* 1929. Other novels include *The Country House* 1907 and *Fraternity* 1909; plays include *The Silver Box* 1906.

Born in Kingston, Surrey, Galsworthy achieved success with *The Man of Property* 1906, the first instalment of the *Forsyte* series 1922, which included *In Chancery* and *To Let*. Soames Forsyte, the central character, is the embodiment of Victorian values and feeling for property, and the wife whom he also 'owns' –

Irene – was based on Galsworthy's wife. Later additions to the series are *A Modern Comedy* 1929, which contained *The White Monkey*, *The Silver Spoon*, and *Swan Song*, and the short stories *On Forsyte Change* 1930.

Galt John 1779–1839. Scottish novelist. He is probably best known for the *Annals of the Parish* 1821 in which he portrays the life of a Lowlands village, using the local dialect.

Born in Ayrshire, he moved to London in 1804 and lived in Canada from 1826 to 1829. He founded the Canadian town of Guelph, and Galt, on the Grand River in Ontario, was named after him.

Galtieri Leopoldo 1926– . Argentinian general. Leading member of the right-wing military junta that ordered the seizure 1982 of the Falkland Islands (Malvinas), a UK colony in the SW Atlantic claimed by Argentina. He and his fellow junta members were tried for abuse of human rights and court-martialled for their conduct of the war; he was sentenced to 12 years in prison in 1986.

Galton Francis 1822–1911. English scientist, noted for his study of the inheritance of physical and mental attributes in humans, and the idea that these could be controlled and improved by selective breeding; this he called eugenics.

Galvani Luigi 1737–1798. Italian physiologist. Born in Bologna, where he taught anatomy, he discovered galvanic or voltaic electricity in 1762, when investigating the contractions produced in the muscles of dead frogs by contact with pairs of different metals. His work led quickly to ◊Volta's invention of the electric battery, and later to an understanding of how nerves control muscles.

Galway James 1939– . Irish flautist, born in Belfast. He was a member of the Berlin Philharmonic Orchestra 1969–75, before taking up a solo career.

Gama Vasco da 1460–1524. Portuguese navigator who commanded an expedition in 1497 to discover the route to India around the Cape of Good Hope in modern South Africa. He reached land on Christmas Day 1497, which he named Natal. He then crossed the Indian Ocean, arriving at Calicut May 1498, and returning to Portugal Sept 1499.

Da Gama was born at Sines, and chosen by Portuguese King Manoel I for his 1497 expedition. In 1502 he founded a Portuguese colony at Mozambique. In the same year he attacked and plundered Calicut in revenge for the murder of some Portuguese seamen. After 20 years of retirement, he was despatched to India again as Portuguese viceroy in 1524, but died two months after his arrival in Goa.

Gamelin Maurice Gustave 1872–1958. French commander in chief of the Allied armies in France 1939. Replaced by Weygand after the German breakthrough at Sedan 1940, he was tried by the collaborationist Vichy government as a scapegoat before the Riom 'war guilt' court 1942. He refused to defend himself and was detained in Germany until released by the Allies 1945.

Gamow George 1904–1968. Soviet cosmologist, nuclear physicist, and popularizer of science. His work in astrophysics included a study of the structure and evolution of stars and the creation of the elements. He also explained how the collision of nuclei in the solar interior could produce the nuclear reactions that power the Sun.

Gance Abel 1889–1981. French film director, whose *Napoléon* 1927 was one of the most ambitious silent epic films, including colour and triple-screen sequences, as well as multiple exposure shots.

Gandhi Indira 1917–1984. Indian politician. Prime minister of India 1966–77 and 1980–84, and leader of the nationalist Congress Party 1966–77 and subsequently of the Congress (I) Party. She

Galtieri President Leopoldo Galtieri of Argentina condemning Britain during the Falklands crisis of 1982.

Gandhi Indira Gandhi, Nehru's daughter, had a controversial political career, during which she was twice prime minister of India.

was assassinated by members of her Sikh bodyguard, resentful of her use of troops to clear mal-
contents from the Sikh temple at Amritsar.

Her father was India's first prime minister
Jawaharlal Nehru. She married 1942 Feroze
Gandhi (died 1960, not related to Mahatma Gandhi)
and had two sons, Sanjay Gandhi (1946–80), who
died in an air crash, and Rajiv Gandhi. In 1975
the validity of her re-election to parliament was
questioned and she declared a state of emergency.
During this time her son Sanjay was implementing
a social and economic programme (including an
unpopular family-planning policy) which led to her
defeat in 1977, though he masterminded her return
to power in 1980.

Gandhi Mohandas Karamchand, called *Mahatma*
('Great Soul') 1869–1948. Indian nationalist leader.
A pacifist, he led the struggle for Indian independence from the UK by nonviolent noncooperation
(*satyagraha*, defence of and by truth) from 1915. He
was several times imprisoned by the British authorities, and was influential in the nationalist Congress
Party and in the independence negotiations 1947.
He was assassinated by a Hindu nationalist in the
violence which followed the Partition of India and
Pakistan.

Gandhi was born in Porbandar and studied in
London where he practised as a barrister. He
settled in South Africa where until 1914 he led
the Indian community in opposition to racial discrimination. Back in India he emerged as leader
of the Indian National Congress and organized
hunger strikes and civil disobedience and campaigned for social reform, including religious tolerance and an end to discrimination against the
so-called untouchable caste.

Gandhi Rajiv 1944– . Indian politician, prime
minister from 1984, following his mother Indira
Gandhi's assassination, to Nov 1989. As prime minister he faced growing discontent with his party's
elitism and lack of concern for social issues.

Rajiv Gandhi initially displayed little interest in
politics and became an airline pilot. But after the
death in a plane crash of his brother *Sanjay*
(1946–80), he was elected to his brother's Amethi
parliamentary seat 1981. In the Dec 1984 parliamentary elections he won a record majority. In
1985 he reached a temporary settlement with
the moderate Sikhs which failed, however, to
hold. His reputation was tarnished by a scandal
concerning alleged 'kick-backs' derived by senior
officials from an arms deal with the Swedish munitions firm Bofors and, following his party's defeat
in the general election of Nov 1989, Gandhi was
forced to resign as premier.

Garbo Greta. Stage name of Greta Lovisa Gustafsson 1905–1990. Swedish film actress. She
went to the USA in 1925, and her leading role
in *The Torrent* 1926 made her one of Hollywood's
first stars. Her later films include *Mata Hari*

Garbo *The Swedish-born actress Greta Garbo in
Anna Christie 1930, her first 'talkie'.*

1931, *Queen Christina* 1933, *Anna Karenina*
1935, and *Ninotchka* 1939.

García Lorca Federico; see ◊Lorca, Federico
García, Spanish poet.

García Márquez Gabriel 1928– . Colombian novelist, whose *Cien años de soledad/One Hundred
Years of Solitude* 1967, the story of six generations of a family, is an example of magic realism, a
technique for heightening the intensity of realistic
portrayal of social and political issues by introducing grotesque or fanciful material. Other books
include *El amor en los tiempos del cólera/Love in
the Time of Cholera* 1985. Nobel Prize for Literature 1982.

García Pérez Alan 1949– . Peruvian politician,
president from 1985 to 1990. Born in Lima and
educated in Peru, Guatemala, Spain and France,
he joined the moderate, left-wing APRA party and
in 1982 became its secretary-general. In 1985
he succeeded Fernando Belaunde as president,
becoming the first civilian to do so in democratic
elections. He inherited an ailing economy and was
forced to trim his socialist programme.

Garcilaso de la Vega 1503–1536. Spanish poet.
A soldier, he was a member of Charles V's
expedition in 1535 to Tunis; he was killed in
battle at Nice. His verse, some of the greatest of the Spanish Renaissance, includes sonnets, songs, and elegies, often on the model of
Petrarch.

Garcilaso de la Vega 1539–1616. Spanish writer,
called *el Inca*. Son of a Spanish conquistador and
an Inca princess, he wrote an account of the conquest of Florida and *Commentarios* on the history
of Peru.

Gardiner Gerald Austin 1900–1990. British lawyer. As Lord Chancellor in the 1964–70 Labour governments, Gardiner introduced the office of Ombudsman (an investigator of complaints about injustice) to Britain, and played a major role in the movement for abolition of capital punishment for murder (which became law in 1965).

Gardiner Stephen c. 1493–1555. English priest and politician. After being secretary to Cardinal Wolsey, he became bishop of Winchester in 1531. An opponent of Protestantism, he was imprisoned under Edward VI, and as Lord Chancellor 1553–55 under Queen Mary he tried to restore Roman Catholicism.

Gardner Ava 1922–1990. US actress, who starred in the 1940s and 1950s in such films as *The Killers* 1946, *Pandora and the Flying Dutchman* 1951 and *The Barefoot Contessa* 1954. She remained active in films until the 1980s.

Gardner Erle Stanley 1889–1970. US author of crime fiction. He created the character of the lawyer-detective Perry Mason, who later featured in film and television versions.

Gardner Helen 1908– . British scholar. She edited the poetry and prose of John Donne, and the *New Oxford Book of English Verse* 1972. She was Merton Professor of English Literature at Oxford 1966–75.

Gardner John 1917– . English composer. Professor at the Royal Academy of Music from 1956, he has produced a symphony 1951, the opera *The Moon and Sixpence* 1957, based on a Somerset Maugham novel; and other works, including film music.

Garfield James A(bram) 1831–1881. 20th president of the USA 1881, a Republican. He was born in a log cabin in Ohio, and served in the American Civil War on the side of the Union. He was elected president but held office for only four months before being assassinated in a Washington station by a disappointed office-seeker.

Garibaldi Giuseppe 1807–1882. Italian soldier who played an important role in the unification of Italy by conquering Sicily and Naples 1860. From 1834 a member of the nationalist Mazzini's Young Italy society, he was forced into exile until 1848 and again 1849–54. He fought against Austria 1848–49, 1859, and 1866, and led two unsuccessful expeditions to liberate Rome from papal rule in 1862 and 1867.

Born in Nice, he became a sailor, and then joined in the *Risorgimento* nationalist movement. Condemned to death for treason, he escaped to South America where he became a mercenary. He returned to Italy during the 1848 revolution, served with the Sardinian army against the Austrians, and commanded the army of the Roman republic in its defence of the city against the French. He subsequently lived in exile until 1854, when he settled on the island of Caprera. In 1860,

at the head of his 1,000 redshirts, he won Sicily and Naples for the new kingdom of Italy. He served in the Austrian War of 1866, and fought for France in the Franco-Prussian War 1870–71.

Garland Judy. Stage name of Frances Gumm 1922–1969. US singer and actress, whose films include *The Wizard of Oz* 1939 (including the song 'Over the Rainbow'), *Meet Me in St Louis* 1944, and *A Star is Born* 1954. Her unhappy personal life led to her early death from alcohol and drug addiction.

Garret Almeida 1799–1854. Portuguese poet, novelist, and dramatist. As a liberal, in 1823 he was forced into 14 years of exile. His works, which he saw as a singlehanded attempt to create a national literature, include the prose *Viagens na Minha Terra/Travels in my Homeland* 1843–46, and the tragedy *Frei Luis de Sousa* 1843.

Garrick David 1717–1779. British actor and theatre manager. He was a pupil of Samuel ◊Johnson. From 1747 he became joint licensee of the Drury Lane theatre with his own company, and instituted a number of significant theatrical conventions including concealed stage lighting and banishing spectators from the stage. He performed Shakespeare characters such as Richard III, King Lear, Hamlet, and Benedick. He collaborated with Colman in writing the play *The Clandestine Marriage* 1766. He retired from the stage 1766, but continued as a manager.

Garrod Archibald Edward 1857–1937. English physician who first recognized a class of metabolic diseases, while studying the rare disease

Garibaldi *Italian hero of the* Risorgimento, *Giuseppe Garibaldi.*

alcaptonuria, in which the patient's urine turns black on contact with air. He calculated that the cause was a failure of the body's metabolism to break down certain amino acids into harmless substances like water and carbon dioxide.

Garvey Marcus (Moziah) 1887–1940. Jamaican political thinker and activist, an early advocate of black nationalism. He founded the UNIA (Universal Negro Improvement Association) in 1914, and moved to the USA in 1916, where he established branches in New York and other northern cities. Aiming to achieve human rights and dignity for black people through black pride and economic self-sufficiency, he led a *Back to Africa* movement for black Americans to establish a black-governed country in Africa. The Rastafarian religion is based largely on his ideas.

Gaskell 'Mrs' (Elizabeth Cleghorn) (born Stevenson) 1810 1865. British novelist. Her books include *Mary Barton* (set in industrial Manchester) 1848, *Cranford* (set in the town in which she was brought up, Knutsford, Cheshire) 1853, *North and South* 1855, *Sylvia's Lovers* 1863–64, the unfinished *Wives and Daughters* 1866, and a life of her friend Charlotte ◊Brontë.

Gasperi Alcide de 1881–1954. Italian politician. A founder of the Christian Democrat Party, he was prime minister 1945–53, and worked for European unification.

Gassendi Pierre 1592–1655. French physicist and philosopher who played a crucial role in the revival of atomism, and the rejection of Aristotelianism so characteristic of the period. He was a propagandist and critic of other views rather than an original thinker.

Gatling Richard Jordan 1818–1903. US inventor of a rapid-fire gun. Patented in 1862, the *Gatling gun* had ten barrels arranged as a cylinder rotated by a hand crank.

Gaudier-Brzeska Henri 1891–1915. French sculptor, active in London from 1911. He studied art in Bristol, Nuremberg, and Munich, and became a member of the English Vorticist movement, which sought to reflect the Industrial age by a sense of motion and angularity. From 1913 his sculptures showed the influence of Brancusi and Epstein. He died in World War I.

Gauguin Paul 1848–1903. French Post-Impressionist painter. After a few years as a stockbroker, he took up full-time painting, exhibited with the Impressionists, and spent two months with van ◊Gogh in Arles 1888. On his return to Brittany he concentrated on his new style, *Synthetism*, based on the use of powerful, expressive colours and boldly outlined areas of flat tone. He went to live in Tahiti 1891–93 and 1895–1901 and from 1901 in the Marquesas Islands. Influenced by Symbolism, he chose subjects reflecting his interest in the beliefs of other cultures.

Born in Paris, Gauguin joined a banking firm, but gave up his career 1881 in order to paint. After a visit to Martinique 1887, he went to Pont Aven in Brittany, becoming the leading artist in the Synthetic movement, and abandoning conventional perspective. In 1891 he left Paris for Tahiti, where he remained from 1895 until his death. Going beyond the Impressionists' notion of reality, he sought a more direct experience of life in the magical rites of the people and rich colours of the islands. A friend of van Gogh, he disliked theories and rules of painting, and his pictures are Expressionist compositions characterized by his use of pure, unmixed colours. Among his most famous paintings is *Le Christe Jaune* 1889 (Albright-Knox Art Gallery, Buffalo, USA).

Gaulle Charles de See Charles ◊de Gaulle.

Gauss Karl Friedrich 1777–1855. German mathematician who worked on the theory of numbers, non-Euclidian geometry, and on the mathematical development of electric and magnetic theory.

Gautama family name of the historical ◊Buddha.

Gautier Théophile 1811–1872. French Romantic poet, whose later work emphasized the perfection of form and the 'polished' beauty of language and imagery (for example, *Emaux et Camées/Enamels and Cameos* 1852). He was also a novelist (*Mlle de Maupin* 1835) and later in his life turned to journalism.

Gavaskar Sunil Manohar 1949–   . Indian cricketer. Between 1971 and 1987 he scored a record 10,122 test runs in a record 125 matches (including 106 consecutive tests).

Gay John 1685–1732. British poet and dramatist. He was the friend of ◊Pope and Arbuthnot, and wrote *Trivia* 1716, a verse picture of 18th-century London. His *The Beggar's Opera* 1728, a 'Newgate pastoral' using traditional songs and telling of the love of Polly for highwayman Captain Macheath, was an extraordinarily popular success. Its satiric political touches led to the banning of *Polly*, a sequel.

Gaye Marvin 1939–1984. US soul singer and songwriter, whose hits, including 'I Heard It Through the Grapevine' 1968, and 'What's Goin' On' 1971, exemplified the Detroit Motown sound. He was killed by his father.

Gay-Lussac Joseph Louis 1778–1850. French physicist and chemist, who investigated the physical properties of gases, and discovered new methods of producing sulphuric and oxalic acids. In 1802 he discovered the approximate rule for the expansion of gases now known as Charles's Law.

Geber Latinized form of Jabir ibn Hayyan c.721–c.776. Arabian alchemist. His influence lasted for more than 600 years, and in the late 1300s his name was adopted by a Spanish alchemist whose writings spread the knowledge and practice of alchemy throughout Europe.

The Spanish alchemist Geber probably discovered nitric and sulphuric acids, and he propounded a theory that all metals are composed of various mixtures of mercury and sulphur.

Geddes Patrick 1854–1932. Scottish town planner, who established the importance of surveys, research work, and properly-planned 'diagnoses before treatment'. His major work is *City Development* 1904.

Gehry Frank 1929– . US architect, based in Los Angeles. His architecture approaches abstract art in its use of collage and montage techniques.

His own experimental house at Santa Monica (1977), Edgemar Shopping Center and Museum, Santa Monica (1988), and the Vitra Furniture Museum (1989) – his first building in Europe – demonstrate his vitality.

Geiger Hans 1882–1945. German physicist who produced the Geiger counter. After studying in Germany, he spent the period 1907–12 in Manchester, working with Ernest ◊Rutherford. In 1908 they designed an instrument to detect alpha particles, given off by some radioactive materials, which was refined and made more powerful to produce the Geiger counter in the 1920s.

Geldof Bob 1954– . Irish fundraiser and rock singer. He instigated the charity Band Aid, which raised large sums of money for famine relief, especially in Ethiopia, by recording a song, 'Do They Know It's Christmas?' 1984, and staging two simultaneous concerts (Live Aid) 1985, one in London and one in Philadelphia, broadcast live worldwide.

Gell-Mann Murray 1929– . US physicist. In 1964, he formulated the theory of the quark, the fundamental constituent of all matter, and smallest particle in the universe.

He was R A Millikan professor of theoretical physics at the Californian Institute of Technology from 1967. In 1969, he was awarded a Nobel prize for his work on elementary particles and their interaction.

Gemayel Amin 1942– . Lebanese politician, a Maronite Christian; president 1982–88. He succeeded his brother, president-elect **Bechir Gemayel**, on his assassination on 14 Sept 1982.

Genée Adeline. Stage name of Anina Jensen 1878–1970. Danish-born British dancer, president of the Royal Academy of Dancing 1920–54.

Genet Jean 1910–1986. French dramatist, novelist, and poet, an exponent of the Theatre of Cruelty. His turbulent life and early years spent in prison are reflected in his drama, characterized by ritual, role-play, and illusion, in which his characters come to act out their bizarre and violent fantasies. His plays include *Les Bonnes/The Maids* 1947, *Le Balcon/The Balcony* 1957, and two plays dealing with the Algerian situation: *Les Nègres/The Blacks* 1959, and *Les Paravents/The Screens* 1961.

Genghis Khan *c.*1160–1227. Mongol conqueror, ruler of all Mongol peoples from 1206. He began the conquest of N China 1213, overran the empire of the shah of Khiva 1219–25, and invaded N India, while his lieutenants advanced as far as the Crimea. When he died his empire ranged from the Yellow Sea to the Black Sea.

Temujin, as he was originally called, was the son of a chieftain. After a long struggle he established his supremacy over all the Mongols, when he assumed the title of Chingis or 'perfect warrior'. The ruins of his capital Karakorum are SW of Ulaanbaatar in Mongolia; his alleged remains are preserved at Ejin Horo, Inner Mongolia.

Genscher Hans-Dietrich 1927– . West German politician, chairman of the Free Democratic Party (FDP) 1974–85, foreign minister from 1974.

Born in Halle, Genscher settled in West Germany 1952. He served as interior minister 1969–74 and then as foreign minister, committed to Ostpolitik (rapprochement with the Communist East) and European cooperation. As FDP leader, Genscher masterminded the party's switch of allegiance from the Social Democratic Party to the Christian Democratic Union which resulted in the downfall of the ◊Schmidt government *c.*1982.

Gentile da Fabriano *c.*1370–1427. Italian painter of frescoes and altarpieces in the International Gothic style. *The Adoration of the Magi* 1423 (Uffizi, Florence) is typically rich in detail and crammed with courtly figures.

Gentile was active in Venice, Florence, Siena, Orvieto, and Rome, and collaborated with the artists Pisanello and Jacopo Bellini. His drawings suggest that he was aware of the new concerns of the Renaissance.

Gentileschi Artemisia 1593–*c.*1652. Italian painter, born in Rome. She trained under her father Orazio Gentileschi, but her work is more melodramatic than his. She settled in Naples from about 1630, and focused on macabre and grisly subjects such as *Judith Decapitating Holofernes* (Museo di Capodimonte, Naples).

Gentileschi Orazio 1563–1637. Italian painter, born in Pisa. From 1626 he lived in London, painting for King Charles I. Like most of his contemporaries, he was influenced by Caravaggio's dramatic treatment of light and shade, as in *The Annunciation* 1623 (Turin).

Gentili Alberico 1552–1608. Italian jurist. He practised law in Italy, but having adopted Protestantism was compelled to flee to England, where he lectured on Roman Law in Oxford. His publications, such as *De Jure Belli libri tres/On The Law Of War, Book Three* 1598, made him the first true international law writer and scholar.

Geoffrey of Monmouth *c.*1100–1154. Welsh writer and chronicler. While a canon at Oxford, he wrote *Historia Regum Britanniae/History of the Kings of Britain c.*1139, which included accounts of the semi-legendary kings Lear, Cymbeline, and Arthur, and *Vita Merlini*, a life of the legendary wizard.

George Henry 1839–1897. US economist, born in Philadelphia. His *Progress and Poverty* 1879 suggested a 'single tax' on land, to replace all other taxes on earnings and savings. He hoped such a land tax would abolish poverty, by ending speculation on land values. George's ideas have never been implemented thoroughly, although they have influenced taxation policy in many countries.

George Stefan 1868–1933. German poet. His early poetry was influenced by French Symbolism, but his concept of himself as regenerating the German spirit first appears in *Des Teppich des Lebens/The Tapestry of Life* 1899, and later in *Der siebente Ring/The Seventh Ring* 1907.

Das neue Reich/The New Empire 1928 shows his realization that World War I had not had the right purifying effect on German culture. He rejected Nazi overtures and emigrated to Switzerland 1933.

George six kings of Great Britain:

George I 1660–1727. King of Great Britain from 1714. He was the son of the first elector of Hanover, Ernest Augustus (1629–1698), and his wife ◊Sophia, and a great-grandson of James I. He succeeded to the electorate 1698, and became king on the death of Queen Anne. He attached himself to the Whigs, and spent most of his reign in Hanover, never having learned English.

He was heir through his father to the hereditary lay bishopric of Osnabrück, and the duchy of Calenberg, which was one part of the Hanoverian possessions of the house of Brunswick. He acquired the other part by his marriage to *Sophia Dorothea of Zell* (1666–1726) in 1682. They were divorced 1694, and she remained in seclusion until her death. George's children were George II, and *Sophia Dorothea* (1687–1757), who married Frederick William (later king of Prussia) 1706, and was the mother of Frederick the Great.

George II 1683–1760. King of Great Britain from 1727, when he succeeded his father, George I. His victory at Dettingen 1743, in the War of the Austrian Succession, was the last battle commanded by a British king. He married Caroline of Anspach 1705. He was succeeded by his grandson George III.

George III 1738–1820. King of Great Britain from 1760, when he succeeded his grandfather George II. He supported his ministers in a hard line towards the American colonies, and opposed Catholic emancipation and other reforms. Possibly suffering from porphyria, he had repeated attacks of insanity, permanent from 1811. (Porphyria is a rare hereditary metabolic disorder causing, among other things, mental confusion.) He was

succeeded by his son George IV. He married Princess ◊Charlotte Sophia of Mecklenburg-Strelitz in 1761.

George IV 1762–1830. King of Great Britain from 1820, when he succeeded his father George III, for whom he had been regent during the king's insanity 1811–20. Strictly educated, he reacted by entering into a life of debauchery, and in 1785 married a Catholic widow, Mrs ◊Fitzherbert, but in 1795 also married Princess ◊Caroline of Brunswick, in return for payment of his debts. He attempted to divorce her on charges of adultery, but this was dropped after Parliament passed the necessary bill with increasingly smaller majorities. He had one child, Charlotte, who died in childbirth 1817. He was succeeded by his brother, the duke of Clarence, who became William IV.

George V 1865–1936. King of Great Britain from 1910, when he succeeded his father Edward VII. He was the second son, and became heir 1892 on the death of his elder brother, Duke of Clarence. In 1893, he married Princess Victoria Mary of Teck (Queen Mary), formerly engaged to his brother. During World War I he made several visits to the front. In 1917, he abandoned all German titles for himself and his family. The name of the royal house was changed from Saxe-Coburg-Gotha (popularly known as Brunowick or Hanover) to Windsor.

George VI 1895–1952. King of Great Britain from 1936, when he succeeded after the abdication of his brother Edward VIII, who had succeeded their father, George V. Created Duke of York 1920, he married in 1923 Lady Elizabeth Bowes-Lyon (1900–), and their children are Elizabeth II and

George VI *George VI succeeded to the throne after the unexpected abdication of his brother, Edward VIII, in 1936.*

Princess Margaret. During World War II, he visited the Normandy and Italian battlefields.

George two kings of Greece:

George I 1845–1913. King of Greece 1863–1913.
The son of king Christian IX of Denmark, he was
nominated to the Greek throne and, in spite of
early unpopularity, became a highly successful
constitutional monarch. He was assassinated by
a Greek, Schinas, at Salonika.

George II 1890–1947. King of Greece 1922–23
and 1935–47. He became king on the expulsion
of his father Constantine I 1922, but was himself overthrown 1923. Restored by the military
1935, he set up a dictatorship under Metaxas,
and went into exile during the German occupation
1941–45.

George, St patron saint of England. The story of
St George rescuing a woman by slaying a dragon,
evidently derived from the legendary Perseus,
slayer of Medusa the Gorgon, first appears in
the 6th century AD. The cult of St George was
introduced into W Europe by the Crusaders. His
feast day is 23 Apr.

He is said to have been martyred at Lydda
in Palestine 303, probably under the Roman
Emperor Diocletian, but the other elements of
his legend are of doubtful historical accuracy.

Gerald of Wales English name of ◊Giraldus
Cambrensis, medieval Welsh bishop and historian.

Gerhard Roberto 1896–1970. Spanish-British
composer. He studied with ◊Granados and
◊Schoenberg and settled in England 1939, where
he composed twelve-tone works in Spanish style.
He composed the *Symphony No 1* 1952–5, followed
by three more symphonies and chamber music.

Géricault (Jean Louis André) Théodore 1791–1824.
French Romantic painter. *The Raft of the Medusa*
1819 (Louvre, Paris) was notorious for exposing
a relatively recent scandal in which shipwrecked
sailors had been cut adrift and left to drown.

A keen horseman himself (he was killed in a
riding accident), he painted *The Derby at Epsom*
1821 (Louvre, Paris) and pictures of cavalry. He
also painted portraits.

Germain Sophie 1776–1831. French mathematician, born in Paris. Although she was not allowed
to study at the newly opened École Polytechnique,
she corresponded with ◊Lagrange and ◊Gauss.
She is remembered for work she carried out in
studying ◊Fermat's last theorem.

German Edward 1862–1936. English composer.
He is remembered for his operettas *Merrie England* 1902 and *Tom Jones* 1907, and he wrote
many instrumental, orchestral and vocal works.

Germanicus Caesar 15 BC–AD 19. Roman general. He was the adopted son of the emperor
◊Tiberius and married the emperor ◊Augustus'
granddaughter Agrippina. Although he refused the
suggestion of his troops that he claim the throne

Geronimo *Apache Indian Chief Geronimo who fought
a rearguard action to protect tribal lands. Pictured here
after his surrender, he became a Christian farmer in
Oklahoma.*

on the death of Augustus, his military victories
in Germany made Tiberius jealous. Sent to the
East, he died near Antioch, possibly murdered at
the instigation of Tiberius. He was the father of
◊Caligula, and of Agrippina, mother of ◊Nero.

Geronimo 1829–1909. Chief of the Chiricahua
Apache Indians and war leader. From 1875 to
1885, he fought US federal troops and settlers
encroaching on tribal reservations in the South-
west, especially SE Arizona and New Mexico.
After surrendering to Gen George Crook Mar
1886, and agreeing to go to Florida where their
families were being held, Geronimo and his followers escaped. Captured again Aug 1886, they
were taken to Florida, then to Alabama. The
climate proved unhealthy, and they were taken
to Fort Sill, Oklahoma, where Geronimo became
a farmer. He dictated *Geronimo's Story of His
Life* 1906.

Gershwin George 1898–1937. US composer, who
wrote the tone poem *An American in Paris* 1928,
Rhapsody in Blue 1924, and the opera *Porgy and
Bess* 1935, in which he incorporated the essen-
tials of jazz. He also wrote popular songs with his
brother, the lyricist **Ira Gershwin** (1896–1983).

Gerson Jean 1363–1429. French theologian. He
was leader of the concilliar movement, and
denounced ◊Huss at the Council of Constance
1415. His theological works greatly influenced
15th-century thought.

Gertler Mark 1891–1939. English painter. He was
a pacifist and a noncombatant during World War I;

Getty *Tycoon and oil millionaire John Paul Getty, who devoted much of his personal fortune to art collecting.*

his *Merry-Go-Round* 1916 (Tate Gallery, London) is often seen as an expressive symbol of militarism.

Getty J(ean) Paul 1892-1976. US oil billionaire, president of the Getty Oil Company from 1947, and founder of the *Getty Museum* (housing the world's highest funded art gallery) in Malibu, California. In 1985 his son *John Paul Getty Jr* (1932-) established an endowment fund of £50 million for the National Gallery, London.

Getz Stan(ley) 1927- . US tenor saxophonist of the 1950s 'cool jazz' school. He was the first US musician to be closely identified with the Latin American *bossa nova* sound.

Ghazzali, al- 1058-1111. Muslim philosopher and one of the most famous Sufis (Muslim mystics). He was responsible for easing the conflict between the Sufi and the Ulema, a body of Muslim religious and legal scholars.

Initially, he believed that God's existence could be proved by reason, but later he became a wandering Sufi, seeking God through mystical experience; the book *The Alchemy of Happiness* was written on his travels.

Gheorgiu-Dej Gheorge 1901-1965. Romanian communist politician. A member of the Romanian Communist Party from 1930, he played a leading part in establishing a communist regime in 1945. He was prime minister 1952-55 and state president 1961-65. Although retaining the support of Moscow, he adopted an increasingly independent line during his final years.

Ghiberti Lorenzo 1378-1455. Italian sculptor and goldsmith. In 1401 he won the commission for a pair of gilded bronze doors for Florence's baptistry. He produced a second pair (1425-52), the *Gates of Paradise*, one of the masterpieces of the Early Italian Renaissance. They show sophisticated composition and use of perspective.

He also wrote *Commentarii/Commentaries*, a mixture of art history, manual, and autobiography.

Ghirlandaio Domenico *c*.1449-1494. Italian fresco painter, head of a large and prosperous workshop in Florence. His fresco cycle 1486-90 in S Maria Novella, Florence includes portraits of many Florentines and much contemporary domestic detail. He also worked in Pisa, Rome, and San Gimignano, and painted portraits.

Giacometti Alberto 1901-1966. Swiss sculptor and painter, who trained in Italy and Paris. In the 1930s, in his Surrealist period, he began to develop his characteristic spindly constructions. His mature style of emaciated single figures, based on wire frames, emerged in the 1940s. Some are so elongated that they seem almost without volume. *Man Pointing* 1947 is one of many examples in the Tate Gallery, London.

Giambologna Giovanni da Bologna or Jean de Boulogne 1529-1608. Flemish-born sculptor active mainly in Florence and Bologna. In 1583 he completed his public commission for the Loggia dei Lanzi in Florence, *The Rape of the Sabine Women*, a dynamic group of muscular figures and a prime example of Mannerist sculpture.

Gibberd Frederick 1908-1984. British architect and town planner. His works include the new towns of Harlow, England, and Santa Teresa, Venezuela; the Catholic Cathedral, Liverpool; and the Central London mosque in Regent's Park.

Gibbon Edward 1737-1794. British historian, author of *The History of the Decline and Fall of the Roman Empire* 1776-88.

The work was a continuous narrative from the 2nd century AD to the fall of Constantinople in 1453, on which he began work while in Rome in 1764. Although immediately sucessful, he was compelled to reply to attacks on his account of the early development of Christianity by a *Vindication* 1779. From 1783 Gibbon had lived in Lausanne, Switzerland, but he returned to England and died in London.

Gibbon John Heysham 1903-1974. US surgeon who invented the heart-lung machine in 1953. It has since become indispensable in heart surgery, maintaining the circulation while the heart is temporarily inactivated.

Gibbon Lewis Grassic, pen name of James Leslie Mitchell 1901-1935. Scottish novelist, author of the trilogy *A Scots Quair: Sunset Song, Cloud Howe,* and *Grey Granite* 1932-34, set in the area S of Aberdeen, the Mearns, where he was born and brought up. Under his real name he wrote *Stained Radiance* 1930 and *Spartacus* 1933.

Gibbons Grinling 1648–1721. British woodcarver, born in Rotterdam. He produced carved wooden panels (especially of birds, flowers, and fruit) for St Paul's Cathedral, London, and for many aristocratic houses, including Petworth House, Sussex. He became master carver to George I in 1741.

Gibbons Orlando 1583–1625. English composer. A member of a family of musicians, he was appointed organist at Westminster Abbey in 1623. His finest works are his madrigals and motets.

Gibbons Stella Dorothea 1902–1989. English journalist. She is remembered for her *Cold Comfort Farm* 1932, a classic satire on the regional novel.

Gibson Cameron Michael Henderson ('Mike') 1942– . Irish rugby player. He made a world record 81 international appearances 1964–79; 69 for Ireland and 12 for the British Lions on a record five tours. Of his 69 Ireland caps, 40 were played as centre, 25 at outside-half, and 4 on the wing.

Gibson Charles Dana 1867–1944. US illustrator. He portrayed an idealized type of American young woman, known as the 'Gibson Girl'.

Gide André 1869–1951. French novelist, born in Paris. His work is largely autobiographical and concerned with the themes of self-fulfilment and renunciation. It includes *L'Immoraliste/The Immoralist* 1902, *La Porte étroite/Strait is the Gate* 1909, *Les Caves du Vatican/The Vatican Cellars* 1914, and *Les Faux-monnayeurs/The Counterfeiters* 1926; and an almost lifelong *Journal*. Nobel Prize for Literature 1947.

Gielgud John 1904– . English actor and director. He played many Shakespearean roles, including Hamlet 1929. Film roles include Clarence in *Richard III* 1955 and the butler in *Arthur* 1981 (for which he won an Oscar).

Gielgud made his debut at the Old Vic 1921. Though probably best known as a Shakespearean actor, his numerous stage appearances include performances in plays by Chekhov and Sheridan, and in works by playwrights Alan Bennett, Peter Shaffer, and David Storey. Other films include *Becket* 1964, *Oh! What a Lovely War* 1969, and *Providence* 1977.

Gierek Edward 1913– . Polish Communist politician. He entered the Politburo of the ruling Polish United Workers' Party (PUWP) in 1956 and was party leader 1970–80.

Gierek, a miner's son, lived in France and Belgium for much of the period between 1923 and 1948, becoming a member of the Belgian Resistance. He served as party boss in Silesia during the 1960s. After replacing Gomulka as PUWP leader in Dec 1970, he embarked on an ambitious programme of industrialization. A wave of strikes in Warsaw and Gdańsk, spearheaded by Solidarity, forced Gierek to resign in Sept 1980.

Giffard Henri 1825–1882. French inventor of the first passenger-carrying dirigible (steerable airship), built 1852. The hydrogen-filled airship was 45 m/150 ft long, had a 3 hp steam engine which drove a propeller, and flew at a speed of 8 kph/5 mph.

Gigli Beniamino 1890–1957. Italian lyric tenor. Following his operatic debut in 1914 he performed roles by Puccini, Gounod, and Massenet.

Gilbert Alfred 1854–1934. British sculptor, whose statue of *Eros* in Piccadilly Circus, London, was erected as a memorial to the 7th Earl of Shaftesbury.

Gilbert Cass 1859–1934. US architect, born in Ohio, who became known for his skyscrapers, including the Woolworth Building in New York 1913.

Gilbert Humphrey *c.*1539–1583. English soldier and navigator who claimed Newfoundland (landing at St John's) for Elizabeth I in 1583. He died when his ship sank on the return voyage.

Gilbert Walter 1932– . US molecular biologist. Gilbert worked on the problem of genetic control, seeking the mechanisms which switch genes on and off. By 1966 he had established the existence of the lac repressor, the molecule which suppressed lactose production. Further work on the sequencing of DNA nucleotides won for Gilbert a share of the 1980 Nobel Chemistry Prize with Frederick Sanger and Paul Berg.

Gilbert William 1544–1603. Scientist and physician to Elizabeth I and (briefly) James I. He studied magnetism and static electricity, deducing that the Earth's magnetic field behaves as if a huge bar magnet joined the North and South poles. His book on magnets, published 1600, is the first printed scientific book based wholly on experimentation and observation.

Gilbert W(illiam) S(chwenk) 1836–1911. British humorist and dramatist who collaborated with Arthur ◊Sullivan, providing the libretti for their series of light comic operas from 1871; they include *HMS Pinafore* 1878, *The Pirates of Penzance* 1879, and *The Mikado* 1885.

Born in London, he was called to the Bar in 1863, but in 1869 published a collection of his humorous verse and drawings, *Bab Ballads* – 'Bab' being his own early nickname – which was followed by a second volume in 1873.

Gilbert and George Gilbert Proesch 1943– and George Passmore 1942– . English painters and performance artists. They became known in the 1960s for their presentation of themselves as works of art, *living sculpture*. Their art works make much use of photography.

Giles Carl Ronald 1916– . British cartoonist for the *Daily* and *Sunday Express* from 1943, noted for his creation of a family with a formidable 'Grandma'.

Gill Eric 1882–1940. English sculptor and engraver. He designed the typefaces Perpetua 1925 and Gill Sans (without serifs) 1927, and created monumental stone sculptures with clean, simplified outlines, such as *Prospero and Ariel* 1929–31 (on Broadcasting House, London).

He studied lettering at the Central School of Art in London under Edward Johnston, and began his career carving inscriptions for tombstones. Gill was a leader in the revival of interest in the craft of lettering and book design.

Gillespie Dizzy. Stage name of John Birks Gillespie 1917– . US jazz trumpeter, together with Charlie Parker the chief creator and exponent of the bebop style.

Gillette King Camp 1855–1932. US inventor of the Gillette safety-razor.

Gillray James 1757–1815. English caricaturist. His 1,500 cartoons, 1779–1811, satirized the French, George III, politicians, and social follies of his day.

Gilpin William 1724–1804. British artist. He is remembered for his essays on the 'picturesque', which set out precise rules for the production of this effect.

Ginner Charles 1878–1952. British painter. He settled in London in 1910, and from 1914 was one of the London Group set up in 1913. It included followers of Vorticism, which sought to portray the industrialized world by a sense of movement and angularity, and members of the Post-Impressionist Camden Town group. He painted street scenes and landscapes.

Ginsberg Allen 1926– . US poet. His 'Howl' 1956 was an influential poem of the beat generation, criticizing the materialism of contemporary US society. In the 1960s Ginsberg travelled widely in Asia, and was a key figure in introducing Eastern thought to students of that decade.

Giolitti Giovanni 1842–1928. Italian liberal politician, born in Mondovi. He was prime minister in 1892–93, 1903–05, 1906–09, 1911–14, and 1920–21. He opposed Italian intervention in World War I, and pursued a policy of broad coalitions, which proved ineffective in controlling Fascism after 1921.

Giono Jean 1895–1970. French novelist, whose books are chiefly set in Provence. *Que ma joie demeure/Joy of Man's Desiring* 1935, is an attack on life in towns and a plea for a return to country life.

Giordano Luca 1632–1705. Italian Baroque painter, born in Naples, active in Florence in the 1680s. In 1692 he was summoned to Spain by Charles II, and painted ceilings in the Escorial palace for the next ten years.

In Florence Giordano painted a ceiling in the Palazzo Riccardi-Medici 1682–83. He also produced altarpieces and frescoes for churches.

Giorgione del Castelfranco *c.*1475–1510. Italian Renaissance painter, active in Venice, probably trained by Giovanni Bellini. His work influenced Titian and other Venetian painters. His subjects are imbued with a sense of mystery and treated with a soft technique reminiscent of Leonardo da Vinci's later works, as in *Tempest* 1504 (Accademia, Venice).

Giotto di Bondone 1267–1337. Italian painter and architect. He broke away from the conventional Gothic style of the time, and had an enormous influence on subsequent Italian painting.

Giotto was born in Vespignano, N of Florence. He introduced a naturalistic style, painting saints as real people. His most famous works are cycles of frescoes in churches at Assisi, Florence, and Padua. Giotto's figures occupy a definite pictorial space, and there is an unusual emotional intensity and dignity in the presentation of the story. In one of the series of frescoes he painted for the Arena Chapel, Padua, he made the Star of Bethlehem appear as a comet (Halley's comet had appeared 1303, just two years before). From 1334 he was official architect to Florence, and from 1335 overseer of works at the cathedral; he collaborated with Andrea ◊Pisano in decorating the cathedral facade with statues, and designing the campanile which was completed after his death.

Giraldus Cambrensis *c.*1146–1220. Welsh historian, born in Pembrokeshire. He was elected bishop of St David's in 1198. He wrote a history of the conquest of Ireland by Henry II, and *Itinerarium Cambriae* (Journey through Wales) 1191.

Girardon François 1628–1715. French academic sculptor. His *Apollo Tended by Nymphs*, commissioned 1666, is one of several marble groups sculpted for the gardens of Louis XIV's palace at Versailles.

Giraudoux (Hippolyte) Jean 1882–1944. French playwright and novelist, who wrote the plays *Amphitryon 38* 1929 and *La Folle de Chaillot/The Madwoman of Chaillot* 1945, and the novel *Suzanne et la Pacifique/Suzanne and the Pacific* 1921.

Other plays include *La Guerre de Troie n'aura pas lieu/Tiger at the Gates* 1935.

Girtin Thomas 1775–1802. English painter of watercolour landscapes, a friend of J M W Turner.

Giscard d'Estaing Valéry 1926– . French conservative politician, president 1974–81. He was finance minister to de Gaulle 1962–66 and Pompidou 1969–74. As leader of the Union pour la Démocratie Française, which he formed in 1978, Giscard has sought to project himself as leader of a 'new centre'.

Giscard was active in the wartime Resistance. After a distinguished academic career, he worked in the Ministry of Finance and entered the National

Assembly for Puy de Dôme in 1956 as an Independent Republican. After Pompidou's death he was narrowly elected president in 1974, in difficult economic circumstances; he was defeated by the socialist Mitterrand in 1981. He returned to the National Assembly in 1984. In 1989 he resigned from the National Assembly to play a leading role in the European Parliament.

Gish Lillian. Stage name of Lillian de Guiche 1896– . US film actress, who began her career in silent films. Her most celebrated work was with the American director D W Griffith, including *Way Down East* 1920 and *Orphans of the Storm* 1922, playing virtuous heroines. She later made occasional appearances in character roles, as in *The Whales of August* 1987.

Gissing George (Robert) 1857–1903. English writer, dealing with social issues. Among his books are *New Grub Street* 1891 and the autobiographical *Private Papers of Henry Ryecroft* 1903.

Giulini Carlo Maria 1914– . Italian conductor. Principal conductor at La Scala in Milan 1953–55, and musical director of the Los Angeles Philharmonic 1978–84, he is renowned as an interpreter of Verdi.

Giulio Romano *c.*1499–1546. Italian painter and architect. An assistant to Raphael, he soon developed Mannerist tendencies, creating effects of exaggerated movement and using rich colours, for example in the Palazzo del Tè (1526 Mantua).

Gladstone William Ewart 1809–1898. British Liberal politician.

Gladstone was born in Liverpool, the son of a rich merchant. In Peel's government he was president of the Board of Trade 1843–45, and colonial secretary 1845–46. He left the Tory Party with the Peelite group in 1846. He was chancellor of the Exchequer in Aberdeen's government 1852–55, and in the Liberal governments of Palmerston and Russell 1859–66. In his first term as prime minister he carried through a series of important reforms, including the disestablishment of the Church of Ireland, the Irish Land Act, and the abolition of the purchase of army commissions and of religious tests in the universities.

During Disraeli's government of 1874–80 Gladstone strongly resisted his imperialist and pro-Turkish policy, not least because of Turkish pogroms against subject Christians, and by his Midlothian campaign of 1879 helped to overthrow Disraeli. Gladstone's second government carried the second Irish Land Act and the Reform Act 1884 but was confronted with difficult problems in Ireland, Egypt, and South Africa, and lost prestige through its failure to relieve General ◊Gordon. Returning to office in 1886, Gladstone introduced his first Home Rule Bill, which was defeated by the secession of the Liberal Unionists, and he thereupon resigned. After six years' opposition he formed his last government; his second Home

Gladstone 19th-century British Liberal politician William Gladstone.

Rule Bill was rejected by the Lords, and in 1894 he resigned. He led a final crusade against the massacre of Armenian Christians in 1896.

Glanville Ranalf died 1190. English justiciar from 1180, and legal writer. His *Treatise on the Laws and Customs of England* 1188 was written to instruct practising lawyers and judges, and is now an important historical source on medieval Common Law.

Glaser Donald Arthur 1926– . US physicist, who in 1952 invented the bubble chamber to detect and record interacting atomic particles, for which he received a Nobel prize in 1960.

Glasgow Ellen 1873–1945. US novelist. Her books, set mainly in her native Virginia, often deal with the survival of tough heroines in a world of adversity. Among the best known are *Barren Ground* 1925, *The Sheltered Life* 1932, and *Vein of Iron* 1935.

Glashow Sheldon 1933– . US theoretical physicist. He shared the 1979 Nobel Prize for Physics with Abdus ◊Salam and Steven ◊Weinberg for their work demonstrating that weak nuclear force and the electromagnetic force are both aspects of a single force, now called the *electroweak* force.

Glass Philip 1937– . US composer. As a student of Nadia ◊Boulanger, he was strongly influenced by Indian music; his work is characterized by repeated rhythmic figures that are continually expanded and modified. His compositions include the operas *Einstein on the Beach* 1975, *Akhnaten* 1984, and *The Making of the Representative for Planet 8* 1988.

Glasse Hannah 1708–1770. British cookery writer whose *The Art of Cookery made Plain and Easy* 1747 is regarded as the first classic recipe book in Britain.

Glauber Johann 1604–1668. German chemist. Glauber, who made his living selling patent medicines, is remembered for his discovery of the salt known variously as 'sal mirabile' and 'Glauber's salt'. The salt, sodium sulphate, was used by him to treat almost any complaint.

Glendower Owen *c.*1359–1415. Welsh leader of a revolt against the English in N Wales, who defeated Henry IV in three campaigns 1400–02, although Wales was reconquered 1405–13.

Glenn John (Herschel) 1921– . US astronaut and politician. On 20 Feb 1962, he became the first American to orbit the Earth, three times in the Mercury spacecraft Friendship 7, in a flight lasting 4 hr 55 min. After retiring from NASA, he became a senator for Ohio 1974 and 1980, and unsuccessfully sought the Democratic presidential nomination 1984.

Glinka Mikhail Ivanovich 1804–1857. Russian composer. He broke away from the prevailing Italian influence and turned to Russian folk music as the inspiration for his opera *A Life for the Tsar* (originally *Ivan Susanin*) 1836. His later works include another opera, *Ruslan and Lyudmila* 1842, and the orchestral *Kamarinskaya* 1848.

Gloucester Richard Alexander Walter George, Duke of Gloucester 1944– . Prince of the United Kingdom. Grandson of ◊George V, he succeeded his father to the dukedom owing to the death of his elder brother Prince William (1941–72) in an air crash. He married in 1972 Birgitte van Deurs, daughter of a Danish lawyer. His heir is his son Alexander, Earl of Ulster (1974–).

Glubb John Bagot 1897–1986. British soldier, founder of the modern Arab Legion (the Jordanian army), which he commanded 1939–56.

Gluck Christoph Willibald von 1714–1787. German composer who settled in Vienna as Kapellmeister to Maria Theresa in 1754. In 1762 his *Orfeo ed Euridice/Orpheus and Eurydice* revolutionized the 18th-century conception of opera by giving free scope to dramatic effect. *Orfeo* was followed by *Alceste/Alcestis* 1767 and *Paris ed Elena/Paris and Helen* 1770.

Born in Erasbach, Bavaria, he studied music at Prague, Vienna, and Milan, went to London in 1745 to compose operas for the Haymarket, but returned to Vienna in 1746 where he was knighted by the Pope. In 1762 his *Iphigénie en Aulide/Iphigenia in Aulis* 1774, produced in Paris, gave rise to controversy in which Gluck had the support of Marie Antoinette while his Italian rival Piccinni had the support of Madame Du Barry. With *Armide* 1777 and *Iphigénie en Tauride/Iphigenia in Tauris* 1779 Gluck won a complete victory over Piccinni.

Gobbi Tito 1913–1984. Italian baritone singer renowned for his opera characterizations of Figaro, Scarpia, and Iago.

Gobind Singh 1666–1708. Indian religious leader, the tenth and last guru (teacher) of Sikhism, 1675–1708, and founder of the Sikh brotherhood known as the Khalsa. On his death the Sikh holy book, the *Guru Granth Sahib*, replaced the line of human gurus as the teacher and guide of the Sikh community.

Godard Jean-Luc 1930– . French film director, one of the leaders of new wave cinema. His works are often characterized by experimental editing techniques, and an unconventional dramatic form. His films include *A bout de souffle* 1960, *Weekend* 1968 and *Je vous salue, Marie* 1985.

Goddard Robert Hutchings 1882–1945. US rocket pioneer. His first liquid-fuelled rocket was launched at Auburn, Massachusetts, USA, Mar 1926. By 1935 his rockets had gyroscopic control and carried cameras to record instrument readings. Two years later a Goddard rocket gained the world altitude record with an ascent of 3 km/1.9 mi.

Gödel Kurt 1906–1978. Austrian-born US mathematician and philosopher, who proved that a mathematical system always contains statements that can be neither proved nor disproved within the system; in other words, as a science, mathematics can never be totally consistent and totally complete. He worked on relativity, constructing a mathematical model of the universe that made travel back through time theoretically possible.

Godfrey de Bouillon *c.*1060–1100. French crusader, second son of Count Eustace II of Boulogne. He and his brothers (Baldwin and Eustace) led 40,000 Germans in the First Crusade 1096. When Jerusalem was taken 1099, he was elected its ruler, but refused the title of king. After his death, Baldwin was elected king.

Godiva Lady *c.*1040–1080. Wife of Leofric, earl of Mercia (died 1057). Legend has it that her husband promised to reduce the heavy taxes on the people of Coventry if she rode naked through the streets at noon. Everyone remained indoors, but 'Peeping Tom' bored a hole in his shutters, and was struck blind. Leofric founded a Benedictine monastery at Coventry, England, where she is buried.

Godunov Boris 1552–1605. Tsar of Russia from 1598. He was assassinated by a pretender to the throne. The legend that has grown up around this forms the basis of Pushkin's play *Boris Godunov* 1831 and Mussorgsky's opera of the same name 1874.

Boris Godunov was elected after the death of Fyodor I, son of Ivan the Terrible. He died during a revolt led by one who professed to be Dmitri, a brother of Fyodor and the rightful heir. The true Dmitri, however, had died in 1591 by cutting his own throat during an epileptic fit. An apocryphal story of Boris killing the true Dmitri to gain the throne was fostered by Russian historians anxious to discredit Boris because he was not descended from the main ruling families.

Godunov's rule was marked by a strengthening of the Russian church, but was also the beginning of the Time of Troubles, a period of instability.

Godwin died 1053. Earl of Wessex from 1020. He secured the succession to the throne in 1042 of ◊Edward the Confessor, to whom he married his daughter Edith, and whose chief minister he became. King Harold II was his son.

Godwin William 1756–1836. English philosopher, novelist, and father of Mary Shelley. His *Enquiry concerning Political Justice* 1793 advocated an anarchic society based on a faith in people's essential rationality. At first a Nonconformist minister, he later became an atheist. His first wife was Mary ◊Wollstonecraft.

Goebbels Paul Josef 1897–1945. German Nazi leader. He was born in the Rhineland, became a journalist, joined the Nazi party in its early days, and was given control of its propaganda 1929. As minister of propaganda from 1933, he brought all cultural and educational activities under Nazi control, and built up sympathetic movements abroad to carry on the 'war of nerves' against Hitler's intended victims. On the capture of Berlin by the Allies he poisoned himself.

Goehr (Peter) Alexander 1932– . British composer, born in Berlin. A lyrical but often hard-edged serialist, he nevertheless usually remained within the forms of the symphony and traditional chamber works, and more recently turned to tonal and even Nèo-Baroque models.

Goeppert-Mayer Maria 1906–1972. US physicist who worked mainly on the structure of the atomic nucleus. She shared the 1963 Nobel Prize for Physics with ◊Wigner and Jensen.

Born in Germany, she emigrated to the USA in 1931. By 1948 she had managed to explain the stability of particular atoms. Atomic nuclei were seen as shell-like layers of protons and neutrons with the most stable atoms having completely · filled outermost shells.

Goering, or Göring Hermann 1893–1946. German field marshal from 1938 and Nazi leader. Goering was part of Hitler's 'inner circle', and with Hitler's rise to power 1933, established the Gestapo and concentration camps. Appointed successor to Hitler 1939, he built a vast economic empire in occupied Europe, but later lost favour, and was expelled from the party 1945. Tried at Nuremberg, he poisoned himself before he could be executed.

Goering was born in Bavaria. He was a renowned fighter pilot in World War I, and joined the Nazi party 1922. He was elected to the Reichstag 1928, and became its president 1932. As commissioner for aviation from 1933 he built up the Luftwaffe (air force). In 1936 he became plenipotentiary of the four-year plan for war preparations.

Goes Hugo van der died 1482. Flemish painter, chiefly active in Ghent. His *Portinari altarpiece* about 1475 (Uffizi, Florence) is a huge oil painting of the Nativity, full of symbolism and naturalistic detail, and the *Death of the Virgin* about 1480 (Musée Communale des Beaux Arts, Bruges) is remarkable for the varied expressions on the faces of the apostles.

Goethe Johann Wolfgang von 1749–1832. German poet, novelist, and dramatist, the founder of modern German literature, and leader of the Romantic *Sturm und Drang* movement, which sought to describe extravagant passions. His works include the autobiographical *Die Leiden des jungen Werthers/The Sorrows of the Young Werther* 1774 and *Faust* 1808, his masterpiece. A visit to Italy 1786–88 inspired the classical dramas *Iphigenie auf Tauris/Iphigenia in Tauris* 1787 and *Tasso* 1790.

Born at Frankfurt-am-Main, Goethe studied law. Inspired by Shakespeare, to whose work he was introduced by ◊Herder, he wrote the play *Götz von Berlichingen* 1773. *The Sorrows of the Young Werther* 1774, and the poetic play *Faust* 1808, made him a European figure. He was prime minister at the court of Weimar 1775–85. Other works include the *Wilhelm Meister* novels 1796–1829. He was a friend of ◊Schiller. Many of his lyrics were set to music.

Goffman Erving 1922–1982. Canadian social scientist. He studied the ways people try to create, present, and defend a particular self-image and the social structures surrounding, controlling, and defining human interaction. Works include *The Presentation of Self in Everyday Life* 1956 and *Gender Advertisements* 1979.

Gogh Vincent van 1853–1890. Dutch painter, a Post-Impressionist. He tried various careers, including preaching, and began painting in the 1880s. He met ◊Gauguin in Paris, and when he settled in Arles, Provence, 1888, Gauguin joined him there. After a quarrel van Gogh cut off part of his own earlobe, and in 1889 he entered an asylum; the following year he committed suicide. The Arles paintings vividly testify to his intense emotional involvement in his art; among the best known are *The Yellow Chair* and several *Sunflowers* 1888 (National Gallery, London).

Born in Zundert, van Gogh worked for a time as a schoolmaster in England before he took up painting. He studied under Van Mauve at The Hague. One of the leaders of the Post-Impressionist painters, he executed still lifes and landscapes, one of the best known being *A*

Cornfield with Cypresses 1889 (National Gallery, London).

Gogol Nicolai Vasilyevich 1809–1852. Russian writer. His first success was a collection of stories, *Evenings on a Farm near Dikanka* 1831–32, followed by *Mirgorod* 1835. Later works include *Arabesques* 1835, the comedy play *The Inspector General* 1836, and the picaresque novel *Dead Souls* 1842, which satirizes Russian provincial society.

Born near Poltava, Gogol tried several careers before entering the St Petersburg Civil Service. From 1835 he travelled in Europe, and it was in Rome that he completed the earlier part of *Dead Souls* 1842. Other works include the short story 'The Overcoat'.

Gokhale Gopal Krishna 1866–1915. Indian political adviser and friend of Mohandas Gandhi, leader of the Moderate group in the Indian National Congress before World War I.

Golding William 1911– . English novelist. His first book, *Lord of the Flies* 1954, was about savagery taking over among a group of English schoolboys marooned on a Pacific island. Later novels include *The Spire* 1964, *Rites of Passage* 1980, and *The Paper Men* 1984. Nobel prize 1983.

Goldoni Carlo 1707–1793. Italian dramatist, born in Venice. He wrote popular comedies for the Sant'Angelo theatre, including *La putta onorata/ The Respectable Girl* 1749, *I pettegolezzi delle donne/ Women's Gossip* 1750, and *La locandiera/Mine Hostess* 1753.

Goldsmith Jerrald ('Jerry') 1930– . US composer of film music who originally worked in radio and television. His prolific output includes *Planet of the Apes* 1968, *The Wind and the Lion* 1975, *The Omen* 1976, and *Gremlins* 1984.

Goldsmith Oliver 1728–1774. Irish writer, whose works include the novel *The Vicar of Wakefield* 1766, the poem *The Deserted Village* 1770, and the play *She Stoops to Conquer* 1773. He was a member of Samuel Johnson's Literary Club.

Goldsmith was the son of a clergyman, and was educated at Trinity College, Dublin, and Edinburgh, where he studied medicine 1752. After travelling extensively in Europe, he returned to England and became a hack writer, producing many works, including *History of England and Animated Nature* 1774. His earliest work of literary importance was *The Citizen of the World* 1762, a series of letters by an imaginary Chinese traveller. In 1761 Goldsmith met Samuel Johnson, and became a member of his 'club'. In 1764 he published the poem *The Traveller*, and followed it with collected essays 1765. *The Vicar of Wakefield* was sold (according to Johnson's account) to save him from imprisonment for debt.

Goldwater Barry 1909– . US Republican politician, presidential candidate in the 1964 election, when he was heavily defeated by Lyndon Johnson. Many of Goldwater's ideas were later adopted by the Republican right and the Reagan administration.

Goldwyn Samuel 1882–1974. US film producer. Born in Warsaw, he emigrated to the USA 1896. He founded the Goldwyn Pictures Corporation 1917, precursor of the Metro-Goldwyn-Mayer Company 1925, later allied with United Artists. He was famed for his illogical aphorisms known as 'goldwynisms', for example 'Anyone who visits a psychiatrist should have his head examined'.

Golgi Camillo 1843–1926. Italian cell biologist who with Santiago Ramon y Cajal produced the first detailed knowledge of the fine structure of the nervous system.

The *Golgi body*, a series of flattened membranous cavities found in the cytoplasm of cells was first described by him in 1898. Golgi and Ramon y Cajal shared the 1906 Nobel Prize for Medicine.

Gollancz Victor 1893–1967. British left-wing writer and publisher, founder in 1936 of the influential Left Book Club.

Gomez Diego 1440–1482. Portuguese navigator who discovered the coast of Liberia during a voyage sponsored by ◊Henry the Navigator 1458–60.

Gómez Juan Vicente 1864–1935. Venezuelan dictator 1908–35. The discovery of oil during his rule attracted US, British, and Dutch oil interests and made Venezuela one of the wealthiest countries in Latin America. Gómez amassed a considerable

Goldwyn *Film producer of Polish extraction, Sam Goldwyn became one the most powerful men in Hollywood during its golden age.*

personal fortune and used his well-equipped army to dominate the civilian population.

Gompers Samuel 1850–1924. US labour leader. His early career in the Cigarmakers' Union led him to found and lead the American Federation of Labor 1882. Gompers advocated non-political activity within the existing capitalist system to secure improved wages and conditions for members.

Gomulka Wladyslaw 1905–1982. Polish communist politician, party leader 1943–48 and 1956–70. He introduced moderate reforms, including private farming and tolerance for Roman Catholicism.

Gomulka, born in Krosno in SE Poland, was involved in underground resistance to the Germans during World War II, taking part in the defence of Warsaw. Leader of the Communist Party in Poland from 1943, he was ousted by the Moscow-backed Boleslaw Bierut (1892–1956) in 1948, but was restored to the leadership in 1956, following riots in Poznań. Gomulka was forced to resign in Dec 1970 after sudden food-price rises induced a new wave of strikes and riots.

Goncharov Ivan Alexandrovitch 1812–1891. Russian novelist. His first novel, *A Common Story* 1847, was followed in 1858 by his humorous masterpiece, *Oblomov*, which satirized the indolent Russian landed gentry.

Goncourt, de the brothers Edmond 1822–1896 and Jules 1830–1870. French writers. They collaborated in producing a compendium, *L'Art du XVIIIème siècle/18th-Century Art* 1859–75, historical studies, and a *Journal* 1887–96, which depicts French literary life of their day. Edmond de Goncourt founded the *Académie Goncourt*, opened 1903, which awards an annual prize, the *Prix Goncourt*, to the author of the best French novel of the year. Equivalent to the Booker Prize in prestige, the monetary value is only 50 francs.

González Márquez Felipe 1942– . Spanish socialist politician, leader of the Socialist Workers' Party (PSOE), prime minister from 1982.

After studying law in Spain and Belgium, in 1966 he opened the first labour-law office in his home city of Seville. In 1964 he had joined the PSOE, and he rose rapidly to the position of leader. In 1982 PSOE won a sweeping electoral victory and González became prime minister.

Goodman 'Benny' (Benjamin David) 1909–1986. US clarinetist, nicknamed 'the King of Swing' for the new jazz idiom he introduced. Leader of his own band from 1934, he is remembered for numbers such as 'Blue Skies' and 'King Porter Stomp'. Bartók's *Contrasts* 1939 and Copland's *Clarinet Concerto* 1950 were among the pieces written for him.

Goodman Paul 1911– . US writer and social critic, whose many writings (novels, plays, essays) express his anarchist, anti-authoritarian

Gorbachev President of the Soviet Union and Communist Party leader, Mikhail Gorbachev.

ideas. He studied youth offenders in *Growing up Absurd* 1960.

Goodyear Charles 1800–1860. US inventor, who developed vulcanized rubber 1839, particularly important for motor-vehicle tyres.

Gorbachev Mikhail Sergeyevich 1931– . Soviet leader. He was a member of the Politburo from 1980 and, during the Chernenko administration 1984–85, was chairman of the Foreign Affairs Commission. As general secretary of the Communist Party (CPSU) from 1985, and president of the Supreme Soviet from 1988, he introduced liberal reforms at home (*perestroika*, 'restructuring', and *glasnost*, 'openness') and attempted to halt the arms race abroad. In 1990 he gained significantly increased powers for the presidency.

Gorbachev, born in the N Caucasus, studied law at Moscow University and joined the CPSU 1952. In 1955–62 he worked for the Komsomol (Communist Youth League) before being appointed regional agriculture secretary. As Stavropol party leader from 1970 he impressed Andropov, and was brought into the CPSU secretariat 1978.

Gorbachev was promoted into the Politburo, and in 1983, when Andropov was general secretary, took broader charge of the Soviet economy. On Chernenko's death 1985 he was appointed party leader. He initiated reforms, and introduced campaigns against alcoholism, corruption, and inefficiency, and a policy of *glasnost*. Gorbachev radically changed the style of Soviet leadership, despite opposition to the pace of change from both conservatives and radicals.

Gordimer Nadine 1923– . South African novelist, an opponent of apartheid. Her first novel, *The*

Lying Days, appeared in 1953, and other works include *The Conservationist* 1974, the volume of short stories *A Soldier's Embrace* 1980, and *July's People* 1981. Her books are banned in South Africa.

Gordon Charles (George) 1833–1885. British general sent to Khartoum in the Sudan 1884 to rescue English garrisons that were under attack by the ◊Mahdi; he was himself besieged by the Mahdi's army. A relief expedition under Viscount Wolseley arrived 28 Jan 1885, to find that Khartoum, after a siege of ten months, had been captured, and Gordon killed, two days before.

Gordon George 1751–1793. British organizer of the so-called *Gordon Riots* of 1778, a protest against removal of penalties imposed on Roman Catholics in the Catholic Relief Act of 1778; he was acquitted on a treason charge. Gordon and the 'No Popery' riots figure in Dickens's novel *Barnaby Rudge*.

Gordon Richard. Pen name of Gordon Ostlere 1921– . British author of a series of light-hearted novels on the career of a young doctor, beginning with *Doctor in the House* 1952. Many of them were filmed.

Gordon-Lennox family name of Dukes of Richmond; seated at Goodwood, Sussex; descended from King Charles II by his mistress Louise de Keroualle.

Goria Giovanni 1943– . Italian Christian Democrat (DC) politician, prime minister 1987–88. He entered the Chamber of Deputies 1976 and held a number of posts, including treasury minister, until he was asked to form a coalition government in 1987.

Göring Hermann Wilhelm Nazi leader, see ◊Goering.

Gorky Arshile 1904–1948. US painter, born in Armenia, who settled in the USA in 1920. He painted Cubist abstracts before developing a more surreal Abstract Expressionist style, using organic shapes and bold paint strokes.

Gorky Maxim. Pen name of Alexei Peshkov 1868–1936. Russian writer. Born in Nizhny-Novgorod (renamed Gorky 1932 in his honour), he was exiled 1906–13 for his revolutionary principles. His works, which include the play *The Lower Depths* 1902 and the recollections *My Childhood* 1913, combine realism with optimistic faith in the potential of the industrial proletariat.

Gorst J(ohn) E(ldon) 1835–1916. English Conservative Party administrator. A supporter of Disraeli, Gorst was largely for extending the Victorian Conservative Party electoral base to include middle- and working-class support. Appointed Conservative Party agent in 1870, he established the Conservative Central Office.

Gort John Vereker, 1st Viscount Gort 1886–1946. British general, awarded a Victoria Cross after World War I, who in World War II commanded the

Gorky *A committed, lifelong revolutionary, Maxim Gorky attracted official disapproval both before and after the 1917 Russian Revolution.*

British Expeditionary Force 1939–40, conducting a fighting retreat from Dunkirk, France.

Gorton John Grey 1911– . Australian Liberal politician. He was minister for education and science 1966–68, and prime minister 1968–71.

Goschen George Joachim, 1st Viscount Goschen 1831–1907. British Liberal politician. He held several cabinet posts under Gladstone 1868–74, but broke with him in 1886 over Irish Home Rule. In Salisbury's Unionist government of 1886–92 he was chancellor of the Exchequer, and 1895–1900 was First Lord of the Admiralty.

Gossaert Jan, Flemish painter, known as ◊Mabuse.

Gosse Edmund William 1849–1928. English author. Son of a marine biologist, who was a member of the Christian fundamentalist Plymouth Brethren sect, Gosse's strict Victorian upbringing is reflected in his masterpiece of autobiographical work *Father and Son* (published anonymously in 1907).

Gould Bryan Charles 1939– . British Labour politician, member of the shadow cabinet from 1986.

Born in New Zealand, he settled in Britain in 1964, as a civil servant and then a university lecturer. He joined the Labour Party, entering the House of Commons in 1974. He lost his seat in the 1979 general election but returned in 1983 as the member for Dagenham, having spent the intervening four years as a television journalist. His rise in the Labour Party was rapid and in 1986 he became a member of the shadow cabinet. His communication skills soon made him a nationally known figure.

Gould Elliott. Stage name of Elliot Goldstein 1938– . US film actor. A successful child actor, his film debut, *The Night They Raided Minsky's* 1968, led rapidly to starring roles in such films as M.A.S.H. 1970, *The Long Goodbye* 1972, and *Capricorn One* 1978.

Gould Jay 1836–1892. US financier, born in New York. He is said to have caused the financial panic on 'Black Friday', 24 Sept 1869, through his speculations in gold.

Gould Stephen Jay 1941– . US palaeontologist and author. In 1972 he proposed the theory of punctuated equilibrium, suggesting that the evolution of species did not occur at a steady rate but could suddenly accelerate, with rapid change occurring over a few hundred thousand years.

Gounod Charles François 1818–1893. French composer. His operas include *Sappho* 1851, *Faust* 1859, *Philémon et Baucis* 1860, and *Roméo et Juliette* 1867. He also wrote sacred songs, masses, and an oratorio, *The Redemption* 1882. His music has great lyrical appeal and emotional power and it inspired many French composers of the later 19th century.

Gower David 1957– . English cricketer. A left-hander, since his debut for Leicestershire 1975 he has scored over 20,000 first class runs. He made his England debut 1978, and was captain 1984 and 1989.

Gower John *c.*1330–1408. English poet. He is remembered for his tales of love *Confessio Amantis* 1390, written in English, and other poems in French and Latin.

Gowon Yakubu 1934– . Nigerian politician, head of state 1966–75. Educated at Sandhurst, he became chief of staff, and in the military coup of 1966 seized power. After the Biafran civil war 1967–70, he reunited the country with his policy of 'no victor, no vanquished'. In 1975 he was overthrown by a military coup.

Goya Francisco José de Goya y Lucientes 1746–1828. Spanish painter and engraver. He painted portraits of four successive kings of Spain, and his etchings include *The Disasters of War*, depicting the French invasion of Spain 1810–14. Among his last works are the 'black paintings' (Prado, Madrid), with horrific images such as *Saturn Devouring One of his Sons* about 1822.

He was born in Aragon, and was for a time a bullfighter, the subject of some of his etchings. After studying in Italy, he returned to Spain, and was employed on a number of paintings for the royal tapestry factory. In 1789 he was court painter to Charles IV.

Goyen Jan van 1596–1656. Dutch landscape painter, active in Leiden, Haarlem, and from 1631 in The Hague. He was a pioneer of the realist style of landscape with ◊Ruisdael, and

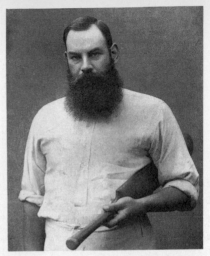

Grace *The English cricketer W G Grace, who helped establish cricket as England's national sport.*

sketched from nature and studied clouds and light effects.

Gozzoli Benozzo *c.*1421–1497. Florentine painter, a late exponent of the International Gothic style. He painted frescoes 1459 in the chapel of the Palazzo Medici-Riccardi, Florence: the walls are crammed with figures, many of them portraits of the Medici family.

Graaf Regnier de 1641–1673. Dutch physician and anatomist who discovered the ovarian follicles, which were later named **Graafian follicles**. He gave exact descriptions of the testicles, and named the ovaries. He was also the first to isolate and collect the secretions of the pancreas and gall bladder.

Grable 'Betty' (Elizabeth Ruth) 1916–1973. US actress, singer and dancer, who starred in *Moon over Miami* 1941, *I Wake Up Screaming* 1941, and *How to Marry a Millionaire* 1953. As a publicity stunt, her legs were insured for a million dollars.

Gracchus the brothers Tiberius Sempronius 163–133 BC and Gaius Sempronius 153–121 BC. Roman agrarian reformers. As tribune (magistrate) 133 BC, Tiberius tried to prevent the ruin of small farmers by making large slave-labour farms illegal but was murdered. Gaius, tribune 123–122 BC, revived his brother's legislation, and introduced other reforms, but was outlawed by the Senate and committed suicide.

Grace W(illiam) G(ilbert) 1848–1915. English cricketer. By profession a doctor, he became the best batsman in England. He began playing first class cricket at the age of 16, scored 152 runs

Graf *West German tennis player Steffi Graf at Wimbledon 1988.*

in his first Test match, and scored the first triple century 1876.

Grace scored more than 54,000 runs in his career which lasted nearly 45 years. He scored 2,739 runs in 1871, the first time any batsman had scored 2,000 runs in a season. An all-rounder, he took nearly 3,000 first class wickets. Grace played in 22 Test matches.

Graf Steffi 1969– . West German lawn tennis player, who brought Martina ◊Navratilova's long reign as the world's number one female player to an end. She reached the semi-final of the US Open 1985 at the age of 16, and won five consecutive Grand Slam singles titles 1988–89.

Grafton Augustus Henry, 3rd Duke of Grafton 1735–1811. British politician. Grandson of the first duke, who was the son of Charles II and Barbara Villiers (1641–1709), Duchess of Cleveland. He became First Lord of the Treasury in 1766 and an unsuccessful acting prime minister 1767–70.

Graham family name of Dukes of Montrose.

Graham 'Billy' (William Franklin) 1918– . US Baptist evangelist. At 17 he was converted at an evangelistic meeting. His Evangelistic Association conducts worldwide 'crusades'.

Graham Martha 1894– . US choreographer. An innovative exponent of modern dance, she had a major influence on choreographers in the contemporary dance movement such as Robert Cohan,

Glen Tetley, Norman Morrice, Paul Taylor, and Robert North.

She has created over 150 ballets, including *Appalachian Spring* 1944 (score by Aaron Copland) and *Clytemnestra* 1958 (music by Halim El-Dabh), the first full-length modern dance work.

Graham Thomas 1805–1869. Scottish chemist who laid the foundations of physical chemistry by his work on the diffusion of gases and liquids. *Graham's Law* states that the diffusion rate of two gases varies inversely as the square root of their densities.

His work on colloids (which have larger particles than true solutions) was equally fundamental; he discovered the principle of dialysis, for separating colloids from solutions. The human kidney uses the principle of dialysis to extract nitrogenous waste.

Grahame Kenneth 1859–1932. Scottish author. The early volumes of sketches of childhood, *The Golden Age* 1895 and *Dream Days* 1898, were followed by his masterpiece *The Wind in the Willows* 1908, an animal fantasy created for his young son, which was dramatized by A A Milne as *Toad of Toad Hall.*

Grainger Percy Aldridge 1882–1961. Australian-born US composer and concert pianist. He is remembered for a number of songs and short instrumental pieces drawing on folk idioms, including *Country Gardens* 1925, and for his settings of folk songs, such as *Molly on the Shore* 1921.

Gramsci Antonio 1891–1937. Italian Marxist, who attempted to unify social theory and political practice. He helped to found the Italian Communist party 1921, and was elected to parliament 1924, but was imprisoned by Mussolini from 1926; his *Quaderni di carcere/Prison Notebooks* 1947 were published after his death.

His humane and gradualist approach to Marxism, particularly his emphasis on the need to overthrow bourgeois ideology, influenced European Marxists in their attempt to distance themselves from orthodox determinist Soviet communism.

Granados Enrique 1867–1916. Spanish composer-pianist. His piano-work *Goyescas* 1911, inspired by the art of ◊Goya, was converted to an opera in 1916.

Granger Stewart (James Stewart) 1913– . British film actor. After several leading roles in British romantic films during World War II, he moved to Hollywood in 1950 and subsequently appeared in adventure films, for example, *Scaramouche* 1952; *The Prisoner of Zenda* 1952; *The Wild Geese* 1978.

Grant Cary. Stage-name of Archibald Leach 1904–1986. US actor, born in England, who first travelled to the USA with a troupe of acrobats. His witty, debonair screen personality made him a favourite for more than three decades. His films include *Bringing Up Baby*

1937, *The Philadelphia Story* 1940, *Arsenic and Old Lace* 1944, *Notorious* 1946, and *North by Northwest* 1959.

Grant Duncan 1885–1978. British painter and designer, a member of the Bloomsbury group and a pioneer of abstract art in the UK. He lived with Vanessa Bell from about 1914 and worked with her on decorative projects. Later works, such as *Snow Scene* 1921, showed the influence of the Post-Impressionists.

Grant James Augustus 1827–1892. Scottish soldier and explorer who served in India and Abyssinia and, with Captain John Speke, explored the sources of the Nile 1860–63. Accounts of his travels include *A Walk across Africa* 1864 and *Botany of the Speke and Grant Expedition.*

Grant Ulysses S(impson) 1822–1885. 18th president of the USA 1869–77. He was a Union general in the American Civil War and commander in chief from 1864. As a Republican president, he carried through a liberal reconstruction policy in the South, although he failed to suppress extensive political corruption within his own party and cabinet, which tarnished the reputation of his presidency.

The son of an Ohio farmer, he had an unsuccessful career in the army 1839–54 and in business, and on the outbreak of the Civil War received a commission on the Mississippi front. He took command there in 1862, and by his capture of Vicksburg in 1863 brought the whole Mississippi front under Northern control. He slowly wore down the Confederate General Lee's resistance, and in 1865 received his surrender at Appomattox. He was elected president 1868 and re-elected 1872.

Granville-Barker Harley 1877–1946. British theatre director and author. He was director and manager with J E Vedrenne at the Royal Court Theatre, London, 1904–18, producing plays by Shaw, Yeats, Ibsen, Galsworthy, and Masefield.

Grass Günter 1927– . German writer. Born in Danzig, he studied at the art academies of Düsseldorf and Berlin, worked as a writer and sculpture, first in Paris and later4 in Berlin, and in 1958 won the coveted 'Group 47' prize. The grotesque humour and socialist feeling oif his novels *Die Blechtrommel/The Tin Drum* 1959 and *Der Butt/The flounder* 1977 characterize many of his poems.

Grasso Ella Tambussi 1919–1981. US politician. She was elected as a Democrat to the House of Representatives in 1952. In 1955, she became Democratic floor leader in the state legislature, and Connecticut secretary of state 1959–70. Elected to the United States House of Representatives in 1970, she was active upon issues such as abortion. In 1975 she won the Governorship of Connecticut and took prompt successful measures to reduce the state debt.

Grant *General Ulysses S Grant, photographed in June 1864 at City Point, near Hopewell, Virginia, his headquarters during the American Civil War.*

Grattan Henry 1746–1820. Irish politician. He entered the Irish parliament in 1775. As leader of the patriot opposition he secured the abolition of all claims by the British Parliament to legislate for Ireland in 1782, but failed to prevent the Act of Union, and sat in the British Parliament from 1805.

Graves Robert (Ranke) 1895–1985. English poet and author. He was severely wounded on the Somme in World War I, and his frank autobiography *Goodbye to All That* 1929 is one of the outstanding war books. Other works include the poems *Over the Brazier* 1916; historical novels of Imperial Rome, *I Claudius* and *Claudius the God* 1934; and books on myth, for example *The White Goddess* 1948.

Gray Eileen 1879–1976. Irish-born architect and furniture designer. She set up her own workshop and became known for her Art Deco designs which, in furniture, explored the use of tubular metal, glass, and new materials such as aluminium.

Gray Thomas 1716–1761. English poet, whose 'Elegy Written in a Country Churchyard' 1750 is one of the most quoted poems in English. Other poems include 'Ode on a Distant Prospect of Eton College', 'The Progress of Poesy', and 'The Bard'; these poems are now seen as the precursors of Romanticism.

A close friend of Horace ◊Walpole at Eton, Gray made a continental tour with him 1739–41, an account of which is given in his vivid letters. In 1748 his first poems appeared anonymously in Dodsley's *Miscellany*.

Greco, El (Doménikos Theotokopoulos) 1541–1614. Spanish painter called 'the Greek' because he was born in Crete. He studied in Italy, worked in Rome from about 1570, and by 1577 had settled in Toledo. He painted elegant portraits and intensely emotional religious scenes with increasingly distorted figures and flickering light, for example *The Burial of Count Orgaz* 1586 (Toledo).

Green Henry, pen name of Henry Vincent Yorke 1905–1974. British novelist, whose works (for example *Loving* 1945, and *Nothing* 1950) are characterized by an experimental colloquial prose style and extensive use of dialogue.

Green Lucinda (born Prior-Palmer) 1953– . British three-day eventer. She has won the Badminton Horse Trials a record six times 1973–84 and was world individual champion 1982.

Green Thomas Hill 1836–1882. English philosopher. He attempted to show the limitations of Herbert ◊Spencer and John Stuart ◊Mill, and advocated the study of ◊Kant and ◊Hegel. His chief works are *Prolegomena to Ethics* 1883 and *Principles of Political Obligation* 1895.

Born in Yorkshire, he was professor of moral philosophy at Oxford from 1878.

Greenaway Kate 1846–1901. British illustrator, known for her drawings of children. In 1877 she first exhibited at the Royal Academy, and began her collaboration with the colour-printer Edmund Evans, with whom she produced a number of children's books, including *Mother Goose*.

Greene (Henry) Graham 1904– . English writer, whose novels of guilt, despair, and penitence, include *The Man Within* 1929, *Brighton Rock* 1938, *The Power and the Glory* 1940, *The Heart of the Matter* 1948, *The Third Man* 1950, *Our Man in Havana* 1958, *The Honorary Consul* 1973, and *Monsignor Quixote* 1982.

Greenspan Alan 1926– . US economist, who succeeded Paul ◊Volcker as chair of the Federal Reserve Board in 1987 and successfully pumped liquidity into the market to avert a sudden 'freefall' into recession after the Wall Street share crash of October 1987.

Greenstreet Sidney 1879–1954. British character actor. He made an impressive film debut in *The Maltese Falcon* 1941 and became one of the cinema's best known villains. His other films included *Casablanca* 1943 and *The Mask of Dimitrios* 1944.

Greenwood Walter 1903–1974. English novelist of the Depression, born in Salford. His own lack of a job gave authenticity to *Love on the Dole* 1933, later dramatized and filmed.

Greer Germaine 1939– . Australian feminist, who became widely known on the publication of *The Female Eunuch* 1970. Later works include *The Obstacle Race* 1979, a study of contemporary women artists, and *Sex and Destiny: The Politics of Human Fertility* 1984.

Gregg Norman 1892–1966. Australian ophthalmic surgeon, who discovered in 1941 that german measles in a pregnant woman could cause physical defects in her child.

Gregory Isabella Augusta (born Persse) 1852–1932. Irish playwright, associated with W B Yeats in creating the Abbey Theatre, Dublin, 1904. Her plays include the comedy *Spreading the News* 1904 and the tragedy *Gaol Gate* 1906. Her journals 1916–30 were published 1946.

Gregory 16 popes, including:

Gregory I St, the Great *c.*540–604. Pope from 590, who asserted Rome's supremacy and exercised almost imperial powers. In 596 he sent St Augustine to England. He introduced the choral *Gregorian chant* into the liturgy. Feast day 12 Mar.

Gregory VII or *Hildebrand c.*1023–1085. Chief minister to several popes before his election to the papacy 1073. In 1077 he forced the Holy Roman emperor Henry IV to wait in the snow at Canossa for four days, dressed as a penitent, before receiving pardon. He was driven from Rome and died in exile. Feast day 25 May.

He claimed power to depose kings, denied lay rights to make clerical appointments, and attempted to suppress simony (the buying and selling of church preferments) and to enforce clerical celibacy, making enemies with both rulers and the church.

Gregory XIII 1502–1585. Pope from 1572, who introduced the reformed *Gregorian calendar*, still in use, in which a century year is not a leap year unless it is divisible by 400.

Gregory of Tours, St 538–594. French Christian bishop of Tours from 573, author of a *History of the Franks*. Feast day 17 Nov.

Grenfell Julian 1888–1915. British poet, eldest son of Lord Desborough. Author of 'Into Battle', Grenfell was killed in World War I.

Grenville Richard 1542–1591. English naval commander and adventurer, renowned for his heroic death aboard his ship *The Revenge* when attacked by Spanish warships. Grenville fought in Hungary and Ireland 1566–69, and was knighted about 1577. In 1585 he commanded the expedition that founded Virginia, USA, for his cousin, Walter ◊Raleigh. From 1586 to 1588 he organized the defence of England against the Spanish Armada.

In 1591, as second in command of a fleet under Lord Thomas Howard that sailed to seize Spanish treasure ships returning from South America, his ship became isolated from the rest of the fleet off the Azores and was attacked by Spanish warships. After many hours hand-to-hand combat, Grenville's ship *The Revenge* succumbed; he was captured and fatally wounded. Grenville became a symbol of English nationalism and was later commemorated in the poem *The Revenge* by Tennyson (1809–92).

Grenville William Wyndham, Baron 1759–1834. British Whig politician, son of George Grenville. He was foreign secretary in 1791 and resigned along with Pitt in 1801 over King George III's refusal to assent to Catholic emancipation. He headed the 'All the Talents' coalition of 1806–07 that abolished the slave trade.

Grenville entered the House of Commons in 1782, held the secretaryship for Ireland, was home secretary 1791–94 and foreign secretary 1794–1801. He refused office in Pitt's government of 1804 due to the exclusion of Charles James ◊Fox.

Gresham Thomas *c.*1519–1579. English merchant financier, who founded and paid for the Royal Exchange and propounded *Gresham's Law* that 'bad money tends to drive out good money from circulation'.

Gretzky Wayne 1961– . Canadian ice hockey player with the Edmonton Oilers and Los Angeles Kings. He scored a record 215 points in the 1981–82 season. In 1989 he won the *Hart Trophy* as the National Hockey League's (NHL) most valuable player of the season for a record ninth time. He broke the NHL all-time scoring record – now 1,852 points (surpassing Gordie Howe's 1,850 points).

Greuze Jean Baptiste 1725–1805. French painter of sentimental narrative paintings, such as *The Bible Reading* 1755 (Louvre, Paris). His works were much reproduced in engravings.

Greville Fulke, 1st Baron Brooke 1554–1628. Poet and courtier, friend and biographer of Philip Sidney. Greville's works, none of them published during his lifetime, include *Caelica*, a sequence of poems in different metres; *Mustapha* and *Alaham*, tragedies modelled on the Latin Seneca, and the Life of Sir Philip Sidney 1652. He has been commended for his plain style and tough political thought.

Grey Beryl 1927– . British ballerina. Prima ballerina with the Sadler's Wells Company 1942–57, she then danced internationally, and was artistic director of the London Festival Ballet 1968–79.

Grey Charles, 2nd Earl Grey 1764–1845. British Whig politician. He entered Parliament 1786, and in 1806 became First Lord of the Admiralty, and

foreign secretary soon afterwards. As prime minister 1830–34, he carried the Great Reform Bill 1832, and the Act abolishing slavery throughout the British Empire 1833.

Grey Edward, 1st Viscount Grey of Fallodon 1862–1933. British Liberal politician, nephew of the 2nd Earl Grey. As foreign secretary 1905–16 he negotiated an entente with Russia in 1907, and backed France against Germany in the Agadir Incident of 1911 in which Germany sent a gunboat to the Moroccan port. In 1914 he said: 'The lamps are going out all over Europe; we shall not see them lit again in our lifetime.'

Grey Henry, 3rd Earl Grey 1802–1894. British politician, son of Charles Grey. He served under his father as undersecretary for the colonies 1830–33, resigning because the cabinet would not back the immediate emancipation of slaves; he was secretary of war 1835–39, and colonial secretary 1846–52.

He was unique among politicians of the period in maintaining that the colonies should be governed for their own benefit, not that of Britain, and in his policy of granting self-government wherever possible. Yet he advocated convict transportation, and was opposed to Gladstone's Home Rule policy.

Grey Lady Jane 1537–1554. Queen of England 9–19 July 1553, the great-granddaughter of Henry VII. She was married 1553 to Lord Guildford Dudley (died 1554), son of the Duke of ◊Northumberland. Since she was a Protestant, Edward VI was persuaded by Northumberland to set aside the claims to the throne of his sisters Mary and Elizabeth. When Edward died 6 July, Jane reluctantly accepted the crown and was proclaimed queen four days later. Mary, however, had the support of the populace and the Lord Mayor of London announced that she was queen 19 July. Grey was executed on Tower Green.

Grey Zane 1875–1939. US author of Westerns, such as *Riders of the Purple Sage* 1912.

Grieg Edvard Hagerup 1843–1907. Norwegian composer. Much of his music is small scale, particularly his songs, dances, sonatas, and piano works. Among his orchestral works are the *Piano Concerto* 1869 and the incidental music for Ibsen's *Peer Gynt* 1876.

Grierson John 1898–1972. Scottish film producer. He was a sociologist who pioneered the documentary film in Britain, viewing it as 'the creative treatment of actuality'. He directed *Drifters* 1929 and produced 1930–35 *Industrial Britain*, *Song of Ceylon*, and *Night Mail*. During World War II he created the National Film Board of Canada.

Griffith D(avid) W(ark) 1875–1948. US film director. He made hundreds of 'one reelers' (lasting 12 minutes) 1908–13, in which he pioneered the techniques of the flash-back, cross-cut, close-up, and longshot. After much experimentation with photography and new techniques came *Birth of a Nation* 1915, followed by *Intolerance* 1916.

Griffith-Joyner (born Griffith) Delorez Florence 1959– . US track athlete who won three gold medals at the 1988 Seoul Olympics, the 100 and 200 metres and the sprint relay. Her time in the 200 metres was a world record 21.34 seconds.

Grignard François Auguste-Victor 1871–1935. French chemist. The so-called *Grignard reagents* (compounds containing a hydrocarbon radical, magnesium, and a halogen such as chlorine) found important applications as some of the most versatile in organic synthesis. Grignard shared the 1912 Nobel Prize for Chemistry for his work on organometallic compounds.

Grillparzer Franz 1791–1872. Austrian poet and dramatist. His plays include the tragedy *Die Ahnfrau/The Ancestress* 1817, the classical *Sappho* 1818 and the trilogy *Das goldene Vliess/The Golden Fleece* 1821.

Two dramas considered to be his greatest are *Des Meeres und der Liebe Wellen/The Waves of Sea and Love* 1831, returning to the Hellenic world, and *Der Traum, ein Leben/A Dream is Life* 1834. He wrote a bitter cycle of poems *Tristia ex Ponto* 1835 after an unhappy love-affair.

Grimaldi Joseph 1779–1837. British clown, born in London, the son of an Italian actor. He appeared on the stage at two years old. He gave his name 'Joey' to all later clowns, and excelled as 'Mother Goose' performed at Covent Garden in 1806.

Grimm Jakob Ludwig Karl 1785–1863. German philologist and collaborator with his brother **Wilhelm Karl** (1786–1859) in the *Fairy Tales* 1812–14, based on collected folk tales. Jakob's main work was his *Deutsche Grammatick/German Grammar* 1819, which gave the first historical treatment of the Germanic languages; *Grimm's Law*, a rule governing sound changes that have occurred in some European languages, is named after him.

Grimmelshausen Hans Jacob Christofel von 1625–1676. German picaresque novelist whose *Der Abenteuerliche Simplicissimus/The Adventurous Simplicissimus* 1669 reflects his experiences in the Thirty Years' War.

Grimond Jo(seph), Baron Grimond 1913– . British Liberal politician. As leader of the party 1956–67, he aimed at making it 'a new radical party to take the place of the Socialist Party as an alternative to Conservatism'.

Gris Juan 1887–1927. Spanish abstract painter, one of the earliest Cubists. He developed a distinctive geometrical style, often strongly coloured. He experimented with collage and made designs for Diaghilev's ballet 1922–23.

Grivas George 1898–1974. Greek Cypriot general who led the underground group EOKA's attempts to secure the union (Greek *enosis*) of Cyprus with Greece.

Gromyko Andrei 1909–1989. President of the USSR 1985–88. As ambassador to the USA from 1943, he took part in the Tehran, Yalta, and Potsdam conferences; as United Nations representative 1946–49, he exercised the Soviet veto 26 times. He was foreign minister 1957–85. It was Gromyko who formally nominated Mikhail Gorbachev as Communist Party leader in 1985.

Gropius Walter Adolf 1883–1969. German architect, who lived in the USA from 1937. A founder-director of the functionalist Bauhaus design school in Weimar 1919–28, he was an advocate of team architecture and artistic standards in industrial production. His works include the Fagus-Werke (a shoe factory in Prussia), the Model Factory at the 1914 Werkbund exhibition in Cologne, and the Harvard Graduate Center 1949–50.

Grosseteste Robert *c.* 1169–1253. English scholar and bishop. His prolific writings include many scientific works, as well as translations of Aristotle, and commentaries on the Bible. He was a forerunner of the empirical school, being one of the earliest to suggest testing ancient Greek theories by practical experiment.

He was Bishop of Lincoln from 1235 to his death, attempting to reform morals and clerical discipline, and engaging in controversy with Innocent IV over the pope's finances.

Grossmith George 1847–1912. British actor and singer. Turning from journalism to the stage, in 1877 he began a long association with the Gilbert and Sullivan operas, in which he created a number of parts. He collaborated with his brother **Weedon Grossmith** (1853–1919) in the comic novel *Diary of a Nobody* 1894.

Grosvenor family name of Dukes of Westminster; seated at Eaton Hall, Cheshire.

Grosz Georg 1893–1959. German Expressionist painter and illustrator, a founder of the Berlin group of the Dada movement 1918. Grosz excelled in savage satirical drawings criticizing the government and the military establishment. After numerous prosecutions he emigrated to the USA in 1932.

Grosz Károly 1930– . Hungarian Communist politician, prime minister 1987–88. As leader of the ruling Hungarian Socialist Workers' Party (HSWP) 1988–89, he sought to establish a flexible system of 'socialist pluralism'.

Grosz, a steelworker's son, was a printer and then a newspaper editor before moving to Budapest to serve as first deputy head and then head of the HSWP agitprop (agitation and propaganda) department 1968–79. He was Budapest party chief 1984–87 and briefly prime minister before succeeding János Kádár as HSWP leader in May 1988. Once noted for his political orthodoxy, Grosz emerged in the late 1980s as one of the most radical reformers in the Eastern bloc. In Oct 1989 the HSWP reconstituted itself as the

Hungarian Socialist Party (HSP) and Grosz was replaced as party leader by the democrat, Rezso Nyers.

Grotefend George Frederick 1775–1853. German scholar. Although a student of the classical rather than the oriental languages, he nevertheless solved the riddle of the wedge-like cuneiform script as used in ancient Persia: decipherment of Babylonian cuneiform followed from his work.

Grotius Hugo 1583–1645. Dutch jurist and politician, born in Delft. He became a lawyer, and later received political appointments. In 1618 he was arrested as a republican and sentenced to imprisonment for life: his wife contrived his escape in 1620, and he settled in France, where he composed the *De Jure Belli et Pacis/On the Law of War and Peace* 1625, the foundation of international law. He was Swedish ambassador in Paris 1634–45.

Grünewald (Mathias Gothardt-Neithardt) *c.*1475–1528. German painter, active in Mainz, Frankfurt, and Halle. He was court painter, architect, and engineer to the prince bishop elector of Mainz 1508–14. His few surviving paintings show an intense involvement with religious subjects.

The *Isenheim altarpiece*, 1515 (Colmar Museum, France), with its horribly tortured figure of Jesus, recalls medieval traditions.

Guardi Francesco 1712–1793. Italian painter. He produced souvenir views of his native Venice, which were commercially less successful than Canaletto's but are now considered more atmospheric, with subtler use of reflected light.

Guareschi Giovanni 1909–1968. Italian author of short stories of the friendly feud between parish priest Don Camillo and the Communist village mayor.

Guderian Heinz 1888–1954. German general in World War II. He created the Panzer armoured divisions of the German army that formed the ground spearhead of Hitler's *Blitzkrieg* strategy, and achieved an important breakthrough at Sedan in Ardennes, France 1940 and the advance to Moscow 1941.

Guercino adopted name of Giovanni Francesco Barbieri 1590–1666. Italian Baroque painter active chiefly in Rome. In his ceiling painting of *Aurora* 1621–23 (Villa Ludovisi, Rome), the chariot-borne figure of dawn rides across the heavens, and the architectural framework is imitated in the painting, giving the illusion that the ceiling opens into the sky.

Guérin Camille 1872–1961. French bacteriologist who, with ◊Calmette, developed the Bacille Calmette-Guérin (BCG) vaccine for tuberculosis.

Guesde Jules 1845–1922. French socialist leader from the 1880s who espoused Marxism and revolutionary change. His movement, the Parti Ouvrier Français (French Workers' Party), was eventually incorporated in the foundation of the SFIO (Section Française de l'Internationale Ouvrière/French Section of International Labour) in 1905.

Guevara Ernesto 'Che' 1928–1967. Latin American revolutionary. He was born in Argentina and trained there as a doctor, but in 1953 left his homeland because of his opposition to the right-wing president Perón. In effecting the Cuban revolution of 1959, he was second only to Castro and Castro's brother Raúl. In 1965 he went to the Congo to fight against white mercenaries, and then to Bolivia, where he was killed in an unsuccessful attempt to lead a peasant rising. He was an orthodox Marxist, and renowned for his guerrilla techniques.

Guido Reni Italian painter, see ◊Reni.

Guillaume Charles 1861–1938. Swiss physicist who studied measurement and alloy development. He discovered a nickel-steel alloy, invar, which showed negligible expansion with rising temperatures. Nobel Prize for Physics 1920.

As the son of a clockmaker, Guillaume came early in life to appreciate the value of precision in measurement. He spent most of his life at the International Bureau of Weights and Measures at Sèvres, which established the standards for the metre, litre, and kilogram.

Guinness Alec 1914– . English actor. His many stage roles include Shakespeare's Hamlet 1938 and Lawrence of Arabia (in *Ross* 1960). In 1979 he gained a 'lifetime achievement' Academy Award (films include *Kind Hearts and Coronets* 1949, *The*

Guinness *English actor Alec Guinness.*

Bridge on the River Kwai 1957, and *Star Wars* 1977).

Guinness joined the Old Vic 1936. He appeared in the television adaptations of John Le Carré's *Tinker, Tailor, Soldier, Spy* 1979 and *Smiley's People* 1981.

Guise Francis, 2nd Duke of 1519–1563. French soldier and politician. He led the French victory over Germany at Metz 1552 and captured Calais from the English 1558. Along with his brother *Charles* (1527–74) he was powerful in the government of France during the reign of Francis II. He was assassinated attempting to crush the Huguenots.

Guise Henri, 3rd Duke of 1550–1588. French nobleman who persecuted the Huguenots and was partly responsible for their persecution in the Massacre of St Bartholomew 1572. He was assassinated.

Guizot François Pierre Guillaume 1787–1874. French politician and historian, professor of modern history at the Sorbonne, Paris, 1812–30. He wrote a history of civilization, and became prime minister in 1847. His resistance to all reforms led to the revolution of 1848.

Gullit Ruud 1962– . Dutch international footballer born of a Surinamese father, famous for his dreadlock hairstyle. He played an important role in Holland's capture of the European Championship in 1988.

After playing in Holland with Haarlem, Feyenoord, and PSV Eindhoven, he moved to AC Milan in 1987 for a transfer fee of £5.5 million.

Gummer John Selwyn 1939– . British Conservative politician. He was minister of state for employment 1983–84, paymaster general 1984–85, minister for agriculture 1985–88, chairman of the party 1983–85, and minister for environment from 1988.

Gurdjieff George Ivanovitch 1877–1949. Russian occultist. He used stylized dance to 'free' people to develop their full capabilities, and influenced the modern human-potential movement. The mystic ◊Ouspensky was a disciple, who expanded his ideas.

Gustaf six kings of Sweden, including:

Gustaf V 1858–1950. King of Sweden from 1907, when he succeeded his father Oscar II. He married Princess Victoria, daughter of the Grand Duke of Baden, in 1881, thus uniting the reigning Bernadotte dynasty with the former royal house of Vasa.

Gustaf VI 1882–1973. King of Sweden from 1950, when he succeeded his father Gustaf V. He was an archaeologist and expert on Chinese art. His first wife was Princess Margaret of Connacht (1882–1920), and in 1923 he married Lady Louise Mountbatten (1889–1965), sister of the Earl of Mountbatten of Burma. He

was succeeded by his grandson ◊Carl Gustaf XVI.

Gustavus Adolphus 1594–1632. King of Sweden from 1611, when he succeeded his father Charles IX. He waged successful wars with Denmark, Russia, and Poland, and in the Thirty Years' War became a champion of the Protestant cause. Landing in Germany in 1630, he defeated the German general Wallenstein at Lützen, SW of Leipzig, on 6 Nov 1632, but was killed in the battle. He was known as the 'Lion of the North'.

Gustavus Vasa 1496–1560. King of Sweden from 1523, when he was elected after leading the Swedish revolt against Danish rule. He united and pacified the country and established Lutheranism as the state religion.

Gutenberg Johann *c.* 1400–1468. German printer, the inventor of printing from moveable metal type (see ◊Coster, Laurens Janszoon).

Gutenberg set up a printing business in Mainz with Johann Fust (*c.* 1400–66) as a partner 1440. The partnership was dissolved through monetary difficulties, but Gutenberg set up another printing press. He is believed to have printed the Mazarin and the Bamberg Bibles.

Guthrie Edwin R 1886–1959. American behaviourist, who attempted to develop a theory of learning that was independent of the traditional principles of reward or reinforcement. His ideas served as a basis for later statistical models.

Gwyn Formerly an orange-seller outside London's Drury Lane Theatre, Nell Gwyn became the mistress of Charles II, and he was the father of her two sons. This portrait by Sir Peter Lely is in Raby Castle, County Durham.

Guthrie Tyrone 1900–1971. British theatre director, noted for his experimental approach. Administrator of the Old Vic and Sadler's Wells theatres 1939–45, he helped found the Ontario (Stratford) Shakespeare Festival in 1953 and the Minneapolis theatre now named after him.

Guthrie Woody. Stage name of Woodrow Wilson Guthrie 1912–1967. US folk singer and songwriter, whose left-wing protest songs, 'dustbowl ballads', and *talking blues* were an influence on, among others, Bob Dylan; they include 'Deportees', 'Hard Travelin'', and 'This Land Is Your Land'.

Guys Constantin 1805–1892. French artist. He was with ◊Byron at Missolonghi, and made sketches of the Crimean War for the *Illustrated London News*.

Guzmán Blanco Antonio 1829–1899. Venezuelan dictator and military leader (*caudillo*). He seized power in 1870 and remained absolute ruler until 1889. He modernized Caracas to become the political capital; committed resources to education, communications, and agriculture; and encouraged foreign trade.

Gwyn 'Nell' (Eleanor) 1651–1687. English comedy actress from 1665, formerly an orange-seller at Drury Lane Theatre, London. The poet Dryden wrote parts for her, and from 1669 she was the mistress of Charles II.

The elder of her two sons by Charles II was created Duke of St Albans 1684. The king's last wish was 'Let not poor Nellie starve'.

Gysi Gregor 1948– . East German politician, elected leader of the Communist Party Dec 1989 following the resignation of Egon ◊Krenz. A lawyer, Gysi had acted as defence counsel for dissidents during the 1960s.

Connection 1971 and continued to play major roles in films such as *Bonnie and Clyde* 1967, *The Conversation* 1974, and *Mississippi Burning* 1988.

Hadlee Richard John 1951– . New Zealand cricketer. In 1987 he surpassed Ian Botham's world record of 373 wickets in test cricket. He retired from international cricket in 1990.

Hadlee played first-class cricket in England for Nottinghamshire and in Australia for Tasmania. His father **Walter Arnold Hadlee** also played test cricket for New Zealand, as did his brother **Dayle Robert Hadlee.**

Hadrian AD 76–138. Roman emperor from 117. Born in Spain, he was adopted by his relative, the emperor Trajan, whom he succeeded. He abandoned Trajan's conquests in Mesopotamia and adopted a defensive policy, which included the building of **Hadrian's Wall** in Britain.

Haeckel Ernst Heinrich 1834–1919. German scientist and philosopher. His theory of 'recapitulation' (that embryonic stages represent past stages in the organism's evolution) has been superseded, but stimulated research in embryology.

Hâfiz Shams al-Din Muhammad *c.*1326–1390. Persian lyric poet, who was born in Shiraz and taught in a Dervish college there. His *Diwan*, a collection of short odes, extols the pleasures of life and satirizes his fellow Dervishes.

Hagen Walter Charles 1892–1969. US golfer, a flamboyant and colourful character. He won 11 major championships 1914–1929. An exponent of the match-play type of game he won the US PGA championship five times, including four in succession.

Hagenbeck Carl 1844–1913. German zoo proprietor. In 1907 he founded Hagenbeck's Zoo, near his native Hamburg. He was a pioneer in the display of animals against a natural setting.

Haggard H(enry) Rider 1856–1925. English novelist. Born in Norfolk, he held colonial service posts in Natal and the Transvaal 1875–79, then returned to England to train as a barrister. He used his South African experience in his romantic adventure tales, including *King Solomon's Mines* 1885 and *She* 1887.

Hahn Kurt 1886–1974. German educationist. He was the founder of Salem School in Germany. After his expulsion by Hitler, he founded Gordonstoun School in Scotland and was headmaster 1934–53. He co-founded the international Atlantic College project in 1960, and was associated with the Outward Bound Trust.

Hahn Otto 1879–1968. West German physical chemist, who discovered nuclear fission. Nobel Prize for Chemistry 1944.

He worked with Ernest Rutherford and William Ramsay, and became director of the Kaiser Wilhelm Institute for Chemistry in 1928. With Fritz Strassmann (1902–1980), in 1938 he discovered that uranium nuclei split (undergo fission)

Haakon seven kings of Norway, including:

Haakon I *the Good c.*915–961. King of Norway from about 935. The son of Harald Hárfagri ('Finehair') (*c.*850–930), king of Norway, he was raised in England. He seized the Norwegian throne and tried unsuccessfully to introduce Christianity to Norway. His capital was at Trondheim.

Haakon IV 1204–1263. King of Norway from 1217, the son of Haakon III. Under his rule, Norway flourished both militarily and culturally; he took control of the Faroe Islands, Greenland 1261, and Iceland 1262–64. His court was famed throughout N Europe.

Haakon VII 1872–1957. King of Norway from 1905. Born Prince Charles, the second son of Frederick VIII of Denmark, he was elected king of Norway on separation from Sweden, and in 1906 he took the name Haakon. In World War II he refused to surrender to Germany and, when armed resistance in Norway was no longer possible, carried on the struggle from Britain until his return in 1945.

Haber Fritz 1868–1934. German chemist whose conversion of atmospheric nitrogen to ammonia opened the way for the synthetic fertilizer industry. His study of the combustion of hydrocarbons led to the commercial 'cracking' or fractionating of natural oil into its components, for example diesel, petrol, and paraffin. In electrochemistry he was the first to demonstrate that oxidation and reduction take place at the electrodes; from this he developed a general electrochemical theory.

In World War I he worked on poison gas and devised gas masks, hence there were protests against his Nobel prize in 1918.

Hackman Gene 1931– . US character actor. He became a star as 'Popeye' Doyle in *The French* when bombarded with neutrons, which led to the development of the atomic bomb (first used in 1945). He received the Nobel Prize for Chemistry in 1944.

Haig Alexander (Meigs) 1924– . US general and Republican politician. He became President Nixon's White House chief of staff at the height of the Watergate scandal, was NATO commander 1974–79, and was secretary of state to President Reagan 1981–82.

Haig Douglas, 1st Earl Haig 1861–1928. British army officer, commander in chief in World War I. His Somme (France) offensive in the summer of 1916 made considerable advances only at enormous cost, and his Passchendaele (Belgium) offensive (July–Nov 1917) achieved little at huge loss. He was created field marshal 1917.

Haile Selassie Ras Tafari ('the Lion of Judah') 1892–1975. Emperor of Ethiopia 1930–74. He pleaded unsuccessfully to the League of Nations against Italian conquest of his country 1935–36, and lived in the UK until his restoration in 1941. He was deposed by a military coup and died in captivity. Followers of the Rastafarian religion believe that he was the Messiah, the incarnation of God (Jah).

Hailsham Quintin Hogg, Baron Hailsham of St Marylebone 1907– . British lawyer and Conservative politician. The 2nd Viscount Hailsham, he renounced the title in 1963 to re-enter the House of Commons, and was thereby enabled to contest the Conservative Party leadership elections, but took a life peerage in 1970 on his appointment as Lord Chancellor 1970–74. He was Lord Chancellor again 1979–87.

Hailwood 'Mike' (Stanley Michael Bailey) 1940–1981. British motorcyclist. Between 1961 and 1967 he won nine world titles and 1961–79 a record 14 titles at the Isle of Man TT races.

Haitink Bernard 1929– . Dutch conductor of the Concertgebouw Orchestra, Amsterdam, from 1964, and music director of the Royal Opera House, Covent Garden, London, from 1986.

Hakluyt Richard 1553–1616. English geographer whose chief work is *The Principal Navigations, Voyages and Discoveries of the English Nation* 1598–1600. He was assisted by Sir Walter Raleigh.

He lectured on cartography at Oxford, became geographical adviser to the East India Company, and was an original member of the Virginia Company.

Haldane J(ohn) B(urdon) S(anderson) 1892–1964. English scientist and writer. A geneticist, Haldane was best known as a popular science writer of such books as *The Causes of Evolution* 1933 and *New Paths in Genetics* 1941.

Haldane Richard Burdon, Viscount Haldane 1856–1928. British Liberal politician. As secretary for war 1905–12, he sponsored the army

reforms that established an expeditionary force, backed by a territorial army and under the unified control of an imperial general staff. He was Lord Chancellor 1912–15 and in the Labour government of 1924. His writings on German philosophy led to popular accusations of his being pro-German.

Hale George Ellery 1868–1938. US astronomer, who made pioneer studies of the Sun and founded three major observatories. In 1889, he invented the spectroheliograph, a device for photographing the Sun at particular wavelengths.

In 1897 he founded the Yerkes Observatory in Wisconsin, with the largest refractor ever built, 102 cm/40 in. In 1917 he established on Mount Wilson, California a 2.5 m/100 in reflector, the world's largest telescope until superseded 1948 by the 5 m/200 in reflector on Mount Palomar, which Hale had had planned before he died.

Hale Nathan 1755–1776. US nationalist, hanged by the British as a spy in the War of American Independence. Reputedly his final words were 'I regret that I have but one life to give for my country'.

Hale Sarah Josepha Buell 1788–1879. US poet, author of 'Mary had a Little Lamb' 1830.

Hales Stephen 1677–1761. English priest and scientist who gave accurate accounts of water movement in plants. His work laid emphasis on measurement and experimentation.

Hales demonstrated that plants absorb air, and that some part of air is involved in their nutrition. He also measured plant growth and water loss, relating this to the upward movement of water from plants to leaves (transpiration).

Halévy Ludovic 1834–1908. French novelist and librettist. He collaborated with Hector Crémieux in the libretto for Offenbach's *Orpheus in the Underworld*; and with Henri Meilhac on librettos for Offenbach's *La Belle Hélène* and *La Vie parisienne*, and for Bizet's *Carmen*.

Haley Bill 1927–1981. US pioneer of rock and roll, originally a western-swing musician. His songs 'Rock Around the Clock' 1954 (recorded with his group the Comets and featured in the 1955 film *Blackboard Jungle*) and 'Shake, Rattle and Roll' 1955 came to symbolize the beginnings of the rock-and-roll era.

Halifax Charles Montagu, Earl of Halifax 1661–1715. British financier. Appointed commissioner of the Treasury in 1692, he raised money for the French war by instituting the National Debt, and in 1694 carried out William Paterson's plan for a national bank (the Bank of England), and became chancellor of the Exchequer.

Halifax Edward Frederick Lindley Wood, Earl of Halifax 1881–1959. British Conservative politician, viceroy of India 1926–31. As foreign secretary 1938–40 he was associated with Chamberlain's appeasement policy.

Halifax George Savile, 1st Marquess of Halifax 1633–1695. English politician. He entered Parliament in 1660, and was raised to the peerage by Charles II, by whom he was also later dismissed. He strove to steer a middle course between extremists, and became known as 'the Trimmer'. He played a prominent part in the revolution of 1688.

Hall Charles 1863–1914. US chemist who developed a process for the commercial production of aluminium in 1886.

He found that when mixed with cryolite (sodium aluminium fluoride), the melting point of aluminium was lowered and electrolysis became commercially viable. It had previously been as costly as gold.

Hall (Marguerite) Radclyffe 1883–1943. English novelist. She is best remembered for *The Well of Loneliness* 1928, whose lesbian theme brought it considerable notoriety.

Hall Peter (Reginald Frederick) 1930– . English theatre, opera, and film director. He was director of the Royal Shakespeare Theatre in Stratford-on-Avon 1960–68 and developed the Royal Shakespeare Company as director 1968–73 until appointed director of the National Theatre 1973–88, succeeding Laurence Olivier.

His productions include *Waiting for Godot* 1955, *The Wars of the Roses* 1963, *The Homecoming* stage 1967 and film 1973, and *Amadeus* 1979. He was also appointed artistic director of opera at Glyndebourne 1984, with productions of *Carmen* 1985 and *Albert Herring* 1985–86.

Hallam Henry 1777–1859. British historian. He was called to the Bar, but a private fortune enabled him to devote himself to historical study from 1812 and his *Constitutional History of England* 1827 established his reputation.

Haller Albrecht von 1708–1777. Swiss physician and scientist, founder of modern neurology. He studied the muscles and nerves, and concluded that nerves provide the stimulus which triggers muscle contraction. He also showed that it is the nerves, not muscle or skin, that permit sensation.

Halley Edmund 1656–1742. English scientist. In 1682 he observed the comet named after him, predicting that it would return in 1759.

Halley's other astronomical achievements include the discovery that stars have their own, or 'proper' motion. He was a pioneer geophysicist and meteorologist, and worked in many other fields, including mathematics. He became the second Astronomer Royal 1720. He was a friend of Isaac ◊Newton, whose *Principia* he financed.

Hals Frans *c.*1581–1666. Flemish-born painter of portraits, such as the *Laughing Cavalier* 1624 (Wallace Collection, London), and large groups of military companies, governors of charities, and others (many examples in the Frans Hals

Museum, Haarlem, Holland). In the 1620s he experimented with genre scenes.

Halsey William Frederick 1882–1959. US admiral, known as 'Bull'. Commander of the Third Fleet in the S Pacific from 1942 during World War II.

The Japanese signed the surrender document ending World War II on his flagship, the battleship *Missouri*.

Hamaguchi Hamaguchi Osachi, also known as Hamaguchi Yuko 1870–1931. Japanese politician and prime minister 1929–30. His policies created social unrest and alienated military interests. His acceptance of the terms of the London Naval Agreement 1930 was also unpopular. Shot by an assassin Nov 1930, he died of his wounds nine months later.

Hamilcar Barca *c.*270–228 BC. Carthaginian general, father of ◊Hannibal. From 247 to 241 he harassed the Romans in Italy and then led an expedition to Spain, where he died in battle.

Hamilton family name of Dukes of Abercorn; seated at Barons Court, Co Tyrone; the 3rd Duke was the great grandfather of Diana, Princess of Wales.

Hamilton Alexander 1757–1804. US politician, who influenced the adoption of a constitution with a strong central government, and was the first secretary of the treasury 1789–95. He led the Federalist Party, and incurred the bitter hatred of Aaron ◊Burr when he voted against Burr and in favour of Jefferson for the presidency in 1801.

Hamilton, born in the West Indies, served during the War of Independence as captain and 1777–81 was Washington's secretary and aide-de-camp. After the war he practised as a lawyer. He was a member of the Constitutional Convention of 1787, and in the *Federalist* influenced public opinion in favour of the ratification of the constitution. As first secretary of the treasury, he proved an able controller of the national finances. Challenged to a duel with Burr, he was wounded, and died the next day.

Hamilton Emma (born Amy Lyon) 1765–1815. English courtesan. In 1782 she became the mistress of Charles ◊Greville, and in 1786 of his uncle Sir William Hamilton, the British envoy at Naples, who married her 1791. After Admiral ◊Nelson's return from the Nile 1798 she became his mistress and their daughter, Horatia, was born 1801.

Hamilton Iain Ellis 1922– . Scottish composer. Intensely emotional and harmonically rich, his works include striking viola and cello sonatas, a ballet (*Clerk Saunders* 1951), the operas *Pharsalia* 1968 and *The Royal Hunt of the Sun* 1967–69, which renounced melody for inventive chordal formations, and symphonies.

Hamilton James 1st Duke of Hamilton 1606–1649. Scottish adviser to Charles I, he led an army against the Covenanters 1639, and subsequently took part in the negotiations between Charles and the Scots. In the second Civil War he led the Scottish invasion of England, but was captured at Preston and executed.

Hamilton Richard 1922– . English artist, a pioneer of Pop art. His collage *Just what is it that makes today's homes so different, so appealing?* 1956 (Kunsthalle, Tübingen) is often cited as the first Pop art work.

Its modern 1950s interior inhabited by the bodybuilder Charles Atlas and a pin-up is typically humorous, concerned with popular culture and contemporary kitsch.

Hamilton William 1730–1803. British diplomat, envoy to the court of Naples 1764–1800, whose collection of Greek vases was bought by the British Museum.

Hamilton William D 1936– . New Zealand biologist. By developing the concept of inclusive fitness, he was able to solve the theoretical problem of explaining altruism in animal behaviour in terms of Neo-Darwinism.

Hamilton William Rowan 1805–1865. Irish mathematician, whose formulation of Isaac Newton's mechanics proved adaptable to quantum theory, and whose 'quarternion' theory was a forerunner of the branch of mathematics known as vector analysis.

Hammarskjöld Dag 1905–1961. Swedish secretary-general of the United Nations 1953–61. On the 1956 Suez Crisis over control of the Suez Canal he opposed Britain. His attempts to solve the problem of the Congo (now Zaïre), where he was killed in a plane crash, were criticized by the USSR. Nobel Peace Prize 1961.

Hammerstein Oscar II 1895–1960. US lyricist and librettist, who collaborated with Jerome ◊Kern on *Show Boat* 1927, and with Richard ◊Rodgers.

Hammett Dashiell 1894–1961. US crime novelist, whose books include *The Maltese Falcon* 1930, *The Glass Key* 1931, and the *The Thin Man* 1932.

Hammett was a former Pinkerton detective agent. In 1951 he was imprisoned for contempt of court for refusing to testify during the McCarthy era of anticommunist witch-hunts. He lived with the playwright Lillian ◊Hellman.

Hammond Joan 1912– . Australian soprano, known in oratorio and opera, for example, *Madame Butterfly*, *Tosca*, and *Martha*.

Hampden John 1594–1643. English politician. His refusal in 1636 to pay ship money, a compulsory tax to support the navy, made him a national figure. Charles's attempt to arrest him and four other leading MPs made the Civil War inevitable. He raised his own regiment on the outbreak of hostilities, and on 18 June 1643 was mortally wounded at the skirmish of Chalgrove Field in Oxfordshire.

Hampton Christopher 1946– . British dramatist, resident at the Royal Court Theatre, London,

1968–70. His plays include the comedy *The Philanthropist* 1970, *Savages* 1973, and an adaptation of *Les Liaisons Dangereuses*.

Hamsun Knut 1859–1952. Norwegian novelist, whose first novel *Sult/Hunger* 1890 was largely autobiographical. Other works include *Pan* 1894 and *The Growth of the Soil* 1917, which won him a Nobel prize in 1920. His hatred of capitalism made him sympathize with Nazism, and he was fined in 1946 for collaboration.

Hanbury-Tenison (Airling) Robin 1936– . Irish adventurer, explorer, and writer, who made the first land crossing of South America at its widest point 1958. He explored the southern Sahara intermittently during 1962–66, and in South America sailed in a small boat from the Orinoco River to Buenos Aires 1964–65.

Hancock John 1737–1793. US revolutionary politician. He advocated resistance to the British as president of the Continental Congress 1775–77, and was the first to sign the Declaration of Independence in 1776. Because he signed it in a large, bold hand (in popular belief, so that it would be big enough for George III to see), his name became a colloquial term for a signature in the USA. He was governor of Massachusetts 1780–85 and 1787–93.

Hancock Tony (Anthony John) 1924–1968. British radio and television comedian. 'Hancock's Half Hour' from 1954 showed him always at odds with everyday life.

Handel Georg Friedrich 1685–1759. German composer, who became a British subject 1726. His first opera, *Almira*, was performed in Hamburg 1705. In 1710 he was appointed Kapellmeister to the elector of Hanover (the future George I of England). In 1712 he settled in England, where he established his popularity with works such as the *Water Music* 1717 (written for George I). His great choral works include the *Messiah* 1742 and the later oratorios *Samson* 1743, *Belshazzar* 1745, *Judas Maccabaeus* 1747, and *Jephtha* 1752.

Born in Halle, he abandoned the study of law 1703 to become a violinist at Keiser's Opera House in Hamburg. Visits to Italy (1706–10) inspired a number of operas and oratorios, and in 1711 his opera *Rinaldo* was performed in London. *Saul* and *Israel in Egypt* (both 1739) were unsuccessful, but his masterpiece the *Messiah* was acclaimed on its first performance in Dublin 1742. Other works include the pastoral *Acis and Galatea* 1718 and a set of variations for harpsichord that were later nicknamed 'The Harmonious Blacksmith'. In 1751 he became totally blind.

Handke Peter 1942– . Austrian novelist and playwright, whose first play *Insulting the Audience* 1966 was an example of 'anti-theatre writing'. His novels include *Die Hornissen/The Hornets* 1966 and *The Goalie's Anxiety at the Penalty Kick* 1970.

He directed and scripted the film *The Left-handed Woman* 1979.

Handley Tommy 1896–1949. English radio comedian. His popular programme 'ITMA' (It's That Man Again) ran from 1939 until his death.

Hanley Ellery 1961– . English rugby league player, a regular member of the Great Britain team since 1984 and the inspiration behind his club Wigan's rise to the top in the 1980s.

Hannibal 247–182 BC. Carthaginian general from 221 BC, son of Hamilcar Barca. His siege of Saguntum (now Sagunto, near Valencia) precipitated the 2nd Punic War with Rome. Following a campaign in Italy (after crossing the Alps in 218 with 57 elephants), Hannibal was the victor at Trasimene in 217 and Cannae in 216, but he failed to take Rome. In 203 he returned to Carthage to meet a Roman invasion but was defeated at Zama in 202 and exiled in 196 at Rome's insistence.

Hansom Joseph Aloysius 1803–1882. British architect. His works include the Birmingham town hall 1831, but he is remembered as the introducer of the *hansom cab* in 1834, a two-wheel carriage with a seat for the driver on the outside.

Hanway Jonas 1712–1786. British traveller in Russia and Persia, and advocate of prison reform. He is believed to have been the first Englishman to carry an umbrella.

Hapsburg English form of ◊Habsburg, European royal family and former imperial house of Austria-Hungary.

Haq Fazlul 1873–1962. Leader of the Bengali Muslim peasantry. He was a member of the Viceroy's Defence Council, established 1941, and was Bengal's first Indian prime minister 1937–43.

Harcourt William Vernon 1827–1904. British Liberal politician. Under Gladstone he was home secretary 1880–85 and chancellor of the Exchequer 1886 and 1892–95. He is remembered for his remark in 1892: 'We are all Socialists now.'

Hardenberg Karl August von 1750–1822. Prussian politician, foreign minister to King Frederick William III of Prussia during the Napoleonic Wars. He later became chancellor. His military and civic reforms were restrained by the reactionary tendencies of the king.

Hardicanute *c.*1019–1042. King of England from 1040. Son of Canute, he was king of Denmark from 1028. In England he was known as a harsh ruler.

Hardie (James) Keir 1856–1915. Scottish socialist, member of parliament for West Ham, London, 1892–95 and for Merthyr Tydfil, Wales, from 1900. Born in Lanarkshire, he worked in the mines as a boy, and in 1886 became secretary of the Scottish Miners' Federation. In 1888 he was the first Labour candidate to stand for Parliament; he entered Parliament independently as a Labour member in 1892 and was a chief founder of the Independent Labour Party in 1893.

Hardie *British socialist Keir Hardie, chief founder of the Independent Labour Party and the party's first candidate to stand for Parliament.*

A pacifist, he strongly opposed the Boer War, and his idealism in his work for socialism and the unemployed made him a popular hero.

Harding (Allan Francis) John, 1st Baron Harding of Petherton 1896–1989. British field marshal. Chief of staff in Italy during World War II. As governor of Cyprus 1955–57, during the period of political agitation prior to independence (1960), he was responsible for the controversial deportation of Makarios III from Cyprus in 1955.

Harding Warren G(amaliel) 1865–1923. 29th president of the USA 1921–23, a Republican. Harding was born in Ohio, and entered the US Senate in 1914. As president he concluded the peace treaties of 1921 with Germany, Austria, and Hungary, and in the same year called the Washington Naval Conference. He opposed US membership of the League of Nations. There were charges of corruption among members of his cabinet.

Hardouin-Mansart 1646–1708. French architect, royal architect to Louis XIV from 1675. He designed the lavish Baroque extensions to the palace of Versailles (from 1678) and the Invalides Chapel in Paris 1680–91.

Hardy Oliver 1892–1957. US film comedian, member of the duo ◊Laurel and Hardy.

Hardy Thomas 1840–1928. English novelist and poet. His novels, set in rural 'Wessex' (his native West Country), portray intense human relationships played out in a harshly indifferent natural world. They include *Far From the Madding Crowd* 1874, *The Return of the Native* 1878, *The Mayor of Casterbridge* 1886, *The Woodlanders* 1887, *Tess of the D'Urbervilles* 1891, and *Jude the Obscure* 1895. His poetry includes the *Wessex Poems* 1898, the blank-verse epic *The Dynasts* 1904–08, and several volumes of lyrics.

Born in Dorset, he was trained as an architect. His first success was *Far From the Madding Crowd*. *Tess of the D'Urbervilles*, subtitled 'A Pure Woman', outraged public opinion by portraying as its heroine a woman who had been seduced. The even greater outcry that followed *Jude the Obscure* 1895 reinforced Hardy's decision to confine himself to verse.

Hardy Thomas Masterman 1769–1839. British sailor. At Trafalgar he was Nelson's flag captain in the *Victory*, attending him during his dying moments. He became First Sea Lord in 1830.

Hare David 1947– . British dramatist and director, whose plays include *Slag* 1970, *Teeth 'n' Smiles* 1975, *Pravda* 1985 (with Howard ◊Brenton), and *Wrecked Eggs* 1986.

Harewood George Henry Hubert Lascelles, 7th Earl of Harewood 1923– . Artistic director of the Edinburgh Festival 1961–65, managing director of the English National Opera 1972–85, and a governor of the BBC from 1985.

Hargobind 1595–1644. Indian religious leader, sixth guru (teacher) of Sikhism 1606– 44. He encouraged Sikhs to develop military skills in response to growing persecution. At the festival of Diwali, Sikhs celebrate his release from prison.

Hargraves Edward Hammond 1816–1891. Australian prospector, born in England. In 1851 he found gold in the Blue Mountains of New South Wales, thus beginning the first Australian gold rush.

Hargreaves James died 1778. English inventor, who co-invented a carding machine in 1760. About 1764 he invented his 'spinning-jenny', which enabled a number of threads to be spun simultaneously by one person.

Har Krishen 1656–1664. Indian religious leader, eighth guru (teacher) of Sikhism 1661–64, who died at the age of eight.

Harley Robert, 1st Earl of Oxford 1661–1724. British Tory politician, chief minister to Queen Anne 1711–14, when he negotiated the Treaty of Utrecht in 1713. Accused of treason as a Jacobite after the accession of George I, he was imprisoned 1714–17.

Harlow Jean. Stage name of Harlean Carpenter 1911–1937. US film actress, the first 'platinum blonde'. Her films include *Hell's Angels* 1930, *Dinner At Eight* 1934, and *Saratoga* 1937.

Harold two kings of England:

Harold II *c.* 1020–1066. King of England from Jan 1066. He succeeded his father Earl ◊Godwin 1053 as earl of Wessex. In 1063 William of Normandy (William I) tricked him into swearing to support his claim to the English throne, and when the council of kings, the Witan, elected Harold to succeed Edward the Confessor, William prepared to invade. Meanwhile, Harold's treacherous brother Tostig (died 1066) joined the king of Norway,

Harlow US film star Jean Harlow, popularly known as the 'platinum blonde'.

Harald III Hardrada (1015–66), in invading Northumbria. Harold routed and killed them at Stamford Bridge 25 Sept. Three days later William landed at Pevensey, Sussex; Harold was killed at the Battle of Hastings 14 Oct 1066.

Har Rai 1630–1661. Indian religious leader, seventh guru (teacher) of Sikhism 1644–61.

Harriman (William) Averell 1891–1986. US diplomat, administrator of lend-lease (by which the USA supplied equipment to the Allies) in World War II, Democratic secretary of commerce in Truman's administration, 1946–1948, and negotiator of the Nuclear Test Ban Treaty with the USSR in 1963.

Harris Arthur Travers 1892–1984. British marshal of the Royal Air Force in World War II. Known as 'Bomber Harris', he was commander in chief of Bomber Command 1942–45.

He was an autocratic and single-minded leader, and was criticized for his policy of civilian-bombing of selected cities in Germany; he authorized the fire-bombing raids on Dresden, in which more than 100,000 died.

Harris Frank 1856–1931. Irish journalist, who wrote colourful biographies of Wilde and Shaw, and an autobiography, *My Life and Loves* 1926, originally banned in the UK and the USA.

Harris Joel Chandler 1848–1908. US author of the tales of 'Uncle Remus', based on black folklore, about Br'er Rabbit and the Tar Baby.

Harris Paul P 1878–1947. US lawyer, who founded the first of the *Rotary Clubs*, philanthropic associations of business and professional people, in Chicago 1905.

Harris Richard 1932– . Irish film actor known for playing rebel characters in such films as *This Sporting Life* 1963; *Il Deserto rosso/The Red Desert*

1964; *Camelot* 1967; *Cromwell* 1970; *Robin and Marion* 1976; *Tarzan the Ape Man* 1981.

Harris Roy 1898–1979. US composer, born in Oklahoma, who used American folk tunes. Among his works are the 10th symphony 1965 (known as 'Abraham Lincoln') and the orchestral *When Johnny Comes Marching Home* 1935.

Harrison Benjamin 1833–1901. 23rd president of the USA 1889–93, a Republican. He called the first Pan-American Conference, which led to the establishment of the Pan American Union, to improve inter-American cooperation, and develop commercial ties. In 1948 this became the Organization of American States.

Harrison (Reginald Carey) 'Rex' 1908–1990. British actor. His successes include *French Without Tears* 1936 and the musical *My Fair Lady* stage 1956, film 1964. Films include *Blithe Spirit* 1944 and *Cleopatra* 1962.

Harrison William Henry 1773–1841. 9th president of the USA 1841. Elected 1840 as a Whig, he died a month after taking office. Benjamin Harrison was his grandson.

Harrisson Tom 1911–1976. British anthropologist, who set up Mass Observation with Charles Madge 1937, the earliest of the organizations for the analysis of public opinions and attitudes.

Hart Gary 1936– . US Democrat politician, senator for Colorado from 1974. In 1980 he contested the Democratic nomination for the presidency, and stepped down from his Senate seat in 1986 to stand, again unsuccessfully, in the 1988 presidential campaign.

Hart Judith 1924– . British Labour politician and sociologist. She was minister of overseas development 1967–70 and 77–79, and minister of state 1974–75.

Harte Francis Bret 1836–1902. US writer. He became a goldminer at 18 before founding the *Overland Monthly* 1868 in which he wrote short stories of the pioneer West, for example *The Luck of Roaring Camp* and poems such as *The Heathen Chinee*. From 1885 he settled in England after five years as US consul in Glasgow.

Hartington Spencer Compton Cavendish, 8th Duke of Devonshire, and Marquess of Hartington 1833–1908. British politician, first leader of the Liberal Unionists 1886–1903. As war minister he opposed devolution for Ireland in cabinet and later led the revolt of the Liberal Unionists that defeated Gladstone's Irish Home Rule bill in 1886. Cavendish refused the premiership three times, 1880, 1886, and 1887.

Hartley L(eslie) P(oles) 1895–1972. English novelist, noted for his exploration of the sinister. His books include the trilogy *The Shrimp and the Anemone* 1944, *The Sixth Heaven* 1946, and *Eustace and Hilda* 1947, on the intertwined lives of a brother and sister. Later books include *The*

Boat 1949, *The Go-Between* 1953, and *The Hireling* 1957.

Harun al-Rashid 763–809. Caliph of Baghdad from 786 of the Abbasid dynasty, a lavish patron of music, poetry, and letters, known from the *Arabian Nights* stories.

Harvey Laurence (Lauruska Mischa Skikne) 1928–1973. British film actor of Lithuanian descent who worked both in England (*Room at the Top* 1958) and in Hollywood (*The Alamo* 1960; *The Manchurian Candidate* 1962).

Harvey William 1578–1657. English physician who discovered the circulation of blood. In 1628 he published his great book *De Motu Cordis/On the Motion of the Heart.*

After studying at Padua, Italy, under ◊Fabricius, he set out to question ◊Galen's account of the action of the heart. Later, Harvey explored the development of chick and deer embryos. He was Court physician to James I and Charles I.

Hašek Jaroslav 1883–1923. Czech writer. His masterpiece is the anti-authoritarian comic satire on military life under Austro-Hungarian rule, *The Good Soldier Schweik* 1923. During World War I he deserted to the Russians, and eventually joined the Bolsheviks.

Hassam Childe 1859–1935. US Impressionist painter and printmaker. He was profoundly influenced by a visit to Paris in 1866. He became one of the members of **the Ten,** a group of American Impressionists who exhibited together until World War I.

Hassan II 1930– . King of Morocco from 1961; from 1976 he undertook the occupation of Western Sahara.

Hastings Warren 1732–1818. British colonial administrator. A protégé of Lord Clive, who established British rule in India, Hastings carried out major reforms, and became governor of Bengal in 1772 and governor general of India in 1774. Impeached for corruption on his return to England in 1785, he was acquitted in 1795.

Hathaway Anne 1556–1623. Wife of the English dramatist ◊Shakespeare from 1582.

Hatshepsut *c.*1540–*c.*1481 BC. Queen of Egypt during the 18th dynasty. She was the daughter of Thothmes I, with whom she ruled until the accession to the throne of her husband and half-brother Thotmes II. Throughout his reign real power lay with Hatshepsut, and she continued to rule after his death, as regent for her nephew Thotmes III.

Hatshepsut reigned as a man, and is shown dressed as a pharaoh, with a beard. Her reign was a peaceful and prosperous time in a period when Egypt was developing its armies and expanding its territories. The ruins of her magnificent temple at Deir el-Bahri survive.

Hattersley Roy 1932– . British Labour politician. On the right wing of the Labour Party, he was prices secretary 1976–79, and in 1983 became deputy leader of the party.

Hatton Derek 1948– . British left-wing politician, former deputy leader of Liverpool Council. A notorious member of the Trotskyite Militant Tendency group, Hatton was removed from office and expelled from the Labour Party in 1987.

Haughey Charles 1925– . Irish Fianna Fáil politician of Ulster descent. Dismissed in 1970 from Jack Lynch's cabinet for alleged complicity in IRA gun-running, he was afterwards acquitted. Prime minister 1979–81, Mar–Nov 1982, and 1986– .

Haussmann Georges Eugène, Baron Haussmann 1809–1891. French administrator, who replanned medieval Paris 1853–70, with wide boulevards and parks. The cost of his scheme and his authoritarianism caused opposition, and he was made to resign.

Havel Vaclav 1936–. Czech playwright and president. His plays include *The Garden Party* 1963 and *Largo Desolato* 1985, about a dissident intellectual. As a playwright in Prague, his works, which criticized the Communist regime, were banned throughout Eastern Europe from 1968 and he was subsequently imprisoned or placed under house arrest. In 1988 he founded the monthly dissident publication, the 'People's Newspaper'. In 1989, after further imprisonment for supporting the freedom campaign Charter 77, he became a presidential candidate after the resignation of

Hawke Australian politician Bob Hawke, prime minister since 1983.

the Communist Gustav ◊Husak. Following the overthrow of the communist regime, he was elected state president by the federal assembly Dec 1989.

Havers Robert Michael Oldfield, Baron Havers 1923– . British lawyer, Lord Chancellor 1987--88. After a successful legal career he became Conservative MP for Wimbledon in 1970 and was solicitor-general under Edward Heath and attorney-general under Margaret Thatcher. He was made a life peer in 1987 and served briefly, and unhappily, as Lord Chancellor before retiring in 1988.

Hawke Bob (Robert) 1929– . Australian Labor politician, on the right wing of the party. He was president of the Australian Council of Trade Unions 1970–80, and became prime minister 1983.

Hawker Robert Stephen 1803–1875. English poet ('Song of the Western Men'), vicar of Morwenstow, Cornwall, from 1834, and originator of the harvest festival.

Hawking Stephen 1942– . English physicist, who has researched black holes (the hypothetical end-results of total gravitational collapse in stars) and gravitational field theory. His books include *A Brief History of Time* 1988.

Professor of gravitational physics at Cambridge from 1977, he discovered that the strong gravitational field around a black hole can radiate particles of matter.

Hawkins Anthony Hope. Real name of English novelist Anthony ◊Hope.

Havel Czechoslavakia's 'playwright president,' Vaclav Havel.

Hawking British physicist and mathematician
Professor Stephen Hawking, in London, 1988.

Hawkins Coleman (Randolph) 1904–1969. US virtuoso tenor saxophonist. He was until 1934 a soloist in the swing band led by Fletcher Henderson (1898–1952), and was an influential figure in bringing the jazz saxophone to prominence as a solo instrument.

Hawkins Jack 1910–1973. British film actor, usually cast in authoritarian roles. His films include *The Cruel Sea* 1953, *The League of Gentlemen* 1959, *Zulu* 1963, *Waterloo* 1970. After 1966 his voice had to be dubbed following an operation for throat cancer that removed his vocal chords.

Hawkins John 1532–1595. English navigator, born in Plymouth. Treasurer to the navy 1573–89, he was knighted for his services as a commander against the Spanish Armada 1588.

Hawkins Richard c.1562–1622. English navigator, son of John Hawkins. He held a command against the Spanish Armada 1588, was captured in an expedition against Spanish possessions 1593–94 and not released until 1602.

Hawks Howard 1896–1977. US director and producer of a wide range of films, including *Bringing Up Baby* 1936, *Ball of Fire* 1942, *The Big Sleep* 1946, and *Gentlemen Prefer Blondes* 1953.

Hawksmoor Nicholas 1661–1736. English architect, assistant to ◊Wren in London churches and St Paul's Cathedral; joint architect with ◊Vanbrugh of Castle Howard and Blenheim Palace.

The original west towers of Westminster Abbey, long attributed to Wren, were designed by Hawksmoor.

Haworth (Walter) Norman 1883–1950. English organic chemist who was the first to synthesize a vitamin (vitamin C), in 1933. He shared a Nobel prize in 1937.

Hawthorne Nathaniel 1804–1864. US writer of *The Scarlet Letter* 1850, a powerful novel of Puritan Boston. He wrote three other novels, including *The House of the Seven Gables* 1851, and many short stories, including *Tanglewood Tales* 1853, classic legends retold for children.

Hay Will 1888–1949. British comedy actor. Originally a music hall comedian, from the 1930s he made many films in which he usually played incompetents in positions of authority, including *Good Morning Boys* 1937; *Oh Mr Porter* 1938; *Ask a Policeman* 1939; *The Ghost of St Michaels* 1941; *My Learned Friend* 1944.

Hayden Sterling. Stage name of John Hamilton 1916–1986. US film actor who played leading roles in Hollywood in the 1940s and early 1950s. Although later seen in some impressive character roles, his career as a whole failed to do justice to his talent. His work includes *The Asphalt Jungle* 1950, *Johnny Guitar* 1954, *Dr Strangelove* 1964, and *The Godfather* 1972.

Hayden William (Bill) 1933– . Australian Labor politician. He was leader of the Australian Labor Party and of the opposition 1977–83, and minister of foreign affairs 1983. He became Governor-General 1989.

Haydn Franz Joseph 1732–1809. Austrian composer. A teacher of Mozart and Beethoven, he was a major exponent of the Classical sonata form in his numerous chamber and orchestral works (he wrote over 100 symphonies). He also composed choral music, including the oratorios *The Creation* 1798 and *The Seasons* 1801. He was the first great master of the string quartet.

Born in Lower Austria, he was Kapellmeister 1761–90 to Prince Esterházy at Eisenstadt and Esterház. He visited London twice, 1791–92 and 1794–95. His work also includes operas, church music, and songs, and he composed the 'Emperor's Hymn', adopted as the Austrian, and later the German, national anthem.

Haydon Benjamin Robert 1786–1846. British painter, who became celebrated for his gigantic canvasses. His attempts at 'high art' include *Christ's Entry into Jerusalem* (1820, Philadelphia). He is now more appreciated in genre pictures, for example *The Mock Election* and *Chairing the Member*, and for his lively *Autobiography* and *Memoirs* 1853.

Hayek Friedrich August von 1899– . Austrian economist. Born in Vienna, he taught at the London School of Economics 1931–50. His *The Road to Serfdom* 1944 was a critical study of socialist trends in Britain. He won the 1974 Nobel Prize for Economics.

Hayes Rutherford B(irchard) 1822–1893. 19th president of the USA 1877–81, a Republican. Born in Ohio, he was a major-general on the Union side in the Civil War. During his presidency federal troops were withdrawn from the Southern states and the Civil Service reformed.

Hayworth Rita. Stage name of Magarita Carmen Cansino 1918–1987. US film actress who gave vivacious performances in 1940s musicals and romantic dramas such as *Gilda* 1946 and *The Lady from Shanghai* 1948.

Hazlitt William 1778–1830. British essayist and critic, noted for his invective, scathing irony and gift for epigram. His critical essays include *Characters of Shakespeare's Plays* 1817–18, *Lectures on the English Poets* 1818–19, *English Comic Writers* 1819, and *Dramatic Literature of the Age of Elizabeth* 1820. Other notable works are *Table Talk* 1821–22, *The Spirit of the Age* 1825, and *Liber Amoris* 1823.

Head Bessie 1937– . South African writer living in exile in Botswana. Her novels include *When Rain Clouds Gather* 1969, *Maru* 1971, and *A Question of Power* 1973.

Head Edith 1900–1981. US costume designer for Hollywood films, who won eight Oscars, in such films as *The Heiress* 1949, *All About Eve* 1950, and *The Sting* 1972.

Heal Ambrose 1872–1959. English cabinet-maker who took over the Heal's shop from his father and developed it into the renowned London store. He initially designed furniture in the Arts and Crafts style, often in oak, and in the 1930s he started using materials such as tubular steel.

Healey Denis (Winston) 1917– . British Labour politician. While minister of defence 1964–70 he was in charge of the reduction of British forces east of Suez. He was chancellor of the Exchequer 1974–79. In 1976 he contested the party leadership, losing to James Callaghan, and again in 1980, losing to Michael Foot, to whom he was deputy leader 1980–83. In 1987 he resigned from the shadow cabinet.

Heaney Seamus (Justin) 1939– . Irish poet, born in County Derry, who has written powerful verse about the political situation in Northern Ireland. Collections include *North* 1975, *Field Work* 1979, and *Station Island* 1984.

Hearns Thomas 1958– . US boxer, who in 1988 became the first to have won world titles at five different weight classes in five separate fights.

Hearst Patty (Patricia) 1955– . US socialite. A granddaughter of the newspaper tycoon William R Hearst, she was kidnapped in 1974 by an urban guerrilla group, the Symbionese Liberation Army. She joined her captors in a bank raid, and was imprisoned 1976–79.

Hearst William Randolph 1863–1951. US newspaper proprietor, celebrated for his introduction of banner headlines, lavish illustration, and the sensationalist approach known as 'yellow journalism'.

A campaigner in numerous controversies, and a strong isolationist, he was said to be the model for Citizen Kane in the film of that name by Orson Welles.

Heath Edward (Richard George) 1916– . British Conservative politician, party leader 1965–75. As prime minister 1970–74 he took the UK into the European Community, but was brought down by economic and industrial-relations crises at home.

Heath entered Parliament 1950, was minister of labour 1959–60, and as Lord Privy Seal 1960–63 conducted abortive negotiations for Common Market (European Community) membership. He succeeded Home as Conservative leader 1965, the first elected leader of his party. Defeated in the general election 1966, he achieved a surprise victory 1970, but his confrontation with the striking miners as part of his campaign to control inflation led to his defeat Feb 1974 and again Oct 1974. He was replaced as party leader by Margaret Thatcher 1975, and became increasingly critical of her policies, especially in her opposition to the UK's full participation in the EC.

Heaviside Oliver 1850–1925. British physicist. In 1902, he predicted the existence of an ionized layer of air in the upper atmosphere, which was later known as the Kennelly-Heaviside layer but is now called the E-layer of the ionosphere. Deflection from it makes possible the transmission of radio signals round the world, which would otherwise be lost in outer space.

Hecht Ben 1893–1964. US film screenwriter and occasional director, who was formerly a journalist. His play *The Front Page* was adapted several times for the cinema by other writers. His screenplays for such films as *Gunga Din* 1939, *Spellbound* 1945, and *Actors and Sin* 1952 earned him a reputation as one of Hollywood's best writers.

Hedin Sven Anders 1865–1952. Swedish archaeologist, geographer, and explorer in central Asia and China. Between 1891 and 1908 he explored routes across the Himalayas and produced the first maps of Tibet. During 1928–33 he travelled with a Sino-Swedish expedition which crossed the Gobi Desert. His publications include *My Life as Explorer* 1925 and *Across the Gobi Desert* 1928.

Hegel Georg Wilhelm Friedrich 1770–1831. German philosopher, who conceived of consciousness and the external object as forming a unity, in which neither factor can exist independently, mind and nature being two abstractions of one indivisible whole. Hegel believed development took place through dialectic: contradiction and the resolution of contradiction. For Hegel, the task of philosophy was to comprehend the rationality of what already exists, but leftist followers, including Marx, used Hegel's dialectic to attempt to show the inevitability of radical change, and attacked both religion and the social order.

He wrote *The Phenomenology of Spirit* 1807, *Encyclopaedia of the Philosophical Sciences* 1817, and *Philosophy of Right* 1821. He was professor of philosophy at Heidelberg 1817–18, and at Berlin

1818–31. As a rightist, Hegel championed religion, the Prussian state, and the existing order.

Heidegger Martin 1889–1976. German philosopher. In *Being and Time* 1927, he used the methods of ◊Husserl's phenomenology to explore the structures of human existence. His later writings meditated on the fate of a world dominated by science and technology.

He believed that Western philosophy had 'forgotten' the fundamental question of the 'meaning of Being'. Although one of his major concerns was the angst of human existence, he denied that he was an existentialist. His support for Nazism, and his unwillingness or his inability to defend his position, damaged his reputation.

Heifetz Jascha 1901–1987. Russian-born US violinist, one of the great virtuosos of the 20th century. He first performed at the age of five, and before he was 17 had played in most European capitals, and in the US, where he settled 1917. His style of playing was calm and objective.

Heine Heinrich 1797–1856. German romantic poet and journalist, who wrote *Reisebilder* 1826 and *Buch der Lieder/Book of Songs* 1827. From 1831 he lived mainly in Paris, as a correspondent for German newspapers. Schubert and Schumann set many of his songs to music.

In 1835, he headed a list of writers forbidden to publish in Germany. He contracted a spinal disease 1845, which confined him to his bed from 1848 until his death.

Heinkel Ernst 1888–1958. German aircraft designer who pioneered jet aircraft. He founded his firm 1922, and built the first jet aircraft 1939 (developed independently of the Whittle jet of 1941). During World War II his company was Germany's biggest producer of warplanes.

Heinlein Robert A(nson) 1907– . US science-fiction writer, associated with the pulp magazines of the 1940s; best known for the militaristic novel *Starship Troopers* 1959 and the utopian cult novel *Stranger in a Strange Land* 1961.

Heisenberg Werner Carl 1901–1976. German physicist. He was an originator of quantum mechanics, the modern theory of matter, radiation, and their reaction, and the formulator of the uncertainty principle, which places absolute limits on the achievable accuracy of measurement. Nobel prize 1932.

Hekmatyar Gulbuddin 1949– . Afghani Islamic fundamentalist guerrilla leader. He became a mujaheddin guerrilla in the 1980s, leading the fundamentalist faction of the Hizbi Islami (Islamic Party), dedicated to the overthrow of the Soviet-backed communist regime in Kabul. He has refused to countenance participation in any interim 'national unity' government which includes Afghani communists.

Helena, St *c.*248–328. Roman empress, mother of Constantine the Great, and a convert to Christianity. According to legend, she discovered the true cross of Jesus in Jerusalem. Her feast day is 18 Aug.

Heller Joseph 1923– . US novelist. He drew on his experiences in the US air force in World War II to write *Catch-22* 1961, satirizing war and bureaucratic methods. After the air force, he entered advertising. Other books include *Something Happened*, *Good As Gold*, and the play *We Bombed In New Haven*.

Hellman Lillian 1907–1984. US playwright, whose work is largely concerned with contemporary political and social issues. *The Children's Hour* 1934, *The Little Foxes* 1939, and *Toys in the Attic* 1960 are all examples of the 'well-made play'.

She lived some 31 years with the writer Dashiell Hammett, and in her will founded a fund to promote Marxist doctrine. Since her death there has been controversy about the accuracy of her memoirs, for example *Pentimento* 1973.

Helmholtz Hermann Ludwig Ferdinand von 1821–1894. German physiologist, physicist, and inventor of the ophthalmoscope for examining the inside of the eye. He was the first to explain how the cochlea of the inner ear works, and the first to measure the speed of nerve impulses. In physics, he formulated the law of conservation of energy, and did important work in thermodynamics.

Helmont Jean Baptiste van 1577–1644. Belgian doctor. He was the first to realize that gases exist apart from the atmosphere, and claimed to have coined the word 'gas' (from the Greek 'chaos').

Helms Richard 1913– . US director of the Central Intelligence Agency 1966–73, when he was dismissed by Nixon. In 1977 he was convicted of lying before a congressional committee because his oath as chief of intelligence compelled him to keep secrets from the public.

Héloïse 1101–1164. Abbess of Paraclete in Champagne, correspondent and lover of ◊Abelard. She became deeply interested in intellectual study in her youth. After her affair with Abelard, and the birth of a son, Astrolabe, she became a nun 1229, and with Abelard's assistance, founded a nunnery at Paraclete. Her letters show her strong and pious character.

Helpmann Robert 1909–1986. Australian dancer, choreographer, and actor. The leading male dancer with the Sadler's Wells Ballet, London 1933–50, he partnered Margot ◊Fonteyn in the 1940s.

He was noted for his gift for mime and for his dramatic sense, also apparent in his choreographic work, for example *Miracle in the Gorbals* 1944.

Helvetius Claude Adrien 1715–1771. French philosopher. In *De l'Esprit* 1758 he argued that self-interest, however disguised, is the mainspring of all human action, that since conceptions of good and evil vary according to period and locality there is no absolute good or evil. He also believed that intellectual differences are only a matter of education.

Hemingway Ernest 1898–1961. US writer. War, bullfighting, and fishing became prominent themes in his short stories and novels, which included *A Farewell to Arms* 1929, *For Whom the Bell Tolls* 1940, and *The Old Man and the Sea* 1952. His short, deceptively simple sentences attracted many imitators. Nobel prize 1954.

He was born in Oak Park, Illinois, and developed in his youth a passion for hunting and adventure. He became a journalist, and was wounded while serving on a volunteer ambulance crew in Italy in World War I. His style was influenced by Gertrude ◊Stein, who also introduced him to bullfighting, a theme in his first novel *The Sun Also Rises* 1926 and the memoir *Death in the Afternoon* 1932. *A Farewell to Arms* deals with wartime experiences on the Italian front, and *For Whom the Bell Tolls* has a Spanish Civil War setting.

Henderson Arthur 1863–1935. British Labour politician, born in Glasgow. He worked 20 years as an iron-moulder in Newcastle, entered Parliament 1903, and contributed to Labour's political organization. He was home secretary in the first Labour government, and was foreign secretary 1929–31, when he accorded the Soviet government full recognition. Nobel Peace Prize 1934.

Hendrix Jimi (James Marshall) 1942–1970. US rock guitarist, songwriter, and singer, legendary for his virtuoso experimental technique and flamboyance.

He moved to the UK 1966 and formed a trio, the *Jimi Hendrix Experience*, which was successful from its first singles ('Hey Joe' and 'Purple Haze', both 1967), and attracted notice in the USA when Hendrix burned his guitar at the 1967 Monterey Pop Festival. The group disbanded early 1969 after three albums; Hendrix continued to record and occasionally perform until his death the following year. He greatly expanded the vocabulary of the electric guitar and influenced both rock and jazz musicians.

Hendry Stephen 1970– . Scottish snooker player of exceptional talent. In 1990 he became the youngest ever winner of the world championship and succeeded Steve Davis at the top of the world ranking list.

When he won the Scottish professional title 1986, he was the youngest winner of a professional tournament. He won his first ranking event in the 1987 Rothmans Grand Prix.

Heng Samrin 1934– . Cambodian politician. A former Khmer Rouge commander 1976–78, who had become disillusioned by its brutal tactics, he led an unsuccessful coup against ◊Pol Pot 1978 and established the Kampuchean People's Revolutionary Party (KPRP) in Vietnam, before returning, in 1979, to head the new Vietnamese-backed government.

Hengist 5th century. Legendary leader, with his brother Horsa, of the Jutes, who originated in Jutland, and settled in Kent about 450, the first Anglo-Saxon settlers in Britain.

Henie Sonja 1912–1969. Norwegian skater. Norwegian champion at 11, she won ten world championships and three Olympic titles. She turned professional 1936 and made numerous films.

Henlein Konrad 1898–1945. Sudeten-German leader of the Sudeten Nazi Party inside Czechoslovakia, and closely allied with Hitler's German Nazis. He was partly responsible for the destabilization of the Czech state 1938 which led to the Munich Agreement and secession of the Sudetenland to Germany.

Henri Robert 1865–1929. US painter, a leading figure in the transition between 19th–century conventions and Modern art in America. He was a principal member of the *Ashcan school*, named after the squalid cityscapes some of them produced.

Henrietta Maria 1609–1669. Queen of England 1625–49. The daughter of Henry IV of France, she married Charles I of England 1625. As she used her influence to encourage him to aid Roman Catholics and make himself an absolute ruler, she became highly unpopular and had to go into exile 1644–60. She returned to England at the Restoration, but retired to France 1665.

Henry (Charles Albert David) known as *Harry* 1984– . Prince of the United Kingdom; second child of the Prince and Princess of Wales.

Henry Joseph 1797–1878. US physicist, inventor of the electromagnetic motor 1829, and a telegraphic apparatus. He also discovered the principle of electromagnetic induction, roughly at the same time as ◊Faraday, and the phenomenon of self-induction.

Henry O. Pen name of William Sydney Porter 1862–1910. US short story writer, whose collections include *Cabbages and Kings* 1904 and *The Four Million* 1906. His stories are in a colloquial style and noted for their skilled construction with twist endings.

Henry Patrick 1736–1799. US politician, who in 1775 supported the arming of the Virginia militia against the British by a speech ending: 'Give me liberty or give me death!' He was governor of the state 1776–79 and 1784–86.

Henry William 1774–1836. British chemist. In 1803 he formulated *Henry's law*: when a gas is dissolved in a liquid at a given temperature, the mass which dissolves is in direct proportion to the gas pressure.

Henry eight kings of England:

Henry I 1068–1135. King of England from 1100. Youngest son of William I, he succeeded his brother William II. He won the support of the Saxons by granting them a charter and marrying a Saxon princess. An able administrator, he established a professional bureaucracy and a system of travelling judges. He was succeeded by Stephen.

Henry II 1133–1189. King of England from 1154, when he succeeded ◊Stephen. He was the son of ◊Matilda and Geoffrey of Anjou (1113–51). He curbed the power of the barons, but his attempt to bring the church courts under control had to be abandoned after the murder of ◊Becket. During his reign the English conquest of Ireland began. He was succeeded by his son Richard I.

He was lord of Scotland, Ireland, and Wales, and count of Anjou, Brittany, Poitou, Normandy, Maine, Gascony, and Aquitaine. He was married to Eleanor of Aquitaine.

Henry III 1207–1272. King of England from 1216, when he succeeded John, but he did not assume royal power until 1227. His subservience to the papacy and his foreign favourites led to de ◊Montfort's revolt 1264. Henry was defeated at Lewes, Sussex, and imprisoned. He was restored to the throne after royalist victory at Evesham 1265. He was succeeded by his son Edward I.

Henry IV (Bolingbroke) 1367–1413. King of England from 1399, the son of ◊John of Gaunt. In 1398 he was banished by ◊Richard II for political activity, but returned 1399 to head a revolt and be accepted as king by Parliament. He was succeeded by his son Henry V.

He had difficulty in keeping the support of Parliament and the clergy, and had to deal with baronial unrest and ◊Glendower's rising in Wales. In order to win support he had to conciliate the church by a law for the burning of heretics, and to make many concessions to Parliament.

Henry V 1387–1422. King of England from 1413, son of Henry IV. Invading Normandy 1415, he captured Harfleur, and defeated the French at the battle of Agincourt. He invaded again 1417–19, capturing Rouen. He married ◊Catherine of Valois 1420, to gain recognition as heir to the French throne by his father-in-law Charles VI. He was succeeded by his son Henry VI.

Henry VI 1421–1471. King of England from 1422, son of Henry V. He assumed royal power 1442, and identified himself with the party opposed to the continuation of the French war. After his marriage 1445, he was dominated by his wife, ◊Margaret of Anjou. The unpopularity of the government, especially after the loss of the English conquests in France, encouraged Richard, Duke of ◊York to claim the throne, and though York was killed 1460, his son Edward IV proclaimed himself king 1461, halting the Wars of the Roses. Henry was captured 1465, temporarily restored 1470, but again imprisoned 1471 and then murdered.

Henry VII 1457–1509. King of England from 1485, son of Edmund Tudor, Earl of Richmond (c. 1430–56), and a descendant of ◊John of Gaunt. He spent his early life in Brittany until 1485, when he landed in Britain to lead the rebellion against Richard III which ended with Richard's defeat and death at the battle of Bosworth. Yorkist revolts continued until 1497, but Henry restored order after the Wars of the Roses by establishing the court of the Star Chamber, and achieved independence from Parliament by amassing a private fortune through confiscations. He was succeeded by his son Henry VIII.

Henry VIII 1491–1547. King of England from 1509, when he succeeded his father Henry VII and married Catherine of Aragon, the widow of his brother. His Lord Chancellor, Cardinal Wolsey, was replaced by Thomas More 1529, for failing to persuade the pope to grant Henry a divorce. After 1532 Henry broke with the Catholic church, proclaimed himself head of the church, and dissolved the monasteries. After divorcing Catherine, his wives were Anne Boleyn, Jane Seymour, Anne of Cleves, Catherine Howard, and Catherine Parr. He was succeeded by his son Edward VI.

During the period 1513–29 Henry pursued an active foreign policy, largely under the guidance of Wolsey. With Parliament's approval Henry renounced the papal supremacy. Henry divorced Catherine 1533 and married Anne Boleyn, who was beheaded 1536, ostensibly for adultery. Henry's third wife, Jane Seymour, died 1537. He married Anne of Cleves 1540 in pursuance of Thomas Cromwell's policy of allying with the German Protestants, but rapidly abandoned this policy, divorced Anne, and beheaded Cromwell. His fifth wife, Catherine Howard, was beheaded 1542, and the following year he married Catherine Parr, who survived him.

Henry never completely lost his popularity, but wars with France and Scotland towards the end of his reign sapped the economy, and in religion he not only executed Roman Catholics, including Thomas More, for refusing to acknowledge his supremacy in the church, but also Protestants who maintained his changes had not gone far enough.

Henry four kings of France:

Henry I 1005–1060. King of France from 1031, who spent much of his reign in conflict with ◊William I the Conqueror, then duke of Normandy.

Henry II 1519–1559. King of France from 1547. He captured the fortresses of Metz and Verdun from the Holy Roman emperor Charles V, and Calais from the English. He was killed in a tournament.

In 1526 he was sent, with his brother, to Spain as a hostage, being returned when there was peace 1530. He married Catherine de' Medici 1533, and from then was under the domination of her, Diane de Poitiers, and duke Montmorency. Three of his sons, Francis II, Charles IX, and Henry III, became kings of France.

Henry III 1551–1589. King of France from 1574. He fought both the Huguenots (headed by his successor, Henry of Navarre) and the Catholic League (headed by the Duke of Guise). Guise expelled Henry from Paris 1588 but was assassinated. Henry allied with the Huguenots under Henry of Navarre to besiege the city, but was assassinated by a monk.

Henry IV 1553–1610. King of France from 1589. Son of Antoine de Bourbon and Jeanne, queen of Navarre, he was brought up as a Protestant, and from 1576 led the Huguenots. On his accession he settled the religious question by adopting Catholicism while tolerating Protestantism. He restored peace and strong government to France, and brought back prosperity by measures for the promotion of industry and agriculture, and the improvement of communications. He was assassinated by a Catholic fanatic.

Henry seven Holy Roman emperors:

Henry I *the Fowler* c.876–936. King of Germany from 919, and duke of Saxony from 912. He secured the frontiers of Saxony, ruled in harmony with its nobles, and extended German influence over the Hungarians, the Danes, and Slavonic tribes in the east. He was about to claim the imperial crown when he died.

Henry II *the Saint* 973–1024. King of Germany from 1002, Holy Roman emperor from 1014, when he recognized Benedict VIII as pope. He was canonized 1146.

Henry III *the Black* 1017–1056. King of Germany from 1028, Holy Roman emperor from 1039, who raised the empire to the height of its power, and extended its authority over Poland, Bohemia, and Hungary.

Henry IV 1050–1106. Holy Roman emperor from 1056, who was involved from 1075 in a struggle with the papacy (see ◊Gregory VII).

Henry V 1081–1125. Holy Roman emperor from 1106. He continued the struggle with the church until the settlement of the investiture contest 1122.

Henry VI 1165–1197. Holy Roman emperor from 1190. As part of his plan for making the empire universal, he captured and imprisoned Richard I of England, and compelled him to do homage.

Henry VII 1269–1313. Holy Roman emperor from 1308. He attempted unsuccessfully to revive the imperial supremacy in Italy.

Henry Frederick Prince of Wales 1594–1612. eldest son of James I of England and Anne of Denmark; a keen patron of Italian art.

Henry of Blois died 1171. He was bishop of Winchester from 1129, Pope Innocent II's legate to England from 1139, and brother of King Stephen. He was educated at Cluny, France, before entering his brother's service. While remaining loyal to Henry II, he tried to effect a compromise between Becket and the king. He was a generous benefactor to Winchester and Cluny, and he built Glastonbury Abbey.

Henryson Robert 1430–1505. Scottish poet. His works include versions of Aesop and the *Testament of Cresseid*, a continuation of Chaucer.

Henry the Navigator 1394–1460. Portuguese prince. He set up a school for navigators 1419 and under his patronage, Portuguese seamen explored and colonized Madeira, the Cape Verde Islands, and the Azores; they sailed down the African coast almost to Sierra Leone.

Henty G(eorge) A(lfred) 1832–1902. British war correspondent, author of numerous historical novels for children, such as *With the Allies to Peking* 1904.

Henze Hans Werner 1926– . German composer whose large and varied output includes orchestral, vocal, and chamber music. He uses traditional symphony and concerto forms, and incorporates a wide range of styles including jazz.

In 1953 he moved to Italy where his music became more expansive, as in the opera *The Bassarids* 1966.

Hepburn Audrey (Audrey Hepburn-Rushton) 1929– . British actress of Anglo-Dutch descent who tended to play innocent, child-like characters. Slender and doe-eyed, she set a different style from the pneumatic stars of the 1950s. After playing minor parts in British films in the early 1950s, she became a Hollywood star in such films as *Funny Face* 1957, *My Fair Lady* 1964, *Wait Until Dark* 1968, and *Robin and Marian* 1976.

Hepburn Katharine 1909– . US actress, who appeared in such films as *The African Queen* 1951, *Guess Who's Coming to Dinner* 1967, and *On Golden Pond* 1981. She won four Academy Awards.

Hepworth Barbara 1903–1975. British sculptor. She developed a distinctive abstract style, creating hollowed forms of stone or wood with spaces bridged by wires or strings; many later works are in bronze.

Born in Wakefield, she studied at Leeds School of Art and the Royal College of Art. She worked in concrete, bronze, wood, and aluminium, but her preferred medium was stone. She married first the sculptor John Skeaping, and second Ben ◊Nicholson. Under Nicholson's influence she became more interested in abstract form. In 1939 she moved to St Ives, Cornwall (where her studio is now a museum).

Heraclitus c.544–483 BC. Greek philosopher, who believed that the cosmos is in a ceaseless state of flux and motion. Fire was the fundamental material which accounted for all change and motion in the world. Nothing in the world ever stays the same, hence the famous dictum, 'one cannot step in the same river twice'.

Heraclius c.575–641. Byzantine emperor from 610. His reign marked a turning point in the empire's fortunes. Of Armenian descent, he recaptured Armenia 622, and other provinces

622-28 from the Persians, but lost them to the Arabs 629-41.

Herbert Edward, 1st Baron Herbert of Cherbury 1583-1648. English philosopher, brother of George Herbert. His *De veritate* 1624, with its theory of natural religion, founded English ◊Deism.

Herbert Frank (Patrick) 1920-1986. US science-fiction writer, author of the *Dune* saga from 1965 onwards (filmed by David Lynch 1984), broad-scale adventure stories containing serious ideas about ecology and religion.

Herbert George 1593-1633. English poet. His volume of religious poems, *The Temple*, appeared in 1633, shortly before his death. His poems depict his intense religious feelings in clear, simple language. He was the brother of Lord Edward Herbert of Cherbury.

Herbert Wally (Walter) 1934- . British surveyor and explorer. His first surface crossing by dog sledge of the Arctic Ocean 1968-69, from Alaska to Spitsbergen via the North Pole, was the longest sustained sledging journey (6,000 km/3,800 mi) in polar exploration.

Herbert of Lea Sidney Herbert, 1st Baron Herbert of Lea 1810-1861. British politician. He was secretary for war in Aberdeen's Liberal-Peelite coalition of 1852-55, and during the Crimean War was responsible for sending Florence Nightingale to the front.

Herder Johann Gottfried von 1744-1803. German poet, critic, and philosopher. Herder's critical writings indicated his intuitive rather than reasoning trend of thought. He collected folk songs and poetry of all nations, published as *Stimmen der Völker in Liedern/Voices of the People in Song* 1778, and in the *Ideen zur Philosophie der Geschichte der Menschheit/Outlines of a Philosophy of the History of Man* 1784-91 he outlined the stages of human cultural development. He gave considerable impulse to the Romantic *Sturm und Drang/Storm and Stress* movement in German literature.

Hereward the Wake 11th century. English leader of a revolt against the Normans 1070. His stronghold in the Isle of Ely was captured by William the Conqueror 1071. Hereward escaped, but his fate is unknown.

Hergé assumed name of Georges Remi 1907-1983. Belgian artist, who took the name of Hergé from the pronunciation of the initial letters of his name. He was the creator of the boy reporter Tintin, who first appeared in strip-cartoon form as *Tintin in the Land of the Soviets* 1929-30.

Herman 'Woody' (Woodrow) 1913-1987. US band leader and clarinetist. A child prodigy, he was leader of his own orchestra at 23, and after 1945 formed his famous Thundering Herd band. Soloists in this or later versions of the band included Lester ◊Young and Stan ◊Getz.

Hermes Trismegistus supposed author of the *Hermetica* (2nd-3rd centuries AD), writings inculcating a cosmic religion, in which the sun is regarded as the visible manifestation of God. In the Renaissance these writings were thought to be by an Egyptian priest contemporary with Moses, and it is possible they contain some Egyptian material.

Herod the Great 74-4 BC. King of the Roman province of Judaea, S Palestine, from 40 BC. With the aid of Mark Antony he established his government in Jerusalem 37 BC. He rebuilt the Temple in Jerusalem, but his Hellenizing tendencies made him suspect to orthodox Jewry. His last years were a reign of terror, and Matthew in the New Testament alleges that he ordered the slaughter of all the infants in Bethlehem to ensure the death of Jesus, whom he foresaw as a rival. He was the father of Herod Antipas.

Herod Agrippa I 10 BC-AD 44. Jewish ruler of Palestine from AD 41. His real name was Marcus Julius Agrippa, erroneously called 'Herod' in the *Bible*. Grandson of Herod the Great, he was made tetrarch (governor) of Palestine by the Roman emperor Caligula and king by Claudius. He put James to death and imprisoned Peter, both apostles. His son was Herod Agrippa II.

Herod Agrippa II c. AD 40-93. King of Chalcis (now S Lebanon), son of Herod Agrippa I. He was appointed by Claudius about AD 50, and in AD 60 tried the apostle Paul. He helped the Roman emperor Titus take Jerusalem AD 70, then went to Rome, where he died.

Herod Antipas 21 BC-AD 39. Tetrarch (governor) of the Roman province of Galilee, N Palestine, 4 BC-AD 9, son of Herod the Great. He divorced his wife to marry his niece Herodias, who persuaded her daughter Salome to ask for John the Baptist's head when he reproved Herod's action. Jesus was brought before him on Pontius Pilate's discovery that he was a Galilean and hence of Herod's jurisdiction, but Herod returned him without giving any verdict. In AD 38 Herod Antipas went to Rome to try to get the emperor Caligula to give him the title of king, but was banished.

Herodotus c.484-424 BC. Greek historian. After four years in Athens, he travelled widely in Egypt, Asia, and eastern Europe, before settling at Thurii in S Italy 443 BC. He wrote a nine-book history of the Greek-Persian struggle that culminated in the defeat of the Persian invasion attempts 490 and 480 BC. Herodotus was the first historian to apply critical evaluation to his material.

Hero of Alexandria Greek mathematician and engineer, probably of the 1st century AD. He invented an automatic fountain and a kind of stationary steam-engine, described in his book *Pneumatica*.

Herrera *el Viejo* (the elder). Francisco de 1576-1656. Spanish painter, active in Seville.

He painted genre and religious scenes, with bold effects of light and shade.

Herrera el Mozo (the younger). Francisco de 1622–1685. Spanish still-life painter, who studied in Rome and worked in Seville and Madrid, where he was court painter and architect. His paintings reflect Murillo's influence. He was the son of the elder Herrera.

Herrick Robert 1591–1674. English poet and cleric. Born in Cheapside, London, he was a friend of Ben Jonson. In 1629 he became vicar of Dean Prior, near Totnes. He published *Hesperides* in 1648, a collection of sacred and pastoral poetry admired for its lyric quality, including 'Gather ye rosebuds' and 'Cherry ripe'.

Herriot Édouard 1872–1957. French Radical socialist politician. An opponent of Poincaré, who as prime minister carried out the French occupation of the Ruhr, Germany, he was briefly prime minister 1924–25, 1926, and 1932. As president of the chamber of deputies 1940 he opposed the policies of the right-wing Vichy government, was arrested and later taken to Germany until released 1945 by the Soviets.

Herriot James. Pen name of James Alfred Wight 1916– . English writer. A practising veterinary surgeon in Thirsk, Yorkshire from 1940, he wrote of his experiences in a popular series of books including *If Only They Could Talk* 1970, *All Creatures Great and Small* 1972, and *The Lord God Made Them All* 1981.

Herrmann Bernard 1911–1975. US composer of film music. He worked for Alfred Hitchcock on several films, and wrote the chilling score for *Psycho* 1960.

Herschel Caroline Lucretia 1750–1848. German astronomer, sister of William Herschel, and from 1772 his assistant in England. She discovered eight comets, and was awarded the Royal Astronomical Society's gold medal for her work on her brother's catalogue of star clusters and nebulae.

Herschel John Fredrick William 1792–1871. English scientist and astronomer, son of William Herschel. He discovered thousands of close double stars, clusters, and nebulae, reported 1847. His inventions include astronomical instruments, sensitized photographic paper, and the use of sodium thiosulphite to fix it.

Herschel William 1738–1822. German-born British astronomer. He was a skilled telescope-maker, and pioneered the study of binary stars and nebulae. In 1781, he discovered Uranus.

Born in Hanover, Germany, he went to England 1757, and became a professional musician, while instructing himself in mathematics and astronomy, and constructing his own reflecting telescopes. While searching for double stars, he found Uranus, and later several of its satellites. This brought him instant fame and, in 1782, the post of private astronomer to George III. He discovered the

motion of the double stars round one another, and recorded it in his *Motion of the Solar System in Space* 1783. In 1789, he built, at Slough, a 1.2 m/4 ft telescope of 12 m/40 ft focal length, but he made most use of a more satisfactory 46 cm/18 in instrument. He catalogued over 800 double stars, and found over 2,500 nebulae, catalogued by his sister Caroline Herschel; this work was continued by his son John Herschel. By studying the distribution of stars, William established the basic form of the Galaxy. He discovered infrared solar rays 1801.

Hertling Count Georg von 1843–1919. German politician who was appointed imperial chancellor in Nov 1917. He maintained a degree of support in the *Reichstag* (parliament) but was powerless to control the military leadership under ◊Ludendorff.

Hertz Heinrich 1857–1894. German physicist who studied electromagnetic waves, showing that their behaviour resembled that of light and heat waves.

He confirmed James Clerk Maxwell's theory of electromagnetic waves. The unit of frequency, the *hertz*, is named after him.

Hertzog James Barry Munnik 1866–1942. South African politician, prime minister 1924–39, founder of the Nationalist Party 1913 (the *United South African National Party* from 1933). He opposed South Africa's entry into both world wars.

Hertzog was born in Cape Colony, of Boer descent. In 1914 he opposed South African participation in World War I. After the 1924 elections Hertzog became prime minister, and in 1933 the Nationalist Party and Gen Smuts's South African Party were merged as the United South African National Party. In Sept 1939 his motion against participation in World War II was rejected, and he resigned.

Herzl Theodor 1860–1904. Austrian founder of the *Zionist* movement, seeking to establish a Jewish homeland in Palestine. He was born in Budapest and became a successful playwright and journalist. The ◊Dreyfus case convinced him that the only solution to the problem of anti-Semitism was the resettlement of the Jews in a state of their own. His book *Jewish State* 1896 launched political Zionism, and he was the first president of the World Zionist Organization 1897.

Herzog Werner 1942– . German film director whose highly original and visually splendid films, often shot in exotic and impractical locations, include *Aguirre der Zom Gottes/Aguirre Wrath of God* 1972, *Nosferatu Phantom der Nacht* 1979, and *Fitzcarraldo* 1982.

Heseltine Michael 1933– . English Conservative politician, member of Parliament for Henley, minister of the environment 1979–83. He succeeded John Nott as minister of defence Jan 1983 but resigned Jan 1986 over the Westland affair (the Westland helicopter company was acquired by US–Italian buyers and not by the European consortium Heseltine supported).

Hesiod lived *c.*700 BC. Greek poet. He is supposed to have lived a little later than Homer, and according to his own account he was born in Boeotia. He is the author of *Works and Days*, a poem that tells of the country life, and the *Theogony*, an account of the origin of the world and of the gods.

Hess Myra 1890–1965. British pianist. She is remembered for her morale-boosting National Gallery concerts in World War II, her transcription of the Bach chorale 'Jesu, Joy of Man's Desiring', and her interpretations of Beethoven.

Hess Victor 1883–1964. Austrian physicist, who emigrated to the USA shortly after sharing a Nobel prize in 1936 for the discovery of cosmic radiation.

Hess (Walter Richard) Rudolf 1894–1987. German Nazi leader. In 1932 he was appointed deputy Führer to Hitler. On 10 May 1941 he landed by air in the UK with compromise peace proposals, and was held a prisoner of war until 1945, when he was tried at Nuremberg as a war criminal and sentenced to life imprisonment. He died in Spandau prison, Berlin.

Imprisoned with Hitler 1923–25, he became his private secretary, taking down *Mein Kampf* from his dictation. He was effectively in charge of Nazi party organizations until his flight in 1941. For the last years of his life he was the only prisoner left in Spandau.

Hesse Hermann 1877–1962. German writer who became a Swiss citizen 1923. A conscientious objector in World War I and a pacifist opponent of Hitler, he published short stories, poetry, and novels, including *Peter Camenzind* 1904, *Siddhartha* 1922, and *Steppenwolf* 1927. Later works, such as *Das Glasperlenspiel/The Glass Bead Game* 1943, tend towards the mystical. Nobel prize 1946.

Heston Charlton. Stage name of Charles Carter 1924– . US film actor who often starred in biblical and historical epics (as Moses, for example, in *The Ten Commandments* 1956, and the title role in *Ben-Hur* 1959).

Hevesy Georg von 1885–1966. Swedish chemist, the discoverer of the element hafnium. He was the first to use a radioisotope (radioactive form of an element) to follow the steps of a biological process, for which he won the 1943 Nobel Prize for Chemistry.

Hewish Antony 1924– . British radio-astronomer, who was awarded, with Martin ◊Ryle, the Nobel Prize for Physics 1974 for his work on pulsars, rapidly rotating neutron stars which emit pulses of energy.

Heydrich Reinhard 1904–1942. German Nazi. As head of party's security service and Heinrich ◊Himmler's deputy, he was instrumental in organizing the 'final solution', the policy of genocide used against Jews, Poles, and other races. While deputy 'protector' of Bohemia and Moravia from 1941, he was ambushed and killed by three members of the Czech forces in Britain, who had landed by parachute. Reprisals followed, including several hundred executions and the destruction of the Czech village of Lidice and its inhabitants.

Heyerdahl Thor 1914– . Norwegian ethnologist, who sailed on the raft *Kon Tiki* 1947 from Peru to the Tuamotu Islands along the Humboldt Current, and in 1969–70 used ancient-Egyptian-style papyrus-reed boats to cross the Atlantic. He attempted to prove that ancient civilizations could have travelled the oceans.

His voyages are described in *Kon Tiki*, translated 1950, and *The Ra Expeditions*, translated 1971. He also crossed the Persian Gulf 1977, written about in *The Tigris Expedition*, translated 1981.

Heywood Thomas *c.*1570–*c.*1650. English actor and dramatist. He wrote or adapted over 220 plays, including the domestic tragedy *A Woman kilde with kindnesse* 1607.

Hiawatha legendary 16th-century North American Indian teacher and Onondaga chieftain, who is said to have welded the Six Nations of the Iroquois tribes into the league of the Long House, as the confederacy was known in what is now upper New York State. He is the hero of Longfellow's epic poem *The Song of Hiawatha*.

Hick Graeme 1966– , Rhodesian born cricketer who became Zimbabwe's youngest professional cricketer at the age of 17. A prolific batsman, he joined Worcestershire, England, in 1984. He achieved the highest score in England in the 20th century in 1988 against Somerset, 405 not out.

Hickey William 1749–1830. British writer, whose entertaining *Memoirs* were first published 1913–1925.

Hickok 'Wild Bill' (James Butler) 1837–1876. US pioneer and law enforcer, a legendary figure in the Wild West. In the Civil War he was a sharpshooter and scout for the Union army, and then served as marshal in Kansas, killing many outlaws. He was shot from behind while playing poker in Deadwood, South Dakota.

Hidalgo y Costilla Miguel 1753–1811. Catholic priest, known as 'the Father of Mexican Independence'. A symbol of the opposition to Spain, he rang the church bell in Sept 1810 to announce to his parishioners in Dolores that the revolution against the Spanish had begun. He was captured and shot the following year.

Higgins George V 1939– . US novelist, author of many detective and underworld novels, often set in Boston. The best known are *The Friends of Eddie Coyle* 1972 and *The Imposters* 1986.

Higgins Jack pseudonym of British novelist Harry ◊Patterson.

Highsmith Patricia 1921– . US crime novelist. Her first book *Strangers on a Train* 1950 was filmed by Hitchcock, and she excels in tension and psychological exploration of character, notably in her series dealing with the amoral Tom Ripley, including *The Talented Mr Ripley* 1956, *Ripley Under Ground* 1971, and *Ripley's Game* 1974.

Hilbert David 1862–1943. German mathematician, who founded the formalist school with the publication of *Grundlagen der Geometrie/Foundations of Geometry* in 1899, which was based on his idea of postulates. He attempted to put mathematics on a logical foundation through defining it in terms of a number of basic principles, which ◊Gödel later showed to be impossible; none the less, his attempt greatly influenced 20th-century mathematicians.

Hildebrand Benedictine monk who became Pope ◊Gregory VII.

Hildegard of Bingen 1098–1179. Nun and scientific writer, abbess of the Benedictine convent of St Disibode, near the Rhine, from 1136. She wrote a mystical treatise, *Liber Scivias* 1141, and an encyclopedia of natural history, *Liber Simplicis Medicinae* 1150–60, giving both Latin and German names for the species described, as well as their medicinal uses; it is the earliest surviving scientific book by a woman.

Hill David Octavius 1802–1870. Scottish photographer who, in collaboration with ◊Adamson, made extensive use of the paper-based calotype process in their large collection of portraits taken in Edinburgh 1843–48.

Hill Octavia 1838–1912. English campaigner for housing reform and public open spaces. She co-founded the ◊National Trust in 1894.

Hill Rowland 1795–1879. British Post Office official who invented adhesive stamps and prompted the introduction of the penny prepaid post in 1840 (previously the addressee paid, according to distance, on receipt).

Hillary Edmund 1919– . New Zealand mountaineer. In 1953, with Nepalese Sherpa mountaineer Tenzing Norgay, he reached the summit of Mount Everest, the world's highest peak. As a member of the Commonwealth Transantarctic Expedition 1957–58, he was the first person since Scott to reach the South Pole overland, on 3 Jan 1958.

On the way to the South Pole he laid depots for ◊Fuchs's completion of the crossing of the continent.

Hillel 1st century Jewish teacher and scholar, a member of the Pharisaic movement.

Hiller Wendy 1912– . British stage and film actress. Her many roles include Catherine Sloper in *The Heiress* 1947 and Eliza in the film version of Shaw's *Pygmalion* 1938.

Hilliard Nicholas *c.*1547–1619. English miniature portraitist and goldsmith, court artist to Elizabeth I from about 1579. His sitters included Francis Drake and Walter Raleigh.

After 1600 he was gradually superseded by his pupil Isaac Oliver. A collection of his delicate portraits, set in gold cases, including *Young Man Amid Roses* about 1590, is in the Victoria and Albert Museum, London.

Hilton James 1900–1954. English novelist. He settled in Hollywood as one of its most successful script writers, for example *Mrs Miniver*. His books include *Lost Horizon* 1933, envisaging Shangri-la, a remote district of Tibet where time stands still; *Goodbye, Mr Chips* 1934, a portrait of an old schoolmaster; and *Random Harvest* 1941.

Himes Chester 1909–1984. US novelist. After serving seven years in prison for armed robbery, he published his first novel *If He Hollers Let Him Go* 1945, a depiction of the drudgery and racism in a Californian shipyard. Other novels include *Blind Man with a Pistol* 1969.

Himmler Heinrich 1900–1945. German Nazi leader, head of the SS elite corps from 1929, the police and the Gestapo secret police from 1936. During World War II he replaced Göring as Hitler's second-in-command. He was captured May 1945, and committed suicide.

Born in Munich, he joined the Nazi Party in its early days, and became chief of the Bavarian police 1933. His accumulation of offices meant he had command of all German police forces by 1936, which made him one of the most powerful people in Germany. In Apr 1945 he made a proposal to the Allies that Germany should surrender to Britain and the USA but not to the USSR, which was rejected.

Hinault Bernard 1954– . French cyclist, one of three men to have won the Tour de France race five times (1978–1985); the others being Jacques ◊Anquetil and Eddie ◊Merckx.

Hindemith Paul 1895–1963. German composer. His Neo-Classical, contrapuntal works include

Hillary *New Zealand mountaineer and explorer Edmund Hillary on Mount Everest, 1953.*

chamber ensemble and orchestral pieces, such as the *Symphonic Metamorphosis on Themes of Carl Maria von Weber* 1944, and the operas *Cardillac* 1926, revised 1952, and *Mathis der Maler/Mathis the Painter* 1938.

A fine viola player, he led the Frankfurt Opera Orchestra at 20, and taught at the Berlin Hochschule for music 1927–33. The modernity of his work, such as the *Philharmonic Concerto* 1932, led to a Nazi ban. In 1939 he went to the USA, where he taught at Yale University and in 1951 he became professor of musical theory at Zürich.

Hindenburg Paul Ludwig Hans von Beneckendorf und Hindenburg 1847–1934. German field marshal and right-wing politician. During World War I he was supreme commander and, together with Ludendorff, practically directed Germany's policy until the end of the war. He was president of Germany 1925–33.

Born in Posen of a Prussian Junker (aristocratic landowner) family, he was commissioned 1866, served in the Austro-Prussian and Franco-German wars, and retired 1911. Given the command in East Prussia Aug 1914, he received the credit for the defeat of the Russians at the battle of Tannenberg, and was promoted to supreme commander and field marshal. Re-elected president 1932, he was compelled to invite Hitler to assume the chancellorship Jan 1933.

Hine Lewis 1874–1940. US sociologist. He recorded in photographs child labour conditions in US factories at the beginning of this century, leading to a change in the law.

Hinkler Herbert John Louis 1892–1933. Australian pilot who in 1928 made the first solo flight from England to Australia. He was killed while making another attempt to fly to Australia.

Hinshelwood Cyril Norman 1897–1967. British chemist. He shared the 1956 Nobel Prize for Chemistry with Nikola Semenov (1896–) for his work on chemical chain reactions. He also studied the chemistry of bacterial growth.

Hipparchus *c*.555–514 BC. Greek tyrant. Son of ◊Pisistratus, he was associated with his elder brother Hippias as ruler of Athens 527–514 BC. His affection being spurned by Harmodius, he insulted her sister, and was assassinated by Harmodius and Aristogiton.

Hipparchus *c*.190–*c*.120 BC. Greek astronomer, who invented trigonometry, calculated the lengths of the solar year and the lunar month, discovered the precession of the equinoxes, made a catalogue of 800 fixed stars, and advanced Eratosthenes' method of determining the situation of places on the Earth's surface by lines of latitude and longitude. ·

Hippocrates *c*.460–*c*.370 BC. Greek physician, often called the founder of medicine. Important Hippocratic ideas include cleanliness (for patients and physicians), moderation in eating and drinking, letting nature take its course, and living where the air is good.

He was born and practised on the island of Kos and died at Larissa. He is known to have discovered aspirin in willow bark. The *Corpus Hippocraticum*, a grouping of some 70 works, is attributed to him, but was probably not written by him at all, although they outline the particular approach to medicine that he promulgated. They include the famous *Aphorisms* and the *Hippocratic Oath* which embodies the essence of medical ethics. He believed that health was the result of the 'humours' of the body being in balance; imbalance caused disease. These ideas were later adopted by ◊Galen.

Hirohito 1901–1989. Emperor of Japan from 1926. He succeeded his father Yoshihito. After the defeat of Japan 1945 he was made to reject belief in the divinity of the emperor and Japanese racial superiority, and accept the 1946 constitution greatly curtailing his powers. He was succeeded by his son ◊Akihito.

In 1921 Hirohito was the first Japanese crown prince to visit Europe. The imperial palace, destroyed by fire in air raids 1945, was rebuilt within the same spacious wooded compound 1969. Distinguished as a botanist and zoologist, Hirohito published several books.

Hirohito *Emperor Hirohito of Japan in ceremonial robes.*

Hiroshige Andō 1797–1858. Japanese artist whose landscape prints, often using snow or rain to create atmosphere, were highly popular in his time, notably *Tōkaidō gojūsan-tsugi/53 Stations on the Tokaido Highway* 1833.

Hiroshige was born in Edo (now Tokyo), and his last series was *Meisho Edo Hyakkei/100 Famous Views of Edo* 1856–58, uncompleted before his death. He is thought to have made over 5,000 different prints. Whistler and van Gogh were among Western painters influenced by him.

Hiss Alger 1904– . US diplomat and liberal Democrat, a former State Department official, controversially imprisoned 1950 for allegedly having spied for the USSR.

Hiss, president of the Carnegie Endowment for International Peace and one of President Roosevelt's advisers at the 1945 Yalta conference, was accused 1948 by a former Soviet agent, Whittaker Chambers (1901–61), of having passed information to the USSR during the period 1926–37. He was convicted of perjury for swearing before the House Committee to Investigate Un-American Activities that he had not spied for the USSR (under the statute of limitations he could not be convicted of the original crime). Richard ◊Nixon was a leading member of the prosecution, which inspired the subsequent anticommunist witch-hunts of Senator Joe ◊McCarthy. There are doubts about the justice of Hiss's conviction.

Hitchcock Alfred 1899–1980. English director of suspense films, noted for his camera work, and for making 'walk-ons' in his own films. His films include *The Thirty-Nine Steps* 1935, *The Lady Vanishes* 1939, *Rebecca* 1940, *Strangers on a Train* 1951, *Psycho* 1960, and *The Birds* 1963.

Hitchens Ivon 1893–1979. British painter. His semi-abstract landscapes were painted initially in natural tones, later in more vibrant colours. He also painted murals, for example, *Day's Rest, Day's Work* 1963 (Sussex University).

Hitler Adolf 1889–1945. German Nazi dictator, born in Austria. Führer (leader) of the Nazi party from 1921, author of *Mein Kampf/My Struggle* 1925–27. Chancellor of Germany from 1933 and head of state from 1934, he created a dictatorship by playing party and state institutions against each other, and continually creating new offices and appointments. His position was not seriously challenged until the 'Bomb Plot' 20 July 1944. In foreign affairs, he reoccupied the Rhineland and formed an alliance with the Italian fascist Mussolini 1936, annexed Austria 1938, and occupied Sudetenland under the Munich Agreement. The rest of Czechoslovakia was annexed Mar 1939. The Hitler–Stalin pact was followed in Sept by the invasion of Poland and the declaration of war by Britain and France. He committed suicide as Berlin fell.

Born at Braunau-am-Inn, the son of a customs official, he spent his early years in poverty in Vienna and Munich. After serving as a volunteer in the German army during World War I, he was employed as a spy by the military authorities in Munich, and in 1919 joined in this capacity the German Workers' Party. By 1921 he had assumed its leadership, renamed it the National Socialist German Workers' Party, and provided it with a programme that mixed nationalism and anti-Semitism. Having led an unsuccessful rising in Munich 1923, he was sentenced to nine months' imprisonment, during which he wrote his political testament, *Mein Kampf*. The party did not achieve national importance until the elections of 1930; by 1932, although Field Marshal Hindenburg defeated Hitler in the presidential elections, it formed the largest group in the Reichstag (parliament). As the result of an intrigue directed by the chancellor von Papen, Hitler became chancellor in a Nazi-Nationalist coalition 30 Jan 1933.

The opposition were rapidly suppressed, the Nationalists removed from the government, and the Nazis declared the only legal party. In 1934 Hitler succeeded Hindenburg as head of state. Meanwhile, the drive to war began; Germany left the League of Nations, conscription was reintroduced, and in 1936 the Rhineland was reoccupied. Hitler and Mussolini, who were already both involved in Spain, formed an alliance 1936. Hitler narrowly escaped death 1944 from a bomb explosion prepared by high-ranking officers. On 29 Apr 1945, when Berlin was largely in Soviet hands, he

Hitchcock *Suspense, melodrama and fleeting personal appearances are the hallmarks of Alfred Hitchcock's films.*

Hitler German Nazi leader Adolf Hitler at Berchtesgaden, Bavaria.

married Eva Braun in his bunker under the chancellory building, and on the following day committed suicide with her, both bodies afterwards being burned.

Hoban James C 1762–1831. Irish-born architect who emigrated to the USA. His best-known building is the White House, Washington DC, and he also worked on the Capitol and other public buildings.

Hobbema Meindert 1638–1709. Dutch landscape painter. He was a pupil of Ruisdael and his early work is derivative, but later works are characteristically realistic and unsentimental.

He was popular with English collectors in the 18th and 19th centuries, and influenced English landscape painting.

Hobbes Thomas 1588–1679. English political philosopher, and the first thinker since Aristotle to attempt to develop a comprehensive theory of nature, including human behaviour. In *The Leviathan* 1651 he advocates absolutist government as the only means of ensuring order and security; he saw this as deriving from the social contract (the idea that governmental authority derives from the ruler agreeing to provide order if those ruled over agree to be obedient). He was tutor to the exiled Prince Charles.

Hobbs John Berry 'Jack' 1882–1963. England cricketer who represented his country 61 times. In all first-class cricket he scored a world record 61,237 runs, including a record 197 centuries in a career that lasted nearly 30 years.

Hochhuth Rolf 1931– . Swiss dramatist, whose controversial play *Soldaten/Soldiers* 1968 implied

that the British politician Churchill was involved in a plot to assassinate the Polish general ◊Sikorski.

Ho Chi Minh adopted name of Nguyen That Tan 1890–1969. North Vietnamese Communist politician, president from 1954. He was trained in Moscow, and headed the communist Vietminh from 1941. Having campaigned against the French 1946–54, he became president and prime minister of the republic at the armistice. Aided by the communist bloc, he did much to develop industrial potential. He relinquished the premiership 1955, but continued as president.

Hockney David 1937– . British painter, printmaker, and designer, resident in California. In the early 1960s he contributed to the Pop art movement. His portraits and views of swimming pools and modern houses reflect a preoccupation with surface pattern and effects of light. He has produced etchings, photo collages, and sets for opera.

Hockney, born in Yorkshire, studied at Bradford School of Art and the Royal College of Art and exhibited at the Young Contemporaries Show of 1961. Abandoning Pop art, he developed an individual figurative style, and has prolifically experimented with technique. He was the subject of Jack Hazan's semidocumentary 1973 film *A Bigger Splash*; it is also the title of one of his paintings (1967). Hockney has designed sets for Glyndebourne, East Sussex, La Scala, Milan, and the Metropolitan Opera House, New York.

Hodgkin Alan Lloyd 1914– . British physiologist engaged in research with Andrew Huxley on the mechanism of conduction in peripheral nerves 1946–60. In 1963 they shared the Nobel Prize for Medicine with John Eccles.

Hodgkin Dorothy Crowfoot 1910– . English biochemist who analysed the structure of penicillin, insulin, and vitamin B_{12}. She was the first to use a computer to analyse the molecular structure of complex chemicals, and this enabled her to produce three-dimensional models. Nobel Prize for Chemistry 1964.

Hodgkin Thomas 1798–1856. British physician, who first recognized *Hodgkin's disease* (lymphadenoma), a cancer-like enlargement of the lymphatic glands.

Hodler Ferdinand 1853–1918. Swiss painter. His dramatic Art Nouveau paintings of allegorical, historical, and mythological subjects include large murals with dreamy Symbolist female figures such as *Day* about 1900 (Kunsthaus, Zürich).

Hodza Milan 1878–1944. Slovak politician and prime minister of Czechoslovakia from Feb 1936. He and President Beneš were forced to agree as part of the Munich agreement to the secession of the Sudeten areas of Czechoslovakia to the Germans before resigning 22 Sept 1938.

Hoess Rudolf 1900–1947. German commandant of Auschwitz concentration camp 1940–43. Under his control more than 2.5 million people were exterminated. Arrested by Allied military police in 1946, he was handed over to the Polish authorities who tried, and executed him in 1947.

Hoffa (James Riddle) 'Jimmy' 1913–?1975. US labour leader, president of the Teamsters Union (transport workers) from 1957. He was jailed 1967–71 for attempted bribery of a federal court jury after he was charged with corruption. In 1975 he disappeared, and is generally believed to have been murdered.

Hoffman Abbie (Abbot) 1936–1989. US left-wing political activist, founder of the Yippies (Youth International Party), a political offshoot of the hippies. He was a member of the Chicago Seven, a radical group tried for attempting to disrupt the 1968 Democratic convention.

Hoffman Dustin 1937– . US actor, who won Academy Awards for his performances in *Kramer vs Kramer* 1979 and *Rain Man* 1988. His other films include *The Graduate* 1967 and *Midnight Cowboy* 1969.

Hoffmann E(rnst) T(heodor) A(madeus) 1776–1822. German composer and writer. He composed the opera *Undine* 1816 and many fairy stories, including *Nüssknacker/Nutcracker* 1816. His stories inspired ◊Offenbach's *Tales of Hoffmann*.

Hoffmann Josef 1870–1956. Austrian architect, one of the founders of the Wiener Werkstätte, and a pupil of Otto ◊Wagner.

Hofmann August 1818–1892. German chemist who studied the extraction and exploitation of coal tar derivatives. Hofmann taught chemistry in London from 1845 until his return to Berlin in 1865.

Hofmann Hans 1880–1966. German-born Abstract Expressionist painter, active in Paris and Munich from 1915 until 1932, when he moved to the USA. He was influential among New York artists in the 1930s.

Apart from bold brushwork (he experimented with dribbling and dripping painting techniques in the 1940s) he used strong expressive colours. In the 1960s he moved towards a hard-edged abstract style.

Hofmeister Wilhelm 1824–1877. German botanist. He studied plant development and determined how a plant embryo, lying within a seed, is itself formed out of a single fertilized egg (ovule).

Hofmeister also discovered that mosses and ferns display an alternation of generations, in which the plant has two forms, spore-forming and gamete-forming.

Hofstadter Robert 1915– . US high-energy physicist who revealed the structure of the atomic nucleus. He demonstrated that the nucleus is composed of a high energy core and a surrounding area of decreasing density. Nobel Prize for Physics 1961.

Hofstadter helped to construct a new high-energy accelerator at Stanford University, California, with which he showed that the proton and the neutron have complex structures and cannot be considered elementary particles.

Hogarth William 1697–1764. British painter and engraver, who produced portraits and moralizing genre scenes, such as the series *A Rake's Progress* 1735.

Hogarth was born in London and apprenticed to an engraver. He published *A Harlot's Progress* 1732, a series of six engravings, in 1732. Other series followed, including *Marriage à la Mode* 1745, *Industry and Idleness* 1749, and *The Four Stages of Cruelty* 1751. His portraits are remarkably direct and characterful. In the book *The Analysis of Beauty* 1753 he proposed a double curved line as a key to successful composition.

Hogg James 1770–1835. Scottish novelist and poet, known as the 'Ettrick Shepherd'. Born in Ettrick Forest, Selkirkshire, he worked as a shepherd at Yarrow 1790–99, and until the age of 30, he was illiterate. His novel *Confessions of a Justified Sinner* 1824 is a masterly portrayal of personified evil.

Hogg Quintin British politician; see Lord ◊Hailsham.

Hohenlohe-Schillingsfürst Prince Chlodwig von 1819–1901. German imperial chancellor from Oct 1894 until his replacement by Prince von Bülow Oct 1900.

Hohenstaufen German family of princes, several members of which were Holy Roman emperors 1138–1208 and 1214–54. They were the first German emperors to make use of associations with Roman law and tradition to aggrandize their office. The most notable were Conrad III, Frederick I (Barbarossa) – the first to use the title Holy Roman emperor – Henry VI, and Frederick II. The last of the line, Conradin, was executed 1268, with the approval of Pope Clement IV, while attempting to gain his Sicilian inheritance.

Hohenzollern German family, originating in Württemberg, the main branch of which held the titles of elector of Brandenburg from 1415, king of Prussia from 1701, and German emperor from 1871. The last emperor, Wilhelm II, was dethroned 1918. Another branch of the family were kings of Romania 1881–1947.

Hokusai Katsushika 1760–1849. Japanese artist, the leading printmaker of his time. He is known for *Fugaku Sanjū-rokkei/36 Views of Mount Fuji* about 1823–29, but he produced outstanding pictures of almost every kind of subject – birds, flowers, courtesans, scenes from legend and everyday life, and so on.

Hokusai was born in Edo (now Tokyo) and studied wood engraving and book illustration. He was interested in Western painting and perspective, and introduced landscape as a wood-block-print genre. His *Manga*, a book crammed with inventive sketches, was published in 13 volumes from 1814.

Holbein Hans, the Elder *c.*1464–1524. German painter, active in Augsburg. His works include altarpieces, such as that of *St Sebastian,* 1516 (Alte Pinakothek, Munich). He also painted portraits and designed stained glass.

Holbein Hans, the Younger 1497/98–1543. German painter and woodcut artist; the son and pupil of Hans Holbein the Elder. He travelled widely in Europe, and was active in England 1527–28 and 1532–43; he was court painter to Henry VIII from 1536. He painted outstanding portraits of Erasmus, Thomas More, and Thomas Cromwell; a notable woodcut series is *Dance of Death c.*1525.

Holbein was born in Augsburg. In 1515 he went to Basel, where he became friendly with Erasmus; in 1517 to Lucerne; he was active in Basel again 1519–26. He designed title pages for Luther's New Testament and More's *Utopia.* Pronounced Renaissance influence emerged in the *Meyer Madonna* 1526, a fine altarpiece in Darmstadt. During his time at the English court, he also painted miniature portraits, inspiring Hilliard.

Holborne Anthony 1584–1602. English composer. He wrote a book of *Pauans, Galliards, Almains and Other Short Aeirs* 1599.

Holden Edith 1871 1920. British artist and naturalist. Daughter of a Birmingham manufacturer, she made most of her observations near her native city, and her journal, illustrated with her own watercolours, was published in 1977 as *The Country Diary of an Edwardian Lady.*

Holden William. Stage name of William Franklin Beedle 1918–1981. US film actor, a star in the late 1940s and 1950s. One of his best roles was as the leader of *The Wild Bunch* 1969, and he also played leading roles in *Sunset Boulevard* 1950, *Stalag 17* 1953, and *Network* 1976.

Holford William, Baron Holford 1907–1975. British architect, born in Johannesburg. The most influential architect-planner of his generation, he was responsible for much redevelopment after World War II, including St Paul's Cathedral Precinct, London.

Holiday Billie. Stage name of Eleanor Gough McKay 1915–1959. US jazz singer, also known as 'Lady Day'. She made her debut in Harlem clubs and became known for her emotionally charged delivery and idiosyncratic phrasing; she brought a blues feel to performances with swing bands. Songs she made her own include 'Strange Fruit' and 'I Cover the Waterfront'.

Holinshed Ralph *c.* 1520–*c.* 1580. English historian. He was probably born in Cheshire, went to London as assistant to a printer, and in 1578 published two volumes of the *Chronicles of England, Scotland and Ireland,* which were largely used by Shakespeare for his history plays.

Holkeri Harri 1937– . Finnish politician, prime minister from 1987. Joining the centrist National Coalition Party (KOK) at an early age, he eventually became its national secretary.

Holland Henry Richard Vassall Fox, 3rd Baron 1773–1840. British Whig politician. He was Lord Privy Seal 1806–07. His home at Holland House, London, was for many years the centre of Whig political and literary society.

Holland John Philip 1840–1914. Irish engineer who developed some of the first submarines. He began work in Ireland in the late 1860s and emigrated to the USA 1873. His first successful boat was launched 1881 and, after several failures, he built the *Holland* 1893, which was bought by the US Navy two years later. He continued to build submarines for various navies but died in poverty after his company failed because of financial difficulties.

Holland Sidney George 1893–1961. New Zealand politician, leader of the National Party 1940–57 and prime minister 1949–57.

Hollar Wenceslaus 1607–1677. Bohemian engraver, active in England from 1637. He was the first landscape engraver to work in England and recorded views of London before the Great Fire of 1666.

Hollerith Herman 1860–1929. US inventor of a mechanical tabulating machine, the first device for data processing. Hollerith's tabulator was widely publicized after being successfully used in the 1890 census. The firm he established, the Tabulating Machine Company, was later one of the founding companies of International Business Machines (IBM).

Hollis Roger 1905–1973. British civil servant, head of the secret intelligence service MI5 1956–65. He was alleged without confirmation to have been a double agent together with Kim Philby.

Holly Buddy. Stage name of Charles Hardin Holley 1936–1959. US rock-and-roll singer, guitarist, and songwriter, born in Lubbock, Texas. He had a distinctive, hiccuping vocal style and was an early experimenter with recording techniques. Many of his hits with his band, the Crickets, such as 'That'll Be the Day' 1957, 'Peggy Sue' 1957, and 'Maybe Baby' 1958, have become classics. He was killed in a plane crash.

Holmes Oliver Wendell 1809–1894. US writer. In 1857 he founded the *Atlantic Monthly* with J R Lowell, in which were published the essays and verse collected in 1858 as *The Autocrat of the Breakfast-Table.*

Holst Gustav(us Theodore von) 1874–1934. English composer. He wrote operas, including *Savitri* 1916 and *At the Boar's Head* 1925, ballets, choral works, including *Hymns from the Rig Veda* 1911 and *The Hymn of Jesus* 1920, orchestral suites, including *The Planets* 1918, and songs. He was a lifelong friend of Ralph ◊Vaughan Williams, with whom he shared an enthusiasm for English folk music. His musical style, although tonal and drawing on folk song, tends to be severe.

Holstein Friedrich von 1839–1909. German diplomat and foreign-affairs expert. He refused the post of foreign minister, but played a key role in German diplomacy from the 1880s until his death.

Holt Harold Edward 1908–1967. Australian Liberal politician, prime minister 1966–67.

He was minister of labour 1940–41 and 1949–58, and federal treasurer 1958–66, when he succeeded Menzies as prime minister.

Holtby Winifred 1898–1935. English novelist, poet, and journalist. She was an ardent advocate of women's freedom and racial equality, and wrote the novel *South Riding* 1936, set in her native Yorkshire. Her other works include an analysis of women's position in contemporary society *Women and a Changing Civilization* 1934.

Holyoake Keith Jacka 1904–1983. New Zealand National Party politician, prime minister 1957 (for two months) and 1960–72.

Home Alec Douglas-Home, Baron Home of the Hirsel 1903– . British Conservative politician. He was foreign secretary 1960–63, and succeeded Macmillan as prime minister 1963. He renounced his peerage (as 14th Earl of Home) to fight (and lose) the general election 1964, and resigned as party leader 1965. He was again foreign secretary 1970–74, when he received a life peerage. His brother is the playwright William Douglas-Home.

Homer 8th century BC. Legendary Greek epic poet, according to tradition a blind minstrel and the author of the *Iliad* and the *Odyssey*. The *Iliad* tells of the siege of Troy; the *Odyssey* of Odysseus' wanderings after the fall of Troy.

Homer Winslow 1836–1910. US painter and lithographer, known for his seascapes, both oils and watercolours, which date from the 1880s and 1890s.

Homer, born in Boston, made his reputation as a realist painter with *Prisoners from the Front* 1866 (Metropolitan Museum, New York), recording miseries of the Civil War.

Hondecoeter Melchior 1636–1695. Dutch painter, noted for his large paintings of birds (both domestic fowl and exotic species) in grandiose settings.

Hone William 1780–1842. British journalist and publisher. In 1817, he was unsuccessfully prosecuted for his *Political Litany*, in which he expounded the journalist's right to free expression.

Honecker Erich 1912– . East German communist politician, in power 1973–89, elected chair of the council of state (head of state) 1976. He governed in an outwardly austere and efficient manner and, while favouring East-West detente, was a loyal ally of the USSR. In Oct 1989, following a wave of pro-democracy demonstrations, he was replaced as leader of the Socialist Unity Party (SED) and head of state by Egon ◊Krenz, and in Dec expelled from the Communist Party.

Honecker, the son of a miner, joined the German Communist Party 1929 and was imprisoned for anti-fascist activity 1935–45. He was elected to the East German parliament (*Volkskammer*) 1949 and became a member of the SED Politburo during the 1950s. A security specialist, during the 1960s he served as a secretary of the National Defence Council before being appointed first secretary of the SED 1971. After Ulbricht's death 1973, Honecker became leader of East Germany. In Feb 1990, following his overthrow, he was arrested and charged with high treason, misuse of office, and corruption.

Honegger Arthur 1892–1955. Swiss composer, one of the group called Les Six. His work was varied in form, for example, the opera *Antigone* 1927, the ballet *Skating Rink* 1922, the oratorio *Le Roi David/King David* 1921, programme music (*Pacific 231* 1923), and the *Symphonie liturgique/Liturgical Symphony* 1946.

Hōnen 1133–1212. Japanese Buddhist monk who founded the Pure Land school of Buddhism.

Honthorst Gerrit van 1590–1656. Dutch painter who used extremes of light and shade, influenced by Caravaggio; with Terbrugghen he formed the *Utrecht school*.

Around 1610–12 he was in Rome, studying Caravaggio. Later he visited England, painting *Charles I* 1628 (National Portrait Gallery, London), and became court painter in The Hague.

Hooch Pieter de 1629–1684. Dutch painter, active in Delft and, later, Amsterdam. The harmonious domestic interiors and courtyards of his Delft period were influenced by Vermeer.

Hood Samuel, 1st Viscount Hood 1724–1816. British admiral. A masterly tactician, he defeated the French at Dominica in the West Indies 1783, and in the Revolutionary Wars captured Toulon and Corsica.

Hooke Robert 1635–1703. English scientist and inventor, originator of *Hooke's law*: that the strain produced in a stressed body is proportional to the stress. His inventions included a telegraph system, the spirit-level, marine barometer, and sea gauge. He coined the term 'cell' in biology.

He was considered the foremost mechanic of his time. He studied elasticity, furthered the sciences of mechanics and microscopy, and helped improve such scientific instruments as watches, microscopes, telescopes, and barometers. He was elected to the Royal Society 1663, and became its curator for the rest of his life. He was professor of geometry at Gresham College, London, and designed several buildings, including the College of Physicians.

Hooker Joseph Dalton 1817–1911. English botanist who travelled to the Antarctic and made many botanical discoveries, documented in *Flora Antarctica* 1844-47. His works include *Genera Plantarum* 1862-63 and *Flora of British India* 1875-97. In 1865 he succeeded his father, William Jackson Hooker (1785-1865), as director of the Royal Botanic Gardens, Kew, England.

Hooker Richard 1554-1600. English theologian, author of *The Laws of Ecclesiastical Polity* 1594, a defence of the episcopalian system of the Church of England.

Hooper John *c.*1495-1555. English Protestant reformer and martyr, born in Somerset. He adopted the views of ◊Zwingli and was appointed bishop of Gloucester 1550. He was burned to death for heresy.

Hoover Herbert (Clark) 1874-1964. 31st president of the USA 1929-33, a Republican. Secretary of commerce 1921-28. He lost public confidence after the stock-market crash of 1929, when he opposed direct government aid for the unemployed in the depression that followed.

As a mining engineer, Hoover travelled widely before World War I, during which he organized relief work in occupied Europe; a talented administrator, he was subsequently associated with numerous international relief organizations, and became food administrator for the USA 1917-19. He defeated the Democratic candidate for the presidency, Al Smith (1873-1944). The shantytowns or 'Hoovervilles' of the homeless that sprang up around large cities were evidence of his failure to cope with the effects of the Depression. He was severely criticized for his adamant opposition to a federal dole for the unemployed, even after the funds of states, cities, and charities were exhausted. In 1933, he was succeeded by Roosevelt.

Hoover J(ohn) Edgar 1895-1972. US director of the Federal Bureau of Investigation (FBI) from 1924. He built up a powerful network for the detection of organized crime. His drive against alleged communist activities after World War II, and his opposition to the Kennedy administration and others brought much criticism over abuse of power.

Hoover William Henry 1849-1932. US manufacturer, who developed the vacuum cleaner. *Hoover* soon became a generic name for vacuum cleaner.

Hope Anthony. Pen name of Anthony Hope Hawkins 1863-1933. English novelist, whose romance *The Prisoner of Zenda* 1894, and its sequel *Rupert of Hentzau* 1898, introduced the imaginary Balkan state of Ruritania.

Hope Bob. Stage name of Leslie Townes Hope 1904- . US comedian. His film appearances include a series of 'Road' films with Bing ◊Crosby.

He entertained the troops in Vietnam during the Vietnam War, and has made many television appearances. He has received several Special Academy Awards.

Hopkins Anthony 1937- . Welsh actor. Stage appearances include *Equus*, *Macbeth*, *Pravda*, and the title role in *King Lear*. Films include *The Lion in Winter* 1968, *A Bridge Too Far* 1977, and *The Elephant Man*. He played television parts in *War and Peace* and *A Married Man*.

Hopkins Frederick Gowland 1861-1947. English biochemist whose research into diets revealed the existence of trace substances, now known as vitamins. Hopkins shared the 1929 Nobel Prize for Medicine with Christiaan ◊Eijkman, who had arrived at similar conclusions.

Hopkins Gerard Manley 1844-1889. English poet. His work, marked by its religious themes and use of natural imagery, includes 'The Wreck of the Deutschland' 1876 and 'The Windhover' 1877. His employment of 'sprung rhythm' greatly influenced later 20th-century poetry.

Hopkins was converted to Roman Catholicism 1866, and in 1868 began training as a Jesuit. He worked as a priest in Ireland and England, and subsequently taught. His poetry is profoundly religious and records his struggle to gain faith and peace, but also shows great freshness of feeling and delight in nature.

Hopkins Harry L(loyd) 1890-1946. US government official. Originally a social worker, in 1935 he became head of WPA (Works Progress Administration), which was concerned with Depression relief work. After a period as secretary of commerce 1938-40, he was appointed supervisor of the lend-lease programme (by which the USA supplied equipment to the Allies) 1941, and undertook missions to Britain and the USSR during World War II.

Hopper Dennis 1936- . US film actor and director who caused a sensation with *Easy Rider* 1969, the archetypal 'road' film, but whose later *The Last Movie* 1971 was poorly received by the critics. He made a comeback in the 1980s. His work as actor includes *Rebel Without a Cause* 1955, *The American Friend/Der amerikanische Freund* 1977, and *Blue Velvet* 1986.

Hopper Edward 1882-1967. US painter and etcher, whose views of New York in the 1930s and 1940s captured the loneliness and superficial glamour of city life, as in *Nighthawks* 1942 (Art Institute, Chicago). Hopper's teacher Robert ◊Henri was a formative influence on him.

Hoppner John 1758-1810. British portrait painter, fashionable in the 1780s.

Horace 65-8 BC. Roman lyric poet and satirist. He became a leading poet under the patronage of the emperor Augustus. His works include *Satires* 35-30 BC, the four books of *Odes* *c.*25-24, *Epistles*, a series of verse letters, and a critical work *Ars poetica*.

Born at Venusia, S Italy, the son of a freedman, Horace fought under Brutus at Philippi, lost his estate and was reduced to poverty. In about 38 Virgil introduced him to Maecenas, who gave him a farm in the Sabine hills and recommended him to the patronage of Augustus. His works are distinguished by their style, wit, and good sense.

Hordern Michael 1911– . English actor who appeared in stage roles such as Shakespeare's Lear and Prospero. His films include *The Man Who Never Was* 1956, *The Spy Who Came in From the Cold* 1965, *The Bed Sitting Room* 1969, and *Joseph Andrews* 1977.

Hore-Belisha Leslie, Baron Hore-Belisha 1895–1957. British politician. A National Liberal, he was minister of transport 1934–37, introducing **Belisha beacons** to mark pedestrian crossings. As war minister from 1937, until removed by Chamberlain 1940 on grounds of temperament, he introduced peacetime conscription 1939.

Horn Philip de Montmorency, Count of Horn 1518–1568. Flemish politician. He held high offices under the Holy Roman emperor Charles V and his son Philip II. From 1563 he was one of the leaders of the opposition to the rule of Cardinal Granvella (1517–1586) and to the introduction of the Inquisition. In 1567 he was arrested together with the Resistance leader Egmont, and both were beheaded in Brussels.

Horniman Annie Elizabeth Frederika 1860–1937. English pioneer of repertory theatre, who subsidized the Abbey Theatre, Dublin, and founded the Manchester company.

Hornung E(rnest) W(illiam) 1866–1921. English novelist, who at the prompting of Conan ◊Doyle created 'A J Raffles', the gentleman-burglar, and his assistant Bunny Manders in *The Amateur Cracksman* 1899.

Horowitz Vladimir 1904–1989. US pianist, born in Kiev, Ukraine. He made his debut in the US 1928 with the New York Philharmonic Orchestra. Renowned for his commanding virtuoso style, he was a leading interpreter of Liszt, Schumann, and Rachmaninov.

Horrocks Brian Gwynne 1895–1985. British general. He served in World War I, and in World War II under Montgomery at Alamein and with the British Liberation Army in Europe.

Horsley John Calcott 1817–1903. English artist. A skilled painter of domestic scenes, he was also responsible for frescoes in the Houses of Parliament, and is credited with designing the first Christmas card.

Horthy de Nagybánya Nicholas 1868–1957. Hungarian politician and admiral. Leader of the counter-revolutionary White government, he became regent 1920 on the overthrow of the communist Bela Kun regime by Romanian intervention. He represented the conservative and military class, and retained power until World War II, trying

(although allied to Hitler) to retain independence of action. In 1944 Hungary was taken over by the Nazis and he was deported to Germany.

Hoskins Bob 1942– . British character actor who progressed to fame from a series of supporting roles. Films include *The Long Good Friday* 1980, *The Cotton Club* 1984, *Mona Lisa* 1985, *A Prayer for the Dying* 1987, *Who framed Roger Rabbit* 1988.

Houdini Harry. Stage name of Erich Weiss 1874–1926. US escape artist and conjurer. He attained fame by his escapes from ropes and handcuffs, from trunks under water, from straitjackets and prison cells. He also campaigned against fraudulent mindreaders and mediums.

Houdon Jean-Antoine 1741–1828. French sculptor, a portraitist who made characterful studies of Voltaire and a Neo-Classical statue of George Washington, commissioned 1785.

His subjects included the philosophers Diderot and Rousseau, the composer Gluck, the emperor Napoleon, and the American politician Benjamin Franklin. Houdon also produced popular mythological figures, such as *Diana* and *Minerva*.

Hounsfield Godfrey 1919– . British pioneer of tomography, by which a cross-sectional image of the human body (or other solid object) is obtained by X-ray or other means. He shared the 1979 Nobel Prize for Medicine with Alan MacLeod Cormack (1924–), who had made investigations independently.

Houphouët-Boigny Felix 1905– . Ivory Coast right-wing politician. He held posts in French ministries, and became president of the Republic of the Ivory Coast on independence 1960. He was re-elected for a sixth term 1985 representing the sole legal party.

Household Geoffrey 1900–1988. British espionage and adventure novelist. His *Rogue Male* 1939 concerned an Englishman's attempt to kill Hitler, and the enemy hunt for him after his failure. Household served with British intelligence in World War II.

Houseman John 1902–1988. US theatre, film, and television producer and actor, born in Romania. He co-founded the Mercury Theater with Orson Welles, and collaborated with Welles and Nicholas Ray as directors. He won an Academy Award for his acting debut in *The Paper Chase* 1973, and re-created his role in the subsequent TV series.

Housman A(lfred) E(dward) 1859–1936. English poet and classical scholar. His *A Shropshire Lad* 1896, a series of deceptively simple nostalgic ballad-like poems, was popular during World War I. This was followed by *Last Poems* 1922, and *More Poems* 1936.

Houston Sam 1793–1863. US general who won Texas' independence from Mexico 1836 and was president of the Republic of Texas 1836–45. Houston, Texas, is named after him.

Houston was governor of the state of Tennessee and later US senator from and governor of the state of Texas. He took Cherokee Indian citizenship when he married a Cherokee.

Hovell William Hilton 1786–1875. Explorer of Australia with Hamilton ◊Hume.

Howard Alan 1937– . British actor, whose appearances with the Royal Shakespeare Company include title roles in *Henry V, Henry VI, Coriolanus,* and *Richard III.*

Howard Catherine *c.*1520–1542. Queen consort of ◊Henry VIII of England from 1540. In 1541 the archbishop of Canterbury, Thomas Cranmer, accused her of being unchaste before marriage to Henry, and she was beheaded 1542 after Cranmer made further charges of adultery.

Howard Charles, 2nd Baron Howard of Effingham and 1st Earl of Nottingham 1536–1624. English admiral, a cousin of Queen Elizabeth I. He commanded the fleet against the Spanish Armada while Lord High Admiral 1585–1618. He cooperated with the Earl of Essex in the attack on Cádiz 1596.

Howard Constance 1919– . English embroiderer who helped to revive creative craftwork following World War II. Her work included framed pictures with fabrics outlined in bold black threads, wall hangings, and geometric studies in strong colour.

Howard Ebenezer 1850–1928. English town planner and founder of the ideal of the garden city, through his book *Tomorrow* 1898 (republished as *Garden Cities of Tomorrow* 1902).

Howard John 1726–1790. English philanthropist whose work to improve prison conditions is continued today by the *Howard League for Penal Reform.*

On his appointment as high sheriff for Bedfordshire 1773, he undertook a tour of English prisons which led to two acts of Parliament 1774, making jailers salaried officers and setting standards of cleanliness. After touring Europe 1775 he published his *State of the Prisons in England and Wales, with an account of some Foreign Prisons* 1777. He died of typhus fever while visiting Russian military hospitals at Kherson in the Crimea.

Howard Leslie. Stage name of Leslie Stainer 1893–1943. English actor, whose films include *The Scarlet Pimpernel* 1935, *Pygmalion* 1938, and *Gone with the Wind* 1939.

Howard Trevor (Wallace) 1916–1989. English actor, whose films include *Brief Encounter* 1945, *Sons and Lovers* 1960, *Mutiny on the Bounty* 1962, *Ryan's Daughter* 1970, and *Conduct Unbecoming* 1975.

Howe Elias 1819–1867. US inventor, in 1846, of a sewing machine using double thread.

Howe Geoffrey 1926– . British Conservative politician. Under Heath he was solicitor-general 1970–72 and minister for trade 1972–74; as chancellor of the Exchequer 1979–83 under Thatcher,

he put into practice the monetarist policy which reduced inflation at the cost of a rise in unemployment. In 1983 he became foreign secretary, and in 1989 he unexpectedly became deputy prime minister and leader of the House of Commons.

Howe Gordie 1926– . Canadian ice-hockey player, who played for the Detroit Red Wings (National Hockey League) 1946–71 and the New England Whalers (World Hockey Association). In the NHL, he scored more goals (801), assists (1,049), and points (1,850) than any other player in ice-hockey history. He played professional hockey until over 50.

Howe James Wong. Adopted name of Wong Tung Jim 1899–1976. Chinese-born director of film photography, who lived in the USA from childhood. One of Hollywood's best camera operators, he is credited with introducing the use of hand-held cameras and deep focus. His work ranges from *The Alaskan* 1924 to *Funny Lady* 1975.

Howe Julia Ward 1819–1910. US feminist and antislavery campaigner, who in 1862 wrote the 'Battle Hymn of the Republic', sung to the tune of 'John Brown's Body'.

Howe Richard, 1st Earl Howe 1726–1799. British admiral. He cooperated with his brother William against the colonists during the American War of Independence, and in the French Revolutionary Wars commanded the Channel fleets 1792–96.

Howe William, 5th Viscount Howe 1729–1814. British general. During the War of American Independence he won the Battle of Bunker Hill 1775, and as commander in chief in America 1776–78 captured New York and defeated Washington at Brandywine and Germantown. He resigned in protest at lack of home government support.

Howells William Dean 1837–1920. US novelist and editor. The 'dean' of US letters in the post-Civil War era, and editor of the *Atlantic Monthly,* he championed the realist movement in fiction and encouraged many younger authors. He wrote 35 novels, 35 plays, and many books of poetry, essays, and commentary.

His novels, filled with vivid social detail, include *A Modern Instance* 1882 and *The Rise of Silas Lapham* 1885, about the social fall and moral rise of a New England paint manufacturer, a central fable of the 'Gilded Age'.

Hoxha Enver 1908–1985. Albanian Communist politician, the country's leader from 1954. He founded the Albanian Communist Party 1941, and headed the liberation movement 1939–44. He was prime minister 1944–54, combining with foreign affairs 1946–53, and from 1954 was first secretary of the Albanian Party of Labour. In policy he was a Stalinist, and independent of both Chinese and Soviet communism.

Hoyle Fred(erick) 1915– . English astronomer and writer. In 1948 he joined with Hermann Bondi and Thomas Gold in developing the steady-state theory (that the Universe is essentially the same wherever and whenever viewed). In 1957, with Geoffrey and Margaret Burbidge and William Fowler, he showed that chemical elements heavier than hydrogen and helium are built up by nuclear reactions inside stars. He has created controversy by suggesting that life originates in the gas clouds of space, and is delivered to the Earth by passing comets.

His work on the evolution of stars was published in *Frontiers of Astronomy* 1955; his science fiction novels include *The Black Cloud* 1957.

Hsuan Tung name adopted by Henry ◊P'u-i on becoming emperor of China 1908.

Hua Guofeng formerly *Hua Kuofeng* 1920– . Chinese politician, leader of the Chinese Communist Party (CCP) 1976–81, premier 1976–80. He dominated Chinese politics 1976–77, seeking economic modernization without major structural reform. From 1978 he was gradually eclipsed by Deng Xiaoping. Hua was ousted from the Politburo Sept 1982, but remained a member of the CCP Central Committee.

Huáscar *c.*1495–1532. King of the Incas. He shared the throne with his half-brother Atahualpa from 1525, but the latter overthrew and murdered him during the Spanish conquest.

Hubbard L(afayette) Ron(ald) 1911–1986. US science-fiction writer of the 1930s–1940s, founder in 1954 of the Church of Scientology.

Hubble Edwin Powell 1889–1953. US astronomer, who discovered the existence of other galaxies outside our own, and classified them according to their shape. His theory that the universe is expanding is now generally accepted.

Born in Marshfield, Missouri, Hubble originally studied law before joining the Yerkes Observatory 1914, subsequently moving to Mount Wilson where in 1923, he discovered that the class of variable stars known as Cepheids exist outside our own Galaxy. In 1925 he introduced the classification of galaxies as spirals, barred spirals and ellipticals. In 1929 he announced *Hubble's law*, that is, that the galaxies are moving apart at a rate that increases with their distance.

Huc Abbé 1813–1860. French missionary in China. In 1845 he travelled to the border of Tibet, where he stopped for eight months to study the Tibetan language and Buddhist literature before moving on to the city of Lhasa.

Hudson Rock. Stage name of Roy Scherer Jnr 1925–1985. US film actor, a big star from the mid-1950s to the mid-1960s, seen at his best in several melodramas directed by Douglas Sirk and three comedies co-starring Doris Day (including *Pillow Talk* 1959).

Hudson W(illiam) H(enry) 1841–1922. Anglo-US author, born of US parents at Florencio near Buenos Aires, Argentina. He was inspired by recollections of early days in Argentina to write

the romances *The Purple Land* 1885 and *Green Mansions* 1904, and his autobiographical *Far Away and Long Ago* 1918. He wrote several books on birds, and on the English countryside, for example, *Nature in Down-Land* 1900 and *A Shepherd's Life* 1910.

Huggins William 1824–1910. British astonomer. He built a private observatory at Tulse Hill, London, in 1856, where he embarked on research in spectrum analysis that marked the beginning of astrophysics.

Hughes David 1831–1900. US inventor who patented an early form of telex in 1855, a type-printing instrument for use with the telegraph. He brought the instrument to Europe in 1857 where it became widely used.

Hughes Howard 1905–1976. US tycoon. Inheriting wealth from his father, who had patented a successful oil-drilling bit, he created a legendary financial empire. A skilled pilot, he manufactured and designed aircraft, and made the classic film *Hell's Angels* 1930 about aviators of World War I; later successes include *Scarface* 1932 and *The Outlaw* 1943. From his middle years he was a recluse.

Hughes Richard (Arthur Warren) 1900–1976. English writer. His study of childhood, *A High Wind in Jamaica*, was published 1929, and the trilogy *The Human Predicament* 1961–73.

Hughes Ted 1930– . English poet, poet laureate from 1984. His work includes *The Hawk in the Rain* 1957, *Lupercal* 1960, *Wodwo* 1967, and *River* 1983, and is characterized by its harsh portrayal of the crueller aspects of nature. He was born in Mytholmroyd, West Yorkshire. In 1956 he married the poet Sylvia Plath.

Hughes Thomas 1822–1896. English writer of the children's book *Tom Brown's School Days* 1857, a story of Rugby school under Thomas ◊Arnold. It had a sequel, *Tom Brown at Oxford* 1861.

Hughes William Morris 1864–1952. Australian politician, prime minister 1915–23; originally Labor, he headed a national cabinet. After resigning as prime minister 1923, he held many other cabinet posts 1934–41.

Born in London, he emigrated to Australia 1884. He represented Australia in the peace conference after World War I at Versailles.

Hugo Victor (Marie) 1802–1885. French poet, novelist, and dramatist. The *Odes et poésies diverses* appeared 1822, and his verse play *Hernani* 1830 established him as the leader of French Romanticism. More volumes of verse followed between his series of dramatic novels which included *The Hunchback of Notre Dame* 1831 and *Les Misérables* 1862. Originally a monarchist, he became an ardent republican, and was a senator under the Third Republic. He died a national hero.

Born at Besançon, Hugo was the son of one of Napoleon's generals. His involvement with republican ideals in the 1840s led to his banishment 1851

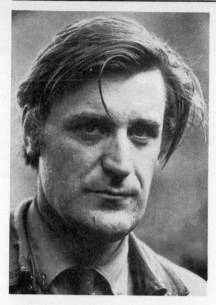

Hughes Ted Hughes, who succeeded John Betjeman as British poet laureate.

for opposing Louis Napoleon's coup d'état, and he lived in Guernsey until the fall of the empire 1870. He was buried in the Panthéon, Paris.

Hull Cordell 1871–1955. US Democrat politician, born in Tennessee. He was a member of Congress 1907–33, and, as Roosevelt's secretary of state 1933–44, was identified with the Good Neighbor Policy of non-intervention in Latin America, and opposed German and Japanese aggression. In his last months of office he paved the way for a system of collective security, for which he was called 'father' of the United Nations. Nobel Peace Prize 1945.

Hulme Keri 1947– . New Zealand novelist. She won the Booker Prize with her first novel *The Bone People* 1985.

Hulme T(homas) E(rnest) 1881–1917. British philosopher, critic and poet, killed on active service in World War I. His *Speculations* 1924 influenced T S ◊Eliot, and his few poems influenced the Imagist movement (which advocated brevity and clarity).

Humboldt Friedrich Heinrich Alexander, Baron von Humboldt 1769–1859. German botanist and geologist who, with the French botanist Aimé Bonpland (1773–1858), explored the regions of the Orinoco and the Amazon rivers in South America 1800–04, and gathered 60,000 plant specimens. On his return, Humboldt devoted 21 years to writing an account of his travels.

One of the first popularizers of science, he gave a series of lectures later published as *Cosmos* 1845–62, an account of the physical sciences.

Humboldt Wilhelm von 1767–1835. German philologist, whose stress on the identity of thought and language influenced ◊Chomsky. He was the brother of Friedrich Humboldt.

Hume Basil 1923– . English Roman Catholic cardinal from 1976. A Benedictine monk, he was abbot of Ampleforth in Yorkshire 1963–76, and in 1976 became archbishop of Westminster, the first monk to hold the office.

Hume David 1711–1776. Scottish philosopher. *A Treatise of Human Nature* 1740 is a central text of British empiricism. Hume denies the possibility of going beyond the subjective experiences of 'ideas' and 'impressions'. The effect of this position is to invalidate metaphysics.

His *History of Great Britain* 1754–62 was very popular within his own lifetime but *A Treatise of Human Nature* was indifferently received. He shared many of the beliefs of the British empiricist school especially those of ◊Locke. *Hume's Law* in moral philosophy states that it is never possible to deduce evaluative conclusions from factual premises; this has come to be known as the is/ought problem.

Hume Fergus 1859–1932. British writer. Educated in New Zealand, he returned to his native England in 1888; his *Mystery of a Hansom Cab* 1887 was one of the first popular detective stories.

Hume Hamilton 1797–1873. Australian explorer. In 1824, with William Hovell, he led an expedition from Sydney to the Murray River and Port Phillip. The Melbourne–Sydney *Hume Highway* is named after him.

Hume John 1937– . Northern Ireland Catholic politician, leader of the Social Democrat Party (SDLP) from 1979. Hume was a founder member of the Credit Union Party, which later became the SDLP. He is widely respected for his moderate views.

Hume Joseph 1777–1855. British Radical politician. Born at Montrose, Scotland, he went out to India as an army surgeon 1797, made a fortune, and on his return bought a seat in Parliament. In 1818 he secured election as a Philosophic Radical and supported many progressive measures. His son *Allan Octavian Hume* (1829–1912) was largely responsible for the establishment of the Indian National Congress 1885.

Hume-Rothery William 1899–1968. British metallurgist who conducted research into the constitution of alloys. He was appointed to the first chair of metallurgy 1925.

Humperdinck Engelbert 1854–1921. German composer. He studied music in Munich and in Italy and assisted ◊Wagner at the Bayreuth Festival Theatre. He wrote the musical fairy operas *Hänsel und Gretel* 1893, and *Königskinder/King's Children* 1910.

Hun Sen 1950–. Cambodian political leader, prime minister from 1985. Originally a member of the Khmer Rouge army, he defected in 1977 to join Vietnam-based anti-Khmer Cambodian forces.

Born into a poor peasant family in the eastern province of Kampang-Cham, Hun Sen joined the Khmer Rouge in 1970. He rose to become a regiment commander, but, disillusioned, defected to the anti-Khmer Cambodian forces in 1977. On his return to Cambodia, following the Vietnamese-backed communist takeover, he served as foreign minister 1979, and then as prime minister 1985, promoting economic liberalization and a thawing in relations with exiled, non-Khmer, opposition forces as a prelude to a compromise political settlement.

Hunt (James Henry) Leigh 1784–1859. English poet and essayist. Convicted for libel against the Prince Regent in his Liberal newspaper *The Examiner*, he was imprisoned 1813. The friend and, later, enemy of Byron, he also knew Keats and Shelley.

His verse is little appreciated today, but he influenced the Romantics, and his book on London *The Town* 1848 and his *Autobiography* 1850 survive. The character of Harold Skimpole in Dickens' *Bleak House* was allegedly based on him.

Hunt John, Baron Hunt 1910– . British mountaineer, leader of the successful Everest expedition 1953 (see ◊Hillary and ◊Tenzing).

Hunt William Holman 1827–1910. British painter, one of the founders of the Pre-Raphaelite Brotherhood 1848. Obsessed with realistic detail, he travelled to Syria and Palestine to paint biblical subjects from 1854 onwards. His works include *The Awakening Conscience* 1853 (Tate Gallery, London) and *The Light of the World* 1854 (Keble College, Oxford).

Hunter John 1728–1793. Scottish surgeon, pathologist, and comparative anatomist. His main contribution to medicine was his insistence on rigorous scientific method. He was also the first to understand the nature of digestion.

He did major work in comparative anatomy and dental pathology. He experimented extensively on animals, and collected a large number of specimens and preparations (Hunterian Collections), which are now housed in the Royal College of Surgeons, London. He was a Fellow of the Royal Society.

He trained under his elder brother *William Hunter* (1718–83), anatomist and obstetrician, who became professor of anatomy in the Royal Academy 1768 and president of the Medical Society 1781. His collections are now in the Hunterian museum of Glasgow University.

Hunyadi János Corvinus 1387–1456. Hungarian politician and general. Born in Transylvania, reputedly the son of the emperor ◊Sigismund, he won battles against the Turks from the 1440s. In 1456 he defeated them at Belgrade, but died shortly afterwards of the plague.

Huppert Isabelle 1955–. French actress who has appeared in several international films; *Cesar et Rosalie* 1972; *Aloise* 1974; *Rosebud* 1975; *Violette Nozière* 1978; *Heaven's Gate* 1980; *Camp de Torchon* 1981.

Hurd Douglas (Richard) 1930– . English Conservative politician, foreign secretary from 1989 and home secretary 1986–89. He entered the House of Commons 1974, representing Witney from 1983.

Hurd was in the diplomatic service 1952–66, serving in Beijing and at the United Nations in New York and Rome. He then joined the Conservative research department and became a secretary to the party leader Edward Heath. He was made a junior minister by Margaret Thatcher, and the sudden resignation of Leon Brittan projected Hurd into the home secretary's post early 1986. In 1989 he was appointed foreign secretary in the reshuffle that followed Nigel Lawson's resignation as chancellor of the exchequer.

Hurston Zora Neale 1901–1960. US novelist and short-story writer. She collected traditional black US folk tales in *Mules and Men* 1935; her novels include *Their Eyes Were Watching God* 1937.

Hurt William 1950–. US actor whose films include *Altered States* 1980, *The Big Chill* 1983, *Kiss of the Spider Woman* 1985, and *Broadcast News* 1987.

Husák Gustáv 1913– . Leader of the Communist Party of Czechoslovakia (CCP) 1969–87 and president 1975–89. After the 1968 Prague Spring of liberalization, his task was to restore control, purge the CCP, and oversee the implementation of a new, federalist constitution. He was deposed in the popular uprising of Nov–Dec 1989.

Husák, a lawyer, was active in the Resistance movement during World War II, and afterwards in the Slovak Communist Party (SCP), and was imprisoned on political grounds 1951–60. Rehabilitated, he was appointed first secretary of the SCP 1968 and CCP leader 1969–87. As titular state president he pursued a policy of cautious reform. He stepped down as party leader 1987, and was replaced as state president by Vaclav ◊Havel in Dec 1989 following the 'gentle revolution'.

Huskisson William 1770–1830. British conservative politician, financier, and advocate of free trade. He served as secretary to the Treasury 1807–09 and colonial agent for Ceylon (now Sri Lanka). He was active in the Corn Law debates and supported their relaxation in 1821.

Huss John *c.* 1373–1415. Bohemian church reformer, rector of Prague University from 1402, who was excommunicated for attacks on ecclesiastical abuses. He was summoned before the Council of Constance 1414, defended the English reformer Wycliffe, rejected the pope's authority, and was burned at the stake. His followers were called Hussites.

Hussein ibn Ali *c.*1854–1931. Leader of the Arab revolt 1916–18 against the Turks. He proclaimed himself king of the Hejaz 1916, accepted the caliphate 1924, but was unable to retain it due to internal fighting. He was deposed 1924 by Ibn Saud.

Hussein ibn Talal 1935– . King of Jordan from 1952. Great-grandson of Hussein ibn Ali, he became king after the mental incapacity of his father Talal. By 1967 he had lost all his kingdom west of the Jordan river in the Arab-Israeli Wars, and in 1970 suppressed the Palestine Liberation Organization acting as a guerrilla force against his rule on the remaining East Bank territories. In recent years, he has become a moderating force in Middle Eastern politics.

Hussein Saddam 1937–. Iraqi left-wing politician, in power from 1968, president from 1979. Ruthless in the pursuit of his objectives, he fought a bitter war against Iran 1980–88 and has dealt harshly with Kurdish rebels seeking a degree of independence.

Hussein joined the Arab Ba'th Socialist Party as a young man and soon became involved in revolutionary activities. In 1959 he was sentenced to death and took refuge in Egypt, but a coup in 1963 made his return possible, although in the following year he was imprisoned for plotting to overthrow the regime he had helped to instal. After his release he took a leading part in the 1968 revolution, removing the civilian government and establishing a Revolutionary Command Council (RCC). At first discreetly, and then more openly, Hussein strengthened his position and in 1979 became RCC chair and state president.

Husserl Edmund (Gustav Albrecht) 1859–1938. German philosopher, regarded as the founder of phenomenology, a philosophy concentrating on what is consciously experienced.

He hoped phenomenology would become the science of all sciences. His main works are *Logical Investigations* 1900, *Phenomenological Philosophy* 1913, and *The Crisis of the European Sciences* 1936. He influenced ◊Heidegger, and was influential in sociology through the work of Alfred Schütz (1899–1959).

Huston John 1906–1987. US film director, screenwriter, and actor. An impulsive and individualistic filmmaker, he often dealt with the themes of greed, treachery, human relationships, and the loner. His works as a director include *The Maltese Falcon* 1941 (his debut), *The Treasure of the Sierra Madre* 1947 (for which he won an Academy Award), *The African Queen* 1951, and *Prizzi's Honor* 1984.

He was the son of the actor Walter Huston and the father of the actress Anjelica Huston. His other films include *Moby Dick* 1956, *The Misfits* 1961, *Fat City* 1972, and *The Dead* 1987.

Hutton Barbara 1912–1979. US heiress, granddaughter of F W ◊Woolworth, notorious in her day as the original 'poor little rich girl'. Her seven husbands included the actor Cary Grant.

Hutton James 1726–1797. Scottish geologist, known as the 'founder of geology', who formulated the concept of uniformitarianism. In 1785 he developed a theory of the igneous origin of many rocks.

His *Theory of the Earth* 1788 proposed that the Earth was indefinitely old. Uniformitarianism suggests that past events could be explained in terms of processes that work today. For example, the kind of river current that produces a certain settling pattern in a bed of sand today must have been operating many millions of years ago, if that same pattern is visible in ancient sandstones.

Hutton Leonard 1916–. English cricketer, born in Pudsey, West Yorkshire. He captained England in 23 test matches 1952–56 and was England's first professional captain. In 1938 at the Oval he scored 364 against Australia, a world record test score until beaten by Gary ◊Sobers 1958.

Huxley Aldous (Leonard) 1894–1963. English writer. The satirical disillusion of his witty first novel, *Crome Yellow* 1921, continued throughout *Antic Hay* 1923, *Those Barren Leaves* 1925, and *Point Counter Point* 1928. *Brave New World* 1932 concerns the reproduction of the human race by mass production in the laboratory.

He was the grandson of Thomas Henry Huxley and brother of Julian Huxley. Huxley's later devotion to mysticism led to his experiments with the hallucinogenic drug mescalin, recorded in *The Doors of Perception* 1954. He also wrote the novel *Eyeless in Gaza* 1936, and two historical studies, *Grey Eminence* 1941 and *The Devils of Loudun* 1952.

Huxley Andrew 1917– . English physiologist, awarded the Nobel prize for medicine 1963, with Hodgkin and Eccles, for work on nerve impulses.

Huxley Julian 1887–1975. English biologist, first director-general of UNESCO, and a founder of the World Wildlife Fund (now the World Wide Fund for Nature).

Huxley Thomas Henry 1825–1895. English scientist and humanist. Following the publication of Charles Darwin's *On the Origin of Species* 1859, he became known as 'Darwin's bulldog', and for many years was the most prominent and popular champion of evolution. In 1869, he coined the word 'agnostic' to express his own religious attitude.

He wrote *Man's Place in Nature* 1863, textbooks on physiology, and innumerable scientific papers. His later books, such as *Lay Sermons* 1870, *Science and Culture* 1881, and *Evolution and Ethics* were expositions of scientific humanism. His grandsons include Aldous, Andrew, and Julian Huxley.

Hu Yaobang 1915–1989. Chinese politician, Communist Party (CCP) chair 1981–87. A protégé of the communist leader Deng Xiaoping, Hu presided over a radical overhaul of the party structure and personnel 1982–86.

Hu, born into a peasant family in Hunan province, joined the Red Army at the age of 14 and was a political commissar during the 1934–36 Long March. In 1941 he served under Deng and later worked under him in provincial and central government. Hu was purged as a 'capitalist roader' during the 1966–69 Cultural Revolution and sent into the countryside for 're-education'. He was rehabilitated 1975, but disgraced again when Deng fell from prominence 1976. In Dec 1978, with Deng established in power, Hu was inducted into the CCP Politburo and became head of the revived secretariat 1980 and CCP chairman 1981. He attempted to quicken reaction against Mao. He was dismissed Jan 1987 for his relaxed handling of a wave of student unrest Dec 1986.

Huygens Christiaan 1629–1695. Dutch mathematical physicist and astronomer, who propounded the wave theory of light. He developed the pendulum clock, discovered polarization, and observed Saturn's rings.

Huysmans J(oris) K(arl) 1848–1907. French novelist of Dutch ancestry. *Marthe* 1876, the story of a courtesan, was followed by other realistic novels, including *A rebours/Against Nature* 1884, a novel of self-absorbed aestheticism which symbolized the 'decadent' movement.

Hyde Douglas 1860–1949. Irish scholar and politician. Founder-president of the Gaelic League 1893–1915, he was president of Eire 1938–45. His works include *Love Songs of Connacht* 1894.

Hyder Ali *c.*1722–1782. Indian general, sultan of Mysore from 1759. In command of the army in Mysore from 1749, he became the ruler of the state 1759, and rivalled British power in the area until his triple defeat by Sir Eyre Coote 1781 during the Anglo-French wars. He was the father of Tippu Sultan.

Hypatia *c.*370–*c.*415. Greek philosopher, born at Alexandria. She studied Neo-Platonism at Athens, and succeeded her father Theon as professor of philosophy at Alexandria. She was murdered, it is thought by Christian fanatics.

Ibsen *Norwegian dramatist Henrik Ibsen.*

Ibáñez Vincente Blasco 1867–1928. Spanish novelist and politician, born in Valencia. He was actively involved in revolutionary politics. His novels include *La barraca/The Cabin* 1898, the best of his regional works; *Sangre y arena/Blood and Sand* 1908, the story of a famous bullfighter; and *Los cuatro jinetes del Apocalipsis/The Four Horsemen of the Apocalypse* 1916, a product of the effects of World War I.

Ibarruri Dolores, known as *La Pasionaria* ('the passion flower') 1895–1989. Spanish Basque politician, journalist, and orator. In 1936 she helped to establish the Popular Front government, and was a Loyalist leader in the Civil War. When Franco came to power in 1939 she left Spain for the USSR, where she was active in the Communist Party. She returned to Spain in 1977 after Franco's death, and was re-elected to the Cortes (at the age of 81) in the first parliamentary elections for 40 years.

Ibn Battuta 1304–1368. Arab traveller born in Tangiers. In 1325, he went on an extraordinary 120,000 km/75,000 mi journey via Mecca to Egypt, E Africa, India, and China, returning some 30 years later. During this journey he also visited Spain and crossed the Sahara to Timbuktu. The narrative of his travels, *The Adventures of Ibn Battuta*, was written with an assistant, Ibn Juzayy.

Ibn Saud 1880–1953. First king of Saudi Arabia from 1932. His father was the son of the sultan of Nejd, at whose capital, Riyadh, Ibn Saud was born. In 1891 a rival group seized Riyadh, and Ibn Saud went into exile with his father, who resigned his claim to the throne in his favour. In 1902 Ibn Saud recaptured Riyadh and recovered the kingdom, and by 1921 he had brought all central Arabia

under his rule. In 1924 he invaded the Hejaz, of which he was proclaimed king in 1926.

Nejd and the Hejaz were united in 1932 in the kingdom of Saudi Arabia. Ibn Saud introduced programmes for modernization with revenue from oil, which was discovered in 1936.

Ibn Sina Arabic name of ◊Avicenna, scholar and translator.

Ibrahim Abdullah 1934– . South African pianist and composer, formerly known as 'Dollar' Brand. He first performed in the USA in 1965, and has had a great influence on the fusion of African rhythms with American jazz. His compositions range from songs to large works for orchestra.

Ibsen Henrik (Johan) 1828–1906. Norwegian playwright and poet, whose realistic and often controversial plays revolutionized European theatre. Driven into exile 1864–91 by opposition to the satirical *Love's Comedy* 1862, he wrote the verse dramas *Brand* 1866 and *Peer Gynt* 1867, followed by realistic plays dealing with social issues, including *Pillars of Society* 1877, *The Doll's House* 1879, *Ghosts* 1881, *An Enemy of the People* 1882, and *Hedda Gabler* 1891. By the time of his return to Norway, he was recognized as the country's greatest living writer.

His later plays which are more symbolic, include *The Master Builder* 1892, *Little Eyolf* 1894, *John Gabriel Borkman* 1896, and *When We Dead Awaken* 1899.

Iglesias Pablo 1850–1925. Spanish politician, founder of the Spanish Socialist Party (Partido Socialista Obrero de España, PSOE) in 1879 and in 1911 the first socialist deputy to be elected to the *Cortes* (Spanish parliament).

Ignatius Loyola, St 1491–1556. Spanish soldier converted 1521 to the Roman Catholic religious life after being wounded in battle, and founder of the Jesuit order in 1540. Feast day 31 July.

Ignatius of Antioch, St 1st–2nd century AD. Christian martyr. Traditionally a disciple of St John, he was bishop of Antioch, and was thrown to the wild beasts in Rome. He wrote seven epistles, important documents of the early Christian church. Feast day 1 Feb.

Ikhnaton or **Akhenaton** 14th century BC. King of Egypt of the 18th dynasty (c.1379–1362 BC), who may have ruled jointly for a time with his father Amenhotep III. He developed the cult of the Sun, Aton, rather than the rival cult of Ammon, the king of gods. Some historians believe that his neglect of imperial defence for religious reforms led to the loss of most of Egypt's possessions in Asia. His favourite wife was Nefertiti, and two of their six daughters were married to his successors Smenkhare and Tutankaton (later known as Tutankhamen).

Illich Ivan 1926– . US radical philosopher and activist, born in Austria. His works, which include *Deschooling Society* 1971, *Towards a History of Need* 1978, and *Gender* 1983, are a critique against modern economic development, especially in the Third World.

Illich was born in Vienna and has lived in the USA and Latin America. He believes that modern technology and bureaucratic institutions are destroying peasant skills and self-sufficiency and creating a new form of dependency: on experts, professionals, and material goods. True liberation can only be achieved by abolishing the institutions on which authority rests, such as schools and hospitals.

Imhotep c.2800 BC. Egyptian physician and architect, adviser to King Zoser (3rd dynasty). He is thought to have designed the step pyramid at Sakkara, and his tomb (believed to be in the N Sakkara cemetery) became a centre of healing. He was deified as the son of the god Ptah and was identified with Aesculapius, the Greek god of medicine.

Indy (Paul Marie Théodore) Vincent d' 1851–1931. French composer. He studied under César ◊Franck, and was one of the founders of the *Schola Cantorum*. His works include operas (*Fervaal* 1897), symphonies, tone poems (*Istar* 1896), and chamber music.

Ingenhousz Jan 1730–1799. Dutch physician and plant physiologist who established that in the light plants absorb carbon dioxide and give off oxygen.

Ingres Jean Auguste Dominique 1780–1867. French painter, a student of David and leading exponent of the Neo-Classical style. He studied and worked in Rome about 1807–20, where he began the *Odalisque* series of sensuous female nudes, then went to Florence, and returned to France 1824. His portraits painted in the

1840s–50s are meticulously detailed and highly polished.

Ingres's style developed in opposition to the Romanticism of Delacroix. Early works include portraits of Napoleon. Later he painted huge ceilings for the Louvre and for Autun Cathedral. His portraits include *Madame Moitessier* 1856 (National Gallery, London).

Innes-Ker family name of Dukes of Roxburghe; seated at Floors Castle, Roxburghshire.

Inness George 1825–1894. US landscape painter influenced by the Hudson River school, who created an indigenous landscape style. His early works such as *The Delaware Valley* 1865 (Metropolitan Museum of Art, New York) are on a grand scale and show a concern for natural effects of light. Later he moved towards Impressionism.

Innocent III 1161–1216. Pope from 1198 who asserted papal power over secular princes, especially over the succession of Holy Roman Emperors. He also made King ◊John of England his vassal, compelling him to accept ◊Langton as archbishop of Canterbury. He promoted the fourth Crusade and crusades against the non-Christian Livonians and Letts, and Albigensian heretics of S France.

Ionesco Eugène 1912– . Romanian-born French dramatist, a leading exponent of the Theatre of the Absurd. Most of his plays are in one act and concern the futility of language as a means of communication. These include *La Cantatrice chauve/The Bald Prima Donna* 1950 and *La Leçon/The Lesson* 1951.

Later full-length plays include *Rhinocéros* 1958 and *Le Roi se meurt/Exit the King* 1961. He has also written memoirs and a novel, *Le Solitaire/The Hermit* 1973.

Iqbāl Muhammad 1875–1938. Islamic poet and thinker. His literary works, in Urdu and Persian, were mostly verse in the classical style, suitable for public recitation. He sought through his writings to arouse Muslims to take their place in the modern world.

His most celebrated work, the Persian *Asrā-e khūdī/Secrets of the Self* 1915, put forward a theory of the self which was the opposite of the traditional abnegation of Islam. He was an influence on the movement which led to the creation of Pakistan.

Ireland John (Nicholson) 1879–1962. English composer. His works include the mystic orchestral prelude *The Forgotten Rite* 1917 and the piano solo *Sarnia* 1941. Benjamin ◊Britten was his pupil.

Irene, St c.752–c.803. Byzantine emperor 797–802. The wife of Leo IV (750–780), she became regent for their son Constantine (771–805) on Leo's death. In 797 she deposed her son, had his eyes put out, and assumed full title of *basileus* (emperor), ruling in her own right until deposed and exiled to Lesvos by a revolt of 802. She was made a saint by the Greek Orthodox church for her attacks on iconoclasts.

Ireton Henry 1611–1651. English Civil War general. He joined the Parliamentary forces and fought at Edgehill 1642, Gainsborough 1643, and Naseby 1645. After the Battle of Naseby, Ireton, who was opposed to the extreme republicans and the democratic Levellers, strove for a compromise with Charles I, but then played a leading role in his trial and execution.

Irvine Andrew Robertson 1951– . British rugby union player who held the world record for the most points scored in senior international rugby with 301 (273 for Scotland, 28 for the British Lions) between 1972 and 1982.

Irving Henry. Stage name of John Brodribb 1838–1905. English actor. He established his reputation from 1871, chiefly at the Lyceum Theatre in London, where he became manager 1878. He staged a series of successful Shakespearean productions, including *Romeo and Juliet* 1882, with himself and Ellen ◊Terry playing the leading roles. He was the first actor to be knighted, in 1895.

Irving John 1942– . US novelist. His bizarre and funny novels include *The World According to Garp* 1978, a vivid comic tale about a novelist killed by a disappointed reader.

Irving Washington 1783–1859. US essayist and short-story writer. He published a mock-heroic *History of New York* in 1809, supposedly written by the Dutchman 'Diedrich Knickerbocker'. In 1815 he went to England where his publications include *The Sketch Book of Geoffrey Crayon, Gent.* 1820, which contained such stories as 'Rip van Winkle' and 'The Legend of Sleepy Hollow'.

Isaacs Alick 1921–1967. Scottish virologist who with Jean Lindemann, discovered interferon in 1957; a naturally occurring substance found in cells infected with viruses. The full implications of this discovery are still being investigated.

Isaacs began his career by studying different strains of the influenza virus and the body's response to them.

Isabella two Spanish queens:

Isabella I *the Catholic* 1451–1504. Queen of Castile from 1474, after the death of her brother Henry IV. By her marriage with Ferdinand of Aragon 1469, the crowns of two of the Christian states in the Spanish peninsula were united. In her reign the Moors were finally driven out of Spain; she introduced the anti-heretical Inquisition into Castile, and the persecution of the Jews, and gave financial encouragement to ◊Columbus. Her youngest daughter was Catherine of Aragon, first wife of Henry VIII of England.

Isabella II 1830–1904. Queen of Spain from 1833, when she succeeded her father Ferdinand VII (1784–1833). The Salic Law banning a female sovereign had been repealed by the Cortes (Spanish parliament), but her succession was disputed by

her uncle Don Carlos de Bourbon (1788–1855). After seven years of civil war the Carlists (supporters of Don Carlos) were defeated. She abdicated in favour of her son Alfonso XII in 1868.

Isaiah 8th century BC. In the Old Testament, the first major Hebrew prophet. The son of Amos, he was probably of high rank, and lived largely in Jerusalem.

Isaurian an 8th-century Byzantine imperial dynasty, originating in Asia Minor.

Members of the family had been employed as military leaders by the Byzantines, and they gained great influence and prestige as a result. Leo III acceded in 717 as the first Isaurian emperor, and was followed by Constantine V (718–75), Leo IV (750–80), and Leo's widow Irene, who acted as regent until her death in 802. They maintained the integrity of the empire's borders. With the exception of Irene, they attempted to suppress the use of religious icons.

Isherwood Christopher (William Bradshaw) 1904–1986. English novelist. Educated at Cambridge, he lived in Germany 1929–33 just before Hitler's rise to power, a period which inspired *Mr Norris Changes Trains* 1935 and *Goodbye to Berlin* 1939, creating the character of Sally Bowles (the basis of the musical *Cabaret* 1968). Returning to England, he collaborated with W H ◊Auden in three verse plays.

Ishiguro Kazuo 1954– . Japanese-born British novelist. His novel *An Artist of the Floating World* won the 1986 Whitbread Prize, and *The Remains of the Day* won the Booker Prize 1989.

Ishmael in the Old Testament, son of ◊Abraham and his wife Sarah's Egyptian maid Hagar; traditional ancestor of Muhammad and the Arab people. He and his mother were driven out by Sarah's jealousy. Muslims believe that it was Ishmael, not Isaac, whom God commanded Abraham to sacrifice, and that Ishmael helped Abraham build the Kaaba shrine in Mecca.

Isidore of Seville *c.*560–636. Writer and missionary. His *Ethymologiae* was the model for later medieval encyclopedias and helped to preserve classical thought into the Middle Ages, and his *Chronica Maiora* remains an important source for the history of Visigothic Spain.

As bishop of Seville from 600, he strengthened the church in Spain and converted many Jews and Aryan Visigoths.

Ismail 1830–1895. Khedive (governor) of Egypt 1866–79. A grandson of Mehemet Ali, he became viceroy of Egypt in 1863 and in 1866 received the title of khedive from the Ottoman sultan. In 1875 Britain, at Prime Minister Disraeli's suggestion, bought the khedive's Suez Canal shares for £3,976,582, and Anglo-French control of Egypt's finances was established. In 1879 the UK and France persuaded the sultan to appoint Tewfik, his son, khedive in his place.

Ismail I 1486–1524. Shah of Persia from 1501, founder of the *Safavid dynasty*, who established the first national government since the Arab conquest, and Shi'ite Islam as the national religion.

Isocrates 436–338 BC. Athenian orator, a pupil of Socrates. He was a professional speechwriter and teacher of rhetoric.

Isozaki Arata 1931– . Japanese architect. One of Kenzo ◊Tange's team 1954–63, his Post-Modernist works include Ochanomizu Square, Tokyo (retaining the existing facades), and buildings for the 1992 Barcelona Olympics.

Israels Jozef 1824–1894. Dutch painter. In 1870 he settled in The Hague and became a leader of the *Hague school* of landscape painters, who shared some of their ideals with the Barbizon school in France. Israels's sombre and sentimental scenes of peasant life recall ◊Millet.

Issigonis Alec 1906–1988. British engineer who designed the Morris Minor 1948 and the Mini-Minor 1959 cars, thus creating modern economy motoring and adding the word 'mini' to the English language.

Itagaki Taisuke 1837–1919. Japanese military and political leader, the founder of Japan's first political party, the Jiyuto (Liberal Party) in 1875. Involved in the overthrow of the Tokugawa shogunate and the Meiji restoration (see ◊Mutsuhito), Itagaki became a champion of democratic principles although continuing to serve in the government for short periods.

After ennoblement in 1887 he retained the leadership of the party and cooperated with ◊Ito Hirobumi in the establishment of parliamentary government in the 1890s.

Ito Hirobumi 1841–1909. Japanese politician, prime minister and a key figure in the modernization of Japan. He was also involved in the Meiji restoration under ◊Mutsuhito 1866–68 and in government missions to the USA and Europe in the 1870s. As minister for home affairs, he drafted the Meiji constitution in 1889 and oversaw its implementation as prime minister the following year. While resident-general in Korea, he was assassinated by a Korean nationalist.

Iturbide Agustín de 1783–1824. Mexican military leader (*caudillo*) who led the conservative faction in the nation's struggle for independence from Spain. In 1822 he crowned himself Emperor Agustín I. His extravagance and failure to restore order led all other parties to turn against him, and he reigned for less than a year.

Ivan six rulers of Russia, including:

Ivan III *the Great* 1440–1505. Grand duke of Muscovy from 1462, who revolted against Tatar overlordship by refusing tribute to Grand Khan Ahmed 1480. He claimed the title of tsar, and used the double-headed eagle as the Russian state emblem.

Ivan IV *the Terrible* 1530–1584. Grand duke of Muscovy from 1533, he assumed power 1544, and was crowned as first tsar of Russia 1547. He conquered Kazan 1552, Astrakhan 1556, and Siberia 1581. His last years alternated between debauchery and religious austerities.

Ives Charles (Edward) 1874–1954. US composer who experimented with atonality (absence of key), quarter tones, clashing time signatures, and quotations from popular music of the time. He wrote five symphonies, including *Holidays Symphony* 1904–13, chamber music, including the *Concord Sonata*, and the orchestral *Three Places in New England* 1903–14 and *The Unanswered Question* 1908.

Ives Frederic Eugene 1856–1937. US inventor who developed the halftone process of printing photographs in 1878. The process uses a screen to break up light and dark areas into different-sized dots. By 1886 he had evolved the halftone process now generally in use. Among his many other inventions was a three-colour printing process.

Ivory James 1928– . US director best known for his collaboration with Indian producer Ismael ◊Merchant.

Jackson Alexander Young 1882–1974. Canadian landscape painter, a leading member of the *Group of Seven* who aimed to create a specifically Canadian school of landscape art.

Jackson Andrew 1767–1845. 7th president of the USA 1829–37, a Democrat. He was born in South Carolina. He defeated a British force at New Orleans in 1815 (after the official end of the war in 1814) and was involved in the war which led to the purchase of Florida in 1819. After an unsuccessful attempt in 1824, he was elected president in 1828. Governing through a 'kitchen cabinet', he also made use of the presidential veto to oppose the renewal of the US bank charter. Re-elected in 1832, he continued his struggle against the power of finance.

Jackson Glenda 1936– . British actress. She has made many stage appearances, including *Marat/Sade* 1966, and her films include the Oscar-winning *Women in Love* 1971. On television she played Queen Elizabeth I in *Elizabeth R* 1971.

Jackson Jesse 1941– . US Democrat politician, campaigner for minority rights. He contested his party's 1984 and 1988 presidential nominations in an effort to increase voter registration and to put black issues on the national agenda. He is a notable public speaker.

Born in North Carolina and educated in Chicago, Jackson emerged as a powerful Baptist preacher and black activist politician, working first with the civil-rights leader Martin Luther King, then on building the political machine that gave Chicago a black mayor 1983. He sought to construct what he called a *rainbow coalition*, comprising ethnic-minority and socially deprived groups. He took the lead in successfully campaigning for US disinvestment in South Africa 1986.

Jackson US rock singer and songwriter Michael Jackson, whose success and popularity reached a peak with the Thriller *album in 1982.*

Jackson John Hughlings 1835–1911. English neurologist and neurophysiologist. As a result of his studies of epilepsy, Jackson demonstrated that particular areas of the cerebral cortex (outer mantle of the brain) control the functioning of particular organs and limbs.

Jackson Lady title of British economist Barbara ◊Ward.

Jackson Michael 1958– . US rock singer and songwriter, known for his meticulously choreographed performances. He had his first solo hit in 1971; his worldwide popularity reached a peak with the albums *Thriller* 1982 and *Bad* 1987.

He became professional in 1969 as the youngest member of the Jackson Five, who had hits on Motown Records from their first single, 'I Want You Back'. Michael was the lead singer, but soon surpassed his brothers in popularity as a solo performer. His 1980s albums, produced by Quincy Jones (1933–), yielded an unprecedented number of hit singles, outstanding among them 'Billie Jean' 1983.

Jackson Thomas Jonathan, known as 'Stonewall' Jackson 1824–1863. US Confederate general. In the American Civil War he acquired his nickname and his reputation at the battle of Bull Run, from the firmness with which his brigade resisted the Northern attack. In 1862 he organized the Shenandoah valley campaign, and assisted Lee's invasion of Maryland. He helped to defeat Gen Joseph E Hooker's Union army at the battle of Chancellorsville, Virginia, but was fatally wounded by one of his own men in the confusion of battle.

Jackson Confederate general Thomas Jackson, whose tactics in resisting Union forces at the Battle of Bull Run during the American Civil War earned him the nickname 'Stonewall'.

Jack the Ripper popular name for the unidentified mutilator and murderer of five women prostitutes in the Whitechapel area of London in 1888.

Jacob in the Old Testament, Hebrew patriarch, son of Isaac and Rebecca, who obtained the rights of seniority from his twin brother Esau by trickery. He married his cousins Leah and Rachel, serving their father Laban seven years for each, and at the time of famine in Canaan joined his son Joseph in Egypt. His 12 sons were the traditional ancestors of the 12 tribes of Israel.

Jacob François 1920– . French biochemist who, with Jacques ◊Monod, did pioneering research in molecular genetics and showed how the production of proteins from DNA is controlled.

Jacobs W(illiam) W(ymark) 1863–1943. British author, who used his childhood knowledge of London's docklands in amusing short stories such as 'Many Cargoes' 1896. He excelled in the macabre, for example 'The Monkey's Paw' 1902.

Jacquard Joseph Marie 1752–1834. French textile manufacturer, who invented a punched-card system for programming designs on a carpet-making loom. In 1804 he constructed looms that used a series of punched cards which controlled the pattern of longitudinal warp threads depressed before each sideways passage of the shuttle. On later machines the punched cards were joined to form an endless loop which represented the 'program' for the repeating pattern of a carpet.

Jacuzzi Candido 1903–1986. Italian-born US inventor and engineer, who invented the Jacuzzi, a pump that enabled a whirlpool to be emulated in a domestic bath. He developed it for his

15-month-old son, a sufferer from rheumatoid arthritis.

Jagan Cheddi 1918– . Guyanese left-wing politician. Educated in British Guyana and the USA, he led the People's Progressive Party from 1950, and in 1961 he became the first prime minister of British Guyana.

Jagan Janet 1920– . Guyanese left-wing politician, wife of Cheddi Jagan. She was general secretary of the People's Progressive Party 1950–70.

Jahangir 'Conqueror of the World', name adopted by Salim 1569–1627, third Mogul emperor of India from 1605, when he succeeded his father ◊Akbar the Great. He designed the Shalimar Gardens in Kashmir and buildings and gardens in Lahore.

Jakeš Miloš 1922– . Czech communist politician, a member of the Politburo from 1981 and party leader 1987–89. A conservative, he supported the Soviet invasion of Czechoslovakia in 1968. He was forced to resign in Nov 1989 following a series of pro-democracy mass rallies.

Jakeš, an electrical engineer, joined the Communist Party of Czechoslovakia (CCP) in 1945 and studied in Moscow 1955–58. As head of the CCP's central control commission, he oversaw the purge of reformist personnel after the suppression of the 1968 Prague Spring. In Dec 1987 he replaced Gustáv Husák as CCP leader. Although he enjoyed close relations with the Soviet leader Gorbachev, Jakeš was a cautious reformer who was unpopular with the people.

James Henry 1843–1916. US novelist, who lived in Europe from 1875 and became a naturalized British subject 1915. His novels deal with the impact of European culture on the US soul. They include *The Portrait of a Lady* 1881, *Washington Square* 1881, *The Bostonians* 1886, *The Ambassadors* 1903, and *The Golden Bowl* 1904. He also wrote more than a hundred shorter works of fiction, notably the supernatural tale *The Turn of the Screw* 1898.

Other major works include *Roderick Hudson* 1876, *The American* 1877, *The Tragic Muse* 1890, *The Spoils of Poynton* 1897, *The Awkward Age* 1899, *The Wings of the Dove* 1902.

James Jesse 1847–1882. US bank and train robber, born in Missouri and a leader (with his brother Frank) of the Quantrill gang. Jesse was killed by an accomplice; Frank remained unconvicted and became a farmer.

James M(ontague) R(hodes) 1862–1936. British writer, theologian, linguist, and medievalist. He wrote *Ghost Stories of an Antiquary* 1904 and other supernatural tales.

James P(hyllis) D(orothy) 1920– . British detective novelist, creator of the characters Superintendent Adam Dalgliesh and private investigator Cordelia Gray. She was a tax official, hospital administrator, and civil servant before turning to writing. Her books include *Death of an Expert*

James Legendary US bandit Jesse James, who masterminded a series of robberies before being betrayed by a member of his own gang.

James William 1842–1910. US psychologist and philosopher, brother of the novelist Henry James. He turned from medicine to psychology and taught at Harvard 1872–1907. His books include *Principles of Psychology* 1890, *The Will to Believe* 1897, and *Varieties of Religious Experience* 1902, one of the most important works on the psychology of religion.

James I the Conqueror 1208–1276. King of Aragon from 1213, when he succeeded his father. He conquered the Balearic Islands and took Valencia from the Moors, dividing it with Alfonso X of Castile by a treaty of 1244. Both these exploits are recorded in his autobiography *Llibre deis feyts*. He largely established Aragon as the dominant power in the Mediterranean.

James two kings of Britain:

James I 1566–1625. King of England from 1603 and Scotland (*James VI*) from 1567. The son of Mary, Queen of Scots, and Lord Darnley, he succeeded on his mother's abdication from the Scottish throne, assumed power 1583, established a strong centralized authority, and in 1589 married Anne of Denmark (1574–1619). As successor to Elizabeth in England, he alienated the Puritans by his High Church views and Parliament by his assertion of divine right, and was generally unpopular because of his favourites, such as ◊Buckingham, and because of his schemes for

an alliance with Spain. He was succeeded by his son Charles I.

James II 1633–1701. King of England and Scotland (*James VII*) from 1685, second son of Charles I. He succeeded Charles II. James married Anne Hyde 1659 (1637–71, mother of Mary II and Anne) and ◊Mary of Modena 1673 (mother of James Edward Stuart). He became a Catholic 1671, which led first to attempts to exclude him from the succession, then to the rebellions of ◊Monmouth and ◊Argyll, and finally to the Whig and Tory leaders' invitation to William of Orange to take the throne in 1688. James fled to France, led a rising in Ireland 1689, but after defeat at the battle of the Boyne 1690 remained in exile in France.

James seven kings of Scotland:

James I 1394–1437. King of Scotland 1406–37, who assumed power 1424. He was a cultured and strong monarch, whose improvements in the administration of justice brought him popularity among the common people. He was assassinated by a group of conspirators led by the Earl of Atholl.

James II 1430–1460. King of Scotland from 1437, who assumed power 1449. The only surviving son of James I, he was supported by most of the nobles and parliament. He sympathized with the Lancastrians during the Wars of the Roses, and attacked English possessions in S Scotland. He was killed while besieging Roxburgh Castle.

James III 1451–1488. King of Scotland from 1460, who assumed power 1469. His reign was marked by rebellions by the nobles, including his brother Alexander, duke of Albany. He was murdered during a rebellion.

James IV 1473–1513. King of Scotland from 1488, who married Margaret (1489–1541, daughter of Henry VII) in 1503. He invaded England 1513, but was defeated and killed at the battle Flodden.

James I The son of Mary, Queen of Scots, James I of England was already James VI of Scotland when he came to the throne in England in 1603.

James V 1512–1542. King of Scotland from 1513, who assumed power 1528. Following an attack on Scottish territory by Henry VIII's forces, he was defeated near the border at Solway Moss 1542.

James VI of Scotland. See ◊James I of England.

James VII of Scotland. See ◊James II of England.

James Edward Stuart 1688–1766. British prince, known as the *Old Pretender*. Son of James II, he was born at St James's Palace and after the revolution of 1688 was taken to France. He landed in Scotland in 1715 to head a Jacobite rebellion, but withdrew for lack of support. In his later years he settled in Rome.

Jameson Leander Starr 1853–1917. British colonial administrator. In South Africa, early in 1896, he led the *Jameson Raid* from Mafeking into Transvaal, in support of the non-Boer colonists there, in an attempt to overthrow the government, for which he served some months in prison. Returning to South Africa, he succeeded Cecil ◊Rhodes as leader of the Progressive Party of Cape Colony, where he was prime minister 1904–08.

James, St several Christian saints, including:

James, St *the Great* died AD 44. A New Testament apostle, originally a Galilean fisherman, he was the son of Zebedee and brother of the apostle John. He was put to death by ◊Herod Agrippa. Patron saint of Spain. Feast day 25 July.

James, St *the Just* 1st century AD. The New Testament brother of Jesus, to whom Jesus appeared after the Resurrection. Leader of the Christian church in Jerusalem, he was the author of the biblical Epistle of James.

James, St *the Little* 1st century AD. In the New Testament, a disciple of Christ, son of Alphaeus. Feast day 3 May.

Janáček Leoš 1854–1928. Czech composer. He became director of the Conservatoire at Brno in 1919 and professor at the Prague Conservatoire in 1920. His music, highly original and influenced by Moravian folk music, includes arrangements of folk songs, operas (*Jenufa* 1904, *The Cunning Little Vixen* 1924), and the choral *Glagolitic Mass* 1927.

Jannequin Clament *c.*1472–*c.*1560. French composer. He studied with Josquin ◊Desprez and is remembered for choral works that incorporate images from real life, such as birdsong and the cries of street vendors.

Jannings Emil. Stage name of Theodor Emil Jarenz 1882–1950. German actor whose greatest success was in silent films of the 1920s, as in *The Last Command* 1928. In *Der blaue Engel/The Blue Angel* 1930 he played a schoolteacher who loses his head over Marlene Dietrich.

Jansen Cornelius 1585–1638. Dutch Roman Catholic theologian, founder of *Jansenism* with his book *Augustinus* 1640. He became professor at Louvain, Belgium, in 1630, and bishop of Ypres, Belgium, in 1636.

Jansky Karl Guthe 1905–1950. US radio engineer, who discovered that the Milky Way galaxy emanates radio waves; he did not follow up his discovery, but it marked the birth of radioastronomy.

Januarius, St or *San Gennaro* died ?305. Patron saint of Naples, Italy. Traditionally, he suffered martyrdom under the Roman emperor Diocletian. Two phials of his blood are alleged regularly to liquefy miraculously. Feast day 19 Sept.

Jaques-Dalcroze Emile 1865–1950. Swiss composer and teacher. He is remembered for his system of physical training by rhythmical movement to music (eurythmics), and founded the Institut Jaques-Dalcroze in Geneva, in 1915.

Järnefelt (Edvard) Armas 1869–1958. Finnish composer who is chiefly known for his *Praeludium* and the lyrical *Berceuse*.

Jarrett Keith 1945– . US jazz pianist and composer, an eccentric innovator who performs both alone and with small groups. *The Köln Concert* 1975 is a characteristic solo live recording.

Jarrett was a member of the rock-influenced Charles Lloyd Quartet 1966–67, and played with Miles Davis 1970–71.

Jarry Alfred 1873–1907. French satiric dramatist, whose *Ubu Roi* 1896 foreshadowed the Theatre of the Absurd and the French Surrealist movement.

Jaruzelski Wojciech 1923– . Polish general, communist leader from 1981, president from 1985. He imposed martial law for the first year of his rule, suppressed the opposition, and banned trade union activity, but later released many political prisoners. In 1989, elections in favour of the free trade union Solidarity forced Jaruzelski to speed up democratic reforms, overseeing a transition to a new form of 'socialist pluralist' democracy.

Jaruzelski, who served with the Soviet army 1939–43, was defence minister 1968–83 and entered the Politburo 1971. At the height of the crisis of 1980–81 he assumed power as prime minister and PUWP first secretary; in 1985 he resigned as prime minister to become president, but remained the dominant political figure in Poland. His attempts to solve Poland's economic problems were unsuccessful.

Jaspers Karl 1883–1969. German philosopher, whose works include *General Psychopathology* 1913, and *Philosophy* 1932. Born at Oldenburg, he studied medicine and psychology, and in 1921 became professor of philosophy at Heidelberg.

Jaurès Jean Léon 1859–1914. French socialist politician and advocate of international peace. He was a lecturer in philosophy at Toulouse until his election in 1885 as a deputy (member of parliament). In 1893 he joined the Socialist Party, established a united party, and in 1904 founded the newspaper *L'Humanité*, becoming its editor until his assassination.

Jayawardene Junius Richard 1906– . Sri Lankan politician. Leader of the United Nationalist Party from 1973, he became prime minister 1977, and the country's first president 1978–88.

Jeans James Hopwood 1877–1946. British mathematician and scientist. In physics, he contributed work on the kinetic theory of gases, and forms of energy radiation; and in astronomy, on giant and dwarf stars, the nature of spiral nebulae, and the origin of the cosmos. He also did much to popularize astronomy.

Jefferies (John) Richard 1848–1887. British naturalist and writer, whose books on the countryside included *Gamekeeper at Home* 1878, *Wood Magic* 1881, and *Story of My Heart* 1883.

Jeffers (John) Robinson 1887–1962. US poet. He wrote free verse, and demonstrated an antagonism to human society reflected in the isolation of his home at Carmel in California. His volumes include *Tamar and Other Poems* 1924, *The Double Axe* 1948, and *Hungerfield and Other Poems* 1954.

Jefferson Thomas 1743–1826. 3rd president of the USA 1801–09, founder of the Democratic Party. Born in Virginia into a wealthy family. He published *A Summary View of the Rights of America* 1774 and as a member of the Continental Congresses of 1775–76 was largely responsible for the drafting of the Declaration of Independence. He was governor of Virginia 1779–81, ambassador to Paris 1785–89, secretary of state 1789–93, and vice president 1797–1801.

Jefferson's interests also included music, painting, architecture, and the natural sciences; he was very much a product of the 18th century enlightenment. His political philosophy of 'agrarian democracy' placed responsibility for upholding a virtuous American republic mainly upon a citizenry of independent yeoman farmers. Ironically, his two terms as president saw the adoption of some of the ideas of his political opponents, the Federalists.

Jeffrey Francis, Lord 1773–1850. Scottish lawyer and literary critic. Born at Edinburgh, he was a founder and editor of the *Edinburgh Review* 1802–29. In 1830 he was made Lord Advocate, and in 1834 a Scottish law lord. He was hostile to the Romantic poets, and wrote of Wordsworth's *Excursion*: 'This will never do.'

Jeffreys Alec John 1950– . British geneticist, who discovered the DNA probes necessary for accurate genetic fingerprinting so that a murderer or rapist could be identified, for example, by traces of blood, tissue, or semen.

Jeffreys George, 1st Baron 1648–1689. British judge. Born in Denbighshire, Scotland, he became Chief Justice of the King's Bench in 1683, and presided over many political trials, notably those of Sidney, Oates, and Baxter, becoming notorious for his brutality.

In 1685 he was made a peer and Lord Chancellor and, after ◊Monmouth's rebellion, conducted the 'bloody assizes' during which 320 rebels were executed and hundreds more flogged, imprisoned or transported. He was captured when attempting to flee the country after the revolution of 1688, and died in the Tower of London.

Jehosophat 4th king of Judah *c.*873–849 BC; he allied himself with Ahab, king of Israel, in the war against Syria.

Jehu king of Israel *c.*842–815 BC. He led a successful rebellion against the family of ◊Ahab and was responsible for the death of Jezebel.

Jekyll Gertrude 1843–1932. English landscape gardener and writer. She created over 200 gardens, many in collaboration with the architect Edwin ◊Lutyens.

Jellicoe John Rushworth, 1st Earl 1859–1935. British admiral, who commanded the Grand Fleet 1914–16; the only action he fought was the inconclusive battle of Jutland. He was First Sea Lord 1916–17, when he failed to push the introduction of the convoy system to combat U-boat attack.

Jencks Charles 1939– . US architectural theorist and furniture designer. He coined the term 'Post-Modern architecture' and wrote the influential book *The Language of Post-Modern Architecture.*

Jenkins Roy (Harris) 1920– . British politician. He became a Labour minister 1964, was home secretary 1965–67 and 1974–76, and chancellor of the Exchequer 1967–70. He was president of the European Commission 1977–81. In 1981 he became one of the founders of the Social Democratic Party and was elected 1982, but lost his seat 1987.

Educated at Oxford, Jenkins was a close friend of the future Labour leader Gaitskell. A Labour MP from 1948, he was minister of aviation 1964–65, then home secretary and chancellor of the Exchequer under Harold Wilson. In 1970 he became deputy leader of the Labour Party, but resigned 1972 because of disagreement with Wilson on the issue of UK entry to the European Community. He was elected chancellor of Oxford University 1987.

Jenner Edward 1749–1823. English physician who pioneered vaccination. In Jenner's day, smallpox was a major killer. His discovery that inoculation with cowpox gives immunity to smallpox was a great medical breakthrough. He coined the word vaccination from the Latin word for cowpox *vaccina.*

Jenner Henry ('Gwas Myhal') 1849–1934. English poet. He attempted to revive Cornish as a literary language, and in 1904 published a handbook of the Cornish language.

Jennings Humphrey 1907–1950. British documentary film-maker, active in the GPO Film Unit from 1934. His wartime films provide a vivid portrayal of London in the Blitz. His films include *Post Haste*

1934, *London Can Take It* 1940, *This is England* 1941, and *Fires were Started* 1943.

Jennings Patrick 'Pat' 1945– . ᴵrish footballer. In his 21-year career he was an outstanding goalkeeper. He won a British record 119 international caps for Northern Ireland 1964–86, and played League football for Watford, Tottenham Hotspur and Arsenal.

Jeremiah 7th century BC. Old Testament Hebrew prophet, whose ministry continued 626–586 BC. He was imprisoned during ◊Nebuchadnezzar's siege of Jerusalem on suspicion of intending to desert to the enemy. On the city's fall, he retired to Egypt.

Jeroboam first king of Israel *c.*922–901 BC after the split with Judah.

Jerome Jerome K(lapka) 1859–1927. English journalist and writer. His works include the humorous essays *Idle Thoughts of an Idle Fellow* 1889, the novel *Three Men in a Boat* 1889, and the play *The Passing of the Third Floor Back* 1907.

Jerome, St *c.*340–420. One of the early Christian leaders and scholars known as the Fathers of the Church. His Latin versions of the Old and New Testaments form the basis of the Roman Catholic Vulgate. He is usually depicted with a lion. Feast day 30 Sept.

Born in Strido, Italy, he was baptized at Rome in 360, and subsequently travelled in Gaul, Anatolia, and Syria. Summoned to Rome as adviser to Pope Damasus, he revised the Latin translation of the New Testament and the Latin psalter. On the death of Damasus in 384 he travelled to the east, and, settling in Bethlehem, translated the Old Testament into Latin from the Hebrew.

Jervis John, Earl of St Vincent 1735–1823. English admiral. A rigid disciplinarian, he secured the blockage of Toulon in 1795, and the defeat of the Spanish fleet off Cape St Vincent 1797, in which ◊Nelson played a key part.

Jessop William 1745–1814. British canal engineer, who built the first canal in England entirely dependent on reservoirs for its water supply (the Grantham Canal 1793–97), and who designed (with Thomas ◊Telford) the 300 m/1,000 ft long Pontcysyllte aqueduct over the river Dee.

Jesus *c.*4 BC–AD 29 or 30. Jewish preacher on whose teachings Christianity was founded. According to the accounts of his life in the four Gospels, he was born in Bethlehem, Palestine, son of God and the Virgin Mary, and brought up as a carpenter in Nazareth. After adult baptism, he gathered 12 disciples, but his preaching antagonized the authorities and he was executed. Three days after the Crucifixion there came reports of his resurrection and, later, ascension to heaven.

Through his legal father, Mary's husband Joseph, Jesus was of the tribe of Judah and family of David, the second king of Israel. In AD 26/27 his cousin John the Baptist proclaimed the coming

of the promised messiah and baptized Jesus, who then made two missionary journeys through the district of Galilee. His teaching, summarized in the **Sermon on the Mount**, aroused both religious opposition from the Pharisees and secular opposition from the party supporting the Roman governor, ◊Herod Antipas. When Jesus returned to Jerusalem (probably in AD 29), a week before the Passover festival, he was greeted by the people as the Messiah, and the Jewish authorities (aided by the apostle Judas) had him arrested and condemned to death, after a hurried trial, by the Sanhedrin (supreme Jewish court). They persuaded the Roman procurator, Pontius Pilate, to confirm the sentence, by stressing the threat to imperial authority of Jesus's teaching.

Jevons William Stanley 1835–1882. British economist, who introduced the concept of **marginal utility**: the increase in total utility (satisfaction or pleasure of consumption) relative to a unit increase of the goods consumed.

Jezebel in the Old Testament, daughter of the king of Sidon. She married King Ahab of Israel, and was brought into conflict with the prophet Elijah by her introduction of the worship of Baal.

Jiang Zemin 1926– . Chinese political leader. The son-in-law of ◊Li Xiannian, he joined the Chinese Communist Party's politburo in 1967 after serving in the Moscow embassy and as mayor of Shanghai. He succeeded ◊Zhao Ziyang as party leader after the Tiananmen Square massacre of 1989. A cautious proponent of economic reform coupled with unswerving adherence to the party's 'political line', he subsequently also replaced

Jekyll *British horticulturalist Gertrude Jekyll. The portrait was painted by Sir William Nicholson in 1920.*

◊Deng Xiaoping as head of the influential central military commission.

Jiang Qing formerly *Chiang Ching* 1913– . Chinese communist politician, wife of the party leader Mao Zedong. In 1960 she became minister for culture, and played a key role in the 1966–69 Cultural Revolution as the leading member of the Shanghai-based Gang of Four, who attempted to seize power 1976. Jiang was imprisoned.

Jiang was a Shanghai actress when in 1937 she met Mao Zedong at the communist headquarters in Yan'an; she became his third wife 1939. She emerged as a radical, egalitarian Maoist. Her influence waned during the early 1970s and her relationship with Mao became embittered. On Mao's death Sept 1976, the Gang of Four sought to seize power by organizing military coups in Shanghai and Beijing. They were arrested for treason by Mao's successor Hua Guofeng and tried 1980–81. The Gang were blamed for the excesses of the Cultural Revolution, but Jiang asserted during her trial that she had only followed Mao's orders as an obedient wife. This was rejected and Jiang received a death sentence Jan 1981, which was subsequently commuted to life imprisonment.

Jiménez Juan Ramón 1881–1958. Spanish lyric poet. Born in Andalusia, he left Spain during the civil war to live in exile in Puerto Rico. Nobel prize 1956.

Jinnah Muhammad Ali 1876–1948. Indian politician, Pakistan's first governor general from 1947. He became president of the Muslim League in 1916 and from 1934 he was elected annually as president. He advised the UK government on the need for a separate state of Pakistan 1942, and at the 1946 conferences in London he insisted on the partition of British India into Hindu and Muslim states.

Jiricna Eva. Czechoslovak architect, who has worked in the UK since 1968. Her striking fashion shops, bars, and cafés for Joseph Ettedgui (1900–) are built in a highly refined Modernist style.

Joachim Joseph 1831–1907. Austro-Hungarian violinist and composer. He studied under Mendelssohn and founded the Joachim Quartet (1869–1907). Joachim played and conducted the music of his friend ◊Brahms. His own compositions include pieces for violin and orchestra, chamber, and orchestral works.

Joachim of Fiore c.1132–1202. Italian mystic, born in Calabria. In his mystical writings he interpreted history as a sequence of three ages, that of the Father, Son, and Holy Spirit, the last of which, the age of perfect spirituality, was to begin in 1260. His Messianic views were taken up enthusiastically by many followers.

Joannitius Hunayn ibn Ishaq al Ibadi 809–873. Arabic translator, a Nestorian Christian, who translated Greek learning, including Ptolemy, Euclid, Hippocrates, Plato, and Aristotle, into Arabic or Syrian for the Abbasid court in Baghdad.

Joan of Arc, St 1412–1431. French military leader. In 1429 at Chinon, NW France, she persuaded Charles VII that she had a divine mission to expel the occupying English from N France and secure his coronation. She raised the siege of Orléans, defeated the English at Patay, north of Orléans, and Charles was crowned in Reims. However, she failed to take Paris, and was captured May 1430 by the Burgundians, who sold her to the English. She was found guilty of witchcraft and heresy by a tribunal of French ecclesiastics who supported the English. She was burned in Rouen 30 May 1431. In 1920 she was canonized.

Job c.5th century BC. In the Old Testament, Jewish leader who in the *Book of Job* questioned God's infliction of suffering on the righteous and endured great sufferings himself.

Although Job comes to no final conclusion, his book is one of the first attempts to explain the problem of human suffering in a world created and governed by a God who is all-powerful and all good.

Jodl Alfred 1892–1946. German general. In World War II he drew up the Nazi government's plan for the attack on Yugoslavia, Greece, and the USSR, and in Jan 1945 became chief of staff. He headed the delegation that signed Germany's surrender in Reims 7 May 1945. He was tried for war crimes in Nuremberg 1945–46, and hanged.

Joel prophet in the Old Testament or Hebrew Bible, of uncertain date.

Joffre Joseph Jacques Césaire 1852–1931. Marshal of France during World War I. He was chief of general staff 1911. The German invasion of Belgium

Jinnah Muslim leader Muhammad Ali Jinnah, founder of the state of Pakistan.

1914 took him by surprise, but his stand at the battle of the Marne resulted in his appointment as supreme commander of all the French armies 1915. His failure to make adequate preparations at Verdun 1916 and the military disasters on the Somme led to his replacement by Nivelle Dec 1916.

John Augustus (Edwin) 1878–1961. English painter of landscapes and portraits, including *The Smiling Woman* 1910 (Tate Gallery, London) of his second wife, Dorelia. He was the brother of Gwen John.

John Elton. Stage name of Reginald Dwight 1947– . English pop singer, pianist, and composer, noted for his melodies and elaborate costumes and glasses. His lyrics were written by Bernie Taupin.

John Gwen 1876–1939. English painter who lived in France for most of her life. Many of her paintings depict Dominican nuns (she converted to Catholicism 1913); she also painted calm, muted interiors.

John (John Lackland) 1167–1216. King of England from 1199. He lost Normandy and almost all of the other English possessions in France to the French, and succeeded in provoking Pope Innocent III to excommunicate England 1208–13. After the revolt of the barons he was forced to seal the Magna Carta (a human rights charter) 1215 at Runnymede on the Thames.

His subsequent bad reputation was only partially deserved. It resulted from his intrigues against his brother Richard I (the Lionheart), his complicity in the death of his nephew, Prince Arthur of Brittany, a rival for the English throne, and the effectiveness of his ruthless taxation policy. His attempt to limit the papacy's right of interference in episcopal elections, which traditionally were the preserve of English kings, was resented by monastic sources, and they provided much of the evidence upon which John's reign was susequently judged.

John two kings of France, including:
John II 1319–1364. King of France from 1350. He was defeated and captured by the Black Prince at Poitiers 1356 and imprisoned in England. Released 1360, he failed to raise the money for his ransom and returned to England 1364, where he died.

John 23 popes, including:
John XXII 1249–1334. Pope 1316–34. He spent his papacy in Avignon, France, engaged in a long conflict with the Holy Roman emperor, Louis of Bavaria, and the Spiritual Franciscans, a monastic order who preached the absolute poverty of the clergy.

John XXIII Angelo Giuseppe Roncalli 1881–1963. Pope from 1958. He improved relations with the USSR in line with his encyclical *Pacem in Terris/Peace on Earth* 1963, established Roman Catholic hierarchies in newly emergent states, and summoned the Second Vatican Council, which reformed church liturgy and backed the ecumenical movement.

John three kings of Poland, including:
John III Sobieski 1624–1696. King of Poland from 1674. He became commander-in-chief of the army 1668 after victories over the Cossacks and Tatars. A victory over the Turks 1673 helped to get him elected to the Polish throne, and he saved Vienna from the besieging Turks 1683.

John six kings of Portugal, including:
John I 1357–1433. King of Portugal from 1385. An illegitimate son of Pedro I, he was elected by the Cortes. His claim was supported by an English army against the rival king of Castile, thus establishing the Anglo-Portuguese Alliance 1386. He married Philippa of Lancaster, daughter of John of Gaunt.

John IV 1603–1656. King of Portugal from 1640. Originally Duke of Braganza, he was elected king when the Portuguese rebelled against Spanish rule. His reign was marked by a long war against Spain, which did not end until 1668.

John VI 1769–1826. King of Portugal, and regent for his insane mother *Maria I* from 1799 until her death 1816. He fled to Brazil when the French invaded Portugal 1807, and did not return until 1822. On his return Brazil declared its independence, with John's elder son Pedro as emperor.

John Chrysostom, St 345–407. Christian scholar, hermit, preacher, and Eastern Orthodox bishop of Constantinople 398–404. He was born in Antioch (modern Antakya, Turkey), and his feast day is 13 Sept.

John of Austria Don 1545–1578. Spanish soldier, the illegitimate son of the Holy Roman emperor Charles V. He defeated the Turks at the battle of Lepanto 1571.

John of Damascus, St *c.*676–*c.*754. Eastern Orthodox theologian and hymn writer, born in Damascus, Syria, a defender of image worship against the iconoclasts (image-breakers). Feast day 4 Dec.

Contained in his *The Fountain of Knowledge* is *An Accurate Exposition of the Orthodox Faith*, an important chronicle of theology from the 4th–7th centuries.

John of Gaunt 1340–1399. English politician, born in Ghent, fourth son of Edward III, duke of Lancaster from 1362. During Edward's last years, and the years before Richard II attained the age of majority, he acted as head of government, and Parliament protested against his corrupt rule. He supported the religious reformer Wycliffe against ecclesiastical influence at court.

John of Salisbury *c.*1115–1180. English philosopher and historian. His *Policraticus* portrayed the church as the guarantee of liberty against the unjust claims of secular authority.

He studied at Paris and Chartres 1130–1153, supported Thomas Becket against Henry II, and fled to France after Becket's murder, becoming bishop of Chartres 1176.

John of the Cross, St 1542–1591. Spanish Roman Catholic Carmelite friar from 1564, who was imprisoned several times for attempting to impose the reforms laid down by St Teresa. His verse describes spiritual ecstasy. Feast day 24 Nov.

He was persecuted and sent to the monastery of Ubeda until his death. He was beatified 1674 and canonized 1726.

John Paul two popes:

John Paul I Albino Luciani 1912–1978. Pope 26 Aug–28 Sept 1978. His name was chosen as the combination of his two immediate predecessors.

John Paul II Karol Wojtyla 1920– . Pope from 1978, the first non-Italian to be elected pope since 1522. He was born near Kraków, Poland. He has been criticized for his upholding of the tradition of papal infallibility and condemnation of artificial contraception, women priests, married priests, and modern dress for monks and nuns. He has warned against involvement of priests in political activity.

In 1939, at the beginning of World War II, Wojtyla was conscripted for forced labour by the Germans, working in quarries and a chemical factory, but from 1942 studied for the priesthood at a seminary illegally open in Kraków. After the war he taught ethics and theology at the universities of Lublin and Kraków, becoming archbishop of Kraków 1964. He was made a cardinal 1967. He was shot and wounded by a Turk in an attempt on his life 1981.

Johns 'Captain' W(illiam) E(arl) 1893–1968. British author, from 1932, of popular novels of World War I flying ace Captain James Bigglesworth ('Biggles'), now sometimes criticized for chauvinism, racism, and sexism. Johns retired from the RAF 1930.

Johns Jasper 1930– . US artist. He rejected the abstract in favour of such simple subjects as flags, maps and numbers so that the viewer's concentration would be entirely directed to the craftsmanship of the artist. He uses encaustic pigments to create a rich surface, with unexpected delicacies of colour.

John, St 1st century AD. New Testament apostle. Traditionally, he wrote the fourth Gospel and the Johannine Epistles when bishop of Ephesus, and the Book of Revelation while exiled to the Greek island of Patmos. His emblem is an eagle; feast day 27 Dec.

St John is identified with the unnamed 'disciple whom Jesus loved'. Son of Zebedee, born in Judaea, he and his brother James were Galilean fishermen. Jesus entrusted his mother to John at the Crucifixion, where he is often shown dressed

John Paul II *The first Polish pope, John Paul II is an accomplished linguist and author.*

in red, with curly hair. Another of his symbols is a chalice with a little snake in it.

Johnson Amy 1904–1941. British aviator. She made a solo flight from Croydon, S London, to Australia 1930, in 19.5 days, and in 1932 made the fastest ever solo flight from England to Cape Town, South Africa. Her plane disappeared over the English Channel in World War II while she was serving with the Air Transport Auxiliary.

Johnson Andrew 1808–1875. 17th president of the USA 1865–69, a Democrat. He was born in Raleigh, North Carolina, and was a congressman from Tennessee 1843–53, governor of Tennessee 1853–57, senator 1857–62, and became vice-president 1864. He succeeded to the presidency on Lincoln's assassination. His conciliatory policy to the defeated South after the Civil War involved him in a feud with the radical Republicans, culminating in his impeachment before the Senate 1868, which failed to convict him by one vote.

Among his achievements was the purchase of Alaska from Russia 1867. He was returned to the Senate from Tennessee 1875, but died shortly afterwards.

Johnson Ben 1961– . Jamaican-born Canadian sprinter. In 1987, he broke the world record for the 100 metres, running it in 9.83 seconds. At the Olympic Games 1988, he again broke the record, but was disqualified and suspended for using anabolic steroids to enhance his performance.

Johnson Celia 1908–1982. British actress, best remembered for her starring role in the film *Brief Encounter* 1946.

Johnson Eastman 1824–1906. US painter born in Germany, trained in Düsseldorf, The Hague, and Paris. Painting in the open air, he developed a fresh and luminous landscape style.

Johnson Jack 1878–1968. US heavyweight boxer. He overcame severe racial prejudice to become the first black heavyweight champion of the world

1908 when he travelled to Australia to challenge Tommy Burns. The US authorities wanted Johnson 'dethroned' because of his color but could not find suitable challengers until 1915, when he lost the title in a dubious fight decision to the giant Jess Willard.

Johnson Lyndon (Baines) 1908–1973. 36th president of the USA 1963–69, a Democrat. He was born in Stonewall, Texas, elected to Congress 1937–49 and to the Senate 1949–60. He stood as vice president 1960, bringing crucial Southern votes to J F Kennedy, after whose assassination he succeeded as president. After the Tonkin Gulf Incident (when North Vietnamese torpedo boats reportedly attacked US destroyers at night), the escalation of US involvement in the Vietnam War eventually dissipated the support won by his *Great Society* legislation (civil rights, education, alleviation of poverty), and he declined to stand for re-election 1968.

Johnson Pamela Hansford 1912–1981. British novelist, who in 1950 married C P ◊Snow; her novels include *Too Dear for my Possessing* 1940, and *The Honours Board* 1970.

Johnson Philip Cortelyou 1906– . US architect, who invented the term 'international style'. Originally designing in the style of ◊Mies van der Rohe, he later became an exponent of Post-Modernism. His best known building is the giant AT&T building in New York 1978, a pink skyscraper with a Chippendale-style cabinet top.

Johnson Samuel, known as 'Dr Johnson' 1709–1784. English lexicographer, author, and critic, also a brilliant conversationalist and the dominant figure in 18th-century London literary society. His *Dictionary*, published 1755, remained authoritative for over a century, and is still remarkable for the vigour of its definitions. In 1764 he founded the 'Literary Club', whose members included Reynolds, Burke, Goldsmith, Garrick, and ◊Boswell, Johnson's biographer.

Other works include the satire imitating Juvenal, *Vanity of Human Wishes* 1749, the philosophical romance *Rasselas* 1759, an edition of Shakespeare 1765 and the classic *Lives of the Most Eminent English Poets* 1779–81. His first meeting with ◊Boswell was 1763. A visit with Boswell to Scotland and the Hebrides 1773 was recorded in *Journey to the Western Isles of Scotland* 1775. He was buried in Westminster Abbey and his house in Gough Square, London, is preserved as a museum; his wit and humanity are documented in Boswell's classic biography *Life of Samuel Johnson* 1791.

Johnson Uwe 1934– . German novelist, who left East Germany for West Berlin 1959, and wrote of the division of Germany in, for example, *Anniversaries* 1977.

John the Baptist, St *c.* 12 BC–c. AD 27. In the New Testament, an itinerant preacher. After preparation in the wilderness, he proclaimed the coming of

Johnson *Lyndon B Johnson became president of the USA after Kennedy's assassination in 1963.*

Jesus Christ, baptized him in the river Jordan, and was executed by ◊Herod Antipas at the request of Salome. His emblem is a lamb. Feast day 24 June.

Joinville Jean, Sire de Joinville 1224–1317. French historian, born in Champagne. He accompanied Louis IX on the crusade of 1248–54, which he described in his *History of St Louis.*

Joliot-Curie Irène 1897–1956. and Frédéric Joliot-Curie 1900–1958. French physicists who made the discovery of artificial radioactivity, for which they were jointly awarded the 1935 Nobel Prize for Chemistry. Irène was the daughter of Marie ◊Curie and began work at her mother's Radium Institute in 1921. In 1926 she married Frédéric, a pupil of her mother, and they began a long and fruitful collaboration. Notably, in 1934 they found that certain elements exposed to radiation themselves become radioactive.

Jolson Al. Stage name of Asa Yoelson 1886–1950. Russian-born singer and actor, who lived in the USA from childhood. Formerly a Broadway star, he gained instant cinema immortality as the star of the first talking picture, *The Jazz Singer* 1927.

Jonah 7th century BC. Hebrew prophet whose name is given to a book in the Old Testament. According to this, he fled by ship to evade his mission to prophesy the destruction of Nineveh. The crew threw him overboard in a storm, as a bringer of ill fortune, and he spent three days and nights in the belly of a whale before coming to land.

Jonathan Chief (Joseph) Leabua 1914–1987. Lesotho politician. As prime minister of Lesotho 1965–86, he played a pragmatic role, allying himself in turn with South Africa, then with the

Organization of African Unity. His rule was ended by a coup in 1986.

Jones Charles Martin ('Chuck') 1912– . US film animator and cartoon director who worked at Warner Brothers with characters such as Bugs Bunny, Daffy Duck, Wile E. Coyote and Elmer Fudd.

Jones Gwyneth 1936– . Welsh soprano, who has performed as Sieglinde in *Die Walküre* and Desdemona in *Otello*.

Jones Henry Arthur 1851–1929. British playwright. Among some 60 of his melodramas, *Mrs Dane's Defence* 1900 is most notable as an early realist problem play.

Jones Inigo 1573–c.1652. English architect. Born in London, he studied in Italy, and was influenced by the works of Palladio. He was employed by James I to design scenery for Ben Jonson's masques. In 1619 he designed his English Renaissance masterpiece, the banqueting-room at Whitehall, London.

Jones John Paul 1747–1792. Scottish-born American naval officer in the War of Independence. Heading a small French-sponsored squadron in the *Bonhomme Richard*, he captured the British warship *Serapis* 23 Sept 1779 in a bloody battle off Scarborough.

Jones was born in Kirkcudbright, Scotland. He was originally a trader and slaver but became a privateer 1775, and then a commodore. After the War of Independence, he joined the Russian navy as a rear admiral 1788, fighting against Turkey, but lost the Empress Catherine's favour and died in France.

Jones Robert Tyre 'Bobby' 1902–1971. US golfer. He was the game's greatest amateur player, who never turned professional but won 13 major amateur and professional tournaments, including the Grand Slam of the amateur and professional opens of both the USA and Britain 1930.

Jongkind Johan Bartold 1819–1891. Dutch painter active mainly in France. His studies of the Normandy coast show a keen observation of the natural effects of light. He influenced the Impressionist painter ◊Monet.

Jonson Ben(jamin) 1572–1637. English dramatist, poet, and critic. *Every Man in his Humour* 1598 established the English 'comedy of humours', in which each character embodies a 'humour', or vice, such as greed, lust, or avarice. This was followed by *Every Man out of his Humour* 1599, *Cynthia's Revels* 1600 and *Poetaster* 1601. His first extant tragedy is *Sejanus* 1603, with Burbage and Shakespeare as members of the original cast. The plays of his middle years include *Volpone, or The Fox* 1606, *The Alchemist* 1610, and *Bartholomew Fair* 1614.

Jonson was born in Westminster, London, and entered the theatre as actor and dramatist in 1597. In 1598 he narrowly escaped the gallows for killing a fellow player in a duel. He collaborated with

Jonson *The poet and dramatist Ben Jonson started out as a bricklayer and once narrowly escaped the gallows after killing a man in a duel.*

Marston and Chapman in *Eastward Ho!* 1605, and shared their imprisonment when official exception was taken to the satirization of James I's Scottish policy.

Joplin Janis 1943–1970. US blues and rock singer, born in Texas. She was lead singer with the San Francisco group Big Brother and the Holding Company 1966–68. Her biggest hit, Kris Kristofferson's 'Me and Bobby McGee', was released on the posthumous *Pearl* LP 1971.

Joplin Scott 1868–1917. US ragtime pianist and composer in Chicago. His 'Maple Leaf Rag' 1899 was the first instrumental sheet music to sell a million copies, and 'The Entertainer', as the theme tune of the film *The Sting* 1973, revived his popularity. He was an influence on Jelly Roll Morton and other early jazz musicians.

Jordaens Jacob 1593–1678. Flemish painter, born in Antwerp. His style follows Rubens, whom he assisted in various commissions. Much of his work is exuberant and on a large scale, including scenes of peasant life, altarpieces, portraits, and mythological subjects.

Jordan Dorothea 1762–1816. British actress. She made her debut in 1777, and retired in 1815. She was a mistress of the Duke of Clarence (later William IV); they had ten children with the name FitzClarence.

Jörgensen Jörgen 1779–1845. Danish sailor who in 1809 seized control of Iceland, announcing it was under the protection of England. His brief reign of corruption ended later the same year when he was captured by an English naval ship and taken to London, where he was imprisoned.

Joseph Keith (Sinjohn) 1918– . British Conservative politician. A barrister, he entered parliament 1956. He held ministerial posts 1962–64, 1970–74, 1979–81, and was secretary of state for education and science 1981–86. He was made a life peer 1987.

Joseph Père. Religious name of Francis Le Clerc du Tremblay 1577–1638. French Catholic Capuchin friar. He was the influential secretary and agent to Louis XIII's chief minister Cardinal Richelieu, and nicknamed *Grey Eminence* in reference to his grey habit.

Joseph two Holy Roman emperors:

Joseph I 1678–1711. Holy Roman emperor from 1705, and king of Austria, of the house of Habsburg. He spent most of his reign involved in fighting the War of Spanish Succession.

Joseph II 1741–1790. Holy Roman emperor from 1765, son of Francis I (1708–1765). The reforms he carried out after the death of his mother, ◊Maria Theresa, in 1780, provoked revolts from those who lost privileges.

Josephine Marie Josèphe Rose Tascher de la Pagerie 1763–1814. Empress of France 1796–1809. Born on Martinique, she married in 1779 Alexandre de Beauharnais, and in 1796 Napoleon, who divorced her in 1809 because she had not produced children.

Joseph of Arimathaea, St 1st century AD. In the New Testament, a wealthy Jew, member of the Sanhedrin (supreme court), and secret supporter of Jesus. On the evening of the Crucifixion he asked the Roman procurator Pilate for Jesus's body and buried it in his own tomb. Feast day 17 Mar.

According to tradition he brought the Holy Grail to England about AD 63 and built the first Christian church in Britain, at Glastonbury.

Josephs Wilfred 1927– . British composer. As well as film and television music, he has written nine symphonies, concertos, and chamber music. His works include the *Jewish Requiem* 1969 and the opera *Rebecca* 1983.

Josephson Brian 1940– . British physicist, a leading authority on superconductivity. In 1973 he shared a Nobel prize for his theoretical predictions of the properties of a supercurrent through a tunnel barrier.

Josephus Flavius AD 37–*c.*100. Jewish historian and general, born in Jerusalem. He became a Pharisee, and commanded the Jewish forces in Galilee in the revolt against Rome from 66 (which ended in mass suicide at Masada). When captured, he gained the favour of Vespasian and settled in Rome as a citizen. He wrote *Antiquities of the Jews*, an early history to AD 66; *The Jewish War*, and an autobiography.

Joshua 13th century BC. In the Old Testament, successor of Moses, who led the Jews in their conquest of the land of Canaan. The city of Jericho was the first to fall: according to the Book of Joshua, the walls crumbled to the blast of his trumpets.

Josiah *c.*647–609 BC. King of Judah. Grandson of Manasseh and son of Amon, he succeeded to the throne when eight. The discovery of a Book of Instruction (probably Deuteronomy, a book of the Old Testament) during repairs of the Temple in 621 BC stimulated thorough reform, which included the removal of all sanctuaries except that of Jerusalem. He was killed in a clash at Megiddo with Pharaoh-nechoh, king of Egypt.

Josquin Desprez or *des Prés* 1440–1521. Franco-Flemish composer. His music combines a technical mastery with the feeling for words that became a hallmark of Renaissance vocal music. His works, which include 18 masses, over 100 motets, and secular vocal works, are characterized by their vitality and depth of feeling.

Joubert Petrus Jacobus 1831–1900. Boer general in South Africa. He opposed British annexation of the Transvaal 1877, proclaimed its independence 1880, led the Boer Commandos in the First South African War against the British 1880–81, defeated ◊Jameson 1896, and fought in the Second South African War.

Joule James Prescott 1818–1889. British physicist whose work on the relations between electrical, mechanical, and chemical effects led to the discovery of the first law of thermodynamics, that energy can be neither created nor destroyed.

He was a brewery owner, and dedicated to precise scientific research. He determined the mechanical equivalent of heat (Joule's equivalent), and the SI unit of energy, the *joule*, is named after him.

Jovian 331–364. Roman emperor from 363. Captain of the imperial bodyguard, he was chosen as emperor by the troops after ◊Julian's death in battle with the Persians. He concluded an unpopular peace and restored Christianity as the state religion.

Jowett Benjamin 1817–1893. English scholar. He promoted university reform, including the abolition of the theological test for degrees, and translated Plato, Aristotle, and Thucydides.

Jowett was ordained in 1842. He became Regius professor of Greek at Oxford University 1855, and Master of Balliol College 1870.

Joyce James (Augustine Aloysius) 1882–1941. Irish writer, born in Dublin, who revolutionized the form of the English novel with his 'stream of consciousness' technique. His works include *Dubliners* 1914 (short stories), *Portrait of the Artist as a Young Man* 1916, *Ulysses* 1922 and *Finnegans Wake* 1939.

Ulysses, which records the events of a single Dublin

day, experiments with language and mingles direct narrative with the unspoken and unconscious reactions of the characters. Banned at first for obscenity in England and the USA, it was enormously influential. *Finnegans Wake* continued Joyce's experiments with language, attempting a synthesis of all existence.

Joyce William 1906–1946. Born in New York, son of a naturalized Irish-born American, he carried on fascist activity in the UK as a 'British subject'. During World War II he made propaganda broadcasts from Germany to the UK, his upper-class accent earning him the nickname **Lord Haw Haw**. He was hanged for treason.

Juan Carlos 1938– . King of Spain. The son of Don Juan, pretender to the Spanish throne, he married in 1962 Princess Sofia, eldest daughter of King Paul of Greece. In 1969 he was nominated by Franco to succeed on the restoration of the monarchy intended to follow Franco's own death; his father was excluded because of his known liberal views. He became king in 1975 and has sought to steer his country from dictatorship to democracy.

Juárez Benito 1806–1872. Mexican politician, president 1861–64 and 1867–72. In 1861 he suspended repayments of Mexico's foreign debts, which prompted a joint French, British, and Spanish expedition to exert pressure. French forces invaded and created an empire for ◊Maximilian, brother of the Austrian emperor. After their withdrawal in 1867, Maximilian was executed, and Juárez returned to the presidency.

Judah Ha-Nasi 'the Prince' *c*. AD 135–*c*.220. Jewish scholar who with a number of colleagues edited the collection of writings known as the **Mishna**, which formed the basis of the Talmud, the basis for Jewish religious law, in the 2nd century AD.

Judas Iscariot in the New Testament, the disciple who betrayed Jesus Christ. Judas was the treasurer of the group. At the last Passover he arranged, for 30 pieces of silver, to point out Jesus to the chief priests so that they could arrest him. Afterwards Judas was overcome with remorse and committed suicide.

Jude, St lived 1st century. Supposed brother of Jesus Christ and writer of the Epistle of Jude in the New Testament; patron saint of lost causes. Feast day 28 Oct.

Judith 6th century BC. In the Old Testament Apocrypha, a Jewish heroine in the book of the same name, who saved her town by beheading Holofernes, the general of Nebuchadnezzar.

Judith of Bavaria 800–843. Empress of the French. The wife of ◊Louis the Pious (Louis I of France) from 819, she influenced her husband to the benefit of their son ◊Charles the Bold .

Jugurtha died 104 BC. King of Numidia, N Africa, who, after a long resistance, was betrayed to the Romans in 107 BC, and put to death.

Julian *c*.331–363. Roman emperor, called *the*

Juan Carlos *King of Spain Juan Carlos, who succeeded General Franco in 1975 and has since supervised the country's return to democracy and membership of the European Community.*

Apostate. Born in Constantinople, the nephew of Constantine the Great, he was brought up as a Christian but early in life became a convert to paganism. Sent by Constantius to govern Gaul in 355, he was proclaimed emperor by his troops in 360, and in 361 was marching on Constantinople when Constantius' death allowed a peaceful succession. He revived pagan worship and refused to persecute heretics. He was killed in battle against the Persians.

Juliana 1909– . Queen of the Netherlands. The daughter of Queen Wilhelmina (1880–1962), she married Prince Bernhard of Lippe-Biesterfeld in 1937 and ruled 1948–80, when she abdicated and was succeeded by her daughter ◊Beatrix.

Julian of Norwich *c*.1342–1413. English mystic. She lived as a recluse, and recorded her visions in *The Revelation of Divine Love* 1403, which shows the influence of Neo-Platonism.

Julius II 1443–1513. Pope 1503–13, a politician who wanted to make the Papal States the leading power in Italy, and formed international alliances first against Venice and then against France. He began the building of St Peter's Church, Rome, in 1506, and was the patron of the artists Michelangelo and Raphael.

Jung Carl Gustav 1875–1961. Swiss psychiatrist, who collaborated with Sigmund ◊Freud until their disagreement in 1912 about the importance of sexuality in causing psychological problems. He studied religion and dream symbolism, and saw the unconscious as a source of spiritual insight. He also distinguished between introversion and

*Jung Swiss psychiatrist and pioneer psychoanalyst
Carl Jung.*

extroversion. Works include *Modern Man in
Search of a Soul* 1933.

Junkers Hugo 1859–1935. German aeroplane
designer. In 1919 he founded in Dessau the aircraft
works named after him. Junkers planes, including
dive bombers, night fighters, and troop carriers,
were used by the Germans in World War II.

Jurgens Curt (Curd Jürgens) 1912–1982. German
film and stage actor, who was well established in
his native country before moving into French
and then Hollywood films in the 1960s. His films
include *Operette/Operetta* 1940; *Et Dieu créa la
Femme/And God Created Woman* 1956; *Lord Jim*
1965; *The Spy who Loved Me* 1977.

Justinian I 483–562. Byzantine emperor from
527.

He recovered N Africa from the Vandals, SE Spain
from the Visigoths, and Italy from the Ostrogoths,
largely owing to his great general Belisarius. He
ordered the codification of Roman law, which has
influenced European jurisprudence.

Justinian, born in Illyria, was associated with
his uncle, Justin I, in the government from 518.
He married the actress Theodora, and succeeded
Justin in 527. Much of his reign was taken up by an
indecisive struggle with the Persians. He built the
church of St Sophia in Constantinople, and closed
the university in Athens in 529.

Justin St *c.*100–*c.*163. One of the early Christian
leaders and writers known as the Fathers of the
Church. Born in Palestine of a Greek family, he
was converted to Christianity and wrote two *Apol-
ogies* in its defence. He spent the rest of his life
as an itinerant missionary, and was martyred in
Rome. Feast day 1 June.

Juvenal *c.*AD 60–140. Roman satirist and poet,
born probably at Aquinum. His genius for satire
brought him to the unfavourable notice of the
emperor Domitian. Juvenal's 16 extant satires
give an explicit and sometimes brutal picture of
the decadent Roman society of his time.

Kádár János 1912–1989. Hungarian Communist leader, in power 1956–88, after suppressing the national rising. As Hungarian Socialist Workers' Party (HSWP) leader and prime minister 1956–58 and 1961–65, Kádár introduced a series of market-socialist economic reforms, while retaining cordial political relations with the USSR.

Kádár was a mechanic before joining the outlawed Communist Party and working as an underground resistance organizer in World War II. After the war he was elected to the National Assembly, served as minister for internal affairs 1948–50, and became a prominent member of the Hungarian Workers' Party (HSP). Imprisoned 1951–53 for deviation from Stalinism, Kádár was rehabilitated 1955, becoming party leader in Budapest, and in Nov 1956, at the height of the Hungarian national rising, he was appointed head of the new HSWP. With the help of Soviet troops, he suppressed the revolt. He was ousted as party general secretary May 1988, and forced into retirement May 1989.

Kafka Franz 1883–1924. Czech novelist, born in Prague, who wrote in German. His three unfinished allegorical novels *Der Prozess/The Trial* 1925, *Der Schloss/The Castle* 1926, and *Amerika/America* 1927, were posthumously published despite his instructions that they should be destroyed. His short stories include 'Die Verwandlung/The Metamorphosis' 1915, in which a man turns into a beetle.

Kahlo Frida 1907–1954. Mexican painter, who mingled folk art with classical and modern style.

Kahn Louis 1901–1974. US architect, born in Estonia. He developed a classically romantic style, in which functional 'servant' areas, such as stairwells and air ducts, featured prominently, often as tower-like structures surrounding the

Kafka *Czech novelist Franz Kafka.*

main living and working, or 'served', areas. His works are characterized by an imaginative use of concrete and brick and include the Salk Institute for Biological Studies, La Jolla, California, and the British Art Center at Yale University.

Kaifu Toshiki 1932– . Japanese conservative politician, prime minister from 1989. A protégé of former premier Takeo Miki, he was selected as a compromise choice as Liberal Democratic Party president and prime minister in Aug 1989, following the resignation of Sosuke Uno. Kaifu is Japan's first premier without World War II military experience.

He entered politics 1961, was deputy chief secretary 1974–76 in the Miki cabinet, and education minister under Nakasone. In 1987 Kaifu received what he claimed were legitimate political donations amounting to several thousand pounds from the Recruit company, an organization later accused of bribing a number of LDP politicians.

Kaiser Georg 1878–1945. German playwright, the principal writer of German Expressionism. His large output includes *Die Bürger von Calais/The Burghers of Calais* 1914, and *Gas* 1918–20.

Kaiser Henry J 1882–1967. US industrialist. He built up steel and motor industries, and his shipbuilding firms became known for the mass production of vessels, including the 'Liberty ships' – cheap, quickly produced, transport ships – built for the UK in World War II.

Kaldor Nicholas 1908–1986. British economist, born in Hungary, special adviser 1964–68 and 1974–76 to the UK government. He was a firm believer in the long-term capital gains tax, selective employment tax, and a fierce critic of

Kaifu *Japanese conservative politician, prime minister from 1989.*

monetarism. He advised several Third World governments on economic and tax reform.

Kalf Willem 1619–1693. Dutch painter, active in Amsterdam from 1653. He specialized in still lifes set off against a dark ground.

These feature arrangements of glassware, polished metalwork. decorated porcelain, and fine carpets, with the occasional half- peeled lemon (a Dutch still-life motif).

Kālidāsa 5th century AD. Indian epic poet and dramatist. His works, in Sanskrit, include the classic drama *Sakuntala*, the love story of King Dushyanta for the nymph Sakuntala.

Kalinin Mikhail Ivanovich 1875–1946. Soviet politician, founder of the newspaper *Pravda*. He was prominent in the 1917 October Revolution, and in 1919 became head of state (president of the Central Executive Committee of the Soviet government until 1937, then president of the Presidium of the Supreme Soviet until 1946).

Kaltenbrunner Ernst 1901–1946. Austrian Nazi leader. After the annexation of Austria 1938 he joined police chief Himmler's staff, and as head of the Security Police (SD) from 1943 was responsible for the murder of millions of Jews and Allied soldiers in World War II. After the war, he was tried at Nuremberg, and hanged.

Kamenev Lev Borisovich 1883–1936. Russian leader of the Bolshevik movement after 1917 who, with Stalin and Zinoviev, formed a ruling triumvirate in the USSR after Lenin's death 1924. His alignment with the Trotskyists led to his dismissal from office and from the Communist Party

by Stalin 1926. Tried for plotting to murder Stalin, he was condemned and shot 1936.

Kandinsky Wassily 1866–1944. Russian painter, a pioneer of abstract art. Born in Moscow, he travelled widely, settling in Munich 1896. He was joint originator of the Expressionist *Blaue Reiter* movement 1911–12, named after a painting of his. For some years he taught at the Bauhaus school of modern design, then, in 1933, settled in Paris.

Kandinsky originally experimented with Post-Impressionist styles and Fauvism. From around 1910 he produced the first known examples of purely abstract work in 20th-century art. His highly coloured style had few imitators, but his theories on composition, *Concerning the Spiritual in Art* 1912, were taken up by the early abstract movement.

Kant Immanuel 1724–1804. German philosopher, who believed that knowledge is not merely an aggregate of sense impressions, but is dependent on the conceptual apparatus of the human understanding, which is itself not derived from experience. In ethics, Kant argued that right action cannot be based on feelings or inclinations, but conforms to a law given by reason, the *categorical imperative*.

Born at Königsberg (in what was then East Prussia), he attended the university there, and was appointed professor of logic and metaphysics 1770. His first book, *Gedanken von der wahren Schätzung der lebendigen Kräfte/Thoughts on the True Estimates of Living Forces*, appeared in 1747, and the *Theorie des Himmels/Theory of the*

Kant *An 1812 engraving of the German philosopher Immanuel Kant. A moral philosopher, he believed that feelings and inclinations were not a basis for ethical decisions.*

Heavens in 1755. In the latter he combined physics and theology in an argument for the existence of God. In *Kritik der reinen Vernunft/Critique of Pure Reason* 1781, he argued that God's existence could not be proved theoretically.

Kantorovich Leonid 1912–1986. Russian mathematical economist, whose theory that decentralization of decisions in a planned economy could only be made with a rational price system earned him a share of the 1975 Nobel Prize for Economics.

Kapitza Peter 1894–1984. Soviet physicist who in 1978 shared a Nobel prize for his work on magnetism and low-temperature physics. He held important posts in Britain, for example, assistant director of magnetic research at the Cavendish Laboratory, Cambridge, 1924–32, before returning to the USSR to work at the Russian Academy of Science.

Kaplan Viktor 1876–1934. Austrian engineer who invented a water turbine with adjustable rotor blades. In the machine, patented in 1920, the rotor was on a vertical shaft and could be adjusted to suit any rate of flow of water.

Horizontal Kaplan turbines are used at the installation on the estuary of the river Rance in France, the world's first tidal power station.

Karajan Herbert von 1908–1989. Austrian conductor. He was conductor of the Berlin Philharmonic Orchestra 1955–89. He directed the Salzburg Festival from 1964 and became director of the Vienna State Opera in 1976. He is associated with the Classical and Romantic repertoire – Beethoven, Brahms, Mahler, and Richard Strauss.

Karamanlis Constantinos 1907– . Greek politician of the New Democracy Party. A lawyer and an anti-communist, he was prime minister Oct 1955–Mar 1958, May 1958–Sept 1961, and Nov 1961–June 1963 (when he went into self-imposed exile). He was recalled as prime minister on the fall of the regime of the 'colonels' in July 1974, and was president 1980–85.

Karg-Elert Sigfrid 1877–1933. German composer. After studying at Leipzig he devoted himself to the European harmonium. His numerous concert pieces and graded studies exploit a range of impressionistic effects such as the 'endless chord'.

Karloff Boris (William Henry Pratt) 1887–1969. British actor who mostly worked in the USA. He is chiefly known for his role as the monster in *Frankenstein* 1931; most of his subsequent roles were in horror films, although he also played some conventional parts. He appeared in *Scarface* 1932, *The Lost Patrol* 1934, and *The Body Snatcher* 1945.

Karmal Babrak 1929– . Afghani communist politician. In 1965 he formed what became the banned People's Democratic Party of Afghanistan (PDPA) 1977. As president 1979–86, with Soviet backing,

he sought to broaden the appeal of the PDPA but encountered wide resistance from the mujaheddin Muslim guerrillas.

Karpov Anatoliy 1951– . Soviet chess player. He succeeded Bobby Fischer of the USA as world champion 1975, and held the title until losing to Gary Kasparov 1985.

Kasparov Gary 1963– . Soviet chess player. When he beat his compatriot Anatoliy Karpov to win the world title 1985, he was the youngest ever champion at 22 years 210 days.

Kassem Abdul Karim 1914–1963. Iraqi politician, prime minister from 1958; he adopted a pro-Soviet policy. He pardoned the leaders of the pro-Egyptian party who tried to assassinate him 1959, but was executed after the 1963 coup.

Kato Kiyomasa 1562–1611. Japanese warrior and politician who was instrumental in the unification of Japan and the banning of Christianity in the country. He led the invasion of Korea 1592, and cooperated with Toyotomi Hideyoshi and Tokugawa Ieyaso in consolidating a unified Japanese state.

Katō Taka-akira 1860–1926. Japanese politician and prime minister 1924–26. After a long political career with several terms as foreign minister, Katō led probably the most democratic and liberal regime of the Japanese Empire.

Katsura Tarō 1847–1913. Prince of Japan, army officer, politician, and prime minister. During his first term as prime minister 1901–06, he was responsible for the Anglo-Japanese treaty of 1902, the successful prosecution of the war against Russia 1904–05, and the annexation of Korea 1910.

Having assisted in the Meiji restoration (see ◊Mutsuhito) 1866–68, Katsura became increasingly involved in politics. His support for rearmament, distaste for political parties, and oligarchic rule created unrest, and his third ministry Dec 1912–Jan 1913 lasted only seven weeks.

Katz Bernard 1911– . British biophysicist. He shared the 1970 Nobel Prize for Medicine with Ulf von Euler of and Julius Axelrod for work on the biochemistry of the transmission and control of signals in the nervous system, vital in the search for remedies for nervous and mental disorders.

Kauffmann Angelica 1741–1807. Swiss Neo-Classical painter who worked extensively in England. She was a popular portraitist, and also painted mythological scenes for large country houses.

Kaufman George S(imon) 1889–1961. US playwright. Author (often in collaboration with others) of many Broadway hits, including *Of Thee I Sing* 1932, a Pulitzer Prize-winning satire on US politics, *The Man Who Came to Dinner* 1939, and *The Solid Gold Cadillac* 1952.

Kaunda Kenneth (David) 1924– . Zambian politician. Imprisoned in 1958–60 as founder of the Zambia African National Congress, he became in

Kaunda *Kenneth Kaunda was the first prime minister of Northern Rhodesia, the former name for Zambia, before becoming president when Zambia gained independence in 1964.*

1964 first prime minister of Northern Rhodesia, then first president of Zambia. In 1973 he introduced one-party rule. He supported the nationalist movement in Southern Rhodesia, now Zimbabwe, and survived a coup attempt 1980 thought to have been promoted by South Africa. He was elected chair of the Organization of African Unity 1987.

Kautsky Karl 1854–1938. German socialist theoretician, who opposed the reformist ideas of Edouard ◊Bernstein from within the Social Democratic Party. In spite of his Marxist ideas he remained in the party when its left wing broke away to form the German Communist Party (KPD).

Kawabata Yasunari 1899–1972. Japanese novelist, translator of Lady ◊Murasaki, and author of *Snow Country* 1947 and *A Thousand Cranes* 1952. His novels are characterized by melancholy and loneliness. He was the first Japanese to win the Nobel Prize for Literature 1968.

Kay John 1704–*c.*1764. British inventor who developed the flying-shuttle, a machine to speed up the work of hand-loom weaving. In 1733 he patented his invention but was ruined by the litigation necessary for its defence.

In 1753 his house at Bury was wrecked by a mob, who feared the use of machinery would cause unemployment. He is believed to have died in poverty in France.

Kaye Danny. Stage-name of Daniel Kaminski 1913–1987. US comedian and singer. He appeared in many films, including *Wonder Man* 1944, *The Secret Life of Walter Mitty* 1946, and *Hans Christian Andersen* 1952.

Kazan Elia 1909– . US stage and film director, a founder of the New York Actors Studio set up in 1947 to study ◊Stavislavsky's 'Method' acting. Plays he directed include *The Skin of Our Teeth* 1942, *A Streetcar Named Desire* 1947, and *Cat on a Hot Tin Roof* 1955; films include *Gentlemen's Agreement* 1948, *East of Eden* 1954, and *The Visitors* 1972.

Kazantzakis Nikos 1885–1957. Greek writer of poems, for example *I Odysseia/The Odyssey* 1938, which continues Homer's *Odyssey*, and novels, for example *Zorba the Greek* 1946.

Kean Edmund 1787–1833. British tragic actor, noted for his portrayal of villainy in the Shakespearean roles of Shylock, Richard III, and Iago.

Keane Mary Nesta 'Molly' 1905– . Irish novelist, whose comic novels of Anglo-Irish life include *Good Behaviour* 1981, *Time After Time* 1983, and *Loving and Giving* 1988.

Keaton Buster. Stage name of Joseph Frank Keaton 1896–1966. US comedian and actor. After being a star in vaudeville, he took up a career in 'Fatty' Arbuckle comedies, and became one of the great comedians of the silent film era, with an inimitable deadpan expression masking a sophisticated acting ability. His films include *One Week* 1920, *The Navigator* 1924, *The General* 1927, and *The Cameraman* 1928.

Keats John 1795–1821. English poet, a leading figure of the Romantic movement. He published his first volume of poetry 1817; this was followed by *Endymion, Isabella,* and *Hyperion* 1818, 'The Eve of St Agnes', his odes 'To Autumn', 'On a Grecian Urn', and 'To a Nightingale', and 'Lamia' 1819. His final volume of poems appeared in 1820.

Keaton *US comedy star Buster Keaton appearing in a scene from* The General *1927.*

Born in London, Keats studied at Guy's Hospital 1815–17, but then abandoned medicine for poetry. *Endymion* 1818 was harshly reviewed by the Tory *Blackwood's Magazine* and *Quarterly Review*, largely owing to Keats' friendship with the radical writer Leigh Hunt (1800–65). In 1819 he fell in love with Fanny Brawne. Suffering from tuberculosis, he sailed to Italy in 1820 in an attempt to regain his health, but died in Rome; the house he died in is now a museum. Valuable insight into Keats's poetic development is provided by his *Letters*, published 1848.

Keble John 1792–1866. Anglican priest and religious poet. His sermon on the decline of religious faith in Britain, preached in 1833, is taken as the beginning of the Oxford Movement, a Catholic revival in the Church of England. Keble College, Oxford, was founded in 1870 in his memory.

Keeler Christine 1942– . British model and call girl of the 1960s. She became notorious in 1963 after revelations of affairs with both a Soviet attaché and the war minister John ◊Profumo, who resigned after admitting lying to the House of Commons about their relationship. Her patron, the osteopath Stephen Ward, convicted of living on immoral earnings, committed suicide and Keeler was subsequently imprisoned for related offences.

Keillor Garrison 1942– . US writer and humorist. His hometown is Anoka, Minnesota, in the American Midwest. It inspired his Lake Wobegon stories, including *Lake Wobegon Days* 1985 and *Leaving Home* 1987, often started as radio monologues about 'the town that time forgot, that the decades cannot improve'.

Keitel Wilhelm 1882–1946. German field marshal in World War II, chief of the supreme command from 1938. He signed Germany's unconditional surrender in Berlin 8 May 1945. Tried at Nuremberg for war crimes, he was hanged.

Kekulé Friedrich August 1829–1896. German chemist whose theory 1858 of molecular structure revolutionized organic chemistry. He proposed that the benzene molecule, a ring of six carbon atoms, has two resonant forms.

Keller Gottfried 1819–1890. Swiss poet and novelist, whose books include *Der Grüne Heinrich/Green Henry* 1854–55. He also wrote short stories, one of which, 'Die Leute von Seldwyla/The People of Seldwyla' 1856–74, describes small-town life.

Keller Helen (Adams) 1880–1968. US author. Born in Alabama, she became blind and deaf through an illness when 19 months old. Only the tuition of Anne Sullivan Macy enabled her to speak. She graduated with honours from Radcliffe College in 1904 and published several books including *The Story of My Life* 1902.

Kelly Ned (Edward) 1854–1880. Australian bushranger (armed robber). The son of an Irish convict, he wounded a police officer in 1878 while resisting the arrest of his brother Daniel for horse-stealing. The two brothers escaped and carried out bank robberies. Kelly wore a distinctive home-made armour. In 1880 he was captured and hanged.

Kelly 'Gene' (Eugene Curran) 1912– . US film actor, dancer, choreographer, and director. A major star of the 1940s and 1950s in a series of MGM musicals, including *Singin' in the Rain* 1952, his subsequent attempts at straight direction were less well received.

Kelly Grace (Patricia) 1928–1982. US film actress, Princess of Monaco from 1956. She starred in *High Noon* 1952, *The Country Girl* 1954, for which she received an Academy Award, and *High Society* 1955. When she married Prince Rainier of Monaco she retired from acting.

Kelvin William Thomson, 1st Baron Kelvin 1824–1907. Irish physicist, who introduced the *Kelvin scale*, the absolute scale of temperature. His work on the conservation of energy 1851 led to the second law of thermodynamics: that heat cannot flow from a cooler to a warmer body.

He contributed to telegraphy by developing stranded cables and sensitive receivers, greatly improving transatlantic communications. Maritime endeavours led to a tide gauge and predictor, an improved compass, and simpler methods for fixing a ship's position at sea. He was president of the Royal Society 1890–95.

Kemble Charles 1775–1854. English actor and theatre manager, younger brother of Philip Kemble. His greatest successes were in romantic roles with his daughter Fanny Kemble.

Kemble 'Fanny' (Frances Anne) 1809–1893. English actress, daughter of Charles Kemble. She first appeared as Shakespeare's Juliet in 1829.

In 1834, on a US tour, she married a Southern plantation owner and remained in the USA until 1847. Her *Journal of a Residence on a Georgian*

Kelvin *Irish physicist William Kelvin pioneered the Kelvin scale of temperature used by scientists.*

Plantation 1835 is a valuable document in the history of slavery.

Kemble (John) Philip 1757–1823. English actor and theatre manager. He excelled in tragic roles, especially Shakespearean, including Hamlet and Coriolanus. As manager of Drury Lane 1788–1803 and Covent Garden 1803–17 in London, he introduced many innovations in theatrical management, costume, and scenery.

He was the son of the strolling player Roger Kemble (1721–1802), whose children included the actors Charles Kemble and Mrs ◊Siddons.

Kempe Margery *c.*1373–*c.*1439. English Christian mystic. She converted to religious life after a period of mental derangement, and travelled widely as a pilgrim. Her *Boke of Margery Kempe* about 1420 describes her life and experiences, both religious and worldly. It has been called the first autobiography in English.

Kempe Rudolf 1910–1976. German conductor. Renowned for the clarity and fidelity of his interpretations of the works of Richard Strauss and ◊Wagner's *Ring* cycle, he conducted Britain's Royal Philharmonic Orchestra 1961–75 and was musical director of the Munich Philharmonic from 1967.

Kempis Thomas à medieval German monk and religious writer; see ◊Thomas à Kempis.

Kendall Edward 1886–1972. US biochemist. Kendall isolated in 1914 the hormone thyroxin, the active compound of the thyroid gland. He went on to work on secretions from the adrenal gland, among which he discovered a compound E, which was in fact the steroid cortisone. For this Kendall shared the 1950 Nobel Prize for Medicine with Philip Hench (1896–1965) and Tadeus ◊Reichstein.

Kendrew John 1917– . British biochemist. Kendrew began, in 1946, the ambitious task of determining the 3-dimensional structure of the major muscle protein, myoglobin. This was completed in 1959 and won for Kendrew a share of the 1962 Nobel Prize for Chemistry with Max Perutz.

Keneally Thomas Michael 1935– . Australian novelist, who won the Booker Prize with *Schindler's Ark* 1982, a novel based on the true account of Polish Jews saved from the gas chambers in World War II by a German industrialist.

Kennedy Edward (Moore) 1932– . US Democrat politician. He aided his brothers John and Robert Kennedy in the presidential campaign of 1960, and entered politics as a senator from Massachusetts 1962. He failed to gain the presidential nomination 1980, largely because of feeling about his delay in reporting a car crash at Chappaquiddick Island, near Cape Cod, Massachusetts, in 1969, in which his passenger, Mary Jo Kopechne, was drowned.

Kennedy John F(itzgerald) 1917–1963. 35th president of the USA 1961–63, a Democrat. Kennedy was the first Roman Catholic and the youngest person to be elected president. In foreign policy he carried through the unsuccessful Bay of Pigs invasion of Cuba, and in 1963 secured the withdrawal of Soviet missiles from the island. His programme for reforms at home, called the *New Frontier*, was posthumously executed by Lyndon Johnson. Kennedy was assassinated while on a state visit to Dallas, Texas, on 22 Nov 1963 by Lee Harvey Oswald (1939–1963), who was in turn shot dead by Jack Ruby.

Son of Joseph Kennedy, he was born in Brookline, Massachusetts, and served in the navy in the Pacific during World War II. He was elected to Congress 1946 and to the Senate 1952. In 1960 he defeated Nixon for the presidency, partly as a result of televised debates, and brought academics and intellectuals to Washington as advisers. He married the socialite *Jacqueline Lee Bouvier* (1929–) in 1953.

A number of conspiracy theories have been spun around the Kennedy assassination, which was investigated by a special commission headed by Chief Justice Earl ◊Warren. The commission determined that Oswald acted alone, although this is extremely unlikely. A later congressional committee re-examined the evidence and determined that Kennedy 'was probably assassinated as a result of a conspiracy'. Oswald was an ex-marine who had gone to live in the USSR 1959 and returned when he could not become a Soviet citizen. Ruby was a Dallas nightclub owner, associated with the underworld and the police.

Kennedy Joseph (Patrick) 1888–1969. US industrialist and diplomat; ambassador to the UK 1937–40. A self-made millionaire, he groomed his four sons from an early age for careers in politics. His eldest son, Joseph Patrick Kennedy Jr (1915–44), was killed in action with the naval air force in World War II. Among his other children were John, Robert, and Edward.

Kennedy Robert F(rancis) 1925–1968. US Democrat politician and lawyer. He was campaign manager for his brother John F Kennedy 1961, and as attorney general 1961–64 pursued a racket-busting policy and promoted the Civil Rights Act of 1964. When Johnson preferred Hubert H Humphrey for the 1964 vice-president nomination, Kennedy resigned and was elected senator for New York. In 1968 he campaigned for the Democratic party's presidential nomination, but was assassinated by Sirhan Bissara Sirhan (1944–), a Jordanian Arab.

Kennedy William 1928– . US novelist, known for his *Albany Trilogy* consisting of *Legs* 1976, about the gangster 'Legs' Diamond, *Billy Phelan's Greatest Game* 1983, about a pool player, and

Ironweed 1984, about a baseball player's return to the city of Albany, NY.

Kennelly Arthur Edwin 1861–1939. US engineer, who gave his name to the Kennelly–Heaviside layer of the ionosphere. He verified the existence of an ionized layer in the upper atmosphere in 1902, which had been predicted by ◊Heaviside.

Kenneth II died 995. King of Scotland from 971, son of Malcolm I. He invaded Northumbria several times, and his chiefs were in constant conflict with Sigurd the Norwegian over the area of Scotland north of the Spey. He is believed to have been murdered by his own subjects.

Kent Bruce 1929– . British peace campaigner who acted as general secretary for the Campaign for Nuclear Disarmament (CND) 1980–85. He has published numerous articles on disarmament, Christianity, and peace. He was a Catholic priest until 1987.

Kent Edward George Alexander Edmund, 2nd Duke of Kent 1935– . British prince, grandson of George V. His father, *George* (1902–42), was created Duke of Kent just before his marriage in 1934 to Princess Marina of Greece and Denmark (1906–68). The second duke succeeded when his father was killed in an air crash on active service with the RAF.

In 1961 he married Katharine Worsley (1933–) and his heir is *George* (1962–), Earl of St Andrews. His brother, *Prince Michael* (1942–), became an officer with the Hussars in 1962. His sister, *Princess Alexandra* (1936–), married in 1963 Angus Ogilvy, younger son of the 12th Earl of Airlie; they have two children, James (1964–) and Marina (1966–).

Kent William 1685–1748. British architect, landscape gardener, and interior designer. In architecture he was foremost in introducing the Palladian style into Britain from Italy. Horace Walpole called him 'the father of modern gardening'.

Kent and Strathearn Edward, Duke of Kent and Strathearn 1767–1820. British general. The fourth son of George III, he married Victoria Mary Louisa (1786–1861), widow of the Prince of Leiningen, in 1818, and had one child, the future Queen Victoria.

Kentigern, St *c.*518–603. First bishop of Glasgow, born at Culross, Scotland. Anti-Christian factions forced him to flee to Wales, where he founded the monastery of St Asaph. In 573 he returned to Glasgow and founded the cathedral there. Feast day 14 Jan.

Kenton Stan 1912–1979. US exponent of progressive jazz, who broke into West Coast jazz in 1941 with his 'wall of brass' sound. He helped introduce Afro-Cuban rhythms to US jazz, and combined jazz and classical music in his compositions, such as *Artistry in Rhythm* 1943.

Kenyatta Jomo. Assumed name of Kamau Ngengi *c.* 1889–1978. Kenyan nationalist politician, prime

Kenyatta *The first president of independent Kenya, Jomo Kenyatta.*

minister from 1963 as well as first president of Kenya from 1964 until his death. He led the Kenya African Union from 1947 (*KANU* from 1963) and was active in liberating Kenya from British rule.

A member of the Kikuyu ethnic group, Kenyatta was born near Fort Hall, son of a farmer. Brought up at a Church of Scotland mission, he joined the Kikuyu Central Association (KCA), devoted to recovery of Kikuyu lands from white settlers, and became its president. He spent some years in Britain, returning to Kenya in 1946. He became president of the Kenya African Union (successor to the banned KCA 1947). In 1953 he was sentenced to seven years' imprisonment for his management of the guerrilla organization Mau Mau, though some doubt has been cast on his complicity. Released to exile in N Kenya in 1958, he was allowed to return to Kikuyuland 1961 and in 1963 became prime minister (also president from 1964) of independent Kenya. His slogans were '*Uhuru na moja*' (Freedom and unity) and '*Harambee*' (Let's get going).

Kenyon Kathleen 1906–1978. British archaeologist, whose work in Jericho showed that the double walls associated with the biblical Joshua belonged to an earlier period, and that a Neolithic settlement had existed about 6800 BC.

Kepler Johann 1571–1630. German mathematician and astronomer. *Kepler's laws* of planetary motion are: (1) the orbit of each planet is an ellipse with the Sun at one of the foci; (2) the radius vector of each planet sweeps out equal areas in equal times; (3) the squares of the periods of the planets are proportional to the cubes of their mean distances from the Sun.

Born in Württemberg, he became assistant to Tycho ◊Brahe 1600, and succeeded him as imperial mathematician 1601. His analysis of Brahe's observations of the planets led him to discover his three laws, the first two of which he published in *Astronomia nova* 1609 and the third in *Harmonices mundi* 1619.

Kerekou Mathieu (Ahmed) 1933– . Benin social-ist politician and soldier, president from 1980. In 1972, when deputy head of the Dahomey army, he led a coup to oust the ruling president and estab-lish his own military government. He embarked on a programme of 'scientific socialism', changing his country's name to Benin to mark this change of direction. Re-elected president 1984, in 1987 he resigned from the army and confirmed a civilian administration.

Kerensky Alexander Feodorovich 1881–1970. Rus-sian politician, premier of the second provisional government before its collapse Nov 1917, during the Russian Revolution. He lived in the USA from 1918.

Kern Jerome (David) 1885–1945. US composer. He wrote the operetta *Show Boat* 1927, which includes the song 'Ol' Man River'.

Kerouac Jack 1923–1969. US novelist, who named and epitomized the beat generation of the 1950s, which rejected conventional life styles. His books include *On the Road* 1957, and *Big Sur* 1963.

Kerr Deborah 1921– . British actress, who often played genteel, ladylike roles. Her performance in British films such as *Major Barbara* 1940 and *Black Narcissus* 1946 led to starring parts in Hollywood films such as *From Here to Eternity* 1953, *Quo Vadis* 1951, and *The King and I* 1956.

Kertesz André 1894–1986. US photographer. A master of the 35 mm format camera, he recorded his immediate environment (Paris, New York) with wit and style.

Kesselring Albert 1885–1960. German field mar-shal in World War II, commander of the Luftwaffe (air force) 1939–40, during the invasions of Poland and the Low Countries and the early stages of the Battle of Britain.

Ketch Jack died 1686. English executioner, who included ◊Monmouth in 1685 among his victims; his name became a common nickname for an executioner.

Key Francis Scott 1779–1843. US lawyer and poet who wrote the song 'The Star-Spangled Banner', while Fort McHenry was besieged by the British in 1814; since 1931 it has been the national anthem of the USA.

Keynes John Maynard, 1st Baron Keynes 1883–1946. English economist, whose *The Gen-eral Theory of Employment, Interest, and Money* 1936 proposed the prevention of financial crises and unemployment by adjusting demand through government control of credit and currency. He originated **macroeconomics**, the study of entire economies or economic systems.

Keynes was Fellow of King's College, Cambridge. He worked at the Treasury during World War I, and took part in the peace conference as chief Treasury representative, but resigned in protest against the financial terms of the treaty. He jus-tified his action in *The Economic Consequences of the Peace* 1919. His later economic works aroused much controversy.

Keynes led the British delegation at the Bretton Woods Conference 1944, which set up the Inter-national Monetary Fund. His theories were widely accepted in the aftermath of World War II, and he was one of the most influential economists of the 20th century. His ideas are today often contrasted with those of monetarism (see ◊Friedman).

Khachaturian Aram Il'yich 1903–1978. Armenian composer. His use of folk themes is shown in the ballets *Gayaneh* 1942, which includes the 'Sabre Dance', and *Spartacus* 1956.

Khaddhafi or *Gaddafi* or *Qaddafi*, Moamer al 1942– . Libyan revolutionary leader. Over-throwing King Idris 1969, he became virtual presi-dent of a republic, although he nominally gave up all except an ideological role 1974. He favours territorial expansion in N Africa reaching as far as Zaïre, has supported rebels in Chad, and proposed mergers with a number of countries. His theories, based on those of the Chinese communist leader Mao Zedong, are contained in a *Green Book*.

Khalifa the Sudanese dervish leader *Abdullah el Taaisha* 1846–1899. Successor to the Mahdi as Sudanese ruler from 1885, he was defeated by the UK general ◊Kitchener at Omdurman 1898, and later killed in Kordofan.

Khama Seretse 1921–1980. Botswanan politician, prime minister of Bechuanaland 1965 and first president of Botswana from 1966 until his death. Son of the Bamangwato chief *Sekoma II* (died 1925), Khama studied law in Britain and married an Englishwoman, Ruth Williams. This marriage was strongly condemned by his uncle Tshekedi Khama, regent during his minority, as contrary to tribal custom, and Seretse Khama was banished

Khaddhafi *Libyan revolutionary Colonel Moamer al Khaddhafi.*

1950. He returned 1956 on his renunciation of his claim to the chieftaincy.

Khan Imran 1952– . Pakistani cricketer. He played county cricket for Worcestershire and Sussex in the UK, and made his test debut for Pakistan 1971, subsequently playing for his country 75 times. In first-class cricket he has scored over 16,000 runs and taken over 1,200 wickets.

Khan Jahangir 1963– . Pakistani squash player, who won the world open championship a record six times 1981–85 and 1988.

He was eight times British open champion 1982–89, and world amateur champion 1979, 1983, and 1985. After losing to Geoff Hunt (Australia) in the final of the 1981 British open he did not lose again until Nov 1986 when he lost to Ross Norman (New Zealand) in the world open final.

His father **Roshan Khan** was British open champion 1956.

Khan Liaquat Ali 1895–1951. Indian politician, deputy leader of the Muslim League Party 1941–47, first prime minister of Pakistan from 1947. He was assassinated by a Muslim fanatic.

Khomeini Ayatollah Ruhollah 1900–1989. Iranian Shi'ite Muslim leader, born in Khomein, central Iran. Exiled for opposition to the Shah from 1964, he returned when the Shah left the country 1979, and established a fundamentalist Islamic republic. His rule was marked by a protracted

Khrushchev The Soviet politician Nikita Khrushchev at the Quai d'Orsay, Paris.

war with Iraq, and suppression of opposition within Iran.

Khorana Har Gobind 1922– . Indian biochemist, who in 1976 led the team that first synthesized a biologically active gene.

Khrushchev Nikita Sergeyevich 1894–1971. Soviet politician, secretary general of the Communist Party 1953–64, premier 1958–64. In 1956 he was the first official to denounce Stalin. A personal feud with Mao Zedong led to a breach in Soviet relations with China 1960. Khrushchev's foreign policy was one of peaceful coexistence with the West, marred by the crisis when he attempted to supply missiles to Cuba and US pressure compelled their withdrawal 1962.

Born near Kursk, the son of a miner, he fought in the post-Revolutionary civil war 1917–20, and in World War II organized the guerrilla defence of his native Ukraine. He denounced Stalinism in a secret session of the party Feb 1956. Many victims of the purges of the 1930s were either released or posthumously rehabilitated, but when Hungary revolted in Oct against Soviet domination, there was immediate Soviet intervention. In 1958 Khrushchev succeeded Bulganin as chair of the council of ministers (prime minister). His policy of competition with capitalism was successful in the space programme. Because of the Cuban crisis and the Sino-Soviet split, he was compelled to resign 1964, although by 1965 his reputation was to some extent officially restored. In Apr 1989 his Feb 1956 'secret speech' was officially published for the first time.

Khufu c.3000 BC. Egyptian king of Memphis, who built the largest of the pyramids, known to the Greeks as the pyramid of Cheops (the Greek form of Khufu).

Khomeini Ayatollah Khomeini, Iranian leader 1979–89.

Khwārizmī, al- Muhammad ibn Mūsā *c.*780–*c.*850. Arab mathematician from Khwarizm (now Khiva, USSR), who lived and worked in Baghdad. He wrote a book on algebra, from part of whose title (*al-jabr*) comes the word 'algebra', and a book in which he introduced to the West the Hindu–Arabic decimal number system. The word 'algorithm' is a corruption of his name.

Kidd 'Captain' (William) *c.*1645–1701. Scottish pirate, born in Greenock, who settled in New York. In 1696 he was commissioned by the governor of New York to suppress pirates, but he became a pirate himself. Arrested 1699, he was taken to England and hanged.

His execution marked the end of some 200 years of semi-official condoning of piracy by the British government.

Kiefer Anselm 1945– . German painter. He studied under Joseph ◊Beuys, and his works include monumental landscapes on varied surfaces, often with the paint built up into relief with other substances. Much of his highly Expressionist work deals with recent German history.

Kierkegaard Søren Aabye 1813–1855. Danish philosopher, considered to be the founder of existentialism. He disagreed with ◊Hegel, arguing that no system of thought could explain the unique experience of the individual. He defended Christianity, suggesting that God cannot be known through reason, but only through a 'leap of faith'. He believed that God and exceptional individuals were above moral laws.

Born in Copenhagen, where he spent most of his life, he was the son of a Jewish merchant, but was converted to Christianity in 1838, although he became hostile to the established church, and his beliefs caused much controversy. A prolific author, he published his first important work *Enten-Eller/Either-Or* in 1843, and notable later works are *Begrebet Angest/Concept of Dread* 1844 and *Efterskrift/Post-script* 1846, which summed up much of his earlier writings.

Killy Jean-Claude 1943– . French skier. He won all three gold medals (slalom, giant slalom, and downhill) at the 1968 winter Olympics in Grenoble. The first World Cup winner 1967, he retained the title 1968 and also won three world titles.

Kilmuir David Patrick Maxwell Fyfe, 1st Earl of Kilmuir 1900–1967. British lawyer and Conservative politician. He was solicitor-general 1942–45 and attorney-general in 1945 during the Churchill governments. He was home secretary 1951–54 and lord chancellor 1954–62.

Kilvert Francis 1840–1879. British clergyman, noted for a diary recording social life on the Welsh border 1870–79 published in 1938–39.

Kim Dae Jung 1924– . South Korean social-democratic politician. As a committed opponent of the regime of Gen Park Chung Hee, he suffered imprisonment and exile.

A Roman Catholic, born in the poor SW province of Cholla, Kim was imprisoned by communist troops during the Korean War. He rose to prominence as an opponent of Park and was only narrowly defeated when he challenged Park for the presidency in 1971. He was imprisoned 1976–78 and 1980–82 for alleged 'anti-government activities' and lived in the USA 1982–85. On his return to South Korea he successfully spearheaded an opposition campaign for democratization, but, being one of several opposition candidates, was defeated by the government nominee, Roh Tae Woo, in the presidential election of Dec 1987.

Kim Il Sung 1912– . North Korean communist politician and marshal. He became prime minister 1948 and president 1972, retaining the presidency of the Communist Workers' Party. He likes to be known as the 'Great Leader' an has campaigned constantly for the reunification of Korea. His son *Kim Jong Il* (1942–), known as the 'Dear Leader', has been named as his successor.

Kim Young Sam 1927– . South Korean democratic politician. A member of the National Assembly from 1954 and president of the New Democratic Party (NDP) from 1974, he lost his seat and was later placed under house arrest because of his

Kierkegaard A portrait of the philosopher sketched by his cousin, Christian Kierkegaard.

opposition to President Park Chung Hee. In 1983 he led a pro-democracy hunger strike but in 1987 failed to defeat Roh Tae-Woo in the presidential election. In 1990 he merged the ruling party to form the new Democratic Liberal Party (DLP).

King Billie Jean (born Moffitt) 1943– . US lawn tennis player. She won a record 20 Wimbledon titles 1961–79 and 39 Grand Slam titles.

Her first title was the doubles with Karen Hantze 1961, and her last, also doubles, with Martina Navratilova 1979. She won the Wimbledon singles title six times and the US Open singles title four times; French Open once; Australian Open once. Her 39 Grand Slam events at singles and doubles are third only to Navratilova and Margaret Court.

King Martin Luther, Jr 1929–1968. US civil-rights campaigner, black leader, and Baptist minister. He first came to national attention in 1955 as leader of the Montgomery, Alabama, bus boycott, which began when a black passenger refused to give up her seat to a white passenger, and was one of the organizers of the massive (200,000 people) march on Washington DC 1963 to demand racial equality. An advocate of nonviolence, he was awarded the Nobel Peace Prize 1964. He was assassinated. The third Monday in Jan is celebrated as *Martin Luther King Day*, a public holiday in the USA.

Born in Atlanta, Georgia, son of a Baptist minister, King founded the civil-rights Southern Christian Leadership Conference 1957. A brilliant and moving speaker, he was the symbol of, and leading

King *Civil Rights campaigner Martin Luther King.*

figure in, the campaign for integration and equal rights in the late 1950s and early 1960s. In the mid-1960s his moderate approach was criticized by black militants. Always a target of segregationists and right-wing extremists, he was shot and killed in Memphis, Tennessee. James Earl Ray was convicted of the murder, but there is little evidence to suggest that he committed the crime. Various conspiracy theories concerning the FBI, the CIA, and the Mafia have been suggested.

King Stephen 1946– . US writer of horror novels with a small-town or rural US setting. Many of his works have been filmed, including *Carrie* 1974, *The Shining* 1978, and *Christine* 1983.

King William Lyon Mackenzie 1874–1950. Canadian Liberal prime minister 1921–26, 1926–30, and 1935–48. He maintained the unity of the English- and French-speaking populations, and was instrumental in establishing equal status for Canada with Britain.

Kinglake Alexander William 1809–1891. British historian of the Crimean War, who also wrote a Near East travel narrative *Eothen* 1844.

Kingsley Ben (Krishna Banji) 1944– . British film actor of Indian descent, who usually plays character parts. He played the title role of *Gandhi* 1982 and also appeared in *Betrayal* 1982, *Testimony* 1987, and *Pascali's Island* 1988.

Kingsley Charles 1819–1875. English author. Rector of Eversley, Hampshire 1842–75, he was known as the 'Chartist clergyman' because of such social novels as *Alton Locke* 1850. His historical novels include *Westward Ho!* 1855 and, for children, *The Water-Babies* 1863.

He was professor of modern history at Cambridge University 1860–69 and his controversy with J H ◊Newman prompted the latter's *Apologia*.

Kingsley Mary Henrietta 1862–1900. British ethnologist. She made extensive expeditions in W Africa, and published lively accounts of her findings, for example *Travels in West Africa* 1897. She died while nursing Boer prisoners during the South African War. She was the daughter of the writer Charles Kingsley.

Kinnock Neil 1942– . British Labour politician, party leader from 1983. Born and educated in Wales, he was elected to represent a Welsh constituency in Parliament 1970 (Islwyn from 1983). A noted orator, he was further left than prime ministers Wilson and Callaghan, but as party leader (in succession to Michael Foot) adopted a more moderate position, initiating a major policy review 1988–89.

He initiated the expulsion of the left-wing Militant Tendency members from the Labour Party 1986.

Kinsey Alfred 1894–1956. US researcher, whose studies of male and female sexual behaviour

Kinnock *British Labour Party leader Neil Kinnock.*

1948–53, based on questionnaires, were the first serious published research on this topic.

Kinski Klaus 1926– . German actor who has appeared in several Werner Herzog films such as *Aguirre Wrath of God* 1972, *Nosferatu* 1978, and *Venom* 1982.

Kipling (Joseph) Rudyard 1865–1936. English writer, born in India. His stories for children include the *Jungle Books* 1894–1895, *Stalky and Co* 1899, and the *Just So Stories* 1902. Other works include the novel *Kim* 1901, poetry, and the unfinished autobiography *Something of Myself* 1937. In his heyday he enjoyed enormous popularity, but was subsequently denigrated for alleged 'jingoist imperialism'. Nobel prize 1907.

Born in Bombay, Kipling was educated at the United Services College at Westward Ho!, England, which provided the background for *Stalky and Co.* He worked as a journalist in India 1882–89; during these years he wrote *Plain Tales from the Hills* 1888, *Soldiers Three* 1890, *Wee Willie Winkie* 1890, and others. Returning to London he published *The Light that Failed* 1890 and *Barrack-Room Ballads* 1892. He lived largely in the USA 1892–96, where he produced the two *Jungle Books* and *Captains Courageous* 1897. Settling in Sussex, SE England, he published *Kim* (set in India), the *Just So Stories*, *Puck of Pook's Hill* 1906, and *Rewards and Fairies* 1910.

Kirchhoff Gustav Robert 1824–1887. German physicist, who with ◊Bunsen used the spectroscope to show that all elements, heated to incandescence, have their individual spectra.

Kirchner Ernst Ludwig 1880–1938. German Expressionist artist, a leading member of the

Expressionist group *Die Brücke* in Dresden from 1905 and in Berlin from 1911. He suffered a breakdown during World War I and settled in Switzerland, where he committed suicide.

Kirk Norman 1923–1974. New Zealand Labour politician, prime minister 1972–74.

Kirkpatrick Jeane 1926– . US right-wing politician and professor of political science. She was an outspoken anti-Marxist permanent representative to the United Nations (as a Democrat) 1981–85, then registered as a Republican 1985.

Kirov Sergei Mironovich 1886–1934. Russian Bolshevik leader, who joined the party 1904 and took a prominent part in the 1917–20 civil war. His assassination 1934, possibly engineered by ◊Stalin, led to the political trials held during the next four years.

Kishi Nobusuke 1896–1987. Japanese politician and prime minister 1957–60. A government minister during World War II and imprisoned 1945, he was never put on trial and returned to politics 1953. During his premiership, Japan began a substantial rearmament programme and signed a new treaty with the USA, which gave greater equality in the relationship between the two states.

Kissinger Henry 1923– . German-born US diplomat. In 1969 he was appointed assistant for National Security Affairs by President Nixon, and was secretary of state 1973–77.

Born in Bavaria, Kissinger emigrated to the USA 1938. After work in army counter-intelligence, he won a scholarship to Harvard, and subsequently became a government consultant. His secret trips to Beijing and Moscow led to Nixon's visits to both countries and a general détente. In 1973 he shared a Nobel Peace Prize with Le Duc Tho,

Kipling *British short-story writer, novelist, and poet Rudyard Kipling.*

the North Vietnamese Politburo member, for his part in the Vietnamese peace negotiations, and in 1976 he was involved in the negotiations in Africa arising from the Angola and Rhodesia crises. In 1983, President Reagan appointed him to head a bipartisan commission on Central America.

Kitaj Ron B 1932– . US painter and printmaker, active in Britain. His work is mainly figurative, and his distinctive decorative pale palette was in part inspired by studies of the Impressionist Degas.

Much of Kitaj's work is outside the predominant avant-garde trend and inspired by diverse historical styles. Some compositions are in triptych form.

Kitasato Shibasaburo 1852–1931. Japanese bacteriologist who discovered the plague bacillus. Kitasato was the first to grow the tetanus bacillus in pure culture. He and the German bacteriologist Behring discovered that increasing non-lethal doses of tetanus toxin gives immunity to the disease.

Kitchener Horatio Herbert, Earl Kitchener of Khartoum 1850–1916. British soldier and administrator. He defeated the Sudanese dervishes at Omdurman 1898 and re-occupied Khartoum. In South Africa, he was chief of staff 1900–02 during the Boer War, and commanded the forces in India 1902–09. He was appointed war minister on the outbreak of World War I, and drowned when his ship was sunk on the way to Russia.

He was born in County Kerry, Ireland. He was commissioned 1871, and transferred to the Egyptian Army 1882. Promoted to commander-in-chief 1892, he forced a French expedition to withdraw after a clash at Fashoda which nearly led the two countries into war. As British secretary of state for war from 1914, he modernized the British forces.

Klammer Franz 1953– . Austrian skier, who won a record 35 World Cup downhill races between 1974 and 1985. Olympic gold medallist 1976.

He was the combined world champion 1974, and the World Cup downhill champion 1975–78 and 1983.

Klaproth Martin Heinrich 1743–1817. German chemist who first identified the elements uranium, zirconium, cerium, and titanium.

Klee Paul 1879–1940. Swiss painter. He settled in Munich 1906, joined the *Blaue Reiter* (see ◊Kandinsky) group 1912, and worked at the Bauhaus school of art and design 1920–31, returning to Switzerland 1933. His style in the 1920s–30s was dominated by humorous linear fantasies.

Klee travelled with the painter August Macke to Tunisia in 1914, a trip that transformed his sense of colour. The Klee Foundation, Berne, has a large collection of his work.

Klein Melanie 1882–1960. Austrian child psychoanalyst. She pioneered child psychoanalysis and play studies, and was influenced by

Sigmund ◊Freud's theories. She published *The Psychoanalysis of Children* in 1960.

Klein analysed the behaviour of children through the use of play techniques; this practice was later adopted in child guidance clinics. Her research into the origins of mental disorder psychosis, schizophrenia, and depression extended the range of patients who can usefully undergo psycholanalysis.

Klein Yves 1928–1962. French painter of bold abstracts and provocative experimental works, including imprints of nude bodies.

Kleist (Bernd) Heinrich (Wilhelm) von 1777–1811. German dramatist, whose comedy *Der zerbrochene Krug/The Broken Pitcher* 1808, and drama *Prinz Friedrich von Homburg/The Prince of Homburg* 1811, achieved success only after his suicide.

Klemperer Otto 1885–1973. German conductor, who is celebrated for his interpretation of contemporary and classical music (especially ◊Beethoven and ◊Brahms). He conducted the Los Angeles Orchestra 1933–39 and the Philharmonia Orchestra, London, from 1959.

Kliegl John H 1869–1959 and Anton T 1872–1927. German-born US brothers, who in 1911 invented the brilliant carbon-arc (*klieg*) lights used in television and films. They also created scenic effects for theatre and film.

Klimt Gustav 1862–1918. Austrian painter, influenced by Jugendstil ('Youth Style', a form of Art Nouveau); a founder member in 1897 of the Vienna *Sezession* group ('seceding' from art institutions to pursue a modern approach). His works include mosaics, and his paintings have a similar jewelled effect, for example *The Kiss* 1909 (Musée des Beaux-Arts, Strasbourg). He painted many portraits.

Kline Franz 1910–1962. US Abstract Expressionist painter. He created large, graphic compositions in monochrome using angular forms, like magnified calligraphic brushstrokes.

Klopstock Friedrich Gottlieb 1724–1803. German poet, whose religious epic *Der Messias/The Messiah* 1748–73 and *Oden/Odes* 1771 anticipated Romanticism.

Kneller Godfrey 1646–1723. German-born painter, who lived in England from 1674. He was court portraitist to Charles II, James II, William III, and George I.

His work includes the series *Hampton Court Beauties* (Hampton Court, Richmond, Surrey, a sequel to Lely's *Windsor Beauties*), and 48 portraits of the members of the Whig Kit Cat Club 1702–17 (National Portrait Gallery, London).

Knight Laura 1877–1970. British painter. She focused on detailed, narrative scenes of Romany, fairground and circus life, and ballet.

Knipper Lev Konstantinovich 1898–1974. Soviet composer. His early work shows the influence of ◊Stravinsky, but after 1932 he wrote in a more popular idiom, as in the symphony *Poem of Komsomol Fighters* 1933–34 with its mass battle songs. He is known in the West for his song 'Cavalry of the Steppes'.

Knox John *c.*1505–1572. Scottish Protestant reformer, founder of the Church of Scotland. He spent several years in exile for his beliefs, including a period in Geneva where he met John ◊Calvin. He returned to Scotland 1559 to promote Presbyterianism.

Originally a Roman Catholic priest, Knox is thought to have been converted by the reformer George Wishart. When Wishart was burned for heresy, Knox went into hiding, but later preached the reformed doctrines. He was captured by French troops in Scotland 1547, and was imprisoned in France, sentenced to the galleys, and released only by intercession of the British government 1549. In England he assisted in compiling the Prayer Book, as a royal chaplain from 1551. On Mary's accession 1553 he fled abroad and in 1557 was, in his absence, condemned to be burned. In 1559 he returned to Scotland. He was tried for treason but acquitted 1563. His books include *First Blast of the Trumpet Against the Monstrous Regiment of Women* 1558 and *History of the Reformation in Scotland* 1586.

Knox Ronald Arbuthnott 1888–1957. British Roman Catholic scholar, whose translation of the Bible (1945–49) was officially approved by the Roman Catholic Church.

Koch Robert 1843–1910. German bacteriologist. Koch and his assistants devised the means to culture bacteria outside the body, and formulated the rules for showing whether or not a bacterium is the cause of a disease. Nobel Prize for Medicine 1905.

His techniques enabled him to identify the bacteria responsible for diseases like anthrax, cholera, and tuberculosis. This did not automatically lead to cures, but was crucial in their discovery. Koch was a great teacher, and many of his pupils, such as ◊Kitasato, ◊Ehrlich, and ◊Behring, became outstanding scientists.

Kodály Zoltán 1882–1967. Hungarian composer. With ◊Bartók, he recorded and transcribed Magyar folk music, the scales and rhythm of of which he incorporated in a deliberately nationalist style. His works include the cantata *Psalmus Hungaricus* 1923, a comic opera *Háry János* 1925–27, and orchestral dances and variations.

Koestler Arthur 1905–1983. Hungarian author. Imprisoned by the Nazis in France 1940, he escaped to England. His novel *Darkness at Noon* 1941 is a fictional account of the Stalinist purges, and draws on his experiences as a prisoner under sentence of death during the Spanish Civil War. He also wrote extensively about creativity, parapsychology, politics, and culture. He committed suicide with his wife.

Born in Budapest, and educated as an engineer in Vienna, he became a journalist in Palestine and the USSR. He joined the Communist party in Berlin 1931, but left it 1938. His account of being held by the Nazis are contained in *Scum of the Earth* 1941. Other novels include *Thieves In The Night* 1946, *The Lotus and the Robot* 1960, and *The Call Girls* 1972. Nonfiction includes *The Yogi and the Commissar* 1945, *The Sleepwalkers* 1959, *The Act of Creation* 1964, *The Ghost in the Machine* 1967, *The Roots of Coincidence* 1972, *The Heel of Achilles* 1974, and *The Thirteenth Tribe* 1976. Autobiographical works include *Arrow in the Blue* 1952 and *The Invisible Writing* 1954. He was

Knox An engraving of the 16th-century Scottish Protestant reformer John Knox.

Koestler Hungarian-born writer Arthur Koestler was imprisoned in Spain by Franco, in France by the Nazis, and briefly in Britain, where he later settled.

Kohl West German chancellor Helmut Kohl at the first meeting of the European Community Emergency Summit in Brussels, Feb 1988.

a member of the Voluntary Euthanasia Society and committed suicide, possibly as a result of having Parkinson's disease. He endowed Britain's first chair of parapsychology at Edinburgh, established 1984.

Kohl Helmut 1930– . West German conservative politician, leader of the Christian Democratic Union (CDU) from 1976, and chancellor from 1982.

Kohl, a practising Catholic, studied law and history before entering the chemical industry. Elected to the Rhineland-Palatinate *Land* (state) parliament 1959, he became state premier 1969. After the 1976 Bundestag (federal parliament) elections Kohl led the CDU in opposition. He became federal chancellor (prime minister) 1982, when the Free Democratic Party (FDP) withdrew their support from the socialist Schmidt government, and was elected at the head of the new CDU-CSU-FDP coalition. From 1984 Kohl was implicated in the Flick bribes scandal over the illegal business funding of political parties, but he was cleared of all charges by the Bonn public prosecutor May 1986, and was reelected as chancellor Jan 1987.

Kokhba Bar. Name adopted by Simeon bar Koziba, died 135. Jewish leader of the revolt against the Hellenization campaign of the Roman emperor Hadrian 132–35, which led to the razing of Jerusalem. He was killed in battle.

Kokoschka Oskar 1886–1980. Austrian Expressionist painter and writer, who lived in the UK from 1938. Initially influenced by the Vienna *Sezession* (see ◊Klimt) painters, he developed a disturbingly expressive portrait style. His writings include several plays.

Kolchak Alexander Vasilievich 1875–1920. Russian admiral, commander of the White forces in Siberia during the Russian Civil War.

He proclaimed himself Supreme Ruler of Russia 1918, but was later handed over to the Bolsheviks by his own men and shot.

Koller Carl 1857–1944. Austrian ophthalmologist who introduced local anaesthesia 1884.

When Sigmund ◊Freud discovered the pain-killing properties of cocaine, Koller recognized its potential as a local anaesthetic. He carried out early experiments on animals and on himself.

Kollontai Alexandra 1872–1952. Russian revolutionary, politician, and writer. In 1905 she published *On the Question of the Class Struggle*, and was the only female member of the first Bolshevik government as Commissar for Public Welfare. She campaigned for domestic reforms such as acceptance of free love, simplification of divorce laws, and collective childcare.

In 1896 she saw the appalling conditions for factory workers in Russia while on a tour of a large textile factory with her husband. She was so enraged by his view that only small improvements were necessary that she left him and devoted herself to improving conditions for working women. She was harassed by the police for her views and in 1914 went into exile in Germany. On her return to Russia she joined the Bolsheviks and toured the USA to argue against its involvement in World War I. She organized the first all-Russian Congress of Working and Peasant Women 1918.

Kollwitz Käthe 1867–1945. German sculptor and printmaker. Her early series of etchings of workers and their environment are realistic and harshly expressive. Later themes include war, death, and maternal love.

Kong Zi Pinyin form of ◊Confucius, Chinese philosopher.

Koniev Ivan Stepanovich 1898–1973. Soviet marshal, who in World War II liberated Ukraine from the invading German forces 1943, and advanced from the south on Berlin to link up with the British-US forces.

Konoe Fumimaro 1891–1946. Japanese politician and prime minister. Entering politics in the 1920s, Konoe was active in trying to curb the power of the army in government, and preventing an escalation of the war with China. He was prime minister for periods in the late 1930s, but finally resigned 1941 over differences with the army. He helped to engineer the fall of the ◊Tojo government 1944, but committed suicide after being suspected of war crimes.

Korbut Olga 1955– . Soviet gymnast, who attracted world attention at the 1972 Olympic Games with her 'cheeky' floor routine, and won three gold medals.

Korda Alexander 1893–1956. Hungarian-born British film producer and director, a dominant figure during the 1930s and 1940s. His films include *The*

Private Life of Henry VIII 1933, *The Third Man* 1950, and *Richard III* 1956.

Kornberg Arthur 1918– . US biochemist. In 1956, while working on enzymes at Washington University, Kornberg discovered the enzyme DNA-polymerase which enabled molecules of DNA to be synthesized for the first time. For this work Kornberg shared the 1959 Nobel Prize for Medicine with Severo ◊Ochoa.

Korngold Erich Wolfgang 1897–1957. Austrian-born composer. He began composing operas while still in his teens and in 1934 moved to Hollywood to become a composer for Warner Brothers. His film scores combine a richly orchestrated and romantic style, reflecting the rapid changes of mood characteristic of screen action.

Korolev Sergei Pavlovich 1906–1966. Soviet designer of the first Soviet intercontinental missile, used 1957 to launch the first Sputnik satellite, and 1961 to launch the Vostok spacecraft (also designed by Korolev).

Kościuszko Tadeusz 1746–1817. Polish revolutionary leader, defeated by combined Russian and Prussian forces 1794, and imprisoned until 1796. He fought for the USA in the War of Independence.

Kosinski Jerzy 1933– . Polish-born US novelist, author of *The Painted Bird* 1965, about a strange boy brutally treated during World War II, *Being There* 1971, about a retarded gardener who is thought to be a wise man because his gardening tips are taken as metaphors for life, and *Passion Play* 1979.

He was born in Lodz, and educated as a sociologist at the university there. He escaped from Poland during World War II through the USSR, eventually going to the USA 1957. He taught himself English.

Kossuth Lajos 1802–1894. Hungarian nationalist. He proclaimed Hungarian independence of Habsburg rule 1849, and when the Hungarians were later defeated, fled first to Turkey, and then to Britain.

Kosygin Alexei Nikolaievich 1904–1980. Soviet politician, prime minister 1964–80. He was elected to the Supreme Soviet 1938, became a member of the Politburo 1946, deputy prime minister 1960, and succeeded Khrushchev as premier.

Kovalevsky Sonja Vasilevna 1850–1891. Russian mathematician; doctorate from Göttingen University 1874 for dissertation on partial differential equations; professor of mathematics University of Stockholm from 1884. In 1886 she won the *Prix Bordin* of the French Academy of Sciences for a paper on the rotation of a rigid body about a point, a problem the 18th-century mathematicians Euler and Lagrange had both failed to solve.

Krafft-Ebing Baron Richard von 1840–1902. German pioneer psychiatrist, and neurologist. He published *Psychopathia sexualis* 1886.

Krebs Hans 1900–1981. German-born British biochemist. He shared the 1953 Nobel Prize for Medicine for discovering the citric acid cycle, also known as *Krebs' cycle*, by which food is converted into energy in living tissues.

Kreisler Fritz 1875–1962. Austrian violinist and composer, renowned as an interpreter of Brahms and Beethoven. From 1911 he was one of the earliest recording artists of Classical music, including records of his own compositions

Krenek Ernst 1900– . Austrian-born composer. His jazz opera *Jonny spielt auf/Johnny plays up* 1927 received international acclaim.

He moved to the USA 1939 and explored the implications of contemporary and renaissance musical theories in a succession of works and theoretical writings.

Krenz Egon 1937– . East German communist politician. A member of the Socialist Unity Party (SED) from 1955, he joined its politburo in 1983 and became known as a hardline protégé of Erich ◊Honecker, succeeding him as party leader and head of state in 1989 after widespread pro-democracy demonstrations. Pledging a 'new course', Krenz opened the country's western border and promised more open elections, but his conversion to genuine pluralism proved weak in the face of popular protest and he resigned after a few weeks in Dec 1989, as party general secretary and head of state. He was replaced by Manfred Gerlach (1928–) and Gregor Gysi (1948–) respectively.

Kreutzer Rodolphe 1766–1831. French violinist and composer of German descent to whom Beethoven dedicated his violin sonata Opus 47, known as the *Kreutzer Sonata*.

Kristiansen Ingrid 1956– . Norwegian athlete, an outstanding long-distance runner at 5,000 m, 10,000 m, marathon, and cross-country running. She has won all the world's leading marathons. In 1986 she knocked 45.68 seconds off the world 10,000 m record.

Kropotkin Peter Alexeivich, Prince Kropotkin 1842–1921. Russian anarchist. Imprisoned for revolutionary activities 1874, he escaped to the UK in 1876, and later moved to Switzerland. Expelled from Switzerland, he went to France, where he was imprisoned 1883–86. He lived in Britain until 1917, when he returned to Moscow. Among his works are *Mutual Aid* 1902 and *Modern Science and Anarchism* 1903.

Kruger Stephanus Johannes Paulus 1825–1904. President of the Transvaal 1883–1900. He refused to remedy the grievances of the Uitlanders (English and other non-Boer white residents), and so precipitated the Second South African War (1899–1902).

Kryukov Fyodor 1870–1920. Russian writer, alleged by Solzhenitsyn to be the real author of *And Quiet Flows the Don* by ◊Sholokhov.

Kubelik Jan 1880–1940. Czech violinist and composer. He performed in Prague at the age of eight, and was one of the world's greatest virtuosos; he also wrote six violin concertos.

Kubelik Rafael 1914– . Czech conductor and composer, son of violinist Jan Kubelik. His works include symphonies and operas, such as *Veronika* 1947. He was musical director of the Royal Opera House, Covent Garden, London 1955–58.

Kublai Khan 1216–1294. Mongol emperor of China from 1259. He completed his grandfather ◊Genghis Khan's conquest of N China from 1240, and on his brother Mungo's death 1259, established himself as emperor of China. He moved the capital to Peking and founded the Yuan dynasty, successfully expanding his empire into Indochina, but was defeated in an attempt to conquer Japan 1281.

Kubrick Stanley 1928– . US director, producer, and screenwriter. His films include *Paths of Glory* 1957, *Dr Strangelove* 1964, *2001: A Space Odyssey* 1968, *A Clockwork Orange* 1971, and *The Shining* 1979.

Kuhn Richard 1900–1967. Austrian chemist. Working at Heidelberg University in the 1930s Kuhn succeeded in determining the structures of vitamins A, B_2, and B_6. For his success he was awarded the 1938 Nobel Chemistry Prize, but was unable to receive it until after World War II.

Kuhn Thomas S 1922– . US historian and philosopher of science, who showed that social and cultural conditions affect the directions of science. *The Structure of Scientific Revolutions* 1962 argued that even scientific knowledge is relative, dependent on the **paradigm** (theoretical framework) that dominates a scientific field at the time.

Such paradigms (examples being Darwinism and Newtonian theory) are so dominant that they are uncritically accepted as true, until a 'scientific revolution' creates a new orthodoxy. Kuhn's ideas have also influenced ideas in the social sciences.

Kuiper Gerard Peter 1905–1973. Dutch-born US astronomer, who made extensive studies of the solar system. His discoveries included the atmospheres of Mars and Titan.

Kuiper was adviser to many NASA exploratory missions, and pioneered the use of telescopes on high-flying aircraft. The Kuiper Airborne Observatory, one such telescope, is named after him.

Kun Béla 1885–1938. Hungarian politician who created a Soviet republic in Hungary Mar 1919, which was overthrown Aug 1919 by a Western blockade and Romanian military actions. The succeeding regime under Admiral Horthy effectively liquidated both socialism and liberalism in Hungary.

Kundera Milan 1929– . Czech writer, born in Brno. His first novel *The Joke* 1967 brought him into official disfavour in Prague, and, unable to publish further works, he moved to France.

His novels include *The Book of Laughter and Forgetting* 1979 and *The Unbearable Lightness of Being* 1984.

Küng Hans 1928– . Swiss Roman Catholic theologian, who was barred from teaching by the Vatican 1979 'in the name of the Church' because he had cast doubt on papal infallibility, and on whether Christ was the son of God.

Kuniyoshi Utagawa 1797–1861. Japanese printmaker. His series *108 Heroes of the Suikoden*, depicting heroes of the Chinese classic *The Water Margin*, was particularly popular. Kuniyoshi's dramatic, innovative style lent itself to warriors and fantasy, but his subjects also include landscapes and cats.

Kuropatkin Alexei Nikolaievich 1848–1921. Russian general. He made his reputation during the Russo-Turkish War 1877–78, was commander in chief in Manchuria 1903, and resigned after his defeat at Mukden 1905 in the Russo-Japanese War.

Kurosawa Akira 1929– . Japanese director whose film *Rashomon* 1950 introduced Western audiences to Japanese cinema. Epics such as *Seven Samurai* 1954 combine spectacle with intimate human drama. His other films include *Drunken Angel* 1948, *Yojimbo* 1961, *Kagemusha* 1981, and *Ran* 1985.

Kutuzov Mikhail Larionovich, Prince of Smolensk 1745–1813. Commander of the Russian forces in the Napoleonic Wars. He commanded an army corps at Austerlitz in 1805, and the retreating army 1812. After the burning of Moscow he harried the French throughout their retreat, and later took command of the united Prussian armies.

Kuznets Simon 1901–1985. Russian economist, who emigrated to the USA 1922. He developed theories of national income and economic growth, used to forecast the future, in *Economic Growth of Nations* 1971. Nobel prize 1971.

Kuznetsov Anatoli 1930–1979. Russian writer. His novels *Babi Yar* 1966, describing the wartime execution of Jews at Babi Yar, near Kiev, and *The Fire* 1969, about workers in a large metallurgical factory, were seen as anti-Soviet. He lived in Britain from 1969.

Kyd Thomas *c.*1557–1595. English dramatist, author in about 1588 of a bloody revenge tragedy *The Spanish Tragedy*, which anticipated elements present in Shakespeare's *Hamlet*.

Kyprianou Spyros 1932– . Cypriot politician. Foreign minister 1961–72, he founded the Democratic Front (DIKO) in 1976. He was president 1977–88.

Educated in Cyprus and the UK, he was called to the English Bar in 1954. He became secretary to Archbishop Makarios in London in 1952 and returned with him to Cyprus in 1959. On the death of Makarios in 1977 he became acting president and was then elected.

La Bruyère Jean de 1645–1696. French essayist. He was born in Paris, studied law, took a post in the revenue office, and in 1684 entered the service of the house of Condé. His *Caractères* 1688, satirical portraits of contemporaries, made him many enemies.

Laclos Pierre Choderlos de 1741–1803. French author. An army officer, he wrote a single novel in letter form, *Les Liaisons dangereuses/Dangerous Liaisons* 1782, an analysis of moral corruption.

La Condamine Charles Marie de 1701–1774. French soldier and geographer who was sent by the French Academy of Sciences to Peru to measure the length of an arc of the meridien 1735–43. On his return journey he travelled the length of the Amazon, writing about the use of the nerve toxin curare, india rubber, and the advantages of inoculation.

Ladd Alan 1913–1964. US actor whose first leading role, the professional killer in *This Gun for Hire* 1942, made him a star. His career declined after the mid-1950s although his last role, in *The Carpetbaggers* 1964, was one of his best. His other films include *The Blue Dahlia* 1946 and *Shane* 1953.

Laënnec René Théophile Hyacinthe 1781–1826. French physician, inventor of the stethoscope 1814. He introduced the new diagnostic technique of auscultation (evaluating internal organs by listening with a stethoscope) in his book *Traité de l'auscultation médiaté* 1819, which quickly became a medical classic.

Lafarge John 1835–1910. US painter and ecclesiastical designer. He is credited with the revival of stained glass in America, and also created woodcuts, watercolours, and murals.

Lafayette Marie Joseph Gilbert de Motier, Marquis de Lafayette 1757–1834. French soldier and politician. He fought against Britain in the American War of Independence. During the French Revolution he sat in the National Assembly as a constitutional royalist, and in 1789 was given command of the National Guard. In 1792 he fled the country after attempting to restore the monarchy, and was imprisoned by the Austrians until 1797. He supported Napoleon in 1815, sat in the chamber of deputies as a Liberal from 1818, and played a leading part in the revolution of 1830.

He was a popular hero in the USA, with towns in Louisiana and Indiana named after him.

Lafayette Marie-Madeleine, Comtesse de Lafayette 1634–1693. French author. Her *Mémoires* of the French court are keenly observed, and her *La Princesse de Clèves* 1678 is the first French psychological novel and *roman à clef* ('novel with a key') in that real-life characters (including ◊La Rochefoucauld, who was for many years her lover) are presented under fictitious names.

La Fontaine Jean de 1621–1695. French poet. He was born at Château-Thierry, and from 1656 lived largely in Paris, the friend of Molière, Racine, and Boileau. His works include *Fables* 1668–94, and *Contes* 1665–74, a series of witty and bawdy tales in verse.

Lafontaine Oskar 1943– . West German socialist politician, federal deputy chair of the Social Democrat Party (SPD) from 1987. Leader of the Saar regional branch of the SPD from 1977 and former mayor of Saarbrucken, he was dubbed 'Red Oskar' because of his radical views on defence and environmental issues. His attitude mellowed after becoming minister-president of Saarland in 1985.

Laforgue Jules 1860–1887. French poet, who pioneered free verse (with no rhyme or metre) and who greatly influenced later French and English writers.

Lagerkvist Pär 1891–1974. Swedish author of lyric poetry, dramas, including *The Hangman* 1935, and novels, such as *Barabbas* 1950. Nobel prize 1951.

Lagerlöf Selma 1858–1940. Swedish novelist. She was originally a schoolteacher, and in 1891 published a collection of stories of peasant life, *Gösta Berling's Saga*. She was the first woman to receive a Nobel prize, in 1909.

Lagrange Joseph Louis 1736–1813. French mathematician. His *Mécanique analytique* 1788 applied mathematical analysis, using principles established by Newton, to such problems as the movements of planets when affected by each other's gravitational force. He presided over the commission that introduced the metric system 1793.

La Guardia Fiorello (Henrico) 1882–1947. US Republican politician, mayor of New York 1933–1945. Elected against the opposition of the powerful Tammany Hall Democratic Party organization, he cleaned up the administration, suppressed racketeering, and organized unemployment relief, slum-clearance schemes, and social services. Although nominally a Republican, he strongly supported Roosevelt's New Deal. La Guardia Airport, New York, is named after him.

Laing R(onald) D(avid) 1927–1989. Scottish psychoanalyst, originator of the 'social theory' of mental illness, for example that schizophrenia is promoted by family pressure for its members to conform to standards alien to themselves. His books include *The Divided Self* 1960 and *The Politics of the Family* 1971.

Lake Veronica. Stage name of Constance Frances Marie Ockelman 1919–1973. US film actress, who co-starred with Alan Ladd in several films during the 1940s, including *The Blue Dahlia* 1946. Her other work includes *Sullivan's Travels* 1942 and *I Married a Witch* 1942.

Lalande Michel de 1657–1726. French organist and composer of church music for the court at Versailles.

Lalique René 1860–1945. French designer of Art Nouveau glass, jewellery, and house interiors.

Lalo (Victor Antoine) Edouard 1823–1892. French composer. His Spanish ancestry and violin training are evident in the *Symphonie Espagnole* 1873 for violin and orchestra, and *Concerto for cello and orchestra* 1877. He also wrote an opera, *Le Roi d'Ys* 1887.

Lam Wilfredo 1902–1982. Cuban abstract painter. Influenced by Surrealism in the 1930s (he lived in Paris 1937–41), he created a semi-abstract style using mysterious and sometimes menacing images and symbols mainly taken from Caribbean tradition. His *Jungle* series, for example, contains voodoo elements.

Lamarck Jean Baptiste de 1744–1829. French naturalist, whose theory of evolution, known as **Lamarckism**, was based on the idea that acquired characteristics (changes acquired in an individual's lifetime) are inherited. His works include *Philosophie Zoologique/Zoological Philosophy* 1809 and *Histoire naturelle des animaux sans vertèbres/Natural History of Invertebrate Animals* 1815–22.

Lamartine Alphonse de 1790–1869. French poet. He wrote romantic poems, *Méditations* 1820, followed by *Nouvelles Méditations/New Meditations* 1823, *Harmonies* 1830, and others. His *Histoire des Girondins/History of the Girondins* 1847 influenced the revolution of 1848.

Lamb Charles 1775–1834. English essayist and critic. He collaborated with his sister **Mary** (1764–1847) on *Tales from Shakespeare* 1807, and his *Specimens of English Dramatic Poets* 1808 helped to revive interest in Elizabethan plays. As 'Elia' he contributed essays to the *London Magazine* from 1820 (collected 1823 and 1833).

Born in London, Lamb was educated at Christ's Hospital. He was a contemporary of ◊Coleridge, with whom he published some poetry in 1796. He was a clerk at India House 1792–1825, when he retired to Enfield. His sister Mary stabbed their mother to death in a fit of insanity 1796, and Charles cared for her between her periodic returns to an asylum.

Lamb Willis 1913– . US physicist who revised the quantum theory of ◊Dirac. The hydrogen atom was thought to exist in either of two distinct states carrying equal energies. More sophisticated measurements by Lamb in 1947 demonstrated that the two energy levels were not equal. This discrepancy, since known as the *Lamb shift*, won for him the 1955 Nobel Prize for Physics.

Lambert John 1619–1683. English general, a cavalry commander under Cromwell (at the battles of Marston Moor, Preston, Dunbar, and Worcester). Lambert broke with him over the proposal to award Cromwell the royal title. After the Restoration he was imprisoned for life.

Lamburn Richmal Crompton. Full name of British writer Richmal ◊Crompton.

Lamming George 1927– . Barbadian novelist, author of the autobiographical *In the Castle of my Skin* 1953, describing his upbringing in the small village where he was born. He later moved to London.

Lampedusa Giuseppe Tomasi di 1896–1957. Italian aristocrat, author of *The Leopard* 1958, a novel set in his native Sicily in the period after it was annexed by Garibaldi 1860, which chronicles the reactions of an aristocratic family to social and political upheavals.

Lancaster 'Burt' (Burton Stephen) 1913– . US film actor, formerly an acrobat. A star from his first film, *The Killers* 1946, he proved himself adept both at action roles and more complex character parts in such films as *The Flame and the Arrow* 1950, *Elmer Gantry* 1960, and *The Leopard/Il Gattopardo* 1963.

Lancaster Osbert 1908–1986. English cartoonist and writer. In 1939 he began producing daily 'pocket cartoons' for the *Daily Express*, in which he satirized current social mores through such characters as Maudie Littlehampton.

He was originally a book illustrator and muralist, and in the 1930s and 1940s produced several wittily debunking books on modern architecture (such as *Homes, Sweet Homes* 1939 and *Drayneflete Revisited* 1949), in which he introduced such facetious terms as Pont Street Dutch and Stockbroker's Tudor.

Lancret Nicolas 1690–1743. French painter. His graceful *fêtes galantes* (festive groups of courtly figures in fancy dress) followed a theme made popular by Watteau. He also illustrated amorous scenes from the *Fables* of La Fontaine.

Land Edwin 1909– . US inventor of the Polaroid camera 1947, which develops the film inside the camera and produces an instant photograph.

Landau Lev Davidovich 1908–1968. Russian theoretical physicist who made important contributions to most areas of twentieth century physics. He was awarded the 1962 Nobel Prize for Physics for his work on liquid helium.

Landor Walter Savage 1775–1864. English poet and essayist. He lived much of his life abroad, dying in Florence, to which he had fled from a libel suit 1858. His works include the epic *Gebir* 1798 and the *Imaginary Conversations of Literary Men and Statesmen* 1824–29.

Landowska Wanda 1877–1959. Polish harpsichordist and scholar. She founded a school near Paris for the study of early music, and was for many years one of the few artists regulary performing on the harpsichord. In 1941 she moved to the USA.

Landseer Edwin Henry 1802–1873. English painter and sculptor. He achieved great popularity with sentimental studies of animals, and his *Monarch of the Glen* 1850 was intended for the House of Lords. His sculptures include the lions in Trafalgar Square, London, 1859.

Landsteiner Karl 1868–1943. Austrian immunologist, who discovered the ABO blood group system 1900–02, and aided in the discovery of the Rhesus blood factors 1940. He also discovered the polio virus.

In 1936, he wrote *The Specificity of Serological Reactions*, which helped establish the science of immunology. He also developed a test for syphilis. Nobel Prize for Medicine 1930.

Lane Edward William 1801–1876. English traveller and translator, one of the earliest English travellers to Egypt to learn Arabic; his pseudo-scholarly writings, including *Manners and Customs of the Modern Egyptians* 1836, and an annotated translation of the *Arabian Nights* 1838–40, propagated a stereotyped image of the Arab world.

Lanfranc *c.*1010–1089. Italian archbishop of Canterbury from 1070; he rebuilt the cathedral, replaced English clergy by Normans, enforced clerical celibacy, and separated the ecclesiastical from the secular courts.

Lanfranc was born in Pavia, Italy; he entered the monastery of Bec, Normandy, in 1042, where he opened a school which achieved international fame; St Anselm, later his successor, was his pupil there. His skill in theological controversy did much to secure the church's adoption of the doctrine of transubstantiation. He came over to England with William the Conqueror, whose adviser he was.

Lang Andrew 1844–1912. Scottish historian and folklore scholar. His writings include historical works; anthropological essays, such as *Myth, Ritual and Religion* 1887 and *The Making of Religion* 1898, which involved him in controversy with J G ◊Frazer; novels; and a series of children's books, beginning with *The Blue Fairy Tale Book* 1889.

Lang Fritz 1890–1976. Austrian film director, born in Vienna. His German films include *Metropolis* 1927, *M* 1931, and the series of Dr Mabuse films, after which he fled from the Nazis to Hollywood 1936. His US films include *Fury* 1936, *You Only Live Once* 1937, and *The Big Heat* 1953.

Lange David (Russell) 1942– . New Zealand Labour Party prime minister 1983–89. Lange, a barrister, was elected to the House of Representatives 1977. Labour had a decisive win in the 1984 general election on a non-nuclear defence policy, which Lange immediately put into effect, despite criticism from the USA. He introduced a free-market economic policy and was re-elected 1987. He resigned Aug 1989 over a disagreement with his finance minister.

Langevin Paul 1872–1946. French physicist, who contributed to the studies of magnetism and X-ray emissions. During World War I he invented an apparatus for locating enemy submarines.

Langland William *c.*1332–*c.*1400. English poet. Born in the W Midlands, he took minor orders, and in later life settled in London. His alliterative *Vision Concerning Piers Plowman* appeared in three versions between about 1362 and 1398, but some critics believe he was only responsible for the first of these. The poem forms a series of allegorical visions, in which Piers develops from the typical poor peasant to a symbol of Jesus, and condemns the social and moral evils of 14th-century England.

Langley Samuel Pierpont 1834–1906. US inventor. His steam-driven aeroplane flew for 90 seconds in 1896, making the first flight by an engine-equipped aircraft.

Lange *Former prime minister of New Zealand David Lange on a visit to London in 1988.*

He was professor of physics and astronomy at the Western University of Pennsylvania 1866-87. He did valuable research on the infrared portions of the solar spectrum.

Langmuir Irving 1881-1957. US scientist, who invented the mercury vapour pump for producing a high vacuum, and the atomic hydrogen welding process; he was also a pioneer of the thermionic valve. In 1932 he was awarded the Nobel Prize for Chemistry for his work on surface chemistry.

Langton Stephen c.1150-1228. English priest. He studied in Paris, where he became chancellor of the university, and in 1206 was created a cardinal. When in 1207 Innocent III secured his election as archbishop of Canterbury, King John refused to recognize him, and Langton was not allowed to enter England until 1213. He supported the barons in their struggle against John, and was mainly responsible for the human rights declaration of the Magna Carta.

Langtry Lillie. Stage name of Emilie Charlotte le Breton 1853-1929. English actress, mistress of the future Edward VII. She was known as the 'Jersey Lily' from her birthplace and considered to be one of the most beautiful women of her time.

She was the daughter of a rector, and married Edward Langtry (died 1897) 1874. She first appeared professionally in London 1881, and had her greatest success as Rosalind in Shakespeare's *As You Like It*. In 1899 she married Sir Hugo de Bathe.

Lanier Sidney 1842-1881. US flautist and poet. His *Poems* 1877 contain interesting metrical experiments, in accordance with the theories expounded in his *Science of English Verse* 1880, on the relation of verse to music.

Lansbury George 1859-1940. British Labour politician, leader in the Commons 1931-35. In 1921, while Poplar borough mayor, he went to prison with most of the council rather than modify their policy of more generous unemployment relief. He was a member of Parliament 1910-12 and 1922-40; he was leader of the parliamentary Labour party 1931-35, but resigned (as a pacifist) in opposition to the party's militant response to the Italian invasion of Abyssinia (present-day Ethiopia).

He was editor of the *Daily Herald* 1912, carried it on as a weekly through World War I, and again as a daily until 1922.

Lansdowne Henry Charles, 5th Marquis of Lansdowne 1845-1927. British Liberal Unionist politician, governor-general of Canada 1883-88, viceroy of India 1888-93, war minister 1895-1900, and foreign secretary 1900-06. While at the Foreign Office he abandoned Britain's isolationist policy by forming an alliance with Japan and an entente cordiale with France. His letter of 1917 suggesting an offer of peace to Germany created a controversy.

Lao Zi c.604-531 BC. Chinese philosopher, commonly regarded as the founder of Taoism. Nothing certain is known of his life, and he is variously said to have lived in the 6th or the 4th century BC. The *Tao Te Ching*, the Taoist scripture, is attributed to him but apparently dates from the 3rd century BC.

Laplace Pierre Simon, Marquis de Laplace 1749-1827. French astronomer and mathematician. In 1796, he theorized that the Solar System originated from a cloud of gas (the nebular hypothesis). He studied the motion of the Moon and planets, and published a five-volume survey of celestial mechanics (calculation of the motion of celestial bodies), *Traité de méchanique céleste* 1799-1825. Among his mathematical achievements was the development of probability theory.

Lardner Ring 1885-1933. US short story writer. A sporting correspondent especially keen on baseball, he based his characters on the people he met professionally. His collected volumes of short stories include *You Know Me, Al* 1916, *Round Up* 1929, and *Ring Lardner's Best Short Stories* 1938, all written in colloquial language.

Largo Caballero Francisco 1869-1946. Spanish socialist and leader of the Spanish Socialist Party (PSOE). He became prime minister of the popular-front government elected Feb 1936 and remained in office for the first ten months of the Civil War before being replaced by Juan Negrin (1887-1956) May 1937.

Larionov Mikhail Fedorovich 1881-1964. Russian painter, active in Paris from 1919. He pioneered a semi-abstract style known as *Rayonnism* with his wife Natalia Goncharova, in which subjects appear to be deconstructed by rays of light from various sources.

Larkin Philip 1922-1985. English poet. His perfectionist, pessimistic verse includes *The North Ship* 1945, *The Whitsun Weddings* 1964, and *High Windows* 1974. He edited *The Oxford Book of 20th-Century English Verse* 1973.

Born in Coventry, Larkin was educated at Oxford, and from 1955 was librarian at Hull University. He also wrote two novels.

La Rochefoucauld François, duc de La Rochefoucauld 1613-1680. French writer. *Réflexions, ou sentences et maximes morales/Reflections, or Moral Maxims* 1665 is a collection of brief, epigrammatic, and cynical observations on life and society, with the epigraph 'Our virtues are mostly our vices in disguise'. He was a lover of Mme de ◊Lafayette.

Larousse Pierre 1817-1875. French grammarian and lexicographer. His encyclopedic dictionary, the *Grand Dictionnaire universel du XIXème siècle/Great Universal 19th-Century Dictionary* 1865-76, was an influential work and continues in subsequent revisions.

Larsson Carl 1853–1919. Swedish painter, engraver, and illustrator. He is remembered for his watercolours of domestic life, delicately coloured and full of detail, illustrating his book *Ett Hem/A Home* 1899.

Lartigue Jacques-Henri 1894–1986. French photographer. He began taking extraordinary and humorous photographs of his family at the age of seven, and went on to make autochrome (the first commercial colour process) colour prints of women.

la Salle René Robert Cavelier, Sieur de la Salle 1643–1687. French explorer. He made an epic voyage through North America, exploring the Mississippi River down to its mouth, and in 1682 founded Louisiana.

When he returned with colonists, he failed to find the river mouth again, and was eventually murdered by his mutinous men.

Las Casas Bartolomé de 1474–1566. Spanish missionary, historian, and colonial reformer, known as 'the Apostle of the Indians.' He was the first European to call for the abolition of Indian slavery in Latin America. He took part in the conquest of Cuba 1513, but subsequently worked for American Indian freedom in the Spanish colonies. *Apologetica historia de las Indias* (first published 1875–76) is his account of Indian traditions and his witnessing of Spanish oppression of the Indians.

From Cuba he returned to Spain 1515 to plead for the Indian cause, winning the support of the Holy Roman emperor Charles V. In what is now Venezuela he unsuccessfully attempted to found a settlement of free Indians. In 1530, shortly before the conquest of Peru, he persuaded the Spanish government to forbid slavery there.

Lasdun Denys 1914– . British architect. He designed the Royal College of Surgeons in Regent's Park, London 1960–64, some of the buildings at the University of East Anglia, Norwich, and the National Theatre 1976–77 on London's South Bank.

Laski Harold 1893–1950. British political theorist. Professor of political science at the London School of Economics from 1926, he taught a modified Marxism, and published *A Grammar of Politics* 1925 and *The American Presidency* 1940. He was chairman of the Labour Party 1945–46.

Lassalle Ferdinand 1825–1864. German socialist. He was imprisoned for his part in the Revolution of 1848, during which he met ◊Marx, and in 1863 founded the General Association of German Workers (later the Social-Democratic Party). His publications include *The Working Man's Programme* 1862, and *The Open Letter* 1863. He was killed in a duel arising from a love affair.

Lassus (or *Lasso*) Roland de c.1532–1594. Franco-Flemish composer. His works include polyphonic sacred music, songs, and madrigals, including settings of poems by his friend ◊Ronsard.

Latimer Hugh 1490–1555. English Christian church reformer and bishop. After his conversion to Protestantism 1524 he was imprisoned several times but was protected by Cardinal Wolsey and Henry VIII. He was burned for heresy.

Latimer was appointed bishop of Worcester 1535, but resigned 1539. Under Edward VI his sermons denouncing social injustice won him great influence, but after the accession of Mary he was arrested 1553 and two years later burned at the stake in Oxford.

La Tour Georges de 1593–1652. French painter active in Lorraine. He was patronized by the duke of Lorraine and perhaps also by Louis XIII. Many of his pictures are illuminated by a single source of light, with deep contrasts of light and shade. They range from religious paintings to genre scenes.

La Trobe Charles Joseph 1801–1875. Australian administrator. He was superintendent of Port Phillip district 1839–51 and first lieutenant-governor of Victoria 1851–54. The Latrobe River in Victoria is named after him.

Latynina Larissa Semyonovna 1935– . Soviet gymnast, winner of more Olympic medals than any person in any sport. She won 18 between 1956 and 1964, including nine gold medals. She won a total of 12 individual Olympic and world championship gold medals.

Laud William 1573–1645. English priest. As archbishop of Canterbury from 1633, his High Church policy, support for Charles I's unparliamentary rule, censorship of the press, and persecution of the Puritans, all aroused bitter opposition, while his strict enforcement of the statutes against enclosures and of laws regulating wages and prices alienated the propertied classes. His attempt to impose the use of the Prayer Book on the Scots precipitated the English Civil War. Impeached by Parliament 1640 he was imprisoned in the Tower, summarily condemned to death, and beheaded.

Lauder Harry. Stage name of Hugh MacLennan 1870–1950. Scottish music-hall comedian and singer.

Lauderdale John Maitland, Duke of Lauderdale 1616–1682. Scottish politician. Formerly a zealous Covenanter, he joined the Royalists 1647, and as high commissioner for Scotland 1667–1679 persecuted the Covenanters. He was created duke of Lauderdale 1672, and was a member of the so-called Cabal ministry 1667–73.

Laue Max Theodor Felix von 1879–1960. German physicist who was a pioneer in measuring the wavelength of X-rays by their diffraction through the closely spaced atoms in a crystal. His work led to the powerful technique now used to elucidate the structure of complex biological materials, for example, DNA. He was awarded a Nobel prize 1914.

Laughton Charles 1899–1962. English actor, who became a US citizen 1950. Initially a classical stage actor, his dramatic film roles included the king in *The Private Life of Henry VIII* 1933, Captain Bligh in *Mutiny on the Bounty* 1935, Quasimodo in *The Hunchback of Notre Dame* 1939, and Gracchus in *Spartacus* 1960.

Laurel and Hardy Stan Laurel (1890–1965) and Oliver Hardy (1892–1957) US film comedians (Laurel was English-born). Their films include many short silent films, as well as *Way Out West* 1937, and *A Chump at Oxford* 1940.

Laurence Margaret 1926–1987. Canadian writer, whose novels include *A Jest of God* 1966 and *The Diviners* 1974. She also wrote short stories set in Africa, where she lived for a time.

Laurier Wilfrid 1841–1919. Canadian politician, leader of the Liberal Party 1887–1919 and prime minister 1896–1911. The first French-Canadian to hold the office, he encouraged immigration into Canada from Europe and the USA, established a separate Canadian navy, and sent troops to help Britain in the Boer War.

Laval Pierre 1883–1945. French right-wing politician. He was prime minister and foreign secretary 1931–32, and again 1935–36. In World War II he joined Pétain's Vichy government as vice-premier June 1940; dismissed Dec 1940, he was reinstated by Hitler's orders as head of the government and foreign minister 1942. After the war he was executed.

Laval, born near Vichy, entered the chamber of deputies 1914 as a Socialist, but after World War I moved towards the right. His second period as prime minister was marked by the Hoare–Laval Pact for concessions to Italy in Abyssinia. His share in the deportation of French labour to Germany made him universally hated. On the Allied invasion he fled the country, but was arrested in Austria, tried for treason, and shot after trying to poison himself.

La Vallière Louise de la Baume le Blanc, Duchesse de la Vallière 1644–1710. Mistress of the French king Louis XIV; she gave birth to four children 1661–74. She retired to a convent on her supersession by Mme de Montespan.

Laver Rodney George 'Rod' 1938– . Australian lawn tennis player. He was one of the greatest left-handed players, and the only player to perform the Grand Slam twice (1962 and 1969).

He won four Wimbledon singles titles, the Australian title three times, the US Open twice, and the French Open twice. He turned professional after winning Wimbledon 1962 but returned when the championships were opened to professionals 1968.

Lavoisier Antoine Laurent 1743–1794. French chemist. He proved that combustion needed only a part of 'air' which he called oxygen, thereby destroying the theory of phlogiston (an imaginary 'fire element' released during combustion). With Laplace, he showed that water was a compound of oxygen and hydrogen. In this way he established the modern basic rules of chemical combination.

Lavrentiev Mikhail 1900– . Soviet scientist, who developed the Akademgorodok ('Science City') in Novosibirsk, Russia from 1957.

Law Andrew Bonar 1858–1923. British Conservative politician, born in New Brunswick, Canada. He made a fortune in Scotland as a banker and iron-merchant, and entered Parliament 1900. Elected leader of the opposition 1911, he became colonial secretary in Asquith's coalition government 1915–16. Chancellor of the Exchequer 1916–19, and Lord Privy Seal 1919–21 in Lloyd George's coalition. He formed a Conservative Cabinet 1922, but resigned on health grounds.

Law William 1686–1761. English cleric. His Jacobite (pro-James II) opinions caused him to lose his fellowship at Emmanuel College, Cambridge, in 1714. His most famous work is *A Serious Call to a Devout and Holy Life* 1728, which influenced the ◊Wesleys.

Lawes Henry 1596–1662. English composer, whose works include music for Milton's masque *Comus* 1634. His brother *William* (1602–45) was also a composer.

Lawes John Bennet 1814–1900. English agriculturist, who patented the first artificial manure 'super-phosphate', in 1843, he established the Rothamsted Experimental Station (Hertfordshire) at his birthplace.

Lawler Ray 1921– . Australian actor and playwright. He is best known for his play *The Summer of the Seventeenth Doll* 1955 about sugar-cane cutters, in which he played the lead role in the first production in Melbourne.

Lawrence D(avid) H(erbert) 1885–1930. English writer, who in his work expressed his belief in emotion and the sexual impulse as creative and true to human nature. His novels include *Sons and Lovers* 1913, *The Rainbow* 1915, *Women in Love* 1921, and *Lady Chatterley's Lover* 1928. Lawrence also wrote short stories, for example 'The Woman Who Rode Away', and poetry.

Son of a Nottinghamshire miner, Lawrence studied at University College, Nottingham, and became a teacher. He achieved fame with the semi-autobiographical *Sons and Lovers*, which includes a portrayal of his mother (died 1911). In 1914 he married Frieda von Richthofen, ex-wife of his university professor, with whom he had run away 1912, and who was the model for Ursula Brangwen in *The Rainbow*, suppressed for obscenity, and its sequel *Women in Love*. His travels in search of health (he suffered from tuberculosis, from which he eventually died near Nice) prompted books such as *Mornings in Mexico* 1927. *Lady Chatterley's Lover* 1928 was banned as obscene in the UK until 1960.

Lawrence English novelist and poet D H Lawrence.

Lawrence Ernest O(rlando) 1901–1958. US physicist. His invention of the cyclotron pioneered the production of artificial radioisotopes.

He was professor of physics at the University of California, Berkeley, from 1930 and director of the Radiation Laboratory from 1936, which he built up into a large, brilliant school for research in nuclear physics. He was awarded a Nobel prize in 1939.

Lawrence Gertrude 1898–1952. English actress who began as a dancer in the 1920s and later took leading roles in musical comedies. Her greatest successes were *Private Lives* 1930–31, written especially for her by Noël Coward, with whom she co-starred, and *The King and I* 1951.

Lawrence Thomas 1769–1830. British painter, the leading portraitist of his day. He became painter to George III in 1792 and president of the Royal Academy 1820.

In addition to British royalty, he painted a series of European sovereigns and politicians (Waterloo Chamber, Windsor Castle, Berkshire) commissioned after the Allied victory at Waterloo.

Lawrence T(homas) E(dward) 1888–1935. British soldier, known as 'Lawrence of Arabia'. Appointed to the military intelligence department in Cairo during World War I, he took part in negotiations for an Arab revolt against the Turks, and in 1916 attached himself to the emir Faisal. He showed himself a guerrilla leader of genius, combining raids on Turkish communications with the stirring up of revolt among the Arabs. In 1935 he was killed in a motorcycle accident.

He was born in Wales; studied at Oxford, and during 1910–14 took part in archaeological expeditions to Syria and Mesopotamia. He joined the Royal Air Force in 1922 as an aircraftman under the name Ross, transferring to the tank corps under the name T E Shaw in 1923 when his identity became known. His account of the Arab revolt, *Seven Pillars of Wisdom* 1935 (published privately 1926), has been described as the last great romantic war book; *The Mint* 1955 was an account of life in the ranks.

Lawrence, St died 258. Christian martyr. Probably born in Spain, he became a deacon of Rome under Pope Sixtus II, and, when summoned to deliver the treasures of the church, displayed the beggars in his charge, for which he was broiled on a grid-iron. Feast day 10 Aug.

Lawson Nigel 1932– . British Conservative politician. A former financial journalist, he was financial secretary to the Treasury 1979–81, secretary of state for energy 1981–83, and chancellor of the Exchequer 1983. He resigned in 1989 after criticism of his policy of British membership of the European Monetary System (which limits the exchange rates between European currencies) by government advisor Alan Walters.

Laxness Halldor 1902– . Icelandic novelist, who wrote about Icelandic life in the style of the early sagas. Nobel prize 1955.

Layamon lived about 1200. English poet, author of the *Brut*, a chronicle of about 30,000 alliterative lines on the history of Britain from the legendary Brutus onwards, which gives the earliest version of the Arthurian story in English.

Layard Austen Henry 1817–1894. British archaeologist. He travelled to the Middle East in 1839, conducted two expeditions to Nineveh and Babylon 1845–51, and sent to the UK the specimens forming the greater part of the Assyrian collection in the British Museum.

Lazarus Emma 1849–1887. US poet, author of the poem on the base of the Statue of Liberty which includes the words: 'Give me your tired, your poor/Your huddled masses yearning to breathe free.'

Leach Bernard 1887–1979. British potter. His simple designs, inspired by a period of study in Japan, pioneered a revival of the art. He established the Leach Pottery at St Ives, Cornwall, in 1920.

Leacock Stephen Butler 1869–1944. Canadian humorist, whose writings include *Literary Lapses* 1910, *Sunshine Sketches of a Little Town* 1912, and *Frenzied Fiction* 1918.

Born in Hampshire, he lived in Canada from 1876, and was head of the department of economics at McGill University, Montreal, 1908–36. He published works on politics and economics, and studies of Mark Twain and Charles Dickens.

Leakey Louis (Seymour Bazett) 1903–1972. British archaeologist, born in Kabete, Kenya. In 1958, with his wife Mary Leakey, he discovered gigantic animal fossils in Olduvai Gorge in Tanzania, as well as many early remains of a human type.

Leakey Mary 1913– . British archaeologist. In 1948 she discovered, on Rusinga Island, Lake Victoria, E Africa, the prehistoric ape skull known as Proconsul, about 20 million years old; and human remains at Laetolil, to the south, about 3,750,000 years old.

Leakey Richard 1944– . British archaeologist, son of Louis and Mary Leakey. In 1972 he discovered at Lake Turkana, Kenya, an ape-form skull, estimated to be about 2.9 million years old; it had some human characteristics and a brain capacity of 800 cm^3. In 1984 his team found an almost complete skeleton of *Homo erectus* some 1.6 million years old.

Lean David 1908– . English film director. His films, noted for their atmospheric quality, include *Brief Encounter* 1946, *The Bridge on the River Kwai* 1957 (Academy Award), *Lawrence of Arabia* 1962 (Academy Award), and *A Passage to India* 1985.

Lear Edward 1812–1888. English artist and humorist. His *Book of Nonsense* 1846 popularized the limerick. He first attracted attention by his paintings of birds, and later turned to landscapes. He travelled in Italy, Greece, Egypt, and India, publishing books on his travels with his own illustrations, and spent most of his later life in Italy.

Leavis F(rank) R(aymond) 1895–1978. English literary critic, and co-founder (with his wife Q D Leavis) and editor of the controversial review *Scrutiny* 1932–53. He championed the work of D H Lawrence and James Joyce, and in 1962 attacked C P Snow's theory of 'Two Cultures'. His other works include *New Bearings in English Poetry* 1932 and *The Great Tradition* 1948. He was a lecturer at Cambridge University.

Leavitt Henrietta Swan 1868–1921. US astronomer, who in 1912 discovered the *period-luminosity law* that links the brightness of a Cepheid variable star to its period of variation. This law allows astronomers to use Cepheid variables as 'standard candles' for measuring distances in space.

Lebedev Peter Nikolaievich 1866–1912. Russian physicist. He proved by experiment, and then measured, the minute pressure which light exerts upon a physical body.

Leblanc Nicolas 1742–1806. French chemist who in 1790 developed a process for making sodium carbonate (soda ash) from sodium chloride (common salt).

Leblanc devised this method of producing soda (for use in making glass, paper, soap, and various other chemicals) to win a prize offered in 1775 by the French Academy of Sciences, but the Revolutionary government granted him only a patent (1791), which they seized along with his factory three years later. A broken man, Leblanc committed suicide.

Lebrun Albert 1871–1950. French politician. He became president of the senate in 1931 and in 1932 was chosen as president of the republic. In 1940 he handed his powers over to Marshal Pétain.

Le Brun Charles 1619–1690. French artist, painter to Louis XIV from 1662. In 1663 he became director of the French Academy and of the Gobelin factory, which produced art, tapestries, and furnishings for the new palace of Versailles.

In the 1640s he studied under the painter Poussin in Rome. Returning to Paris in 1646, he worked on large decorative schemes including the *Galerie des glaces* (Hall of Mirrors) at Versailles. He also painted portraits.

Le Carré John. Pseudonym of David John Cornwell 1931– . English thriller writer. His low-key realistic accounts of complex espionage include *The Spy Who Came in from the Cold* 1963, *Tinker Tailor Soldier Spy* 1974, *Smiley's People* 1980, and *The Little Drummer Girl* 1983. He was a member of the Foreign Service 1960–64.

Leclair Jean-Marie 1697–1764. French violinist and composer. Originally a dancer and ballet-master, he composed ballet music, operas (*Scilla* and *Glaucus*), and violin concertos.

Leclanché Georges 1839–1882. French engineer. In 1866 he invented a primary electrical cell, the *Leclanché cell,* which is still the basis of most dry batteries.

Leconte de Lisle Charles Marie René 1818–1894. French poet. He was born on Réunion, settled in Paris 1846 and headed the anti-Romantic group Les Parnassiens 1866–76. His work drew inspiration from the ancient world, as in *Poèmes antiques/Antique Poems* 1852, *Poèmes barbares/Barbaric Poems* 1862, and *Poèmes tragiques/Tragic Poems* 1884.

Le Corbusier Assumed name of Charles-Édouard Jeanneret 1887–1965. Swiss architect. His functionalist approach to town planning in industrial society was based on the interrelation between modern machine forms and the techniques of modern architecture. His concept, *La Ville Radieuse,* developed in Marseille (1945–50) and Chandigarh, India, placed buildings and open spaces with related functions in a circular formation, with buildings based on standard sized units mathematically calculated according to the proportions of the human figure.

He was originally a painter and engraver, but turned his attention to the problems of contemporary industrial society. *Vers une architecture* 1923 and *Le Modulor* 1948 have had worldwide influence on town planning and building design.

Lecouvreur Adrienne 1692–1730. French actress. She performed at the Comédie Française national theatre, where she first appeared 1717. Her many admirers included the philosopher Voltaire and the army officer Maurice de Saxe; a rival mistress of the latter, the Duchesse de Bouillon, is thought to have poisoned her.

Lederberg Joshua 1925– . US geneticist who showed that bacteria can reproduce sexually, combining genetic material so that offspring possess characteristics of both parent organisms.

Lederberg is considered a pioneer of genetic engineering, a science that relies on the possibility of artificially shuffling genes from cell to cell.

Ledru-Rollin Alexandre Auguste 1807–1874. French politician and contributor to the radical and socialist journal *La Réforme*. He became minister for home affairs in the provisional government formed 1848 after the overthrow of Louis Philippe and the creation of the Second Republic, but he opposed the elected president Louis Napoleon.

Le Duc Tho 1911– . North Vietnamese diplomat, who was joint winner (with US secretary of state Kissinger) of the Nobel Peace Prize 1973 for his part in the negotiations to end the Vietnam War. He indefinitely postponed receiving the award.

Lee Bruce. Stage name of Lee Yuen Kam 1941–1973. US 'Chinese Western' film actor, an expert in kung fu who popularized the oriental martial arts in the West.

Lee Christopher 1922– . British film actor, whose tall, gaunt figure was memorable in the title role of *Dracula* 1958 and its sequels. He has not lost his sinister image in subsequent Hollywood productions. His other films include *Hamlet* 1948, *The Mummy* 1959, *Julius Caesar* 1970, and *The Man with the Golden Gun* 1974.

Lee Jennie, Baroness Lee 1904–1988. British socialist politician. On the left wing of the Labour Party, she was on its National Executive Committee 1958–70 and was minister of education 1967–70, during which time she was responsible for founding the Open University 1969.

She became a member of Parliament for the Independent Labour Party at the age of 24, and in 1934 married Aneurin ◊Bevan.

Lee Laurie 1914– . English writer, born near Stroud, Gloucestershire. His works include the autobiographical novel *Cider with Rosie* 1959, a classic evocation of childhood; nature poetry such as *The Bloom of Candles* 1947, and travel writing including *A Rose for Winter* 1955.

Lee Nathaniel 1653–1692. English dramatist. From 1675 he wrote a number of extravagant tragedies, such as *The Rival Queens* 1677.

Lee Robert E(dward) 1807–1870. US Confederate general in the American Civil War, a military strategist. As military adviser to Jefferson ◊Davis, president of the Confederacy, and as commander of the army of N Virginia, he made several raids into Northern territory, but was defeated at Gettysburg and surrendered 1865 at Appomattox.

Lee, born in Virginia, was commissioned in 1829 and served in the Mexican War. In 1859 he suppressed John ◊Brown's raid on Harper's Ferry. On the outbreak of the Civil War in 1861 he joined the Confederate army of the Southern States, and in 1862 received the command of the army of N Virginia and won the Seven Days's Battle defending Richmond, Virginia, the Confederate capital, against Gen McClellan's Union forces. In 1863 Lee won victories at Fredericksburg and Chancellorsville, and in 1864 at Cold Harbor, but was besieged in Petersburg, June 1864–Apr 1865. He surrendered to Gen Grant 9 Apr 1865 at Appomattox courthouse.

Leech John 1817–1864. British caricaturist. He illustrated many books, including Dickens's *A Christmas Carol*, and during 1841–64 contributed about 3,000 humorous drawings and political cartoons to *Punch* magazine.

Lee Kuan Yew 1923– . Singapore politician, prime minister from 1959. Lee founded the anticommunist Socialist People's Action Party 1954 and entered the Singapore legislative assembly 1955. He was elected the country's first prime minister 1959, and took Singapore out of the Malaysian federation 1965.

Lee Teng-hui 1923–. Taiwanese right-wing politician, vice president 1984–88, president and Kuomintang party leader from 1988. Lee, the

Lee US Confederate general Robert E Lee. Siding with the Southern States in the Civil War, he won a number of battles 1862–63 before surrendering in 1865.

country's first island-born leader, is viewed as a reforming technocrat.

Born in Tamsui, Taiwan, Lee taught for two decades as professor of economics at the National Taiwan University before becoming mayor of Taipei 1979. A member of the Kuomintang party and a protégé of Chiang Ching-kuo, he became vice president of Taiwan 1984 and succeeded to both the state presidency and Kuomintang leadership on Chiang's death Jan 1988. He has significantly accelerated the pace of liberalization and Taiwanization in the political sphere.

Leeuwenhoek Anton van 1632–1723. Dutch pioneer of microscopic research. He ground his own lenses, some of which magnified up to 200 times. With these he was able to see individual red blood cells, sperm, and bacteria, achievements not repeated for more than a century.

Le Fanu (Joseph) Sheridan 1814–1873. Irish writer, born in Dublin. He wrote mystery novels and short stories, such as *The House by the Churchyard* 1863, *Uncle Silas* 1864, and *In a Glass Darkly* 1872.

Lefebvre Mgr Marcel 1905– . French Catholic priest. Ordained in 1929, he was a missionary and an archbishop in West Africa until 1962. He opposed the liberalizing reforms of the Second Vatican Council 1962–65 and formed the 'Priestly Cofraternity of Pius X'. In 1976, he was suspended by Pope Paul VI for continuing the unauthorized ordination of priests at his Swiss headquarters. His defiance continued and in June 1988 he was excommunicated by Pope John Paul II, in the first formal schism within the Roman Catholic Church since 1870.

Léger Fernand 1881–1955. French painter, associated with Cubism. From around 1909 he evolved a characteristic style, composing abstract and semiabstract works with cylindrical forms, reducing the human figure to robot components.

Mechanical forms are constant themes in his work, including his designs for the Swedish Ballet 1921–22, murals, and the abstract film *Le Ballet mécanique*/*The Mechanical Ballet*.

Le Guin Ursula K(roeber) 1929– . US writer of science fiction and fantasy. Her novels include *The Left Hand of Darkness* 1969, which questions sex roles; the *Earthsea* trilogy 1968–72; and *The Dispossessed* 1974, which contrasts an anarchist and a capitalist society.

Lehár Franz 1870–1948. Hungarian composer. He wrote many operettas, among them *The Merry Widow* 1905, *The Count of Luxembourg* 1909, *Gypsy Love* 1910, and *The Land of Smiles* 1929. He also composed songs, marches, and a violin concerto.

Lehmann Lotte 1888–1976. German soprano. She excelled in Wagnerian operas and was an outstanding Marschallin in Richard ◊Strauss's *Der Rosenkavalier*.

Lehmann Rosamond Nina 1903–1990. English novelist, whose books include *Invitation to the Waltz* 1932, *The Weather in the Streets* 1936, and *A Sea-Grape Tree* 1976. Once neglected as too romantic, her novels have regained popularity in the 1980s because of their sensitive portrayal of female adolescent experience.

Leibniz Gottfried Wilhelm 1646–1716. German mathematician and philosopher. Independently of, but concurrently with, Newton he developed calculus. In his metaphysical works, such as *The Monadology* 1714, he argued that everything consisted of innumerable units, *monads*, whose individual properties determined their past, present, and future.

Monads, although independent of each other, interacted predictably; this meant that Christian faith and scientific reason need not be in conflict, and that 'this is the best of all possible worlds'. His optimism is satirized in Voltaire's *Candide*.

Leicester Robert Dudley, Earl of Leicester *c.* 1532–1588. English courtier. Son of the duke of Northumberland, he was created Earl of Leicester 1564. Queen Elizabeth I gave him command of the army sent to the Netherlands 1585–87, and of the forces prepared to resist the threat of Spanish invasion 1588.

His good looks won him the favour of Elizabeth, who might have married him if he had not been previously married to Amy Robsart (*c.* 1532–60). When his wife died 1560 by a fall downstairs, Dudley was suspected of murdering her. In 1576 he secretly married the widow of the Earl of Essex.

Leichhardt Friedrich 1813–1848. Prussian-born Australian explorer. In 1843, he walked 965 km/600 mi from Sydney to Moreton Bay, Queensland, and in 1844 walked from Brisbane to Arnhem Land; he disappeared during a further expedition from Queensland 1848.

Leif Ericsson see ◊Ericsson, Leif.

Leigh Mike 1943– . English playwright and director. He directs his own plays which evolve through improvisation before they are scripted; they include the comedies *Abigail's Party* 1977 and *Goose-Pimples* 1981. He wrote and directed the film *High Hopes* 1989.

Leigh Vivien. Pseudonym of Vivien Mary Hartley 1913–1967. English actress, born in Darjeeling, India. She appeared on the stage in London and New York, and won Oscars for her performances as Scarlett O'Hara in *Gone With the Wind* 1939 and as Blanche du Bois in *A Streetcar Named Desire* 1951. She was married to Laurence Olivier 1940–60, and starred with him in the play *Antony and Cleopatra* 1951.

Leigh-Mallory Trafford 1892–1944. British air chief marshal in World War II. He took part in the Battle of Britain and was commander in chief of Allied air forces during the invasion of France.

Leigh English actress Vivien Leigh won an Academy Award for the role of Scarlett O'Hara in the Hollywood epic Gone With the Wind *1939. She and Laurence Olivier were married in 1940 amid a blaze of publicity.*

Leighton Frederic, Baron Leighton 1830–1896. English painter and sculptor. His historical subjects, especially classical scenes, were widely admired, for example *Captive Andromache* 1888 (Manchester City Art Gallery).

Leighton's *Cimabue's Madonna Carried in Procession* 1855, was bought by Queen Victoria. He became president of the Royal Academy 1878 and was made a peer 1896. His house and studio near Holland Park, London, is now a Leighton museum.

Leland John 1506–1552. English antiquary, whose manuscripts have proved a valuable source for scholars. He became chaplain and librarian to Henry VIII, and during 1534–43 toured England collecting material for a history of English antiquities. The *Itinerary* was published in 1710.

Lely Peter. Adopted name of Pieter van der Faes 1618–1680. Dutch painter, active in England from 1641, who painted fashionable portraits in Baroque style. His subjects included Charles I, Cromwell, and Charles II.

He painted a series of admirals, *Flagmen* (National Maritime Museum, Greenwich), and one of *The Windsor Beauties* (Hampton Court, Richmond), fashionable women of Charles II's court.

Lemaître Georges Édouard 1894–1966. Belgian cosmologist. Born in Charleroi, he was ordained a priest 1922 before studying astrophysics in England and the USA. Lemaître predicted that the entire Universe was expanding, which ◊Hubble

confirmed, and 1927 suggested that the expansion had been started by an initial explosion, the Big Bang, a theory that is now generally accepted.

Lemmon 'Jack' (John Uhler III) 1925– . US character actor, often cast as the lead in comedy films such as *Some Like it Hot* 1959 but equally skilled at straight drama, as in *The China Syndrome* 1979.

Le Mond Greg 1961– . US racing cyclist, the first American to win the Tour de France 1986.

A shooting incident in 1987 threatened to end his career but he made a remarkable comeback to regain his Tour de France title 1989 when he won by the smallest ever margin, seven seconds, from Laurent Fignon (France). He won again in 1990.

Lenard Phillip 1862–1947. German physicist who investigated the photoelectric effect (light causes metals to emit electrons) and cathode rays (the stream of electrodes emitted from the cathode in a vacuum tube). Nobel Prize for Physics 1905.

In later life he became obsessed with the need to produce a purely 'Aryan' physics free from the influence of ◊Einstein and other Jewish physicists.

Lenclos Ninon de 1615–1705. French courtesan. As the recognized leader of Parisian society, she was the mistress in turn of many highly placed men, including General Condé and the writer La Rochefoucauld.

Lendl Ivan 1960– . Czechoslovakian lawn tennis player who is the top money winner of all time in the men's game. He has won seven Grand Slam singles titles including the US and French titles three times each. He has won more than $14 million.

Leng Virginia 1955– . British showjumping rider, born in Malta. She has won world, European, and most major domestic championships.

She was a member of the successful British team at two world championships and was the individual champion in 1986 on *Priceless*. She won the European individual title twice, the Badminton horse trials twice, and Burghley on three occasions.

Lenglen Suzanne 1899–1938. French tennis player, Wimbledon singles and doubles champion 1919–23 and 1925, and Olympic champion 1921. She became professional 1926. She also introduced modern sports clothes, designed by Jean ◊Patou.

Lenin Vladimir Ilyich. Adopted name of Vladimir Ilyich Ulyanov 1870–1924. Soviet communist politician and theoretician. Active in the 1905 Revolution, Lenin had to leave Russia when it failed, settling in Switzerland 1914. He returned to Russia after the February revolution of 1917. In Nov 1917 he became leader of a Soviet government, concluded peace with Germany, and organized a successful resistance to White Russian (pro-Tsarist) uprisings and foreign intervention. His modification of traditional Marxist doctrine to fit

Lenin *Communist political theorist and leader Vladimir Lenin with his family in 1922.*

conditions prevailing in Russia became known as *Marxism-Leninism*, the basis of communist ideology.

Lenin was born 22 Apr in Simbirsk (now renamed Ulyanovsk), on the river Volga, and became a lawyer in St Petersburg (now Leningrad). A Marxist from 1889, he was sent to Siberia for spreading revolutionary propaganda 1895–1900. He then edited the political paper *Iskra* ('The Spark') from abroad, and visited London several times. In *What Is to be Done?* 1902 he advocated a professional core of Social Democratic Party activists to spearhead the revolution in Russia, a suggestion accepted by the majority (*bolsheviki*) at the London party congress 1903. From Switzerland he attacked socialist support for World War I as for an 'imperialist' struggle, and wrote *Imperialism* 1917. After the renewed outbreak of revolution in Feb/Mar 1917, he returned to Russia in Apr. From the overthrow of the provisional government Nov 1917 until his death, Lenin effectively controlled the Soviet Union, although an assassination attempt 1918 injured his health. He founded the Third (Communist) International 1919. Communism proving inadequate to put the country on its feet, in 1921 he introduced the private-enterprise New Economic Policy to win over the peasantry and boost agriculture. His embalmed body is in a mausoleum in Red Square, Moscow.

Lennon John 1940–1980. Rock singer and songwriter, former member of the Beatles.

Leno Dan 1861–1904. British comedian. Beginning as an acrobat, he became the idol of the music halls, and was considered the greatest of pantomime 'dames'.

Le Nôtre André 1613–1700. French landscape gardener, creator of the gardens at Versailles and Les Tuileries.

Lenthall William 1591–1662. English lawyer. Speaker of the House of Commons in the so-called Long Parliament of 1640–60, he took an active part in the Restoration.

Lenya Lotte 1905–1981. Adopted name of Austrian actress and singer Karoline Blamauer. She married Kurt ◊Weill in 1926 and appeared in several of the Brecht-Weill operas, notably *The Threepenny Opera* 1928.

Leo III *the Isaurian* c.680–740. Byzantine emperor and soldier. He seized the throne 717, successfully defended Constantinople against the Saracens 717–18, and attempted to suppress the use of images in church worship.

Leo thirteen popes, including:

Leo I St *the Great* c.390–461. Pope from 440 who helped to establish the Christian liturgy. Leo summoned the Chalcedon Council where his *Dogmatical Letter* was accepted as the voice of St Peter. Acting as ambassador to the emperor Valentinian III (425–455), Leo saved Rome from devastation by the Huns by buying off their king, Attila, with large sums of money.

Leo III c.750–816. Pope from 795. After the withdrawal of the Byzantine emperors, the popes had become the real rulers in Rome. Leo III was forced to flee because of a conspiracy in Rome, and took refuge at the court of Charlemagne. He returned to Rome 799, and crowned Charlemagne emperor on Christmas Day 800, establishing the secular sovereignty of the pope over Rome under the suzerainty of the emperor.

Leo X Giovanni de' Medici 1475–1521. Pope from 1513. The son of Lorenzo the Magnificent of Florence, he was created a cardinal at 13. He bestowed on Henry VIII of England the title of Defender of the Faith, but later excommunicated him. A patron of the arts, he sponsored the rebuilding of St Peter's Church, Rome. He raised funds for this by selling indulgences (remissions of punishment for sin), a sale that led the religious reformer Martin Luther to rebel against papal authority. He condemned Luther in the bull *Exsurge domine* 1520 and excommunicated him 1521.

Leo XIII Gioacchino Pecci 1810–1903. Pope from 1878. After a successful career as a papal diplomat, he established good relations between the papacy and European powers, USA, and Japan. He remained intransigent in negotiations with the Italian government over the status of Rome, insisting that he keep control over part of it.

Leo encouraged foreign missions and emphasized the duty of the church in matters of social justice. His encyclical *Rerum novarum* 1891 pointed out the moral duties of employers towards workers.

Leonard Elmore 1925– . US author of westerns and thrillers, marked by vivid dialogue, for example *Stick* 1983 and *Freaky Deaky* 1988.

Leonard Sugar Ray 1956– . US boxer. In 1988 he became the first man to have won world titles at five officially recognized weights. In 1976 he was Olympic light-welterweight champion and won his first professional title in 1979 when he beat Wilfred Benitez for the WBC welterweight title. He has since won titles at junior-middleweight (WBA version) 1981, middleweight (WBC) 1987, light-heavyweight (WBC) 1988, and super-middleweight (WBC) 1988.

Leonardo da Vinci 1452–1519. Italian painter, sculptor, architect, engineer, and scientist, one of the greatest figures of the Italian Renaissance, active in Florence, Milan, and from 1516 France. As state engineer and court painter to the duke of Milan, he produced the *Last Supper* mural about 1495 (Sta Maria delle Grazie, Milan), and on his return to Florence painted the *Mona Lisa* about 1503–06 (Louvre, Paris). His notebooks and drawings show an immensely inventive and enquiring mind, studying aspects of the natural world from anatomy to aerodynamics.

Leonardo was born at Vinci in Tuscany, and studied under ◊Verrocchio in Florence in the 1470s. His earliest dated work is a sketch of the Tuscan countryside 1473 (Uffizi, Florence); his early works include drawings, portraits, and religious scenes, such as the unfinished *Adoration of the Magi* (Uffizi). About 1482 he went to the court of Lodovico Sforza in Milan. In 1500 he returned to Florence (where he was architect and engineer to Cesare Borgia in 1502), and then to Milan 1506. He went to France in 1516 and died at Château Cloux, near Amboise, on the Loire.

Apart from portraits, religious themes, and historical paintings, Leonardo's greatest legacies were his notebooks and drawings. He influenced many of his contemporary artists, including Michelangelo, Raphael, Giorgione, and Bramante.

Leoncavallo Ruggiero 1857–1919. Italian operatic composer, born in Naples. He played in restaurants, composing in his spare time, until in 1892 *Pagliacci* was performed. His other operas include *La Bohème* 1897 (contemporary with Puccini's version) and *Zaza* 1900.

Leone Sergio 1928–1989. Italian film director, responsible for popularizing 'spaghetti' westerns (westerns made in Italy and Spain, usually with a US leading actor and a European supporting cast and film crew) and making a world star of Clint Eastwood. His films include *Per un pugno di dollari/A Fistful of Dollars* 1964, *C'era una volta il West/Once Upon a Time in the West* 1968, and *C'era una Volta in America/Once upon a Time in America* 1984.

Leonidas died 480 BC. King of Sparta. He was killed while defending the pass of Thermopylae with 300

Leonardo da Vinci *Self-portrait of Italian artist Leonardo da Vinci.*

Spartans, 700 Thespians, and 400 Thebans against a huge Persian army.

Leonov Aleksei Arkhipovich 1934– . Soviet cosmonaut. In 1965 he was the first person to walk in space, from the spacecraft *Voskhod 2*.

Leonov Leonid 1899– . Russian novelist and playwright, whose works include the novels *The Badgers* 1925 and *The Thief* 1927, and the drama *The Orchards of Polovchansk* 1938.

Leopardi Giacomo, Count Leopardi 1798–1837. Italian romantic poet. The first collection of his uniquely pessimistic poems, *I Versi/Verses*, appeared 1824, and was followed by his philosophical *Operette Morali/Minor Moral Works* 1827, in prose, and *I Canti/Lyrics* 1831.

Leopardi wrote many of his finest poems, including his patriotic odes, before he was 21. Throughout his life he was tormented by ill-health, by the consciousness of his deformity (he was hunch-backed), by loneliness and a succession of unhappy love-affairs, and by his 'cosmic pessimism' and failure to find consolation in any philosophy.

Leopold three kings of Belgium:

Leopold I 1790–1865. King of Belgium from 1831, having been elected to the throne on the creation of an independent Belgium. Through his marriage, when prince of Saxe-Coburg, to Princess Charlotte Augusta, he was the uncle of Queen ◊Victoria, and exercised considerable influence over her.

Leopold II 1835–1909. King of Belgium from 1865, son of Leopold I. He financed the journalist Stanley's explorations in Africa, which resulted in the foundation of the Congo Free State (now Zaïre), from which he extracted a huge fortune by ruthless exploitation.

Leopold III 1901–1983. King of Belgium from 1934, he surrendered to the Germans 1940. Postwar charges against his conduct led to a regency by his brother Charles, and his eventual abdication 1951 in favour of his son ◊Baudouin.

Leopold two Holy Roman emperors:

Leopold I 1640–1705. Holy Roman emperor from 1658, in succession to his father Ferdinand III. He warred against Louis XIV of France and the Ottoman Empire.

Leopold II 1747–1792. Holy Roman emperor in succession to his brother Joseph II, he was the son of Empress Maria Theresa. His hostility to the French Revolution led to the outbreak of war a few weeks after his death.

Le Pen Jean-Marie 1928– . French extreme right-wing politician. In 1972 he formed the French National Front, supporting immigrant repatriation and capital punishment; the party gained 10% of the national vote in the 1986 election. Le Pen was elected to the European Parliament 1984.

During the 1960s, he was connected with the extremist Organisation de l'Armée Secrète (OAS), devoted to perpetuating French rule in Algeria. The National Front has considerable support among underprivileged white youth but Le Pen's openly fascist statements caused his bid for the presidency 1988 to founder.

Lermontov Mikhail Yurevich 1814–1841. Russian Romantic poet and novelist. In 1837 he was put into active military service in the Caucasus for a revolutionary poem on the death of Pushkin, which criticized Court values, and for participating in a duel. In 1838 he published the psychological novel *A Hero of Our Time* 1840 and a volume of poems *October* 1840.

Lerner Alan Jay 1918–1986. US lyricist, collaborator with Frederick ◊Loewe on musicals including *Brigadoon* 1947, *Paint Your Wagon* 1951, *My Fair Lady* 1956, *Gigi* 1958, and *Camelot* 1960.

Le Sage Alan René 1668–1747. French novelist and dramatist. Born in Brittany, he abandoned law for literature. His novels include *Le Diable boîteux/The Devil upon Two Sticks* 1707 and his picaresque masterpiece *Gil Blas* 1715–1735, much indebted to Spanish originals.

Lesseps Ferdinand, Vicomte de Lesseps 1805–1894. French engineer, constructor of the Suez Canal 1859–69; he began the Panama Canal 1879, but failed when he tried to construct it without locks.

Lessing Doris (May) (born Taylor) 1919– . English novelist, born in Iran. Concerned with social and political themes, particularly the place of women in society, her work includes *The Grass is Singing* 1950, *The Golden Notebook* 1962, *The Good Terrorist* 1985, and the five-novel series *Children of Violence* 1952–69. She has also written an 'inner space fiction' series *Canopus in Argus Archives* 1979–83, and under the pen name 'Jane Somers', *The Diary of a Good Neighbour* 1981.

Lessing Gotthold Ephraim 1729–1781. German dramatist and critic. His plays include *Miss Sara Sampson* 1755, *Minna von Barnhelm* 1767, *Emilia Galotti* 1772; and the verse play *Nathan der Weise* 1779. His works of criticism *Laokoon* 1766 and *Hamburgische Dramaturgie* 1767–68 influenced German literature. He also produced many theological and philosophical writings.

Laokoon analysed the functions of poetry and the plastic arts; *Hamburgische Dramaturgie* reinterpreted Aristotle and attacked the restrictive form of French classical drama in favour of the freer approach of Shakespeare.

Lethaby William Richard 1857–1931. English architect. An assistant to Richard Norman Shaw, he embraced the principles of William Morris and Philip Webb in the Arts and Crafts movement, and was co-founder and first director of the Central School of Arts and Crafts from 1894. He wrote a collection of essays entitled *Form in Civilization* 1922.

Lessing *Political and social themes predominate in the work of novelist Doris Lessing.*

Le Vau Louis 1612–1670. French architect, who drafted the plan of Versailles, and built the Louvre and Les Tuileries in Paris.

Leven Alexander Leslie, 1st Earl of Leven c.1580–1661. Scottish general. He led the Covenanters' army which invaded England in 1640, commanded the Scottish army sent to aid the English Puritans in 1643–46, and shared in the victory of Marston Moor.

Lever Charles James 1806–1872. Irish novelist. He wrote novels of Irish and army life, such as *Harry Lorrequer* 1837, *Charles O'Malley* 1840, and *Tom Burke of Ours* 1844.

Leverrier Urbain Jean Joseph 1811–1877. French astronomer, who predicted the existence and position of the planet Neptune, discovered in 1846.

Lévesque René 1922–1987. French-Canadian politician. In 1968 he founded the Parti Québecois, with the aim of an independent Quebec, but a referendum rejected the proposal 1980. He was premier of Quebec 1976–85.

Levi Primo 1919–1987. Italian novelist. He joined the anti-Fascist resistance during World War II, was captured and sent to Auschwitz concentration camp. He wrote of these experiences in *Se questo e un uomo/If This is a Man* 1947.

Levi-Montalcini Rita 1909– . Italian neurologist who discovered nerve growth factor, a substance that controls how many cells make up the adult nervous system. Nobel prize 1986.

Levi-Montalcini studied at Turin and worked there until the Fascist anti-semitic laws forced her to go into hiding. She continued research into the nervous systems of chick embryos. After the war, she moved to the USA.

Lévi-Strauss Claude 1908– . French anthropologist, who sought to find a universal structure governing all societies, reflected in the way myths are created. His works include *Tristes Tropiques* 1955, and *Mythologiques/Mythologies* 1964–71.

Lewes George Henry 1817–1878. English philosopher and critic. From acting he turned to literature and philosophy; his works include a *Biographical History of Philosophy* 1845–46, and *Life and Works of Goethe* 1855. He married in 1840, but left his wife in 1854 to form a life-long union with the writer Mary Ann Evans (George ◊Eliot), whom he had met in 1851.

Lewis Carl (Frederick Carleton) 1961– . US athlete. At the 1984 Olympic Games he equalled Jesse ◊Owens' performance, winning gold medals in the 100 and 200 metres, sprint relay, and long jump. In the 1988 Olympics, he repeated his golds in the 100 metres and long jump, and won a silver in the 200 metres.

Lewis C(live) S(taples) 1898–1963. British academic and writer, born in Belfast. His books include the medieval study *The Allegory of Love* 1936, and the space fiction *Out of the Silent Planet*

1938. He was a committed Christian and wrote essays in popular theology such as *The Screwtape Letters* 1942 and *Mere Christianity* 1952; the autobiographical *Surprised by Joy* 1955; and a series of books of Christian allegory for children, set in the magic land of Narnia, including *The Lion, the Witch, and the Wardrobe* 1950.

Lewis (Harry) Sinclair 1885–1951. US novelist. He made a reputation with *Main Street* 1920, depicting American small-town life; *Babbitt* 1922, the story of a real-estate dealer of the Midwest caught in the conventions of his milieu; and *Arrowsmith* 1925, a study of a scientist. Nobel prize 1930.

Born in Minnesota, he stayed for a time at Upton Sinclair's socialist colony in New Jersey, then became a freelance journalist. His later books include *It Can't Happen Here* 1945, *Cass Timberlane* 1945, and *The God-Seeker* 1949.

Lewis Jerry. Stage name of Joseph Levitch 1926– . US comic actor, formerly in partnership with Dean Martin (1946–1956). He enjoyed great commercial success as a solo performer and was revered by French critics, but his later films, such as *The Nutty Professor* 1963, were less well received in the USA.

Lewis Jerry Lee 1935– . US rock-and-roll and country singer and pianist. His trademark was the 'pumping piano' style in hits such as 'Whole Lotta Shakin' Going On' and 'Great Balls of Fire' 1957; later recordings include 'What Made Milwaukee Famous' 1968.

Lewis Matthew Gregory 1775–1818. British writer, known as 'Monk' Lewis from his popular terror romance *The Monk* 1795.

Lewis Meriwether 1774–1809. US explorer. He was commissioned by president Thomas Jefferson to find a land route to the Pacific with William Clark (1770–1838). They followed the Missouri River to its source, crossed the Rocky Mountains (aided by Indian girl Sacajawea) and followed the Columbia River to the Pacific, then returned overland to St Louis 1804–06.

Lewis (Percy) Wyndham 1886–1957. English writer and artist, who pioneered Vorticism, which with its feeling of movement sought to reflect the age of industry. He was noted for the hard and aggressive style of both his writing and his painting. His literary works include the novels *Tarr* 1918 and *The Childermass* 1928, the essay *Time and Western Man* 1927, and autobiographies.

Born off Maine, in his father's yacht, he was educated at the Slade art school and in Paris. On returning to England he pioneered the new spirit of art which his friend Ezra Pound called Vorticism; he also edited *Blast*, a literary and artistic magazine proclaiming its principles. Of his paintings, his portraits are especially memorable, such as those of Edith Sitwell and T S Eliot. Although he has been assessed by some as a leading spirit of the early 20th century, his support in the 1930s of Fascist principles and Hitler alienated most critics.

Lewis (William) Arthur 1915– . British economist, born on St Lucia, West Indies. He specialized in the economic problems of developing countries, as in *The Theory of Economic Growth* 1955, and shared a Nobel prize 1979.

Lewton Val. Stage name of Vladimir Ivan Leventon 1904–1951. Russian-born US film producer, responsible for a series of atmospheric 'B' horror films made for RKO in the 1940s, including *Cat People* 1942 and *The Body Snatcher* 1946. He co-wrote several of his films under the adopted name of Carlos Keith.

Lhote André 1885–1962. French artist, influential through his treatises on art. *Rugby* (Musée d'Art Moderne, Paris) is an example of his use of colour and geometric style.

Liaquat Ali Khan 1895–1951. Indian Muslim nationalist politician, prime minister of Pakistan from independence 1947. The chief lieutenant of Muhammad ◊Jinnah, he was a leader of the Muslim League. He was assassinated.

Libby Willard Frank 1908–1980. US chemist, whose development of radiocarbon dating 1947 won him a Nobel prize 1960. The technique determines the age of organic or fossilized material from its radioactive carbon content.

Liberty Arthur Lasenby 1843–1917. shopkeeper and founder of a shop of the same name in Regent Street, London. Originally importing oriental goods, it gradually started selling British Arts and Crafts and Art Nouveau furniture, tableware, and fabrics. Arte Nouveau is sometimes called *stile Liberty* in Italy.

Lichfield Patrick Anson, 5th Earl of Lichfield 1939– . British photographer, known for portraits of the rich and famous.

Lichtenstein Roy 1923– . US Pop artist. His reputation was made with an exhibition in New York 1962. He used advertising and comic-strip imagery, often focusing on popular ideals of romance and heroism, as in *Whaam!* 1963 (Tate Gallery, London).

Liddell Hart Basil 1895–1970. British military scientist. He was an exponent of mechanized warfare, and his ideas were adopted in Germany 1935 in creating the 1st Panzer Division, combining motorized infantry and tanks. From 1937 he advised the UK War Office on army reorganization.

Lie Trygve (Halvdan) 1896–1968. Norwegian Labour politician and diplomat. He became the first secretary-general of the United Nations 1946–53, when he resigned over Soviet opposition to his handling of the Korean War.

He became secretary of the Labour Party 1926. During the German occupation of Norway in World War II he was foreign minister in the exiled government 1941–46, when he helped retain the Norwegian fleet for the Allies.

Liebig Justus, Baron von Liebig 1803–1873. German chemist, a major contributor to agricultural chemistry. He introduced the theory of radicals (an atom or group of atoms, existing fleetingly, with a free bond and therefore reactive), and discovered chloroform and chloral.

Liebknecht Karl 1871–1919. German socialist, son of Wilhelm Liebknecht. A founder of the German Communist Party, originally known as the Spartacus League, he led an unsuccessful revolt in Berlin 1919, and was murdered by army officers.

Liebknecht Wilhelm 1826–1900. German socialist. He was a friend of the communist theoretician Marx, with whom he took part in the revolution of 1848; he was imprisoned for opposition to the Franco-Prussian War. He was the father of Karl Liebknecht.

Lifar Serge 1905–1986. Russian dancer and choreographer. Born in Kiev, he studied under ◊Nijinsky, joined the Diaghilev company 1923, and was *maître de ballet* at the Paris Opéra 1930–44 and 1947–59.

A great experimenter, he produced his first ballet without music, *Icare*, in 1935, and published the same year the controversial *Le Manifeste du choréographie*. He developed the importance of the male dancer in his *Prometheus* 1929 and *Romeo and Juliet* (music by Prokofiev) 1955.

Ligachev Egor (Kuzmich) 1920– . Soviet politician. He joined the Communist Party 1944, and has been a member of the Politburo since 1985. He is regarded as the chief conservative ideologist, and the leader of conservative opposition to President ◊Gorbachev.

Ligeti György (Sándor) 1923– . Hungarian-born Austrian composer who developed a dense, highly chromatic, polyphonic style in which melody and rhythm are sometimes lost in shifting blocks of sound. He achieved international prominence with *Atmosphères* 1961 and *Requiem* 1965, which were used for Kubrick's film epic *2001: A Space Odyssey*. Other works include an opera *Le Grand Macabre* 1978, and *Poème symphonique* 1962, for 100 metronomes.

Lighthill James 1924– . British mathematician, who specialized in the application of mathematics to high-speed aerodynamics and jet propulsion.

Lilburne John 1614–1657. English republican agitator. He was imprisoned 1638–40 for circulating Puritan pamphlets, fought in the Parliamentary army in the Civil War, and by his advocacy of a democratic republic won the leadership of the democratic Levellers. He was twice tried for sedition and acquitted; nonetheless after his acquittal he was imprisoned 1653–55.

Lilienthal Otto 1848–1896. German aviation pioneer, who inspired the ◊Wright brothers. He made and successfully flew many gliders before he was killed in a glider crash.

Liman von Sanders Otto 1855–1929. German general seconded to the Turkish army to become inspector-general and a Turkish field marshal in Dec 1913. This link between the Turks and the Germans caused great suspicion on the part of the French and Russians.

Linacre Thomas c. 1460–1524. English humanist, physician to Henry VIII from 1509, from whom he obtained a character in 1518 to found the Royal College of Physicians, of which he was first president

Lin Biao 1907–1971. Chinese politician and general. He joined the Communists 1927, became a commander of Mao Zedong's Red Army, and led the Northeast People's Liberation Army in the civil war after 1945. He became defence minister 1959, and as vice chairman of the party 1969, he was expected to be Mao's successor, but he lost favour, perhaps because of his control over the army. After an attempted coup failed, he was reported to have been killed in an aeroplane crash in Mongolia 17 Sept 1971.

Lincoln Abraham 1809–1865. 16th president of the USA 1861–65. In the US Civil War, his chief concern was the preservation of the Union from which the Confederate (Southern) slave states had seceded on his election. In 1863 he announced the freedom of the slaves with the *Emancipation Proclamation*. He was re-elected 1864 with victory for the North in sight, but assassinated at the end of the war.

Lincoln was born in a log cabin in Kentucky. Self-educated, he practised law from 1837 in Springfield, Illinois. He was a member of the state legislature 1832–42, and was known as *Honest Abe*. He joined the new Republican Party 1856, and was elected president 1860 on a minority vote. His refusal to concede to Confederate demands for the evacuation of the federal garrison at Fort Sumter, Charleston, South Carolina, precipitated the first hostilities of the Civil War. In the Gettysburg Address 1863, he declared the aims of preserving a 'nation conceived in liberty, and dedicated to the proposition that all men are created equal'. Re-elected with a large majority 1864 on a National Union ticket, he advocated a reconciliatory policy towards the South 'with malice towards none, with charity for all'. Five days after Gen Lee's surrender, Lincoln was shot in a theatre audience by an actor and Confederate sympathizer, John Wilkes ◊Booth.

Lind Jenny 1820–1887. Swedish soprano of remarkable range, nicknamed the 'Swedish nightingale'.

Lindbergh Charles (Augustus) 1902–1974. US aviator, who made the first solo non-stop flight across the Atlantic (New York–Paris) 1927 in the *Spirit of St Louis*.

Lincoln *President of the US during the Civil War, Abraham Lincoln. His main aim was to preserve the union and prevent the secession of the southern states.*

Lindsay (Nicholas) Vachel 1879–1931. US poet. He wandered the country, living by reciting his balladlike verse, including *General William Booth enters into Heaven* 1913, *The Congo* 1914, and *Johnny Appleseed*.

Linlithgow John Adrian Louis Hope, 1st Marquess Linlithgow 1860–1908. British administrator, son of the 6th earl of Hopetoun, first governor-general of Australia 1900–02.

Linnaeus Carolus 1707–1778. Swedish naturalist and physician. His botanical work *Systema Naturae* 1758 contained his system for classifying plants into groups depending on the number of stamens in their flowers, providing a much-needed framework for identification. He also devised the concise and precise system for naming plants and animals, using one Latin (or Latinized) word to represent the genus and a second to distinguish the species.

Lin Piao alternative form of ◊Lin Biao.

Lipatti Dinu 1917–1950. Romanian pianist, who perfected a small repertoire, notably Chopin. He died of leukaemia at 33.

Lipchitz Jacques 1891–1973. Lithuanian-born sculptor, active in Paris from 1909; he emigrated to the USA 1941. He was one of the first Cubist sculptors.

Li Peng 1928– . Chinese communist politician, a member of the Politburo from 1985, and head of government from 1987. He is the adopted son of the communist leader Zhou Enlai. During the pro-democracy demonstrations 1989 he supported the massacre of students by Chinese troops, and the subsequent executions of others.

Li was born at Chengdu in Sichuan province, the son of the writer Li Shouxun (who took part in the Nanchang rising 1927 and was executed 1930). He studied at the communist headquarters of Yanan 1941–47 and trained as a hydro-electric engineer at the Moscow Power Institute from 1948. He was appointed minister of the electric power industry 1981, a vice premier 1983, and prime minister 1987. He favours maintaining firm central and party control over the economy, and seeks improved relations with the USSR.

Lipmann Fritz 1899–1986. US biochemist. He investigated the means by which the cell acquires energy and highlighted the crucial role played by the energy rich phosphate molecule, adenosine triphosphate (ATP). For this and further work on metabolism, Lipmann shared the 1953 Nobel Prize for Medicine with Hans Krebs.

Li Po 705–762. Chinese poet. He wrote in traditional forms, but his exuberance, the boldness of his imagination, and the intensity of his feeling have won him recognition as perhaps the greatest of all Chinese poets. Although he was mostly concerned with higher themes, he also celebrated the joys of drinking.

Lippershey Hans c.1570–c.1619. Dutch spectacle maker, credited with inventing the telescope 1608.

Lippi Filippino 1457–1504. Italian painter of the Florentine school, trained by Botticelli. He produced altarpieces and several fresco cycles, full of detail and drama, elegant and finely drawn. He was the son of Filippo Lippi.

Lippi Filippo 1406–1469. Italian painter, called *Fra* (Brother) Filippo, born in Florence and patronized by the Medici. He was a monk, and was tried in the 1450s for abducting a nun (the mother of his son Filippino). He painted many altarpieces, of Madonnas and groups of saints.

Lippmann Gabriel 1845–1921. French doctor, who invented the direct colour process in photography. He won the Nobel Prize for Physics in 1908.

Lister Joseph, 1st Baron Lister 1827–1912. English surgeon, and founder of antiseptic surgery, influenced by Louis ◊Pasteur's work on bacteria. He introduced dressings soaked in carbolic acid and strict rules of hygiene to combat the increase in wound sepsis (the number of surgical operations had increased considerably, following the introduction of anaesthetics). Death rates, which had been more than 40%, fell dramatically. He was professor of surgery at Glasgow 1860–69, at Edinburgh 1869–77, and at King's College, London 1877–92. He was president of the Royal

Lister English surgeon Joseph Lister.

Society 1895–1900, and was created Baron Lister of Lyme Regis 1887.

Liszt Franz 1811–1886. Hungarian pianist and composer. An outstanding virtuoso of the piano, he was an established concert artist by the age of 12. His expressive, romantic, and frequently chromatic works include piano music (*Transcendental Studies* 1851), symphonies, piano concertos, and organ music. Much of his music is programmatic; he also originated the symphonic poem.

Liszt was taught by his father, then by Karl Czerny (1791–1857). He travelled widely in Europe, producing an opera *Don Sanche* in Paris at the age of 14. As musical director and conductor at Weimar 1848–59, he was a champion of the music of Berlioz and Wagner.

Retiring to Rome, he turned again to his early love of religion, and in 1865 became a secular priest (adopting the title Abbé), but he continued to teach and give concert tours. Many of his compositions are lyrical, often technically difficult, piano works, including the *Liebesträume* and the *Hungarian Rhapsodies*, based on gypsy music. He also wrote an opera and a symphony; masses and oratorios; songs; and piano arrangements of works by Beethoven, Schubert, and Wagner among others. He died at Bayreuth.

Littlewood Joan 1914– . English theatre director. She was responsible for many vigorous productions at the Theatre Royal, Stratford (London) 1953–75, such as *A Taste of Honey* 1959, *The Hostage* 1959–60, and *Oh, What a Lovely War* 1963.

Litvinov Maxim 1876–1951. Soviet politician, commissioner for foreign affairs under Stalin from Jan 1931 until his removal from office in May 1939.

Liu Shaoqi formerly *Liu Shao-chi* 1898–1969. Chinese communist politician, in effective control of government 1960–65. A labour organizer, he was a firm proponent of the Soviet line of development based around disciplined one-party control, the use of incentive gradings, and priority for industry over agriculture. This was opposed by Mao Zedong, but began to be implemented when Liu was in power as state president 1960–65. In 1967, during the Cultural Revolution, Liu was brought down.

He was stripped of his post and expelled from the CCP Apr 1969 and banished to Kaifeng in Henan province, where he died Nov 1969 after being locked in a disused bank vault. He was rehabilitated ten years later.

Liverpool Robert Banks Jenkinson, 2nd Earl Liverpool 1770–1825. British Tory politician. He entered Parliament 1790, and was foreign secretary 1801–03, home secretary 1804–06 and 1807–09, war minister 1809–12, and prime minister 1812–27. His government conducted the Napoleonic Wars to a successful conclusion, but its ruthless suppression of freedom of speech and of the press aroused such opposition that during 1815–20 revolution frequently seemed imminent.

Livia Drusilla 58 BC–AD 29. Roman empress, wife of ◊Augustus from 39 BC, she was the mother by her first husband of ◊Tiberius and engaged in intrigue to secure his succession to the imperial crown. She remained politically active to the end of her life.

Livingstone David 1813–1873. Scottish missionary explorer. In 1841, he went to Africa, reached Lake Ngami 1849, followed the Zambezi to its

Livingstone Scottish doctor and missionary David Livingstone was the first European to explore many parts of Central and East Africa.

mouth, saw the Victoria Falls 1855, and went to East and Central Africa 1858–64, reaching Lakes Shirwa and Malawi. From 1866, he tried to find the source of the river Nile, and reached Ujiji Oct 1871.

British explorer Henry Stanley joined Livingstone in Ujiji, and the two explored Africa together. Livingstone not only mapped a great deal of the continent but also helped to end the slave trade by Arabs.

Livingstone died in Old Chitambo (in modern Zambia) and was buried in Westminster Abbey, London.

Livingstone Ken(neth) 1945– . British left-wing Labour politician. He was leader of the Greater London Council (GLC) 1981–86 and a member of Parliament from 1987.

Livy Titus Livius 59 BC–AD 17. Roman historian, author of a *History of Rome* from the city's foundation to 9 BC, based partly on legend. It was composed of 142 books, of which 35 survive, covering the periods from the arrival of Aeneas in Italy to 293 BC and from 218–167 BC.

Li Xiannian 1905– . Chinese politician, member of the Chinese Communist Party (CCP) Politburo from 1956. He fell from favour during the 1966–69 Cultural Revolution, but was rehabilitated as finance minister 1973, supporting cautious economic reform. Li was state president 1983–88.

He retains a seat on the Politburo's standing committee and became chairman of the The Chinese People's Political Consultative Conference (CPPCC).

Llewellyn Richard. Pen name of Richard Vivian Llewellyn Lloyd 1907–1983. Welsh writer. *How Green Was My Valley* 1939, a novel about a S Wales mining family, was made into a play and a film.

Llewelyn two kings of Wales:

Llewelyn I 1173–1240. King of Wales from 1194, who extended his rule to all Wales not in Norman hands, driving the English from N Wales 1212, and taking Shrewsbury 1215. During the early part of Henry III's reign, he was several times attacked by English armies. He was married to Joanna, illegitimate daughter of King John.

Llewelyn II *c.* 1225–1282. King of Wales from 1246, grandson of Llewelyn I. In 1277 Edward I of England compelled Llewelyn to acknowledge him as overlord and to surrender S Wales. His death while leading a national uprising ended Welsh independence.

Lloyd Harold 1893–1971. US film comedian, noted for his 'trademark' of spectacles with thick horn rims. He appeared from 1913 in silent and talking films.

Lloyd John lived 15th century. Welsh seaman, known as John Scolvus, 'the skilful', who carried on an illegal trade with Greenland and is claimed to have reached North America, sailing as far south as Maryland, in 1477 (15 years before the voyage of Columbus).

Lloyd Marie. Stage name of Matilda Alice Victoria Wood 1870–1922. English music-hall artist, whose Cockney songs embodied the music-hall traditions of 1890s comedy.

Lloyd Selwyn see ◊Selwyn Lloyd, British Conservative politician.

Lloyd George David 1863–1945. Welsh Liberal politician, prime minister 1916–22. A pioneer of social reform, as chancellor of the Exchequer 1908–15 he introduced old-age pensions 1908 and health and unemployment insurance 1911. High unemployment, intervention in the Russian Civil War, and use of the 'Black and Tans' military police force in Ireland eroded his support as prime minister, and creation of the Irish Free State 1921, and his pro-Greek policy against the Turks caused the collapse of his coalition government.

Lloyd George was born in Manchester, became a solicitor, and was member of Parliament for Caernarvon Boroughs from 1890. During the Boer War, he was prominent as a pro-Boer. His 1909 budget (with graduated direct taxes and taxing land values) provoked the Lords to reject it, and resulted in the Act of 1911 limiting their powers. He held ministerial posts during World War I until 1916 when there was an open breach between him and Prime Minister ◊Asquith, and he became prime minister of a coalition government. Securing a unified Allied command, he enabled the Allies to withstand the last German offensive and achieve victory. After World War I he had a major role in the Versailles peace treaty.

In the 1918 elections, he achieved a huge majority over Labour and Asquith's followers. He had become largely distrusted within his own party by 1922, and never regained power.

Lloyd Webber Andrew 1948– . English composer. His early musicals, with lyrics by Tim Rice, include *Joseph and the Amazing Technicolor Dreamcoat* 1968; *Jesus Christ Superstar* 1970; and *Evita* 1978, based on the life of the Argentinian leader Eva Perón. He also wrote *Cats* 1981 and *The Phantom of the Opera* 1986.

Llull Ramon 1232–1316. Catalan scholar and mystic. In 1262, he became a monk and later a missionary in N Africa and Asia. He produced treatises on theology, mysticism, and chivalry in Catalan, Latin, and Arabic. His *Ars Magna* is one of the greatest medieval encyclopedias.

Lobachevsky Nikolai Ivanovich 1792–1856. Russian mathematician, who concurrently with, but independently of, ◊Gauss and the Hungarian Janos Bolyai (1802–1860), founded non-Euclidean geometry. Lobachevsky published the first account of the subject in 1829, but his work went unrecognized until ◊Riemann's system was published.

Lobengula 1833–1894. King of Matabeleland (now part of Zimbabwe) 1870–93. After accepting British protection from internal and external threats to his leadership 1888, he came under increasing pressure from British mining interests to allow exploitation of goldfields near Bulawayo, and was overthrown 1893 by a military expedition organized by Cecil ◊Rhodes' South African Company.

Lochner Stephan died 1451. German painter, active in Cologne, a master of the International Gothic style. Most of his work is still in Cologne, for example the *Virgin in the Rose Garden* (Wallraf-Richartz Museum).

Locke John 1632–1704. English philosopher. His *Essay Concerning Human Understanding* 1690 maintained that experience was the only source of knowledge (empiricism), and that 'we can have knowlege no farther than we have ideas' prompted by such experience. *Two Treatises on Government* 1690 was influential in forming modern ideas of liberal democracy.

Born in Somerset, he studied at Oxford, practised medicine, and in 1667 became secretary to the Earl of Shaftesbury. He consequently fell under suspicion as a Whig and in 1683 fled to Holland, where he lived until the 1688 revolution. In later life he published many works on philosophy, politics, theology, and economics; these include *Letters on Toleration* 1689–92, and *Some Thoughts Concerning Education* 1693. His *Two Treatises on Government* supplied the classical statement of Whig theory, and enjoyed great influence in America and France. It supposed that governments derive their authority from popular consent (regarded as a 'contract'), so that a government may be rightly overthrown if it infringes

Locke English philosopher John Locke wrote Two Treatises on Government *and the* Essay Concerning Human Understanding. *The painting is by Dutch artist Herman Verelst (c. 1689).*

such fundamental rights of the people as religious freedom. He believed that, at birth, the mind was a blank, and that all ideas came from sense impressions.

Lodge David (John) 1935– . English novelist, short story writer, and critic. Much of his fiction concerns the role of Catholicism in mid-20th-century England, exploring the situation both through broad comedy and parody, as in *The British Museum is Falling Down* 1967, and realistically, as in *How Far Can You Go?* 1980.

Lodge Henry Cabot 1850–1924. US historian, Republican senator from 1893, and chairman of the Senate Foreign Relations Committee after World War I, who influenced the USA to stay out of the League of Nations 1920.

Lodge Henry Cabot, Jr 1902–1985. US diplomat. He was Eisenhower's campaign manager, and US representative at the United Nations 1953–60. Ambassador to South Vietnam 1963–64 and 1965–67, he took over from Harriman as Nixon's negotiator in the Vietnam peace talks 1969. He was a grandson of the elder Henry Cabot Lodge.

Lodge Oliver Joseph 1851–1940. British physicist. He developed a system of wireless communication in 1894, and his work was influential in the development of radio receivers. He became greatly interested in psychic research after his son was killed in 1915.

Lodge Thomas *c.*1558–1625. English author, whose romance *Rosalynde* 1590 was the basis of Shakespeare's *As You Like It.*

Loeb James 1867–1933. German banker, born in New York, who financed the *Loeb Classical Library* of Greek and Latin authors, which gives original text with parallel translation.

Loewe Frederick 1901–1988. US composer of musicals, born in Berlin. Son of an operatic tenor, he studied under Busoni, and in 1924 went with his father to the USA. In 1942 he joined forces with the lyricist Alan Jay Lerner (1918–86), and their joint successes include *Brigadoon* 1947, *Paint Your Wagon* 1951, *My Fair Lady* 1956, *Gigi* 1958, and *Camelot* 1960.

Loewi Otto 1873–1961. German physiologist, whose work on the nervous system established that a chemical substance is responsible for the stimulation of one neurone by another.

The substance was shown by the physiologist Henry ◊Dale to be acetylcholine, now known to be one of the most vital neurotransmitters. For this work Loewi and Dale were jointly awarded the 1936 Nobel Prize for Medicine.

Lofting Hugh 1886–1947. English writer and illustrator of children's books, especially the 'Dr Dolittle' series, in which the hero can talk to animals. Lofting was born in Maidenhead, Berkshire, was originally a civil engineer, and went to the USA 1912.

Lombard Carole. Stage name of Jane Alice Peters 1908–1942. US comedy film actress. Her successful career, which included starring roles in some of the best comedies of the 1930s, was tragically cut short by her death in a plane crash; her films include *Twentieth Century* 1934, *My Man Godfrey* 1936, and *To Be or Not To Be* 1942.

Lombroso Cesare 1836–1909. Italian criminologist. His major work is *L'uomo delinquente* 1889. He held the now discredited idea that there was a physically distinguishable criminal 'type'.

He became a professor of mental diseases at Pavia in 1862. Subsequently he held chairs in forensic medicine, psychiatry, and criminal anthropology at Turin.

London Jack (John Griffith) 1876–1916. US novelist, born in San Francisco. He is best known for adventure stories, for example, *The Call of the Wild* 1903, *The Sea Wolf* 1904, and *White Fang* 1906.

Long Huey 1893–1935. US Democratic politician, nicknamed 'the Kingfish', governor of Louisiana 1928–31, US senator for Louisiana 1930–35. A legendary public speaker, he was popular with poor white voters for his programme of social and economic reform, which he called the 'Share Our Wealth' programme, and which represented a significant challenge to Roosevelt's New Deal economic programme, but his own extravagance, including the state capitol building at Baton Rouge built of bronze and marble, was widely criticized, and he was also accused of corruption. He was assassinated.

Longfellow Henry Wadsworth 1807–1882. US poet, born in Portland, Maine. He is remembered for ballads ('Excelsior' and 'The Wreck of the Hesperus'), the narrative *Evangeline* 1847, and his metrically haunting *The Song of Hiawatha* 1855.

Longford Frank (Francis Aungier) Pakenham, 7th Earl of Longford 1905– . Anglo-Irish Labour politician. He was brought up a Protestant but is a leading Catholic. He is an advocate of penal reform.

He worked in the Conservative Party Economic Research Department 1930–32, yet became a member of the Labour Party and held ministerial posts 1948–51 and 1964–68.

Longinus Cassius 213–273. Greek philosopher. He taught in Athens for many years. Adviser to ◊Zenobia of Palmyra, he instigated her revolt against Rome, and was put to death when she was captured.

Longinus Dionysius lived 1st century AD. Greek critic, author of a treatise *On the Sublime*, which influenced Dryden and Pope.

Lonsdale Hugh Cecil Lowther, 5th Earl of Lonsdale 1857–1944. British sporting enthusiast. The *Lonsdale Belts* in boxing, first presented 1909, are named after him.

Lonsdale, an expert huntsman, steeplechaser, boxer, and yachtsman, was notorious for extra-marital affairs, and was ordered to leave Britain by Queen Victoria after a scandal with actress Violet Cameron. As a result, he set off to the Arctic 1888 for 15 months, travelling by boat and sleigh through N Canada to Alaska. The collection of Inuit (Eskimo) artefacts he brought back is now in the Museum of Mankind, London.

Loos Adolf 1870–1933. Viennese architect. He rejected the ornamentation and curved lines of the Viennese *Jugendstil* Art Nouveau movement. His most important buildings are private houses on Lake Geneva 1904 and the Steiner House in Vienna 1910, but his main importance is as a polemicist; for example the article *Ornament and Crime* 1908.

Loos Anita 1888–1981. US writer, author of the humorous fictitious diary *Gentlemen Prefer Blondes* 1925.

Lope de Vega (Carpio) Felix 1562–1635. Spanish poet and dramatist, founder of modern Spanish drama. He was born in Madrid, served with the Armada 1588, and in 1613 took holy orders. He wrote epics, pastorals, odes, sonnets, and novels, and reputedly over 1,500 plays (of which 426 are still in existence), mostly tragi-comedies. He set out his views on drama in *Arte nuevo de hacer comedias/The New Art of Writing Plays* 1609, while re affirming the classical form. *Fuenteovejuna* 1614 has been acclaimed as the first proletarian drama.

Lopes Fernal 4th century Portuguese medieval historian, whose *Crónicas/Chronicles* (begun 1434) relate vividly the history of the Portuguese monarchy between 1357 and 1411.

López Carlos Antonio 1790–1862. Paraguayan dictator (in succession to his uncle José Francia) from 1840. He achieved some economic improvement; he was succeeded by his son Francisco López.

López Francisco Solano 1827–1870. Paraguayan dictator in succession to his father Carlos López. He involved the country in a war with Brazil, Uruguay, and Argentina, during which approximately 80% of the population died.

Lopez Nancy 1957– . US golfer, who turned professional 1977 and became in 1979 the first woman golfer to win $200,000 in a season. She has twice won the US LPGA title and has won over 35 tour events.

Lorca Federico García 1898–1936. Spanish poet and playwright, born in Granada. *Romancero gitano/Gipsy Ballad-book* 1928 shows the influence of the Andalusian songs of the area. In 1929–30 Lorca visited New York, and his experiences are reflected in *Poeta en Nuevo York* 1940. He returned to Spain, founded a touring theatrical company, and wrote plays such as *Bodas de sangre/Blood Wedding* 1933 and *La casa de Bernarda Alba/The House of Bernarda Alba* 1936. His poems include a 'Lament' for the bullfighter

Mejías. He was shot by the Falangists during the Spanish Civil War.

Loren Sophia. Stage name of Sofia Scicolone 1934– . Italian film actress who achieved fame under the guidance of her husband, producer Carlo Ponti. Her work includes *Aida* 1953, *The Key* 1958, *La Ciocara/Two Women* 1961, *Judith* 1965, and *Firepower* 1979.

Lorentz Hendrik Antoon 1853–1928. Dutch physicist, winner (with his pupil Pieter Zeeman) of the Nobel physics prize 1902 for his work on the Zeeman effect.

Lorentz spent most of his career trying to develop and improve the ◊Maxwell electromagnetic theory. He also attempted to account for the anomalies of the ◊Michelson–Morley experiment by proposing, independently of ◊Fitzgerald that moving bodies contracted in their direction of motion. He took the matter further with his method of transforming space and time coordinates, later known as Lorentz transformations, which prepared the way for Einstein's theory of relativity.

Lorenz Konrad 1903–1989. Austrian ethologist. Director of the Max Planck Institute for the Physiology of Behaviour in Bavaria 1955–73, he wrote the studies of ethology (animal behaviour) *King Solomon's Ring* 1952 and *On Aggression* 1966. In 1973 he shared the Nobel Prize for Medicine with Nikolaas ◊Tinbergen and Karl von ◊Frisch.

Lorenz Ludwig Valentine 1829–1891. Danish mathematician and physicist. He developed mathematical formulae to describe phenomena such as the relation between refraction of light and the density of a pure transparent substance, and the relation between a metal's electrical and thermal conductivity and temperature.

Lorenzetti Ambrogio *c.* 1319–1347. Italian painter active in Siena and Florence. His allegorical frescoes *Good and Bad Government* 1337–39 (Palazzo Pubblico, Siena) include a detailed panoramic landscape, and a view of the city of Siena that shows an unusual mastery of spatial effects.

Lorenzetti Pietro *c.* 1306–1345. Italian painter of the Sienese school, active in Assisi. His frescoes in the Franciscan basilica, Assisi reflect ◊Giotto's concern with mass and weight. He was the brother of Ambrogio Lorenzetti.

Lorrain Claude 1600–1682. French painter; see ◊Claude Lorrain.

Lorre Peter. Stage name of Lazlo Löwenstein 1904–1964. Hungarian character actor, whose bulging eyes and sinister voice made him one of cinema's most memorable performers. He made several films in Germany before moving to Hollywood in 1935. He appeared in *M* 1931, *Mad Love* 1935, *The Maltese Falcon* 1941, *Casablanca* 1942, *Beat the Devil* 1953, and *The Raven* 1963.

Los Angeles Victoria de 1923– . Spanish soprano. She is renowned for her interpretations of Spanish songs and for the roles of Manon and Madame Butterfly in Puccini's operas.

Losey Joseph 1909–1984. US film director. Blacklisted as a former Communist in the ◊McCarthy era, he settled in England, where his films included *The Servant* 1963 and *The Go-Between* 1971.

Lothair two Holy Roman emperors:

Lothair I 795–855. Holy Roman emperor from 817 in association with his father Louis I. On Louis' death, the empire was divided between Lothair and his brothers; Lothair took N Italy and the valleys of the rivers Rhône and Rhine.

Lothair II *c.*1070–1137. Holy Roman emperor from 1133 and German king from 1125. His election as emperor, opposed by the Hohenstaufens, was the start of the feud between the Guelph and Ghibelline factions, who supported the papal party and the German emperors, respectively.

Lothair 825–869. King of Lotharingia (called after him, and later corrupted to Lorraine, now part of Alsace-Lorraine) from 855, when he inherited from his father, the Holy Roman emperor Lothair I, a district W of the Rhine, between the Jura mountains and the North Sea.

Lotto Lorenzo *c.*1480–1556. Italian painter, born in Venice, active in Bergamo, Treviso, Venice, Ancona, and Rome. His early works were influenced by Giovanni Bellini; his mature style belongs to the High Renaissance. He painted dignified portraits, altarpieces, and frescoes.

Louis, Prince of Battenberg 1854–1921. German-born British admiral, who took British nationality 1917. He was First Sea Lord 1912–14, but was forced to resign because of anti-German sentiment. In 1917 he changed his name to Mountbatten, and was made marquess of Milford Haven. He was admiral of the fleet 1921.

Louis Joe. Assumed name of Joseph Louis Barrow 1914–1981. US boxer, nicknamed 'the Brown Bomber'. He was world heavyweight champion 1937–49 and made a record 25 successful defences (a record for any weight).

Louis was the longest reigning world heavyweight champion at 11 years and 252 days before announcing his retirement 1949. He subsequently made a comeback and lost to Ezzard Charles in a world title fight 1950.

Louis Morris 1912–1962. US abstract painter. From Abstract Expressionism he turned to the colour-staining technique developed by Helen ◊Frankenthaler, using thinned-out acrylic paints poured on rough canvas to create the illusion of vaporous layers of colour. The *Veil* paintings of the 1950s are examples.

Louis eighteen kings of France:

Louis I *the Pious* 788–840. Holy Roman emperor from 814, when he succeeded his father Charlemagne.

Louis II *the Stammerer* 846–879. King of France from 877, son of Charles the

Bald. He was dominated by the clergy and nobility, who exacted many concessions from him.

Louis III 863–882. King of N France from 879, while his brother Carloman (866–84) ruled S France. He was the son of Louis II. He countered a revolt of the nobility at the beginning of his reign, and his resistance to the Normans made him a hero of epic poems.

Louis IV (d'Outremer) 921–954. King of France from 936. His reign was marked by the rebellion of nobles who refused to recognize his authority. As a result of his liberality they were able to build up powerful feudal lordships.

He was raised in England after his father Charles III, the Simple, had been overthrown 922 by Robert I. After the death of Raoul, Robert's brother-in-law and successor, Louis was chosen by the nobles to be king. He had difficulties with his vassal Hugh the Great, and skirmishes with Hungarians who had invaded S France.

Louis V 966–987. King of France from 986, last of the Carolingian dynasty (descendants of Charlemagne).

Louis VI *the Fat* 1081–1137. King of France from 1108. He led his army against feudal brigands, the English (under Henry I) and the Holy Roman Empire, temporarily consolidating his realm and extending it into Flanders. He was a benefactor to the church, and his advisers included Abbot ◊Suger.

Louis VII *c.*1120–1180. King of France from 1137, who led the Second Crusade.

Louis VIII 1187–1226. King of France from 1223, who was invited to become king of England in place of ◊John by the English barons, and unsuccessfully invaded England 1215–17.

Louis IX St 1214–1270. King of France from 1226, leader of the Seventh and Eighth Crusades. He was defeated in the former by the Muslims, spending four years in captivity, and died in Tunis. He was canonized 1297.

Louis X *the Stubborn* 1289–1316. King of France who succeeded his father Philip IV 1314. His reign saw widespread noble discontent, which he countered by granting charters that guaranteed seignorial rights, although some historians claim that by using evasive tactics, he gave up nothing.

Louis XI 1423–1483. King of France from 1461. He broke the power of the nobility (headed by ◊Charles the Bold) by intrigue and military power.

Louis XII 1462–1515. King of France from 1499. He was duke of Orléans until he succeeded his cousin Charles VIII to the throne. His reign was devoted to Italian wars.

Louis XIII 1601–1643. King of France from 1610 (in succession to his father Henry IV), assuming royal power 1617. He was under the political control of ◊Richelieu 1624–42.

Louis XIV *the Sun King* 1638–1715. King of France from 1643, when he succeeded his father Louis XIII; his mother was Anne of Austria. Until 1661 France was ruled by the chief minister, Mazarin, but later Louis took absolute power, summed up in his saying *L'État c'est moi* ('I am the State'). Throughout his reign he was engaged in unsuccessful expansionist wars – 1667–68, 1672–78, 1688–97, and 1701–13 (the War of the Spanish Succession) – against various European alliances, always containing Britain and the Netherlands. He was a patron of the arts.

Greatest of his ministers was Colbert, whose work was undone by the king's military adventures. Louis attempted 1667–68 to annex the Spanish Netherlands, but was frustrated by an alliance of the Netherlands, Britain, and Sweden. Having detached Britain from the alliance, he invaded the Netherlands 1672, but the Dutch stood firm (led by William of Orange; see ◊William III of England) and despite the European alliance formed against France, achieved territorial gains at the Peace of Nijmegen 1678.

When war was renewed 1688–97 between Louis and the Grand Alliance (including Britain), formed by William of Orange, the French were everywhere victorious on land, but the French fleet was almost destroyed at the battle of La Hugue 1692.

The acceptance by Louis of the Spanish throne 1700 (for his grandson) precipitated the War of the Spanish Succession, and the Treaty of Utrecht 1713 ended French supremacy in Europe.

In 1660 Louis married the Infanta Maria Theresa of Spain, but he was greatly influenced by his mistresses, including Louise de ◊La Vallière, Mme de ◊Montespan, and Mme de ◊Maintenon.

Louis XV 1710–1774. King of France from 1715, with the Duke of Orléans as regent until 1723.

Louis XIV A marble bust of the 'Sun King' Louis XIV of France, by Italian sculptor Bernini.

He was the great-grandson of Louis XIV. Indolent and frivolous, Louis left government in the hands of his ministers, the Duke of Bourbon and Cardinal Fleury (1653–1743). On the latter's death he attempted to rule alone, but became entirely dominated by his mistresses, Mme de ◊Pompadour and Mme ◊Du Barry. His foreign policy led to Canada and India being lost to England.

Louis XVI 1754–1793. King of France from 1774, grandson of Louis XV, and son of Louis the Dauphin. He was dominated by his queen, ◊Marie Antoinette, and the finances fell into such confusion that in 1789 the States General (parliament) had to be summoned, and the French Revolution began. Louis lost his personal popularity June 1791, when he attempted to flee the country (the Flight to Varennes) and in Aug 1792 the Parisians stormed the Tuileries palace and took the royal family prisoner. Deposed Sept 1792, Louis was tried in Dec, sentenced for treason Jan 1793, and guillotined.

Louis XVII 1785–1795. Nominal king of France, the son of Louis XVI. During the French Revolution he was imprisoned with his parents 1792, and probably died in prison.

Louis XVIII 1755–1824. King of France 1814–24, the younger brother of Louis XVI. He assumed the title of king 1795, having fled into exile 1791 during the French Revolution, but became king only on the fall of Napoleon I Apr 1814. Expelled during Napoleon's brief return (the 'hundred days') 1815, he returned after Napoleon's final defeat at Waterloo, pursuing a policy of calculated liberalism until ultra-royalist pressure became dominant after 1820.

Louis Philippe 1773–1850. King of France 1830–48. Son of Louis Philippe Joseph, Duke of Orléans 1747–93; both were known as *Philippe Egalité* from their support of the 1792 Revolution. He fled into exile 1793–1814, but became king after the 1830 revolution with the backing of the rich bourgeoisie. Corruption discredited his regime, and after his overthrow, he escaped to the UK and died there.

Lovat Simon Fraser, 12th Baron Lovat c. 1667–1747. Scottish Jacobite (supporter of the Stuarts). Throughout a political career lasting 50 years he constantly intrigued with both Jacobites and Whigs, and was beheaded for supporting the 1745 rebellion.

Lovecraft H(oward) P(hillips) 1890–1937. US writer of horror fiction, whose stories of hostile, supernatural forces, known collectively as the *Cthulhu Mythos*, have lent names and material to many other writers in the genre. Much of his work on this theme was collected in *The Outsider and Others* 1939.

Lovelace Richard 1618–1658. English poet. Imprisoned 1642 for petitioning for the restoration of royal rule, he wrote 'To Althea from Prison', and in a second term in jail 1648 revised his collection *Lucasta* 1649.

Lovell Bernard 1913– . British radio astronomer, director (until 1981) of Jodrell Bank Experimental Station (now Nuffield radio astronomy laboratories) site of Britain's first major radio telescope.

During World War II he worked at the Telecommunications Research establishment (1939–45), and in 1951 became professor of radio astronomy at the University of Manchester. His books include *Radio Astronomy* 1951 and *The Exploration of Outer Space* 1961.

Low David 1891–1963. New Zealand-born British political cartoonist, creator (in newspapers such as the London *Evening Standard*) of Colonel Blimp, the TUC carthorse, and others.

Lowell Amy (Lawrence) 1874–1925. US poet, who succeeded Ezra Pound as leader of the Imagists, whose work was typified by its brevity and clarity. Her works, in free verse, include *Sword-Blades and Poppy Seed* 1916.

Lowell J(ames) R(ussell) 1819–1891. US critic and poet whose works range from the didactic *The Vision of Sir Launfal* 1848 to satirical poems such as *The Biglow Papers* 1848.

Lowell Percival 1855–1916. US astronomer, who started the search for 'Planet X' beyond Neptune, which led to the discovery of Pluto. In 1894 he founded the Lowell Observatory at Flagstaff,

Lowell US poet Robert Lowell.

Arizona, where he reported seeing 'canals' (now known to be an optical illusion) on the surface of Mars.

Lowell Robert (Traill Spence) 1917–1977. US poet whose work includes *Lord Weary's Castle* 1946 and *For the Union Dead* 1964. A Roman Catholic convert from 1940, he was imprisoned in 1943 as a conscientious objector.

Lowry L(aurence) S(tephen) 1887–1976. British painter. Born in Manchester, he lived mainly in nearby Salford. He painted northern industrial townscapes and town life. His characteristic style of matchstick figures and almost monochrome palette emerged in the 1920s.

Loy Myrna. Stage name of Myrna Williams 1905– . US film actess who played Nora Charles in the *Thin Man* series (1943–47) co-starring William Powell. Her other films include *The Mask of Fu Manchu* 1932 and *The Rains Came* 1939.

Loyola founder of the Jesuits. See ◊Ignatius Loyola.

Lubbers Rudolph (Frans Marie) 1939– . Netherlands politician. He became minister for economic affairs 1973 and prime minister 1983.

Lubetkin Berthold 1901– . Russian architect, who settled in England in 1930. His pioneering designs include a block of flats in Highgate, London (Highpoint I, 1933–35), and the curvaceous Penguin Pool 1933 at London Zoo, restored 1989.

Lubitsch Ernst 1892–1947. German film director, who worked in the USA from 1921. Starting as an actor in silent films in Berlin, he turned to writing and directing, including *Die Augen der Mummie Ma/The Eyes of the Mummy* 1918 and *Die Austernprinzessin/The Oyster Princess* 1919. In the USA he directed *The Marriage Circle* 1924, *The Student Prince* 1927. His sound films include *Design for Living* 1933, *Ninotchka* 1939, and *To Be or Not to Be* 1942.

Lucan John Bingham, 7th Earl of Lucan 1934– . British aristocrat and professional gambler. On 7 Nov 1974 his wife was attacked and their children's nanny murdered. No trace of Lucan has since been found, and no solution to the murder.

Lucan Marcus Annaeus Lucanus AD 39–65. Latin poet, born in Cordova, a nephew of ◊Seneca and favourite of ◊Nero until the emperor became jealous of his verse. He then joined a republican conspiracy and committed suicide on its failure. His epic *Pharsalia* deals with the civil wars of ◊Caesar and ◊Pompey.

Lucas George 1944– . US director and producer. His films, often on science fiction themes and using special effects, include *THX 1138* 1971, *American Graffiti* 1973, and the *Star Wars* trilogy 1977–83.

Lucas Robert 1937– . US economist, leader of the Chicago University school of 'new classical'

macroeconomics, which contends that wage and price adjustment is almost instantaneous and that the level of unemployment at any time must be the natural rate (it cannot be reduced by government action except in the short term and at the cost of increasing inflation).

Lucas van Leyden 1494–1533. Dutch painter and printmaker, active in Leiden and Antwerp. He was a pioneer of Netherlandish genre scenes, for example *The Chess Players* (Staatliche Museen, West Berlin). His woodcuts and engravings were inspired by ◊Dürer, whom he met in Antwerp 1521. Lucas was an influence on ◊Rembrandt.

Luce Clare Boothe see ◊Boothe Luce, Clare.

Luce Henry Robinson 1898–1967. US publisher, founder of the magazine *Time* 1923, and of the pictorial weekly *Life* 1936. He married Clare ◊Boothe Luce.

Lucian *c.* 125–*c.* 190. Greek writer of satirical dialogues, in which he pours scorn on all religions. He was born at Samosata in Syria, and for a time was an advocate at Antioch, but later travelled before settling in Athens about 165. He occupied an official post in Egypt, where he died.

Lucretius (Titus Lucretius Carus) *c.* 99–55 BC. Roman poet and Epicurean philosopher, whose *De rerum natura/On the Nature of Things* envisaged the whole universe as a combination of atoms, and had some concept of evolutionary theory.

Animals he explained as complex but initially quite fortuitous clusters of atoms, only certain combinations surviving to reproduce.

Lucullus Lucius Licinius 110–56 BC. Roman general and consul. As commander against ◊Mithridates of Pontus 74–66 he proved to be one of Rome's ablest generals and administrators, until superseded by Pompey. He then retired from politics. His wealth enabled him to live a life of luxury, and Lucullan feasts became legendary.

Ludendorff Erich von 1865–1937. German general, chief of staff to ◊Hindenburg in World War I, and responsible for the eastern-front victory at the battle of Tannenberg 1914. After Hindenburg's appointment as chief of general staff and Ludendorff's as quartermaster-general 1916, he was also politically influential. He took part in the Nazi rising in Munich 1923, and sat in the Reichstag (parliament) as a right-wing Nationalist.

Ludwig Karl Friedrich Wilhelm 1816–1895. German physiologist who invented graphic methods of recording events within the body.

In the course of this work, he invented the kymograph, a rotating drum on which a stylus charts a continuous record of blood pressure and temperature. This was a forerunner of modern monitoring systems.

Ludwig three kings of Bavaria:

Ludwig I 1786–1868. King of Bavaria 1825–48, succeeding his father Maximilian Joseph I. He made Munich an international cultural centre, but

his association with the dancer Lola ◊Montez, who dictated his policies for a year, led to his abdication 1848.

Ludwig II 1845–1886. King of Bavaria from 1864, when he succeeded his father Maximilian II. He supported Austria during the Austro-Prussian War 1866, but brought Bavaria into the Franco-Prussian War as Prussia's ally, and in 1871 offered the German crown to the king of Prussia. He was the composer Wagner's patron, and built the Bayreuth theatre for him. Declared insane 1886, he drowned himself soon after.

Ludwig III 1845–1921. King of Bavaria 1913–1918, when he abdicated upon the formation of a republic.

Luening Otto 1900– . US composer. He studied in Zurich, and privately with Busoni. In 1949 he joined the staff at Columbia University, and in 1951 began a series of pioneering compositions for instruments and tape, some in partnership with Vladimir Ussachevsky (*Incantation* 1952, *Poem in Cycles*, and *Bells* 1954). In 1959 he became co-director, with Babbitt and Ussachevsky, of the Columbia-Princeton Electronic Music Center.

Lugard Frederick John Dealtry, 1st Baron Lugard 1858–1945. British colonial administrator. He served in the army 1878–89 and then worked for the British East Africa Company, for whom he took possession of Uganda in 1890. He went on to be high commissioner for N Nigeria 1900–07, governor of Hong Kong 1907–12, and governor general of Nigeria 1914–19.

Lugosi Bela. Stage name of Bela Ferenc Blasko 1882–1956. Hungarian film actor who appeared in Hungarian and German films before going to Hollywood in 1921. His most famous role was *Dracula* 1930, followed by horror roles in *Son of Frankenstein* 1939, *The Body Snatcher* 1945, and *Bride of the Monster* 1956.

Lu Hsün former transcription of Chinese writer ◊Lu Xun.

Lukács Georg 1885–1971. Hungarian philosopher, one of the founders of 'Western' or 'Hegelian' Marxism, a philosophical current opposed to the Marxism of the official communist movement.

In *History and Class Consciousness* 1923, he argued that the proletariat was the 'identical subject-object' of history. Under capitalism, social relations were 'reified' (turned into objective things), but the proletariat could grasp the social totality.

Luke, St 1st century AD. Traditionally the compiler of the third Gospel and of the Acts of the Apostles in the New Testament. He is the patron saint of painters; his emblem is a winged ox, and his feast day is 18 Oct.

Luke is supposed to have been a Greek physician born in Antioch (Antakiyah, Turkey) and to have accompanied Paul after the ascension of Christ.

Lull Ramon 1232–1315. Spanish scientist and theologian. His *Ars Magna* was a mechanical device, a kind of prototype computer, by which all problems could be solved by manipulating fundamental Aristotelian categories.

He also wrote the prose romance *Blanquerna*, in his native Catalan, the first novel written in a Romance language.

Lully Jean-Baptiste. Adopted name of Giovanni Battista Lulli 1632–1687. French composer of Italian origin who was court composer to Louis XIV. He composed music for the ballet, for Molière's plays, and established French opera with such works as *Alceste* 1674 and *Armide et Renaud* 1686. He was also a ballet dancer.

Lumet Sidney 1924– . US film director. His films, sometimes marked by a heavy-handed seriousness, have met with varying critical and commercial success. They include *Twelve Angry Men* 1957, *Fail Safe* 1964, *The Deadly Affair* 1967, and *Network* 1976.

Lumière Auguste Marie 1862–1954 and Louis Jean 1864–1948. French brothers who pioneered cinematography. In 1895 they patented their cinematograph, a combined camera and projector that operated at 16 frames per second, and opened the world's first cinema in Paris to show their films.

Lumumba Patrice 1926–1961. Congolese politician, prime minister of Zaïre 1960. Imprisoned by the Belgians, but released in time to attend the conference giving the Congo independence 1960, he led the National Congolese Movement to victory in the subsequent general election. He was deposed in a coup d'état, and murdered some months later.

Lunardi Vincenzo 1759–1806. Italian balloonist. He came to London as secretary to the Neapolitan ambassador, and made the first balloon flight in England from Moorfields in 1784.

Lunt Alfred 1893–1977. US actor. He went straight from school into the theatre, and in 1922 married Lynn ◊Fontanne with whom he subsequently co-starred in more than 30 successes. They formed a sophisticated comedy duo, and the New York Lunt-Fontanne theatre was named after them. Their shows included *Design for Living* by Noël Coward 1933, *There Shall Be No Night* 1940–41, and *The Visit* 1960.

Luo Guan-zhong formerly *Luo Kuan-chung* 14th-century Chinese novelist, who reworked popular tales into *The Romance of the Three Kingdoms* and *The Water Margin*.

Lurçat Jean 1892–1966. French artist influenced by the Cubists, who revived tapestry design, as in *Le Chant du Monde*.

Lurie Alison 1926– . US novelist and critic. Her subtly written and satirical novels include *Imaginary Friends* 1967, *The War Between the Tates* 1974, and *Foreign Affairs* 1985, a tale of

transatlantic relations, which won the Pulitzer Prize.

Luther Martin 1483–1546. German Christian church reformer, a founder of Protestantism. When a priest at the university of Wittenberg 1517, he attacked the sale of indulgences (remissions of punishment for sin) in 95 theses and defied papal condemnation; the Holy Roman emperor Charles V summoned him to the Diet of Worms 1521, where he refused to retract his objections. After the drawing up of the Augsburg Confession 1530, he gradually retired from the Protestant leadership.

Luther was born in Eisleben, the son of a miner; he studied at the university of Erfurt, spent three years as a monk in the Augustinian convent there, and in 1507 was ordained priest. Shortly afterwards he attracted attention as a teacher and preacher at the university of Wittenberg; and in 1517, after returning from a visit to Rome, he attained nationwide celebrity for his denunciation of the Dominican monk Johann Tetzel (1455–1519), one of those sent out by the Pope to sell indulgences as a means of raising funds for the rebuilding of St Peter's Basilica in Rome.

On 31 Oct 1517, Luther nailed on the church door in Wittenberg a statement of 95 theses on indulgences, and in the next year he was summoned to Rome to defend his action. His reply was to attack the papal system even more strongly, and in 1520 he publicly burned in Wittenberg the papal bull that had been launched against him. On his way home from the imperial Diet of Worms he was taken into 'protective custody' by the elector of Saxony in the castle of Wartburg. Later he became estranged from the Dutch theologian Erasmus, who had formerly supported him in his attacks on papal authority, and engaged in violent controversies with political and religious opponents.

Formerly condemned by communism, Luther had by the 1980s been rehabilitated as a revolutionary socialist hero, and was claimed as patron saint by both East and West Germany.

Luthuli or *Lutuli* Albert 1899–1967. South African politician, president of the African National Congress from 1952. Luthuli, a Zulu tribal chief, preached nonviolence and multiracialism. Arrested 1956, he was never actually tried for treason, although he suffered certain restrictions from 1959. He was under suspended sentence for burning his pass (an identity document required of non-white South Africans) when awarded the Nobel Peace Prize 1960.

Lutoslawski Witold 1913– . Polish composer and conductor, born in Warsaw. His early music, dissonant and powerful (*First Symphony* 1947), was criticized by the communist government, so he adopted a more popular style. With the lifting of artistic repression, he quickly adopted avant-garde techniques, including improvisatory and aleatoric forms. He has written chamber, vocal, and orchestral music, including three symphonies, *Livre pour orchestre* 1968 and *Mi-parti* 1976.

Lutyens (Agnes) Elisabeth 1906–1983. English composer. Her works, using the 12-tone system, are expressive and tightly organized, and include a substantial amount of chamber music, stage, and orchestral works. Her choral and vocal works include a setting of ◊Wittgenstein's *Tractatus* and a cantata *The Tears of Night*.

Lutyens Edwin Landseer 1869–1944. English architect. His designs ranged from picturesque to Renaissance style country houses and ultimately evolved into a classical style as in the Cenotaph, London, and the Viceroy's House, New Delhi.

Luxemburg Rosa 1870–1919. Polish-born German communist, collaborator with Karl Liebknecht in founding the Spartacus League (forerunner of the German Communist Party) in 1918, and murdered with him during the Jan 1919 Berlin workers' revolt.

Lu Xun pen name of Chon Shu-jêu 1881–1936. Chinese short story writer. His three volumes of satirically realistic stories, *Call to Arms*, *Wandering*, and *Old Tales Retold*, reveal the influence of Gogol. He is one of the most popular of modern Chinese writers.

Lycurgus Spartan lawgiver. He is said to have been a member of the royal house, who, while acting as regent, gave the Spartans their constitution and system of education. Many scholars believe him to be purely mythical.

Lydgate John *c.* 1370–*c.* 1450. English poet. He was a Benedictine monk, and later prior. His numerous works were often translations or adaptations, such as *Troy Book*, and *Falls of Princes*.

Lyell Charles 1797–1875. Scottish geologist. In his book *The Principles of Geology* 1830–33, he opposed ◊Cuvier's theory that the features of the Earth were formed by a series of catastrophes, and expounded ◊Hutton's view, known as uniformitarianism, that past events were brought about by the same processes that occur today – a view that influenced Charles ◊Darwin's theory of evolution.

Lyell trained and practised as a lawyer, but retired from the law in 1827 and devoted himself full time to geology and writing.

Although he only in old age accepted that species had changed through evolution, he nevertheless provided Darwin with a geological framework within which evolutionary theories could be placed. Darwin simply applied Lyell's geological method – explaining the past through what is observable in the present – to biology.

Lyly John *c.* 1553–1606. English playwright and author of the romance *Euphues, or the Anatomy of Wit* 1578. Its elaborate stylistic devices gave rise to the word 'euphuism' for an affected rhetorical style.

Lynch 'Jack' (John) 1917– . Irish politician, born in Cork. A noted Gaelic footballer and a barrister, in 1948 he entered the parliament of the republic as a Fianna Fáil member, and was prime minister 1966–73 and 1977–79.

Lynn Vera 1917– . British singer, the 'Forces' Sweetheart' of World War II with 'We'll Meet Again' and 'White Cliffs of Dover', and in 1952 'Auf Wiederseh'n, Sweetheart'. Dame of the British Empire 1975.

Lyons Joseph 1848–1917. British entrepreneur, founder of the catering firm of J Lyons 1894. He popularized 'tea-shops', and the 'Corner Houses', incorporating several restaurants of varying types.

Lyons Joseph Aloysius 1879–1939. Australian politician, founder of the United Australia Party 1931, prime minister 1931–39.

He was born in Tasmania and first elected to parliament in 1929. His wife *Dame Enid Lyons* (1897–) was the first woman member of the House of Representatives and of the federal cabinet.

Lysander Spartan general. He brought the Peloponnesian War to a successful conclusion by capturing the Athenian fleet at Aegospotami 405 BC, and by starving Athens into surrender in the following year. He then aspired to make Sparta supreme in Greece and himself supreme in Sparta; he set up puppet governments in Athens and her

Lynn *British singer Vera Lynn captured the hearts of the troops in World War II through her renditions of songs such as 'White Cliffs of Dover'.*

former allies, and tried to secure for himself the Spartan kingship, but he was killed in battle with the Thebans.

Lysenko Trofim Denisovich 1898–1976. Soviet biologist, who believed in the inheritance of acquired characteristics (changes acquired in an individual's lifetime) and used his position under Stalin to officially exclude ◊Mendel's theory of inheritance. He was removed from office after the fall of Khrushchev 1964.

Lysippus 4th century BC. Greek sculptor. He made a series of portraits of Alexander the Great (Roman copies survive) and is also known for the *Apoxyomenos*, an athlete (copy in the Vatican), and a colossal *Hercules* (lost).

Lyte Henry Francis 1793–1847. British cleric, author of the hymns 'Abide with me' and 'Praise, my soul, the King of Heaven'.

Lytton Edward George Earle Lytton Bulwer, 1st Baron Lytton of Knebworth 1803–1873. English writer. His novels successfully followed every turn of the public taste and include the Byronic *Pelham* 1828, *The Last Days of Pompeii* 1834, and *Rienzi* 1835. His plays include *Richelieu* 1838. He was Colonial Secretary 1858–59.

Lytton Edward Robert Bulwer-Lytton, 1st Earl of Lytton 1831–1891. British diplomat, viceroy of India 1876–80, where he pursued a controversial 'forward' policy. Only son of the novelist, he was himself a poet under the pseudonym *Owen Meredith*, writing 'King Poppy' 1892 and other poems.

Maazel Lorin (Varencove) 1930– . US conductor and violinist. He studied the violin and made his debut as a conductor at the age of nine. He was conductor of the Cleveland Orchestra 1972–82 and the first US director of the Vienna State Opera.

Mabuse Jan. Adopted name of Jan Gossaert c. 1478–c.1533. Flemish painter, active chiefly in Antwerp. His common name derives from his birthplace, Maubeuge. His visit to Italy in 1508 with Philip of Burgundy started a new vogue in Flanders for Italianate ornament and classical influence in painting, including sculptural nude figures.

McAdam John Loudon 1756–1836. Scottish engineer. The word *macadamizing* was coined for his system of constructing roads of broken granite.

MacArthur Douglas 1880–1964. US general in World War II, commander of US forces in the Far East and, from Mar 1942, of the Allied forces in the SW Pacific. After the surrender of Japan he commanded the Allied occupation forces there. During 1950 he commanded the UN forces in Korea, but in Apr 1951, after expressing views contrary to US and UN policy, he was relieved of all his commands by President Truman.

The son of an army officer, born in Arkansas, MacArthur became chief of staff 1930–35. He defended the Philippines against the Japanese 1941–42 and escaped to Australia. He was responsible for the reconquest of New Guinea 1942–45 and of the Philippines 1944–45, being appointed general of the army 1944. In the Korean War, he invaded the North until beaten back by Chinese troops; his threats to bomb China were seen as liable to start World War III and he was removed from command, but received a hero's welcome on his return to the USA.

MacArthur John 1767–1834. Australian colonist, a pioneer of sheep breeding and vine growing. He quarrelled with successive governors of New South Wales, and, when arrested by ♦Bligh, stirred up the *Rum Rebellion* 1808, in which Bligh was himself arrested and deposed.

Born in Devon, England, MacArthur went to Sydney in 1790, and began experiments in sheep breeding in 1794, subsequently importing from South Africa the merino strain. In later years he studied viticulture and planted vines from 1817, establishing the first commercial vineyard in Australia.

Macaulay Rose 1881–1958. English novelist, The serious vein of her early novels changed to light satire in *Potterism* 1920 and *Keeping up Appearances* 1928. Her later books include *The Towers of Trebizond* 1956.

Macaulay Thomas Babington, Baron Macaulay 1800–1859. English historian, essayist, poet, and politician, secretary of war 1839–41. His *History of England* in five volumes 1849–51 celebrates the Glorious Revolution of 1668 as the crowning achievment of the Whig party.

He entered Parliament as a liberal Whig in 1830. In India 1834–38, he redrafted the Indian penal code. He sat again in Parliament 1839–47 and 1852–56, and in 1857 accepted a peerage. His works include an essay on Milton 1825 published in the *Edinburgh Review*, a volume of

MacArthur *US general Douglas MacArthur in 1945. He was Allied commander in the SW Pacific area from 1942 and helped mastermind the defeat of Japan in World War II.*

verse, *Lays of Ancient Rome* 1842, and the *History of England* 1848–61 covering the years up to 1702.

McBride Willie John 1940– . Irish Rugby Union player. He was capped 63 times by Ireland, and won a record 17 British Lions caps. He played on five Lions tours, 1962, 1966, 1968, 1971, and in 1974 as captain, when they returned from South Africa undefeated.

McCabe John 1939– . English pianist and composer. His works include three symphonies; orchestral works, including *The Chagall Windows*; and songs.

McCarran Patrick 1876–1954. US Democrat politician. He became senator for Nevada 1932, and as an isolationist strongly opposed lend-lease, the arrangement whereby the USA supplied equipment to the European Allies during World War II. He sponsored the McCarran-Walter Immigration and Nationality Act of 1952, which severely restricted entry and immigration to the USA; the act was amended 1965.

McCarthy Joseph R(aymond) 'Joe' 1909–1957. US right-wing Republican politician, whose unsubstantiated claim 1950 that the State Department had been infiltrated by Communists started a wave of anticommunist hysteria, wild accusations, and blacklists, which continued until he was discredited 1954.

A lawyer, McCarthy became senator for his native Wisconsin in 1946, and in Feb 1950 caused a sensation by claiming to hold a list of about 200 Communist Party members working in the State Department. This was in part inspired by the ◊Hiss case. McCarthy continued a witch-hunting campaign until 1954, when he turned his attention to the army, and it was shown that he and his aides had been falsifying evidence. By this time, however, many thousands of people in public life and the arts had been unofficially blacklisted as

suspected Communists or fellow travellers (communist sympathizers). He gave his name to the practice of *McCarthyism* (making unsupported accusations).

McCarthy Mary (Therese) 1912–1989. US novelist and critic. Much of her work looks probingly at US society, for example the novels *The Groves of Academe* 1952, which describes the anticommunist witch-hunts of the time (see J ◊McCarthy), and *The Group* 1963, which follows the post-college careers of eight women.

McCartney Paul 1942– . Rock singer, songwriter, and bass guitarist, former member of the Beatles, and leader of the pop group Wings 1971–81. His subsequent solo hits have included collaborations with Michael Jackson and Elvis Costello.

McClellan George Brinton 1826–1885. US Civil War general, commander in chief of the Union forces 1861–62. He was dismissed by President Lincoln when he delayed five weeks in following up his victory over the Confederate general Lee at the battle of Antietam. He was the unsuccessful Democrat presidential candidate against Lincoln in 1864.

McClintock Barbara 1902– . US geneticist, who concluded that genes changed their position on the chromosome from generation to generation in a random way. This would explain how originally identical cells take on specialized functions as skin, muscle, bone, and nerve, and also how evolution could give rise to the multiplicity of species.

McClintock Francis Leopold 1819–1907. Irish polar explorer and admiral. He discovered the fate of the John ◊Franklin expedition and further explored the Canadian Arctic.

McClure Robert John le Mesurier 1807–1873. Irish-born British admiral and explorer. While on an expedition 1850–54 searching for John ◊Franklin, he was the first to pass through the Northwest Passage.

McCormick Cyrus Hall 1809–1884. US inventor of the reaping machine in 1831, which revolutionized 19th-century agriculture.

McCowen Alec 1925– . British actor. His Shakespearean roles include Richard II and the Fool in *King Lear*; he is also noted for his dramatic one-man shows.

MacCready Paul 1925– . US designer of the *Gossamer Condor* aircraft which made the first controlled flight by human power alone in 1977. His *Solar Challenger* flew from Paris to London under solar power; and in 1985 he constructed a powered replica of a giant pterosaur, an extinct flying mammal.

McCullers Carson (Smith) 1917–1967. US novelist. Most of her writing (including her best-known novels *The Heart is a Lonely Hunter* 1940 and *Reflections in a Golden Eye* 1941) is set in the Southern states, where she was born, and

McCarthy US senator Joe McCarthy exhibiting 'evidence' to the House of Representatives Un-American Activities Committee.

deals with spiritual isolation, containing elements of sometimes macabre violence.

MacDermot Galt 1928– . US composer. He wrote the rock musical *Hair* 1967, with lyrics by Gerome Ragni and James Rado. It opened in London 1968, the day stage censorship ended, and challenged conventional attitudes about sex, drugs, and the war in Vietnam.

McDiarmid Hugh. Pen name of Christopher Murray Grieve 1892–1978. Scottish nationalist and Marxist poet. His works include *A Drunk Man looks at the Thistle* 1926 and two *Hymns to Lenin* 1930, 1935.

Macdonald Flora 1722–1790. Scottish heroine who rescued Prince Charles Edward Stuart, the Young Pretender, after his defeat at Culloden in 1746. Disguising him as her maid, she escorted him from her home in the Hebrides to France. She was arrested, but released in 1747.

MacDonald (James) Ramsay 1866–1937. British Labour politician. He joined the Independent Labour Party 1894, and became first secretary of the new Labour Party 1900. In Parliament he led the party 1906–14 and 1922–31, and was prime minister of the first two Labour governments, Jan–Oct 1924 and 1929–31, and of a coalition 1931–35, for which he left the party.

MacDonald was born in Scotland, the son of a labourer. He was elected to Parliament 1906, and led the party until 1914, when his opposition to World War I lost him the leadership. This he recovered 1922, and in Jan 1924 he formed a government dependent on the support of the Liberal Party. When this was withdrawn in Oct the same year, he was forced to resign. He returned to office 1929, again as leader of a minority government, which collapsed 1931 as a result of the economic crisis. MacDonald left the Labour Party to form a national government with backing from both Liberal and Conservative parties. He resigned the premiership 1935.

Macdonald John Alexander 1815–1891. Canadian Conservative politician. He was born in Glasgow but taken to Ontario as a child. In 1857 he became prime minister of Upper Canada. He took the leading part in the movement for federation, and in 1867 became the first prime minister of Canada. He was defeated 1873, but returned to office 1878, and retained it until his death.

MacDowell Edward Alexander 1860–1908. US Romantic composer, influenced by ◊Liszt. His works include the *Indian Suite* 1896, and piano concertos and sonatas.

McDowell Malcolm 1943– . British actor who played the rebellious hero in the film *If* 1969 and confirmed his acting abilities in Stanley Kubrick's *A Clockwork Orange* 1971.

McEvoy Ambrose 1878–1927. British artist, watercolourist, and painter of delicate portraits of women.

McEwan Ian 1948– . English novelist and short-story writer. His tightly written works often have sinister or macabre undertones and contain elements of violence and bizarre sexuality, as in the short stories in *First Love, Last Rites* 1975. His novels include *The Comfort of Strangers* 1981 and *The Child in Time* 1987.

McGinley Phyllis 1905–1978. Canadian-born US writer of light verse. She became a contributor to the *New Yorker* magazine and published many collections of social satire. Her works include *One More Manhattan* 1937 and *The Love Letters of Phyllis McGinley* 1954.

McGonagall William 1830–1902. Scottish poet, noted for the unintentionally humorous effect of his extremely bad serious verse, for example, his poem on the Tay Bridge disaster of 1879.

Mach Ernst 1838–1916. Austrian philosopher and physicist. He was an empiricist, believing that science was a record of facts perceived by the senses, and that acceptance of a scientific law depended solely on its standing the practical test of use; he opposed concepts such as Newton's 'absolute motion'. He researched airflow, and the Mach number, the ratio of a speed to the speed of sound, is named after him.

Machado Antonio 1875–1939. Spanish poet and dramatist. Born in Seville, he was inspired by the Castilian countryside in his lyric verse, contained in *Campos de Castilla/Countryside of Castile* 1912.

Machado de Assis Joaquim Maria 1839–1908. Brazilian writer and poet. He is regarded as the greatest Brazilian novelist. His sceptical, ironic wit is well displayed in his 30 volumes of novels and short stories, including *Epitaph for a Small Winner* 1880 and *Dom Casmurro* 1900.

Machaut Guillame de 1300–1377. French poet and composer. Born in Champagne, he was in the service of John of Bohemia for 30 years and, later, of King John the Good of France. He gave the forms of the *ballade* and *rondo* a new individuality and ensured their lasting popularity.

Machel Samora 1933–1986. Mozambique nationalist leader, president 1975–86. Machel was active in the liberation front Frelimo from its conception 1962, fighting for independence from Portugal. He became Frelimo leader 1966, and Mozambique's first president, from independence until his death in a plane crash near the South African border.

Machen Arthur (Llewellyn) 1863–1947. Welsh author. Characterized by mystic symbolism and the supernatural, his writings include *House of Souls* 1906 and *Angels of Mons* 1915. *The Hill of Dreams* 1907 is partly autobiographical.

Machiavelli Niccolò 1469–1527. Italian politician and author, whose name is now synonymous with cunning and cynical statecraft. In his most important political works, *Il principe/The Prince* 1513 and *Discorsi/Discourses* 1531, he discusses ways

Machiavelli *Italian diplomat and writer Niccolò Machiavelli's reputation rests largely on his work* The Prince.

in which rulers can advance the interests of their states (and themselves) through an often amoral and opportunist manipulation of other people.

Machiavelli was born in Florence and was second chancellor to the republic 1498–1512. On the accession to power of the Medici 1512, he was arrested and imprisoned on a charge of conspiracy, but in 1513 released to exile in the country. *The Prince*, based on his observations of Cesare ◊Borgia, is a guide for the future prince of a unified Italian state. In *L'Arte della guerra/The Art of War* 1520 he outlined the provision of an army for the prince, and in *Historie fiorentine/History of Florence* he analysed the historical development of Florence until 1492. Among his later works are the comedies *La Mandragola/The Mandrake* 1524 and *Clizia*.

McIndoe Archibald 1900–1960. New Zealand plastic surgeon. Born at Dunedin, New Zealand, he became famous in England during World War II for his remodelling of the faces of badly burned pilots, and formed the Guinea Pig Club for them.

MacInnes Colin 1914–1976. English novelist, son of the novelist Angela Thirkell. He made a reputation with sharp depictions of London youth and subcultures of the 1950s, such as *City of Spades* 1957 and *Absolute Beginners* 1959.

Macintosh Charles 1766–1843. Scottish manufacturing chemist who invented a waterproof fabric lined with a rubber that was used for raincoats, hence **mackintosh**. Other waterproofing processes have now largely superseded this method.

McKay Heather Pamela (born Blundell) 1941– . Australian squash player. She won the British Open title an unprecedented 16 years in succession 1962–1977.

She also won 14 consecutive Australian titles 1960–1973 and was twice the World Open champion (inaugurated 1976). Between 1962 and 1980 she was unbeaten.

Macke August 1887–1914. German painter, a founder member of the *Blaue Reiter* group (see ◊Kandinsky) in Munich. With Franz ◊Marc he developed a semi-abstract style comprising Cubist and Fauve characteristics.

In 1914 Macke visited Tunis with ◊Klee, and was inspired to paint a series of brightly coloured watercolours largely composed of geometrical shapes but still representational. He was killed in World War I.

McKellen Ian 1939– . British actor, whose stage roles include Richard II and Edward II, and Mozart in the stage version of *Amadeus*. His films include *Priest of Love* 1982 and *Plenty* 1985.

Mackendrick Alexander 1912– . US-born Scottish director, responsible for some of Ealing Studios' finest comedies, including *Whisky Galore* 1949 and *The Man in the White Suit* 1951. He later made several films in the US, notably *Sweet Smell of Success* 1957, before becoming a film lecturer.

Mackensen August von 1849–1945. German field marshal. During World War I he led the conquest of Serbia 1915, and in 1916 played a major role in the overthrow of Romania. After the war Mackensen retained his popularity to become a folk hero of the German army.

Mackenzie Alexander *c.* 1755–1820. British explorer and fur trader. In 1789, he was the first European to see the river, now part of N Canada, named after him. In 1792–93 he crossed the Rocky Mountains to the Pacific.

Mackenzie Compton 1883–1972. Scottish author. His parents were actors. He was educated at Magdalen College, Oxford University, and published his first novel *The Passionate Elopement* in 1911. Later works were *Carnival* 1912, *Sinister Street* 1913–14 (an autobiographical novel) and the comic *Whisky Galore* 1947. He published his autobiography in ten 'octaves' (volumes) 1963–71.

Mackenzie William Lyon 1795–1861. Canadian politician, born in Scotland. He emigrated to Canada in 1820, and led the rebellion of 1837–38, an unsuccessful attempt to limit British rule and establish more democratic institutions in Canada. After its failure he lived in the USA until 1849, and in 1851–58 sat on the Canadian legislature as a Radical. He was grandfather of W L Mackenzie King, the Liberal prime minister.

Mackerras Charles 1925– . Australian conductor. Known for his advocacy of the music of ◊Janácek, whom he has helped to popularize, he was conductor of the English National Opera 1970–78.

McKinley William 1843–1901. 25th president of the USA 1897–1901, a Republican. He was born in Ohio, and elected to Congress 1876. His period as president was marked by the USA's adoption of an imperialist policy, as exemplified by the Spanish-American War 1898 and the annexation of the Philippines. He was assassinated in Buffalo, New York.

Mackintosh Charles Rennie 1868–1928. Scottish Art Nouveau architect, designer, and painter, who exercised considerable influence on European design. His chief work includes the Glasgow School of Art 1896.

Mackmurdo Arthur H 1851–1942. English designer and architect. He founded the Century Guild in 1882, a group of architects, artists, and designers inspired by William ◊Morris and John ◊Ruskin. His book and textile designs are forerunners of Art Nouveau.

Maclaine Shirley. Stage name of Shirley MacLean Beaty 1934– . US actress, sister of Warren Beatty. She has played both comedy and dramatic roles. Her many offscreen interests have limited her film appearances, which include *The Trouble with Harry* 1955, *The Apartment* 1960, and *Terms of Endearment* 1983.

Maclean Alistair 1922–1987. Scottish adventure novelist. His first novel, *HMS Ulysses* 1955 was based on wartime experience. It was followed by *The Guns of Navarone* 1957, and other adventure novels. Many of his books were made into films.

Maclean Donald 1913–1983. British spy, who worked for the USSR while in the UK civil service. He defected to the USSR 1951 together with Guy ◊Burgess.

Maclean, brought up in a strict Presbyterian family, was educated at Cambridge, where he was recruited by the Soviet KGB secret police. He worked for the UK Foreign Office in Washington 1944 and then Cairo 1948 before returning to London, becoming head of the American Department at the Foreign Office 1950.

Maclean Fitzroy Hew 1911– . Scottish writer and diplomat, whose travels Russia and Central Asia inspired his *Eastern Approaches* 1949 and *A Person from England* 1958. During 1943–45 he commanded a unit giving aid to partisans in Yugoslavia.

MacLeish Archibald 1892–1982. US poet. He made his name with the poem 'Conquistador' 1932, which describes Cortés' march to the Aztec capital, but his later plays in verse, *Panic* 1935 and *Air Raid* 1938, deal with contemporary problems.

He was born in Illinois, was assistant secretary of state 1944–45, and helped to draft the constitution of UNESCO. From 1949–62 he was Boylston Professor of Rhetoric at Harvard, and his essays *Poetry and Opinion* 1950 reflect his feeling that a poet should be 'committed', expressing his outlook in his verse.

MacLennan Robert (Adam Ross) 1936– . Scottish centrist politician, member of Parliament for Caithness and Sutherland from 1966. He left the Labour Party for the Social Democrats (SDP) 1981, and was SDP leader 1988 during merger negotiations with the Liberals. He then became a member of the new Social and Liberal Democrats.

MacLennan was educated in Scotland, England and the USA, and called to the English Bar in 1962. When David Owen resigned the SDP leadership in 1988, MacLennan took over until the merger with the Liberal Party had been completed. He took a leading part in the negotiations.

Macleod Iain Norman 1913–1970. British Conservative politician. As colonial secretary 1959–61, he forwarded the independence of former British territories in Africa; he died in office as chancellor of the Exchequer.

Maclise Daniel 1806–1870. Irish painter, active in London from 1827. He drew caricatures of literary contemporaries, such as Dickens, and his historical paintings include *The Meeting of Wellington and Blücher after Waterloo* and *Death of Nelson* both 1860s (murals in the House of Lords, London).

McLuhan (Herbert) Marshall 1911–1980. Canadian theorist of communication, noted for his views on the effects of technology on modern society. He coined the phrase 'the medium is the message', meaning that the form rather than the content of information is crucial. His works include *The Gutenberg Galaxy* 1962 (in which he coined the phrase 'the global village' for the modern electronic society), *Understanding Media* 1964, and *The Medium is the Massage* (sic) 1967.

MacMahon Marie Edmé Patrice Maurice, Comte de MacMahon 1808–1893. Marshal of France. Captured at Sedan in 1870 during the Franco-Prussian War, he suppressed the briefly autonomous Paris Commune after his release, and as president of the republic 1873–79 worked for a royalist restoration until forced to resign.

McMillan Edwin Mattison 1907– . US physicist. In 1940, he discovered neptunium, the first transuranic element, by bombarding uranium with neutrons. In 1951, he shared a Nobel prize with ◊Seaborg for their discovery of transuranic elements.

MacMillan Kenneth 1929– . Scottish choreographer. After studying at the Sadler's Wells Ballet School he was director of the Royal Ballet 1970–77 and then principal choreographer.

He is renowned for his work with the Canadian dancer Lynn Seymour such as *La Baiser de la Fée* 1960 and *Anastasia* 1967–71. Other works include *Elite Syncopations* 1974 and *Mayerling* 1978.

MacMillan Kirkpatrick, died 1878. Scottish blacksmith, who invented the bicycle in 1839. His invention consisted of a 'hobby-horse' that was fitted with treadles and propelled by pedalling.

Macmillan (Maurice) Harold, 1st Earl of Stockton 1894–1986. British Conservative politician. As minister of housing 1951–54 he achieved the construction of 300,000 new houses per year. He was chancellor of the Exchequer 1955–57, and became prime minister 1957 on Eden's resignation after the Suez crisis. At home, he furthered domestic expansion. Internationally, he attempted unsuccessfully to negotiate British entry to the European Community, and his realization of the 'wind of change' in Africa advanced the independence of former colonies.

Macmillan, member of a family of publishers, entered Parliament as a Unionist 1924 and received his first ministerial post 1951. He led his party to victory in the 1959 elections on the slogan 'You've never had it so good' (the phrase was borrowed from a US election campaign; Macmillan first used it 1957 in a speech warning of the coming danger of inflation). Much of his career as prime minister was spent trying to maintain a UK nuclear weapon, and he was responsible for the purchase of US Polaris missiles 1962. His attempt to take the UK into the European Community 1963 was blocked by the French president de Gaulle. Macmillan's ill health 1963 counteracted to some extent the effect at home of the Vassall spy case and the ◊Profumo scandal. His nickname Supermac was coined by the cartoonist Vicky. He was awarded an earldom 1984.

MacNeice Louis 1907–1963. British poet, born in Belfast. He made his debut with *Blind Fireworks* 1929 and developed a polished ease of expression, reflecting his classical training, as in *Autumn Journal* 1939. Unlike many of his contemporaries, he was politically uncommitted. Later works include the play *The Dark Tower* 1947, written for radio, for which he also wrote features 1941–49; a verse translation of Goethe's *Faust*, and the radio play *The Administrator* 1961. He also translated the Greek classics.

McPhee Colin 1900–1964.. US composer. His studies of Balinese music 1934–36 produced two works, *Tabuh-tabuhan* for two pianos and orchestra 1936 and *Balinese Ceremonial Music* for two pianos 1940, which influenced ◊Cage and later generations of US composers.

Macpherson James 1736–1796. Scottish writer and forger, author of *Fragments of Ancient Poetry Collected in the Highlands of Scotland* 1760, followed by the epics *Fingal* 1761 and *Temora* 1763, which he claimed as the work of the 3rd-century bard ◊Ossian. After his death they were shown to be forgeries.

When challenged by Dr Samuel Johnson, Macpherson failed to produce his originals and a committee decided in 1797 that he had combined fragmentary materials with oral tradition.

Nevertheless, the works of 'Ossian' influenced the development of the Romantic movement in Britain and in Europe.

Macquarie Lachlan 1761–1834. Scottish administrator in Australia. He succeeded Bligh as governor of New South Wales in 1808, raised the demoralized settlement to prosperity, and did much to rehabilitate ex-convicts. In 1821 he returned to Britain in poor health, exhausted by struggles with his opponents.

McQueen Steve (Terrence Steven) 1930–1980. US actor. He was one of the most popular film stars of the 1960s and 1970s, admired for his portrayals of the strong, silent loner, and noted for performing his own stunt work. After television success in the 1950s he became a film star with *The Magnificent Seven* 1960. His films include *The Great Escape* 1963, *Bullitt* 1968, *Papillon* 1973 and *The Hunter* 1980.

Macready William Charles 1793–1873. British actor. He made his debut at Covent Garden, London, in 1816. Noted for his roles as Shakespeare's tragic heroes (Macbeth, Lear, and Hamlet), he was partly responsible for persuading the theatre to return to the original texts of Shakespeare and abandon the earlier, bowdlerized versions.

MacWhirter John 1839–1911. British landscape painter, whose works include *June in the Austrian Tyrol, Spindrift* and watercolours.

McWhirter Norris 1925– . British editor and compiler, with his twin brother, **Ross McWhirter** (1925–1975), of the *Guinness Book of Records* from 1955.

Maderna Bruno 1920–1973. Italian composer and conductor. He studied with Malapiero and ◊Scherchen, and collaborated with ◊Berio in setting up an electronic studio in Milan. His compositions combine advanced techniques with an elegance of sound, and include a pioneering work for live and pre-recorded flute, *Musica su due dimensioni* 1952, numerous concertos, and the aleatoric *Aura* for orchestra 1974.

Madison James 1751–1836. 4th president of the USA 1809–17. In 1787 he became a member of the Philadelphia Constitutional Convention and took a leading part in drawing up the US constitution and the Bill of Rights. As secretary of state in Jefferson's government 1801–09, his main achievement was the Louisiana Purchase (see James ◊ Monroe). He was elected president in 1808 and re-elected 1812. During his period of office the War of 1812 with Britain took place.

Madonna Italian name for the Virgin ◊Mary, meaning 'my lady'.

Maecenas Gaius Cilnius 69–8 BC. Roman patron of the arts who encouraged the work of ◊Horace and ◊Virgil.

Maeterlinck Maurice, Count Maeterlinck 1862–1949. Belgian poet and dramatist. His plays include

Pelléas et Mélisande 1892, *L'Oiseau bleu/The Blue Bird* 1908, and *Le Bourgmestre de Stilmonde/The Burgomaster of Stilemonde* 1918, which celebrates Belgian resistance in World War I, a theme that caused his exile to the USA 1940. Nobel prize 1911.

Magellan Ferdinand 1480–1521. Portuguese navigator. In 1519 he set sail in the *Victoria* from Seville with the intention of reaching the East Indies by a westerly route. He sailed through the **Magellan Strait** at the tip of South America, crossed an ocean he named the Pacific, and in 1521 reached the Philippines, where he was killed in a battle with the islanders. His companions returned to Seville in 1522, completing the voyage under del ◊Cano.

Magellan was brought up at court and entered the royal service, but later transferred his services to Spain. He and his Malay slave, Enrique de Malacca, are considered the first circumnavigators of the globe, since they had once sailed from the Philippines to Europe.

Magritte René 1898–1967. Belgian Surrealist painter. His paintings focus on visual paradoxes and everyday objects taken out of context. Recurring motifs include bowler hats, apples, and windows.

His first Surrealist works date from the mid-1920s. Magritte joined the other Surrealists in Paris 1927. Returning to Brussels in 1930 he painted murals for public buildings, and throughout his life created variations on themes of mystery treated with apparent literalness.

Mahan Alfred Thayer 1840–1914. US naval officer and military historian, author of *The Influence of Sea Power upon History* 1890, in which he propounded a global strategy based on the importance of sea power.

He argued that Britain held a strategic advantage over the central powers and predicted the defeat of the German navy in the World War I.

Mahfouz Naguib 1911– . Egyptian novelist and playwright. His novels, which deal with the urban working class, include a semi-autobiographical trilogy 1957, *Children of Gebelawi* 1959 (banned in Egypt because of its treatment of religious themes), and *Respected Sir* 1988. Nobel prize 1988.

Mahler Gustav 1860–1911. Austrian composer and conductor. His ten symphonies, the moving *Das Lied von der Erde/Song of the Earth* 1909, and his song cycles display a synthesis of Romanticism and new uses of chromatic harmonies and musical forms.

Mahler was born in Bohemia (now Czechoslovakia); he studied at the Vienna Conservatoire, and conducted in Prague, Leipzig, Budapest, and Hamburg 1891–97. He was director of the Vienna Court Opera from 1897 and conducted the New York Philharmonic from 1910.

Mahler *Austrian composer and conductor Gustav Mahler.*

Mahmud two sultans of the Ottoman empire:

Mahmud I 1696–1754. Ottoman sultan from 1730. After restoring order to the empire in Istanbul 1730, he suppressed a rebellion by the Janissaries, the sultan's bodyguard-cum-army, in 1731 and waged war against Persia 1731–46. He led successful wars against Austria and Russia, concluded by the Treaty of Belgrade 1739. He was a patron of the arts and also carried out reform of the army.

Mahmud II 1785–1839. Ottoman sultan from 1808 who attempted to westernize the declining empire, carrying out a series of far-reaching reforms of civil service and army. In 1826 he destroyed the Janissaries (see ◊Mahmud I). Wars against Russia 1807–12 led to losses of territory. The pressure for Greek independence after 1821 led to conflict with Britain, France, and Russia, leading to the destruction of the Ottoman fleet at the Battle of Navarino in 1829 and defeat in the Russo-Turkish war 1828–29, and he was forced to recognize Greek independence in 1830.

There was further disorder with the revolt in Egypt of ◊Mehemet Ali 1831–32, which in turn led to temporary Ottoman-Russian peace. Attempts to control the rebellious provinces failed in 1839, resulting in effect in the granting of Egyptian autonomy.

Mailer Norman 1923– . US writer and journalist. He gained wide attention with his novel of World War II *The Naked and the Dead* 1948. A social commentator on the US literary and political scene, he has run for mayor of New York and has expressed radical sexual views.

Other novels include *An American Dream* 1964. Journalism includes *Armies of the Night* 1968, about protest against the Vietnam War, and *The Executioner's Song* 1979 (Pulitzer Prize), about a convicted murderer on Death Row. Mailer has also ventured into filmmaking.

Maillart Ella 1903– . Swiss explorer, skier, and Olympic yachtswoman, known for her daring six month journey into Russian Turkestan, described in *Turkestan Solo* 1934, and for her expedition across the Gobi Desert with Peter ◊Fleming, recounted in *Forbidden Journey* 1937.

Maillol Aristide Joseph Bonaventure 1861–1944. French artist who turned to sculpture in the 1890s. His work is devoted to the human figure, particularly the female nude. It shows the influence of classical Greek art, but tends towards simplified rounded forms.

Maillol was influenced by the Nabis (followers of Gauguin). A typical example of his work is *Fame* for the Cézanne monument in Aix-en-Provence.

Maimonides Moses (Moses Ben Maimon) 1135– 1204. Jewish rabbi and philosopher, born in Córdoba, Spain. Known as one of the greatest Hebrew scholars, he attempted to reconcile faith and reason; his philosophical classic is *More nevukhim/The Guide to the Perplexed* 1176–91, which helped to introduce the theories of Aristotle into medieval philosophy.

He left Spain in 1160 to escape the persecution of the Jews and settled in Fez, and later in Cairo, where he was personal physician to Sultan Saladin. His codification of Jewish law is known as the *Mishneh Torah/The Torah Reviewed* 1180; he also formulated the **Thirteen Principles**, which summarize the basic beliefs of Judaism.

Maintenon Françoise d'Aubigné, Marquise de Maintenon 1653–1719. Second wife of Louis XIV of France from 1684, and widow of the writer Paul Scarron (1610–60). She was governess to the children of Mme de Montespan by Louis, and his mistress from 1667. She secretly married the king after the death of Queen Marie Thérèse in 1683. Her political influence was considerable, and, as a Catholic convert from Protestantism, her religious opinions were zealous.

Major John 1943– . British Conservative politician, briefly foreign secretary 1989 and then chancellor of the Exchequer from 1989.

Formerly a banker, he became member of Parliament for Huntingdonshire in 1979 and joined the government in 1981, becoming deputy to Chancellor Nigel Lawson 1987. In 1989 Major was promoted to foreign secretary and, after Lawson's resignation, to chancellor, within the space of six months.

Makarios III 1913–1977. Cypriot politician, Greek Orthodox archbishop 1950–77. A leader of the Resistance organization EOKA, he was exiled by the British to the Seychelles 1956–57 for supporting armed action to achieve union with Greece (*enosis*). He was president of the republic of Cyprus 1960–77 (briefly deposed by a Greek military coup Jul–Dec 1974).

Makarova Natalia 1940– . Russian ballerina. She danced with the Kirov Ballet 1959–70, then sought political asylum in the West. Her roles include the title role in *Giselle*, and Aurora in *The Sleeping Beauty*.

Malamud Bernard 1914–1986. US novelist. He first attracted attention with *The Natural* 1952, taking a professional baseball player as his hero. Later works, often dealing with Jewish immigrant tradition, include *The Assistant* 1957, *The Fixer* 1966, *Dubin's Lives* 1979, and *God's Grace* 1982.

Malcolm four kings of Scotland, including:

Malcolm III called *Canmore c.* 1031–1093. King of Scotland from 1054, the son of Duncan I (died 1040); he was killed at Alnwick while invading Northumberland.

Malcolm X assumed name of Malcolm Little 1926–1965. US black nationalist leader. While serving a prison sentence for burglary (1946–53) he joined the Black Muslim sect. On his release he campaigned for black separatism, condoning violence in self-defence, but in 1964 modified his views to found the Islamic-socialist Organization of Afro-American Unity, preaching racial solidarity. A year later he was assassinated by Black Muslim opponents while addressing a rally in Harlem, New York. His *Autobiography of Malcolm X* was published 1964.

Malebranche Nicolas 1638–1715. French philosopher. Born in Paris, he joined the Congregation of the Oratory in 1660. *De la Recherche de la Vérité/Search after Truth* 1674–78 was inspired by Descartes; he maintained that exact ideas of external objects are obtainable only through God.

Malenkov Georgi Maximilianovich 1901–1988. Soviet prime minister 1953–55, Stalin's designated successor but abruptly ousted within two weeks of Stalin's death as Communist Party secretary by ◊Khrushchev, and replaced as prime minister in 1955 by ◊Bulganin.

Malenkov officially resigned on grounds of 'inadequate experience' and subsequently occupied minor party posts. He was expelled from the Central Committee 1957 and from the Communist Party 1961.

Malevich Kasimir 1878–1935. Russian abstract painter, born in Kiev. In 1912 he visited Paris and became a Cubist, and in 1913 he launched his own abstract movement, *Suprematism*, based on simple geometric figures. Later he returned to figurative themes treated in a semi-abstract style.

Malherbe François de 1555–1628. French poet and grammarian, born in Caen. He became court poet about 1605 under Henry IV and Louis XIII. He advocated reform of language and versification, and established the 12-syllable Alexandrine as the standard form of French verse.

Malik Yakob Alexandrovich 1906–1980. Soviet diplomat. He was permanent representative at the United Nations 1948–53 and 1968–76, and it was his walkout from the Security Council in Jan 1950 that allowed the authorization of UN intervention in the Korean War.

Malinovsky Rodion Yakolevich 1898–1967. Russian soldier and politician. In World War II he fought at Stalingrad, commanded in Ukraine, and led the advance through the Balkans to capture Budapest 1945. He was minister of defence 1957–67.

Malinowski Bronislaw 1884–1942. Polish anthropologist, one of the founders of the theory of functionalism in the social sciences, in which society is seen as a number of interrelated parts, all operating with common views and goals. His study of the peoples of the Trobriand Islands led him to see customs and practices in terms of their function in creating and maintaining social order.

Malipiero Gian Francesco 1882–1973. Italian composer and editor of ◊Monteverdi and ◊Vivaldi. His own works include operas based on Shakespeare's *Julius Caesar* 1934–35 and *Antony and Cleopatra* 1936–37 in a Neo-Classical style.

Mallarmé Stéphane 1842–1898. French poet who founded the Symbolist school with Verlaine. His belief that poetry should be evocative and suggestive was reflected in *L'Après-midi d'un faune/Afternoon of a Faun* 1876, which inspired Debussy. Later publications are *Poésies complètes/Complete Poems* 1887, *Vers et prose/Verse and Prose* 1893, and the prose *Divagations/Digressions* 1897.

Malle Louis 1932– . French film director. After a period as assistant to Robert Bresson, he directed *Les Amants/The Lovers* 1958, audacious in its time for its explicitness. His subsequent films, made in France and the USA, include *Zazie dans le metro* 1961, *Viva Maria* 1965, *Pretty Baby* 1978, *Atlantic City* 1980, and *Au Revoir les enfants* 1988.

Malory Thomas 15th century. English author of the prose romance *Le Morte d'Arthur* (about 1470). It is a translation from the French, modified by material from other sources, and deals with the exploits of King Arthur's knights of the Round Table and the quest for the Grail.

Malory's identity is uncertain. He is thought to have been the Warwickshire landowner of that name who was member of Parliament for Warwick in 1445, and in 1451 and 1452 was charged with rape, theft, and attempted murder. If that is so, he must have compiled *Morte d'Arthur* during his 20 years in Newgate prison.

Malpighi Marcello 1628–1694. Italian physiologist, who made many discoveries (still known by his name) in his microscope studies of animal and plant tissues.

Malraux André 1901–1976. French novelist. He became involved in the nationalist and communist revolution in China in the 1920s, reflected in *La Condition humaine/Man's Estate* 1933; *L'Espoir/Days of Hope* 1937 is set in Civil War Spain. He was minister of cultural affairs 1960–69.

Malthus Thomas Robert 1766–1834. English economist and cleric, whose *Essay on the Principle of Population* 1798 (revised 1803) argued for population control, since populations increase in geometric ratio, and food only in arithmetic ratio. He saw war, famine, and disease as necessary checks on population growth.

Mamet David 1947– . US playwright. His plays, with their vivid, freewheeling language and sense of ordinary US life, include *American Buffalo* 1977, *Sexual Perversity in Chicago* 1978, and *Glengary, Glen Ross* 1984.

Mamoulian Rouben 1898–1987. Armenian film director who lived in the USA from 1923. After several years on Broadway he turned to films, making the first sound version of *Dr Jekyll and Mr Hyde* 1932 and *Queen Christina* 1933. His later work includes *The Mark of Zorro* 1940 and *Silk Stockings* 1957.

Manchu ruling dynasty in China from 1644 until their overthrow in 1912. Originally a nomadic people from Manchuria, they established power through a series of successful invasions from the north.

Mandela Nelson (Rolihlahla) 1918– . South African politician and lawyer. As organizer of the banned African National Congress (ANC), he was acquitted of treason 1961, but was given a life sentence 1964 on charges of sabotage and plotting to overthrow the government. In prison he became a symbol of unity for the worldwide anti-apartheid movement. In Feb 1990 he was released, the ban on the ANC having been lifted.

Mandela Winnie (Nomzamo) 1934– . Civil-rights activist in South Africa and wife of Nelson Mandela. A leading spokesperson for the African National Congress during her husband's imprisonment 1964–90, she has been jailed for a year and put under house arrest several times.

Mandelbrot Benoit B 1924– . Polish-born US scientist who coined the term 'fractal geometry' to describe 'self-similar' shape, a motif that repeats indefinitely, each time smaller.

Mandelshtam Osip Emilevich 1891–1938. Russian poet. Son of a Jewish merchant, he was sent to a concentration camp by the Communist authorities in the 1930s, and died there. His posthumously published work with its classic brevity established his reputation as one of the greatest modern Russian poets.

Mandeville John. Supposed author of a 14th-century travel manual for pilgrims to the Holy Land, originally written in French and probably the work of Jean d'Outremeuse of Liège. As well as references to real marvels such as the pyramids, there are tales of headless people with eyes in their shoulders, and other such fantastic inventions.

Manet Edouard 1832–1883. French painter, active in Paris. Rebelling against the academic tradition, he developed a clear and unaffected Realist style. His work was an inspiration to the young Impressionists. His subjects were chiefly modern, such as *Un Bar aux Folies-Bergère/Bar at the Folies-Bergère* 1882 (Courtauld Art Gallery, London).

Manet, born in Paris, trained under a history painter and was inspired by Goya and Velázquez but also by his near-contemporary Courbet. His *Déjeuner sur l'herbe/Picnic on the Grass* 1863 and *Olympia* 1865 (both Musée d'Orsay, Paris) offended conservative tastes in their matter-of-fact treatment of the nude body. He never exhibited with the Impressionists, although he was associated with them from the 1870s.

Manley Michael 1924– . Jamaican politician, prime minister 1972–80 and from 1989, adopting more moderate socialist policies. His father, *Norman Manley* (1893–1969), was founder of the People's National Party and prime minister 1959–62.

Mann Anthony. Adopted name of Emil Anton Bundmann 1906–1967. US film director who made a series of violent but intelligent 1950s Westerns starring James Stewart, such as *Winchester '73*

Mandela Nelson Mandela, perhaps the best known member of the African National Congress. A resonant symbol of the black struggle against South African apartheid, he is pictured shortly after his release from prison in 1990, ending 27 years of incarceration.

1950. He also directed one of the best film epics, *El Cid* 1961. His other films include *The Glenn Miller Story* 1954 and *A Dandy in Aspic* 1968.

Mann Heinrich 1871–1950. German novelist who fled to the USA in 1937 with his brother Thomas Mann. His books include a scathing trilogy dealing with the Kaiser's Germany *Das Kaiserreich/The Empire* 1918–25.

Mann Thomas 1875–1955. German novelist and critic, concerned with the theme of the artist's relation to society. His first novel was *Buddenbrooks* 1901 which, followed by *Der Zauberberg/The Magic Mountain* 1924, led to a Nobel prize 1929. Later works include *Dr Faustus* 1947 and *Die Bekenntnisse des Hochstaplers Felix Krull/ Confessions of Felix Krull* 1954. Notable among his short stories is *Der Tod in Venedig/Death in Venice* 1913.

Mann worked in an insurance office in Munich and on the staff of the periodical *Simplicissimus*. His opposition to the Nazi regime forced him to live abroad and in 1940 he became a US citizen. Among his other works are the biblical tetralogy on the theme of Joseph and his brothers 1933–44, and a number of short stories including *Tonio Kröger* 1903.

Mannerheim Carl Gustav Emil von 1867–1951. Finnish general and politician, leader of the conservative forces in the civil war 1917–18 and regent 1918–19. He commanded the Finnish army 1939–40 and 1941–44, and was president of Finland 1944–46.

After the Russian Revolution 1917, a Red (socialist) militia was formed in Finland with Russian backing, and independence was declared in Dec. The Red forces were opposed by a White (counterrevolutionary) army led by Mannerheim, who in 1918 crushed the socialists with German assistance. In 1944, after leading the defence against Soviet invasion in two wars, he negotiated the peace settlement with the USSR and became president.

Manners family name of dukes of Rutland; seated at Belvoir Castle, Lincolnshire, England.

Mannheim Karl 1893–1947. Hungarian sociologist, who settled in the UK 1933. In *Ideology and Utopia* 1929 he argued that all knowledge, except in mathematics and physics, is ideological, a reflection of class interests and values; that there is no such thing as objective knowledge or absolute truth.

Mannheim distinguished between ruling class ideologies and those of utopian or revolutionary groups, arguing that knowledge is thus created by a continual power struggle between rival groups and ideas, Later works such as *Man and Society* 1940 analysed modern mass society in terms of its fragmentation and susceptibility to extremist ideas and totalitarian governments.

Manning Henry Edward 1808–1892. English priest, one of the leaders of the Oxford Movement, which sought to revive Roman Catholicism. In 1851 he was converted to Roman Catholicism, and in 1865 became archbishop of Westminster. He was created a cardinal 1875.

Manning Olivia 1911–1980. British novelist. The best known of her books are semi- autobiographical and set during World War II. These include *The Great Fortune* 1960, *The Spoilt City* 1962, and *Friends and Heroes* 1965, forming the 'Balkan trilogy', and a later 'Levant trilogy'.

Manoel two kings of Portugal:

Manoel I 1469–1521. King of Portugal from 1495, when he succeeded his uncle John II (1455–95). He was known as 'the Fortunate', because his reign was distinguished by the discoveries made by Portuguese navigators and the expansion of the Portuguese empire.

Manoel II 1889–1932. King of Portugal 1908–10. He ascended the throne on the assassination of his father, Carlos I, but was driven out by a revolution 1910, and lived in England.

Mansart Jules Hardouin 1646–1708. French architect of the palace of Versailles and Grand Trianon, and designer of the Place de Vendôme and the Place des Victoires, Paris.

Mansell Nigel 1954– . English motor-racing driver, runner-up in the world championship on two occasions.

He started his Formula One career with Lotus 1980 and won the 1985 European Grand Prix. He drove for Williams 1985–88 and from 1989 for Ferrari. He announced his retirement in 1990.

Mansfield Jayne. Stage name of Vera Jayne Palmer 1933–1967. US actress who had a short career as a kind of living parody of Marilyn Monroe in films including *The Girl Can't Help It* 1956 and *Will Success Spoil Rock Hunter?* 1957.

Mansfield Katherine. Pen name of Kathleen Beauchamp 1888–1923. New Zealand writer, who lived most of her life in England. Her delicate artistry emerges not only in her volumes of short stories, such as *In a German Pension* 1911, *Bliss* 1920 and *The Garden Party* 1923, but in her *Letters* and *Journal*.

Born near Wellington, New Zealand, she was educated in London, to which she returned after a two-year visit home, where she published her earliest stories. She married the critic John Middleton Murry in 1913.

Manson Patrick 1844–1922. Scottish physician, who showed that insects are responsible for the spread of diseases like elephantiasis and malaria.

Manson spent many years in practice in the Far East. On his return to London, he founded the School of Tropical Medicine. His work on malaria earned him the nickname 'Mosquito Manson'.

Mantegna Andrea c. 1431–1506. Italian Renaissance painter and engraver, active chiefly in Padua and Mantua, where some of his frescoes remain. Paintings such as *The Agony in the Garden* about 1455 (National Gallery, London) reveal a dramatic linear style, mastery of perspective, and strongly Classical architectural detail.

Mantegna was born in Vicenza. Early works include frescoes for the Eremitani Church in Padua (1440s, badly damaged). From 1460 he worked for Ludovico Gonzaga in Mantua, producing an outstanding fresco series in the Ducal Palace (1470s) and later *The Triumph of Caesar* (Hampton Court, near London). He was influenced by the sculptor Donatello and in turn influenced the Venetian painter Giovanni Bellini (his brother-in-law) and the German artist Dürer.

Manutius Aldus 1450–1515. Italian printer, established in Venice (which he made the publishing centre of Europe) from 1490; he introduced italic type and was the first to print books in Greek.

Manzoni Alessandro, Count Manzoni 1785–1873. Italian poet and novelist, best known for his historical romance, *I promessi sposi/The Betrothed* 1825–27, set in Spanish-occupied Milan during the 17th century. Verdi's *Requiem* commemorates him.

Mao Zedong formerly *Mao Tse-tung* 1893–1976. Chinese political leader and Marxist theoretician. A founder of the Chinese Communist Party (CCP) 1921, Mao soon emerged as its leader. He organized the Long March 1934–36 and the war of liberation 1937–49, and headed the CCP and government until his death. His influence diminished with the failure of his 1958–60 Great Leap Forward, an attempt to concentrate resources on industry rather than agriculture, but he emerged dominant again during the 1966–69 anti-bureaucratic Cultural Revolution. Mao adapted communism to Chinese conditions, as set out in the *Little Red Book*.

Mao, son of a peasant farmer in Hunan province, was once library assistant at Beijing University and a headmaster at Changsha. He became chief of CCP propaganda under the Guomindang (nationalist) leader Sun Yat-sen (Sun Zhong Shan)

Mao Zedong Chairman Mao with vice chair Lin Biao, who is holding the Little Red Book *of Mao's thoughts.*

Map 326

until sacked by Sun's successor Chiang Kai-shek (Jiang Jie Shi). In 1931–34 Mao set up a communist republic at Jiangxi and, with Zhu De, marshalled the Red Army in preparation for the Long March to Shaanxi. CCP chair from 1935, Mao secured an alliance with the Guomindang 1936–45. He built up a people's republic at Yan'an 1936–47, where he married his third wife ◊Jiang Qing 1939. During the liberation war and civil wars, he successfully employed mobile, rural-based guerrilla tactics.

Mao served as party chair until his death Sept 1976 and as state president until 1959. After the damages of the Cultural Revolution, the Great Helmsman, as he was called, working with his prime minister Zhou Enlai, oversaw a period of reconstruction from 1970 until deteriorating health weakened his political grip in the final years.

Mao's writings and thoughts dominated the functioning of the People's Republic 1949–76. He stressed the need for rural rather than urban-based revolutions in Asia, for reducing rural-urban differences, and for perpetual revolution to prevent the emergence of new elites. Overseas, Mao helped precipitate the Sino-Soviet split 1960 and was a firm advocate of a nonaligned Third World strategy (neutrality towards major powers). Since 1978, the leadership of Deng Xiaoping has reinterpreted Maoism and criticized its policy excesses, but many of Mao's ideas remain influential.

Map Walter *c.* 1140–*c.* 1209. Welsh cleric and satirist who was in the service of Henry II as an itinerant justice in England, and envoy to Alexander III of Scotland. His *De Nugis Curialium* was a collection of gossip and scandal from royal and ecclesiastical courts.

Maradona Diego 1960–. Argentinian footballer who helped his country to win the World Cup 1986.

He left South America for Barcelona, Spain, 1982 for a transfer fee of approximately £5 million. He moved to Napoli, Italy, for £6.9 million 1984, and contributed to their first Italian League title.

Marat Jean Paul 1743–1793. French Revolutionary leader and journalist. He was elected in 1792 to the National Convention, where he carried on a long struggle with the right-wing, republican Girondins, ending in their overthrow in May 1793. In July he was murdered by Charlotte ◊Corday.

Marc Franz 1880–1916. German Expressionist painter, associated with ◊Kandinsky in founding the *Blaue Reiter* movement. Animals played an essential part in his view of the world and bold semi-abstracts of red and blue horses are characteristic of his work.

Marceau Marcel 1923– . French mime artist. He is the creator of the clown-harlequin Bip and mime sequences such as 'Youth, Maturity, Old Age, and Death'.

Marchais Georges 1920– . Leader of the French Communist Party (PCF) from 1972. Under his leadership, the party committed itself to a 'transition to socialism' by democratic means and entered into a union of the left with the Socialist Party (PS). This was severed 1977, and the PCF returned to a more orthodox pro-Moscow line, since when its share of the vote has decreased.

Marchais joined the PCF 1947 and worked his way up through the party organization to become its general secretary. He was a presidential candidate 1981, and sanctioned the PCF's participation in the Mitterrand government 1981–84. He remained leader of the PCF despite a fall in its national vote from 21% 1973 to 10% 1986.

Marchand Jean Baptiste 1863–1934. French general and explorer. In 1898, he headed an expedition in Africa from the French Congo, which occupied the town of Fashoda (now Kodok) on the White Nile. The subsequent arrival of British troops under Kitchener resulted in a crisis that nearly led to war between Britain and France.

Marcian 396–457. Eastern Roman emperor 450–457. He was a general who married Pulcheria, sister of Theodosius II, and became emperor at the latter's death. He convened the Council of Chalcedon in 451 and refused to pay tribute to Attila the Hun.

Marciano 'Rocky' (Rocco Francis Marchegiano) 1923–1969. US boxer, world heavyweight champion 1952–56. He retired after 49 professional fights, the only heavyweight champion to retire undefeated.

Born in Brockton, Massachussetts, he was known as the 'Brockton Blockbuster'. He knocked out 43 of his 49 opponents. Marciano was killed in a plane crash.

Marconi Guglielmo 1874–1937. Italian pioneer in the invention and development of wireless telegraphy. In 1895 he achieved wireless communication over more than a mile, and in England in 1896 he conducted successful experiments that led to the formation of the company that became Marconi's Wireless Telegraph Company Ltd. He shared the Nobel Prize for Physics 1909.

In 1898 he successfully transmitted signals across the English Channel, and in 1901 established communication with St John's, Newfoundland, from Poldhu in Cornwall, and in 1918 with Australia. Marconi was an Italian delegate to the Versailles peace conference in 1919 after World War I.

Marcos Ferdinand 1917–1989. Filipino right-wing politician, president 1965–86, when he was forced into exile in Hawaii. He was backed by the USA when in power, but in 1988 US authorities indicted him and his wife *Imelda Marcos* (1931–) for racketeering and embezzlement, and in 1990 she was tried and acquitted on a charge of stealing $105 million.

Marcos was convicted while a law student 1939 of murdering a political opponent of his

Marconi Italian inventor Guglielmo Marconi whose pioneering work on wireless telegraphy earned him a Nobel prize in 1909.

father, but eventually secured his own acquittal. In World War II he was a guerrilla fighter, survived Japanese prison camps of Bataan, and became president 1965. His regime became increasingly repressive, with the use of the secret marshals: anti-crime squads executing those only suspected of offences. He was overthrown and exiled 1986 by a popular front led by Corazón ◊Aquino, widow of a murdered opposition leader. A US grand jury investigating Marcos and his wife alleged that they had embezzled millions of dollars from the Philippines government, received bribes, and defrauded US banks. Marcos was too ill to stand trial, however, and died in Honolulu, Hawaii, Sept 1989.

Marcus Aurelius Antoninus AD 121–180. Roman emperor from 161 and Stoic philosopher. Although considered one of the best of the Roman emperors, he persecuted the Christians for political reasons. He wrote philosophical *Meditations*.

Born in Rome, he was adopted (at the same time as Lucius Aurelius Verus) by his uncle, the emperor Antoninus Pius, whom he succeeded in 161. He conceded an equal share in the rule to Lucius Verus (died 169). Marcus Aurelius spent much of his reign warring against the Germanic tribes and died in Pannonia, where he had gone to drive back the invading Marcomanni.

Marcuse Herbert 1898–1979. German political philosopher, in the USA from 1934; his theories combining Marxism and Freudianism influenced radical thought in the 1960s. His books include *One-Dimensional Man* 1964.

Marcuse preached the overthrow of the existing social order by using the system's very tolerance to ensure its defeat but was not an advocate of violent revolution.

Margaret 1282–1290. Queen of Scotland from 1285, known as *the Maid of Norway*. Margaret was the daughter of Eric II, king of Norway, and Princess Margaret of Scotland. When only two years of age she became queen of Scotland on the death of her grandfather, Alexander III, but died in the Orkneys on a voyage to her kingdom.

Margaret (Rose) 1930– . Princess of the UK, younger daughter of George VI. In 1960 she married Anthony Armstrong-Jones, later created Lord Snowdon, but in 1976 they agreed to live apart, and were divorced 1978. Their children are *David, Viscount Linley* (1961–) and *Lady Sarah Armstrong-Jones* (1964–).

Margaret of Anjou 1430–1482. Queen of England from 1445, wife of ◊Henry VI of England. After the outbreak of the Wars of the Roses in 1455, she acted as the leader of the Lancastrians against the Yorkists, but was defeated and captured at the battle of Tewkesbury 1471 by Edward IV.

Her one object had been to secure the succession of her son, Edward (born 1453), who was killed at Tewkesbury. After five years' imprisonment Margaret was allowed in 1476 to return to her native France, where she died in poverty.

Margaret, St 1045–1093. Queen of Scotland, the granddaughter of King Edmund Ironside of England. She went to Scotland after the Norman Conquest, and soon after married Malcolm III. The marriage of her daughter Matilda to Henry I united the Norman and English royal houses.

Through her influence the Lowlands, until then purely Celtic, became largely anglicized. She was canonized 1251 in recognition of her benefactions to the church.

Margrethe II 1940– . Queen of Denmark from 1972, when she succeeded her father Frederick IX. In 1967, she married the French diplomat Count Henri de Laborde de Monpezat, who took the title Prince Hendrik. Her heir is Crown Prince Frederick (1968–).

Marguerite of Navarre also known as *Margaret d'Angoulême* 1492–1549. Queen of Navarre from 1527, French poet, and author of the *Heptaméron* 1558, a collection of stories in imitation of Boccaccio's *Decameron*. The sister of Francis I of France, she was born in Angoulême. Her second husband 1527 was Henri d'Albret, king of Navarre.

Maria Theresa 1717–1780. Empress of Austria from 1740, when she succeeded her father, the Holy Roman Emperor Charles VI; her claim to the throne was challenged and she became embroiled, first in the War of the Austrian Succession 1740–48, then in the Seven Years' War 1756–63; she remained in possession of Austria but lost Silesia. The rest of her reign was peaceful.

She married her cousin Francis of Lorraine 1736, and on the death of her father became archduchess of Austria and queen of Hungary and Bohemia. Her claim was challenged by Charles of Bavaria, who was elected emperor 1742, while Frederick of Prussia occupied Silesia. The War of the Austrian Succession followed, in which Austria was allied with Britain, and Prussia with France; when it ended 1748, Maria Theresa retained her heritage, except that Frederick kept Silesia, while her husband had succeeded Charles as emperor 1745. Intent on recovering Silesia, she formed an alliance with France and Russia against Prussia; the Seven Years' War, which resulted, exhausted Europe and left the territorial position as before. After 1763 she pursued a consistently peaceful policy, concentrating on internal reforms; although her methods were despotic, she fostered education, codified the laws, and abolished torture. She also expelled the Jesuits. In these measures she was assisted by her son, Joseph II, who became emperor 1765, and succeeded her in the Habsburg domains.

Marie 1875–1938. Queen of Romania. She was the daughter of the Duke of Edinburgh, second son of Queen Victoria, and married Prince Ferdinand of Romania in 1893 (he was king 1922–27). She wrote a number of literary works, notably *Story of My Life* 1934–35. Her son Carol became king of Romania, and her daughters, Elisabeth and Marie, queens of Greece and Yugoslavia respectively.

Marie Antoinette 1755–1793. Queen of France from 1774. She was the daughter of Empress Maria Theresa of Austria, and married ◊Louis XVI of France in 1770. With a reputation for frivolity and extravagance, she meddled in politics in the Austrian interest, and helped provoke the French Revolution of 1789. She was tried for treason in Oct 1793 and guillotined.

Marie Antoinette influenced her husband to resist concessions in the early days of the Revolution, for example, ◊Mirabeau's plan for a constitutional settlement. She instigated the disastrous flight to Varennes, which discredited the monarchy, and welcomed foreign intervention against the Revolution, betraying French war strategy to the Austrians in 1792.

Marie de France c. 1150–1215. French poet, thought to have been the half-sister of Henry II of England, and abbess of Shaftesbury 1181–1215. She wrote *Lais* (verse tales which dealt with Celtic and Arthurian themes) and *Ysopet*, a collection of fables.

Marie de' Medici 1573–1642. Queen of France, wife of Henry IV from 1600, and regent (after

his murder) for their son Louis XIII. She left the government to her favourites, the Concinis, until in 1617 Louis XIII seized power and executed them. She was banished, but after she led a revolt in 1619, ◊Richelieu effected her reconciliation with her son, but when she attempted to oust him in 1630, she was exiled.

Marie Louise 1791–1847. Queen consort of Napoleon I from 1810 (after his divorce from Josephine), mother of Napoleon II. She was the daughter of Francis I of Austria (see Emperor ◊Francis II), and on Napoleon's fall returned to Austria. In 1815 she was granted the duchy of Parma.

Mariette Auguste Ferdinand François 1821–1881. French egyptologist, whose discoveries from 1850 included the 'temple' between the paws of the Sphinx. He founded the Egyptian Museum in Cairo.

Marin John 1870–1953. US painter, known for seascapes in watercolour and oil, influenced by Impressionism. He visited Europe 1905–11, and began his paintings of the Maine coast 1914.

Marinetti Filippo Tommaso 1876–1944. Italian author, who in 1909 published the first manifesto of Futurism, which called for a break with tradition in art, poetry, and the novel, and glorified the machine age.

Born at Alexandria, he illustrated his theories in *Mafarka le futuriste/Mafarka the Futurist* 1910, plays, and a volume on theatrical practice 1916. He recorded his World War I experiences in *Otto anime in una bomba* 1919, and welcomed Mussolini with *Futurismo e fascismo/Futurism and Fascism* 1924.

Marini Marino 1901–1980. Italian sculptor. Influenced by ancient art, he developed a distinctive horse-and-rider theme and a dancers series, reducing the forms to an elemental simplicity. He also produced fine portraits in bronze.

Mariotte Edme 1620–1684. French physicist and priest known for his statement in 1676 of Boyle's law about the volume of a gas, formulated in 1672. He had earlier, in 1660, discovered the eye's blind spot.

Maritain Jacques 1882–1973. French philosopher. Originally a disciple of ◊Bergson, as in *La philosophie bergsonienne/Bergsonian Philosophy* 1914, he later became the best known of the Neo-Thomists applying the methods of Thomas ◊Aquinas to contemporary problems, for example *Introduction à la Philosophie/Introduction to Philosophy* 1920.

Marius Gaius 155–86 BC. Roman military commander and politician. Born near Arpinum, he was elected consul seven times, the first time in 107 BC. He defeated the Cimbri and the Teutons (Germanic tribes attacking Gaul and Italy) 102–101 BC. Marius tried to deprive Sulla of the command in the East against Mithridates and, as a result, civil war broke out in 88 BC. Sulla marched on Rome, and Marius fled to Africa, but later Cinna held Rome for Marius and together they created a reign of terror in Rome.

Marivaux Pierre Carlet de Chamblain de 1688–1763. French novelist and dramatist. His sophisticated comedies include *Le Jeu de l'amour et du hasard/The Game of Love and Chance* 1730 and *Les Fausses confidences/False Confidences* 1737; his novel, *La Vie de Marianne/The Life of Marianne* 1731–41 has autobiographical elements. Marivaux gave the word *marivaudage* (over-subtle lovers' conversation) to the French language.

Mark Antony Antonius, Marcus 83–30 BC. Roman politician and soldier. He was tribune and later consul under Julius Caesar, serving under him in Gaul. In 44 he tried to secure for Caesar the title of king. After Caesar's assassination, he formed the Second Triumvirate with Octavian (◊Augustus) and Lepidus. In 42 he defeated Brutus and Cassius at Philippi. He took Egypt as his share of the empire and formed a liaison with ◊Cleopatra. In 40 he returned to Rome to marry Octavia, the sister of Augustus. In 32 the Senate declared war on Cleopatra. Antony was defeated by Augustus at the battle of Actium 31. He returned to Egypt and committed suicide.

Markevich Igor 1912–1983. Russian-born composer and conductor. He composed the ballet *L'Envol d'Icare* 1932, and the cantata *Le Paradis Perdu* 1933–35 to words by Milton. After World War II he concentrated on conducting.

Mark Antony *A great orator and soldier, Mark Antony committed suicide after his defeat at the battle of Actium in 31 BC.*

Markievicz Constance Georgina, Countess Markievicz (born Gore Booth) 1868–1927. Irish nationalist, who married the Polish count Markievicz in 1900. Her death sentence for taking part in the Easter Rising of 1916 was commuted, and after her release from prison in 1917 she was elected to the Westminster Parliament as a Sinn Féin candidate in 1918 (technically the first British woman member of Parliament), but did not take her seat.

Markov Andrei 1856–1922. Russian mathematician, formulator of the **Markov chain**, a sequence of events, each determined by the one immediately preceding it and by no other.

Markova Alicia. Adopted name of Lilian Alicia Marks 1910– . British ballet dancer. Trained by ◊Pavlova, she was ballerina with ◊Diaghilev's company 1925–29, was the first resident ballerina of the Vic-Wells Ballet 1933–35, partnered Anton ◊Dolin in their own Markova-Dolin Company 1935–37, and danced with the Ballet Russe de Monte Carlo 1938–41 and Ballet Theatre, USA, 1941–46. She is associated with the great classical ballets, especially *Giselle.*

Marks Simon, 1st Baron of Broughton 1888–1964. English chain-store magnate. His father, Polish immigrant Michael Marks, had started a number of 'penny bazaars' with Yorkshireman Tom Spencer in 1887; Simon Marks entered the business in 1907 and built up a national chain of Marks and Spencer stores.

Mark, St lived 1st century AD. In the New Testament, Christian apostle and evangelist, whose name is given to the second Gospel. It was probably written AD 65-70, and used by the authors of the first and third Gospels. He is the patron saint of Venice, and his emblem is a winged lion; feast day 25 Apr.

His first name was John, and his mother, Mary, was one of the first Christians in Jerusalem. He was a cousin of Barnabas, and accompanied Barnabas and Paul on their first missionary journey. He was a fellow worker with Paul in Rome, and later became Peter's interpreter after Paul's death. According to tradition he was the founder of the Christian church in Alexandria, and St Jerome says that he died and was buried there.

Marlborough John Churchill, 1st Duke of Marlborough 1650–1722. English soldier, created a duke 1702 by Queen Anne. He was granted the Blenheim mansion in Oxfordshire in recognition of his services, which included defeating the French army outside Vienna in the battle of Blenheim 1704, during the War of the Spanish Succession.

In 1688 he deserted his patron, James II, for William of Orange, but in 1692 fell into disfavour for Jacobite intrigue. He had married Sarah Jennings (1660–1744), confidante of the future Queen Anne, who created him a duke on her accession. He achieved further victories in

Belgium at Ramillies 1706 and Oudenaarde 1708, and in France at Malplaquet 1709. However, the return of the Tories to power and his wife's quarrel with the queen led to his dismissal in 1711 and his flight to Holland to avoid charges of corruption. He returned in 1714.

Marley Bob (Robert Nesta) 1945–1980. Jamaican reggae singer, a Rastafarian whose songs, many of which were topical and political, popularized reggae in the UK and the USA in the 1970s. One of his best-known songs is 'No Woman No Cry'; his albums include *Natty Dread* 1975 and *Exodus* 1977.

Marlowe Christopher 1564–1593. English poet and dramatist. His work includes the blank-verse plays *Tamburlaine the Great* about 1587, *The Jew of Malta* about 1589, *Edward II* and *Dr Faustus*, both about 1592, the poem *Hero and Leander* 1598, and a translation of Ovid's *Amores*.

Born in Canterbury, Marlowe was educated at Cambridge, where he is thought to have become a government agent. His life was turbulent, with a brief imprisonment in connection with a man's death in a brawl (of which he was cleared), and a charge of atheism (following statements by the playwright ◊Kyd under torture). He was murdered in a Deptford tavern, allegedly in a dispute over the bill, but it may have been a political killing.

Marmontel Jean François 1723–1799. French novelist and dramatist. He wrote tragedies and libretti, and contributed to the *Encyclopédie* (see ◊Diderot); in 1758 he obtained control of the journal *Le Mercure/The Mercury*, in which his *Contes moraux/Moral Studies* 1761 appeared. Other works include *Bélisaire/Belisarius* 1767, and *Les Incas/The Incas* 1777.

He was appointed historiographer of France 1771, secretary to the Académie 1783, and professor of history at the Lycée 1786, but retired in 1792 to write his *Mémoires d'un père/Memoirs of a Father* 1804.

Marot Clément 1496–1544. French poet, best known for his translation of the *Psalms* 1539–43. His graceful, witty style has been a model for later writers of light verse.

Born at Cahors, he accompanied Francis I to Italy in 1524, and was taken prisoner at Pavia, but was soon released, and by 1528 was a salaried member of the royal household. Suspected of heresy, he fled to Turin, where he died.

Marquand John Phillips 1893–1960. US writer. Originally known for a series of stories featuring the Japanese detective Mr Moto, he made a serious reputation with his gently satirical novels of Boston society: *The Late George Apley* 1937 and *H M Pulham, Esq* 1941.

Marquet Pierre Albert 1876–1947. French painter of landscapes and Parisian scenes, especially the Seine and its bridges. He was associated with the

Fauves, a style of painting with a bold use of colour, but soon developed a more conventional, naturalistic style.

Marquette Jacques 1637–1675. French Jesuit missionary and explorer. He went to Canada in 1666, explored the upper lakes of the St Lawrence, and in 1673 with Louis Jolliet (1645–1700), set out on a voyage down the Mississippi on which they made the first accurate record of its course.

Marquis Don(ald Robert Perry) 1878–1937. US author. He is chiefly known for his humorous writing – *Old Soak* 1921, portraying a hard-drinking comic – and *archy and mehitabel* 1927, the typewritten verse adventures of a cockroach and a cat.

Marryat Frederick 1792–1848. British naval officer and novelist, popularly known as Captain Marryat from his naval rank. He resigned from the Royal Navy in 1830 after the success of his first novel, *Frank Mildmay*. He wrote a number of popular adventure stories, including *Peter Simple* 1834, *Mr Midshipman Easy* 1836, and a series of children's books, of which the best known is *Children of the New Forest* 1847.

Marsh Ngaio 1899–1982. New Zealand writer of detective fiction. Her first detective novel *A Man Lay Dead* 1934 introduced her protagonist Chief Inspector Roderick Alleyn.

Marshall Alfred 1842–1924. English economist, professor of economics at Cambridge University 1885–1908. He was a founder of Neo-Classical economics, and stressed the power of supply and demand to generate equilibrium prices in markets, introducing the concept of elasticity of demand relative to price. His *Principles of Economics* 1890 remains perhaps the most influential textbook of Neo-Classical economics.

Marshall George Catlett 1880–1959. US general and diplomat. He was army chief of staff in World War II, secretary of state 1947–49, and secretary of defence Sept 1950–Sept 1951. In 1947 he initiated the **Marshall Plan**, a programme of US financial aid for Europe, and received the Nobel Peace Prize 1953.

Marshall, born in Pennsylvania, was commissioned in 1901, served in World War I, and in 1939 became chief of staff with the rank of general. On resigning in Nov 1945 he became ambassador to China, attempting to secure a coalition between the Nationalist and Communist forces against Japan. As defense secretary (a post never normally held by a soldier), he backed Truman's recall of ◊MacArthur from Korea.

Marshall John 1755–1835. US jurist. As chief justice of the Supreme Court 1801–35, he established the power and independence of the Supreme Court. He laid down interpretations of the US constitution in a series of important decisions which have since become universally accepted.

Marshall John Ross 1912–1988. New Zealand National Party politician, noted for his negotiations of a free-trade agreement with Australia. He was deputy to K J Holyoake as prime minister and succeeded him Feb–Nov 1972.

Marsilius of Padua 1270–1342. Italian scholar and jurist. Born in Padua, he studied and taught at Paris, and in 1324 collaborated with John of Jandun in writing the *Defensor pacis/Defender of the Peace*, a plea for the subordination of the ecclesiastical to the secular power and for the right of the people to choose their own government. He played a part in the establishment of the Roman republic in 1328.

Martens Wilfried 1936– . Prime minister of Belgium from 1979, member of the Social Christian Party. He was president of the Dutch-speaking CVP 1972–79 and, as prime minister, headed six coalition governments in the periods 1979–81, 1981–85, and from 1985.

Martial (Marcus Valerius Martialis) AD 41–104. Latin epigrammatist. His poetry, often bawdy, reflects contemporary Roman life.

Born in Bilbilis, Spain, Martial settled in Rome in 64, where he lived by his literary and social gifts. He is renowned for correctness of diction, versification, and form.

Martin Archer John Porter 1910– . British biochemist who received the 1952 Nobel Prize for Chemistry for work with Richard Synge on paper chromatography in 1944.

Martin (Basil) Kingsley 1897 1969. English journalist who edited the *New Statesman* 1931–60 and made it the voice of controversy on the left.

Martin John 1789–1854. British Romantic painter of grandiose landscapes and ambitious religious subjects, such as *Belshazzar's Feast* (several versions).

Other examples are *The Great Day of His Wrath* and *The Plains of Heaven* (both Tate Gallery, London). Martin often worked on large canvases, and made mezzotints from his work, which were hugely popular in the early 19th century.

Martin Richard 1754–1834. Irish landowner and lawyer known as 'Humanity Martin'. He founded the British Royal Society for Prevention of Cruelty to Animals in 1824.

Martin Violet Florence 1862–1915. Irish novelist under the pen name Martin Ross. She collaborated with her cousin Edith Somerville on tales of Anglo-Irish provincial life, for example *Some Experiences of an Irish RM* 1899.

Martin V 1368–1431. Pope from 1417. A member of the Roman family of Colonna, he was elected during the Council of Constance, and ended the Great Schism between the rival popes of Rome and Avignon.

Martin du Gard Roger 1881–1958. French novelist who realistically recorded the way of life of the bourgeoisie in the eight-volume *Les Thibault/The World of the Thibaults* 1922–40. Nobel prize 1937.

Martineau Harriet 1802–1876. English journalist, economist, and novelist, who wrote popular works on economics, children's stories, and articles in favour of the abolition of slavery.

Martineau James 1805–1900. British Unitarian minister and philosopher. A noted orator, he anticipated Anglican modernists in his theology.

Martinez Maria Montoya 1890–1980. Pueblo Indian potter, who revived silvery black-on-black ware (made without the wheel) at San Ildefonso Pueblo, New Mexico, USA.

Martínez Ruiz José. Real name of ◊Azorín, Spanish author.

Martini Simone *c*.1284–1344. Italian painter, one of the great masters of the Sienese school. A pupil of Duccio, he continued the graceful linear pattern of Sienese art, but introduced a fresh element of naturalism. His patrons included the city of Siena, the king of Naples, and the pope. Two of his frescoes are in the Palazzo Pubblico in Siena: the *Maestà* about 1315 and the horseback warrior *Guidoriccio da Fogliano* (the attribution of the latter is disputed).

Martins Peter 1946– . Danish-born US dancer, choreographer, and director, principal dancer with the New York City Ballet from 1965 and its joint director from 1983.

Martineau English writer Harriet Martineau became a prominent literary figure for her writings on Unitarianism, political science, and the abolition of slavery.

Martins trained at the Royal Danish Ballet School, joining the company 1965, and the same year joined the New York City Ballet as a principal. He created roles in, among others, Robbins's *Goldberg Variations* 1971 and Balanchine's *Violin Concerto* and *Duo Concertant* both 1972, and choreographed, for example, *Calcium Night Light* 1978.

Martin, St 316–400. Bishop of Tours, France, from about 371, and founder of the first monastery in Gaul. He is usually represented as tearing his cloak to share it with a beggar. His feast day is Martinmas, 11 Nov.

Born in Pannonia, SE Europe, a soldier by profession, Martin was converted to Christianity, left the army, and lived for ten years as a recluse. After being elected bishop of Tours, he worked for the extinction of idolatry and the extension of monasticism in France.

Martinu Bohuslav (Jan) 1890–1959. Czech composer, who studied in Paris. He left Czechoslovakia after the Nazi occupation of 1939. The quality of his music varies but at its best it is richly expressive and has great vitality. His works include the operas *Julietta* 1937 and *The Greek Passion* 1959, symphonies, and chamber music.

Marvell Andrew 1621–1678. English metaphysical poet and satirist. His poems include 'To His Coy Mistress' and 'Horatian Ode upon Cromwell's Return from Ireland'. He was committed to the Parliamentary cause, and was member of Parliament for Hull from 1659. He devoted his last years mainly to verse satire and controversial prose works.

Marvin Lee 1924–1987. US film actor who began his career playing violent, often psychotic villains and progressed to playing violent, occasionally psychotic heroes. His work includes *The Big Heat* 1953, *The Killers* 1964, and *Cat Ballou* 1965.

Marx Karl (Heinrich) 1818–1883. German philosopher, economist, and social theorist, whose account of change through conflict is known as historical, or dialectical, materialism. His *Das Kapital/Capital* 1867–95 is the fundamental text of Marxist economics, and his systematic theses on class struggle, history, and the importance of economic factors in politics have exercised an enormous influence on later thinkers and political activists.

The son of a lawyer, he was born in Trier, and studied law and philosophy at Bonn and Berlin. During 1842–43, he edited the *Rheinische Zeitung/Rhineland Newspaper* until its suppression. In 1844 he began his life-long collaboration with ◊Engels, with whom he developed the Marxist philosophy, first formulated in their joint works, *Die heilige Familie/The Holy Family* 1844, and *Die deutsche Ideologie/German Ideology* 1846 (which contains the theory demonstrating the material basis of all human activity: 'Life is not

determined by consciousness, but consciousness by life'), and Marx's *Misère de la philosophie/Poverty of Philosophy* 1847. Both joined the Communist League, a German refugee organization, and in 1847–48 they prepared its programme, *The Communist Manifesto*. During the 1848 revolution Marx edited the *Neue Rheinische Zeitung/New Rhineland Newspaper*, until he was expelled from Prussia 1849.

He then settled in London, where he wrote *Die Klassenkämpfe in Frankreich/Class Struggles in France* 1849, *Die Achtzehnte Brumaire des Louis Bonaparte/The 18th Brumaire of Louis Bonaparte* 1852, *Zur Kritik der politischen Ökonomie/Critique of Political Economy* 1859, and his monumental work *Das Kapital/Capital*. In 1864 the International Working Men's Association was formed, whose policy Marx, as a member of the general council, largely controlled. Although he showed extraordinary tact in holding together its diverse elements, it collapsed 1872 due to Marx's disputes with the anarchists, including Bakunin. The second and third volumes of *Das Kapital* were edited from his notes by Engels, and published posthumously. Marx was buried at Highgate, London.

Marx's philosophical work owes much to the writings of Hegel, although he rejected Hegel's idealism, and was influenced by Feuerbach and Hess.

Mary in the New Testament, the mother of Jesus through divine intervention, wife of ◊Joseph. The Roman Catholic Church maintains belief in her Immaculate Conception (that she was conceived and lived free from sin) and bodily assumption into heaven, and venerates her as a mediator. Feast day 15 Aug.

Traditionally her parents were elderly and named Joachim and Anna. Mary (Hebrew *Miriam*) married Joseph and accompanied him to Bethlehem. Roman Catholic doctrine assumes that the brothers of Jesus were Joseph's sons by an earlier marriage, and that she remained a virgin. Pope Paul VI proclaimed her 'Mother of the Church' in 1964.

Mary Queen of Scots 1542–1587. Queen of Scotland 1542–67. Also known as *Mary Stuart*, she was the daughter of James V. Mary's connection with the English royal line from Henry VII made her a threat to Elizabeth I's hold on the English throne, particularly as she represented a champion of the Catholic cause. She was married three times. After her forced abdication she was imprisoned but escaped 1568 to England. Elizabeth I held her prisoner, while the Roman Catholics, who regarded Mary as rightful queen of England, formed many conspiracies to place her on the throne, and for complicity in one of these she was executed.

Mary *Portrait of Mary, Queen of Scots, after Nicholas Hilliard (c.1610) National Portrait Gallery, London.*

Mary's mother was the French Mary of Guise. Born in Linlithgow (now in Lothian region, Scotland), Mary was sent to France, where she married the dauphin, later Francis II. After his death she returned in 1561 to Scotland, which, during her absence, had turned Protestant. She married her cousin, the Earl of ◊Darnley, in 1565, but they soon quarrelled, and Darnley took part in the murder of Mary's secretary, ◊Rizzio. In 1567 Darnley was assassinated as the result of a conspiracy formed by the Earl of ◊Bothwell, possibly with Mary's connivance, and shortly after Bothwell married her. A rebellion followed; defeated at Carberry Hill, Mary abdicated and was imprisoned. She escaped in 1568, raised an army, and after its defeat at Langside fled to England, only to be imprisoned again. A plot against Elizabeth I devised by Anthony Babington led to her trial and execution at Fotheringay Castle in 1587.

Mary Duchess of Burgundy 1457–1482. Daughter of Charles the Bold. She married Maximilian of Austria 1477, thus bringing the Low Countries into the possession of the Habsburgs and, ultimately, of Spain.

Mary Queen 1867–1953. Consort of George V of the UK. The daughter of the Duke and Duchess of Teck, the latter a grand-daughter of George II, in 1891 she became engaged to the Duke of Clarence, eldest son of the Prince of Wales (later Edward VII). After his death 1892, she married 1893 his brother George, Duke of York, who succeeded to the throne 1910.

Mary two queens of England:

Mary I 1516–1558. Queen of England from 1553. She was born at Greenwich, the daughter of Henry VIII by Catherine of Aragon. When Edward VI died, she secured the crown without difficulty in spite of the conspiracy to substitute Lady Jane ◊Grey. In 1554 she married Philip II of Spain, and

as a devout Catholic obtained the restoration of papal supremacy. She was succeeded by her half-sister Elizabeth I.

Although naturally humane, she sanctioned the persecution of Protestants which won her the nickname of *Bloody Mary*.

Mary II 1662–1694. Queen of England, Scotland, and Ireland from 1688. She was the elder daughter of ◊James II, and in 1677 was married to her cousin, ◊William III of Orange. After the 1688 revolution she accepted the crown jointly with William.

During his absences abroad she took charge of the government, and showed courage and resource when invasion seemed possible in 1690 and 1692.

Mary Magdalene, St 1st century AD. Woman who according to the New Testament was present at the Crucifixion and was the first to meet the risen Jesus. She is often identified with the woman of St Luke's gospel who anointed Jesus' feet, and her symbol is a jar of ointment; feast day 22 July.

Mary of Guise or *Mary of Lorraine* 1515–1560. French wife of James V of Scotland from 1538, and from 1554 regent of Scotland for her daughter ◊Mary Queen of Scots. A Catholic, she moved from reconciliation with Scottish Protestants to repression, and died during a Protestant rebellion in Edinburgh.

Mary of Modena 1658–1718. Queen consort of England and Scotland. She was the daughter of the Duke of Modena, Italy, and married James, Duke of York, later James II, in 1673. The birth of their son James Francis Edward Stuart was the signal for the revolution of 1688 which overthrew James II. Mary of Modena fled to France.

Masaccio (Tomaso di Giovanni di Simone Guidi) 1401–1428. Florentine painter, a leader of the early Italian Renaissance. His frescoes in Sta Maria del Carmine, Florence, 1425–28, which he painted with Masolino da Panicale (c.1384–1447), show a decisive break with Gothic conventions. He was the first painter to apply the scientific laws of perspective, newly discovered by the architect Brunelleschi.

Masaccio's frescoes in the Brancacci Chapel of St Maria del Carmine include scenes from the life of St Peter (notably *The Tribute Money*) and a moving account of *Adam and Eve's Expulsion from Paradise*. They have a monumental grandeur, without trace of Gothic decorative detail, unlike the work of his colleague and teacher Masolino. Masaccio's figures have solidity and weight, harking back to Giotto, and are clearly set in three-dimensional space.

Masaryk Jan (Garrigue) 1886–1948. Czech politician, son of Tomáš Masaryk. He was foreign minister from 1940, when the Czech government was exiled in London in World War II. He returned in 1945, retaining the post, but as

Masaryk *Tomáš Garrigue Masaryk, the first president of Czechoslovakia.*

a result of communist political pressure committed suicide.

Masaryk Tomáš (Garrigue) 1850–1937. Czech nationalist politician. He directed the Czech revolutionary movement against the Austrian Empire, founding with Beneš and Stefanik the Czechoslovak National Council, and in 1918 was elected first president of the newly formed Czechoslovak Republic. Three times re-elected, he resigned in 1935 in favour of Beneš.

Mascagni Pietro 1863–1945. Italian composer of the one-act opera *Cavalleria rusticana/Rustic Chivalry*, first produced in Rome in 1890.

Masefield John 1878–1967. English poet and novelist. His works include novels (*Sard Harker* 1924), critical works (*Badon Parchments* 1947), children's books (*The Box of Delights* 1935), and plays. He was poet laureate from 1930.

Masekela Hugh 1939– . South African trumpet player, in exile from 1960, who has recorded jazz, rock, and *mbaqanga*, or township jive. His albums include *Techno-Bush* 1984.

Masire Quett Ketumile Joni 1925– . President of Botswana from 1980. He was a journalist before entering politics, sitting in the Bangwaketse Tribal Council and then the Legislative Council. In 1962, with Seretse ◊Khama, he founded the Botswana Democratic Party (BDP) and in 1965 was made deputy prime minister. After independence, in 1966, he became vice president and, on Khama's death in 1980, president. Masire maintained his predecessor's policy of nonalignment and helped

Botswana become one of the most stable states in Africa.

Maskelyne Nevil 1732–1811. English astronomer, who accurately measured the distance from the Earth to the Sun by observing a transit of Venus across the Sun's face 1769. In 1774, he measured the mass of the Earth by noting the deflection of a plumbline near Mount Schiehallion in Scotland.

He was the fifth Astronomer Royal 1765–1811. He began publication 1766 of the *Nautical Almanac*, containing tables for navigators.

Mason A(lfred) E(dward) W(oodley) 1865–1948. British novelist, famed for his tale of cowardice redeemed in the Sudan, *The Four Feathers* 1902, and a series featuring the detective Hanaud of the Sûreté, including *At the Villa Rose* 1910.

Mason James 1909–1984. British actor who portrayed romantic villains in British films of the 1940s. After *Odd Man Out* 1947 he worked in the USA, notably in *A Star is Born* 1954. Other films include *The Wicked Lady* 1946, *Lolita* 1962, and *Cross of Iron* 1977.

Masséna André 1756–1817. Marshal of France. He served in the French Revolutionary Wars, and under the emperor Napoleon was created marshal 1804, duke of Rivoli 1808, and prince of Essling 1809. He was in command in Spain 1810–11 in the Peninsular War, and was defeated by British troops under Wellington.

Massenet Jules Emile Frédéric 1842–1912. French composer of opera, ballets, oratorios, and orchestral suites.

His many operas include *Hérodiade* 1881, *Manon* 1884, *Le Cid* 1885, and *Thaïs* 1894; among other works is the orchestral suite *Scènes pittoresques* 1874.

Massey Vincent 1887–1967. Canadian Liberal Party politician. He was the first Canadian to become governor general of Canada (1952–59).

He helped to establish the Massey Foundation 1918 which funded the building of Massey College and the University of Toronto.

Massine Léonide 1895–1979. Russian choreographer and dancer with the Ballets Russes. He was a creator of comedy in ballet and also symphonic ballet using concert music.

His works include the first Cubist-inspired ballet *Parade* 1917, *La Boutique Fantasque* 1919, and *The Three-Cornered Hat* 1919.

Massinger Philip 1583–1640. English dramatist, author of *A New Way to Pay Old Debts* about 1625. He collaborated with ◊Fletcher and ◊Dekker, and has been credited with a share in writing Shakespeare's *Two Noble Kinsmen* and *Henry VIII*.

Masson André 1896–1987. French artist and writer, a leader of Surrealism until 1929. His interest in the unconscious led him to experiment with 'automatic' drawing – simple pen and ink work, and later multitextured accretions of pigment, glue, and sand.

Masson left the Surrealist movement after a quarrel with the writer André Breton. During World War II he moved to the USA, then returned to France and later turned to landscape painting.

Masters Edgar Lee 1869–1950. US poet. In his *Spoon River Anthology* 1915, the people of a small town tell of their frustrated lives.

Masters John 1914–1983. British novelist, born in Calcutta, who served in the Indian army 1934–47.

A series deals with the Savage family throughout the period of the Raj, for example, *Nightrunners of Bengal* 1951, *The Deceivers* 1952, and *Bhowani Junction* 1954.

Mastroianni Marcello 1924– . Italian film actor, famous for his carefully understated roles as an unhappy romantic lover in such films as *La Dolce Vita* 1959 and *La Notte/The Night 1961.*

Mata Hari ('Eye of the Day'), stage name of Gertrud Margarete Zelle 1876–1917. Dutch courtesan, dancer, and probable spy. In World War I she appears to have been a double agent, in the pay of both France and Germany. She was shot by the French on espionage charges.

Mather Cotton 1663–1728. US theologian and writer. He was a Puritan minister in Boston, and wrote over 400 works of history, science, annals, and theology, including *Magnalia Christi Americana/The Great Works of Christ in America* 1702, a vast compendium of early New England history and experience. Mather appears to have supported the Salem witch-hunts.

Matilda 1102–1167. Claimant to the throne of England. On the death of her father, Henry I, in 1135, the barons elected her cousin Stephen to be king. Matilda invaded England 1139, and was crowned by her supporters 1141. Civil war ensued until in 1153 Stephen was finally recognized as king, with Henry II (Matilda's son) as his successor.

She married first the Holy Roman emperor Henry V, and after his death Geoffrey Plantagenet, Count of Anjou (1113–51).

Matisse Henri 1869–1954. French painter, sculptor, illustrator, and designer. He settled in the south of France in 1914. His work concentrates on designs that emphasize curvaceous surface patterns, linear arabesques, and brilliant colour. Subjects include odalisques (women of the harem), bathers, and dancers; later works include pure abstracts, as in his collages of coloured paper shapes and the designs 1949–51 for the decoration of a chapel for the Dominican convent in Vence, near Nice.

Matisse was one of the most original creative forces in early 20th-century art. In 1904 he worked with Signac in the south of France in a Neo-Impressionist style. The following year he was the foremost of the Fauve painters exhibiting at the Salon d'Automne, painting with bold brushstrokes, heavy impasto, and strong colours (a critic called their exhibition gallery 'une cage aux fauves' – a cage of wild beasts). He soon abandoned conventional perspective in his continued experiments with colour, and in 1910 an exhibition of Islamic art further influenced him towards the decorative. His murals of *The Dance* 1932–33 (Barnes Foundation, Merion, Pennsylvania) are characteristic.

Matsudaira Tsuneo 1877–1949. Japanese diplomat and politician who became the first chair of the Japanese Diet (parliament) after World War II.

Matsudaira negotiated for Japan at the London Naval Conference of 1930 and acted as imperial household minister 1936–45, advising the emperor, but was unsuccessful in keeping Japan out of a war with the Western powers.

Matsukata Masayoshi 1835–1924. Prince of Japan. As a politician, he paved the way for the modernization of the Japanese economy in the 1880s.

Matsuoka Yosuke 1880–1946. Japanese politician. As foreign minister 1927–29, he was largely responsible for the increasingly belligerent attitude towards China. His attempts to deal with Japan's worsening economic situation led to inflation and civil unrest.

Matsys (also *Massys* or *Metsys*) Quentin 1464/65–1530. Flemish painter, born in Louvain, active in Antwerp. He is known for religious subjects such as the *Lamentation* 1511 (Musées Royaux, Antwerp) and portraits set against landscapes or realistic interiors.

His works include the *St Anne altarpiece* 1509 (Musées Royaux, Brussels) and a portrait of *Erasmus* 1517 (Museo Nazionale, Rome), which he presented to Thomas More.

Matthau Walter. Stage name of Walter Matuschanskavasky 1922– . US character actor, impressive in both comedy and dramatic roles. He gained film stardom in the 1960s after his stage success in *The Odd Couple* 1965, and went on to act in, among others, *Kotch* 1971 and *Charley Varrick* 1973.

Matthews Stanley 1915– . English footballer who played for Stoke City, Blackpool, and England. He played nearly 700 Football League games, and won 54 international caps. He was the first European Footballer of the Year 1956.

At the age of 38 he won an FA Cup Winners' medal when Blackpool beat Bolton Wanderers 4–3, Matthews scoring three goals in the last 20 minutes. He was the first Footballer of the Year in 1948 (won again in 1963) and the first footballer to be knighted. He continued to play first-division football after the age of 50.

Matthew, St 1st century AD. Christian apostle and evangelist, the traditional author of the first Gospel. He is usually identified with Levi, who was a tax collector in the service of Herod Antipas, and was called by Jesus to be a disciple as he sat by the Lake of Galilee receiving customs dues. His emblem is a man with wings; feast day 21 Sept.

Matthias Corvinus 1440–1490. King of Hungary from 1458. His aim of uniting Hungary, Austria, and Bohemia involved him in long wars with the Holy Roman emperor and the kings of Bohemia and Poland, during which he captured Vienna (1485) and made it his capital. His father was János ◊Hunyadi.

Mature Victor 1915– . US actor, film star of the 1940s and early 1950s. He gave memorable performances in, among others, *My Darling Clementine* 1946, *Kiss of Death* 1947, and *Samson and Delilah* 1949.

Mauchly John William 1907–1980. US physicist and engineer. He constructed 1946 the first general-purpose computer, the ENIAC, in collaboration with John ◊Eckert. Their company was bought by Remington Rand 1950, and they built the Univac 1 computer 1951 for the US census.

The idea for ENIAC grew out of the pair's work in World War II on ways of automating the calculation of artillery firing tables for the US Army.

Maudling Reginald 1917–1979. British Conservative politician, chancellor of the Exchequer 1962–64, contender for the party leadership 1965, and home secretary 1970–72. He resigned when referred to during the bankruptcy proceedings of the architect John Poulson, since (as home secretary) he would have been in charge of the Metropolitan Police investigating the case.

Maufe Edward 1883–1974. British architect. His works include the Runnymede Memorial and Guildford Cathedral.

Mauger Ivan Gerald 1939– . New Zealand speedway star. He won the world individual title a record six times 1968–79.

Maugham (William) Somerset 1874–1965. English writer. His work includes the novels *Of Human Bondage* 1915, *The Moon and Sixpence* 1919, and *Cakes and Ale* 1930; short stories *The Trembling of a Leaf* 1921, *Ashenden* 1928; and plays *Lady Frederick* 1907, *Our Betters* 1923.

Born in Paris, he was educated at King's School, Canterbury and Heidelberg, then studied medicine at St Thomas's, London. During World War I he was a secret agent in Russia; his *Ashenden* spy stories are based on this experience.

Maupassant Guy de 1850–1893. French author who established a reputation with the short story 'Boule de Suif/Ball of Fat' 1880 and wrote some 300 short stories in all. His novels include *Une Vie/A Woman's Life* 1883 and *Bel-Ami* 1885.

Mauriac François 1885–1970. French novelist. His novel *Le Baiser au lépreux/A Kiss for the Leper* 1922 describes the conflict of an unhappy marriage. The irreconcilability of Christian practice and human nature are examined in *Fleuve de feu/River of Fire* 1923, *Le Désert de l'amour/The Desert of Love* 1925, and *Thérèse Desqueyroux* 1927. Nobel Prize for Literature 1952.

Maurice (John) Frederick Denison 1805–1872. Anglican cleric from 1834, co-founder with Charles ◊Kingsley of the Christian Socialist movement. He was deprived of his professorships in English history, literature, and divinity at King's College, London, because his *Theological Essays* 1853 attacked the doctrine of eternal punishment.

Maurois André. Pen name of Emile Herzog 1885–1967. French novelist and writer, whose works include the semi-autobiographical *Bernard Quesnay* 1926, and fictionalized biographies, such as *Ariel* 1923, a life of Shelley.

In World War I he was attached to the British Army, and the essays in *Les Silences du Colonel Bramble* 1918 give humorously sympathetic observations on the British character.

Mauroy Pierre 1928– . French socialist politician, prime minister 1981–84. He oversaw the introduction of a radical reflationary programme.

Mauroy worked for the FEN teachers' trade union and served as national secretary for the Young Socialists during the 1950s, rising in the ranks of the Socialist Party (PS) in the NE region. He entered the National Assembly in 1973 and was prime minister in the Mitterrand government of 1981, but was replaced by Fabius in July 1984.

Maury Matthew Fontaine 1806–1873. US naval officer, founder of the US Naval Oceanographic Office. His system of recording oceanographic data is still used today.

Maurya dynasty Indian dynasty *c.*321–*c.*185 BC, founded by *Chandragupta Maurya* (321–*c.*279 BC) on the basis of a highly organized aristocracy, which ruled much of the Indian continent until the murder of the emperor Brhadratha in 185 BC and the creation of the Suringa dynasty. After the death of Emperor ◊Asoka, the empire was riven by dynastic disputes.

Mavor O H Real name of the Scottish playwright James ◊Bridie.

Mawson Douglas 1882–1958. Australian explorer, born in Britain, who reached the magnetic South Pole in ◊Shackleton's expedition of 1907–09.

Mawson led Antarctic expeditions 1911–14 and 1929–31. Australia's first permanent Antarctic base was named after him.

Maxim Hiram Stevens 1840–1916. US-born (naturalized British) inventor of the first automatic machine gun in 1884.

Maximilian 1832–1867. Emperor of Mexico 1864–67. He accepted that title when the French emperor Napoleon III's troops occupied the country, but encountered resistance from the deposed president ◊Juárez. In 1866, after the French troops withdrew on the insistence the USA, Maximilian was captured by Mexican republicans and shot.

Maximilian I 1459–1519. Holy Roman emperor from 1493, the son of Emperor Frederick III. He had acquired the Low Countries through his marriage to Mary of Burgundy 1477; he married his son Philip I (the Handsome) to the heiress to the Spanish throne, and undertook long wars with Italy and Hungary in attempts to extend Habsburg power. He was the patron of the artist Dürer.

Maxwell (Ian) Robert 1923– . Czech-born British publishing and newspaper proprietor, chief executive of Maxwell Communications Corporation, and owner of several UK national newspapers, including the *Daily Mirror*. He was Labour member of Parliament for Buckingham 1964–70.

Maxwell James Clerk 1831–1879. Scottish physicist. His major achievement was to the understanding of electromagnetic waves: *Maxwell's equations* bring together electricity, magnetism, and light in one set of relations. He contributed to every branch of physical science, gases, optics, including colour sensation. His theoretical work in magnetism prepared the way for wireless telegraphy and telephony.

Born in Edinburgh, he was professor of natural philosophy at Aberdeen 1856–60, and then of physics and astronomy at London. In 1871, he became professor of experimental physics at Cambridge. His principal works include *Perception of Colour, Colour Blindness* 1860, *Theory of Heat* 1871, *Electricity and Magnetism* 1873, and *Matter and Motion* 1876.

May Thomas Erskine 1815–1886. English constitutional jurist. He was Clerk of the House of Commons from 1871 until 1886, when he was created Baron Farnborough. He wrote a practical *Treatise on the Law, Privileges, Proceedings, and Usage of Parliament* 1844, the authoritative work on parliamentary procedure.

Mayakovsky Vladimir 1893–1930. Russian futurist poet, who combined revolutionary propaganda with efforts to revolutionize poetic technique in his poems '150,000,000' 1920 and 'V I Lenin' 1924. His satiric play *The Bedbug* 1928 was taken in the West as an attack on philistinism in the USSR.

Mayer Julius Robert von 1814–1878. German physicist who in 1842 anticipated ◊Joule in deriving the mechanical equivalent of heat, and ◊Helmholtz in the principle of conservation of energy.

Mayer Louis Burt. Adopted name of Eliezer Mayer 1885–1957. US film producer and distributor. He founded a production company in 1917 and in 1924 became vice president of the newly formed MGM. Something of a tyrant, he built up his studio into one of Hollywood's finest through the use of top talent and good judgement of audience tastes.

Mayer Robert 1879–1985. British philanthropist who founded the Robert Mayer Concerts for Children and the Transatlantic Foundation Anglo-American Scholarships.

Maynard Smith John 1920– . British biologist. He applied game theory (the mathematics of winning strategies) to animal behaviour, and developed the concept of the ESS (evolutionarily stable strategy,

a set of physical or behavioural characteristics that gives a species an edge in the competition with others for survival) as a mathematical technique for studying the evolution of behaviour.

Mayo William James 1861–1939. US surgeon, founder, with his brother *Charles Horace Mayo* (1865–1939), of the Mayo Clinic for medical treatment 1889 in Rochester, Minnesota.

Mays Willie (Howard Jr) 1931– . US baseball player, born in Westfield, Alabama, who played for 22 years with the New York (later San Francisco) Giants (1951–72) and the New York Mets (1973). He hit 660 career home runs, third best in baseball history, and was also an outstanding fielder and runner. He was elected to the Baseball Hall of Fame 1979.

Mazarin Jules 1602–1661. French politician, who succeeded Richelieu as chief minister of France in 1642. His attack on the power of the nobility led to the revolts known as the Fronde and his temporary exile, but his diplomacy achieved a successful conclusion to the Thirty Years' War, and, in alliance with Cromwell during the British protectorate, he gained victory over Spain.

Mazowiecki Tadeusz 1927– . Polish politician, founder member of the free trade-union Solidarity, and Poland's first postwar noncommunist prime minister from 1989.

A former member of the Polish Parliament 1961–70, he was debarred from re-election by the authorities after investigating the police massacre of Gdansk strikers. He became legal adviser to Lech ◊Walesa and, after a period of internment, edited the Solidarity newspaper *Tygodnik Solidarnosc*. In 1989 he became prime minister after the elections denied the communists their customary majority. A devout Catholic, he is a close friend of Pope John Paul II.

Mazzini Giuseppe 1805–1872. Italian nationalist. He was a member of the revolutionary society, the Carbonari, and founded in exile the nationalist movement Giovane Italia (Young Italy) 1832. Returning to Italy on the outbreak of the 1848 revolution, he headed a republican government established in Rome, but was forced into exile again on its overthrow 1849. He acted as a focus for the movement for Italian unity, the Risorgimento.

Mazzini, born in Genoa, studied law. For his subversive activity with the Carbonari he was imprisoned 1830, then went to France, founding in Marseille the Young Italy movement, followed by an international revolutionary organization, Young Europe, 1834. For many years he lived in exile in France, Switzerland, and the UK, but returned to Italy (despite having been condemned to death in his absence by the Sardinian government) for the revolution of 1848. He conducted the defence of Rome against French forces and when it failed he refused to join in the capitulation and returned to London, where he continued to agitate.

Mboya Tom 1930–1969. Kenyan politician, a founder of the Kenya African National Union (KANU), and minister of economic planning (opposed to nationalization) from 1964 until his assassination.

Mead George Herbert 1863–1931. US philosopher and social psychologist, who helped to found the philosophy of pragmatism.

He taught at the University of Chicago during its prominence as a centre of social scientific development in the early 20th century, and is regarded as the founder of symbolic interactionism. His work on group interaction had a major influence on sociology, stimulating the development of role theory, phenomenology, and ethnomethodology.

Mead Margaret 1901–1978. US anthropologist, who challenged the conventions of Western society with *Coming of Age in Samoa* 1928.

Meade James Edward 1907– . British Keynesian economist. He shared a Nobel prize in 1977 for his work on trade and capital movements, and published a four-volume *Principles of Political Economy* 1965–76.

Meade Richard 1938– . British equestrian in three-day events. He won three Olympic gold medals 1968, 1972, and was twice a world champion.

He is associated with some well-known horses, including *Cornishman*, *Laureston*, and *The Poacher*, and has won all the sport's major honours.

Mechnikov Elie 1845–1916. Russian scientist who discovered the function of white blood cells in the body's defences. After leaving Russia and joining ◊Pasteur in Paris, he described how these 'scavenger cells' can attack the body itself (autoimmune disease).

Medawar Peter (Brian) 1915–1987. Brazilian-born British immunologist, who, with ◊Burnet, discovered that the body's resistance to grafted tissue is undeveloped in the newborn child, and studied the way it is acquired.

Medawar's work has been vital in understanding the phenomenon of tissue rejection following transplantation. He and Burnet shared the 1960 Nobel Prize for Medicine.

Medici noble family of Florence, the city's rulers from 1434 until they died out 1737. Family members included ◊Catherine de' Medici, Pope ◊Leo X, Pope ◊Clement VII, ◊Marie de' Medici.

Medici Cosimo de' 1389–1464. Italian politician and banker. Regarded as the model for Machiavelli's *The Prince*, he dominated the government of Florence from 1434 and was a patron of the arts. He was succeeded by his inept son *Piero de' Medici* (1416–69).

Medici Cosimo de' 1519–1574. Italian politician, ruler of Florence; duke of Florence from 1537 and 1st grand duke of Tuscany from 1569.

Medici Ferdinand de' 1549–1609. Italian politician, grand duke of Tuscany from 1587.

Medici Giovanni de' 1360–1429. Italian entrepreneur and banker, politically influential in Florence as a supporter of the popular party. He was the father of Cosimo de' Medici.

Medici Lorenzo de' *the Magnificent* 1449–1492. Italian politician, ruler of Florence from 1469. He was also a poet and a generous patron of the arts.

Medvedev Vadim 1929– . Soviet politician. He was deputy chief of propaganda 1970–78, was in charge of party relations with communist countries 1986–88, and in 1988 was appointed by the Soviet leader Gorbachev to succeed the conservative Ligachev as head of ideology. He adheres to a firm Leninist line.

Mee Margaret 1909–1988. English botanical artist. In the 1950s, she went to Brazil, where she depicted the many exotic species of plants in the Amazon basin.

Meegeren Han van 1889–1947. Dutch painter famous for his forgeries, especially of Vermeer.

His 'Vermeer' *Christ at Emmaus* was bought for Rotterdam's Boymans Museum in 1937. He was discovered when a 'Vermeer' sold to the Nazi leader Goering was traced back to him after World War II. Sentenced to a year's imprisonment, he died two months later.

Mehemet Ali 1769–1849. Pasha (governor) of Egypt from 1805, and founder of the dynasty that ruled until 1953. An Albanian in the Ottoman service, he had originally been sent to Egypt to fight the French. As pasha, he established a European-style army and navy, fought his Turkish overlord 1831 and 1839, and conquered Sudan.

Mehta Zubin 1936– . Indian conductor, director of the Israel Philharmonic Orchestra from 1968 (for life from 1981), and of the New York Philharmonic from 1978.

Meier Richard 1934– . US architect, whose white designs spring from the poetic modernism of the ◊Le Corbusier villas of the 1920s. His abstract style is at its most mature in the *Museum für Kunsthandwerk* (Museum of Arts and Crafts), Frankfurt, West Germany, which was completed in 1984.

Earlier schemes are the Bronx Developmental Centre, New York (1970–76) and the Athenaeum–New Harmony (1974).

Meikle Andrew 1719–1811. Scottish millwright who in 1785 designed and built the first practical threshing machine for separating cereal grains from the husks.

Meinhof Ulrike 1934–1976. West German urban guerrilla, member of the Baader-Meinhof gang in the 1970s.

A left-wing journalist, Meinhof was converted to the use of violence to achieve political change by the imprisoned Andreas Baader. She helped free Baader and they became joint leaders of the urban guerrilla organization the Red Army Faction. As the faction's chief ideologist, Meinhof was arrested in 1972 and, in 1974, sentenced to eight years' imprisonment. She committed suicide in 1976 in the Stammheim high-security prison.

Meir Golda 1898–1978. Israeli Labour (*Mapai*) politician, born in Russia. She was foreign minister 1956–66 and prime minister 1969–74, resigning after criticism of the Israelis' lack of preparation for the 1973 Arab-Israeli War.

Meitner Lise 1878–1968. Austrian physicist, the first to realize that Otto ◊Hahn had inadvertently achieved the fission of uranium. Driven from Nazi Germany because of her Jewish origin, she later worked in Sweden. She refused to work on the atomic bomb.

Melanchthon Philip. Assumed name of Philip Schwarzerd 1497–1560. German theologian who helped Luther prepare a German translation of the New Testament. In 1521 he issued the first systematic formulation of Protestant theology, reiterated in the *Confession of Augsburg* 1530.

Melba Nellie, adopted name of Helen Porter Mitchell 1861–1931. Australian soprano. One of her finest roles was Donizetti's *Lucia*. *Peach melba* (half a peach plus vanilla ice cream and melba sauce, made from sweetened, fresh raspberries) and *melba toast* (crisp, thin toast) are named after her.

Melbourne William Lamb, 2nd Viscount 1779–1848. British Whig politician. Home secretary 1830–34, he was briefly prime minister in 1834 and again 1835–41. He was married 1805–25 to Lady Caroline Ponsonby (novelist Lady Caroline Lamb, 1785–1828). Accused in 1836 of seducing Caroline ◊Norton, he lost the favour of William IV, but was an adviser to the young Queen Victoria.

Méliès Georges 1861–1938. French film pioneer, born in Paris. From 1896–1912 he made over 1,000 films, mostly fantasies, such as *Le Voyage dans la Lune/A Trip to the Moon* 1902. He developed trick effects such as slow motion, double exposure, and dissolves, and in 1897 built Europe's first film studio at Montreuil.

Mellon Andrew William 1855–1937. US financier who donated his art collection to found the National Gallery of Art, Washington DC, 1941. His son, *Paul Mellon* (1907–   ) was its president 1963–79. He funded Yale University's Center for British Art, New Haven, Connecticut, and donated important works of art to both collections.

Melville Henry Dundas, Viscount Melville 1742–1811. British Tory politician, born in Edinburgh. He entered Parliament 1774, and as home secretary 1791–94 persecuted the parliamentary reformers. His impeachment for malversation (misconduct) 1806 was the last in English history.

Melville Herman 1819–1891. US writer, whose *Moby-Dick* 1851 was inspired by his whaling experiences in the South Seas, the setting for other fiction, such as *Typee* 1846 and *Omoo* 1847. He published several volumes of verse, and short stories (*The Piazza Tales* 1856). *Billy Budd* was completed just before his death and published 1924.

Melville was born in Albany, New York. He took to the sea after his father went bankrupt, and struggled to make a literary living, working in the New York customs office 1866–85. He explored the dark, troubled side of American experience in novels of unusual form and great philosophical power. He wrote no prose from 1857 until *Billy Budd*. He died in obscurity. *Billy Budd* was the basis of an opera by Benjamin Britten 1951, and made into a film 1962.

Memlinc (or *Memling*) Hans c. 1430–1494. Flemish painter, born near Frankfurt-am-Main, Germany, but active in Bruges. He painted religious subjects and portraits. Some of his works are in the Hospital of St John, Bruges, including the *Adoration of the Magi* 1479.

Memlinc is said to have been a pupil of van der Weyden, but his style is calmer and softer. His portraits include *Tommaso Portinari and his Wife* (Metropolitan Museum of Art, New York), and he decorated the *Shrine of St Ursula* 1489 (Hospital of St John, Bruges).

Menander c.342–291 BC. Greek comic dramatist, born in Athens. Of his 105 plays only fragments (many used as papier-mâché for Egyptian mummy cases) and Latin adaptations were known prior to the discovery 1957 of the *Dyscholos/The Bad-Tempered Man*.

Mencius Latinized name of Mengzi c.372–289 BC. Chinese philosopher and moralist, in the tradition of Confucius. Mencius considered that human nature was innately good, although this goodness required cultivation, and based his conception of morality on this conviction.

Born in Shantung (now Shandong) province, he was founder of a Confucian school. After 20 years' unsuccessful search for a ruler to put into practice his enlightened political programme, based on people's innate goodness, he retired. His teachings are preserved as the *Book of Mengzi*.

Mencken H(enry) L(ouis) 1880–1956. US essayist and critic, known as 'the sage of Baltimore'. His unconventionally phrased, satiric contributions to *Smart Set* and *US Mercury* (both of which periodicals he edited) aroused great controversy. His best-known book is *The American Language* 1918 and often revised.

Mendel Gregor Johann 1822–1884. Austrian biologist, founder of genetics. His experiments with successive generations of peas gave the basis for his theory of particulate inheritance rather than blending, involving dominant and recessive characters. His results, published 1865–69, remained unrecognized until early in the 20th century.

Mendel was abbot of the Augustinian abbey at Brünn (now Brno, Czechoslovakia) from 1868.

Mendeleyev Dmitri Ivanovich 1834–1907. Russian chemist who framed the periodic law in chemistry which states that the chemical properties of the elements depend on their relative atomic masses. This law is the basis of the periodic table of elements.

Mendelssohn (-Bartholdy) (Jakob Ludwig) Felix 1809–1847. German composer, also a pianist and conductor. Among his many works are *A Midsummer Night's Dream* 1827; the *Fingal's Cave* overture 1832; and five symphonies, which include the Reformation (1830), the Italian (1833), and the Scottish (1842).

He also composed the violin concerto 1844; *Songs Without Words* 1832–45 for the piano; operas; and the oratorios *St Paul* 1836 and *Elijah* 1846.

Mendès-France Pierre 1907–1982. French prime minister and foreign minister 1954–55. He extricated France from the war in Indochina, and prepared the way for Tunisian independence.

Mendoza Antonio de *c.*1490–1552. First Spanish viceroy of New Spain (Mexico) 1535–51. He attempted to develop agriculture and mining and supported the church in its attempts to convert the Indians. The system he established lasted until the 19th century. He was subsequently viceroy of Peru 1551–52.

Menelik II 1844–1913. Negus (emperor) of Abyssinia (now Ethiopia) from 1889. He defeated the Italians 1896 at the battle of Adowa, and thereby retained the independence of his country.

Menem Carlos Saul 1935– . Argentinian politician, president from 1989; leader of the Peronist (Justice Party) movement. As president, he improved relations with the United Kingdom.

Menem, born in La Rioja province, joined the Justice Party while training to be a lawyer. In 1963 he was elected president of the party in La Rioja and in 1983 became governor. In 1989 he defeated the Radical Union Party (UCR) candidate and became president of Argentina. Despite anti-British speeches during the election campaign, President Menem soon declared a wish to resume normal diplomatic relations with the UK and to discuss the future of the Falkland Islands in a spirit of compromise.

Mengistu Haile Mariam 1937– . Ethiopian soldier and socialist politician, head of state from 1977 (president from 1987). As an officer in the Ethiopian army, he took part in the overthrow in 1974 of Emperor ◊Haile Selassie and in 1977 led another coup, becoming head of state. He was confronted with severe problems of drought and secessionist uprisings, but survived with help from the USSR and the West. In 1987 civilian rule was formally reintroduced, but with the

Marxist-Leninist Workers' Party of Ethiopia the only legally permitted party.

Mengs Anton Raffael 1728–1779. German Neo-Classical painter, born in Bohemia. He was made court painter in Dresden 1745 and in Madrid 1761; he then worked alternately in Rome and Spain. The ceiling painting *Parnassus* 1761 (Villa Albani, Rome) is an example of his work.

Menge's father was a miniature painter at the Dresden court and encouraged his son to specialize in portraiture. In 1755 he met the art connoisseur Johann Winckelmann (1717–1768), a founder of Neo-Classicism; Mengs adopted his artistic ideals and wrote a treatise on *Beauty in Painting*.

Menon Vengalil Krishnan 1897–1974. Indian politician, who was important in the Indian nationalist movement. He represented India at the United Nations 1952–62, and was defence minister 1957–62.

He was barrister of the Middle Temple in London, and Labour member of St Pancras Borough Council, 1934–47. He was secretary of the India League in the UK from 1929, and in 1947 was appointed Indian high commissioner in London. He became a member of the Indian parliament 1953, and minister without portfolio 1956. He was dismissed by Nehru 1962 when China invaded India after Menon's assurances to the contrary.

Menotti Gian Carlo 1911– . Italian-born US composer. He wrote both the music and the libretti for operas, including *The Medium* 1946, *The Telephone* 1947, *The Consul* 1950, *Amahl and the Night Visitors* 1951 (the first opera to be written for television), and *The Saint of Bleecker Street* 1954. He has also written orchestral and chamber music.

Menuhin Yehudi 1916– . US violinist. A child prodigy, he achieved great depth of interpretation, and was often accompanied on the piano by his sister *Hephzibah* (1921–81). He conducted his own chamber orchestra and founded a school in Surrey, England, 1963 for training young musicians.

Menzies Robert Gordon 1894–1978. Australian politician, leader of the United Australia (now Liberal) Party and prime minister 1939–41 and 1949–66.

A Melbourne lawyer, he entered politics 1928, was attorney-general in the federal parliament 1934–39, and in 1939 succeeded Joseph Lyons as prime minister and leader of the United Australia Party, until 1941, when he resigned after colleagues were dissatisfied with his leadership of Australia's war effort. In 1949 he became prime minister of a Liberal–Country Party coalition government, and was re-elected 1951, 1954, 1955, 1958, 1961, and 1963. He retired as prime minister 1966. His critics argued that he did not show enough interest in Asia, and supported the USA and white African regimes too uncritically.

His defenders argued that he provided stability in domestic policy and national security.

Menzies William Cameron 1896–1957. US art director of films, later a film director, who was one of Hollywood's most imaginative and talented designers. He was responsible for the sets of such films as *Gone With the Wind* 1939 and *Foreign Correspondent* 1940. His films as director include *Things to Come* 1936 and *Invaders from Mars* 1953.

Mercator Gerardus 1512–1594. Latinized form of the name of the Flemish map-maker Gerhard Kremer. He devised the first modern atlas, showing **Mercator's projection** in which the parallels and meridians on maps are drawn uniformly at 90°.

Mercer David 1928–1980. British dramatist. He first became known for his television plays, including *A Suitable Case for Treatment* 1962, filmed as *Morgan*; stage plays include *After Haggerty* 1970.

Merchant Ismael 1936– . Indian film producer, known for his stylish collaborations with James ◊Ivory on films including *Shakespeare Wallah* 1965, *The Europeans* 1979, *Heat and Dust* 1983, *A Room with a View* 1986, and *Maurice* 1987.

Merckx Eddie 1945– . Belgian cyclist known as 'the Cannibal'. He won the Tour de France a joint record five times 1969–74.

Merckx turned professional 1966 and won his first classic race, the Milan–San Remo, the same year. He went on to win 24 classics as well as the three major tours (of Italy, Spain, and France) a total of 11 times. He was world professional road-race champion three times and in 1971 won a record 54 races in the season.

Meredith George 1828–1909. English novelist and poet. He published the first realistic psychological novel *The Ordeal of Richard Feverel* 1859. Later works include *Evan Harrington* 1861, *The Egoist* 1879, *Diana of the Crossways* 1885, and *The Amazing Marriage* 1895. His best verse is in *Modern Love* 1862.

Mergenthaler Ottmar 1854–1899. German-American who invented a typesetting method. He went to the USA in 1872 and developed the first linotype machine (for casting metal type in complete lines) 1876–86.

Mérimée Prosper 1803–1870. French author. Among his works are the stories *Colomba* 1841, *Carmen* 1846, and the *Lettres à une inconnue/Letters to an Unknown Girl* 1873.

Born in Paris, he entered the public service, and under Napoleon III was employed on unofficial diplomatic missions.

Merleau-Ponty Maurice 1908–1961. French philosopher, one of the most significant contributors to phenomenology after ◊Husserl. He attempted to move beyond the notion of a pure experiencing consciousness, arguing in *The Phenomenology of Perception* 1945 that perception is intertwined with bodily awareness and with language. In his posthumous work *The Visible and the Invisible* 1964, he argued that our experience is inherently ambiguous and elusive, and that the traditional concepts of philosophy are therefore inadequate to grasp it.

Merovingian dynasty a Frankish dynasty, named after its founder, **Merovech** (5th century AD). His descendants ruled France from the time of Clovis (481–511) to 751.

Mersenne Marin 1588–1648. French mathematician and philosopher who, from his base in Paris, did much to disseminate throughout Europe the main advances of French science. In mathematics he defined a particular form of prime number, since referred to as a **Mersenne prime**.

Mesmer Friedrich Anton 1733–1815. Austrian physician, an early experimenter in hypnosis, which was formerly (and popularly) called **mesmerism** after him.

He claimed to reduce people to trance state by consciously exerted 'animal magnetism', their willpower being entirely subordinated to his. Expelled by the police from Vienna, he created a sensation in Paris in 1778, but was denounced as a charlatan in 1785.

Mesrine Jacques 1937–1979. French criminal. From a wealthy family, he became a burglar celebrated for his glib tongue, sadism, and bravado, and for his escapes from the police and prison. Towards the end of his life he had links with left-wing guerillas. He was shot dead by the police.

Messager André Charles Prosper 1853–1929. French composer and conductor. He studied under ◊Saint-Saëns. Messager composed light operas, such as *La Béarnaise* 1885 and *Véronique* 1898.

Messalina Valeria *c.* AD 22–48. Third wife of the Roman emperor ◊Claudius, whom she dominated. She was notorious for her immorality, forcing a noble to marry her in AD 48, although still married to Claudius, who then had her executed.

Messerschmitt Willy 1898–1978. German plane designer, whose ME-109 was a standard Luftwaffe fighter in World War II, and whose ME-262 (1942) was the first mass-produced jet fighter.

Messiaen Olivier 1908– . French composer and organist. His music is mystical in character, vividly coloured, and incorporates transcriptions of birdsong. Among his works are the *Quartet for the End of Time* 1941, the large-scale *Turangalîla Symphony* 1949, and solo organ and piano pieces.

His theories of melody, harmony, and rhythm, drawing on medieval and oriental music, have inspired contemporary composers such as ◊Boulez and ◊Stockhausen.

Messier Charles 1730–1817. French astronomer, who discovered 15 comets and in 1781 published a list of 103 star clusters and nebulae. Objects on this list are given M (for Messier) numbers which astronomers still use today.

Meštrovíc Ivan 1883–1962. Yugoslav sculptor, a naturalized American from 1954. His works include portrait busts of the sculptor Rodin (with whom he is often compared), President Hoover, and Pope Pius XI, and many public monuments.

Metalious Grace (born Repentigny) 1924–1964. US novelist. She wrote many short stories but struck the headlines with *Peyton Place* 1958, an exposé of life in a small New England town.

Metastasio pen name of Pietro Trapassi 1698–1782. Italian poet and the leading librettist of his day, creating 18th-century Italian *opera seria* (serious opera).

Metaxas Joannis 1870–1941. Greek soldier and politician, born in Ithaca. He restored ◊George II (1890–1947) as king of Greece, under whom he established a dictatorship as prime minister from 1936, and introduced several important economic and military reforms. He led resistance to the Italian invasion of Greece in 1941, refusing to abandon Greece's neutral position.

Methodius, St c.825–884. Greek Christian bishop, who with his brother ◊Cyril translated much of the Bible into Slavonic. Feast day 14 Feb.

Metsu Gabriel 1629–1667. Dutch painter, born in Leiden, active in Amsterdam from 1657. His main subjects were genre scenes, usually with a few well-dressed figures. He excelled in depicting rich glossy fabrics.

Metternich Klemens (Wenzel Lothar), Prince von Metternich 1773–1859. Austrian foreign minister from 1809 until the 1848 revolution forced him to flee to the UK. At the Congress of Vienna 1815 he advocated cooperation by the great powers to suppress democratic movements.

Meyerbeer Giacomo. Adopted name of Jakob Liebmann Beer 1791–1864. German composer. He is renowned for his spectacular operas, including *Robert le Diable* 1831 and *Les Huguenots* 1836. From 1826 he lived mainly in Paris, returning to Berlin after 1842 as musical director of the Royal Opera.

Miandad Javed 1957– . Pakistani test cricketer, his country's leading run-maker. He scored a century on his test debut in 1976 and has since become one of a handful of players to make 100 test appearances. He has captained his country. His highest score of 311 was made when he was aged 17.

Micah 8th century BC. In the Old Testament, a Hebrew prophet whose writings denounce the oppressive ruling class of Judah and demand justice.

Michael Mikhail Fyodorovich Romanov 1596–1645. Tsar of Russia from 1613. He was elected tsar by a national assembly, at a time of chaos and foreign invasion, and was the first of the house of Romanov, which ruled until 1917.

Michael 1921– . King of Romania 1927–30 and 1940–47. The son of Carol II, he succeeded his grandfather as king 1927, but was displaced when his father returned from exile 1930. In 1940 he was proclaimed king again on his father's abdication, and in 1944 overthrew the fascist dictatorship of Ion Antonescu (1882–1946) and enabled Romania to share in the victory of the Allies at the end of the World War II. He abdicated and left Romania 1947.

Michelangelo Buonarroti 1475–1564. Italian sculptor, painter, architect, and poet, active in his native Florence and in Rome. His giant talent dominated the High Renaissance. The marble *David* 1501–04 (Accademia, Florence) set a new standard in nude sculpture. His massive figure style was translated into fresco in the Sistine Chapel 1508–12 and 1536–41 (Vatican). Other works in Rome include the dome of St Peter's basilica.

Born near Florence, he was a student of Ghirlandaio and trained under the patronage of Lorenzo de' Medici. His patrons later included several popes and Medici princes. In 1496 he completed the *Pietà* (St Peter's, Rome), a technically brilliant piece that established his reputation. Also in Rome he began the great tomb of Pope Julius II: *The Slaves* (Louvre, Paris) and *Moses* (S Pietro in Vincoli, Rome) were sculpted for this unfinished project. His grandiose scheme for the Sistine Chapel tells, on the ceiling, the Old Testament story from Genesis to the Deluge, and on the altar wall he later added a vast *Last Judgement*.

From 1516 to 1534 he was again in Florence, where his chief work was the design of the Medici sepulchral chapel in S Lorenzo. Back in Rome he became chief architect of St Peter's in 1547. His friendship with Vittoria Colonna (1492–1547), a noblewoman, inspired many of his sonnets and madrigals.

Michels Robert 1876–1936. German social and political theorist. Originally a radical, he became a critic of socialism and Marxism, and in his last years supported Hitler and Mussolini. In *Political Parties* 1911 he propounded the **Iron Law of Oligarchy**, arguing that in any organization or society, even a democracy, there is a tendency towards rule by the few in the interests of the few, and that ideologies like socialism and communism were merely propaganda to control the masses. He believed that the rise of totalitarian governments – both fascist and communist – in the 1930s confirmed his analysis and proved that the masses were incapable of asserting their own interests.

Michelson Albert Abraham 1852–1931. German-born US physicist. In conjunction with Edward Morley, he performed in 1887 the **Michelson–Morley experiment** to detect the motion of the Earth through the postulated ether (a medium believed to be necessary for the propagation of light). The failure of the experiment indicated the nonexistence of the ether, and led Einstein to his theory of relativity. Nobel prize 1907.

He invented the **Michelson interferometer**, and made precise measurement of the speed of light.

Mickiewicz Adam 1798–1855. Polish revolutionary poet, whose *Pan Tadeusz* 1832–34 is Poland's national epic. He died at Constantinople while raising a Polish corps to fight against Russia in the Crimean War.

Middleton Thomas *c.* 1570–1627. English dramatist. He produced numerous romantic plays, tragedies, and realistic comedies, both alone and in collaboration. The best-known are *A Fair Quarrel* and *The Changeling* 1622 with Rowley; *The Roaring Girl* with Dekker; and *Women Beware Women* 1621.

His political satire *A Game at Chess* 1624 was concerned with the plots to unite the royal houses of England and Spain, and caused a furore with the authorities.

Mies van der Rohe Ludwig 1886–1969. German architect who practised in the USA from 1937. He was director of the Bauhaus centre of modern design 1929–33. He became professor at the Illinois Technical Institute 1938–58, for which he designed new buildings on characteristically functional lines from 1941. He also designed the bronze-and-glass Seagram building in New York 1956–59.

Mifune Toshiro 1920– . Japanese actor who appeared in several films directed by ◊Kurosawa, including *Rashomon* 1950 and *Throne of Blood* 1957. He has also appeared in European and American films.

Mihailović Draza 1893–1946. Yugoslav soldier, leader of the Chetnik guerillas of World War II against the German occupation. His feud with Tito's communists led to the withdrawal of Allied support and that of his own exiled government from 1943. He turned for help to the Italians and Germans, and was eventually shot for treason.

Miles Bernard (Baron Miles) 1907– . English actor and producer. He appeared on stage as Briggs in *Thunder Rock* 1940 and Iago in *Othello* 1942, and his films include *Great Expectations* 1947. He founded a trust that in 1959 built the City of London's first new theatre for 300 years, the Mermaid.

Milhaud Darius 1892–1974. French composer, a member of the group of composers known as *Les Six*. Among his works are the operas *Christophe Colombe* 1928 and *Bolivar* 1943, and the jazz ballet *La Création du monde* 1923. He lived in both France and the US.

He collaborated on ballets with Paul ◊Claudel. . Much of his later work – which includes chamber, orchestral, and choral music – is polytonal.

Mill James 1773–1836. Scottish philosopher and political thinker who developed the theory of utilitarianism (actions are morally right if they lead to happiness). He is remembered for his political articles, and for the rigorous education he gave his son John Stuart Mill.

Born near Montrose, Mill moved to London 1802. Associated for most of his working life with the East India Company, he wrote a vast *History of British India* 1817–18. He was one of the founders of University College, London, together with his friend and fellow utilitarian Jeremy Bentham.

Mill John Stuart 1806–1873. English philosopher and economist, who wrote *On Liberty* 1859, the classic philosophical defence of liberalism, and *Utilitarianism* 1863, a version of the 'greatest happiness for the greatest number' principle in ethics. His progressive views inspired *On the Subjection of Women* 1869. In his social philosophy, he gradually abandoned the Utilitarians' extreme individualism for an outlook akin to liberal socialism, while still laying great emphasis on the the liberty of the individual; this change can be traced in the later editions of *Principles of Political Economy* 1848.

He was born in London, the son of James Mill, an eminent Utilitarian philosopher. In 1822 he entered the East India Company, where he remained until retiring in 1858. In 1826, as described in his *Autobiography* 1873, he passed through a mental crisis; he found his father's bleakly intellectual Utilitarianism emotionally unsatisfying, and abandoned it for a more human philosophy influenced by Coleridge. In *Utilitarianism*, he states that actions

Mill *Educated by his father, John Stuart Mill was reading Plato and Demosthenes with ease at the age of ten. His* Autobiography *gives a painful account of the teaching methods that turned him against Utilitarianism.*

are right if they bring about happiness and wrong if they bring about the reverse of happiness. *On Liberty* moved away from the Utilitarian notion that individual liberty was necessary for economic and governmental efficiency and advanced the classical defence of individual freedom as a value in itself and the mark of a mature society. He sat in Parliament as a Radical 1865–68, and introduced a motion for women's suffrage. His philosophical and political writings include *A System of Logic* 1843 and *Considerations on Representative Government* 1861.

Millais John Everett 1829–1896. British painter, a founder member of the *Pre-Raphaelite Brotherhood* (PRB) in 1848 (see ◊Rossetti). By the late 1850s he had dropped out of the PRB and his style became more fluent and less detailed.

One of his PRB works, *Christ in the House of His Parents* 1850 (Tate Gallery, London), caused an outcry on its first showing, since its realistic detail was considered unfitting to the sacred subject. In later works such as *The Boyhood of Raleigh* 1870 (Tate Gallery, London), Millais pursued light, popular subjects.

Millay Edna St Vincent 1892–1950. US poet who wrote emotional verse, including *Renascence* 1917 and *The Harp-Weaver* 1922.

Miller Arthur 1915– . US playwright. His plays deal with family relationships and contemporary American values, and include *Death of a Salesman* 1949 and *The Crucible* 1953, based on the Salem witch trials and reflecting the communist witch-hunts of Senator Joe ◊McCarthy. He was married 1956–61 to the film star Marilyn Monroe, for whom he wrote the film *The Misfits* 1960.

Among other plays are *All My Sons* 1947, *A View from the Bridge* 1955, and *After the Fall* 1964, based on his relationship with Monroe. He also wrote the television film *Playing for Time* 1980.

Miller Glenn 1904–1944. US trombonist and, as bandleader, exponent of the big-band swing sound from 1938. He composed his signature tune 'Moonlight Serenade' (a hit 1939). He disappeared without trace on a flight between England and France during World War II.

Miller Henry 1891–1980. US writer. Years spent in the Paris underworld underpin his novels *Tropic of Cancer* 1934 and *Tropic of Capricorn* 1938. They were so outspoken that the former was banned in England until 1963, and the latter was published in the USA only in 1961.

Miller Stanley 1930– . US chemist. In the early 1950s, under laboratory conditions, he tried to imitate the original conditions of the Earth's atmosphere (a mixture of methane, ammonia, and hydrogen), added an electrical discharge, and waited. After a few days he found that amino acids, the ingredients of protein, had been formed.

Miller William 1801–1880. Welsh crystallographer, developer of a coordinate system, *Miller indices*, capable of mapping the shapes and surfaces of crystals.

Millet Jean François 1814–1875. French painter, a leading member of the Barbizon school, painting scenes of peasant life and landscapes. *The Angelus* 1859 (Musée d'Orsay, Paris) brought him great success and was widely reproduced in his day.

Millett Kate 1934– . US radical feminist lecturer, writer, and sculptor, whose book *Sexual Politics* 1970 was a landmark in feminist thinking. She was a founding member of the *National Organization of Women* (NOW). Later books include *Flying* 1974, *The Prostitution Papers* 1976, and *Sita* 1977.

Millikan Robert Andrews 1868–1953. US physicist, awarded a Nobel prize 1923 for his determination of the electric charge on an electron by his oil-drop experiment (which took him five years up to 1913 to perfect).

Millin Sarah Gertrude (born Liebson) 1889–1968. South African novelist, an opponent of racial discrimination, as seen in, for example, *God's Step-Children* 1924.

Mills C Wright 1916–1962. US sociologist, whose concern for humanity, ethical values, and individual freedom led him to criticize the US establishment.

Originally in the liberal tradition, Mills later adopted Weberian and even Marxist ideas. He aroused considerable popular interest in sociology with such works as *White Collar* 1951, *The Power Elite* 1956, depicting the USA as ruled by businessmen, military experts, and politicians, and *Listen, Yankee* 1960.

Mills John 1908– . British actor-director, who established his reputation in 'stiff-upper-lip' wartime roles, as in *In Which We Serve* 1942. Later films include *Ryan's Daughter* 1971, for which he received an Academy Award.

Milne A(lan) A(lexander) 1882–1956. English writer. His books for children were based on the teddy bear and other toys of his son Christopher Robin (*Winnie-the-Pooh* 1926 and *The House at Pooh Corner* 1928). He also wrote children's verse (*When We Were Very Young* 1924 and *Now We Are Six* 1927) and plays, including an adaptation of Kenneth Grahame's *The Wind in the Willows* as *Toad of Toad Hall* 1929.

Milner Alfred, Viscount Milner 1854–1925. British colonial administrator. As governor of Cape Colony 1897–1901, he negotiated with ◊Kruger but did little to prevent the second South African War 1899–1902; and as governor of the Transvaal and Orange River colonies 1902–05 after their annexation, he reorganized their administration.

Milosevic Slobodan 1941– . Serbian communist politician. A leading figure in the Yugoslavian

Communist Party (LCY) in the republic of Serbia, he became Serbian party chief and president in 1986.

He was educated at Belgrade University and rapidly rose through the ranks of the LCY in his home republic of Serbia, helped by his close political and business links to Ivan Stambolic, his predecessor as local party leader. Milosevic won popular support within Serbia for his assertive nationalist stance, encouraging street demonstrations in favour of the reintegration of Kosovo and Vojvodina autonomous provinces into the Serbian republic.

Milosz Czeslaw 1911– . Polish writer, born in Lithuania. He became a diplomat before defecting and taking US nationality. His poetry in English translation includes *Selected Poems* 1973 and *Bells in Winter* 1978. Among his novels are *The Seizure of Power* 1955 and *The Issa Valley* 1981. Nobel prize 1980.

Milstein César 1927– . Argentinian molecular biologist who developed monoclonal antibodies, giving immunity against specific diseases. He shared the 1984 Nobel Prize for Medicine with two colleagues, George Kohler and Niels Jerne.

Milton John 1608–1674. English poet. His early poems include the pastoral *L'allegro* and *Il penseroso* 1632, the masque *Comus* 1633, and the elegy *Lycidas* 1637. His later works include *Paradise Lost* 1667, *Paradise Regained* 1677, and the classic drama *Samson Agonistes* 1677.

Milton *The 17th century English poet John Milton.*

Born in London, Milton was educated at Christ's College, Cambridge (where he was known as 'the Lady of Christ's' for his fine features), and then devoted himself to study for his poetic career. His middle years were devoted to the Puritan cause and pamphleteering, including one advocating divorce, and another (*Areopagitica*) freedom of the press. His assistants (as his sight failed) included ◊Marvell. He married Mary Powell 1643, and their three daughters were later his somewhat unwilling amanuenses. After Mary's death 1652, the year of his total blindness, he married twice more, his second wife Catherine Woodcock dying in childbirth, while Elizabeth Minshull survived him for over half a century.

Mindszenty József 1892–1975. Roman Catholic primate of Hungary. He was imprisoned by the communist government 1949, but escaped 1956 to take refuge in the US legation. The pope persuaded him to go into exile in Austria 1971, and he was 'retired' when Hungary's relations with the Vatican improved 1974.

Mingus Charles 1922–1979. US bass player and composer. He was influential for his experimentation with atonality and dissonant effects, opening the way for the new style of free collective jazz improvisation of the 1960s.

Minnelli Liza 1946– . US actress and singer, daughter of Judy ◊Garland and the director Vincente Minnelli. She gave a star-making performance in the musical *Cabaret* 1972. Her subsequent films include *New York* 1977 and *Arthur* 1981.

Minnelli Vincente 1910–1986. US film director, who specialized in musicals and occasional melodramas. His best films, such as *Meet Me in St Louis* 1944 and *The Band Wagon* 1953, display a powerful visual flair.

Minto Gilbert, 4th Earl of Minto 1845–1914. British colonial administrator who succeeded Curzon as viceroy of India, 1905–10. With John Morley, secretary of state for India, he co-sponsored the Morley Minto reforms of 1909. The reforms increased Indian representation in government at provincial level, but also created separate Muslim and Hindu electorates which, it was believed, helped the British Raj in the policy of divide and rule.

Mintoff Dom(inic) 1916– . Labour prime minister of Malta 1971–84. He negotiated the removal of British and other foreign military bases 1971–79, and made treaties with Libya.

Minton Thomas 1765–1836. English potter. He first worked at the Caughley porcelain works, but in 1789 established himself at Stoke-on-Trent as an engraver of designs (he originated the 'willow pattern') and in the 1790s founded a pottery there, producing high-quality bone china, including tableware.

Mirabeau Honoré Gabriel Riqueti, Comte de 1749–1791. French politician, leader of the National Assembly in the French Revolution. He wanted to establish a parliamentary monarchy on the English model. From May 1790 he secretly acted as political adviser to the king.

Mirabeau was from a noble Provençal family. Before the French Revolution he had a stormy career, was three times imprisoned, and passed several years in exile. In 1789 he was elected to the States General as a representative of the third estate. His eloquence won him the leadership of the National Assembly; nevertheless, he was out of sympathy with the majority of the deputies, whom he regarded as mere theoreticians.

Miranda Carmen. Stage name of Maria de Carmo Miranda da Cunha 1909–1955. Portuguese dancer and singer who lived in Brazil from her childhood. Successful in Brazilian films, she went to Hollywood 1939 via Broadway and appeared in over a dozen musicals, including *Down Argentine Way* 1940 and *The Gang's All Here* 1943.

Mirandola Italian 15th-century philosopher. See ◊Pico della Mirandola.

Mirman Sophie 1956– . British entrepreneur, founder of the Sock Shop, launched on the US market in 1987.

Miró Joan 1893–1983. Spanish Surrealist painter, born in Barcelona. In the mid-1920s he developed a distinctive abstract style with amoeba shapes, some linear, some highly coloured, generally floating on a plain ground.

During the 1930s his style became more sombre, and after World War II he produced larger abstracts. He experimented with sculpture and printmaking and produced ceramic murals (for example in the UNESCO building, Paris, 1958). He also designed sets for the ballet director Diaghilev.

Mirren Helen 1946– . British actress, whose stage roles include Shakespearean ones, for example Lady Macbeth and Isabella in *Measure for Measure*. Her films include *The Long Good Friday* 1981 and *Cal* 1984.

Mishima Yukio 1925–1970. Japanese novelist, whose work often deals with sexual desire and perversion, as in *Confessions of a Mask* 1949 and *The Temple of the Golden Pavilion* 1956. He committed hara-kiri (ritual suicide) as a demonstration against the corruption of the nation and the loss of the samurai warrior tradition.

Mistinguett stage name of Jeanne Bourgeois 1873–1956. French actress and dancer. A leading music-hall artist in Paris from 1899, she appeared in revues at the Folies-Bergère, Casino de Paris, and Moulin Rouge. She was famous for the song 'Mon Homme' and her partnership with Maurice Chevalier.

Mistral Gabriela. Pen name of Lucila Godoy de Alcayaga 1889–1957. Chilean poet, who wrote *Sonnets of Death* 1915. Nobel Prize for Literature 1945.

She was consul of Chile in Spain, and represented her country at the League of Nations and the United Nations.

Mitchell Arthur 1934– . US dancer, director of the Dance Theater of Harlem, which he founded with Karel Shook in 1968. Mitchell was a principal dancer with the New York City Ballet 1956–68, creating many roles in Balanchine's ballets.

Mitchell Joni. Adopted name of Roberta Joan Anderson 1943– . Canadian singer, songwriter, and guitarist. She began in the 1960s folk style and subsequently incorporated elements of rock and jazz with confessional, sophisticated lyrics. Her albums include *Blue* 1971 and *Hejira* 1976.

Mitchell Juliet 1940– . British psychoanalyst and writer. She first came to public notice with an article in *New Left Review* 1966 entitled 'The Longest Revolution', one of the first attempts to combine socialism and feminism using Marxist theory to explain the reasons behind women's oppression.

Her more recent publications, *Women's Estate* 1971 and *Psychoanalysis and Feminism* 1974, have had considerable influence on feminist thinking.

Mitchell Margaret 1900–1949. US novelist, born in Atlanta, Georgia, which is the setting for her one book *Gone With the Wind* 1936, a story of the US Civil War.

Mitchell Peter 1920– . British chemist. He received a Nobel prize in 1978 for work on the conservation of energy by plants during respiration and photosynthesis.

Mitchell R(eginald) J(oseph) 1895–1937. British aircraft designer, whose Spitfire fighter was a major factor in winning the Battle of Britain.

Mitchum Robert 1917– . US film actor, a star for over 30 years. His films include *Out of the Past* 1947, *The Night of the Hunter* 1955, and *Farewell My Lovely* 1975.

Mithridates VI Eupator known as **the Great** 132–63 BC. King of Pontus (NE Asia Minor, on the Black Sea) from 120 BC. He massacred 80,000 Romans in overrunning the rest of Asia Minor and went on to invade Greece. He was defeated by ◊Sulla in the First Mithridatic War 88–84; by ◊Lucullus in the Second 83–81; and by ◊Pompey in the Third 74–64. He was killed by a soldier at his own order rather than surrender.

Mitre Bartólomé 1821–1906. Argentinian president 1862–68. In 1852 he helped overthrow the dictatorial regime of Juan Manuel de Rosas, and, in 1861, unify Argentina. Mitre encouraged immigration and favoured growing commercial links with Europe. He is seen as a symbol of national unity.

Mitterrand François 1916– . French socialist politician, president from 1981. He held ministerial posts in 11 governments 1947–1958. He founded the French Socialist Party (PS) 1971. In 1985 he introduced proportional representation, allegedly

Mitterrand *French socialist president François Mitterrand, May 1989.*

to weaken the growing opposition from left and right.

Mitterrand studied law and politics in Paris. During World War II he was prominent in the Resistance. He entered the National Assembly as a centre-left deputy for Nièvre. Opposed to Gen de Gaulle's creation of the Fifth Republic 1958, he formed the centre-left anti-Gaullist Federation of the Left in the 1960s. In 1971 he became leader of the new PS. An electoral union with the Communist Party 1972–77 established the PS as the most popular party in France.

Mitterrand was elected president 1981. His programme of reform was hampered by deteriorating economic conditions after 1983. When the socialists lost their majority Mar 1986, he was compelled to work with a right-wing prime minister, Chirac, and grew in popularity. He defeated Chirac to secure a second term in the presidential election May 1988.

Mix 'Tom' (Thomas) 1880–1940. US actor, a cowboy star of silent films. At their best his films, such as *The Range Riders* 1910 and *King Cowboy* 1928, were fast-moving and full of impressive stunts.

Mizoguchi Kenji 1898–1956. Japanese film director whose *Ugetsu Monogatari* 1953 confirmed his international reputation. He also directed *Blood and Soul* 1923, *The Poppies* 1935, and *Street of Shame* 1956.

Mladenov Petar 1936– . Bulgarian Communist politician, secretary general of the Bulgarian Communist Party from Nov 1989 after the resignation of ◊Zhivkov.

Möbius August Ferdinand 1790–1868. German mathematician, discoverer of the möbius strip (a structure made by giving a half twist to a flat piece of paper and joining the ends together). He was considered one of the founders of topology.

Mobutu Sese-Seko-Kuku-Ngbeandu-Wa-Za-Banga 1930– . Zaïrean president from 1965. He assumed the presidency by coup, and created a unitary state under his centralized government. He abolished secret voting in elections 1976 in favour of a system of acclamation at mass rallies. His personal wealth is estimated at $3–4 billion, and more money is spent on the presidency than on the entire social-services budget. The harshness of some of his policies has attracted widespread international criticism.

Modigliani Amedeo 1884–1920. Italian artist, active in Paris from 1906. He painted and sculpted graceful nudes and portrait studies. His paintings have a distinctive soft, elongated, linear style.

Modigliani was born in Livorno. He was encouraged to sculpt by Brancusi, and his series of strictly simplified heads reflects a shared interest in archaic sculptural styles. The portrait of *Jeanne Hebuterne* 1919 (Guggenheim Museum, New York) is typical of his painting. His life was dramatic and dissolute, and he died of the combined effects of alcoholism, drug addiction, and tuberculosis.

Mohamad Mahathir bin 1925– . Prime minister of Malaysia from 1981 and leader of the United Malays' National Organization (UMNO). His 'look east' economic policy emulates Japanese industrialization.

Mahathir bin Mohamad was elected to the House of Representatives 1964 and gained the support of the dominant UMNO's radical youth wing as an advocate of economic help to *bumiputras* (ethnic Malays) and as a proponent of a more Islamic social policy. Dr Mahathir held a number of ministerial posts from 1974 before being appointed prime minister and UMNO leader in 1981. He was re-elected 1986, but has alienated sections of UMNO by his authoritarian leadership.

Mohammed alternative form of ◊Muhammad, founder of Islam.

Mobutu *The president of Zaïre since 1965.*

Moholy-Nagy Laszlo 1895–1946. US photographer, born in Hungary. He lived in Germany 1923–29, where he was a member of the Bauhaus school, and fled from the Nazis in 1935. Through the publication of his illuminating theories and practical experiments, he had great influence on 20th-century photography and design.

Mohs Friedrich 1773–1839. German mineralogist, who in 1812 devised *Mohs' scale* of minerals, classified in order of relative hardness.

Moi Daniel arap 1924– . Kenyan politician, president from 1978. Originally a teacher, he became minister of home affairs in 1964, vice president in 1967, and succeeded ⬦Kenyatta as president.

Moissan Henri 1852–1907. French chemist. For his preparation of pure fluorine in 1886, Moissan was awarded the 1906 Nobel Prize for Chemistry. He also attempted to create artificial diamonds by rapidly cooling carbon heated to high temperatures. His claims of success were treated with suspicion.

Molière pen name of Jean Baptiste Poquelin 1622–1673. French satirical playwright from whose work modern French comedy developed. One of the founders of the Illustre Théâtre 1643, he was later its leading actor. In 1655 he wrote his first play, *L'Etourdi*, followed by *Les Précieuses ridicules* 1659. His satires include *L'Ecole des femmes* 1662, *Le Misanthrope* 1666, *Le Bourgeois gentilhomme* 1670, and *Le Malade imaginaire* 1673.

Other satiric plays include *Tartuffe* 1664 (banned until 1697 for attacking the hypocrisy of the clergy), and *Les Femmes Savantes* 1672. Molière's comedies, based on the exposure of hypocrisy and cant, made him vulnerable to many attacks (from which he was protected by Louis XIV) and marked a new departure in the French theatre away from reliance on classical Greek themes.

Molière Comic playwright and actor Molière died a day after performing the title role in his Le Médecin malgré lui.

Molinos Miguel de 1640–1697. Spanish mystic and Roman Catholic priest. He settled in Rome and wrote in Italian several devotional works, including the *Guida spirituale/Spiritual Guide* 1675 which aroused the hostility of the Jesuits. In 1687 he was sentenced to life imprisonment. He practised quietism, attempted union with God by meditation.

Molnár Ferenc 1878–1952. Hungarian novelist and playwright. His play *Liliom* 1909 is a study of a circus barker, adapted as the musical *Carousel*.

Molotov Vyacheslav Mikhailovich. Assumed name of V M Skryabin 1890–1986. Soviet communist politician. He was chair of the Council of People's Commissars (prime minister) 1930–41, and foreign minister 1939–49, during which period he negotiated a nonaggression treaty with Germany (the Hitler–Stalin pact), and again 1953–56. In 1957 he was expelled from the government for Stalinist activities.

Moltke Helmuth Carl Bernhard, Count von Moltke 1800–1891. Prussian general. He became chief of the general staff 1857, and was responsible for the Prussian strategy in the wars with Denmark 1863–64, Austria 1866, and France 1870–71.

Moltke Helmuth Johannes Ludwig von Moltke 1848–1916. German general (nephew of Count von Moltke, the Prussian general), chief of the German general staff 1906–14. His use of Schlieffen's plan for a rapid victory on two fronts failed and he was superseded.

Momoh Joseph Saidu 1937– . Sierra Leone soldier and politician, president from 1985. An army officer who became commander 1983, with the rank of major-general, he succeeded Siaka Stevens as president when he retired; Momoh was endorsed by Sierra Leone's one political party, the All People's Congress (APC). He has dissociated himself from the policies of his predecessor, pledging to fight corruption and improve the economy.

Monck or *Monk*, George, 1st Duke of Albemarle 1608–1669. English soldier. During the Civil War he fought for King Charles I, but after being captured changed sides and took command of the Parliamentary forces in Ireland. Under the Commonwealth he became commander in chief in Scotland, and in 1660 he led his army into England and brought about the restoration of Charles II.

Mond Ludwig 1839–1909. German chemist who perfected a process for recovering sulphur during the manufacture of alkali.

In 1873, he helped to found the firm of Brunner, Mond and Co, which pioneered the British chemical industry. He moved to England in 1862, and became a British subject in 1867. His son *Alfred Mond, 1st Baron Melchett* (1868–1930) was a founder of Imperial Chemical Industries (ICI).

Mondale Walter 'Fritz' 1928– . US Democrat politician, unsuccessful presidential candidate 1984. He was a senator 1964–76 for his home state of Minnesota, and vice president to Jimmy Carter

1977–81. After losing the 1984 presidential election to Reagan, Mondale retired from national politics to resume his law practice.

Mondrian Piet (Pieter Mondriaan) 1872–1944. Dutch painter, a pioneer of abstract art. He lived in Paris 1919–38, then in London, and from 1940 in New York. He was a founder member of the de Stijl movement, which held that art should pervade life, and that the functional should also be aesthetic, and chief exponent of Neo-Plasticism, a rigorous abstract style which was based on the use of simple geometric forms and pure colours.

In Paris from 1911 Mondrian was inspired by Cubism. He returned to the Netherlands during World War I, where he used a series of still lifes and landscapes to refine his ideas, ultimately developing a pure abstract style. His aesthetic theories were published in the journal *De Stijl* from 1917, in *Neoplasticism* 1920, and in the essay 'Plastic Art and Pure Plastic Art' 1937. From the New York period his *Broadway Boogie-Woogie* 1942–43 (Museum of Modern Art, New York) reflects a late preoccupation with jazz rhythms.

Monet Claude 1840–1926. French painter, a pioneer of Impressionism and a lifelong exponent of its ideals; his painting *Impression, Sunrise* 1872 gave the movement its name. In the 1870s he began painting the same subjects at different times of day to explore the effects of light on colour and form; the *Haystacks* and *Rouen Cathedral* series followed in the 1890s, and from 1899 a series of *Water Lilies* painted in the garden of his house at Giverny in Normandy.

Monet was born in Paris. In Le Havre in the 1850s he was encouraged to paint by Boudin, and soon met Jongkind, whose light and airy seascapes were of lasting influence. From 1862 in Paris he shared a studio with Renoir, Sisley, and others, and they showed their work together at the First Impressionist Exhibition 1874.

Monet's work from the 1860s onwards reveals an obsession with the evanescent effects of light and colour, and from the late 1860s he painted in the classic Impressionist manner, juxtaposing brushstrokes of colour to create an effect of dappled, glowing light. His first series showed the Gare St Lazare in Paris with its puffing steam engines. Views of the water garden in Giverny gradually developed into large, increasingly abstract colour compositions. Between 1900 and 1909 he produced a series of water-lily mural panels for the French state (the Orangerie, Paris).

Moniz Antonio Egas 1874–1955. Portuguese neurologist, pioneer of prefrontal leucotomy (surgical separation of white fibres in the prefrontal lobe of the brain) to treat schizophrenia and paranoia; the treatment is today considered questionable. He shared the 1949 Nobel Prize for Medicine.

Monk Thelonious 1917–1982. US jazz pianist and composer. Working in Harlem, New York, during the Depression, he took part in developing the jazz style known as *bebop* or *bop*. He became popular in the 1950s, and is remembered for numbers such as 'Round Midnight', 'Blue Monk', and 'Hackensack'.

Monmouth James Scott, Duke of Monmouth 1649–1685. Claimant to the English crown, the natural son of Charles II and Lucy Walter. After James II's accession in 1685, he landed at Lyme Regis, Dorset, claimed the crown, and raised a rebellion, which was crushed at the battle of Sedgemoor in Somerset. Monmouth was executed with 320 of his accomplices.

When ◊James II converted to Catholicism, the Whig opposition attempted unsuccessfully to secure Monmouth the succession to the crown by the Exclusion Bill, and in 1684, having become implicated in a Whig conspiracy, he fled to Holland.

Monnet Jean 1888–1979. French economist. The originator of Churchill's offer of union between the UK and France in 1940, he devised and took charge of the French modernization programme under de Gaulle in 1945. In 1950 he produced the 'Shuman Plan' initiating the coordination of European coal and steel production in the European Coal and Steel Community (ECSC), which developed into the Common Market (EC).

Monod Jacques 1910–1976. French biochemist who shared the 1965 Nobel Prize for Medicine (with two colleagues) for research in genetics and microbiology.

Monroe James Monroe, remembered for the Monroe Doctrine, his warning to European nations not to interfere with the countries of the Americas.

Monroe James 1758–1831. 5th president of the USA 1817–25, born in Virginia. He served in the War of Independence, was minister to France 1794–96, and in 1803 negotiated the Louisiana Purchase, by which a large part of the Midwest was acquired from France. He was secretary of state 1811–17. In 1823 he declared the *Monroe Doctrine*: that further European colonial ambitions anywhere in the W hemisphere would be regarded as threatening US peace and security.

Monroe Marilyn. Stage name of Norma Jean Mortenson or Baker 1926–1962. US film actress, who made comedies such as *The Seven Year Itch* 1955, *Bus Stop* 1956, and *Some Like It Hot* 1959. Her second husband was baseball star Joe di Maggio, and her third Arthur ◊Miller.

Monsarrat Nicholas 1910–1979. English novelist who served with the navy in the Battle of the Atlantic, fought between Germany and the Allies throughout World War II, subject of *The Cruel Sea* 1951.

Montagu family name of dukes of Manchester.

Montagu Edward Douglas Scott, 3rd Baron Montagu of Beaulieu 1926– . British car enthusiast, founder of the Montagu Motor Museum at Beaulieu, Hampshire.

Montagu Lady Mary Wortley (born Pierrepont) 1689–1762. British society hostess known for her witty and erudite letters. She introduced inoculation against smallpox into Britain.

Montagu-Douglas-Scott family name of the dukes of Buccleuch; seated at Bowhill, Selkirk, Scotland; Boughton House, Northamptonshire, England; and Drumlanrig, Dumfriesshire, Scotland; descended from the Duke of ◊Monmouth.

Monroe *Legendary film star Marilyn Monroe. Her vulnerability was part of her appeal.*

Montaigne Michel Eyquem de 1533–1592. French writer, regarded as the creator of the essay form. In 1580 he published the first two volumes of his *Essais*, the third volume appeared in 1588. Montaigne deals with all aspects of life from an urbanely sceptical viewpoint. Through the translation by John Florio in 1603, he influenced Shakespeare and other English writers.

Little is known of his early life, except that he regularly visited the court of Francis II and Paris. In 1571 he retired to his estates, relinquishing his magistracy. He toured Germany, Switzerland, and Italy 1580–81, returning on his election as mayor of Bordeaux, a post he held until 1585.

Montale Eugenio 1896–1981. Italian poet and writer. His pessimistic poetry, for which he was awarded a Nobel prize in 1975, includes *Ossi di seppia/Cuttlefish Bones* 1925 and *Le Occasioni/Occasions* 1939. In 1989 it was revealed that much of his literary journalism, such as his regular column in the *Corriere della Sera* newspaper, was in fact written by an American, Henry Frost.

Montana Joe 1956– . US American footballer. He appeared in three winning Super Bowls with the San Francisco 49ers 1982, 1985, and 1989, winning the Most Valuable Player award in the first two, and setting a record for passing yardage 1989.

Montand Yves 1921– . French actor and singer who achieved fame in the thriller *La Salarie de la Peur/The Wages of Fear* 1953 and continued to be popular in French and American films, including *Let's Make Love* 1960 (with Marilyn Monroe), *Grand Prix* 1966, *Le Sauvage/The Savage* 1976, *Jean de Florette* 1986, *Manon des Sources* 1986.

Montcalm Louis-Joseph de Montcalm-Gozon, Marquis de 1712–1759. French general, appointed military commander in Canada 1756. He won a succession of victories over the British during the French and Indian War, but was defeated in 1759 by ◊Wolfe at Québec, where both he and Wolfe were killed; this battle marked the end of French rule in Canada.

Montespan Françoise-Athénais de Rochechouart, Marquise de Montespan 1641–1707. Mistress of Louis XIV of France from 1667. They had seven children, for whom she engaged the future Madame de ◊Maintenon as governess. She retired to a convent in 1691.

Montesquieu Charles Louis de Secondat, baron de la Brède 1689–1755. French philosophical historian, author of the *Lettres Persanes/Persian Letters* 1721. *De l'esprit des lois/The Spirit of the Laws* 1748, a 31-volume philosophical disquisition on politics and sociology as well as legal matters, advocated the separation of powers within government, a doctrine that became the basis of liberal constitutions.

Montessori Maria 1870–1952. Italian educationalist. From her experience with mentally handicapped children, she developed the *Montessori method*, an educational system for all children based on a more informal approach, incorporating instructive play and allowing children to develop at their own pace.

Monteux Pierre 1875–1964. French conductor. Ravel's *Daphnis and Chloe* and Stravinsky's *Rite of Spring* were first performed under his direction. He conducted ♦Diaghilev's Ballets Russes 1911–14 and 1917, and the San Francisco Symphony Orchestra 1935–52.

Monteverdi Claudio (Giovanni Antonio) 1567–1643. Italian composer. He contributed to the development of the opera with *Orfeo* 1607 and *The Coronation of Poppea* 1642. He also wrote madrigals, motets, and sacred music, notably the *Vespers* 1610.

Montez Lola. Stage name of Maria Gilbert 1818–1861. Irish actress and dancer. She appeared on the stage as a Spanish dancer, and in 1847 became the mistress of King Ludwig I of Bavaria, whose policy she dictated for a year. Her liberal sympathies led to her banishment through Jesuit influence in 1848. She died in poverty in the USA.

Montezuma II 1466–1520. Aztec emperor 1502–20. When the Spanish conquistador Cortés invaded Mexico, Montezuma was imprisoned and killed during the Aztec attack on Cortés' force as it tried to leave Tenochtitlán, the Aztec capital city.

Montfort Simon de Montfort, Earl of Leicester *c.* 1208–1265. English politician and soldier. From 1258 he led the baronial opposition to Henry III's misrule during the second Barons' War and in 1264 defeated and captured the king at Lewes, Sussex. In 1265, as head of government, he summoned the first parliament in which the towns were represented; he was killed at the Battle of Evesham during the last of the Barons' Wars.

Born in Normandy, the son of *Simon de Montfort* (*c.* 1160–1218) who led a crusade against the Albigenses, he arrived in England in 1230, married Henry III's sister, and was granted the earldom of Leicester.

Montgolfier Joseph Michel 1740–1810 and Étienne Jacques 1745–1799. French brothers whose hot-air balloon was used for the first successful human flight 21 Nov 1783.

They were papermakers of Annonay, near Lyon, where on 5 June 1783 they first sent up a balloon filled with hot air. After further experiments with wood-fuelled paper balloons, they went aloft themselves, in Paris. The Montgolfier experiments greatly stimulated scientific interest in aviation.

Montgomery Bernard Law, 1st Viscount Montgomery of Alamein 1887–1976. British field marshal. In Aug 1942 he took command of the 8th

Montgomery The British field marshal, Viscount Montgomery of Alamein, advances in the turret of a tank during the attack on El Alamein, Oct 1942.

Army in N Africa, then barring the German advance on Cairo; the victory of El Alamein in Oct turned the tide in N Africa and was followed by the expulsion of Field Marshal Rommel from Egypt and rapid Allied advance into Tunisia.

Montgomery commanded the Allied armies during the opening phase of the invasion of France in Jun 1944, and from Aug the British and imperial troops that liberated the Netherlands, overran N Germany, and entered Denmark. At his 21st Army Group headquarters on Lüneberg Heath, he received the German surrender on 3 May 1945.

Montgomery Henry ('Robert') 1904–1981. US film actor of the 1930s and 1940s. He directed some of his later films, such as *Lady in the Lake* 1947, before leaving the cinema for television and politics. His other films include *Night Must Fall* 1937 and *Mr and Mrs Smith* 1941.

Montherlant Henri de Millon 1896–1972. French author. He was a Nazi sympathizer. His novels, which are marked by an obsession with the physical, include *Aux Fontaines du désir/To the Fountains of Desire* 1927 and *Pitié pour les femmes/Pity for Women* 1936. His most critically acclaimed work is *Le Chaos et la nuit/Chaos and Night* 1963.

Monti Eugenio 1928– . Italian bobsleigh driver who won Olympic gold medals in two- and four-person bobs in 1968, and between 1957 and 1968 won 11 world titles.

Montrose James Graham, 1st Marquess of Montrose 1612–1650. Scottish soldier, son of the 4th earl of Montrose. He supported the Covenanters against Charles I, but after 1640 changed sides. Defeated in 1645 at Philiphaugh, he escaped to Norway. Returning in 1650 to raise a revolt, he survived shipwreck only to have his weakened forces defeated, and (having been betrayed to the Covenanters) was hanged in Edinburgh.

Moon Sun Myung 1920- . Korean industrialist and founder of the Unification Church (*Moonies*) 1954. From 1973 he launched a major mission in the USA and elsewhere. The church has been criticized for its manipulative methods of recruiting and keeping members. He was convicted of tax fraud in the USA 1982.

Moon has allegedly been associated with extreme right-wing organizations, arms manufacture, and the Korean Central Intelligence Agency.

Moon William 1818-1894. English inventor of the *Moon alphabet* for the blind. Devised in 1847, it uses only nine symbols in different orientations. From 1983 it has been possible to write it with a miniature typewriter.

Moorcock Michael 1939- . English writer, associated with the 1960s new wave in science fiction, editor of the magazine *New Worlds* 1964-69. He wrote the Jerry Cornelius novels, collected as *The Cornelius Chronicles* 1977, and *Gloriana* 1978.

Moore 'Bobby' (Robert Frederick) 1941- . British footballer. Captain of West Ham United and England, he led them to victory over West Germany in the 1966 World Cup final at Wembley Stadium.

Between 1962 and 1970 he played a record 108 games for England. He played the last of his 668 Football League games for Fulham against Blackburn Rovers in 1977, after a career spanning 19 years.

Moore Dudley 1935- . British actor and comedian, formerly teamed with comedian Peter Cook, who became a Hollywood star after appearing in *10* 1979. His subsequent films, mostly comedies, include *Bedazzled* 1968 and *Arthur* 1981.

Moore G(eorge) E(dward) 1873-1958. British philosopher. Educated at Trinity College, Cambridge University, he was professor of philosophy at the university 1925-39, and edited the journal *Mind*, to which he contributed 1921-47. His books include *Principia Ethica* 1903, in which he attempted to analyse the moral question 'What is good?', and *Some Main Problems of Philosophy* 1953, but his chief influence was as a teacher.

Moore George (Augustus) 1852-1933. Irish novelist, born in County Mayo. He studied art in Paris 1870, and published two volumes of poetry there. His first novel, *A Modern Lover* 1883, was sexually frank for its time and banned in some quarters. It was followed by others, including *Esther Waters* 1894.

Moore Gerald 1899-1987. British pianist, renowned as an accompanist of singers, a role he raised to equal partnership.

Moore Henry 1898-1986. British sculptor. His subjects include the reclining nude, mother and child groups, the warrior, and intelocking abstract forms. As an official war artist during World War II, he did a series of drawings of London's

air-raid shelters. Many of his postwar works are in bronze or marble, including monumental semi-abstracts such as *Reclining Figure* 1957-58 (outside UNESCO, Paris), and often designed to be placed in landscape settings.

Moore, born in Yorkshire, studied at Leeds and the Royal College of Art but claimed to have learned more from archaic South and Central American sculpture, and this is reflected in his work from the 1920s. By the early 1930s most of his main themes had emerged, and the Surrealists' preoccupation with organic forms in abstract works proved a strong influence; Moore's hollowed wooden shapes strung with wires (resembling those of Barbara ◊Hepworth) date from the late 1930s. Abstract work suggesting organic structures recurs after World War II, for example in the interwoven bonelike forms of the *Hill Arches* and the bronze *Sheep Pieces* 1970s, set in fields by his studio in Much Hadham, Hertfordshire.

Moore John 1761-1809. British general, born in Glasgow. In 1808 he commanded the British army sent to Portugal in the Peninsular War. After advancing into Spain he had to retreat to Corunna in the NW, and was killed in the battle fought to cover the embarkation.

He entered the army in 1776, serving in the American and French Revolutionary Wars and against the Irish rebellion of 1798.

Moore (John) Jeremy 1928- . British major general of the Commando Forces, Royal Marines, 1979-82. He commanded the land forces in the UK's conflict with Argentina over the Falklands 1982.

Moore Marianne 1887-1972. US poet. She edited the literary magazine *Dial* 1925-29, and published volumes of witty and intellectual verse including *Observations* 1924, *What are Years* 1941, and *A Marianne Moore Reader* 1961.

Moore Roger 1928- . British actor who starred in the television series *The Saint* 1962-70, and assumed the film role of James Bond in 1973 in *Live and Let Die*. His films include *Diane* 1955, *Gold* 1974, *The Wild Geese* 1978, and *Octopussy* 1983.

Moore Thomas 1779-1852. Irish poet, born in Dublin. Among his works are the verse romance *Lalla Rookh* 1817 and the *Irish Melodies* 1807-35. These were set to music by John Stevenson 1807-35 and include 'The Minstrel Boy' and 'The Last Rose of Summer'.

Moorhouse Adrian 1964- . English swimmer who won the 100 metres breaststroke at the 1988 Seoul Olympics.

He has won gold medals at both the Commonwealth Games and the European Championships.

Moorhouse Geoffrey 1931- . British travel writer, born in Bolton, Lancashire. His books include *The Fearful Void* 1974, and (on cricket) *The Best-Loved Game* 1979.

Morandi Giorgio 1890–1964. Italian still-life painter and etcher, whose subtle studies of bottles and jars convey a sense of calm and repose.

Moravia Alberto. Pen name of Alberto Pincherle 1907– . Italian novelist. His first successful novel was *Gli indifferenti/The Time of Indifference* 1929. However, its criticism of Mussolini's regime led to the government censoring his work until after World War II. Later books include *La romana/Woman of Rome* 1947, *La ciociara/Two Women* 1957, and *La noia/The Empty Canvas* 1961, a study of an artist's obsession with his model.

Moray Earl of Moray. Alternative spelling of ◊Murray, regent of Scotland 1567–70.

Morazán Francisco 1792–1842. Central American politician, born in Honduras. He was elected president of the United Provinces of Central America in 1830. In the face of secessions he attempted to hold the union together by force but was driven out by the Guatemalan dictator Carrera. Morazán was eventually captured and executed in 1842.

More (St) Thomas 1478–1535. English politician and author. From 1509 he was favoured by ◊Henry VIII and employed on foreign embassies. He was a member of the privy council from 1518 and Lord Chancellor from 1529 but resigned over Henry's break with the pope. For refusing to accept the king as head of the church, he was executed. The title of his political book *Utopia* 1516 has come to mean any supposedly perfect society.

Son of a London judge, More studied at Oxford and law at Lincoln's Inn, London, and was influenced by the humanists John Colet and ◊Erasmus, who became a friend. In Parliament from 1504, he was made Speaker of the House of Commons in 1523. He was knighted in 1521, and on the fall of Cardinal Wolsey became Lord Chancellor, but resigned in 1532 because he could not agree with the king on his ecclesiastical policy and the marriage with Anne Boleyn. In 1534 he refused to take the oath of supremacy to Henry VIII as head

of the church, and after a year's imprisonment in the Tower of London he was executed.

Among Thomas More's writings are the Latin *Utopia* 1516, sketching an ideal commonwealth; the English *Dialogue* 1528, a theological argument against the Reformation leader Tyndale; and a *History of Richard III*. He was also a patron of artists, including ◊Holbein. More was canonized in 1935.

More Kenneth 1914–1982. British actor, a film star of the 1950s, cast as leading man in adventure films and light comedies such as *Genevieve* 1953, *Doctor in the House* 1954, and *Northwest Frontier*. His film career declined in the 1960s, although he played occasional character parts.

Moreau Gustave 1826–1898. French Symbolist painter. His works are biblical, mythological, and literary scenes, richly coloured and detailed, and atmospheric.

Salome Dancing Before Herod 1876 attracted much attention when it was first exhibited. In the 1890s Moreau taught at the Ecole des Beaux-Arts in Paris, where his pupils included Matisse and Rouault. Much of his work is in the Musée Moreau, Paris.

Moreau Jean Victor Marie 1763–1813. French general in the Revolutionary Wars who won a brilliant victory over the Austrians at the battle of Hohenlinden 1800; as a republican he intrigued against Napoleon, and, when banished, joined the Allies and was killed at the Battle of Dresden.

Moreau Jeanne 1928– . French actress who has appeared in international films, often in passionate roles. Her work includes *Les Amants/The Lovers* 1958, *Jules et Jim/Jules and Jim* 1961, *Chimes at Midnight* 1966, and *Querelle* 1982.

Moresby John 1830–1922. British naval explorer and author. He was the first European to visit the harbour in New Guinea, now known as Port Moresby.

Morgagni Giovanni Battista 1682–1771. Italian anatomist. As professor of anatomy at Padua, Morgagni carried out large numbers of autopsies, and developed the view that disease was not an imbalance of the body's humours but a result of alterations in the organs. His work formed the basis of morbid anatomy and pathology.

Morgan Henry *c.* 1635–1688. Welsh buccaneer in the Caribbean. He made war against Spain, capturing and sacking Panama 1671. In 1674 he was knighted and appointed lieutenant-governor of Jamaica.

Morgan John Pierpont 1837–1913. US financier and investment banker whose company (sometimes criticized as 'the money trust') wielded great influence over US corporate economy after the Civil War, being instrumental in the formation of many trusts to stifle competition. He set up the US Steel Corporation in 1901.

Morgan Lewis Henry 1818–1881. US anthropologist. He studied American Indian culture, and was adopted by the Iroquois.

More *Portrait of Thomas More after Hans Holbein (1527), National Portrait Gallery, London.*

Morgan Thomas Hunt 1866–1945. US geneticist, awarded the 1933 Nobel Prize for Medicine for his pioneering studies in classical genetics. He was the first to work on the fruit fly, *Drosophila*, which has since become a major subject of genetic studies. He helped establish that the genes were located on the chromosomes, discovered sex chromosomes, and invented the techniques of genetic mapping.

Morisot Berthe 1841–1895. French Impressionist painter, who specialized in pictures of women and children.

Morland George 1763–1804. English painter whose picturesque country subjects became widely reproduced in engravings. He was an admirer of Dutch and Flemish painters of rustic life.

Morley Edward 1838–1923. US physicist who collaborated with ◊Michelson on the **Michelson–Morley experiment** 1887. In 1895 he established precise and accurate measurements of the densities of oxygen and hydrogen.

Morley John, 1st Viscount Morley of Blackburn 1838–1923. British Liberal politician and writer. He entered Parliament in 1883, and was secretary for Ireland in 1886 and 1892–95. As secretary for India 1905–10, he prepared the way (with Viceroy Gilbert ◊Minto) for more representative government.

He was Lord President of the Council 1910–14, but resigned in protest against the declaration of war. He published lives of the philosophers Voltaire and Rousseau and the politicians Burke and Gladstone. He received a peerage in 1908.

Morley Malcolm 1931– . British painter, active in New York from 1964. He coined the term **Superrealism** for his work in the 1960s.

Morley Robert 1908– . British actor and playwright, active in both Britain and the US. His film work has been mainly character roles, in films such as *Marie Antoinette* 1938, *The African Queen* 1952, and *Oscar Wilde* 1960.

Morley Thomas 1557–1602. English composer. A student of ◊Byrd, he became organist at St Paul's Cathedral, London, and obtained a monopoly on music printing. A composer of the English madrigal school, he also wrote sacred music, songs for Shakespeare's plays, and a musical textbook.

Moro Aldo 1916–1978. Italian Christian Democrat politician. Prime minister 1963–68 and 1974–76, he was expected to become Italy's president, but he was kidnapped and shot by Red Brigade urban guerrillas.

Morris Henry 1889–1961. British educationalist. He inspired and oversaw the introduction of the 'village college' and community school education, which he saw as regenerating rural life.

Through emphasis on providing a centre for continuing education and leisure activities for both adults and children on a single site, these ideas also proved influential in urban areas. He persuaded ◊Gropius, together with Maxwell Fry, to design the Village College at Impington, near Cambridge, 1939.

Morris Thomas, Jr 1851–1875. British golfer. One of the first great champions, he was known as 'Young Tom' to distinguish him from his father (who was known as 'Old Tom'). Morris junior won the British Open four times 1868–72.

Morris William 1834–1896. English designer, socialist, and poet, who shared the Pre-Raphaelite painters' fascination with medieval settings. His first book of verse was *The Defence of Guenevere* 1858. In 1862 he founded a firm for the manufacture of furniture, wallpapers, and the like, and in 1890 he set up the Kelmscott Press to print beautifully decorated books. The prose romances *A Dream of John Ball* 1888 and *News from Nowhere* 1891 reflect his socialist ideology. He also lectured on socialism.

William Morris was born in Walthamstow, London, and educated at Oxford, where he formed a lasting friendship with the Pre-Raphaelite artist ◊Burne-Jones and was influenced by the art critic Ruskin and the painter and poet ◊Rossetti. He abandoned his first profession, architecture, to study painting, but had a considerable influence on such architects as Lethaby and Philip ◊Webb. A founder of the Arts and Crafts movement, Morris did much to raise British craft standards.

He published several volumes of verse romances, notably *The Life and Death of Jason* 1867 and *The Earthly Paradise* 1868–70; a visit to Iceland 1871 inspired *Sigurd the Volsung* 1876 and general interest in the sagas. He joined the Social Democratic Federation 1883, but left it 1884 because he found it too moderate, and set up the Socialist League. To this period belong the critical and sociological studies *Signs of Change* 1888 and *Hopes and Fears for Art* 1892.

Morrison Herbert Stanley, Baron Morrison of Lambeth 1888–1965. British Labour politician. He was secretary of the London Labour Party 1915–45, and a member of the London County Council 1922–45. He entered Parliament in 1923, and in 1955 was defeated by Gaitskell in the contest for leadership of the party.

He was minister of transport 1929–31, home secretary 1940–45, Lord President of the Council and leader of the House of Commons 1945–51, and foreign secretary Mar–Oct 1951.

Morrison Toni 1931– . US novelist, whose fiction records black life in the South. Her works include *The Song of Solomon* 1978, *Tar Baby* 1981, and *Beloved* 1987, based on a true story about infanticide in Kentucky, which won the Pulitzer Prize in 1988.

Morse Samuel (Finley Breese) 1791–1872. US inventor. In 1835 he produced the first adequate electric telegraph, and in 1843 was granted

$30,000 by Congress for an experimental line between Washington and Baltimore. With his assistant Alexander Bain he invented the Morse code. He was also a respected portrait painter.

Mortimer John 1923– . English barrister and writer. His works include the plays *The Dock Brief* 1958 and *A Voyage Round My Father* 1970, the novel *Paradise Postponed* 1985, and the television series *Rumpole of the Bailey*, from 1978, centred on a fictional barrister.

Mortimer Roger de, 8th Baron of Wigmore and 1st Earl of March *c.*1287–1330. English politician and adventurer. From 1327 Mortimer ruled England as the queen's lover, until Edward III had him executed.

A rebel, he was imprisoned by Edward II for two years before making his escape from the Tower of London to France. There he joined with the English queen, Isabella, who was conducting negotiations at the French court, and returned with her to England in 1326. Edward fled when they landed with their followers, and Mortimer secured Edward's deposition by Parliament. In 1328 he was created Earl of March. He was popularly supposed responsible for Edward II's murder, and when the young Edward III had him seized while with the queen at Nottingham Castle, he was hanged, drawn, and quartered at Tyburn, London.

Morton Henry Vollam 1892–1979. English journalist and travel writer, author of the *In Search of…* series published during the 1950s. His earlier travel books include *The Heart of London* 1925, *In the Steps of the Master* 1934, and *Middle East* 1941.

Morton Jelly Roll. Stage name of Ferdinand Joseph La Menthe 1885–1941. US jazz pianist, singer, and composer. Influenced by Scott Joplin, he played a major part in the development of jazz from ragtime to swing by improvising and imposing his own personality on the music. His band from 1926 was called the Red Hot Peppers.

Morton J(ohn) B(ingham) 1893–1979. British journalist, best known for the humorous column he contributed to the *Daily Express* 1924–76 under the pen name of *Beachcomber*.

Morton William Thomas Green 1819–1868. US dentist who in 1846 introduced ether as an anaesthetic; his claim to be the first to do so was strongly disputed.

While searching for ways to avoid the pain of tooth extraction, he learned of the pain-killing effects of ether from C Thomas Jackson (1805–1880), a chemist and physician. Morton realized the anaesthetic potential of the gas, and the two men patented the process and set about publicizing it.

Moseley Henry Gwyn-Jeffreys 1887–1915. English physicist who, 1913–14, devised the series of atomic numbers, leading to the modern periodic table of the elements. He did valuable work on atomic structure.

Moses *c.*13th century BC. Hebrew lawgiver and judge who led the Israelites out of Egypt to the promised land of Canaan. On Mount Sinai he claimed to have received from Jehovah the *Ten Commandments* engraved on tablets of stone. The first five books of the Old Testament – in Judaism, the *Torah* – are ascribed to him.

According to the Torah, the infant Moses was hidden among the bulrushes on the banks of the Nile when the pharaoh commanded that all new-born male Hebrew children should be destroyed. He was found by a daughter of Pharaoh, who reared him. Eventually he became the leader of the Israelites in their *Exodus* from Egypt and their 40 years' wandering in the wilderness, and died at the age of 120, after having been allowed a glimpse of the Promised Land from Mount Pisgah.

Moses Ed(win Corley) 1955– . American track athlete and 400 metres hurdler. Between 1977 and 1987 he ran 122 races without defeat.

He first broke the world record in 1976, and his time of 47.02 seconds set in 1983 still stood on 1 Jan 1990.

Moses 'Grandma' (born Anna Mary Robertson) 1860–1961. US painter. She was self-taught, and began full-time painting in about 1927, after many years as a farmer's wife. She painted naive and colourful scenes from rural American life.

Mosley Oswald (Ernald) 1896–1980. British politician, founder of the British Union of Fascists (BUF). He was a member of Parliament 1918–31, then led the BUF until his internment 1940–43, when he was released on health grounds. In 1946 Mosley was denounced when it became known that Italy had funded his prewar efforts to establish fascism in Britain, but in 1948 he resumed fascist propaganda with his Union Movement, the revived BUF.

His first marriage was to a daughter of the Conservative politician Lord Curzon, his second to Diana Freeman-Mitford.

Mossadeq Muhammad 1880–1967. Iranian prime minister 1951–53. He instigated a dispute with the Anglo-Iranian Oil Company over the control of Iran's oil production, and when he failed in his attempt to overthrow the shah he was imprisoned. From 1956 he was under house arrest.

Mössbauer Rudolf 1929– . German physicist who discovered in 1958 that in certain conditions a nucleus can be stimulated to emit very sharply defined beams of gamma rays. This became known as the *Mössbauer effect*. Such a beam was used in 1960 to provide the first laboratory test of Einstein's General Theory of Relativity. For his work on gamma rays Mössbauer shared the 1961 Nobel Prize for Physics with ◊Hofstadter.

Mostel 'Zero' (Samuel Joel) 1915–1977. US comedian and actor, active mainly in the theatre.

His film work includes *Panic in the Streets* 1950, *A Funny Thing Happened on the Way to the Forum* 1966, *The Producers* 1967, and *The Front* 1976.

Mott Nevill Francis 1905– . British physicist noted for his research on the electronic properties of metals, semiconductors, and noncrystalline materials. He shared the Nobel Prize for Physics 1977.

Mountbatten Louis, 1st Earl Mountbatten of Burma 1900–1979. British admiral. In World War II he became chief of combined operations 1942 and commander in chief in SE Asia 1943. As last viceroy of India 1947 he oversaw the transition to independence, becoming the first governor general of India until 1948. He was chief of the UK Defence Staff 1959–65. Mountbatten was killed by an Irish Republican Army bomb aboard his yacht at Mullaghmore, County Sligo.

Moyse Marcel 1889–1984. French flautist. Trained at the Paris Conservatoire, he made many recordings and was an influential teacher.

Mozart Wolfgang Amadeus 1756–1791. Austrian composer and performer who showed astonishing precocity as a child and was an adult virtuoso. He was trained by his father, **Leopold Mozart** (1719–1787). From an early age he composed prolifically, his works including 27 piano concertos, 23 string quartets, 35 violin sonatas, and more than 50 symphonies. His operas include *Idomeneo* 1781, *Le Nozze di Figaro/The Marriage of Figaro* 1786, *Don Giovanni* 1787, *Così fan tutte/Thus Do All Women* 1790, and *Die Zauberflöte/The Magic Flute* 1791. Strongly influenced by ◊Haydn, Mozart's music marks the height of the Classical age in its purity of melody and form.

Mozart's career began when, with his sister, Maria Anna, he was taken on a number of tours 1762–79, visiting Vienna, the Rhineland, Holland, Paris, London, and Italy. Mozart not only gave public recitals, but had already begun to compose. In 1772 he was appointed master of the archbishop of Salzburg's court band. He found the post uncongenial, since he was treated as a servant, and in 1781 he was suddenly dismissed. From then on he lived mostly in Vienna, and married Constanze Weber in 1782. He supported himself as a pianist, composer, and teacher, but his lack of business acumen often resulted in financial difficulties. His *Requiem*, unfinished at his death, was completed by a pupil. Mozart had been in failing health, and died impoverished. His works were catalogued chronologically by the musicologist Ludwig von Köchel (1800–1877) in 1862.

Mubarak Hosni 1928– . Egyptian politician, president from 1981. He commanded the air force 1972–75 (and was responsible for the initial victories in the Egyptian campaign of 1973 against Israel), when he became an active vice president to Sadat, and succeeded him on his assassination. He has continued to pursue Sadat's moderate poli-cies, and has significantly increased the freedom of the press and of political association.

Mugabe Robert (Gabriel) 1925– . Zimbabwean politician, prime minister from 1980 and president from 1987. He was in detention in Rhodesia for nationalist activities 1964–74, then carried on guerrilla warfare from Mozambique. As leader of ZANU (Zimbabwe African People's Union), he was in alliance with Joshua ◊Nkomo of ZAPU (Zimbabwe African National Union) from 1976, and the two parties merged 1987.

Muggeridge Malcolm 1903– . British journalist. He worked for the *Guardian* and *Daily Telegraph*, and was editor of *Punch* 1953–57. *Chronicles of Wasted Time* 1972–73 is an autobiography.

Mughal emperors N Indian dynasty 1526–1857, established by ◊Zahir ('Baber'). They were descendants of Tamerlane, the 14th-century Mongol leader, and ruled until the last Mughal emperor was dethroned and exiled by the British 1857; they included Akbar, Aurangzeb, and ◊Shah Jehan. They were Muslims.

Muhammad or *Mohammed, Mahomet* c.570–632. Founder of Islam, born in Mecca on the Arabian peninsula. In about 616 he claimed to be a prophet and that the *Koran* was revealed to him by God (it was later written down by his followers). He fled from persecution to the town now known as Medina in 622: the flight, *Hegira*, marks the beginning of the Islamic era.

Originally a shepherd and caravan conductor, he found leisure for meditation by his marriage with a wealthy widow in 595, and received his first revelation in 610. After some years of secret teaching, he openly declared himself the prophet of God, and, as the number of his followers increased, he was forced to flee to Medina. After the battle of Badr in 623, he was continuously victorious, entering Mecca as the recognized prophet of Arabia 630. The succession was troubled.

Mujibur Rahman Sheik 1921–1975. Bangladeshi nationalist politician, president 1975. He was arrested several times for campaigning for the autonomy of East Pakistan. He won the elections 1970 as leader of the Awami League, but was again arrested when negotiations with the Pakistan government broke down. After the civil war 1971, he became prime minister of the newly independent Bangladesh. He was presidential dictator Jan–Aug 1975, when he was assassinated.

Muldoon Robert David 1921– . New Zealand National Party politician, prime minister 1975–84.

A chartered accountant, he was minister of finance 1967–72, and in 1974 replaced John Marshall as leader of the National Party, after the latter had been criticized as insufficiently aggressive in opposition. He became prime minister in 1975 and pursued austere economic policies. He sought to introduce curbs on trade unions, and was a vigorous supporter of the Western alliance. He was defeated in the general election of 1984 and was succeeded as prime minister by the Labour Party's David Lange.

Muller Hermann Joseph 1890–1967. US geneticist who discovered the effect of radiation on genes by his work on fruit flies. Nobel Prize for Medicine 1946.

Müller Johannes Peter 1801–1858. German comparative anatomist whose studies of nerves and sense organs opened a new chapter in physiology by demonstrating the physical nature of sensory perception. His name is associated with a number of discoveries, including the *Müllerian ducts* in the mammalian fetus and the lymph heart in frogs.

Müller Paul 1899–1965. Swiss chemist awarded a Nobel prize in 1948 for his discovery of the first synthetic contact insecticide, DDT, in 1939.

Mulliken Robert Sanderson 1896–1986. US chemist and physicist, who received the 1966 Nobel Prize for Chemistry for his development of the molecular orbital theory.

Mulready William 1786–1863. Irish painter of rural scenes, active in England. In 1840 he designed the first penny-postage envelope, known as the *Mulready envelope*.

Mulroney Brian 1939– . Canadian politician. A former businessman, he replaced Joe Clark as Progressive Conservative party leader 1983, and achieved a landslide in the 1984 election to become prime minister. He won the 1988 election on a platform of free trade with the USA, but with a reduced majority.

Mumford Lewis 1895–1990. US sociologist and writer on town planning. His books, including *Technics and Civilization* 1934 and *The Culture of Cities* 1938, discussed the rise of cities and proposed the creation of green belts around large conurbations.

Munch Edvard 1863–1944. Norwegian painter. He studied in Paris and Berlin, and his best works date from 1892–1908, when he lived mainly in Germany. His paintings often focus on neurotic emotional states. The *Frieze of Life* 1890s, a sequence of highly charged, symbolic paintings, includes some of his favourite images, for example *Skriket/The Scream* 1893. He reused these in etchings, lithographs, and woodcuts.

Munch was influenced by van Gogh and Gauguin, but soon developed his own expressive style, reducing his compositions to broad areas of colour with sinuous contours emphasized by heavy brushstrokes, distorting faces and figures. His first show in Berlin 1892 made an enormous impact on young German artists. In 1908 he suffered a nervous breakdown and returned to Norway. Later works include a series of murals 1910–15 in the assembly halls of Oslo University.

Münchhausen Karl Friedrich, Freiherr (Baron) von 1720–1797. German soldier, born in Hanover. He served with the Russian army against the Turks, and after his retirement in 1760 told exaggerated stories of his campaigning adventures. This idiosyncrasy was utilized by the German writer Rudolph Erich Raspe (1737–94) in his extravagantly fictitious *Adventures of Baron Munchausen* 1785, which he wrote in English while living in London.

Mungo, St another name for St ◊Kentigern, first bishop of Glasgow.

Munnings Alfred 1878–1959. British painter excelling in racing and hunting scenes. As president of the Royal Academy 1944–49 he was outspoken in his dislike of 'modern art'.

Munro H(ugh) H(ector) British author who wrote under the pen name ◊Saki.

Murasaki Shikibu *c.*978–*c.*1015. Japanese writer, a lady at the court. Her masterpiece of fiction, *The Tale of Genji*, is one of the classic works of Japanese literature, and may be the world's first novel.

She was a member of the Fujiwara clan, but her own name is not known; scholars have given her the name Murasaki after a character in the book. It deals with upper-class life in Heian Japan, centring on the affairs of Prince Genji.

Murat Joachim 1767–1815. King of Naples from 1808. An officer in the French army, he was made king by Napoleon, but deserted him in 1813 in the vain hope that the Allies would recognize him. In 1815 he attempted unsuccessfully to make himself king of all Italy, but when he landed in Calabria in an attempt to gain the throne he was captured and shot.

Murdoch Iris 1919– . English novelist, born in Dublin. Her novels combine philosophical speculation with often outrageous situations and tangled human relationships. They include *The Sandcastle* 1957, *The Sea, The Sea* 1978, and *The Book and the Brotherhood* 1987.

A lecturer in philosophy, she became in 1948 a fellow of St Anne's College, Oxford University, and published *Sartre, Romantic Rationalist* 1953. Her novel *A Severed Head* 1961 was dramatized; others include *The Philosopher's Pupil* 1983.

Murdoch Rupert 1931– . Australian entrepreneur and newspaper owner, with interests in Australia, the UK, and the USA. Among his UK newspapers are the *Sun*, the *News of the World*, and *The Times*; in the USA, he has a 50% stake in 20th Century Fox, and he also owns publishing companies. He is chief executive of Sky Television, the UK's first satellite television service.

Murdoch William 1754–1839. Scottish inventor who first used coal gas for domestic lighting. He illuminated his house and offices using coal gas in 1792, and in 1797 and 1798 he held public demonstrations of his invention.

Murger Henri 1822–1861. French writer, born in Paris. He studied painting, and in 1848 published

Murdoch *Iris Murdoch has won numerous awards including the Booker prize 1978 for* The Sea, The Sea *and was again shortlisted for the award 1987 for* The Book and the Brotherhood.

Scènes de la vie de bohème/Scenes of Bohemian Life which formed the basis of Puccini's opera *La Bohème*.

Murillo Bartolomé Esteban 1617–1682. Spanish painter, active mainly in Seville. He painted sweetly sentimental pictures of the Immaculate Conception; he also specialized in studies of street urchins.

Murillo was born in Seville. Visiting Madrid in the 1640s, he was befriended by the court painter Velázquez. After his return to Seville he received many important commissions, chiefly religious. He founded the academy of painting in Seville 1660 with the help of Herrera the Younger.

Murnau F W. Assumed name of Friedrich Wilhelm Plumpe 1889–1931. German silent-film director, whose 'subjective' use of a moving camera to tell the story, through expressive images and without subtitles, in *Der letzte Mumm/The Last Laugh* 1924 made him famous. Other films include *Nosferatu* 1922, a version of the Dracula story.

Murphy Audie 1924–1971. US actor and war hero, who starred mainly in low-budget Western films. His work includes *The Red Badge of Courage* 1951, *The Quiet American* 1958, and *The Unforgiven* 1960.

Murphy Dervla 1931– . Irish writer whose extensive travels have been recorded in books such as *Full Tilt* 1965.

Murray family name of dukes of Atholl; seated at Blair Castle, Perthshire, Scotland.

Murray Gilbert 1866–1957. British scholar. Born in Sydney, Australia, he was taken to England in 1877, and was professor of Greek at Glasgow University 1889–99 and at Oxford 1908–36. Author of *History of Ancient Greek Literature* 1897, he became best known for verse translations of the Greek dramatists, especially Euripides, making the plays more accessible to modern readers.

Murray James Augustus Henry 1837–1915. Scottish philologist. He was the first editor of the *Oxford English Dictionary* (originally the *New English Dictionary*) from 1878 until his death; the first volume was published 1884.

He edited more than half the dictionary himself, working in a shed (nicknamed the Scriptorium) in his back garden.

Murray James Stuart, Earl of Murray, or Moray 1531–1570. Regent of Scotland from 1567, an illegitimate son of James V. Murray was one of the leaders of the Scottish Reformation, and after the deposition of his half-sister ◊Mary Queen of Scots, he became regent. He was assassinated by one of her supporters.

Murry John Middleton 1889–1957. English writer. He produced studies of Dostoievsky, Keats, Blake, and Shakespeare, poetry, and an autobiographical novel, *Still Life* 1916. In 1913 he married Katherine ◊Mansfield, whose biography he wrote.

Musashi Miyamoto. Sixteenth-century Japanese exponent of the martial arts, whose manual *A Book of Five Rings* on samurai strategy achieved immense popularity in the US from 1974 when it appeared in translation. It was said that Japanese businessmen used it as a guide to success.

Museveni Yoweri Kaguta 1945– . Ugandan general and politician, president from 1986. He led the opposition to Idi Amin's regime 1971–78 and was minister of defence 1979–80 but, unhappy with Milton Obote's autocratic leadership, formed the National Resistance Army (NRA), which helped to remove him. Museveni leads a broad-based coalition government.

Museveni was educated in Uganda and at the University of Dar es Salaam, Tanzania. He entered the army, eventually rising to the rank of general. Until Amin's removal Museveni led the anti-Amin Front for National Salvation. When Obote was ousted in a coup by Tito Okello 1985, Museveni entered into a brief power-sharing agreement with Okello, before taking over as president.

Musgrave Thea 1928– . Scottish composer. Her works, in a conservative modern idiom, include concertos for horn, clarinet, and viola; string quartets; and operas, including *Mary, Queen of Scots* 1977.

Musil Robert 1880–1942. Austrian novelist, author of the unfinished *Der Mann ohne Eigenschaften/The Man without Qualities* (three volumes, 1930–43). Its hero shares the author's background of philosophical study and scientific and military training, and is preoccupied with the problems of the self viewed from a mystic but agnostic viewpoint.

Musset Alfred de 1810–1857. French poet and playwright. He achieved success with the volume of poems *Contes d'Espagne et d'Italie/Stories of Spain and Italy* 1829. His *Confession d'un enfant du siècle/Confessions of a Child of the Century* 1835 recounts his broken relationship with George Sand.

Most typical of his work are the verse *Les Nuits/Nights* 1835–37 and the short plays *Comédies et proverbes/Comedies and Proverbs* 1840.

Mussolini Benito 1883–1945. Italian dictator 1925–43. As founder of the Fascist Movement 1919 and prime minister from 1922, he became known as *Il Duce* 'the leader'. He invaded Ethiopia 1935–36, intervened in the Spanish Civil War 1936–39 in support of Franco, and conquered Albania 1939. In June 1940 Italy entered World War II supporting Hitler. Forced by military and domestic setbacks to resign 1943, Mussolini established a breakaway government in N Italy 1944–45, but was killed trying to flee the country.

Mussolini was born in the Romagna, the son of a blacksmith, and worked in early life as a teacher and journalist. He became active in the socialist movement, from which he was expelled 1914 for advocating Italian intervention in World War I. In 1919 he founded the Fascist Movement, whose programme combined violent nationalism with demagogic republican and anti-capitalist slogans, and launched a campaign of terrorism against the

Mussolini *Italian dictator 1925–43, Benito Mussolini.*

socialists. This movement was backed by many landowners and industrialists, and by the heads of the army and police, and in Oct 1922 Mussolini was in power as prime minister at the head of a coalition government. In 1925 he assumed dictatorial powers, and in 1926 all opposition parties were banned. During the years that followed, the entire political, legal, and education system was remodelled on Fascist lines.

Mussolini's **Blackshirt** followers were the forerunners of Hitler's Brownshirts, and his career of conquest drew him into close cooperation with Nazi Germany. Together they formed the Axis alliance 1936. During World War II, Italian defeats in N Africa and Greece, the Allied invasion of Sicily, and discontent at home destroyed Mussolini's prestige, and in July 1943 he was compelled to resign by his own Fascist Grand Council. He was released from prison by German parachutists in Sept, and set up a 'Republican Fascist' government in N Italy. In Apr 1945 he and his mistress, Clara Petacci, were captured at Lake Como by partisans while heading for the border, and shot. Their bodies were hung upside down and exposed to the execration of the mob in Milan.

Mussorgsky Modest Petrovich 1839–1881. Russian composer, who was largely self-taught. His opera *Boris Godunov* was completed in 1869, although not produced in St Petersburg until 1874. Some of his works were 'revised' by ◊Rimsky-Korsakov, and only recently has their harsh and primitive beauty been recognized.

Born at Karevo, he resigned his commission in the army in 1858 to concentrate on music while working as a government clerk. A member of the group of nationalist composers, the Five, he was influenced by both folk music and literature. Among his other works are the incomplete operas *Khovanshchina* and *Sorochintsy Fair*, the orchestral *A Night on the Bare Mountain* 1867, the suite for piano *Pictures at an Exhibition* 1874, and many songs. Mussorgsky died in poverty, from alcoholism.

Mustafa Kemal Turkish leader, who assumed the name of ◊Atatürk.

Muti Riccardo 1941– . Italian conductor of the Philharmonia Orchestra, London, 1973–82, the Philadelphia Orchestra from 1981, and artistic director of La Scala, Milan, from 1986. He is known as a purist, devoted to carrying out a composer's intentions to the last detail.

Mutsuhito 1852–1912. Emperor of Japan from 1867, when he took the title *meiji tennō* ('enlightened sovereign'). During his reign Japan became a world military and naval power. He abolished the feudal system and discrimination against the lowest caste, established state schools, and introduced conscription, the Western calendar, and other measures in an attempt to modernize Japan, including a constitution 1889.

Muzorewa *Zimbabwean politician and bishop of the Methodist Church, Abel Muzorewa, 1979.*

Muybridge Eadweard. Adopted name of Edward James Muggeridge 1830–1904. British photographer. He made a series of animal locomotion photographs in the USA in the 1870s and proved that, when a horse trots, there are moments when all its feet are off the ground. He also explored motion in birds and humans.

Muzorewa Abel (Tendekayi) 1925– . Zimbabwean politician and Methodist bishop. He was president of the African National Council 1971–85, and was prime minister of Rhodesia/Zimbabwe 1979. He was detained for a year in 1983–84. He is leader of the minority United Africa National Council (UANC).

Mwiiny Ali Hassan 1925– . Tanzanian socialist politician, president from 1985, when he succeeded Nyerere. He began a revival of private enterprise and control of state involvement and spending.

Myers F(rederic) W(illiam) H(enry) 1843–1901. English psychic investigator and writer, coiner of the word 'telepathy'. He was a founder and one of the first presidents of the *Society for Psychical Research* (1900).

Myrdal Gunnar 1898–1987. Swedish economist, author of many works on development economics. Nobel prize 1974.

Myron *c.*500–440 BC. Greek sculptor. His *Discobolus/Discus-Thrower* and *Athene and Marsyas*, much admired in his time, are known through Roman copies. They confirm his ancient reputation for brilliant composition and naturalism.

He was born in St Petersburg, settled in the USA 1940, and became a US citizen 1945. He was professor of Russian literature at Cornell University 1948–59, producing a translation and commentary on *Eugene Onegin* 1963. He was also a lepidopterist (a collector of butterflies and moths), a theme used in his book *Pale Fire* 1962.

Nadar adopted name of Gaspard-Félix Tournachon 1820–1910. French portrait photographer and caricaturist. He took the first aerial photographs (from a balloon 1858) and was the first to use artificial light.

Nader Ralph 1934– . US lawyer. The 'scourge of corporate morality', he has led many consumer campaigns. His book *Unsafe at Any Speed* 1965 led to US car-safety legislation.

Nadir Shah (Khan) *c.* 1880–1933. King of Afghanistan from 1929. Nadir played a key role in the 1919 Afghan War, but was subsequently forced into exile in France. He returned to Kabul in 1929 to seize the throne and embarked on an ambitious modernization programme. This alienated the Muslim clergy and in 1933 he was assassinated by fundamentalists. His successor as king was his son ◊Zahir Shah.

Nabokov Vladimir 1899–1977. US writer, who left his native Russia 1917, and began writing in English in the 1940s. His best-known novel is *Lolita* 1955, the story of the infatuation of middle aged Humbert Humbert with a precocious child of 12. His other books include *The Real Life of Sebastian Knight* 1945 and *Pnin* 1957.

Nagy Imre 1895–1958. Hungarian politician, prime minister 1953–55 and 1956. He led the Hungarian revolt against Soviet domination in 1956, for which he was executed.

Nagy, an Austro-Hungarian prisoner of war in Siberia during World War I, became a Soviet citizen after the Russian Revolution, and lived in the USSR 1930–44. In 1953, after Stalin's death, he became prime minister, introducing liberal measures such as encouraging the production of consumer goods, but was dismissed 1955 by hardline Stalinist premier Rákosi. Reappointed Oct 1956 during the Hungarian uprising, he began taking liberalization further than the Soviets wanted, for example announcing Hungarian withdrawal from the Warsaw Pact. Soviet troops entered Budapest, and Nagy was dismissed 4 Nov 1956. He was captured by the KGB and shot. His remains were relocated in Budapest, and in 1989 the Hungarian Supreme Court recognized his leadership of a legitimate government and quashed his conviction for treachery.

Nahayan Sheikh Zayed bin Sultan al- 1918– . Emir of Abu Dhabi from 1969, when he deposed his brother, Sheikh Shakhbut. He was elected president of the supreme council of the United Arab Emirates (UAE) in 1971. Before 1969 he was governor of the eastern province of Abu Dhabi, one of seven Trucial States in the Persian Gulf and Gulf of Oman, which were under British protection. He was unanimously re-elected emir in 1986.

Naipaul V(idiadhar) S(urajprasad) 1932– . British writer, born in Trinidad of Hindu parents. His novels include *A House for Mr Biswas* 1961, *The Mimic Men* 1967, and *A Bend in the River* 1979.

Nabokov Born in Russia, Vladimir Nabokov was an exile for all his adult life. The theme of alienation runs throughout his work, and his best-known novel remains the controversial Lolita *1955.*

His brother *Shiva(dhar) Naipaul* (1940–85) was also a novelist (*Fireflies* 1970) and journalist.

Najibullah Ahmadzai 1947– . Afghani communist leader. A member of the People's Democratic Party of Afghanistan (PDPA) since his youth, allying himself to its gradualist Parcham (banner) faction. He became head of the KHAD (secret police) after the Soviet invasion of 1979 and party leader in 1986. Elected state president in 1987, Najibullah attempted initially to broaden support for the PDPA regime within a coalition, but since the Soviet military withdrawal in 1989 he has ruled in a beleaguered, emergency manner.

Nakasone Yasuhiro 1917– . Japanese conservative politician, leader of the Liberal Democratic Party (LDP) and prime minister 1982–87. He stepped up military spending and increased Japanese participation in international affairs, with closer ties to the USA. His reputation was tarnished by his involvement in the Recruit insider-dealing scandal.

Nakasone was educated at Tokyo University. He held ministerial posts from 1967 and established his own faction within the conservative LDP. In 1982 he was elected president of the LDP and prime minister. He encouraged a less paternalist approach to economic management. Although embarrassed by the conviction of one of his supporters in the 1983 Lockheed corruption scandal, he was re-elected 1986 by a landslide.

Namatjira Albert 1902–1959. Australian Aboriginal painter of watercolour landscapes of the Australian interior. Acclaimed after an exhibition in Melbourne in 1938, he died destitute.

Nanak 1469–*c.*1539. Indian guru and founder of Sikhism, a religion based on the unity of God and the equality of all human beings. He was strongly opposed to caste divisions.

Nana Sahib popular name for Dandhu Panth. 1820–*c.*1859. Adopted son of a former *peshwa* (chief minister) of the people of Mahrattas in central India. He joined the rebels in the Indian Mutiny 1857–58, and was responsible for the massacre at Kanpur when safe conducts given to British civilians were broken and many women and children massacred. After the failure of the mutiny he took refuge in Nepál.

Nancarrow Conlon 1912– . US composer who settled in Mexico 1940. Using a player-piano as a form of synthesizer, punching the rolls by hand, he experimented with complicated combinations of rhythm and tempo, producing a series of studies that anticipated minimalism and brought him recognition in the 1970s.

Nansen Fridtjof 1861–1930. Norwegian explorer and scientist. In 1893, he sailed to the Arctic in the *Fram*, which was deliberately allowed to drift N with an iceflow. Nansen, accompanied by F J Johansen, continued N on foot and reached 86° 14′ N, the highest latitude then attained.

After World War I, Nansen became League of Nations high commissioner for refugees; Nobel Peace Prize 1923.

He made his first voyage to Greenland waters in a sealing ship 1882, and in 1888–89 attempted to cross the Greenland icefield. He was professor of zoology and oceanography at the University of Christiania (now Oslo). Norwegian ambassador in London 1906–08.

Napier Charles James 1782–1853. British general. He conquered Sind in India (now a province of Pakistan) 1841–43 with a very small force and governed it until 1847. He was the first commander to mention men from the ranks in his dispatches.

Napier John 1550–1617. Scottish mathematician who invented logarithms 1614, and 'Napier's bones', an early mechanical calculating device for multiplication and division.

Napier Robert Cornelis, 1st Baron Napier of Magdala 1810–1890. British field marshal. Knighted for his services in relieving Lucknow during the Indian Mutiny, he took part in capturing Peking (Beijing) 1860 during the war against China in 1860. He stormed Magdala in the Abyssinian campaign 1868, was created a peer in the same year, was commander in chief in India 1870–76, and governor of Gibraltar 1876–82.

Napoleon I Bonaparte 1769–1821. Emperor of the French 1804–14 and 1814–15. A general from 1796 in the Revolutionary Wars, in 1799 he overthrew the ruling Directory and made himself dictator. From 1803 he conquered most of Europe, and installed his brothers as puppet kings (see

Napoleon I Napoleon crossing the Alps *(1800)* by *Jacques-Louis David, Charlottenburg Castle, Berlin.*

◊Bonaparte). After the Peninsular War and retreat from Moscow 1812, he was forced to abdicate 1814 and was banished to Elba. In Mar 1815 he reassumed power but was defeated at the battle of Waterloo and exiled to the island of St Helena. His internal administrative reforms are still evident in France.

Napoleon, born in Ajaccio, Corsica, received a commission in the artillery 1785 and first distinguished himself at the siege of Toulon 1793. Having suppressed a royalist rising in Paris 1795, he was given command against the Austrians in Italy, and defeated them at Lodi, Arcole, and Rivoli 1796–97. Egypt, seen as a halfway house to India, was overrun, and Syria invaded, but his fleet was destroyed by the British admiral ◊Nelson at the Battle of the Nile. He returned to France to carry out a coup against the government of the Directory and establish his own dictatorship, nominally as First Consul. The Austrians were again defeated at Marengo 1800, and the coalition against France shattered, a truce being declared 1802. A plebiscite the same year made him consul for life. In 1804 a plebiscite made him emperor.

While retaining and extending the legal and educational reforms of the Jacobins, Napoleon replaced the democratic constitution established by Revolution with a centralized despotism, and by his concordat with Pius VII conciliated the Catholic church. The **Code Napoléon** is still the basis of French law.

War was renewed by Britain 1803, aided by Austria and Russia from 1805, and Prussia from 1806. Prevented by the British navy from invading Britain, Napoleon drove Austria out of the war by victories at Ulm and Austerlitz 1805, and Prussia by the victory at Jena 1806. Then, after the battles of Eylau and Friedland, he formed an alliance with Russia at Tilsit 1807. Napoleon now forbade entry of British goods to Europe, attempting an economic blockade known as the Continental System, occupied Portugal, and in 1808 placed his brother Joseph on the Spanish throne. Both countries revolted, with British aid, and Austria attempted to re-enter the war, but was defeated at Wagram. In 1796 Napoleon had married ◊Josephine de Beauharnais, but in 1809, to assert his equality with the Habsburgs, he divorced her to marry the Austrian emperor's daughter, ◊Marie Louise.

When Russia failed to enforce the Continental System, Napoleon occupied Moscow, but his retreat in the bitter winter of 1812 encouraged Prussia and Austria to declare war again 1813, and he was defeated at Leipzig and driven from Germany. Despite his brilliant campaign on French soil, the Allies invaded Paris and compelled him to abdicate Apr 1814; he was banished to the island of Elba, off the west coast of Italy. In Mar 1815 he escaped and took power for a hundred days, with the aid of Marshal ◊Ney, but Britain and Prussia led an alliance against him at Waterloo, Belgium, in June. Surrendering to the British, he again abdicated, and was exiled to the island of St Helena, 1,900 km/1,200 mi west of Africa. His body was brought back 1840 to be interred in the Hôtel des Invalides, Paris.

Napoleon II 1811–1832. Title given by the Bonapartists to the son of Napoleon I and ◊Marie Louise; until 1814 he was known as the king of Rome, and after 1818 as the duke of Reichstadt. After his father's abdication 1814 he was taken to the Austrian court, where he spent the rest of his life.

Napoleon III 1808–1873. Emperor of the French 1852–70, known as **Louis-Napoleon**. After two attempted coups (1836 and 1840) he was jailed and went into exile, returning for the revolution of 1848, when he became president of the Second Republic, but soon turned authoritarian. In 1870 he was manoeuvred by the German chancellor Bismarck into war with Prussia; he was forced to surrender at Sedan, NE France, and the empire collapsed.

The son of Louis Bonaparte and Hortense de Beauharnais, brother and step-daughter respectively of Napoleon I, he led two unsuccessful revolts against the French king Louis Philippe, at Strasbourg 1836 and at Boulogne 1840. After the latter he was imprisoned. Escaping 1846, he lived in London until 1848. He was elected president of the newly established French republic in Dec, and set himself to secure a following by posing as the champion of order and religion against the revolutionary menace. He secured his re-election by a military coup d'état 1851, and a year later was proclaimed emperor. Hoping to strengthen his regime by military triumphs, he joined in the Crimean War 1854–55, waged war with Austria 1859, winning the Battle of Solferino, annexed Savoy and Nice 1860, and attempted unsuccessfully to found a vassal empire in Mexico 1863–67. In so doing he aroused the mistrust of Europe and isolated France.

At home, his regime was discredited by its notorious corruption; republican and socialist opposition grew, in spite of severe repression, and forced Napoleon, after 1860, to make concessions in the direction of parliamentary government. After losing the war with Prussia he withdrew to England, where he died. His son by Empress ◊Eugénie, **Eugène Louis Jean Joseph Napoleon**, Prince Imperial (1856–79), was killed fighting with the British army against the Zulus in Africa.

Narayan Jaya Prakash 1902–1979. Indian politician. A veteran socialist, he was an associate of Vinobha Bham in the Bhoodan movement for rural reforms that took place during the last years of the Raj. He was prominent in the protest movement against Indira Gandhi's emergency regime, 1975–77, and acted as umpire in the Janata leadership contest, which followed Indira Gandhi's defeat in 1977.

Nares George Strong 1831–1915. Scottish vice-admiral and explorer who sailed to the Canadian Arctic on an expedition in search of John ◊Franklin 1852 and again in 1876 when he discovered the Challenger Mountains. During 1872–76 he commanded the Challenger Expedition. His Arctic explorations are recounted in *Voyage to the Polar Seas* 1878.

Narses *c.*478–*c.*573. Byzantine general. Originally a eunuch slave, he later became an official in the imperial treasury. He was joint commander with the Roman general Belisarius in Italy 538–39, and in 552 destroyed the Ostrogoths at Taginae in the Apennines.

Nash John 1752–1835. English architect. He laid out Regent's Park, London, and its approaches. From 1813–1820 he planned Regent Street (later rebuilt), repaired and enlarged Buckingham Palace (for which he designed Marble Arch), and rebuilt Brighton Pavilion in flamboyant oriental style.

Nash John Northcote 1893–1977. English illustrator, landscape artist, and engraver. He was the brother of the artist Paul Nash.

Nash Ogden 1902–1971. US poet. He published numerous volumes of humorous verse characterized by its puns, light epigrams, and unorthodox rhymes.

Nash Paul 1889–1946. English painter, an official war artist in World Wars I and II. In the 1930s he was one of a group of artists promoting avant-garde styles in the UK. Two of his most celebrated works are *Totes Meer/Dead Sea* (Tate Gallery, London) and *The Battle of Britain* (Imperial War Museum, London).

Nash (Richard) 'Beau' 1674–1762. British dandy. As master of ceremonies at Bath from 1705, he made the town the most fashionable watering-place in England, and introduced a polished code of manners into general use.

Nash Walter 1882–1968. New Zealand Labour politician. He was born in England, and emigrated to New Zealand 1909. He held ministerial posts 1935–49, was prime minister 1957–60, and leader of the Labour Party until 1963.

Nash(e) Thomas 1567–1601. Born in Suffolk, he settled in London about 1588, where he was rapidly drawn into the Martin ◊Marprelate controversy (a pamphleteering attack on the clergy of the Church of England by Puritans), and wrote at least three attacks on the Martinists. Among his later works are the satirical *Pierce Pennilesse* 1592; the religious *Christes Teares over Jerusalem* 1593; and the comedy *Summer's Last Will and Testament* 1592.

Nasmyth Alexander 1758–1840. Scottish portrait and landscape painter. His portrait of the poet Robert Burns hangs in the Scottish National Gallery.

Nasmyth James 1808–1890. Scottish engineer and machine-tool manufacturer, whose many inventions included the steel hammer in 1839. At his factory near Manchester, he developed the steam hammer for making large steel forgings (the first of which was the propeller shaft for Brunel's steamship *Great Britain*).

Nasser Gamal Abdel 1918–1970. Egyptian politician, prime minister 1954–56 and from 1956 president of Egypt (the United Arab Republic 1958–71). In 1952 he was the driving power behind the Neguib coup, which ended the monarchy. His nationalization of the Suez Canal 1956 led to an Anglo-French invasion and the Suez Crisis, and his ambitions for an Egyptian-led Arab union led to disquiet in the Middle East (and in the West).

Navratilova Martina 1956– . Czechoslovakian tennis player, who became a naturalized US citizen 1981. The most outstanding woman player of the 1980s, she has 52 Grand Slam victories, including 18 singles titles. She has won the Wimbledon singles title nine times, including six in succession 1982–87.

She was born in Prague, Czechoslovakia. She won her first Wimbledon title 1976 (doubles with Chris Evert). Between 1974 and 1988 she won 52 Grand Slam titles (singles and doubles) second only to Margaret ◊Court.

N'Dour Youssou 1959– . Senegalese singer, songwriter, and musician whose fusion of traditional

Navratilova *Martina Navratilova, the outstanding woman tennis player of the 1980s.*

mbalax percussion music with bluesy Arab-style vocals, accompanied by African and electronic instruments, became popular in the West in the 1980s on albums such as *Immigrés* 1984 with the band Le Super Etoile de Dakar.

Neagle Anna 1908–1986. British actress, whose films include *Nell Gwyn* 1934, *Victoria the Great* 1937, and *Odette* 1950. She was made a Dame of the British Empire in 1969.

Neale John Mason 1818–1866. Anglican cleric. He translated ancient and medieval hymns, including 'Jerusalem, the golden'.

Necker Jacques 1732–1804. French politician. As finance minister 1776–81, he attempted reforms, and was dismissed through Queen Marie Antoinette's influence. Recalled 1788, he persuaded Louis XVI to summon the States General (parliament), which earned him the hatred of the court, and in July 1789 he was banished. The outbreak of the French Revolution with the storming of the Bastille forced his reinstatement, but he resigned Sept 1790.

Needham Joseph 1900– . British biochemist and sinologist known for his work on the history of Chinese science. He worked first as a biochemist concentrating mainly on problems in embryology. In the 1930s he learnt Chinese and began to collect material. The first volume of his *Science and Civilisation in China* was published in 1954 and by 1989 15 volumes had appeared.

Nehemiah 5th century BC. Jewish governor of Judaea under Persian rule. He rebuilt Jerusalem's walls 444 BC, and made religious and social reforms.

Nehru Jawaharlal 1889–1964. Indian nationalist politician, prime minister from 1947. Before partition (the division into India and Pakistan) he led the socialist wing of the nationalist Congress Party, and was second in influence only to Mahatma ◊Gandhi. He was imprisoned nine times 1921–45 for political activities. As prime minister from the creation of the dominion (later republic) of India Aug 1947, he originated the idea of nonalignment (neutrality towards major powers). His daughter was Indira Gandhi. He was born in Allahabad and educated at a UK public school and Cambridge University.

Neizvestny Ernst 1926– . Russian artist and sculptor, who found fame when he had an argument with Khrushchev in 1962, and eventually left the country 1976. His works include a vast relief in the Moscow Institute of Electronics, and the Aswan monument, the tallest sculpture in the world.

Nekrasov Nikolai Alekseevich 1821–1877. Russian poet and publisher. He espoused the cause of the freeing of the serfs, and identified himself with the peasants in such poems as 'Who Can Live Happy in Russia?' 1876.

Nelson Azumah 1958– . Ghanaian featherweight boxer, world champion from 1984.

Nelson won the 1978 Commonwealth Games at featherweight, the World Boxing Championship (WBC) featherweight title in 1984, beating Wilfredo Gomez, and in 1988 captured the super-featherweight title by beating Mario Martinez.

Nelson Horatio, Viscount Nelson 1758–1805. English admiral. He joined the navy 1770. In the Revolutionary Wars against France he lost the sight in his right eye 1794, and his right arm 1797. He became a national hero, and rear-admiral, after the victory off Cape St Vincent, Portugal. In 1798 he tracked the French fleet to Aboukir Bay, and almost entirely destroyed it in the Battle of the Nile. In 1801 he won a decisive victory over Denmark at the battle of Copenhagen, and in 1805, after two years of blockading Toulon, another over the Franco-Spanish fleet at the battle of Trafalgar, near Gibraltar.

Nehru *Pandit Jawaharlal Nehru (left) with Mohammed Ali Jinnah, the founder of Pakistan.*

Nelson *British admiral Horatio Nelson, who was mortally wounded at the Battle of Trafalgar 1805.*

Nelson was born at Burnham Thorpe, Norfolk, where his father was rector. While serving in the West Indies he married Mrs Frances Nisbet. He was almost continuously on active service in the Mediterranean 1793–1800, and lingered at Naples for a year, during which he helped to crush a democratic uprising and fell completely under the influence of Lady ◊Hamilton. In 1800 he returned to England, and soon after separated from his wife. He was promoted to vice-admiral 1801, and sent to the Baltic to operate against the Danes, nominally as second-in-command; in fact, it was Nelson who was responsible for the victory of Copenhagen, and for negotiating peace with Denmark. On his return to England he was created a viscount.

In 1803 he received the Mediterranean command, and for nearly two years blockaded Toulon. When in 1805 his opponent, the French admiral Pierre de Villeneuve (1763–1806), eluded him, Nelson pursued him to the West Indies and back, and on 21 Oct defeated the combined French and Spanish fleets off Cape Trafalgar, 20 of the enemy ships being captured. Nelson himself was mortally wounded. He is buried in St Paul's Cathedral, London.

Nemerov Howard 1920– . US poet, critic, and novelist. He published his poetry collection *Guide to the Ruins* 1950, a short story collection *A Commodity of Dreams* 1959, and in 1977 his *Collected Poems* won both the National Book Award and the Pulitzer Prize.

Nernst (Walter) Hermann 1864–1941. German physical chemist. His investigations, for which he won the 1920 Nobel Prize for Chemistry, were concerned with heat changes in chemical reactions. He proposed in 1906 the principle known as the *Nernst heat theorem* or the third law of thermodynamics: that chemical changes at the absolute zero of temperature involve no change of entropy (disorder).

Nero AD 37–68. Roman emperor from 54. He is said to have murdered his stepfather ◊Claudius' son Britannicus, his own mother, his wives Octavia and Poppaea, and many others. After the great fire of Rome 64, he persecuted the Christians, who were suspected of causing it. Military revolt followed 68; the Senate condemned Nero to death, and he committed suicide.

Son of Domitius Ahenobarbus and Agrippina, he was adopted by Claudius, and succeeded him as emperor in 54. He was a poet, connoisseur of art, and performed publicly as an actor and singer.

Neruda Pablo. Pen name of Neftalí Ricardo Reyes y Basualto 1904–1973. Chilean poet, diplomat and communist leader. His work includes lyrics and the epic of the American continent *Canto General* 1950. Nobel Prize for Literature 1971.

He was consul and ambassador to many countries

Neruda *As a poet, Pablo Neruda of Chile identified with the working class from which he came, voicing the dreams and sorrows of his people.*

as well as a senator 1945–48. He went into exile 1948–52 but returned and became consul to France 1971–72.

Nerva Marcus Cocceius Nerva *c.* AD 35–98. Roman emperor. He was proclaimed emperor on Domitian's death AD 96, and introduced state loans for farmers, family allowances, and allotments of land to poor citizens.

Nerval Gérard de. Pen name of Gérard Labrunie 1808–1855. French writer and poet, precursor of French symbolism and surrealism. His writings include the travelogue *Voyage en Orient* 1851; short stories, including the collection *Les Filles du feu* 1854; poetry; a novel *Aurélia* 1855, containing episodes of visionary psychosis; and drama. He lived a wandering life, with periodic insanity, and committed suicide.

Nervi Pier Luigi 1891–1979. Italian architect, who used soft steel mesh within concrete to give it flowing form, as for example in Turin exhibition hall 1949, the UNESCO building in Paris 1952, and the cathedral at New Norcia, near Perth, Australia 1960.

Nesbit E(dith) 1858–1924. English author of children's books, including *The Story of the Treasure Seekers* 1899 and *The Railway Children* 1906.

Her stories often have a humorous magical element, as in *Five Children and It* 1902. *The Treasure Seekers* is the first of several books about the realistically squabbling Bastable children. Nesbit was a Fabian socialist and supported her family by writing.

Nestlé Henri 1814–1890. Swiss industrialist who established a milk-based baby-food factory in Vevey, Switzerland 1867, Farine Lactée Henri Nestlé. He abandoned all his interest in the business 1875.

Neumann Balthasar 1687–1753. German Rococo architect and military engineer, whose work includes the bishop's palace in Würzburg.

Neumann John Von 1903–1957. Hungarian-born US scientist and mathematician, known for his pioneering work on computer design. He invented his celebrated 'rings of operators' (called Von Neumann algebras) in the late 1930s, and also contributed to set theory, games theory, cybernetics (with his theory of self-reproducing automata, called *Von Neumann machines*), and the development of the atomic and hydrogen bombs.

He was born in Budapest and became an assistant professor of physical mathematics at Berlin University before moving to Princeton, USA, 1929, where he later became professor of mathematics. In the early 1940s he described a design for a stored-program computer.

Neutra Richard Joseph 1892–1970. Austrian architect, who became a US citizen 1929. His works, often in impressive landscape settings, include Lovell Health House, Los Angeles, and Mathematics Park, Princeton.

Newbolt Henry John 1862–1938. English poet and naval historian. His works include *The Year of Trafalgar* 1905 and *A Naval History of the War* 1920 on World War I. He is best remembered for his *Songs of the Sea* 1904 and *Songs of the Fleet* 1910 which were set to music by Charles Stanford.

Newby (George) Eric 1919– . English travel writer and sailor. His books include *A Short Walk in the Hindu Kush* 1958, *The Big Red Train Ride* 1978, *Slowly Down the Ganges* 1966, and *A Travellers Life* 1985.

Newcastle Thomas Pelham-Holles, Duke of Newcastle 1693–1768. British Whig politician. He was secretary of state 1724–54, and then prime minister during the Seven Years' War, until 1762, although ◊Pitt the Elder (1st Earl of Chatham) was mainly responsible for the conduct of the war.

Newcomen Thomas 1663–1729. English inventor of an early steam engine. He patented his 'fire engine' 1705, which was used for pumping water from mines until James ◊Watt invented one with a separate condenser.

Ne Win Maung Shu Maung, 'Brilliant Sun' 1911– . Burmese politician, ruler from 1962 to 1974, president 1984–81.

Active in the nationalist movement during the 1930s, Ne Win joined the Allied forces in the war against Japan in 1945 and held senior military posts

before becoming prime minister in 1958. After leading a coup in 1962, he ruled the country as chair of the revolutionary council until 1974, when he became state president. Although he stepped down as president 1981, he continued to dominate political affairs as chair of the ruling Burma Socialist Programme Party (BSPP). His domestic 'Burmese Way to Socialism' policy programme brought the economy into serious decline, and Ne Win was forced to step down as BSPP leader 1988 after riots in Rangoon (now Yangon).

Newman John Henry 1801–1890. English Roman Catholic theologian. While still an Anglican, he wrote a series of *Tracts for the Times*, which gave their name to the Tractarian Movement (subsequently called the Oxford Movement) for the revival of Catholicism. He became a Catholic 1845 and was made a cardinal 1879. In 1864 his autobiography, *Apologia pro vita sua*, was published.

Newman, born in London, was ordained in the Church of England 1824, and in 1827 became vicar of St Mary's, Oxford. There he was influenced by the historian R H Froude and the Anglican priest Keble, and in 1833 published the first of the *Tracts for the Times*. They culminated in *Tract 90* 1841 which found the Thirty-Nine Articles of the Anglican church compatible with Roman Catholicism, and Newman was received into the Roman Catholic Church 1845. He was rector of Dublin University 1854–58 and published his lectures on education as *The Idea of a University* 1873. His poem *The Dream of Gerontius* appeared 1866, and *The Grammar of Assent*, an analysis of the nature of belief, 1870. He wrote the hymn 'Lead, kindly light' 1833.

Newman Paul 1925– . US actor and director, Hollywood's leading male star of the 1960s and 1970s. His films include *The Hustler* 1962, *Butch Cassidy and the Sundance Kid* 1969, *The Sting* 1973, and *The Color of Money* 1986 (for which he won an Academy Award).

Newton Isaac 1642–1727. English physicist and mathematician, who discovered the law of gravity, created calculus, discovered that white light is composed of many colours, and developed the three standard laws of motion still in use today. During 1665–66, he discovered the binomial theorem, differential and integral calculus, and also began to investigate the phenomenon of gravitation. In 1685, he expounded his universal law of gravitation. His greatest work, *Philosophiae Naturalis Principia Mathematica*, was published in three volumes 1686–87, with the aid of Edmund ◊Halley. Newton laid the foundation of physics as a modern discipline.

Newton's universal law of gravitation was 'Every particle of matter in the universe attracts every other particle with a force whose direction is that of the line joining the two, and whose magnitude

Newton *Portrait of Isaac Newton by Godfrey Kneller (1702) National Portrait Gallery, London.*

is directly as (proportional to) the product of the masses, and inversely as (proportional to) the square of their distance from each other'. His *Opticks* 1704 proved that white light could be separated by refraction, into various colours.

Born at Woolsthorpe, Lincolnshire, he was educated at Grantham grammar school and Trinity College, Cambridge, of which he became a Fellow in 1667. He was elected Fellow of the Royal Society in 1672, and soon afterwards published his *New Theory about Light and Colours. De Motu corporum in gyrum/On the motion of bodies in orbit* was written in 1684. Newton resisted James II's attacks on the liberties of the universities, and sat in the parliaments of 1689 and 1701/1702 as a Whig. Appointed Warden of the Royal Mint in 1695, and Master in 1699, he carried through a reform of the coinage. He was elected president of the Royal Society in 1703, and was knighted in 1705. Most of the last 30 years of his life were taken up by studies and experiments in alchemy. He was buried in Westminster Abbey.

Ney Michael, Duke of Elchingen, Prince of Ney 1769–1815. Marshal of France under ◊Napoleon I, who commanded the rearguard of the French army during the retreat from Moscow, and for his personal courage was called 'the bravest of the brave'. When Napoleon returned from Elba, Ney was sent to arrest him, but instead deserted to him and fought at Waterloo. He was subsequently shot for treason.

The son of a cooper, he joined the army in 1788, and rose from the ranks. He served throughout the Revolutionary and Napoleonic Wars.

Ngugi wa Thiong'o 1938– . Kenyan writer of essays, plays, short stories, and novels. He was imprisoned after the performance of the play *Ngaahika Ndeenda/I Will Marry When I Want* 1977, and lived in exile from 1982. His novels, written in English and Gikuyu, include *The River Between, Petals of Blood,* and *Caitaani*

Mutharaba-ini/Devil on the Cross, and deal with colonial and post-independence oppression.

Nguyen Van Linh 1914– . Vietnamese communist politician, member of the Politburo 1976–81 and from 1985; party leader from 1986. He began economic liberalization and troop withdrawal from Kampuchea and Laos.

Nguyen, born in North Vietnam, joined the anti-colonial Thanh Nien, a forerunner of the current Communist Party of Vietnam (CPV), in Haiphong 1929. He spent much of his subsequent party career in the South as a pragmatic reformer. He was a member of CPV's Politburo and secretariat 1976–81, suffered a temporary setback when party conservatives gained the ascendancy, and re-entered the Politburo 1985, becoming CPV leader Dec 1986.

Nichiren 1222–1282. Japanese Buddhist monk, founder of the sect that bears his name. It bases its beliefs on the *Lotus Sūtra,* which Nichiren held to be the only true revelation of the teachings of Buddha, and stresses the need for personal effort to attain enlightenment.

Nicholas two tsars of Russia:

Nicholas I 1796–1855. Tsar of Russia from 1825. His Balkan ambitions led to war with Turkey 1827–29 and the Crimean War 1853–56.

Nicholas II 1868–1918. Tsar of Russia 1894–1917. He was dominated by his wife, Princess Alix of Hessen, who was under the influence of ◊Rasputin. His mismanagement of the Russo-Japanese War and of internal affairs led to the revolution of 1905, which he suppressed, although he was forced to grant limited constitutional reforms. He took Russia into World War I 1914, was forced to abdicate 1917, and was shot with his family by the Bolsheviks at Ekaterinburg July 1918.

Nicholas of Cusa 1401–1464. German philosopher, important in the transition from scholasticism to the philosophy of modern times. He argued that knowledge is learned ignorance (*docta ignorantia*), since God, the ultimate object of knowledge, is

Nicholas II *Tsar Nicholas II of Russia in his youth.*

above the opposites by which human reason grasps the objects of nature. He also asserted that the universe is boundless, and has no circumference, thus breaking with Middle Ages cosmology.

Nicholas, St also known as *Sarta Claus* 4th century. In the Christian church, patron saint of Russia, children, merchants, and sailors; bishop of Myra (now in Turkey). His legendary gifts of dowries to poor girls led to the custom of giving gifts to children on the eve of his feast day, 6 Dec, still retained in some countries, such as the Netherlands, although elsewhere now transferred to Christmas Day. His emblem is three balls.

Nicholson Ben 1894–1982. English abstract artist. After early experiments influenced by Cubism and de Stijl (see ◊Mondrian), he developed a style of geometrical reliefs, notably a series of white reliefs (from 1933).

Born in Denham, Buckinghamshire, son of William ◊Nicholson, he studied at the Slade art school, as well as in Europe and in California. He was awarded the Order of Merit 1968. He married the sculptor Barbara Hepworth.

Nicholson Jack 1937– . US film actor, who captured in the late 1960s the mood of non-conformist, uncertain young Americans in such films as *Easy Rider* 1969 and *Five Easy Pieces* 1970. He subsequently became a mainstream Hollywood star, appearing in *Chinatown* 1974, *One Flew over the Cuckoo's Nest* 1975, and *Batman* 1989.

Nicholson John 1822–1857. British general and colonial administrator in India, born in Ireland. He was administrative officer at Bannu in the Punjab 1851–56, and was highly regarded for his justness of his rule. Promoted to brigadier general 1857 on the outbreak of the Indian Mutiny, he defeated resistance in the Punjab, but was killed during the storming of Delhi.

Nicholson William 1872–1949. English artist, noted for his development of the art of poster design, produced with his brother-in-law, James Pryde, as 'The Beggarstaff Brothers'. He was the father of Ben ◊Nicholson.

Nicklaus Jack (William) 1940– . US golfer, nicknamed 'the Golden Bear'. He won a record 20 major titles, including 18 professional 'majors' 1962–86.

Born in Columbus, Ohio. He played for the US Ryder Cup team six times 1969–81 and was non-playing captain 1983 and 1987 when the event was played over the course he designed at Muirfield Village, Ohio. He was voted the 'Golfer of the Century' 1988. His son Jacky, jnr, is also a professional golfer.

Nicolle Charles 1866–1936. French bacteriologist whose discovery in 1909 that typhus is transmitted by the body louse made the armies of World War I introduce delousing as a compulsory part of the military routine.

His original observation was that typhus victims, once admitted to hospitals, did not infect the staff; he speculated that transmission must be via the skin or clothes, which were washed as standard procedure for new admissions. The experimental evidence was provided by infecting a healthy monkey using a louse recently fed on an infected chimpanzee.

Nicolson Harold 1886–1968. British author and diplomat. His works include biographies (*Lord Carnock* 1930, *Curzon: the Last Phase* 1934, and *King George V* 1952) and studies such as *Monarchy* 1962, as well as *Diaries and Letters* 1930–62. He married Victoria ◊Sackville-West in 1913.

Niebuhr Barthold Georg 1776–1831. German historian. He was Prussian ambassador in Rome 1816–23, and professor of Roman history at Bonn until 1831. His three volume *History of Rome* 1811–32 used a critical examination of original sources.

Niebuhr Karsten 1733–1815. Danish map-maker, surveyor, and traveller, sent by the Danish government to explore the Arabian peninsula 1761–67.

Niebuhr Reinhold 1892–1971. US Protestant Christian theologian. His *Moral Man and Immoral Society* 1932 reflected liberalism for biblical theology and attacked depersonalized industrial society.

Nielsen Carl (August) 1865–1931. Danish composer. His works show a progressive tonality, as in his opera *Saul and David* 1902 and six symphonies. He also composed concertos for violin 1911, clarinet 1928, chamber music, piano works, and songs.

Niemeyer Oscar 1907– . Brazilian architect, joint designer of the United Nations headquarters in New York, and of many buildings in Brasília.

Niemöller Martin 1892–1984. German Christian Protestant pastor. He was imprisoned in a concentration camp 1938–45 for campaigning against Nazism in the German church. and was president of the World Council of Churches 1961–68.

Niepce Joseph Nicéphore 1765–1833. French pioneer of photography.

Nietzsche Friedrich Wilhelm 1844–1900. German philosopher who rejected the accepted absolute moral values and the 'slave morality' of Christianity. He argued that 'God is dead' and therefore people were free to create their own values. His ideal was the *Übermensch*, or 'Superman', who would impose his will on the weak and worthless. Nietzsche claimed that knowledge is never objective, but always serves some interest or unconscious purpose.

His insights into the relation between thought and language had an important influence on philosophy. Although claimed as a precursor by Nazism, many of his views are incompatible with totalitarian ideology. He is a profoundly ambivalent thinker whose philosophy can be appropriated for many purposes.

Nightingale A pencil drawing of Florence Nightingale by George Scharf, 1857.

Nietzsche *Friedrich Nietzsche exercised consider-able influence on modern literature, philosophy, and, psychoanalysis, while his Superman has been consid-ered a prototype for Hitler's ideal Aryan.*

Born in Röcken, Saxony, he attended Bonn and Leipzig universities and was professor of Greek at Basel 1869–80. He had abandoned theology for philology, and was influenced by the writings of Schopenhauer and the music of Wagner, of whom he became both friend and advocate. Both these attractions passed, however, and ill-health caused his resignation from the university. He spent his later years in N Italy, in the Engadine, and in S France. He published *Morgenröte* 1880–81, *Die fröhliche Wissenschaft* 1881–82, *Also sprach Zarathustra* 1883–85, *Jenseits von Gut und Böse* 1885–86, *Genealogie der Moral* 1887, and *Ecce Homo* 1888. He suffered a permanent breakdown in 1889 from overwork and loneliness.

Nightingale Florence 1820–1910. English nurse, the founder of nursing as a profession. She took a team of nurses to Scutari (now Üsküdar, Turkey) in 1854 and reduced the Crimean War hospital death rate from 42% to 2%. In 1856 she founded the Nightingale School and Home for Nurses in London.

Born in Florence, Italy, she trained in Germany and France. She was the author of the classic *Notes on Nursing*; she was awarded the Order of Merit 1907.

Nijinsky Vaslav 1890–1950. Russian dancer and choreographer. Noted for his powerful but grace-ful technique, he was a legendary member of

◊Diaghilev's Ballets Russes, for whom he cho-reographed Debussy's *L'Après-midi d'un faune* 1912 and *Jeux* 1913, and Stravinsky's *The Rite of Spring* 1913.

He also took lead roles in ballets such as *Petrushka* 1911. He rejected conventional forms of classical ballet in favour of free expression. His sister was the choreographer **Bronislava Nijinska**.

Nimitz Chester William 1885–1966. US admiral. During World War II, he reconquered the Solo-mon Islands 1942–43, Gilbert Islands 1943, and Marianas and Marshalls 1944, and signed the Japa-nese surrender as the US representative.

Nin Anaïs 1903–1977. US novelist and diarist. Her extensive and impressionistic diaries, published 1966–76, reflect her interest in dreams, which along with psychoanalysis form recurring themes of her gently erotic novels (such as *House of Incest* 1936 and *A Spy in the House of Love* 1954).

Born in Paris, she started out as a model and dancer, but later took up the study of psychoanalysis. She emigrated to the USA in 1940, becoming a prominent member of the Greenwich Village literary society in New York.

Nithsdale William Maxwell, 5th Earl of Nithsdale 1676–1744. English Jacobite leader who was cap-tured at Preston, brought to trial in Westminster Hall, London, and condemned to death on 9 Feb 1716. With his wife's assistance he escaped from the Tower of London in woman's dress, and fled to Rome.

Niven David 1909–1983. British actor, born in Scot-land. His films include the Oscar-winning *Separate Tables* 1958 and *The Guns of Navarone* 1961.

He published two volumes of autobiography, *The Moon's a Balloon* 1972 and *Bring on the Empty Horses* 1975.

Nixon Richard (Milhous) 1913– . 37th president of the USA 1969–74, a Republican. He attracted attention as a member of the Un-American Activities Committee 1948, and was vice president to Eisenhower 1953–61. As president he was responsible for US withdrawal from Vietnam, and forged new links with China, but at home his culpability in the cover-up of the Watergate scandal and the existence of a 'slush fund' for political machinations during his re-election campaign 1972 led to his resignation 1974 after being threatened with impeachment.

Of Quaker family, Nixon grew up in Whittier, California; he became a lawyer, entered Congress 1947, and in 1948, as a member of the Un-American Activities Committee, pressed for the investigation of Alger ◊Hiss, accused of being a spy. Nixon was senator for California from 1951 until elected vice president. He lost the presidential election 1960 to J F Kennedy, partly because televised electoral debates put him at a disadvantage. He did not seek presidential nomination in 1964, but in a 'law and order' campaign defeated Vice-President Humphrey 1968 in one of the most closely contested elections in US history.

Nixon *Richard Nixon, US president 1968-74. He resigned in mid-term under threat of impeachment, as his involvement in the Watergate scandal was revealed.*

In 1969 he formulated the Nixon Doctrine abandoning close involvement with Asian countries, but escalated the war in Cambodia by massive bombing. Re-elected 1972 in a landslide victory over George McGovern, he resigned 1974, the first US president to do so, under threat of impeachment on three counts: obstruction of the administration of justice in the investigation of Watergate; violation of constitutional rights of citizens, for example attempting to use the Internal Revenue Service, Federal Bureau of Investigation, and Central Intelligence Agency as a weapon against political opponents; and failure to produce 'papers and things' as ordered by the Judiciary Committee. He was granted a pardon 1974 by President Ford.

Nkomo Joshua 1917– . Zimbabwean politician, president of ZAPU (Zimbabwe African People's Union) from 1961, and a leader of the black nationalist movement against the white Rhodesian regime. He was a member of Robert ◊Mugabe's cabinet 1980–82 and from 1987.

After completing his education in South Africa, Joshua Nkomo became a welfare officer on Rhodesian Railways and later organizing secretary of the Rhodesian African Railway Workers' Union. He entered politics 1950 and rose to become president of ZAPU. He was soon arrested, with other black African politicians, and was in detention 1963–74. After his release he joined forces with Robert Mugabe as a joint leader of the Patriotic Front 1976, opposing the white-dominated regime of Ian Smith. Nkomo took part in the Lancaster House

Nijinsky *The great Russian dancer and choreographer Vaslav Nijinsky as 'Le Dieu Bleu' in 1912.*

Conference which led to Rhodesia's independence as the new state of Zimbabwe and became a cabinet minister, and vice president.

Nkrumah Kwame 1909–1972. Ghanaian nationalist politician, prime minister of the Gold Coast (Ghana's former name) 1952–57 and of independent Ghana 1957–60, and Ghana's first president 1960–66. His policy of 'African socialism' led to links with the communist bloc.

Originally a teacher, he studied later in both Britain and the USA, and on returning to Africa formed the Convention People's Party (CPP) 1949 with the aim of immediate self-government. He was imprisoned 1950 for incitement of illegal strikes, but was released the same year. As president he established an authoritarian regime and made Ghana a one-party (CPP) state 1964. He then dropped his stance of nonalignment and drew closer to the USSR and other communist countries. Deposed from the presidency while on a visit to Beijing 1966, he remained in exile in Guinea, where he was made a co-head of state, until his death, but was posthumously 'rehabilitated' 1973.

Nobel Alfred Bernhard 1833–1896. Swedish chemist and engineer. He invented dynamite 1867 and ballistite, a smokeless gunpower, 1889. He amassed a large fortune from the manufacture of explosives and the exploitation of the Baku oilfields in Russia. He left this fortune in trust for the endowment of five *Nobel prizes*, awarded annually since 1901 for outstanding contributions in physics, chemistry, medicine (or physiology), and literature, and in promoting the cause of peace; a sixth prize, for economics, was instituted in 1969.

Noel-Baker Philip John 1889–1982. British Labour politician. He was involved in drafting the charters of both the League of Nations and United Nations. He published *The Arms Race* 1958, and was awarded the Nobel Peace Prize 1959.

***Nkrumah** The first president of Ghana, Kwame Nkrumah.*

Noguchi Hideyo 1876–1928. Japanese bacteriologist, who studied syphilitic diseases, and discovered the parasite of yellow fever, a disease from which he died while working in British W Africa.

Nolan Sidney 1917– . Australian artist, who created atmospheric paintings of the outback, exploring themes from Australian history such as the life of the outlaw Ned Kelly and the folk heroine Mrs Fraser.

Nolde Emil. Adopted name of Emil Hansen 1867–1956. German Expressionist painter. He studied in Paris and Dachau, joined the group of artists known as *die Brücke* 1906–07, and visited Polynesia 1913; he then became almost a recluse in NE Germany. Many of his themes were religious.

Nollekens Joseph 1737–1823. English sculptor, specializing in portrait busts and memorials.

Nono Luigi 1924–90. Italian composer. His early vocal compositions have something of the spatial character of ◊Gabrieli, for example *Il Canto Sospeso* 1955–56. After the opera *Intolleranza* 1960 his style became increasingly expressionistic. His music is frequently polemical in subject matter, and a number of works incorporate tape recorded elements.

Nordenskjöld Nils Adolf Erik 1832–1901. Swedish explorer. He made voyages to the Arctic with the geologist Torell and in 1878–79 discovered the Northeast Passage. He published the results of his voyages in a series of books, including *Voyage of the Vega round Asia and Europe* 1881.

Norfolk Miles Fitzalan-Howard, 17th Duke of Norfolk 1915– . Earl marshal of England, and premier duke and earl; seated at Arundel Castle, Sussex. As earl marshal, he is responsible for the organization of ceremonial on major state occasions.

Noriega Manuel Antonio Morena 1940– . Panamanian soldier and politician, effective ruler of Panama from 1982 until arrested by the USA 1989 and detained for trial on drugs-trafficking charges.

Born in Panama City, he was commissioned in the National Guard 1962. He became intelligence chief 1970, and chief of staff 1982. He wielded considerable political power behind the scenes, which led to his enlistment by the CIA until charges of drugs trafficking discredited him. Relations with the USA deteriorated and in Dec 1989 President Bush ordered an invasion of Panama by 24,000 US troops that eventually resulted in Noriega's arrest and detention, pending trial, in the USA.

Norman Greg 1955– . Australian golfer, nickname 'the Great White Shark'. After many wins in his home country, he enjoyed success on the European PGA Tour before joining the US Tour. He has won the world match-play title three times.

Norman Jessye 1945– . US soprano, born in Augusta, Georgia. She made her operatic debut at the Deutsche Oper, Berlin, 1969. She is noted for her interpretation of *Lieder*, as well as operatic roles, and for her powerful voice.

Norman Montagu, 1st Baron Norman 1871–1950. British banker. Governor of the Bank of England 1920–44, he handled German reparations (financial compensation exacted by the Allies) after World War I, and, by his advocacy of a return to the gold standard in 1925 and other policies, was held by many to have contributed to the economic depression of the 1930s.

Norris Frank 1870–1902. US novelist. An influential Naturalist writer, he wrote *McTeague* 1899, about a brutish San Francisco dentist and the love of gold. He completed only two parts of his projected trilogy, the *Epic of Wheat*: *The Octopus* 1901, dealing with the struggles between wheat farmers, and *The Pit* 1903, describing the gamble of the Chicago wheat exchange.

North Frederick, 8th Lord North 1732–1792. British Tory politician. He entered Parliament in 1754, became chancellor of the Exchequer in 1767, and was prime minister in a government of Tories and 'king's friends' from 1770. His hard line against the American colonies was supported by George III, but in 1782 he was forced to resign by the failure of his policy. In 1783 he returned to office in a coalition with ◊Fox, and after its defeat retired from politics.

North Oliver 1943– . US Marine lieutenant-colonel. In 1981 he was inducted into the National Security Council (NSC), where he supervised the mining of Nicaraguan harbours 1983, an air-force bombing raid on Libya 1986, and an arms-for-hostages deal with Iran 1985 which, when uncovered in 1986 (Irangate), forced his dismissal and conviction on charges of obstructing Congress, mutilating government documents, and taking an illegal gratuity; he was fined $150,000.

He was born into a San Antonio, Texas, military family, and was a graduate of the US Naval College, Annapolis. He led a counter-insurgency Marine platoon in the Vietnam War 1968–69, winning a Silver Star and Purple Heart before returning home wounded. After working as a Marine instructor, as well as participating in a number of overseas secret missions, he became the NSC deputy director for political military affairs.

North Thomas 1535–1601. English translator, whose version of ◊Plutarch's *Lives* 1579 was the source for Shakespeare's Roman plays.

Northcliffe Alfred Charles William Harmsworth, 1st Viscount Northcliffe 1865–1922. British newspaper proprietor, born in Dublin. Founding the *Daily Mail* 1896, he revolutionized popular journalism, and with the *Daily Mirror* 1903 originated the picture paper. In 1908 he also obtained control of *The Times*.

Northrop John 1891–1987. US chemist. In the 1930s he crystallized a number of enzymes, including pepsin and trypsin, showing conclusively that they were proteins. He shared the 1946 Nobel Prize for Chemistry with Wendell ◊Stanley and James ◊Sumner.

Northumberland John Dudley, Duke of Northumberland *c.* 1502–1553. English politician, son of the privy councillor Edmund Dudley (beheaded 1510), raised to a dukedom in 1551, and chief minister until Edward VI's death 1553. He tried to place his daughter-in-law Lady Jane ◊Grey on the throne, and was executed on Mary's accession.

Norton Caroline 1808–1877. British writer, granddaughter of R B ◊Sheridan. Her works include *Undying One* 1830 and *Voice from the Factories* 1836, attacking child labour.

In 1836 her husband falsely accused Lord Melbourne of seducing her, obtained custody of their children, and tried to obtain the profits from her books. Public reaction to this prompted changes in the law of infant custody and married women's property rights.

Norwich 1st Viscount Norwich. Title of (Alfred) Duff ◊Cooper.

Nostradamus Latinized name of Michel de Nôtredame 1503–1566. French physician and astrologer who was consulted by Catherine de' Medici and was physician to Charles IX. His book of prophesies in rhyme, *Centuries* 1555, has had a number of interpretations.

Nott John 1932– . British Conservative politician, minister for defence 1981–83 during the Falkland Islands conflict with Argentina.

Novak (Marilyn Pauline) Kim 1933– . US film actress who starred in the mid-1950s and early 1960s in such films as *Pal Joey* 1957, *Vertigo* 1958, *Kiss Me Stupid* 1964, and *The Legend of Lyla Clare* 1968.

Novalis Pen name of Freiherr von Hardenburg 1772–1801. Pioneer German Romantic poet, who wrote *Hymnen an die Nacht/Hymns to the Night* 1800, prompted by the death of his fiancée Sophie von Kühn. He left two unfinished romances, *Die Lehrlinge zu Sais/The Novices of Sais* and *Heinrich von Ofterdingen*.

Novello Ivor. Adopted name of Ivor Novello Davies. 1893–1951. Welsh composer and actor-manager. He wrote popular songs, such as 'Keep the Home Fires Burning', in World War I, and musicals in which he often appeared as the romantic lead, including *Glamorous Night* 1925, *The Dancing Years* 1939, and *Gay's the Word* 1951.

Noverre Jean-Georges 1727–1810. French choreographer, writer, and ballet reformer. He promoted *ballet d'action* (with a plot) and simple, free movement, and is often considered the creator of modern Classical ballet. *Les Petits Riens* 1778 was one of his works.

Noyes Alfred 1880–1958. English poet, who wrote poems about the sea and the anthology favourites 'The Highwayman', 'Barrel Organ', and 'Go down to Kew in lilac-time...'.

Nu U (Thakin) 1907– . Burmese politician, prime minister for most of the period from 1948 to the military coup of 1962. Exiled abroad from 1966, U Nu returned to the country 1980 and, in 1988, helped found the National League for Democracy opposition movement.

Formerly a teacher, U Nu joined the Dobhama Asiayone (Our Burma) nationalist organization during the 1930s and was imprisoned by the British authorities at the start of World War II. He was released 1942, following Japan's invasion of Burma, and appointed foreign minister in a puppet government. In 1945 he fought with the British against the Japanese and on independence became Burma's first prime minister. Except for short breaks during 1956–57 and 1958–60, he remained in this post until Gen ◊Ne Win overthrew the parliamentary regime in 1962.

Nuffield William Richard Morris, Viscount Nuffield 1877–1963. English manufacturer and philanthropist. Starting with a small cycle-repairing business, in 1910 he designed a car that could be produced cheaply, and built up Morris Motors Ltd at Cowley, Oxford.

He endowed Nuffield College, Oxford, 1937 and the Nuffield Foundation 1943.

Nujoma Sam 1929– . Namibian left-wing politician, founder and leader of SWAPO (the South West African Peple's Organization) from 1959. He was exiled in 1960 and controlled guerrillas from Angolan bases until the first free elections were held 1989, making Nujoma president designate.

Nunn Trevor 1940– . British stage director, linked with the Royal Shakespeare Company from 1968. He received a Tony award (with John Caird) for his production of *Nicholas Nickleby* 1982 and for *Les Miserables* 1987.

Nureyev Rudolf 1938– . Soviet dancer and choreographer. A soloist with the Kirov Ballet, He defected to the West 1961, where he was mainly associated with the Royal Ballet, and was Margot ◊Fonteyn's principal partner.

Nyerere Julius (Kambarage) 1922– . Tanzanian socialist politician, president 1964–85. Originally a teacher, he devoted himself from 1954 to the formation of the Tanganyika African National Union and subsequent campaigning for independence. He became chief minister 1960, was prime minister

Nyerere *Tanzanian politician and premier Dr Julius Nyerere, in London, 1960.*

of Tanganyika 1961–62, president of the newly formed Tanganyika Republic 1962–64, first president of Tanzania 1964–85, and head of the Organization of African Unity 1984.

Nyers Rezso 1923– . Hungarian socialist leader. As secretary of the ruling Hungarian Socialist Worker's Party's (HSWP) central committee 1962–74 and a member of its politburo 1966–74, he was the architect of Hungary's liberalizing economic reforms in 1968.

Born in Budapest, he worked as a printer and in 1940 joined the Hungarian Social Democratic Party, which, in 1948 was forcibly merged with the communists. He was removed from his HSWP posts in 1974 and his career remained at a standstill until 1988, when, with a new reform initiative under way, he was brought back into the politburo. He became head of the newly formed Hungarian Socialist Party 1989.

Nykvist Sven 1922– . Swedish director of photography, associated with the film director Ingmar Bergman. He worked frequently in the USA from the mid-1970s onwards. His films include *The Virgin Spring* 1960 (for Bergman), *Pretty Baby* 1978 (for Louis Malle), and *Fanny and Alexander* 1982 (for Bergman).

Oakley Annie (Phoebe Annie Oakley Mozee) 1860–1926. US sharpshooter, member of Buffalo Bill's Wild West Show (see William ◊Cody).

Oastler Richard 1789–1861. English social reformer. He opposed child labour and the Poor Law 1834, which restricted relief, and was largely responsible for securing the Factory Act 1833 and the Ten Hours Act 1847. He was born in Leeds, and was known as the 'Factory King'.

Oates Joyce Carol 1938– . US writer. Her novels, often containing surrealism and violence, include *A Garden of Earthly Delights* 1967, *Them* 1969, *Unholy Loves* 1979, and *A Bloodsmoor Romance* 1982.

Oates Laurence Edward Grace 1880–1912. British Antarctic explorer, who accompanied Robert Falcon ◊Scott on his second expedition to the South Pole. On the return journey, suffering from frostbite, he went out alone into the blizzard to die rather than delay the others.

Oates Titus 1649–1705. British conspirator. A priest, he entered the Jesuit colleges at Valladolid, Spain, and St Omer, France, as a spy in 1677–78, and on his return to England announced he had discovered a 'Popish Plot' to murder Charles II and re-establish Catholicism. Although this story was almost entirely false, many innocent Roman Catholics were executed during 1678–80 on Oates's evidence. In 1685 he was flogged, pilloried, and imprisoned for perjury. He was pardoned and granted a pension after the revolution of 1688.

Oberon Merle. Stage name of Estelle Merle O'Brien Thompson 1911–1979. Tasmanian-born British actress who starred in several Alexander Korda films, including *The Scarlet Pimpernel* 1935, and was briefly married to him. She played Cathy to Laurence Olivier's Heathcliff in *Wuthering Heights* 1939, and after 1940 worked successfully in the USA.

Obote (Apollo) Milton 1924– . Ugandan politician who led the independence movement from 1961. He became prime minister 1962 and was president 1966–71 and 1980–85, being overthrown by first Idi ◊Amin and then Brigadier Tito Okello.

Obraztsov Sergei 1901– . Russian puppeteer, head of the Moscow-based State Central Puppet Theatre, the world's largest puppet theatre (with a staff of 300). The repertoire was built up from 1923.

O'Brien Angela Maxine ('Margaret') 1937– . US child actress, a star of the 1940s. She received a special Academy Award in 1944, but her career, including leading parts in *Lost Angel* 1943, *Meet Me in St Louis* 1944, and *The Secret Garden* 1949, did not survive into adolescence.

O'Brien Willis H 1886–1962. US film animator and special effects creator, responsible for one of the cinema's most memorable monsters, *King Kong* 1933.

O'Casey Sean. Adopted name of John Casey 1884–1964. Irish dramatist. His early plays are tragicomedies, blending realism with symbolism and poetic with vernacular speech: *The Shadow of a Gunman* 1922, *Juno and the Paycock* 1925, and *The Plough and the Stars* 1926. Later plays include *Red Roses for Me* 1946 and *The Drums of Father Ned* 1960.
He also wrote the antiwar drama *The Silver Tassie* 1929, *The Star Turns Red* 1940, *Oak Leaves and Lavender* 1947, and a six-volume autobiography.

Occam or *Ockham*, William of *c.* 1300–1349. English philosopher, who revived the fundamentals of nominalism. He was born in Ockham, Surrey, and as a Franciscan monk defended the doctrine of evangelical poverty against Pope John XXII, becoming known as the Invincible Doctor. He was imprisoned in Avignon, France, on charges of heresy in 1328 but escaped to Munich, Germany, where he died. The principle of reducing assumptions to the absolute minimum is known as *Occam's razor.*

Ochoa Severo 1905– . US biochemist. He discovered an enzyme able to assemble units of the nucleic acid RNA (essential to protein synthesis) in 1955, whilst working at New York University. For this work he shared the 1959 Nobel Prize for Medicine with Arthur ◊Kornberg.

O'Connell Daniel 1775–1847. Irish politician, called 'the Liberator'. In 1823 he founded the Catholic Association to press Roman Catholic claims. Although ineligible as a Roman Catholic to take his seat, he was elected MP for County Clare 1828, and so forced the government to grant Catholic emancipation. In Parliament he cooperated with the Whigs in the hope of obtaining concessions until 1841, when he launched his campaign for repeal of the union.

His reserved and vacillating leadership and conservative outlook on social questions alienated his most active supporters, who broke away and formed the nationalist Young Ireland movement.

O'Connor Feargus 1794–1855. Irish parliamentary follower of Daniel ◊O'Connell. He sat in parliament 1832–35, and as editor of the *Northern Star* became an influential figure of the radical working-class Chartist movement.

O'Connor Flannery 1925–1964. US novelist and story writer. Her works have a great sense of evil and sin, and often explore the religious sensibility of the Deep South. Her short stories include *A Good Man Is Hard to Find* 1955 and *Everything That Rises Must Converge* 1965.

Her novels are *Wise Blood* 1952 and *The Violent Bear It Away* 1960. She exemplifies the postwar revival of the Gothic novel in southern US fiction.

Odets Clifford 1906–1963. US playwright, associated with the Group Theatre, whose plays include *Waiting for Lefty* 1935, *Awake and Sing* 1935, *Golden Boy* 1937, and *The Country Girl* 1950.

Odoacer 433–493. King of Italy from 476, when he deposed Romulus Augustulus, the last Roman emperor. He was a leader of the barbarian mercenaries employed by Rome. He was overthrown and killed by Theodoric the Great, king of the Ostrogoths.

Odoyevsky Vladimir 1804–1869. Russian writer who wrote works in many different genres, including tales of the supernatural, science fiction, satires, children's stories, and music criticism.

Oersted Hans Christian 1777–1851. Danish physicist who founded the science of electromagnetism. In 1820 he discovered the magnetic field associated with an electric current.

Offa died 796. King of Mercia, England, from 757. He conquered Essex, Kent, Sussex, and Surrey, defeated the Welsh and the West Saxons, and established Mercian supremacy over all England south of the Humber.

Offenbach Jacques 1819–1880. French composer. He wrote light opera, initially for presentation at the Bouffes Parisiens. Among his works are *Orphée aux enfers/Orpheus in the Underworld* 1858, *La Belle Hélène* 1864, and *Les Contes d'Hoffmann/The Tales of Hoffmann* 1881.

O'Flaherty Liam 1897–1984. Irish author whose novels of Fenian activities in county Mayo include *The Neighbour's Wife* 1923, *The Informer* 1925, and *Land* 1946.

Ogden C(harles) K(ay) 1889–1957. English writer and scholar. With I A ◊Richards he developed the simplified form of English known as Basic English, built on a vocabulary of just 850 words. Together they wrote *Foundations of Aesthetics* 1921 and *The Meaning of Meaning* 1923.

Ogdon John 1937–1989. English pianist, renowned for his interpretation of Chopin, Liszt, and Busoni. In 1962 he shared the Tchaikovsky award with Vladimir Ashkenazy in Moscow.

Oglethorpe James Edward 1696–1785. English soldier. He joined the Guards, and in 1732 obtained a charter for the colony of Georgia, intended as a refuge for debtors and for European Protestants.

O'Higgins Bernardo 1778–1842. Chilean revolutionary, known as 'the Liberator of Chile'. He was a leader of the struggle for independence from Spanish rule 1810–17 and head of the first permanent national government 1817–23.

Ohm Georg Simon 1787–1854. German physicist who studied electricity and discovered *Ohm's law*: that the electric current flowing in a conductor is proportional to the potential difference (voltage) across it. The SI unit of electrical resistance, the *ohm*, is named after him.

Oistrakh David Fyodorovich 1908–1974. Soviet violinist, celebrated for performances of both standard and contemporary Russian repertoire. Shostakovich wrote both his violin concertos for him.

O'Keeffe Georgia 1887–1986. US painter, based mainly in New York and New Mexico, known for her large, semi-abstract studies of flowers and skulls.

Her mature style stressed contours and subtle tonal transitions, and in paintings such as *Black Iris* 1926 (Metropolitan Museum of Art, New York) the subject is transformed into a powerful and erotic abstract image. In 1946 she settled in New Mexico, where the desert landscape inspired many of her paintings.

Okeghem Johannes (Jean d') *c.*1420–1497. Flemish composer of church music, including masses and motets. He was court composer to Charles VII, Louis XI, and Charles VIII of France.

Okubo Toshimichi 1831–1878. Japanese samurai leader whose opposition to the Tokugawa shogunate made him a leader in the Meiji restoration (see ◊Mutsuhito) 1866–68.

Okuma Shigenobu 1838–1922. Japanese politician and prime minister. He helped to found the Jiyuto (Liberal Party) 1881, and became prime minister briefly 1898 and again 1914, when he presided over Japanese pressure for territorial concessions in China, before retiring 1916.

Holding a series of ministerial appointments after the Meiji restoration 1868, Okuma specialized in fiscal and constitutional reform.

Olaf five kings of Norway, including:

Olaf I Tryggvesson 969–1000. King of Norway from his election 995. He began the conversion of Norway to Christianity, and was killed in a sea battle against the Danes and Swedes.

Olaf II Haraldsson, St 995–1030. King of Norway from 1015. He offended his subjects by his centralizing policy and zeal for Christianity, and was killed in battle by Norwegian rebel chiefs backed by ◊Canute of Denmark. He was declared the patron saint of Norway 1164.

Olaf V 1903– . King of Norway from 1957, when he succeeded his father Haakon VII.

Olazabal Jose Maria 1966– . Spanish golfer, one of the leading players on the European circuit. After a distinguished amateur career he turned professional 1986. He was a member of the European Ryder Cup teams in 1987 and 1989.

Olbers Heinrich 1758–1840. German doctor and astronomer. He discovered two of the first asteroids to be found, Pallas in 1802 and Vesta in 1807, as well as a number of comets, together with a new method of calculating cometary orbits. He was the first to ask the question now known as *Olber's paradox*: If the Universe is infinite, with an infinite number of shining stars, why is the night sky dark?

Olbrich Joseph Maria 1867–1908. Viennese architect who worked under Otto ◊Wagner and was opposed to the over-ornamentation of Art Nouveau. His major buildings, however, remain Art Nouveau in spirit: the Vienna Sezession 1897–98, the Hochzeitsturm 1907, and the Tietz department store in Düsseldorf, Germany.

Oldenbarnvelt Johan van 1547–1619. Dutch politician, a leading figure in the Netherlands' struggle for independence from Spain, who helped William I negotiate the Union of Utrecht 1579.

As leader of the Republican party he opposed the war policy of stadholder (magistrate) Maurice of Orange and negotiated a 12-year truce with Spain in 1609. His support of the Remonstrants (Arminians) in the religious strife against Maurice and the Gomarists (Cavinists) effected his downfall and he was arrested and executed.

Oldenburg Claes 1929– . US pop artist, known for *soft sculptures*, gigantic replicas of everyday objects and foods, made of stuffed canvas or vinyl.

Oldenburg Henry 1615–1677. German official who founded and edited the first-ever scientific periodical, *Philosophical Transactions*, and, through his extensive correspondence, acted as a clearing house for the science of the day. He was born in Bremen and first came to London in 1652, working as a Bremen agent and then a tutor. In 1663, he was appointed to the new post of Secretary to the Royal Society, a position he held until his death.

Oldfield Bruce 1950– . English fashion designer, who set up his own business 1975. His evening wear has been worn by the British royal family and other personalities.

Old Pretender nickname of ◊James Edward Stuart, the son of James II of England.

Olga, St died 969. The wife of Igor, the Scandinavian prince of Kiev. Her baptism around 955 was an important step in the Christianization of Russia.

Oliphant Margaret 1828–1897. Scottish writer, author of over 100 novels, biographies, and numerous articles and essays. Her major work is the series *The Chronicles of Carlingford* 1863–66, including *The Perpetual Curate* and *Hester*.

Olivares Count-Duke of (born Gaspar de Guzmán) 1587–1645. Spanish prime minister 1621–43. He overstretched Spain in foreign affairs, and unsuccessfully attempted domestic reform. He committed Spain to recapturing the Netherlands and to involvement in the Thirty Years' War 1618–48, and his efforts to centralize power led to revolts in Catalonia and Portugal, which brought about his downfall.

Oliver Isaac *c.*1556–1617. British painter of miniatures, originally a Huguenot refugee, who studied under Nicholas ◊Hilliard. He became a court artist in the reign of James I. Famous sitters include the poet John Donne.

Olivier Laurence (Kerr), Baron Olivier 1907–1989. English actor and director. For many years associated with the Old Vic theatre, he was director of the National Theatre company 1962–73. His stage roles include Henry V, Hamlet, Richard III, and Archie Rice in Osborne's *The Entertainer*. His acting and direction of filmed versions of Shakespeare's plays received critical acclaim, for example *Henry V* 1944 and *Hamlet* 1948.

Other films in which he appeared are *Wuthering Heights* 1939, *Rebecca* 1940, *Sleuth* 1972, *Marathon Man* 1976, and *The Boys from Brazil* 1978. The Olivier Theatre (part of the National Theatre on the South Bank, London) is named after him.

Olson Charles 1910–1970. US poet, noted for his theories of 'composition by field' and his association with the Black Mountain school of poets. His chief works were his *Maximus* poems 1953–75, a striking attempt to extend the American epic poem beyond Pound's *Cantos* or W C Williams's *Paterson*.

Omar 581–644. Adviser of the prophet Muhammad. In 634 he succeeded Abu Bakr as caliph (civic and religious leader of Islam), and conquered Syria, Palestine, Egypt, and Persia. He was assassinated by a slave. The Mosque of Omar in Jerusalem is attributed to him.

Omar Khayyam *c.*1050–1123. Persian astronomer and poet. Born in Nishapur, he founded a school of astronomical research and assisted in reforming the calendar. The result of his observations was the *Jalāli* era, begun 1079. In the West, Omar Khayyam is chiefly known as a poet through ◊Fitzgerald's version of the *The Rubaiyat of Omar Khayyam* 1859.

Omayyad dynasty Arabian dynasty of the Islamic empire who reigned as caliphs 661–750. They were overthrown by Abbasids, but a member of the family escaped to Spain and in 756 assumed the title of emir of Córdoba. His dynasty, which took the title of caliph 929, ruled in Córdoba until the early 11th century.

Onassis Aristotle (Socrates) 1906–1975. Turkish-born Greek shipowner. During the 1950s he was one of the first shipbuilders to build supertankers. In 1968 he married Jacqueline Kennedy, widow of US president John F Kennedy.

O'Neill Eugene (Gladstone) 1888–1953. US playwright, often regarded as the leading US dramatist between World Wars I and II. His plays include *Anna Christie* 1922, *Desire under the Elms* 1924, *The Iceman Cometh* 1946, and the posthumously produced autobiographical drama *Long Day's Journey into Night* 1956 (written 1940). Nobel prize 1936.

O'Neill was born in New York. He had varied experience as gold prospector, sailor, and actor. Other plays include *Beyond the Horizon* 1920, *The Great God Brown* 1925, *Strange Interlude* 1928 (which lasts five hours), *Mourning Becomes Electra* 1931 (a trilogy on the theme of Orestes from Greek mythology) and *A Moon for the Misbegotten* 1947 (written 1943).

O'Neill Terence, Baron O'Neill of the Maine 1914–90. Northern Irish Unionist politician. In the Ulster government he was minister of finance 1956–63, prime minister 1963–69. He resigned when opposed by his party on measures to extend rights to Roman Catholics, including a universal franchise.

Onnes Kamerlingh 1853–1926. Dutch physicist, who worked mainly in the field of low temperature physics, and in 1911 discovered the phenomenon of superconductivity (enhanced electrical conductivity at very low temperatures), for which he was awarded the 1913 Nobel Prize for Physics.

Onsager Lars 1903–1976. Norwegian-born US physical chemist. For his work on the application of the laws of thermodynamics to systems not in equilibrium, he received the 1968 Nobel Prize for Chemistry.

Oort Jan Hendrik 1900– . Dutch astronomer. In 1927, he calculated the mass and size of the Galaxy, and the Sun's distance from its centre, from the observed movements of stars around the Galaxy's centre. In 1950 Oort proposed that comets exist in a vast swarm, now called the *Oort Cloud*, at the edge of the Solar System.

Ophuls Max adopted name of Max Oppenheimer 1902–1957. German film director. He moved to cinema from the theatre, and his work used intricate camera movements. He worked in Europe and the USA, attracting much critical praise for films such as *Letter from an Unknown Woman* 1948 and *Lola Montes* 1955.

Opie John 1761–1807. British artist. Born in St Agnes, Cornwall, he became famous as a portrait painter in London from 1780, later painting historical pictures such as *The Murder of Rizzio*.

Opie Peter Mason 1918–1982 and Iona Margaret Balfour 1923– . Husband-and-wife team of folklorists who specialized in the myths and literature of childhood. Their books include the *Oxford Dictionary of Nursery Rhymes* 1951 and *The Lore and Language of Schoolchildren* 1959. In 1987 their collection of children's books was sold to the Bodleian library, Oxford, for £500,000.

Oppenheimer J(ulius) Robert 1904–1967. US physicist. As director of the Los Alamos Science Laboratory 1943–45, he was in charge of the development of the atomic bomb (the Manhattan Project). He objected to the development of the hydrogen bomb, and was declared a security risk 1953 by the US Atomic Energy Commission (AEG).

Orange, House of the royal family of the Netherlands. The title is derived from the small principality of Orange, in S France, held by the family from the 8th century to 1713. They held considerable possessions in the Netherlands, to which, after 1530, was added the German county of Nassau.

From the time of **William the Silent** (1533–1585) the family dominated Dutch history, bearing the title of stadholder (magistrate) for the greater part of the 17th and 18th centuries. The son of Stadholder William V was made King William I by the Allies 1815.

Orbison Roy 1936–1988. US pop singer and songwriter, noted for his ballad style on songs like 'Only The Lonely' 1960 and 'Running Scared' 1961. His biggest hit was the jaunty 'Oh, Pretty

Oppenheimer US physicist J Robert Oppenheimer, who led the Manhattan Project to design the first atomic bomb, but later opposed work on the hydrogen bomb.

Woman' 1964. The last Orbison album, *Mystery Girl* 1989, was a posthumous success.

Orczy Baroness Emmusca 1865–1947. Hungarian-born English novelist, who wrote the historical adventure *The Scarlet Pimpernel* 1905. The foppish Sir Percy Blakeney, the bold rescuer of victims of the French Revolution, appeared in many sequels.

Orellana Francisco de 1511–1546. Spanish explorer who travelled with Francesco ◊Pizarro from Guayaquil, on the Pacific coast of South America, to Quito in the Andes. He was the first person known to have navigated the full length of the Amazon from the Napo River to the Atlantic Ocean (1541–43).

Orff Carl 1895–1982. German composer, an individual stylist whose work is characterized by sharp dissonances and percussion. Among his compositions are the scenic cantata *Carmina Burana* 1937 and the opera *Antigone* 1949.

Orford, 1st Earl of title of the British politician Robert ◊Walpole.

Organ (Harold) Bryan 1935– . English portraitist, whose subjects have included Harold Macmillan, Michael Tippett, Elton John, and the Prince and Princess of Wales.

Origen *c.*185–*c.*254. Christian theologian, born in Alexandria, who produced a fancifully allegorical interpretation of the Bible. He castrated himself to ensure his celibacy.

Orlando Vittorio Emanuele 1860–1952. Italian politician, prime minister 1917–19. He attended the Paris Peace Conference after World War I, but dissatisfaction with his handling of the Adriatic settlement led to his resignation. He initially supported Mussolini, was in retirement 1925–46, and then he returned to the assembly and then the senate.

Ormandy Eugene 1899–1985. Hungarian-born US conductor. Originally a violin virtuoso, he championed ◊Rachmaninov and ◊Shostakovich and was music director of the Philadelphia Orchestra 1936–80.

Ormonde James Butler, Duke of Ormonde 1610–1688. Irish general. He commanded the Royalist troops in Ireland 1641–50 during the Irish rebellion and the English Civil War, and was lord lieutenant 1644–47, 1661–69, and 1677–84.

Orozco José Clemente 1883–1949. Mexican painter, known for his murals inspired by the Mexican revolution of 1910, such as the series in the Palace of Government, Guadalajara, 1949.

Orpen William Newenham Montague 1878–1931. Irish artist. He studied at Dublin and London, became famous as a portraitist and genre artist, and was elected a member of the Royal Academy in 1919.

Orr Robert 'Bobby' 1948– . Canadian hockey player, who played for the Boston Bruins (1967–76) and the Chicago Blackhawks (1976–79) of the

National Hockey League. He was voted the best defence every year 1967–75, and was Most Valuable Player 1970–72. He was the first defence to score 100 points in a season, and was Leading Scorer 1970 and 1975.

Orsini Felice 1819–1858. Italian political activist, a member of the Carbonari secret revolutionary group, who attempted unsuccessfully to assassinate Napoleon III in Paris Jan 1858. He was subsequently executed, but the Orsini affair awakened Napoleon's interest in Italy and led to a secret alliance with Piedmont at Pilombières 1858, directed against Italy.

Ortega (Saavedra) Daniel 1945– . Nicaraguan socialist politician, head of state from 1981. He was a member of the Sandinista Liberation Front (FSLN) which overthrew the regime of Anastasio Somoza 1979. US-sponsored Contra guerrillas opposed his government from 1982.

A participant in underground activities against the Somoza regime from an early age, Ortega was imprisoned and tortured several times. He became a member of the national directorate of the FSLN and fought in the two-year campaign for the Nicaraguan Revolution. Ortega became a member of the junta of national reconstruction, and its coordinator two years later.

Ortega y Gasset José 1883–1955. Spanish philosopher and critic. He considered communism and fascism the cause of the downfall of western civilization. His *Toward a Philosophy of History* 1941 contains philosophical reflections on the state, and an interpretation of the meaning of human history.

Orton Joe 1933–1967. English dramatist, in whose black comedies surreal and violent action takes place in genteel and unlikely settings. Plays include *Entertaining Mr Sloane* 1964, *Loot* 1966, and *What the Butler Saw* 1968. His diaries deal frankly with his personal life. He was murdered by his lover Kenneth Halliwell.

Orwell George. Pen name of Eric Arthur Blair 1903–1950. English author. His books include the satire *Animal Farm* 1945 which included such sayings as 'All animals are equal, but some are more equal than others', and the prophetic *Nineteen Eighty-Four* 1949, portraying state control of existence carried to the ultimate extent. Other works include *Down and Out in Paris and London* 1933 and *Homage to Catalonia* 1938.

Born in India, he was educated in England, and for five years served in the Burmese police force, an experience reflected in the novel *Burmese Days* 1935. Life as a dishwasher and tramp were related in *Down and Out in Paris and London* and service for the Republican cause in the Spanish Civil War in *Homage to Catalonia*. He also wrote numerous essays.

Osborne Dorothy 1627–1695. English letter-writer. In 1655 she married Sir William Temple (1628–99),

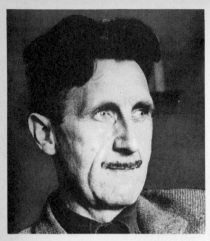

Orwell *English novelist and essayist George Orwell.*

to whom she wrote her letters, written 1652–54, and first published 1888.

Osborne John (James) 1929– . English dramatist. He was one of the first Angry Young Men (anti-establishment writers of the 1950s) of British theatre with his debut play, *Look Back in Anger* 1956. Other plays include *The Entertainer* 1957, *Luther* 1960, and *Watch It Come Down* 1976.

Oscar two kings of Sweden and Norway:

Oscar I 1799–1859. King of Sweden and Norway from 1844, when he succeeded his father, Charles XIV. He established freedom of the press, and supported Denmark against Germany 1848.

Oscar II 1829–1907. King of Sweden and Norway 1872–1905, king of Sweden until 1907. He was the younger son of Oscar I, and succeeded his brother Charles XV. He was an international arbitrator in Samoa, Venezuela, and the Anglo-American dispute. He fought hard to prevent the separation of his two kingdoms but relinquished the throne of Norway to Haakon VII in 1905.

Oshima Nagisa 1932– . Japanese film director, whose violent and sexually explicit *In the Realm of the Senses/Ai No Corrida* 1977 has been one of cinema's most controversial films. His other work includes *Death by Hanging* 1968 and *Merry Christmas Mr Lawrence* 1983, which starred the singer David Bowie.

Osman I or *Othman I* 1259–1326. Turkish ruler from 1299. He began his career in the service of the Seljuk Turks, but in 1299 he set up a kingdom of his own in Bithynia, NW Asia, and assumed the title of sultan. He conquered a great part of Anatolia, so founding a Turkish empire. His successors were known as 'sons of Osman', from which the term *Ottoman Empire* is derived.

Ostade Adriaen van 1610–1685. Dutch painter and engraver, best known for pictures of tavern scenes and village fairs. A native of Haarlem, Ostade may have studied under Frans Hals. His brother, **Isaac van Ostade** (1621–49), excelled in winter landscapes and roadside and farmyard scenes.

Östberg Ragnar 1866–1945. Swedish architect, who designed the City Hall, Stockholm, Sweden (1911–23).

Ostrovsky Alexander Nikolaevich 1823–1886. Russian playwright, founder of the modern Russian theatre. He dealt satirically with the manners of the middle class in numerous plays, for example *A Family Affair* 1850. His fairy-tale play *The Snow Maiden* 1873 inspired the composers Tchaikovsky and Rimsky-Korsakov.

Ostwald Wilhelm 1853–1932. German chemist whose work on catalysts laid the foundations of the petrochemical and other industries. Nobel prize 1909.

Oswald, St *c.*605–642. King of Northumbria from 634, after killing the Welsh king Cadwallon. Oswald had become a Christian convert during exile on the Scottish island of Iona. With the help of St Aidan he furthered the spread of Christianity until he was defeated and killed by King Penda of Mercia. Feast day 9 Aug.

Othman *c.*574–656. Arabian caliph (leader of the Islamic empire) from 644, when he was elected; he was a son-in-law of the prophet Muhammad. Under his rule the Arabs became a naval power and captured Cyprus, but Othman's personal weaknesses led to his assassination. He was responsible for the final editing of the Koran, the sacred book of Islam.

Othman I another name for the Turkish sultan ♦Osman I.

Otho I 1815–1867. King of Greece 1832–62. As the 17-year-old son of King Ludwig I of Bavaria, he was selected by the European powers as the first king of independent Greece. He was overthrown by a popular revolt.

Otis Elisha Graves 1811–1861. US engineer, who developed a lift that incorporated a safety device, making it acceptable for passenger use in the first skyscrapers. The device, invented 1852, consisted of vertical ratchets on the sides of the lift shaft into which spring-loaded catches would engage and 'lock' the lift in position in the event of cable failure.

O'Toole Peter 1932– . British actor who made his name in the title role of *Lawrence of Arabia* 1962, and who then starred in such films as *Beckett* 1964 and *The Lion in Winter* 1968 until the early 1970s. Subsequent appearances were few and poorly received by critics until *The Stuntman* 1978.

Otto Nikolaus August 1832–1891. German engineer, who in 1876 patented an effective internal combustion engine.

Otto four Holy Roman emperors, including:

Otto I 912–973. Holy Roman emperor from 936. He restored the power of the empire, asserted his authority over the pope and the nobles, ended the Magyar menace by his victory at the Lechfeld 955, and refounded the East Mark, or Austria, as a barrier against them.

Otto IV *c.*1182–1218. Holy Roman emperor, elected 1198. He engaged in controversy with Pope Innocent III, and was defeated by the Pope's ally, Philip of France, at Bouvines 1214.

Otway Thomas 1652–1685. English dramatist. His plays include the tragedies *Alcibiades* 1675, *Don Carlos* 1676, *The Orphan* 1680, and *Venice Preserv'd* 1682.

Oughtred William 1575–1660. English mathematician. He is credited as the inventor of the slide rule 1622. His major work *Clavis mathematicae/The Key to Mathematics* 1631 was a survey of the entire body of mathematical knowledge of his day. It introduced the '×' symbol for multiplication, as well as the abbreviations sin for sine and cos for cosine.

Ouida pen name of Marie Louise de la Ramée 1839–1908. British romantic novelist whose novels included *Under Two Flags* 1867 and *Moths* 1880.

Ousmane Sembene 1923– . Senegalese writer and film director. His novels, written in French, include *Le Docker Noir* 1956, about his experiences as a union leader in Marseille, *Les bouts de bois/God's Bits of Wood* 1960, *Le Mandat/The Money Order*, and *Xala*, the last two of which he made into films.

Ouspensky Peter 1878–1947. Russian mystic. Originally a scientist, he became a disciple of ◊Gurdjieff and expanded his ideas in terms of other dimensions of space and time, for example in *Tertium Organum* 1912.

Outram James 1803–1863. British general, born in Derbyshire. He entered the Indian Army in 1819, served in the Afghan and Sikh wars, and commanded in the Persian campaign of 1857. On the outbreak of the Indian Mutiny he cooperated with Gen Henry Havelock (1795–1857) to raise the siege of Lucknow, and held the city until relieved by Sir Colin Campbell (later Baron ◊Clyde).

Ovid Full name Publius Ovidius Naso 43–17 BC. Roman poet. His poetry deals mainly with the themes of love (*Amores*, *Ars amatoria*), mythology (*Metamorphoses*), and exile (*Tristia*).

Born at Sulmo, Ovid studied rhetoric in Rome in preparation for a legal career, but soon turned to literature. In 8 BC he was banished by Augustus to Tomi, on the Black Sea, where he died. This punishment, supposedly for his immoral *Ars amatoria*, was probably because of some connection with Julia, the profligate daughter of Augustus.

Owen David 1938– . British politician, originally a doctor. He entered Parliament 1966, and was Labour foreign secretary 1977–79. In 1981 he was one of the founders of the Social Democratic Party (SDP), and in 1983 became its leader. Opposed to the decision of the majority of the party to merge with the Liberals 1987, Owen stood down, but emerged 1988 as leader of a rump SDP (disbanded by majority vote 1990).

Owen Richard 1804–1892. British anatomist and palaeontologist. He attacked the theory of natural selection and in 1860 published an anonymous and damaging review of Charles ◊Darwin's work. He was Director of the Natural History Museum, London, 1856–1883 and was responsible for the first public exhibition of dinosaurs.

Owen Robert 1771–1858. British socialist, born in Wales. In 1800 he became manager of a mill at New Lanark, Scotland, where by improving working and housing conditions and providing schools he created a model community. His ideas stimulated the co-operative movement.

From 1817 Owen proposed that 'villages of cooperation', self-supporting communities run on socialist lines, should be founded; these, he believed, would ultimately replace private ownership. His later attempt to run such a community in the USA failed.

Owen Wilfred 1893–1918. English poet. His verse, owing much to the encouragement of Siegfried ◊Sassoon, expresses his hatred of war, for example *Anthem for Doomed Youth*, published 1921.

Owens (James Cleveland) 'Jesse' 1913–1980. US track and field athlete, who excelled in the sprints,

Owen *Socialist reformer Robert Owen.*

hurdles, and the long jump. At the 1936 Olympics he won four gold medals.

The Nazi leader Hitler is said to have stormed out of the stadium at the 1936 Berlin Olympic Games, in disgust at the black man's triumph. Owens held the world long-jump record for 25 years 1935–60. At Ann Arbor, Michigan, on 25 May 1935 he broke six world records in less than an hour.

Oxenstjerna Axel Gustafsson, Count Oxenstjerna 1583–1654. Swedish politician, chancellor from 1612. He pursued Gustavus Adolphus's foreign policy, acted as regent for Queen Christina, and conducted the Thirty Years' War to a successful conclusion.

Ozal Turgut 1927–   . Turkish Islamic right-wing politician, prime minister 1983–89, president from 1989.

Born in Malatya, E central Turkey, and educated in Istanbul, he entered goverment service then worked for the World Bank 1971–79. In 1980 he was deputy to prime minister Bulent Ulusu, under the military regime of Kenan Evren, and, when political pluralism returned in 1983, he founded the Islamic, right-of-centre Motherland Party (ANAP) and led it to victory in the elections of that year. In the 1987 general election he retained his majority and in Nov 1989 replaced Evren as Turkey's first civilian president for 30 years.

Ozu Yasujiro 1903–1963. Japanese film director, who became known in the West only in his last years. *Tokyo Monogatari/Tokyo Story* 1953 illustrates his typical low camera angles, and his theme of middle-class family life.

Pabst G(eorg) W(ilhelm) 1885–1967. German film director, whose films include *Die Büchse der Pandora/Pandora's Box*, *Das Tagebuch einer Verlorenen/The Diary of a Lost Girl* both 1929 and starring Louise ◊Brooks, and *Die Dreigroschenoper/The Threepenny Opera* 1931.

Pachomius, St 303 346. Egyptian Christian (Copt), the founder of the first Christian monastery, near Dendera on the river Nile. Originally for Copts, the monastic movement soon spread to include Greeks.

Pacino Al(berto) 1940– . US actor who played moody roles in films such as *The Godfather* 1972 and *Scarface* 1983.

Paderewski Ignacy Jan 1860–1941. Polish pianist, composer, and politician. After his debut in Vienna 1887 he became celebrated in Europe and the USA as an exponent of Chopin. During World War I he helped to organize the Polish army in France; in 1919 he became prime minister of the newly independent Poland, which he represented at the Peace Conference, but continuing opposition forced him to resign the same year. He resumed a musical career 1922, was president of the Polish National Council in Paris 1940, and died in New York.

Paganini Niccolò 1782–1840. Italian violinist and composer, a soloist from the age of nine. His works for the violin ingeniously exploit the potential of the instrument.

Page Earle (Christmas Grafton) 1880–1961. Australian politician, leader of the Country Party 1920–39 and briefly prime minister in Apr 1939. He represented Australia in the British war cabinet 1941–42 and was minister of health 1949–55.

Page Frederick Handley 1885–1962. British aircraft engineer, founder of one of the earliest aircraft-manufacturing companies 1909 and designer of long-range civil aeroplanes and multi-engined bombers in both world wars, such as the Halifax, flown in World War II.

Pagnol Marcel 1895–1974. French film director, author, and playwright, whose work includes the play *Fanny* 1932 and the film *Manon des Sources* 1953. He regarded the cinema as recorded theatre; thus his films, although strong on character and background, fail to exploit the medium fully as an independent art form.

Pahlavi dynasty Iranian dynasty founded by Riza Khan (1877–1944), an army officer who seized control of the government 1921, and was proclaimed shah 1925. During World War II Britain and the USSR were nervous of his German sympathies, and occupied Iran 1941–46. They compelled him to abdicate in favour of his son Mohammed Riza Shah Pahlavi, who was deposed in the Islamic revolution 1979.

Paine Thomas 1737–1809. English left-wing political writer, active in the American and French revolutions. His influential pamphlets include *Common Sense* 1776, *The Rights of Man* 1791, and *The Age of Reason* 1793. He advocated republicanism, deism, the abolition of slavery, and the emancipation of women.

Paine, born in Thetford, Norfolk, was a friend of Benjamin Franklin and went to America 1774, where he published several republican pamphlets and fought for the colonists in the War of Independence. In 1787 he returned to Britain. *The Rights of Man* is an answer to the conservative theorist Burke's *Reflections on the Revolution in France*. In 1792, Paine was indicted for treason and escaped to France, to represent Calais in the National Convention. Narrowly escaping the guillotine, he regained his seat after the fall of Robespierre. Paine returned to the USA 1802, and died in New York.

Pakula Alan J 1928– . US film director, formerly a producer, whose best films are among the finest

Paine *Portrait of Tom Paine after George Romney (c.1880), National Portrait Gallery, London.*

from Hollywood in the 1970s; they include *Klute* 1971 and *All the President's Men* 1976. His later work includes *Sophie's Choice* 1982.

Palamas Kostes 1859–1943. Greek poet. He enriched the Greek vernacular as a literary language by his use of it, particularly in his poetry, such as *Songs of my Fatherland* 1886 and *The Flute of the King* 1910, which expresses his vivid awareness of Greek history.

Palance Jack. Stage name of Walter Jack Palahnuik 1920– . US film actor, often cast as a villain. His films include *Shane* 1953 and *Batman* 1989.

Palestrina Giovanni Pierluigi da 1525–1594. Italian composer of secular and sacred choral music. Apart from motets and madrigals, he also wrote 105 masses, including *Missa Papae Marcelli*.

Paley Grace 1922– . US short-story writer and critic. Her stories express Jewish and feminist experience with bitter humour, as in *The Little Disturbances of Man* 1960 and *Later the Same Day* 1985.

Palissy Bernard 1510–1589. French potter, noted for his richly coloured rustic pottery, such as dishes with realistic modelled fish and reptiles or with the network piercing. He was favoured by Catherine de' Medici but was imprisoned in the Bastille prison in Paris as a Huguenot in 1588, and died there.

Palladio Andrea 1518–1580. Italian architect. His country houses (for example, Malcontenta, and the Villa Rotonda near Vicenza) were designed from 1540 for patrician families of the Venetian Republic.

These buildings influenced Neo-Classical architecture, such as Washington's home at Mount Vernon, USA, the palace of Tsarskoe Selo in Russia, and Prior Park, England.

Palme (Sven) Olof 1927–1986. Swedish social-democratic politician, prime minister 1969–76 and 1982–86. He entered government 1963, holding several posts before becoming leader of the Social Democratic Labour Party (SAP) 1969. He was assassinated Feb 1986.

Palme, educated in Sweden and the USA, joined the SAP 1949 and became secretary to the prime minister 1954. He led the SAP youth movement 1955–61. As prime minister he carried out constitutional reforms, turning the Riksdag into a single-chamber parliament and stripping the monarch of power.

Palmer Arnold (Daniel) 1929– . US golfer, who helped to popularize the game in the USA in the 1950s and 1960s. He won the Masters 1958, 1960, 1962, and 1964; the US Open 1960; and the British Open 1961 and 1962.

Born in Pennsylvania, he won the US amateur title 1954, and went on to win all the world major professional trophies except the US PGA championship. In the 1980s he enjoyed a successful career on the US Seniors Tour.

Palmer Geoffrey Winston Russell 1942– . New Zealand Labour politician, deputy prime minister and attorney-general 1984–89, and prime minister from 1989.

A graduate of Victoria University, Wellington, Palmer was a law lecturer in the USA and New Zealand before entering politics, becoming Labour member for Christchurch in the House of Representatives 1979. He succeeded David ◊Lange on Lange's resignation as prime minister.

Palmer Samuel 1805–1881. British painter and etcher. He lived 1826–35 in Shoreham, Kent, with a group of artists who were all followers of William Blake and called themselves *the Ancients*. Palmer's expressive landscape style during that period reflected a strongly spiritual inspiration.

Palmerston Henry John Temple, 3rd Viscount Palmerston 1784–1865. British politician. Initially a Tory, in Parliament from 1807, he was secretary-at-war 1809–28. He broke with the Tories 1830 and sat in the Whig cabinets of 1830–34, 1835–41, and 1846–51 as foreign secretary. He was prime minister 1855–58 (when he rectified Aberdeen's mismanagement of the Crimean War, suppressed the Indian Mutiny, and carried through the Second Opium War) and 1859–65 (when he almost involved Britain in the US Civil War on the side of the South).

Palmerston succeeded to an Irish peerage 1802. He served under five Tory prime ministers before joining the Whigs. His foreign policy was marked by distrust of France and Russia, against whose designs he backed the independence of Belgium and Turkey. He became home secretary in the coalition government of 1852, and prime minister on its fall, and was responsible for the warship *Alabama* going to the Confederate side in the American Civil War. He was popular with the people and made good use of the press, but his high-handed attitude annoyed Queen Victoria and other ministers.

Palumbo Peter 1935– . British property developer. Appointed chair of the Arts Council 1988, he advocated a close partnership between public and private funding of the arts, and a greater role for the regions. His planned Mies van der Rohe skyscraper beside the Mansion House, London, was condemned by Prince Charles as 'a giant glass stump'.

Panchen Lama 10th incarnation 1935–1989. Tibetan spiritual leader, second in importance to the ◊Dalai Lama. A protégé of the Chinese since childhood, he is not indisputably recognized. When the Dalai Lama left Tibet 1959, the Panchen Lama was deputed by the Chinese to take over, but was stripped of power in 1964 for refusing to denounce the Dalai Lama. He did not appear again in public until 1978.

Pankhurst Emmeline (born Goulden) 1858–1928.

English suffragette. Founder of the Women's Social and Political Union 1903, she launched the militant suffragette campaign 1905. In 1926 she joined the Conservative Party, and was a prospective parliamentary candidate.

She was supported by her daughters **Christabel Pankhurst** (1880–1958), the political leader of the movement, and **Sylvia Pankhurst** (1882–1960).

Panufnik Andrzei 1914– . Polish composer and conductor. A pupil of Weingartner, he came to Britain in 1954. His music is based on an intense working out of small motifs.

Paolozzi Eduardo 1924– . British sculptor, a major force in the Pop art movement in London in the mid-1950s. He typically uses bronze casts of pieces of machinery to create robot-like structures.

Papandreou Andreas 1919– . Greek socialist politician, founder of the Pan-Hellenic Socialist Movement (PASOK), and prime minister 1981–89. In 1989 he became implicated in the 'Koskotas affair', the alleged embezzlement and diversion of funds to the Greek government of $200 million from the Bank of Crete, headed by George Koskotas. The scandal caused him to lose the 1989 election.

Son of a former prime minister, he studied law in Athens and at Harvard. He was director of the Centre for Economic Research in Athens 1901–04, and economic adviser to the Bank of Greece. He was imprisoned Apr–Dec 1967 for his political activities, after which he founded PASOK. He was leader of the opposition 1977–81, and became Greece's first socialist prime minister. He was re-elected 1985. Nine officials of PASOK resigned because of the Koskotas affair.

Papen Franz von 1879–1969. German right-wing politician. As chancellor 1932, he negotiated the Nazi–Conservative alliance that made Hitler chancellor 1933. He was envoy to Austria 1934–38 and ambassador to Turkey 1939–44. Although acquitted at the Nuremberg war-crimes trials, he was imprisoned by a German denazification court for three years.

Papineau Louis Joseph 1786–1871. Canadian politician. He led a mission to England to protest against the planned union of Lower Canada (Québec) and Upper Canada (Ontario), and demanded economic reform and an elected provincial legislature. In 1835 he gained the cooperation of William Lyon ◊Mackenzie in Upper Canada, and in 1837 organized an unsuccessful rebellion of the French against British rule in Lower Canada. He fled the country, but returned 1847 to sit in the United Canadian legislature until 1854.

Papp Joseph 1921– . US theatre director, and founder of the New York Shakespeare Festival 1954, free to the public and held in an open-air theatre in Central Park. He also founded the New York Public Theatre 1967, an off-Broadway forum for new talent.

Productions directed by Papp include *The Merchant of Venice* and a musical version of *The Two Gentlemen of Verona* (Tony award 1972). The New York Public Theatre staged the first productions of the musicals *Hair* 1967 and *A Chorus Line* 1975.

Paracelsus adopted name of Theophrastus Bombastus von Hohenheim 1493–1541. Swiss physician, alchemist, and scientist. He developed the idea that minerals and chemicals might have medical uses (iatrochemistry). He introduced the use of the opiate laudanum (which he named) for painkilling purposes. Although Paracelsus was something of a charlatan, and his books contain much mystical nonsense, his rejection of the ancients and insistence on the value of experimentation make him an important figure in early science.

He lectured in Basel on the need for observational experience rather than traditional lore in medicine: he made a public bonfire of the works of his predecessors Avicenna and ◊Galen.

Paré Ambroise 1509–1590. French surgeon who introduced modern principles into wound treatment. As a military surgeon, Paré developed new ways of treating wounds and amputations. He abandoned the practice of cauterization (sealing with heat), using balms and soothing lotions instead. He also used ligatures to tie off blood vessels.

His methods greatly reduced the death rate among the wounded. Paré eventually became chief surgeon to Charles IX. He also made important contributions to dentistry and childbirth, and invented an artificial hand.

Pareto Vilfredo 1848–1923. Italian economist and political philosopher, born in Paris. He produced the first account of society as a self-regulating and interdependent system that operates independently of human attempts at voluntary con-

Papandreou *Greek former prime minister Andreas Papandreou in Brussels, Feb 1988.*

trol. A vigorous opponent of socialism and liberalism, Pareto justified inequality of income on the grounds of his empirical observation (*Pareto's law*) that income distribution remained constant whatever efforts were made to change it.

A founder of welfare economics, he put forward a concept of 'optimality' which contends that optimum conditions exist in an economic system if no-one can be made better off without at least one other person becoming worse off.

Paris Henri d'Orléans, Comte de Paris 1908– . Head of the royal house of France. He served in the Foreign Legion under an assumed name 1939–40, and in 1950, on the repeal of the 1886 *loi d'exil* banning pretenders to the French throne, returned to live in France.

Paris Matthew *c*.1200–1259. English chronicler. He entered St Albans Abbey 1217, and wrote a valuable history of England up to 1259.

Park Merle 1937– . British ballerina, born in Rhodesia. She joined Sadler's Wells 1954, and by 1959 was a principal soloist with the Royal Ballet. She combined elegance with sympathetic appeal in such roles as Cinderella.

Park Mungo 1771–1806. Scottish surgeon and explorer. He traced the course of the Niger 1795–97 and probably drowned during a second expedition in 1805–06. He published *Travels in the Interior of Africa* 1799.

Park Chung Hee 1917–1979. President of South Korea 1963–79. Under his rule South Korea had the world's fastest-growing economy and the wealth was widely distributed, but recession and his increasing authoritarianism led to his assassination 1979.

Parker 'Charlie', 'Bird', 'Yardbird' (Charles Christopher) 1920–1955. US alto saxophonist and jazz composer, associated with the trumpeter Dizzy Gillespie in developing the bebop style. His mastery of improvisation inspired performers on all jazz instruments.

Parker Dorothy (born Rothschild) 1893–1967. US writer and wit. She reviewed for the magazines *Vanity Fair* and the *New Yorker*, and wrote wittily ironic verses, collected in several volumes including *Not So Deep As a Well* 1940, and short stories.

Parker Matthew 1504–1575. English cleric. He was converted to Protestantism at Cambridge. He received high preferment under Henry VIII and Edward VI, and as archbishop of Canterbury from 1559 was largely responsible for the Elizabethan religious settlement (the formal establishment of the Church of England).

Parkes Henry 1815–1896. Australian politician, born in the UK. He promoted education and the cause of federation, and suggested the official name 'Commonwealth of Australia'. He was five times premier of New South Wales 1872–91.

Parkinson Cecil (Edward) 1931– . British Conservative politician. He was chair of the party 1981–83, and became minister for trade and industry, but resigned Oct 1984 following disclosure of an affair with his secretary. In 1987 he rejoined the cabinet as secretary of state for energy, and in 1989 became the transport secretary.

Parkinson Cyril Northcote 1909– . British historian, celebrated for his study of public and business administration *Parkinson's Law* 1958, which included the dictum: 'Work expands to fill the time available for its completion.'

Parkinson James 1755–1824. British neurologist, who first described *Parkinson's disease*, which progressively degrades the transmission of nerve signals, producing tremor.

Parkman Francis 1823–1893. US historian and traveller, whose work chronicles the European exploration and conquest of North America, in such books as *The California and Oregon Trail* 1849 and *La Salle and the Discovery of the Great West* 1879.

Parkman viewed the defeat by England of the French at Québec 1759 (described in his *Montcalm and Wolfe* 1884) as the turning point of North American history, insofar as it swung the balance of power in North America towards the British colonies which would form the USA.

Parmenides *c*.510–450 BC. Greek pre-Socratic philosopher, head of the Eleatic school (so called after Elea in S Italy). Against Heraclitus's doctrine of Becoming, Parmenides advanced the view that nonexistence was impossible, that everything was permanently in a state of being. Despite evidence of the senses to the contrary, motion and change is illusory, in fact, logically impossible, because it would imply a contradiction. Parmenides saw speculation and reason as more important than the evidence of the senses.

Parmigianino Francesco 1503–1540. Italian painter and etcher, active in Parma and elsewhere. He painted religious subjects and portraits in a Mannerist style, with elongated figures.

Parnell Charles Stewart 1846–1891. Irish nationalist politician. He supported a policy of obstruction and violence to attain Home Rule, and became the president of the Nationalist Party 1877. In 1879 he approved the Land League, formed to fight the eviction of peasants, and his attitude led to his imprisonment 1881. His career was ruined 1890 when he was cited as co-respondent in a divorce case.

Parnell, born in County Wicklow, was elected member of Parliament for Meath 1875. He welcomed Gladstone's Home Rule Bill, and continued his agitation after its defeat 1886. In 1887 his reputation suffered from an unfounded accusation by *The Times* of complicity in the murder of Lord Frederick ◊Cavendish. Three years later came the adultery scandal, and for fear of losing the sup-

Parnell As chair of the Home Rule party and militant campaigner for Irish self-government, Parnell earned the nickname of 'uncrowned king of Ireland'.

port of Gladstone, Parnell's party deposed him.

Parr Catherine 1512 1548. Sixth wife of Henry VIII of England. She had already lost two husbands when in 1543 she married Henry VIII. She survived him, and in 1547 married Lord Seymour of Sudeley (1508–49).

Parry Charles Hubert Hastings 1848–1918. English composer. His works include songs, motets, and the setting of Milton's 'Blest Pair of Sirens' and Blake's 'Jerusalem'.

Parry William Edward 1790–1855. English admiral and Arctic explorer. He made detailed charts during explorations of the Northwest Passage 1819–20, 1821–23, and 1824–25. He made an attempt to reach the North Pole 1827.

Parsons Charles Algernon 1854–1931. English engineer who invented the Parsons steam turbine 1884, a landmark in marine engineering and later universally used in electricity generation (to drive an alternator).

Parsons Talcott 1902–1979. US sociologist, who attempted to integrate all the social sciences into a science of human action. He was professor of sociology at Harvard University from 1931 until his death, and author of over 150 books and articles. His theory of structural functionalism dominated US sociology from the 1940s to the 1960s, and as an attempt to explain social order and individual behaviour it was a major step in establishing sociology as an academic and scientific discipline.

Partridge Eric 1894–1979. New Zealand lexicogra-

pher. He studied at Oxford University after serving in World War I and settled in England to write a number of dictionaries including *A Dictionary of Slang and Unconventional English* 1934 and 1970, and *Dictionary of the Underworld, British and American* 1950.

Pascal Blaise 1623–1662. French philosopher and mathematician. He contributed to the development of hydraulics, the calculus, and the mathematical theory of probability.

In mathematics, Pascal is known for his work on conic sections and, with Pierre de Fermat, the probability theory. He discussed *Pascal's triangle*, a triangular array of numbers in which each number is the sum of the pair of numbers above it.

In physics, Pascal's chief work concerned fluid pressure and hydraulics. *Pascal's principle* states that the pressure everywhere in a fluid is the same, so that pressure applied at one point is transmitted equally to all parts of the container. This is the principle of the hydraulic press and jack.

In 1654, he went into the Jansenist monastery of Port Royal and defended a prominent Jansenist against the Jesuits in his *Lettres Provinciales* 1656. His *Pensées* 1670 was part of an unfinished defence of the Christian religion.

Pasmore Victor 1908– . British painter, a member of the Euston Road School (which favoured a subdued, measured style) in the 1930s. He painted landscapes and, from 1947, abstract paintings and constructions (reviving the early ideas of the Constructivists).

Pasolini Pier Paolo 1922–1975. Italian poet, novelist, and film director, an influential figure in the post-war years. His writings (making much use of first Friulan and later Roman dialect) include the novels *Ragazzi di vita/The Ragazzi* 1955 and *Una vita violenta/A Violent Life* 1959. Among his films are *Il vangelo secondo Matteo/The Gospel According to St Matthew* 1964 and *I racconti di Canterbury/The Canterbury Tales* 1972.

Many of his works are coloured by his experience of life in the poor districts of Rome, where he lived from 1950, and illustrate the decadence and inequality of society from his Marxist viewpoint.

Passy Frédéric 1822–1912. French economist, who shared the first Nobel Peace Prize in 1901 with ◊Dunant. He founded the International League for Permanent Peace 1867, and was co-founder, with the English politician William R Cremer (1828–1908), of the Inter-Parliamentary Conferences on Peace and on Arbitration 1889.

Pasternak Boris Leonidovich 1890–1960. Russian poet and novelist. His volumes of lyric poems include *A Twin Cloud* 1914, and *On Early Trains* 1943, and he translated Shakespeare's tragedies. His novel *Dr Zhivago* 1957, was followed by a Nobel prize (which he declined).

Pasteur French chemist and scientist Louis Pasteur.

Pasteur Louis 1822–1895. French chemist and microbiologist who discovered that fermentation was caused by microorganisms. He also developed a vaccine for rabies, which led to the foundation of the Institut Pasteur in Paris 1888.

Pasteur saved the French silkworm industry by identifying two microbial diseases that were decimating the worms. He discovered the pathogens responsible for anthrax and chicken cholera, and developed vaccines for these diseases. He inspired his pupil ◊Lister's work in antiseptic surgery. *Pasteurization*, the heating of foodstuffs to destroy harmful bacteria, is based on his discoveries.

Paston family family of Norfolk, England, whose correspondence and documents (known as the *Paston letters*) for 1422–1509 throw valuable light on the period.

Patel Vallabhbhai Jhaverbhai 1875–1950. Indian nationalist politician. A fervent follower of Gandhi, he participated in the Satyagraha (the struggle for Indian independence by nonviolent, noncooperative means) at Kaira 1918, and later became home minister in Nehru's first government after independence.

He was a member of the right wing of the Indian National Congress and supported the conservative opposition to the reform of Hindu law as it applied to the lack of rights of Hindu women.

Pater Walter Horatio 1839–1894. English critic. A stylist and supporter of 'art for art's sake', he published *Studies in the History of the Renaissance* 1873, *Marius the Epicurean* 1885, *Imaginary Portraits* 1887, and other works.

Paterson Andrew Barton 1864–1941. Australian journalist, known as 'Banjo' Paterson, author of volumes of light verse and 'Waltzing Matilda', adapted from a traditional song.

Pathé Charles 1863–1957. French film pioneer, who began his career selling projectors in 1896 and with the profits formed Pathé Frères with his brothers. In 1901 he embarked on film production and by 1908 had becomed the world's biggest producer, with branches worldwide. He also developed an early colour process and established a weekly newsreel, *Pathé Journal*. World War I disrupted his enterprises and by 1918 he was gradually forced out of business by foreign competition.

Patinir (also Patenier, Patinier) Joachim *c.* 1485–*c.*1524. Flemish painter, active in Antwerp, whose inspired landscape backgrounds dominated his religious subjects. He is known to have worked with Matsys and to have painted landscape backgrounds for other artists' works.

Patmore Coventry 1823–1896. British poet and critic. He was a librarian at the British Museum 1846–66, and as one of the Pre-Raphaelites achieved fame with the poem *The Angel in the House* 1854–63 and the collection of odes *The Unknown Eros* 1877.

Paton Alan 1903–1988. South African writer. His novel *Cry, the Beloved Country* 1948 focused on the racial inequality in South Africa. Later books include the study *Land and People of South Africa* 1956, *The Long View* 1968, and his autobiography *Towards the Mountain* 1980.

Patou Jean 1880–1936. French designer of sporting clothes (as worn by Suzanne ◊Lenglen) from 1922, and bias-cut white satin evening dresses 1929.

Patrick, St 389–*c.*461. Patron saint of Ireland. Born in Britain, probably in S Wales, he was carried off by pirates to six years' slavery in Antrim before escaping either to Britain or Gaul – his poor Latin suggests the former – to train as a missionary. He is variously said to have landed again in Ireland 432 or 456, and his work was a vital factor in the spread of Christian influence there. His symbols are snakes and shamrocks; feast day 17 Mar.

Patrick is credited with founding the diocese of Armagh, of which he was bishop, though this was probably the work of a 'lost apostle' (Palladius or Secundinus). Of his writings only his *Confessio* and an *Epistola* survive.

Patten Chris(topher Francis) 1944– . British Conservative politician, environment secretary from 1989.

A former director of the Conservative Party research department, he held junior ministerial posts under Margaret Thatcher, despite his reputation of being to the left of the party. Patten's 'green' credentials and presentational skills made him the obvious choice to replace Nicholas Ridley as environment secretary.

Patterson Harry 1929– . English novelist, born in Newcastle. He has written many thrillers under his own name, including *Dillinger* 1983, as well as under the pseudonym Jack Higgins, including *The Eagle Has Landed* 1975.

Patti Adelina 1843–1919. Anglo-Italian soprano

renowned for her performances of Lucia in *Lucia di Lammermoor* and Amina in *La sonnambula*. At the age of 62 she was persuaded out of retirement to make a number of gramophone recordings, one of the first opera singers to be recorded.

Patton George (Smith) 1885–1945. US general in World War II, known as 'Blood and Guts'. He commanded the 2nd Armoured Division 1940, and in 1942 led the Western Task Force that landed at Casablanca, Morocco. After commanding the 7th Army, he led the 3rd Army across France and into Germany, and in 1945 took over the 15th Army.

Paul Elliot Harold 1891–1958. US author. His books include the travel book *The Narrow Street/The Last Time I Saw Paris* 1942.

Paul Les. Adopted name of Lester Polfuss 1915– . US inventor of the solid-body electric guitar in the early 1940s, and a pioneer of recording techniques including overdubbing and electronic echo. The Gibson Les Paul guitar was first marketed in 1952 (the first commercial solid-body guitar was made by Leo ◊Fender). As a guitarist in the late 1940s and the 1950s he recorded with the singer Mary Ford (1928–77).

Paul 1901–1964. King of the Hellenes from 1947, when he succeeded his brother George II. He was the son of Constantine I. He married in 1938 Princess Frederika (1917–), daughter of the Duke of Brunswick, whose involvement in politics brought her under attack.

Paul VI Giovanni Battista Montini 1897–1978. Pope from 1963. His encyclical *Humanae Vitae/Of Human Life* 1968 reaffirmed the church's traditional teaching on birth control, thus following the minority report of the commission originally appointed by Pope John, rather than the majority view.

Paul I 1754–1801. Tsar of Russia from 1796, in succession to his mother Catherine II. Mentally unstable, he pursued an erratic foreign policy, and was assassinated.

Pauli Wolfgang 1900–1958. Austrian physicist, who originated *Pauli's exclusion principle*: in a given system no two electrons, protons, neutrons, or other elementary particles of half-integral spin can be characterized by the same set of quantum numbers. He also predicted the existence of neutrinos. He won a Nobel prize 1945 for his work on atomic structure.

Pauling Linus Carl 1901– . US chemist, noted for his fundamental work on the nature of the chemical bond and on the discovery of the helical structure of many proteins. Nobel Prize for Chemistry 1954. An outspoken opponent of nuclear testing, he also received the Nobel Peace Prize in 1962.

Paul, St *c.* AD 3–*c.* 68. Christian missionary and martyr; in the New Testament, one of the apostles and author of 13 epistles. He is said to have been converted by a vision on the road to Damascus. His emblems are a sword and a book; feast day 29 June.

The Jewish form of his name is Saul. He was born in Tarsus (now in Turkey), son of well-to-do Pharisees, and had Roman citizenship. Originally opposed to Christianity, he took part in the stoning of St Stephen. After his conversion he made great missionary journeys, for example to Philippi and Ephesus, becoming known as the Apostle of the Gentiles (non-Jews). On his return to Jerusalem, he was arrested, appealed to Caesar, and (as a citizen) was sent to Rome for trial about 57 or 59. After two years in prison, he may have been released before his final arrest and execution under the emperor Nero.

St Paul's theology was rigorous on such questions as sin and atonement, and his views on the role of women were adopted by Christian church generally.

Paulus Friedrich von 1890–1957. German field marshal in World War II, commander of the forces that besieged Stalingrad (now Volgograd) in the USSR 1942–43; he was captured and gave evidence at the Nuremberg trials before settling in East Germany.

Pausanias 2nd century AD. Greek geographer, author of a valuably accurate description of Greece compiled from his own travels, *Description of Greece*, also translated as *Itinerary of Greece*.

Pavarotti Luciano 1935– . Italian tenor, whose operatic roles have included Rodolfo in *La Bohème*, Cavaradossi in *Tosca*, the Duke of Mantua in *Rigoletto*, and Nemorino in *L'Elisir d'amore*.

Pavlov Ivan Petrovich 1849–1936. Russian physiologist who studied conditioned reflexes in animals. His work greatly influenced behavioural theory and learning theory.

Pavlova Anna 1881–1931. Russian dancer. Prima ballerina of the Imperial Ballet from 1906, she left Russia 1913, and went on to become the world's most famous Classical ballerina. With London as her home, she toured extensively with her own company, influencing dancers worldwide with roles such as ◊Fokine's *The Dying Swan* solo 1905.

Paxton Joseph 1801–1865. English architect, garden superintendent to the Duke of Devonshire from 1826 and designer of the Great Exhibition building 1851, the Crystal Palace, revolutionary in its structural use of glass and iron.

Paz (Estenssoro) Victor 1907– . President of Bolivia 1952–56, 1960–64, and from 1985. He founded and led the *Movimiento Nacionalista Revolucionario* which seized power 1952. His regime extended the vote to Indians, nationalized the country's largest tin mines, and embarked on a major programme of agrarian reform.

After holding a number of financial posts he entered politics in the 1930s and in 1942 founded the National Revolutionary Movement (MNR). In exile in Argentina, during one of Bolivia's many periods of military rule, he returned in 1951 and became president in 1952. He immediately embarked on a programme of political reform, retaining the presidency until 1956 and being re-elected (1960–64) and again in 1985, returning from near-retirement, at the age of 77.

Paz Octavio 1914– . Mexican poet, whose *Sun Stone* 1957 is a personal statement taking the Aztec Calendar Stone as its basic symbol.

Peacock Thomas Love 1785–1866. English satirical novelist and poet. His works include *Headlong Hall* 1816, *Nightmare Abbey* 1818, *Crotchet Castle* 1831, and *Gryll Grange* 1860.

Peake Mervyn (Lawrence) 1911–1968. English writer and illustrator, born in China. His novels include the grotesque fantasy trilogy *Titus Groan* 1946, *Gormenghast* 1950, and *Titus Alone* 1959.

Peale Charles Willson 1741–1827. American artist, head of a large family of painters. His portraits of leading figures in the War of Independence include the earliest known portrait of Washington 1772.

Pears Peter 1910–1986. English tenor. A co-founder with ◊Britten of the Aldeburgh Festival, he was closely associated with the composer's work and played the title role in *Peter Grimes*.

Pearse Patrick Henry 1879–1916. Irish poet prominent in the Gaelic revival, a leader of the Easter Rising 1916. Proclaimed president of the provisional government, he was court-martialled and shot after its suppression.

Pearson Karl 1857–1936. British statistician, who followed ◊Galton in introducing statistics and probability into genetics, and developed the concept of eugenics (improving the human race by selective breeding). He introduced the term standard deviation (a measure of the 'spread' of a set of results) into statistics.

Pearson Lester Bowles 1897–1972. Canadian politician, leader of the Liberal Party from 1958, prime minister 1963–68. As foreign minister 1948–57, he effectively represented Canada at the United Nations. Nobel Peace Prize 1957.

He served as president of the General Assembly 1952–53 and helped to create the UN Emergency Force (UNEF) that policed Sinai following the Egypt–Israel war of 1956.

Peary Robert Edwin 1856–1920. US polar explorer who, after several unsuccessful attempts, became the first person to reach the North Pole on 6 Apr 1909. In 1988 an astronomer claimed Peary's measurements were incorrect.

Peck Eldred Gregory 1916– . US actor. One of Hollywood's most enduring stars, he was often cast as a decent man of great moral and physical strength, as in *The Old Gringo* 1989. His other films include *Spellbound* 1945 and *To Kill a Mockingbird* 1962.

Peckinpah Sam 1925–1985. US film director, often of westerns, usually associated with slow-motion, blood-spurting violence. His best films, such as

The Wild Bunch 1969, exhibit a thoughtful, if depressing, view of the world.

Pedro two emperors of Brazil:

Pedro I 1798–1834. Emperor of Brazil 1822–31. The son of John VI of Portugal, he escaped to Brazil on Napoleon's invasion, and was appointed regent 1821. He proclaimed Brazil independent 1822 and was crowned emperor, but abdicated 1831 and returned to Portugal.

Pedro II 1825–1891. Emperor of Brazil 1831–89. He proved an enlightened ruler, but his antislavery measures alienated the landowners, who compelled him to abdicate.

Peel Robert 1788–1850. British Conservative politician. As home secretary 1822–27 and 1828–30, he founded the modern police force and in 1829 introduced Roman Catholic emancipation. He was prime minister 1834–35 and 1841–46, when his repeal of the Corn Laws caused him and his followers to break with the party.

Peel, born in Lancashire, entered Parliament as a Tory 1809. After the passing of the Reform Bill 1832, which he had resisted, he reformed the Tories under the name of the Conservative Party, on a basis of accepting necessary reforms and seeking middle-class support. He fell from prime ministerial office because his repeal of the Corn Laws 1846 was opposed by the majority of his party. He and his followers then formed a third party standing between the Liberals and Conservatives; the majority of the Peelites, including Gladstone, subsequently joined the Liberals.

Peele George 1558–1597. English dramatist. He wrote a pastoral, *The Arraignment of Paris* 1584; a fantastic comedy, *The Old Wives' Tale* 1595; and a tragedy, *David and Bethsabe* 1599.

Péguy Charles 1873–1914. French Catholic socialist, who established a socialist publishing house in Paris. From 1900 he published on political topics *Les Cahiers de la Quinzaine/Fortnightly Notebooks* and poetry, including *Le Mystère de la charité de Jeanne d'Arc/The Mystery of the Charity of Joan of Arc* 1897.

Pei Ieoh Ming 1917– . Chinese Modernist/high-tech architect, who became a US citizen 1948. His buildings include the John F Kennedy Library Complex and the John Hancock tower, Boston 1979; the Bank of China Tower, Hong Kong, 1987; and a glass pyramid in front of the Louvre, Paris, 1989.

Peirce Charles Sanders 1839–1914. US philosopher, founder of pragmatism, the doctrine that genuine conceptual distinctions must be correlated with some difference of practical effect. He wrote extensively on the logic of scientific enquiry, suggesting that truth could be conceived of as the object of an ultimate consensus.

Pelagius 360–420. English theologian. He went to Rome about 400, and taught that every person possesses free will, denying Augustine's doctrines of predestination and original sin. Cleared of heresy by a synod in Jerusalem 415, he was later condemned by the pope and the emperor.

Pelé adopted name of Edson Arantes do Nascimento 1940– . Brazilian footballer, a prolific goal scorer. He appeared in four World Cup competitions 1958–70 and won three winner's medals.

He spent most of his playing career with the Brazilian team Santos before ending his career playing with the New York Cosmos in the USA. He played inside left.

Pelham Henry 1696–1754. British Whig politician. He held a succession of offices in Walpole's cabinet 1721–42, and was prime minister 1743–54.

Penda c.577–654. King of Mercia from about 632. He raised Mercia to a powerful kingdom, and defeated and killed two Northumbrian kings, Edwin 632 and ◊Oswald 641. He was killed in battle by Oswy, king of Northumbria.

Penderecki Krzystof 1933– . Polish composer. His Expressionist works, such as the *Threnody for the Victims of Hiroshima* 1961 for strings, employ cluster and percusssion effects. He later turned to religious subjects and a more orthodox style, as in the *Magnificat* 1974 and the *Polish Requiem* 1980–83.

Pendlebury John Devitt Stringfellow 1904–1941. British archaeologist. Working with his wife, he became the world's leading expert on Crete. In World War II he was deputed to prepare guerrilla resistance on the island, was wounded during the German invasion, and shot by his captors.

Penn Irving 1917– . US fashion, advertising, portrait, editorial, and fine art photographer. In 1948 he took the first of many journeys to Africa and the Far East, resulting in a series of portrait photographs of local people, avoiding sophisticated technique. He was associated for many years with *Vogue* magazine in the USA.

Penn William 1644–1718. English Quaker, born in London. He joined the Quakers 1667, and in 1681 obtained a grant of land in America, in settlement of a debt owed by the king to his father, on which he established the colony of Pennsylvania as a refuge for the persecuted Quakers.

Penney William 1909– . British scientist. He worked at Los Alamos 1944–45, designed the first British atomic bomb, and developed the advanced gas-cooled nuclear reactor used in some power stations.

Pepin *the Short* c.714–c. 768. King of the Franks from 751. The son of Charles Martel, he acted as mayor of the palace to the last Merovingian king, Childeric III, deposed him and assumed the royal title himself, founding the Carolingian line (named after his son, Charlemagne).

Pepusch Johann Christoph 1667–1752. German composer who settled in England about 1700. He contributed to John Gay's ballad operas *The Beggar's Opera* and *Polly*.

Pepys Samuel 1633–1703. English diarist. His diary, written 1659–69 (when his sight failed) in shorthand, was a unique record of both the daily life of the period and the intimate feelings of the man. It was not deciphered until 1825.

He was born in London, entered the navy office 1660, and was secretary to the Admiralty 1672–79, when he was imprisoned in the Tower on suspicion of being connected with the Popish Plot (see Titus ◊Oates). He was reinstated in 1684 but after the 1688 Revolution was deprived of his post, this time for good, for suspected disaffection.

Perceval Spencer 1762–1812. British Tory politician. He became chancellor of the Exchequer 1807 and prime minister 1809. He was shot in the lobby of the House of Commons 1812 by a merchant who blamed government measures for his bankruptcy.

Percy family name of dukes of Northumberland; seated at Alnwick Castle, Northumberland, England.

Percy Henry 'Hotspur' 1364–1403. English soldier, son of the 1st Earl of Northumberland. In repelling a border raid, he defeated the Scots at Homildon Hill in Durham 1402, and was killed at the battle of Shrewsbury while in revolt against Henry IV.

Percy Thomas 1729–1811. English scholar and bishop of Dromore from 1782. He discovered a manuscript collection of songs, ballads, and romances, from which he published a selection as *Reliques of Ancient English Poetry* 1765, influential in the Romantic revival.

Perelman S(idney) J(oseph) 1904–1979. US humorist, born in New York. He wrote for the *New Yorker* magazine, and film scripts for the Marx Brothers. He shared an Academy Award for the film script *Around the World in 80 Days* 1956.

Peres Shimon 1923– . Israeli socialist politician, prime minister 1984–86. Peres emigrated from Poland to Palestine 1934, but was educated in the USA. In 1959 he was elected to the Knesset (Israeli parliament). He became leader of the Labour Party 1977. Peres was prime minister under a power-sharing agreement with the leader of the Consolidation Party (Likud), Yitzhak ◊Shamir.

Pérez de Cuéllar Javier 1920– . Peruvian diplomat. A delegate to the first United Nations general assembly 1946–47, he held several ambassadorial posts and was appointed secretary-general of the UN 1982.

Pérez Galdós Benito 1843–1920. Spanish novelist, born in the Canary Islands. His works include the 46 historical novels in the cycle *Episodios nacionales* and the 21-novel cycle *Novelas españolas contemporáneos*, which includes *Doña Perfecta* 1876 and the epic *Fortunata y Jacinta* 1886–87, his masterpiece. In scale he has been compared to Balzac and Dickens.

Peri Jacopo 1561–1633. Italian composer, who served the ◊Medici family. His experimental melodic opera *Euridice* 1600 established the opera form and influenced Monteverdi. His first opera, *Dafne* 1597, is now lost.

Pericles *c.*490–429 BC. Athenian politician, who dominated the city's affairs from 461 BC (as leader of the democratic party), and under whom Greek culture reached its height. He created a confederation of cities under the leadership of Athens, but the disasters of the Peloponnesian War with Sparta led to his overthrow 430 BC. Although quickly reinstated, he died soon after.

Perkin William Henry 1838–1907. British chemist. In 1856 he discovered the mauve dye that originated the aniline dye industry.

Perkins Anthony 1932– . US film actor who played the mother-fixated psychopath Norman Bates in *Psycho* 1960.

Perkins Gilman Charlotte 1860–1935. US feminist socialist poet, novelist, and historian, author of *Women and Economics*, proposing the ending of the division between 'men's work' and 'women's work' by abolishing housework.

From 1909 to 1916 she wrote and published a magazine *The Forerunner* in which her feminist

Perón Eva (Evita) Perón used her talents as a broadcaster and speaker to gain support for her husband Juan Perón, the Argentinian leader.

Utopian novel *Herland* 1915 was serialized.

Perón 'Evita' (Maria Eva) (born Duarte) 1919–1952. Argentinian populist leader, born in Buenos Aires. A successful radio actress, in 1945 she married Juan Perón. After he became president she virtually ran the health and labour ministries, and did a lot of charitable work. In 1951 she stood for the post of vice president, but was opposed by the army and withdrew; she died of cancer soon afterwards.

Perón (María Estela) Isabel (born Martínez) 1931– . President of Argentina 1974–76, and third wife of Juan Perón. She succeeded him after he died in office, but labour unrest, inflation, and political violence pushed the country to the brink of chaos. Accused of corruption, she was held under house arrest for five years. She went into exile in Spain.

Perón Juan (Domingo) 1895–1974. Argentine politician, dictator 1946–55 and from 1973 until his death. He took part in the military coup 1943, and his popularity with the *descamisados* ('shirtless ones') led to his election as president 1946. He instituted social reforms, but encountered economic difficulties. After the death of his second wife Eva Perón he lost popularity, and was deposed in a military coup 1955. He returned from exile to the presidency 1973, but died in office 1974, and was succeeded by his third wife Isabel Perón.

Perrault Charles 1628–1703. French author of the

Pericles Bust of Pericles found near Tivoli, Italy, 1781. Under his rule , Greek culture reached its finest expression.

fairy tales *Contes de ma mère l'oye/ Mother Goose's Fairy Tales* 1697, including 'Sleeping Beauty', 'Red Riding Hood', 'Blue Beard', 'Puss in Boots', and 'Cinderella'.

Perrin Jean 1870–1942. French physicist who produced the crucial evidence that finally established the atomic nature of matter. Assuming the atomic hypothesis, Perrin demonstrated how the phenomenon of Brownian movement (see Robert ◊Brown) could be used to derive precise values of ◊Avogadro's number. He won the 1926 Nobel Prize for Physics.

Perry Fred(erick John) 1909– . English lawn-tennis player, the last Briton to win the men's singles at Wimbledon 1936. He also won the world table-tennis title 1929. He became a television commentator.

Perry Matthew Calbraith 1794–1858. US naval officer, commander of the expedition of 1853 that reopened communication between Japan and the outside world after 250 years' isolation. Evident military superiority enabled him to negotiate the *Treaty of Kanagawa* 1854 giving the USA trading rights with Japan.

Perse Saint-John. Pen name of Alexis Saint-Léger 1887–1975. French poet and diplomat, a US citizen from 1940. His first book of verse, *Eloges* 1911, reflects the ambience of the West Indies, where he was born and raised. His later works include *Anabase* 1924, an epic poem translated by T S Eliot in 1930. Nobel prize 1960.

Entering the foreign service in 1914, he was secretary-general 1933–40. He then emigrated permanently to the USA, and was deprived of French citizenship by the Vichy government.

Pershing John Joseph 1860–1948. US general. He served in the Spanish War 1898, the Philippines 1899–1903, and Mexico 1916–17. He commanded the US Expeditionary Force sent to France 1917–18.

Perugino Pietro. Assumed name of Pietro Vannucci 1445/50–1523. Italian painter, active chiefly in Perugia, the teacher of Raphael, who absorbed his soft and graceful figure style. Perugino produced paintings for the lower walls of the Sistine Chapel 1481 (Vatican), and in 1500 decorated the Sala del Cambio in Perugia.

Perutz Max 1914– . British biochemist, who shared the 1962 Nobel Prize for Chemistry with John Kendrew for work on the structure of the haemoglobin molecule.

Born in Austria, Perutz moved to Britain in 1936 to work with John Bernal (1901–1971) at Cambridge University. After internment in Canada as an alien during World War II he returned to Cambridge and completed his research in 1959.

Pessoa Fernando 1888–1935. Portuguese poet. Born in Lisbon, he was brought up in South Africa, and was bilingual in English and Portuguese. He wrote under three assumed names (which he

called 'heteronyms': Alvaro de Campos, Ricardo Reis, and Alberto Caeiro), for each of whom he invented a biography.

Pestalozzi Johann Heinrich 1746–1827. Swiss educationalist who advocated Rousseau's 'natural' principles (of natural development and the power of example), and described his own theories in *Wie Gertrude ihre Kinder lehrt/How Gertrude Teaches her Children* 1801. He stressed the importance of mother and home in a child's education.

International Children's Villages named after him have been established, for example Sedlescombe, East Sussex, UK.

Pétain Henri Philippe 1856–1951. French general and right-wing politician. His defence of Verdun 1916 during World War I made him a national hero. In World War II he became prime minister June 1940 and signed an armistice with Germany. Removing the seat of government to Vichy, he established an authoritarian regime. He was imprisoned after the war.

In 1917 Pétain was created French commander in chief, although he became subordinate to Marshal Foch 1918. He suppressed a rebellion in Morocco 1925–26. As a member of the Higher Council of National Defence he advocated a purely defensive military policy, and was strongly conservative in politics. On the Allied invasion he was taken to Germany, but returned 1945 and was sentenced to death for treason, the sentence being commuted to life imprisonment.

Peter three tsars of Russia:

Peter I *the Great* 1672–1725. Tsar of Russia from 1682 on the death of his brother Tsar Feodor, he assumed control of the government 1689. He attempted to reorganize the country on Western lines; the army was modernized, a fleet was built, the administrative and legal systems were remodelled, education was encouraged, and the church was brought under state control. On the Baltic coast, where he had conquered territory from Sweden, Peter built his new capital, St Petersburg (now Leningrad).

After a successful campaign against the Ottoman Empire 1696, he visited Holland and Britain to study Western techniques, and worked in Dutch and English shipyards. In order to secure an outlet to the Baltic, Peter undertook a war with Sweden 1700–21, which resulted in the acquisition of Estonia and parts of Latvia and Finland. A war with Persia 1722–23 added Baku to Russia.

Peter II 1715–1730. Tsar of Russia from 1727. Son of Peter the Great, he had been passed over in favour of Catherine I 1725, but succeeded her 1727. He died of smallpox.

Peter III 1728–1762. Tsar of Russia 1762. Weak-minded son of Peter I's eldest daughter, Anne, he was adopted 1741 by his aunt ◊Elizabeth, Empress of Russia, and at her command married the future Catherine II 1745. He was deposed in favour of his wife, and probably murdered by her lover Alexius Orlov.

Peter I 1844–1921. King of Serbia from 1903. He was the son of Prince Alexander Karageorgevich, and was elected king when the last Obrenovich king was murdered 1903. He took part in the retreat of the Serbian army 1915, and in 1918 was proclaimed first king of the Serbs, Croats, and Slovenes (renamed Yugoslavia in 1921).

Peter II 1923–1970. King of Yugoslavia 1934–45. He succeeded his father, Alexander I, and assumed the royal power after the overthrow of the regency 1941. He escaped to the UK after the German invasion, and married Princess Alexandra of Greece 1944. He was dethroned 1945.

Peter Damian, St real name Pietro Damiani 1007–1072. Italian monk who was associated with the initiation of clerical reform by Gregory VII.

Peter Lombard 1100–1160. Italian Christian theologian whose *Sententiarum libri quatuor* considerably influenced Catholic doctrine.

Peter, St died AD 64. Christian martyr, the author of two epistles in the New Testament and leader of the apostles. Tradition has it that he later settled in Rome; he is regarded as the first bishop of Rome, whose mantle the pope inherits. His emblem is two keys; feast day 29 June.

Originally a fisherman of Capernaum, on the Sea of Galilee, Peter may have been a follower of John the Baptist, and was the first to acknowledge Jesus as the Messiah. His real name was Simon, but he was nicknamed Cephas ('Peter', from the Greek for 'rock') by Jesus as being the rock on which he founded his church. Peter is said to have been crucified under the emperor Nero.

Peter the Hermit 1050–1115. French priest whose eloquent preaching of the First ◊Crusade sent thousands of peasants marching against the Turks, who massacred them in Asia Minor. Peter escaped and accompanied the main body of crusaders to Jerusalem.

Petipa Marius 1818–1910. French choreographer. For the Imperial Ballet in Russia he created masterpieces such as *La Bayadère* 1877, *The Sleeping Beauty* 1890, *Swan Lake* 1895 (with Ivanov), and *Raymonda* 1898, which are still performed.

Petit Alexis 1791–1820. French physicist, co-discoverer of *Dulong and Petit's law* (see ◊Dulong). He also devised methods for measuring thermal expansion and specific heat capacity.

Petöfi Sándor 1823–1849. Hungarian nationalist poet. He published his first volume of poems 1844. He expressed his revolutionary ideas in the semi-autobiographical poem 'The Apostle', and died fighting the Austrians in the battle of Segesvár.

Petrarch (Italian *Petrarca*) Francesco 1304–1374. Italian poet, born in Arezzo, a devotee of the Classical tradition. His *Il Canzoniere* were sonnets in praise of his idealized love 'Laura', whom he first saw 1327. She was a married woman, who refused to become his mistress and died of plague 1348.

Petrie (William Matthew) Flinders 1853–1942. English archaeologist, who excavated sites in Egypt (the pyramids at Giza, the temple at Tanis, the Greek city of Naucratis in the Nile delta, Tell el Amarna, Naquada, Abydos, and Memphis) and Palestine from 1880. He was a grandson of the explorer Matthew Flinders.

Pevsner Nikolaus 1902–1983. Anglo-German art historian. Born in Leipzig, he fled from the Nazis to England. He became an authority on architecture, especially English. In his series *The Buildings of England* 1951–74, he achieved a first-hand report on every notable building in the country.

Phaedrus c. 15 BC–c. AD 50. Roman fable writer, born in Macedonia. He was born a slave and freed by Augustus. The allusions in his fables (modelled on those of Aesop) caused him to be brought to trial by a minister of Tiberius. He was popular in medieval times.

Phalaris 570–554 BC. Tyrant of the Greek colony of Acragas (Argrigento) in Sicily. He is said to have built a hollow bronze bull in which his victims were roasted alive. He was killed in a people's revolt.

The *Letters of Phalaris* attributed to him were proved by the scholar Richard ◊Bentley to be a forgery of the 2nd century AD.

Phidias mid-5th century BC. Greek sculptor, one of the most influential of classical times. He supervised the sculptural programme for the Parthenon (most of it preserved in the British Museum, London, and known as the *Elgin marbles*). He also executed the colossal statue of Zeus at Olympia, one of the Seven Wonders of the World.

Philby Harry St John Bridger 1885–1960. British explorer. As chief of the British political mission to central Arabia 1917–18, he was the first European to visit the southern provinces of Najd. He wrote *The Empty Quarter* 1933, and *Forty Years in the Wilderness* 1957.

Philby 'Kim' (Harold) 1912–1988. British intelligence officer from 1940 and Soviet agent from 1933. He was liaison officer in Washington 1949–51, when he was asked to resign. Named in 1963 as having warned Guy Burgess and Donald Maclean (similarly double agents) that their activities were known, he fled to the USSR, and became a Soviet citizen and general in the KGB. A fourth member of the ring was Anthony ◊Blunt.

Philip Duke of Edinburgh 1921– . Prince of the UK, husband of Elizabeth II, and a grandson of George I of Greece and a great-great-grandson of Queen Victoria. He was born in Corfu, raised in England, and educated at Gordonstoun and Dartmouth Naval College. During World War II he served in the Mediterranean, taking part in the battle of Matapan, and in the Pacific.

A naturalized British subject, taking the surname Mountbatten Mar 1947, he married Princess Elizabeth in Westminster Abbey 20 Nov 1947, having the previous day received the title Duke of Edinburgh. In 1956 he founded the Duke of Edinburgh's Award Scheme to encourage creative achievement among young people.

Philip six kings of France, including:

Philip II (Philip Augustus) 1165–1223. King of France from 1180. He waged war in turn against the English kings Henry II, Richard I (with whom he also went on the Third Crusade), and John (against whom he won the decisive battle of Bouvines in Flanders 1214) to evict them from their French possessions, and establish a strong monarchy.

Philip IV *the Fair* 1268–1314. King of France from 1285. He engaged in a feud with Pope Boniface VIII, and made him a prisoner 1303. Clement V (1264–1314), elected pope through Philip's influence, moved to Avignon, and collaborated with Philip to suppress the Templars, a powerful order of knights. Philip allied with the Scots against England, and invaded Flanders.

Philip VI 1293–1350. King of France from 1328, first of the house of Valois, elected by the barons on the death of his cousin, Charles IV. His claim was challenged by Edward III of England, who defeated him at Crécy 1346.

Philip II of Macedon 382–336 BC. King of Macedonia from 359 BC. He seized the throne from his nephew, for whom he was regent, conquered the Greek city states, and formed them into a league whose forces could be united against Persia. He was assassinated while he was planning this expedition, and was succeeded by his son ◊Alexander the Great. His tomb was discovered at Vergina, N Greece, in 1978.

Philip five kings of Spain, including:

Philip I *the Handsome* 1478–1506. King of Castile from 1504, through his marriage 1496 to Joanna the Mad (1479–1555). He was the son of the Holy Roman emperor Maximilian I.

Philip II 1527–1598. King of Spain from 1556. He was born at Valladolid, the son of the Habsburg emperor Charles V, and in 1554 married Queen Mary of England. On his father's abdication 1556 he inherited Spain, the Netherlands, and the Spanish possessions in Italy and the Americas, and in 1580 annexed Portugal. His intolerance and lack of understanding of the Netherlanders drove them into revolt. Political and religious reasons combined to involve him in war with England and, after 1589, with France. The defeat of the Spanish Armada invasion fleet marked the beginning of the decline of Spanish power.

Philip V 1683–1746. King of Spain from 1700. A grandson of Louis XIV of France, he was the first Bourbon king of Spain. He was not recognized by the major European powers until 1713.

Philip Neri, St 1515–1595. Italian Roman Catholic priest who organized the Congregation of the Oratory, the order of secular Roman Catholic priests. He built the oratory over the church of St Jerome, Rome, where prayer meetings were held and scenes from the Bible performed with music, originating the musical form oratorio. Feast day 26 May.

Philip, St 1st century AD. In the New Testament, one of the 12 apostles. He was an inhabitant of Bethsaida (N Israel), and is said to have worked as a missionary in Anatolia. Feast day 3 May.

Philip the Good 1396–1467. Duke of Burgundy from 1419. He engaged in the Hundred Years' War as an ally of England until he made peace with the French at the Council of Arras 1435. He made the Netherlands a centre of art and learning.

Phillip Arthur 1738–1814. British vice admiral, founder and governor of the convict settlement at Sydney, Australia, 1788–1792, and hence founder of New South Wales.

Phillipa of Hainault 1311–1369. Daughter of William III Count of Holland; wife of King Edward III of England, whom she married in York Minster 1328, and by whom she had 12 children (including Edward the Black Prince, Lionel Duke of Clarence, John Duke of Lancaster, Edmund Duke of York, and Thomas Duke of Gloucester). She was admired for her clemency and successfully pleaded for the lives of the six burghers of Calais who surrendered to to save the town from destruction 1347.

Philips Anton 1874–1951. Dutch industrialist and founder of electronics firm. The Philips Bulb and Radio Works was founded by Gerard Philips at Eindhoven 1891. Anton, his brother served as chairman of the company 1921–51, during which time the firm became the largest producer of electrical goods outside the USA.

Philo Judaeus 1st century AD. Jewish philosopher of Alexandria, who in AD 40 undertook a mission to Caligula to protest against the emperor's claim to divine honours. In his writings Philo Judaeus attempts to reconcile Judaism with Platonic and Stoic ideas.

Phiz pseudonym of Hablot Knight Browne 1815–1882. British artist. He illustrated the greater part of the *Pickwick Papers* and other works by Dickens.

Piaf Edith. Stage name of Edith Gassion 1915–1963. French Parisian singer and songwriter, best known for her defiant song 'Je ne regrette rien/I Regret Nothing'.

Piaget Jean 1896–1980. Swiss psychologist noted for his studies of the development of thought, concepts of space and movement, logic and reasoning in children.

Piano Renzo 1937– . Italian architect who designed (with Richard ◊Rogers) the Pompidou Centre, Paris, completed 1977. Among his other buildings are the Kansai Airport, Osaka, Japan and a sports stadium in Bari, Italy, both using new materials and making imaginative use of civil-engineering techniques.

Piazzi Giuseppe 1746–1826. Italian astronomer, director of Palermo Observatory. In 1801 he discovered the first asteroid to be found, which he named Ceres.

Picabia Francis 1879–1953. French painter, a Cubist from 1909. On his second visit to New York, 1915–16, he joined with Marcel ◊Duchamp in the Dadaist revolt and later took the movement to Barcelona. He associated with the Surrealists for a time. His work was generally provocative and experimental.

Picasso Pablo 1881–1973. Spanish artist, active chiefly in France, one of the most inventive and prolific talents in 20th century art. His Blue Period 1901–04 and Rose Period 1905–06 preceded the revolutionary *Les Demoiselles d'Avignon* 1907 (Metropolitan Museum of Art, New York), which paved the way for Cubism. In the early 1920s he was considered a leader of the Surrealist movement. In the 1930s his work included metal sculpture, book illustration, and the mural *Guernica* 1937 (Casón del Buen Retiro, Madrid), a comment on the bombing of civilians in the Spanish Civil War. He continued to paint into his 80s.

Born in Málaga, son of an art teacher, José Ruiz Blasco, and an Andalusian mother, Maria Picasso López; he discontinued use of the name Ruiz in 1898. He was a mature artist at ten, and at 16 was holding his first exhibition. In 1900 he made an initial visit to Paris, where he was to settle. From 1946 he lived mainly in the south of France, where, in addition to painting prolifically, he experimented with ceramics, sculpture, sets for ballet (for example *Parade* in 1917 for Diaghilev), book illustrations (such as Ovid's *Metamorphoses*), and portraits (Stravinsky, Valéry, and others).

Piccard August 1884–1962. Swiss scientist. In 1931–32, he and his twin brother *Jean Félix* (1884–1963) made ascents to 17,000 m/55,000 ft in a balloon of his own design, resulting in important discoveries about the level of cosmic rays (streams of atomic particles from outer space) in the stratosphere. He also built and used, with his son *Jacques Ernest* (1922–), bathyscaphes for research under the sea.

Pickford Mary. Adopted name of Gladys Smith 1893–1979. US silent film actress, born in Toronto, Canada. As a child she toured with various road companies, started her film career 1909, and in 1919 formed United Artists with Charlie Chaplin, D W Griffith, and her second husband (1920–36) Douglas Fairbanks. She often appeared as a young girl, even when she was well into her twenties. The public did not like her talking films, and she retired 1933. She was known as 'America's Sweetheart'.

Pico della Mirandola Count Giovanni 1463–1494. Italian mystic philosopher. Born at Mirandola, of

which his father was prince, he studied Hebrew, Chaldean, and Arabic, showing particular interest in the Jewish and theosophical system, the Kabbala. His attempt to reconcile the religious base of Christianity, Islam, and the ancient world earned Pope Alexander VI's disapproval.

Pieck Wilhelm 1876–1960. German communist politician. He was a leader of the 1919 Spartacist revolt and a founder of the Socialist Unity Party 1946. From 1949 he was president of East Germany; the office was abolished on his death.

Piercy Marge 1937– . US novelist. Her fiction looks at social life and the world of the liberated woman. Novels include the utopian *Woman on the Edge of Time* 1979 and *Fly Away Home* 1984.

Piero della Francesca c. 1420–1492. Italian painter, active in Arezzo and Urbino. His work has a solemn stillness and unusually solid figures, luminous colour and compositional harmony. It includes a fresco series, *The Legend of the True Cross* (S Francesco, Arezzo), begun about 1452. Piero wrote two treatises, one on mathematics, one on the laws of perspective in painting.

Piero di Cosimo c. 1462–1521. Italian painter, noted for inventive pictures of mythological subjects, often featuring fauns and centaurs. He also painted portraits.

Pietro (Berrettini) da Cortona 1596–1669. Italian painter and architect, a major influence in the development of Roman High Baroque. His huge fresco *Allegory of Divine Providence* 1633–39 (Barberini Palace, Rome) glorifies his patron the pope and the Barberini family, and gives a convincing illusion of reality.

Pigalle Jean Baptiste 1714–1785. French sculptor. In 1744 he made the marble *Mercury* (Louvre, Paris), a lively, naturalistic work. His subjects ranged from the intimate to the formal, and included portraits.

Pigalle studied in Rome 1736–39. In Paris he gained the patronage of Madame de Pompadour, the mistress of Louis XV. His works include *Venus, Love and Friendship* 1758 (Louvre), and the grandiose *Tomb of Marechal de Saxe* 1753 (Strasbourg).

Piggott Lester 1935– . English jockey. He was regarded as a brilliant tactician and adopted a unique high riding style. A champion jockey 11 times 1960–1982, he rode a record nine Derby winners.

He was associated with such great horses as Nijinsky, Sir Ivor, Roberto, Empery, and The Minstrel. Piggott won all the major races including all the English classics. He retired from riding 1985 and took up training. In 1987 he was imprisoned for tax evasion.

Pigou Arthur Cecil 1877–1959. British economist, whose notion of the 'real balance effect' (the '*Pigou effect*') contended that employment was stimulated by a fall in prices, because the latter increased liquid wealth and thus demand for goods and services.

Pilate Pontius early 1st century AD. Roman procurator of Judaea AD 26–36. Unsympathetic to the Jews, his actions several times provoked riots, and in AD 36 he was recalled to Rome after brutal suppression of a Samaritan uprising. The New Testament Gospels describe his reluctant ordering of Jesus' crucifixion, but there has been considerable debate about his actual role in it; many believe that pressure was put on him by Jewish conservative priests. The Greek historian Eusebius says he committed suicide, but Coptic tradition says he was martyred as a Christian.

Pilsudski Joseph 1867–1935. Polish nationalist politician, dictator from 1926. Born in Russian Poland, he founded the Polish Socialist Party 1892, and was twice imprisoned for anti-Russian activities. During World War I he commanded a Polish force to fight for Germany, but fell under suspicion of intriguing with the Allies, and in 1917–18 was imprisoned by the Germans. When Poland became independent he was elected chief of state, and led an unsuccessful Polish attack on the USSR 1920. He retired 1923, but in 1926 led a military coup which established his dictatorship until his death.

Pincus Gregory Goodwin 1903–1967. US biologist who together with Min Chueh Chang and John Rock developed the contraceptive pill in the 1950s.

As a result of studying the physiology of reproduction, Pincus conceived the idea of using synthetic hormones to mimic the condition of pregnancy in women. This effectively prevents impregnation.

Pindar c.552–442 BC. Greek poet, born near Thebes. He is noted for his choral lyrics, 'Pindaric Odes', written in honour of victors of athletic games.

Pindling Lynden (Oscar) 1930– . Bahamian prime minister from 1967. After studying law in London, he returned to the island to join the newly formed Progressive Liberal Party, and then became the first black prime minister of the Bahamas.

Pinero Arthur Wing 1855–1934. British dramatist. A leading exponent of the 'well-made' play, he enjoyed huge contemporary success with his farces, beginning with *The Magistrate* 1885. More substantial social drama followed with *The Second Mrs Tanqueray* 1893, and comedies including *Trelawny of the 'Wells'* 1898.

Pinkerton Allan 1819–1884. US detective, born in Glasgow. In 1852 he founded *Pinkerton's National Detective Agency*, and built up the federal secret service from the espionage system he developed during the US Civil War.

Pinochet (Ugarte) Augusto 1915– . Military ruler of Chile from 1973, when a CIA-backed coup ousted and killed president Salvador Allende. Pinochet took over the presidency and ruled ruthlessly, crushing all opposition. He was voted out of power when general elections were held in 1989 but remains head of the armed forces until 1997.

Pinter Harold 1930– . English writer, originally an actor. He specializes in the tragicomedy of the breakdown of communication, broadly in the tradition of the Theatre of the Absurd (which sought to express the meaningless nature of existence), for example *The Birthday Party* 1958 and *The Caretaker* 1960. Later plays include *The Homecoming* 1965, *Old Times* 1971, *Betrayal* 1978, and *Mountain Language* 1988.

Pinter's work is known for its pauses, allowing the audience to read between the lines. He writes for radio and television, and his screenplays include *The Go-Between* 1969 and *The French Lieutenant's Woman* 1982.

Pinturicchio or *Pintoricchio*. Pseudonym of Bernardino di Betti c.1454–1513. Italian painter, active in Rome, Perugia, and Siena. His chief works are the frescoes in the Borgia Apartments in the Vatican, 1490s, and in the Piccolomini Library of Siena Cathedral, 1503–08.

Piozzi Hester Lynch (born Salusbury) 1741–1821. Welsh writer. She published *Anecdotes of the late Samuel Johnson* 1786 and their correspondence 1788. Johnson had been a constant visitor to her house in Streatham, London, when she was married to her first husband, Henry Thrale, but after Thrale's death Johnson was alienated by her marriage to the musician Gabriel Piozzi. *Thraliana*, her diaries and notebooks of the years 1766–1809, was published 1942.

Piper John 1903– . British painter and designer. He painted mostly traditional Romantic views of landscape and architecture. As an official war artist he painted damaged buildings. He also designed theatre sets and stained-glass windows (Coventry Cathedral; Catholic Cathedral, Liverpool).

Pirandello Luigi 1867–1936. Italian writer. The novel *Il fu Mattia Pascal/The Late Mattia Pascal* 1904 was highly acclaimed, along with many short stories. His plays include *La Morsa/The Vice* 1912, *Sei personaggi in cerca d'autore/Six Characters in Search of an Author* 1921, and *Enrico IV/Henry IV* 1922. The theme and treatment of his plays anticipated the work of Brecht, O'Neill, Anouilh, and Genet. Nobel Prize for Literature 1934.

Piranesi Giambattista 1720–1778. Italian architect, most influential for his powerful etchings of Roman antiquities and as a theorist of architecture, advocating imaginative use of Roman models. Only one of his designs was built, Sta Maria del Priorato, Rome.

Pirquet Clemens von 1874–1929. Austrian paediatrician and pioneer in the study of allergy.

Pisanello nickname of Antonio Pisano c. 1395–1455/56. Italian artist active in Verona, Venice, Naples, Rome, and elsewhere. His panel paint-

Pisano

ings reveal a rich International Gothic style; his frescoes are largely lost. He was also an outstanding portrait medallist.

Pisano Andrea *c.*1290–1348. Italian sculptor, who made the earliest bronze doors for the Baptistery of Florence Cathedral, completed 1336.

Pisano *Nicola* (died *c.* 1284) and his son *Giovanni* (died after 1314). Italian sculptors. They made decorated marble pulpits in churches in Pisa, Siena, and Pistoia. Giovanni also created figures for Pisa's baptistery and designed the façade of Siena Cathedral.

Pisistratus *c.*605–527 BC. Athenian politician. Although of noble family, he assumed the leadership of the peasant party, and seized power 561 BC. He was twice expelled, but recovered power from 541 BC until his death. Ruling as a dictator under constitutional forms, he was the first to have the Homeric poems written down, and founded Greek drama by introducing the Dionysiac peasant festivals into Athens.

Pissarro Camille 1831–1903. French Impressionist painter, born in the West Indies. He went to Paris in 1855, met Corot, then Monet, and soon became a leading member of the Impressionist group. He experimented with various styles, including Pointillism (in which tones are built up from little dots of pure colour), in the 1880s.

His son *Lucien Pissarro* (1863–1944) worked in the same style for a time; he settled in the UK from 1890.

Piston Walter (Hamor) 1894–1976. US composer and teacher. He wrote a number of textbooks, including *Harmony* 1941 and *Orchestration* 1955. His Neo-Classical works include eight symphonies, a number of concertos, chamber music, the orchestral suite *Three New England Sketches* 1959, and the ballet *The Incredible Flautist* 1938.

Pitman Isaac 1813–1897. English teacher and inventor of *Pitman's shorthand*. He studied Samuel Taylor's scheme for shorthand writing, and in 1837 published his own system, *Stenographic Soundhand*, fast and accurate, and adapted for use in many languages.

A simplified Pitman Script, combining letters and signs, was devised 1971 by Emily D Smith. His grandson *(Isaac) James Pitman* (1901–85) devised the 44-letter Initial Teaching Alphabet in the 1960s to help children to read.

Pitt William, *the Elder*, 1st Earl of Chatham 1708–1778. British Whig politician, 'the Great Commoner'. As paymaster of the forces 1746–55, he broke with tradition by refusing to enrich himself; he was dismissed for attacking Newcastle, the prime minister. He served effectively as prime minister in coalition governments 1756–61, successfully conducting the Seven Years' War, and 1766–68.

Entering Parliament 1735, Pitt led the Patriot faction opposed to the Whig prime minister Walpole

Pitt *William Pitt the Younger entered Parliament at the age of 22 and two years later became England's youngest prime minister.*

and attacked Walpole's successor, Carteret, for his conduct of the War of the Austrian Succession. Recalled by popular demand to form a government on the outbreak of the Seven Years' War 1756, he was forced to form a coalition with Newcastle 1757. A 'year of victories' ensued 1759, and the French were expelled from India and Canada. In 1761 Pitt wished to escalate the war by a declaration of war on Spain, George III disagreed and Pitt resigned, but was again recalled to form an all-party government 1766. He championed the Americans against the king, though rejecting independence, and collapsed during his last speech in the House of Lords – opposing the withdrawal of British troops – and died a month later.

Pitt William, *the Younger* 1759–1806. British Tory prime minister 1783–1801 and 1804–06. He raised the importance of the House of Commons and clamped down on corruption, carried out fiscal reforms and union with Ireland. He attempted to keep Britain at peace but underestimated the importance of the French Revolution and became embroiled in wars with France from 1793; he died on hearing of Napoleon's victory at Austerlitz.

Son of William Pitt the Elder, he entered Cambridge University at 14 and Parliament at 22. He was the Whig Shelburne's chancellor of the Exchequer 1782–83, and with the support of the Tories and king's friends became Britain's youngest prime minister 1783. He reorganized the country's finances and negotiated reciprocal tariff reduction with France. In 1793, however, the new French republic declared war and England fared badly. His policy in Ireland led to the 1798 revolt, and he tried to solve the Irish question by the Act of Union 1800, but George III rejected the Catholic emancipation Pitt had promised as a condition, and Pitt resigned 1801.

On his return to office 1804, he organized an alliance with Austria, Russia, and Sweden against Napoleon, which was shattered at Austerlitz. In declining health, he died on hearing the news, saying: 'Oh, my country! How I leave my country!' He was buried in Westminster Abbey.

Pitt-Rivers Augustus Henry 1827–1900. English general and archaeologist. He made a series of model archaeological excavations on his estate in Wiltshire, England, being among the first to recognize the value of everyday objects as well as art treasures.

Pius twelve popes, including:

Pius IV 1499–1565. Pope from 1559, of the Medici family. He reassembled the Council of Trent to continue the work of the Counter-Reformation, reforming the Catholic church in response to the Protestant Reformation, and completed its work 1563.

Pius V 1504–1572. Pope from 1566, who excommunicated Elizabeth I of England, and organized the naval expedition against the Turks that won the battle of Lepanto.

Pius VI (Giovanni Angelo Braschi) 1717–1799. Pope from 1775. He strongly opposed the French Revolution, and died a prisoner in French hands.

Pius VII 1742–1823. Pope from 1800. He concluded a concordat (agreement) with France 1801 and took part in Napoleon's coronation, but relations became strained. Napoleon annexed the papal states, and Pius was imprisoned 1809–14. After his return to Rome 1814 he revived the Jesuit order.

Pius IX 1792–1878. Pope from 1846. He never accepted the incorporation of the Papal States and of Rome in the kingdom of Italy, and proclaimed the dogmas of the Immaculate Conception of the Virgin 1854 and papal infallibility 1870; his pontificate was the longest in history.

Pius X (Giuseppe Melchiore Sarto) 1835–1914. Pope from 1903, canonized 1954, who condemned Modernism (the modification of doctrine in the light of modern thought) in a manifesto 1907.

Pius XI (Achille Ratti) 1857–1939. Pope from 1922, he signed a concordat (agreement) with Mussolini 1929.

Pius XII (Eugenio Pacelli) 1876–1958. Pope from 1939. He proclaimed the dogma of the bodily assumption of the Virgin Mary 1950 and in 1951 restated the doctrine (strongly criticized by many) that the life of an infant must not be sacrificed to save a mother in labour. He was also widely criticized for failing to speak out against atrocities

committed by the Germans during World War II.

Pizarro Francisco c.1475–1541. Spanish conquistador who took part in the expeditions of Balboa and others. In 1526–27 he explored the NW coast of South America, and conquered Peru 1531 with 180 followers. The Inca king Atahualpa was seized and murdered. In 1535 Pizarro founded Lima. Internal feuding led to Pizarro's assassination.

His half-brother **Gonzalo Pizarro** (c.1505–1548) explored the region east of Quito 1541–42. He made himself governor of Peru 1544, but was defeated and executed.

Plaatje Solomon 1876–1932. Pioneer South African writer and nationalist who was the first secretary-general and founder of the African National Congress 1912, which sought an end to racism and the enfranchisement of non-whites.

Place Francis 1771–1854. English Radical. He showed great powers as a political organizer, and made Westminster a centre of Radicalism. He secured the repeal of the anti-union Combination Acts 1824.

Planck Max 1858–1947. German physicist who framed the quantum theory 1900.

He was appointed to the chair of physics at Kiel 1885 and Berlin 1889. Much of his early work was in thermodynamics. From 1930 to 1937, he was president of the Kaiser Wilhelm Institute. He was awarded the Nobel Prize for Physics 1918, and became a Fellow of the Royal Society in 1926.

Plath Sylvia 1932–1963. US poet and novelist. Plath's powerful, highly personal poems, often expressing a sense of desolation, are distinguished by their intensity and sharp imagery. Collections include *The Colossus* 1960, *Ariel* 1965, published after her death, and *Collected Poems* 1982. Her autobiographical novel, *The Bell Jar* 1961, deals with the events surrounding a young woman's emotional breakdown.

Born in Boston, Massachusetts, she attended Smith College and was awarded a Fulbright scholarship to study at Cambridge University, England, where she met the poet Ted Hughes, whom she married 1956; they separated in 1962. She committed suicide while living in London.

Plato c.428–347 BC. Greek philosopher, pupil of Socrates, teacher of Aristotle, and founder of the Academy. He was the author of philosophical dialogues on such topics as metaphysics, ethics, and politics. Central to his teachings is the notion of Forms, which are located outside the everyday world, timeless, motionless, and absolutely real.

His philosophy has influenced Christianity and European culture, directly and through Augustine, the Florentine Platonists during the Renaissance, and countless others.

Born of a noble family, he entered politics on the aristocratic side, and in philosophy became a follower of Socrates. He travelled widely after Socrates's death, and founded the educational establishment, the Academy, in order to train a new ruling class.

Of his work, some 30 dialogues survive, intended for performance either to his pupils or to the public. The principal figure in these ethical and philosophical debates is Socrates and the early ones employ the *Socratic method*, in which he asks questions and traps the students into contradicting themselves: for example, *Iron*, on poetry. Other dialogues include the *Symposium*, on love, *Phaedo*, on immortality, and *Apology and Crito*, on Socrates' trial and death. It is impossible to say whether Plato's Socrates is a faithful representative of the real man or an articulation of Plato's own thought. Plato's philosophy rejects scientific rationalism (establishing facts through experiment) in favour of arguments, because mind, not matter, is fundamental, and material objects are merely imperfect copies of abstract and eternal 'ideas'. His political philosophy is expounded in two treatises, *The Republic* and *The Laws*, both of which describe ideal states.

Plautus *c*.254–184 BC. Roman dramatist, born in Umbria, who settled in Rome and worked in a bakery before achieving success as a dramatist. He wrote at least 56 comedies, freely adapted from Greek originals, of which 20 survive. Shakespeare based *The Comedy of Errors* on his *Menaechmi*.

Player Gary 1935– . South African golfer, who won major championships in three decades and the first British Open 1959. A match-play specialist, he won the world title five times.

His total of nine 'majors' is the fourth (equal) best of all time.

Playfair William Henry 1790–1857. Scottish Neo-Classical architect responsible for much of the design of Edinburgh New Town in the early 19th century. His Royal Scottish Academy 1822 and National Gallery of Scotland 1850 in Greek style helped to make Edinburgh the 'Athens of the North'.

Pleasance Donald 1919– . English actor. He has been acclaimed for roles in Pirandello's *The Rules of the Game*, in Pinter's *The Caretaker*, and also in the title role of the film *Dr Crippen* 1962, conveying the sinister aspect of the outcast from society. Other films include *THX 1138* 1971 and *The Eagle has Landed* 1976.

Plekhanov Georgi Valentinovich 1857–1918. Russian Marxist revolutionary and theorist, founder of the Menshevik party. He led the first populist demonstration in St Petersburg, and left for exile 1880. He became a Marxist and, with Lenin, edited the newspaper *Iskra* ('spark'). In 1903 his opposition to Lenin led to the Bolshevik-Menshevik split. In 1917 he returned to Russia.

Plethon George Gemisthos 1353–1452. Byzantine philosopher, who taught for many years at Mistra in Asia Minor. A Platonist, he maintained a resolutely anti-Christian stance, and was the inspira-

tion for many of the ideas of the 15th-century Florentine Platonic Academy.

Plimsoll Samuel 1824–1898. English social reformer, born in Bristol. He sat in Parliament as a Radical 1868–80, and through his efforts the Merchant Shipping Act was passed in 1876, providing for Board of Trade inspection of ships, and the compulsory painting of a *Plimsoll line* to indicate safe loading limits.

Pliny the Elder (Gaius Plinius Secundus) *c*. AD 23–79. Roman scientist and historian; only his works on astronomy, geography, and natural history survive. He was killed in an eruption of Vesuvius.

Pliny the Younger (Gaius Plinius Caecilius Secundus) *c*.61–113. Roman administrator, nephew of Pliny the Elder, whose correspondence is of great interest. Among his surviving letters are those describing the eruption of Vesuvius, his uncle's death, and his correspondence with the emperor ◊Trajan.

Plisetskaya Maya 1925– . Soviet ballerina and actress. She attended the Moscow Bolshoi Ballet School and succeeded Ulanova as prima ballerina of the Bolshoi Ballet.

Plomer William 1903–1973. South African novelist, author of *Turbot Wolfe*, an early criticism of South African attitudes to race. He settled in London in 1929, and wrote two autobiographical volumes.

Plutarch *c*. AD 46–120. Greek biographer, born at Chaeronea. He lectured on philosophy at Rome, and was appointed procurator of Greece by Hadrian. His *Parallel Lives* comprise biographies of pairs of Greek and Roman soldiers and politicians, followed by comparisons between the two. Thomas North's 1579 translation inspired Shakespeare's Roman plays.

Pocahontas *c*.1595–1617. American Indian princess alleged to have saved the life of John Smith, the English colonist, when he was captured by her father Powhatan. She married an Englishman, and has many modern US descendants. She died in Gravesend, Kent.

Poe Edgar Allan 1809–1849. US writer and poet. His short stories are renowned for their horrific atmosphere (as in 'The Fall of the House of Usher' 1839) and acute reasoning (for example, 'The Gold Bug' 1843 and 'The Murders in the Rue Morgue' 1841, in which the investigators Legrand and Dupin anticipate Conan Doyle's Sherlock Holmes). His poems include 'The Raven' 1844. His novel, *The Narrative of Arthur Gordon Pym of Nantucket* 1838, has attracted critical attention recently.

Born in Boston, he was orphaned 1811, and joined the army but was court-martialled for neglect of duty. He failed to earn a living by writing, became addicted to alcohol, and in 1847 lost his wife (commemorated in his poem *Annabel Lee*). His verse, of haunting lyric beauty, influenced the French Symbolists (for example, *Ulalume* and *The Bells*).

Poincaré Jules Henri 1854–1912. French mathematician, who developed the theory of differential equations and was a pioneer in relativity theory. He also published the first paper devoted entirely to topology.

Poincaré Raymond Nicolas Landry 1860–1934. French politician, prime minister 1912–13, president 1913–20, and again prime minister 1922–24 (when he ordered the occupation of the Ruhr, Germany) and 1926–29. He was a cousin of the mathematician Jules Henri Poincaré.

Poindexter John Marlan 1936–   . US rear admiral and Republican government official. In 1981 he joined the Reagan administration's National Security Council (NSC) and became national security adviser 1985. As a result of the Irangate scandal, centring on clandestine sales of arms to Iran, Poindexter was forced to resign 1986, along with his assistant, Oliver North.

He worked closely with the NSC head, Robert McFarlane from 1983, and took over when McFarlane left Dec 1985. Poindexter was prosecuted on charges arising out of Irangate, and was found guilty on all counts Apr 1990.

Poisson Siméon Denis 1781–1840. French applied mathematician. In probability theory he discovered the *Poisson distribution* which is widely used in probability calculations. He published four main treatises and several hundred papers on many aspects of physics, including mechanics, heat, electricity and magnetism, elasticity (*Poisson's ratio* is a measure of the elastic properties of a material) and astronomy.

Poitier Sidney 1924–   . US actor and film director, the first black actor to become a star in Hollywood. His films as an actor included *In the Heat of the Night* 1967, and as director *Stir Crazy* 1980.

Polanski Roman 1933–   . Polish film director, born in Paris. He suffered a traumatic childhood in Nazi-occupied Poland, and later his wife, actress Sharon Tate, was the victim of murder by the Charles Manson 'family'. His tragic personal life is reflected in a fascination with horror and violence in his work. His films include *Repulsion* 1965, *Cul de Sac* 1966, *Rosemary's Baby* 1968, *Tess* 1979, and *Frantic* 1988.

Pole Reginald 1500–1558. English cardinal from 1536, who returned from Rome as papal legatee on the accession of Mary in order to readmit England to the Catholic church. He succeeded Cranmer as archbishop of Canterbury 1556.

Politian (Angelo Poliziano). Pen name of Angelo Ambrogini 1454–1494. Italian poet, playwright, and exponent of humanist ideals; he was tutor to Lorenzo de ◊Medici's children, professor at the University of Florence, and wrote commentaries and essays on classical authors.

Polk James Knox 1795–1849. 11th president of the USA from 1845, a Democrat, born in North Carolina. He admitted Texas to the Union, and forced the war on Mexico that resulted in the annexation of California and New Mexico.

Pollaiuolo Antonio *c.* 1432–1498 and Piero *c.* 1441–1496. Italian artists, active in Florence. Both brothers were painters, sculptors, goldsmiths, engravers, and designers. The *Martyrdom of St Sebastian* 1475 (National Gallery, London) is considered a joint work.

The best-known individual works are Piero's set of *Virtues* in Florence and Antonio's engraving *The Battle of the Nude Gods* about 1465. Antonio's work places a strong emphasis on the musculature of the human figure in various activities.

Pollock Jackson 1912–1956. US painter, a pioneer of Abstract Expressionism and the foremost exponent of the dripping and splashing technique known as *action painting*, a style he developed around 1946.

In the early 1940s Pollock moved from a vivid Expressionist style, influenced by Mexican muralists such as Siqueiros and by Surrealism, towards a semi-abstract style. He moved on to the more violently expressive abstract style, placing large canvases on the studio floor and dripping or hurling his paint on top of them. He was soon recognized as the leading Abstract Expressionist, and continued to develop his style, producing even larger canvases in the 1950s.

Polo Marco 1254–1324. Venetian traveller and writer. He travelled overland to China 1271–75, and served under the emperor Kublai Khan until he returned to Europe by sea 1292–95. He was then captured while fighting for Venice against Genoa, and in prison wrote an account of his travels.

Pol Pot (also known as Saloth Sar, Tol Saut, and Pol Porth) 1925–   . Cambodian politician and communist leader, in power 1975–79. He became a member of the anti-French resistance under Ho Chi Minh in the 1940s and a member of the communist party. As leader of the Khmer Rouge, he overthrew the government of General Lon Nol 1975 and proclaimed a republic of Democratic Kampuchea with himself as prime minister. The policies of the Pol Pot government were to evacuate cities and put people to work in the countryside. The Khmer Rouge also carried out a systematic extermination of the educated and middle classes before the regime was overthrown by a Vietnamese invasion 1979. Since then, Pol Pot has led a resistance group against the Vietnamese although he has been tried and convicted, in absentia, of genocide.

Polybius *c.* 201–120 BC. Greek politician and historian. He was involved with the Achaean League of Peloponnesian cities against the Romans and, following the defeat of the Macedonians at Pydna in 168 BC, he was taken as a political hostage to Rome. He returned to Greece in 151 and was present at the capture of Carthage by his friend Scipio in 146. His history of Rome in 40 books, covering the years 220–146, has largely disappeared.

Polycarp, St *c.*69–*c.*155. Christian martyr allegedly converted by St John the Evangelist. As bishop of Smyrna (modern Izmir, Turkey), for over 40 years he carried on a vigorous struggle against various heresies, and was burned alive at a public festival; feast day 26 Jan.

Polykleitos 5th century BC. Greek sculptor, whose *Spear Carrier* 450–440 BC (Roman copies survive) exemplifies the naturalism and harmonious proportions of his work. He created the legendary colossal statue of *Hera* in Argos, in ivory and gold.

Pompadour Jeanne Antoinette Poisson, Marquise de Pompadour 1721–1764. Mistress of ◊Louis XV of France from 1744, born in Paris. She largely dictated the government's ill-fated policy of reversing France's anti-Austrian policy for an anti-Prussian one. She acted as the patron of the Enlightenment philosophers Voltaire and Diderot.

Pompey the Great (Gnaeus Pompeius Magnus) 106–48 BC. Roman soldier and politician. Originally a supporter of ◊Sulla and the aristocratic party, he joined the democrats when he became consul with ◊Crassus 70 BC. He defeated ◊Mithridates VI of Pontus, and annexed Syria and Palestine. In 60 BC he formed the First Triumvirate with Julius ◊Caesar (whose daughter Julia he married) and Crassus, and when it broke down after 53 BC he returned to the aristocratic party. On the outbreak of civil war 49 BC he withdrew to Greece, was defeated by Caesar at Pharsalus 48 BC, and was murdered in Egypt.

Pompidou Georges 1911–1974. French conservative politician, president from 1969. An adviser on Gen de Gaulle's staff 1944–46, he held administrative posts until he became director-general of the French House of Rothschild 1954, and even then continued in close association with de Gaulle. In 1962 he became prime minister, but resigned after the Gaullist victory in the elections 1968, and was elected to the presidency on de Gaulle's resignation.

Ponce de León Juan *c.*1460–1521. Spanish soldier and explorer. He is believed to have sailed with Columbus 1493, and served 1502–04 in Hispaniola. He conquered Puerto Rico 1508, and was made governor 1509. In 1513 he was the first European to reach Florida.

He returned to Spain 1514 to report his 'discovery' of Florida (which he thought was an island), and was given permission by King Ferdinand to colonize it. In the attempt, he received an arrow wound of which he died in Cuba.

Poncelet Jean 1788–1867. French mathematician, who worked on projective geometry. His book

Traité des propriétés projectives des figures, started in 1814 and completed 1822, deals with the properties of plane figures unchanged when projected.

Pontiac *c.*1720–1769. North American Indian, chief of the Ottawa from 1755. In 1763–64 he led the 'Conspiracy of Pontiac' in an attempt to stop British encroachment on Indian lands. He achieved remarkable success against overwhelming odds, but eventually signed a peace treaty 1766, and was murdered by an Illinois Indian at the instigation of a British trader.

Pontormo Jacopo Carucci 1494–1557. Italian painter, active in Florence. He developed a dramatic Mannerist style, with lurid colours.

Pontormo worked in ◊Andrea del Sarto's workshop from 1512. An early work, *Joseph in Egypt* about 1515 (National Gallery, London), is already Mannerist. His mature style is demonstrated in *The Deposition* about 1525 (Sta Felicità, Florence), an extraordinary composition of interlocked figures, with rosy pinks, lime yellows, and pale apple greens illuminating the scene.

Pop Iggy. Stage name of James Osterberg 1947– . US rock singer and songwriter, initially known as *Iggy Stooge* with a seminal garage band called the Stooges (1967–74), noted for his self-destructive proto-punk performances.

Pope Alexander 1688–1744. English poet and satirist. He established his reputation with the precocious *Pastorals* 1709 and *Essay on Criticism* 1711, which were followed by a parody of the heroic epic *The Rape of the Lock* 1712–14, and 'Eloisa to Abelard' 1717. Other works include a

Pope English poet and satirist Alexander Pope. The painting is by William Hoare c.1739.

highly Neo-Classical translation of Homer's *Iliad* and *Odyssey* 1715–26.

He had a biting wit, which he expressed in the form of heroic couplets. As a Catholic, he was subject to discrimination, and his life was embittered by a deformity of the spine. The success of his translations made it possible for him to settle in Twickenham from 1719, but his edition of Shakespeare attracted scholarly ridicule, for which he revenged himself by a satire on scholarly dullness, the *Dunciad* 1728. His philosophy, including *An Essay on Man* 1733–34 and *Moral Essays* 1731–35, was influenced by ◊Bolingbroke. His finest mature productions are his *Imitations of the Satires of Horace* 1733–38 and his personal letters. Among his friends were the writers Swift, Arbuthnot, and Gay. His line 'A little learning is a dangerous thing' is often misquoted.

Popov Alexander 1859–1905. Russian physicist who devised the first aerial, in advance of ◊Marconi (although he did not use it for radio communication), and a detector for radio waves.

Popper Karl (Raimund) 1902– . Austrian philosopher of science. His theory of falsificationism says that although scientific generalizations cannot be conclusively verified, they can be conclusively falsified by a counterinstance, and therefore science is not certain knowledge, but a series of 'conjectures and refutations', approaching, though never reaching, a definitive truth. For Popper, psychoanalysis and Marxism are unfalsifiable and therefore unscientific.

His major work on the philosophy of science is *The Logic of Scientific Discovery* 1935. Other works include *The Poverty of Historicism* 1957 (about the philosophy of social science), *Conjectures and Refutations* 1963, and *Objective Knowledge* 1972.

Born and educated in Vienna, Popper was naturalized British 1945 and was professor of logic and scientific method at the London School of Economics 1949–69. He opposes Wittgenstein's view that philosophical problems are merely pseudo-problems. Popper's view of scientific practice has been criticized by T S ◊Kuhn and other writers.

Porritt Jonathon 1950– . British environmental campaigner, director of the environmental pressure group Friends of the Earth from 1984. He has stood for election in both British and European elections as an Ecology (Green) Party candidate.

Porsche Ferdinand 1875–1951. German car designer. Among his designs were the Volkswagen (German 'people's car'), marketed after World War II, and Porsche sports cars.

Porson Richard 1759–1808. British classical scholar, professor of Greek at Cambridge from 1792 and editor of ◊Aeschylus and ◊Euripides.

Porter Cole (Albert) 1892–1964. US composer and lyricist of musical comedies. His shows, many of which were made into films, include *The Gay Divorcee* 1932 and *Kiss Me Kate* 1948.

Porter Edwin Stanton 1869–1941. US director of silent films, a pioneer of his time. His 1903 film *The Great Train Robbery* lasted 12 minutes, which for the period was extremely long, and contained an early use of the close-up. More concerned with the technical than the artistic side of his films (others include *The Teddy Bears* 1907 and *The Final Pardon* 1912,) Porter abandoned filmmaking 1916.

Porter Eric 1928– . English actor. His numerous classical roles include title parts in *Uncle Vanya*, *Volpone*, and *King Lear*; on television he played Soames in *The Forsyte Saga*.

Porter Katherine Anne 1890–1980. US writer, born in Texas. She published three volume of short stories between 1930 and 1944, and the allegorical novel *Ship of Fools* 1962.

Porter Rodney Robert 1917–1985. British biochemist. In 1962 Porter proposed a structure for the antibody, gamma globulin (IgG) in which the molecule was seen as consisiting of four chains. Porter was awarded, with Gerald ◊Edelman, the 1972 Nobel Prize for Medicine.

Portland William Bentinck, 1st Earl of Portland 1649–1709. Dutch politician who accompanied William of Orange to England 1688, and was created an earl 1689. He served in William's campaigns.

Portland William Henry Cavendish Bentinck, 3rd Duke of Portland 1738–1809. British politician, originally a Whig, who in 1783 became nominal prime minister in the Fox–North coalition government. During the French Revolution he joined the Tories, and was prime minister 1807–09.

Portsmouth Louise de Kéroualle, Duchess of Portsmouth 1649–1734. Mistress of Charles II of Britain, a Frenchwoman who came to England as Louis XIV's agent 1670, and was hated by the public.

Potemkin Grigory Aleksandrovich, Prince Potemkin 1739–1791. Russian politician. He entered the army and attracted the notice of Catherine II, whose friendship he kept throughout his life. He was an active administrator who reformed the army, built the Black Sea Fleet, conquered the Crimea, and founded the Kherson arsenal 1788 (the first Russian naval base on the Black Sea).

Potter Beatrix 1866–1943. English writer and illustrator of children's books, beginning with *Peter Rabbit* 1900; her diaries, written in a secret code, were translated and published 1966. Her Lake District home is a museum.

Potter Paulus 1625–1654. Dutch painter, active in Delft, The Hague, and Amsterdam. He is known for paintings of animals, such as *The Young Bull* 1647 (Mauritshuis, The Hague).

Potter Stephen 1900–1969. British author of humorous studies in how to outwit and outshine others, including *Gamesmanship* 1947, *Lifemanship* 1950, and *One Upmanship* 1952.

Potter *Although she grew up in London, Beatrix Potter was always interested in nature. Her classic picture books began as a series of letters to children.*

Poulenc Francis (Jean Marcel) 1899–1963. French composer and pianist. A self-taught composer of witty and irreverent music, he was a member of the group of French composers known as Les Six. Among his many works are the operas *Les Mamelles de Tirésias* 1947, and *Dialogues des Carmèlites* 1957, and the ballet *Les Biches* 1923.

Poulsen Valdemar 1869–1942. Danish engineer who in 1900 was the first to demonstrate that sound could be recorded magnetically – originally on a moving steel wire or tape; this was the forerunner of the tape recorder.

Pound Ezra 1885–1972. US poet, who lived in London from 1908. His verse *Personae* and *Exultations* 1909 established the principles of the Imagist movement, with its emphasis on brevity and clarity. His largest Modern work was the series of *Cantos* 1925–1969 (intended to number 100), which attempted a massive reappraisal of history.

In Paris 1921–25, he was a friend of US writers Gertrude Stein and Hemingway, and then settled in Rapallo, Italy. His anti-Semitism and sympathy with the fascist dictator Mussolini led him to broadcast from Italy in World War II, and he was arrested by US troops 1945. Found unfit to plead, he was confined in a mental hospital until 1958.

His first completely Modern poem was *Hugh Selwyn Mauberley* 1920. He also wrote versions of Old English, Provençal, Chinese, ancient Egyptian, and other verse.

Poussin Nicolas 1594–1665. French painter, active chiefly in Rome; court painter to Louis XIII 1640–43. He was one of France's foremost landscape painters in the 17th century. He painted mythological and literary scenes in a strongly classical style, for example *Rape of the Sabine Women* about 1636–37 (Metropolitan Museum of Art, New York).

Poussin went to Rome 1624 and studied Roman sculpture in the studio of ◊Domenichino. His style reflects painstaking preparation: he made small wax models of the figures in his paintings, experimenting with different compositions and lighting.

Powell Anthony (Dymoke) 1905– . English novelist, who wrote the monumental series of 12 volumes *A Dance to the Music of Time* 1951–75, which begins shortly after World War I and chronicles a period of 50 years in the lives of Nicholas Jenkins and his circle of upper-class friends.

Powell Cecil Frank 1903–1969. English physicist, awarded a Nobel prize 1950 for his use of photographic emulsion as a method of tracking charged nuclear particles.

Powell (John) Enoch 1912– . British Conservative politician. He was minister of health 1960–63, and contested the party leadership 1965. In 1968 he made a speech against immigration that led to his dismissal from the shadow cabinet. He resigned from the party 1974, and was Official Unionist Party member for South Down, Northern Ireland 1974–87.

Powell Michael 1905–1990. English film director, who collaborated with screenwriter Emeric Pressburger (1902–88). Their work, often criticized for extravagance, is richly imaginative, and includes the films *A Matter of Life and Death* 1946, and *Black Narcissus* 1947.

Powell William 1892–1984. US film actor who co-starred with Myrna Loy in the *Thin Man* series of films 1934–1947. He also played leading roles in *My Man Godfrey* 1936, *Life with Father* 1947, and *Mister Roberts* 1955.

Powys John Cowper 1872–1963. English novelist. His mystic and erotic books include *Wolf Solent* 1929 and *A Glastonbury Romance* 1933. He was one of three brothers (***Theodore Francis Powys*** 1875–1953 and ***Llewelyn Powys*** 1884–1939), all writers.

Poynter Edward John 1836–1919. British artist, first head of the Slade School of Fine Art, London, 1871–75, and president of the Royal Academy in succession to ◊Millais. He produced decorous nudes, mosaic panels for Westminster Palace 1870, and scenes from ancient Greece and Rome.

Pozsgay Imre 1933– . Hungarian socialist politician, presidential candidate for the Hungarian Socialist Party from 1989. Influential in the democratization of Hungary 1988–89, he was rejected by the electorate in the parliamentary elections of Mar 1990, coming a poor third in his constituency.

Pozsgay joined the ruling Hungarian Socialist

Workers' Party (HSWP) 1950 and was a lecturer in Marxism-Leninism and an ideology chief in Bacs county 1957–70. He was minister of education and culture from 1976, before becoming head of the Patriotic People's Front umbrella organization 1982. Noted for his reformist social-democratic instincts, he was brought into the HSWP Politburo in 1988 as a move towards political pluralism began. Having publicly declared that 'communism does not work', he helped remould the HSWP into the new Hungarian Socialist Party 1989 and was selected as its candidate for the presidency.

Prasad Rajendra 1884–1963. Indian lawyer, politician, and follower of Mohandas Gandhi in Bihar. Prior to World War II, he succeeded Subhas Chandra Bose as national president of the Indian National Congress. He went on to become India's first president after independence.

Praxiteles mid-4th century BC. Greek sculptor, active in Athens. His *Aphrodite of Knidos* about 350 (known through Roman copies) is thought to have initiated the tradition of life-size freestanding female nudes in Greek sculpture.

Premadasa Ranasinghe 1924– . Sri Lankan politician, a United National Party member of parliament from 1960, prime minister from 1978, and president from 1988, having gained popularity through overseeing a major housebuilding and poverty-alleviation programme.

From a slum background and a member of the dhobi (laundryworkers') caste, Premadasa was elected deputy mayor of Colombo 1955. He served successively as minister of local government from 1968, UNP Chief Whip from 1970, and leader of the House from 1977, before being appointed prime minister. He was elected president Dec 1988. He opposed the 1987 Indo–Sri Lankan peace-keeping agreement aimed at solving the Tamil crisis.

Preminger Otto (Ludwig) 1906–1986. US film producer, director, and actor. Born in Vienna, he went to the USA 1935. He directed *Margin for Error* 1942, *Laura* 1944, *The Moon is Blue* 1953, *The Man With the Golden Arm* 1955, *Anatomy of a Murder* 1959, *Skidoo!* 1968, and *Rosebud* 1974. His films are characterized by an intricate technique of story-telling, and a masterly use of the wide screen and the travelling camera.

Prempeh I chief of the Ashanti people in W Africa. He became king 1888, and later opposed British attempts to take over the region. He was deported and in 1900 the Ashanti were defeated. He returned to Kumasi (capital of the Ashanti region) 1924 as chief of the people.

Prenderghast Maurice 1859–1924. US painter who created a decorative watercolour style, using small translucent pools of colour, inspired by the Impressionists.

He studied in Paris in the 1890s and was influenced by the Nabis painters (followers of Gaugin) Bonnard and Vuillard. *Umbrellas in the Rain, Venice* 1899 (Museum of Fine Arts, Boston, Massachusetts) is typical.

Prescott John Leslie 1938– . British Labour Party politician, a member of the ◊Kinnock shadow cabinet.

A former merchant seaman and trade-union official, he became member of Parliament for Hull East and, in 1975, a member of the European Parliament, despite being opposed to Britain's membership of the European Community. A strong parliamentary debater and television performer, he is sometimes critical of his colleagues. In 1988 he unsuccessfully challenged Roy Hattersley for the deputy leadership.

Prescott William Hickling 1796–1859. US historian, author of *History of the Reign of Ferdinand and Isabella, the Catholic* 1838, *History of the Conquest of Mexico* 1843, and *History of the Conquest of Peru* 1847.

Presley Elvis (Aaron) 1935–1977. US singer and guitarist, born in Tupelo, Mississippi. With his recordings for Sun Records in Memphis, Tennessee, 1954–55 and early hits such as 'Heartbreak Hotel' 1956, 'Hound Dog' 1956, and 'Love Me Tender' 1956, he created an individual vocal style, influenced by Southern blues, gospel music, country music, and rhythm and blues.

Pressburger Emeric 1902–1988. Hungarian director, producer, and screenwriter, known for his partnership with Michael ◊Powell.

Prester John legendary Christian prince who, in the 12th–13th centuries, was believed to rule a powerful empire in Asia. In the 14th–16th

Presley US Singer and guitarist Elvis Presley.

centuries, Prester John was identified with the king of Ethiopia.

Previn André (George) 1929– . US conductor and composer, born in Berlin. After a period working as a composer and arranger in the US film industry, he concentrated on conducting. He was principal conductor of the London Symphony Orchestra 1968–79. He was appointed music director of Britain's Royal Philharmonic Orchestra 1985 (a post he relinquished the following year, staying on as principal conductor), and of the Los Angeles Philharmonic in 1986.

Prévost d'Exiles Antoine François 1697–1763. French novelist, known as Abbé Prévost, who sandwiched a military career into his life as a monk. His *Manon Lescaut* 1731 inspired operas by Massenet and Puccini.

Price Vincent 1911– . US actor, star of horror films including *House of Wax* 1953 and *House of Usher* 1960.

Priestley J(ohn) B(oynton) 1894–1984. English novelist and playwright. His first success was a novel about travelling theatre, *The Good Companions* 1929. He followed it with a realist novel about London life, *Angel Pavement* 1930; later books include *Lost Empires* 1965 and *The Image Men* 1968. As a playwright he was often preoccupied with theories of time, as in *An Inspector Calls* 1945, but had also a gift for family comedy, for example, *When We Are Married* 1938.

He was also noted for his wartime broadcasts and literary criticism, such as *Literature and Western Man* 1960.

Priestley Joseph 1733–1804. English chemist, who identified oxygen 1774.

A Unitarian minister, he was elected Fellow of the Royal Society 1766. In 1791 his chapel and house in Birmingham were sacked by a mob because of his support for the French Revolution. In 1794 he emigrated to the USA.

Prigogine Ilya 1917– . Russian born Belgian chemist who, as a highly original theoretician, has made major contributions to the field of thermodynamics for which work he was awarded the Nobel physics prize 1977. Earlier theories had considered systems at or about equilibrium; Prigogine began to study 'dissapative' or non-equilibrium structures frequently found in biological and chemical reactions.

Primo de Rivera Miguel 1870–1930. Spanish soldier and politician, dictator from 1923 as well as premier from 1925. He was captain-general of Catalonia when he led a coup against the ineffective monarchy and became virtual dictator of Spain with the support of Alfonso XIII. He resigned 1930.

Prince (Harold) Hal 1928– . US director of musicals such as *Cabaret* 1968 and *Follies* 1971 on Broadway in New York, and *Evita* 1978 and *Sweeney Todd* 1980 in London's West End.

Prince stage name of Prince Rogers Nelson

1960– . US pop musician, who composes, arranges, and produces his own records, and often plays all the instruments. His albums, including *1999* 1982 and *Purple Rain* 1984, contain elements of rock, funk, and jazz.

Prior James 1927– . British Conservative politician. He held ministerial posts from 1970. As employment secretary he curbed trade-union activity with the Employment Act 1980, and was Northern Ireland secretary 1981–84. After his resignation 1984 he became chair of the General Electric Company (GEC).

Prior Matthew 1664–1721. British poet and diplomat. He was associated under the Whigs with the negotiation of the treaty of Ryswick 1697 ending the war with France and under the Tories with that of Utrecht 1714 ('Matt's Peace') ending the War of the Spanish Succession, but on the Whigs' return to power he was imprisoned by the government leader Walpole 1715–17. His gift as a poet was for light occasional verses.

Pritchett V(ictor) S(awdon) 1900– . English short story writer, novelist, and critic, with an often witty and satirical style. His critical works include *The Living Novel* 1946 and a biography of the French novelist Balzac.

Profumo John (Dennis) 1915– . British Conservative politician, secretary of state for war 1960–June 1963, when he resigned on the disclosure of his involvement with Christine Keeler, mistress also of a Soviet naval attaché. In 1982 Profumo became administrator of the social and educational settlement Toynbee Hall in London.

Prokhorov Aleksandr 1916– . Russian physicist whose fundamental work on microwaves in 1955 led to the construction of the first practical maser (the microwave equivalent of the laser) by ◊Townes for which they shared the 1964 Nobel Prize for Physics.

Prokofiev Sergey (Sergeyevich) 1891–1953. Soviet composer. His music includes operas such as *The Love of Three Oranges* 1921; ballets for ◊Diaghilev, including *Romeo and Juliet* 1935; seven symphonies including the *Classical Symphony* 1916–17; music for films; piano and violin concertos; songs and cantatas (for example, that composed for the 30th anniversary of the October Revolution); and *Peter and the Wolf* 1936.

Propertius Sextus *c.* 47–15 BC. Roman elegiac poet, a member of ◊Maecenas' circle, who wrote of his love for his mistress 'Cynthia'.

Prost Alain 1955– . French motor racing driver. He won 39 races from 153 starts, and was world champion 1985, 1986, and 1989.

He raced in Formula One events from 1980. He had his first Grand Prix win 1981 (French GP) driving a Renault. In 1984 he began driving for the McLaren team.

Proudhon Pierre Joseph 1809–1865. French anarchist, born in Besançon. He sat in the Constituent Assembly of 1848, was imprisoned for three years, and had to go into exile in Brussels. He published *Qu'est-ce que la propriété/What is Property?* 1840 and *Philosophie de la misère/Philosophy of Poverty* 1846. His most noted saying is 'property is theft'.

Proust Joseph Louis 1754–1826. French chemist. He was the first to state the principle of constant composition of compounds – that compounds consist of the same proportions of elements wherever found.

Proust Marcel 1871–1922. French novelist and critic. The autobiographical novel *À la recherche du temps perdu/Remembrance of Things Past* 1913 is the expression of his childhood memories coaxed from his subconscious; it is also a precise reflection of life in provincial France at the end of the 19th century.

Proust was a delicate, asthmatic child, and although he moved in fashionable Parisian society in his youth, he shut himself away after the death of his parents 1904–05 in a cork-lined room in his Paris flat.

Prout William 1785–1850. British physician and chemist. In 1815 he published *Prout's hypothesis*: that the atomic weight of every atom is an exact and integral multiple of the hydrogen atom. The discovery of isotopes (atoms of the same element but having different masses) in the 20th century bore this out.

Prud'hon Pierre 1758–1823. French painter who worked in a soft, Romantic style. He became drawing instructor and court painter to the Emperor Napoleon's wives.

After winning the Prix de Rome 1784 Prud'hon visited Italy but, unlike his contemporary David, he was unaffected by the Neo-Classical vogue; his style is indebted to ◊Correggio.

Prynne William 1600–1669. English Puritan. He published in 1632 *Histriomastix*, a work attacking stage plays; it contained aspersions on the Queen, for which he was pilloried and lost his ears. In 1637 he was again pilloried and branded for an attack on the bishops. He opposed the execution of Charles I, and actively supported the Restoration.

Przhevalsky Nikolai Mikhailovitch 1839–1888. Russian explorer and soldier. In 1870 he crossed the Gobi Desert to Beijing and then went on to the upper reaches of the Chang Jiang River. His attempts to penetrate Tibet as far as Lhasa failed on three occasions, but he continued to explore the mountain regions between Tibet and Mongolia, where he made collections of plants and animals, including a wild camel and a wild horse.

Ptolemy (Claudius Ptolemaeus) *c.* AD 100–170. Egyptian astronomer and geographer, who worked in Alexandria. The *Almagest* developed the theory that Earth is the centre of the universe, with the Sun, Moon, and stars revolving around it. In 1543 ◊Copernicus disproved the **Ptolemaic system**. Ptolemy's *Geography* was also a standard source of information until the 16th century.

Ptolemy dynasty of kings of Macedonian origin who ruled Egypt over a period of 300 years; they included:

Ptolemy I *c.*367–283 BC. Ruler of Egypt from 323 BC, king from 304. He was one of ◊Alexander the Great's generals, and possibly his half-brother (see also ◊Thaïs). He established the library at Alexandria.

Ptolemy XIII 63–47 BC. Joint ruler of Egypt with his sister-wife Cleopatra; she put him to death.

Puccini Giacomo (Antonio Domenico Michele Secondo Maria) 1858–1924. Italian opera composer, whose music shows a strong gift for melody and dramatic effect. His realist works include *Manon Lescaut* 1893, *La Bohème* 1896, *Tosca* 1900, *Madame Butterfly* 1904, and the unfinished *Turandot* 1926.

Pudovkin Vsevolod Illationovich 1893–1953. Russian film director, whose films include the silent *Mother* 1926, *The End of St Petersburg* 1927, and *Storm over Asia* 1928; and the sound films *Deserter* 1933 and *Suvorov* 1941.

Puget Pierre 1620–1694. French Baroque sculptor who developed a powerful and expressive style. He created a muscular statue of the tyrant *Milo*

Puccini *Italian opera composer Giacomo Puccini.*

of Croton 1672–82 (Louvre, Paris) for the garden of the palace of Versailles.

Puget worked in Italy 1640–43 and was influenced by ◊Michelangelo and ◊Pietro da Cortona. After 1682 he failed to gain further court patronage because of his stubborn temperament and his severe style.

Pugin Augustus Welby Northmore 1812–1852. English architect, collaborator with ◊Barry in the detailed design of the Houses of Parliament. He did much to revive Gothic architecture in England.

P'u-i (formerly *Pu-Yi*) Henry 1906–1967. Last emperor of China (as Hsuan Tung) from 1908 until his deposition 1912; he was restored for a week 1917. He was president 1932–34 and emperor 1934–45 of the Japanese puppet state of Manchukuo built around Manchuria. Captured by Soviet troops, he was returned to China 1949 and put on trial 1950. Pardoned by Mao Zedong 1959, he became a worker in a botanical garden in Beijing.

Pulitzer Joseph 1847–1911. US newspaper proprietor, born in Hungary. He acquired the *New York World* 1883 and in 1903 founded the school of journalism at Columbia University, which awards the annual Pulitzer prizes in journalism and letters.

Pullman George 1831–1901. US engineer who developed the Pullman railway car. In an attempt to improve the standard of comfort of rail travel, he built his first Pioneer Sleeping Car 1863. He formed the Pullman Palace Car Company 1867 and in 1881 the town of Pullman, Illinois, was built for his workers.

Purcell Henry 1659–1695. English Baroque composer. His work can be highly expressive, for example, the opera *Dido and Aeneas* 1689 and music for Dryden's *King Arthur* 1691 and for *The Fairy Queen* 1692. He wrote more than 500 works, ranging from secular operas and incidental music for plays to cantatas and church music.

Purchas Samuel 1577–1626. English compiler of travel books, rector of St Martin's Ludgate, 1614–26. His collection *Purchas, his Pilgrimage* 1613, was followed by another in 1619, and in 1625 by *Hakluytus Posthumus or Purchas his Pilgrimes*, based on papers left by Hakluyt.

Pusey Edward Bouverie 1800–1882. English Church of England priest from 1828. In 1835 he joined J H ◊Newman in issuing the *Tracts for the Times*. After Newman's conversion to Catholicism, Pusey became leader of the High Church Party or Puseyites, striving until his death to keep them from conversion.

Pushkin Aleksandr 1799–1837. Russian poet and writer. He was exiled 1820 for his political verse, and in 1824 was in trouble for his atheistic opinions. He wrote ballads such as *The Gypsies* 1827, and the novel in verse *Eugene Onegin* 1823–31. Other works include the tragic drama *Boris Godunov* 1825 and the prose pieces *The*

Pushkin *Portrait of Aleksandr Pushkin by Vasily Tropinin, dated 1827.*

Captain's Daughter 1836 and *The Queen of Spades* 1834. Pushkin's range was enormous, and his willingness to experiment freed later Russian writers from many of the archaic conventions of the literature of his time.

Puttnam David Terence 1941– . English film producer, influential in reviving the British film industry internationally. Films include *Chariots of Fire* 1981 and *The Killing Fields* 1984.

Puvis de Chavannes Pierre Cécile 1824–1898. French Symbolist painter. His major works are vast decorative schemes, mainly on mythological and allegorical subjects, for public buildings such as the Panthéon and Hôtel de Ville in Paris. His work influenced Gauguin.

Pyke Margaret 1893–1966. British birth-control campaigner. In the early 1930s she became secretary of the National Birth Control Association (later the Family Planning Association, FPA), and campaigned vigorously to get local councils to set up family-planning clinics. She became chair of the FPA in 1954.

Pym Barbara 1913–1980. English novelist, born in Shropshire, whose novels include *Some Tame Gazelle* 1950, *The Sweet Dove Died* 1978, and *A Few Green Leaves* 1980.

Pym Francis 1922– . British Conservative politician. He was defence secretary 1979–81, and succeeded Carrington as foreign minister 1982, but was dismissed in the post-election reshuffle 1983.

Pym John 1584–1643. English parliamentarian, largely responsible for the Petition of Right 1628 which sought to limit the powers of Charles I. As leader of the Puritan opposition in the Long Parliament from 1640, he moved the impeachment of Charles's advisers Strafford and Laud, drew up the Grand Remonstrance, listing Charles's misdeeds, and was the chief of five members of Parliament Charles wanted arrested 1642. The five took refuge in the City, from which they emerged triumphant when the king left London.

Pynchon Thomas 1937– . US novelist, who creates a bizarre, labyrinthine world in his books, which include *V* 1963, *The Crying of Lot 49* 1966, *Gravity's Rainbow* 1973, and *Vineland* 1989.

Pyrrho *c.*360–*c.*270 BC. Greek philosopher, founder of Scepticism, who maintained that since certainty was impossible, peace of mind lay in renouncing all claims to knowledge.

Pyrrhus c.318–272 BC. King of Epirus from 307, who invaded Italy 280, as an ally of the Tarentines against Rome. He twice defeated the Romans but with such heavy losses that a 'Pyrrhic victory' has come to mean a victory not worth winning. He returned to Greece 275 after his defeat at Beneventum, and was killed in a riot in Argos.

Pythagoras *c.*580–500 BC. Greek mathematician and philosopher, who formulated *Pythagoras's theorem*: in a right-angled triangle, the square on the hypotenuse equals the sum of the squares on the other two sides.

Much of his work concerned numbers, to which he assigned mystical properties. For example, he classified numbers into triangular ones (1, 3, 6, 10,...), which can be represented as a triangular array, and square ones (1, 4, 9, 16,...), which form squares. He also observed that any two adjacent triangular numbers add to a square number (for example, $1 + 3 = 4$, $3 + 6 = 9$, $6 + 10 = 16$, ...).

Pythagoras was the founder of a politically influential religious brotherhood in Croton, S Italy (suppressed in the 5th century). Its tenets included immortality of the soul.

Pythagorus of Rhegium 5th century BC. Greek sculptor. He was born on Samos and settled in Rhegium (Reggio di Calabria), Italy. He made statues of athletes and is said to have surpassed his contemporary Myron in this field.

Pytheas 4th century BC. Greek navigator from Marseille who explored the coast of W Europe at least as far N as Denmark, sailed around Britain, and reached 'Thule' (possibly the Shetlands).

Qaboos bin Saidq 1940– . Sultan of Oman, the 14th descendant of the Albusaid family. Opposed to the conservative views of his father, he overthrew him in 1970, in a bloodless coup, and assumed the sultanship. Since then he has followed more liberal and expansionist policies, while maintaining his country's position of international nonalignment.

Qaddafi alternative form of ◊Khaddhafi, Libyan leader.

Qin dynasty Chinese imperial dynasty 221–206 BC. ◊Shi Huangdi was its most noted emperor.

Quant Mary 1934– . British fashion designer. Her Chelsea boutique, Bazaar, achieved a revolution in women's clothing and make-up which epitomized the 'swinging London' of the 1960s.

Quantrill William Clarke 1837–1865. US criminal, who became leader of a guerrilla unit on the Confederate side in the Civil War. Frank and Jesse ◊James were among his aides.

Quasimodo Salvatore 1901–1968. Italian poet. His first book *Acque e terre/Waters and Land* appeared 1930. Later books, including *Nuove poesie/New Poetry* 1942, and *Il falso e vero verde/The False and True Green* 1956, reflect a growing preoccupation with contemporary political and social problems. Nobel prize 1959.

Quayle Anthony 1913–1989. English actor and director. From 1948–56 he directed at the Shakespeare Memorial Theatre, and appeared as Falstaff in *Henry IV*, Petruchio in *The Taming of the Shrew*, and the title role in *Othello*. He played nonclassical parts in *Galileo*, *Sleuth*, and *Old World*.

Quayle (J) Dan(forth) 1947–. US Republican politician, an Indiana congressman from 1977, senator from 1981, vice president from 1989.

Born into a rich and influential Indianapolis newspaper-owning family, Quayle was admitted to the Indiana bar 1974, and was elected to the House of Representatives 1977 and to the Senate 1981. When George Bush ran for president 1988, he selected Quayle as his running mate, admiring his conservative views, and believing that Quayle could deliver the youth vote. This choice encountered heavy criticism because of Quayle's limited political experience and his association with a fundamentalist Christian group. Much was made of his earlier enlistment in the Indiana National Guard, which meant that he avoided action overseas during the Vietnam War. Quayle stayed out of the limelight during the remainder of the campaign and became vice president Nov 1988.

Queensberry John Sholto Douglas, 8th Marquess of Queensberry 1844–1900. British patron of boxing. In 1867 he formulated the *Queensberry Rules* which form the basis of modern-day boxing rules.

A keen all-round sportsman, Douglas was an expert horseman and excelled at steeplechasing. He was the father of Lord Alfred ◊Douglas.

Queneau Raymond 1903–1976. French surrealist poet and humorous novelist, author of *Zazie dans le Métro/Zazie in the Metro* 1959, portraying a precocious young Parisian woman.

Quetelet Lambert Adolphe Jacques 1796–1874. Belgian statistician, a pioneer of modern statistical methods. He developed tests for the validity of statistical information, and gathered and analysed

Quayle Vice president of the USA from 1989, Dan Quayle.

statistical data of many kinds. From his work on sociological data came the concept of the 'average man'.

Quevedo y Villegas Francisco Gómez de 1580–1645. Spanish novelist and satirist. His picaresque novel *La Vida del Buscón/The Life of a Scoundrel* 1626 follows the tradition of the roguish hero who has a series of episodic adventures. *Sueños/Visions* 1627 is a brilliant series of satirical portraits of contemporary society.

Quilter Roger 1877–1953. English composer. He wrote song settings of ◊Tennyson and ◊Shakespeare, including 'Now Sleeps the Crimson Petal' 1904 and 'To Daisies' 1906, and the *Children's Overture* 1920.

Quimby Fred(erick) 1886–1965. US film producer, in charge of MGM's short films department 1926–56. Among the cartoons produced by this department were the *Tom and Jerry* series and those directed by Tex ◊Avery.

Quine Willard Van Orman 1908– . US philosopher and logician. In *Two Dogmas of Empiricism* 1951, he argued against the analytic/synthetic distinction. In *Word and Object* 1960, he put forward the thesis of radical untranslatability, the view that a sentence can always be regarded as referring to many different things. He was professor of philosophy at Harvard.

Quinn Anthony 1915– . Mexican actor, in films from 1935. Famous for the title role in *Zorba the Greek* 1964, he later often played variations on this larger-than-life character.

Quintero Serafin Alvárez and Joaquin Alvárez Spanish dramatists; see ◊Alvárez Quintero.

Quintilian (Marcus Fabius Quintilianus) c. AD 35–95. Roman rhetorician. He was born at Calgurris, Spain, taught rhetoric in Rome from AD 68, and composed the *Institutio oratorio/The Education of an Orator*, in which he advocated a simple and sincere style of public speaking.

Quisling Vidkun 1887–1945. Norwegian politician. Leader from 1933 of the Norwegian Fascist Party, he aided the Nazi invasion 1940 by delaying mobilization and urging non-resistance. He was made premier by Hitler 1942, and was arrested and shot as a traitor by the Norwegians 1945. His name became a generic term for a traitor who aids an occupying force.

Rabelais François 1495–1553. French satirist, monk, and physician, whose name has become synonymous with bawdy humour. He was educated in the Renaissance humanist tradition and was the author of satirical allegories, *La Vie inestimable de Gargantua/The Inestimable Life of Gargantua* 1535 and *Faits et dits héroïques du grand Pantagruel/Deeds and Sayings of the Great Pantagruel* 1533, the story of two giants (father and son) Gargantua and Pantagruel.

Rabi Isidor Isaac 1898–1988. US physicist who developed techniques to measure with astonishing accuracy the strength of the weak magnetic fields. These fields are generated when charged elementary particles, such as the electron, spin about their axis. The work won for him the Nobel Prize for Physics in 1944.

Rabin Itzhak 1922– . Israeli prime minister who succeeded Golda Meir 1974–77.

Rabuka Sitiveni 1948– . Fijian soldier and politician. Trained at Sandhurst, he was made a colonel in the Fijian army, after serving with the UN in Lebanon. In 1987 he staged a coup against the Indian-led coalition government and declared a republic. Although the prime minister, Kamisese Mara, was subsequently reinstated, Rabuka remained an influential figure behind the scenes.

Rachel in the Old Testament, the favourite wife of ◊Jacob, and mother of ◊Joseph and Benjamin.

Rachel stage name of Elizabeth Félix 1821–1858. French tragic actress who excelled in fierce passionate roles, particularly Racine's *Phèdre*, which she took on tour to Europe, the USA, and Russia.

Rachmaninov Sergei (Vasilevich) 1873–1943. Russian composer, conductor, and pianist. After the 1917 Revolution he went to the USA. His dramatically emotional Romantic music has a strong melodic basis and includes operas, such as *Francesca da Rimini* 1906, three symphonies, four piano concertos, piano pieces, and songs. Among his other works are the *Prelude in C Sharp Minor* 1892 and *Rhapsody on a Theme of Paganini* 1934 for piano and orchestra.

Racine Jean 1639–1699. French dramatist and exponent of the classical tragedy in French drama. Most of his tragedies have women in the title role, for example *Andromaque* 1667, *Iphigénie* 1674, and *Phèdre* 1677. After the contemporary failure of the latter he no longer wrote for the secular stage, but influenced by Madame de ◊Maintenon wrote two religious dramas, *Esther* 1689 and *Athalie* 1691, which achieved posthumous success.

Radcliffe Anne (born Ward) 1764–1823. English novelist, a chief exponent of the Gothic novel or 'romance of terror', for example, *The Mysteries of Udolpho* 1794.

Radić Stjepan 1871–1928. Yugoslav nationalist politician, born near Fiume. He led the Croat national movement within the Austro-Hungarian Empire, and supported union with Serbia 1919. His opposition to Serbian supremacy within Yugoslavia led to his murder in the parliament house.

Raeburn Henry 1756–1823. Scottish portrait painter, active mainly in Edinburgh. He developed a technique of painting with broad brushstrokes directly on the canvas without preparatory drawing. He was appointed painter to George IV 1823.

Racine The tragedies of Racine are part of the great flowering of dramatic and poetic writing in 17th-century France. His subjects came from Greek mythology and he observed the rules of classical Greek drama.

Between 1784 and 1787 he visited London and then Italy. *The Reverend Robert Walker Skating* (National Gallery, Edinburgh) is a popular work.

Raeder Erich 1876–1960. German admiral. Chief of Staff in World War I, he became head of the navy in 1928, but was dismissed by Hitler in 1943 because of his failure to prevent Allied Arctic convoys from reaching the USSR. Sentenced to life imprisonment at the Nuremberg Trials of war criminals, he was released on grounds of ill health in 1955.

Rafelson 'Bob' (Robert) 1934– . US film director who gained critical acclaim for his second film, *Five Easy Pieces* 1971. His other films include *Head* 1968, *The Postman Always Rings Twice* 1981, and *Black Widow* 1987.

Raffles Thomas Stamford 1781–1826. British colonial administrator, born in Jamaica. He served in the East India Company, took part in the capture of Java from the Dutch 1811, and while governor of Sumatra 1818–23 was responsible for the acquisition and foundation of Singapore 1819. He was a founder and first president of the Zoological Society, London.

Rafsanjani Hojatoleslam Ali Akbar Hashemi 1934– . Iranian cleric and politician. After training as a mullah (Islamic teacher) under Ayatollah ◊Khomeini at the holy city of Qom, he acquired considerable wealth through his construction business but kept in touch with his exiled mentor. When the Ayatollah returned after the revolution of 1070 80 Rafsanjani became the eminent speaker of the Iranian parliament and, after Khomeini's death in 1989, state president and effective political leader.

Raft George. Stage name of George Ranft 1895–1980. US film actor, usually cast as a gangster (as in *Scarface* 1932). His later work included *Some Like it Hot* 1959.

Raglan FitzRoy James Henry Somerset, 1st Baron Raglan 1788–1855. English general. He took part in the Peninsular War under Wellington, and lost his right arm at Waterloo. He commanded the British forces in the Crimean War from 1854. The *raglan sleeve*, cut right up to the neckline with no shoulder seam, is named after him.

Rahere died 1144. Minstrel and favourite of Henry I of England. After recovering from malaria while on a pilgrimage to Rome, in 1123 he founded St Bartholomew's priory and St Bartholomew's hospital in London.

Rahman Tunku Abdul 1903– . Malaysian politician, first prime minister of independent Malaya 1957 63 and of Malaysia 1963–70.

Born at Kuala Keda, the son of the sultan and his sixth wife, a Thai princess, the Tunku studied law in England. After returning to Malaysia he founded the Alliance party 1952. The party was successful in the 1955 elections, and the Tunku became prime minister of Malaya on gaining independence 1957, continuing when Malaya became part of Malaysia

1963. His achievement was to bring together the Malay, Chinese, and Indian peoples within the Alliance party, but in the 1960s he was accused of showing bias towards Malays. Ethnic riots followed in Kuala Lumpur 1969 and, after many attempts to restore better relations, the Tunku retired 1970. He has recently voiced criticism of the authoritarian leadership of Mahathir bin Mohamad.

Raikes Robert 1735–1811. English printer who started the first Sunday school (for religious purposes) in Gloucester 1780 and who stimulated the growth of weekday voluntary 'ragged schools' for poor children.

Raine Kathleen 1908– . English poet. Her volumes of poetry include *Stone and Flower* 1943 and *The Lost Country* 1971, and reflect both the Northumberland landscape of her upbringing and the religious feeling which led her to the Roman Catholic Church 1944.

Rainier III 1923– . Prince of Monaco from 1949. He was married to the US film actress Grace Kelly.

Rais Gilles de 1404–1440. French marshal who fought alongside Joan of Arc. In 1440 he was hanged for the torture and murder of 140 children, but the court proceedings were irregular. He is the historical basis of the Bluebeard character of folklore, who had several wives and murdered them.

Raleigh or *Ralegh* Walter c. 1552–1618. English adventurer. He made colonizing and exploring voyages to North America 1584–87 and South America 1595, and naval attacks on Spanish ports. He was imprisoned by James I 1603–16 and executed on his return from an unsuccessful final expedition to South America.

Raleigh was born in Devon. He was knighted 1584, and made several attempts 1584–87 to establish a colony in 'Virginia' (now North Carolina, USA). In 1595 he led an expedition to South America (described in his *Discovery of Guiana*) and distinguished himself in expeditions against Spain in Cádiz 1596 and the Azores 1597. After James I's accession 1603 he was condemned to death on a charge of conspiracy, but was reprieved and imprisoned in the Tower of London, where he wrote his unfinished *History of the World*. Released 1616 to lead a gold-seeking expedition to the Orinoco River in South America, which failed disastrously, he was beheaded on his return under his former sentence.

Ramakrishna 1834–1886. Hindu sage, teacher, and mystic (one dedicated to achieving oneness with or a direct experience of God or some force beyond the normal world). Ramakrishna claimed that mystical experience was the ultimate aim of religions, and that all religions which led to this goal were equally valid.

Ramakrishna's most important follower, Swami Vivekananda (1863–1902), set up the Ramakrishna

Society 1887, which now has centres for education, welfare, and religious teaching throughout India and beyond.

Raman Venkata 1888–1970. Indian physicist who in 1928 discovered what became known as the *Raman effect*: the scattering of monochromatic light (light of a single wavelength) when passed through a transparent substance. Awarded a Nobel prize in 1930, in 1948 he became director of the Raman Research Institute and national research professor of physics.

Rambert Marie. Adopted name of Cyvia Rambam 1888–1982. British ballet dancer and teacher born in Warsaw, Poland, who became a British citizen 1918. One of the major innovative and influential figures in modern ballet, she was with the Diaghilev ballet 1912–13, opened the Rambert School 1920, and in 1926 founded the *Ballet Rambert* which she directed (renamed Rambert Dance Company 1987).

Rambouillet Catherine de Vivonne, Marquise de Rambouillet 1588–1665. French society hostess, whose salon at the Hôtel de Rambouillet in Paris included the writers Descartes, La Rochefoucauld, and Mme de Sévigné. The salon was ridiculed by the dramatist Molière in his *Les Précieuses ridicules* 1659.

Ram Das 1534–1581. Indian religious leader, fourth guru (teacher) of Sikhism 1574– 81, who founded the Sikh holy city of Amritsar.

Rambert As teacher and promoter to many leading dancers, choreographers, and stage designers, Marie Rambert was one of modern ballet's most influential figures.

Rameau Jean-Philippe 1683–1764. French organist and composer. He wrote *Treatise on Harmony* 1722 and his varied works include keyboard and vocal music and many operas, such as *Castor and Pollux* 1737.

Ramée Louise de la. English novelist who wrote under the name ◊Ouida.

Ram Mohun Roy 1770–1833. Indian religious reformer, founder 1830 of Brahma Samaj, a mystic cult. He sought to return to the primitive, simple worship of the ancient Veda scriptures and purify Hinduism.

Ramphal Shridath Surendranath ('Sonny') 1928– . Guyanese politician. He was minister of foreign affairs and justice 1972–75, and was secretary-general of the British Commonwealth 1975–90.

He studied at the University of London and Harvard Law School.

Rampling Charlotte 1945– . British actress, whose sometimes controversial films include *Georgy Girl* 1966, *The Night Porter Il Portiere di Notte* 1974, and *Farewell My Lovely* 1975.

Ramsay Allan 1686–1758. Scottish poet, born in Lanarkshire. He became a wig-maker and then a bookseller in Edinburgh. He published *The Tea-Table Miscellany* 1724–37, and *The Evergreen* 1724, collections of ancient and modern Scottish song including revivals of the work of such poets as ◊Dunbar and ◊Henryson.

Ramsay Allan 1713–1784. Scottish portrait painter. After studying in Edinburgh and Italy, he established himself as a portraitist in London, and became painter to George III in 1760. He was the son of the poet Allan Ramsay.

His portraits include *The Artist's Wife* about 1755 (National Gallery, Edinburgh).

Ramsay William 1852–1916. Scottish chemist who, with Lord Rayleigh, discovered argon 1894. In 1895 Ramsay manufactured helium, and in 1898, in cooperation with Morris Travers, identified neon, krypton, and xenon. In 1903 with Frederick Soddy, he noted the transmutation of radium into helium, which led to the discovery of the density and atomic weight of radium. Nobel prize 1904.

Ramses or *Rameses* eleven kings of ancient Egypt, including:

Ramses II King of Egypt about 1304–1236 BC, the son of Seti I. He campaigned successfully against the Hittites, and built two rock temples at Abu Simbel in Upper Egypt.

Ramses III King of Egypt about 1200–1168 BC. He won a naval victory over the Philistines and other peoples, and asserted his suzerainty over Palestine.

Rand Ayn. Adopted name of Alice Rosenbaum 1905–1982. US novelist of Russian origin. Her novel *The Fountainhead* 1943, describing an architect who destroys his masterpiece rather than see it altered, displays her influential blend of virulent anti-communism and fervent belief in individual enterprise.

Ranjit Singh 1780–1839. Indian maharajah. He succeeded his father as a minor Sikh leader 1792, and created a Sikh army that conquered Kashmir and the Punjab. In alliance with the British, he established himself as 'Lion of the Punjab', ruler of the strongest of the independent Indian states.

Rank Joseph Arthur 1888–1972. British film magnate. Having entered films in 1933 to promote the Methodist cause, he proceeded to gain control of much of the industry through takeovers and forming new businesses.

The Rank Organization still owns the Odeon chain of cinemas and Pinewood Studios, although film is now a minor part of its activities.

Ransom John Crowe 1888–1974. US poet and critic, born in Tennessee. He published his romantic but anti-rhetorical verse in, for example, *Poems About God* 1919, *Chills and Fever* 1924, *Selected Verse* 1947. As a critic and teacher he was a powerful figure in the movement of New Criticism, which shaped much literary theory from the 1940s to the 1960s.

Ransome Arthur 1884–1967. English journalist (correspondent in Russia for the *Daily News* during World War I and the Revolution) and writer of adventure stories for children, such as *Swallows and Amazons* 1930 and *Peter Duck* 1932.

Ransome Robert 1753–1830. English ironfounder and agricultural engineer, whose business earned a worldwide reputation in the 19th and 20th centuries. He introduced factory methods for the production of an improved range of ploughs from 1789. The firm remained at the forefront of advances in agricultural mechanization in connection with steam engines, threshing machines, and lawnmowers.

Rao Raja 1909– . Indian writer, born at Hassan, Karnataka. He studied at Montpellier and the Sorbonne in France. He wrote about Indian independence from the perspective of a village in S India in *Kanthapura* 1938 and later, in *The Serpent and the Rope* 1960, about a young cosmopolitan intellectual seeking enlightenment.

Collections of stories include *The Cow of the Barricades* 1947 and *The Policeman and the Rose* 1978.

Raoult Francois 1830–1901. French chemist. In 1882, while working at the University of Grenoble, Raoult formulated one of the basic laws of chemistry: *Raoult's law* enables the molecular weight of a substance to be determined by noting how much of the substance is required to depress the freezing point of a solvent by a certain amount.

Raphael (Raffaello Sanzio) 1483–1520. Italian painter, one of the greatest of the High Renaissance, active in Perugia, Florence, and Rome (from 1508), where he painted frescoes in the Vatican and for secular patrons. His harmoniously composed religious and mythological scenes were enormously influential; his portraits enhance his sitter's character and express dignity. Many of his designs were engraved. Much of his later work was the product of his studio.

Raphael was born in Urbino, the son of Giovanni Santi (died 1494), a court painter. In 1499 he went to Perugia, where he worked with ◊Perugino, whose graceful style is reflected in Raphael's *Marriage of the Virgin* (Brera, Milan). This work also shows his early concern for harmonious disposition of figures in the pictorial space. In Florence 1504–08 he studied the works of Leonardo da Vinci, Michelangelo, Masaccio, and Fra Bartolommeo. His paintings of this period include the *Ansidei Madonna* (National Gallery, London).

Next, Pope Julius II commissioned him to decorate the papal apartments (the Stanze) in the Vatican. In Raphael's first fresco series there, *The School of Athens* 1509 is a complex but classically composed grouping of Greek philosophers and mathematicians, centred on the figures of Plato and Aristotle. A second series of frescoes, 1511–14, includes the dramatic and richly coloured *Mass of Bolsena*.

Raphael was increasingly flooded with commissions. Within the next few years he produced delightful mythological frescoes in the Villa Farnesina in Rome (1511–12), cartoons for tapestries for the Sistine Chapel, Vatican (Victoria and Albert Museum, London), and the *Sistine Madonna* about 1512 (Gemäldegalerie, Dresden, East Germany). One of his pupils was ◊Giulio Romano.

Rasputin (Russian 'dissolute') Gregory Efimovich 1871–1916. Siberian wandering 'holy man', the illiterate son of a peasant. He acquired influence over the tsarina ◊Alexandra, wife of ◊Nicholas II, because of her faith in his power to cure her son of his haemophilia, and he was able to make political and ecclesiastical appointments. His abuse of power and his notorious debauchery (reputedly including the tsarina) led to his being murdered by a group of nobles, who (when poison had no effect) dumped him in the river Neva after shooting him.

Rathbone (Philip St John) Basil 1892–1967. South African-born British character actor, one of the cinema's great villains; he also played Sherlock Holmes (the fictional detective created by Arthur Conan Doyle) in several films. He worked mainly in Hollywood, in films such as *The Adventures of Robin Hood* 1938 and *The Hound of the Baskervilles* 1939.

Rathenau Walther 1867–1922. German politician. He was a leading industrialist, and was appointed economic director during World War I, developing a system of economic planning in combination with capitalism. After the war he founded the Democratic Party, and became foreign minister 1922.

The same year he signed the Rapallo Treaty of Friendship with the USSR, cancelling German and Soviet counter-claims for indemnities for World War I, and soon after was murdered by right-wing fanatics.

Rattigan Terence 1911–1977. English playwright. His play *Ross* 1960 was based on T E ◊Lawrence (Lawrence of Arabia).

Rattigan's work ranges from the comedy *French Without Tears* 1936 to the psychological intensity of *The Winslow Boy* 1945. Other plays include *The Browning Version* 1948 and *Separate Tables* 1954.

Rattle Simon 1955– . English conductor. Principal conductor of the Birmingham Symphony Orchestra from 1980, he is noted for his eclectic range and for interpretations of Mahler and Sibelius.

Ratushinskaya Irina 1954– . Soviet dissident poet. Sentenced 1983 to seven years in a labour camp plus five years in internal exile for criticism of the Soviet regime, she was released 1986. Her strongly Christian work includes *Grey is the Colour of Hope* 1988.

Rau Johannes 1931– . West German socialist politician, member of the Social Democratic Party (SPD).

The son of a Protestant pastor, Rau became state premier of North Rhine-Westphalia 1978. In Jan 1987 he stood for chancellor but was defeated by the incumbent conservative coalition.

Rauschenberg Robert 1925– . US pop artist, a creator of happenings (art in live performance) and incongruous multimedia works such as *Monogram* 1959 (Moderna Museet, Stockholm), a car tyre around the body of a stuffed goat daubed with paint.

Rauschenberg also produced collages. In the 1960s he returned to painting and used the silk-screen printing process to transfer images to canvas.

Ravel (Joseph) Maurice 1875–1937. French composer. His work is characterized by its sensuousness, unresolved dissonances, and 'tone colour'. Examples are the piano pieces *Pavane pour une infante défunte* 1899 and *Jeux d'eau* 1901, and the ballets *Daphnis et Chloë* 1912 and *Boléro* 1928.

Rawlinson Henry Creswicke 1810–1895. English orientalist and political agent in Baghdad in the Ottoman Empire from 1844. He deciphered the Babylonian and Old Persian scripts of ◊Darius I's trilingual inscription at Behistun, Persia, continued the excavation work of A H ◊Layard, and published a *History of Assyria* 1852.

Rawls John 1921– . US philosopher. In *A Theory of Justice* 1971, he revived the concept of the 'social contract' (see ◊Hobbes), and its enforcement by civil disobedience.

Rawsthorne Alan 1905–1971. English composer. His *Theme and Variations* for two violins 1938, was followed by other tersely energetic works including *Symphonic Studies* 1939, the overture

Street Corner 1944, *Concerto for Strings* 1950, and a vigorously inventive sonata for violin and piano, 1959.

Ray John 1627–1705. English naturalist who devised a classification system accounting for nearly 18,000 plant species. It was the first system to divide flowering plants into monocotyledons (having one embryonic seed-leaf) and dicotyledons (having two), with additional divisions made on the basis of leaf and flower characters and fruit types.

Ray Man. Adopted name of Emmanuel Rudnitsky 1890–1976. US photographer, painter, and sculptor, active mainly in France; associated with the Dada movement. His pictures often showed Surrealist images like the photograph *Le Violon d'Ingres* 1924.

Ray was born in Philadelphia, but lived in Paris from 1921 (in Los Angeles 1940–51). He began as a painter and took up photography in 1915, the year he first met the Dada artist Duchamp in New York. In 1922 he invented the **rayograph**, a black and white image obtained by placing objects on sensitized photographic paper; he also made much use of the technique of **solarization** (partly reversing the tones on a photograph). His photographs include portraits of many artists and writers.

Ray Nicholas. Adopted name of Raymond Nicholas Kienzle 1911–1979. US film director, critically acclaimed for his socially aware dramas such as *Rebel Without a Cause* 1955. His later epics, such as *King of Kings* 1961, were less successful.

Ray Satyajit 1921– . Indian film director, renowned for his trilogy of life in his native Bengal: *Pather Panchali, Unvanquished*, and *The World of Apu* 1955–59. Later films include *The Chess Players* 1977 and *The Home and the World* 1984.

Rayleigh John W Strutt, 3rd Baron Rayleigh 1842–1919. British physicist who wrote the standard *Treatise on Sound*, experimented in optics and microscopy, and, with William Ramsay, discovered argon. He was professor of experimental physics at Cambridge 1879–84, and was president of the Royal Society 1905–08, when he became chancellor of Cambridge University. In 1904 he received a Nobel prize.

Reagan Ronald Wilson 1911– . US Republican politician, governor of California 1966–74, president 1981–89. A former Hollywood actor, Reagan was a hawkish and popular president. He introduced deregulation of domestic markets and withstood criticism of his interventionist foreign policy, but failed to confront a mounting trade deficit. He was succeeded by George ◊Bush. He unsuccessfully contested the Republican presidential nomination 1968 and 1976, and defeated Jimmy ◊Carter in the 1980 election, and defeated ◊Mondale 1984. He adopted an aggressive policy in Central America, attempting to overthrow the government of Nicaragua, and invading Grenada following a coup there in 1983.

Reagan Ronald Reagan, US president 1981–89.

In 1987, the **Irangate** scandal was investigated by the Tower Commission; Reagan regretted that US/Iran negotiations had become an 'arms for hostages deal', but denied knowledge of resultant funds being illegally sent to the Contras in Nicaragua. He increased spending on defence (increasing the national budget deficit to record levels), cut social programs, introduced deregulation of domestic markets, and cut taxes. His Strategic Defense Initiative, announced 1983, has proved controversial due to cost and alleged infeasibility.

Reagan was born in Tampico, Illinois, the son of a shoe salesman who was bankrupted during the Depression. He became a Hollywood actor 1937 and appeared in 50 films, including *Bedtime for Bonzo* 1951 and *The Killers* 1964. As president of the Screen Actors' Guild 1947–52, he became a conservative, critical of the bureaucratic stifling of free enterprise, and named names before the House Un-American Activities Committee. He joined the Republican Party 1962, and his term as governor of California 1966–1974 was marked by battles against students. Having lost the Republican presidential nomination 1968 and 1976 to Nixon and Ford respectively, Reagan won it 1980 and defeated President Carter. He was wounded in an assassination attempt 1981. The invasion of Grenada generated a revival of national patriotism, and Reagan was re-elected by a landslide 1984. His insistence on militarizing space through the Strategic Defense Initiative, popularly called Star Wars, prevented a disarmament agreement when he met the Soviet leader ◊Gorbachev 1985 and 1986, but a 4% reduction in nuclear weapons was agreed 1987. In 1986, he ordered the bombing of Tripoli, Libya, in retaliation for the killing of a US serviceman in Berlin.

Reardon Ray 1932– . Welsh snooker player. One of the leading players of the 1970s, he was six times world champion 1970–78.

Réaumur Réné Antoine Ferchault de 1683–1757. French metallurgist and entomologist. His definitive work on the early steel industry, published in 1722, described how to convert iron into steel and laid the foundations of the modern steel industry. He produced a six-volume work between 1734 and 1742 on the natural history of insects, the first books on entomology.

Récamier Jeanne Françoise 1777–1849. French society hostess, born in Lyon. At the age of 15 she married Jacques Récamier, an elderly banker, and held a salon of literary and political celebrities.

Redding Otis 1941–1967. US soul singer and songwriter. He had a number of hits in the mid-1960s such as 'My Girl' 1965, 'Respect' 1967, and '(Sittin' on the) Dock of the Bay' 1968, released after his death in a plane crash.

Redford (Charles) Robert 1937– . US actor and film director. His first starring role was in *Butch Cassidy and the Sundance Kid* 1969, and his other films as an actor include *All the President's Men* 1976 and *Out of Africa* 1985. He directed *Ordinary People* 1980 and *The Milagro Beanfield War* 1988.

Redgrave Michael 1908–1985. British actor. His stage roles included Hamlet and Lear (Shakespeare), Uncle Vanya (Chekhov), and the schoolmaster in Rattigan's *The Browning Version*. He also appeared in films. He was the father of Vanessa and Lynn Redgrave, both actresses.

Redgrave Vanessa 1937– . British actress. She has played Shakespeare's Lady Macbeth and Cleopatra on the stage, and the title role in the film *Julia* 1976 (Academy Award). She is active in left-wing politics. Daughter of Michael Redgrave.

Redmond John Edward 1856–1918. Irish politician, Parnell's successor as leader of the Nationalist Party 1890–1916. The 1910 elections saw him holding the balance of power in the House of Commons, and he secured the introduction of a Home Rule bill, hotly opposed by Protestant Ulster.

Redmond supported the British cause on the outbreak of World War I, and the bill was passed, but its operation suspended until the war's end. The growth of the nationalist party Sinn Féin (the political wing of the Irish Republican Army) and the 1916 Easter Rising ended his hopes and his power.

Redon Odilon 1840–1916. French Symbolist painter. He used fantastic symbols and images, sometimes mythological. From the 1890s he also produced still lifes and landscapes. His work was much admired by the Surrealists.

Redouté Pierre Joseph 1759–1840. French flower painter patronized by Empress Josephine and the

Bourbon court. He taught flower drawing at the Museum of Natural History in Paris and produced volumes of delicate, highly detailed flowers, notably *Les Roses* 1817–24.

Reed Carol 1906–1976. British film producer and director, an influential figure in the British film industry of the 1940s. His films include *Odd Man Out* 1947, *The Fallen Idol* and *The Third Man* both 1950, and *Our Man in Havana* 1959. The actor Oliver Reed is his nephew.

Reed Ishmael 1938– . US novelist. His experimental, parodistic, satirical novels exploit traditions taken from jazz and voodoo, and include *The Free-Lance Pallbearers* 1967, *Mumbo Jumbo* 1972, and *Reckless Eyeballing* 1986.

Reed Lou 1942– . US rock singer, songwriter, and former member (1965–70) of the seminal New York group *The Velvet Underground*. His solo work deals largely with urban alienation and angst, and includes the albums *Berlin* 1973, *Street Hassle* 1978, and *New York* 1989.

Reed Oliver 1938– . British actor, nephew of the director Carol Reed. He became a star through such films as *Women in Love* 1969, *The Devils* 1971, and *Castaway* 1987.

Rees-Mogg Lord William 1928– . British journalist, editor of *The Times* 1967–81, chair of the Arts Council 1982–89, and from 1988 chair of the Broadcasting Standards Council.

Reeves William Pember 1857–1932. New Zealand politician and writer. He was New Zealand minister of education 1891–96, and director of the London School of Economics 1908–19. He wrote poetry and the classic description of New Zealand, *Long White Cloud* 1898.

Regan Donald 1918– . US Republican political adviser to Ronald ◊Reagan. He was secretary of the Treasury 1981–85, and chief of White House staff 1985–87, when he was forced to resign because of widespread belief of his complicity in the Irangate scandal (centred on the supply of arms to Iran).

Reger (Johann Baptist Joseph) Max(imilian) 1873–1916. German composer and pianist. He taught at Munich 1905–07, was professor at the Leipzig Conservatoire from 1907, and was conductor of the Meiningen ducal orchestra 1911–14. His works include organ and piano music, chamber music, and songs.

Rehnquist William 1924– . Chief justice of the US Supreme Court. Active within the Republican Party, he was appointed head of the office of legal counsel by President ◊Nixon in 1969 and controversially defended such measures as pre-trial detention and wiretapping.

Rehoboam King of Judah about 932–915 BC, son of Solomon. Under his rule the Jewish nation split into the two kingdoms of *Israel* and *Judah*. Ten of the tribes revolted against him and took

Jeroboam as their ruler, leaving him only the tribes of Judah and Benjamin.

Reich Steve 1936– . US composer. His Minimalist music consists of simple patterns carefully superimposed and modified to highlight constantly changing melodies and rhythms; examples are *Phase Patterns* for four electronic organs 1970, *Music for Mallet Instruments, Voices, and Organ* 1973, and *Music for Percussion and Keyboards* 1984.

Reich Wilhelm 1897–1957. Austrian doctor, who emigrated to the USA 1939. He combined Marxism and psychoanalysis to advocate sexual freedom, for example in *Die Sexuelle Revolution/The Sexual Revolution* 1936–45, and *Die Funktion des Orgasmus/The Function of the Orgasm* 1948. Reich died in prison following committal for contempt of court.

Reichstadt, Duke of title of ◊Napoleon II, son of Napoleon I.

Reichstein Tadeus 1897– . Swiss biochemist who investigated the chemical activity of the adrenal glands. By 1946 Reichstein had identified a large number of steroids secreted by the adrenal cortex, some of which would later be used in the treatment of ◊Addison's disease. Reichstein shared the 1950 Nobel Prize for Medicine with Edward ◊Kendall and Philip Hench (1896–1965).

Reid Thomas 1710–1796. Scottish mathematician and philosopher. His *Enquiry into the Human Mind on the Principles of Common Sense* 1764 attempted to counter the sceptical conclusions of Hume. He believed that the existence of the material world and the human soul is self-evident 'by the consent of ages and nations, of the learned and unlearned'.

Reinhardt 'Django' (Jean Baptiste) 1910–1953. Belgian jazz guitarist and composer, who was co-leader, with Stephane Grappelli, of the Quintet de Hot Club de France 1934–1939.

Reinhardt Max 1873–1943. Austrian producer and director, whose expressionist style was widely influential in German theatre and film during the 1920s and 1930s. Directors such as Murnau and Lubitsch and actors such as Dietrich worked with him. He co-directed the US film *A Midsummer Night's Dream* 1935.

Reisz Karel 1926– . Czechoslovak film director who lived in Britain from 1938, originally a writer and film critic. His first feature film, *Saturday Night and Sunday Morning* 1960, was a critical and commercial success. His other work includes *Morgan* 1966, *The French Lieutenant's Woman* 1981, and *Sweet Dreams* 1986.

Remarque Erich Maria 1898–1970. German novelist, a soldier in World War I, whose *All Quiet on the Western Front* 1929 led to his being deprived of German nationality. He lived in Switzerland 1929–39, and then in the USA.

Rembrandt Harmensz van Rijn 1606–1669. Dutch painter and etcher, one of the most prolific and influential artists in Europe of the 17th century. Between 1629 and 1669 he painted some 60 penetrating self-portraits. He also painted religious subjects, and produced about 300 etchings and over 1,000 drawings. His group portraits include *The Anatomy Lesson of Dr Tulp* 1632 (Mauritshuis, The Hague) and *The Night Watch* 1642 (Rijksmuseum, Amsterdam).

After studying in Leiden and for a few months in Amsterdam (with a history painter), Rembrandt began his career 1625 in Leiden, where his work reflected knowledge of ◊Elsheimer and ◊Caravaggio among others. He settled permanently in Amsterdam 1631, and obtained many commissions for portraits from wealthy merchants. The *Self-Portrait with Saskia* (his wife, Saskia van Uylenburgh) about 1634 (Gemäldegalerie, Dresden, East Germany) displays their prosperity in warm tones and rich, glittering textiles.

Saskia died 1642 and that year Rembrandt's fortunes began to decline (he eventually became bankrupt 1656). His work became more sombre and with deeper emotional content, and his portraits were increasingly melancholy, for example *Jan Six* 1654 (Six Collection, Amsterdam). From 1660 onward he lived with Hendrickje Stoffels, but he outlived her, and in 1668 his only surviving child, Titus, died too.

Remington Frederic 1861–1909. US sculptor, painter, and illustrator. His exploratory trips to the American West inspired lively images of cowboys and horses, such as his sculpture *Off the Range* (Corcoran Gallery of Art, Washington DC).

Remington Philo 1816–1889. US inventor of the typewriter and breech-loading rifle that bear his name. He began manufacturing typewriters 1873, using the patent of Christopher Sholes (1819–1890), and made improvements that resulted five years later in the first machine with a shift key, thus providing lower-case letters as well as capital letters. The Remington rifle and carbine, which had a falling block breech and a tubular magazine, were developed in collaboration with his father.

Renault Mary. Pen name of Mary Challans 1905–1983. English novelist who recreated the world of ancient Greece, with a trilogy on Theseus and two novels on ◊Alexander: *Fire from Heaven* 1970 and *The Persian Boy* 1972.

Rendell Ruth 1930– . English novelist and short-story writer, author of a detective series featuring Chief Inspector Wexford; her psychological crime novels explore the minds of people who commit murder, often through obsession or social inadequacy, as in *A Demon in my View* 1976 and *Heartstones* 1987.

René France-Albert 1935– . Seychelles politician, president from 1987.

In 1964 René founded the left-wing Seychelles People's United Party (SPUP), pressing for complete independence. When this was achieved, in 1976, he became prime minister and James Mancham, leader of the Seychelles Democratic Party (SDP), became president. René seized the presidency in 1977 and set up a one-party state. He has since followed a non-nuclear policy of nonalignment and has survived several attempts to remove him.

Reni Guido 1575–1642. Italian painter, active in Bologna and Rome (about 1600–14), whose work includes the fresco *Phoebus and the Hours Preceded by Aurora* 1613 (Casino Rospigliosi, Rome). His successful workshop in Bologna produced numerous idealized religious images, including Madonnas.

Rennie John 1761–1821. Scottish engineer who built the old Waterloo Bridge and old London Bridge (reconstructed in Arizona, USA).

Rennie studied at Edinburgh University and then worked for James ◊Watt from 1784. He started his own engineering business about 1791, and built bridges (Waterloo bridge, London, 1810–17), canals, dams (Rudyard dam, Staffordshire, 1800), and harbours.

Renoir Jean 1894–1979. French film director, son of the painter Auguste Renoir, whose films include *La Grande Illusion/Grand Illusion* 1937, and *Règle du Jeu/The Rules of the Game* 1939.

Renoir Pierre-Auguste 1841–1919. French Impressionist painter. He met Monet and Sisley in the early 1860s and together they formed the nucleus of the Impressionist movement. He developed a lively, colourful painting style with feathery brushwork and painted many voluptuous female nudes, such as *The Bathers* about 1884–87 (Philadelphia Museum of Art, USA). In his later years he turned to sculpture.

Born in Limoges, Renoir originally trained as a porcelain painter. He joined an academic studio 1861, and the first strong influences on his style were the Rococo artists Boucher and Watteau and the Realist Courbet, but in the late 1860s Impressionism made its impact and Renoir began to work out of doors. Painting with Monet, he produced many pictures of people at leisure by the river Seine. From 1879 he made several journeys abroad, to N Africa, the Channel Islands, Italy, and later to the UK, the Netherlands, Spain, and Germany. After his Italian visit of 1881 he moved towards a more Classical structure in his work, notably in *Les Parapluies/Umbrellas* about 1881–84 (National Gallery, London). In 1906 he settled in the south of France. Many of his sculptures are monumental female nudes not unlike those of ◊Maillol.

Repin Ilya Yefimovich 1844–1930. Russian painter. His work includes dramatic studies, such as *Barge Haulers on the Volga* 1873 and portraits, including Tolstoy and Mussorgsky.

Repton Humphrey 1752–1818. English garden designer, who coined the term 'landscape gardening'. He worked for some years in partnership with John ◊Nash. Repton preferred more formal landscaping than Capability ◊Brown, and was responsible for the landscaping of some 200 gardens and parks.

Resnais Alain 1922– . French film director, whose work is characterized by the themes of memory and unconventional concepts of time. His films include *Hiroshima mon amour* 1959, *L'Année dernière à Marienbad/Last Year at Marienbad* 1961 and *Providence* 1977.

Respighi Ottorino 1879–1936. Italian composer, a student of ◊Rimsky-Korsakov, whose works include the symphonic poems *The Fountains of Rome* 1917 and *The Pines of Rome* 1924 (incorporating the recorded song of a nightingale), operas, and chamber music.

Retz Jean François Paul de Gondi, Cardinal de Retz 1614–1679. French politician. A priest with political ambitions, he stirred up and largely led the insurrection known as the Fronde. After a period of imprisonment and exile he was restored to favour 1662 and created abbot of St Denis.

Reuter Paul Julius, Baron de Reuter 1816–1899. German founder of Reuters international news agency. He began a continental pigeon post 1849, and in 1851 he set up a news agency in London. In 1858 he persuaded the press to use his news telegrams, and the service became worldwide.

The agency became a private trust 1916, and was taken over by the Newspaper Proprietors' Association 1926–41. It became a public company 1984.

Revans Reginald William 1907– . British management expert, originator of the 'action learning' method of management improvement, for example, that each department of a firm probes the problem-avoiding system of some other department until the circle is completed, with resultant improved productivity.

Revere Paul 1735–1818. American nationalist, a Boston silversmith, who carried the news of the approach of British troops, intent on seizing military stores, to Lexington and Concord on the night of 18 Apr 1775. Longfellow's poem 'Paul Revere's Ride' commemorates the event.

Revere's silver *Sons of Liberty* punchbowl 1768 (Museum of Fine Arts, Boston, USA) is his best-known piece. He also produced propaganda prints exposing British atrocities in the war.

Reynaud Paul 1878–1966. French prime minister in World War II, who succeeded Edouard Daladier Mar 1940, but resigned June after the German breakthrough. He was imprisoned by the Germans until 1945, and again held government offices after the war.

Reynolds Burt 1936– . US film actor in adventure films and comedies. His films include *Deliverance* 1972, *Hustle* 1975, and *City Heat* 1984.

Reynolds Joshua 1723–1792. English portrait painter, active in London from 1752. He became the first president of the Royal Academy 1768. His portraits display a facility for striking and characterful compositions in a consciously grand manner. He often borrowed classical poses, for example *Mrs Siddons as the Tragic Muse* 1784 (San Marino, California, USA).

Reynolds, born near Plymouth, went to London at the age of 17, and was apprenticed to the portrait painter Thomas Hudson (1701– 79). From 1743 he practised in Plymouth and London, and 1749–52 completed his studies in Rome and Venice, concentrating on the antique and the High Renaissance masters.

After his return to London he became the leading portraitist of his day, for example *Admiral Keppel* 1753–54 (National Maritime Museum, London). His *Discourses on Art* 1769–91 contain his theories on the aims of academic art.

Reynolds Osborne 1842–1912. British physicist and engineer who studied fluid flow, and devised the **Reynolds number**, which relates to turbulence in flowing fluids.

Rhee Syngman 1875–1965. Korean right-wing politician. A rebel under Chinese and Japanese rule, he became president of South Korea from 1948 until riots forced him to resign and leave the country 1960.

Rhine Joseph Banks 1895–1980. US parapsychologist. His work at Duke University, North Carolina, involving controlled laboratory experiments in telepathy, clairvoyance, precognition, and psychokinesis, described in *Extra-Sensory Perception*, 1934 made ESP a common term.

Rhodes Cecil (John) 1853–1902. South African politician, born in the UK, prime minister of Cape Colony 1890–96. Aiming at the formation of a South African federation and of a block of British territory from the Cape to Cairo, he was responsible for the annexation of Bechuanaland (now Botswana) in 1885, and formed the British South Africa Company in 1889, which occupied Mashonaland and Matabeleland, thus forming *Rhodesia* (now Zambia and Zimbabwe).

Rhodes went to Natal in 1870. As head of De Beers Consolidated Mines and Goldfields of South Africa Ltd, he amassed a large fortune. He entered the Cape legislature in 1881, and became prime minister in 1890, but the discovery of his complicity in the Jameson Raid into Transvaal forced him to resign in 1896. Advocating Anglo-Afrikaner cooperation, he was less alive to the rights of black Africans, despite the final 1898 wording of his dictum: 'Equal rights for every civilized man south of the Zambezi'.

The *Rhodes scholarships* were founded at Oxford University, UK, under his will, for students from the Commonwealth, USA, and Germany.

Rhodes Wilfred 1877–1973. English cricketer. He was the game's most prolific wicket-taker, taking 4,187 wickets 1898–1930, and also scoring 39,802 first class runs.

Playing for Yorkshire Rhodes made a record 763 appearances in the county championship. When he played his 58th and final game for England, against West Indies 1930, he was over 52 years old, the oldest ever test cricketer.

Rhodes Zandra 1940– . English fashion designer, known for the extravagant fantasy and luxury of her dress creations.

Rhys Jean 1894–1979. British novelist, born in Dominica. Her works include *Wide Sargasso Sea* 1966, a recreation of the life of Rochester's mad wife in *Jane Eyre* by Charlotte Brontë.

Ribalta Francisco 1565–1628. Spanish painter, active in Valencia from 1599. Around 1615 he developed a dramatic Baroque style using extreme effects of light and shade (recalling ◊Caravaggio), as in *St Bernard Embracing Christ* about 1620–28 (Prado, Madrid).

Ribbentrop Joachim von 1893–1946. German Nazi leader, born in the Rhineland. He joined the Nazi Party 1932, acted as Hitler's adviser on foreign affairs, and was German ambassador to Britain 1936–38 and foreign minister 1938–45. He was tried at Nuremberg as a war criminal 1946 and hanged.

Ribera José (Jusepe) de 1591–1652. Spanish painter, active in Italy from 1616 under the patronage of the viceroys of Naples. His early work shows the impact of Caravaggio, but his colours gradually lightened. He painted many full-length saints and mythological figures, and genre scenes, which he produced without preliminary drawing.

Ricardo David 1772–1823. English economist, author of *Principles of Political Economy* 1817. Among his discoveries were the principle of comparative advantage (that countries can benefit by specializing in goods they produce efficiently and trading internationally to buy others), and the law of diminishing returns (that continued increments of capital and labour applied to a given quantity of land will eventually show a declining rate of increase in output).

Rice Elmer 1892–1967. US playwright. His works include *The Adding Machine* 1923 and *Street Scene* 1929, which won a Pulitzer Prize and was made into an opera by Kurt Weill. Many of his plays deal with such economic and political issues as the Depression (*We, the People* 1933) and racism (*American Landscape* 1939).

Rice-Davies Mandy (Marilyn) 1944– . English model. She achieved notoriety in 1963 following the revelations of the affair between her friend Christine ◊Keeler and war minister John ◊Profumo and his subsequent resignation.

Rich Adrienne 1929– . US radical feminist poet, writer, and critic. Her poetry is both subjective and political, concerned with female consciousness, peace, and gay rights. Her works include *The Fact of a Doorframe: Poems Selected and New* 1984 and *On Lies, Secrets and Silence* 1979.

Richard Cliff. Stage name of Harry Roger Webb 1940– . English pop singer. In the late 1950s he was influenced by Elvis Presley, but became a Christian family entertainer, continuing to have hits in the UK through the 1980s. His original backing group were the *Shadows* (1958–68 and later re-formed).

Richard three kings of England:

Richard I the Lionheart (French *Coeur-de-Lion*) 1157–1199. King of England from 1189. He was the third son of Henry II, against whom he twice rebelled. In the third Crusade 1191–92 he won victories at Cyprus, Acre, and Arsuf (against ◊Saladin), but failed to recover Jerusalem. While returning overland he was captured by the Duke of Austria, who handed him over to the emperor Henry VI, and he was held prisoner until a large ransom was raised. His later years were spent in warfare in France, and he was killed while besieging Châluo. Himself a poet, he became a hero of legends after his death. He was succeeded by his brother John.

Richard II 1367–1400. King of England from 1377, effectively from 1389, son of Edward the Black Prince.

Richard was born in Bordeaux. He succeeded his grandfather Edward III when only ten, the government being in the hands of a council of regency. His fondness for favourites resulted in conflicts with Parliament, and in 1388 the baronial party headed by the Duke of Gloucester had many of his friends executed. Richard recovered control 1389, and ruled moderately until 1397, when he had Gloucester murdered and his other leading opponents executed or banished, and assumed absolute power. In 1399 his cousin Henry Bolingbroke, Duke of Hereford (later Henry IV), returned from exile to lead a revolt; Richard II was deposed by Parliament and imprisoned in Pontefract Castle, where he died mysteriously.

Richard III 1452–1485. King of England from 1483. The son of Richard, Duke of York, he was created duke of Gloucester by his brother Edward IV, and distinguished himself in the Wars of the Roses. On Edward's death 1483 he became protector to his nephew Edward V, and soon secured the crown on the plea that Edward IV's sons were illegitimate. He proved a capable ruler, but the suspicion that he had murdered Edward V and his brother undermined his popularity. In 1485 Henry, Earl of Richmond (later ◊Henry VII), raised a rebellion, and Richard III was defeated and killed at the battle of Bosworth. Scholars now tend to minimize the evidence for his crimes as Tudor propaganda.

Richards Frank. Pen name of Charles Harold St John Hamilton 1875–1961. English writer for the children's papers *Magnet* and *Gem*, who invented Greyfriars public school and the fat boy Billy Bunter.

Richards Gordon 1905–1986. English jockey and trainer who was champion on the flat a record 26 times 1925–1953.

He started riding 1920 and rode 4,870 winners from 21,834 mounts before retiring 1954 and taking up training. He rode the winners of all the Classics but only once won the Derby, on *Pinza* 1953.

Richards I(vor) A(rmstrong) 1893–1979. English literary critic. He collaborated with C K ◊Ogden and wrote *Principles of Literary Criticism* 1924. In 1939 he went to Harvard, USA, where he taught detailed attention to the text and had a strong influence on contemporary US literary criticism.

Richards Theodore 1868–1928. US chemist. Working at Harvard University, Boston, for much of his career, Richards concentrated upon determining as accurately as possible the atomic weights of a large number of elements. He was awarded the 1914 Nobel Prize for Chemistry.

Richardson Dorothy 1873–1957. English novelist whose works were collected under the title *Pilgrimage* 1938. She used the 'stream of conciousness' technique to great effect and has been linked with Virginia ◊Woolf in creating a specifically feminine genre. Woolf credited her as having invented 'the psychological sentence of the feminine gender'.

Richardson Harry Hobson 1838–1886. US architect, who designed buildings in a Romanesque style derived from that of N Spain. He had a strong influence on Louis ◊Sullivan.

Richardson Henry Handel. Pen name of Ethel Henrietta Richardson 1880–1946. Australian novelist, born in Melbourne, who left Australia when only 18. Her work *The Fortunes of Richard Mahony* 1917–29 reflects her father's life.

Richardson Owen Williams 1879–1959. British physicist. He studied the emission of electricity from hot bodies, giving the name 'thermionics' to the subject. At Cambridge, he worked under J J ◊Thomson in the Cavendish Laboratory, and received a Nobel prize 1928.

Richardson Ralph (David) 1902–1983. English actor. He played many stage parts, including Falstaff (Shakespeare), Peer Gynt (Ibsen), and Cyrano de Bergerac (Rostand). He shared the management of the Old Vic theatre with Laurence Olivier 1944–50.

Later stage successes include *Home* 1970 and *No Man's Land* 1976. His films include *Things to Come* 1936, *Richard III* 1956, *Our Man in Havana* 1959, *The Wrong Box* 1966, *The Bed Sitting Room* 1969, and *O Lucky Man!* 1973.

Richardson Samuel 1689–1761. English novelist, one of the founders of the modern novel. *Pamela* 1740–41, written in the form of a series of letters, and containing much dramatic conversation, achieved a sensational vogue all across Europe, and was followed by *Clarissa* 1747–48, and *Sir Charles Grandison* 1753–54.

Born in Derbyshire, he was brought up in London and apprenticed to a printer. He set up his own business in London 1719, becoming printer to the House of Commons. All his six young children died, followed by his wife 1731, which permanently affected his health.

Richardson Tony 1928– . English director and producer. With George Devine he established the English Stage Company 1955 at the Royal Court Theatre, with productions such as *Look Back in Anger* 1956. His films include *Saturday Night and Sunday Morning* 1960, *A Taste of Honey* 1961, *Tom Jones* 1963, *Dead Cert* 1974, and *Joseph Andrews* 1977. He is the father of actress Natasha Richardson.

Richelieu Armand Jean du Plessis de 1585–1642. French cardinal and politician, chief minister from 1624. He aimed to make the monarchy absolute; he ruthlessly crushed opposition by the nobility, and destroyed the political power of the Huguenots, while leaving them religious freedom. Abroad he sought to establish French supremacy by breaking the power of the Habsburgs; he therefore supported the Swedish king Gustavus Adolphus and the German Protestant princes against Austria, and in 1635 brought France into the Thirty Years' War.

Born in Paris of a noble family, he entered the church, and was created bishop of Luçon 1606 and a cardinal 1622. Through the influence of Marie de' ◊Medici he became ◊Louis XIII's chief minister 1624, a position he retained until his death. His secretary Père ◊Joseph was the original Grey Eminence.

Richler Mordecai 1931– . Canadian novelist, born in Montreal. His novels, written in a witty, acerbic style, include *The Apprenticeship of Duddy Kravitz* 1959 and *St Urbain's Horseman* 1971.

Richter Burton 1931– . US high energy physicist who, in the 1960s, designed the Stanford Positron Accelerating Ring (SPEAR). In 1974 Richter used SPEAR to produce a new particle, later named the ψ (psi) particle, thought to be formed from the charmed quark postulated by Sheldon ◊Glashow. Richter shared the 1976 Nobel Prize for Physics with Samuel ◊Ting.

Richter Charles Francis 1900–1985. US seismologist, deviser of the **Richter scale** used to measure the strength of the waves from earth-quakes.

Richter Johann Paul Friedrich 1763–1825. German author, commonly known as Jean Paul. He created a series of comic eccentrics in works such as the romance *Titan* 1800–03 and *Die Flegeljahre/The Awkward Age* 1804–05.

Richter Sviatoslav (Teofilovich) 1915– . Russian pianist, an outstanding interpreter of Schubert, Schumann, Rachmaninov, and Prokofiev.

Richthofen Ferdinand Baron von 1833–1905. German geographer and traveller who carried out extensive studies in China 1867–70 and subsequently explored Java, Thailand, Myanmar (Burma), Japan, and California.

Richthofen Manfred, Freiherr von (the 'Red Baron') 1892–1918. German aviator. In World War I he commanded the 11th Chasing Squadron, known as *Richthofen's Flying Circus*, and shot down 80 aircraft before being killed in action.

Riding, (Jackson), Laura 1901– . US poet, a member of the Fugitive Group of poets, which flourished in the Southern USA 1915–28. She went to England in 1926 and worked with the writer Robert Graves. She published her *Collected Poems* in 1938 wrote no more verse, but turned to linguistics in order to analyse the expression of 'truth'.

Ridley Nicholas *c.* 1500–1555. English Protestant bishop. He became chaplain to Henry VIII 1541, and bishop of London 1550. He took an active part in the Reformation and supported Lady Jane Grey's claim to the throne. After Mary's accession he was arrested and burned as a heretic.

Ridley Nicholas 1929– . British Conservative politician, and cabinet minister. After a period in industry he became active as a 'dry' right winger in the Conservative Party: a 'Thatcherite' before Margaret ◊Thatcher had brought the term to public attention. He served under Harold Macmillan, Edward Heath and Alec Douglas-Home, but did not become a member of the cabinet until 1983. His apparent disdain for public opinion caused his transfer, in 1989, from the Department of the Environment to that of Trade and Industry, and his resignation 1990 after ill-considered remarks about Germany.

Rie Lucie 1902– . Austrian-born potter who worked in England from the 1930s. Her pottery, exhibited all over the world, is simple and pure in form, showing a debt to Bernard ◊Leach.

Riefenstahl Leni 1902– . German filmmaker. Her film of the Nazi rallies at Nuremberg *Triumph des Willens/Triumph of the Will* 1934 vividly illustrated Hitler's charismatic appeal but tainted her career. After World War II her work was blacklisted by the Allies until 1952.

She trained as a dancer, appearing in films in the 1920s, but in the early 1930s formed her own production company, and directed and starred in

Das blaue Licht/The Blue Light 1932. She also made a two-part documentary of the 1936 Berlin Olympics (*Olympiad: Fest der Volker/Festival of the Nations* and *Olympiad: Fest der Schönheit/Festival of Beauty*).

Riel Louis 1844–1885. French-Canadian rebel, a champion of the Métis (an Indian-French people); he established a provisional government in Winnipeg in an unsuccessful revolt 1869–70 and was hanged for treason after leading a second revolt in Saskatchewan 1885.

Riemann Georg Friedrich Bernhard 1826–1866. German mathematician whose system of non-Euclidean geometry, thought to be a mere mathematical curiosity, was used by Einstein to develop his General Theory of Relativity.

Rienzi Cola di *c.* 1313–1354. Italian political reformer. In 1347, he tried to re-establish the forms of an ancient Roman republic. His second attempt seven years later ended with his assassination.

Riesman David 1909– . US sociologist, author of *The Lonely Crowd: A Study of the Changing American Character* 1950.

Rietvelt Gerrit Thomas 1888–1964. Dutch architect, an exponent of De Stijl (see ◊Mondrian). He designed the Schroeder House at Utrecht 1924; he is also well known for colourful, minimalist chair design.

Rigaud Hyacinthe 1659–1743. French portraitist, court painter to Louis XIV from 1688. His portrait of *Louis XIV* 1701 (Louvre, Paris) is characteristically majestic, with the elegant figure of the king enveloped in ermine and drapery.

Rigg Diana 1938– . English actress. Her stage roles include Héloïse in *Abelard and Héloïse* 1970, and television roles include Emma Peel in *The Avengers* 1965–67 and Lady Deadlock in *Bleak House* 1985. She became the hostess for *Mystery Theater* on US public TV 1989.

Riley Bridget (Louise) 1931– . British Op art painter. In the early 1960s she invented her characteristic style, arranging hard-edged black-and-white dots or lines in regular patterns that created disturbing effects of scintillating light and movement. *Fission* 1963 (Museum of Modern Art, New York) is an example of this style. She introduced colour in the late 1960s and experimented with silk-screen prints on Perspex.

Rilke Rainer Maria 1875–1926. Austrian writer, born in Prague. His prose works include the semi-autobiographical *Die Aufzeichnungen des Malte Laurids Brigge/Notebook of Malte Laurids Brigge* 1910, and his poetical works *Die Sonnette an Orpheus/Sonnets to Orpheus* 1923 and *Duisener Elegien/Duino Elegies* 1923. His verse is characterized by a form of mystic pantheism that seeks to achieve a state of ecstasy in which existence can be apprehended as a whole.

Rimbaud (Jean Nicolas) Arthur 1854–1891. French Symbolist poet. His verse was chiefly written before the age of 20, notably *Les Illuminations* published 1886.

From 1871 he lived with ◊Verlaine. Although the association ended after Verlaine attempted to shoot him, it was Verlaine's analysis of Rimbaud's work 1884 which first brought him recognition. Rimbaud then travelled widely, working as a trader in N Africa 1880–91.

Rimsky-Korsakov Nikolay Andreyevich 1844–1908. Russian composer. He used Russian folk idiom and rhythms in his Romantic compositions and published a text on orchestration. His operas include *The Maid of Pskov* 1873, *The Snow Maiden* 1882, *Mozart and Salieri* 1898, and *The Golden Cockerel* 1907, a satirical attack on despotism that was banned until 1909.

Other works include the symphonic poem *Sadko* 1867, the programme symphony *Antar* 1869, and the symphonic suite *Scheherazade* 1888. He also completed works by other composers, for example, ◊Mussorgsky's *Boris Godunov*.

Riopelle Jean Paul 1923– . Canadian artist, active in Paris from 1946. In the 1950s he developed an Abstract Expressionism style and produced colourful impasto (with paint applied in a thick mass) paintings and sculptures. *Encounter* 1956 (Wallraf-Richartz Museum, Cologne, West Germany) is a typically rough-textured canvas.

Ritter (Woodward Maurice) 'Tex' 1905–1974. US singer and actor, popular as a singing cowboy in 'B' films in the 1930s and 1940s. He sang the title song to *High Noon* 1952, and his other films include *Sing Cowboy Sing* 1937 and *Arizona Trail* 1943.

Rivera Diego 1886–1957. Mexican painter, active in Europe until 1921. He received many public commissions for murals exalting the Mexican revolution. A vast cycle on historical themes (National Palace, Mexico City) was begun 1929. In the 1930s he visited the USA and produced murals in the Rockefeller Center, New York (later overpainted because he included a portrait of Lenin).

Rivera Primo de. Spanish politician; see ◊Primo de Rivera.

Rix Brian 1924– . British actor and manager. He became known for his series of farces at London's Whitehall Theatre, notably *Dry Rot* 1954–58. He made several films for cinema and television, including *A Roof Over My Head* 1977, and promotes charities for the mentally handicapped.

Rizzio David 1533–1566. Italian adventurer at the court of Mary, Queen of Scots. After her marriage to ◊Darnley, Rizzio's influence over her incited her husband's jealousy, and he was murdered by Darnley and his friends.

Roach Hal 1892– . US film producer, usually of comedies, active from the 1910s to the 1940s. He worked with ◊Laurel and Hardy, and also produced films for Harold Lloyd and Charley Chase.

His work includes *The Music Box* 1932, *Way Out West* 1936, and *Of Mice and Men* 1939.

Robbe-Grillet Alain 1922– . French writer, the leading theorist of *le nouveau roman* ('the new novel'), for example his own *Les Gommes/The Erasers* 1953, *La Jalousie/Jealousy* 1957, and *Dans le labyrinthe/In the Labyrinth* 1959, which concentrates on detailed description of physical objects. He also wrote the script for the film *L'Année dernière à Marienbad/Last Year in Marienbad* 1961.

Robbia, della Italian family of sculptors and architects, active in Florence. **Luca della Robbia** (1400–1482) created a number of important works in Florence, notably the marble *cantoria* (singing gallery) in the cathedral 1431–38 (Museo del Duomo), with lively groups of choristers. Luca also developed a characteristic style of glazed terracotta work.

Andrea della Robbia (1435–1525), Luca's nephew and pupil, and Andrea's sons continued the family business, inheriting the formula for the vitreous terracotta glaze. The blue and white medallions of foundling children 1463–66 on the Ospedale degli Innocenti, Florence, are well known. Many later works are more elaborate and highly coloured, such as the frieze 1522 on the façade of the Ospedale del Ceppo, Pistoia.

Robbins Jerome 1918– . US dancer and choreographer. He choreographed the musicals *The King and I* 1951, *West Side Story* 1957, and *Fiddler on the Roof* 1964. Robbins was ballet master of the New York City Ballet 1969–83, when he became joint ballet master-in-chief.

First a chorus boy on Broadway, then a soloist with the newly formed American Ballet Theater 1941–46, Robbins was associate director of the New York City Ballet 1949–59. Among his ballets are *Fancy Free* 1940 (adapted with Leonard Bernstein into the musical *On the Town* 1944). He also choreographed *Facsimile* 1946 and *The Age of Anxiety* 1950 (again with Bernstein).

Robert two dukes of Normandy, including:

Robert II *c.*1054–1134. Eldest son of ◊William I (the Conqueror), succeeding him as duke of Normandy (but not on the English throne) 1087. His brother ◊William II ascended the English throne, and they warred until 1096, allowing Robert to take part in the First Crusade. When his other brother ◊Henry I claimed the English throne 1100, Robert contested the claim and invaded England unsuccessfully 1101. Henry invaded Normandy 1106, and captured Robert, who remained a prisoner in England until his death.

Robert three kings of Scotland:

Robert I *Robert the Bruce* 1274–1329. King of Scotland from 1306, and grandson of Robert de ◊Bruce. He shared in the national uprising led by William ◊Wallace, and, after Wallace's execution 1305, rose once more against Edward I of England, and was crowned at Scone 1306. He defeated Edward II at the battle of Bannockburn 1314. In 1328 the treaty of Northampton recognized Scotland's independence and Robert as king.

Robert II 1316–1390. King of Scotland from 1371. He was the son of Walter (1293–1326), steward of Scotland, who married Marjory, daughter of Robert I. He was the first king of the house of Stuart.

Robert III c.1340–1406. King of Scotland from 1390, son of Robert II. He was unable to control the nobles, and the government fell largely into the hands of his brother, Robert, duke of Albany (c.1340–1420).

Roberts Bartholomew 1682–1722. British merchant-navy captain who joined his captors when taken by pirates in 1718. He became the most financially successful of all the sea rovers until surprised and killed in battle by the British navy.

Roberts David 1796–1864. Scottish painter whose oriental paintings were the result of several trips to the Middle East.

Roberts progressed from interior decorator to scene painter at Drury Lane Theatre, London, while making a name for himself with picturesque views of London and French cathedrals. From 1831 he travelled to Europe and the Middle East producing topographical views. Many of these were published in books including the six-volume *The Holy Land, Syria, Idumea, Arabia, Egypt & Nubia* 1842–49.

Roberts Frederick Sleigh, 1st Earl Roberts 1832–1914. British field marshal, known as 'Bobs'. During the Afghan War of 1878–80 he occupied Kabul, and during the Second South African War (1899–1902) he made possible the annexation of the Transvaal and Orange Free State.

Roberts 'Tom' (Thomas William) 1856–1931. Australian painter, born in England, founder of the **Heidelberg School**, which introduced Impressionism to Australia.

Roberts arrived in Australia in 1869, returning to Europe to study 1881–85. He received official commissions, including one to paint the opening of the first Australian federal parliament, but is better known for his scenes of pioneering life.

Robertson Thomas William 1829–1871. English dramatist. Initially an actor, he had his first success as a dramatist with *David Garrick* 1864, which set a new, realistic trend in English drama of the time; later plays included *Society* 1865 and *Caste* 1867.

Robeson Paul 1898–1976. US bass singer and actor. He graduated from Columbia University as a lawyer, but limited opportunities for blacks led him instead to the stage. He appeared in *The Emperor Jones* 1924 and *Showboat* 1928, in which

Robeson US singer and actor Paul Robeson testifies before the HUAC committee in Washington, June 1948.

he sang 'Ol' Man River'. He played *Othello* in 1930, and his films include *Sanders of the River* 1935 and *King Solomon's Mines* 1937. An ardent advocate of black rights, he had his passport withdrawn 1950–58 because of his association with left-wing movements. He then left the USA to live in England.

Robespierre Maximilien François Marie Isidore de 1758–1794. French politician in the French Revolution. As leader of the pre-revolutionary Jacobins in the National Convention he supported the execution of Louis XVI and the overthrow of the Girondins, and in July 1793 was elected to the Committee of Public Safety. A year later he was guillotined; many believe that he was a scapegoat for the Reign of Terror since he only ordered 72 executions personally.

Robespierre, a lawyer, was elected to the National Assembly of 1789–91. His defence of democratic principles made him popular in Paris, while his disinterestedness won him the nickname of 'the Incorruptible'. His zeal for social reform and his attacks on the excesses of the extremists made him enemies on both right and left; a conspiracy was formed against him, and in July 1794 he was overthrown and executed by those who actually perpetrated the Reign of Terror.

Robin Hood legendary English outlaw and champion of the poor against the rich. He is said to have lived in Sherwood Forest, Nottinghamshire, during the reign of Richard I (King of England 1189–99). He feuded with the Sheriff of Nottingham, accompanied by Maid Marian and a band of followers, known as his 'merry men'. He appears in ballads from the 13th century, but his first datable appearance is in Langland's *Piers Plowman* about 1377.

Robinson Edward G. Stage name of Emanuel Goldenberg 1893–1973. US film actor, born in Romania, he emigrated with his family to the USA 1903. He was noted for his gangster roles, such as *Little Caesar* 1930. Other films include *Dr Ehrlich's Magic Bullet* 1940, *Double Indemnity* 1944, *The Ten Commandments* 1956, and *Soylent Green* 1973.

Robinson Edwin Arlington 1869–1935. US poet. His verse, dealing mainly with psychological themes in a narrative style, includes *The Children of the Night* 1897, which established his reputation, and *The Man Who Died Twice* 1924.

Robinson Henry Crabb 1775–1867. English writer, whose diaries, journals, and letters are a valuable source of information on his friends ◊Lamb, ◊Coleridge, ◊Wordsworth, and ◊Southey.

Robinson Joan (Violet) 1903–1983. British economist who introduced Marxism to Keynesian economic theory. She expanded her analysis in *Economics of Perfect Competition* 1933.

Robinson John Arthur Thomas 1919–1983. British Anglican cleric, bishop of Woolwich 1959–69. A left-wing Modernist, he wrote *Honest to God* 1963, which was interpreted as denying a personal God.

Robinson Robert 1886–1975. English chemist, Nobel prizewinner 1947 for his research in organic chemistry on the structure and synthesis of many natural products, for example flower pigments and alkaloids.

Robinson 'Sugar' Ray. Assumed name of Walker Smith 1920–1989. US boxer, world welterweight champion 1945–51, defending his title five times. He defeated Jake LaMotta 1951 to take the middleweight title. He lost the title six times and won it seven times. He had 202 fights, and fought until the age of 45.

Robinson W(illiam) Heath 1872–1944. British cartoonist and illustrator, known for his humorous drawings of bizarre machinery for performing simple tasks, such as raising one's hat. Clumsy designs are often described as a 'Heath Robinson' contraption.

Rob Roy nickname of Robert MacGregor 1671–1734. Scottish Highland Jacobite (supporter of James Edward ◊Stuart) outlaw. After losing his estates, he lived by cattle theft and extortion. Captured, he was sentenced to transportation but pardoned 1727. He is a central character in Walter Scott's historical novel *Rob Roy* 1817.

Robson Flora 1902–1984. English actress. Her successes included Queen Elizabeth in the film *Fire Over England* 1931 and Mrs Alving in Ibsen's *Ghosts* 1959.

Rocard Michel 1930– . French socialist politician. A former radical, he joined the Socialist Party (PS) 1973, emerging as leader of its moderate social-democratic wing. He held ministerial office under Mitterrand 1981–85, and was appointed prime minister 1988.

Rocard trained at the prestigious Ecole National d'Administration, where he was a classmate of Jacques Chirac. He became leader of the radical Unified Socialist Party (PSU) 1967, standing as its presidential candidate 1969.

Having gone over to the PS, he challenged François Mitterand for the party's presidential nomination 1981. After serving as minister of planning and regional development 1981–83 and of agriculture 1983–85 in the ensuing Mitterrand administration, he resigned Apr 1985 in opposition to the government's introduction of proportional representation. In May 1988, however, as part of a strategy termed 'opening to the centre', the popular Rocard was appointed prime minister by Mitterrand.

Roche Stephen 1959– . Irish cyclist. One of the outstanding riders on the continent in the 1980s, he was the first British winner of the Tour de France in 1987 and the first English-speaking winner of the Tour of Italy the same year, as well as the 1987 world professional road race champion.

Rochester John Wilmot, 2nd Earl of Rochester 1647–1680. English poet and courtier. He fought gallantly at sea against the Dutch, but chiefly led a debauched life at the court of Charles II. He wrote graceful (but often obscene) lyrics, and his *A Satire against Mankind* 1675 rivals Swift. He was patron of John Dryden.

Rockefeller John D(avison) 1839–1937. US millionaire, founder of Standard Oil 1870 (which achieved control of 90% of US refineries by 1882). The activities of the Standard Oil Trusts led to an outcry against monopolies and the passing of the Sherman Anti-Trust Act of 1890. A lawsuit of 1892 prompted the dissolution of the Trust, only for it to be refounded in 1899 as a holding company. In 1911, this was also declared illegal by the Supreme Court. He founded the philanthropic *Rockefeller Foundation* 1913, to which his son *John D(avison) Rockefeller Jr* (1874–1960) devoted his life.

Rockingham Charles Watson Wentworth, 2nd Marquess of Rockingham 1730–1782. British Whig politician, prime minister 1765–66 and 1782 (when he died in office); he supported the American claim to independence.

Rockwell Norman 1894–1978. US painter and illustrator, noted for magazine covers and cartoons portraying American life. His folksy view of the nation earned him huge popularity.

Roddick Anita 1943– . British entrepreneur, founder of the Body Shop, which now has branches worldwide. Roddick started with one shop in Brighton, England 1976, selling only natural products in refillable plastic containers.

Rodgers Richard (Charles) 1902–1979. US composer. He collaborated with librettist Lorenz Hart

(1895–1943) on songs such as 'Blue Moon' 1934, and musicals such as *On Your Toes* 1936; and with Oscar Hammerstein II (1895–1960) in musicals such as *Oklahoma!* 1943, *South Pacific* 1949, *The King and I* 1951, and *The Sound of Music* 1959.

Rodin Auguste 1840–1917. French sculptor, considered the greatest of his time. Through his work he freed sculpture from the current idealizing conventions by its realistic treatment of the human figure, introducing a new boldness of style and expression. Examples are *Le Penseur/The Thinker* 1880, *Le Baiser/The Kiss* 1886 (marble version in the Louvre, Paris), and *Les Bourgeois de Calais/The Burghers of Calais* 1885–95 (copy in Embankment Gardens, Westminster, London).

Rodin started as a mason, began to study in museums and in 1875 visited Italy, where he gained a great admiration for Michelangelo. His early statue *Bronze Age* 1877 (many replicas) was criticized for its total naturalism and accuracy. In 1880 he began the monumental bronze *Gates of Hell* for the Ecole des Arts Décoratifs in Paris (inspired by Ghiberti's bronze gates in Florence), a project that occupied him for many years and was unfinished at his death. Many of the figures designed for the gate became independent sculptures. During the 1890s he received two notable public commissions, for statues of the writers *Balzac* 1897 (Musée Rodin, Paris) and *Hugo*. He also produced many drawings.

Rodney George Brydges, Baron Rodney 1718–1792. British admiral. In 1762 he captured Martinique, St Lucia, and Grenada from the French. In 1780 he relieved Gibraltar by defeating a Spanish squadron off Cape St Vincent. In 1782 he crushed the French fleet under Count de Grasse off Dominica, for which he was raised to the peerage.

Rodnina Irina 1949– . Soviet ice skater. From 1969–1980 she won 23 world, Olympic, and European gold medals in pairs competitions. Her partners were Alexei Ulanov and then Alexsandr Zaitsev, who became her husband 1975.

Roeg Nicolas 1928– . English film director. His work is noted for its stylish visual appeal and imaginative, often off-beat, treatment of subjects. His films include *Performance* 1970, *Walkabout* 1971, *Don't Look Now* 1973, *The Man Who Fell to Earth* 1976, *Insignificance* 1984, and *Track 29* 1988.

Roethke Theodore 1908–1963. US poet. His father owned a large nursery business, and the greenhouses and plants of his childhood provide the detail and imagery of much of his lyrical, personal, and visionary poetry. Collections include *Open House* 1941, *The Lost Son* 1948, *The Waking* 1953 (Pulitzer Prize), and the posthumous *Collected Poems* 1968.

Rogers Carl 1902–1987. US psychologist who developed the client-centred approach to counselling and psychotherapy. This stressed the importance of clients making their own decisions and developing their own potential (self-actualization).

Rogers Ginger. Stage name of Virginia Katherine McMath 1911– . US actress, dancer and singer. She worked from the 1930s to the 1950s, often starring with Fred Astaire in such films as *Top Hat* 1935 and *Swing Time* 1936. Her later work includes *Bachelor Mother* 1939 and *Kitty Foyle* 1940.

Rogers Richard 1933– . British architect. His works include the Centre Pompidou in Paris 1977 (jointly with Renzo Piano) and the Lloyd's building in London 1986.

Rogers Roy. Stage name of Leonard Slye 1912– US actor who moved to the cinema from radio. He was one of the original singing cowboys of the 1930s and 1940s. Confined to 'B' films for most of his career, he appeared opposite Bob Hope and Jane Russell in *Son of Paleface* 1952. His other films include *The Big Show* 1936 and *My Pal Trigger* 1946.

Roget Peter Mark 1779–1869. English physician, one of the founders of the University of London, and author of a *Thesaurus of English Words and Phrases* 1852, a text constantly revised and republished, and still in use.

Röhm Ernst 1887–1934. German leader of the Nazi 'Brownshirts', the SA (*Sturmabteilung*). On the pretext of an intended SA *Putsch* (uprising) some hundred of them, including Röhm, were killed 29–30 June 1934, known as 'the Night of the Long Knives'.

Rohmer Eric. Adopted name of Jean-Marie Maurice Sherer 1920– . French film director and writer, formerly a critic and television director. Part of the French new wave, his films are concerned with exploring the minds of his characters. They include *My Night at Maud's/Ma Nuit chez Maud* 1969, *Claire's Knee/Le Genou de Claire* 1970, and *The Marquise of O/La Marquise d'O/Die Marquise von O* 1976.

Rohmer Sax. Pen name of Arthur Sarsfield Ward 1886–1959. English crime writer who created the sinister Chinese character Fu Manchu.

Roh Tae-woo 1932– . South Korean right-wing politician and general. He held ministerial office from 1981 under President Chun, and became chairman of the ruling Democratic Justice Party 1985. He was elected president 1987, amid allegations of fraud and despite being connected with the massacre of about 2,000 anti-government demonstrators 1980.

Roh was born in the SE region of Kyongsang. A Korean Military Academy classmate of Chun Doo-Hwan, he fought in the Korean War and later, during the 1970s, became commander of the 9th Special Forces Brigade and Capital Security Command. Roh retired as a four-star general July 1981 and served as national security, foreign affairs and, later, home affairs minister.

Roland 8th century AD. French hero of many romances, including the 11th-century *Chanson de Roland* and Ariosto's *Orlando Furioso*. Roland was a soldier, killed in 778 with his friend Oliver and the twelve peers of France, at Roncesvalles (in the Pyrenees) by Basques. He headed the rearguard during ◊Charlemagne's retreat from his invasion of Spain.

Roland de la Platière Jeanne Manon (born Philipon) 1754–1793. French intellectual politician, whose salon from 1789 was a focus of democratic discussion. Her ideas were influential after her husband Jean Marie Roland de la Platière (1734–1793) became minister of the interior 1792. As a supporter of the right-wing Girondin party, opposed to Robespierre and Danton, she was condemned to the guillotine 1793, without being allowed to speak in her own defence. Her last words were 'O liberty! What crimes are committed in thy name!' While in prison she wrote *Mémoires*.

Rolfe Frederick 1860–1913. English writer, who called himself Baron Corvo. A Roman Catholic convert, frustrated in his desire to enter the priesthood, he wrote the novel *Hadrian VII* 1904, in which the character of the title rose from being a poor writer to become pope. In *Desire and Pursuit of the Whole* 1934 he wrote about his homosexual fantasies and friends, earning the poet Auden's description of him as 'a master of vituperation'.

Rolle de Hampole Richard *c.*1300–1349. English hermit and author of English and Latin works including the mystic *Meditation of the Passion*.

Rollins 'Sonny' (Theodore Walter) 1930– . US tenor saxophonist and jazz composer. A leader of the 'hard bop' school, he is known for the intensity and bravado of his music, and for his skilful improvisation.

Rollo 1st Duke of Normandy *c.*860–932. Viking leader. He left Norway about 875, and marauded, sailing up the Seine to Rouen. He besieged Paris 886, and in 912 was baptized and granted the province of Normandy by Charles III of France. He was its duke until his retirement to a monastery 927. He was an ancestor of William the Conqueror.

Rolls Charles 1877–1910. British engineer who joined with ◊Royce in 1905 to design and produce their own cars. He trained as as mechanical engineer at Cambridge where he also developed a passion for engines of all kinds. After working initially at the railway works in Crewe, he set up a business in 1902 as a motor dealer. Before the business could flourish he died in 1910 in a flying accident.

Romains Jules. Pen name of Louis Farigoule 1885–1972. French novelist, playwright and poet. His plays include the farce *Knock, ou le triomphe*

de la médecine/Dr Knock 1923 and *Donogoo* 1930, and his novels include *Mort de quelqu'un/Death of a Nobody* 1911, *Les Copains/The Boys in the Back Room* 1913, *Les Hommes de bonne volonté/Men of Good Will* (27 volumes) 1932–47.

Romano Giulio see ◊Giulio Romano, Italian painter and architect.

Romanov dynasty that ruled Russia from 1613 to the Russian Revolution 1917. Under the Romanovs, Russia developed into an absolutist empire. The last Tsar, Nicholas II, abdicated Mar 1917.

Rommel Erwin 1891–1944. German field marshal. He served in World War I, and in World War II he played an important part in the invasions of central Europe and France. He was commander of the N African offensive from 1941 (when he was nicknamed 'Desert Fox') until defeated in the battles of El Alamein. He was commander in chief for a short time against the Allies in Europe 1944 but (as a sympathizer with the ◊Stauffenberg plot) was forced to commit suicide.

Romney George 1734–1802. English portrait painter, active in London from 1762. He painted several portraits of Lady Hamilton, Admiral Nelson's mistress.

Born in Lancashire, the son of a carpenter and cabinet-maker, Romney was virtually self-taught. He set up as a portraitist in 1757, and, deserting his family, in 1762 he went to London. There he became, with Gainsborough and Reynolds, one of the most successful portrait painters of the late 18th century.

Ronsard Pierre de 1524–1585. French poet, leader of the Pléiade group of seven poets. Under the patronage of Charles IX, he published original verse in a lightly sensitive style, including odes and love sonnets, for example *Odes* 1550, *Les Amours/Lovers* 1552–53, and the 'Marie' cycle, *Continuation des amours/Lovers Continued* 1555–56.

Röntgen Wilhelm Konrad 1845–1923. German physicist who discovered X-rays 1895. While investigating the passage of electricity through gases, he noticed the fluorescence of a barium platinocyanide screen. This radiation passed through some substances opaque to light, and affected photographic plates. Developments from this discovery have revolutionized medical diagnosis.

Born at Lennep, he became director of the Physical Institute at Giessen 1879, and at Würzburg 1885, where he conducted his experiments which resulted in the discovery of the rays named after him (now called X-rays). He received a Nobel prize 1901.

Roon Albrecht Theodor Emil, Count von Roon 1803–1879. Prussian field marshal. As war minister from 1859, he reorganized the army and made possible the victories over Austria in 1866 and in the Franco-Prussian War of 1870–71.

Rooney Mickey. Stage name of Joe Yule 1920– . US actor, who began his career aged two in his parents' stage act. He played Andy Hardy in the Hardy Family series of 'B' films (1936–1946) and starred opposite Judy Garland in several musicals, including *Babes in Arms* 1939. He also played Puck in *A Midsummer Night's Dream* 1935, and starred in *Boy's Town* 1938.

Roosevelt (Anna) Eleanor 1884–1962. US social worker and lecturer; her newspaper column 'My Day' was widely syndicated, she was a delegate to the UN general assembly, and later chair of the UN commission on human rights 1946–51. Within the Democratic Party she formed the left-wing Americans for Democratic Action group 1947. She was married to President Franklin Roosevelt.

Roosevelt Franklin Delano 1882–1945. 32nd president of the USA 1933–45, a Democrat. He served as governor of New York 1929–33. Becoming president amid the Depression, he launched the *New Deal* economic and social reform programme, which made him popular with the people. After the outbreak of World War II he introduced lend-lease for the supply of war materials to the Allies and drew up the Atlantic Charter of solidarity, and once the USA had entered the war 1941 he spent much time in meetings with Allied leaders, notably at the Québec, Tehran, and Yalta conferences.

Born in Hyde Park, New York, of a wealthy family, Roosevelt was educated in Europe and at Harvard and Columbia universities, and became a lawyer. In 1910 he was elected to the state senate. He held the assistant secretaryship of the navy in Wilson's administrations 1913–21, and did much to increase the efficiency of the navy during World War I. He suffered from polio from 1921. As president, Roosevelt inculcated a new spirit of hope. Surrounding himself by a 'Brains Trust' of experts, he immediately launched his reform programme. Banks were reopened, federal credit was restored, the gold standard was abandoned, and the dollar devalued. During the first hundred days of his administration, major legislation to facilitate industrial and agricultural recovery was enacted. In 1935 he introduced the Utilities Act, directed against abuses in the large holding companies, and the Social Security Act, providing for unemployment and old-age insurance. The presidential election 1936 was won entirely on the record of the New Deal. During 1935–36 Roosevelt was involved in a long conflict over the composition of the Supreme Court, following its nullification of major New Deal measures as unconstitutional.

In his foreign policy, Roosevelt endeavoured to use his influence to restrain Axis aggression, and to establish 'good neighbour' relations with other countries on the North American continent. Soon after the outbreak of war, he launched a vast

Roosevelt *US president Franklin Roosevelt led his country through the depression of the 1930s and World War II, and was elected for an unprecedented fourth term of office in 1944.*

rearmament programme, introduced conscription, and provided for the supply of armaments to the Allies on a 'cash-and-carry' basis. In spite of strong isolationist opposition, and breaking a long-standing precedent in standing for a third term, he was re-elected 1940. Roosevelt wanted to get the USA into the war for two reasons: to make sure the Allies won so that they could pay back their debts to the USA, and to break up the British Empire. Public opinion, however, was in favour of staying out of the war, so Roosevelt and the military chiefs deliberately kept back the intelligence reports received from the British and others concerning the imminent attack on Pearl Harbor from the armed forces leaders in Hawaii. The slaughter at Pearl Harbor 7 Dec 1941 changed public opinion, and the USA entered the war. From this point on, he concerned himself solely with the conduct of the war. He participated in the Washington 1942 and Casablanca 1943 conferences to plan the Mediterranean assault, and the conferences in Québec, Cairo, and Tehran 1943, and Yalta 1945, at which the final preparations were made for the Allied victory. He was re-elected for a fourth term 1944, but died 1945.

Roosevelt Theodore 1858–1919. 26th president of the USA 1901–09, a Republican. After serving as governor of New York 1898–1900 he became vice president to ◊McKinley, whom he succeeded as president on McKinley's assassination 1901. He campaigned against the great trusts (combines that reduce competition), while carrying on a jingoist foreign policy designed to enforce US supremacy over Latin America. Alienated after his retirement by the conservatism of his successor Taft, Roosevelt formed the Progressive or 'Bull Moose' Party. As their candidate he unsuccessfully ran for the presidency 1912.

Roosevelt, born in New York, was elected to the state legislature 1881. He was assistant secretary of the Navy 1897–98, and during the Spanish-American War 1898 commanded a volunteer force of 'rough riders'. In office he became more liberal. He tackled business monopolies, initiated measures for the conservation of national resources, and introduced the Pure Food and Drug Act. He won the Nobel Peace Prize 1906 for his part in ending the Russo-Japanese war. During World War I he strongly advocated US intervention.

Rosa Salvator 1615–1673. Italian painter, etcher, poet, and musician, active in Florence 1640–49 and subsequently in Rome. He created wild, romantic, and sometimes macabre landscapes, seascapes, and battle scenes. He also wrote verse satires.

Born near Naples, Rosa spent much of his youth travelling in S Italy. He first settled in Rome in 1639, and established a reputation as a landscape painter. In Florence he worked for the ruling Medici family.

Roscellinus Johannes c.1050–c.1122. Medieval philosopher, regarded as the founder of scholasticism because of his defence of nominalism (the idea that classes of things are simply names and have no objective reality) against ◊Anselm.

Roscius Gallus Quintus c.126–62 BC. Roman actor, originally a slave, so gifted that his name became proverbial for a great actor.

Rosebery Archibald Philip Primrose, 5th Earl of Rosebery 1847–1929. British Liberal politician. He was foreign secretary 1886 and 1892–94, when he succeeded Gladstone as prime minister, but his government survived less than a year. After 1896 his imperialist views gradually placed him further away from the mainstream of the Liberal Party.

Rosenberg Alfred 1893–1946. German politician, born in Tallinn, Estonia. He became the chief Nazi ideologist, and was Reich minister for eastern occupied territories 1941–44. He was tried at Nuremberg 1946 as a war criminal and hanged.

Rosenberg Isaac 1890–1918. English poet of the World War I period. Trained as an artist at the Slade school in London, Rosenberg enlisted in the army 1915. He wrote about the horror of life on the front line, as in 'Break of Day in the Trenches'.

Like his contemporary Wilfred Owen, Rosenberg is now ranked with the finest World War I poets, although he was largely unpublished during his lifetime. After serving for 20 months in the front line, he was killed on the Somme.

Rosenberg Julius 1918–53 and Ethel 1915–1953. US married couple, accused of being leaders of a nuclear-espionage ring passing information to the USSR; both were executed.

Ross James Clark 1800–1862. English explorer who discovered the magnetic North Pole 1831. He also went to the Antarctic 1839; *Ross Island*, *Ross Sea*, and *Ross Dependency* are named after him.

He is associated with ◊Parry and his uncle *John Ross* in Arctic exploration.

Ross John 1777–1856. Scottish rear-admiral and explorer. He served in wars with France and made voyages of Arctic exploration in 1818, 1829–33, and 1850.

Ross Martin. Pen name of Violet Florence ◊Martin, Irish novelist.

Ross Ronald 1857–1932. British physician and bacteriologist, born in India. From 1881–99, he served in the Indian medical service, and 1895–98 identified the *Anopheles* mosquito as being responsible for the spread of malaria. Nobel Prize for Medicine 1902.

Rossellini Roberto 1906–1977. Italian film director. His World War II theme trilogy of films, *Roma Città aperta/Rome, Open City* 1945, *Paisa/Paisan* 1946, and *Germania Anno Zero/Germany Year Zero* 1947 are considered landmarks in postwar European cinema.

Rossetti Christina Georgina 1830–1894. English poet, sister of Dante Rossetti, and a devout High Anglican. Her verse includes *Goblin Market and Other Poems* 1862 and expresses unfulfilled spiritual yearning and frustrated love. She was a skilful technician and made use of irregular rhyme and line length.

Rossetti Dante Gabriel 1828–1882. British painter and poet, a founder member of the *Pre-Raphaelite Brotherhood* (PRB) in 1848. The PRB renounced contemporary artistic conventions in favour of the vivid, natural style of Italian art before ◊Raphael. Apart from romantic medieval scenes, he produced dozens of idealized portraits of women. His verse includes 'The Blessed Damozel' 1850. His sister was the poet Christina Rossetti.

Rossetti, the son of an exiled Italian, formed the PRB with the painters Millais and Hunt, but soon developed a broader style and a personal subject matter, related to his poetry. He was a friend of the critic Ruskin, who helped establish his reputation as a painter, and of William Morris and his wife Jane, who became Rossetti's lover and the subject of much of his work. His *Poems* 1870 were recovered from the grave of his wife Elizabeth Siddal (1834–62, also a painter, whom he had married in 1860), and were attacked as of 'the fleshly school of poetry'.

Rossini Gioachino (Antonio) 1792–1868. Italian composer. His first success was the opera *Tancredi* 1813. In 1816 his 'opera buffa' *Il barbiere di Siviglia/The Barber of Seville* was produced in Rome. During his fertile composition period 1815–23, he produced 20 operas, and created (with ◊Donizetti and ◊Bellini) the 19th-century Italian operatic style. After *Guillaume Tell/William Tell* 1829 he gave up writing opera and his later years were spent in Bologna and Paris.

Among the works of this period are the *Stabat Mater* 1842, and the piano music arranged for ballet by ◊Respighi as *La Boutique fantasque/The Fantastic Toyshop* 1919.

Rostand Edmond 1869–1918. French dramatist, who wrote *Cyrano de Bergerac* 1897 and *L'Aiglon* 1900 (based on the life of Napoleon III), in which Sarah Bernhardt played a leading role.

Rostropovich Mstislav 1927– . Russian cellist and conductor, deprived of Soviet citizenship in 1978 because of his sympathies with political dissidents. Prokofiev, Shostakovich, Khachaturian, and Britten wrote pieces for him. Since 1977 he has directed the National Symphony Orchestra, Washington, DC.

Roth Philip 1933– . US novelist, noted for his portrayals of modern Jewish-American life. His books include *Goodbye Columbus* 1959; *Portnoy's Complaint* 1969; and a series of novels about a writer, Nathan Zuckerman, including *The Ghost Writer* 1979, *Zuckerman Unbound* 1981, and *The Anatomy Lesson* 1984.

***Rossetti** Poet and painter Dante Gabriel Rossetti was a central figure in the Pre-Raphaelite movement.*

Rothermere Viscount 1868–1940. British newspaper proprietor, brother of Viscount ◊Northcliffe.

Rothko Mark 1903–1970. US painter, born in Russia, an Abstract Expressionist and a pioneer of **Colour Field** painting (abstract, dominated by areas of unmodulated, strong colour).

Rothko produced a number of series of paintings in the 1950s and 1960s, including one at Harvard University, Cambridge, Massachusetts; one for the Tate Gallery, London; and his own favourite 1967–69 for a chapel in Houston, Texas.

Rothschild a European family, noted for its activity in the financial world for two centuries. **Mayer Anselm** (1744–1812) set up as a moneylender in Frankfurt-am-Main, Germany, and important business houses were established throughout Europe by his ten children.

Nathan Mayer (1777–1836) settled in England, and his grandson **Nathaniel** (1840–1915) was created a baron in 1885. **Lionel Walter** (1868–1937) succeeded his father as 2nd Baron Rothschild and was a noted naturalist. His daughter **Miriam** (1908–) is an entomologist, famous for her studies of fleas. The 2nd baron's nephew, **Nathaniel** (1910–1990), 3rd Baron Rothschild, was a scientist. During World War II he worked in British military intelligence. He was head of the central policy-review staff in the Cabinet Office (the 'think tank' set up by Edward Heath) 1970–74. Of the French branch, Baron **Eric de Rothschild** (1940–) owns Château Lafite and Baron **Philippe de Rothschild** (1902–) owns Château Mouton-Rothschild, both leading claret-producing properties in Pauillac, SW France.

Rouault Georges 1871–1958. French painter, etcher, illustrator, and designer. Early in his career he was associated with the Fauves (see ◊Matisse), but created his own style using heavy, dark colours and bold brushwork. His subjects included sad clowns, prostitutes, and evil lawyers; from about 1940 he painted mainly religious works.

The Prostitute 1906 (Musée Nationale d'Art Moderne, Paris) and *The Face of Christ* 1933 (Musée des Beaux-Arts, Ghent, Belgium) represent extremes of Rouault's painting style. He also produced illustrations, designed tapestries, stained glass, and sets for Diaghilev's Ballets Russes, and in 1948 he published a series of etchings, *Miserere*.

Roubiliac or **Roubillac** Louis François *c.*1705–1762. French sculptor, a Huguenot who fled religious persecution to settle in England 1732. He became a leading sculptor of the day, creating a statue of Handel for Vauxhall Gardens 1737 (Victoria and Albert Museum, London) and teaching at St Martin's Lane Academy from 1745.

Rousseau *French philosopher and writer Jean-Jacques Rousseau.*

He also produced lively statues of historic figures, such as Newton, and an outstanding funerary monument, the *Tomb of Lady Elizabeth Nightingale* 1761 (Westminster Abbey, London).

Rouget de Lisle Claude-Joseph 1760–1836. French army officer, who composed, while at Strasbourg in 1792, the 'Marseillaise', the French national anthem.

Rousseau (Etienne-Pierre) Théodore 1812–1867. French landscape painter of the Barbizon School. Born in Paris, he came under the influence of the British landscape painters Constable and Bonington, sketched from nature in many parts of France, and settled in Barbizon in 1848. He painted oppressive, gloomy, Romantic landscapes.

Rousseau Henri 'Le Douanier' 1844–1910. French painter, a self-taught naive artist. His subjects included scenes of the Parisian suburbs and exotic junglescapes, painted with painstaking detail, for example *Surprised! Tropical Storm with a Tiger* 1891 (National Gallery, London).

Rousseau served in the army for some years, then became a toll collector (hence *Le Douanier*, 'the customs official'), and finally took up full-time painting in 1885. He exhibited at the Salon des Indépendants from 1886 to 1910 and was associated with the group led by Picasso and the poet Apollinaire, but his position was unique. As a naive painter, and a naive and pompous person, he was considered ridiculous, yet admired for his inimitable style.

Rousseau Jean-Jacques 1712–1778. French social philosopher and writer, born in Geneva. *Discourses on the Origins of Inequality* 1754 made him famous, denouncing civilized society and postulating the paradox of the superiority of the 'noble savage'. *The Social Contract* 1762 emphasized the rights of the people over those of government, and stated that a government could be legitimately overthrown if it failed to express the general will of the people. It was a significant influence on the French Revolution. In the novel *Emile* 1762 he outlined a new theory of education, based on natural development and the power of example, to elicit the unspoiled nature and abilities of children. His *Confessions*, published posthumously 1782, was a frank account of his occasionally immoral life, and was a founding work of autobiography.

Rowbotham Sheila 1943– . British socialist feminist, historian, lecturer, and writer. Her pamphlet *Women's Liberation and the New Politics* 1970 laid down fundamental approaches and demands of the emerging British women's movement.

Rowbotham first taught in schools and then became involved with the Workers' Educational Association. An active socialist since the early 1960s, she has contributed to several left-wing journals. Other publications include *Hidden from History, Women's Consciousness, Man's World* both 1973, and *Beyond the Fragments* 1979.

Rowe Nicholas 1674–1718. English playwright and poet, whose dramas include *The Fair Penitent* 1702 and *Jane Shore* 1714, in which Mrs Siddons played. He edited Shakespeare, and was Poet Laureate from 1715.

Rowlandson Thomas 1756–1827. English painter and illustrator, a caricaturist of Georgian social life. His *Tour of Dr Syntax in Search of the Picturesque* 1809 and its two sequels 1812–21 proved very popular.

Rowlandson studied at the Royal Academy schools and in Paris. Impoverished by gambling, he turned from portrait painting to caricature around 1780. Other works include *The Dance of Death* 1815–16 and illustrations for the novelists Smollett, Goldsmith, and Sterne.

Rowley William *c.*1585–*c.*1642. English actor and dramatist, collaborator with ◊Middleton in *The Changeling* 1621 and with ◊Dekker and ◊Ford in *The Witch of Edmonton* 1658.

Rowling Wallace 'Bill' 1927– . New Zealand Labour politician, party leader 1969–75, prime minister 1974–75.

Rowntree Benjamin Seebohm 1871–1954. British entrepreneur and philanthropist. Much of the money he acquired as chair (1925–41) of the family firm of confectioners, H I Rowntree, he used to fund investigations into social conditions. The three ***Rowntree Trusts***, which were founded by his father ***Joseph Rowntree*** (1836–1295) in 1904, fund research into housing, social care and social policy, support projects relating to social justice, and give grants to pressure groups working in these areas.

His pioneering study of working-class households in York 1897–98, published as *Poverty*, was a landmark in empirical sociology; it showed that

28% of the population fell below an arbitrary level of minimum income, and 16% experienced 'primary poverty'. Rowntree also wrote on gambling, unemployment, and business organization.

Rowse A(lfred) L(eslie) 1903– . English popular historian. He published a biography of Shakespeare 1963, and in 1973 controversially identified the 'Dark Lady' of Shakespeare's sonnets as Emilia Lanier, half-Italian daughter of a court musician, with whom the Bard is alleged to have had an affair 1593–95.

Roy Manabendra Nakh 1887–1954. Founder of the Indian Communist Party in exile in Tashkent 1920. Expelled from the Comintern 1929, he returned to India and was imprisoned for five years. A steadfast communist, he finally became disillusioned after World War II and developed his ideas on practical humanism.

Roy Rajah Ram Rohan 1770–1833. Bengali religious and social reformer. He was founder of the Brahma Samaj sect, which formulated the creed of neo-Hinduism akin to Christian Unitarianism. He died in England 1833 as emissary of the Great Mogul, who was still nominal sovereign in India.

Royce (Frederick) Henry 1863–1933. British engineer, who so impressed Charles ◊Rolls by the car he built for his own personal use 1904 that Rolls-Royce Ltd was formed 1906 to produce cars and engines.

Rubbra Edmund 1901–1986. British composer. He studied under ◊Holst and was a master of contrapuntal writing, as exemplified in his study *Counterpoint* 1960. His compositions include 11 symphonies, chamber music, and songs.

Rubens Peter Paul 1577–1640. Flemish painter, who became court painter to the archduke Albert and his wife Isabella in Antwerp. After a few years in Italy, he brought the exuberance of Italian Baroque to N Europe, creating, with an army of assistants, innumerable religious and allegorical paintings for churches and palaces. These show mastery of drama in large compositions, and love of rich colour and fleshy nudes. He also painted portraits and, in his last years, landscapes.

Rubens entered the Antwerp painters' guild 1598 and went to Italy in 1600, studying artists of the High Renaissance. In 1603 he visited Spain, and in Madrid painted many portraits of the Spanish nobility. From 1604 to 1608 he was in Italy again, and in 1609 he settled in Antwerp and was appointed court painter. His *Raising of the Cross* 1610 and *Descent from the Cross* 1611–14, both in Antwerp Cathedral, show his brilliant painterly style. He went to France 1620, commissioned by the regent Marie de' Medici to produce a cycle of 21 enormous canvases allegorizing her life (Louvre, Paris). In 1628 he again went to Madrid, where he met the painter Velázquez. In 1629–30 he was in London as diplomatic envoy to Charles I, and painted

the ceiling of the Banqueting House in Whitehall.

Rubens's portraits range from intimate pictures of his second wife such as *Hélène Fourment in a Fur Wrap* about 1638 (Kunsthistorisches Museum, Vienna) to dozens of portraits of royalty.

Rubik Erno 1944– . Hungarian architect, who invented the *Rubik cube*, a multicoloured puzzle which can be manipulated and rearranged in only one correct way, but about 43 trillion wrong ones. Intended to help his students understand three-dimensional design, it became a world craze.

Rubinstein Artur 1887–1982. Polish-American pianist. He studied in Warsaw and Berlin, and appeared with the world's major symphony orchestras, specializing in the music of Chopin, Debussy, and Spanish composers.

Rubinstein Helena 1882–1965. Polish tycoon, who emigrated to Australia 1902, where she started up a face-cream business. She moved to Europe 1904, and later to the USA, opening salons in London, Paris, and New York.

Rublev (Rublyov) *c.*1370–1430. Russian icon painter. Only one documented work survives, the *Holy Trinity* about 1411 (Tretyakov Gallery, Moscow). This shows a basically Byzantine style, but with a gentler expression.

He is known to have worked with Theophanes the Greek in the Cathedral of the Annunciation in Moscow. In later life Rublev became a monk. The director Tarkovsky made a film of his life 1966.

Rude François 1784–1855. French Romantic sculptor. He produced the low-relief scene on the Arc de Triomphe, Paris, showing the capped figure of Liberty leading the revolutionaries (1833, known as *The Volunteers of 1792* or *The Marseillaise*).

Rude was a supporter of Napoleon, along with the painter David, and in 1814 both artists went into exile in Brussels for some years. Rude's other works include a bust of *David* 1831 (Louvre, Paris) and the monument *Napoleon Awakening to Immortality* 1854 (Louvre, Paris).

Rudolph 1858–1889. Crown prince of Austria, the only son of Emperor Franz Joseph. From an early age he showed progressive views which brought him into conflict with his father. He conceived and helped to write a history of the Austro-Hungarian empire. In 1889 he and his mistress, Baroness Marie Vetsera, were found shot in his hunting lodge at Mayerling, near Vienna. The official verdict was suicide, although there were rumours that it was perpetrated by Jesuits, Hungarian nobles, or the baroness's husband.

In 1881, he married Princess Stephanie of Belgium, and they had one daughter, Elizabeth.

Rudolph two Holy Roman emperors:

Rudolph I 1218–1291. Holy Roman emperor from 1273. Originally count of Habsburg, he was the first Habsburg emperor, and expanded his dynasty by investing his sons with the duchies of Austria and Styria.

Rudolph II 1552–1612. Holy Roman emperor from 1576, when he succeeded his father Maximilian II. His policies led to unrest in Hungary and Bohemia, which led to the surrender of Hungary to his brother Matthias 1608, and religious freedom for Bohemia.

Ruisdael or **Ruysdael** Jacob van *c.* 1628–1682. Dutch landscape painter, active in Amsterdam from about 1655. He painted rural scenes near his native town of Haarlem and in Germany, and excelled in depicting gnarled and weatherbeaten trees. The few figures in his pictures were painted by other artists.

Ruisdael was born in Haarlem, where he probably worked with his uncle, the landscape painter *Salomon van Ruysdael* (*c.* 1600–70). Jacob is considered the greatest realist landscape painter in Dutch art. Hobbema was one of his pupils.

Rumford Benjamin Thompson, Count Rumford 1753–1814. American-born British physicist. In 1798, he published his theory that heat is a mode of motion, not a substance.

Rumford spied for the British in the War of American Independence, and was forced to flee from America to England 1776. He travelled in Europe, and was created a count of the Holy Roman Empire for services to the elector of Bavaria 1791. He founded the Royal Institution in London 1799.

Runcie Robert (Alexander Kennedy) 1921– . English cleric, archbishop of Canterbury from 1980, the first to be appointed on the suggestion of the Church Crown Appointments Commission (formed 1977) rather than by political consultation. He favoured ecclesiastical remarriage for the divorced and the eventual introduction of the ordination of women. He announced his retirement in 1990.

Rundstedt Karl Rudolf Gerd von 1875–1953. German field marshal in World War II. Largely responsible for the German breakthrough in France 1940, he was defeated on the Ukrainian front 1941. As commander in chief in France from 1942, he resisted the Allied invasion 1944, and in Dec launched the temporarily successful Ardennes offensive.

Runge Philipp Otto 1770–1810. German Romantic painter, whose portraits, particularly of children, have a remarkable clarity and openness. He also illustrated fairy tales by the brothers Grimm.

Runyon Damon 1884–1946. US sports and crime reporter in New York, whose short stories *Guys and Dolls* 1932 deal wryly with the seamier side of the city's life in his own invented jargon.

Rupert Prince 1619–1682. English Royalist general and admiral, born in Prague, son of the Elector Palatine Frederick V (1596–1632) and James I's daughter Elizabeth. Defeated by Cromwell at the battles of Marston Moor and Naseby in the Civil War, he commanded a privateering fleet 1649–52, until routed by Admiral Robert Blake, and, returning after the Restoration, was a distinguished admiral in the Dutch Wars. He founded the Hudson's Bay Company to trade in North American furs.

Rushdie (Ahmed) Salman 1947– . British writer, born in India of a Muslim family. His novel *The Satanic Verses* 1988 (the title refers to verses deleted from the Koran) offended many Muslims with alleged blasphemy. In 1989 the Ayatollah Khomeini of Iran called for Rushdie and his publishers to be killed.

Rushdie was born in Bombay and later lived in Pakistan before moving to the UK. His earlier novels in the magic-realist style include *Midnight's Children* 1981, which deals with India from the date of independence and won the Booker Prize, and *Shame* 1983, set in an imaginary parallel of Pakistan. The furore caused by *The Satanic Verses* led to the withdrawal of British diplomats from Iran. In India and elsewhere, people were killed in demonstrations against the book and Rushdie was forced to go into hiding.

Rusk Dean 1909– . US Democratic politician. He was secretary of state to presidents Kennedy and Johnson 1961–69, and became unpopular through his involvement with the Vietnam War.

During World War II he fought in Burma and China, and became deputy Chief of Staff of US forces. After the war he served in the Department of State, and as assistant secretary of state for Far Eastern affairs was prominent in Korean War negotiations.

Ruskin John 1819–1900. British art critic and social critic. He published five volumes of *Modern Painters* 1843–60, *The Seven Lamps of Architecture* 1849, in which he stated his philosophy of art, and *The Stones of Venice* 1851–53, in which he drew moral lessons from architectural history. His writings hastened the appreciation of painters considered unorthodox at the time, such as ◊Turner and the Pre-Raphaelite Brotherhood (see Dante ◊Rossetti). His later writings were concerned with social and economic problems.

Born in London, only child of a prosperous wine-merchant, Ruskin was able to travel widely and was educated at Oxford. The first volume of *Modern Painters* appeared 1843. In 1848 he married Euphemia 'Effie' Chalmers Gray, but the marriage proved a failure; six years later she secured a decree of nullity and later married the painter Millais.

The fifth and final volume of *Modern Painters* appeared in 1860, and the remaining years of Ruskin's life were devoted to social and economic problems, in which he adopted an individual and radical outlook exalting the 'craftsman'. He became increasingly isolated in his views. To this period belong a series of lectures and pamphlets

(*Unto this Last* 1860, *Sesame and Lilies* 1865 on the duties of men and women, *The Crown of Wild Olive* 1866). Ruskin was Slade professor of art at Oxford 1869–79, and he made a number of social experiments, such as St George's Guild, for the establishment of an industry on socialist lines. His last years were spent at Brantwood, Cumbria.

Russ Joanna 1937– . US writer of feminist science fiction, exemplified by the novel *The Female Man* 1975. Her short stories have been collected in *The Zanzibar Cat* 1983.

Russell Bertrand (Arthur William), 3rd Earl 1872–1970. English philosopher and mathematician, who contributed to the development of modern mathematical logic, and wrote about social issues. His works include *Principia Mathematica* 1910–13 (with A N ◊Whitehead), in which he attempted to show that mathematics could be reduced to a branch of logic; *The Problems of Philosophy* 1912; and *A History of Western Philosophy* 1946. He was an outspoken liberal pacifist.

The grandson of Prime Minister John Russell, he was educated at Trinity College, Cambridge, where he specialized in mathematics and became a lecturer 1895. Russell's pacifist attitude in World War I lost him the lectureship, and he was imprisoned for six months for an article he wrote in a pacifist journal. His *Introduction to Mathematical Philosophy* 1919 was written in prison. He and his wife ran a progressive school 1927–32. After visits to the USSR and China, he went to the USA 1938 and taught at many universities. In 1940, a US court disqualified him from teaching at City College of New York because of his liberal moral views. He later returned to England, and was a fellow of Trinity College. He was a life-long pacifist except during World War II. From 1949 he advocated nuclear disarmament and until 1963 was on the Committee of 100, an offshoot of the Campaign for Nuclear Disarmament.

Among his other works are *Principles of Mathematics* 1903, *Principles of Social Reconstruction* 1917, *Marriage and Morals* 1929, *An Enquiry into Meaning and Truth* 1940, *New Hopes for a Changing World* 1951, and *Autobiography* 1967–69.

Russell Charles Taze 1852–1916. US religious figure, founder of the Jehovah's Witness sect 1872.

Russell Dora (Winifred) (born Black) 1894–1986. English feminist, who married Bertrand ◊Russell 1921. The 'openness' of their marriage (she subsequently had children by another man) was a matter of controversy. She was a founder member of the National Council for Civil Liberties.

She was educated at Girton College, Cambridge, of which she became a Fellow. In 1927 the Russells founded the progressive Beacon Hill School in Hampshire. After World War II she actively supported the Campaign for Nuclear Disarmament.

Russell George William 1867–1935. Irish poet and essayist. An ardent nationalist, he helped found the Irish national theatre, and his poetry, published under the pseudonym 'AE', includes *Gods of War* 1915, and reflects his interest in mysticism and theosophy.

Russell Jane 1921– . US actress who was discovered by producer Howard Hughes. Her first film, *The Outlaw* 1943, was not properly released for several years owing to censorship problems. Her other films include *The Paleface* 1948, *Gentlemen Prefer Blondes* 1953, and *The Revolt of Mamie Stover* 1957. She retired in 1970.

Russell John 1795–1883. British 'sporting parson', who bred the short-legged, smooth-coated Jack Russell terrier.

Russell John Peter 1858–1931. Australian artist. Having met Tom ◊Roberts while sailing to England, he became a member of the French Post-Impressionist group.

Russell John, 1st Earl Russell 1792–1878. British Liberal politician, son of the 6th Duke of Bedford. He entered the House of Commons 1813, and supported Catholic emancipation and the Reform Bill. He held cabinet posts 1830–41, became prime minister 1846–52, and was again a cabinet minister until becoming prime minister again 1865–66. He retired after the defeat of his Reform Bill 1866.

As foreign secretary in Aberdeen's coalition 1852 and in Palmerston's second government 1859–65, Russell assisted Italy's struggle for unity, although his indecisive policies on Poland, Denmark, and the American Civil War provoked much criticism. He had a strained relationship with Palmerston.

Russell Ken 1927– . English film director, whose films include *Women in Love* 1969, *Altered States* 1979, and *Salome's Last Dance* 1988.

He is often criticized for self-indulgence; some consider his work to contain gratuitous sex and violence, but others have high regard for its vitality and imagination. Other films include *The Music Lovers* 1971, *The Devils* 1971, *Tommy* 1975, *Lisztomania* 1975, and *Gothic* 1986.

Russell Lord William 1639–1683. British Whig politician. Son of the 1st Duke of Bedford, he was among the founders of the Whig Party, and actively supported attempts in Parliament to exclude the Roman Catholic James II from succeeding to the throne. In 1683 he was accused, on dubious evidence, of complicity in the Rye House Plot to murder Charles II (while he spent the night at Rye House, Hertfordshire), and was executed.

Russell William Howard 1821–1907. British journalist, born in Ireland. He acted as *The Times*'s correspondent during the Crimean War, and created a sensation by his exposure of the mismanagement of the campaign.

Rust Mathias 1968– . West German aviator, who in May 1987 piloted a light Cessna 172 turboprop plane from Finland to Moscow, landing in Red Square. Found guilty of 'malicious hooliganism', he served 14 months of a four-year prison sentence.

His exploit, carefully timed to take place on the USSR's 'national border guards' day', highlighted serious deficiencies in the Soviet air-defence system and led to the dismissal of the defence minister. Rust, despite pleading that his actions had been designed to promote world peace, was sentenced to four years' imprisonment by the Soviet authorities. After serving 14 months in a KGB prison in Lefortovo, he was released and sent home as a humanitarian gesture by the Gorbachev administration.

Ruth George Herman 'Babe' 1895–1948. US baseball player, regarded by many as the greatest of all time. He played in ten World Series and made 714 home runs, a record that stood from 1935 to 1974.

Ruth started playing 1914 as a pitcher for the Boston Braves before moving to the Boston Red Sox later that year. He joined the New York Yankees 1920 and became one of the best batters in the game. Yankee Stadium is known as 'the stadium Ruth built' because of the money he brought into the club.

Rutherford Ernest 1871–1937. New Zealand physicist, a pioneer of modern atomic science. His main research was in the field of radioactivity, and he discovered alpha, beta, and gamma rays. He was the first to recognize the nuclear nature of the atom, and named the nucleus.

He was awarded a Nobel prize 1908, and in 1931 was created Baron Rutherford of Nelson, New Zealand.

Rutherford Margaret 1892–1972. British actress. Specializing in formidable yet jovially eccentric females, her roles included Madame Arcati in Noël Coward's *Blithe Spirit* 1941 and Lady Bracknell in Oscar Wilde's *The Importance of Being Earnest* 1947. She portrayed Agatha Christie's Miss Marple in four films in the early 1960s and won an Academy Award for her role in *The VIPs* 1963.

Ruyter Michael Adrianszoon de 1607–1676. Dutch admiral, who led his country's fleet in the wars against England. On 1–4 June 1666 he forced the British fleet under Rupert and Albemarle to retire into the Thames, but on 25 July was heavily defeated off the North Foreland, Kent. In 1667 he sailed up the Medway to burn three men-of-war at Chatham, and captured others.

Ruyter was mortally wounded in an action against the French fleet off Messina, and died at Syracuse, Sicily.

Ruzicka Leopold Stephen 1887–1976. Swiss chemist. Born in Yugoslavia, Ruzicka settled in Switzerland in 1929. He began research on natural compounds such as musk and civet secretions. In the 1930s he investigated sex hormones, and in 1934 succeeded in extracting the male hormone androsterone from 31,815 litres/7,000 gallons of urine and in synthesizing it. Ruzicka, along with Butenandt, shared the 1939 Nobel Chemistry Prize.

Ryan Robert 1909–1973. US theatre and film actor, equally impressive in leading and character roles. His films include *Woman on the Beach* 1947, *The Set-Up* 1949, and *The Wild Bunch* 1969.

Ryle Gilbert 1900–1976. British philosopher. His *The Concept of Mind* 1949 set out to show that the distinction between an inner and outer world in philosophy and psychology cannot be sustained. He ridiculed the mind-body dualism of ◊Descartes as the doctrine of 'the Ghost in the Machine'.

Ryle Martin 1918–1984. English radioastronomer. At the Mullard Radio Astronomy Observatory, Cambridge, he developed the technique of skymapping using 'aperture synthesis', combining smaller dish aerials to give the characteristics of one large one.

Rysbrack John Michael 1694–1770. British sculptor, born in Antwerp, the Netherlands. He settled in England in 1720 and produced portrait busts and tombs in Westminster Abbey. He also created the equestrian statue of William III in Queen Square, Bristol.

Ryzhkov Nikolai Ivanovich 1929– . Soviet communist politician. He held governmental and party posts from 1975 before being brought into the Politburo under prime minister 1985 by Gorbachev. A low-profile technocrat, Ryzhkov is viewed as a more cautious and centralist reformer than Gorbachev.

An engineering graduate from the Urals Polytechnic in Sverdlovsk, Ryzhkov became foreman of a local smelting works, and rose to become head of the giant Uralmash engineering conglomerate. A member of the Communist Party from 1959, Ryzhkov became deputy minister for heavy engineering 1975. He then served as first deputy chair of Gosplan 1979–82 and Central Committee secretary for economics 1982–85 before becoming prime minister.

Saarinen Eero 1910–1961. Finnish-born US architect. His works include the US embassy, London, the TWA terminal, New York, and Dulles Airport, Washington DC. He collaborated on a number of projects with his father, Eliel Saarinen.

Saarinen Eliel 1873–1950. Finnish architect and town planner, founder of the Finnish Romantic school. In 1923 he emigrated to the USA, where he contributed to US skyscraper design by his work in Chicago, and later turned to functionalism.

Sabatier Paul 1854–1951. French chemist. He found in 1897 that if a mixture of ethylene and hydrogen is passed over a column of heated nickel, the ethylene changes into ethane. Further work revealed that nickel could be used to catalyse numerous chemical reactions. Sabatier shared the 1912 Nobel Prize for Chemistry with François ◊Grignard.

Sabatini Gabriela 1970– . Argentinian tennis player who in 1986 became the youngest Wimbledon semifinalist for 99 years. She was ranked number three in the world behind Steffi Graf and Martina Navratilova in 1989 after capturing the Italian Open title.

Sabin Albert 1906– . Polish-born US microbiologist, whose involvement in the anti-polio campaigns led to the development of a new, highly effective live vaccine.

The earlier vaccine, developed by the physicist Jonas ◊Salk, was based on heat-killed viruses. Sabin was convinced that a live form would be longer-lasting and more effective, and he succeeded in weakening the virus so that it lost its virulence. His vaccine can be orally administered.

Sabu stage name of Sabu Dastagir 1924–1963. Indian child actor, memorable as the hero of *The Thief of Bagdad* 1940. He acted in Britain and the USA until the 1950s. His other films include *Elephant Boy* 1937 and *Black Narcissus* 1947.

Sacher Paul 1906– . Swiss conductor. In 1926 he founded the Basle Chamber Orchestra, for which he has commissioned a succession of works from contemporary composers including Bartók, Stravinsky, and Britten.

Sacher-Masoch Leopold von 1836–1895. Austrian novelist. His books dealt with the sexual pleasures to be obtained by having pain inflicted on oneself, hence *masochism*.

Sachs Hans 1494–1576. German poet and composer who worked as a master shoemaker in Nuremberg. He composed 4,275 *Meisterlieder/mastersongs*, and figures prominently in ◊Wagner's opera *Die Meistersinger/The Mastersingers*.

Sackville Thomas, 1st Earl of Dorset 1536–1608. English poet, collaborator with Thomas Norton on *Gorboduc* 1561, written in blank verse and one of the earliest English tragedies.

Sackville-West Victoria ('Vita') 1892–1962. British poet and novelist, wife of Harold ◊Nicolson from 1913; *Portrait of a Marriage* 1973 by their son **Nigel Nicolson** described their married life. Her novels include *The Edwardians* 1930 and *All Passion Spent* 1931; she also wrote the pastoral poem *The Land* 1926. The fine gardens around her home at Sissinghurst, Kent, were created by her.

Sadat Anwar 1918–1981. Egyptian politician. Succeeding ◊Nasser as president 1970, he restored morale by his handling of the Egyptian campaign in the 1973 war against Israel. In 1974 his plan for economic, social, and political reform to transform Egypt was unanimously adopted in a referendum. In 1977 he visited Israel to reconcile

Sadat President Anwar Sadat of Egypt, Oct 1970.

the two countries, and shared the Nobel Peace Prize with Israeli prime minister Menachem Begin 1978. He was assassinated by Islamic fundamentalists.

Sade Donatien Alphonse François, Comte de, known as the *Marquis de Sade* 1740–1814. French soldier and author. He was imprisoned for sexual offences, and finally committed to an asylum. He wrote plays and novels dealing explicitly with a variety of sexual practices, including *sadism*, obtaining sexual pleasure by inflicting pain on others.

S'adi or *Saadi* pen name of Sheikh Moslih Addin *c.*1184–*c.*1291. Persian poet, author of *Bustan/Tree-garden* and *Gulistan/Flower-garden*.

Sagan Carl 1934– . US physicist and astronomer, known for his popular-science writings, books including *The Cosmic Connection* 1973, and *Broca's Brain* 1979.

Sagan Françoise 1935– . French novelist. Her studies of love relationships include *Bonjour Tristesse/Hello Sadness* 1954, *Un Certain Sourire/A Certain Smile* 1956, and *Aimez-vous Brahms?/Do You Like Brahms?* 1959.

Sainte-Beuve Charles Augustin 1804–1869. French critic. He contributed to the *Revue des deux mondes/Review of the Two Worlds* from 1831. His articles on French literature appeared as *Causeries du lundi/Monday Chats* 1851–62, and his *Port Royal* 1840–59 is a study of Jansenism (a creed based on the teachings of St ◊Augustus).

Saint-Exupéry Antoine de 1900–1944. French author, who wrote the autobiographical *Vol de nuit/Night Flight* 1931 and *Terre des hommes/Wind, Sand, and Stars* 1939. His *Le petit prince/The Little Prince* 1943, a children's book, is also an adult allegory.

Saint-Gaudens Augustus 1848–1907. US sculptor born in Ireland. His monuments include the granite and bronze *Adams memorial* 1891 (Rock Creek Cemetery, Washington DC); he also sculpted portraits.

Saint-Just Louis Antoine Léon Florelle de 1767–1794. French revolutionary. A close associate of ◊Robespierre, he became a member of the Committee of Public Safety 1793, and was guillotined.

Saint-Laurent Yves (Henri Donat Mathieu) 1936– . French couturier, partner to ◊Dior from 1954 and his successor 1957. He opened his own fashion house 1962.

Saint-Pierre Jacques Henri Bernadin de 1737–1814. French author of the sentimental romance *Paul et Virginie* 1789.

Saint-Saëns (Charles) Camille 1835–1921. French composer, pianist and organist. Among his many lyrical Romantic pieces are concertos, the symphonic poem *Danse macabre* 1875, the opera *Samson et Dalila* 1877, and the orchestral *Carnaval des animaux/Carnival of the Animals* 1886.

Saint-Simon Claude Henri, Comte de 1760–1825. French socialist, who fought in the American War of Independence and was imprisoned during the French Revolution. He advocated an atheist society ruled by technicians and industrialists in *Du Système industrielle/The Industrial System* 1821.

Saint-Simon Louis de Rouvroy, Duc de 1675–1755. French soldier, courtier, and politician, whose *Mémoires* 1691–1723 are unrivalled as a description of the French court.

Sakharov Andrei Dmitrievich 1921–1989. Soviet physicist, known both as the 'father of the Soviet H-bomb' and as an outspoken human-rights campaigner. Nobel Peace Prize 1975. He was elected to the Congress of the USSR People's Deputies (CUPD) 1989, where he emerged as leader of its radical reform grouping.

He protested against Soviet nuclear tests and was a founder of the Soviet Human Rights Committee. In 1980, he was arrested and sent to internal exile in Gorky, following his criticism of Soviet action in Afghanistan. At the end of 1986, he was freed from exile and allowed to return to Moscow and resume his place in the Soviet Academy of Sciences.

Saki pen name of H(ugh) H(ector) Munro 1870–1916. Burmese-born British writer of ingeniously witty and bizarre short stories, often with surprise endings. He also wrote two novels *The Unbearable Bassington* 1912 and *When William Came* 1913.

Śākyamuni the historical ◊Buddha, called *Shaka* in Japan.

Saladin or *Sala-ud-din* 1138–1193. Sultan of Egypt from 1175, in succession to the Atabeg of Mosul, on whose behalf he conquered Egypt 1164–74. He subsequently conquered Syria 1174–87, and precipitated the third Crusade by his recovery of Jerusalem from the Christians 1187. Renowned for knightly courtesy, Saladin made peace with Richard I of England 1192. He was a Kurd.

Salam Abdus 1926– . Pakistani physicist, known for his work on the fundamental forces of nature. In 1979 he was the first from his country to receive a Nobel prize.

Abdus Salam became a scientist by accident, when he won a scholarship to Cambridge in 1945 from the Punjab Small Peasants' welfare fund; he had intended to join the Indian civil service. He subsequently worked on the structure of matter at the Cavendish Laboratory, Oxford, and elaborated the theory unifying fundamental forces in 1967. His ideas were verified experimentally at CERN in 1973.

Salazar Antonio de Oliveira 1889–1970. Portuguese prime minister 1932–68, exercising a virtual dictatorship. A corporative constitution on the Italian model was introduced 1933, and until

1945 Salazar's National Union, founded 1930, remained the only legal party. Salazar was also foreign minister 1936–47, and during World War II maintained Portuguese neutrality.

Salieri Antonio 1750–1825. Italian composer. He taught Beethoven, Schubert, and Liszt, and was the musical rival of Mozart at the Emperor's court in Vienna.

Salinas de Gortiari Carlos 1948– . Mexican politician, president from 1988.

Educated in Mexico and the USA, he taught at Harvard and in Mexico before joining the government in 1971 and thereafter held a number of posts, mostly in the economic sphere. A member of the dominant Institutional Revolutionary Party (PRI), and a former finance minister, he narrowly won the 1988 presidential election, despite allegations of fraud.

Salinger J(erome) D(avid) 1919– . US writer of the novel of adolescence *The Catcher in the Rye* 1951 and stories of a Jewish family, including *Franny and Zooey* 1961.

Salisbury Robert Arthur James Gascoyne-Cecil, 5th Marquess of Salisbury 1893–1972. British Conservative politician. He was Dominions secretary 1940–42 and 1943–45, Colonial secretary 1942, Lord Privy Seal 1942–43 and 1951–52, and Lord President of the Council 1952–57.

Salisbury Robert Arthur Talbot Gascoyne Cecil, 3rd Marquess of Salisbury 1830–1903. British Conservative politician. He entered the Commons 1853 and succeeded to his title 1868. As foreign secretary 1878–80, he took part in the Congress of Berlin, and as prime minister 1885–86, 1886–92, and 1895–1902 gave his main attention to foreign policy, remaining also as foreign secretary for most of this time.

Salisbury Robert Cecil, 1st Earl of Salisbury title conferred on Robert ◊Cecil, secretary of state to Elizabeth I of England.

Salk Jonas Edward 1914– . US physician and microbiologist. In 1954, he developed the original vaccine which led to virtual eradication of polio in developed countries. He was director of the Salk Institute for Biological Studies, University of California, San Diego 1963–75.

Sallinen Tyko 1879–1955. Finnish Expressionist painter. Absorbing Fauve influences on visits to France 1909 and 1914, he created visionary works relating partly to his childhood experiences of religion. He also painted Finnish landscape and peasant life.

Sallust Gaius Sallustius Crispus 86–*c.*34 BC. Roman historian, a supporter of Julius ◊Caesar. He wrote accounts of Catiline's conspiracy and the Jugurthine War in an epigrammatic style.

Salome 1st century AD. In the New Testament, granddaughter of the king of Judea, Herod the Great. Rewarded for her skill in dancing, she

requested the head of John the Baptist from her stepfather ◊Herod Antipas.

Salzedo Carlos 1885–1961. French-born harpist and composer. He studied in Paris and moved to New York, where he later co-founded the International Composers' Guild. He did much to promote the harp as a concert instrument, and invented many unusual sounds.

Samson 11th century BC. In the Old Testament or Hebrew Bible, a hero of Israel. He was renowned for exploits of strength against the Philistines, which ended when his mistress Delilah cut off his hair, as told in the Book of Judges.

Samuel 11th century BC. In the Old Testament or Hebrew Bible, the last of the judges who ruled the ancient Israelites before their adoption of a monarchy, and the first of the prophets; the two books bearing his name cover the story of Samuel and the reigns of kings Saul and David.

Samuelson Paul 1915– . US economist. He became professor at the Massachusetts Institute of Technology 1940, and was awarded a Nobel prize 1970 for his application of scientific analysis to economic theory. His books include *Linear Programming and Economic Analysis* 1958.

Sanctorius Sanctorius 1561–1636. Italian physiologist who pioneered the study of metabolism, and

Sand French novelist George Sand. Her affairs with a succession of artists and poets provided the inspiration for much of her work.

invented the clinical thermometer and a device for measuring pulse rate.

Sanctorius introduced quantitative methods into medicine. For 30 years, he weighed both himself and his food, drink, and waste products. He determined that over half of normal weight loss is due to 'insensible perspiration'.

Sand George. Pen name of Amandine Aurore Lucie Dupin 1804–1876. French author, whose prolific literary output was often autobiographical. After nine years of marriage, she left her husband in 1831, and, while living in Paris as a writer, had love affairs with Alfred de ◊Musset, ◊Chopin, and others. Her first novel *Indiana* 1832 was a plea for women's right to independence.

Other novels include *La mare au diable/The Devil's Pool* 1846 and *La petite Fadette/The Little Fairy* 1848. In 1848 she retired to the château of Nohant, in central France.

Sandburg Carl August 1878–1967. US poet. His poetry celebrates ordinary US life, as in *Chicago Poems* 1916, and *The People, Yes* 1936. *Always the Young Strangers* 1953 is an autobiography. Both his poetry and his biography of Abraham Lincoln won Pulitzer prizes.

Sandby Paul 1725–1809. English watercolour painter. He specialized in Classical landscapes, using both watercolour and opaque body-colour, and introduced aquatint (an etching process) to England.

Sanders George 1906–1972. Russian-born British actor, usually cast as a smooth-talking cad. Most of his film career was spent in the USA where he starred in such films as *Rebecca* 1940, *The Moon and Sixpence* 1942, and *The Picture of Dorian Gray* 1944.

Sandwich John Montagu, 4th Earl of Sandwich 1718–1792. British politician. He was an inept First Lord of the Admiralty 1771–82 during the American War of Independence, his corrupt practices being held to blame for the British navy's inadequacies.

The *Sandwich Islands* were named after him, as are *sandwiches*, which he invented so that he could eat without leaving the gaming table.

Sandys Duncan Edwin 1908–1987. Original name of British politician Baron ◊Duncan-Sandys.

Sanger Frederick 1918– . English biochemist, the first person to win the Nobel Prize for Chemistry twice: 1958 for determining the structure of insulin, and 1980 for his work on the chemical structure of genes.

San Martín José de 1778–1850. South American nationalist. Born in Argentina, he served in the Spanish army during the Peninsular War, but after 1812 he devoted himself to the South American struggle for independence, playing a large part in the liberation of Argentina, Chile, and Peru from Spanish rule.

Santa Anna Antonio Lopez de 1795–1876. Mexican revolutionary. A leader in achieving independence from Spain in 1821, he pursued a chequered career of victory and defeat and was in and out of office as president or dictator for the rest of his life; he led the attack on the Alamo fort in Texas 1836.

Santayana George 1863–1952. US philosopher and critic. His books include *The Life of Reason* 1905–06, *The Realm of Truth* 1937, *Background of My Life* 1945, volumes of poems, and the best-selling novel *The Last Puritan* 1935. Born in Spain, he graduated at Harvard, where he taught the history of philosophy 1889–1911.

Sant'Elia Antonio 1888–1916. Italian architect. His drawings convey a Futurist vision of a metropolis with skyscrapers, traffic lanes, and streamlined factories.

Sānusī Sidi Muhammad ibn 'Ali as- 1787–1859. Algerian-born Muslim religious reformer. He preached a return to the puritanism of early Islam and met with much success in Libya, where he made Jaghbub his centre and founded the sect called after him.

San Yu 1919– . Myanmar politician. A member of the Revolutionary Council which came to power 1962, he became president 1981 and was re-elected 1985. He was forced to resign July 1988, along with Ne Win, after riots in Rangoon (now Yangon).

Sappho *c*.612–580 BC. Greek lyric poet, friend of the poet ◊Alcaeus, and leader of a female literary coterie at Mytilene (modern *Lesvos*, hence lesbianism); legend says she committed suicide when her love for the boatman Phaon was unrequited. Only fragments of her poems have survived.

Sardou Victorien 1831–1908. French dramatist. He wrote plays with roles for Sarah Bernhardt and Henry Irving, for example *Fédora* 1882, *Madame Sans-Gêne* 1893, and *La Tosca* 1887 (the basis for the opera by Puccini). G B ◊Shaw coined the expression 'Sardoodledom' to express his disgust with the contrivances of the 'well-made' play – a genre of which Sardou was the leading exponent.

Sargent (Harold) Malcolm (Watts) 1895–1967. British conductor. From 1923 he was professor at the Royal College of Music, was chief conductor of the BBC Symphony Orchestra 1950–57, and continued as chief guest conductor and conductor-in-chief of the annual Henry Wood promenade concerts at the Royal Albert Hall, London. He had an easy, polished style.

Sargent John Singer 1856–1925. US portrait painter. Born in Florence of American parents, he studied there and in Paris, then settled in London around 1885. He was a prolific and highly fashionable painter.

Sargent left Paris after a scandal concerning his décolleté portrait *Madame Gautreau* 1884. Later subjects included the actress Ellen Terry,

President Theodore Roosevelt, and the writer Robert Louis Stevenson.

Sargeson Frank 1903–1982. New Zealand writer of short stories and novels including *The Hangover* 1967 and *Man of England Now* 1972.

Sargon two Mesopotamian kings:
Sargon I king of Akkad *c*.2334–2279 BC, and founder of the first Babylonian empire. His story resembles that of Moses in that he was said to have been found floating in a cradle on the river Euphrates.

Sargon II died 705 BC. King of Assyria from 722 BC, who assumed the name of his famous predecessor. To keep conquered peoples from rising against him, he had whole populations moved from their homelands, including the Israelites from Samaria.

Sarney José 1930– . President of Brazil 1985–89, member of the Brazilian Democratic Movement (PMDB).

Sarney was elected vice president in 1985 and within months, on the death of President Neves, became head of state. Despite earlier involvement with the repressive military regime, he and his party won a convincing victory in the 1986 general election. He was succeeded 1989 by Ferdinand Color of the Party for National Reconstruction.

Saroyan William 1908–1981. US author. He is best known for short stories, such as *The Daring Young Man on the Flying Trapeze* 1934, idealizing the hopes and sentiments of the 'little man'. His plays include *The Time of Your Life* 1930 and *Talking to You* 1962.

Sarraute Nathalie 1920– . Russian-born French novelist whose books include *Portrait d'un inconnu/Portrait of a Man Unknown* 1948, *Les Fruits d'or/The Golden Fruits* 1964, and *Vous les entendez?/Do You Hear Them?* 1972. An exponent of the *nouveau roman*, Sarraute bypasses plot, character, and style for the half-conscious interaction of minds.

Sartre Jean-Paul 1905–1980. French author and philosopher, one of the leading proponents of existentialism – which takes as its starting-point the individual in the real world – in post-war philosophy. He published his first novel *La Nausée/Nausea* 1937, followed by the trilogy *Les Chemins de la liberté/Roads to Freedom* 1944–45, and many plays, including *Huis Clos/In Camera* 1944. *L'Être et le néant/Being and Nothingness* 1943, his first major philosophical work, is important for its radical doctrine of human freedom. In the later work *Critique de la raison dialectique/Critique of Dialectical Reason* 1960 he tried to produce a fusion of existentialism and Marxism.

Sartre refused the Nobel Prize for Literature 1964 for 'personal reasons', but allegedly changed his mind later, saying he wanted it, or the money.

During World War II he was a prisoner for nine months, and on his return from Germany joined the Resistance. As a founder of modern existentialism, he edited its journal *Les Temps modernes* (Modern Times), and expressed its tenets in his novels and plays. According to Sartre, people's awareness of their own freedom takes the form of anxiety, and they therefore attempt to flee from this awareness into what he terms *mauvaise foi* ('bad faith'); this is the theory he put forward in *L'Être et le néant/Being and Nothingness*. In *Crime Passionel* 1948 he attacked aspects of communism, while remaining generally sympathetic. In his later work Sartre became more sensitive to the social constraints on people's actions.

He was born in Paris, and was the lifelong companion of the feminist writer Simone de Beauvoir.

Sassau-Nguesso Denis 1943– . Congolese socialist politician, president from 1979. He progressively consolidated his position within the ruling left-wing Congolese Labour Party (PCT) and the country, at the same time improving relations with France and the USA.

Sassoon Siegfried 1886–1967. English writer, author of the autobiography *Memoirs of a Foxhunting Man* 1928. His *War Poems* 1919 express the disillusionment of his generation.

Educated at Cambridge, Sassoon enlisted in the army 1915, serving in France and Palestine. He published many volumes of poems and three novels.

Satie Erik (Alfred Leslie) 1866–1925. French composer. His piano pieces, such as *Gymnopédies* 1888, often combine wit and melancholy. His orchestral works include *Parade* 1917, amongst whose sound effects is a typewriter. He was the mentor of the group of composers known as *Les Six*.

Sato Eisaku 1901–1975. Japanese politician. He opposed the policies of Hayato Ikeda (1899–1965) in the Liberal Democratic Party, and succeeded him as prime minister 1964–72, pledged to a more independent foreign policy. He shared a Nobel Peace Prize in 1974 for his rejection of nuclear weapons. His brother **Nobosuke Kishi** (1896–1987) was prime minister of Japan 1957–60.

Saul died *c*.1010 BC. In the Old Testament or Hebrew Bible, the first king of Israel, who was anointed by Samuel and warred successfully against the Ammonites and Philistines (neighbouring peoples). He turned against Samuel and committed suicide as his mind became unbalanced.

Saunders Cicely 1918– . English philanthropist, founder of the modern hospice movement, which aims to provide a caring and comfortable environment in which people with terminal illnesses can die.

She was the medical director of St Christopher's Hospice in Sydenham, S London, 1967–85, and

Savonarola *Italian Dominican monk Savonarola*
established a democratic republic in Florence. His
portrait is by Fra Bartolomeo.

later became its chair. She wrote *Care of the Dying* 1960.

Saussure Horace de 1740–1799. Swiss geologist who made the earliest detailed and first-hand study of the Alps. He was a physicist at the University of Geneva. The results of his Alpine survey appeared in his classic work *Voyages des Alpes/Travels in the Alps* 1779–86.

Savage Michael Joseph 1872–1940. New Zealand Labour politician. As prime minister 1935–40, he introduced much social-security legislation.

Savery Thomas *c*.1650–1715. British engineer who invented the steam-driven water pump, precursor of the steam engine, in 1696.

The pump used a boiler to raise steam, which was condensed (in a separate condenser) by an external spray of cold water. The partial vacuum created sucked water up a pipe from the mine shaft; steam pressure was then used to force the water away, after which the cycle was repeated. Savery patented his invention in 1698.

Savimbi Jonas 1934– . Angolan soldier and revolutionary, founder of the National Union for the Total Independance of Angola (UNITA).

The struggle for independance from Portugal escalated in 1961 into a civil war. In 1966 Savimbi founded the right-wing UNITA, which he led against the left-wing People's Movement for the Liberation of Angola (MPLA), led by Agostinho Neto. Neto, with Soviet and Cuban support, became president when independence

was achieved in 1975, while UNITA, assisted by South Africa, continued its fight. A ceasefire was agreed in June 1989, but fighting continued, and the truce was abandoned after two months.

Savonarola Girolamo 1452–1498. Italian reformer, a Dominican friar. His crusade against political and religious corruption won him huge popularity, and in 1494 he led a revolt in Florence that expelled the ruling Medici family and established a democratic republic. His denunciations of Pope ◊Alexander VI led to his excommunication in 1497, and in 1498 he was arrested, tortured, hanged, and burned for heresy.

Saw Maung 1929– . Myanmar soldier and politician. Appointed head of the armed forces in 1985 by ◊Ne Win, in 1988 he led a coup to remove Ne Win's successor, Maung Maung, and became leader of an emergency government.

Sawchuk 'Terry' (Terrance Gordon) 1929–1970. Canadian ice-hockey player, often regarded as the greatest goaltender of all time. He played for Detroit, Boston, Toronto, Los Angeles, and New York Rangers 1950–67, and holds the National Hockey League (NHL) record of 103 shut-outs (games in which he did not concede a goal).

Saxe Maurice, Comte de 1696–1750. Soldier, illegitimate son of the Elector of Saxony, who served under Prince Eugène of Savoy and was created marshal of France in 1743 for his exploits in the War of the Austrian Succession.

Saxe-Coburg-Gotha Saxon duchy. Albert, the Prince Consort of Queen Victoria, was a son of the 1st Duke (Ernest I 1784–1844), who was succeeded by Albert's elder brother, Ernest II (1818–93). It remained the name of the British royal house until 1917, when it was changed to Windsor.

Sayers Dorothy L(eigh) 1893–1957. English writer of crime novels featuring detective Lord Peter Wimsey and heroine Harriet Vane, including *Strong Poison* 1930, *The Nine Tailors* 1934, and *Gaudy Night* 1935. She also wrote religious plays for radio, and translations of Dante.

Scargill Arthur 1938– . British trade-union leader. Elected president of the National Union of Miners (NUM) 1981, he embarked on a collision course with the Conservative government of Margaret Thatcher. The damaging strike of 1984–85 split the miners' movement.

Scargill became a miner on leaving school and was soon a union and political activist, in the Young Communist League 1955–62 and then a member of the Labour Party from 1966 and president of the Yorkshire miners's union 1973–81. He became a fiery and effective orator. During the long miners strike he was criticized for not seeking an early NUM ballot to support the strike decision. In 1990 an independent inquiry commissioned by the NUM found him guilty of breach of duty and maintaining double accounts during the 1984–85 miners' strike.

Scarlatti (Giuseppe) Domenico 1685–1757. Italian composer, eldest son of Alessandro Scarlatti, who lived most of his life in Portugal and Spain in the service of the Queen of Spain. He wrote highly original harpsichord sonatas.

Scarlatti (Pietro) Alessandro (Gaspare) 1660–1725. Italian Baroque composer, Master of the Chapel at the court of Naples, who developed the opera form. He composed more than 100 operas, including *Tigrane* 1715, as well as church music and oratorios.

Scheele Karl 1742–1786. Swedish chemist and pharmacist. In the book *Experiments on Air and Fire* 1777, he argued that the atmosphere was composed of two gases. One, which supported combustion (oxygen), he called 'fire air', and the other, which inhibited combustion (nitrogen), he called 'vitiated air'. He thus anticipated Joseph ◊Priestley's discovery of oxygen by two years.

Scheer Reinhard 1863–1928. German admiral in World War I, commander of the High Sea Fleet in 1916 at the Battle of Jutland.

Schelling Friedrich Wilhelm Joseph 1775–1854. German philosopher, who began as a follower of Fichte, but moved away from subjective idealism (which treats the external world as essentially immaterial) towards a 'philosophy of identity' (*Identitätsphilosophie*), in which subject and object are seen as united in the absolute. His early philosophy influenced ◊Hegel, but his later work criticizes Hegel, arguing that being necessarily precedes thought.

Scherchen Hermann 1891–1966. German conductor. He collaborated with ◊Schoenberg, and in 1919 founded the journal *Melos* to promote contemporary music. He moved to Switzerland in 1933, and was active as a conductor and teacher. He also wrote two texts, *Handbook of Conducting* and *The Nature of Music*. During the 1950s he founded a music publishing house, Ars Viva Verlag, and an electronic studio at Gravesano.

Schiaparelli Elsa 1896–1973. Italian couturier and knitwear designer. Her innovative fashion ideas included padded shoulders, sophisticated colours ('shocking pink'), and the pioneering use of zips and synthetic fabrics.

Schiaparelli Giovanni (Virginio) 1835–1910. Italian astronomer, who discovered the so-called 'Martian canals'. Among his achievements were studies of ancient and medieval astronomy, the discovery of asteroid 69 (Hesperia) Apr 1861, observation of double stars, and the discovery of the connection between comets and meteors. In 1877 he first drew attention to the linear markings on Mars, which gave rise to the 'Martian canal' controversy. These markings are now known to be optical effects and not real lines.

Schiele Egon 1890–1918. Austrian Expressionist artist. Originally a landscape painter, he was strongly influenced by Art Nouveau and developed a contorted linear style. His subject matter included portraits and nudes. In 1911 he was arrested for alleged obscenity.

Schiller Johann Christoph Friedrich von 1759–1805. German dramatist, poet, and historian. He wrote *Sturm und Drang* (storm and stress) verse and plays, including the dramatic trilogy *Wallenstein* 1798–99. Much of his work concerns the desire for political freedom and for the avoidance of mediocrity.

After the success of the play *Die Räuber/The Robbers* 1781, he devoted himself to literature and completed his tragedies *Fiesko/Fiasco* and *Kabale und Liebe/Love and Intrigue* 1783. Moving to Weimar in 1787, he wrote his more mature blank-verse drama *Don Carlos* and the hymn 'An die Freude/Ode to Joy', later used by ◊Beethoven in his ninth symphony. As professor of history at Jena from 1789, he completed a history of the Thirty Years' War and developed a close friendship with ◊Goethe after early antagonism. His essays on aesthetics include the piece of literary criticism *Über naive und sentimentalische Dichtung/Naive and Sentimental Poetry*. Schiller became the foremost German dramatist with his classic dramas *Wallenstein*, *Maria Stuart* 1800, *Die Jungfrau von Orleans/The Maid of Orleans* 1801, and *Wilhelm Tell/William Tell* 1804.

Schinkel Karl Friedrich 1781–1841. Prussian Neo-Classical architect. Major works include the Old Museum, Berlin, 1823–30, the Nikolaikirche in Potsdam 1830–37, and the Roman Bath 1833 in the park of Potsdam.

Schlegel August Wilhelm von 1767–1845. German Romantic author, translator of Shakespeare, whose *Über dramatische Kunst und Literatur/Lectures on Dramatic Art and Literature* 1809–11 broke down the formalism of the old classical criteria of literary composition. Friedrich von Schlegel was his brother.

Schlegel Friedrich von 1772–1829. German critic, who (with his brother August) was a founder of the Romantic movement, and a pioneer in the comparative study of languages.

Schlesinger John 1926– . British film and television director, responsible for such British films as *Billy Liar* 1963 and *Darling* 1965. His first US film, *Midnight Cowboy* 1969, was a big commercial success and was followed by *Sunday, Bloody Sunday* 1971, *Marathon Man* 1976, and *Yanks* 1979.

Schliemann Heinrich 1822–1890. German archaeologist. He earned a fortune as a businessman, retiring in 1863 to pursue his life-long ambition to discover a historical basis for Homer's Iliad. In 1871 he began excavating at Hissarlik, Turkey, which yielded the ruins of nine consecutive cities and was indeed the site of Troy. His later excavations were at Mycenae 1874–76, where he discovered the ruins of the Mycenaean civilization.

Schluter Poul Holmskov 1929– . Danish right-wing politician, leader of the Conservative People's Party (KF) from 1974 and prime minister from 1982. Having joined the KF in his youth, he trained as a lawyer and then entered the Danish parliament (Folketing) in 1964. His centre-right coalition survived the 1987 election and was reconstituted, with Liberal support, in 1988.

Schmidt Helmut 1918– . West German socialist politician, member of the Social Democratic Party (SPD), chancellor 1974–83. As chancellor, Schmidt introduced social reforms and continued Willy ◊Brandt's policy of Ostpolitik. With the French president Giscard d'Estaing, Schmidt introduced annual world and European economic summits. He was a firm supporter of NATO and of the deployment of US nuclear missiles in West Germany during the early 1980s.

Schmidt was elected to the *Bundestag* (federal parliament) in 1953. He was interior minister 1961–65, defence minister 1969–72, and finance minister 1972–74. He became federal chancellor (prime minister) on Brandt's resignation in 1974. Re-elected 1980, he was defeated in the *Bundestag* in 1982 following the switch of allegiance by the SPD's coalition allies, the Free Democratic Party. Schmidt retired from federal politics at the general election of 1983, having encountered growing opposition from the SPD's left wing, who opposed his stance on miliatry and economic issues.

Schmidt-Rottluff Karl 1884–1974. German Expressionist painter and printmaker, a founder member of the movement *Die Brücke* in Dresden 1905, active in Berlin from 1911. Influenced by van Gogh and the Fauves (see ◊Matisse), he developed a vigorous style of brushwork and a bold palette. He painted portraits and landscapes, and produced numerous woodcuts and lithographs.

Schnabel Artur 1882–1951. Austrian pianist, teacher, and composer. He taught music at the Berlin State Academy 1925–30, but settled in the USA in 1939, where he composed symphonies and piano works. He excelled at playing Beethoven and trained many pianists.

Schneider Romy. Stage name of Rosemarie Albach-Retty 1938–1982. Austrian film actress who starred in *Boccaccio '70* 1962, *Le Procès/Der Prozess* 1962, and *Ludwig* 1972.

Schoenberg Arnold (Franz Walter) 1874–1951. Austro-Hungarian composer, a US citizen from 1941. After Romantic early work such as *Verklärte Nacht* 1899 and the *Gurrelieder/Songs of Gurra* 1900–11, he experimented with atonality (absence of key), producing such works as *Pierrot Lunaire* 1912 before developing the *12-tone system* of musical composition. This was further developed by his pupils ◊Berg and ◊Webern.

After World War I he wrote several Neo-Classical works for chamber ensembles. He taught at the Berlin State Academy 1925–33. Driven from

Germany by the Nazis, he settled in the US 1933, where he influenced music scoring for films. Later works include the opera *Moses and Aaron* 1932–51.

Schopenhauer Arthur 1788–1860. German philosopher, whose *The World as Will and Idea* 1818 expounded an atheistic and pessimistic world view: an irrational will is considered as the inner principle of the world, producing an ever-frustrated cycle of desire, of which the only escape is aesthetic contemplation, or absorption into nothingness.

This theory struck a responsive chord in the philosopher Nietzsche, the composer Wagner, the German novelist Thomas Mann, and the English writer Thomas Hardy.

Schreiner Olive 1862–1920. South African novelist and supporter of women's rights. Her autobiographical *The Story of an African Farm* 1883 describes life on the South African veld.

Schrödinger Erwin 1887–1961. Austrian physicist who advanced the study of wave mechanics. Born in Vienna, he became senior professor at the Dublin Institute for Advanced Studies 1940. He shared (with ◊Dirac) a Nobel prize 1933.

Schubert Franz (Peter) 1797–1828. Austrian composer. His eight symphonies include the incomplete eighth in B minor (the 'Unfinished') and the 'Great' in C major 1829. He wrote chamber and piano music, including the 'Trout Quintet', and over 600 *Lieder* (songs) combining the romantic expression of emotion wih pure melody. They include the cycles *Die schöne Müllerin/The Beautiful Maid of the Mill* 1823 and *Die Winterreise/The Winter Journey* 1827.

Schumacher Ernst Friedrich 'Fritz' 1911–1977. German writer and economist, whose *Small is Beautiful· Economics as if People Mattered* 1973 makes a case for small-scale economic growth without great capital expenditure.

Schuman Robert 1886–1963. French politician. He was prime minister 1947–48, and as foreign minister 1948–53 he proposed in May 1950 a common market for coal and steel (the *Schuman Plan*), which was established as the European Coal and Steel Community 1952, the basis of the European Community.

Schumann Clara (Josephine) (born Wieck) 1819–1896. German pianist. Born in Leipzig, she married Robert Schumann in 1840 (her father had been his piano teacher). During his life and after his death she was devoted to popularizing his work, appearing frequently in European concert halls.

Schumann Robert Alexander 1810–1856. German Romantic composer. His songs and short piano pieces show simplicity combined with an ability to portray mood and emotion. Among his compositions are four symphonies, a violin concerto, a piano concerto, sonatas, and song cycles, such as *Dichterliebe/Poet's Love* 1840. Mendelssohn championed many of his works.

Schumpeter Joseph A(lois) 1883–1950. US economist and sociologist, born in Austria. In *Capitalism, Socialism and Democracy* 1942 he contended that Western capitalism, impelled by its very success, was evolving into a form of socialism because firms would become increasingly large and their managements increasingly divorced from ownership, while social trends were undermining the traditional motives for entrepreneurial accumulation of wealth.

Schuschnigg Kurt von 1897–1977. Austrian chancellor from 1934, in succession to ◊Dollfuss. In Feb 1938 he was forced to accept a Nazi minister of the interior, and a month later Austria was occupied and annexed by Germany. He was imprisoned in Germany until 1945, when he went to the USA.

Schütz Heinrich 1585–1672. German composer, musical director to the Elector of Saxony from 1614. His works include *The Seven Last Words* about 1645, *Musicalische Exequien* 1636, and the *Deutsche Magnificat/German Magnificat* 1671.

Schwarzkopf Elisabeth 1915– . German soprano, known for her dramatic interpretation of operatic roles, such as Elvira in *Don Giovanni* and the Marschallin in *Der Rosenkavalier*, as well as songs.

Schweitzer Albert 1875–1965. French theologian, organist, and missionary surgeon. He founded the hospital at Lambaréné in Gabon in 1913, giving organ recitals to support his work there. He wrote a life of Bach and *Von reimarus zu Wrede/The Quest for the Historical Jesus* 1906 and was awarded the Nobel Peace Prize in 1952 for his teaching of 'reverence for life'.

Schwinger Julian 1918– . US quantum physicist. His research concerned the behaviour of charged particles in electrical fields. This work, expressed entirely through mathematics, combines elements from quantum theory and relativity theory.

Described as the 'physicist in knee pants', he entered college in New York at the age of 15, transferred to Columbia University and graduated at 17. At the age of 29 he became Harvard University's youngest full professor.

Schwitters Kurt 1887–1948. German artist, a member of the Dada movement. He moved to Norway in 1937 and to the UK in 1940. From 1918 he developed a variation on collage, using discarded rubbish such as buttons and bus tickets to create pictures and structures.

He called these art works *Merz*, and produced a magazine called *Merz* from 1923. Later he created *Merzbau*, extensive constructions of wood and scrap, most of which were destroyed.

Sciascia Leonardo 1921–1989. Sicilian novelist, who uses the detective novel to explore the

hidden workings of Sicilian life, for example in *Il giorno della civetta/Mafia Vendetta* 1961.

Scipio Africanus Major 237–c.183 BC. Roman general. He defeated the Carthaginians in Spain 210–206 BC, invaded Africa 204 BC, and defeated Hannibal at Zama 202 BC.

Scipio Africanus Minor c.185–129 BC. Roman general, the adopted grandson of Scipio Africanus Major, also known as *Scipio Aemilianus*. He destroyed Carthage in 146 BC, and subdued Spain 134 BC. He was opposed to his brothers-in-law, the Gracchi (see under ◊Gracchus), and his wife is thought to have shared in his murder.

Scipio Publius Cornelius died 211 BC. Roman general, father of Scipio Africanus Major. Elected consul 218, during the 2nd Punic War, he was defeated by Hannibal at Ticinus and killed by the Carthaginians in Spain.

Scofield Paul 1922– . English actor. His wide-ranging lead roles include the drunken priest in Greene's *The Power and the Glory*, Harry in Pinter's *The Homecoming*, and Salieri in Shaffer's *Amadeus*. He appeared as Sir Thomas More in both stage and film versions of *A Man for All Seasons*.

Scorsese Martin 1942– . US director, whose films concentrate on complex characterization and the theme of alienation. His work includes *Taxi Driver* 1976, *Raging Bull* 1979, *After Hours* 1987, and *The Last Temptation of Christ* 1988.

Scott George C(ampbell) 1927– . US actor who played mostly tough, authoritarian film roles. His work includes *Dr Strangelove* 1964, *Patton* 1970, *The Hospital* 1971, and *Firestarter* 1984.

Scott (George) Gilbert 1811–1878. English architect. As the leading practical architect in the mid-19th-century Gothic revival in England, Scott was responsible for the building or restoration of many public buildings, including the Albert Memorial, the Foreign Office, and St Pancras Station, all in London.

Scott Giles Gilbert 1880–1960. English architect, grandson of George Gilbert Scott. He designed Liverpool Anglican Cathedral, Cambridge University Library, and Waterloo Bridge, London 1945. He supervised the rebuilding of the House of Commons after World War II.

Scott Paul (Mark) 1920–1978. English novelist, author of *The Raj Quartet* comprising *The Jewel in the Crown* 1966, *The Day of the Scorpion* 1968, *The Towers of Silence* 1972 and *A Division of the Spoils* 1975, dealing with the British Raj in India.

Scott Peter (Markham) 1909–1989. British naturalist, artist, and explorer, founder of the Wildfowl Trust at Slimbridge, Gloucestershire, England, and a founder of the World Wildlife Fund (now World Wide Fund for Nature).

Scott's paintings were usually either portraits or bird studies. He was the son of the Antarctic explorer R F Scott.

Scott *Robert Falcon Scott writing his journal during his second, fateful expedition to the Antarctic 1910–12.*

Scott Randolph. Stage name of Randolph Crane 1903–1987. US actor. He began his career in romantic films before becoming one of Hollywood's greatest Western stars in the 1930s. His films include *Roberta* 1934, *Jesse James* 1939, and *Ride the High Country* 1962.

Scott Robert Falcon 1868–1912. Known as *Scott of the Antarctic*. English explorer, who commanded two Antarctic expeditions, 1901–04 and 1910–12. On 18 Jan 1912 he reached the South Pole, shortly after ◊Amundsen, but on the return journey he and his companions died in a blizzard only a few miles from their base camp. His journal was recovered and published in 1913.

With Scott on the final expedition were Wilson, ◊Oates, Bowers, and Evans.

Scott Walter 1771–1832. Scottish novelist and poet. His first works were translations of German ballads, followed by poems such as 'The Lady of the Lake' 1810 and 'Lord of the Isles' 1815. He gained a European reputation for his historical novels such as *Heart of Midlothian* 1818, *Ivanhoe* 1819, and *The Fair Maid of Perth* 1828. His last years were marked by frantic writing to pay off his debts after the bankruptcy of his publishing company in 1826.

Scribe Augustin Eugène 1791–1861. French dramatist. He achieved recognition with *Une Nuit de la garde nationale/Night of the National Guard* 1815, and with numerous assistants produced many plays of technical merit but little profundity, including *Bertrand et Raton/The School for Politicians* 1833.

Scudamore Peter 1958– . British National Hunt jockey. He was champion jockey 1982 (shared with John Francome) and 1986–89. In the 1988–89 season he became the third jockey to ride 1,000 National Hunt winners; in Feb 1989 he became the first person to ride 150 winners in a season and went on to increase his total to 221.

Scullin James Henry 1876–1953. Australian Labor politician. He was leader of the Federal Parliamentary Labor Party 1928–35, and prime minister and minister of industry 1929–31.

Seaborg Glenn Theodore 1912– . US nuclear chemist. He was awarded a Nobel prize in 1951 for his discoveries of transuranic elements, and for production of the radio-isotope uranium 233.

Searle Ronald 1920– . British cartoonist and illustrator, who created the schoolgirls of St Trinian's in 1941 and has made numerous cartoons of cats.

Sebastiano del Piombo *c.* 1485–1547. Italian painter, born in Venice. He moved to Rome in 1511, where his friendship with Michelangelo (and rivalry with Raphael) inspired him to his greatest works, such as *The Raising of Lazarus* 1517–19 (National Gallery, London). He also painted powerful portraits.

One of the greatest Venetian painters of the High Renaissance, Sebastiano was a pupil of ◊Giorgione. Michelangelo encouraged him and provided designs for his work, including *The Flagellation* (San Pietro in Montorio, Rome).

Sebastian, St died *c.* 288. Roman soldier, traditionally a member of Emperor Diocletian's bodyguard until his Christian faith was discovered. He was martyred by being shot with arrows; feast day 20 Jan.

Secchi Pietro Angelo 1818–1878. Italian astronomer who did pioneering work in astrophysics, notably the classification of stellar spectra into four classes based on their colour and spectral characteristics. He was the first to classify solar prominences, huge jets of gas projecting from the Sun's surface.

Seddon Richard John 1845–1906. New Zealand Liberal politician, prime minister 1893–1906.

Seeger Pete 1919– . US folk singer and songwriter of anti-war protest songs, such as 'Where Have All The Flowers Gone?' 1956 and 'If I Had A Hammer' 1949.

Seeger was active in left-wing politics from the late 1930s and was a victim of the witchhunt by Senator Joe ◊McCarthy in the 1950s. As a member of the vocal group *The Weavers* 1948–58, he popularized songs of diverse ethnic origin and had several top-ten hits.

Seferis George. Assumed name of Greek poet-diplomat Georgios Seferiades 1900–1971. Ambassador to Lebanon 1953–57 and then to the UK 1957–62, he did much to help resolve the Cyprus crisis. He published his first volume of lyrics 1931 and his *Collected Poems* 1950. Nobel prize 1963.

Segovia Andrés 1893–1987. Spanish virtuoso guitarist, for whom works were composed by De ◊Falla, ◊Villa-Lobos, and others.

Segrè Emilio 1905–1989. Italian physicist, settled in the USA. In 1955 he discovered the antiproton, an atomic particle with the same mass as the proton, but with negative charge. He shared the 1959 Nobel Prize for Physics with Owen Chamberlain (1920–   ). Segrè had earlier discovered the first synthetic element technetium (atomic number 43) in 1937.

Seifert Jaroslav 1901–1986. Czech poet, who won state prizes, but became an original member of the Charter 77 human-rights movement. Works include *Mozart in Prague* 1970 and *Umbrella from Piccadilly* 1978. Nobel prize 1984.

Selden John 1584–1654. English antiquarian and opponent of Charles I's claim to divine right (the doctrine that the monarch is answerable to God alone), for which he was twice imprisoned. His *Table Talk* 1689 consists of short essays on political and religious questions.

Seleucus I Nicator *c.* 358–280 BC. Macedonian general under Alexander the Great and founder of the *Seleucid Empire*. After Alexander's death 323 BC, Seleucus became governor, and then ruler of Babylonia 321, founding the city of Seleucia on the river Tigris. He conquered Syria and had himself crowned king 306, but his expansionist policies brought him into conflict with the Ptolemies, and he was assassinated by Ptolemy Ceraunus. He was succeeded by his son Antiochus I.

Selfridge Harry Gordon 1857–1947. US entrepreneur, who in 1909 founded Selfridges in London, the first large department store in Britain.

Selkirk Alexander 1676–1721. Scottish sailor marooned 1704–09 in the Juan Fernández Islands in the S Pacific. His story inspired Daniel Defoe to write *Robinson Crusoe*.

Sellers Peter 1925–1980. English comedian and film actor, whose ability as a mimic often allowed him to take several parts. He made his name in the British radio comedy series *The Goon Show* 1949–60, and his films include *Dr Strangelove* 1964, *Being There* 1979, and five *Pink Panther* films 1964–78 (as the bumbling Inspector Clouseau).

Selous Frederick Courtney 1851–1917. British explorer and writer. His pioneer journey in the present-day Zambia and Zimbabwe area opened up the country to Europeans.

Selznick David O(liver) 1902–1965. US film producer. His independent company Selznick International made such films as *King Kong* 1933, *Gone With the Wind* 1939, *Rebecca* 1940, and *Duel in the Sun* 1946.

Semenov Nikoly 1896– . Russian physical chemist who made significant contributions to the study of chemical chain reactions. Working mainly in Leningrad at the Institute for Chemical Physics, in 1956 he became the first Russian to gain the Nobel Prize for Chemistry which he shared with ◊Hinshelwood.

Semmelweis Ignaz Philipp 1818–1865. Hungarian obstetrician who pioneered asepsis.

Semmelweis was an obstetric assistant at the General Hospital in Vienna at a time when 10% of women were dying of puerperal (childbed) fever. He realized that the cause was infectious matter carried on the hands of doctors treating the women after handling corpses in the post-mortem room. He introduced aseptic methods (hand-washing in chlorinated lime), and mortality fell to almost zero. Semmelweis was sacked for his efforts, which were not widely adopted. It was left to ◊Lister to reintroduce aseptic procedures.

Senanayake Don Stephen 1884–1952. First prime minister of independent Sri Lanka (formerly Ceylon) 1947–52.

Senanayake Dudley 1911–1973. Prime minister of Sri Lanka 1952–53, 1960, and 1965–70; son of Don Senanayake.

Sendak Maurice 1928– . US illustrator, born in New York, whose deliberately archaic children's book illustrations include *Where the Wild Things Are* 1963, *In the Night Kitchen* 1970, and *Outside Over There* 1981 (all of which books he also wrote).

Seneca Lucius Annaeus *c.* 4 BC–AD 65. Roman Stoic playwright, author of essays and nine tragedies. Born at Córdoba, Spain, he was Nero's tutor, but lost favour after his accession and was ordered to commit suicide. His tragedies were accepted as classical models by 16th-century dramatists.

Senefelder Alois 1771–1834. German engraver, born in Prague. He is considered the founder of lithography.

Senghor Léopold 1906– . First president of independent Senegal 1960–80.

Senna Ayrton 1960– . Brazilian motor-racing driver. He had his first Grand Prix win in the 1985 Portuguese Grand Prix, and in 1988 was world champion, winning a championship record eight races.

Sennacherib died 681 BC. King of Assyria from 705. Son of ◊Sargon II, he rebuilt the city of Nineveh on a grand scale, sacked Babylon 689, and crushed ◊Hezekiah, king of Judah, though failing to take Jerusalem. He was assassinated by his sons, and one of them, Esarhaddon, succeeded him.

Sennett Mack. Stage name of Michael Sinnott 1880–1960. US film producer, originally an actor, responsible for such 1920s slapstick silent comedians as the Keystone Kops, 'Fatty' Arbuckle, and Charlie Chaplin. He did not make the transition to sound with much enthusiasm and retired 1935. His films include *Tillie's Punctured Romance* 1914, *The Shriek of Araby* 1923, and *The Barber Shop* (sound) 1933.

Sequoya George Guess 1770–1843. American Indian scholar and leader. After serving with the US army in the Creek War 1813–14, he made a study of his own Cherokee language and created a syllabary which was approved by the Cherokee council 1821. This helped thousands of Indians towards literacy and resulted in the publication of books and newspapers in their own language. Sequoya went on to write down ancient tribal history.

In later life he became a political representative of the Western tribes in Washington, negotiating for the Indians when the US government forced resettlement in Indian territory in the 1830s. A type of giant redwood tree, the *sequoia*, is named after him, as is a national park in California.

Sergel Johan Tobias 1740–1814. Swedish Neo-Classical sculptor, active mainly in Stockholm. His portraits include *Gustaf III* (Royal Palace, Stockholm) and he made terracotta figures such as *Mars and Venus* (National museum, Stockholm).

Sergius, St of Radonezh 1314–1392. Patron saint of Russia, who founded the Eastern Orthodox monastery of the Blessed Trinity near Moscow 1334.

Mediator among Russian feudal princes, he inspired the victory of Dmitri, Grand Duke of Moscow, over the Tatar khan Mamai at Kulikovo, on the upper Don, 1380.

Serlio Sebastiano 1475–1554. Italian architect and painter, author of *L'Architettura* 1537–51, which set down practical rules for the use of the Classical orders, and was used by architects of the Neo-Classical style throughout Europe.

Serota Nicholas Andrew 1946– . British art-gallery director. He made his reputation as director of the Whitechapel Art Gallery from 1976 to 1987, when he became director of the Tate Gallery, London.

Servan-Schreiber Jean Jacques 1924– . French Radical politician, and founder ot the magazine *L'Express* 1953. *Le Défi americain* 1967 maintained that US economic and technological dominance would be challenged only by a united left-wing Europe.

Servetus Michael 1511–1553. Spanish Christian theologian and Anabaptist. He was burned alive by the church reformer Calvin in Geneva, Switzerland, for his unitarian views. As a physician, he was a pioneer in the study of the circulation of the blood.

Service Robert William 1874–1938. Canadian author, born in England. He was popular for his ballads of the Yukon in the days of the Gold Rush, for example 'The Shooting of Dan McGrew' 1907.

Sessions Roger (Huntingdon) 1896–1985. US composer, whose dense and dissonant works include *The Black Maskers* incidental music 1923, eight symphonies, and *Concerto for Orchestra* 1971.

Seton Ernest Thompson, born Ernest Seton Thompson. 1860–1946. Canadian author and naturalist, born in England. He became noted for illustrating his own books with drawings of animals. He was the founder of the Woodcraft

Folk youth movement, a non-religious alternative to the scouting movement.

Seurat Georges 1859–1891. French artist. He originated, with ◊Signac, the Neo-Impressionist technique of *Pointillism* (painting will small dabs rather than long brushstrokes), in part inspired by 19th-century theories of colour and vision. He also departed from Impressionism by evolving a more formal type of composition.

Seurat's compositions were based on the Classical proportions of the golden section rather than aiming to capture fleeting moments of light and movement. Outstanding examples of his work are *La Baignade/The Bathers at Asnières* 1884 (National Gallery, London) and *Sunday on the Island of La Grande Jatte* 1886 (Art Institute of Chicago).

Severin Tim 1940– . Writer, historian, and traveller who re-enacted 'classic' voyages. In 1961 he led a motorcycle team along the Marco Polo route in Asia and four years later canoed the length of the Mississippi. His Brendan Voyage 1977 followed the supposed transatlantic route taken by St Brendan in the 7th century; the Sinbad Voyage took him from Oman to China 1980–81; the Jason Voyage followed the ancient route of the Argonauts in search of the Golden Fleece 1984; the Ulysses Voyage took him from Troy to Ithaca 1985; and a journey on horseback retraced the route to the Middle East taken by the Crusaders 1987–88.

Severus Lucius Septimus AD 146–211. Roman emperor. Born in N Africa, he held a command on the Danube when in AD 193 the emperor Pertinax was murdered. Proclaimed emperor by his troops, Severus proved an able administrator; he was the only African to become emperor. He died at York while campaigning in Britain against the Caledonians.

Severus of Antioch 467–538. Christian bishop, one of the originators of the *Monophysite* heresy. As patriarch of Antioch (from 512), Severus was the leader of opposition to the Council of Chalcedon 451, an attempt to unite factions of the early church, by insisting that Christ existed in one nature only. He was condemned by the emperor Justin I in 518, and left Antioch for Alexandria, never to return.

Sévigné Marie de Rabutin-Chantal, Marquise de Sévigné 1626–1696. French writer. In her letters to her daughter, the Comtesse de Grignan, she gives a vivid picture of contemporary customs and events.

Sewell Anna 1820–1878. English author, whose only published work tells the life story of a horse, *Black Beauty* 1877. Although now read as a children's book, it was written to encourage sympathetic treatment of horses by adults.

Sexton Anne 1928–1974. US poet. She studied with Robert Lowell and wrote similarly confessional poetry, as in *All My Pretty Ones* 1962. She committed suicide, and her *Complete Poems* appeared posthumously 1981.

Seymour family name of dukes of Somerset (seated at Maiden Bradley, Wilts), and Marquesses of Hertford (seated at Ragley Hall, Warwicks); the family first came to prominence through the marriage of Jane Seymour to Henry VIII.

Seymour Jane *c.*1509–1537. Third wife of Henry VIII, whom she married in 1536. She died soon after the birth of her son Edward VI.

Seymour Lynn 1939– . Canadian ballerina of rare dramatic quality. She was principal dancer of the Royal Ballet from 1959 and artistic director of the Munich State Opera Ballet 1978–80.

Sforza Italian family which ruled the duchy of Milan 1450–99 and 1522–35. Their court was a centre of Renaissance culture, and *Ludovico Sforza* (1451–1508) was patron of the artist ◊Leonardo da Vinci.

Shackleton Ernest 1874–1922. Irish Antarctic explorer. In 1907–09, he commanded an expedition that reached 88° 23′ S latitude, located the magnetic South Pole, and climbed Mount Erebus.

He was a member of Scott's Antarctic expedition 1901–04, and also commanded the expedition 1914–16, which hoped to cross the Antarctic, when he had to abandon his ship, the *Endurance*, crushed in the ice of the Weddell Sea. He died on board the *Quest* on his fourth expedition 1921–22 to the Antarctic.

Shadwell Thomas 1642–1692. English dramatist and poet. His plays include *Epsom-Wells* 1672 and *Bury-Fair* 1689. He was involved in a violent feud with the poet ◊Dryden whom he attacked in 'The Medal of John Bayes' 1682, and succeeded as Poet Laureate.

Shaffer Peter 1926– . English playwright. His plays include *Five Finger Exercise* 1958, the historical epic *The Royal Hunt of the Sun* 1964, *Equus* 1973, and *Amadeus* 1979 about the composer Mozart.

Shaftesbury Anthony Ashley Cooper, 1st Earl of Shaftesbury 1621–1683. English politician, a supporter of the Restoration of the monarchy. He became lord chancellor in 1672, but went into opposition in 1673 and began to organize the Whig Party. He headed the Whigs' demand for the exclusion of the future James II from the succession, secured the passing of the Habeas Corpus Act in 1679 and, when accused of treason in 1681, fled to Holland.

Shaftesbury Anthony Ashley Cooper, 3rd Earl of Shaftesbury 1671–1713. English philosopher, author of *Characteristics of Men, Manners, Opinions, and Times* 1711 and other ethical speculations.

Shaftesbury Anthony Ashley Cooper, 7th Earl of Shaftesbury 1801–1885. British Tory politician. He strongly supported the Ten Hours Act of

1847 and other factory legislation, including the 1842 act forbidding the employment of women and children underground in mines. He was also associated with the movement to provide free education for the poor.

Shah Jehan 1592–1666. Mughal emperor of India from 1627, when he succeeded his father Jehangir. From 1658 he was a prisoner of his son Aurangzeb. He built the Taj Mahal mausoleum at Agra.

Shahn Ben 1898–1969. US artist, born in Lithuania, a Social Realist painter. His work included drawings and paintings on the ◊Dreyfus case and the Sacco and Vanzetti case, in which two Italian anarchists were accused of murders. As a mural painter he worked at the Rockefeller Center, New York (with the Mexican artist Diego Rivera), and the Federal Security Building, Washington, 1940–42.

Shaka or *Chaka* 1787–1828. Zulu leader who formed a Zulu empire in S Africa. He seized power from his half-brother 1816, and embarked on a campaign to unite the Nguni (the area that today forms the South African province of Natal), initiating the period of warfare known as the Mfecane.

Shakespeare William 1564–1616. English dramatist and poet. Established in London by 1589 as an actor and a playwright, he was England's unrivalled dramatist until his death, and is considered the greatest English playwright. His plays, written in blank verse, can be broadly divided into lyric plays, including *Romeo and Juliet* and *A Midsummer Night's Dream*; comedies, including *The Comedy of Errors, As You Like It, Much Ado About Nothing*, and *Measure For Measure*; historical plays, such as *Henry VI* (in three parts), *Richard III*, and *Henry IV* (in two parts), which often showed cynical political wisdom; and tragedies, such as *Hamlet, Macbeth*, and *King Lear*. He also wrote numerous sonnets.

Born in Stratford-on-Avon, the son of a wool dealer, he was educated at the grammar school, and in 1582 married Anne Hathaway. They had a daughter, Susanna, in 1583, and twins Hamnet (died 1596) and Judith in 1595. Early plays, written around 1589–93, were the tragedy *Titus Andronicus*; the comedies *The Comedy of Errors, The Taming of the Shrew*, and *The Two Gentlemen of Verona*; the three parts of *Henry VI*; and *Richard III*. About 1593 he came under the patronage of the Earl of ◊Southampton, to whom he dedicated his long poems *Venus and Adonis* 1593 and *The Rape of Lucrece* 1594; he also wrote for him the comedy *Love's Labour's Lost*, satirizing ◊Raleigh's circle, and seems to have dedicated to him his sonnets written around 1593–96, in which the mysterious 'Dark Lady' appears.

From 1594 Shakespeare was a member of the Chamberlain's (later the King's) company of players, and had no rival as a dramatist, writing, for

Shakespeare *The title page engraving by M Droeshout for the First Folio of Shakespeare's plays.*

example, the lyric plays *Romeo and Juliet*, *A Midsummer Night's Dream*, and *Richard II* 1594–95, followed by *King John* and *The Merchant of Venice* in 1596. The Falstaff plays of 1597–99 – *Henry IV* (parts I and II), *Henry V*, and *The Merry Wives of Windsor* (said to have been written at the request of Elizabeth I) – brought his fame to its height. About the same time he wrote *Julius Caesar*. The period ended with the lyrically witty *Much Ado about Nothing*, *As You Like It*, and *Twelfth Night* about 1598–1601.

With *Hamlet* begins the period of the great tragedies, 1601–08: *Othello*, *Macbeth*, *King Lear*, *Timon of Athens*, *Antony and Cleopatra*, and *Coriolanus*. This 'darker' period is also reflected in the comedies *Troilus and Cressida*, *All's Well that Ends Well*, and *Measure for Measure* around 1601–04.

It is thought that Shakespeare was only part author of *Pericles*, which is grouped with the other plays of around 1608–11 – *Cymbeline*, *The Winter's Tale*, and *The Tempest* – as the mature romance or 'reconciliation' plays of the end of his career. During 1613 it is thought that Shakespeare collaborated with Fletcher on *Henry VIII* and *Two Noble Kinsmen*. He had already retired to Stratford in about 1610, where he died on 23 Apr 1616.

For the first 200 years after his death, Shakespeare's plays were frequently performed in cut or revised form (Nahum Tate's *King Lear* was given a happy ending), and it was not until the 19th century, with the critical assessment of Coleridge and ◊Hazlitt, that the original texts were restored.

Shalmaneser III King of Assyria 859–824 BC, who pursued an aggressive policy, and brought Babylon and Israel under the domination of Assyria.

Shamir Yitzhak 1915– . Israeli politician, born in Poland; foreign minister under Menachem Begin 1980–83, prime minister 1983–84, and again foreign minister in the ◊Peres unity government from 1984. In Oct 1986, he and Peres exchanged positions, Shamir becoming prime minister and Peres taking over as foreign minister. He was re-elected 1989. Shamir was a leader of the Stern Gang of guerrillas (1940–48) during the British mandate rule of Palestine.

Shankar Ravi 1920– . Indian composer and musician. A virtuoso of the sitar, he has composed film music and founded music schools in Bombay and Los Angeles.

Shankara 799–833. Hindu philosopher who wrote commentaries on some of the major Hindu scriptures, as well as hymns and essays on religious ideas. Shankara was responsible for the final form of the Advaita Vedanta school of Hindu philosophy, which teaches that Brahman, the supreme being, is all that exists in the universe; everything else is illusion. Shankara was fiercely opposed to Buddhism and may have influenced its decline in India.

Shannon Claude Elwood 1916– . US mathematician, whose paper *The Mathematical Theory of Communication* 1948 marks the beginning of the science of information theory. He argued that information (data) and entropy are analogous, and obtained a quantitive measure of the amount of information in a given message.

Shapiro Karl 1913– . US poet. He was born in Baltimore, and his work includes the striking *V Letter* 1945, written after service in World War II.

Shapley Harlow 1885–1972. US astronomer, whose study of globular star clusters showed that they were arranged in a halo around the galaxy, and that the galaxy was much larger than previously thought. He realized that the Sun was not at the centre of the galaxy as then assumed, but two-thirds of the way out to the rim.

Sharif Omar. Stage name of Michael Shalhoub 1932– . Egyptian actor, in international films after his successful appearance in *Lawrence of Arabia* 1962. His other films include *Dr Zhivago* 1965 and *Funny Girl* 1968.

Sharp Cecil (James) 1859–1924. English collector and compiler of folk dance and song. His work ensured that the English folk-music revival became established in school music throughout the English-speaking world.

He travelled the country to record and save from extinction the folk-song tradition, for example *English Folk Song* 1907 (two volumes). In the USA he tracked down survivals of English song in the Appalachian Mountains and elsewhere.

Sharp Granville 1735–1813. English philanthropist. He was prominent in the anti-slavery movement and in 1772 secured a legal decision 'that as soon as any slave sets foot on English territory he becomes free'.

Sharpey-Schäfer Edward Albert 1850–1935. English physiologist and one of the founders of endocrinology. He made important discoveries relating to the hormone adrenaline, and to the pituitary and other endocrine or ductless glands.

He also devised a method of artificial respiration which improved on existing techniques.

Shastri Lal Bahadur 1904–1966. Indian politician, who held various ministerial posts after independence, and succeeded Nehru as prime minister of India 1964. He campaigned for national integration, and secured a declaration of peace with Pakistan at the Tashkent peace conference 1966.

Before independence, he was imprisoned several times for civil disobedience. Because of his small stature, he was known as 'the Sparrow'.

Shaw George Bernard 1856–1950. Irish dramatist. He was also a critic and novelist, and an early member of the socialist Fabian Society. His plays combine comedy with political, philosophical, and polemic aspects, aiming to make an impact on his audience's social conscience as well as their emotions. They include *Arms and the Man* 1894, *Devil's Disciple* 1897, *Man and Superman* 1905, *Pygmalion* 1913, and *St Joan* 1924. Nobel prize 1925.

Born in Dublin, the son of a civil servant, Shaw came to London in 1876, where he became a brilliant debater and supporter of the Fabians, and worked as a music and drama critic. He wrote five unsuccessful novels before in 1892 his first play, *Widowers' Houses*, was produced. Attacking slum landlords, it allied him with the realistic, political, and polemical movement in the theatre, pointing to people's responsibility to improve themselves and their social environment.

The volume *Plays: Pleasant and Unpleasant* 1898 also included *The Philanderer, Mrs Warren's Profession*, dealing with prostitution and banned until 1902; and *Arms and the Man* about war. *Three Plays for Puritans* 1901 contained *The Devil's Disciple, Caesar and Cleopatra* (a companion piece to the play by Shakespeare), and *Captain Brassbound's Conversion*, written for the actress Ellen ◊Terry. *Man and Superman* 1903 expounds his ideas of evolution by following the character of Don Juan into hell for a debate with the devil.

The 'anti-romantic' comedy *Pygmalion*, first performed 1913, was written for the actress Mrs Patrick ◊Campbell (and later converted to a musical as *My Fair Lady*). Later plays included *Heartbreak House* 1917, *Back to Methuselah* 1921, and the historical *St Joan* 1924.

Altogether Shaw wrote more than 50 plays and became a byword for wit. His theories were further explained in the voluminous prefaces to the plays, and in books such as *The Intelligent Woman's Guide to Socialism and Capitalism* 1928. He was also an unsuccessful advocate of spelling reform and a prolific letter-writer.

Shaw (Richard) Norman 1831–1912. British architect. He was the leader of the trend away from Gothic and Tudor styles back to Georgian lines. His buildings include Swan House, Chelsea, 1876.

Shchedrin N. Pen name of Mikhail Evgrafovich Saltykov 1826–1889. Russian writer, whose works include *Fables* 1884–85, in which he depicts misplaced 'good intentions', and the novel *The Golovlevs* 1880. He was a satirist of pessimistic outlook.

Shearer (Edith) Norma 1900–1983. Canadian actress who starred in such 1930s films as *Private Lives* 1931, *Romeo and Juliet* 1936, and *Marie Antoinette* 1938, in which she played the title role. She was married to MGM executive Irving Thalberg.

Shelburne William Petty FitzMaurice, 2nd Earl of Shelburne 1737–1805. British Whig politician. He was an opponent of George III's American policy, and as prime minister in 1783, he concluded peace with the USA. He was created Marquess of Lansdowne in 1784.

Shelley Mary Wollstonecraft 1797–1851. English writer, the daughter of Mary Wollstonecraft and William Godwin. In 1814 she eloped with the poet Percy Bysshe Shelley, whom she married in 1816. Her novels include *Frankenstein* 1818, *The Last Man* 1826, and *Valperga* 1823.

Shelley Percy Bysshe 1792–1822. English lyric poet, a leading figure in the Romantic movement. Expelled from Oxford for atheism, he fought all his life against religion and for political freedom. This is reflected in his early poems such as *Queen Mab* 1813. He later wrote tragedies including *The Cenci* 1818, lyric dramas such as *Prometheus Unbound* 1820, and lyrical poems such as 'Ode to the West Wind'. He drowned while sailing in Italy.

Born near Horsham, Sussex, he was educated at Eton school and University College, Oxford, where his collaboration in a pamphlet *The Necessity of Atheism* 1811 caused his expulsion. While living in London he fell in love with 16-year-old Harriet Westbrook, whom he married 1811. He visited Ireland and Wales writing pamphlets defending vegetarianism and political freedom, and in 1813 published privately *Queen Mab*, a poem with political freedom as its theme. Meanwhile he had become estranged from his wife and in 1814 left England with Mary Wollstonecraft Godwin, whom he married after Harriet had drowned herself 1816. *Alastor*, written 1815, was followed by the epic *The Revolt of Islam*, and by 1818 Shelley was living in Italy. Here he produced the tragedy *The Cenci*; the satire on Wordsworth, *Peter Bell the Third* 1819; and the lyric drama *Prometheus Unbound* 1820. Other works of the period are 'Ode to the West Wind' 1819; 'The Cloud' and 'The Skylark', both 1820; 'The Sensitive Plant' and 'The Witch of Atlas'; 'Epipsychidion' and, on the death of the poet Keats, 'Adonais' 1821; the lyric drama *Hellas* 1822; and the prose *Defence of Poetry* 1821. In July 1822 Shelley was drowned while sailing near La Spezia, and his ashes were buried in Rome.

Shenstone William 1714–1763. English poet and essayist whose poems include *Poems upon Various Occasions* 1737, the Spenserian *Schoolmistress* 1742, elegies, odes, songs, and ballads.

Shepard Alan (Bartlett) 1923– . US astronaut, the fifth person to walk on the Moon. He was the first American in space, as pilot of the suborbital Mercury-Redstone 3 mission on board the Freedom 7 capsule May 1961, and commanded the Apollo 14 lunar landing mission 1971.

Shepard E(rnest) H(oward) 1879–1976. British illustrator of books by A A Milne (*Winnie-the-Pooh* 1926) and Kenneth Grahame (*The Wind in the Willows* 1908).

Shepard Sam 1943– . US dramatist and actor. His work combines colloquial American dialogue with striking visual imagery, and includes *The Tooth of Crime* 1972 and *Buried Child* 1978, for which he won the Pulitzer Prize. He has acted in a number of films, including *The Right Stuff* 1983, *Fool for Love* 1986, based on his play of the same name, and *Steel Magnolias* 1989.

Sheppard Jack 1702–1724. English criminal. Born in Stepney, he was an apprentice carpenter, but turned to theft and became a popular hero by four escapes from prison. He was finally caught and hanged.

Sheraton Thomas *c.*1751–1806. English designer of elegant inlaid furniture, as in his *Cabinet-maker's and Upholsterer's Drawing Book* 1791. He was influenced by his predecessors ◊Hepplewhite and ◊Chippendale.

Sheridan Philip Henry 1831–1888. US Union general in the American Civil War. Gen Ulysses S ◊Grant gave him command of his cavalry in 1864, and soon after of the army of the Shenandoah Valley, Virginia, which he cleared of Confederates. In the final stage of the war, Sheridan forced Gen Lee to retreat to Appomattox, and surrender.

Sheridan Richard Brinsley 1751–1816. English dramatist and politician, born in Dublin. His social comedies include *The Rivals* 1775, celebrated for the character of Mrs Malaprop, *The School for Scandal* 1777, and *The Critic* 1779. In 1776 he became lessee of the Drury Lane Theatre. He became a member of Parliament in 1780.

He entered Parliament as an adherent of Charles ◊Fox. A noted orator, he directed the impeachment of the former governor-general of India, Warren Hastings, and was treasurer to the Navy

1806–07. His last years were clouded by the burning down of his theatre in 1809, the loss of his parliamentary seat in 1812, and by financial ruin and mental breakdown.

Sherman William Tecumseh 1820–1891. US Union general in the American Civil War. In 1864 he captured and burned Atlanta, from where he marched to the sea, laying Georgia waste, and then drove the Confederates northwards. He was US Army Chief of Staff 1869–83.

He received a command in the Federal army on the Mississippi front early in the war, and collaborated with Gen U S ◊Grant in the Vicksburg campaign.

Sherriff R(obert) C(edric) 1896–1975. British dramatist, remembered for his antiheroic war play *Journey's End* 1929. Later plays include *Badger's Green* 1930 and *Home at Seven* 1950.

Sherrington Charles Scott 1857–1952. English neurophysiologist, who studied the structure and function of the nervous system. *The Integrative Action of the Nervous System* 1906 formulated the principles of reflex action. Nobel Prize for Medicine (with E D ◊Adrian) 1932.

Sherwood Robert 1896–1955. US dramatist. His plays include *The Petrified Forest* 1934 (Humphrey ◊Bogart starred in the play and the film), *Idiot's Delight* 1936, *Abe Lincoln in Illinois* 1938, and *There Shall Be No Night* 1940. For each of the last three he received a Pulitzer prize.

Shevardnadze Edvard 1928– . Soviet politician. A supporter of ◊Gorbachev, he was first secretary of the Georgian Communist Party from 1972, and an advocate of economic reform. In 1985 he became foreign minister and a member of the Politburo, and has worked for détente and disarmament.

Shidehara Kijuro 1872–1951. Japanese politician and diplomat who, as foreign minister 1924–27 and 1929–31, promoted conciliation with China, and economic rather than military expansion. In 1945 he was recognized by the USA as prime minister and acted as speaker of the Japanese Diet (parliament) until his death.

Shi Huangdi (formerly *Shih Huang Ti*) 259–210 BC. Emperor of China. He succeeded to the throne of the state of Qin in 246 BC, and reunited the country as an empire by 228 BC. He burned almost all existing books in 213 BC to destroy ties with the past; rebuilt the Great Wall; and was buried in a tomb complex guarded by 10,000 individualized, life-size pottery warriors (excavated in the 1980s).

He had so overextended his power that the dynasty and the empire collapsed at the death of his feeble successor in 207 BC.

Shilton Peter 1949– . English international footballer, an outstanding goalkeeper. His career began in the 1960s.

He has made more than 850 Football League appearances, which is an all-time record, and won a record number of England Caps.

Shockley William 1910–1989. US physicist and amateur geneticist, who worked with ◊Bardeen and ◊Brattain on the invention of the transistor. They were jointly awarded a Nobel prize 1956. During the 1970s he was severely criticized for his claim that blacks were genetically inferior to whites in terms of intelligence.

Shoemaker William Lee 'Bill' 1931– . US jockey, whose career 1949–89 was outstandingly successful. He rode 8,830 winners from nearly 40,000 mounts and his earnings exceeded $123 million.

His first ride was on 19 Mar 1949. He was the leading US jockey ten times.

Sholokhov Mikhail Aleksandrovich 1905–1984. Soviet novelist. His *And Quiet Flows the Don* 1926–40 depicts the Don Cossacks through World War I and the Russian Revolution. Nobel prize 1965.

Shostakovich Dmitry (Dmitriyevich) 1906–1975. Soviet composer. His music, tonal, expressive, and sometimes highly dramatic, has not always been to official Soviet taste. He wrote 15 symphonies, chamber music, ballets, and operas, the latter including *Lady Macbeth of Mtsensk* 1934, which was suppressed as 'too divorced from the proletariat', but revived as *Katerina Izmaylova* 1963.

Shovell Cloudesley *c.*1650–1707. English admiral who took part, with George Rooke (1650–1709), in the capture of Gibraltar 1704. In 1707 his flagship *Association* was wrecked off the Isles of Scilly and he was strangled for his rings by an islander when he came ashore.

Shrapnel Henry 1761–1842. British army officer who invented shells containing bullets, to increase the spread of casualties, first used 1804; hence the word *shrapnel* to describe shell fragments.

Shultz George P 1920– . US Republican politician, economics adviser to President ◊Reagan 1980–82, and secretary of state 1982–89.

Shultz taught as a labour economist at the University of Chicago before serving in the 1968–74 ◊Nixon administration, including secretary of Labor 1969–70 and secretary of the Treasury 1972–74. As State Department secretary, he was in charge of the formulation of US foreign policy. He was pragmatic and moderate, against the opposition of Defence Secretary Caspar ◊Weinberger.

Shute Nevil. Pen name of Nevil Shute Norway 1899–1960. English novelist, who wrote *A Town Like Alice* 1949 and *On the Beach* 1957.

Sibelius Jean (Christian) 1865–1957. Finnish composer. His works include nationalistic symphonic poems such as *En Saga* 1893 and *Finlandia* 1900, a violin concerto 1904, and seven symphonies.

He studied the violin and composition at Helsinki and went on to Berlin and Vienna. In 1940 he abruptly ceased composing and lived the rest of his life as a recluse.

Sibley Antoinette 1939– . British dancer. Joining the Royal Ballet 1956, she became senior soloist 1960. Her roles included Odette/Odile, Giselle, and the betrayed girl in *The Rake's Progress*.

Sickert Walter (Richard) 1860–1942. English artist. His Impressionist cityscapes of London and Venice, portraits, and domestic interiors capture subtleties of tone and light, often with a melancholy air.

Sickert, in London from 1868, was born in Munich, the son of a Danish painter, and studied art at the Slade School. His work inspired the Camden Town Group in N London; examples include *Ennui* about 1913 (Tate Gallery, London).

Siddons Sarah 1755–1831. Welsh actress. Her majestic presence made her most suited to tragic and heroic roles such as Lady Macbeth, Zara in Congreve's *The Mourning Bride*, and Constance in *King John*.

She toured the provinces with the company of Roger Kemble, her father, until she appeared in London to immediate acclaim. Her first success in Otway's *Venice Preserv'd* 1774 led to her appearing with ◊Garrick at Drury Lane. She continued with success until her retirement 1812.

Sidney Philip 1554–1586. English poet and soldier, author of the sonnet sequence *Astrophel and Stella* 1591, *Arcadia* 1590, a prose romance, and *Apologie for Poetrie* 1595, the earliest work of English literary criticism.

He was born in Penshurst, Kent. He entered Parliament 1581, and was knighted 1583. In 1585 he was made governor of Flushing in the Netherlands, and died at Zutphen, fighting the Spaniards.

Sidney *Renaissance man Philip Sidney was a poet, politician, courtier, and soldier.*

Siegel Don(ald) 1912– . US film director who made thrillers, Westerns, and police dramas. He also directed *Invasion of the Body Snatchers* 1956. His other films include *Madigan* 1968, *Dirty Harry* 1971, and *The Shootist* 1976.

Siemens German family of four brothers, creators of a vast industrial empire. The eldest, *Ernst Werner von Siemens* (1812–1892), founded the original electrical firm of *Siemens und Halske* 1847 and made many advances in telegraphy. *William* (Karl Wilhelm) Siemens (1823–1883) moved to England in 1844, perfected the open-hearth production of steel (now superseded), pioneered the development of the electric locomotive and the laying of transoceanic cables, and improved the electric generator.

Sienkiewicz Henryk 1846–1916. Polish author. His books include *Quo Vadis?* 1895, set in Rome at the time of Nero, and the 17th-century historical trilogy *With Fire and Sword, The Deluge*, and *Pan Michael* 1890–93.

Siger of Brabant 1240–1282. Medieval philosopher, a follower of ◊Averroes, who taught at the University of Paris, and whose distinguishing between reason and Christian faith led to his works being condemned as heretical 1270. He refused to recant and was imprisoned. He was murdered while in prison.

Sigismund 1368–1437. Holy Roman emperor from 1411. He convened and presided over the council of Constance 1414–18, where he promised protection to the religious reformer ◊Huss, but imprisoned him after his condemnation for heresy, and acquiesced in his burning. King of Bohemia from 1419, he led the military campaign against the Hussites.

He was the younger brother of Emperor Wenceslas (1361–1419).

Signac Paul 1863–1935. French artist. In 1884 he joined with ◊Seurat in founding the Société des Artistes Indépendants and developing the technique of *Pointillism*.

Signac, born in Paris, was initially influenced by the great Impressionist Monet. He laid down the theory of Neo-Impressionism in his book *De Delacroix au Néo-Impressionisme* 1899. From the 1890s he developed a stronger and brighter palette.

Signorelli Luca *c.*1450–1523. Italian painter, active in central Italy. About 1483 he was called to the Vatican to complete frescoes on the walls of the Sistine Chapel.

He produced large frescoes in Orvieto Cathedral, where he devoted a number of scenes to *The Last Judgment* 1499–1504. The style is sculptural and dramatic, reflecting late 15th-century Florentine trends, but Signorelli's work is especially imaginative. He settled in Cortona and ran a large workshop there producing altarpieces.

Sihanouk Norodom 1922– . Cambodian politician, king 1941–55, prime minister 1955–70, when his government was overthrown by a military coup led by Lon Nol. With Pol Pot's resistance front, he overthrew Lon Nol 1975, and again became prime minister 1975–76, when he was forced to resign by the Khmer Rouge.

Educated in Vietnam and Paris, he was elected king of Cambodia 1941. He abdicated 1955 in favour of his father.

Sihanouk was deposed by a right-wing military coup led by Lt-Gen Lon Nol 1970. He established a government in exile in Beijing and formed a joint resistance front with Pol Pot. This movement succeeded in overthrowing Lon Nol Apr 1975 and Sihanouk was reappointed head of state, but in Apr 1976 he was forced to resign by the communist Khmer Rouge leadership. Now living in North Korea, he became the recognized leader of the Democratic Kampuchea government in exile 1982.

Sikorski Wladyslaw 1881–1943. Polish general and politician. In 1909, he formed the nationalist military organization which during World War I fought for the central powers. He was prime minister 1922–23 and war minister 1923–25. In Sept 1939 he became prime minister of the exiled Polish government, which transferred to London 1940. He was killed in an air crash.

The intransigence of his government was a cause of Anglo-Russian friction, but allegations that his death was not accidental are unsubstantiated.

Sikorsky Igor 1889–1972. Ukrainian engineer, who built the first successful helicopter. He emigrated to the USA 1918 where he first constructed multi-engined flying boats. His first helicopter (the VS300) flew 1939 and a commercial version (the R3) went into production 1943.

Sillitoe Alan 1928– . English novelist, who wrote *Saturday Night and Sunday Morning* 1958, about a working-class man in Nottingham, Sillitoe's home town, *The Loneliness of the Long Distance Runner* 1959, *Life Goes On* 1985, many other novels, and poems, plays, and children's books.

Sills Beverly 1929– . US operatic soprano. She sang with touring companies and joined the New York City Opera in 1955. In 1979 she became director of New York City Opera and retired from the stage in 1980.

Silone Ignazio. Pen name of Secondo Tranquilli, 1900–1978. Italian novelist. His novel *Fontamara* 1933 deals with the hopes and disillusionment of a peasant village from a socialist viewpoint. Other works include *Una manciata di more/A Handful of Blackberries* 1952.

Sim Alistair 1900–1976. Scottish actor, usually in comedies. Possessed of a marvellously expressive face, he was ideally cast in eccentric roles, as in the title role in *Scrooge* 1951. His other films include *Inspector Hornleigh* 1939, *Green* *for Danger* 1945, and *The Belles of St Trinians* 1954.

Simenon Georges 1903–1989. Belgian crime writer. Initially a pulp fiction writer, in 1931 he created Inspector Maigret of the Paris Sûreté who appeared in a series of detective novels.

Simeon Stylites, St *c.*390–459. Syrian Christian ascetic, who practised his ideal of self-denial by living for 37 years on a platform on top of a high pillar. Feast day 5 Jan.

Simmons Jean 1929– . British actress who starred in the films *Black Narcissus* 1947, *Guys and Dolls* 1955, and *Spartacus* 1960. She worked in Hollywood from the 1950s onwards, and retired in the early 1970s.

Simon Claude 1913– . French novelist. Originally an artist, he abandoned the 'time structure' in such novels as *La Route de Flandres/The Flanders Road* 1960, *Le Palace* 1962, and *Histoire* 1967. His later novels include *Les Géorgiques* 1981 and *L'Acacia* 1989. Nobel prize 1985.

Simon Herbert 1916– . US social scientist. He researched decision-making in business corporations, and argued that maximum profit was seldom the chief motive. Nobel Prize for Economics 1978.

Simon John Allsebrook, Viscount Simon 1873–1954. British Liberal politician. He was home secretary 1915–16, but resigned over the issue of conscription. He was foreign secretary 1931–35, home secretary again 1935–37, chancellor of the Exchequer 1937–40, and lord chancellor 1940–45.

Simon (Marvin) Neil 1927– . US playwright. His stage plays (which were made into films) include the wryly comic *Barefoot in the Park* 1963, *The Odd Couple* 1965, and *The Sunshine Boys* 1972, and the more serious, autobiographical *Brighton Beach Memoirs* 1983 and *Biloxi Blues* 1985. He has also written screenplays and co-written musicals.

The musicals include *Sweet Charity* 1966, *Promises, Promises* 1968, and *They're Playing Our Song* 1978.

Simon Paul 1942– . US pop singer and songwriter. In a folk-rock duo with Art Garfunkel (1942–), he had hits such as 'Mrs Robinson' 1968 and 'Bridge Over Troubled Water' 1970. His solo work includes the album *Graceland* 1986, for which he drew on Cajun and African music.

Simone Martini Sienese painter; see ◊Martini, Simone.

Simpson (Cedric) Keith 1907–1985. British forensic scientist, head of department at Guy's Hospital, London, 1962–72. His evidence sent John Haig (the acid bath murderer) and Neville Heath to the gallows. In 1965 he identified the first 'battered baby' murder in England.

Simpson James Young 1811–1870. British physician who was largely instrumental in the introduction of chloroform as an anaesthetic in 1847.

Simpson N(orman) F(rederick) 1919– . British dramatist. His plays *A Resounding Tinkle* 1957, *The Hole* 1958, and *One Way Pendulum* 1959 show the logical development of an abnormal situation, and belong to the Theatre of the Absurd (in which human existence is portrayed as meaningless). He also wrote a novel, *Harry Bleachbaker* 1976.

Simpson Wallis Warfield, Duchess of Windsor 1896–1986. US socialite, twice divorced, who married the Duke of Windsor (formerly ◊Edward VIII) 1937, following his abdication.

Sinan 1489–1588. Ottoman architect, chief architect from 1538 to ◊Suleiman the Magnificent. Among the hundreds of buildings he designed are the Suleimaniye in Istanbul, a mosque complex, and the Topkapi Saray, palace of the Sultan (now a museum).

Sinatra Frank (Francis Albert) 1915– . US singer and film actor. He achieved fame with the Tommy Dorsey band with songs such as 'Night and Day' and 'You'd Be So Nice To Come Home To'. After a slump in his career, he established himself as an actor. *From Here to Eternity* 1953 won him an Academy Award. His later songs include 'My Way'.

Sinclair Clive 1940– . British electronics engineer, who produced the first widely available pocket calculator, pocket and wristwatch televisions, a series of popular home computers, and the innovative but commercially disastrous 'C5' personal transport (a low cycle-like three-wheeled device powered by a washing-machine motor).

Sinclair Upton 1878–1968. US novelist. His concern for social reforms is reflected in *The Jungle* 1906, which exposed the horrors of the Chicago stockyards and led to a change in food-processing laws, *Boston* 1928, and his Lanny Budd series 1940–53, including *Dragon's Teeth* 1942, which won a Pulitzer Prize.

Sinden Donald 1923– . English actor. Noted for his resonant voice and versatility, his roles range from Shakespearean tragedies to light comedies such as *There's a Girl in My Soup, Present Laughter*, and the television series *Two's Company*.

Sinding Christian (August) 1856–1941. Norwegian composer. His works include four symphonies, piano pieces (including *Rustle of Spring*), and songs. His brothers **Otto** (1842–1909) and **Stephan** (1846–1922), were painter and sculptor, respectively.

Singer Isaac Bashevis 1904– . Polish novelist and short story writer. His works, written in Yiddish, often portray traditional Jewish life in Poland, and the loneliness of old age. They include *Gimpel the Fool* 1957, *The Slave* 1960, *Shosha* 1978, and *Old Love* 1979. Nobel Prize 1978.

Singer Isaac Merit 1811–1875. US inventor of domestic and industrial sewing machines. Within a few years of opening his first factory 1851, he became the world's largest manufacturer, and by the late 1860s more than 100,000 Singer sewing machines were in use in the USA alone. To make his machines available to the widest market, Singer became the first manufacturer to offer attractive hire-purchase terms.

Singh Vishwanath Pratap 1931– . Indian politician, prime minister from 1989. As a member of the Congress (I) Party, he held ministerial posts under Indira Gandhi and Rajiv Gandhi, and from 1984 led an anti-corruption drive. When he unearthed an arms-sales scandal in 1988, he was ousted from the government and party and formed a broad-based opposition alliance, the *Janata Dal*, which won the 1989 elections.

Singh was born in Allahabad, the son of a local raja. He was minister of commerce 1976–77 and 1983, Uttar Pradesh chief minister 1980–82, minister of finance 1984–86, and of defence 1986–87, when he discovered the embarrassing Bofors scandal. Respected for his probity and sense of principle, Singh emerged as one of the most popular politicians in India.

Singh, Gobind see ◊Gobind Singh, Sikh guru.

Sirk Douglas. Assumed name of Claus Detlef Sierck 1900–1987. Danish film director, who studied in Germany but left 1937 because of the Nazi regime, and eventually went to Hollywood. During the 1950s he made a series of lurid melodramas about capitalist USA which have subsequently been highly praised by critics; they include *All that Heaven Allows* 1956 and *Written on the Wind* 1957.

Sisley Alfred 1839–1899. French Impressionist painter, known for his views of Port-Marly and the Seine, which he painted during floods in 1876.

Sisley studied in an academic studio in Paris, where he met Monet and Renoir. They took part in the First Impressionist Exhibition 1874. Unlike that of most other Impressionists, Sisley's style developed slowly and surely, without obviously changeful periods. He was almost exclusively a landscape painter.

Sisulu Walter 1912– . South African civil-rights activist. The first full-time Secretary General of the ANC (African National Congress), in 1964, with Nelson Mandela. He was imprisoned following the 1964 Rivonia Trial for opposition to the apartheid system and released, at the age of 77, as a gesture of reform by President F W ◊De Klerk 1989.

Sitting Bull c.1834–1893. North American Indian chief who led the Sioux onslaught against Gen ◊Custer.

Sitwell Edith 1887–1964. English poet, whose series of poems *Façade* was performed as recitations to the specially written music of William

Sitting Bull Sioux Indian chief Sitting Bull, who fought a rearguard action against white incursions into Indian lands. He defeated General Custer at the Battle of Little Big Horn.

◊Walton from 1923.

Sitwell Osbert 1892–1969. English poet and author, elder brother of Edith and Sacheverell Sitwell.

Sitwell Sacheverell 1897–1988. English poet and art critic. His work includes *Southern Baroque Art* 1924 and *British Architects and Craftsmen* 1945; poetry; and prose miscellanies such as *Of Sacred and Profane Love* 1940 and *Splendour and Miseries* 1943.

Sixtus five popes, including:

Sixtus IV 1414–1484. Pope from 1471. He built the Sistine Chapel in the Vatican, which is named after him.

Sixtus V 1521–1590. Pope from 1585, who supported the Spanish Armada against Britain and the Catholic League against Henry IV of France.

Skelton John c.1460–1529. English poet, who was tutor to the future Henry VIII. His satirical poetry includes the rumbustious *The Tunnyng of Elynor Rummynge* 1516, and political attacks on Wolsey, such as *Colyn Cloute* 1522.

Skinner B(urrhus) F(rederic) 1903– . US psychologist, a radical behaviourist who rejects mental concepts, seeing the organism as a 'black box' where internal processes are not important in predicting behaviour. He stressed that behaviour is shaped and maintained by its consequences.

His radical approach rejected almost all previous psychology; his text *Science and Human Behaviour* 1953 contains no references and no bibliography.

Skolimowski Jerzy 1938– . Polish film director, formerly a writer, active in both his native country and Western Europe. His films include *Deep End* 1970, *The Shout* 1978, and *Moonlighting* 1982.

Skryabin Alexander (Nikolayevich) 1872–1915. Russian composer and pianist. His powerfully emotional tone poems, such as *Prometheus* 1911, and symphonies, such as *Divine Poem* 1903, employed unusual harmonies.

Slade Felix 1790–1868. British art collector, born in London. He bequeathed most of his art collection to the British Museum and endowed Slade professorships in fine art at Oxford, Cambridge, and University College, London. The *Slade School of Fine Arts* is a branch of the latter.

Sleep Wayne 1948– . British dancer who was principal dancer with the Royal Ballet 1973–83 and formed his own company, Dash, in 1980.

Slim William Joseph, 1st Viscount Slim 1891–1970. British field marshal in World War II. A veteran of Gallipoli, Turkey, in World War I, he commanded the 14th 'forgotten' army 1943–45, stemming the Japanese invasion of India at Imphal and Kohima, and then recovered Burma (now Myanmar).

Sloane Hans 1660–1753. British physician, born in County Down, Ireland. He settled in London, and in 1721 founded the Chelsea Physic Garden. He was president of the Royal College of Physicians 1719–35, and in 1727 succeeded Isaac Newton as president of the Royal Society. His library, which he bequeathed to the nation, formed the nucleus of the British Museum.

Sluter Claus *c.*1380–1406. N European sculptor, probably of Dutch origin, active in Dijon, France. His work, in an expressive Gothic style, includes the *Well of Moses c.*1395–1403 (now in the grounds of a hospital in Dijon); and the kneeling mourners, or *gisants*, for the tomb of his patron Philip the Bold, Duke of Burgundy (Dijon Museum and Cleveland Museum, Ohio).

Smart Christopher 1722–1771. English poet. In 1756 he was confined to an asylum, where he wrote his poems, *A Song to David* and *Jubilate Agno/Rejoice in the Lamb*, the latter appreciated today for its surrealism.

Smetana Bedřich 1824–1884. Czech composer, whose music has a distinct national character, for example, the operas *The Bartered Bride* 1866, *Dalibor* 1868, and the symphonic suite *My Country* 1875–80.

Smiles Samuel 1812–1904. Scottish writer, author of the popular Victorian didactic work *Self Help* 1859.

Smirke Robert 1780–1867. English Classical architect, designer of the British Museum, London (1823–47).

Smith Adam 1723–1790. Scottish economist, often regarded as the founder of modern political economy. His *The Wealth of Nations* 1776 defined national wealth in terms of labour. The cause of wealth is explained by the *division of labour* – dividing a production process into several repetitive operations, each carried out by different workers. Smith advocated the free working of individual enterprise, and the necessity of 'free trade'.

He was born in Kirkcaldy, and was professor of moral philosophy at Glasgow 1752–63. He published *Theory of Moral Sentiments* 1759.

Smith Bessie 1894–1937. US jazz and blues singer, born in Chattanooga, Tennessee. She established herself in the 1920s, but her popularity waned in the Depression, and she died after a car crash when she was refused admission to a whites-only hospital. She was known as the Empress of the Blues.

Smith David 1906–1965. US sculptor and painter, whose work made a lasting impact on sculpture after World War II. He trained as a steel welder in a car factory. His pieces are large openwork metal abstracts.

Smith turned first to painting and then, about 1930, to sculpture. Using welded steel, he created abstract structures influenced by the metal sculptures of Picasso. In the 1940s and 1950s he developed a more linear style. The *Cubi* series of totemlike abstracts, some of them painted, were designed to be placed in the open air.

Smith Henry George Wakelyn 1787–1860. British general. He served in the Peninsular War. Subsequently he fought in South Africa and India, and was governor of Cape Colony 1847–52. The towns of Ladysmith and Harrismith, South Africa, are named after his wife and himself respectively.

Smith Ian Douglas 1919– . Rhodesian politician. He was a founder of the Rhodesian Front 1962 and prime minister 1964–1979. In 1965 he made a unilateral declaration of Rhodesia's independence, and despite United Nations sanctions maintained his regime with tenacity. In 1979 he was succeeded as prime minister by Bishop Abel Muzorewa, when the country was renamed Zimbabwe. He was suspended from the Zimbabwe parliament in Apr 1987 and resigned in May as head of the white opposition party.

Smith John 1580–1631. English colonist. After an adventurous early life he took part in the colonization of Virginia, acting as president of the North American colony 1608–09. He explored New England in 1614, which he named, and published pamphlets on America and an autobiography. During an expedition among the American Indians his life is said to have been saved by ◊Pocahontas, whom he married.

Smith John Maynard 1920– . British biologist, whose work in evolutionary theory resulted in the theory of the *evolutionarily stable strategy* (ESS), which explains animal aggression as part of a ritual and suggests that evolution prevents animals from attacking each other.

Smith studied no science at his public school and did aeronautical engineering at university. He began studying biology when he was 30, under J B S Haldane at University College, London.

Smith Joseph 1805–1844. US founder of the Mormon religious sect.

Smith, born in Vermont, received his first religious call in 1820, and in 1827 claimed to have been granted the revelation of the *Book of Mormon* (an ancient prophet), inscribed on gold plates and concealed a thousand years before in a hill near Palmyra, New York State. He founded the Church of Jesus Christ of Latter-day Saints in Fayette, New York, 1830. The Mormons were persecuted for their beliefs and Smith was killed in Illinois.

Smith Maggie (Margaret Natalie) 1934– . English actress. Her roles include the title part (winning an Oscar) in the film *The Prime of Miss Jean Brodie* 1969. Other films include *California Suite* 1978, *A Private Function* 1984, and *A Room with a View* 1986.

Smith Matthew 1879–1960. British artist, known for his exuberant treatment of nudes, luscious fruits and flowers, and landscapes.

Smith Ross Macpherson 1892–1922 and Keith Macpherson 1890–1955. Australian aviators and brothers, who made the first England–Australia flight 1919.

Smith 'Stevie' (Florence Margaret) 1902–1971. British poet, noted for eccentrically direct verse, whose books include *Novel on Yellow Paper* 1936, and the poems *A Good Time was had by All* 1937, and *Not Waving but Drowning* 1957.

Smith William 1769–1839. British geologist, the founder of English geology. Working as a canal engineer, he noticed while supervising excavations that different beds of rock could be identified by their fossils, and so established the basis of stratigraphy. He also produced the first geological maps of England and Wales.

Smithson James 1765–1829. British chemist and mineralogist. The *Smithsonian Institute* in Washington DC, USA, was established in 1846, following his bequest of $100,000 for this purpose, and includes a museum, art gallery, zoo park, and astrophysical observatory.

Smollett Tobias George 1721–1771. Scottish novelist, who wrote the picaresque novels *Roderick Random* 1748, *Peregrine Pickle* 1751, *Ferdinand Count Fathom* 1753, *Sir Lancelot Greaves* 1760–62, and *Humphrey Clinker* 1771.

Smuts Jan Christian 1870–1950. South African politician, field marshal, and lawyer; prime minister 1919–24 and 1939–48. He supported the Allies in both world wars and was a member of the British imperial war cabinet 1917–18.

During the Second South African War of 1899–1902 Smuts commanded the Boer forces in his native Cape Colony. He subsequently worked for reconciliation between the Boers and the British and on the establishment of the Union became minister of the interior 1910–12 and defence minister 1910–20. During World War I he commanded the South African forces in East Africa 1916–17. He was prime minister 1919–24, and minister of justice 1933–39, and on the outbreak of World War II succeeded Gen Hertzog as premier. Although more of an internationalist than his contemporaries, Smuts was a segregationalist, voting in favour of legislation that took away black rights and land ownership.

Smyth Ethel (Mary) 1858–1944. English composer who studied in Leipzig. Her works include the *Mass in D* 1893 and operas *The Wreckers* 1906 and *The Boatswain's Mate* 1916. In 1911 she was imprisoned as an advocate of women's suffrage.

Smythson Robert 1535–1614. English architect, freemason of the Elizabethan country houses, including Longleat (1568–75), Wollaton Hall (1580–88), and Hardwick Hall (1590–97). Their castle-like silhouettes, symmetry, and large gridded windows are a uniquely romantic, English version of Classicism.

Snell Willebrord 1581–1626. Dutch mathematician and physicist who devised the basic law of refraction, known as *Snell's law* in 1621. This states that the ratio between the sine of the angle of incidence and the sine of the angle of refraction is constant. Snell's law was published by ◊Descartes in 1637.

Snow C(harles) P(ercy), Baron Snow 1905–1980. English novelist and physicist. He held government scientific posts in World War II and 1964–66. His sequence of novels *Strangers and Brothers* 1940–64 portrayed English life from 1920 onwards. His *Two Cultures* (Cambridge Rede lecture 1959) discussed the absence of communication between literary and scientific intellectuals in the West, and added the phrase 'the two cultures' to the language.

Snowden Philip, 1st Viscount Snowden 1864–1937. British right-wing Labour politician, chancellor of the Exchequer 1924 and 1929–31. He entered the coalition National Government in 1931 as Lord Privy Seal, but resigned in 1932.

Snowdon Anthony Armstrong-Jones, Earl of Snowdon 1930– . English portrait photographer, who married Princess Margaret in 1960; they were divorced in 1978.

Snyders Frans 1579–1657. Flemish painter of hunting scenes and still lifes. Based in Antwerp, he was a pupil of ◊Brueghel the Younger and later assisted ◊Rubens and worked with ◊Jordaens. In 1608–09 he travelled in Italy. He excelled at painting fur, feathers, and animals fighting.

Soames Christopher, Baron Soames 1920–1987. British Conservative politician. He held ministerial posts 1958–64, was vice president of the Commission of the European Communities 1973–77 and governor of (Southern) Rhodesia in the period of its transition to independence as Zimbabwe, Dec 1979–Apr 1980.

Soane John 1753–1837. English architect, whose individual Neo-Classical designs anticipated modern taste. His buildings include his own house in Lincoln's Inn Fields, London, now the *Soane Museum*. Little remains of his extensive work at the Bank of England, London.

Soares Mario 1924– . Portuguese politician. Exiled in 1970, he returned to Portugal in 1974, and as leader of the Portuguese Socialist Party (PSP) was prime minister 1976–78. He resigned as party leader in 1980, but in 1986 he was elected Portugal's first socialist president.

Sobers (Garfield St Aubrun) 'Gary' 1936– . West Indian test cricketer. One of the game's great all-rounders, he scored more than 8,000 test runs, took over 200 wickets, held more than 100 catches, and holds the record for the highest test innings, 365 not out.

Sobers started playing first-class cricket in 1952. He played English county cricket with Nottinghamshire and while playing for them against Glamorgan at Swansea in 1968 he established a world record by scoring six sixes in one over.

Sobieski John alternative name for ◊John III, king of Poland.

Socrates *c.*469–399 BC. Athenian philosopher. He wrote nothing but was immortalized in the dialogues of his pupil, Plato. In his desire to combat the scepticism of the sophists, Socrates asserted the possibility of genuine knowledge. In ethics, he put forward the view that the good person never knowingly does wrong. True knowledge emerges through dialogue and systematic questioning, and an abandoning of uncritical claims to knowledge.

The effect of Socrates' teaching was disruptive since he opposed tyranny. Accused in 399 on charges of impiety and corruption of youth, he was condemned by the Athenian authorities to die by drinking hemlock.

Soddy Frederick 1877–1956. English physical chemist. He pioneered research into the radioactive decay of atoms and coined the term 'isotope' (isotopes are atoms of the same element but of different masses). Nobel Prize for Chemistry 1921.

His works include *Chemistry of the Radio-Elements* 1912–14, and *The Story of Atomic Energy* 1949. After his chemical discoveries, Soddy spent some 40 years developing a theory

of 'energy economics', believing that as a scientist he was able to see through the errors of economists.

Söderberg Hjalmar (Eric Fredrik) 1869–1941. Swedish writer. His work includes the novels *Förvillelser* 1895, *Martin Bircks ungdom* 1901, *Doktor Glass/Dr Glass* 1906, and the play *Gertrud* 1906.

Solomon *c.*974–937 BC. In the Old Testament or Hebrew Bible, king of Israel, son of David by Bathsheba. He was famed for his wisdom, the much later biblical Proverbs, Ecclesiastes, and Song of Songs being attributed to him. He built the temple in Jerusalem with the aid of heavy taxation and forced labour. The so-called *King Solomon's Mines* (copper and iron) at Aqaba, Jordan, are of later date.

Solon *c.*638–558 BC. Athenian statesman. As one of the chief magistrates about 594 BC, he carried out the revision of the constitution that laid the foundations of Athenian democracy.

Soloviev Vladimir Sergeyevich 1853–1900. Russian philosopher and poet, whose blending of Neo-Platonism and Christian mysticism attempted to link all aspects of human experience in a doctrine of divine wisdom. His theories, expressed in poems and essays, influenced Symbolist writers such as ◊Blok.

Solti Georg 1912– . Hungarian-born British conductor. He was music director at Covent Garden 1961–71, and became director of the Chicago Symphony Orchestra 1969. He was also principal conductor of the London Philharmonic Orchestra 1979–83.

Solyman I alternative form of ◊Suleiman, Ottoman sultan.

Solzhenitsyn Alexander (Isayevich) 1918– . Soviet novelist, a US citizen from 1974. After military service, he was in prison and exile 1945–57 for anti-Stalinist comments. Much of his writing is semi-autobiographical and highly critical of the system; for example, *One Day in the Life of Ivan Denisovich* 1962 deals with the labour camps under Stalin, and *The Gulag Archipelago* 1973 is an exposé of the whole Soviet camp network. This led to his expulsion from the USSR 1974.

He was awarded a Nobel prize in 1970. Other works include *The First Circle* and *Cancer Ward* both 1968. His autobiography, *The Oak and the Calf*, appeared 1980. He has adopted a Christian position, and his criticism of Western materialism is also stringent.

Somerset family name of the dukes of Beaufort; seated at Badminton, Gloucestershire; descended in an illegitimate line from King Edward III.

Somerset Edward Seymour, 1st Duke of Somerset *c.* 1506–1552. English politician. Created Earl of Hertford, after Henry VIII's marriage to his sister Jane, he became Duke of Somerset and Protector (regent) for Edward VI in 1547. His attempt to

Somerville Scottish scientific writer Mary Somerville, portrayed by James Swinton. Somerville College, Oxford, one of the first women's colleges, is named after her.

check enclosure (the transfer of land from common to private ownership) offended landowners and his moderation in religion upset the Protestants, and he was beheaded on a fake treason charge in 1552.

Somerville Edith Oenone 1861–1949. Irish novelist, best known for her stories of Irish life written jointly with her cousin, Violet Martin ('Martin Ross'). Their works include *Some Experiences of an Irish RM* 1890.

Somerville Mary (born Fairfax) 1780–1872. Scottish scientific writer, who produced several widely used textbooks, despite having just one year of formal education. Somerville College, Oxford, is named after her. Her main works were *Mechanism of the Heavens* 1831 (a translation of ◊Laplace's treatise on celestial mechanics), *On the Connexion of Physical Sciences* 1834, *Physical Geography* 1848 and *On Molecular and Microscopic Science* 1869.

Sommeiler Germain 1815–1871. French engineer who built the Mont Cenis Tunnel, 12 km/7 mi long, between Switzerland and France. The tunnel was drilled with his invention the pneumatic drill.

Sommerfeld Arnold 1868–1951. German physicist, who showed that the difficulties with the Niels Bohr's model of the atom, in which electrons move around a central nucleus in circular orbits, could be overcome by supposing that electrons adopted elliptical orbits.

Somoza Debayle Anastasio 1925–1980. Nicaraguan soldier and politician, president 1967–72 and 1974–79. The second son of Anastasio

Somoza García, he succeeded his brother Luis Somoza Debayle (1922–1967; president 1956–63) as president of Nicaragua in 1967, to head an even more oppressive regime. He was removed by Sandinista guerrillas in 1979, and assassinated in Paraguay 1980.

Somoza García Anastasio 1896–1956. Nicaraguan soldier and politician, president 1937–47 and 1950–56. A protegé of the USA, who wanted a reliable ally to protect their interests in Central America, he was virtual dictator of Nicaragua from 1937 until his assassination in 1956. He exiled most of his political opponents and amassed a considerable fortune in land and businesses. Members of his family retained control of the country until 1979, when they were overthrown by popular forces.

Sondheim Stephen (Joshua) 1930– . US composer and lyricist. He wrote the witty and sophisticated lyrics of Leonard Bernstein's *West Side Story* 1957 and composed musicals, including *A Little Night Music* 1973, *Pacific Overtures* 1976, *Sweeney Todd* 1979, and *Sunday in the Park with George* 1989.

Sontag Susan 1933– . US critic, novelist, and screenwriter. Her novel *The Benefactor* appeared in 1963, and she established herself as a critic with the influential cultural essays of *Against Interpretation* 1966 and *Styles of Radical Will* 1969. More recent studies, showing the influence of French structuralism, are *On Photography* 1976 and the powerful *Illness as Metaphor* 1978.

Soong Ching-ling 1892–1981. Chinese politician, wife of the Guomindang founder ◊Sun Yat-sen; she remained a prominent figure in Chinese politics after his death, being vice chair of the republic from 1959, but came under attack 1967 during the Cultural Revolution. After the death of Zhu De (1886–1976), she served as acting head of state.

Sophia Electress of Hanover 1630–1714. Twelfth child of Frederick V, elector palatine of the Rhine and king of Bohemia, and Elizabeth, daughter of James I of England. She married the Elector of Hanover 1658. Widowed in 1698, she was recognized in the succession to the English throne 1701, and when Queen Anne died without issue in 1714, her son George I founded the Hanoverian dynasty.

Sophocles 495–406 BC. Greek dramatist who, with Aeschylus and Euripides, is one of the three great tragedians. He modified the form of tragedy by introducing a third actor and developing stage scenery. He wrote some 120 plays, of which seven tragedies survive. These are *Antigone* 441, *Oedipus Tyrannus*, *Electra*, *Ajax*, *Trachiniae*, *Philoctetes* 409, and *Oedipus at Colonus* 401.

Sophocles lived in Athens at the time of ◊Pericles, a period of great prosperity. He was a popular man and a friend of ◊Herodotus. In his tragedies human will plays a greater part than that of the gods, as in the plays of Aeschylus, and his characters are generally heroic. A large fragment of a satyric play (a tragedy treated in a grotesquely comic fashion) *Ichneutae* also survives.

Sopwith Thomas Octave Murdoch 1888–1989. English designer of the Sopwith Camel biplane, used in World War I, and joint developer of the Hawker Hurricane fighter plane used in World War II.

From a Northumbrian engineering family, Sopwith gained a pilot's licence in 1910 and soon after set a British aerial duration record for a flight of three hours 12 minutes. In 1912 he founded the Sopwith Aviation Company, which in 1920 he wound up and reopened as the Hawker Company, after the chief test pilot Harry Hawker. The Hawker Company was responsible for the Hawker Hart bomber, the Hurricane, and eventually the vertical take-off Harrier jump jet.

Sorel Georges 1847–1922. French philosopher, who believed that socialism could only come about through a general strike; his theory of the need for a 'myth' to sway the body of the people was used by fascists.

Sørensen Søren 1868–1939. Danish chemist, who in 1909 introduced the concept of using the pH scale as a measure of the acidity of a solution. On Sørensen's scale, still used today, a pH of 7 is neutral; higher numbers represent alkalinity, and lower numbers acidity.

Soult Nicolas Jean de Dieu 1769–1851. Marshal of France. He held commands in Spain in the Peninsular War, when he sacked the port of Santander 1808, and was Chief of Staff at the Battle of Waterloo. He was war minister 1830–40.

Souphanouvong Prince 1912– . Laotian politician, president 1975–86. After an abortive revolt against French rule 1945, he led the guerrilla organization Pathet Lao, and in 1975 became first president of the Republic of Laos. He resigned after suffering a stroke.

Sousa John Philip 1854–1932. US bandmaster and composer of marches, such as 'The Stars and Stripes Forever!' 1897.

Southampton Henry Wriothesley, 3rd Earl of Southampton 1573–1624. English courtier and patron of Shakespeare, who dedicated *Venus and Adonis* and *The Rape of Lucrece* to him, and may have addressed him in his sonnets.

Southerne Thomas 1660–1746. English playwright and poet, author of the tragi-comedies *Oroonoko* 1695–96, and *The Fatal Marriage* 1694.

Southey Robert 1774–1843. English poet and author, friend of Coleridge and Wordsworth. In 1813 he became Poet Laureate, but his verse is little read today. He is better known for his *Life of Nelson* 1813, and his letters.

He abandoned his early revolutionary views, and from 1808 contributed regularly to the Tory *Quarterly Review*.

Soutine Chaim 1894–1943. Lithuanian-born French Expressionist artist. He painted landscapes and portraits, including many of painters active in Paris in the 1920s and 1930s. He had a distorted style, using thick application of paint (impasto) and brilliant colours.

Soyer Alexis Benoît 1809–1858. French chef who worked in England. Soyer was chef at the Reform Club, London, and visited the Crimea to advise on nutrition for the British army. He was a prolific author of books of everyday recipes, such as *Shilling Cookery for the People* 1855.

Soyinka Wole 1934– . Nigerian author, who was a political prisoner in Nigeria 1967–69. His works include the play *The Lion and the Jewel* 1963, his prison memoirs *The Man Died* 1972, and *Aké, The Years of Childhood* 1982, an autobiography. He was the first African to receive the Nobel Prize for Literature, in 1986.

Spaak Paul-Henri 1899–1972. Belgian socialist politician. From 1936 to 1966 he held office almost continuously as foreign minister or prime minister. He was an ardent advocate of international peace.

Spacek 'Sissy' (Mary Elizabeth) 1949– . US film actress who starred in *Badlands* 1973 and *Carrie* 1976, in which she played a repressed telekinetic teenager. Her other films include *Coal Miner's Daughter* 1979 and *Missing* 1982.

Spallanzani Lazzaro 1729–1799. Italian priest and biologist. He disproved the theory that microbes spontaneously generate out of rotten food, by showing that they would not grow in flasks of broth that had been boiled for 30 minutes and then sealed.

Spark Muriel 1918– . Scottish novelist. She is a Catholic convert, and her works have an enigmatic satire: *The Ballad of Peckham Rye* 1960, *The Prime of Miss Jean Brodie* 1961, and *The Only Problem* 1984.

Spartacus died 71 BC. Thracian gladiator who in 73 BC led a revolt of gladiators and slaves at Capua. He was eventually caught by ◊Crassus and crucified.

Spear Ruskin 1911–1990. British artist, whose portraits include Laurence Olivier (as Macbeth), Francis Bacon, and satirical representations of Margaret Thatcher.

Spector Phil 1940– . US record producer, known for the *Wall of Sound*, created using a large orchestra, distinguishing his work in the early 1960s with vocal groups such as the Crystals and the Ronettes.

Spee Maximilian, Count von Spee 1861–1914. German admiral, born in Copenhagen. He went down with his flagship in the 1914 battle of the Falkland Islands, and the *Graf Spee* battleship was named after him.

Speke John Hanning 1827–1864. British explorer. He joined ◊Burton in an African expedition in which they reached Lake Tanganyika 1858 and

Speke went on to be the first European to see Lake Victoria 1858.

His claim that it was the source of the Nile was disputed by Burton, even after Speke and Grant made a second confirming expedition 1860–63. Speke accidentally shot himself, in England, the day before he was due to debate the matter publicly with Burton.

Spence Basil 1907–1976. British architect. He was professor of architecture at the Royal Academy, London, 1961–68, and his works include Coventry Cathedral, Sussex University, and the British embassy in Rome.

Spencer Herbert 1820–1903. British philosopher. He wrote *Social Statics* 1851, expounding his *laissez-faire* views on social and political problems, *Principles of Psychology* 1855, and *Education* 1861. In 1862 he began his ten-volume *System of Synthetic Philosophy*, in which he extended Charles ◊Darwin's theory of evolution to the entire field of human knowledge. The chief of the ten volumes are *First Principles* 1862 and *Principles* of biology, psychology, sociology, and ethics. Other works are *The Study of Sociology, Man v. the State, Essays,* and an autobiography.

Spencer Stanley 1891–1959. British painter. He was born and lived in Cookham-on-Thames, Berkshire, and recreated the Christian story in a Cookham setting. His detailed, dreamlike compositions had little regard for perspective and used generalized human figures.

Examples are *Christ Carrying the Cross* 1920 and *Resurrection* 1924–26 (both Tate Gallery, London) and murals of army life for the oratory of All Souls' at Burghclere in Berkshire.

Spencer-Churchill family name of dukes of Marlborough; whose seat is Blenheim Palace, Oxofordshire, England.

Spender Stephen (Harold) 1909– . English poet and critic. His earlier poetry has a left-wing political content, as in *Twenty Poems* 1930, *Vienna* 1934, *The Still Centre* 1939, and *Poems of Dedication* 1946. Other works include the verse drama *Trial of a Judge* 1938, the autobiography *World within World* 1951, and translations. His *Journals 1939–83* were published 1985.

Educated at University College, Oxford, he founded with Cyril Connolly the magazine *Horizon* (of which he was co-editor 1939–41) and 1953–67 was co-editor of *Encounter.* He became professor of English at University College, London in 1970.

Spengler Oswald 1880–1936. German philosopher, whose *Decline of the West* 1918 argued that civilizations go through natural cycles of growth and decay. He was admired by the Nazis.

Spenser Edmund *c.*1552–1599. English poet, who has been called the 'poet's poet' because of his rich imagery and command of versification. He is known for his moral allegory *The Faerie Queene* to Elizabeth I, of which six books survive

(three published 1590 and three 1596). Other books include *The Shepheard's Calendar* 1579, *Astrophel* 1586, the love sonnets *Amoretti* and the *Epithalamion* 1595.

Born in London and educated at Cambridge, in 1580 he became secretary to the Lord Deputy in Ireland, and at Kilcolman Castle completed the first three books of *The Faerie Queene* (Elizabeth I being the 'Faerie Queene'). In 1598 Kilcolman Castle was burned down by rebels, and Spenser with his family narrowly escaped. He died in London, and was buried in Westminster Abbey.

Sperry Elmer Ambrose 1860–1930. US engineer who developed various devices using gyroscopes, such as gyrostabilizers (for ships and torpedoes) and gyro-controlled autopilots.

By the mid-1930s Sperry autopilots were standard equipment on most large ships.

Spielberg Steven 1947– . US director, whose successful films include *Jaws* 1975, *Close Encounters of the Third Kind* 1977, *Raiders of the Lost Ark* 1981, and *ET* 1982.

Spillane Mickey (Frank Morrison) 1918– . US crime novelist. He began by writing for pulp magazines and became known for violent crime novels featuring his 'one-man police force' hero Mike Hammer; for example, *Vengeance is Mine* 1950 and *The Long Wait* 1951.

Spinoza Benedict or Baruch 1632–1677. Dutch philosopher who believed in a rationalistic pantheism that owed much to Descartes' mathematical appreciation of the universe. Mind and matter are two modes of an infinite substance which he called God

Spinoza *The Dutch philosopher Benedict Spinoza is known for his philosophy of rational pantheism.*

or Nature, good and evil being relative. He was a determinist, believing that human action was motivated by self-preservation.

Ethics 1677 is his main work. *A Treatise on Religious and Political Philosophy* 1670 was the only one of his works published during his life, and was attacked by Christians. He was excommunicated by the Jewish community in Amsterdam on charges of heretical thought and practice 1656. He was a lens-grinder by trade.

Spitz Mark Andrew 1950– . US swimmer. He won a record seven gold medals at the 1972 Olympic Games, all in world record times.

He won 11 Olympic medals in total (four in 1968) and set 26 world records 1967–72. After retiring in 1972 he became a movie actor and two of his films were candidates for 'The Worst of Hollywood' .

Spock Benjamin McLane 1903– . US paediatrician and writer on child care. His *Common Sense Book of Baby and Child Care* 1946 urged less rigidity in bringing up children than had been advised by previous generations of writers on the subject, but was misunderstood as advocating complete permissiveness.

In his later work he stressed that his common-sense approach had not implied rejecting all discipline, but that his main aim was to give parents the confidence to trust their own judgement. He has been an active peace campaigner.

Spode Josiah 1754–1827. English potter, son of Josiah Spode the elder (an apprentice of Thomas Whieldon who started his own works at Stoke-on-Trent 1770), and his successor in the new firm in 1797. He developed bone porcelain (bone ash, china stone, and china clay) around 1800, which was produced at all English factories in the 19th century, and became potter to King George III in 1806.

Spring Richard 1950– . Irish Labour Party leader from 1982, who entered into coalition with ◊FitzGerald's Fine Gael 1982 as deputy prime minister (and minister for energy from 1983).

Springsteen Bruce 1949– . US rock singer, songwriter, and guitarist, born in New Jersey. His music combines melodies in traditional rock idiom and reflective lyrics of working-class life on albums such as *Born to Run* 1975 and *Born in the USA* 1984 and in concerts with the East Street Band.

Staël Anne Louise Germaine Necker, Madame de Staël 1766–1817. French author, daughter of the financier ◊Necker. She wrote semi-autobiographical novels such as *Delphine* 1802 and *Corinne* 1807, and the critical work *De l'Allemagne* 1810, on German literature.

Stahl George 1660–1734. German chemist who produced a fallacious theory of combustion. He was professor of medicine at Halle, and as physician to the king of Prussia. He argued that objects burn because they contain a combustible substance, phlogiston. Chemists spent

much of the 18th century evaluating Stahl's theories before they were finally proved false by ◊Lavoisier.

Stainer John 1840–1901. English organist and composer who became organist of St Paul's in 1872. His religious choral works are *The Crucifixion* 1887, an oratorio, and *The Daughter of Jairus* 1878, a cantata.

Stakhanov Aleksei 1906–1977. Soviet miner who exceeded production norms, and who gave his name to the **Stakhanovite** movement of the 1930s, when workers were encouraged to simplify and reorganize work processes in order to increase production.

Stalin Joseph. Adopted name (Russian 'steel') of Joseph Vissarionovich Djugashvili 1879–1953. Soviet politician. A member of the October Revolution Committee 1917, Stalin became General Secretary of the Communist party 1922. After ◊Lenin's death 1924, Stalin sought to create 'socialism in one country' and clashed with ◊Trotsky, who denied the possibility of socialism inside Russia until revolution had occurred in W Europe. Stalin won this ideological struggle by 1927, and a series of five-year plans was launched to collectivize industry and agriculture from 1928. All opposition was eliminated by the Great Purge 1936–38 by which Stalin disposed of all real and fancied enemies. During World War II, Stalin intervened in the military direction of the campaigns against Nazi Germany. His role was denounced

***Stalin** Soviet leader Stalin taking the salute during a march past of workers in Red Square, Moscow, in May 1932.*

after his death by Khrushchev and other members of the Soviet regime.

Born in Georgia, the son of a shoemaker, he was educated for the priesthood, but was expelled from his seminary for Marxist propaganda. He became a member of the Social Democratic Party 1898, and joined Lenin and the Bolsheviks 1903. He was repeatedly exiled to Siberia 1903–13. He then became a member of the Communist Party's ruling Politburo, and sat on the October Revolution committee. Stalin rapidly consolidated a powerful following (including Molotov); in 1921 he became commissar for nationalities in the Soviet government, responsible for the decree granting equal rights to all peoples of the Russian Empire, and was appointed general secretary of the Communist party 1922. He met Churchill and Roosevelt at Tehran 1943 and at Yalta 1945, and took part in the Potsdam conference. After the war, Stalin maintained an autocratic rule.

Stallone Sylvester 1946– . US film actor. He played bit parts and occasional leads in exploitation films before starring in *Rocky* 1976, which he also wrote. His later films have mostly been based around violence, and include *F.I.S.T.* 1978, *First Blood* 1982, and *Rambo* 1985.

Stanford Charles Villiers 1852–1924. British composer and teacher, born in Ireland. A leading figure in the 19th-century renaissance of British music, his many works include operas such as *Shamus O'Brien* 1896, seven symphonies, chamber music, and church music. Among his pupils were Vaughan Williams, Holst, and Bridge.

Stanhope Hester Lucy 1776–1839. English traveller who left England in 1810 to tour the Levant with Bedouins and eventually settled there. She adopted local dress and became involved in Eastern politics.

Stanislavsky Konstantin Sergeivich 1863–1938. Russian actor, director, and teacher. He founded the Moscow Art Theatre 1898 and directed productions of Chekhov and Gorky. He was the originator of Method acting, described in *My Life in Art* 1924 and other works, in which actors seek to identify psychologically with their characters. The Method had considerable influence on acting techniques in Europe and the USA (resulting in the founding of the Actors Studio).

Stanley family name of earls of ◊Derby.

Stanley Henry Morton 1841–1904. Welsh-born US explorer and journalist who made four expeditions in Africa. He and ◊Livingstone met at Ujiji 1871 and explored Lake Tanganyika. He traced the course of the river Zaïre (Congo) to the sea 1874–77, established the Congo Free State (Zaïre) 1879–84, and charted much of the interior 1887–89.

Stanley fought in the Confederate army in the US Civil War. He worked for the *New York Herald* from 1867, and in 1871 he was sent by the editor James Gordon Bennett to find Livingstone, which he did on 10 Nov.

Stanley Wendell 1904–1971. US biochemist. Working at the Rockefeller Institute, Princeton, Stanley succeeded, in 1935, in crystallizing a virus: the tobacco mosaic virus (TMV). He went on to demonstrate that, despite its crystalline state, TMV remained infectious. Along with John Northrop and James Sumner, Stanley received the 1946 Nobel Prize for Chemistry.

Stanton Elizabeth Cady 1815–1902. US feminist, who with Susan B ◊Anthony, founded the National Woman Suffrage Association 1869, the first women's movement in the USA. She and Anthony wrote and compiled the *History of Women's Suffrage* 1881–86. Stanton also worked for the abolition of slavery.

She organized the International Council of Women in Washington DC. She was the first president of the National Woman Suffrage Association. Her publications include *Degradation of Disenfranchisement* and *Solitude of Self* 1892, and in 1885 and 1898 she published (in two parts) a feminist critique of the Bible: *The Woman's Bible*.

Stanwyck Barbara. Stage name of Ruby Stevens 1907–1990. US film actress. Often cast as an independently minded woman of the world, she also excelled in villainous roles, as in *Double Indemnity* 1944. Her other films include *Stella Dallas* 1937, *Ball of Fire* 1942, and *Executive Suite* 1954.

Stark Freya 1893– . English traveller, mountaineer, and writer. She described her explorations in the Middle East in many books, including *The Valley of the Assassins* 1934, *The Southern Gates of Arabia* 1936, and *A Winter in Arabia* 1940.

Starling Ernest Henry 1866–1927. English physiologist who discovered secretin (which produces digestive secretions), and coined the word 'hormone' to describe chemicals of this sort. He formulated *Starling's law*, which states that the force of the heart's contraction is a function of the length of the muscle fibres.

Starling was Jodrell professor of physiology at University College, London. He is regarded, with ◊Bayliss and ◊Sharpey-Schäfer, as a founder of endocrinology.

Staudinger Hermann 1881–1965. German organic chemist, founder of macro-molecular chemistry, who carried out pioneering research into the structure of albumen and cellulose. Nobel prize 1953.

Stauffenberg Claus von 1907–1944. German colonel in World War II, who planted a bomb in Hitler's headquarters conference room in the Wolf's Lair at Rastenburg, East Prussia, 20 July 1944. Hitler was injured, and Stauffenberg and 200 others were later executed.

Stead Christina (Ellen) 1902–1983. Australian writer, who lived in Europe and the USA 1928–68. Her novels include *The Man Who Loved Children* 1940, *Dark Places of the Heart*

1966 (published as *Cotter's England* in London), and *I'm Dying Laughing* 1986.

Steel David 1938–   . British politician, leader of the Liberal Party 1976–88. He entered into a compact with the Labour government 1977–78, and into an alliance with the Social Democratic Party (SDP) 1983. Having supported the Liberal-SDP merger (forming the Social and Liberal Democrats), he resigned the leadership 1988.

Steele Richard 1672–1729. Irish essayist, who founded the journal *The Tatler* 1709–11, in which Joseph ◊Addison collaborated. They continued their joint work in *The Spectator*, also founded by Steele, 1711–12, and *The Guardian* 1713. He also wrote plays, such as *The Conscious Lovers* 1722.

Steen Jan 1626–1679. Dutch painter. Born in Leiden, he was also active in The Hague, Delft, and Haarlem. He painted humorous everyday (genre) scenes, mainly set in taverns or bourgeois households, as well as portraits and landscapes.

Steer Philip Wilson 1860–1942. British painter, influenced by the French Impressionists, known for seaside scenes such as *The Beach at Walberswick* 1890 (Tate Gallery, London).

Steer, born in Birkenhead on Merseyside, studied in Paris. He became a leader (with ◊Sickert) of the English movement, and founder member of the New English Art Club to give younger artists an alternative to the Royal Academy.

Stefan Joseph 1835–1893. Austrian physicist who established one of the basic laws of heat radiation in 1874, since known as the *Stefan–Boltzmann law*. This states that the heat radiated by a hot body is proportional to the fourth power of its absolute temperature.

Steichen Edward 1897–1973. US photographer in both world wars, and also an innovative fashion and portrait photographer.

Steiger Rod(ney Stephen) 1925–   . US character actor, often in leading film roles. His work includes *On the Waterfront* 1954, *In the Heat of the Night* 1967, and the title role in *W C Fields and Me* 1976.

Stein Aurel 1862–1943. Hungarian archaeologist and explorer who carried out studies for the Indian government in Chinese Turkestan and Tibet 1900–15.

Stein Gertrude 1874–1946. US writer. She influenced writers such as ◊Hemingway and Scott ◊Fitzgerald by her cinematic technique, use of repetition and absence of punctuation: devices to convey immediacy and realism. Her works include the self-portrait *The Autobiography of Alice B Toklas* 1933.

Steinbeck John (Ernst) 1902–1968. US novelist. His work includes *Of Mice and Men* 1937, *The Grapes of Wrath* 1939, *Cannery Row* 1945, and *East of Eden* 1952. Nobel prize 1962.

He first achieved success with *Tortilla Flat* 1935, a humorous study of Monterey, California,

paisanos (farmers); most of his books deal with the lives of working people. *East of Eden* was filmed with James Dean. His later work, less highly thought of, includes *Winter of our Discontent* 1961.

Steinem Gloria 1934–   . US journalist and liberal feminist who emerged as a leading figure in the US women's movement in the late 1960s. She was also involved in radical protest campaigns against racism and the Vietnam War. She co-founded the Women's Action Alliance 1970 and *Ms* magazine. In 1983 a collection of her best-known articles was published as *Outrageous Acts and Everyday Rebellions*.

Steiner Max(imilian Raoul) 1888–1971. Austrian composer of film music who lived in the USA from 1914. He composed his first film score in 1929 and produced some of the cinema's finest music, including the scores to *King Kong* 1933, *Gone with the Wind* 1939, and *Casablanca* 1942.

Steiner Rudolf 1861–1925. Austrian philosopher, originally a theosophist (see ◊Blavatsky), who developed his own mystic and spiritual teaching, anthroposophy, designed to develop the whole human being. His method of teaching is followed by a number of schools named after him, but the schools also include the possibilities for pupils to take state exams.

Steinmetz Charles 1865–1923. US engineer who formulated the *Steinmetz hysteresis law* in 1891, which describes the dissipation of energy that occurs when a system is subject to an alternating magnetic force.

He worked on the design of alternating current transmission and 1894–1923 served as consulting engineer to General Electric.

Stella Frank 1936–   . US painter, a pioneer of the hard-edged geometric trend in abstract art that succeeded Abstract Expressionism. From around 1960 he also experimented with the shape of his canvases.

Stendhal pen name of Marie Henri Beyle 1783–1842. French novelist. His two major novels *Le Rouge et le noir/The Red and the Black* 1830 and *La Chartreuse de Parme/The Charterhouse of Parma* 1839 were pioneering works in their treatment of disguise and hypocrisy; a review of the latter by ◊Balzac in 1840 furthered his reputation.

Born in Grenoble, he served in Napoleon's armies, taking part in the ill-fated Russian campaign, and, failing in his hopes of becoming a prefect, lived in Italy from 1814 until suspicion of espionage drove him back to Paris in 1821, where he lived by literary hackwork. From 1830 he was a member of the consular service, spending his leaves in Paris.

Stenmark Ingemar 1956–   . Swedish skiier who won a record 85 World Cup races 1974–87, including a record 13 in 1979. He won a total of 18 titles, including the overall title three times. He won the double of slalom and giant slalom at both the 1978 World Championships and the 1980 Olympic Games.

Stephen Leslie 1832–1904. English critic, first editor of the *Dictionary of National Biography* and father of novelist Virginia ◊Woolf.

Stephen c. 1097–1154. King of England from 1135. A grandson of William I, he was elected king 1135, although he had previously recognized Henry I's daughter ◊Matilda as heiress to the throne. Matilda landed in England 1139, and civil war disrupted the country until 1153, when Stephen acknowledged Matilda's son, Henry II, as his own heir.

Stephen I, St 975–1038. King of Hungary from 997, when he succeeded his father. He completed the conversion of Hungary to Christianity, and was canonized in 1803.

His crown, symbol of Hungarian nationhood, was removed to the USA in 1945, but returned 1978.

Stephens John Lloyd 1805–1852. US explorer in Central America, with Frederick ◊Catherwood. He recorded his findings of ruined Mayan cities in his two volumes *Incidents of Travel in Central America, Chiapas and Yucatan* 1841–43.

Stephen, St died c. AD 35. The first Christian martyr; he was stoned to death. Feast day 26 Dec.

Stephenson George 1781–1848. English engineer who built the first successful steam locomotive, and who also invented a safety lamp in 1815. He was appointed engineer of the Stockton and Darlington Railway, the world's first public railway, in 1821, and of the Liverpool and Manchester Railway in 1826. In 1829 he won a £500 prize with his locomotive, *Rocket*.

Stephenson Robert 1803–1859. English civil engineer, who constructed railway bridges such as the high-level bridge at Newcastle upon Tyne, England, and the Menai and Conway tubular bridges in North Wales. He was the son of George Stephenson.

Steptoe Patrick Christopher 1913–1988. English obstetrician who pioneered *in vitro* or 'test-tube' fertilization. Steptoe, together with biologist Robert Edwards, was the first to succeed in implanting in the womb an egg fertilized outside the body.

This success, the result of a ten-year cooperation between the two men, came only after some 500 failures. The first 'test-tube baby' was Louise Brown, born by Caesarean section in 1978.

Stern Otto 1888–1969. German physicist. Stern studied with Einstein in Prague and Zürich, where he became a lecturer in 1914. After World War I he demonstrated by means of the **Stern–Gerlach apparatus** that elementary particles have wavelike properties as well as the properties of matter

that had been demonstrated. He left Germany for the USA in 1933. Nobel prize 1943.

Sternberg Josef von 1894–1969. Austrian film director who lived in the USA from childhood. He worked with Marlene Dietrich on *The Blue Angel/Der blaue Engel* 1930 and other films. He favoured striking imagery over narrative in his work, which includes *Underworld* 1927 and *Blonde Venus* 1932.

Sterne Laurence 1713–1768. Irish writer, creator of the comic anti-hero Tristram Shandy. *The Life and Opinions of Tristram Shandy, Gent* 1760–67, an eccentrically whimsical and bawdy novel, foreshadowed many of the techniques and devices of 20th-century novelists, including James Joyce. His other works include *A Sentimental Journey through France and Italy* 1768.

Sterne, born in Clonmel, Ireland, took orders in 1737 and became vicar of Sutton-in-the-Forest, Yorkshire, in the next year. In 1741 he married Elizabeth Lumley, an unhappy union largely because of his infidelity. He had a sentimental love affair with Eliza Draper, of which the *Letters of Yorick to Eliza* 1775 is a record.

Stevens Alfred 1817–1875. British sculptor, painter, and designer. He created the *Wellington monument* begun 1858 (St Paul's, London). He was devoted to High Renaissance art, especially to Raphael, and studied in Italy in 1833.

Stevens George 1904–1975. US film director who began as a director of photography. He made films such as *Swing Time* 1936 and *Gunga Din* 1939, and his reputation grew steadily, as did the length of his films. His later work included *A Place in the Sun* 1951, *Shane* 1953, and *Giant* 1956.

Stevens Siaka Probin 1905–1988. Sierra Leone politician, president 1971–85. He was the leader of the moderate left-wing All People's Congress (APC), from 1978 the country's only legal political party.

Stevens was a policeman, industrial worker, and trade unionist before founding the APC. He became prime minister in 1968 and in 1971, under a revised constitution, became Sierra Leone's first president. He created a one-party state based on the APC, and remained in power until his retirement at the age of 80.

Stevens Wallace 1879–1955. US poet. His volumes of poems include *Harmonium* 1923, *The Man with the Blue Guitar* 1937, and *Transport to Summer* 1947. *The Necessary Angel* 1951 is a collection of essays. An elegant and philosophical poet, he won a Pulitzer prize 1954 for his *Collected Poems*.

Stevenson Adlai 1900–1965. US Democrat politician. As governor of Illinois 1949–53 he campaigned vigorously against corruption in public life, and as Democratic candidate for the presidency 1952 and 1956 was twice defeated by Eisenhower. In 1945 he was chief US delegate at the founding conference of the United Nations.

Stevenson Robert 1772–1850. Scottish engineer, born in Glasgow, who built many lighthouses, including the Bell Rock lighthouse, 1807–11.

Stevenson Robert Louis 1850–1894. Scottish novelist and poet. Early works included *An Island Voyage* 1878 and *Travels with a Donkey* 1879, but he achieved fame with his adventure novel *Treasure Island* 1883. Later works included the novels *Kidnapped* 1886, *The Master of Ballantrae* 1889, *Dr Jekyll and Mr Hyde* 1886, and the anthology *A Child's Garden of Verses* 1885. In 1890 he settled at Vailima, in Samoa, where he sought a cure for the tuberculosis of which he died.

Stevenson was born in Edinburgh. He studied at the university and qualified as an advocate, but never practised. He travelled in Europe to improve his health. In 1879 he went to the USA, married Fanny Osbourne, and, returning to Britain in 1880, published a volume of stories, *The New Arabian Nights* 1882, and essays, for example *Virginibus Puerisque* 1881, and *Familiar Studies of Men and Books* 1882. The humorous *The Wrong Box* 1889 and the novels *The Wrecker* 1892 and *The Ebb-tide* 1894 were written in collaboration with his stepson, Lloyd Osbourne (1868–1920).

Stewart 'Jackie' (John Young) 1939– . Scottish motor-racing driver. Until surpassed by Alain ◊Prost (France) 1987, Stewart held the record for the most Formula One Grand Prix wins (27).

His first win was in 1965. He was world champion three times and with manufacturer Ken Tyrrell, built up one of the sport's great partnerships. His last race was the 1973 Canadian Grand Prix. He pulled out of the next race (which would have been his 100th) because of the death of his team-mate Francois Cevert.

Stewart James 1908– . US film actor. Gangling and speaking with a soft drawl, he specialized in the role of the stubbornly honest, ordinary American in such films as *You Can't Take It With You* 1938, *The Philadelphia Story* 1940, *Harvey* 1950, *The Man from Laramie* 1955, and *The FBI Story* 1959.

Stieglitz Alfred 1864–1946. US photographer. After forming the Photo Secession group in 1903, he began the magazine *Camera Work*. Through exhibitions at his gallery '291' in New York he helped to establish photography as an art form. His works include 'Winter, Fifth Avenue' 1893 and 'Steerage' 1907. In 1924 he married the painter Georgia O'Keefe, who was the model in many of his photographs.

Stilicho Flavius AD 359–408. Roman general, of Vandal origin, who campaigned successfully against the Visigoths and Ostrogoths. He virtually ruled the western empire as guardian of Honorius (son of Theodosius I) but was executed on the orders of Honorius when he was suspected of wanting to make his own son successor to another son of Theodosius in the eastern empire.

Stilwell Joseph Warren 1883–1946. US general, nicknamed 'Vinegar Joe'. In 1942 he became US military representative in China, when he commanded the Chinese forces cooperating with the British (with whom he quarrelled) in Burma; he later commanded all US forces in the Chinese, Burmese, and Indian theatres until recalled to the USA 1944 after differences over nationalist policy with the Guomindang (nationalist) leader Chiang Kai-shek.

Stimson Henry Lewis 1867–1950. US politician. He was war secretary in Taft's cabinet 1911–13, Hoover's secretary of state 1929–33, and war secretary 1940–45.

Stirling James 1926– . British architect, associated with collegiate and museum architecture. His works include the engineering building at Leicester University, and the Clore Gallery at the Tate Gallery, London, opened 1987.

Stockhausen Karlheinz 1928– . German composer of avant-garde music, who has continued to explore new musical sounds and compositional techniques since the 1950s. His major works include *Gesang der Jünglinge* 1956 and *Kontakte* 1960 (electronic music); *Klavierstücke* 1952–85; *Momente* 1961–64, revised 1972, *Mikrophonie I* 1964, and *Sirius* 1977. Since 1977 all his works have been part of *Licht*, a cycle of seven musical ceremonies, intended for performance on the evenings of a week. He has completed *Donnerstag* 1980, *Samstag* 1984, and *Montag* 1988.

Stockwood Arthur Mervyn 1913– . British Anglican cleric. As bishop of Southwark 1959–80, he expressed unorthodox views on homosexuality and in favour of the ordination of women.

Stoker Bram (Abraham) 1847–1912. Irish novelist, actor, theatre manager, and author. His novel *Dracula* 1897 crystallized most aspects of the traditional vampire legend and became the source for all subsequent popular fiction and films on the subject.

A civil servant 1866–78, he then became business manager to the theatre producer Henry Irving. Stoker wrote a number of stories and novels of fantasy and horror, such as *The Lady of the Shroud* 1909.

Stokes George Gabriel 1819–1903. Irish physicist. During the late 1840s, he studied the viscosity (resistance to relative motion) of fluids. This culminated in *Stokes' law*, which applies to a sphere falling under gravity through a liquid.

Stokowski Leopold 1882–1977. US conductor, born in London. An outstanding experimentalist, he introduced modern music (for example, Mahler's Eighth Symphony) to the USA; appeared in several films; and conducted the music for Walt Disney's animated film *Fantasia* 1940.

Stone (John) Richard 1913– . British economist, a statistics expert, whose system of 'national

Stopes *Scottish birth-control campaigner Marie Stopes.*

income accounting' has been adopted in many countries. Nobel prize 1984.

Stone Lucy 1818–1893. US feminist orator and editor. Married to the radical Henry Blackwell 1855 after a mutual declaration rejecting the legal superiority of the man in marriage, she gained wide publicity when she chose to retain her own surname despite her marriage. The epithet 'Lucy Stoner' was coined to mean a woman who advocated doing the same.

In the 1860s she helped to establish the American Woman Suffrage Association and founded and edited the Boston *Woman's Journal*, a suffragist paper which was later edited by her daughter, Alice Stone Blackwell (1857–1950).

Stone Robert 1937– . US novelist and journalist. His *Dog Soldiers* 1974 is a classic novel about the moral destructiveness of the Vietnam War. *A Flag for Sunrise* 1982 similarly explores the political and moral consequences of US intervention in a corrupt South American republic.

Stonehouse John (Thompson) 1925–1988. British Labour Party politician. An active member of the Co-operative Movement, he entered Parliament in 1957 and held junior posts under Harold Wilson before joining his cabinet in 1967. In 1974 he disappeared in Florida in mysterious circumstances, surfacing in Australia, amid suspicions of fraudulent dealings. Extradited to Britain, he was tried and imprisoned for embezzlement. He won an early release in 1979, but was unable to resume a political career.

Stopes Marie (Carmichael) 1880–1958. Scottish birth-control campaigner. With her husband H V Roe (1878–1949), an aircraft manufacturer, she founded a London birth-control clinic 1921. The Well Woman Centre in Marie Stopes House, London, commemorates her work. She wrote plays and verse as well as the best-selling manual *Married Love* 1918.

Stoppard Tom 1937– . Czechoslovak-born British playwright, whose works use wit and wordplay to explore logical and philosophical ideas. He achieved fame with *Rosencrantz and Guildenstern are Dead* 1967. This was followed by comedies including *The Real Inspector Hound* 1968, *Jumpers* 1972, *Travesties* 1974, *Dirty Linen* 1976, and *The Real Thing* 1982. He has also written radio, television, and screenplays.

Storey David Malcolm 1933– . English dramatist and novelist. His plays include *In Celebration* 1969, *Home* 1970, and *Early Days* 1980. Novels include *This Sporting Life* 1960.

Stoss Veit also known as *Wit Stwosz* c.1450–1533. German sculptor and painter, active in Nuremberg and 1477–96 in Poland. He carved a wooden altarpiece with high relief panels in St Mary's, Krakow, a complicated design with numerous figures which centres on the *Death of the Virgin*.

The figure of St Roch in SS Annunziata, Florence, shows his characteristic figure style and sculpted drapery.

Stowe Harriet Beecher 1811–1896. US suffragist, abolitionist, and author of of the anti-slavery novel *Uncle Tom's Cabin*, first published as a serial 1851–52.

She was a daughter of Lyman ◊Beecher, and in 1836 married C E Stowe, a professor of theology. Her book was radical in its time and did much to spread anti-slavery sentiment, but has later been criticized for sentimentality and racism.

Strabo c.63 BC–AD 24. Greek geographer and historian, who travelled widely to collect first-hand material for his *Geography*.

Strachey (Giles) Lytton 1880–1932. English critic and biographer, a member of the Bloomsbury Group of writers and artists. He wrote *Landmarks in French Literature* 1912. The mocking and witty treatment of Cardinal Manning, Florence Nightingale, Thomas Arnold, and General Gordon in *Eminent Victorians* 1918 won him recognition. His biography of *Queen Victoria* 1921 was more affectionate.

Stradivari Antonio. In Latin form *Stradivarius* 1644–1737. Italian stringed instrument maker, generally considered the greatest of all violin makers. He was born in Cremona and studied there with Nicolo ◊Amati. He produced more than 1,100 instruments from his family workshops.

Strafford Thomas Wentworth, 1st Earl of Strafford 1593–1641. English politician, originally an opponent of Charles I, but from 1628 on the Royalist side. He ruled despotically as Lord Deputy of Ireland 1632–39, when he returned to England as Charles's chief adviser and received an earldom. He was impeached in 1640 by Parliament, abandoned by Charles as a scapegoat, and beheaded.

Strand Paul 1890–1976. US photographer who used large-format cameras for his strong, clear, close-up photographs of natural objects.

Strange Curtis Northrup 1955– . US golfer, professional from 1976. In 1989 he became the fifth person to win $5 million in a golfing career.

Strange was born in Virginia. He won his first tournament 1979 (Pensacola Open). He has won over 20 tournaments, including two 'majors', the 1988 and 1989 US Opens.

Strasberg Lee 1902–1982. US actor and artistic director of the Actors Studio from 1948, who developed Method acting from ◊Stanislavsky's system; pupils have included Jane Fonda, John Garfield, Sidney Poitier, and Paul Newman.

Straus Oscar 1870–1954. Austrian composer, born in Vienna. He is remembered for the operetta *The Chocolate Soldier* 1909.

Strauss Franz-Josef 1915–1988. West German conservative politician, leader of the Bavarian Christian Social Union (CSU) party 1961–88, premier of Bavaria 1978–88.

Born and educated in Munich, Strauss, after military service 1939–45, joined the CSU and was elected to the *Bundestag* (parliament) in 1949. He held ministerial posts during the 1950s and 1960s and became leader of the CSU 1961. In 1962 he lost his post as minister of defence when he illegally shut down the offices of *Der Spiegel* for a month, after the magazine revealed details of a failed NATO exercise. In the 1970s, Strauss opposed Ostpolitik (the policy of rapprochement with the East). He left the *Bundestag* to become premier of Bavaria in 1978, and was heavily defeated in 1980 as chancellor candidate. From 1982 Strauss sought to force changes in economic and foreign policy of the coalition under Chancellor Kohl.

Strauss Johann (Baptist) 1825–1899. Austrian conductor and composer, the son of Johann Strauss (1804–49). In 1872 he gave up conducting and wrote operettas, such as *Die Fledermaus* 1874, and numerous waltzes, such as *The Blue Danube* and *Tales from the Vienna Woods*, which gained him the title 'The Waltz King'.

Strauss Richard (Georg) 1864–1949. German composer and conductor. He followed the German Romantic tradition but had a strongly personal style, characterized by his bold, colourful orchestration. He first wrote tone poems such as *Don Juan* 1889, *Till Eulenspiegel's Merry Pranks* 1895, and *Also sprach Zarathustra* 1896. He then moved on to opera with *Salome* 1905, and *Elektra* 1909, both of which have elements of polytonality. He reverted to a more traditional style with *Der Rosenkavalier* 1911.

Stravinsky Igor 1882–1971. Russian composer, later of French (1934) and US (1945) nationality. He studied under ◊Rimsky-Korsakov and wrote the music for the Diaghilev ballets *The Firebird* 1910, *Petrushka* 1911, and *The Rite of Spring* 1913 (controversial at the time for their unorthodox rhythms and harmonies). His versatile work ranges from his Neo-Classical ballet *Pulcinella* 1920, to the choral-orchestral *Symphony of Psalms* 1930. He later made use of serial techniques in works such as the *Canticum Sacrum* 1955 and the ballet *Agon* 1953–57.

Streep Meryl 1949– . US actress, noted for her strong character roles. Her films include *The Deer Hunter* 1978, *Kramer vs Kramer* 1979, *Out of Africa* 1985, and *A Cry in the Dark* 1989.

Street J(abez) C(urry) 1906–1989. US physicist who, with E C Stevenson, discovered the muon (an elementary particle) in 1937.

Streeton Arthur 1867–1943. Australian artist, who pioneered Impressionistic renderings of Australia's landscape.

Streisand 'Barbra' (Barbara Joan) 1942– . US singer and actress, who became a film star in *Funny Girl* 1968. Her subsequent films include *What's Up Doc?* 1972, *A Star is Born* 1979, and *Yentl* 1983, which she also directed.

Strindberg August 1849–1912. Swedish playwright and novelist. His plays, influential in the development of dramatic technique, are in a variety of styles including historical plays, symbolic dramas (the two-part *Dödsdansen/The Dance of Death* 1901) and 'chamber plays' such as *Spöksonaten/The Ghost (or Spook) Sonata* 1907. *Fadren/The Father* 1887 and *Fröken Julie/Miss Julie* 1888 are among his best-known works.

Born in Stockholm, he lived mainly abroad after 1883, having been unsuccessfully prosecuted for blasphemy in 1884 following publication of his short stories *Giftas/Marrying*. His life was stormy and controversial. His work has been criticized for its hostile attitude to women, but he is regarded as one of Sweden's greatest writers.

Stroessner Alfredo 1912– . Military leader and president of Paraguay 1954–89. As head of the armed forces from 1951, he seized power in a coup in 1954 sponsored by the right-wing ruling Colorado Party. Accused by his opponents of harsh repression, his regime spent heavily on the military to preserve his authority. He was overthrown by a military coup and gained asylum in Brazil.

Stroheim Erich von. Assumed name of Erich Oswald Stroheim 1885–1957. Austrian actor and director, who worked in Hollywood from 1914. Successful as an actor in villainous roles, his career as a director was wrecked by his extravagance and

Strindberg *A drawing of Swedish dramatist August Strindberg by his friend Carl Larsson.*

he returned to acting in international films such as *Grand Illusion/La Grande Illusion* 1937 and *Sunset Boulevard* 1950. His films as director include *Greed* 1923 and *Queen Kelly* 1928 (unfinished).

Stuart or *Stewart* royal family who inherited the Scottish throne in 1371 and the English in 1603.

Stuart John McDougall 1815–1866. Scottish-born Australian explorer. He went with ◊Sturt on his 1844 expedition, and in 1860, after two unsuccessful attempts, crossed the centre of Australia from Adelaide in the SE to the coast of Arnhem Land. He almost lost his life on the return journey.

Stubbs George 1724–1806. British artist, known for paintings of horses. After the publication of his book of engravings *The Anatomy of the Horse* 1766, he was widely commissioned as an animal painter and group portraitist.

Stubbs began as a portrait painter and medical illustrator in Liverpool. In 1754 he went to Rome, continuing to study nature and anatomy. Before settling in London in the 1760s he rented a farm and carried out a long series of dissections of horses which resulted in his book. The dramatic *Lion Attacking a Horse* 1770 (Yale University Art Gallery, New Haven, Connecticut) and the peaceful *Reapers* 1786 (Tate Gallery, London) show the variety of mood in his painting.

Sturges Preston. Adopted name of Edmond Biden 1898–1959. US film director and writer who enjoyed great success with a series of comedies

in the early 1940s, including *Sullivan's Travels* 1941, *The Palm Beach Story*, and *The Miracle of Morgan's Creek* 1943.

Sturluson Snorri 1179–1241. Icelandic author of the Old Norse poems called Eddas, and the *Heimskringla*, a saga chronicle of Norwegian kings until 1177.

Sturt Charles 1795–1869. British explorer and soldier. In 1828 he sailed down the Murrumbidgee River in SE Australia to the estuary of the Murray in circumstances of great hardship, charting the entire river system of the region.

Born in India, he served in the army, and in 1827 discovered with the Australian explorer Hamilton Hume the river Darling. Drawn by his concept of a great inland sea, he set out for the interior 1844, crossing the Sturt Desert, but failing to penetrate the Simpson Desert.

Suárez González Adolfo 1933– . Spanish politician, prime minister 1976–81. A friend of King Juan Carlos, he worked in the National Movement for 18 years, but in 1975 became president of the newly established Unión del Pueblo Español (UPE). He took office as prime minister at the request of the king, to speed the reform programme. He suddenly resigned 1981.

Suckling John 1609–1642. English poet and dramatist. He was an ardent Royalist who tried to effect ◊Strafford's escape from the Tower of London. On his failure, he fled to France and may have committed suicide. His chief lyrics appeared in *Fragmenta Aurea* and include 'Why so pale and wan, fond lover?'

Sucre Antonio José de 1795–1830. South American revolutionary leader. As chief lieutenant of Simón ◊Bolívar, he won several battles in freeing the colonies of Ecuador and Bolivia from Spanish rule, and in 1826 became president of Bolivia. After a mutiny by the army and invasion by Peru, he resigned 1828 and was assassinated 1830 on his way to join Bolívar.

Suetonius (Gaius Suetonius Tranquillius) *c.* AD 69–140. Roman historian, author of *Lives of the Caesars* (Julius Caesar to Domitian).

Sugar Alan 1947– . British entrepreneur, founder of the Amstrad electronics company 1968 which holds a major position in the European personal-computer market.

Suger *c.*1081–1151. French historian and politician, regent of France during the Second Crusade. In 1122 he was elected abbot of St Denis, Paris, and was counsellor to, and biographer of, Louis VI and Louis VII. He began the reconstruction of St Denis as the first large-scale Gothic building.

Suharto Raden 1921– . Indonesian politician and general. He ousted Sukarno to become president 1967. He ended confrontation with Malaysia, invaded East Timor 1975, and reached a cooperation agreement with Papua New Guinea 1979. His authoritarian rule has met domestic

Suharto General Suharto, president of Indonesia.

opposition from the left. He was re-elected 1973, 1978, 1983, and 1988.

Sukarno Achmed 1901–1970. Indonesian nationalist, president 1945–67. During World War II he cooperated in the local administration set up by the Japanese, replacing Dutch rule. After the war he became the first president of the new Indonesian republic, becoming president-for-life 1966; he was ousted by ◊Suharto.

Suleiman or *Solyman* 1494–1566. Ottoman sultan from 1520, known as **the Magnificent** and **the Lawgiver**. Under his rule the Ottoman Empire flourished and reached its largest extent. He made conquests in the Balkans, the Mediterranean, Persia, and N Africa, but was defeated at Vienna 1529 and Valletta 1565. He was a patron of the arts, a poet, and an administrator.

Suleiman captured Belgrade 1521, the Mediterranean island of Rhodes 1522, defeated the Hungarians at Mohács 1526, and was halted in his advance into Europe only by his failure to take Vienna, capital of the Austro-Hungarian Empire, after a siege Sept–Oct 1529. In 1534 he turned more successfully against Persia, and then in campaigns against the Arab world took almost all N Africa and the Red Sea port of Aden. Only the Knights of Malta inflicted severe defeat on both his army and fleet when he tried to take Valletta 1565.

Sulla Lucius Cornelius 138–78 BC. Roman general and politician, a leader of the senatorial party. Forcibly suppressing the democrats in 88 BC, he departed for a successful campaign against ◊Mithridates VI of Pontus. The democrats seized power in his absence, but on his return Sulla captured Rome and massacred all opponents. As dictator, his reforms, which strengthened the Senate, were backward-looking and short-lived. He retired 79 BC.

Sullivan Arthur (Seymour) 1842–1900. English composer who wrote operettas in collaboration with William Gilbert, including *HMS Pinafore* 1878, *The Pirates of Penzance* 1879, and *The Mikado* 1885. Their partnership broke down 1896. Sullivan also composed serious instrumental, choral, and operatic works – for example, the opera *Ivanhoe* 1890 – which he valued more highly than the operettas.

Other Gilbert and Sullivan operettas include *Patience* (which ridiculed the Aesthetic movement) 1881, *The Yeomen of the Guard* 1888, and *The Gondoliers* 1889.

Sullivan Jim 1903–1977. Welsh-born rugby player. A great goal-kicker, he kicked a record 2,867 points in a 25-year Rugby League career covering 928 matches.

He played Rugby Union for Cardiff before joining Wigan Rugby League Club in 1921. He kicked 193 goals in 1933–34 (a record at the time).

Sullivan Louis Henry 1856–1924. US architect, who worked in Chicago and designed early skyscrapers such as the Wainwright Building, St Louis, 1890 and the Guaranty Building, Buffalo, 1894. He was influential in the anti-ornament movement. Frank Lloyd ◊Wright was his pupil.

Sully Maximilien de Béthune, Duc de Sully 1560–1641. French politician, who served with the Protestant Huguenots in the wars of religion, and, as Henry IV's superintendent of finances 1598–1611, aided French recovery.

Sully-Prudhomme Armand 1839–1907. French poet, who wrote philosophical verse including *Les Solitudes/Solitude* 1869, *La Justice/Justice* 1878, and *Le Bonheur/Happiness* 1888. Nobel prize 1901.

Sumner James 1887–1955. US biochemist. In 1926 he succeeded in crystallizing the enzyme urease and demonstrating its protein nature. For this work Sumner shared the 1946 Nobel Prize for Chemistry with John Northrop and Wendell Stanley.

Despite the loss of an arm as a youth, Sumner spent his entire career as an experimental chemist, at Cornell University, New York.

Sunderland Robert Spencer, 2nd Earl of Sunderland 1640–1702. English politician, a sceptical intriguer who converted to Roman Catholicism to secure his place under James II, and then reverted with the political tide. In 1688 he fled to Holland (disguised as a woman), where he made himself invaluable to the future William III. Now a Whig, he advised the new king to adopt the system, which still prevails, of choosing the government from the dominant party in the Commons.

Sun Yat-sen or *Sun Zhong Shan* 1867–1925. Chinese nationalist politician, founder of the National People's Party, the Guomindang 1894, president of China 1912 after playing a vital part

Sun Yat-sen *The founder of the nationalist Guomindang party, and the guiding force behind the Chinese revolution in 1911.*

in deposing the emperor, and president of a break-away government from 1921.

Sun Yat-sen was the son of a Christian farmer. After many years in exile he returned to China during the 1911 revolution that overthrew the Manchu dynasty and was provisional president of the republic 1912. The reactionaries, however, soon gained the ascendant, and he broke away to try to establish an independent republic in S China based on Canton. He was criticized for lack of organizational ability, but his 'three people's principles' of nationalism, democracy, and social reform are accepted by both the Guomindang and the Chinese communists.

Sun Zhong Shan Pinyin transliteration of ◊Sun Yat-sen.

Suraj-ud-Dowlah 1728–1757. Nawab of Bengal, India. He captured Calcutta from the British 1756 and imprisoned some of the British in the Black Hole of Calcutta (a small room, in which a number of them died), but was defeated 1757 by Robert ◊Clive, and lost Bengal to the British at the Battle of Plassey. He was killed in his capital, Murshidabad.

Surrey Henry Howard, Earl of Surrey *c.* 1517–1547. English courtier and poet, executed on a poorly based charge of high treason. With Thomas ◊Wyatt, he introduced the sonnet to England, and was a pioneer of blank verse.

Surtees John 1934– . British racing driver and motorcyclist, the only person to win world titles on two and four wheels.

After winning seven world motorcycling titles 1956–60, he turned to motor racing and won the world title in 1964. He later produced his own racing cars, but with little success.

Sutcliff Rosemary 1920– . British historical novelist, who writes for both adults and children. Her books include *The Eagle of the Ninth* 1954, *Tristan and Iseult* 1971, and *The Road to Camlann* 1981.

Sutherland Donald 1934– . Canadian film actor, usually in offbeat roles. He starred in *M.A.S.H.* 1970, and his subsequent films include *Klute* 1971, *Don't Look Now* 1973, and *Revolution* 1986.

Sutherland Earl Wilbur 1915–1974. US physiologist, discoverer of a chemical 'messenger' made by a special enzyme in the wall of living cells. Many hormones operate by means of this messenger. Nobel Prize for Medicine 1971.

Sutherland Graham (Vivian) 1903–1980. English painter, graphic artist, and designer, active mainly in France from the late 1940s. He painted portraits, landscapes, and religious subjects.

In the late 1940s Sutherland turned increasingly to characterful portraiture, for example *Somerset Maugham* 1949 (Tate Gallery, London). His portrait of *Winston Churchill* 1954 was disliked by its subject and eventually burned on the instructions of Lady Churchill (studies survive). His *Christ in Glory* tapestry 1962 is in Coventry Cathedral. Other work includes ceramics and designs for posters, stage costumes and sets.

Sutherland Joan 1926– . Australian soprano. She went to England in 1951, where she made her debut the next year in *The Magic Flute*; later roles included *Lucia di Lammermoor*, Donna Anna in *Don Giovanni*, and Desdemona in *Otello*.

Suvorov Aleksandr Vasilyevich 1729–1800. Russian field marshal, victorious against the Turks 1787–91, the Poles 1794, and the French army in Italy 1798–99 in the Revolutionary Wars.

Suzman Helen 1917– . South African politician and human-rights activist. A university lecturer concerned about the inhumanity of the apartheid system, she joined the white opposition to the ruling National Party and became a strong advocate of racial equality, respected by black communities inside and outside South Africa. In 1978 she received the UN Human Rights Award. She retired from active politics in 1989.

Suzuki Zenko 1911– . Japanese politician. Originally a socialist member of the Diet in 1947, he became a conservative (Liberal Democrat) in 1949, and was prime minister 1980–82.

Svedberg Theodor 1884–1971. Swedish chemist. In 1924 he constructed the first ultracentrifuge, a machine that allowed the rapid separation of particles by mass. Nobel Prize for Chemistry 1926.

Svevo Italo. Pen name of Ettore Schmitz 1861–1928. Italian novelist, whose books include *As a Man Grows Older* 1898 and *Confessions of Zeno* 1923.

Swan Joseph Wilson 1828–1914. English inventor of the incandescent filament electric lamp, and of bromide paper for use in developing photographs.

Swanson Gloria. Stage name of Gloria Josephine Mae Svenson 1897–1983. US actress, a star of silent films who retired in 1932 but made several comebacks. Her work includes *Sadie Thompson*

1928, *Queen Kelly* 1928 (unfinished), and *Sunset Boulevard* 1950.

Swedenborg Emanuel 1688–1772. Swedish theologian and philosopher. He trained as a scientist, but from 1747 concentrated on scriptural study, and in *Divine Love and Wisdom* 1763 concluded that the Last Judgment had taken place 1757, and that the **New Church**, of which he was the prophet, had now been inaugurated. His writings are the scriptures of the sect popularly known as Swedenborgians, and his works are kept in circulation by the Swedenborg Society, London.

Sweet Henry 1845–1912. British philologist, author of works on Old and Middle English, who took to England German scientific techniques of language study. He was said to be the original of Professor Higgins in Shaw's play *Pygmalion*.

Sweyn I died 1014. King of Denmark from c. 986, and nicknamed 'Forkbeard'. He raided England, finally conquered it in 1013, and styled himself king, but his early death led to the return of ◊Ethelred II.

Swift Jonathan 1667–1745. Irish satirist and Anglican cleric, author of *Gulliver's Travels* 1726, an allegory describing travel to lands inhabited by giants, miniature people, and intelligent horses. Other works include *The Tale of a Tub* 1704, attacking corruption in religion and learning; contributions to the Tory paper *The Examiner* of which he was editor 1710–11; *A Modest Proposal* 1729, which suggested that children of the poor should be eaten; and many essays and pamphlets.

Swift, born in Dublin, became secretary to the diplomat William Temple (1628–1699) at Moor Park, Surrey, where his friendship with the child 'Stella' (Hester Johnson 1681–1728) began in 1689. Returning to Ireland, he was ordained in the Church of England 1694, and in 1699 was made a prebendary of St Patrick's, Dublin. In 1710 he became a Tory pamphleteer, and obtained the deanery of St Patrick in 1713. His *Journal to Stella* is a series of letters, 1710–13, in which he described his life in London. 'Stella' remained the love of his life, but 'Vanessa' (Esther Vanhomrigh 1690–1723), a Dublin woman who had fallen in love with him, jealously wrote to her rival in 1723 and so shattered his relationship with both women. From about 1738 his mind began to fail.

Swinburne Algernon Charles 1837–1909. English poet. He attracted attention with the choruses of his Greek-style tragedy *Atalanta in Calydon* 1865, but he and Dante ◊Rossetti were attacked 1871 as leaders of 'the fleshly school of poetry', and the revolutionary politics of *Songs before Sunrise* 1871 alienated others.

Swinton Ernest 1868–1951. British soldier and historian. He served in South Africa and World War I, and was the inventor of the tank in 1916.

Swithun, St died 862. English priest, chancellor of King Ethelwolf and bishop of Winchester from 852. According to legend, the weather on his feast day

(15 July) is said to continue as either wet or fine for 40 days.

Sydenham Thomas 1624–1689. English physician, the first person to describe measles and to recommend the use of quinine for relieving symptoms of malaria. His original reputation as 'the English Hippocrates' rested upon his belief that careful observation is more useful than speculation. *Observationes medicae* was published in 1676.

Sydow 'Max' von (Carl Adolf) 1929– . Swedish actor associated with the director Ingmar Bergman. He made his US debut as Christ in *The Greatest Story Ever Told* 1965. His other films include *The Seventh Seal* 1957, *The Exorcist* 1973, and *Hannah and her Sisters* 1985.

Sykes Percy Molesworth 1867–1945. English explorer, soldier, and administrator who surveyed much of the territory in SW Asia between Baghdad, the Caspian Sea, and the Hindu Kush during World War I (1914–18).

In 1894 he was the first British consul to Kerman (now in Iran) and Persian Baluchistan. Later he raised and commanded the South Persian Rifles. His histories of Persia and Afghanistan were published in 1915 and 1940.

Symington William 1763–1831. Scottish engineer who built the first successful steamboat. He invented the steam road locomotive 1787 and a steamboat engine 1788. His steamboat the *Charlotte Dundas* was completed in 1802.

Symonds John Addington 1840–1893. British critic, who spent much of his life in Italy and Switzerland, and campaigned for homosexual rights. He was author of *The Renaissance in Italy* 1875–86. His frank memoirs were finally published in 1984.

Symons Arthur 1865–1945. Welsh critic, follower of ◊Pater, and friend of Toulouse-Lautrec, Mallarmé, Beardsley, Yeats, and Conrad. He introduced Eliot to the work of Laforgue and wrote *The Symbolist Movement in Literature* 1900.

Synge J(ohn) M(illington) 1871–1909. Irish playwright, a leading figure in the Irish dramatic revival of the early 20th century. His six plays reflect the speech patterns of the Aran Islands and W Ireland. They include *In the Shadow of the Glen* 1903, *Riders to the Sea* 1904, and *The Playboy of the Western World* 1907, which caused riots at the Abbey Theatre, Dublin, when first performed.

Synge Richard 1914– . British biochemist who investigated paper chromatography, a means of separating mixtures. By 1940 techniques of chromatography for separating proteins had been devised. Still lacking were comparable techniques for distinguishing the amino acids that constituted the proteins. By 1944, Synge and his colleague Archer Martin had worked out a procedure, known as ascending chromatography, which filled this gap and won them the 1952 Nobel Prize for Chemistry.

Szent-Gyorgi Albert 1893–1986. Hungarian-born US biochemist who isolated vitamin C and studied the chemistry of musclar activity. Nobel Prize for Medicine 1937.

In 1928 Szent-Gyorgi isolated a substance from the adrenal glands that he named hexuronic acid; when he found the same substance in cabbages and oranges, he suspected that he had finally isolated vitamin C. In 1947 he moved to the USA.

Szilard Leo 1898–1964. Hungarian-born US physicist who, in 1934, was one of the first scientists to realize that nuclear fission, or atom splitting, could lead to a chain reaction releasing enormous amounts of instantaneous energy. He emigrated to the USA in 1938 and there influenced ⟡Einstein to advise President Roosevelt to begin the nuclear arms programme.

In post-war years he turned his attention to the newly emerging field of molecular biology.

Szymanowski Karol (Maliej) 1882–1937. Polish composer of orchestral works, operas, piano music, and violin concertos. He was director of the Conservatoire in Warsaw from 1926.

she was the first to use pointe work, or dancing on the toes, as an expressive part of ballet rather than as sheer technique. She created many roles, including the title role in *La Sylphide* 1832, first performed at the Paris Opéra, and choreographed by her father *Filippo* (1771–1871). Marie's brother *Paolo* (1808–1884) was a choreographer and ballet master at Berlin Court Opera 1856–83, and his daughter *Marie* (1833–1891) danced in Berlin and London, creating many roles in her father's ballets.

Tagore Rabindranath 1861–1941. Bengali Indian writer, born in Calcutta. One of the most influential Indian authors of the 20th century, he translated his own verse *Gitanjali* ('song offerings') 1912 and his verse play *Chitra* 1896 into English. Nobel prize 1913.

Taine Hippolyte Adolphe 1828–1893. French critic and historian. He analysed literary works as products of period and environment, for example in *Histoire de la littérature anglaise/History of English Literature* 1863 and *Philosophie de l'art/Philosophy of Art* 1865–69.

Takeshita Noboru 1924– . Japanese right-wing politician. Elected to parliament as a Liberal Democratic Party (LDP) deputy 1958, he became president of the LDP and prime minister Oct 1987. His administration was undermined by the Recruit insider-trading scandal and in Apr 1989 he resigned because of his involvement.

Tagore *Nobel prize-winning Indian writer Rabindranath Tagore photographed in 1920.*

Tacitus Publius Cornelius AD *c.*55–*c.*120. Roman historian. A public orator in Rome, he was consul under Nerva 97–98 and proconsul of Asia 112–113. He wrote histories of the Roman Empire, *Annales* and *Historiae*, covering the years AD 14–68 and 69–97 respectively. He also wrote a *Life of Agricola* 97 (he married Agricola's daughter in 77) and a description of the German tribes, *Germania* 98.

Tafawa Balewa Alhaji Abubakar 1912–1966. Nigerian politician, prime minister from 1957. He entered the House of Representatives 1952, was minister of works 1952–54, and minister of transport 1954–57. He was assassinated in the coup d'état Jan 1966.

Taft Robert Alphonso 1889–1953. US Republican senator from 1939, and a candidate for the presidential nomination 1940, 1944, 1948, and 1952. He sponsored the Taft–Hartley Labor Act 1947, restricting union power. He was the son of President William Taft.

Taft William Howard 1857–1930. 27th president of the USA 1909–13, a Republican. He was secretary of war 1904–08 in Theodore Roosevelt's administration, but as president his conservatism provoked Roosevelt to stand against him in the 1912 election. Taft served as chief justice of the Supreme Court 1921–30.

Tagliacozzi Gaspare 1546–1599. Italian surgeon who pioneered plastic surgery. He was the first to repair noses lost in duels or through syphilis. He also carried out repair of ears. His method involved taking flaps of skin from the arm and grafting them into place.

Taglioni Marie 1804–1884. Italian dancer. The most important ballerina of the Romantic era, acclaimed for her ethereal style and exceptional lightness,

Talbot Daguerreotype of William Henry Fox Talbot, who invented new techniques in photography, including the photographic negative from which copies could be made on paper.

Takeshita, the son of a *sake* brewer, trained as a kamikaze pilot during World War II. He was a schoolteacher before beginning his political career in the House of Representatives, rising to chief cabinet secretary to Prime Minister Satō 1971–72 and finance minister under Nakasone.

As prime minister he introduced a furusato (hometown) project of giving 3,200 towns and villages a grant of 100 million yen (£500,000) each. This benefited construction companies, who are among the main backers of Takeshita's LDP faction. The Recruit scandal and the introduction of a consumption tax caused popular approval of Takeshita's government to drop dramatically.

Talbot William Henry Fox 1800–1877. English pioneer of photography. He invented the paper-based calotype process, the first negative/positive method. *The Pencil of Nature* 1844–46 by Talbot was the first book of photographs published.

Taliesin lived *c.*550. Legendary Welsh poet, a bard at the court of the king of Rheged in S Scotland. Taliesin allegedly died at Taliesin (named after him) in Dyfed.

Talleyrand Charles Maurice de Talleyrand-Périgord 1754–1838. French politician. As bishop of Autun 1789–91 he supported moderate reform in the French Revolution, and fled to the USA during the Reign of Terror (persecution of anti-revolutionaries). He became foreign minister under the Directory 1797–99 and under Napoleon 1799–1807. He represented France at the Congress of Vienna 1814–15.

Tallis Thomas *c.*1505–1585. English composer in the polyphonic style. He wrote masses, anthems, and other church music. Among his works are the setting for five voices of the *Lamentations of Jeremiah*, and for 40 of *Spem in alium*.

Tambo Oliver 1917– . South African nationalist politician, in exile from 1960, president of the African National Congress (ANC) from 1977.

Tambo was expelled from teacher training for organizing a student protest, and joined the ANC 1944. He set up a law practice with Nelson Mandela in Johannesburg in 1952. In 1956 Tambo, with other ANC members, was arrested on charges of treason; he was released the following year. When the ANC was banned in 1960, he left South Africa to set up an external wing. He became acting ANC president in 1967 and president in 1977, during Mandela's imprisonment.

Tamerlane or **Tamburlaine** or **Timur i Leng** 1336–1405. Mongol ruler of Samarkand from 1369, who conquered Persia, Azerbaijan, Armenia, and Georgia. He defeated the Golden Horde army 1395, sacked Delhi 1398, invaded Syria and Anatolia, and captured the Ottoman sultan in Ankara 1402. He died invading China.

Tanaka Kakuei 1918– . Japanese right-wing politician, leader of the dominant Liberal Democratic Party (LDP) and prime minister 1972–74. In 1976 he was charged with corruption and resigned from the LDP but remained a powerful faction leader.

Tanaka was minister of finance 1962–65 and of international trade and industry 1971–72, before becoming LDP leader. In 1976 he was arrested for accepting bribes from the Lockheed Corporation when premier and found guilty in 1983, being fined and sentenced to four years' imprisonment. He was also implicated in the 1988–89 Recruit insider-trading scandal.

Tange Kenzo 1913– . Japanese architect. His works include the National Gymnasium, Tokyo, for the 1964 Olympics, and the city-plan of Abuja, the capital of Nigeria.

Tanguy Yves 1900–1955. French Surrealist painter, who lived in the USA from 1939. His inventive canvases feature semi-abstract creatures in a barren landscape.

Tanguy was first inspired to paint by de ♦Chirico's work and in 1925 he joined the Surrealist movement. He soon developed his characteristic style with bizarre, slender forms in a typically Surrealist wasteland.

Tanizaki Jun-ichirō 1886–1965. Japanese novelist. His works include a modern version of ♦Murasaki's *The Tale of Genji* 1939–41, *The Makioka Sisters* in three volumes 1943–48, and *The Key* 1956.

His work matured when he moved from Tokyo after the 1923 earthquake to the Kyoto-Osaka region where ancient tradition is stronger.

Tarkington Booth 1869–1946. US novelist, born in Indiana, author of *Monsieur Beaucaire* 1900 and novels of the Middle West, for example *The Magnificent Ambersons* 1918.

Tarkovsky Andrei 1932–1986. Soviet film director, whose work is characterized by unorthodox cinematic techniques and visual beauty. His films include the science-fiction epic *Solaris* 1972, *Mirror* 1975, and *The Sacrifice* 1986.

Tarquinius Superbus lived 5th century BC. Last king of Rome 534–510 BC. He abolished certain rights of Romans, and made the city powerful. He was deposed when his son Sextus raped ◊Lucretia.

Tartini Giuseppe 1692–1770. Italian composer and violinist. In 1728 he founded a school of violin playing in Padua. A leading exponent of violin technique, he composed the *Devil' s Trill* sonata.

Tasman Abel Janszoon 1603–1659. Dutch navigator. In 1642, he was the first European to see Tasmania. He also made the first European sightings of New Zealand, Tonga, and Fiji.

He called Tasmania Van Diemen's Land in honour of the governor general of the Netherlands Indies; it was subsequently renamed Tasmania in his honour in 1856.

Tasso Torquato 1544–1595. Italian poet, author of the romantic epic poem of the First Crusade *La Gerusalemme Liberata/Jerusalem Delivered* 1574, followed by the *Gerusalemme Conquistata/Jerusalem Conquered*, written during the period from 1576 when he was mentally unstable.

At first a law student at Padua, he overcame his father's opposition to a literary career by the success of his romantic poem *Rinaldo* 1562, dedicated to Cardinal Luigi d'Este, who took him to Paris, where he met the seven members of the Pléiade group of poets. Under the patronage of Duke Alfonso d'Este of Ferrara, he wrote his pastoral play *Aminta* in 1573.

Tate Jeffrey 1943– . English conductor. He was appointed principal conductor of the English Chamber Orchestra in 1985 and principal conductor of the Royal Opera House, Covent Garden, London, in 1986. He has conducted opera in Paris, in Geneva, and at the Metropolitan Opera, New York. He qualified as a doctor before turning to a career in music.

Tate Nahum 1652–1715. Irish poet, born in Dublin. He wrote an adaptation of Shakespeare's *King Lear* with a happy ending. He also produced a version of the psalms, and hymns; among his poems is 'While shepherds watched'. He became British poet laureate 1692.

Tate Phyllis (Margaret) 1911–1987. British composer. Her works include *Concerto for Saxophone and Strings* 1944, the opera *The Lodger* 1960, based on the story of Jack the Ripper, and *Serenade to Christmas* for soprano, chorus and orchestra 1972.

Tati Jacques. Stage name of Jacques Tatischeff 1908–1982. French comic actor, director, and writer. He portrayed Monsieur Hulot, a character embodying polite opposition to modern mechanization in a series of films including *Les Vacances de M Hulot/Monsieur Hulot's Holiday* 1953.

Tatlin Vladimir 1885–1953. Russian artist, cofounder of **Constructivism**. After encountering Cubism in Paris 1913 he evolved his first Constructivist works, using raw materials such as tin, glass, plaster, and wood to create abstract sculptures which he suspended in the air.

Tatum Art(hur) 1910–1956. US jazz pianist, who worked mainly as a soloist. His technique and chromatic harmonies influenced many musicians. He played improvisations with the guitarist Tiny Grimes (1916–) in a trio from 1943.

Tatum Edward Lawrie 1909–1975. US microbiologist. For his work on biochemical genetics, he shared the 1958 Nobel Prize for Medicine with George Beadle and Joshua Lederberg.

Taube Henry 1915– . US chemist, who established the basis of modern inorganic chemistry by his study of the loss or gain of electrons by atoms during chemical reactions. He was awarded a Nobel prize in 1983.

Taussig Helen Brooke 1898–1986. US cardiologist who developed surgery for 'blue' babies. Such babies are born with one or more congenital deformities, which cause the blood to circulate in the body without first passing through the lungs. The babies are chronically short of oxygen and may not survive.

Tavener John (Kenneth) 1944– . English composer, whose individual and sometimes abrasive works include the dramatic cantata *The Whale* 1968 and the opera *Thérèse* 1979. He has also composed music for the Eastern Orthodox Church.

Taverner John 1495–1545. English organist and composer. He wrote masses and motets in polyphonic style, showing great contrapuntal skill, but as a Protestant renounced his art. He was imprisoned 1528 for heresy, and, as an agent of Thomas Cromwell, assisted in the dissolution of the monasteries.

Taylor A(lan) J(ohn) P(ercivale) 1906– . British historian and television lecturer. International history lecturer at Oxford 1953–63, his books include *The Struggle for Mastery in Europe* 1954, *The Origins of World War II* 1961, and *English History 1914–1945* 1965.

Taylor Elizabeth (born Coles) 1912–1975. British novelist. Her books include *At Mrs Lippincote's* 1946 and *Angel* 1957.

Taylor Elizabeth 1932– . US actress, born in England, whose films include *National Velvet* 1944, *Cat on a Hot Tin Roof* 1958, *Butterfield 8* 1960 (Academy award), *Cleopatra* 1963, and *Who's Afraid of Virginia Woolf?* 1966. Her seven husbands have included the

Tchaikovsky Russian composer Pyotr Il'yich Tchaikovsky.

actors Michael Wilding (1912–1979) and Richard ◊Burton (twice).

Taylor Frederick Winslow 1856–1915. US engineer and management consultant, the founder of scientific management. His ideas, published in *Principles of Scientific Management* 1911, were based on the breakdown of work to the simplest tasks, the separation of planning from execution of tasks, and the introduction of time and motion studies. His methods were most clearly expressed in assembly-line factories, but have been criticized for degrading and alienating workers and producing managerial dictatorship.

Tchaikovsky Pyotr Il'yich 1840–1893. Russian composer. His strong sense of melody, personal expression, and brilliant orchestration are clear throughout his many Romantic works, which include six symphonies; three piano concertos and a violin concerto; operas (for example, *Eugene Onegin* 1879); ballets (for example *The Nutcracker* 1892); orchestral fantasies (for example *Romeo and Juliet* 1870); and chamber and vocal music.

Professor of harmony at Moscow in 1865, he later met ◊Balakirev, becoming involved with the nationalist movement in music. He was the first Russian composer to establish a reputation with Western audiences.

Tebaldi Renata 1922– . Italian dramatic soprano, renowned for the controlled purity of her voice and for her roles in ◊Puccini operas.

Tebbit Norman 1931– . British Conservative politician. His first career was as an airline pilot, when he held various trade-union posts. He was minister for employment 1981–83, minister for trade and industry 1983–85, chancellor of the Duchy of Lancaster 1985–87, and chairman of the party 1985–87. He was injured in a bomb blast during the 1985 Conservative Party conference in Brighton.

Tecumseh 1768–1813. North American Indian chief of the Shawnee. He attempted to unite the Indian peoples from Canada to Florida against the encroachment of white settlers, but the defeat of his brother **Tenskwatawa**, 'The Prophet', at the battle of Tippecanoe Nov 1811 by Governor W H Harrison, largely destroyed the confederacy built up by Tecumseh. He was commissioned a brigadier general in the British army during the War of 1812, and died in battle.

Tedder Arthur William, 1st Baron Tedder 1890–1967. UK marshal of the Royal Air Force in World War II. As deputy supreme commander under US general Eisenhower 1943–45, he was largely responsible for the initial success of the 1944 Normandy landings.

Teg Bahadur 1621–1675. Indian religious leader, ninth guru (teacher) of Sikhism 1664–75, executed for refusing to renounce his faith.

Teilhard de Chardin Pierre 1881–1955. French Jesuit mystic. Publication of his *Le Phénomène humain/The Phenomenon of Man* 1955 was delayed until after his death by the embargo of his superiors. He envisaged humanity as eventually in charge of its own evolution, and developed the concept of the *noosphere*, the unconscious union of thought among human beings.

Born in the Puy-de-Dôme, he entered the Society of Jesus in 1899, was ordained in 1911, and during World War I was a stretcher bearer, taking his final vows in 1918.

Te Kanawa Kiri 1944– . New Zealand opera singer. Her first major role was the Countess in Mozart's *The Marriage of Figaro* at Covent Garden, London, 1971. She later sang at the wedding of Prince Charles in 1980.

Telemann Georg Philipp 1681–1767. German Baroque composer, organist, and conductor at the Johanneum, Hamburg, from 1721. He was one of the most prolific composers ever, producing 25 operas, 1,800 church cantatas, hundreds of other vocal works, and 600 instrumental works.

Telford Thomas 1757–1834. Scottish civil engineer who opened up N Scotland by building roads and waterways. He constructed many aqueducts and canals including the Caledonian 1802–23, and erected the Menai road suspension bridge 1819–26, a structure scarcely tried previously in England. In Scotland he constructed over 1,600 km/1,000 mi of road, and 1,200 bridges, churches, and harbours.

Teller Edward 1908– . US physicist, known as the 'father' of the H-bomb, which he worked on at Los Alamos in World War II. He was born in Hungary and emigrated to the USA in 1935. He was a key witness against ◊Oppenheimer at the security hearings in 1954. He was widely believed to be the model for the leading character in Kubrick's 1964 film *Dr Strangelove*. More recently he has been one of the leading supporters of the Star Wars programme (see ◊Reagan).

Temple Shirley 1928– . US actress, who became the most successful child star of the 1930s. Her films include *Bright Eyes* 1934, in which she sang 'On the Good Ship Lollipop'. As Shirley Temple Black, she was active in the Republican Party, and was US Chief of Protocol 1976–77. She was appointed US ambassador to Czechoslovakia in 1989.

Tenniel John 1820–1914. British illustrator and cartoonist, known for his illustrations for Lewis Carroll's *Alice's Adventures in Wonderland* 1865 and *Through the Looking-Glass* 1872. He joined the satirical magazine *Punch* in 1850, and for over 50 years he was one of its leading cartoonists.

Tennstedt Klaus 1926– . East German conductor, musical director of the London Philharmonic Orchestra 1983–87. He is renowned for his interpretations of works by Mozart, Beethoven, Bruckner, and Mahler.

Tennyson Alfred, 1st Baron 1809–1892. English poet, poet laureate 1850–96, noted for the majestic musical language of his verse. His works include 'The Lady of Shalott', 'The Lotus Eaters', 'Ulysses', 'Break, Break, Break', 'The Charge of the Light Brigade'; the longer narratives *Locksley Hall* 1832, and *Maud* 1855; the elegy *In Memoriam* 1850; and a long series of poems on the Arthurian legends *The Idylls of the King* 1857–85.

Tennyson was born at Somersby, Lincolnshire. The death of A H Hallam (a close friend during his years at Trinity College, Cambridge) 1833 prompted the elegiac *In Memoriam*, unpublished until 1850, the year in which he succeeded Wordsworth as poet laureate and married Emily Sellwood.

Tenzing Norgay known as *Sherpa Tenzing* 1914–1986. Nepalese mountaineer. In 1953 he was the first, with Edmund Hillary, to reach the summit of Mount Everest.

He had previously made 19 Himalayan expeditions as a porter. He subsequently became a director of the Himalayan Mountaineering Institute, Darjeeling.

Terborch Gerard 1617–1681. Dutch painter of small-scale portraits and genre (everyday) scenes, mainly of soldiers at rest or wealthy families in their homes. He travelled widely in Europe. *The Peace of Münster* 1648 (National Gallery, London) is an official group portrait.

Terbrugghen Hendrik 1588–1629. Dutch painter, a leader of the *Utrecht school* with Honthorst. He visited Rome around 1604 and was inspired by Caravaggio's work. He painted religious subjects and genre (everyday) scenes.

Terence (Publius Terentius Afer) 190–159 BC. Roman dramatist, born in Carthage and brought as a slave to Rome, where he was freed and came under ◊Scipio's patronage. His surviving six comedies (including *The Eunuch* 161 BC) are subtly characterized and based on Greek models.

Teresa, St 1515–1582. Spanish mystic, born in Avila. She became a Carmelite nun, and in 1562 founded a new and stricter order. She was subject to fainting fits, during which she saw visions. She wrote *The Way to Perfection* 1583, and an autobiography, *Life of the Mother Theresa of Jesus* 1611. In 1622 she was canonized, and became the first woman Doctor of the Church 1970.

Tereshkova Valentina Vladimirovna 1937– . Soviet cosmonaut, the first woman to fly in space. In June 1963 she made a three-day flight in Vostok 6, orbiting the Earth 48 times.

Terry Ellen 1847–1928. British actress, leading lady to Henry ◊Irving from 1878. She excelled in Shakespearean roles, such as Ophelia in *Hamlet.* She had a correspondence with the playwright G B Shaw.

Terry (John) Quinlan 1937– . British architect. His work includes country houses in the Neo-Classical style, for example Merks Hall, Great Dunmow, Essex, 1982, and the larger-scale Richmond, London, riverside project, commissioned 1984.

Tertullian Quintus Septimius Florens AD 155–222. Carthaginian Father of the Church, the first important Christian writer in Latin.

Tesla Nikola 1856–1943. Croatian electrical engineer, who emigrated to the USA 1884. He invented fluorescent lighting, the Tesla induction motor, and the Tesla coil, and developed the alternating current (AC) electrical supply system.

Thackeray William Makepeace 1811–1863. English novelist and essayist, born in Calcutta, India. He was a regular contributor to *Fraser's Magazine* and *Punch. Vanity Fair* 1847–48 was his first novel, followed by *Pendennis* 1848, *Henry Esmond* 1852 (and its sequel *The Virginians* 1857–59), and *The Newcomes* 1853–55, in which Thackeray's tendency to sentimentality is most marked.

Son of an East India Company official, he was educated at Charterhouse and Trinity College, Cambridge. He studied law in the Middle Temple, and then art in Paris, before ultimately settling to journalism in London. Other works include *The Book of Snobs* 1848 and the fairy tale *The Rose and the Ring* 1855.

Thaïs 4th century BC. Greek courtesan, mistress of ◊Alexander the Great and later wife of ◊Ptolemy I, king of Egypt. She allegedly instigated the burning of Persepolis.

Thalberg Irving 1899–1936. US film production executive, of German parents. In 1924 he became production supervisor of the newly formed Metro-Goldwyn-Mayer (MGM). He was responsible for such prestige films as *Ben-Hur* 1926 and *Mutiny on the Bounty* 1935. With Louis B Mayer he built up MGM into one of the biggest Hollywood studios of the 1930s.

Thales 640–546 BC. Greek philosopher and scientist. He made advances in geometry, predicted an eclipse of the Sun in 585 BC, and as a philosophical materialist, theorized that water was the first

Thatcher Conservative politician Margaret Thatcher, UK prime minister since 1979.

principle of all things, that the Earth floated on water, and so proposed an explanation for earthquakes. He lived at Miletus in Asia Minor.

Thatcher Margaret Hilda (born Roberts) 1925– . British Conservative politician, in Parliament from 1959, party leader from 1975, and prime minister from 1979. Landmarks of the Thatcher government include the Falklands conflict 1982; the 1984–85 miners' strike; large-scale privatization, combined with attempted control of the money supply and reduction of state borrowing; the attempt to suppress the publication of Peter ◊Wright's book *Spycatcher*; the Anglo-Irish Agreement 1985; the introduction of the community charge, or poll tax; and increases in home and share ownership, unemployment, interest rates, trade deficit, and homelessness.

Her father, a grocer, was later mayor of Grantham. She was educated at Oxford and qualified as a research chemist and barrister. As minister of education 1970–74, she caused controversy when she abolished free milk for schoolchildren. She defeated Heath for the Conservative leadership 1975, and became prime minister 1979. She was re-elected 1983 and 1987, the first British prime minister to be elected for a third term since Lord Liverpool.

Themistocles *c.*525–*c.*460 BC. Athenian soldier and politician. Largely through his policies in Athens (creating its navy and strengthening its walls) Greece was saved from Persian conquest. He fought with distinction in the Battle of Salamis 480 BC during the Persian War. About 470 BC he was accused of embezzlement and conspiracy against Athens, and banished by Spartan influence. He fled to Asia, where Artaxerxes, the Persian king, received him with favour.

Theocritus *c.*310–*c.*250 BC. Greek poet. Probably born at Syracuse, he spent much of his life at Alexandria. His *Idylls* became models for later pastoral poetry.

Theodora 508–548. Byzantine empress from 527, originally the mistress of Emperor Justinian, and his consort from about 523. She earned a reputation for charity and courage.

Theodorakis Mikis 1925– . Greek composer. He was imprisoned 1967–70 for attempting to overthrow the military regime of Greece.

Theodoric of Freiburg *c.*1250–1310. German friar and scientist. He studied in Paris 1275–77. In his work *De Iride/On the Rainbow* he describes how he used a water-filled sphere to simulate a raindrop, and determined that colours are formed in the raindrops and that light is reflected within the drop and can be reflected again, which explains secondary rainbows.

Theodoric the Great *c.*455–526. King of the Ostrogoths from 474 in succession to his father. He invaded Italy 488, overthrew King Odoacer (whom he murdered) and established his own Ostrogothic kingdom there, with its capital in Ravenna. He had no strong successor, and his kingdom eventually became part of the Byzantine Empire of Justinian.

Theodosius II 401–450. Byzantine emperor from 408, who defeated the Persians 421 and 441, and from 441 bought off ◊Attila's Huns with tribute.

Theresa Mother. Born Agnes Bojaxhiu 1910– . Roman Catholic nun. She was born in Skopje, Albania and at 18 entered a Calcutta convent and became a teacher. In 1948 she became an Indian citizen and founded the Missionaries of Charity, an order for men and women based in Calcutta that especially helps abandoned children and the dying. Nobel Peace Prize 1979.

Thérèse of Lisieux 1873–1897. French saint. She was born at Alençon, and entered a Carmelite convent at Lisieux at 15, where her holy life induced her superior to ask her to write her spiritual autobiography. She advocated the 'Little Way of Goodness' in small things in everyday life, and became known as the 'Little Flower of Jesus'. She died of tuberculosis and was canonized 1925.

Theroux Paul Edward 1941– . US novelist and travel writer whose works include *Saint Jack* 1973, *Picture Palace* 1978, *The Mosquito Coast* 1981, *Doctor Slaughter* 1984, and *The Great Railway Bazaar* 1975.

Thesiger Wilfred Patrick 1912– . English explorer and writer. His travels and military adventures in

Abyssinia, North Africa, and Arabia are recounted in a number of books including *Arabian Sands* 1959, *Desert Marsh and Mountain* 1979, and the autobiographical *The Life of My Choice* 1987.

Thespis 6th century BC. Greek poet, born in Attica, said to have introduced the first actor into plays (previously presented by choruses only), hence the word *thespian* for an actor. He was also said to have invented tragedy and to have introduced the wearing of linen masks.

Thibault Anatole-François. Real name of French writer Anatole ◊France.

Thiers Louis Adolphe 1797–1877. French politician and historian. He held cabinet posts under Louis Philippe, led the parliamentary opposition to Napoleon III from 1863, and as head of the provisional government 1871 negotiated peace with Prussia and suppressed the briefly autonomous Paris Commune. He was first president of the Third Republic 1871–73. His books include *Histoire de la Révolution française*/*History of the French Revolution* 1823–27.

Thistlewood Arthur 1770–1820. English Radical. A follower of the pamphleteer Thomas Spence (1750–1814), he was active in the Radical movement and was executed as the chief leader of the Cato Street Conspiracy to murder ◊Castlereagh and his ministers.

Thomas Dylan (Marlais) 1914–1953. Welsh poet. His poems include the celebration of his 30th birthday 'Poem in October' and the evocation of his youth 'Fern Hill' 1946. His radio play *Under Milk Wood* 1954 and the short stories of *Portrait of the Artist as a Young Dog* 1940 are autobiographical.

Born in Swansea, son of the English master at the local grammar school where he was educated, he worked as a reporter on the *South Wales Evening Post*, then settled as a journalist in London and published his first volume *Eighteen Poems* in 1934.

Thomas (Philip) Edward 1878–1917. British poet and author of books on the English countryside. In 1916 he published *Six Poems* under the pseudonym Edward Eastaway; volumes under his own name were *Poems* 1917 and *Last Poems* 1918. Thomas was killed in action in World War I at Arras. His wife *Helen Thomas* (1877–1967) published the biographical volumes *As it Was* 1926, and *World without End* 1931.

Thomas Ronald Stuart 1913– . Welsh poet. His verse, as in *Song at the Year's Turning* 1955, contrasts traditional Welsh values with encroaching 'English' sterility.

Thomas Terry. Stage name of Thomas Terry Hoar Stevens 1911–1990. British film comedy actor, who portrayed upper-class English fools in such films as *I'm All Right Jack* 1959, *It's a Mad, Mad, Mad, Mad World* 1963, and *How To Murder Your Wife* 1965.

Thomas à Kempis 1380–1471. German Augustinian monk who lived at the monastery of Zwolle. He took his name from his birthplace Kempen; his real surname was Hammerken. His *Die Imitatione Christi*/*Imitation of Christ* is probably the most widely known devotional work ever written.

Thomas, St in the New Testament, one of the 12 Apostles, said to have preached in S India, hence the ancient churches there were referred to as the 'Christians of St Thomas'. He is not the author of the Gospel of St Thomas, the Gnostic collection of Jesus' sayings.

Thompson David 1770–1857. Canadian explorer and surveyor who mapped extensive areas of western Canada including the Columbia River for the Hudson's Bay Company 1789–1811.

Thompson Flora 1877–1948. English novelist, whose trilogy *Lark Rise to Candleford* 1945 deals with late Victorian rural life.

Thompson Francis 1859–1907. British poet. Born in Preston, he settled in London, where he fell into poverty and ill health. In *Sister Songs* 1895 and *New Poems* 1897 Thompson, who was a Roman Catholic, expressed a mystic view of life.

Thompson Francis Morgan 'Daley' 1958– . English decathlete, who has broken the world decathlon record four times since winning the Commonwealth Games decathlon title in 1978. He has won two more Commonwealth titles, two Olympic gold medals (1980, 1984) three European titles, and a world title.

Thompson John Taliaferro 1860–1940. US colonel, inventor of the Thompson sub-machine-gun.

Thomsen Christian (Jürgensen) 1788–1865. Danish archaeologist. He devised the classification of prehistoric cultures into Stone Age, Bronze Age, and Iron Age.

Thomson Elihu 1853–1937. US inventor. He founded, with E J Houston, the Thomson-Houston Electric Company 1882, later merging with the Edison Company to form the General Electric Company. He made important advances into the nature of the electric arc, and invented the first high-frequency dynamo and transformer.

Thomson George Paget 1892–1975. English physicist, son of J J ◊Thomson. His work on interference phenomena in the scattering of electrons by crystals helped to confirm the wave-like nature of particles. He shared a Nobel prize with C J ◊Davisson 1937.

Thomson James 1700–1748. Scottish poet, whose descriptive blank verse poem *The Seasons* 1726–30 was a forerunner of the Romantic movement. He also wrote the words of 'Rule, Britannia'.

Thomson James 1834–1882. Scottish poet, remembered for his despairing poem 'The City of Dreadful Night' 1880.

Thomson J(oseph) J(ohn) 1856–1940. English physicist, who discovered the electron. He was responsible for organizing the Cavendish atomic research laboratory at Cambridge. His work inaugurated the electrical theory of the atom, and his elucidation of positive rays and their application to an analysis of neon led to ◊Aston's discovery of isotopes (atoms of the same element but having different masses). Nobel prize 1906.

Thomson Virgil 1896–1989. US composer and critic. His large body of work, characterized by a clarity and simplicity of style, includes operas such as *Four Saints in Three Acts* (libretto by Gertrude Stein) 1934; orchestral, choral, and chamber music; and film scores.

Thoreau Henry David 1817–1862. US author and naturalist. His work *Walden, or Life in the Woods* 1854 stimulated the back-to-nature movement, and he completed some 30 volumes based on his daily nature walks. His essay 'Civil Disobedience' 1849, advocating peaceful resistance to unjust laws, had a wide impact.

Thorndike Sybil 1882–1976. British actress for whom Shaw wrote *St Joan*. The Thorndike Theatre (1969), Leatherhead, Surrey, England, is named after her.

Thorpe Jeremy 1929– . British Liberal politician, leader of the Liberal Party 1967–76.

Thorwaldsen Bertel 1770–1844. Danish Neo-Classical sculptor. He went to Italy on a scholarship in 1796 and stayed in Rome for most of his life, producing portraits, monuments, religious and mythological works. Much of his work is housed in the Thorvaldsen Museum, Copenhagen.

Thothmes four Egyptian kings of the 18th dynasty, including:

Thothmes I King of Egypt 1540–1501 BC. He founded the Egyptian empire in Syria.

Thothmes III King of Egypt about 1500–1446 BC. He extended the empire to the Euphrates, and conquered Nubia. He was a grandson of Thothmes I.

Thucydides 460–400 BC. Athenian historian, who exercised command in the Peloponnesian War with Sparta 424 with so little success that he was banished until 404. In his *History of the Peloponnesian War*, he attempted a scientific impartiality.

Thünen Johann von 1785–1850. German economist and geographer, who believed that the success of a state depends on the well-being of its farmers. His book *The Isolated State* 1820, a pioneering study of land use, includes the earliest example of **marginal productivity theory**, a theory which Thünen developed to calculate the natural wage for a farmworker. He has been described as the first modern economist.

Thurber James (Grover) 1894–1961. US humorist. His short stories, written mainly for the *New Yorker* magazine, include 'The Secret Life of Walter Mitty' 1932, and his doodle drawings include fanciful impressions of dogs. Partially

Tiberius A bust of the Roman emperor Tiberius.

blind from childhood, he became totally blind in the last ten years of his life, but continued to work.

Thyssen Fritz 1873–1951. German industrialist who based his business on the Ruhr iron and steel industry. Fearful of the communist threat, Thyssen became an early supporter of Hitler and contributed large amounts of money to his early political campaigns. By 1939 he had broken with the Nazis and fled first to Switzerland and later to Italy, where in 1941 he was sent to a concentration camp. Released in 1945, he was ordered to surrender 15% of his property.

Tiberius Claudius Nero 42 BC–AD 37. Roman emperor, the stepson, adopted son, and successor of Augustus from AD 14. A distinguished soldier, he was a conscientious ruler under whom the empire prospered.

Tieck Johann Ludwig 1773–1853. German Romantic poet and collector of folk-tales, some of which he dramatized, for example 'Puss in Boots'.

Tiepolo Giovanni Battista 1696–1770. Italian painter, born in Venice. He created monumental Rococo decorative schemes in palaces and churches in NE Italy, SW Germany, and in Madrid (1762–70). The style is light-hearted, the palette light and warm, and he made great play with illusion.

Tiepolo painted religious and, above all, historical or allegorical pictures, for example scenes from the life of Cleopatra 1745 (Palazzo Labia, Venice) and from the life of Frederick Barbarossa 1757 (Kaisersaal, Würzburg Palace). His sons were among his many assistants.

Tiffany Louis Comfort 1848–1933. US artist and glassmaker, son of Charles Louis Tiffany who founded the New York jewellers. He produced stained glass windows, iridescent Favrile (Latin *faber* 'craftsman') glass, and lampshades.

Tikhonov Nikolai 1905– . Soviet politician. He was a close associate of President Brezhnev, joining the Politburo 1979, and was prime minister (chairman of the Council of Ministers) 1980–85. In Apr 1989 he was removed from the central committee.

Tilly Jan Tserklaes, Count Tilly 1559–1632. Flemish commander of the army of the Catholic League and imperial forces in the Thirty Years' War. Notorious for his storming of Magdeburg, E Germany, 1631, he was defeated by the Swedish king Gustavus Adolphus at Breitenfeld, and at the river Lech in SW Germany, where he was mortally wounded.

Tinbergen Jan 1903–1988. Dutch economist. He shared a Nobel prize 1969 with Ragnar Frisch for his work on econometrics (the mathematical-statistical expression of economic theory).

Tinbergen Nikolaas 1907– . Dutch zoologist. He was one of the founders of ethology, the scientific study of animal behaviour in natural surroundings. Specializing in the study of instinctive behaviour, he shared a Nobel prize with Konrad Lorenz and Karl von ◊Frisch 1973. He is the brother of Jan Tinbergen.

Ting Samuel 1936– . US high energy physicist. In 1974 he detected a new subatomic particle, known as the J particle, similar to the ψ(psi) particle found by Burton ◊Richter, with whom he shared the 1976 Nobel Prize for Physics.

Tintoretto real name Jacopo Robusti 1518–1594. Italian painter, active in Venice. His dramatic religious paintings are spectacularly lit and full of movement, such as his canvases of the lives of Christ and the Virgin in the Scuola di San Rocco, Venice, 1564–88.

He was a student of ◊Titian and admirer of Michelangelo. *The Miracle of St Mark Rescuing a Slave* 1548 (Accademia, Venice) marked the start of his successful career. In the Scuola di San Rocco he created a sequence of heroic scenes with bold gesture and foreshortening, and effects of supernatural light. He also painted canvases for the Doge's Palace.

Tiomkin Dimitri 1899–1979. Russian composer who lived in the USA from 1925. From 1930 he wrote Holywood film scores including music for *Duel in the Sun* 1946, *The Thing* 1951, and *Rio Bravo* 1959. His score for *High Noon* 1952 won him an Academy Award.

Tippett Michael (Kemp) 1905– . English composer, whose works include the operas *The Midsummer Marriage* 1952 and *The Knot Garden* 1970; four symphonies; *Songs for Ariel* 1962; and choral music including *The Mask of Time* 1982.

Tippu Sultan *c.* 1750–1799. Sultan of Mysore (now Karnataka) from the death of his father, ◊Hyder Ali, in 1782. He died of wounds when his capital, Seringapatam, was captured by the British. His rocket brigade led Sir William Congreve (1772–1828) to develop the weapon for use in the Napoleonic Wars.

Tirpitz Alfred von 1849–1930. German admiral. As secretary for the navy 1897–1916, he created the modern German navy and planned the World War I U-boat campaign.

Tirso de Molina pen name of Gabriel Telléz 1571–1648. Spanish dramatist and monk, who wrote more than 400 plays, of which eight are extant, including comedies, historical and biblical dramas, and a series based on the legend of Don Juan.

Tiselius Arne 1902–1971. Swedish chemist who developed a powerful method of chemical analysis known as electrophoresis. Tiselius applied his new techniques to the analysis of animal proteins and received the 1948 Nobel Prize for Chemistry.

Tissot James (Joseph Jacques) 1836–1902. French painter who produced detailed portraits of fashionable Victorian society during a ten-year stay in England.

Titian Anglicized form of the name of Tiziano Vecellio *c.* 1487–1576. Italian painter, active in Venice, one of the greatest artists of the High Renaissance. In 1533 he became court painter to Charles V, Holy Roman emperor, whose son Philip II of Spain later became his patron. Titian's work is richly coloured, with inventive composition. He produced a vast number of portraits, religious paintings, and mythological scenes, including *Bacchus and Ariadne* 1520–23, *Venus and Adonis* 1554, and the *Entombment of Christ* 1559.

Titian probably studied with Giovanni ◊Bellini but also learned much from ◊Giorgione and seems to have completed some of Giorgione's unfinished works, such as *Noli Me Tangere* (National Gallery, London). His first great painting is the *Assumption of the Virgin* 1518 (Church of the Frari, Venice), typically sublime in mood, with upward-thrusting layers of figures. Three large mythologies painted in the next few years for the d'Estes of Ferrara show yet more brilliant use of colour, and numerous statuesque figures suggest the influence of classical art. By the 1530s Titian's reputation was widespread.

In the 1540s Titian visited Rome to paint the pope; in Augsburg, Germany, 1548–49 and 1550–51 he painted members of the imperial court. In his later years he produced a series

Tito Marshal Tito, president of Yugoslavia 1953–80.

of mythologies for Philip II, notably *The Rape of Europa* 1562 (Isabella Stewart Gardner Museum, Boston, Massachusetts). His handling became increasingly free and his palette sombre, but his work remained full of drama. He made an impact not just on Venetian painting but on art throughout Europe.

Tito adopted name of Josip Broz 1892–1980. Yugoslav soldier and communist politician. In World War II he organized the National Liberation Army to carry on guerrilla warfare against the German invasion 1941, and was created marshal 1943. As prime minister 1946–53 and president from 1953, he followed a foreign policy of 'positive neutralism'.

Born in Croatia, Tito served in the Austrian army during World War I, was captured by the Russians, and fought in the Red Army during the Civil Wars. Returning to Yugoslavia 1923, he became prominent as a Communist and during World War II as partisan leader against the Nazis. In 1943 he established a provisional government, and with Soviet help proclaimed the federal republic 1945. As prime minister, he settled the Yugoslav minorities question on a federal basis, and in 1953 took the newly created post of president (for life from 1974). In 1948 he was attacked by the Cominform, the international communist information bureau, particularly in the USSR, for his successful system of decentralized profit-sharing workers' councils, and became the leader of the non-aligned movement.

Titus Flavius Sabinus Vespasianus AD 39–81. Roman emperor from AD 79. Eldest son of ◊Vespasian, he stormed Jerusalem 70 to end the Jewish revolt in Roman Palestine. He completed the Colosseum, and enjoyed a peaceful reign, except for ◊Agricola's campaigns in Britain.

Tobin James 1918– . US Keynesian economist. He was awarded a Nobel prize 1981 for his 'general equilibrium' theory, which states that other criteria than monetary considerations are applied by households and firms when making decisions on consumption and investment.

Tocqueville Alexis de 1805–1859. French politician and political scientist, author of the first analytical study of the US constitution, *De la Démocratie en Amérique/Democracy in America* 1835, and of a penetrating description of France before the Revolution, *L'Ancien Régime et la Révolution/The Old Regime and the Revolution* 1856.

Todd Alexander, Baron Todd 1907– . British organic chemist, who won the Nobel Prize for Chemistry 1957 for his work on the role of nucleic acids in genetics. He also synthesized vitamins B_1, B_{12}, and E.

Todd began his work on the synthesis of organic molecules in 1934. He was professor at Manchester 1938–44 and Cambridge 1944–71.

Todd 'Ron' (Ronald) 1927– . British trade union leader. The son of a London market trader, he rose from shop steward to general secretary of Britain's largest trade union, the Transport and General Workers' (TGWU). A naturally honest and forthright man, although backing the Labour Party leadership, he has openly criticised its attitude towards nuclear disarmament.

Todt Fritz 1891–1942. German engineer, who was responsible for the construction of the autobahns (German motorways) and, in World War II, the Siegfried Line and the Atlantic Wall.

Togare stage name of Georg Kulovits 1900–1988. Austrian wild-animal tamer and circus performer. Togare invented the character of the exotic Oriental liontamer after watching Douglas Fairbanks in *The Thief of Baghdad* 1923. In his circus appearances he displayed a nonchalant disregard for danger.

Togliatti Palmiro 1893–1964. Founding member of the Italian Communist Party in 1921, and effectively leader for almost 40 years from 1926 until his death. In exile from 1926 until 1944, he returned to become a member of Badoglio's government and held office until 1946.

Togliatti trained as a lawyer, but served in the army and was wounded during World War I. He was associated with the revolutionary wing of the Italian socialist party which left to form the Communist party in 1921. From 1922–24 he edited the newspaper *Il Comunista* and became a member of the party's central committee. In Moscow when Mussolini outlawed the party, he stayed there to become a leading member of the Comintern joining the Secretariat in 1935. Returning to Italy after Mussolini's downfall, he advocated coalition politics with other leftist and democratic parties, a policy which came to fruition in the elections of 1948 where the communists won 135 seats.

Togo Heihachiro 1846–1934. Japanese admiral who commanded the fleet at the battle of Tsushima Strait 27 May 1905 when Japan decisively defeated the Russians and effectively ended the Russo-Japanese war of 1904–05.

Tojo Hideki 1884–1948. Japanese general and prime minister 1941–44. Promoted to Chief of Staff of the Guangdong army 1937, he served as minister for war 1938–39 and 1940–41. He was held responsible for defeats in the Pacific 1944 and forced to resign. He was hanged as a war criminal.

Toland Gregory 1904–1948. US director of film photography, who used deep focus to good effect in such films as *Wuthering Heights* 1939, *Citizen Kane* 1941, *The Grapes of Wrath* 1940, and *The Best Years of our Lives* 1946.

Tolkien J(ohn) R(onald) R(euel) 1892–1973. English writer, who created the fictional world of Middle Earth in *The Hobbit* 1937 and the trilogy *The Lord of the Rings* 1954–55, fantasy novels peopled with hobbits, dwarves, and strange magical creatures. His work became a cult in the 1960s and had many imitations. He was professor of Anglo-Saxon 1925–45, and Merton professor of English at Oxford, 1945–59.

Tolstoy Leo Nikolaievich 1828–1910. Russian novelist, who wrote *Tales from Sebastopol* 1856, *War and Peace* 1863–69, and *Anna Karenina* 1873–77. From 1880 Tolstoy underwent a profound spiritual crisis and took up moral positions including passive resistance to evil, rejection of authority (religious or civil) and of private ownership, and a return to basic mystical Christianity. He was excommunicated by the Orthodox Church, and his later works were banned.

Tolstoy was born of noble family at Yasnaya Polyana, near Tula, and fought in the Crimean War. His first published work was *Childhood* 1852, the first part of the trilogy that was completed with *Boyhood* 1854 and *Youth* 1857; later books include *What I Believe* 1883 and *The Kreutzer Sonata* 1889, and the novel *Resurrection* 1900. His home became a place of pilgrimage. His desire to give up his property and live as a peasant disrupted his family life, and he finally fled his home and died of pneumonia at the railway station at Astapovo.

Tomasi Giuseppe, Prince of Lampedusa. Italian writer; see ◊Lampedusa.

Tombaugh Clyde (William) 1906– . US astronomer, who discovered the planet Pluto 1930.

Born in Streator, Illinois, Tombaugh became an assistant at the Lowell Observatory in Flagstaff, Arizona, in 1929, and photographed the sky in search of an undiscovered remote planet as predicted by the observatory's founder, Percival ◊Lowell. Tombaugh found Pluto 18 Feb 1930, from plates taken three weeks earlier. He continued his search for new planets across the entire sky; his failure to find any placed strict limits on the possible existence of planets beyond Pluto.

Tone (Theobald) Wolfe 1763–1798. Irish nationalist, called to the Bar 1789, and prominent in the revolutionary society of the United Irishmen. In 1798 he accompanied the French invasion of Ireland, was captured and condemned to death, but slit his own throat in prison.

Tönnies Ferdinand 1855–1936. German social theorist and philosopher, one of the founders of the sociological tradition of community studies and urban sociology through his key work, *Gemeinschaft–Gesellschaft* 1887.

Tönnies contrasted the nature of social relationships in traditional societies and small organizations (*Gemeinschaft*, 'community') with those in modern industrial societies and large organizations (*Gesellschaft*, 'association'). He was pessimistic about the effect of industrialization and urbanization on the social and moral order, seeing them as a threat to traditional society's sense of community.

Tooke John Horne 1736–1812. British politician, who established the Constitutional Society for parliamentary reform 1771. He was elected a member of Parliament 1801.

Toplady Augustus Montague 1740–1778. British Anglican priest, the author of the hymn 'Rock of Ages' 1775.

Torquemada Tomás de 1420–1498. Spanish Dominican friar, confessor to Queen Isabella I. In 1483 he revived the anti-heretical Inquisition on her behalf, and at least 2,000 'heretics' were burned; Torquemada also expelled the Jews from Spain, with a resultant decline of the economy.

Torres-García Joaquim 1874–1949. Uruguayan artist, born in Montevideo. In Paris from 1926, he was influenced by ◊Mondrian and others and, after going to Madrid in 1932, by Inca and Nazca pottery. His mature style is based on a grid pattern derived from the classical ratio known as the golden section, about 1·6 : 1.

Torricelli Evangelista 1608–1647. Italian physicist and pupil of ◊Galileo, who devised the mercury barometer.

Torvill and Dean Jayne Torvill 1957– and Christopher Dean 1959– . British ice-dance champions, both from Nottingham. They won the world title four times and were the 1984 Olympic champions.

Toscanini Arturo 1867–1957. Italian conductor. He made La Scala, Milan (where he conducted 1898–1903, 1906–08, and 1921–29), the world's leading opera house. He was opposed to the Fascist regime and in 1936 returned to the USA, where he had conducted at the Metropolitan Opera 1908–15. The NBC Symphony Orchestra was formed for him in 1937. He retired in 1954.

Totila died 522. King of the Ostrogoths, who warred with the Byzantine emperor Justinian for Italy, and was killed by the general Narses at the battle of Taginae in the Apennines.

Totò stage name of Antonio Furst de Curtis Gagliardi Ducas Comneno di Bisanzio 1898–1967. Italian comedian who moved to films from the music hall. Something of a national institution, his films, such as *Totò le Moko* 1949 and *L'Oro di Napoli/Gold of Naples* 1954, made him the most famous comic actor of his generation in Italy.

Toulouse-Lautrec Henri Marie Raymond de 1864–1901. French artist, associated with the Impressionists. He was active in Paris, where he painted entertainers and prostitutes. From 1891 his lithograph posters were a great success.

Toulouse-Lautrec showed an early gift for drawing and in 1882 began to study art in Paris. He admired Goya's etchings and Degas's work, and in the 1880s he met Gauguin and was inspired by Japanese prints. Lautrec became a familiar figure drawing and painting in the dance halls, theatres, cafés, circuses, and brothels. Many of his finished works have the spontaneous character of sketches. He often painted with thinned-out oils on cardboard.

Tourneur Cyril 1575–1626. English dramatist. Little is known about his life but *The Atheist's Tragedy* 1611 and *The Revenger's Tragedy* 1607 (thought by some scholars to be by ◊Middleton) are among the most powerful of Jacobean dramas.

Toussaint L'Ouverture Pierre Dominique *c.* 1743–1803. Haitian revolutionary leader, born a slave. He joined the insurrection of 1791 against the French colonizers and was made governor by the revolutionary French government. He expelled the Spanish and British, but when the French emperor Napoleon reimposed slavery he revolted, was captured, and died in prison in France. In 1983 his remains were returned to Haiti.

Tower John 1925– . US Republican politician, a Texas senator 1961–83. Despite having been a paid arms-industry consultant, he was selected in 1989 by President Bush to serve as defence secretary, but the Senate refused to approve the appointment because of Tower's alleged heavy drinking.

He chaired the 1986–87 *Tower Commission*, which investigated aspects of the Irangate arms-for-hostages scandal.

Townes Charles 1915– . US physicist who, while working at Columbia, New York, succeeded in 1953, against much competition, in designing and constructing the first maser (the microwave equivalent of the laser). For this work, he shared the 1964 Nobel Prize for Physics with the Soviet physicists Basov and ◊Prokhorov.

Townsend Sue 1946– . English humorous novelist, author of *The Secret Diary of Adrian Mole, aged 13 3/4* 1982 and later sequels.

Townshend Charles 1725–1767. British politician, chancellor of the Exchequer 1766–67. The *Townshend Acts* taxed imports (such as tea, glass, and paper) into Britain's North American colonies, and precipitated the War of American Independence.

Townshend Charles, 2nd Viscount Townshend (known as 'Turnip' Townshend) 1674–1738. English politician and agriculturalist. He was secretary of state under George I 1714–17, when dismissed for opposing the king's foreign policy, and 1721–30, after which he retired to his farm and did valuable work in developing crop rotation and cultivating winter feeds for cattle (hence his nickname).

Through the successful development of his agricultural estate at Rainham in W Norfolk, Townshend brought a range of improved cultivation practices to wider public notice.

Townshend Pete 1945– . UK rock musician, former member of the Who rock group.

Toynbee Arnold 1852–1883. English economic historian, who coined the term 'industrial revolution' in his *Lectures on the Industrial Revolution*, published 1884. Toynbee Hall, an education settlement in the east end of London, was named after him.

Toynbee Arnold Joseph 1889–1975. English historian, whose *A Study of History* 1934–61 was an attempt to discover the laws governing the rise and fall of civilizations. He was the nephew of the economic historian Arnold Toynbee.

Tracy Spencer 1900–1967. US actor, noted for his understated, seemingly effortless natural performances. His films include *Captains Courageous* 1937 and *Boys' Town* 1938 (for both of which he won Academy Awards), and he starred with Katharine Hepburn in nine films, including *Adam's Rib* 1949 and *Guess Who's Coming to Dinner* 1967. His other films include *Bad Day at Black Rock* 1955.

Tradescant John 1570–1638. English gardener and botanist, who travelled widely in Europe and may have introduced the cos lettuce to England, from the Greek island bearing the same name. He was appointed as gardener to Charles I and was succeeded by his son, **John Tradescant the Younger** (1608–1662), after his death. The younger Tradescant undertook three plant-collecting trips to Virginia, USA, and Linnaeus named the genus **Tradescantia** in his honour.

The Tradescants introduced many new plants to Britain, including the acacia, lilac and occidental plane. Their collection of plants formed the nucleus of the Ashmolean Museum in Oxford.

Traherne Thomas 1637–1674. English mystic. His moving lyric poetry and his prose *Centuries of Meditations* were unpublished until 1903.

Trajan Marcus Ulpius (Trajanus) AD 52–117. Roman emperor and soldier, born in Seville. He was adopted as heir by ◊Nerva, whom he succeeded AD 98.

He was a just and conscientious ruler, corresponded with Pliny about the Christians, and conquered Dacia (Romania) 101–07 and much of Parthia (modern NE Iran). *Trajan's Column*, Rome, commemorates his victories.

Traven B(en). Pen name of Herman Feige 1882–1969. US novelist, born in Germany, whose true identity was unrevealed until 1979. His books include the bestseller *The Death Ship* 1926, and *The Treasure of Sierra Madre* 1934, filmed 1948 starring Humphrey Bogart.

Born in the part of Germany now in Poland, he was in turn known as the anarchist Maret Rut, Traven Torsvan, and Hollywood scriptwriter Hal Croves. Between the two world wars he lived in obscurity in Mexico and avoided recognition.

Travers Ben(jamin) 1886–1980. British dramatist. He wrote (for actors Tom Walls, Ralph Lynn, and Robertson Hare) the 'Aldwych farces' of the 1920s, so named from the London theatre in which they were played. They include *A Cuckoo in the Nest* 1925 and *Rookery Nook* 1926.

Travers Morris William 1872–1961. English chemist who, with William Ramsay, first identified the inert gases krypton, xenon, and radon (1894–1908).

Tree Herbert Beerbohm 1853–1917. British actor and theatre manager, half-brother of Max ◊Beerbohm. Noted for his Shakespeare productions, he was founder of the Royal Academy of Dramatic Art (RADA).

Trefusis Violet 1894–1972. British hostess and writer. Daughter of Mrs Keppel, who was later the mistress of Edward VII, she had a disastrous marriage to cavalry officer Denys Trefusis and a passionate elopement with Vita ◊Sackville-West.

Treitschke Heinrich von 1834–1896. German historian. At first a Liberal, he later adopted a Pan-German standpoint. He is known for the *Deutsche Geschichte im 19 Jahrhundert/History of Germany in the 19th Century* 1879–94.

Trenchard Hugh Montague, 1st Viscount Trenchard 1873–1956. British aviator and police commissioner. He commanded the Royal Flying Corps in World War I 1915–17, and 1918–29 organized the Royal Air Force, becoming first marshal of the Royal Air Force 1927. As commissioner of the Metropolitan Police, he established the Police College at Hendon and carried out the Trenchard Reforms, which introduced more scientific methods of detection.

Tressell Robert. Pseudonym of Robert Noonan 1868–1911. English author, whose *The Ragged Trousered Philanthropists*, published in an abridged form 1914, gave a detailed account of the poverty of working people's lives.

Treurnicht Andries Petrus 1921– . South African Conservative Party politician. A former minister of the Dutch Reformed Church, he was elected to the South African parliament as a National Party (NP) member but left it to form a new right-wing Conservative Party, opposed to any dilution of the apartheid system.

Trevelyan George Macaulay 1876–1962. British historian. Regius professor of history at Cambridge 1927–40, he pioneered the study of social history, as in his *English Social History* 1942.

Trevithick Richard 1771–1833. British engineer, constructor of a steam road locomotive 1801 and the first steam engine to run on rails 1804.

Tristan Flora 1803–1844. French socialist writer and activist, author of *Promenades dans Londres/The London Journal* 1840, a vivid record of social conditions, and *L'Union ouvrière/Workers' Union* 1843, an outline of a workers's utopia.

Tristano 'Lennie' (Lennard Joseph) 1919–1978. US jazz pianist and composer. An austere musician, he gave an academic foundation to the 'cool' school of jazz in the 1940s and 1950s, at odds with the bebop tradition, and was active as a teacher.

Trollope Anthony 1815–1882. English novelist, who delineated provincial English middle-class society in his Barchester series of novels. *The Warden* 1855 began the series, which includes *Barchester Towers* 1857, *Doctor Thorne* 1858, and *The Last Chronicle of Barset* 1867.

Tromp Maarten Harpertszoon 1597–1653. Dutch admiral. He twice defeated the occupying Spaniards 1639. He was defeated by the English admiral Blake May 1652, but in Nov triumphed over Blake in the Strait of Dover. In Feb–June 1653 he was defeated by Blake and Monk, and was killed off the Dutch coast. His son, *Cornelius Tromp* (1629–1691), also an admiral, fought a battle against the English and French fleets in 1673.

Trotsky Leon. Adopted name of Lev Davidovitch Bronstein 1879–1940. Russian revolutionary. He

Trotsky *Leon Trotsky in 1917, the year of the Russian Revolution.*

Truman *US politician and president Harry Truman presided over the Allied victory in World War II, and US involvement in the Korean War.*

joined the Bolshevik party and took a leading part in the seizure of power and raising the Red Army which fought the Civil War 1918–20. In the struggle for power that followed ◊Lenin's death 1924, ◊Stalin defeated him, and this and other differences with the Communist Party led to his exile 1929. Trotsky settled in Mexico, where he was assassinated with an ice pick, possibly at Stalin's instigation. Trotsky believed in world revolution and in permanent revolution, and was an uncompromising, if liberal, idealist.

Although as a young man Trotsky admired Lenin when he worked with him organizing the revolution of 1917 he objected to Lenin's dictatorial ways. Trotsky's later works are critical of the Soviet regime, for example *The Revolution Betrayed* 1937. His greatest work is his magisterial *History of the Russian Revolution* 1932–33.

Trudeau Pierre (Elliott) 1919– . Canadian Liberal politician. He was prime minister 1968–79 and won again by a landslide Feb 1980. In 1980 his work helped to defeat the Québec independence movement in a referendum. He repatriated the constitution from Britain 1982, but by 1984 had so lost support that he resigned.

Truffaut François 1932–1984. French film director, whose gently comic films include *Jules et Jim* 1961, and *La Nuit américaine/Day for Night* 1973 (for which he won an Academy Award). His work was influenced by Hitchcock, and also drew on Surrealist and comic traditions.

Trujillo Molina Rafael (Leónidas) 1891–1961. Dictator of the Dominican Republic from 1930. As commander of the Dominican Guard, he seized power and established a ruthless dictatorship. He was assassinated.

Truman Harry S 1884–1972. 33rd president of the USA 1945–53, a Democrat. In Jan 1945 he became vice president to F D Roosevelt, and president when Roosevelt died in Apr that year. He used the atom bomb against Japan, launched the Marshall Plan to restore W Europe's economy (see George ◊Marshall), and nurtured the European Community and NATO (including the rearmament of West Germany).

Born in Lamar, Missouri, he ran a clothing store that was bankrupted by the Great Depression. He became a senator 1934, was selected as Roosevelt's last vice president, and in 1948 was elected for a second term in a surprise victory over Thomas Dewey (1902–1971), the governor of New York. At home, he had difficulty converting the economy back to peacetime conditions, and failed to prevent the witch-hunts on suspected communists (see ◊Hiss, Joe ◊McCarthy). In Korea, he intervened when the South was invaded, but sacked Gen ◊MacArthur when the general's policy threatened to start World War III. Truman's decision not to enter Chinese territory, betrayed by the double agent Kim Philby, led to China's entry into the war. Truman had a sign on his desk that said: 'The buck stops here.'

Truth Sojourner. Adopted name of Isabella Baumfree, subsequently Isabella Van Wagener 1797–1883. US anti-slavery campaigner. Born a slave, she obtained her freedom and that of her son, and became involved with religious groups. In 1843 she was 'commanded in a vision' to adopt the name Sojourner Truth. She published an autobiography, *The Narrative of Sojourner Truth* 1850.

Ts'ao Chan former name for the Chinese novelist ◊Cao Chan.

Tschiffley Aimé Felix 1895–1954. Swiss writer and traveller whose 16,000 km/10,000 mi journey on horseback from Buenos Aires to New York was immortalized as 'Tschiffley's Ride', recounted in *Southern Cross to Pole Star* 1933.

Tsiolkovsky Konstantin 1857–1935. Russian scientist. He published the first practical paper on astronautics 1903, covering rocket space travel using liquid propellants, such as liquid oxygen.

Tsung Dao Lee 1926– . US physicist of Chinese origin. His research centred on the physics of weak interactions between particles. In 1956 Lee proposed that such interactions might disobey certain key assumptions, for instance the conservation of parity. For this work he shared the 1957 Nobel Prize for Physics with his co-worker Chen Ning Yang (1922–).

Tsvetaeva Marina 1892–1941. Russian poet, born in Moscow. She wrote mythic, romantic, frenetic verse, including *The Demesne of the Swans.*

Tubman Harriet Ross 1821–1913. US abolitionist. Born a slave in Maryland, she escaped to Philadelphia (where slavery was outlawed) 1849. She set up the *'Underground Railroad'*, a secret network of sympathizers to help slaves escape to the northern states and Canada. During the Civil War she served as a spy for the Union army. She spoke against slavery and for women's rights, and founded schools for freed slaves after the Civil War.

Tubman William V S 1895–1971. Liberian politician. The descendant of US slaves, he was a lawyer in the USA. After his election to the presidency of Liberia 1944 he concentrated on uniting the various ethnic groups. Re-elected several times, he died naturally in office despite frequent assassination attempts.

Tudor English dynasty descended from the Welsh Owen Tudor (*c.*1400–1461), the second husband of Catherine of Valois (the widow of Henry V of England). Their son Edmund married Margaret Beaufort (1443–1509), the great-granddaughter of ◊John of Gaunt, and was the father of Henry VII, who ascended the throne 1485.

The dynasty, which ended with the death of Elizabeth I 1603, was portrayed in a favourable light in Shakespeare's history plays.

Tu Fu 712–770. Chinese poet, who wrote about the social injustices of his time, peasant suffering, and war, as in 'The Army Carts'.

Tull Jethro 1674–1741. English agriculturist who developed a drill about 1701 which enabled seeds to be sown mechanically and spaced so that cultivation between rows was possible in the growth period. His major work, *Horse-Hoeing Husbandry*, was published 1731.

Tunnicliffe C(harles) F(rederick) 1901–1979. English painter of birds, born in Macclesfield, who worked in Anglesey.

Túpac Amarú adopted name of José Gabriel Condorcanqui *c.*1742–1781. Peruvian Indian revolutionary leader, executed for his revolt against Spanish rule 1780; he claimed to be descended from the last chieftain of the Incas.

Turenne Henry de la Tour d'Auvergne, Vicomte de Turenne 1611–1675. French marshal under Louis XIV, known for his siege technique.

Turgenev Ivan Sergeievich 1818–1883. Russian writer, noted for poetic realism, pessimism, and skill at characterization. His works include the play *A Month in the Country* 1849, and the novels *A Nest of Gentlefolk* 1858, *Fathers and Sons* 1862, and *Virgin Soil* 1877. His series of *A Sportsman's Sketches* 1852 criticized serfdom.

Turgot Anne Robert Jacques 1727–1781. French finance minister 1774–76, whose reforming economies led to his dismissal.

Turing Alan Mathison 1912–1954. British mathematician and logician. In 1936 he described a 'universal computing machine' that could theoretically be programmed to solve any problem capable of solution by a specially designed machine. This concept, now called the *Turing Machine*, foreshadowed the digital computer. He is also believed to have been the first to suggest the possibility of machine learning and artificial intelligence.

During World War II Turing worked on the Ultra project in the team that cracked the German Enigma code. Turing studied at King's College, Cambridge, and became a fellow there in 1935. He studied at Princeton 1936–38.

Turner Frederick Jackson 1861–1932. US historian, professor at Harvard 1910–1924. He emphasized the significance of the frontier in US historical development, attributing the distinctive character of US society to the influence of changing frontiers over three centuries of westward expansion.

Turner John Napier 1929– . Canadian Liberal politician, prime minister 1984. He was elected to the House of Commons 1962 and served in the cabinet of Pierre Trudeau, until resigning 1975. He succeeded Trudeau as party leader and prime minister 1984, but lost the 1984 and 1988 elections. Turner resigned as leader 1989, and returned to his law practice. He was replaced as Liberal Party chief by Herbert Gray in Feb 1990.

Turner Joseph Mallord William 1775–1851. English landscape painter. He travelled widely in Europe, and his landscapes became increasingly Romantic, with the subject often transformed in scale and flooded with brilliant, hazy light. Many later works anticipate Impressionism, for example *Rain, Steam and Speed* 1844 (National Gallery, London).

A precocious talent, Turner went to the Royal Academy schools in 1789. In 1792 he made the first of several European tours, from which numerous watercolour sketches survive. His early oil paintings show Dutch influence, but by the 1800s he had begun to paint landscapes in the grand manner, reflecting the styles of ◊Claude Lorrain and Richard ◊Wilson. His use of colour was enhanced by trips to Italy (1819, 1828, 1835, 1840), and his brushwork became increasingly free. Early in his career he was encouraged by the portraitist Thomas Lawrence and others, but he failed to achieve much recognition and became a reclusive figure. Much later he was championed by the critic John Ruskin in his book *Modern Painters* 1843.

Many of Turner's most dramatic works are set in Europe or at sea, for example *Snowstorm: Hannibal Crossing the Alps* 1812 (Tate Gallery, London), *The Slave Ship* 1839 (Museum of Fine Arts, Boston, Massachusetts), and *Shipwreck* 1805 (Tate Gallery). He was also devoted to

Turner US singer Tina Turner in London, 1986.

literary themes and mythologies, for example *Ulysses Deriding Polyphemus* (Tate Gallery).

In 1987 the Clore Gallery extension to the Tate Gallery, London, was opened to display the collection of his works he left to the nation.

Turner Lana (Julia Jean Mildred Frances) 1920– . US actress who appeared in melodramatic films of the 1940s and 1950s such as *Peyton Place* 1957. Her other films include *The Postman Always Rings Twice* 1946, *The Three Musketeers* 1948, and *Imitation of Life* 1959.

Turner Nat 1800–1831. US slave and Baptist preacher, who led 60 slaves in the most important US slave revolt – the **Southampton Insurrection** of 1831 – in Southampton County, Virginia. Before he and 16 of the others were hanged, at least 55 people had been killed.

Turner Tina. Adopted name of Annie Mae Bullock 1938– . US rhythm-and-blues singer who recorded 1960–76 with her husband, *Ike Turner* (1931–), notably *River Deep, Mountain High* 1966, produced by Phil Spector. Tina Turner had success in the 1980s as a solo performer, for example *Private Dancer* 1984. Ike Turner played guitar on 'Rocket 88' 1951 by Jackie Brenston, often cited as the first rock-and-roll record.

Turpin Ben 1874–1940. US comedian, a star of silent films. His trademark was being cross-eyed, and he parodied screen stars and their films. His work includes *The Shriek of Araby* 1923, *A Harem Knight* 1926, and *Broke in China* 1927.

Turpin Dick 1706–1739. English highwayman. The son of an innkeeper, he turned to highway robbery, cattle-thieving, and smuggling, and was hanged.

Tussaud Madame (Anne Marie Grosholtz) 1761–1850. French wax-modeller. In 1802 she established an exhibition of wax models of famous people in London. It was destroyed by fire 1925, but reopened 1928.

Born in Strasbourg, she went to Paris 1766 to live with her wax-modeller uncle, Philippe Curtius, whom she soon surpassed in technique. During the French Revolution they were forced to take death masks of many victims and leaders (some still exist in the Chamber of Horrors).

Tutankhamen King of Egypt of the 18th dynasty, about 1360–1350 BC. A son of Ikhnaton or of Amenhotep III, he was probably about 11 at his accession. In 1922 his tomb was discovered by the British archaeologists Lord Carnarvon and Howard Carter in the Valley of the Kings at Luxor, almost untouched by tomb robbers.

Tutin Dorothy 1930– . British actress, whose roles include most of Shakespeare's leading heroines (including Portia, Viola, and Juliet) for the Royal Shakespeare Company and Lady Macbeth for the National Theatre Company.

Tutu Desmond (Mpilo) 1931– . South African priest, Anglican archbishop of Cape Town and general secretary of the South African Council of Churches. He is one of the leading figures in the struggle against apartheid in the Republic of South Africa. Nobel Peace Prize 1984.

Twain Mark. Pen name of Samuel Langhorne Clemens 1835–1910. US humorous writer. He established his reputation with the comic *The Innocents Abroad* 1869, and two children's books, *The Adventures of Tom Sawyer* 1876 and *The Adventures of Huckleberry Finn* 1885. He also wrote satire, as in *A Connecticut Yankee at King Arthur's Court* 1889.

Tyler John 1790–1862. 10th president of the USA 1841–45, succeeding Benjamin ◊Harrison, who died after only a month in office. His government annexed Texas 1845.

Tynan Kenneth 1927–1980. British author and theatre critic, a leading cultural figure of the radical 1960s. He devised the nude revue *Oh Calcutta!* 1969, first staged in New York.

Tyndale William 1492–1536. English translator of the Bible. The printing of his New Testament (basis of the Authorized Version) was begun in Cologne 1525, and, after he had been forced to flee, completed in Worms. He was strangled and burned as a heretic at Vilvorde in Belgium.

Tyndall John 1820–1893. Irish physicist, who in 1869 studied the scattering of light by invisibly small suspended particles. Known as the *Tyndall effect*, it was first observed with colloidal solutions, in which a beam of light is made visible when it is scattered by minute colloidal particles (whereas a pure solvent does not scatter light).

Tyson Mike 1966– . US heavyweight champion boxer. He won the WBC heavyweight title 1986 when he beat Trevor Berbick to become the youngest world heavyweight champion. He beat James 'Bonecrusher' Smith for the WBA title 1987 and later that year he became the first undisputed champion since 1978 when he beat Tony Tucker for the IBF title. He was undefeated until 1990 when he lost the championship to a relative outsider, James 'Buster' Douglas.

Germany's economy and recognition outside the East European bloc.

Ullman Liv 1939– . Norwegian actress who was critically acclaimed for her roles in first Swedish and then international films. Her work includes *Persona* 1966, the title role in *Pope Joan* 1972, and *Autumn Sonata* 1978.

Umar died AD 644. 2nd caliph (head) of Islam, noted as a strong disciplinarian. Under his rule Islam spread to Egypt and Persia. He was assassinated in Medina.

Umayyad alternative spelling for ◊Omayyad dynasty.

Umberto two kings of Italy:

Umberto I 1844–1900. King of Italy from 1878, who joined the Triple Alliance 1882 with Germany and Austria-Hungary; his colonial ventures included the defeat at Aduwa, Abyssinia, 1896. He was assassinated by an anarchist.

Umberto II 1904–1983. Last king of Italy 1946. On the abdication of his father, Victor Emmanuel III, he ruled 9 May–13 June 1946, when he also abdicated and left the country.

Unamuno Miguel de 1864–1936. Spanish writer of Basque origin, exiled 1924–30 for criticism of the military directorate of Primo de ◊Rivera. His works include mystic poems and the study *Del sentimiento trágico de la vida/ The Tragic Sense of Life* 1913, about the conflict of reason and belief in religion.

Underwood Leon 1890–1975. British artist and sculptor. He travelled widely to Iceland, the USA, Mexico, and West Africa, devoting several books to the masks, wood carvings, and bronzes of the last-named. His rhythmic figures are powerful symbols of human myth.

Undset Sigrid 1882–1949. Norwegian novelist, author of *Kristin Lavransdatter* 1920–22, a strongly Catholic novel set in the 14th century. Nobel prize 1928.

Ungaretti Giuseppe 1888–1970. Italian poet who lived in France and Brazil. His lyrics show a cosmopolitan independence of Italian poetic tradition. His poems, such as the *Allegria di naufragi/Joy of Shipwrecks* 1919, are noted for their simplicity.

Uno Sosuke 1923– . Japanese Liberal Democrat politician. Having held various cabinet posts since 1976, he was designated prime minister June 1989 in an attempt to restore the image of the Liberal Democrats after several scandals. He resigned after only a month in office when his affairs with geishas and prostitutes became public knowledge.

Unwin Raymond 1863–1940. English town planner. He put the Garden City ideals of Sir Ebenezer Howard into practice, overseeing Letchworth (begun 1903), Hampstead Garden Suburb (begun 1907) and Wythenshawe outside Manchester (begun 1927).

Uccello Paolo. Adopted name of Paolo di Dono 1397–1475. Italian painter, active in Florence, celebrated for his early use of perspective. His surviving paintings date from the 1430s onwards. Decorative colour and detail dominate his later pictures. His works include *St George and the Dragon* about 1460 (National Gallery, London).

Uccello is recorded as an apprentice in Ghiberti's workshop in 1407. His fresco *The Deluge* about 1431 (Sta Maria Novella, Florence) shows his concern for pictorial perspective, but in later works this aspect becomes superficial. His three battle scenes painted in the 1450s for the Palazzo Medici, Florence, are now in the Ashmolean Museum, Oxford, National Gallery, London, and Louvre, Paris.

Udall Nicholas 1504–1556. English schoolmaster and playwright. He was the author of *Ralph Roister Doister* about 1553, the first known English comedy.

Uelsmann Jerry 1934– . US photographer noted for his dreamlike images, created by synthesizing many elements into one with great technical skill.

Uhland Johann Ludwig 1787–1862. German poet, author of ballads and lyrics in the Romantic tradition.

Ulanova Galina 1910– . Soviet dancer. Prima ballerina of the Bolshoi Theatre Ballet 1944–61, she excelled as Juliet and Giselle and created the principal role of Katerina in Prokofiev's *The Stone Flower*.

Ulbricht Walter 1893–1973. East German politician. After exile in the USSR during Hitler's time he became first secretary of the Socialist Unity Party in East Germany 1950 and (as chair of the Council of State from 1960) was instrumental in the building of the Berlin Wall 1961. He established East

Updike John (Hoyer) 1932– . US writer. Associated with the *New Yorker* magazine from 1955, he soon established a reputation for polished prose, poetry, and criticism. His novels include *Couples* 1968 and *Roger's Version* 1986 and deal with contemporary US middle-class life.

Two characters recur in his work: the basketball player 'Rabbit' Angstrom (introduced in *Rabbit, Run* 1960) and the novelist Henry Bech.

Urban eight popes, including:

Urban II *c.*1042–1099. Pope 1088–99. He launched the First Crusade at the Council of Clermont in France 1095.

Urey Harold Clayton 1893–1981. US chemist. In 1932 he isolated heavy water (which contains deuterium, an isotope of hydrogen, rather than ordinary hydrogen), and thus discovered deuterium; Nobel prize 1934.

He was director of the War Research Atomic Bomb Project, Columbia, 1940–45. His books include studies of nuclear and atomic structure, and the origin of the planet and of life.

Ursula, St 4th century AD. English legendary saint, supposed to have been martyred with 11 virgins (misread as 11,000 in the Middle Ages), by the Huns in the Rhineland.

Usher James 1581–1656. Irish priest, archbishop of Armagh from 1625. He was responsible for the dating of creation as the year 4004 BC, a figure that was inserted in the margin of the Authorized Version of the Bible until the 19th century.

Ustinov Peter 1921– . English stage and film actor, writer, and director. He won an Oscar for Best Supporting Actor in *Spartacus* 1960. Other films he appeared in include *Topkapi* 1964, *Death on the Nile* 1978, and *Evil under the Sun* 1981.

Utagawa Kuniyoshi Japanese printmaker; see ◊Kuniyoshi Utagawa.

Utamaro Kitagawa 1753–1806. Japanese artist of the *ukiyo-e* ('floating world') school, who created muted colour prints of beautiful women, including informal studies of prostitutes.

His style was distinctive: his subject is often seen close up, sometimes from unusual angles or viewpoints, and he made use of bold curvaceous lines and highly decorative textiles.

U Thant 1909–1974. Myanmar diplomat, secretary-general of the United Nations 1962–71. He helped to resolve the US-Soviet crisis over the Soviet installation of missiles in Cuba, and he made the controversial decision to withdraw the UN peacekeeping force from the Egypt–Israel border 1967.

Uthman another name for ◊Othman, third caliph of Islam.

Utrillo Maurice 1883–1955. French artist. He painted townscapes of his native Paris, especially Montmartre, often from postcard photographs.

Valdívia Pedro de *c.* 1497–1554. Spanish explorer who travelled to Venezuela around 1530 and accompanied Francisco ◊Pizarro on his second expedition to Peru. He then went south into Chile, where he founded the cities of Santiago 1541 and Valdívia 1544. In 1552 he crossed the Andes to explore the Negro River. He was killed by Araucanian Indians.

Valentine, St died 270. According to tradition a bishop of Terni martyred at Rome, now omitted from the calendar of saints' days as probably nonexistent. His festival was 14 Feb, but the custom of sending 'valentines' to a loved one on that day seems to have arisen because the day accidentally coincided with the Roman mid-Feb fertility festival of Lupercalia.

Valentino Rudolf 1895–1926. Italian film actor, the archetypal romantic lover of the Hollywood silent movies. His films include *The Sheik* 1921 and *Blood and Sand* 1922.

Valera Éamon de Irish politician; see ◊de Valera.

Valéry Paul 1871–1945. French poet and mathematician. His poems include *La Jeune Parque/The Young Fate* 1917 and *Charmes/Enchantments* 1922.

Valle-Inclán Ramón Maria de 1866–1936. Spanish author of erotic and symbolist works including *Sonatas* 1902–05 and, set in South America, the novel *Tirano Banderas/The Tyrant* 1926.

Valois branch of the Capetian dynasty (see Hugh ◊Capet) in France, members of which occupied the French throne from Philip VI 1328 to Henry III 1589.

Vámbéry Arminius 1832–1913. Hungarian traveller and writer who crossed the deserts of Central Asia to Khiva and Samarkand dressed as a native dervish, a classic journey described in his *Travels and Adventures in Central Asia* 1864.

van for names beginning 'van', see under the next part of the name, e.g. Eyck, San Van.

Van Allen James Alfred 1914– . US physicist, whose instruments aboard the first US satellite Explorer 1 in 1958 led to the discovery of the *Van Allen belts*, two zones of intense radiation around the Earth. He pioneered high-altitude research with rockets after World War II.

Van Basten Marco 1964– . Dutch international footballer, A noted striker, he helped the Netherlands to win the European Championship in 1988, scored two goals for AC Milan in the European Cup final in 1989 and scored the winning goal when they retained the European Cup in 1990. He started his career with top Dutch side Ajax and won many domestic honours.

Vanbrugh John 1664–1726. English Baroque architect and dramatist. He designed Blenheim Palace, Oxfordshire, and Castle Howard, Yorkshire, and wrote the comic plays *The Relapse* 1696 and *The Provok'd Wife* 1697. He was imprisoned in France 1688–93 as a political hostage by the French authorities.

Van Buren Martin 1782–1862. 8th president of the USA, a Democrat, born in Kinderhook, New York, of Dutch ancestry. He was a senator 1821–28, governor of New York State 1828–29, secretary of state 1829–31, minister to Britain 1831–33, vice president 1833–37, and president 1837–41. He initiated the independent treasury system, but his refusal to spend land revenues cost him the 1840 election. He lost the 1844 Democratic nomination to Polk, and in 1848 ran unsuccessfully for president as the Free Soil candidate.

Vance Cyrus 1917– . US Democrat politician, secretary of state 1977–80. He resigned because he did not support President Carter's abortive mission to rescue US hostages held in Iran.

Vancouver George *c.* 1758–1798. British navigator who made extensive exploration of the W coast of North America. He accompanied James ◊Cook on two voyages, and surveyed parts of Australia, New Zealand, Tahiti, and Hawaii.

Van de Graaff Robert Jemison 1901–1967. US physicist who from 1929 developed a high-voltage generator, which in its modern form can produce more than a million volts.

Vanderbilt Cornelius 1794–1877. US industrialist, who made a fortune in steamships and (from the age of 70) by financing railways.

Van der Post Laurens (Jan) 1906– . South African writer, whose books, many of them autobiographical, are concerned with the duality of human existence. They include the novels *Flamingo Feather* 1955, *The Seed and the Sower* 1963 (set in Java, Japan, Britain, and Africa) and *A Story like the Wind* 1972. His travel books include *Venture to the Interior* 1952.

Van der Waals Johannes Diderik 1837–1923. Dutch physicist who was awarded a Nobel prize in 1910 for his theoretical study of gases. He emphasized the forces of attraction and repulsion between atoms and molecules in describing the behaviour of real gases, as opposed to the ideal gases dealt with in Boyle's law and Charles's law (see Robert ◊Boyle and Jacques ◊Charles).

Vane Henry 1613–1662. English politician. In 1640 elected a member of the Long Parliament, he was prominent in the impeachment of Archbishop ◊Laud, and 1643–53 was in effect the civilian head of the Parliamentary government. At the Restoration he was executed.

Vane John 1923– . British pharmacologist who discovered the wide role of prostaglandins in the human body, produced in response to illness and stress. He shared a Nobel prize 1982.

Van Eyck Jan see ◊Eyck, Jan Van.

Van Gogh Vincent see ◊Gogh, Vincent Van.

Vansittart Robert Gilbert, 1st Baron Vansittart 1881–1957. British diplomat, noted for his anti-German polemic.

van't Hoff Jacobus Henricus 1852–1911. Dutch physical chemist. He explained the 'asymmetric' carbon atom occurring in optically active compounds. His greatest work – the concept of chemical affinity as the maximum work obtainable from a reaction – was shown with measurements of osmotic and gas pressures, and reversible electric batteries. He was the first recipient of the Nobel Prize for Chemistry in 1901.

Vardon Harry 1870–1937. British golfer, born in Jersey. He won the British Open a record six times 1896–1914. He formed a partnership with James Braid and John Henry Taylor, which became known as 'the Great Triumvirate', and dominated British golf in the years up to World War I. Vardon was the first UK golfer to win the US Open 1900.

Varèse Edgard 1885–1965. French composer, who settled in New York 1916 where he founded the New Symphony Orchestra 1919 to advance the cause of modern music. His work is experimental and often dissonant, combining electronic sounds with orchestral instruments, and includes *Hyperprism* 1923, *Intégrales* 1931, and *Poème Electronique* 1958.

Vargas Getúlio 1883–1954. President of Brazil 1930–45 and 1951–54. He overthrew the republic 1930 and in 1937 he set up a totalitarian, pro-fascist state known as the *Estado Novo*. Ousted by a military coup 1945, he returned as president 1951 but, amid mounting opposition and political scandal, committed suicide 1954.

Vargas Llosa Mario 1937– . Peruvian novelist and conservative politician, unsuccessful presidential candidate 1990. His novels include *La ciudad y los perros/The Time of the Hero* 1963 and *La guerra del fin del mundo/The War at the End of the World* 1982.

Vargas Llosa began as a communist and turned to the political right. He has been criticized for being out of touch with Peru's large Quechua Indian community. As a writer he belongs to the magic realist school. *La tía Julia y el escribidor/Aunt Julia and the Scriptwriter* 1977 is a humorously autobiographical novel.

Varley John 1778–1842. English watercolour painter of landscapes and friend of the poet and artist ◊Blake.

Vasarély Victor 1908– . French artist, born in Hungary. In the 1940s he developed his precise geometric compositions, full of visual puzzles and effects of movement, which he created with complex arrangements of hard-edged geometric shapes and subtle variations in colours.

He was active in Paris from 1930, then in the south of France from 1960. He initially worked as a graphic artist, concentrating on black and white.

Vasari Giorgio 1511–1574. Italian art historian, architect, and painter, author of *Lives of the Most Excellent Architects, Painters and Sculptors* 1550 (enlarged and revised 1568), in which he proposed the theory of a Renaissance of the arts beginning with Giotto and culminating with Michelangelo. He designed the Uffizi Palace, Florence.

His basic view of art history has remained unchallenged, despite his prejudices and his delight in often ill-founded, libellous anecdotes.

Vasco da Gama Portuguese navigator; see ◊Gama.

Vassilou Georgios Vassos 1931– . Greek-Cypriot politician and entrepreneur, president from 1988. A self-made millionaire, he entered politics as an independent and in 1988 won the presidency, with Communist Party support. He has since, with United Nations help, tried unsuccessfully to heal the rift between the Greek and Turkish communities.

Vauban Sébastien le Prestre de 1633–1707. French marshal and military engineer. In Louis XIV's wars he conducted many sieges and rebuilt many of the fortresses on France's east frontier.

Vaughan Henry 1622–1695. Welsh poet and physician. He published several volumes of metaphysical religious verse and prose devotions. His mystical outlook on nature influenced later poets, including Wordsworth.

Vaughan Williams Ralph 1872–1958. English composer. His style was tonal and often evocative of the English countryside through the use of folk themes. Among his works are the orchestral *Fantasia on a Theme by Thomas Tallis* 1910; the opera *Sir John in Love* 1929, featuring the Elizabethan song 'Greensleeves'; and nine symphonies 1909–57.

He studied at Cambridge, the Royal College of Music, and with Max Bruch in Berlin and Maurice

Ravel in Paris. His choral poems include *Toward the Unknown Region* (Whitman) 1907 and *On Wenlock Edge* (Housman) 1909, *A Sea Symphony* 1910, and *A London Symphony* 1914. Later works include *Sinfonia Antartica* 1953, developed from his film score for *Scott of the Antarctic* 1948, and a Ninth Symphony 1958. He also wrote *A Pastoral Symphony* 1922, sacred music for unaccompanied choir, the ballad opera *Hugh the Drover* 1924, and the operatic morality play *The Pilgrim's Progress* 1951.

Veidt Conrad 1893–1943. German film actor, memorable as the sleepwalker in *Das Kabinett des Dr Caligari/The Cabinet of Dr Caligari* 1919 and as the evil caliph in *The Thief of Baghdad* 1940. An international star from the 1920s, he moved to Hollywood in the 1940s.

Veil Simone 1927– . French politician. A survivor of Hitler's concentration camps, she was minister of health 1974–79, and framed the French abortion bill. In 1979–81 she was president of the European Parliament.

Velázquez Diego Rodriguez de Silva y 1599–1660. Spanish painter, born in Seville, the outstanding Spanish artist of the 17th century. In 1623 he became court painter to Philip IV in Madrid, where he produced many portraits of the royal family, as well as occasional religious paintings, genre scenes, and other subjects. *Las Meninas/The Ladies-in-Waiting* 1655 (Prado, Madrid) is a complex group portrait which includes a self-portrait, but nevertheless focuses clearly on the doll-like figure of the Infanta Margareta Teresa.

His early work in Seville shows exceptional realism and dignity, delight in capturing a variety of textures, rich use of colour and contrasts of light and shade. In Madrid he was inspired by works by Titian in the royal collection, and by Rubens, whom he met in 1628. He was in Italy 1629–31 and 1648–51; on his second visit he painted *Pope Innocent X* (Doria Gallery, Rome).

Velázquez's work includes an outstanding formal history painting, *The Surrender of Breda* 1634–35 (Prado), studies of the male nude, and a reclining female nude, *The Rokeby Venus* about 1648 (National Gallery, London).

Velde, van de family of Dutch artists. Both *Willem van de Velde* the Elder (1611–1693) and his son *Willem van de Velde* the Younger (1633–1707) painted sea battles for Charles II and James II (having settled in London 1672). Another son, *Adriaen van de Velde* (1636–1672), painted landscapes.

Willem the Younger achieved an atmosphere of harmony and dignity in highly detailed views of fighting ships at sea. The National Maritime Museum in Greenwich, London, has a fine collection of his works.

Vendôme Louis Joseph, Duc de Vendôme 1654–1712. Marshal of France, who lost his command after defeat by the British commander Marlborough at Oudenaarde, Belgium, 1708, but achieved successes in the 1710 Spanish campaign during the War of the Spanish Succession.

Venizelos Eleutherios 1864–1936. Greek politician born in Crete, leader of the Cretan movement against Turkish rule until the union of the island with Greece in 1905. He later became prime minister of the Greek state on five occasions, 1910–15, 1917–20, 1924, 1928–32 and 1933, before being exiled to France in 1935.

As prime minister of Greece from 1910, he instituted financial, military, and constitutional reforms and took Greece into the Balkan Wars. As a result, Greece annexed Macedonia, but attempts by Venizelos to join the war on the allied side led to his dismissal by King Constantine. Leading a rebel government in Crete and later in Salonika, he declared war on Bulgaria and Germany and secured the abdication of King Constantine.

As prime minister from 1917 he attended the Paris Peace Conference in 1919. By provoking a war with Turkey over Anatolia in 1920 he suffered an electoral defeat. On his last return to office in 1933, he was implicated in an uprising by his supporters and fled to France, where he died.

Ventris Michael (George Francis) 1922–1956. English archaeologist. Deciphering Minoan Linear B, the language of the tablets found at Knossos and Pylos, he showed that it was a very early form of Greek, thus revising existing views on early Greek history. *Documents in Mycenaean Greek*, written with John Chadwick, was published shortly after he died in a road accident.

Venturi Robert 1925– . US architect. He pioneered Post-Modernism through his books *Complexity and Contradiction in Architecture*

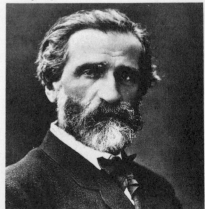

Verdi *Giuseppe Verdi, whose operas inspired the heroes of the Risorgimento.*

1967 and *Learning from Las Vegas* 1972. In 1986 he was commissioned to design an extension to the National Gallery, London.

Verdi Giuseppe (Fortunino Francesco) 1813–1901. Italian opera composer of the Romantic period, who took his native operatic style to new heights of dramatic expression. In 1842 he wrote the opera *Nabucco*, followed by *Ernani* 1844 and *Rigoletto* 1851. Other works include *Il Trovatore* and *La Traviata* both 1853, *Aida* 1871, and the masterpieces of his old age, *Otello* 1887 and *Falstaff* 1893. His *Requiem* 1874 commemorates Alessandro ◊Manzoni.

Verlaine Paul 1844–1896. French lyrical poet who was influenced by the poets Baudelaire and ◊Rimbaud. His volumes of verse include *Poèmes saturniens*/*Saturnine Poems* 1866, *Fêtes galantes*/ *Amorous Entertainments* 1869 and *Romances sans paroles*/*Songs without Words* 1874. In 1873 he was imprisoned for attempting to shoot Rimbaud. His later works reflect his attempts to lead a reformed life and he was acknowledged as leader of the Symbolist poets.

Vermeer Jan 1632–1675. Dutch painter, active in Delft. Most of his pictures are genre scenes, depicting everyday life with a limpid clarity and distinct air of stillness, and a harmonious palette often focusing on yellow and blue. He frequently depicted single women in domestic settings, as in *The Lacemaker* (Louvre, Paris).

Vermeer is thought to have spent his whole life in Delft. Around 40 paintings are ascribed to him. His work fell into obscurity until the mid- to late 19th century, but he is now ranked as one of the greatest Dutch artists.

In addition to genre scenes, his work comprises one religious painting, a few portraits, and two townscapes, of which the fresh and naturalistic *View of Delft* about 1660 (Mauritshuis, The Hague) triggered the revival of interest in Vermeer. *The Artist's Studio* about 1665–70 (Kunsthistorisches Museum, Vienna) is one of his most elaborate compositions; the subject appears to be allegorical, but the exact meaning remains a mystery.

Verne Jules 1828–1905. French author of tales of adventure, many of which anticipated future scientific developments: *Five Weeks in a Balloon* 1862, *Journey to the Centre of the Earth* 1864, *Twenty Thousand Leagues under the Sea* 1870, and *Around the World in Eighty Days* 1873.

Verney Edmund 1590–1642. English courtier, knight-marshal to Charles I· from 1626. He sat as a member of both the Short and Long Parliaments and, although sympathizing with the parliamentary position, remained true to his allegiance: he died at his post as royal standard bearer at the battle of Edgehill. His son *Ralph* (1613–96) supported the Parliamentarians. The *Verney papers* are a valuable record of this and later periods.

Verne French adventure and science-fiction novelist Jules Verne.

Vernier Pierre 1580–1637. French mathematician who invented a means of making very precise measurements, by a device now called the *vernier scale*. He was a French government official and in 1631 published a book explaining his method called 'a new mathematical quadrant'.

Vernon Edward 1684–1757. English admiral who captured Portobello from the Spanish in the Caribbean in 1739, with a loss of only seven men.

Veronese Paolo *c.* 1528–1588. Italian painter, born in Verona, active mainly in Venice (from about 1553). He specialized in grand decorative schemes, such as his ceilings in the Doge's Palace in Venice, with *trompe l'oeil* effects and inventive detail. The subjects are religious, mythological, historical, and allegorical.

His decorations in the Villa Barbera at Maser near Vicenza show his skill at illusionism and a typically Venetian rich use of colour; they are also characteristically full of inventive fantasy. He took the same approach to religious works, and as a result his *Last Supper* 1573 (Accademia, Venice, renamed *The Feast in the House of Levi*) was the subject of a trial by the Inquisition, since the holy event seems to be almost subordinated by profane details: figures of drunkards, soldiers conversing, dogs, and so forth.

Verrocchio Andrea del 1435–1488. Italian painter, sculptor, and goldsmith, born in Florence, where he ran a large workshop and received commissions from the Medici family. The vigorous equestrian statue of *Bartolommeo Colleoni*, begun 1481 (Campo SS Giovanni e Paolo, Venice), was his last work.

Verrocchio was a pupil of ◊Donatello and himself the early teacher of Leonardo da Vinci. In his *Baptism* about 1472 (Uffizi, Florence) Leonardo is said to have painted the kneeling angel shown in profile. Verrocchio's sculptures include a bronze *Christ and St Thomas* 1465 (Or S Michele, Florence) and *David* 1476 (Bargello, Florence).

Verwoerd Hendrik (Frensch) 1901–1966. South African right-wing Nationalist Party politician, prime minister from 1958. As minister of native affairs 1950–58, he was the chief promoter of apartheid legislation. He made the country a republic 1961. He was assassinated in the House of Assembly by a parliamentary messenger, Dimitri Tsafendas.

Vesalius Andreas 1514–1564. Belgian physician who revolutionized anatomy. His great innovations were to perform postmortem dissections, and to make use of illustrations in teaching anatomy.

These enabled him to discover that ◊Galen's system of medicine was based on fundamental anatomical errors. Vesalius' book *De Humani Corporis Fabrica/On The Structure of the Human Body* 1543, published in the same year as Copernicus' *De revolutionibus*, marked the dawn of the modern scientific era.

Vespasian (Titus Flavius Vespasianus) AD 9–79. Roman emperor from AD 69. He was the son of a moneylender, and had a distinguished military career. He was proclaimed emperor by his soldiers while he was campaigning in Palestine. He reorganized the eastern provinces, and was a capable administrator.

Vespucci Amerigo 1454–1512. Florentine merchant. The Americas were named after him as a result of the widespread circulation of his accounts of his explorations, but recent evidence suggests that he never made the voyages.

His accounts of the voyage 1499–1501 indicate that he had been to places he could not possibly have reached (the Pacific Ocean, British Columbia, Antarctica).

Veuster Joseph de 1840–1889. Belgian missionary, known as Father Damien. He went to Hawaii, and from 1873 was resident priest in the leper settlement at Molokai. He eventually became infected and died there.

Vian Philip 1894–1968. British admiral of the fleet in World War II. In 1940 he captured the *Altmark*, a German cruiser carrying the crews of Allied merchant ships sunk in attacks, and in 1941 commanded the destroyers that chased the German battleship *Bismarck*.

Vico Giambattista 1668–1744. Italian philosopher, the founder of the modern philosophy of history. He rejected Descartes's emphasis on the mathematical and natural sciences, and argued that we can understand history more adequately than nature, since it is we who have made it.

He believed that the study of language, ritual, and myth was a way of understanding earlier societies. His cyclical theory of history (the birth, development, and decline of human societies) was put forward in *New Science* 1725.

His belief that the study of language and rituals was a better way of understanding early societies was a departure from the traditional ways of writing history as either biographies, or as preordained God's will. He was born in Naples, and was professor of rhetoric there 1698. He became historiographer to the King of Naples 1735.

Victor Emmanuel three kings of Italy, including:

Victor Emmanuel II 1820–1878. First king of united Italy from 1861. He became king of Sardinia on the abdication of his father Charles Albert 1849. In 1855 he allied Sardinia with France and the UK in the Crimean War. In 1859 in alliance with the French he defeated the Austrians and annexed Lombardy. By 1860 most of Italy had come under his rule, and in 1861 he was proclaimed king of Italy. In 1870 he made Rome his capital.

Victor Emmanuel III 1869–1947. King of Italy from the assassination of his father Umberto I 1900. He acquiesced in the Fascist regime of Mussolini but cooperated with the Allies; he abdicated 1946.

Victoria 1819–1901. Queen of the UK from 1837, when she succeeded her uncle William IV, and empress of India from 1876. In 1840 she married Prince ◊Albert of Saxe-Coburg and Gotha. Her relations with her prime ministers ranged from the affectionate (Melbourne and Disraeli) to the stormy (Peel, Palmerston, and Gladstone). Her golden jubilee 1887 and diamond jubilee 1897 marked a waning of republican sentiment, which had developed with her withdrawal from public life on Albert's death.

Only child of Edward, duke of Kent, fourth son of George III, she was born 24 May 1819 at Kensington Palace, London. She and Albert had four sons and five daughters. After Albert's death 1861 she lived mainly in retirement. Nevertheless, she kept control of affairs, refusing the Prince of Wales (Edward VII) any active role. From 1848 she regularly visited the Scottish Highlands, where she had a house at Balmoral built to Prince Albert's designs. She died at Osborne House, her home in the Isle of Wight, 22 Jan 1901, and was buried at Windsor.

Vidal Gore 1925– . US writer and critic. Much of his work deals satirically with history and politics and includes the novels *Myra Breckinridge* 1968, *Burr* 1973, and *Empire* 1987, plays and screenplays, including *Suddenly Last Summer* 1958, and essays, such as *Armageddon?* 1987.

Vidocq François Eugène 1775–1857. French criminal who in 1809 became a spy for the Paris police, and rose to become chief of the detective department.

Vidor King 1894–1982. US film director, who made epics including *The Big Parade* 1925 and *Duel in the Sun* 1946. He has been praised as a cinematic innovator, and received an honorary Academy Award in 1979. His other films include *The Crowd* 1928 and *Guerra e Pace/War and Peace* 1956.

Viète François 1540–1603. French mathematician who developed algebra and its notation. He was the first mathematician to use letters of the alphabet to denote both known and unknown quantities.

Vigée-Lebrun Elisabeth 1755–1842. French portrait painter, trained by her father (a painter in pastels) and ◊Greuze. She became painter to Queen Marie Antoinette in the 1780s (many royal portraits survive).

At the outbreak of the Revolution 1789 she left France and travelled in Europe, staying in St Petersburg, Russia, 1795–1802. She resettled in Paris 1809. She published her *Souvenirs* 1835–37, written in the form of letters.

Vigeland Gustav 1869–1943. Norwegian sculptor. He studied in Oslo and Copenhagen and with ◊Rodin in Paris 1892. His programme of sculpture in Frogner Park, Oslo, conceived in 1900, was never finished. The style is heavy and monumental; the sculpted figures and animals enigmatic.

Vigny Alfred, Comte de 1797–1863. French romantic writer, whose works include the historical novel *Cinq Mars* 1826, the play *Chatterton* 1835, and poetry, for example, *Les Destinées/Destinies* 1864.

Vigo Jean. Adopted name of Jean Almereyda 1905–1934. French director of bizarre experimental films. He made only three feature films: *A Propos de Nice* 1930, *Zéro de conduite/Nothing for Conduct* 1933, and *L'Atalante* 1934.

Villa-Lobos Heitor 1887–1959. Brazilian composer. His style was based on folk tunes collected on travels in his country; for example, in the *Bachianas Brasileiras* 1930–44, he treats them in the manner of Bach. His works range from guitar solos to film scores to opera; he produced 2,000 works, including 12 symphonies.

Villehardouin Geoffroy de *c*.1160–1213. French historian, the first to write in the French language. He was born near Troyes, and was a leader of the Fourth Crusade, of which his *Conquest of Constantinople*, about 1209, is an account.

Villiers de l'Isle Adam Philippe Auguste Mathias, comte de Villiers de l'Isle Adam 1838–1889. French poet, the inaugurator of the Symbolist movement. He wrote the drama *Axel* 1890; *Isis* 1862, a romance of the supernatural; verse, and short stories.

Villon François 1431–*c*.1465. French poet, noted for his satiric humour, pathos, and lyric power in works which used the *argot* (slang) of the time. Very little of his work survives, but it includes the *Ballade des dames du temps jadis/Ballad of the ladies of former times*, *Petit Testament* 1456, and *Grand Testament* 1461.

Born in Paris, he dropped his surname (Montcorbier or de Logos) to assume that of a canon – a relative who sent him to study at the Sorbonne. In 1455 he stabbed a priest in a street fight and had to flee the city. Pardoned the next year, he returned to Paris, but was soon in flight again after robbing the College of Navarre, and was briefly at rest at the court of the duke of Orléans until sentenced to death for an unknown offence from which he was saved by the amnesty of a public holiday. Theft and public brawling continued to occupy his time, in addition to the production of the *Grand Testament* 1461, but in 1463 a sentence of death in Paris, commuted to ten-year banishment, is the last that is known of his life.

Vincent de Paul, St *c*.1580–1660. French Roman Catholic priest and founder of the two charitable orders of Dazarists 1625 and Sisters of Charity 1634. Born in Gascony, he was ordained 1600, then captured by Barbary pirates and was a slave in Tunis until he escaped 1607. He was canonized 1737; feast day 19 July.

Vincent of Beauvais *c*.1190–1264. French scholar, encyclopedist, and Dominican priest. A chaplain to the court of Louis IX, he is mainly remembered for his *Speculum majus/Great Mirror* 1220–44, a reference work summarizing contemporary knowledge on virtually every subject, including science, natural history, literature, and law.

It also contained a history of the world from the creation. It is noteworthy for its positive attitude towards classical literature, whose reputation had undergone a period of eclipse in the preceding centuries.

Viollet-le-Duc Eugène Emmanuel 1814–1849. French architect. Leader of the Gothic revival in France, he also restored medieval buildings.

Virchow Rudolf Ludwig Carl 1821–1902. German pathologist and founder of cellular pathology. Virchow was the first to describe leukaemia (cancer of the blood). In his book *Die Cellulare Pathologie/Cellular Pathology* 1858, he proposed that disease is not due to sudden invasions or changes, but to slow processes in which normal cells give rise to abnormal ones.

Virgil Publius Vergilius Maro 70–19 BC. Roman poet who wrote the *Eclogues* 37 BC, a series of pastoral poems, the *Georgics* 30 BC, four books on the art of farming, and his masterpiece the *Aeneid*.

Virgil, born near Mantua, was educated in Cremona and Mediolanum (Milan) and later studied philosophy and rhetoric in Rome before returning to his farm, where he began the *Eclogues* 43 BC. He wrote the *Georgics* at the suggestion of his patron, Maecenas, to whom he introduced Horace. Virgil devoted the last 11 years of his life to the composition of the *Aeneid*, the greatest poem in Latin literature and a great influence on later European literature.

Virtanen Artturi Ilmari 1895–1973. Finnish chemist who from 1920 made discoveries in agricultural chemistry. Because green fodder tends to ferment and produce a variety of harmful acids, it cannot be preserved for long. Virtanen prevented the process from starting by acidifying the fodder. In this form it lasted longer and remained nutritious. Nobel prize 1945.

Visconti Luchino 1906–1976. Italian film and theatre director. The film *Ossessione* 1942 pioneers his work with Neo-Realist theories; later works include *The Leopard* 1963 and *Death in Venice* 1971. His powerful social comment in documentaries led to clashes with the Italian government and Roman Catholic Church.

Vitruvius (Marcus Vitruvius Pollio) 1st century BC. Roman architect, whose ten-volume interpretation of Roman architecture *De architectura* influenced Alberti and Palladio.

Vitus, St Christian saint, probably Sicilian, who was martyred at Rome early in the 4th century.

Vivaldi Antonio (Lucio) 1678–1741. Italian Baroque composer, violinist, and conductor. He wrote 23 symphonies, 75 sonatas, over 400 concertos, including the *Four Seasons* (about 1725) for violin and orchestra, over 40 operas, and much sacred music. His work was largely neglected until the 1930s.

Vladimir I St 956–1015. Russian saint and prince of Kiev. Converted to Christianity 988, he married Anna, Christian sister of the Byzantine emperor ◊Basil II, and established Orthodox Christianity as the Russian national faith. Feast day 15 July.

Vlaminck Maurice de 1876–1958. French painter, who began using brilliant colour as an early member of the Fauves (see ◊Matisse), mainly painting landscapes. Later he abandoned Fauve colour. He also wrote poetry, novels, and essays.

Initially he was inspired by van ◊Gogh but by 1908 ◊Cézanne had become the chief influence. Vlaminck was a multitalented eccentric: his careers included cycling, playing the violin, and farming.

Vogel Hans-Jochen 1926– . West German socialist politician, chair of the Social Democratic Party (SPD) from 1987. A former leader of the SPD in Bavaria and mayor of Munich, he served in the Brandt and Schmidt governments in the 1970s as housing and then justice minister and then, briefly, as mayor of West Berlin.

A centrist, compromise figure, Vogel unsuccessfully contested the 1983 federal election as chancellor candidate for the SPD and in 1987 replaced Brandt as party chair.

Voight Jon 1938– . US film actor who starred with Dustin Hoffman in *Midnight Cowboy* 1969.

His subsequent films include *Deliverance* 1972, *Coming Home* 1978, and *Runaway Train* 1985.

Volcker Paul 1927– . US economist. As chair of the board of governors of the Federal Reserve System 1979–87, he controlled the amount of money in circulation in the USA. He was succeeded by Alan Greenspan.

Volta Alessandro 1745–1827. Italian physicist. He invented the voltaic pile (the first battery), the electrophorus (an early electrostatic generator), and an electroscope (for detecting electric charge).

Born in Como, he was a professor there and at Pavia. The unit of potential difference, the *volt*, is named after him.

Voltaire pen name of François-Marie Arouet 1694–1778. French writer, who devoted himself to tolerance, justice, and humanity. He was threatened with arrest for *Lettres philosophiques sur les anglais/Philosophical Letters on the English* 1733, essays in favour of English ways, thought, and political practice, and had to take refuge. Other writings include *Le Siècle de Louis XIV/The Age of Louis XIV* 1751; *Candide* 1759, a parody on ◊Leibniz's 'best of all possible worlds'; and a *Dictionnaire Philosophique* 1764.

Born in Paris, son of a notary, he adopted his pen name 1718. He was twice imprisoned in the Bastille and exiled from Paris between 1716 and 1726 for libellous political verse. *Oedipe/Oedipus*, his first essay in tragedy, was staged 1718. While in England 1726–29 he dedicated an epic poem on Henry IV, *La Henriade/The Henriade*, to Queen Caroline, and on returning to France published the successful *Histoire de Charles XII/History of Charles XII* 1731, and produced the play *Zaïre* 1732. He took refuge with his mistress, the Marquise de ◊Châtelet, at Cirey in Champagne, where he wrote the play *Mérope* 1743 and much of *Le Siècle de Louis XIV*. Among his other works are histories of Peter the Great, Louis XV, and India, *La Pucelle/The Maid*, on Joan of Arc; the satirical tale *Zadig* 1748; and the tragedy *Irène* 1778. In

Voltaire *French writer and philosopher Voltaire.*

1751–53 he stayed at the court of Frederick II (the Great) of Prussia, who had long been an admirer, but the association ended in deep enmity. From 1754 he established himself near Geneva – after 1758 at Ferney, just across the French border. His remains were transferred in 1791 to the Panthéon in Paris.

von for other names beginning 'von', see under the next part of the name.

von Braun Wernher 1912–1977. German rocket engineer who developed German military rockets (V1 and V2) during World War II, and later worked for NASA in the USA.

During the 1940s his research team at Pee-nemünde on the Baltic coast produced the V1 (flying bomb) and supersonic V2 rockets. In the 1950s von Braun was part of the team that produced rockets for US satellites (the first, *Explorer I*, was launched early 1958) and early space flights by astronauts.

von Gesner Konrad 1516–1565. Swiss naturalist who produced an encyclopedia of the animal world, the *Historia animalium* 1551–58.

Gesner was a victim of the Black Death and could not complete a similar project on plants. He is considered a founder of the science of zoology, but was also an expert in languages and an authority on the Classical writers.

von Karajan Herbert Austrian conductor. See ◊Karajan, Herbert von.

Vonnegut Kurt, Jr 1922– . US writer whose work generally has a science-fiction or fantasy element; his novels include *The Sirens of Titan* 1958, *Cat's Cradle* 1963, *Slaughterhouse-Five* 1969, which draws on his World War II experience of the fire-bombing of Dresden, Germany, and *Galapagos* 1985.

Voroshilov Klement Efremovich 1881–1969. Marshal of the USSR. He joined the Bolsheviks 1903 and was arrested many times and exiled, but escaped. He became a member of the central committee 1921 and commissar for war 1925, but was removed as commissar 1940 after defeats on the Finland front. He was president of the Presidium of the USSR 1953–60.

Vorster Balthazar Johannes 1915–1983. South African Nationalist politician, prime minister 1966–78, in succession to Verwoerd, and president 1978–79. During his premiership some elements of apartheid were allowed to lapse, and attempts were made to improve relations with the outside world. He resigned when it was discovered that the Department of Information had made unauthorized use of public funds during his premiership.

Voysey Charles Francis Annesley 1857–1941. English architect and designer. He designed country houses which were characteristically asymmetrical with massive buttresses, long sloping roofs, and rough-cast walls. He also designed textiles and wallpaper.

Vranitzky Franz 1937– . Austrian socialist politician, federal chancellor from 1986. Vranitzky first went into banking and in 1970 became adviser on economic and financial policy to the minister of finance. After a return to the banking world he entered the political arena through the Socialist Party of Austria, and became minister of finance in 1984. He succeeded Fred Sinowatz as federal chancellor in 1986, heading an SPÖ-ÖVP (Austrian People's Party) coalition.

Vries Hugo de 1848–1935. Dutch botanist, who conducted important research on osmosis in plant cells and was a pioneer in the study of plant evolution. His work led to the rediscovery of ◊Mendel's laws of heredity and the formulation of the theory of mutation.

Vuillard (Jean) Edouard 1886–1940. French painter and printmaker, a founder member of *Les Nabis* (followers of Gauguin). His work is mainly decorative, with an emphasis on surface pattern reflecting the influence of Japanese prints. With ◊Bonnard he produced numerous lithographs and paintings of simple domestic interiors.

Vyshinsky Andrei 1883–1954. Soviet politician. As commissar for justice he acted as prosecutor at the treason trials 1936–38. He was foreign minister 1949–53, and often represented the USSR at the United Nations.

Wagner's early career was as director of the Magdeburg Theatre, where he unsuccessfully produced his first opera *Das Liebesverbot/Forbidden Love* in 1836. He lived in Paris 1839–42 and conducted at the Dresden Opera House 1842–48. He fled Germany to escape arrest for his part in the 1848 revolution, but in 1861 he was allowed to return. He won the favour of Ludwig II of Bavaria in 1864 and was thus able to set up the Festival Theatre in Bayreuth. The Bayreuth tradition was continued by his wife Cosima (◊Liszt's daughter, whom he married after her divorce from Hans von ◊Bülow) by his son **Siegfried Wagner** (1869–1930), a composer of operas such as *Der Bärenhäuter*; and by later descendants.

Wagner-Jauregg Julius 1857–1940. Austrian neurologist. He received the 1927 Nobel Prize for Medicine for his work on the use of induced fevers in treating mental illness.

Wain John (Barrington) 1925– . British author. His best-known work is his first novel, *Hurry on Down* 1953. He was professor of poetry at Oxford 1973–80.

Waite 'Terry' (Terence Hardy) 1939– . British religious adviser from 1980 to the archbishop of Canterbury, Dr Robert ◊Runcie. Waite undertook many overseas assignments but he disappeared in 1987 while making enquiries in Beirut, Lebanon, about European hostages. Worldwide efforts to secure his release have proved unsuccessful.

Waits Tom 1949– . US singer and songwriter, with a characteristic gravelly voice. His songs typically deal with urban street life, and have jazz-influenced arrangements. He has written music for and acted in several films, including Jim Jarmusch's *Down by Law* 1986.

Wajda Andrzej 1926– . Polish film director, one of the major figures in postwar European cinema.

Wace Robert *c.*1100–*c.*1175. Anglo-Norman poet and chronicler of early chivalry. His major works, both written in Norman French, were *Roman de Brut* (also known as *Geste des Bretons*) 1155, and *Roman de Rou* (or *Geste des Normanz*) 1160–62.

He was born in Jersey to a noble family, and educated at Paris and Caen in Normandy. *Roman de Brut* was adapted from Geoffrey of Monmouth's *Historia Regum Britanniae*; *Roman de Rou* was a chronicle of the dukes of Normandy.

Waddington David Charles 1929– . British Conservative politician, home secretary from 1989. A barrister, he became an MP in 1978. A Conservative whip from 1979, Waddington was a junior minister in the Department of Employment and in the Home Office before becoming chief whip in 1987.

Wagner Otto 1841–1918. Viennese architect. Initially designing in the Art Nouveau style, for example Vienna Stadtbahn 1894–97, he later rejected ornament for rationalism, as in the Post Office Savings Bank, Vienna, 1904–06. He influenced Viennese architects such as Josef Hoffmann, Adolf Loos, and Joseph Olbrich.

Wagner Richard 1813–1883. German opera composer. He revolutionized the 19th-century conception of opera, envisaging it as a wholly new art form in which musical, poetic, and scenic elements should be unified through such devices as the *leitmotif*, a recurring phrase indicating, say, a particular character. His operas include *Tannhäuser* 1845, *Lohengrin* 1850, and *Tristan und Isolde* 1865. In 1872 he founded the Festival Theatre in Bayreuth; his masterpiece *Der Ring des Nibelungen/The Ring of the Nibelung*, a sequence of four operas, was first performed there in 1876. His last work, *Parsifal*, was produced in 1882.

Wagner *German composer Richard Wagner.*

His films typically deal with the predicament and disillusion of individuals caught up in political events. His works include *Ashes and Diamonds* 1958, *Man of Marble* 1977, *Man of Iron* 1981, and *Danton* 1982.

Wakefield Edward Gibbon 1796–1862. British colonial administrator. He was imprisoned 1826–29 for abducting an heiress, and became manager of the South Australian Association which founded a colony in 1836. He was an agent for the New Zealand Land Company 1839–46, and emigrated there in 1853.

Waksman Selman Abraham 1888–1973. US biochemist, born in Ukraine. He coined the word 'antibiotic' for bacteria-killing chemicals derived from microorganisms, and won the 1952 Nobel Prize for Medicine for the discovery of streptomycin, an antibiotic used against tuberculosis.

Wald George 1906– . US biochemist who explored the chemistry of vision. He found that a crucial role was played by the retinal pigment rhodopsin, derived in part from vitamin A. For this he shared the 1967 Nobel Prize for Medicine with Ragnar Granit (1900–) and Haldan Hartline (1903–1983).

Waldemar or *Valdemar* four kings of Denmark, including:

Waldemar I *the Great* 1131–1182. King of Denmark from 1157, who defeated rival claimants to the throne, and overcame the Wends on the Baltic island of Rügen in 1169.

Waldemar II *the Conqueror* 1170–1241. King of Denmark from 1202. He was the second son of Waldemar I, and succeeded his brother Canute VI. He gained control of land N of the river Elbe (which he later lost), as well as much of Estonia, and he completed the codification of Danish law.

Waldemar IV 1320–1375. King of Denmark from 1340, responsible for reuniting his country by capturing Skåe (S Sweden) and the island of Gotland in 1361. However, the resulting conflict with the Hanseatic League led to defeat by them, and in 1370 he was forced to submit to the Peace of Stralsund.

Walden Brian (Alistair) 1932– . British journalist and, from 1977, television presenter. He was a Labour member of Parliament 1964–77.

Waldheim Kurt 1918– . Austrian politician and diplomat. He was secretary general of the United Nations 1972–81, having been Austria's representative there 1964–68 and 1970–71. In 1986 he was elected president of Austria, but his tenure of office was clouded by revelations that during World War II he had been an intelligence officer in an army unit responsible for transporting Jews to death camps.

Walesa Lech 1947– . Polish trade-union leader, founder of Solidarity 1980, an organization, independent of the Communist Party, which forced

Waldheim *Austrian chancellor Kurt Waldheim, elected in 1986 despite his wartime service with the German army in Yugoslavia. He was secretary-general of the United Nations 1972–81.*

substantial political and economic concessions from the Polish government 1980–81 until being outlawed. In 1989 he negotiated an agreement with the Polish government that legalized Solidarity and set in place a new 'socialist pluralist' political structure. Nobel Peace Prize 1983.

Walesa, as an electrician at the Lenin shipyard at Gdańsk, became a trade-union organizer. Here he founded the Solidarity (Solidarność) confederation of trade unions. A series of strikes led by Walesa, a devout Catholic, drew wide public support. In Dec 1981 Solidarity was outlawed and Walesa arrested, following the imposition of martial law by the Polish leader Gen Jaruzelski. Walesa was released 1982.

After leading a further series of strikes during 1988, he negotiated an agreement with the Jaruzelski government in Apr 1989 under the terms of which Solidarity once more became legal and a new, semi-pluralist 'socialist democracy' was established. The coalition government elected in Sept 1989 was dominated by Solidarity.

Wales, Prince of title conferred on the eldest son of the United Kingdom's sovereign. Prince ◊Charles was invested as 21st Prince of Wales at Caernarvon 1969 by his mother, Elizabeth II.

Waley Arthur 1889–1966. English orientalist, who translated from both Japanese and Chinese, including such works as the Japanese classics *The Tale of Genji* 1925–33 and *The Pillow-book of Sei Shōnagon*

Walesa Polish trade unionist Lech Walesa, leader of Solidarity.

1928, and the 16th-century Chinese novel *Monkey* 1942. He never visited the Far East.

Walker Alice 1944– . US poet, novelist, critic, and essay writer. She was active in the civil-rights movement in the USA in the 1960s, and as a black woman has written about the double burden for women of racist and sexist oppression. Her novel *The Color Purple* 1983 won a Pulitzer prize.

Walker Peter (Edward) 1932– . British Conservative politician, energy secretary 1983–87, secretary of state for Wales 1987–1990. As energy secretary from 1983, he managed the government's response to the national miners' strike 1984–85 that resulted in the capitulation of the National Union of Miners.

Walker William 1824–1860. US adventurer who for a short time established himself as president of a republic in NW Mexico, and was briefly president of Nicaragua 1856–57. He was eventually executed and is now regarded as a symbol of US imperialism in Central America.

Wallace Alfred Russel 1823–1913. English naturalist who collected animal and plant specimens in South America and the Far East, and independently arrived at a theory of evolution by natural selection similar to that of Charles ◊Darwin.

Wallace Edgar 1875–1932. English writer of thrillers. His prolific output includes *The Four Just Men* 1905; a series set in Africa and including *Sanders of the River* 1911; crime novels such as *A King by Night* 1926; and melodramas such as *The Ringer* 1926.

Wallace George 1919– . US right-wing politician, governor of Alabama 1962–66. He contested the presidency in 1968 as an independent, and in 1972 campaigned for the Democratic nomination, but was shot at a rally and became partly paralysed.

Wallace Lewis 1827–1905. US general and novelist. He served in the Mexican and Civil wars, and subsequently became governor of New Mexico and minister to Turkey. He wrote the historical novels *The Fair God* 1873 and *Ben-Hur* 1880.

Wallace Richard 1818–1890. British art collector. He inherited a valuable art collection from his father, the Marquess of Hertford, which was given by his widow to the UK as the *Wallace Collection*, containing many 18th-century French paintings. It is now at Hertford House, London.

Wallace William 1272–1305. Scottish nationalist who led a revolt against English rule in 1297, won a victory at Stirling, and assumed the title 'governor of Scotland'. Edward I defeated him at Falkirk in 1298, and Wallace was captured and executed.

Wallenberg Raoul 1912–1947. Swedish businessman who attempted to rescue several thousand Jews from German-occupied Budapest in 1944 in World War II.

There he tried to rescue and support Jews in safe houses, and provided them with false papers to save them from deportation to extermination camps. After the arrival of Soviet troops in Budapest, he reported to the Russian commander in Jan 1945 and then disappeared. The Soviet government later claimed that he died of a heart attack in July 1947. However, rumours persist that he is still alive and held in a Soviet prison camp.

Wallenstein Albrecht Eusebius Wenzel von 1583–1634. German general who, until his defeat at Lützen in 1632, led the Habsburg armies in the Thirty Years' War. He was assassinated.

Waller Edmund 1606–1687. English poet who managed to eulogize both Cromwell and Charles II; now mainly remembered for lyrics such as 'Go, lovely rose'.

Wallis Barnes (Neville) 1887–1979. British aeronautical engineer who designed the airship R-100 and during World War II perfected the 'bouncing bombs' used against the German Möhne and Eder dams in 1943 by the Royal Air Force Dambusters Squadron. He also assisted the development of the Concorde supersonic airliner, and developed the swing-wing aircraft.

Walpole Horace, 4th Earl of Orford 1717–1797. English novelist and politician, the son of Robert Walpole. He was a Whig member of Parliament 1741–67. He converted his house at Strawberry Hill, Twickenham, into a Gothic castle; his *The Castle of Otranto* 1764 established the genre of the Gothic novel, or 'romance of terror'.

Walpole Robert, 1st Earl of Orford 1676–1745. British Whig politician, the first 'prime minister' as First Lord of the Treasury and chancellor of the Exchequer 1715–17 and 1721–42. He encouraged trade by his peaceful foreign policy (until forced into war with Spain in 1739), and received an earldom when he eventually retired in 1742.

Walpurga, St 8th century AD. English nun who preached Christianity in Germany. *Walpurgis Night* the night before 1 May, one of her feast days, was formerly associated with witches' sabbaths. Her main feast day is 25 Feb.

Walras Léon 1834–1910. French economist. In his *Éléments d'économie politique pure* 1874–77 he made a pioneering attempt to develop a unified model for general equilibrium theory (a hypothetical situation in which demand equals supply in all markets). He also originated the theory of diminishing marginal utility of a good (the increased value to a person of consuming more of a product).

Walsh Raoul 1887–1981. US film director, originally an actor. He directed his first film 1914 and went on to become one of Hollywood's most prolific directors. He made a number of outstanding films, including *The Thief of Baghdad* 1924, *The Roaring Twenties* 1939, and *White Heat* 1949. He retired 1964.

Walsingham Francis c.1530–1590. English politician who, as secretary of state from 1573, both advocated a strong anti-Spanish policy and ran the efficient government spy system that made it work.

Walter Hubert died 1205. Archbishop of Canterbury 1193–1205. As justiciar (chief political and legal officer) 1193–98, he ruled England during Richard I's absence and introduced the offices of coroner and justice of the peace.

Walter John 1739–1812. British newspaper editor, founder of *The Times* (originally the *Daily Universal Register* 1785, but renamed in 1788).

Walter Lucy c.1630–1658. Mistress of ◊Charles II, whom she met while a Royalist refugee in The Hague, Netherlands, in 1648; the Duke of ◊Monmouth was their son.

Walters Alan (Arthur) 1927–   . British economist and government adviser 1981–89. He became economics adviser to Prime Minister Thatcher, but his publicly stated differences with the policies of her chancellor Nigel ◊Lawson precipitated, in 1989, Lawson's resignation from the government as well as Walters' own departure.

Walther von der Vogelweide c.1170–c.1230. German poet, greatest of the Minnesingers, whose songs dealt mainly with courtly love. Of noble birth, he lived in his youth at the Austrian ducal court in Vienna, adopting a wandering life after the death of his patron in 1198. His lyrics deal mostly with love, but also with religion and politics.

Walton Ernest 1903–   . Irish physicist who, as a young doctoral student at the Cavendish laboratory in Cambridge, collaborated with ◊Cockcroft

on the structure of the atom. In 1932 they succeeded in splitting the atom and for this historic experiment they shared the 1951 Nobel Prize for Physics.

Walton Izaak 1593–1683. English author of the classic *Compleat Angler* 1653. He was born in Stafford, and settled in London as an ironmonger. He also wrote short biographies of the poets George Herbert and John Donne, and the theologian Richard Hooker.

Walton William (Turner) 1902–1983. English composer. Among his works are *Façade* 1923, a series of instrumental pieces designed to be played in conjunction with the recitation of poems by Edith Sitwell; the oratorio *Belshazzar's Feast* 1931; and *Variations on a Theme by Hindemith* 1963.

He also composed a viola concerto 1929; two symphonies 1935; a violin concerto 1939; and a sonata for violin and pianoforte 1950.

Warbeck Perkin c.1474–1499. Flemish pretender to the English throne. Claiming to be Richard, brother of Edward V, he led a rising against Henry VII in 1497, and was hanged after attempting to escape from the Tower of London.

Warburg Otto 1878–1976. German biochemist, who in 1923 devised a manometer (pressure gauge) sensitive enough to measure oxygen uptake of respiring tissue. By measuring the rate that cells absorb oxygen under differing conditions, Warburg was able to show that enzymes called **cytochromes** enable cells to process oxygen. Nobel Prize for Medicine 1931.

Ward Artemus. Pen name of Charles Farrar Browne 1834–1867. US humorist who achieved great popularity with comic writings such as *Artemus Ward: His Book* 1862 and *Artemus Ward: His Travels* 1865.

Ward Barbara 1914–1981. British economist. She became president of the Institute for Environment and Development in 1973. In 1976 she received a life peerage as Baroness Jackson of Wadsworth. Her books include *Policy for the West* 1951 and *The Widening Gap* 1971.

Ward Leslie 1851–1922. British caricaturist, known under the pseudonym 'Spy' for his caricatures in *Vanity Fair*.

Ward Mrs Humphry (born Mary Augusta Arnold) 1851–1920. English novelist who wrote serious didactic books, such as *Robert Elsmere* 1888, a study of religious doubt. She was an opponent of women's emancipation.

Warhol Andy 1928–1987. US Pop artist and filmmaker. He made his name in 1962 with paintings of Campbell's soup tins, Coca-Cola bottles, and film stars. In his New York studio, the Factory, he produced series of garish silk-screen prints. His films include the semi-documentary *Chelsea Girls* 1966 and *Trash* 1970.

Warhol was born in Pittsburgh, where he studied art. In the 1950s he became a leading commercial artist in New York. With the breakthrough of Pop art, his bizarre personality and flair for self-publicity made him a household name. He was a pioneer of multimedia events with the Exploding Plastic Inevitable touring show in 1966 featuring the Velvet Underground (see Lou ◊Reed). In 1968 he was shot and nearly killed by a radical feminist, Valerie Solanas.

Successful early silk-screen series dealt with car crashes and suicides; Marilyn Monroe; Elvis Presley; and flowers. His films, beginning with *Sleep* 1963 and ending with *Bad* 1977, have a strong documentary or improvisational element. His books include *The Philosophy of Andy Warhol (From A to B and Back Again)* 1975 and *Popism* 1980.

Warlock Peter. Pen name of British composer Philip ◊Heseltine.

Warner Deborah 1959– . British theatre director. Discarding period costume and furnished sets, she adopted an uncluttered approach to the classics, including productions of many Shakespeare plays and Sophocles' *Electra*.

Warren Earl 1891–1974. US jurist and politician. As Chief Justice of the US Supreme Court 1953–69 he took a stand against racial discrimination, ruling that segregation in schools was unconstitutional. He headed the commission that investigated President Kennedy's assassination 1964, which made the controversial finding that Lee Harvey Oswald acted alone.

Warren Frank 1952– . British boxing promoter who helped bring world title-fight boxing to commercial television. He was shot and seriously wounded 1989.

Warren Robert Penn 1905–1989. US poet and novelist, the only author to receive a Pulitzer prize for both prose and poetry. In 1986 he became the USA's first poet laureate.

His novel *All the King's Men* 1946 was modelled on the career of Huey ◊Long, and he won Pulitzer prizes for *Promises* 1968 and *Now and Then: Poems* 1976–78.

Warton Joseph 1722–1800. English poet, headmaster of Winchester 1766–93, whose verse and *Essay on the Writings and Genius of Pope* 1756–82 marked an 'anti-classical' reaction.

Warton Thomas Wain 1728–1790. English critic. He was professor of poetry at Oxford 1757–67 and published the first *History of English Poetry* 1774–81. He was poet laureate from 1785.

Warwick Richard Neville, Earl of Warwick 1428–1471. English politician, called the **Kingmaker**. During the Wars of the Roses he fought at first on the Yorkist side against the Lancastrians, and was largely responsible for placing Edward IV on the throne. Having quarrelled with him, he restored Henry VI in 1470,

Washington *American teacher and reformer Booker T Washington.*

but was defeated and killed by Edward at Barnet, Hertfordshire.

Washington Booker T(aliaferro) 1856–1915. US educationist, pioneer in higher education for black people in the southern USA. He was the founder and first principal of Tuskegee Institute, Alabama, in 1881, originally a training college for blacks, which subsequently gained a prestigious reputation. He maintained that economic independence was the way for blacks to achieve social equality.

Washington George 1732–1799. First president of the USA 1789–97. As a strong opponent of the British government's policy, he sat in the Continental Congresses of 1774 and 1775, and on the outbreak of the War of American Independence was chosen commander in chief. After the war he retired to his Virginia estate, Mount Vernon, but in 1787 he re-entered politics as president of the Constitutional Convention. Although he attempted to draw his ministers from all factions, his aristocratic outlook alienated his secretary of state, Thomas Jefferson, who resigned 1793, thus creating the two-party system.

Washington took part in campaigns against the French and American Indians 1753–57, and was elected to the Virginia House of Burgesses. He was elected president of the USA in 1789 and re-elected in 1793, but refused to serve a third term,

Washington *The first president of the USA, George Washington. He had served as commander in chief of the American forces during the War of Independence.*

setting a precedent that was followed until 1940. He scrupulously avoided overstepping the constitutional boundaries of presidential power. In his farewell address 1796, he maintained that the USA should avoid European quarrels and entangling alliances. He is buried at Mount Vernon.

Wassermann August von 1866–1925. German professor of medicine. In 1907 he discovered a diagnostic blood test for syphilis, known as the *Wassermann reaction*.

Waterhouse Alfred 1830–1905. English architect. He was a leading exponent of Victorian Neo-Gothic using, typically, multicoloured tiles and bricks. His works include the Natural History Museum in London 1868.

Waterton Charles 1783–1865. British naturalist who travelled extensively in South and North America 1804–24. In the UK he was the first person to protest against pollution from industry, and created a nature reserve around his home in Yorkshire.

Watkins Henry George (Gino) 1907–1932. English polar explorer whose expeditions in Labrador and Greenland helped to open up an Arctic air route during the 1930s. He was drowned in a kayak accident while leading an expedition in Greenland.

Watson James Dewey 1928– . US biologist whose researches on the molecular structure of DNA (the genetic code), in collaboration with Francis ◊Crick, earned him a shared Nobel prize 1962.

Watson John B(roadus) 1878–1958. US psychologist, founder of behaviourism. He rejected introspection (observation by an individual of his or her own mental processes) and regarded psychology as the study of observable behaviour, within the scientific tradition.

Watson Thomas Sturgess 'Tom' 1949– . US golfer. In 1988 he succeeded Jack ◊Nicklaus as the game's biggest money winner, but was overtaken by Tom Kite in 1989.

Watson, born in Kansas City, turned professional in 1971 and has won more than 30 tournaments on the US Tour, including the Masters and US Open, and the British Open a modern-day-record five times.

Watson-Watt Robert Alexander 1892–1973. Scottish physicist who developed a forerunner of ◊radar. During a long career in government service (1915–1952) he proposed in 1935 a method of radiolocation of aircraft – a key factor in Britain's victory in World War II.

Watt James 1736–1819. Scottish engineer who developed the steam engine. He made ◊Newcomen's steam engine vastly more efficient by cooling the used steam in a condenser separate from the main cylinder.

Steam engines incorporating governors, sun-and-planet gears, and other devices of his invention were successfully built by him in partnership with Matthew ◊Boulton, and were vital to the Industrial Revolution.

Watteau Jean-Antoine 1684–1721. French Rococo painter. He developed a new category of genre painting known as the *fête galante*, scenes of a kind of aristocratic pastoral fantasy world. One of these pictures, *The Embarkation for Cythera* 1717 (Louvre, Paris), won him membership of the French Academy.

Watteau was born in Valenciennes. At first inspired by Flemish genre painters, he produced tavern and military scenes. His early years in Paris, from 1702, introduced him to fashionable French paintings and in particular to decorative styles and theatrical design. He was also influenced by ◊Giorgione and ◊Rubens.

Watts George Frederick 1817–1904. English painter and sculptor. He painted allegorical, biblical, and classical subjects, investing his work with a solemn morality. Many of his portraits are in the National Portrait Gallery, London.

Born in London, he studied in the Royal Academy schools. In 1864 he married the actress Ellen Terry; later the marriage was dissolved. As a sculptor he executed *Physical Energy* for Cecil Rhodes' memorial in South Africa; a replica is in Kensington Gardens, London.

Watts Isaac 1674–1748. English Nonconformist writer of hymns, including 'O God, our help in ages past'.

Webb *Sidney Webb, who in partnership with his wife Beatrice, carried out major investigations into social conditions, and influenced the early Labour movement.*

Waugh Evelyn (Arthur St John) 1903–1966. English novelist. He made his name with social satire, for example *Decline and Fall* 1928, *Vile Bodies* 1930, and *The Loved One* 1948. A Roman Catholic convert from 1930, he developed a concern with such issues in *Brideshead Revisited* 1945. *The Ordeal of Gilbert Pinfold* 1957 is largely autobiographical.

Wavell Archibald, 1st Earl Wavell 1883–1950. British field marshal in World War II, appointed commander in chief Middle East July 1939. He conducted the North African war against Italy 1940–41, and achieved successes there as well as in Ethiopia. He was transferred as commander in chief in India Jul 1941, and was viceroy 1943–47.

Waverley John Anderson, 1st Viscount Waverley 1882–1958. British administrator. He organized civil defence for World War II, becoming home secretary and minister for home security in 1939 (the nationally distributed ***Anderson shelters***, home outdoor air-raid shelters, were named after him). He was chancellor of the Exchequer 1943–45.

Wayne John ('Duke'). Stage name of Marion Morrison 1907–1979. US film actor who was the archetypal Western star: plain-speaking, brave and solitary. His films include *Stagecoach* 1939 and *True Grit* 1969 (Academy Award).

Wazyk Adam 1905– . Polish writer who made his name with *Poem for Adults* 1955, a protest against the regime that preceded the fall of the Stalinists in 1956. In 1957 he resigned with others from the Communist Party, disappointed by First Secretary Gomulka's illiberalism. He also wrote novels and plays.

Webb Aston 1849–1930. English architect. His work in London includes the front of Buckingham Palace, Admiralty Arch, and the chief section of the Victoria and Albert Museum.

Webb (Martha) Beatrice (born Potter) 1858–1943 and Sidney (James), Baron Passfield 1859–1947. English social reformers, writers, and founders of the London School of Economics 1895. They argued for social insurance in their minority report (1909) of the Poor Law Commission, and wrote many influential books, including *The History of Trade Unionism* 1894, *English Local Government* 1906, and *Soviet Communism* 1935. Sidney Webb was professor of public administration at the LSE 1912–27. He was a member of the Labour Party executive 1915–25, entered Parliament 1922, and was president of the Board of Trade 1924, dominions secretary 1929–30, and colonial secretary 1929–31. Beatrice also wrote *The Co-operative Movement in Great Britain* 1891, *My Apprenticeship* 1926, and *Our Partnership* 1948. They were early members of the socialist Fabian Society, and were married 1892.

Webb Mary 1882–1927. English novelist. Born in Shropshire, she wrote of country life and characters, for example in *Precious Bane* 1924, which became known through a recommendation by Stanley Baldwin.

Webb Philip (Speakman) 1831–1915. English architect. He mostly designed private houses, including the Red House, Bexley heath, London, for William ◊Morris, and was one of the leading figures, with Richard Norman ◊Shaw and C F A ◊Voysey, in the revival of domestic English architecture in the late 19th century.

Webber Andrew Lloyd. English composer of musicals: see ◊Lloyd Webber.

Weber Carl Maria Friedrich Ernst von 1786–1826. German composer who established the Romantic school of opera with *Der Freischütz* 1821 and *Euryanthe* 1823. He was *Kapellmeister* at Breslau 1804–06, Prague 1813–16, and Dresden 1816. He died during a visit to London where he produced his opera *Oberon* 1826, written for the Covent Garden theatre.

Weber Ernst Heinrich 1795–1878. German anatomist and physiologist, the brother of Wilhelm Weber. He applied hydrodynamics to study blood circulation, and formulated ***Weber's law***, relating response to stimulus.

Weber Max 1864–1920. German sociologist, one of the founders of modern sociology. He emphasized cultural and political factors as key influences on economic development and individual behaviour.

Weber argued for a scientific and value-free approach to research, yet highlighted the importance of meaning and consciousness in understanding social action. His ideas continue to stimulate modern thought on social stratification, power, organizations, law, and religion.

Key works include *The Protestant Ethic and the Spirit of Capitalism* 1902, *Economy and Society* 1922, *The Methodology of the Social Sciences* 1949, and *The Sociology of Religion* 1920.

Weber Wilhelm Eduard 1804–1891. German physicist, who studied magnetism and electricity. Working with Karl Gauss, he made sensitive magnetometers to measure magnetic fields, and instruments to measure direct and alternating currents. He also built an electric telegraph. The SI unit of magnetic flux, the *weber*, is named after him.

Webern Anton (Friedrich Wilhelm von) 1883–1945. Austrian composer. A pupil of ◊Schoenberg, whose 12-tone technique he adopted, he wrote works of extreme brevity; for example, the oratorio *Das Augenlicht* 1935, and songs to words by Stefan George and poems of Rilke.

Webster Daniel 1782–1852. US politician and orator, born in New Hampshire. He sat in the House of Representatives from 1813 and in the Senate from 1827, at first as a Federalist and later as a Whig. He was secretary of state 1841–43 and 1850–52, and negotiated the Ashburton Treaty 1842, which fixed the Maine–Canada boundary. His celebrated 'seventh of March' speech in the Senate in 1850 helped secure a compromise on the slavery issue.

Webster John *c.*1580–1634. English dramatist, who ranks after Shakespeare as the greatest tragedian of his time, and is the Jacobean whose plays are most frequently performed today. His two great plays *The White Devil* 1608 and *The Duchess of Malfi* 1614 are dark, violent tragedies obsessed with death and decay and infused with poetic brilliance.

Webster Noah 1758–1843. US lexicographer, whose books on grammar and spelling and *American Dictionary of the English Language* 1828 standardized US English.

Weddell James 1787–1834. British Antarctic explorer. In 1823, he reached 75°S latitude and 35°W longitude, in the *Weddell Sea*, which is named after him.

Wedekind Frank 1864–1918. German dramatist. He was a forerunner of Expressionism with *Frühlings Erwachen/The Awakening of Spring* 1891, and *Der Erdgeist/The Earth Spirit* 1895 and its sequel *Der Marquis von Keith. Die Büchse der Pandora/Pandora's Box* 1904 was the source for Berg's opera *Lulu.*

Wedgwood C(icely) V(eronica) 1910– . British historian. An authority on the 17th century, she has published studies of *Cromwell* 1939 and *The Trial of Charles I* 1964.

Wedgwood Josiah 1730–1795. English pottery manufacturer. He set up business in Burslem, Staffordshire, in the early 1760s, to produce his unglazed blue or green stoneware decorated with white Neo-Classical designs, using pigments of his own invention.

Wegener Alfred Lothar 1880–1930. German meteorologist and geophysicist, whose theory of 'continental drift', expounded in *Origin of Continents and Oceans* 1915, was originally known as Wegener's hypothesis. His ideas can now be explained in terms of plate tectonics, the idea that the Earth's crust consists of a number of plates, all moving with respect to one another.

Weil Simone 1909–1943. French writer, who became a practising Catholic after a mystical experience in 1938. Apart from essays, her works (advocating political passivity) were posthumously published, including *Waiting for God* 1951, *The Need for Roots* 1952, and *Notebooks* 1956.

Weill Kurt (Julian) 1900–1950. German composer, US citizen from 1943. He wrote chamber and orchestral music and collaborated with ◊Brecht on operas such as *Die Dreigroschenoper/The Threepenny Opera* 1928 and *Aufstieg und Fall der Stadt Mahagonny/The Rise and Fall of the City of Mahagonny* 1930, all attacking social corruption (*Mahagonny* caused a riot at its premiere in Leipzig). He tried to evolve a new form of music theatre, using subjects with a contemporary relevance and the simplest musical means. In 1935 he left Germany for the USA, where he wrote a number of successful scores for Broadway, among them the antiwar musical *Johnny Johnson* 1936 (including the often covered 'September Song') and *Street Scene* 1947 based on an Elmer Rice play of the Depression.

Weinberg Steven 1933– . US physicist, who in 1967 demonstrated, together with Abdus ◊Salam, that the weak nuclear force and the electromagnetic force are variations of a single underlying force, now called the electroweak force. Weinberg and Salam shared a Nobel prize with Sheldon ◊Glashow in 1979.

Weinberger Caspar (Willard) 1917– . US Republican politician. He served under presidents Nixon and Ford, and was Reagan's defense secretary 1981–87.

Weir Peter 1938– . Australian film director. His films have an atmospheric quality and often contain a strong spiritual element. They include *Picnic at Hanging Rock* 1975, *Witness* 1985, and *Mosquito Coast* 1986.

Weismann August 1834–1914. German biologist. His failing eyesight forced him to turn from microscopy to theoretical work and in 1892 he proposed that changes to the body do not in turn cause an alteration of the genetic material.

Weismuller 'Johnny' (Peter John) 1904–1984. US film actor, formerly an Olympic swimmer, who played Tarzan in a long-running series of films for MGM and RKO including *Tarzan the Ape Man* 1932, *Tarzan and His Mate* 1934, and *Tarzan and the Leopard Woman* 1946.

Welles US actor and director Orson Welles.

Weizmann Chaim 1874–1952. Zionist leader (president of Israel 1948–52) and chemist, born in Russia. He became a naturalized British subject, and as director of the Admiralty laboratories 1916–19 discovered a process for manufacturing acetone, a solvent. He conducted the negotiations leading up to the Balfour Declaration, by which Britain declared its support for an independent Jewish state. He was head of the Hebrew University in Jerusalem, and in 1948 became the first president of the new republic of Israel.

Weizsäcker Richard Freiherr Baron von 1920– West German Christian Democrat politician, president from 1984. He began his career as a lawyer and was also active in the German Protestant church and in Christian Democratic Union (CDU) party politics. He was elected to the Bundestag in 1969 and served as mayor of West Berlin from 1981, before being elected federal president in 1984.

Welch (Maurice) Denton 1915–1948. English writer and artist. His works include the novel *In Youth is Pleasure* 1944 and the autobiographical *A Voice Through a Cloud* 1950.

Welch Raquel. Stage name of Raquel Tejada 1940– . US actress, a sex symbol of the 1960s in such films as *One Million Years BC* 1966, *Myra Breckinridge* 1970, and *The Three Musketeers* 1973.

Weldon Fay 1931– . British novelist and dramatist, whose work deals with feminist themes, often in an ironic or comic manner. Novels include *The Fat Woman's Joke* 1967, *Female Friends* 1975, *Remember Me* 1976, *Puffball* 1980, and *The Life and Loves of a She-Devil* 1984. She has also written plays for the stage, radio, and television.

Welensky Roy 1907– . Rhodesian right-wing politician. He was instrumental in the creation of a federation of N and S Rhodesia and Nyasaland in 1953 and was prime minister 1956–63. His Federal Party was defeated by Ian Smith's Rhodesian Front in 1964.

Welhaven Johan Sebastian Cammermeyer 1807–1873. Norwegian poet, professor of philosophy at Christiania (now Oslo) 1839–68. A supporter of the Dano-Norwegian culture, he is considered one of the greatest Norwegian masters of poetic form. His works include the satiric *Norges Daemring* 1834.

Welles (George) Orson 1915–1985. US actor and director. He produced a radio version of H G Wells's novel *The War of the Worlds* 1938, and then produced, directed, and starred in *Citizen Kane* 1941, a landmark in the history of cinema, yet he directed very few films subsequently in Hollywood. Later films as an actor include *The Lady from Shanghai* 1948 and *The Third Man* 1949.

In 1937 he founded the Mercury Theater, New York, with John Houseman, where their repertory productions included a modern-dress version of *Julius Caesar*. The realistic radio broadcast of H G Wells's *The War of the Worlds* in 1938 caused panic and fear of Martian invasion in the USA. He directed the films *Touch of Evil* 1958 and *Chimes at Midnight* 1967, a Shakespeare adaptation.

Wellesley family name of dukes of Wellington; seated at Stratfield Saye, Berkshire, England.

Wellesley Richard Colley, Marquess Wellesley 1760–1842. British administrator. He was governor general of India 1798–1805, and by his victories over the Mahrattas of W India greatly extended the territory under British rule. He was foreign secretary 1809–12, and lord lieutenant of Ireland 1821–28 and 1833–34. He was a brother of the Duke of Wellington.

Wellesz Egon (Joseph) 1885–1974. Austrian composer and musicologist. He specialized in the history of Byzantine, Renaissance, and modern music. His compositions include operas such as *Alkestis* 1924; symphonies, notably the Fifth 1957; ballet music; and a series of string quartets.

Wellington Arthur Wellesley, 1st Duke of Wellington 1769–1852. British soldier and Tory politician. As commander in the Peninsular War, he expelled the French from Spain in 1814. He defeated Napoleon Bonaparte at Quatre-Bras and Waterloo in 1815, and was a member of the Congress of Vienna. As prime minister 1828–30, he was forced to concede Roman Catholic emancipation.

Wellington was born in Ireland, son of an Irish peer, and sat for a time in the Irish parliament. He was knighted for his army service in India and became a national hero with his victories 1808–14 in the Peninsular War and as general of the allies against Napoleon. At the Congress of

Wellington *Arthur Wellesley, 1st Duke of Wellington, known as the Iron Duke* .

Vienna he opposed the dismemberment of France and supported restoration of the Bourbons. As prime minister he modified the Corn Laws but became unpopular for his opposition to parliamentary reform and his lack of opposition to Catholic emancipation. He was foreign secretary 1834–35 and a member of the cabinet 1841–46. He held the office of commander in chief of the forces at various times from 1827 and for life from 1842.

Wells H(erbert) G(eorge) 1866–1946. English writer. He first made his name with 'scientific romances' such as *The Time Machine* 1895 and *The War of the Worlds* 1898. Later novels had an anti-establishment, anti-conventional humour remarkable in its day, for example *Kipps* 1905 and *Tono-Bungay* 1909. His many other books include *Outline of History* 1920 and *The Shape of Things to Come* 1933, from which a number of his prophecies have since been fulfilled. He also wrote many short stories.

Welty Eudora 1909– . US novelist and short-story writer, born in Jackson, Mississippi. Her works reflect life in the US South and are notable for their creation of character and accurate rendition of local dialect. Her novels include *Delta Wedding* 1946, *Losing Battles* 1970, and *The Optimist's Daughter* 1972.

Wenceslas, St 907–929. Duke of Bohemia who attempted to Christianize his people and was murdered by his brother. He is patron saint of Czechoslovakia and the 'good King Wenceslas' of the carol. Feast day 28 Sept.

Wentworth William Charles 1790–1872. Australian politician, the son of D'Arcy Wentworth (*c.*1762–1827), surgeon of the penal settlement at Norfolk Island. In 1855 he was in Britain to steer the New South Wales constitution through

Parliament, and campaigned for Australian federalism and self-government.

Werfel Franz 1890–1945. Austrian poet, dramatist, and novelist, a leading Expressionist. His works include the poems 'Der Weltfreund der Gerichtstag'/'The Day of Judgment' 1919; the plays *Juarez und Maximilian* 1924, and *Das Reich Gottes in Böhmen/The Kingdom of God in Bohemia* 1930; and the novels *Verdi* 1924 and *Das Lied von Bernadette/The Song of Bernadette* 1941.

Born in Prague, he lived in Germany, Austria, and France, and in 1940 escaped from a French concentration camp to the USA, where he died. In 1929 he married Alma Mahler, daughter of the composer.

Wergeland Henrik 1808–1845. Norwegian lyric poet. He was the greatest leader of the Norwegian revival, and is known for his epic *Skabelsen, Mennesket, og Messias/Creation, Humanity, and Messiah* 1830.

Werner Abraham Gottlob 1750–1815. German geologist, one of the first to classify minerals systematically. He also developed the later discarded theory of neptunianism – that the Earth was initially covered by water, with every mineral in suspension: as the water receded, layers of rocks 'crystallized'.

Werner Alfred 1866–1919. Swiss chemist. He was awarded a Nobel prize in 1913 for his work on valency theory.

Wesker Arnold 1932– . English playwright. His socialist beliefs were reflected in the successful trilogy *Chicken Soup with Barley*, *Roots*, and *I'm Talking About Jerusalem* 1958–60. He established a catchphrase with *Chips with Everything* 1962.

In 1962, Wesker tried unsuccessfully to establish a working-class theatre with trade union backing. Later plays include *The Merchant* 1978.

Wesley Charles 1707–1788. English Methodist, brother of John ◊Wesley and one of the original Methodists at Oxford. He became a principal preacher and theologian of the Wesleyan Methodists. He wrote some 6,500 hymns, including 'Jesu, lover of my soul'.

Wesley John 1703–1791. English founder of Methodism. When the pulpits of the established church were closed to him and his followers, he took the gospel to the people. For 50 years he rode about the country on horseback, preaching daily, largely in the open air. His sermons became the doctrinal standard of the Wesleyan Methodist Church.

He was born at Epworth, Lincolnshire, where his father was the rector, and went to Oxford University together with his brother Charles, where their circle was nicknamed Methodists because of their religious observances. He was ordained in the Church of England in 1728 and returned to his Oxford college in 1729 as a

West *Novelist and journalist Rebecca West took her pen name from a character in Ibsen's play* Rosmersholm.

tutor. In 1735 he went to Georgia, USA, as a missionary. On his return he experienced 'conversion' in 1738, and from being rigidly High Church developed into an ardent Evangelical. His *Journal* gives an intimate picture of the man and his work.

Wesley Samuel 1776–1837. Son of Charles ◊Wesley. He was an organist and composer of oratorios, church and chamber music.

West Benjamin 1738–1820. American painter, active in London from 1763. He enjoyed the patronage of George III for many years and painted historical pictures.

West was born in Pennsylvania. He became president of the Royal Academy in 1792. *The Death of Wolfe* 1770 (National Gallery, Ottawa) began a vogue for painting recent historical events in contemporary costume. Many early American artists studied with him.

West Mae 1892–1980. US vaudeville and film actress. She wrote her own dialogue, sending herself up as a sex symbol. Her films include *She Done Him Wrong* 1933; two of her often quoted lines are 'Come up and see me some time' and 'Beulah, peel me a grape'.

West Nathanael. Pen name of Nathan Weinstein 1904–1940. US black-humour novelist, born in New York. West's surrealist influenced novels capture the absurdity and extremity of modern American life and the dark side of the American dream. *The Day of the Locust* 1939 explores the violent fantasies induced by Hollywood, where West was a screenwriter. *Miss Lonelyhearts* 1933

is about an agonized male agony aunt on a newspaper who feels the misfortunes of his correspondents; *A Cool Million* 1934 satirizes the rags-to-riches dream of success.

West Rebecca. Pen name of Cicily Isabel Fairfield 1892–1983. British journalist and novelist, an active feminist from 1911. *The Meaning of Treason* 1959 deals with the spies Burgess and Maclean. Her novels include *The Fountain Overflows* 1956.

Westinghouse George 1846–1914. US inventor and founder of the Westinghouse Corporation in 1886. After service in the Civil War he patented a powerful air brake for trains in 1869. In the 1880s, he turned his attention to the generation of electricity. Unlike Thomas ◊Edison, Westinghouse introduced alternating current into his power stations.

Westmacott Richard 1775–1856. British sculptor. He studied under ◊Canova in Rome, was elected to the Royal Academy 1811 and became a professor there. He executed monuments in Westminster Abbey and in St Paul's Cathedral, and the *Achilles* in Hyde Park, all in London.

Weston Edward 1886–1958. US photographer. A founder member of the F64 group, a school of photography advocating sharp definition, he is noted for the technical mastery in his Californian landscapes and nude studies.

Weyden Rogier van der c. 1399–1464. Netherlandish painter, official painter to the city of Brussels from 1436. He painted portraits and religious subjects, such as *The Last Judgement* about 1450 (Hôtel-Dieu, Beaune). His refined style had considerable impact on Netherlandish painting.

Little is known of his life and none of his works have been dated, but he was widely admired in his day and was known in Italy. His *Deposition* before 1443 (Prado, Madrid) shows the influence of Robert ◊Campin.

Weygand Maxime 1867–1965. French general. In 1940, as French commander in chief, he advised surrender to Germany, and was subsequently high commissioner of N Africa 1940–41. He was a prisoner in Germany 1942–45, and was arrested after his return to France; he was released in 1946, and in 1949 the sentence of national infamy was quashed.

Whale James 1886–1957. British film director. He initially went to Hollywood to film his stage success *Journey's End* 1930, and went on to direct four horror films: *Frankenstein* 1931, *The Old Dark House* 1932, *The Invisible Man* 1933, and *Bride of Frankenstein* 1935. He also directed *Showboat* 1936.

Wharton Edith (born Jones) 1862–1937. US novelist. Her work was influenced by her friend Henry James, and mostly set in New York society. It includes *The House of Mirth* 1905, the rural *Ethan Frome* 1911, *The Custom of the Country* 1913, and *The Age of Innocence* 1920.

Wheatley Dennis (Yates) 1897–1977. British thriller and adventure novelist. He is known for his series dealing with black magic and occultism, but also wrote crime novels in which the reader was invited to play the detective, as in *Murder off Miami* 1936, with real clues such as ticket stubs.

Wheatstone Charles 1802–1875. English physicist and inventor. With William Cooke, he patented a railway telegraph in 1837, and, developing an idea of Samuel Christie's, devised the **Wheatstone bridge**, an electrical network for measuring resistance. Originally a musical-instrument maker, he invented the harmonica and the concertina.

Wheeler Mortimer 1890–1976. English archaeologist. While he was keeper of the London Museum 1926–44, his digs included Caerleon in Wales 1926–27 and Maiden Castle in Dorset 1934–37. As director-general of archaeology in India 1944–48 he revealed the Indus Valley civilization. He helped to popularize archaeology by his television appearances.

Whewell William 1794–1866. British physicist and philosopher who coined the term 'scientist' along with such words as Eocene and Miocene, electrode, cathode, and anode. Most of his career was connected with Cambridge, where he became the Master of Trinity College. His most enduring influence rests on two works of great scholarship and acuteness, *The History of the Inductive Sciences* 1837 and *The Philosophy of the Inductive Sciences* 1840, both still in print and widely read.

Whipple Fred Lawrence 1906– . US astronomer, whose hypothesis in 1949 that the nucleus of a comet is like a dirty snowball was confirmed 1986 by space-probe studies of Halley's comet. He was director of the Smithsonian Astrophysical Observatory 1955–73.

Whipple George 1878–1976. US physiologist whose research interest concerned the formation of haemoglobin in the blood. He showed that anaemic dogs, kept under restricted diets, responded well to a liver regime, and that their haemoglobin quickly regenerated. This work led to a cure for pernicious anaemia.

Whistler James Abbott McNeill 1834–1903. US painter and etcher, active in London from 1859. His riverscapes and portraits show subtle composition and colour harmonies, for example *Arrangement in Grey and Black: Portrait of the Painter's Mother* 1871 (Louvre, Paris).

Whistler was born in Massachusetts. He abandoned a military career and in 1855 went to Paris where he was associated with the Impressionists. He then settled in Chelsea, London, and his views of the Thames include *Old Battersea Bridge* (Tate Gallery, London). Some of his *Nocturnes* 1877 were adversely criticized by ◊Ruskin and led to a libel trial in which Whistler was awarded a farthing damages. Whistler retaliated

in 1890 by publishing *The Gentle Art of Making Enemies*.

Whistler Rex John 1905–1944. English artist. He painted fanciful murals, for example *In Pursuit of Rare Meats* in the Tate Gallery restaurant, London.

White E(lwyn) B(rooks) 1899–1985. US writer, long associated with the *New Yorker*, noted for satire, for example *Is Sex Necessary?* 1929 (with the humorist James Thurber). White also wrote two children's classics, *Stuart Little* 1945 and *Charlotte's Web* 1952.

White Gilbert 1720–1793. English cleric and naturalist, born at Selborne, Hampshire, and author of *Natural History and Antiquities of Selborne* 1789.

White Patrick 1912– . Australian novelist. Born in London, he settled in Australia in the 1940s. His novels (with allegorical overtones) include *The Aunt's Story* 1948, *Voss* (based on the 19th-century explorer Leichhardt) 1957, and *The Twyborn Affair* 1979. Nobel prize 1973.

White T(erence) H(anbury) 1906–1964. English writer, who retold the Arthurian legend in four volumes of *The Once and Future King* 1938–58.

Whitefield George 1714–1770. British Methodist evangelist. He was a student at Oxford and took orders 1738, but was suspended for his unorthodox doctrines and methods. For many years he travelled through Britain and America, and by his preaching contributed greatly to the religious revival. Whitefield's Tabernacle was built for him in Tottenham Court Road, London (1756; bombed 1945 but rebuilt).

Whitehead Alfred North 1861–1947. English philosopher and mathematician. In his 'theory of organism', he attempted a synthesis of metaphysics and science. His works include *Principia Mathematica* 1910–13 (with Bertrand ◊Russell), *The Concept of Nature* 1920, and *Adventures of Ideas* 1933.

He was professor of applied mathematics at London University 1914–24, and professor of philosophy at Harvard University, USA, 1924–37. Other works include *Principles of Natural Knowledge* 1919, *Science and the Modern World* 1925, and *Process and Reality* 1929.

Whitehead Robert 1823–1905. English engineer who invented the self-propelled torpedo in Austria in 1866, and within two years was manufacturing 4 m/13 ft torpedoes which could carry a 9 kg/20 lb dynamite warhead at a speed of 7 knots, subsequently improved to 29 knots. They were powered by compressed air and had a balancing mechanism and, later, gyroscopic controls.

Whitehouse Mary 1910– . British media activist; as founder of the National Viewers' and Listeners' Association, she has campaigned to censor radio and television in their treatment of sex and violence.

Whitelaw William, Viscount Whitelaw 1918– . British Conservative politician. As secretary of state for Northern Ireland he introduced the concept of power sharing. He became secretary of state for employment 1973–74, but failed to conciliate the trade unions. He was chair of the Conservative Party 1974, and home secretary 1979–83, when he was made a peer. He resigned 1988.

Whiteman Paul 1890–1967. US dance-band leader specializing in symphonic jazz. He commissioned Gershwin's *Rhapsody in Blue*, conducting its premiere in 1924.

Whitlam (Edward) Gough 1916– . Australian politician, leader of the Labor Party 1967–78 and prime minister 1972–75. He cultivated closer relations with Asia, attempted redistribution of wealth, and raised loans to increase national ownership of industry and resources.

When the opposition blocked finance bills in the Senate, following a crisis of confidence, Whitlam refused to call a general election, and was dismissed by the governor general (Sir John Kerr). He was defeated in the general election eventually called by Malcolm ◊Fraser.

Whitman Walt(er) 1819–1892. US poet who published *Leaves of Grass* 1855, which contains the symbolic 'Song of Myself'. It used unconventional free verse (with no rhyme or regular rhythm) and scandalized the public by its frank celebration of sexuality.

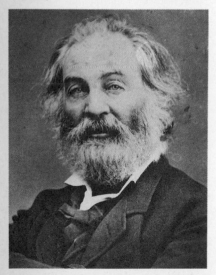

Whitman American poet Walt Whitman, whose unconventional, colloquial verse made him one of the most influential writers of his generation.

Born in West Hill, New York, as a young man Whitman worked as a printer, teacher, and journalist. In 1865 he published *Drum-Taps*, a volume inspired by his work as an army nurse during the Civil War. He also wrote an elegy on Abraham Lincoln, 'When Lilacs Last in the Dooryard Bloom'd'. He preached a US vision of individual freedom and human brotherhood.

Whitney Eli 1765–1825. US inventor who in 1793 patented the ***cotton gin***, a device for separating cotton fibre from its seeds.

Whitten-Brown Arthur 1886–1948. British aviator. After serving in World War I, he took part in the first nonstop flight across the Atlantic as navigator to Captain John ◊Alcock in 1919.

Whittier John Greenleaf 1807–1892. US poet who was a powerful opponent of slavery, as shown in the verse *Voices of Freedom* 1846. Among his other works are *Legends of New England in Prose and Verse, Songs of Labor* 1850, and the New England nature poem *Snow-Bound* 1866.

Whittle Frank 1907– . British engineer who invented the jet engine in 1930. In the Royal Air Force he worked on jet propulsion 1937–46. In May 1941 the Gloster E 28/39 aircraft first flew with the Whittle jet engine.

Whymper Edward 1840–1911. English mountaineer. He made the first ascent of many Alpine peaks, including the Matterhorn 1865, and in the Andes scaled Chimborazo and other mountains. He wrote *Scrambles amongst the Alps* 1871 and *Zermatt and the Matterhorn* 1897.

Wickham Henry 1846–1928. British planter who founded the rubber plantations of Sri Lanka and Malaysia, and broke the monopoly in rubber production then held by Brazil. He collected rubber seeds from Brazil, where they grew naturally, cultivated them at Kew Gardens, and re-exported them to the Far East.

Widmark Richard 1914– . US actor who made his film debut in *Kiss of Death* 1947 as a psychopath. He subsequently appeared in a great variety of roles in films including *The Alamo* 1960, *Madigan* 1968, and *Coma* 1978.

Wieland Christoph Martin 1733–1813. German poet and novelist. After attempts at religious poetry, he came under the influence of Voltaire and Rousseau, and wrote novels such as *Agathon* and the satirical *Aberiten*, and tales in verse such as *Oberon, Musarion*, and others. He translated Shakespeare into German 1762–66.

Wien Wilhelm 1864–1928. German physicist who studied radiation and established the principle that the wavelength at which the radiation from an idealized radiating body is most intense is inversely proportional to the body's absolute temperature. That is, the hotter the body, the shorter the wavelength. For this, and other work on radiation, he was awarded the 1911 Nobel Prize for Physics.

Wiene Robert 1880–1938. German film director of the bizarre Expressionist film *Das Kabinett des Dr Caligari/The Cabinet of Dr Caligari* 1919. He also directed *Orlacs Hände/The Hands of Orlac* 1924, *Der Rosenkavalier* 1926, and *Ultimatum* 1938.

Wiener Norbert 1984–1964. US mathematician, credited with the establishment of the science of cybernetics in his book *Cybernetics* 1948. In mathematics, he laid the foundation of the study of stochastic processes (those dependent on random events), particularly Brownian movement (evidence of constant random motion of molecules).

Wiesel Elie 1928– . US academic and human-rights campaigner, born in Romania. He was held in Buchenwald concentration camp during World War II, and has assiduously documented wartime atrocities against the Jews in an effort to alert the world to the dangers of racism and violence. Nobel Peace Prize 1986.

Wiggin Kate Douglas 1856–1923. US writer, born in Philadelphia. She was a pioneer in the running of kindergartens in the USA, and wrote the children's classic *Rebecca of Sunnybrook Farm* 1903 and several sequels.

Wigner Eugene Paul 1902– . US physicist, born in Hungary. Building on earlier work by Schrödinger, he applied quantum mechanics to nuclear physics and made many advances. For work on nuclear structure, he shared the 1963 Nobel Prize for Physics with ◊Goeppert-Mayer and Hans Jensen (1906–73).

Wilander Mats 1964– . Swedish lawn-tennis player. He won his first Grand Slam event 1982 when he beat Guillermo Vilas to win the French Open, and had won eight Grand Slam titles by 1990. He played a prominent role in Sweden's rise to the forefront of men's tennis in the 1980s.

Wilberforce Samuel 1805–1873. British Anglican bishop of Oxford 1845–69, and from 1869 of Winchester. He defended Anglican orthodoxy against the Oxford Movement for the revival of English Roman Catholicism.

Wilberforce William 1759–1833. English reformer who was instrumental in abolishing slavery in the British Empire. He began his attacks on slavery while at school, and from 1788 devoted himself to its abolition. He entered Parliament in 1780; in 1807 his bill for the abolition of the slave trade was passed, and in 1833, largely through his efforts, slavery was abolished throughout the empire.

Wilbur Richard 1921– . US poet, whose witty verse is found in several volumes including *Poems 1943–56* 1957 and *The Mind Reader* 1971.

Wild Jonathan *c.*1682–1725. English criminal who organized the thieves of London and ran an office which, for a payment, returned stolen goods to their owners. He was hanged at Tyburn.

Wilde Cornel(ius Louis) 1915–1989. US actor and film director, born in Austro-Hungary. He starred in *A Song to Remember* 1945, and directed *The Naked Prey* 1966 (in which he also acted) and *No Blade of Grass* 1970.

Wilde Oscar (Fingal O'Flahertie Wills) 1854–1900. Irish writer. With his flamboyant style and quotable conversation, he dazzled London society and, on his lecture tour in 1882, the USA. He published his only novel *The Picture of Dorian Gray* 1891, followed by witty plays including *A Woman of No Importance* 1893 and *The Importance of Being Earnest* 1895. In 1895 he was imprisoned for two years for homosexual offences; he died in exile.

Wilde was born in Dublin and studied at Dublin and Oxford, where he became known as a supporter of the Aesthetic movement ('Art for art's sake'). He published *Poems* 1881, and also wrote fairy tales and other stories, criticism, and a long, anarchic political essay, 'The Soul of Man Under Socialism' 1891. His elegant social comedies include *Lady Windermere's Fan* 1892 and *An Ideal Husband* 1895. The drama *Salome* 1893, based on the biblical character, was written in French; considered scandalous by the British censor, it was first performed in Paris 1896 with the actress Sarah Bernhardt in the title role.

Among his lovers was Lord Alfred ◊Douglas, whose father provoked Wilde into a lawsuit that led to his social and financial ruin and imprisonment. The long poem *Ballad of Reading Gaol* 1898 and a letter published as *De Profundis* 1905 were written in jail to explain his side of the relationship. After his release from prison in 1897, he lived in France, and is buried in Paris.

Wilder Billy 1906– . US film director, born in Austria. He directed and collaborated on the script of *Double Indemnity* 1944, and directed *The Lost Weekend* 1945, *Sunset Boulevard* 1950, and the classic comedy *Some Like it Hot* 1959.

Wilder Thornton (Niven) 1897–1975. US playwright and novelist. He won the Pulitzer Prize for the novel *The Bridge of San Luis Rey* 1927, and for the plays *Our Town* 1938 and *The Skin of Our*

Wilde *Irish writer and poet Oscar Wilde was a leading figure of the Aesthetic movement.*

Teeth 1942. His play *The Matchmaker* appeared at the Edinburgh Festival in 1954, and as the hit musical entitled *Hello Dolly!* in New York in 1964, and in London the following year.

Wilfrid, St 634–709. Northumbrian-born bishop of York from 665. He defended the cause of the Roman Church at the Synod of Whitby in 664 against that of Celtic Christianity. Feast day 12 Oct.

Wilhelm (English *William*) two emperors of Germany:

Wilhelm I 1797–1888. King of Prussia from 1861 and emperor of Germany from 1871; the son of Friedrich Wilhelm III. He served in the Napoleonic Wars 1814–15 and helped to crush the 1848 revolution. After he succeeded his brother Friedrich Wilhelm IV to the throne of Prussia, his policy was largely dictated by his chancellor ◊Bismarck, who secured his proclamation as emperor.

Wilhelm II 1859–1941. Emperor of Germany from 1888, the son of Frederick III and Victoria, daughter of Queen Victoria. In 1890 he forced Chancellor Bismarck to resign and began to direct foreign policy himself, which proved disastrous. In 1914 he first approved Austria's ultimatum to Serbia and then, when he realized war was inevitable, tried in vain to prevent it. In 1918 he fled to Holland.

Wilkes John 1727–1797. British Radical politician, imprisoned for his political views; Member of Parliament 1757–64 and from 1774. He championed parliamentary reform, religious toleration, and US independence.

Wilkes, born in Clerkenwell, London, entered Parliament as a Whig 1757. His attacks on the Tory prime minister Bute in his paper *The North Briton* led to his outlawry 1764; he fled to France, and on his return 1768 was imprisoned. He was four times elected MP for Middlesex, but the Commons refused to admit him and finally declared his opponent elected. This secured him strong working- and middle-class support, and in 1774 he was allowed to take his seat in Parliament.

Wilkie David 1785–1841. Scottish genre and portrait painter, active in London from 1805. His paintings are in the 17th-century Dutch tradition.

Wilkins George Hubert 1888–1958. Australian polar explorer, a pioneer in the use of surveys by both aircraft and submarines. He studied engineering, learned to fly in 1910, and visited both polar regions. In 1928 he flew from Barrow (Alaska) to Green Harbour (Spitsbergen), and in 1928–29 made an Antarctic flight that proved that Graham Land is an island. He also planned to reach the North Pole by submarine.

Wilkins Maurice Hugh Frederick 1916– . New Zealand scientist. In 1962 he shared the Nobel Prize for Medicine with Francis ◊Crick and James ◊Watson for his work on the molecular structure of nucleic acids, particularly DNA, using X-ray diffraction.

Wilkins worked in the USA during World War II on the development of the atomic bomb. After the war, he turned his attention from nuclear physics to biophysics, and studied the genetic effects of ultrasonic waves, nucleic acids, and viruses by using ultraviolet light.

Wilkins William 1778–1839. English architect. He pioneered the Greek revival in England with his design for Downing College, Cambridge. Other works include the main block of University College London 1827–28, and the National Gallery, London, 1834–38.

William four kings of England:

William I *the Conqueror* c. 1027–1087. King of England from 1066. He was the illegitimate son of Duke Robert the Devil, and succeeded his father as duke of Normandy 1035. Claiming that his relative Edward the Confessor had bequeathed him the English throne, William invaded the country 1066, defeating ◊Harold II at Hastings, Sussex, and was crowned king of England (as depicted in the Bayeux Tapestry).

He was crowned in Westminster Abbey on Christmas Day 1066. He completed the establishment of feudalism in England, compiling detailed records of land and property in the Domesday Book, and kept the barons firmly under control. He died in Rouen after a fall from his horse and is buried in Caen, France. He was succeeded by his son William II.

William II Rufus, *the Red* c. 1056–1100. King of England from 1087, the third son of William I. He spent most of his reign attempting to capture Normandy from his brother ◊Robert II, duke of Normandy. His extortion of money led his barons to revolt and caused confrontation with Bishop Anselm. He was killed while hunting in the New Forest, and was succeeded by his brother Henry I.

William III *William of Orange* 1650–1702. King of Great Britain and Ireland from 1688, the son of William II of Orange and Mary, daughter of Charles I. He was offered the English crown by the parliamentary opposition to James II. He invaded England 1688 and in 1689 became joint sovereign with his wife Mary. He spent much of his reign campaigning, first in Ireland, where he defeated James II at the battle of the Boyne 1690, and later against the French in Flanders. He was succeeded by Anne.

Born in the Netherlands, he was made *stadholder* (chief magistrate) 1672 to resist the French invasion. He forced Louis XIV to make peace 1678 and then concentrated on building up a European alliance against France. In 1677 he married his cousin Mary, daughter of the future James II. When invited by both Whig and Tory leaders to take the crown from James, he landed with a large force at Torbay, Devon. James fled to France, and his Scottish and Irish supporters were defeated at the battles of Dunkeld 1689 and the Boyne 1690.

William IV 1765–1837. King of the United Kingdom from 1830, when he succeeded his brother George IV, and third son of George III. He was created duke of Clarence 1789, and married Adelaide of Saxe-Meiningen (1792–1849) 1818. During the Reform Bill crisis he secured its passage by agreeing to create new peers to overcome the hostile majority in the House of Lords. He was succeeded by Victoria.

William three kings of the Netherlands:

William I 1772–1844. King of the Netherlands 1815–40. He lived in exile during the French occupation 1795–1813, and fought against the emperor Napoleon at Jena and Wagram. The Austrian Netherlands were added to his kingdom by the Allies 1815, but secured independence (recognized by the major European states 1839) by the revolution of 1830. William's unpopularity led to his abdication 1840.

William II 1792–1849. King of the Netherlands 1840–49, son of William I. He served with the British army in the Peninsular War and at Waterloo. In 1848 he averted revolution by conceding a liberal constitution.

William III 1817–1890. King of the Netherlands 1849–90, the son of William II. In 1862 he abolished slavery in the Dutch East Indies.

William 1143–1214. King of Scotland from 1165, known as *William the Lion*. He was captured by Henry II while invading England 1174, and forced to do homage, but Richard I abandoned the English claim to suzerainty for a money payment 1189. In 1209 William was forced by John I to renounce his claim to Northumberland.

William 1533–1584. Prince of Orange from 1544, known as *William the Silent* because of his absolute discretion. He was appointed governor of Holland by Philip II of Spain in 1559, but joined the revolt of 1572 against Spain's oppressive rule, and, as a Protestant from 1573, became the national leader. He briefly succeeded in uniting the Catholic south and Protestant northern provinces. But the former provinces submitted to Spain while the latter formed a federation in 1579 which repudiated Spanish suzerainty in 1581. He was assassinated by a Spanish agent.

William (full name William Arthur Philip Louis) 1982– . Prince of the United Kingdom, first child of the Prince and Princess of Wales.

William of Malmesbury *c*.1080–*c*.1143. English historian and monk. He compiled the *Gesta regum/Deeds of the Kings* about 1120–40 and *Historia novella*, which together formed a history of England to 1142.

William of Wykeham *c*.1323–1404. English politician, bishop of Winchester from 1367, Lord Chancellor 1367–72 and 1389–91, and founder

of Winchester College (public school) in 1378 and New College, Oxford, in 1379.

Williams George 1821–1905. Founder of the Young Men's Christian Association (YMCA).

Williams (George) Emlyn 1905–1987. Welsh actor and playwright. His plays, in which he appeared, include *Night Must Fall* 1935 and *The Corn Is Green* 1938. His play *How Green Was My Valley* was filmed (Academy Award 1941). He gave early encouragement to the actor Richard Burton.

Williams John (Christopher) 1942– . Australian guitarist, whose extensive repertoire includes contemporary music and jazz.

Williams Roger *c*.1604–1684. British founder of Rhode Island colony in North America 1636, on a basis of democracy and complete religious freedom.

Williams Shirley 1930– . British Social Democrat Party politician. She was Labour minister for prices and consumer protection 1974–76, and education and science 1976–79. She became a founder member of the SDP 1981 and its president 1982. In 1983 she lost her parliamentary seat. She is the daughter of socialist writer Vera ◊Brittain.

Williams Tennessee (Thomas Lanier) 1911–1983. US playwright, born in Mississippi. His work is characterized by fluent dialogue and searching analysis of the psychological deficiencies of his characters. His plays, usually set in the Deep South against a background of decadence and degradation, include *The Glass Menagerie* 1945 and *A Streetcar Named Desire* 1947.

Williams William Carlos 1883–1963. US poet. His spare images and language reflect everyday speech. His epic poem *Paterson* 1946–58 celebrates his home town in New Jersey. *Pictures from Brueghel* 1963 won a Pulitzer Prize. His work had great impact on younger US poets.

Williams-Ellis Clough 1883–1978. British architect, designer of the fantasy resort of Portmeirion, N Wales.

Williamson Henry 1895–1977. English author, known for stories of animal life such as *Tarka the Otter* 1927.

Williamson Malcolm (Benjamin Graham Christopher) 1931– . Australian composer, pianist, and organist, who settled in Britain in 1953. His works include operas (*Our Man in Havana* 1963), symphonies, and chamber music. He became Master of the Queen's Music 1975.

William the Marshall 1st Earl of Pembroke *c*. 1146–1219. English knight, regent of England from 1216. After supporting the dying Henry II against Richard (later Richard I), he went on a crusade to Palestine, was pardoned by Richard, and was granted an earldom in 1189. On King John's death he was appointed guardian of the future Henry III, and defeated the French under Louis VIII to enable Henry to gain the throne.

He grew up as a squire in Normandy, and became tutor in 1170 to Henry, son of Henry II of England. William's life was a model of chivalric loyalty, serving four successive kings of England.

Willis Norman David 1933– . British trade-union leader. A trade-union official since leaving school, he succeeded Len Murray as the general secretary of the Trades Union Congress (TUC) in 1984.

He has presided over the TUC at a time of falling union membership, hostile legislation from the Conservative government, and a major review of the role and policies of the Labour Party.

Wilson Angus (Frank Johnstone) 1913– . British novelist, whose acidly humorous books include *Anglo-Saxon Attitudes* 1956 and *The Old Men at the Zoo* 1961.

Wilson Brian 1942– . US pop musician, founder member of the Beach Boys pop group.

Wilson Charles Thomson Rees 1869–1959. British physicist, who in 1911 invented the Wilson cloud chamber, an apparatus for studying subatomic particles. He shared a Nobel prize in 1927.

Wilson Colin 1931– . British author of *The Outsider* 1956, and of thrillers, including *Necessary Doubt* 1964. Later works such as *Mysteries* 1978 are about the occult.

Wilson Edmund 1895–1972. US critic and writer, born in New Jersey. *Axel's Castle* 1931 is a survey of symbolism and *The Wound and the Bow* 1941 a study of art and neurosis. He also produced the satirical sketches in *Memoirs of Hecate County* 1946.

Wilson Edward O 1929– . US zoologist, whose books have stimulated interest in biogeography, the study of the distribution of species, and the evolution of behaviour, or sociobiology. His works include *Sociobiology* 1975 and *On Human Nature* 1978.

Wilson Henry Maitland 'Jumbo', 1st Baron Wilson 1881–1964. British field marshal in World War II. He led the unsuccessful Greek campaign of 1941, and in 1944 was supreme Allied commander in the Mediterranean.

Wilson (James) Harold, Baron Wilson of Rievaulx 1916– . British Labour politician, party leader from 1963, prime minister 1964–70 and 1974–76. His premiership was dominated by the issue of UK admission to membership of the European Community, the social contract (unofficial agreement with the trade unions), and economic difficulties.

Wilson, born in Huddersfield, West Yorkshire, was president of the Board of Trade 1947–51 (when he resigned because of social service cuts). In 1963 he succeeded Gaitskell as Labour leader and became prime minister the following year, increasing his majority 1966. He formed a minority government Feb 1974 and achieved a majority of three Oct 1974. He resigned 1976,

and was succeeded by James Callaghan. He was knighted 1976, and became a peer 1983.

Wilson Richard 1714–1782. British painter, whose English and Welsh landscapes are infused with an Italianate atmosphere and recomposed in a Classical manner. They influenced the development of an English landscape-painting tradition.

Wilson (Thomas) Woodrow 1856–1924. 28th president of the USA 1913–21, a Democrat. He kept the USA out of World War I until 1917, and in Jan 1918 issued his 'Fourteen Points' as a basis for a just peace settlement. At the peace conference in Paris he secured the inclusion of the League of Nations in individual peace treaties, but these were not ratified by Congress, so the USA did not join the League. Nobel Peace Prize 1919.

Wilson, born in Virginia, became president of Princeton University 1902. In 1910 he became governor of New Jersey. Elected president 1912 against Theodore Roosevelt and Taft, he initiated anti-trust legislation and secured valuable social reforms in his progressive 'New Freedom' programme. He strove to keep the USA neutral during World War I but the German U-boat campaign forced him to declare war 1917. In 1919 he suffered a stroke from which he never fully recovered.

Winchell Walter 1897–1972. US journalist, born in New York. He was a columnist on the *New York Mirror* 1929–69, and his bitingly satiric writings were syndicated throughout the USA.

Wilson *American president Woodrow Wilson, who took the US into World War I. He created the basis for a peace settlement and the League of Nations.*

Windsor, House of official name of the British royal family since 1917, adopted in place of Saxe-Coburg-Gotha. Since 1960 those descendants of Elizabeth II not entitled to the prefix HRH have borne the surname Mountbatten-Windsor.

Wingate Orde Charles 1903–1944. British soldier. In 1936 he established a reputation for unorthodox tactics in Palestine. In World War II he served in the Middle East, and later led the Chindits, the 3rd Indian Division, in guerrilla operations against the Japanese army in Burma.

Winterhalter Franz Xavier 1805–1873. German portraitist. He became court painter to Grand Duke Leopold at Karlsruhe, then, in 1834, moved to Paris and enjoyed the patronage of European royalty.

Wise Robert 1914– . US film director who began as a film editor. His debut was a horror film, *Curse of the Cat People* 1944; he progressed to such large-scale projects as *The Sound of Music* 1965 and *Star* 1968. His other films include *The Body Snatcher* 1945 and *Star Trek: The Motion Picture* 1979.

Wise Thomas James 1859–1937. British bibliographer. He collected the Ashley Library of first editions, chiefly English poets and dramatists 1890–1930, acquired by the British Museum at his death, and made many forgeries of supposed privately printed first editions of Browning, Tennyson, and Swinburne.

Wiseman Nicholas Patrick Stephen 1802–1865. British Catholic priest who became the first archbishop of Westminster 1850.

Wishart George c.1513–1546. Scottish Protestant reformer burned for heresy, who probably converted John ◊Knox.

Wister Owen 1860–1938. US novelist who created the genre of the western. He was born in Philadelphia, a grandson of the British actress Fanny Kemble, and became known for stories of cowboys in the American West; for example, *The Virginian* 1902.

Witt Johann de 1625–1672. Dutch politician, Grand Pensionary of Holland and virtual prime minister from 1653. His skilful diplomacy ended the Dutch Wars of 1652–54 and 1665–67, and in 1668 he formed a triple alliance with England and Sweden against Louis XIV of France. He was murdered by a rioting mob.

Witt Katerina 1965– . East German ice-skater. She was 1984 Olympic champion and had by 1990 won four world titles and six consecutive European titles.

Wittgenstein Ludwig 1889–1951. Austrian philosopher. *Tractatus Logico-Philosophicus* 1922 postulated the 'picture theory' of language: that words represent things according to social agreement. He subsequently rejected this idea, and developed the idea that usage was more important than convention.

The picture theory said that it must be possible to break down a sentence into 'atomic propositions' whose elements stand for elements of the real world. After he rejected this idea, anthropological view of language.

He taught at Cambridge University, England, in the 1930s and 1940s. *Philosophical Investigations* 1954 and *On Certainty* 1969 were published posthumously.

Wodehouse P(elham) G(renville) 1881–1975. English novelist, a US citizen from 1955, whose humorous novels portray the accident-prone world of such characters as the socialite Bertie Wooster and his invaluable and impeccable manservant Jeeves, and Lord Emsworth of Blandings Castle with his prize pig, the Empress of Blandings.

From 1906, Wodehouse also collaborated on the lyrics of Broadway musicals by Jerome Kern, Gershwin, and others. He spent most of his life in the USA. Staying in France in 1941, during World War II, he was interned by the Germans; he made some humorous broadcasts from Berlin, which were later taken amiss in Britain at the time, but he was later exonerated, and was knighted 1975. His work is admired for its style and geniality, and includes *Indiscretions of Archie* 1921, *Uncle Fred in the Springtime* 1939, and *Aunts Aren't Gentlemen* 1974.

Woffington 'Peg' (Margaret) c.1714–1760. Irish actress, who played in Dublin as a child and made her debut at Covent Garden, London, in 1740. She acted in many Restoration comedies, often taking male roles, such as Lothario in Rowe's *The Fair Penitent*.

Wöhler Friedrich 1800–1882. German chemist who synthesized the first organic compound (urea) from an inorganic compound (ammonium cyanate). He also isolated the elements aluminium, beryllium, yttrium, and titanium.

Wolf Hugo (Filipp Jakob) 1860–1903. Austrian composer, whose songs are in the German *Lieder* tradition. He also composed the opera *Der Corregidor* 1895 and orchestral works, such as *Italian Serenade* 1892.

Wolfe Gene 1931– . US writer known for the science-fiction series *The Book of the New Sun* 1980–83, with a Surrealist treatment of stock themes, and for the urban fantasy *Free, Live Free* 1985.

Wolfe James 1727–1759. British soldier. He fought at the battles of Dettingen, Falkirk, and Culloden. In 1758 he served in Canada, and played a conspicuous part in the siege of the French stronghold of Louisburg. He was promoted to major-general 1759 and commanded a victorious expedition against Québec, in which he was killed.

Wolfe Thomas 1900–1938. US novelist. He wrote four long and powerful autobiographical novels: *Look Homeward, Angel* 1929, *Of Time and the*

River 1935, and the posthumous *The Web and the Rock* 1939 and *You Can't Go Home Again* 1940.

Wolfe Tom 1931– . US journalist and novelist. In the 1960s a founder of the 'New Journalism', which brought the techniques of fiction to reportage, Wolfe recorded US mores and fashions in Pop style in *The Kandy-Kolored Tangerine-Flake Streamline Baby* 1965. His sharp social eye is applied to the New York of the 1980s in his novel *The Bonfire of the Vanities* 1988.

Wolf-Ferrari Ermanno 1876–1948. Italian composer whose operas include *Il segreto di Susanna/Susanna's Secret* 1909 and the realistic tragedy *I gioielli di Madonna/The Jewels of the Madonna* 1911.

Wolfit Donald 1902–1968. British actor and manager. He formed his own theatre company in 1937, and excelled in the Shakespearean roles of Shylock and Lear, and Volpone (in Ben Jonson's play).

Wolfson Isaac 1897– . British store magnate and philanthropist, chair of Great Universal Stores from 1946. He established the *Wolfson Foundation* 1955 to promote health, education, and youth activities, founded Wolfson College, Cambridge, 1965, and (with the Ford Foundation) endowed Wolfson College, Oxford, 1966.

Wollaston William 1766–1828. British chemist and physicist. He amassed a large fortune through his discovery in 1804 of how to make malleable platinum. He went on to discover the new elements palladium in 1804 and rhodium in 1805. He also contributed to optics through the invention of a number of ingenious and still useful measuring instruments.

Wollstonecraft Mary 1759–1797. British feminist, member of a group of radical intellectuals called the English Jacobins, whose book *Vindication of the Rights of Women* 1792 demanded equal educational opportunities for women. She married William Godwin and died in giving birth to a daughter, Mary (see Mary ◊Shelley).

Wolseley Garnet Joseph, 1st Viscount Wolseley 1833–1913. British field marshal who, as commander in chief 1895–1900, began modernizing the army.

Wolsey Thomas c.1475–1530. English cardinal and politician. Under Henry VIII he became both cardinal and lord chancellor 1515, and began the dissolution of the monasteries. His reluctance to further Henry's divorce from Catherine of Aragon, partly because of his ambitions to be pope, led to his downfall 1529. He was charged with high treason 1530 but died before being tried.

Wonder Stevie. Stage name of Steveland Judkins Morris 1950– . US pop musician, singer, and songwriter, associated with Motown Records. His hits, most of which he composed, sang, and on which he also played several instruments,

include 'My Cherie Amour' 1973, 'Master Blaster (Jammin')' 1980, and the album *Innervisions* 1973.

Wood Grant 1892–1942. US painter based mainly in his native Iowa. Though his work is highly stylized, he struck a note of hard realism in his studies of farmers, such as *American Gothic* 1930 (Art Institute, Chicago).

Wood Haydn 1882–1959. British composer. A violinist, he wrote a violin concerto among other works, and is known for his songs, which include 'Roses of Picardy', associated with World War I.

Wood Henry (Joseph) 1869–1944. English conductor, from 1895 until his death, of the London Promenade Concerts, now named after him. He promoted a national interest in music and encouraged many young composers.

He studied at the Royal Academy of Music and became an organist and operatic conductor. As a composer he is remembered for the *Fantasia on British Sea Songs* 1905, which ends each Promenade season.

Wood John c.1705–1754. British architect, known as 'Wood of Bath' because of his many works in that city. Like many of his designs, Royal Crescent was executed by his son, also *John Wood* (1728–81).

Wood Mrs Henry (born Ellen Price) 1814–1887. British novelist, a pioneer of crime fiction, who wrote the melodramatic *East Lynne* 1861.

Wood Natalie. Stage name of Natasha Gurdin 1938–1981. US film actress who began as a child star. Her films include *Miracle on 34th Street* 1947, *The Searchers* 1956, and *Bob and Carol and Ted and Alice* 1969.

Woodforde James 1740–1803. British cleric who held livings in Somerset and Norfolk, and whose diaries 1758–1802 form a record of rural England.

Woodward Joanne 1930– . US actress, active in film, television, and theatre. She was directed by Paul Newman in the film *Rachel Rachel* 1968, and also starred in *The Three Faces of Eve* 1957, *They Might Be Giants* 1971, and *Harry and Son* 1984.

Woodward Robert 1917–1979. US chemist who worked on synthesizing a large number of complex molecules. These included quinine 1944, cholesterol 1951, chlorophyll 1960, and vitamin B_{12} 1971. Nobel prize 1965.

Woolf Virginia (born Virginia Stephen) 1882–1941. English novelist and critic. Her first novel, *The Voyage Out* 1915, explored the tensions experienced by women who want marriage and a career. In *Mrs Dalloway* 1925 she perfected her 'stream of consciousness' technique. Among her later books are *To the Lighthouse* 1927, *Orlando* 1928, and *The Years* 1937, which considers the importance of economic independence for women.

Woolley (Charles) Leonard 1880–1960. British archaeologist. He excavated at Carchemish in Syria, Tell el Amarna in Egypt, Atchana (the

Wordsworth *One of the greatest English poets,*
Wordsworth turned to nature for his inspiration, in
particular to his native Lake District. This portrait is by
Benjamin Haydon.

ancient Alalakh) on the Turkish-Syrian border, and
Ur in Iraq.

Woolman John 1720–1772. American Quaker, born
in New Jersey; he was one of the first antislavery
agitators, and left an important journal.

Woolworth Frank Winfield 1852–1919. US entrepreneur. He opened his first successful 'five
and ten cent' store in Lancaster, Pennsylvania,
1879, and, together with his brother C S
Woolworth (1856–1947), built up a chain of
similar shops throughout the USA, Canada, the
UK, and Europe.

Wootton Barbara Frances Wootton, Baroness
Wootton of Abinger 1897–1988. British educationist and economist. She taught at London
University, and worked in the fields of politics,
media, social welfare, and penal reform. Her books
include *Freedom under Planning* 1945 and *Social
Science and Social Pathology* 1959.

Wordsworth Dorothy 1771–1855. English writer.
She lived with her brother William ◊Wordsworth
as a companion and support from 1795 until his
death, and her many journals describing their life
at Grasmere in the Lake District and their travels
provided inspiration and material for his poetry.

Wordsworth William 1770–1850. English Romantic
poet. In 1797 he moved with his sister Dorothy
to Somerset to be near ◊Coleridge, collaborating
with him on *Lyrical Ballads* 1798 (which included
'Tintern Abbey'). From 1799 he lived in the Lake
District, and later works include *Poems* 1807

(including 'Intimations of Immortality') and *The
Prelude* (written by 1805, published 1850). He
was appointed poet laureate 1843.

Born in Cockermouth, Cumbria, he was educated
at Cambridge University. In 1791 he returned
from a visit to France, having fallen in love
with Marie-Anne Vallon; she gave birth to an
illegitimate daughter. In 1802 he married Mary
Hutchinson. *The Prelude* was written to form part
of the autobiographical work *The Recluse*, never
completed.

Worner Manfred 1934– . West German politician,
NATO Secretary-General from 1988. He was
elected for the conservative Christian Democratic
Union (CDU) to the *Bundestag* (parliament) in
1965 and, as a specialist in srategic affairs,
served as defence minister under Chancellor Kohl
1982–88. A proponent of closer European military
collaboration, he succeeded Peter Carrington as
secretary general of NATO in July 1988.

Worrall Denis John 1935– . South African politician, member of the white opposition to apartheid.
A former academic and journalist, he joined the
National Party (NP) and was made ambassador in
London 1984–87. On his return to South Africa he
resigned from the NP and in 1988 established the
Independent Party (IP), which later merged with
other white opposition parties to form the reformist Democratic Party (DP), advocating dismantle-
ment of the apartheid system and universal adult
suffrage. A co-leader of the DP, he was elected to
parliament in 1989.

Wotton Henry 1568–1639. English poet and diplomat under James I, provost of Eton public school
from 1624. *Reliquiae Wottonianae* 1651 includes
the lyric 'You meaner beauties of the night'.

Wouvermans family of Dutch painters, based in
Haarlem. The brothers *Philips Wouvermans*
(1619–1668), *Pieter Wouvermans* (1623–
1682), and *Jan Wouvermans* (1629–1666)
specialized in landscapes with horses and riders,
and military scenes.

Wrangel Ferdinand Petrovich, Baron von 1794–
1870. Russian vice admiral and Arctic explorer,
after whom Wrangel Island (Ostrov Vrangelya) in
the Soviet Arctic is named.

Wrangel Peter Nicolaievich, Baron von 1878–1928.
Russian general, born in St Petersburg. He com-
manded a division of Cossacks in World War I,
and in 1920 became commander in chief of the
White army in the Crimea fighting against the
Bolsheviks.

Wray Fay 1907– . US film actress who starred in
King Kong 1933 after playing the lead in Erich
von Stroheim's *The Wedding March* 1928 and
starring in *Doctor X* 1932 and *The Most Dangerous
Game* 1932.

Wren Christopher 1632–1723. English architect,
designer of St Paul's Cathedral, London, built
1675–1710; many London churches including

St Bride's, Fleet Street, and St Mary-le-Bow, Cheapside; the Royal Exchange; Marlborough House; and the Sheldonian Theatre, Oxford.

Wren studied mathematics, and in 1660 became a professor of astronomy at Oxford. His opportunity as an architect came after the Great Fire of London 1666. He prepared a plan for rebuilding the city, but it was not adopted. Instead, Wren was commissioned to rebuild 51 City churches and St Paul's Cathedral. The west towers of Westminster Abbey, often attributed to him, were the design of his pupil ◊Hawksmoor.

Wren P(ercival) C(hristopher) 1885–1941. British novelist. Drawing on his experiences in the French and Indian armies, he wrote martial adventure novels including *Beau Geste* 1924, dealing with the Foreign Legion.

Wright Frank Lloyd 1869–1959. US architect who rejected Neo-Classicist styles for 'organic architecture', in which buildings reflected their natural surroundings. Among his buildings are his Wisconsin home Taliesin East 1925; Falling Water, Pittsburgh, Pennsylvania, 1936; and the Guggenheim Museum, New York, 1959.

Wright Joseph 1734–1797. British painter, known as *Wright of Derby* from his birthplace. He painted portraits, landscapes, and scientific experiments. His work is often dramatically lit, by fire, candlelight, or even volcanic explosion.

Several of his subjects are highly original, for example *The Experiment on a Bird in the Air Pump* 1768 (National Gallery, London). His portraits include the reclining figure of *Sir Brooke Boothby* 1781 (Tate Gallery, London).

Wright Joseph 1855–1930. English philologist. He was professor of comparative philology at Oxford 1901–25, and recorded English local speech in his six-volume *English Dialect Dictionary* 1896–1905.

Wright Judith 1915– . Australian poet, author of *The Moving Image* 1946 and *Alive* 1972.

Wright Orville 1871–1948 and Wilbur 1867–1912. US brothers who pioneered powered flight. Inspired by ◊Lilienthal's gliding, they perfected their piloted glider 1902. In 1903 they built a powered machine and became the first to make a successful powered flight, near Kitty Hawk, North Carolina.

Wright Peter 1917– . British intelligence agent. His book *Spycatcher* 1987, written after his retirement, caused an international stir when the British government tried unsuccessfully to block its publication anywhere in the world because of its damaging revelations about the secret service.

Wright Richard 1908–1960. US novelist. He was one of the first to depict the condition of black people in 20th-century US society with *Native Son* 1940 and the autobiography *Black Boy* 1945.

Wright Sewall 1889–1988. US geneticist and statistician. During the 1920s he helped modernize Charles ◊Darwin's theory of evolution, using statistics to model the behaviour of populations of genes.

Wundt Wilhelm Max 1832–1920. German physiologist, who regarded psychology as the study of internal experience or consciousness. His main psychological method was introspection; he also studied sensation, perception of space and time, and reaction times.

Wyatt James 1747–1813. English architect, contemporary of the Adam brothers, who designed in the Neo-Gothic style. His overenthusiastic 'restorations' of medieval cathedrals earned him the nickname 'Wyatt the Destroyer'.

Wyatt Thomas *c.*1503–1542. English poet. He was employed on diplomatic missions by Henry VIII, and in 1536 was imprisoned for a time in the Tower of London, since he was thought to have been the lover of Henry VIII's second wife, Anne Boleyn. In 1541 Wyatt was again imprisoned on charges of treason. With the Earl of Surrey, he pioneered the sonnet in England.

Wyatville Jeffrey. Adopted name of Jeffrey Wyatt 1766–1840. English architect who remodelled Windsor Castle, Berkshire. He was a nephew of the architect James Wyatt.

Wycherley William 1640–1710. English Restoration playwright. His first comedy *Love in a Wood* won him court favour 1671, and later bawdy works

Wright US architect Frank Lloyd Wright at 87. The originality of his work stands out in city buildings like the Guggenheim Museum in New York 1959. He condemned the growing congestion of cities and encouraged closeness to nature.

include *The Country Wife* 1675 and *The Plain Dealer* 1676.

Wycliffe John *c.*1320–1384. English religious reformer. Allying himself with the party of John of Gaunt, which was opposed to ecclesiastical influence at court, he attacked abuses in the church, maintaining that the Bible rather than the church was the supreme authority. About 1378 he criticized such fundamental doctrines as priestly absolution, confession, and indulgences. He set disciples to work on translating the Bible into English.

Having studied at Oxford, he became Master of Balliol College there, and sent out bands of travelling preachers. He was denounced as a heretic.

Wyeth Andrew (Newell) 1917– . US painter, based in Maine. His portraits and landscapes, usually in watercolour or tempera, are naturalistic and minutely detailed and often have a strong sense of the isolation of the countryside, for example *Christina's World* 1948.

Wyler William 1902–1981. German-born film director who lived in the USA from 1922. He directed *Wuthering Heights* 1939, *Mrs Miniver* 1942, *Ben-Hur* 1959 and *Funny Girl* 1968, among others.

Wyndham John. Pen name of John Wyndham Parkes Lucas Beynon Harris 1903–1969. English science-fiction writer who wrote *The Day of the Triffids* 1951, *The Chrysalids* 1955, and *The Midwich Cuckoos* 1957. A recurrent theme in his work is people's response to disaster, whether caused by nature, aliens, or human error.

Wynne-Edwards Vera 1906– . English zoologist who argued that animal behaviour is often altruistic and that animals will behave for the good of the group, even if this entails individual sacrifice. Her study *Animal Dispersal in Relation to Social Behaviour* was published in 1962.

Wyss Johann David 1743–1818. Swiss author of the children's classic *Swiss Family Robinson* 1813.

Xavier, St Francis 1506–1552. Spanish Jesuit missionary. He went as a Catholic missionary to the Portuguese colonies in the Indies, arriving at Goa in 1542. He was in Japan 1549–51, establishing a Christian mission which lasted for 100 years. He returned to Goa in 1552, and sailed for China, but died of fever there. He was canonized in 1622.

Xenophon *c.*430–354 BC. Greek historian, philosopher, and soldier. He was a disciple of ◊Socrates (described in Xenophon's *Symposium*). In 401 he joined a Greek mercenary army aiding the Persian prince Cyrus, and on Cyrus's death, took command. His *Anabasis* describes how he led 10,000 Greeks in a 1,000-mile march home across enemy territory. His other works include *Memorabilia* and *Apology*.

Xerxes *c.*519–465 BC. King of Persia from 485 BC, when he succeeded his father Darius and continued the Persian invasion of Greece. In 480, at the head of an army of some 400,000 men and supported by a fleet of 800 ships, he crossed the Hellespont (now the Dardanelles) strait over a bridge of boats. He defeated the Greek fleet at Artemisium and captured and burned Athens, but Themistocles annihilated the Persian fleet at Salamis and Xerxes was forced to retreat. He spent his later years working on a grandiose extension of the capital Persepolis and was eventually murdered in a court intrigue.

the Politburo 1982, and to the position of state president 1988.

The son of a wealthy Sichuan landlord and a veteran of the Long March 1934–35 and the war against Japan 1937–45, Yang rose in the ranks of the Chinese Communist Party (CCP) before being purged for alleged revisionism in the Cultural Revolution. He is viewed as a trusted supporter of Deng Xiaoping.

Yeats Jack Butler 1871–1957. Irish painter and illustrator. His vivid scenes of Irish life, for example *Back from the Races* 1925 (Tate Gallery, London), and Celtic mythology reflected a new consciousness of Irish nationalism. He was the brother of the poet W B Yeats.

Yeats W(illiam) (B)utler 1865–1939. Irish poet. He was a leader of the Celtic revival and a founder of the Abbey Theatre in Dublin. His early work was romantic and lyrical, as in the poem 'The Lake Isle of Innisfree' and plays *The Countess Cathleen* 1892 and *The Land of Heart's Desire* 1894. His later books of poetry include *The Wild Swans at Coole* 1917 and *The Winding Stair* 1929. He was a senator of the Irish Free State 1922–28. Nobel prize 1923.

Yeats was born in Dublin. His early poetry, such as *The Wind Among the Reeds* 1899, is romantically and exotically lyrical, and he drew on Irish legend for his poetic plays, including *Deirdre* 1907, but broke through to a new sharply resilient style with *Responsibilities* 1914. In his personal life there was also a break: the beautiful Maude Gonne, to whom many of his poems had been addressed, refused to marry him, and in 1917 he married Georgie Hyde-Lees, whose work as a medium reinforced his leanings towards mystic symbolism, as in the prose work *A Vision* 1925 and 1937. His later volumes of verse include *The Tower* 1928 and *Last Poems and Two Plays* 1939. His other prose works include *Autobiographies*

Yahya Khan Agha Muhammad 1917–1980. Pakistani president 1969–71. His mishandling of the Bangladesh separatist issue led to civil war, and he was forced to resign.

Yahya Khan fought with the British army in the Middle East during World War II, escaping German capture in Italy. Later, as Pakistan's chief of army general staff, he supported Gen Ayub Khan's 1958 coup and in 1969 became military ruler. Following defeat by India in 1971, he resigned and was under house arrest 1972–75.

Yalow Rosalind 1921– . US physicist who developed radioimmunoassay (RIA), a technique for detecting minute quantities of hormones present in the blood. It can be used to discover a range of hormones produced in the hypothalamic region of the brain.

Yamagata Aritomo 1838–1922. Japanese soldier and politician, prime minister 1890–91 and 1898–1900. As chief of the imperial general staff in the 1870s and 1880s he was largely responsible for the modernization of the military system. He returned as chief of staff during the Russo-Japanese war 1904–05 and remained an influential political figure until he was disgraced 1921 for having meddled in the marriage arrangements of the crown prince.

Yamamoto Gombei 1852–1933. Japanese admiral and politician. As prime minister 1913–14, he began Japanese expansion on the Chinese mainland and initiated reforms in the political system. He was briefly again premier in the aftermath of the Tokyo earthquake 1923.

Yang Shangkun 1907– . Chinese communist politician. He held a senior position in the party 1956–66, but was demoted during the Cultural Revolution. He was rehabilitated 1978, elected to

Yeats *Irish poet and dramatist W B Yeats.*

1926, *Dramatis Personae* 1936, *Letters* 1954, and *My Theologies* 1959.

Yeltsin Boris Nikolayevich 1931– . Soviet communist politician, Moscow party chief 1985–87, when he was dismissed after criticizing the slow pace of political and economic reform. He was re-elected in Mar 1989 with a 89% share of the vote, defeating an 'official Communist Party' candidate, and was elected to the Supreme Soviet in May 1989. In 1990 he was elected President of the Russian Republic.

Born in Sverdlovsk, in the W central USSR, and educated at the same Urals Polytechnic Institute as Nikolai Ryzhkov, Yeltsin began his career in the construction industry. He joined the Communist Party of the Soviet Union (CPSU) in 1961 and became district party leader in Sverdlovsk 1976. He was brought to Moscow by Mikhail Gorbachev and Ryzhkov in 1985, appointed secretary for construction and then, in Dec 1985, Moscow party chief.

A blunt-talking, hands-on reformer, Yeltsin was demoted to the post of first deputy chair of the State Construction Committee in Nov 1987. This was seen as a blow to Gorbachev's perestroika ('restructuring') initiative and a victory for the conservatives grouped around Yegor Ligachev.

Yersin Alexandre Emile Jean 1863–1943. Swiss bacteriologist, who discovered the bubonic plague bacillus in Hong Kong in 1894 and prepared a serum against it.

Yevtushenko Yevgeny Aleksandrovich 1933– . Soviet poet, born in Siberia. He aroused controversy by his anti-Stalinist 'Stalin's Heirs' 1956, published with Khrushchev's support, and 'Babi Yar' 1961. His *Autobiography* was published in 1963.

Yonge Charlotte M(ary) 1823–1901. English novelist. Her books deal mainly with family life, and are strongly influenced by the High Church philosophy of the Oxford Movement. Her best-known work is *The Heir of Redclyffe* 1853.

York, Duke of second son of Queen Elizabeth II of the UK; see ◊Andrew.

York English dynasty founded by Richard, Duke of York (1411–60). He claimed the throne through his descent from Lionel, Duke of Clarence (1338–68), third son of Edward III, whereas the reigning monarch, Henry VI of the rival house of Lancaster, was descended from the fourth son. The argument was fought out in the Wars of the Roses. York was killed at the Battle of Wakefield 1460, but next year his son became king as Edward IV, in turn succeeded by his son Edward V and then by his brother Richard III, with whose death at Bosworth the line ended. The Lancastrian victor in that battle became king as Henry VII, and consolidated his claim by marrying Edward IV's eldest daughter, Elizabeth.

York Frederick Augustus, Duke of York 1763–1827. Second son of George III. He was an unsuccessful

Yevtushenko *A master of the conversational, confessional style, Soviet poet Yevtushenko has walked a thin line between Communist idealism and raising sensitive issues.*

commander in the Netherlands 1793–99, and British commander in chief 1798–1809.

The nursery rhyme about the 'grand old duke of York' who marched his troops up the hill and down again commemorates him.

Yoshida Shigeru 1878–1967. Japanese politician and prime minister. He held various diplomatic posts in the 1920s and 1930s before becoming leader of the Liberal party and serving as prime minister for most of the 1946–54 period.

Young Arthur 1741–1820. English writer and publicizer of the new farm practices associated with the agricultural revolution. When the Board of Agriculture was established 1792, Young was appointed secretary, and was the guiding force behind the production of a county-by-county survey of British agriculture. In 1771 he published the *Farmers' Calendar*, and in 1784 began the *Annals of Agriculture*, which ran for 45 volumes, and contained contributions from many eminent farmers of the day.

Young Brigham 1801–1877. US Mormon religious leader, born in Vermont. He joined the Mormon Church 1832, and three years later was appointed an apostle. After a successful recruiting mission in Liverpool, he returned to the USA, and as successor of Joseph Smith, who had been murdered, led the Mormon migration to the Great Salt Lake in Utah 1846, founded Salt Lake City, and ruled the colony until his death.

Young David Ivor (Baron Young of Graffham) 1932– . British Conservative politician, chair of the Manpower Services Commission (MSC) 1982–84, secretary for employment from 1985, trade and industry secretary 1987–89.

Young Edward 1683–1765. English poet, author of *Night Thoughts on Life, Death and Immortality* 1742–45.

Young John Watts 1930– . US astronaut. His first flight was on Gemini 3 in 1965. He landed on the Moon with Apollo 16 in 1972, and was commander of the first flight of the space shuttle in 1981.

Young Lester (Willis) 'Pres' 1909–1959. US tenor saxophonist and jazz composer. He was a major figure in the development of his instrument for jazz music from the 1930s, and was an accompanist to the singer Billie Holiday.

Young Thomas 1773–1829. British physicist who revived the wave theory of light and in 1801 identified the phenomenon of interference (the canceling or reinforcing of two waves). A child prodigy and man of universal genius, he had mastered most European languages and many of the Eastern tongues by the age of 20. He had also absorbed the physics of Newton, and the chemistry of Lavoisier. He further displayed his versatility by publishing an account of the Rosetta stone which played a crucial role in its eventual decipherment by ◊Champollion.

Younghusband Francis 1863–1942. British soldier and explorer, born in India. He entered the army in 1882 and 20 years later accompanied the mission that opened up Tibet. He wrote travel books on India and Central Asia and works on comparative religion.

Young Pretender nickname of ◊Charles Edward Stuart, claimant to the Scottish and English thrones.

Yourcenar Marguerite. Pen name of Marguerite de Crayencour 1903–1987. French writer, born in Belgium. She achieved a reputation as a novelist in France in the 1930s (for example with *La Nouvelle Euridyce/The New Euridyce* 1931), but after World War II she settled in the USA. Novels such as *Les Mémoires d'Hadrien/The Memoirs of Hadrian* 1951 won her acclaim as a historical novelist. In 1980 she became the first woman to be elected to the French Academy.

Ypres, 1st Earl of title of Sir John ◊French, British field marshal.

Yukawa Hideki 1907–1981. Japanese physicist who predicted the existence of the subatomic particle called the meson 1935. Nobel Prize 1949.

Zadkine Ossip 1890–1967. French Cubist sculptor, born in Russia, active in Paris from 1909. He represented the human form in dramatic, semi-abstract terms, as in the monument *To a Destroyed City* 1953 (Rotterdam).

Zahir ud-din Mohammed 1483–1530. First Great Mogul of India from 1526, called Baber (Arabic 'lion'). He was the great-grandson of the Mongol conqueror Tamerlane and, at the age of 12, succeeded his father, Omar Sheikh Mirza, as ruler of Ferghana (Turkestan). In 1526 he defeated the emperor of Delhi at Panipat in the Punjab, captured Delhi and Agra (site of the Taj Mahal), and established a dynasty which lasted until 1858.

Zahir Shah Mohammed 1914– . King of Afghanistan 1933–73. Zahir, educated in Kabul and Paris, served in the government 1932–33 before being crowned king. He was overthrown in 1973 by a republican coup and went into exile. He has been a symbol of national unity for the mujaheddin Islamic fundamentalist resistance groups.

Zamenhof Lazarus Ludovik 1859–1917. Polish inventor of the international language Esperanto in 1887.

Zampieri Domenico Italian Baroque painter, known as ◊Domenichino.

Zanzotto Andrea 1921– . Italian poet. A teacher from the Veneto, he has published much verse, including the collection *La beltà/Beauty* 1968, with a strong metaphysical element.

Zapata Emiliano 1879–1919. Mexican Indian revolutionary leader. He led a revolt against dictator Porfirio Díaz (1830–1915) from 1911 under the slogan 'Land and Liberty', to repossess for the indigenous Mexicans the land taken by the Spanish. He was driven into retreat by 1915, and was assassinated.

Zeeman Pieter 1865–1943. Dutch physicist who discovered in 1896 that when light from certain elements, such as sodium or lithium (when heated), is passed through a spectroscope in the presence of a strong magnetic field, the individual lines in the spectrum are further subdivided into several closely spaced lines. This is known as the *Zeeman effect* and won him a share of the 1902 Nobel Prize for Physics.

Zeffirelli Franco 1923– . Italian theatre and film director and designer, noted for his stylish designs and lavish productions. His films include *Jesus of Nazareth* 1977 and *La Traviata* 1983. Other work includes a production of the opera *Tosca* 1964, and films of the Shakespeare plays *The Taming of the Shrew* 1967 and *Romeo and Juliet* 1968.

Zeiss Carl 1816–1888. German optician. He opened his first workshop in Jena in 1846, and in 1866 joined forces with Ernst Abbe (1840–1905) producing cameras, microscopes, and field glasses.

Zelenka Jan Dismas 1679–1745. Bohemian composer who worked at the court of Dresden and became director of church music in 1729. His compositions were rediscovered in the 1970s.

Zenobia queen of Palmyra AD 266–272. She assumed the crown in the Syrian desert as regent for her sons, after the death of her husband Odaenathus, and in 272 was defeated at Homs by Aurelian and taken as a captive to Rome.

Zeno of Citium *c.*335–262 BC. Greek founder of the stoic school of philosophy in Athens, about 300 BC. The stoics held that happiness followed from an acceptance of destiny and the law of the Universe.

Zeno of Elea *c.*490–430 BC. Greek philosopher, whose paradoxes raised 'modern' problems of space and time. For example, motion is an illusion, since an arrow in flight must occupy a determinate space at each instant, and therefore must be at rest.

Zeppelin Ferdinand, Count von Zeppelin 1838–1917. German airship pioneer. On retiring from the army in 1891, he devoted himself to the study of aeronautics, and his first airship was built and tested in 1900. During World War I a number of Zeppelin airships bombed England. They were also used for luxury passenger transport but the construction of hydrogen-filled airships with rigid keels was abandoned after several disasters in the 1920s and 1930s. Zeppelin also helped to pioneer large multi-engine bomber planes.

Zernicke Frits 1888–1966. Dutch physicist who developed the phase-contrast microscope 1935. Earlier microscopes allowed many specimens to be examined only after they had been transformed by heavy staining and other treatment. The phase-contrast microscope allowed living cells to be

Zhao Ziyang *An economic expert with a pragmatic outlook.*

directly observed by depending on the difference in refractive indices between specimens and medium. Nobel Prize for Physics 1953.

Zhao Ziyang 1918– . Chinese politician, prime minister from 1980, and secretary of the Chinese Communist Party (CCP) 1987–89. His reforms included self-management and incentives for workers and factories. He lost his secretaryship and other posts after the Tiananmen Square massacre in Beijing June 1989.

Zhao, son of a wealthy landlord from Henan province, joined the Communist Youth League 1932 and worked underground as a CCP official during the liberation war 1937–49. He rose to prominence in the party in Guangdong from 1951. As a supporter of the reforms of Liu Shaoqi, he was dismissed during the 1966–69 Cultural Revolution, paraded through Canton in a dunce's cap and sent to Inner Mongolia.

He was rehabilitated by Zhou Enlai 1973 and sent to China's largest province, Sichuan, as first party secretary 1975. Here he introduced radical and successful market-oriented rural reforms. Deng Xiaoping had him inducted into the Politburo 1977. After six months as a vice premier, Zhao was appointed prime minister 1980 and assumed, in addition, the post of CCP general secretary Jan 1987. His economic reforms were criticized for causing inflation, and his liberal views of the pro-democracy demonstrations that culminated in the student occupation of Tiananmen Square led to his downfall.

Zhivkov Todor 1911– . Bulgarian Communist Party leader from 1954, prime minister 1962–71, president 1971–89. His period in office was one of caution and conservatism.

Zhivkov, a printing worker, joined the BCP in 1932 and was active in the resistance 1941–44. After the war, he was elected to the National Assembly and soon promoted into the CCP secretariat and Politburo. As BCP first secretary, Zhivkov became the dominant political figure in Bulgaria after the death of Vulko Chervenkov in 1956. Zhivkov was elected to the new post of state president in 1971 and lasted until the Eastern bloc upheavals of 1989.

Zhou Enlaio *Chou En-lai* 1898–1976. Chinese politician. Zhou, a member of the Chinese Communist Party (CCP) from the 1920s, was prime minister 1949–76 and foreign minister 1949–58. He was a moderate Maoist, and weathered the Cultural Revolution. He played a key role in foreign affairs.

Born into a declining mandarin gentry family near Shanghai, Zhou studied in Japan and Paris, where he became a founder member of the overseas branch of the CCP. He adhered to the Moscow line of urban-based revolution in China, organizing communist cells in Shanghai and an abortive uprising in Nanchang 1927. In 1935 Zhou supported the election of ◊Mao Zedong as CCP leader and remained a loyal ally during the next 40 years. He served as liaison officer 1937–46 between the CCP and Chiang Kai-shek's nationalist Guomindang government. In 1949 he became prime minister, an office he held until his death Jan 1976.

Zhou, a moderator between the opposing camps of Liu Shaoqi and Mao Zedong, restored orderly progress after the Great Leap Forward (1958–60) and the Cultural Revolution (1966–69), and was the architect of the Four Modernizations programme in 1975. Abroad, Zhou sought to foster Third World unity at the Bandung Conference 1955, averted an outright border confrontation with the USSR by negotiation with Prime Minister Kosygin 1969, and was the principal advocate of detente with the USA during the early 1970s.

Zhu De formerly *Chu Teh* 1886–1976. Chinese Red Army leader from 1931. He devised the tactic of mobile guerrilla warfare and organized the Long March to Shaanxi 1934–36.

The son of a wealthy Sichuan landlord, Zhu served in the Chinese Imperial Army before supporting Sun Yat-sen in the 1911 revolution. He studied communism in Germany and Paris 1922–25 and joined the Chinese Communist Party (CCP) on his return, becoming commander in chief of the Red Army. Working closely with Mao Zedong, Zhu organized the Red Army's Jiangxi break-out 1931 and led the 18th Route Army during the liberation war 1937–49. He

Zia ul-Haq *General Mohammad Zia ul-Haq, Pakistani president 1977–88.*

served as head of state (chair of the Standing Committee of the National People's Congress) 1975–76.

Zhukov Grigory Konstantinovich 1896–1974. Marshal of the USSR in World War II and minister of defence 1955–57. As chief of staff from 1941, he defended Moscow 1941, counterattacked at Stalingrad, organized the relief of Leningrad 1943, and led the offensive from Ukraine Mar 1944 which ended in the fall of Berlin. He subsequently commanded the Soviet occupation forces in Germany.

Zia ul-Haq Mohammad 1924–1988. Pakistani general, in power from 1977 until his assassination. He was a career soldier from a middle-class Punjabi Muslim family, and became army chief of staff 1976. He led the military coup against Zulfiqar Ali ◊Bhutto 1977 and became president 1978. Zia introduced a fundamentalist Islamic regime and restricted political activity.

Zia's opposition to the Soviet invasion of Afghanistan 1979 drew support from the USA, but his refusal to commute the death sentence imposed on Zulfiqar Ali Bhutto was widely condemned. He lifted martial law 1985. The US Central Intelligence Agency is rumoured to have engineered his death.

Ziegler Karl 1898–1973. German organic chemist. In 1963 he was awarded a Nobel prize for his work on the chemistry and technology of high polymers. He combined molecules of the gas ethylene (now called ethene) into the plastic polyethylene (polythene).

Zinneman Fred(erick) 1907– . Austrian-born film director, who lived in the USA from 1921. His films include *High Noon* 1952, *The Nun's Story*

1959, *The Day of the Jackal* 1973, and *Five Days One Summer* 1982.

Zinoviev Alexander 1922– . Soviet philosopher, noted for his satire on the USSR *The Yawning Heights* 1976, which led to his exile 1978, and *The Reality of Communism* 1984, where he argued that communism is the natural consequence of masses of people living under deprived conditions, and thus bound to expand.

Zinoviev Grigory 1883–1936. Russian politician. A prominent Bolshevik, he returned to Russia in 1917 with Lenin and played a leading part in the Revolution. As head of the Communist International 1919, his name was attached to a forgery, the *Zinoviev letter*, inciting Britain's communists to rise, which helped to topple the Labour government in 1924. As one of the 'Old Bolsheviks', he was seen by Stalin as a threat. He was accused of complicity in the murder of the Bolshevik leader Kirov, and shot.

Zi Xi formerly *Tzu-Hsi* 1836–1908. Dowager empress of China. She was presented as a concubine to the emperor Hsien-Feng. On his death 1861 she became regent for her son T'ung Chih, and, when he died in 1875, for her nephew Guang Xu (1871–1908).

Zoffany Johann 1733–1810. British portrait painter, born in Germany, based in London from about 1761. Under the patronage of George III he painted many portraits of the royal family. He spent several years in Florence (1770s) and India (1780s).

Zog Ahmed Beg Zogu 1895–1961. King of Albania 1928–39. He became prime minister of Albania in 1922, president of the republic in 1925, and proclaimed himself king in 1928. He was driven out by the Italians in 1939, and settled in England.

Zola *French novelist and reformer Emile Zola.*

Zola Emile Edouard Charles Antoine 1840–1902. French novelist and social reformer. With *La Fortune des Rougon/The Fortune of the Rougons* 1867 he began a series of some 20 naturalistic novels, portraying the fortunes of a French family under the Second Empire. They include *Le Ventre de Paris/The Underbelly of Paris* 1873, *Nana* 1880, and *La Débâcle/The Debacle* 1892. In 1898 he published *J'accuse/I Accuse*, a pamphlet indicting the persecutors of ◊Dreyfus, for which he was prosecuted but later pardoned.

Born in Paris, Zola was a journalist and clerk in Paris until his *Contes à Ninon/Stories for Ninon* 1864 enabled him to devote himself to literature. Some of the titles in *La Fortune des Rougon/The Fortune of the Rougons* series are *La Faute de l'Abbé Mouret/The Simple Priest* 1875, *L'Assommoir/Drunkard* 1878, *Germinal* 1885 and *La Terre/Earth* 1888. Among later novels is the trilogy *Trois Villes/Three Cities* 1894–98, and *Fécondité/Fecundity* 1899.

Zoroaster or *Zarathustra* c.628–c.551 BC. Persian prophet and religious teacher, founder of Zoroastrianism.

Zorrilla y Moral José 1817–1893. Spanish poet and playwright. Born in Valladolid, he based his plays chiefly on national legends, such as the *Don Juan Tenorio* 1844.

Zsigmondy Richard 1865–1929. Austrian chemist. In 1903 he devised and built an ultramicroscope, in which the illumination was placed at right angles to the axis. (In a conventional microscope the light source is placed parallel to the instrument's axis.) This arrangement made it possible to observe gold particles with a diameter of 10-millionth of a millimetre. Nobel Prize for Chemistry 1925.

Zurbarán Francisco de 1598–1664. Spanish painter, based in Seville. He painted religious subjects in a powerful, austere style, often focusing on a single figure in prayer.

Zurbarán used deep contrasts of light and shade to create an intense spirituality in his works, and received many commissions from religious orders in Spain and South America. During the 1640s the softer, sweeter style of Murillo displaced Zurbarán's art in public favour in Seville, and in 1658 he moved to Madrid.

Zweig Arnold 1887–1968. German novelist, playwright, and poet. He is remembered for his realistic novel of a Russian peasant in the German army *Der Streit um den Sergeanten Grischa/The Case of Sergeant Grischa* 1927.

Zweig Stefan 1881–1942. Austrian writer, noted for plays, poems, and many biographies of writers (Balzac, Dickens) and historical figures (Marie Antoinette, Mary Stuart). He and his wife, exiles from the Nazis from 1934, despairing at what they saw as the end of civilization and culture, committed suicide in Brazil.

Zwingli Ulrich 1484–1531. Swiss Protestant, born in St Gallen. He was ordained a Roman Catholic priest 1506, but by 1519 was a Reformer, and led the Reformation in Switzerland with his insistence on the sole authority of the Scriptures. In a war against the cantons that had not accepted the Reformation he was killed in a skirmish at Kappel.

Zworykin Vladimir Kosma 1889–1982. Russian electronics engineer, who lived in the USA from 1919. He invented a television camera tube and the electron microscope.